International Conference on Interfaces and Human Computer Interaction 2019, International Conference on Game and Entertainment Technologies 2019 and International Conference on Computer Graphics, Visualization, Computer Vision and Image Processing 2019

Held at the Multi-Conference on Computer Science and Information Systems (MCCSIS 2019)

Porto, Portugal
16-19 July 2019

Editors:

Katherine Blashki
Yingcai Xiao
Luís Rodrigues

ISBN: 978-1-5108-9242-2

Printed from e-media with permission by:

Curran Associates, Inc.
57 Morehouse Lane
Red Hook, NY 12571

Some format issues inherent in the e-media version may also appear in this print version.

Printed by Curran Associates, Inc. (2019)

For permission requests, please contact International Association for Development of the Information Society (IADIS) at the address below.

International Association for Development of the Information Society (IADIS)
Rua Sao Sebastiao Da Pedreira
No. 100, 30, 1050-209
Lisbon, Portugal

Phone: 351 21 3151373
Fax: 351 21 3151244

secretariat@iadis.org

Additional copies of this publication are available from:

Curran Associates, Inc.
57 Morehouse Lane
Red Hook, NY 12571 USA
Phone: 845-758-0400
Fax: 845-758-2633
Email: curran@proceedings.com
Web: www.proceedings.com

MULTI CONFERENCE ON COMPUTER SCIENCE AND INFORMATION SYSTEMS

MCCSIS 2019

16-19 JULY

PORTO, PORTUGAL

Proceedings of the International Conferences

Interfaces and Human Computer Interaction 2019
Game and Entertainment Technologies 2019
Computer Graphics, Visualization, Computer Vision and Image Processing 2019

Edited by
Katherine Blashki
Yingcai Xiao

iadis
international association for development of the information society

Volume Editors:
Katherine Blashki and Yingcai Xiao

Computer Science and Information Systems Series Editors:
Piet Kommers and Pedro Isaías

Associate Editor: Luís Rodrigues

PROCEEDINGS OF THE INTERNATIONAL CONFERENCES

INTERFACES AND HUMAN COMPUTER INTERACTION 2019

GAME AND ENTERTAINMENT TECHNOLOGIES 2019

and

COMPUTER GRAPHICS, VISUALIZATION, COMPUTER VISION AND IMAGE PROCESSING 2019

Porto, Portugal
JULY 16 - 18, 2019

Organised by

iadis

international association for development of the information society

Co-Organised by

isep Instituto Superior de Engenharia do Porto

INTERNATIONAL CONFERENCES ON

INTERFACES AND HUMAN COMPUTER INTERACTION 2019

GAME AND ENTERTAINMENT TECHNOLOGIES 2019

and

COMPUTER GRAPHICS, VISUALIZATION, COMPUTER VISION AND IMAGE PROCESSING 2019

part of the

MULTI CONFERENCE ON COMPUTER SCIENCE

AND INFORMATION SYSTEMS 2019

TABLE OF CONTENTS

FULL PAPERS

INTERFACES AND HUMAN COMPUTER INTERACTION

GAME AND ENTERTAINMENT TECHNOLOGIES

COMPUTER GRAPHICS, VISUALIZATION, COMPUTER VISION AND IMAGE PROCESSING

SHORT PAPERS

INTERFACES AND HUMAN COMPUTER INTERACTION

GAME AND ENTERTAINMENT TECHNOLOGIES

COMPUTER GRAPHICS, VISUALIZATION, COMPUTER VISION AND IMAGE PROCESSING

REFLECTION PAPERS

INTERFACES AND HUMAN COMPUTER INTERACTION

GAME AND ENTERTAINMENT TECHNOLOGIES

COMPUTER GRAPHICS, VISUALIZATION, COMPUTER VISION AND IMAGE PROCESSING

POSTERS

INTERFACES AND HUMAN COMPUTER INTERACTION

GAME AND ENTERTAINMENT TECHNOLOGIES

COMPUTER GRAPHICS, VISUALIZATION, COMPUTER VISION AND IMAGE PROCESSING

FOREWORD

These proceedings contain the papers and posters of the following conferences: 13th International Conference on Interfaces and Human Computer Interaction 2019, 12th International Conference on Game and Entertainment Technologies 2019 and 13th International Conference on Computer Graphics, Visualization, Computer Vision and Image Processing 2019, which were organised by the International Association for Development of the Information Society, from 16 - 18 July, 2019. These conferences are part of the Multi Conference on Computer Science and Information Systems 2019, 16 - 19 July, which had a total of 926 submissions.

The Interfaces and Human Computer Interaction (IHCI) 2019 conference aims to address the main issues of concern within Interface Culture and Design with a particular emphasis on the affective aspects of design, development and implementation of interfaces and the generational implications for design of human and technology interaction. This conference aims to explore and discuss innovative studies of technology and its application in interfaces and welcomes research in progress, case studies, practical demonstrations and workshops in addition to the traditional submission categories.

This conference seeks to cover both technological as well as non-technological issues related to these developments.

Submissions were accepted under the following topics:

- Affective User-Centred Analysis, Design and Evaluation
- The Value of Affective Interfaces / Systems / Application / Interaction
- Generational differences and technology design
- Measurement of success of emotional technology / interfaces
- Supporting user populations from specific Generations
- Supporting user populations with Physical Disabilities
- Supporting user populations with Intellectual Disabilities
- Creativity Support Systems
- Emotional Design issues / methods / experiences for novel interfaces including tangible, Mobile and Ubiquitous computing, mixed reality interfaces and multi-modal interfaces
- Usability
- User studies and fieldwork
- Methodological implications of Emotional User Studies
- Participatory design and Cooperative design techniques
- Ethical issues in emotional design
- HCI and Design education
- Eliciting User Requirements

The Game and Entertainment Technologies (GET) 2019 conference aims to bring together research and practice from creative, social and business practitioners and researchers in this challenging field. The focus of this conference is on design, development and evaluation of games, entertainment technologies and the nature of play.

Known to have been enjoyed since at least 30 BC, games and entertainment are a universal part of human experience and present in all cultures. Games and entertainment activities contribute to the social, emotional, psychological and physical well-being of human society. As game and entertainment technologies become increasingly more pervasive we are continually challenged in our work, learning and personal life by increased access to virtual spaces and communities that offer opportunities for everyday needs and aesthetic experiences. The 'Creative Industries' require design and development structures, techniques and methodologies that enrich, enhance and encourage new interaction modes, metaphors and in-depth co-creation.

Topics of interest include, but are not limited to the following areas:

- Development methodologies
- Design issues
- Controversial issues – we welcome debate and dissension, for example; games as art, entertainment as purely for monetary returns etc
- Special Effects
- Animation
- Mobile and ubiquitous games and entertainment
- Serious Games –applications, critiques
- Philosophical issues
- Prototypes
- Social and cultural uses of/for Play
- Tools and technologies
- Skills, strategy, rules and chance
- Genre
- Immersiveness and engagement
- Research methodologies in creative practice
- Usability and playability
- User/player centered design
- Psychological, social, and cultural differences in perception and participation
- Communities, networks, social interaction and social capital
- Cross-cultural and intercultural approaches
- Assessment of exploratory learning approaches
- Emerging practices

The Computer Graphics, Visualization, Computer Vision and Image Processing (CGVCVIP) 2019 conference intends to address the research issues in the closely related areas of Computer Graphics, Visualization, Computer Vision and Image Processing.
The conference encourages the interdisciplinary research and applications of these areas.

Submissions were accepted under the following 5 main topics:

- Computer Graphics
- Visualization
- Computer Vision
- Image Processing
- Other Related Topics

These events received 216 submissions from more than 31 countries. Each submission has been anonymously reviewed by an average of five independent reviewers, to ensure that accepted submissions were of a high standard. Consequently, only 37 full papers were published. The overall acceptance rate corresponds to about 17 %. A few more papers were accepted as short papers, reflection papers and posters. An extended version of the best papers will be published in the IADIS International Journal on WWW/Internet (ISSN: 1645-7641) and also in other selected journals, including journals from Inderscience.

Besides the presentation of full papers, short papers, reflection papers and posters, the conferences also included a keynote presentation and one tutorial from internationally distinguished researchers. We would therefore like to express our gratitude to Prof. Paula Escudeiro, Institute of Engineering of Porto, Polytechnic Institute of Porto, Portugal, for accepting our invitation to be the keynote speaker and Rüdiger Heimgärtner for the Tutorial presentation.

This volume has taken shape as a result of the contributions from a number of individuals. We are grateful to all authors who have submitted their papers to enrich these conferences proceedings. We wish to thank all members of the organizing committee, delegates, invitees and guests whose contribution and involvement are crucial for the success of the conference.

Last but not the least, we hope that everybody had a good time in Porto, and we invite all participants for the next years´ edition of these conferences.

Katherine Blashki, Noroff University College, Norway
Interfaces and Human Computer Interaction 2019
& Game and Entertainment Technologies 2019 Program Chair

Yingcai Xiao, The University of Akron, USA
Computer Graphics, Visualization, Computer Vision and Image Processing 2019
Program Chair

Piet Kommers, University of Twente, The Netherlands
Pedro Isaías, The University of Queensland, Australia
MCCSIS 2019 General Conference Co-Chairs

Bertil Marques, ISEP, Portugal
MCCSIS 2019 Local Organising Chair

Porto, Portugal
July 2019

PROGRAM COMMITTEE

INTERFACES AND HUMAN COMPUTER INTERACTION CONFERENCE & GAME AND ENTERTAINMENT TECHNOLOGIES CONFERENCE

PROGRAM CHAIR

Katherine Blashki, Noroff University College, Norway

COMPUTER GRAPHICS, VISUALIZATION, COMPUTER VISION AND IMAGE PROCESSING

PROGRAM CHAIR

Yingcai Xiao, The University of Akron, USA

MCCSIS GENERAL CONFERENCE CO-CHAIRS

Piet Kommers, University of Twente, The Netherlands
Pedro Isaías, The University of Queensland, Australia

MCCSIS LOCAL ORGANISING CHAIR

Bertil Marques, ISEP, Portugal

INTERFACES AND HUMAN COMPUTER INTERACTION CONFERENCE

COMMITTEE MEMBERS

Aidan Rowe, University of Alberta, Canada
Alan Newell, Retired (University of Dundee), United Kingdom
Alexander Gelbukh, Instituto Politécnico Nacional, Mexico
Alexander Kröner, Technische Hochschule Nürnberg Georg Simon Ohm, Germany
Ana Cristina Bicharra Garcia , Universidade Federal Flumninese, Brazil
Andre Constantino da Silva, Instituto Federal de Sao Paulo, Brazil
Arianna D Ulizia, IRPPS-CNR, Italy
Asterios Leonidis, Foundation for Research & Technology - Hellas, Greece
Cecilia Sik-lanyi, University of Pannonia, Hong Kong
Celia Martinie, Universite Paul Sabatier, France
Chee Weng Khong, Multimedia University, Malaysia
Connie Veugen, Vrije Universiteit Amsterdam, Netherlands
Eduardo Tanaka, Eldorado Research Institute, Brazil
Eleni Mangina, University College Dublin (UCD), Ireland
Fang Chen, Chalmers University, Sweden
Fazel Naghdy, University of Wollongong, Australia
Francisco Madera Ramirez, Universidad Autonoma de Yucatan, Mexico
Hiram Calvo, National Polytechnic Institute, Mexico
Jesuk Ko, Gwangju University, Republic of Korea

Jon Preston, Southern Polytechnic State University, USA
José Antonio Macías Iglesias, Universidad Autónoma de Madrid, Spain
Josef Gründler, Fh Joanneum University of Applied Sciences, Austria
Kal Dhou, University of Missouri - St. Louis, USA
Kathia Oliveira, Université de Valenciennes et du Hainaut-Cambrésis, France
Katrina Attwood, University of York, United Kingdom
Keith Nesbitt, University of Newcastle, Australia
Khaled Khankan, Taibah University, Saudi Arabia
Larbi Esmahi, Athabasca University, Canada
Leonelo Almeida, Federal University of Technology, Paraná, Brazil
Marcelo Romero Huertas, Universidad Autonoma del Estado de Mexico, Mexico
Maria Claudia Buzzi , IIT - CNR, Italy
Mark Apperley, University of Waikato, New Zealand
Mathieu Raynal, University of Toulouse, France
Maxim Bakaev, Novosibirsk State Technical University, Russia
Michael Hobbs, Deakin University, Australia
Michael Hohl, HS Anhalt/FB Design, Germany
Nadine Vigouroux, IRIT, CNRS, Paul Sabtier University, France
Nuno Otero, Linnaeus University, Sweden
Otniel Portillo Rodriguez, Universidad Autonóma del Estado de México, Mexico
Roberto Pereira, Federal University of Parana (UFPR), Brazil
Rodica Mocan, Babes-Bolyai University, Romania
Rodrigo Bonacin, Dssd - CTI Renato Archer, Brazil
Rüdiger Heimgärtner, Intercultural User Interface Consulting, Germany
Sebastián Romero López, I.e.s Cañada De La Encina, Spain
Silvio Cazella, UFCSPA, Brazil
Xiaokun Zhang, Athabasca University, Canada
Yacine Bellik, Laboratory Limsi-CNRS, France

GAME AND ENTERTAINMENT TECHNOLOGIES

COMMITTEE MEMBERS

Alessio Ceccherelli, Tor Vergata University, Italy
Alf Inge Wang, Norwegian University of Science and Technology, Norway
Ali Arya, Carleton University, Canada
Carla Hoekendijk, Independant Consultant/Developer, Netherlands
Castulus Kolo, Macromedia University of Applied Sciences, Germany
Christos Bouras, University of Patras and Computer Technology Institute, Greece
Connie Veugen, Vrije Universiteit Amsterdam, Netherlands
Daniel Cermak-Sassenrath, IT University of Copenhagen, Denmark
Ellen Brox, Norut - Northen Research Institute, Norway
Etienne Armand Amato, Gobelins L École de L Image, France
Gabriele D`Angelo, University of Bologna, Italy
Harry Agius, Brunel University London, United Kingdom
Ian Marshall, Coventry University, United Kingdom
Ines Di Loreto, University of Technologies of Troyes, Finland
Isabelle Astic, CNAM, France
Jouni Smed, University of Turku, Finland

Katie Salen, University of California, USA
Marcia Medeiros, UniFANOR (Devry Brasil), Brazil
Michael Katchabaw, University of Western Ontario, Canada
Michel Simatic, Telecom Sudparis, France
Monica Gavrielidou, University of Thessaly, Greece
Panagiotis Kyriakoulakos, University of the Aegean, Greece
Pilar Lacasa, University of Alcala, Spain
Ruck Thawonmas, Ritsumeikan University, Japan
Thrasyvoulos Tsiatsos, Aristotle Univerisity of Thessaloniki, Greece
Ulysses Bernardet, Aston University, United Kingdom
Yoshihiro Okada, Kyushu University, Japan

COMPUTER GRAPHICS, VISUALIZATION, COMPUTER VISION AND IMAGE PROCESSING

COMMITTEE MEMBERS

Aiert Amundarain, CEIT, Spain
Alexander Shoulson, Red Storm Entertainment, USA
Ana Serrano, Universidad de Zaragoza, Spain
Angelica De Antonio, Universidad Politecnica de Madrid, Spain
Anna Lewandowska, Technical University of Szczecin, Poland
Bruce Campbell, Rhode Island School of Design, USA
Carlo Nati, Working Group for the Development of Tecnoscientif, Italy
Celmar Guimarães da Silva, University of Campinas, Brazil
Charalampos Georgiadis, The Aristotle University, Greece
Chong Zhang, ESRI, USA
Creto Vidal, Federal University of Ceará, Brazil
Dalton Lin, National Taipei University, Taiwan
David Wortley, 360in360 Immersive Experiences, United Kingdom
Elefelious Getachew Belay, Università Degli Studi Di Milano, Italy
Fatima Nunes, University of São Paulo, Brazil
Hongchuan Yu, Bournemouth University, United Kingdom
Ingemar Ragnemalm, Linköping University, Sweden
Jian Chang, Bournemouth University, United Kingdom
José Pascual Molina Massó, Universidad de Castilla-la Mancha, Spain
Jose Remo Ferreira Brega, São Paulo State University, Brazil
Josip Almasi, Open Computing Ltd, Ireland
Juan Manuel Gonzalez Calleros, Meritorious Autonomous University of Puebla, Mexico
Julio Marco, Universidad de Zaragoza, Spain
Kadi Bouatouch, Irisa, University of Rennes 1, France
Krzysztof Okarma, West Pomeranian University of Technology, Poland
Krzysztof Walczak, Poznan University of Economics, Poland
Leandro Fernandes, Federal Fluminense University, Brazil
Lihua You, Bournemouth University, United Kingdom
Linda Giannini, ENO National Coordinator, Italy
Luca Grilli, Department of Engineering, University of Perugia, Italy

Luciano Soares, Insper Instituto de Ensino e Pesquisa, Brazil
Marcelo de Paiva Guimaraes, UNIFESP / UNIFACCAMP, Brazil
Matteo Paolo Lanaro, The University of Milan, Italy
Mu-Chun Su, National Central University, Taiwan
Nadia Ambrosetti, Universita Degli Studi di Milano, Italy
Paolo Pingi, CNR - ISTI, Italy
Peter Dannenmann, RheinMain University of Applied Sciences, Germany
Pierre-frederic Villard, University of Lorraine, France
Piotr Lech, West Pomeranian University of Technology, Poland
Quan Wen, University of Electronic Science and Technology, China
Rene Rosenbaum, meeCoda, Germany
Robert Sitnik, Warsaw University of Technology, Poland
Roman Durikovic, Comenius University in Bratislava, Slovakia
Shaun Bangay, Deakin University, Australia
Theresa-Marie Rhyne, Computer Graphics Consultant, USA
Timothy Newman, University of Alabama in Huntsville, USA
Unai Elordi, Vicomtech-ik4, Spain
Xiaogang Jin, Zhejiang University, China
Xiaosong Yang, Bournemouth University, United Kingdom
Xuejun Hao, Columbia University, USA

KEYNOTE LECTURE

INCLUSIVE INTERFACES

Prof. Paula Escudeiro,
Institute of Engineering of Porto, Polytechnic Institute of Porto,
Portugal

ABSTRACT

Promoting equal opportunities and social inclusion of disabled people is a concern of modern society and a key issue in European Education. The evolution of science and the emerging new technologies promote social inclusion and simplify the communication with disabled people. The current status can, however, evolve. In the access of deaf or blind people to public services, for instance, it can be quite complex to communicate. Education is another critical area and a more serious problem. Education impacts citizens lives to a great extent. Barriers to education limit future opportunities. Any contribution to tear these barriers down promotes equity. Deaf people experience significant obstacles in reading. Blind people have no easy access to digital content. These facts severely compromise the development of creative, emotional and social skills in deaf or blind students. The main goal of this research project is to promote the access of deaf or blind people to education and citizenship.

The project addresses research issues raised by Virtual Sign (VS). VS investigated the translation between Portuguese sign language and written Portuguese using desktop devices. It became clear that investigating mobile devices and their ability to empower disabled people with effective communication facilities not depending on desktop devices is necessary. It adds that the number of external devices required to collect the inputs to model gestures should be reduced making the solution more adequate for daily usage, outside the lab or traditional classrooms.

The project investigates the integration of multiple channels (MC) of communication (gesture, speech, text, digital arts) and multiple languages (ML) making them available through desktop and mobile devices in order to promote the communication with/between deaf and blind students.

The purpose of Multi-Channel/Multi-Language Communication (MCMLC) Model and Methodology, is the analysis and design of a model synthesizing the features required to implement a bi-directional converter between gestures and text, a voice-gesture converter and a gesture-voice converter. All these converters will embed language translators. This model should address the communication difficulties and the concrete needs of blind and deaf people on their daily lives.

The user interface plays a very important role, of particular relevance when directed to people with disabilities. User Interface Design will define the protocols, the characteristics and the requirements for interacting via audio, video, gestures and text on desktop and mobile devices. We will create the user interface architecture and define the modes of operation.

The automatic conversion between gestures, text and voice will be based on machine learning processes that learn from examples. In addition, the reproduction of gestures by a 3D avatar is needed when converting text or voice to gestures.

TUTORIAL

METHOD-MIX FOR THE DEVELOPMENT OF INTERCULTURAL USER INTERFACES

Rüdiger Heimgärtner
Intercultural User Interface Consulting (IUIC), R&D HMI
Lindenstraße 9, 93152 Undorf, Germany

ABSTRACT

After a brief introduction to the development of intercultural user interfaces (IUID), a method-mix for IUID is presented and then applied and specifically practiced in groups on the basis of concrete project examples to derive recommendations for IUID from scratch. This tutorial is suitable for everyone, who is interested in a systematic approach to IUID willing to understand the cultural influences on HMI design and how to take them into account in intercultural product development (such as HMI researchers, UI developers, UX designers, students and practitioners).

KEYWORDS

Culture, Human Factors, UX, Usability, Intercultural User Interface Design, IUID, Method Mix, HMI Dimensions

1. OBJECTIVE, CONTENT, AND DIDACTIC CONCEPT

IUID is prerequisite for improving the intercultural UX of software, which in turn is a prerequisite for global sales opportunities. Based on feedback from tutorials and workshops on IUID, the reflections on a model for culture-dependent HMI design and the revised summary of the state of research on IUID, the author proposes a method-mix for IUID (cf. (Heimgärtner, 2019)) lectured in this tutorial. First, a short introduction to intercultural HMI design and the approaches in IUID are given. Then, the most important methods for IUID (method of culture-oriented HMI design as well as the identification of cultural differences and their variables for HMI design (Röse, 2002), user interface characteristics (Marcus, 2006), cultural dimensions (Hofstede, Hofstede, & Minkov, 2010), and HMI dimensions (Heimgärtner, 2012)) are explained and documented using a handout. Sequentially, the IUID method-mix is practiced and applied in groups of 3-10 participants on the basis of practical examples to experience the methodological challenges in cultural contexts and to learn how to overcome them. The discussion of these findings supports intensive reflection and deepening the new (acquired) knowledge. Summary and feedback close this modular tutorial designed for half a day (3 hours) with four blocks of 45 minutes each (and a break after block 2). Depending on the number of participants, previous knowledge, and demand, it can be extended to 6 hours with 90 min. blocks.

REFERENCES

Heimgärtner, R. (2012). *Cultural Differences in Human-Computer Interaction* (Paperback B: Einband - flex.(Paperback) ed. Vol. 1): Oldenbourg Verlag.

Heimgärtner, R. (2019). IUID Method-Mix: Towards a Systematic Approach for Intercultural User Interface Design. *Journal of Computer and Communications.*

Hofstede, G. H., Hofstede, G. J., & Minkov, M. (2010). *Cultures and organizations: software of the mind* (3. ed.). Maidenhead: McGraw-Hill.

Marcus, A. (2006). Cross-Cultural User-Experience Design. In D. Barker-Plummer, R. Cox, & N. Swoboda (Eds.), *Diagrammatic Representation and Inference* (Vol. 4045, pp. 16-24): Springer Berlin Heidelberg.

Röse, K. (2002). *Model of Culture and Their Applicability for Designing User Interfaces.* Paper presented at the Paper presented at the Conference WWDU 2002- World Wide Work, Berchtesgaden.

Full Papers

AN EMPIRICAL STUDY ON GUI-II INTERVIEW METHODS IN PARTICIPATORY DESIGN

Arsineh Boodaghian Asl[1] and Michel Gokan Khan[2]
[1]*Karlstad Business School, Department of Information Systems, Karlstad University, Karlstad, Sweden*
[2]*Department of Mathematics and Computer Science, Karlstad University, Karlstad, Sweden*

ABSTRACT

Graphical user interface interaction interview (GUI-ii), is a recently purposed method in which designers can remotely co-design and review GUI prototypes by eliminating the need for physical presence of co-designers. However, there are some concerns regarding the accuracy of such remote interview methods, as users do not have any physical interaction with the designers during their interview. In this work, for the first time, we compare GUI-ii methods with the traditional face-to-face interview processes to study their effectiveness in various design phases. The result shows that GUI-ii method is most effective when used in Ozlab.

KEYWORDS

Human-Computer Interaction, Participatory Design, Interview Methods, Graphical User Interface, Prototype

1. INTRODUCTION

One of the critical aspects of designing interfaces is to find out what are the most vital end-users' needs. There are multiple cases where it is essential to gather information from the end-user during the designing process. To obtain information from the end-users, as *co-designers* in a *co-design environment*, designers combine participatory design techniques (Simonsen and Robertson, 2013; Spinuzzi, 2005) with interview methods.

There are different interview methods, one of the basic ones is the traditional face-to-face interview, where the designer meets the co-designer face-to-face, and they use paper and pencil to interview and gather information according to the design phase prerequisites. There are other interview methods developed such as think-aloud (Nielsen et al., 2002), post-task, and survey-based (E. Baauw et al., 2004) interviews.

GUI interaction interviews (GUI-ii) (Pettersson et al., 2017) is a new interview method where interviewees are creating user interfaces and interacts with them. It is interesting to evaluate its benefits under different conditions, to find out its limits, advantages, and disadvantages. There are various approaches for using the GUI-ii interview method, such as *face-to-face* interview, interviewing via *screen-sharing* and interviewing using the *Ozlab* web application (Pettersson and Siponen, 2002) which provides Wizard-of-Oz (Steinfeld et al., 2009) functionalities to enhance the interactive experience (Pettersson et al., 2018, 2017).

Majority of designers go through different interview methods to get the necessary information from the users according to their needs. Whether it's remote, face-to-face or even a combination of methods and approaches.

In this research, for the first time, we compare these GUI-ii approaches with traditional face-to-face interview method and analyze the benefits in each design phase according to different parameters, which will be covered later in the research method section.

2. RELATED WORKS

There are researches who did an empirical study on interview methods which are different from the ones covered in this work. The comparison they conclude was whether before starting the design, in information gathering phase, or after it, in the usability test phase. However, none of them covered the importance of choosing a suitable interview method in a co-design environment, especially from the *human-computer interaction* (HCI) perspective.

Dimond et al. (Dimond et al., 2012) did a comparison test on instant messaging, e-mail and phone, in order to find out that different methods have different effects on the test's result; they had used the following parameter for analyzing the result, first *word count* and second the *quality code*. They did not take the difficulty level into consideration that can affect the *willingness to provide information*, and thus on the quality of the test. In this work, we will discuss the *willingness to provide information* and represent its impacts through graphs.

Baauw et al. (Baauw and Markopoulous, 2004) results showed that girls tend to communicate more while they were encountering problems during the usability test than boys. However, all the children in this research were tested for usability testing, and they weren't involved as co-designers.

Brush et al. (Brush et al., 2004) also did a similar comparison. They listed five different issues of usability testing and they also did a survey on users who participated to remote and local tests and asked about their difficulties during the test, and they also recorded their voices and shared screens interactions during the interview. Even though the tools and techniques of their tests are very useful. The test was concentrated on the usability test and not participatory design.

On another empirical study by *Johnathan Gratch et.al. (Gratch et al., 2014)*, four different interview methods such as face-to-face, teleconference, Wizard-of-Oz, and automated character (*Ellie,* a virtual animated character) has been compared. At the first two interview methods, the conductor was a human being, on the third and fourth interview methods the interviewer was Ellie. However, the goal of the research was not related to the participatory design field and not even to usability testing and it focused on supporting psychological conditions.

GUI-ii method has been developed by Pettersson, Wik and Andersson. in a research study called "Wizards of Oz in the Evolving Map of Design Research" (Pettersson et al., 2018, 2017).

3. RESEARCH METHODOLOGY

This research study has used qualitative methodology the main goal is to precisely explain and clarify the efficiency and quality of four different interview methods over one another.

3.1 Interview Methods

This research study will cover the comparison of the following four interview methods:

GUI-ii Face-to-Face: In this method, a *designer*, who is also the *test leader*, and a *co-designer,* who is called *co-designer*, will work together with one computer, in a face-to-face manner. The computer will be mainly accessible by the co-designer, in order to let the co-designer to have the freedom of creativity, the designer will act as a secondary designer.

GUI-ii Screen-Sharing*:* the designer and co-designer do the interview in distance, however, the co-designer is unable to interact with the software and s/he can only see the screen, so the co-designer constantly gives feedback during the test via Skype and the designer applies the necessary changes according to the co-designer's needs.

GUI-ii Ozlab*:* Ozlab's primary use is to perform usability test. Ozlab has different view panels for the designer, co-designer and viewers. In the first view panel, which is called "Test Leader", the designers can add, remove, and edit scenes and GUI elements, and also allows co-designers, to freely move GUI elements and the designer can track their mouse movements. Second view panel, which is called "Test Participant", is for the co-designers in order to interact with the system; and the last panel, which is called "Test Viewer(s)", is for possible viewer(s), just in case another person is going to do the analysis, who would like to monitor the test but not to interact with the test. Unlike previous mentioned interview methods, there are two ways to apply this method, one through a laboratory and the other one via an internet-based remote interview method, which we used in an additional experiment in order to compare the remote results with the lab results. The lab should be facilitated with at least two computers, one for the designer and another one for the co-designer, with a microphone and speaker, where the designer can communicate with the co-designer. The interview starts by pressing the start session button from the designer side and finishes by stop session button. The lab may also be facilitated with a dark glassed wall, for the purpose of observing co-designer's behavior. The second way of running this interview method, is to do it via internet; though, the designer and co-designer should communicate using a phone call or a massaging app.

Traditional Face-to-Face: in this method, the designers and co-designer sit together face-to-face but with paper and pencil. The co-designer is the main person writing and drawing on the paper, and the designer just cooperates with the co-designer as a secondary designer.

3.2 Design Phases

In this research, we applied the four mentioned interview methods, in the following design phases:

Listing interface components: In this phase, the designer prepares a list of interface components to presents it to the co-designer, and starts the interview by an unstructured questionnaire (Preece et al., 2015). Then, the co-designer is asked to edit, delete, combine or add components if necessary.

Sketching: (Rettig, 1994) In this phase, the designer presents the co-designer, with the result of the first phase and asks him/her to review the components list and decide the location/size of them on the interface.

Lo-Fi Prototyping: (Rettig, 1994) In this phase, the co-designer's task is to follow the previous phase's sketch and to replace components with satisfactory GUI elements such as buttons, textboxes, menus, etc.

Hi-Fi Prototyping: (Rettig, 1994) This is the last phase of design, where co-designer choses a convenient way to interact with GUI elements (i.e. if it is best to open a menu by hovering the mouse, or click to open).

3.3 Comparison Parameters

In this paper, we selected four parameters to consider while comparing interview methods in each phase:

Duration per component: it is important for designers to know how long an interview method takes. In some design phases, a short and quick interview method may not extract enough information, as it takes time for them to feel comfortable to give feedback for components. On the contrary, in some other phases, it can be cumbersome to use long interview methods, as the co-designer can get exhausted and may start to give insufficient feedback at the end of interview. The reason for considering duration of interview according to the number of components instead of total duration, is that co-designers list different components at the beginning of the design phase, and depends on number of components they list, the total duration of interviews may vary. So, in order to accurately compare interview methods from the time perspective, we need to compare interview duration based on number of components that has been listed at the beginning of design phase.

Willingness to provide information: we asked co-designers to step-by-step elaborate what they are doing and the reason behind their choices. For this purpose, think-aloud method has been used; however, it is not convenient for the co-designer to be reminded to think-aloud while co-designing, as it may put the co-designer in an awkward and uncomfortable situation. By comparing this parameter, we found out which interview method can make the co-designer to speak more willingly. We analyzed each interview's video records and counted the number of words that the co-designer spoke out regarding each component.

Difficulty: in some interview methods, it can take some time for the co-designer to learn how to interact with the interview environment or the related softwares while co-designing. Sometimes this may cause negative effect on the co-designer's *willingness to provide information*. While the co-designer might need enough time to learn about the interview's environment and related softwares in use, s/he should not go in details while doing a sketch for the first time. This can slow down the interview and may cause longer duration and eventually the co-designer may get bored. This will be measured by the amount of time the co-designer learn how to interact with the environment and asks questions regarding their problems with the interview tools.

Cost: no matter how easy and streightforward an interview method can be, there is always a limited budget for running an interview. Things such as computers, softwares license, renting a lab, etc,

3.4 Software

For the purpose of running this interview methods, during some of the mentioned design phases, we have used *Pencil* and *Sketch* desktop applications, which are both designing tools with GUI elements available for quick interface designing, corresponding to the design phase. Also, we used *Skype*, as our messaging app for internet-based remote interview methods since it has a screen-sharing feature and all the co-designers are familiar how to use it.

3.5 Test Participants

There were in total eight participants. All the test participants (co-designers) were university students from various study fields between the age range of 20 to 40, six males and two females. None of them had ever been in a participatory design, and they weren't familiar with the Sketch and Pencil desktop applications or Ozlab web application. Throughout this research paper, we will refer all the test participants as co-designers.

3.6 Test Leaders

The test leader is responsible for preparing the unstructured questionnaire, orientation script, non-disclosure agreement (Rubin and Chisnell, 2008) and conducting the literature review and observation. He/she is also responsible for analyzing test results, and act as the Wizard-of-Oz method. Throughout this research paper, we refer the main test leader as designer.

3.7 The Participatory Design Test

We have used 4*4 within-subject design experiment, with counterbalancing order (see Table 1). It is an approach to iterate the test subjects into all the phases of design without repeating the same interview method.

In Table 1, the first row represents interview methods, and the first column represents design phases. According to counterbalancing order, all the test subjects who are the co-designers, went through all the phases of design one by one. However, in each phase they were interviewed by different methods and no one has repeated the same phase by the same interview method. On the other hand, they received the results from the same interview method. So that, co-designers didn't work on their own results from the previous design phase.

The reason for choosing within-subject design is that the co-designer is already familiar with the previous design phase results, s/he learned how to act in the interview method already familiar with the test goal.

Table 1. 2*2 with-in subject design with counterbalancing order

Subjects	GUI-ii Face-to-Face	GUI-ii Screen-Sharing at Lab	GUI-ii Ozlab at Lab	Traditional Face-to-Face
Listing Interface Components	1st Subject	2nd Subject	3rd Subject	4th Subject
Sketching	4th Subject	1st Subject	2nd Subject	3rd Subject
Lo-Fi Prototyping	3rd Subject	4th Subject	1st Subject	2nd Subject
Hi-Fi Prototyping	2nd Subject	3rd Subject	4th Subject	1st Subject

For GUI-ii Ozlab remote interview, we used different co-designers group from Stockholm and Uppsala (see Table 2).

Table 2. Order and location of the co-designers for remote GUI-ii Ozlab interview

Subjects	**Remote GUI-ii Ozlab**
Listing Interface Component Phase	5th Subject from Stockholm
Sketching Phase	6th Subject from Uppsala
Lo-Fi Prototyping Phase	7th Subject from Stockholm
Hi-Fi Prototyping Phase	8th Subject Uppsala

In remote based GUI-ii Ozlab interview method, we did not follow within-subject design rule. We added remote interview method to compare the lab environments impacts on co-designers' desire to think-aloud.

In order to reduce the mistakes in real test and increase the accuracy, a pilot test (Rubin and Chisnell, 2008) was performed. As a result, we manage to edit the unstructured questionnaire, be more precise while answering their questions and keep the test simple for the co-designers, i.e. using *Sketch* application for easy learning.

3.8 Test Scenario

In order to run the test, we have decided to perform the participatory design technique on developing an *online synchronous learning system* user interface from the students' perspective, where the teacher and students meet online at the same time. Though, the goal of the research study is to test the interview methods, not the interface. Same test scenario was used for pilot test but with different participants which all of them were males.

3.9 Measurement System

The scales used for the parameters has been categorized as follows: very low, low, below average, average, above average, high, very high. *Duration per component* range is [0.1,350] (in minutes), *willingness to provide information* range is [0,900], *difficulty* range is [0,10], and the *cost* range is [500$,15000$].

4. RESULT

This section is divided into two parts, where the first part will display the scaled-based results tables, and the second part will represent charts to compare interview methods based on parameters.

4.1 Scale-based Tables

Tables 3,4 and 6 show the result of all the interview video tapes and the screen interactions' analysis. The first row in these tables are the interview methods and the first column to the left are the parameters.

Table 3. Test results from interface components listing phase

Listing Interface Components	GUI-ii Face-to-Face	GUI-ii Screen-Sharing at Lab	GUI-ii Ozlab at Lab	GUI-ii Ozlab Remote	Traditional Face-to-Face
Duration Per Component	Low	Below Average	Average	Above Average	High
Willingness to Provide Information	Low	Average	High	Above Average	Below Average
Difficulty	Low	Low	Low	Below Average	Low
Cost	Average	Above Average	Very High	Low	Below Average

In the first phase (see Table 3), considering both *duration per component* and *willingness to provide information,* the GUI-ii face-to-face has the lowest outcome as the co-designers always has the false impression the designer fully understand what they do as they look at the same screen, so they don't usually speak-out.

A few difficulties have been reported on GUI-ii Ozlab remote interview method, and it's due to the extra explanations for co-designer to run the Ozlab web application on his/her device. Regarding *cost*, GUI-ii Ozlab at Usability Lab is the most expensive one, as it requires to rent/own a lab with sophisticated facilities such as dark glassed wall, at least 2 computers, microphones and speakers.

Table 4. Test results from sketching phase

Sketching	GUI-ii Face-to-Face	GUI-ii Screen-Sharing at Lab	GUI-ii Ozlab at Lab	GUI-ii Ozlab Remote	Traditional Face-to-Face
Duration Per Component	High	Average	Average	Above Average	Very High
Willingness to Provide Information	Low	Average	High	Above Average	Below Average
Difficulty	High	Average	Low	Below Average	Low
Cost	Average	Above Average	Very High	Low	Below Average

In the sketching phase (Table 4), once again GUI-ii Ozlab at Usability Lab has the most satisfactory results by merging both *duration per component* and *willingness to provide information*. We also have a huge variation for *difficulty* parameter; especially on GUI-ii face-to-face: it was twice as difficult as GUI-ii screen-sharing as even though the designer is close by during the face-to-face interview, the co-designer supposed to interact with the system alone and requires some basic understanding about the *Pencil* desktop application.

One of the advantages of using GUI-ii Ozlab web application is that you cannot have margins for the components on the sketching phase, which help the designers and developers to cover the empty spaces on the web by resizing existing components. On the down-side, using Ozlab web application remotely, causes a slight delay in viewing the co-designer's interactions.

Table 5 differs from other tables presented. First, GUI-ii Ozlab method is not applicable on this phase, which is an advantage as it has interactive GUI elements and easy to rearrange, which helps the designers to combine both Lo-Fi and Hi-Fi prototypes, and instead of doing the design in four different phases, it can be done in three design phases, by avoiding Lo-Fi prototyping phase. However, if a designer is going to use an interview method other than GUI-ii Ozlab for Lo-Fi prototyping phase, it is better to use GUI-ii screen-sharing as it consumes less time and higher *willingness to provide information* for co-designers. The only disadvantage is that GUI-ii screen-sharing is twice as difficult as GUI-ii face-to-face (Table 4) which has totally the opposite value, by comparing to sketching phase (Table 5); since, in the sketching phase the co-designer only needs to show the location and the size for different components, but for Lo-Fi the co-designer needs to access different GUI elements in the software, which forces them to spend more time on learning during the test.

Table 5. Test results from Lo-Fi prototyping phase

Sketching	GUI-ii Face-to-Face	GUI-ii Screen-Sharing at Lab	GUI-ii Ozlab at Lab	GUI-ii Ozlab Remote	Traditional Face-to-Face
Duration Per Component	High	Average	-	-	Above Average
Willingness to Provide Information	Low	Average	-	-	Below Average
Difficulty	Average	High	-	-	Low
Cost	Average	Above Average	-	-	Below Average

In Hi-Fi prototyping phase (last phase) (Table 6) GUI-ii screen-sharing interview method is exceptionally difficult as the co-designer cannot interact with the software her/him self, and s/he can only see the shared screen via *Skype*. Also, they need to learn and remember the GUI elements in order to ask the designer to add it to the screen, it takes longer to accomplish the test.

Table 6. Test results from Hi-Fi prototyping phase

Sketching	GUI-ii Face-to-Face	GUI-ii Screen-Sharing at Lab	GUI-ii Ozlab at Lab	GUI-ii Ozlab Remote	Traditional Face-to-Face
Duration Per Component	High	Above Average	Average	Average	Very High
Willingness to Provide Information	Low	Average	High	Above Average	Below Average
Difficulty	High	Very High	Low	Below Average	Average
Cost	Average	Above Average	Very High	Low	Below Average

4.2 Comparison Charts

Here, we will demonstrate three comparison charts for interview methods. In Figure 1, y-axis represents the number of words that co-designer spoke out regarding each component in 15 minutes time slice, which represents the *willingness to provide information*. In Figure 2, y-axis is the amount of time co-designer spent to learn about the environment, struggle and/or asks questions regarding their problems with the interview tools on each 15-minute time slice, which represents the *difficulty*.

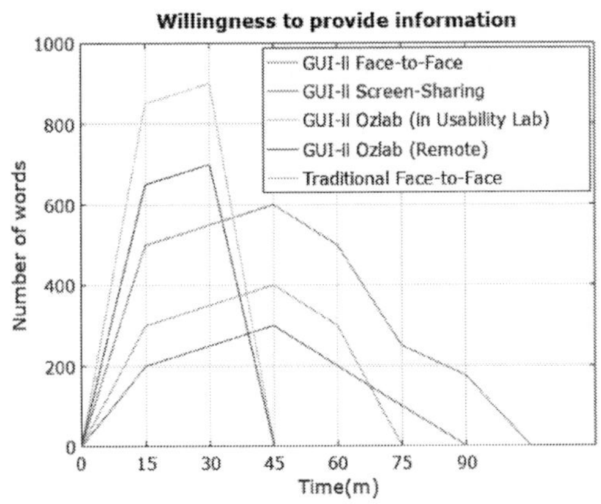

Figure 1. Willingness to talk every 15 minutes

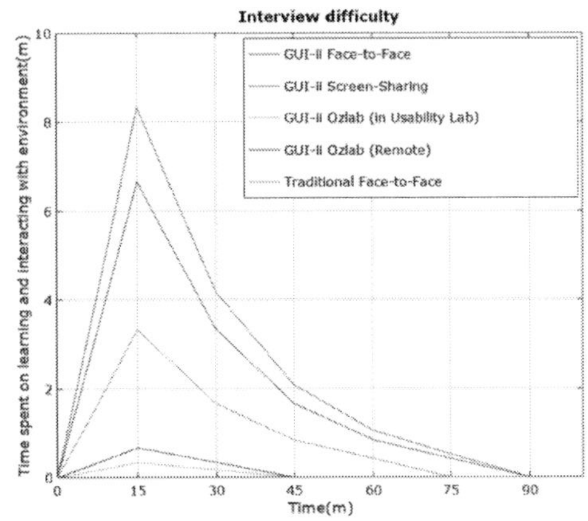

Figure 2. Difficulty every 15 minutes

According to Figure 1, both remote and in-lab approaches in GUI-ii Ozlab interview method has the highest *willingness to provide information* and it doesn't take long to finish the test. We can also see that if the interview takes longer than one hour, the co-designer lost his/her interest to provide more information as they become tired and exhausted. Furthermore, the sudden drop of "number of words" in GUI-ii Ozlab interview method is because even-though the test is finished but co-designers still had willing to provide us with more information.

The data in Figure 2 demonstrates which interview method is the most difficult to accomplish. As we can see GUI-ii screen-sharing method reached the peak point. Thus, on GUI-ii Ozlab method it is easier for the co-designer to interact with the system without frustration. We can also see it was easier for the co-designers to use the Ozlab web application at the Usability Lab, since the application was ready on the browser while they entered the room. For remote co-designers, there had to gain extra information on how the system works and how you should connect the system via the provided link.

With all the interactive GUI elements available today (such as dropdown menus, accordion menus, etc.) it's hard for co-designers to visually present all kinds of GUI elements on a paper. Hence, they choose to design a primitive GUI and it makes their sketch/prototype misleading.

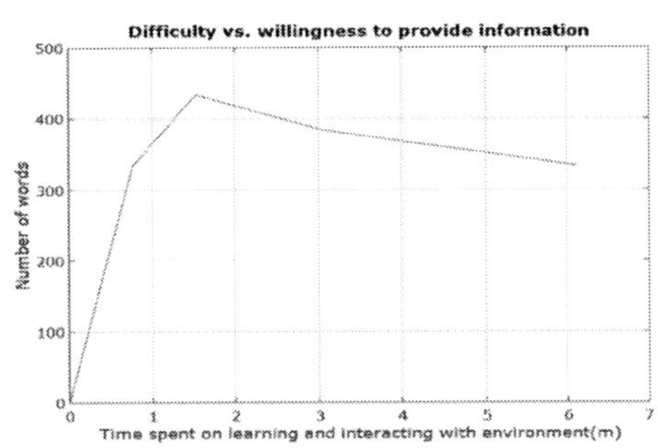

Figure 3. Effect of interview method's difficulty on co-designer's willingness to provide information

In Figure 3, we demonstrated the effect of interview method's *difficulty* versus co-designer's *willingness to provide information.* We can observe that when the duration of learning and interacting with the interview environment increases, the number of words the co-designer spoke out decreases. So, we can easily conclude that co-designer's *willingness to provide information* decreases when interview method's *difficulty* increase.

5. CONCLUSION

We analyzed the effects of three GUI-ii based interview methods as well as traditional face-to-face one, in four different phases of design and also compared the effects of the remote interviews versus lab-based ones. We compared each interview method from different perspective and proposed 4 comparison parameters: *duration per component, willingness to provide information, difficulty* and *cost.*

Besides, we studied the effect of interview method's difficulty on the co-designer's *willingness to provide information*. We also showed that co-designers tend to provide much more fruitful results when they are in a lab rather than during a remote interview. Moreover, during a face-to-face or a lab-based interview, co-designers were more motivated; either through designing or through think-aloud. However, it is important for the designers to check their available resources (i.e., budget, time and place) before conducting interviews.

This research study provides essential scale-based analysis tables and comparison charts to help future designers make more accurate assumptions when choosing different interview methods for each design phase.

ACKNOWLEDGEMENT

We would like to thank Prof. John Sören Pettersson, for his support and generosity to let us use the lab facilities. We would also like to say thanks to Fabian Jaskotka and Kai Langenekert for helping out in running the test.

REFERENCES

Baauw, E., Markopoulous, P., 2004. A comparison of think-aloud and post-task interview for usability testing with children, in: Proceeding of the 2004 Conference on Interaction Design and Children Building a Community - IDC '04. Presented at the Proceeding of the 2004 conference, ACM Press, Maryland, pp. 115–116.

Brush, A.J.B., Ames, M., Davis, J., 2004. A comparison of synchronous remote and local usability studies for an expert interface, in: Extended Abstracts of the 2004 Conference on Human Factors and Computing Systems - CHI '04. Presented at the Extended abstracts of the 2004 conference, ACM Press, Vienna, Austria, p. 1179.

Dimond, J.P., Fiesler, C., DiSalvo, B., Pelc, J., Bruckman, A.S., 2012. Qualitative data collection technologies: a comparison of instant messaging, email, and phone, in: Proceedings of the 17th ACM International Conference on Supporting Group Work - GROUP '12. Presented at the the 17th ACM international conference, ACM Press, Sanibel Island, Florida, USA, p. 277.

Gratch, J., Artstein, R., Lucas, G., Stratou, G., Scherer, S., Nazarian, A., Wood, R., Boberg, J., DeVault, D., Marsella, S., Traum, D., Rizzo, S., Morency, L.-P., 2014. The Distress Analysis Interview Corpus of human and computer interviews, in: Proceedings of the Ninth International Conference on Language Resources and Evaluation (LREC-2014). European Language Resources Association (ELRA), Reykjavik, Iceland.

Nielsen, J., Clemmensen, T., Yssing, C., 2002. Getting access to what goes on in people's heads?: reflections on the think-aloud technique, in: Proceedings of the Second Nordic Conference on Human-Computer Interaction - NordiCHI '02. Presented at the the second Nordic conference, ACM Press, Aarhus, Denmark, p. 101.

Pettersson, J.S., Siponen, J., 2002. Ozlab: a simple demonstration tool for prototyping interactivity, in: Proceedings of the Second Nordic Conference on Human-Computer Interaction - NordiCHI '02. Presented at the the second Nordic conference, ACM Press, Aarhus, Denmark, p. 295.

Pettersson, J.S., Wik, M., Andersson, H., 2018. GUI Interaction Interviews in the Evolving Map of Design Research, in: Paspallis, N., Raspopoulos, M., Barry, C., Lang, M., Linger, H., Schneider, C. (Eds.), Advances in Information Systems Development. Springer International Publishing, Cham, pp. 149–167.

Pettersson, J.S., Wik, M., Andersson, H., 2017. Wizards of Oz in the Evolving Map of Design Research – Trying to Frame GUI Interaction Interviews Supporting Development of Interactive Systems in Interactive Sessions, in: Information Systems Development: Advances in Methods, Tools and Management (ISD2017 Proceedings). Presented at the Information Systems Development: Advances in Methods, Tools and Management (ISD2017), Larnaca, Cyorus.

Preece, J., Rogers, Y., Sharp, H., 2015. Interaction design: beyond human-computer interaction, Fourth edition. ed. Wiley, Chichester.

Rettig, M., 1994. Prototyping for tiny fingers. Commun. ACM 37, 21–27.

Rubin, J.Z., Chisnell, D., 2008. Handbook of usability testing: how to plan, design, and conduct effective tests, 2. ed. ed. Wiley, Indianapolis, Ind.

Simonsen, J., Robertson, T. (Eds.), 2013. Routledge international handbook of participatory design, Routledge international handbooks. Routledge, London.

Spinuzzi, C., 2005. The Methodology of Participatory Design. Soc. Tech. Commun. 52, 163–174.

Steinfeld, A., Jenkins, O.C., Scassellati, B., 2009. The oz of wizard: simulating the human for interaction research, in: Proceedings of the 4th ACM/IEEE International Conference on Human Robot Interaction - HRI '09. Presented at the the 4th ACM/IEEE international conference, ACM Press, La Jolla, California, USA, p. 101.

THE DESIGNER'S ROLE IN REVITALIZED PARTICIPATORY DESIGN AGENDAS

Bernardo Alves Villarinho Lima and Leonelo Dell Anhol Almeida
Postgraduate Program in Technology and Society (PPGTE) - Federal University of Technology, Paraná (UTFPR)
Av. Sete de Setembro, 3165. Curitiba, PR – Brazil

ABSTRACT

Over the last four decades, Participatory Design (PD) gained traction in Human Computer Interaction (HCI) communities around the world. The discipline became recurrent in HCI publications, the tools and methods it offers present alternatives in attempts to design with persons, and not only for them. The PD research community is challenged by the notion that current practices focus on the production of artifacts, rather than designing for democracy and empowerment of partner communities. Countering technocratic trends, researchers around the world seek to renew the discipline by proposing alternative research agendas, towards a critical and politically engaged discipline. Designers present themselves as actors and actresses in these processes, and understanding how they operate can inform future works on how design practices can promote empowerment despite the power gap between participants and designers. This paper explores papers from the 2018 Participatory Design Conference (PDC), seeking state-of-the-art on how researchers perceive themselves in their practices, and proposes a set of suggestions on how to plan participation in a situated manner.

KEYWORDS

Participatory Design, Science, Technology and Society Studies, Critical Theory of Technology

1. INTRODUCTION

Participatory Design (PD) presents itself as an alternative to revert scenarios of disempowerment that entail the introduction of computational artifacts in living and work spaces (Bødker and Kyng 2018). The research field and development approach started in Scandinavian countries with a political commitment, which sought to support workers amidst rapid changes in technology occurring during the seventies (Emspak, 1993). Researchers and developers, referred to as designers, held the conviction that projects guided by strong partnerships between design teams and the communities that are affected by technological change would lead to improvements in the communities' quality of life and work (Bjerknes and Bratteteig, 1995) (Sundblad, 2011). Participation in projects rely on the application of methodological procedures that seek to involve stakeholders actively and directly, the procedures are termed Participatory Practices (Muller et al., 1997).

Among the contributions of the pioneering generations in PD were the use of prototypes of varied fidelities in different stages of development, and techniques for building legitimate spaces for participation and democracy. These contributions carry on to the following generations, and enable designers and partner communities to decide on technology in a meaningful and informed way. Moreover, the original co-design projects also investigated: the impact of computers in operational environments (Kensing and Blomberg, 1998); policies towards regulating technological change in work spaces; and means workers and managers can negotiate changes in productive processes (Ehn, 1990). The original participatory projects were focused on local action towards organizational policies, with an intent to side with the workers and potentially enable them to improve their own quality of life through negotiation and taking a measure of control over technological change from managers and business owners. Often, participation involved negotiation and re-design in order to build industrial spaces which accommodate both production demands and worker rights.

In its history, PD gained notoriety and its practices were appropriated by communities in diverse locales, approaching diverse research and development problems (Sundblad, 2011) (Schuler and Namioka, 1993). However, there are challenges and pitfalls, occasioned by disparities inherent to the roles of professional designer and partner community. According to Muller et al. (1997), designers can use participatory practices to exploit partners' work while giving no returns to their communities, and can deceive the communities in order to push their own design vision towards problems, rather than applying a collective vision.

The different needs of each community (be it designer or partner) change how PD is applied and what research and development matters it seeks. For instance, when imported to the United States from Scandinavia, PD would no longer hold worker's needs as its driving force, and would instead be driven by designing more efficient and more effective artifacts (Muller et al., 1997) (Spinuzzi, 2002). During the nineties in the US, leveraging partners' expertise in order to build better computer systems is justified by agendas that sought to improve results through artifacts, in lieu of changing politics in work environments, such as Contextual Design (Beyer and Holtzblatt, 1998). This approach adapts Scandinavian investigation and prototyping techniques in a way that discards the need to acknowledge conflicts of power inherent to technological change, imposing a technocratic vision over the introduction of new artifacts (Spinuzzi, 2002).

The beginning of the Participatory Design Conference (PDC) in 1990 promoted communication between European and North American designer communities, which contributed to an alignment of research agendas (Halskov and Hansen, 2015). Following the first PDC, the PD community's interest in making political commitments waned, not only because of the commercial results by Contextual Design and similar approaches, but also due to changes in Scandinavian politics (Bødker and Grønbæk 1992). PD during and after the nineties gained traction as a way to produce artifacts, but lost some of its original focus as a political mindset for collaboration and production of better quality of life to partner communities (Spinuzzi, 2002).

Moreover, and in spite of eventual alignments in research agendas, the development of technology and artifacts does not occur homogeneously in every designer community. The way of thinking about technology and design varies according to community and historical moment (Feenberg, 2000). There are movements that resist the alignment of research agendas. PD practitioners during the twenty-tens seek methods for promoting spaces for participation which integrate different cultural and historical situations, conflicts and contradictions as important parts of technological innovation, using disciplines beyond Computer Science and thinking beyond the introduction of artifacts (Björgvinsson et al., 2010) (Pihkala and Karasti, 2018).

Bødker and Kyng (2018) expose participatory and collaborative projects whose results bring a breath of fresh air to the discipline, and proposed a research agenda with the potential to "revitalize" it, returning PD to its roots as a way for taking political action through design. Upon the publication of the 2018 special edition of the ACM Transactions on Computer-Human Interaction, about re-thinking PD, researchers from many locales (e.g. Belgium (Huybrechts et al., 2018), Portugal (Teli et al., 2018), Australia and UK (Akama and Light 2018), China (Thinyane et al. 2018)) declared similar positionings: making a commitment to renew research agendas towards political issues relevant to their locations and communities.

Each research agenda is written in a different locale, since each community has its own thinking about PD (Halskov and Hansen, 2015). However, designers constantly have a primary role in starting PD processes (Kendall and Dearden 2018). In order to think about contextually aware design, it is necessary to consider that designers are submitted to power relations under which the act of designing operates (Feng and Feenberg 2008). Power gaps between designers and partners challenge the authenticity of participatory processes as a space for dialogue and innovation, and are a concern of the discipline (Boy, 1997).

Articulating agendas which situate design spaces and projects in society and culture, in opposition of agendas interlined by technological neutrality, present as an opportunity for the Science, Technology and Society Studies to contribute to Participatory Design (Thinyane et al. 2018) (Feng and Feenberg, 2008). Considering the designer's responsibility to promote democratic spaces, this paper presents an analysis of works from the 2018 edition of the PDC seeking to comprehend, in the state-of-the-art, how designers perceive themselves in their practices. From the findings, we also propose a set of suggestions regarding the planning of participatory practices that are aware of the designer's needs to position themselves politically.

This paper is organized as follows: section 2 exposes a comparative study of how the designer is viewed by authors of the 2018 edition of the PDC; section 3 proposes a set of suggestions for planning participatory practices; and section 4 closes this paper by presenting considerations, opportunities for future work.

2. VISIBLE DESIGNERS IN PARTICIPATORY DESIGN

A research agenda guides short and long term goals in research projects, by means of suggestions on what researchers must think about when making epistemological and methodological choices in their investigations.

Composing and articulating an agenda explicitly is a relevant step on elaborating any research project. An agenda can reinforce researchers to position themselves with precision when deciding actions in investigation. Agendas indicate perspectives and political positions, and are not exempt of reproducing technocratic visions (Feng and Feenberg, 2008). PD communities in many locales sought to re-think their research agendas in order to direct their action not only towards social demands, but also towards theories and technology that enables the exercise of the partners' personal power (Korsgaard, et al., 2016).

Writing an agenda which covers theoretical, methodological and technological questions whilst still being useful is a challenge, when trying to put in perspective every aspect in research, authors leave gaps which must be taken into consideration. In this paper, we focus on the designer's role as an exercise of self-reflection, assuming that the designer has a key role in beginning and sustaining participatory projects, as the designer's expertise guides important aspects of the technology in development. The differences between designer and partner are of interest to PD researchers, since participatory practices may reproduce forms of labor division (e.g. the partner's role in Contextual Design processes), and reducing all actors and actresses in participatory projects to a single category may not be possible in most academic participatory projects, as they may be in distinct groups with diverse needs (Bødker and Kyng, 2018).

For the discussion on the designer's role, we start by the seventeen full papers in the 2018 edition of the PDC (the latest at the time of writing). The conference is a core reference for research in PD, making it representative of the state-of-the-art in PD. The event's impact means that the research agendas discussed are given visibility, and have the potential to be adopted and adapted in future works.

Due to the number of papers, and diversity of topics approached by each work, we begin investigating by reading their abstracts, their introductions, and their last sections, in order to gather a set of works with content related to the designer's role in participatory projects and practices, seeking discussions that approach designers in a directly and explicitly. We present each of the six selected articles briefly:

- **Akama and Light (2018)** analyse their personal experience in preparing for participatory practices, exposing a view on how a designer acts during practice. The work argues that the interactions occurring during practice are unique, and depend on the collaborating people and their cultures. The authors offer two concepts to explain difficult aspects to elucidate in participatory practices: *poise*, which is a practitioner's positioning on the practice; and *punctuation*, which is how a practitioner positions themselves in relation to the partner community;
- **Huybrechts et al. (2018)** explored how Hannah Arendt's reflections on the political dimension of work can be employed in designing participation projects. Arendt's concept of "action", defined as undertaking the role of a politically active citizen in society, is a guide towards discussing and building democratic spaces that outlast the designers' stay;
- **Kendall and Dearden (2018)** assumed that the participatory process is inherently political, and explored a historical question in PD ("Who participates with whom and what and why?"), pointing towards challenges in working with PD in developing countries, eliciting disparities between designers and partners, exposing how participation can lose its purpose due to colonial relations;
- **Lodato and DiSalvo (2018)** work towards stratagems for using PD in public policies, signaling three challenges that restrict the success of PD projects: the design space; economical and budget restrictions; and differences in beliefs among institutions and designers;
- **Spiel et al. (2018)** investigate how designers make ethical decisions in their practices, signaling that each action the designer makes has implications in the practice's results, and suggest ways for power dynamics to compromise the actualization of participation and democracy in PD;
- **Thinyane et al. (2018)** used the Critical Theory of Technology as a lens to discuss PD, and state that practicing the approach without reflecting about socio-economic structures may perpetuate disempowerment even in participatory processes which successfully produce artifacts. The authors expose five barriers to effective participation: language, cultural factors, power dynamics, personality traits, and knowledge of technology.

The eleven works not considered for this discussion did not approach the designer's role explicitly, focusing on other topics, such as methodology for PD projects and practices, technological education, public awareness of science, and project result reports. The texts present and elaborate on the designer's role in participatory practices and projects. Each one has a different focus, the views exposed in each work are exposed on Table 1, which also includes whether the work is oriented towards instances of practice, towards whole project lifecycles, or both.

Table 1. An overview of the designer's role according to the selected papers

Work	Focus	The designer's role
Akama and Light (2018)	Practice	Each designer is unique. Personal histories, experiences, culture, and worldviews shape how they undertake challenges and practice PD. Designers configure the environments for participation, and their relationships with the partner communities (including mutual learning) and with their own research or products change over time during a project, in a way that makes each practice also unique.The uniqueness of each practice may generate unexpected situations, for which the designer must respond, on the risk of compromising the entire practice. A designer's judgement is an important tool, that must be used to give a practice its meaning.
Huybrechts et al. (2018)	Project and Practice	Designers can reintegrate work and social practices, which have become distant due to the current mode of production. The designer's role is to frame, support, and reactivate forms of public engagement and representation.
Kendall and Dearden (2018)	Project	Designers are political actors and actresses, abiding not only by institutional and ethical standards, but also by their own political views. A conscious effort is needed to make designers and their political standpoints visible in design processes. The designer acts under time and budget constraints that limit their stay in a project, but they will influence the direction of the project even after they leave. The designer participates into the world of the partner, and there are important ethical concerns about how much it is allowable for a partner to integrate the designer's world, to prevent participation from becoming exploitation.
Lodato and DiSalvo (2018)	Project	Institutions are constantly framing and constraining PD efforts, and designers need to be aware of how they conduct the research. Strategies for participation present in the literature, such as agonism, may not always be welcome in partner communities. Designers are responsible for developing ways for working with their partners.
Spiel et al. (2018)	Practice	PD is not inherently attentive to ethics, and designers must make explicit efforts in order to make ethical commitments. In conducting participatory practices, unexpected interpersonal situations may happen. The way a designer deals with the unexpected is essential to instancing legitimate participatory practices, as they must be careful in order to avoid contradicting ethical principles. In particular contexts, designers make ethical judgements continuously, as interpersonal interactions have a weight on participatory practice results.
Thinyane et al. (2018)	Practice	The power dynamics between partners and designers, and between individuals and technology are important for understanding the importance and effectiveness of a participatory practice. The designer must interact and engage with partners during practices, but there are barriers for promoting democratic participation and empowerment that must be considered during planning.

The selected works inform and signal perceptions of the PD community about the designer's role as an important political agent in participation, reinforcing that the field leverages the differences between designer and partner as a factor that shapes practice. The texts point that designers positioning themselves politically have the potential to enable meaningful technological innovation by means of participation.

The selection also presents other current and important concerns of the PD community, which are linked to building spaces for participation: the project's durability; ethics in participation; communication barriers between designer and partner. The content in all six works brings a series of recommendations to support designers in thinking technological, ethical, and political matters during participatory practices. The position of each paper approaches a different part of what makes a participatory practice. It is possible, therefore, to gather their decision points and compose a comprehensive set of suggestions on how state-of-the-art PD practices can promote participation in thinking about technology beyond its materialization in artifacts, considering also the way which partners can learn how to make and maintain technology.

3. PRACTICING CO-DESIGN IN REVITALIZED AGENDAS

In a current scenario of disempowerment in relation to the use, adoption and change in technological artifacts, producing technology through PD can be an alternative for communities to improve their lives whilst being out of the technology industry's agenda. Choosing a participatory approach to a problem, however, will not immediately create definitive solutions for disempowerment. Many participatory projects conclude without the desired results, and without the changes to the *status quo* that the approach prescribes (Bødker and Kyng, 2018). The PD community has grown conscious of the limitations in their current agendas, and by thinking about the designer inside practice spaces, it is possible to reckon how to promote participation and empowerment considering disparities between designer and partner. This section presents reflections on the reviewed works, and attempts to articulate them into a set of suggestions on factors they approach.

Upon reading all selected works, we propose a way to organize the suggestions in their agendas. Through the review, we consider three core dimensions for PD agendas: a political dimension; an ethical dimension; and a technological dimension. The dimensions we considered were based on the contents of the papers selected in the review. Bødker and Kyng's (2018) work was a methodological reference in assembling the three dimensions, and each dimension attempts to consider the PD That Matters agenda their work presents. Each dimension presents a set of suggestions towards: promoting the empowerment of partner communities; conscious choice of technology; and participation as a mutual learning process between partners and designers. These suggestions are not prescriptive or final, but may serve as a starting point for discussing the designer's role in projects and practices, and are as follows:

- Political dimension
  - **Building democratic dialogue spaces is as important as building artifacts**: reconnecting PD to improving work and quality of life can be achieved by building democratic spaces for dialogues, that can be made to outlast the designers' stay in a community. The spaces can also be co-designed using participatory practices (Huybrechts et al., 2018b). Tackling the challenge of making a participatory project continue after designers leave the partner community is as relevant to the promotion of legitimate participations as the production of artifacts (Kendall and Dearden 2018). This challenge is a concern to new PD agendas (Bødker and Kyng, 2018) as creating means for people of different hierarchical positions to discuss on an equal footing is never a trivial undertaking, but helps PD contributions along their core goals;
  - **Participatory practices are a conflictual environment**: in a participatory practice, each stakeholder has different needs and goals, making PD a discipline that needs to deal with conflict if it seeks to tension power relations and change who gets to decide technology. Considering conflict as a driving force for change can make designers integrate them to the practices (Kendall and Dearden 2018), though some preparation should always be in order for dealing with them (Akama and Light 2018). Conflicts represent opportunities for mutual learning among people in the practice space, but can also be hurdles for making meaningful change and promoting democracy (Thinyane et al. 2018). Considering conflicts may point to challenges and opportunities for participation, and not taking any conflict into consideration is a means for abstaining from making political commitments, and would be a repetition of historic HCI agendas, that sought to universalize people as "end-users" (Satchell and Dourish, 2009);
- Ethical Dimension
  - **Contextual and cultural differences make or break the practice**: each person, be it designer or partner, has a personal and cultural history, as well as some life experience before participating in a project (Feng and Feenberg 2008). In collaborating with many people, each singular personal history may contribute with information for co-design (Huybrechts et al., 2018b). Thinking about why interpersonal conflicts exist, for example, may direct participation towards a more ethic form, that would fall for PD's historic pitfalls of exploitation, manipulation, and illusion (Muller et al., 1997). For example, Kendall and Dearden (2018) explore how historical processes of colonialism influence PD projects;
  - **Interpersonal interactions in a participatory practice matter**: the way which a designer responds to conflicts and unexpected situations in practice is a point considered in new PD agendas (Akama and Light 2018). Interpersonal relationships which occur during practice influence the results, and building trust is an important part of working with a partner community

(Spiel et al., 2018). Each detail in the practice's procedure influences the relations between people in practice, and it is possible for the designer to prepare for working on the community (Akama and Light 2018). However, this effort of preparation is not a guarantee of success, as some interactions that are not usually documented in technical reports (e.g. appearance) may still change project results (Spiel et al., 2018) (Kendall and Dearden 2018);

- Technological dimension
  - **A participatory project may not fit to paper format**: durability is an important factor for PD projects (Kendall and Dearden 2018), and is key for focusing contributions towards more ambitions societal and technological changes (Bødker and Kyng, 2018). Enabling meaningful and lasting change is a challenge for PD, as research and participation are situated inside extremely complex social systems (Huybrechts et al., 2018b). The surroundings, past issues, practice results, consequences, and people involved in a participatory process may not entirely fit in a paper format, specially considering durable participatory processes are meant to continue without the designer's presence and intervention; and
  - **Mutual learning emerges from practice**: participation is a means for designers and partner communities to mutually learn about technology (e.g. how to build artifacts that make sense and tackle real issues, how to think about the consequences of a technology to a community, what is each community's history, how is their daily lives), these moments of learning can emerge from unexpected moments during conversation (Spiel et al., 2018) (Akama and Light 2018). This unexpected learning can help adjust ongoing and future practices, and can inform partner communities about how to produce technology, even without the designer's say. Technological education is an important form PD researchers have for returning results to the communities.

4. CONSIDERATIONS

This paper sought to comprehend how current PD practitioners perceive themselves in their practices amidst a moment of renewal and re-thinking of participation. The paper places the designer's comprehension in three dimensions, ethics, and exposes important points of reflection in each dimension. We identified that using participation to produce artifacts is losing space in favor of applying PD with shifted core goals, such as building legitimate democratic dialogue spaces and promoting technological education. The durability and sustainability of PD projects is also a prominent issue and concern, and is considered an important factor for making contributions that are meaningful and lasting.

The three dimensions for situating designers in their practices can be used as a lens to approach the issues exposed by Bødker and Kyng (2018). We made an exercise in how thinking in the three dimensions and acting on the suggestions might help counter issues the authors signaled in current PD projects:

1. **The excessive focus on here-and-now** is countered by considering PD as being more than the collaborative production of artifacts, as shown by Thinyane et al. (2018), and by thinking in project durability, as exposed by Huybrechts et al. (2018). Thinking about the future, however, does not abstain designers from co-designing artifacts that work, as working artifacts build trust in the partner community and give more meaning to participatory practices. The technological dimension discussed in the previous section can be an instrument to mitigate this issue, as to help active efforts to consider the consequences of a practice or a project;
2. **The low technological ambitions** emerge as a consequence of thinking about technology as only artifacts, not as a way for employing rationality to think about new ways to transform reality. Considering technological education as an important means for giving back to partners is in itself a higher technological ambition (Lodato and DiSalvo, 2018). PD has the potential to offer more than better artifacts, and it can operate on callings to change politics and technology according to the participants' needs, without the need to design technology that would not necessarily be accessible to them (Thinyane et al., 2018). The technological and political dimensions may be useful towards thinking about this issue, as they relate to recognize technology as more than artifacts;
3. **The non-confrontational do-gooding** is a consequence of an ideology in PD research that considers it as being inherently good, and above discussions about technological neutrality. Thinking about power relations, history, and the surroundings of practice and design may help seeing PD as part of a

productive system where disempowerment occur, breaking the illusion of goodness the field carries (Spiel et al.,2018)) (Lodato and DiSalvo, 2018). The ethical and political dimensions are important to dismiss this ideology, as they consider PD not as inherently good, or even ethical. Promoting empowerment through practice is the responsibility of designers, and understanding where disempowerment stems from is an important consideration for a legitimate process;

4. **The politics being reduced to ethics** is tensioned by thinking about the personal histories of each partner, and about PD as a space for conflict. Approaches with agonistic views are common in PD research (Björgvinsson et al., 2010), and present ways for embracing conflict as a critical and essential part to the quality of a contribution. The political dimension considers participation as a space for contention, and we believe this is a way to disentangle politics and ethics.

The set of suggestions this paper presents indicates that the international PD community has intent to advance their agendas towards renewed political concerns. This paper's contribution is on punctuating them in a concise and practice-oriented way, enabling designers to express their positionings explicitly in relation to their research agendas. In practice, the differences between agendas exist in implementation details, which are important as they influence practice results. The suggestions here presented can be expanded upon when more projects are reported. This renewal of agendas and advancements of the discipline are still only beginning, and we cannot predict where this revitalization is headed towards.

Proposing techniques and participatory practices that consider all dimensions is an opportunity for future works, as the applicability of agendas made by other communities may be limited by cultural and social factors in different locales. Comprehending the current situation of PD agendas in each locale is a need for proposing novel ways for designing with people, building not only computer systems that work according to the partner community's needs, but also dialogue and democracy spaces, as well as education about technological change and its implications.

REFERENCES

Akama, Y. and Light, A., 2018. Practices of readiness: Punctuation, poise and the contingencies of participatory design. *Proceedings of the 15th Participatory Design Conference: Full Papers - Volume 1*. New York, NY, pp. 13:1-13:12.

Beyer, H. and Holtzblatt, K., 1998. *Contextual Design: Defining Customer-centered Systems*. Morgan Kaufmann Publishers Inc., San Francisco, USA.

Bjerknes, G. and Bratteteig, T., 1995. User participation and democracy: A discussion of scandinavian research on systems development. In *Scandinavian Journal of Information Systems*, 7(1):73-98.

Björgvinsson, E. et al, 2010. Participatory design and "democratizing innovation". *Proceedings of the 11th Biennial Participatory Design Conference*, pp. 41-50, New York, USA

Boy, Guy A., 1997. The group elicitation method for participatory design and usability testing. *Interactions*. Vol. 4(2). pp 27-33.

Bødker, S. and Kyng, M., 2018. Participatory design that matters – facing the big issues. *ACM Transactions on Computer-Human Interaction*, Vol. 25(1), pp 4:1-4:31.

Bødker, S. and Grønbæk, K., 1992. Design in action: From prototyping by demonstration to cooperative prototyping. *Design at Work: Cooperative Design of Computer Systems*, pp 197–218.

Ehn, P., 1990. *Work-Oriented Design of Computer Artifacts*. L. Erlbaum Associates Inc., Hillsdale, USA.

Emspak, F., 1993. Workers, unions, and new technology. In *Participatory Design – Principles and Practices*, pp 13-26. CRC Press, Florida, USA.

Feenberg, A., 2000. From essentialism to constructivism: Philosophy of technology at the crossroads. *Technology and the good life*, pp 294–315.

Feng, P. and Feenberg, A., 2008. *Thinking about Design: Critical Theory of Technology and the Design Process*, pp 105-118. Springer Netherlands, Dordrecht.

Halskov, K. and Hansen, N. B., 2015. The diversity of participatory design research practice at PDC 2002–2012. *International Journal of Human-Computer Studies*, Vol. 74, pp 81- 92.

Huybrechts, L. et al, 2018. Work, labour and action: The role of participatory design in (re)activating the political dimension of work. *Proceedings of the 15th Participatory Design Conference: Full Papers - Volume 1*, pp 1–11, New York, USA.

Huybrechts, L. et al, editors, 2018b. PDC '18: *Proceedings of the 15th Participatory Design Conference: Full Papers - Volume 1*, New York, USA.

Kendall, L. and Dearden, A., 2018. Disentangling participatory ict design in socioeconomic development. *Proceedings of the 15th Participatory Design Conference: Full Papers - Volume 1*, pp 1-12, New York, USA.

Kensing, F. and Blomberg, J.,1998. Participatory design: Issues and concerns. *Computer Supported Cooperative Work*, Vol. 7, No. 3, pp 167–185.

Korsgaard, H. et al, 2016. Computational alternatives in participatory design: Putting the t back in socio-technical research. *Proceedings of the 14th Participatory Design Conference: Full Papers - Volume 1*, pp 71–79, New York, USA.

Muller, M. J. et al, 1997. Participatory practices in the software lifecycle. In Helander, M. G., Landauer, T. K., and Prabhu, P. V., editors, *Handbook of human-computer interaction*, pp 256–300. North-Holland.

Pihkala, S. and Karasti, H., 2018. Politics of mattering in the practices of participatory design. *Proceedings of the 15th Participatory Design Conference: Short Papers, Situated Actions, Workshops and Tutorial - Volume 2*, pp 13:1–13:5, New York, USA.

Satchell, C. and Dourish, P., 2009. Beyond the user: Use and non-use in hci. *Proceedings of the 21st Annual Conference of the Australian Computer-Human Interaction Special Interest Group: Design: Open 24/7*, pp 9–16, New York, USA.

Schuler, D. and Namioka, A., editors, 1993. Participatory Design: Principles and Practices. L. Erlbaum Associates Inc., Hillsdale, USA.

Spiel, K. et al, 2018. Microethics for participatory design with marginalised children. *Proceedings of the 15th Participatory Design Conference: Full Papers - Volume 1*, pages 17:1-17:12, New York, USA.

Spinuzzi, C., 2002. A scandinavian challenge, a us response: Methodological assumptions in scandinavian and us prototyping approaches. *Proceedings of the 20th Annual International Conference on Computer Documentation, SIGDOC '02*, pp 208-215, New York, USA.

Sundblad, Y., 2011. Utopia: Participatory design from scandinavia to the world. In Impagliazzo, J., Lundin, P., and Wangler, B., editors, *History of Nordic Computing 3*, pp 176–186. Springer Berlin Heidelberg. Berlin, Heidelberg.

Teli, M. et al, 2018. Institutioning the common: The case of commonfare. *Proceedings of the 15th Participatory Design Conference: Full Papers - Volume 1*, pp 6:1–6:11, New York, USA.

Thinyane, M. et al, 2018. Critical participatory design: Reflections on engagement and empowerment in a case of a community based organization. *Proceedings of the 15th Participatory Design Conference: Full Papers - Volume 1*, pp 2:1–2:10, New York, USA.

'THINKING THROUGH THINGS' TO SUPPORT COOPERATIVE DESIGN IN THE DEVELOPMENT OF TECHNOLOGY TO SUPPORT HEALTH & WELLBEING

Paul Chamberlain[1], Claire Craig[2] and Nick Dulake[3]
[1]*Prof., Sheffield Hallam University*
[2]*Dr., Sheffield Hallam University*
[3]*Sheffield Hallam University*
Cantor building, 153 Arundel Street, Sheffield, S1 2NU, UK

ABSTRACT

Literature highlights that the reason for non-acceptance of health technologies is complex (Sligo et al. 2017, Standing et al. 2018, Bentley et al, 2014). The context where the technologies will operate and how they relate to the end users' lives are key factors to uptake and utilization. A number of researchers have suggested that the poor design of many devices and subsequent non-uptake may be directly attributed to the failure of technologists to engage end users and elicit understanding of their requirements. To date few studies have articulated how this might be achieved. This paper describes the outcomes of the first phase of a Horizon 2020 project, which adopted a participatory design research method, called 'exhibition in a box' developed by the authors which is predicated on 'thinking with things'. Over one hundred older people across four countries participated in the study, which sought to develop a virtual digital coach to support active ageing. This paper discusses the themes that arose in relation to the barriers and enablers to engagement with technology as identified by participants within the study. It critically reflects on the strengths and challenges of the co-design methodology.

KEYWORDS

Design, Co-Design, Design for Health and Wellbeing, Health Technology

1. INTRODUCTION

Declining mortality rates mean higher life expectancies globally. In 2015 there were 901 million people aged 60 years and over worldwide. By 2050 it will have increased to 2.1 billion or 21.3% of the global population (DESA 2017). This ageing population and the resultant pressure on healthcare capacity and changing roles and expectations are driving demand for innovative solutions to support independence at home for people living with long term conditions and disability. Digital technologies are being seen as a way to respond to these challenges and as a consequence the way in which medical and healthcare is delivered is being transformed (EU 2018).

Much of the focus of technology to date has been on medical device development with a particular emphasis on products that measure to record data relating to physical functioning (e.g. blood pressure, heart rate, pulse-oxygen). However, more recently there has been an increased recognition of the link between social isolation, loneliness and reduced life expectancy (Bhatti et al 2017, Holt-Lundstad et al 2015) and this has led to a growing emphasis on policies to address the social dimension of health.

Alongside these changes, a paradigm shift has occurred within health that places greater emphasis on self-management and health promotion. Here responsibility is given to the individual to recognize and manage the symptoms of their condition (Lorig and Holman, 2004). Approaches that support a more pro-active approach and that do not rely on health and social care services are being promoted globally. Models of healthy and active ageing with a focus on the multi-stage life are replacing previous conceptualizations of ageing predicated on decline and withdrawal from society. Within this new paradigm technology can play a key role in offering integrated solutions to promote on-going engagement in meaningful activity and promote community connectedness.

Whilst technology can potentially have a significant impact on health and wellbeing, to date the uptake of digital health technologies has been problematic in a number of wide-scale studies (Steventon et al 2015). Literature highlights that the reason for non-acceptance is complex. Authors have cited confidence, the stigmatizing aesthetics of products, meaningfulness of technology in the broader context of the persons' life, ease of use and integration into everyday routines as important factors (Bentley et al 2014, Hanson et al 2010).

1.1 Aims of the Research

Novel Empowering Solutions and Technologies for Older People to Retain Everyday Life Activities (NESTORE) is a Horizon 2020 funded project focusing on a technological innovation to enable individuals to engage in health promoting activities as they age. The innovation is conceptualized as a 'friend, a companion and coach' seeking to valorize the capabilities of the older person, to recognize and support them in maximizing their abilities and to experience mental, physical and cognitive wellbeing. NESTORE is intended to promote choice, to educate, to signpost to opportunities, to connect individuals to community facilities and resources and to promote on-going social connectedness throughout the life-course. The system is not a medical device. Rather, it seeks to promote wellbeing through enabling the person to identify and reflect on current lifestyle choices and to access opportunities to engage in meaningful health promoting activities. To develop a solution fit for purpose it is therefore necessary to build understanding of what end users identify as being meaningful and the qualities and characteristics the technology needs to possess. The role of the design is to better understand the broader physical and social environments in which services and technologies will operate and how they relate to the contexts of the end-user. These insights are then communicated to the technologists in the development of the end product. The methodological approach followed in NESTORE provided for users to be involved in the design and development of the solution throughout the project duration.

The Consortium responsible for undertaking the research comprises of sixteen partners from eight European countries. Research expertise includes: design, health (psychology, medicine, nutrition), engineering, business and technology. These partners span Higher Education Institutions and Industry. The overall study is divided into 4 distinct phases. Phase one of the research utilizes participatory research methods and is focused on developing cultural and behavioural insights related to technology, initially in the United Kingdom. Phase two extends and develops this participatory methodology to focus on the materiality, interaction and usability issues related to the NESTORE system. Co-design groups in the Netherlands, Italy and Spain extend cultural insights and test the transferability of the methodology. Phase three of the study then supports the development of prototypes and product through an iterative process. Phase four of the research comprises of a pilot study with 60 participants across Italy, Netherlands and Spain.

1.2 Methods of Engagement

Participatory methods are centred on the principle that participant engagement can provide value throughout research planning and implementation, yielding findings that directly reflect on a community's needs and perceptions. Participants are given an active role, allowing them to shape the direction and methods of the research itself. Multiple benefits are associated with the use of participatory methods including developing collaborative and productive partnerships with participants, providing participants with a voice and harnessing participant engagement to stimulate positive change and the design of better products. Within this study, co-design was defined as creativity of designers and people not trained in design working together in the design development process. From the outset of the research it was envisaged that as the project evolved multiple levels of engagement and participation would occur. For instance, in the earlier stages of the research, individuals would be actively involved in the co-design of the products whilst at other points participants would play more of a role in providing feedback and reflections on the products being developed.

The overall study design followed the UK Design Council's Double Diamond with the initial phases of the research interrogating the requirements of the product by adopting a more exploratory approach, asking questions, conceptualizing possibilities rather than offering solutions. (figure 1)

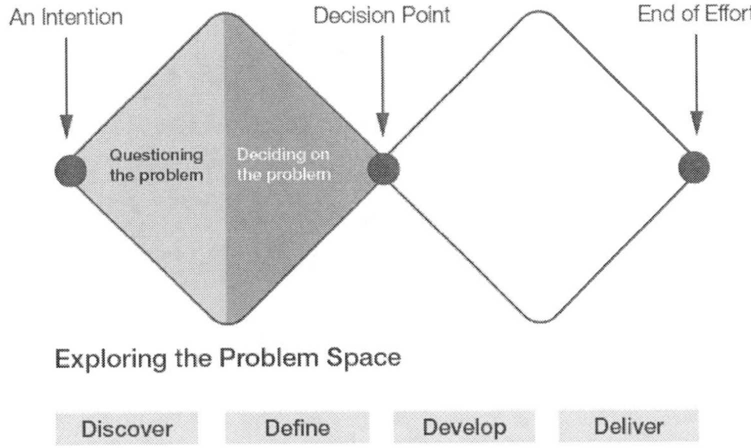

Figure 1. Design Council (UK) Double Diamond

2. DESIGN OF THE RESEARCH

This paper describes phases one and two of the study which sought to explore the problem space. The first of these phases was undertaken in the United Kingdom with the aim of inviting community living older people to engage in a co-design process to build understanding of user requirements of the technology, identify factors that promote and inhibit use and explore potential contexts where technologies would be used.

Phase two of the research was then undertaken in the partner countries of Spain, Italy and the Netherlands. The same co-design methodology was used with groups of community living older people in these countries with the addition that themes from the first phase of the study were shared to build understanding of the potential for transferability. The aims of this phase were therefore to: build understanding of the similarities/differences in requirements of older people in these countries; to test and understand the transferability of the methodology developed.

As part of this element of the study, a group of older people was recruited and actively engaged in analyzing data generated from the research.

3. METHODS

Co-design methods in NESTORE drew on an existing body of work developed by the authors (Chamberlain and Roddis, 2003 Chamberlain and Yoxall 2012, Chamberlain and Craig 2013) which used objects and artefacts as methods to stimulate and scaffold thinking, offering valuable vehicles through which the complexities of lives can be understood. The concept of exhibition is embedded within the culture of art and design and has a long history as a form of gathering employed to prompt academic discourse.

Exhibition in a box (Chamberlain and Craig 2013) takes the form of nine objects defined through user work-shops across multiple research projects. The objects have been carefully selected to code, represent and prompt further discussion on themes that have emerged through earlier research. The objects form the basis of an exhibition, contained in a box (figure 2) a la Duchamp that can be transported to diverse environs including the home. Just as exhibition pieces invite individuals to express ideas and opinions and to articulate deeply held values and opinions so the objects provide an opportunity for participants to express their emotional responses, to respond to and describe things of importance in the context of the research theme.

Figure 2. Exhibition in a box

Whilst traditional qualitative research methods using structured and semi-structured interviews can preference the views of the researcher who can make assumptions about what the issues are, Exhibition in a box offers participants the space to reflect, discuss, explore and define the questions that reflect their priorities. The objects offer scaffolds for communication because at one and the same time they are both concrete and abstract.

4. THE STUDY

4.1 Phase One

Ethical approval for the study was granted from Sheffield Hallam University's Ethics Committee in October 2017. Between October 2017 - January 2018 a convenience sample of 82 older user representatives were recruited from across organizations across the city of Sheffield based in the north of England to participate in a series of NESTORE co-design workshops.

Inclusion criteria for the study were that participants should be community living older people aged 50 and over; Individuals able to give informed consent; people who had some degree of familiarity with the use of technology (reflecting future groups of people who may use NESTORE).

Workshops were facilitated across a number of different venues including community centres, people's homes, and the user-laboratory space within the University. Each workshop lasted on average between one to two hours. The workshops began with a general introduction from the research team and an invitation for participants to share (verbally) activities they engaged in and found meaningful, with a particular focus on hobbies or leisure. Exhibition in a box was then introduced and participants were invited, in turn, to select and use the object to explore their ideas further (this might relate to the objects form, its sensory quality or a more metaphorical use). This was shared with the broader group. Participants were then invited to share associations that came to mind when they heard the word technology. Again, the critical artefacts were used to explore and interrogate these themes further. With permission, each workshop was audio-recorded and then transcribed

These transcriptions were then shared with a group of ten older people in the UK who formed an expert group for NESTORE (figure 3). During a one day workshop these individuals were engaged in a process of identifying the main themes from the overall data collection and identifying the most important factors in relation to considerations and user requirements of NESTORE. These were; Privacy, Empowerment, Fits my life, Personalization, Cost, Freedom, Ergonomics, Reliability, Observation, Connectedness, Security, Infrastructure, Being social, Engaging, Keeping active.

Figure 3. Expert group UK

4.2 Phase Two

A similar methodology was adopted in workshops with older people in each of the partner countries (Milan, Barcelona, Delft). Nominated members of the country partner NESTORE team facilitated each workshop. All took part in earlier briefing meetings with the UK team prior to the workshop and workshops were delivered in the local language. The UK team was present and contributed to the workshop with translation support. A convenience sample of 30 older people across the 3 countries took part in this phase of the research (Figure 4 & 5).

Workshop participants engaged in the thinking through things method with exhibition in a box sharing their personal insights into what is meaningful in their lives and their opinions and relationships with technology. The second part of the workshop focused on the priorities identified from the user workshops conducted in the UK. Participants were collectively asked to reflect on each of these and whether they agreed or disagreed with their validity in the context of what NESTORE should consider in its development and application. In addition the participants were asked if there were any themes they felt were missing from the list.

Figure 4. Co-design workshops Milan

Figure 5. Co-design workshops Delft

5. RESULTS

Findings from phase one of the study were found to be congruent across countries with a few minor differences mainly concerning the politics of how NESTORE might be appropriated (distributed through current health systems and regulations) and a call for NESTORE to be underpinned by research. There were no significant cultural differences however it was noted that climate and environment should be carefully considered in how it might impact on lifestyles. The workshops were conducted during the winter period with extreme cold weather in the UK and the Netherlands in contrast with mild pleasant weather in Italy and Spain. This has significant bearing on the ability for people to engage in outdoor activities.

Attitudes to and responses to technology across all workshops were polarized. Digital technologies were seen as mechanisms through which to access information, and to offer vehicles and opportunities for new learning and to connect to interests. At the same time individuals framed technology as having potential detrimental affects on health and posing a threat to the present way of life. Barriers to engaging in technology included the speed of change leading to challenges in new learning at a point of cognitive decline, questions relating to privacy and trust in terms of who is able to access and use the data generated and the reliability of the technology and the information and readings created. Prohibitive costs and lack of technological infrastructures were also seen as challenges. Design considerations, which were identified as supporting engagement and adoption, included the potential for personalization, portability, durability and considerations in relation to ergonomics. Features that promoted control and the building of self-efficacy were also valued. An aesthetic that was fit for purpose, as according to Dieter Rams 'good design is aesthetic' (Rosenfield 2012). A visual language that expresses reliability and durability for example, was identified as an important aspect in the design of NESTORE.

Above all it was necessary to consider how technology relates to other elements of the person's life and how it fits with self-concept and value system. Specific design considerations identified by individuals participating in the study are described as follows:

The ability to **personalize** the technology was by far the most desirable design consideration expressed in this element of the research This was seen as a way to counter the uniformity of existing technology and to enable participants to create a sense of identity and ownership.

Because one of the things about this tech, which you've just been alluding to then, is that it's identifiable with you, isn't it? You make your decisions on what you'd like.

If personalization and the ability to adapt and shape the technology reflected the owners personality then the opposite was true in relation to the operation of digital devices. Participants identified the need above all for **consistency in design**, in the symbols used on controls across products. The following quote was typical of a number of responses:

you have no idea of what the symbols mean, and the lack of consistency around design, where you suddenly go – is that making it hotter or is that making it colder? I have no idea.

These characteristics both align with and validate existing usability guidelines for IT systems (Rajanen, (Marghescu) 2009).

Portability was another design consideration. Older people in our study enjoyed travel and pursuits in the locality and did not want to be tied to the home or to a particular room in the house. Within this size and weight were both factors as the following quotes reflect:

Fancy carrying that around! When you've got so much shopping and so much else in your life, that you feel as though you must have this huge thing.

Participants valued design features to promote **control and self-efficacy**. Individuals, for instance were clear that not being dependent on others to update the device or change batteries should be a consideration especially if the aim of the technology was to increase self-efficacy. Participants also appreciated the choice and option to have time to disconnect from technology and there was much discussion about feelings in relation to using systems that were completely automated. There were mixed views in terms of whether devices should have multiple functions or whether a single piece of technology should have a single function. This extensive quote encapsulates the dilemma:

I'm not striving to have that mobile phone that can take the best pictures, If I'm taking a photo, I want an ordinary camera. For me a phone is not something that's counting how many steps I do, it's something that when I need to make a call or text something, I do. I like its separateness. I'm not comfortable with this race to have everything on your wrist, sort of social interaction. I don't know, it just doesn't feel right to me.

One unexpected theme that emerged during this phase of the research was discussion across three of the workshops relating to the **potential negative impact technology** may have on health. Concern was expressed as to whether a focus on measurement of health behaviours (pedometers, step counters) could result in the focus being on the behaviour rather than the activity itself.

another woman a couple of weeks ago. She'd got one. And she was saying oh I've only done 7,000 and something, and I really need to fit in... I thought, it's gone 8 o'clock, what the hell? Surely there's something more meaningful that you can do with your life than count up a few more steps, so you get this magic 10,000.

A number of strengths in relation to the exhibition in a box method were identified. The objects transcended boundaries of culture, language and age and whilst the objects remained unchanging the associations they prompted and the stories they elicited were dynamic and ever changing. Across the various workshop/focus groups different objects elicited the same themes of conversation. Particularly powerful were the key which very much related to security and the dice which participants used to talk about parity of access. Participants shared rich descriptions of their attitudes towards and experiences of technology and a depth of information was offered within the first few minutes of the workshop beginning. Older people expressed appreciation of the tangibility of the objects and their sensory qualities, acting as a physical prompt. The method also enabled individuals to achieve some distance when sharing more personal stories by 'speaking through the objects' or using the objects metaphorically. Rather than being dependent on fixed interview schedules whereby the researcher had pre-defined questions the method very much preferenced the views of participants. This is integral to the co-design process. Finally, individuals participating in the workshops expressed enjoyment of the experience and reflected on their learning and the new insights they had gained through the process. This positive experience led to an expressed interest in participating in other elements of the study.

6. DISCUSSION AND CONCLUSION

This research study aimed to inform the design and development of NESTORE a digital platform and tangible interface which seeks to promote wellbeing through enabling the person to identify and reflect on current lifestyle choices and to access opportunities to engage in meaningful health promoting activities. In response to an ageing population and growing pressures on health services digital technologies are seen as a solution to these challenges. However there is to date limited uptake of health technologies with literature suggesting lack of user engagement being a significant reason for this. Whilst the literature is clear in terms of the importance of involving end users from the beginning of the design process in collective imagining, few papers exist of ways to accomplish this. Traditional qualitative research methods using structured and semi-structured interviews can preference the views of the researcher who can make assumptions about what the issues are. This can be particularly challenging when seeking to imagine facets of products that have yet to be created. Within this study, Exhibition in a Box provided a tangible tool to offer participants a space to reflect, discuss, explore and begin to envision the qualities and characteristics NESTORE might need to possess. Finding ways to involve people authentically within research is important and Exhibition in a box offers a useful method for engagement where researcher and participant enter a space on equal terms and individuals are literally able to think and talk through things.

The next phase of the research brings the design team and expert users together with the technologists, and through a series of co-design events creatively translate these user requirements into tangible interactive prototypes.

ACKNOWLEDGEMENT

This research was supported through the European Commission's H2020 programme.

REFERENCES

Bentley C, Powell L, Orrell A, Mountain G. (2014) Addressing design and suitability barriers to telecare use: has anything changed? *Technol Disabil.* 26(4):221–35.

Bhatti A B and Haq A (2017) The pathophysiology of perceived social isolation: effects on health and mortality. *Cureus* Jan 24 doi: 10.7759/cureus.994

Chamberlain, P, Craig, C (2013) Engagingdesign, Methods for Collective Creativity, *Human-Computer Interaction. Human-Centred Design Approaches, Methods, Tools, and Environments*. Volume 8004 of the series Lecture Notes in Computer Science pp 22-31

Chamberlain, P, Roddis, J. (2003) - 'Making sense', *The Design Journal*, Volume 6, issue 1, Ashgate Publications Ltd. England. ISBN 0-7546-0910

Chamberlain, P., Yoxall, A., "Of Mice and Men. The Role of Interactive Exhibitions as Re- search Tools for Inclusive Design". Vol. 15, Issue 1. pp 57-78. Ashgate Publications (2012)

DESA (2017) *World Population Prospects, key findings and advance tables*. New York. United Nations.

EU (2018) *The Silver Economy*: Luxembourg. Publications Office of the European Union.

Hanson V L (2010) Influencing technology adoption of older adults. *Interacting with Computers 22 pp502-509*

Holt-Lundstad J, Sith T B, Baker, M., Harris T and Stephenson D (2015) Loneliness and social Isolation as risk factors for mortality: a meta-analytic review. *Perspectives on Psychological Science vol 10 (2) p227-237.*

Rosenfield. K. "Dieter Rams 10 Principles of "Good Design"" 09 Jan 2012. ArchDaily. Accessed 19 Jun 2019. <https://www.archdaily.com/198583/dieter-rams-10-principles-of-%25e2%2580%259cgood-design%25e2%2580%259d/> ISSN 0719-8884

Lorig K and Holman H (2004) Patient self-management: a key to effectiveness and efficiency in care of chronic diseases. *Public Health Report May-June; 119 (3) pp239-243.*

Rajanen, (Marghescu), D. (2009). Usability Evaluation of Information Systems: A Review of Five International Standards. 10.1007/978-0-387-68772-8_11.

Steventon A et al (2012) Effect of telehealth on use of secondary care and mortality: findings from the Whole System Demonstrator cluster randomised trial. *British Medical Journal* 2012; 344

Sligo J, Gauld R, Roberts V, Villa L. (2017) A literature review for large-scale health information system project planning, implementation and evaluation. *Int J Med Inform*. 97:86–97

Standing C, Standing S, McDermott M, Gururajan R, Kiani Mavi R. (2018) The paradoxes of telehealth: a review of the literature 2000-2015. *Systems Research and Behavioural Science* 35 90-101

CUCKOO – FACILITATING COMMUNICATION FOR PEOPLE WITH MENTAL AND PHYSICAL DISABILITIES IN RESIDENTIAL COMMUNITIES

Victoria Batz[1], Henrik Riess[1,2], Mareike Gabele[3], Dominik Schumacher[1] and Michael Herzog[1]

[1]Magdeburg-Stendal University, Germany
[2]University of Applied Sciences Potsdam, Germany
[3]Otto von Guericke University Magdeburg, Germany

ABSTRACT

Social interaction is a fundamental aspect of human needs. However, people with mental or physical disabilities often lack individual opportunities for socializing. For them, it is hard to initiate social contact in everyday life – even if they share flats and daily rituals. At the same time, digital media cannot be used to create a balance for missing interaction in real life, due to lack of interest and know how. This paper describes a human-centered design process leading to an experimental product solution to address the mentioned communication gap. At first qualitative user research studies including observations and interviews illustrate the social situation of people with disabilities in assisted shared living. Furthermore, it will be shown how user requirements are translated into an experimental interactive prototype that promotes social interaction between people with disabilities. A wall-mounted cuckoo clock represents the installation. The clock proposes either suggestions for shared free-time activities or even allows users to promote their ideas through a playful and intuitive physical user interface. Thereby, it supports the development of family-like welfare and independent decision-making. A subsequent expert survey underlines the relevance and need of the product in facilities for PWD. This interaction design study represents an essential basis for the development of further concepts for the improvement of social interactions. At the same time, long-term research results are to be achieved through the future implementation of the assistance system.

KEYWORDS

Social Interaction, Digital Assistance, People with Disabilities, Tangible Interaction, Prototyping, Gamification, Design Methods

1. INTRODUCTION

"Would you like to have coffee with me?" "Yes, I will be in the kitchen in five minutes." That sounds like a simple social interaction. One roommate knocks on the door of the other one and suggests an activity - this way we signal the need for community. For people with mental and physical disabilities (PWD), this interaction can become a challenge. It is difficult for them to initiate human interactions or to react in an adapted way. It is also tricky for PWD (Combinations of symptoms like: Learning disability, lack of concentration, attention deficit, health problems, limited cognitive ability, mental and neurological disorder, behavioral abnormalities, limited social and emotional development, signs of dementia) to find out how others are feeling and what they are doing (Stangl, 2018). The following work examines the conditions and requirements for an assistance system that promotes social interaction in shared flats for PWD. A large number of PWD grow up in a relationship of dependence. They are relieved of many responsibilities and decisions about their lives. Family members or care staff mostly make these decisions. This type of exclusion leads to isolated behavior and a reduction of already existing abilities, which can be expressed for example, through a lack of willingness to cooperate, negative self-assessment, tantrums or passivity (Fiedler, 2007, p. 26).

Social skills develop through participation in human interaction. PWD need to find a way to solve conflicts and test social behavior. A great incentive is a family-like living environment in a shared apartment - besides not having to do activities alone. At the end of 2015, the Federal Statistical Office counted around 10 million disabled people in Germany, including 7.6 million people with severe disabilities, a share of 9.3% of the total population. About half of all mentally disabled people live in assisted living facilities (Federal Statistical Office, 2018). The Convention of Rights for people with disabilities stimulates the support in their daily lives in a more self-determined manner. So far the support of social skills and interaction among PWD in shared flats has received little attention in literature and research. A digital assistance solution to overcome linguistic, physical, visual and social barriers haven't been found yet.

This paper examines how social barriers between roommates can be overcome through the use of technology. The assistance system uses the metaphor of a cuckoo clock to actively and reflexively initiate communication between PWD. The concept is intended to support human contact to create a development-friendly environment in the living space. The aim is social participation in everyday life, self-determination, and interaction between flatmates in assisted living communities for PWD.

2. RELATED WORK

Playing is a productive process, that trains logical thinking and promotes sociability at the same time (Schell, 2012). It also triggers emotions. Unlike in the real world, games treat all participants like they are equal, regardless of social origin, status, gender or educational level (Sailer et al., 2016). Gamification uses elements which are typically used in games but are inserted in a different, non-game context (Deterding et al., 2011). It increases motivation and performance when fulfilling a task, as well as the fun factor (Sailer et al., 2016, p. 11).

The motivational aspect was demonstrated in the project "Fold it" (Reinhardt, 2015), in which the protein structure of the AIDS virus was deciphered in a short period through a playful implementation of the problem in a Tetris like game setting. For children with cancer, gamification could be used successfully in dealing with pain (Stinson et al., 2015). Most gamification applications focus on promoting, changing or maintaining certain behaviors (Sailer, p. 77). Gamification mainly supports people with disabilities, by aligning their performance and skills (Korn et al., 2013, p. 124). Unlike people without disabilities, mentally impaired people are less able to filter environmental stimuli. That is why PWD quickly feel overwhelmed by too much input. Social failures with human interactions lead to a lack of motivation. This lack of positive experiences in social situations during childhood leads to a lack of self-esteem (Weingärtner et al., 2007). Limited social skills also make it more difficult to establish contact with other people (Stangl, 2018). Partially supervised shared communities offer a protected space for PWD, in which they can meet as equals. The interaction between caregivers and residents, on the other hand, is always subject to a relationship of dependency (Weingärtner et al., 2007, p. 69).

An independent organization of activities and communication with flatmates only occurs in individual cases. The life in institutions for disabled people is characterized by structure and hierarchy (Dennhöfer, p. 348). The ability to communicate is simplified with the use of drawings, photos, pictograms or word cards (Hettinger et al., 1996). The card game "Step into a Conversation" (Meleen, 2018) helps PWD to start a conversation, engage in a dialogue and send non-verbal signs just like eye contact. METACOM (Kitzinger, 2018) is a collection of 10,000 symbols. The collection is divided into categories such as small words, attributes/emotions, verbs, time, conversation/interaction and symbols for questions (Kitzinger, 2108). The symbol library is used for various Ambient Assisted Living systems such as talker, communication books and image boxes. Talker is an electronic communication aid. By touching a button, the user can participate in a conversation, draw attention to him-/herself or express a wish. MetaTalk is an iPad App with questions and phrases to initiate, maintain or end a conversation ("Hello, what's your name?" "That's a beautiful name"). The questions can be answered by pressing a button, which also can be recorded by the user (Kitzinger, 2018).

As part of the AAL initiative, the project CABito has been developed. CABito is a barrier-free information system that is easily accessible for PWD due to visible and audible content. The CABito can be found in homes for the elderly, facilities for PWD, town halls or day-care centers for children. The permanently installed TouchDisplay makes it easy to call up information and display it individually. A multimodal output (text, image, and speech) is provided. The chat and video call function opens unknown communication possibilities for PWD. After several years of use, it is obvious that standard functions are used consistently such as the menu, excursion pictures, and films, current news in easy language, which convey everyday topics and provide impulses for conversations. Time and date announcements are frequently activated. Slightly less than half of all residents and caregivers use CABito daily (Caritas Augsburg, 2018).

Hettinger (1996, p. 212) defined theoretical requirements to promote social skills for people with disabilities. However, there are hardly any concrete pedagogical approaches that support social interaction among disabled people without the influence of care staff in shared flats. Similarly, little scientific studies have been published about the leisure behavior and free time needs of people with mental disabilities. However, PWD show many parallels in leisure behavior with non-disabled people. The care staff is often perceived as supervisors. Their presence is noticed as a lack of freedom in living out their wishes (supervisory authority). Therefore, people living in assisted communities often prefer to spend their free time separately in order to be more self-determined. They want to have as much influence as possible regarding decisions on clothes for example, or when choosing activities (Schröder, 2006). Limited financial possibilities, boredom and lack of ideas, problems in establishing social contacts and limited mobility characterize the main issues for PWD when exercising free time activities (Schröder, 2006, p. 38). Passive activities such as watching television and listening to music often dominate. Sports and social interactions are rarely carried out on individual initiative. Most leisure activities take place at home. The field of action is limited to the possibilities available close by (Schröder, 2006, p. 86). According to their statement, PWD wants to spend more time with family and friends. The flatmates are already the most frequent leisure partners and, according to surveys, the actual desired partners for social interactions (Schröder, 2006, p. 91).

3. DESIGN PROCESS

At first, requirements had to be analyzed to transfer the needs and abilities of the target group into an adequate design concept. The design process was based on a combination of the Design Science Research Model according to Peffers et al. (2006) and a Design Thinking Process (Martin et al., 2013). The development should be practice-oriented, user-centered and offer real added value within the given framework within the current state of research. The assistance system is less a speculative design concept on how PWD can be better integrated into society, than help for independent participation in everyday life nowadays.

In order to gain a better understanding of the housing situation and the daily lives of PWD, their wishes, fears, and abilities, two specialized facilities were involved in the project: The 'Gemeinnützige Werk- und Wohnstätten GmbH (GWW)' and the 'Pfeiffersche Stiftungen' open their doors for visits, observations and interviews with care staff, facility managers and clients (PWD). In addition to the established dormitories, which are usually run 24 hours a day, the shared flats are a rather new housing concept for PWD. PWD quickly develop abilities when they become more independent. They only need help with a few challenges in everyday life like dealing with money. In contrast to the dormitories, the shared flats are close to the city and furnished like regular rented apartments. Usually, two up to six people live together, sharing the living room, the bathrooms, and the kitchen. The support staff is on site certain days of the week for a few hours to help with organizational tasks like shopping or taking care of problems (the Internet connection for example). If there are any difficulties and there is no supervisor around, the flatmates can call for help. Unlike in student flats, the flatmates cannot choose each other. The care staff is not responsible for help in organizing leisure time. However, they motivate residents by telling them about their activities or make suggestions. Based on literature research, observations and interviews, a stakeholder analysis, an opportunity map, the elaboration of personas and scenarios were made, to identify the core requirements: First of all impulses with playful elements and sensual stimuli are to be integrated as an incentive to establish contact. Therefore, different senses and communication channels to overcome inhibitions should be addressed. All effects need to be repeatable to signal reliability of the system. Failure can lead to demotivation. It should create a pleasant initial situation with positive experiences and provide a limited repertoire of possible responses. In advance to the implementation, employees and residents must be trained. Only trusted supervisors can be integrated.

PWD often have feelings of inferiority. Therefore, the exclusion of individual users must be avoided. All users should receive the same information at all times. The free choice to participate in group activity without social pressure must remain. The system may not expose users and consider the interests of every individual (refusal, privacy, data storage, no demands). Possible limitations of PWD in motor skills, communication, and cognition, must be considered when guiding users and selecting activities. Giving and receiving feedback encourages users in their actions. The final product design should be contemporary and not childish - unlike style elements often used for the target group. The exchange between roommates is promoted by joint successes and experiences that trigger a group dynamic: Conversations with roommates about current events, shopping or mutual help. The target group can partly read individual words and understand language, but less frequently uses language itself in a targeted way. Symbols and images should be conventional and iconic. The demands on the user may require turning the gaze, following movements, recognizing figures and forms, hearing and understanding signals. Arm movements and gestures can be integrated such as grasping things, knocking, pulling or pressing buttons. Limited linguistic vocabulary such as "yes" and "no" can also be used for voice input. The content should be adaptable according to individual preferences. The user experience is designed intuitive and easy to install with little use of technology based on familiar principles. Preferably, existing technological possibilities of the facilities are used. Nevertheless, it should be given priority to stationary mounting, as it simplifies implementation and the learning process.

Ideas and concepts were generated during the design phase. Experts tested 3 different approaches with low-fi paper prototypes for user guidance and friendliness. Feedback from the focus group was used to derive the detailed concept and functionality of the prototype. Wireframes were created, and the interface for the display was designed. To implement a functional prototype, a product model was built and the technology integrated.

4. CONCEPT

The most critical point of interaction between roommates is "taking the first step". It does not matter who takes it. Once the contact between roommates has been established and there is a topic to talk about, the foundations have been laid. It is enough to say "hello" - Say "cuckoo" and thereby show a desire for community. This principle is transmitted as a metaphor to the cuckoo clock.

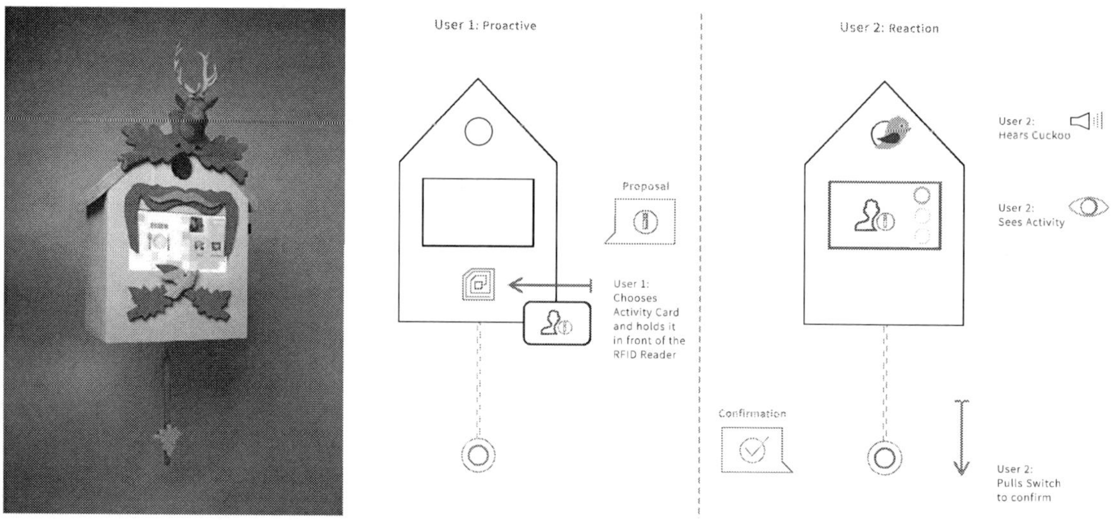

Figure 1. Prototype and function sketch of the assistance system

It should be a communication starter and a source of ideas for interaction among each other to support communication between PWD and thereby motivate them to engage in joint activities. First and foremost, the roommates get in touch with each other without being intrusive or exposing anyone. The roommate does not knock unexpectedly on the door but subtly submits a proposal. The social skills are trained by the conscious decision to contact. In the long run, behavioral patterns can be interpreted better. Habits of living together emerge. Also, roommates are trained in decision-making by participating in an activity or not. This way the user becomes a self-determined actor.

Gamification elements are intended to support the openness too: An incentive to take the initiative to propose an activity to the roommates can be achieved through the fun factor of triggering the "cuckoo" sound among the other rooms. Different interactions are assigned different sounds. Each roommate has a cuckoo clock in its room, and the clocks are wirelessly connected. Either by the roommates or externally by a caregiver the clocks can be activated. Selecting an activity or communication card starts the watch from standby mode.

The card is placed on the clock and held by magnets. All clocks in the apartment receive a signal: The cuckoo calls. The suggested activity will be shown on a display in all rooms where the clock is turned on. If a roommate wants to rest, the clock can be switched off at any time. The activity appears as a pictogram for all roommates on display. The picture representation is inspired by clear contours and good contrasts of the METACOM library. Besides, the proposal will appear in textual form and phonetic language. This way, language comprehension can also be trained. In addition to the spoken language, a suitable sound for the activity is conceivable (clattering plates, clicking of a camera) and passively tell the roommates, which interaction was proposed. In addition to the activity, a picture of the initiator appears. The cuckoo begins and ends the communication. A period of time is initiated (ticking), in which the roommates can decide, whether they feel like participating in the activity or not. To confirm the pendulum is pulled. All clocks receive a signal that there is a new participant and their image appear on display. An active rejection does not take place. If a roommate does not want to participate, no reaction will be shown during the decision period. When the decision period has expired, the cuckoo calls four times. The activity begins. The display automatically goes to sleep as soon as the initiator removes its cards from the clock or the decision period ends. A new activity card and a new proposal can be submitted. A pre-programmed night's sleep makes sure that the cuckoo does not wake anyone intentionally or unintentionally at night. During this period, no suggestions can be made to the roommates, and the cuckoo closes its door.

5. IMPLEMENTATION

The interface is divided into the activity and the participant area. The activity area displays the interaction proposed in real time. The participant area informs about who has initiated the interaction and which participants confirm the activity. The two areas are positioned centrally on the interface. Visual elements have been reduced to not overwhelm the user. Text is limited to terms of activities and names of the roommates.

The countdown of the decision process is visually and audibly displayed. A synchronized animation is used, which depicts the period. The tile pattern selected for the background is initially hidden. Once the roommates agree, the focus shifts from the activity to the participant area. Like a mosaic, the tiles begin to fill up until the decision period has expired. A new proposal can be made.

Figure 2. Activity Cards

The system can be used without additional technology or a change of settings. The clock only needs a regular power supply and a WLAN connection. It was deliberately dispensed with the operation of the touch screen since some users could be biased in dealing with a sensitive surface and the precise hand gesture. Sensory perceptions are broadly used. The auditory perception is addressed via the cuckoo sound and the speech output. The visual perception is addressed with the representation of the activities and the recognition of the roommates on the screen. Haptic is needed to select and place the interaction cards or to confirm activities by pulling the pendulum. The user interface has three stages: Proposal of activity, awareness of the proposal. Reacting to the proposal and the activity starts. The relevant information for each stage is highlighted. Animations, acoustic or visual stimuli guide the user experience.

The model of the cuckoo clock was made of wood. The back of the model is removable, so the electronics can be placed and removed flexibly. For the interface, a 7 inch LCD touch screen is used, which is controlled by a Raspberry Pi 3. The graphical user interface is programmed via the Python platform Tkinter. The activities are saved on an RFID chip. The user selects an activity which is symbolized on a magnetic image card (RFID Chip). The card can be attached to the front of the cuckoo clock. The RFID reader inside the clock detects the respective ID and sends the signal to the Raspberry Pi. Implementing acoustic signals to the system, an expansion board for the Raspberry Pi has been integrated. The sound module has a recording device (microphone) and a speaker for playback. The confirmation of each activity takes place through a pull switch, which users can use to express their preference. The switch is turned on or off with the pull cord. The signal is routed to the Raspberry Pi when the switch snaps into place. The pull switch itself was screwed into the clock.

6. EVALUATION

The study aimed to give people with disabilities the opportunity to overcome personal barriers and to initiate social interaction. As a basis, a guided interview was conducted with two managers of a housing facility for PWD. The concept was explained and demonstrated with PowerPoint and video simulation. Two experts, a facility manager of the care sector and the head of Partially Assisted Living, were invited and interviewed together after the presentation followed by an open discussion. The interview was conducted over video telephony and not recorded. A transcript of the interview was written down during and after the interview. The study had a total duration of one hour. The answers were sorted and summarized according to relevance for the further development of the prototype and the most essential content to the interview partners. The open feedback was clustered and assigned to the interview questions. The core questions related to practical challenges, extensions and possible areas of application of the assistance system. (1) Is there a need for the use of such a system? (2) How would your residents handle it? (3) How could the way, joint activities are proposed to each other, affect the behavior of the roommates? (4) Is it possible to include supervisors? (5) Which initial stimuli would please the residents most (light, sound, animations, countdown, ...) and thus encourage social activities? (6) Is the system too complicated? (7) To what extent can the concept be implemented and which aspects need to be adapted?

Results: (1) The concept is beneficial for shared flat and also for dormitories. There is a need for this kind of assistance. The communication channels between roommates can be shortened in this way. Such a system could help to structure everyday life by planning meals or birthdays together. At the same time, it helps to organize the daily routine. (2) At first, some users may be afraid of the complexity. Users are often afraid of failing when it comes to new applications and don't even want to try. It is helpful if very little interaction with the system is needed - limited to one or two buttons pressed. In an implementation phase, an editor can submit proposals for activities adapted to the needs and habits of the residents and save them in the system as standard settings. Initially, familiar standards from residents could be used, as their sports activities. At the same time, free activities can be selected. A help button should be available to contact a staff member. (3) The number of activities should not occur too big, otherwise the users will be overwhelmed. The choice of activities could be individually tailored to each shared apartment. During the learning process, the library of activity cards can be customized and expanded according to individual needs. If the device is accepted, which is very likely as our residents partly use smartphones, tablets, and messengers, it will increase the interaction between roommates. The idea of taking the initiative, knock on the door and addressing someone directly does not arise. That's why many people sit alone in their room without really wanting to. If communication is simplified this way, there could be more exchange. (4) Activities should divide into categories and distinguishable by color or shape. A survey could be carried out to find out what associations residents associate with certain activities. Resident inquiries are green and round, employee inquiries orange and square for example. Additionally, an editor for supervisors is important, so the use of the system can be guided and controlled. On-Call service for questions would also be helpful. (5) A clear visual classification of interactions into different categories (sports, music, food, birthdays, etc.) would further simplify user guidance for the target group. In order to start an activity, new and saved activities can set an initial stimulus. At the same time, the system helps the residents to do routines together, such as having dinner together or shopping ("It's time for dinner, do you want to eat together?). In this way, different initial stimuli can be automatically distributed throughout the day. As soon as the system is fun to use, it will be utilized more often. Initial sparks like flash, light and sound effects, music, vibrations make you want to interact. (6) It is already reduced to core functions and no more complicated than other devices used by roommates in everyday life, such as the microwave. It is beneficial that the Cuckoo clock does not look like a technological device and large gestures can be used to control it. (7) The concept is conceivable in all forms of living and could make an essential contribution to make free time more independent. Visual and acoustic stimuli have to shine very conspicuous and well defined - intense colors, well distinguishable tones, different shapes, and eye-catching animation. Smooth Interaction and access for PWD will be provided.

7. CONCLUSION AND OUTLOOK

The cuckoo clock installation is a design study that clearly minimizes the communication gap in shared flats for PWD by triggering conversations and social activities on a daily basis. This work identifies a problem area through background research in missing social interactions between PWD, defined a solution concept by using different design methods, developed a functional prototype for stimulating these interactions of PWD which fits into a time where 24/7 assisted living is being transformed into partially assisted shared living communities. The full functional artifact was demonstrated and evaluated with professionals in the application context. The need for assistance in different housing situations showed relevance for PWD, indicated by the experts within the feedback group. The need for supervisor suggestions points out that promoting self-employment is an ongoing process for the social interaction of PWD. For this purpose, an onboarding process can be integrated. It introduces the system and dynamically expand the level of self-employment depending on the development of the residents. It should be aimed, that clients get the assistance they need at any time. Then again, they should be gently challenged depending on their abilities. The artifact could accomplish both. Individualizing the system is an essential aspect for residents.

The setting of the initial stimulus at the beginning of social interaction evolved as a core function of the system. As a result, the physical prototype mirrors the possibilities of networking in online social media platforms. The concept creates a combination of current desires of users while encouraging the development of social interaction between PWD. This outcome addresses a gap in existing research and shows the potential to close it. As a supplement to the clock, storage for the activity cards would be necessary in the living room, e.g. a magnetic strip. Another extension of the system is that the activity cards only trigger the interaction and a concrete suggestion can be selected on display itself, just like the introduced talker. This way, the selection is kept up to date and adapts to the conditions of the environment and seasons.

The reward for the use of the system can be the extension of gamification elements, which have been neglected so far. Some concept ideas provide that users could acquire "social points" through proposed activities or participation in proposals. A social high score can be achieved. For this integration, it should be evaluated which particular elements provide enough incentive to trigger behavior and which tend to have a demotivating effect. Constructed videos and animations from pictures, which are put together to a personal film as a memory album, are well conceivable. A further feature would be the integration of routines for interactions like joint dinners to create traditions. This function can also include a noticeable countdown for the roommates, which defines a starting point for the concerning activity. In a continuation of the concept, it is quite conceivable to make a cross-apartment application available for selection. In both institutions were several shared flats in the same building. Therefore it makes sense to create a communication network within one building.

For a long-term evaluation, at least three prototypes have to be produced and implemented in a flat-sharing community, with the possibility to access the system from outside by software. The two experts stated that about half a year of familiarization time had to be planned to analyze the appropriateness of permanent use. Then an iteration of the system is necessary. Continuing, results of this study will be used as a basis for further development of the prototype. A long-term study on the effectiveness of the concept must be conducted. It can also reveal which activities are more relevant and whether a cluster or ranking can be created. By networking with an app, caregivers can be integrated as initiators in the early stages. A guaranteed error-free technical operation is relevant in order to stabilize the self-confidence of the users. Empirical research clearly showed how much value the audience attaches to storytelling and photo-taking. These reminders bring the memory and the feelings back to the experience. Such a feature can also be integrated into the system in the future. Further steps will need to integrate a broader scope of stakeholders to ensure a holistic integration and implementation in existing / future service models, accompanied by long-term testing and evaluation. This fact given the design and research team is convinced that shifting this idea from an applied research level in the direction of a market-ready product is an important contribution to society.

REFERENCES

Caritas Augsburg. *CABito – Das barrierefreie Informationssystem.* Available at: https://www.cab-b.de/produkte/cabito/cabito/cabito (Accessed: 16 June 2018).

Deterding, S., Khaled, R., Nacke, L., Dixon, D., 2011. *Gamification: Toward a Definitio'*, CHI 2011 Gamification Workshop Proceedings, Vancouver, BC, Canada.

Dennhöfer, J., 2004. Leben in Gruppen und Einrichtungen für Menschen mit geistiger Behinderung. *In Soziale Probleme von Menschen mit geistiger Behinderung.* Stuttgart: Kohlhammer GmbH, p. 348.

Federal Statistical Office. *Behinderte Menschen.* Available at: https://www.destatis.de/DE/ZahlenFakten/GesellschaftStaat/Gesundheit/Behinderte/BehinderteMenschen.html. (Accessed: 31 May 2018).

Fiedler, D., 2007. *Soziale Kompetenz bei Menschen mit geistiger Behinderung.* Julius Klinkhardt Verlag KG, Bad Heilbrunn, Germany, p. 26.

Hettinger, J., 1996. *Selbstverletzendes Verhalten, Stereotyping und Kommunikation.* Universitätsverlag Winter GmbH - Edition Schindele, Heidelberg, Germany, p. 212.

Kitzinger, A. *Wie sich Metas Kommunikation entwickelte.* Available at: http://www.metakommuniziert.de/meta_kommunikation/ukmeta.html (Accessed: 14. June 2018).

Korn, O., Abele, S., Schmidt, A. and Hörz, T., 2013. Augmentierte Produktion. Assistenzsysteme mit Projektion und Gamification für leistungsgeminderte und leistungsgewandelte Menschen. *In Proceedings of Mensch & Computer,* pp. 119-128.

Martin, B., Hanington, B., 2013. *Designmethoden.* Stiebner Verlag GmbH, München.

Meleen, M. *Printable Games for Autistic Children.* Available at: https://autism.lovetoknow.com/Games_for_Autistic_Children (Accessed: 14 April 2018).

Peffers, K., Tuunanen, T., Rothenberger, M.A. and Chatterjee, S., 2007. A design science research methodology for information systems research. *In Journal of management information systems*, 24(3), pp. 45-77.

Reinhardt, A. 'Motivation & Manipulation im Alltag'. Available at: https://www.deutschlandfunk.de/spieltheorie-gamification-motivation-und-manipulation-im.724.de.html?dram:article_id=312668 (Accessed: 15. January 2018).

Robinson, D. and Bellotti, V., 2013. A preliminary taxonomy of gamification elements for varying anticipated commitment. *In Proceedings of CHI 2013 Workshop on Designing Gamification: Creating Gameful and Playful Experiences.* ACM.

Sailer, M., 2016. *Die Wirkung von Gamification auf Motivation und Leistung.* Springer Verlag, Germany.

Schell, J., 2012. *Die Kunst des Game Designs: Bessere Games konzipieren und entwickeln.* mitp-Verlag, Germany.

Schröder, K., 2006. *Freizeitverhalten und Freizeiterleben von Jugendlichen mit geistiger Behinderung.* Dissertation University Dortmund, Germany.

Stangl, W., *Geistige Behinderung und Soziale Kompetenz.* Available at: http://arbeitsblaetter.stangltaller.at/KOMMUNIKATION/SozialeKompetenz.shtml. (Accessed: 13. May 2018).

Stinson, J.N., Jibb, L.A., Nguyen, C., Nathan, P.C., Maloney, A.M., Dupuis, L.L., Gerstle, J.T., Hopyan, S., Alman, B.A., Strahlendorf, C., Portwine, C., 2015. Construct validity and reliability of a real-time multidimensional smartphone app to assess pain in children and adolescents with cancer. *In PAIN - The Journal of the International Association for the study of Pain.* Vol. 156, No. 12, pp. 2607-2615.

Weingärtner, C. 2007. *Schwer geistig behindert und selbstbestimmt: Eine Orientierung für die Praxis.* Lambertus, Germany.

ON THE USE OF A CONTINUOUS ACCESSIBILITY ASSESSMENT PROCESS FOR DEALING WITH WEBSITE EVOLUTION

Aline Bossi Pereira da Silva, Celmar Guimarães da Silva and Regina Lúcia de Oliveira Moraes
School of Technology, University of Campinas, Limeira, São Paulo, Brazil

ABSTRACT

The accessibility of the websites is important to ensure the full access of relevant information to people with disabilities. Website evolution impacts the website accessibility, as the amount of accessibility faults in websites tend to increase during this phase. Normally, the accessibility evaluation is done before deployment but there is a lack of accessibility maintenance after evolution. Although legislation has been established for government websites, updates are not always conducted. This paper hypothesizes that adopting a continuous validation process of website accessibility could facilitate accessibility maintenance after each evolution. For this end, a tool was adapted to support developers on finding and fixing the accessibility faults. We invited governmental websites managers to participate on our evaluation procedure that was based on failures report by email, questionnaire and direct contact, to make them aware of the regulation and the faults found in the websites under their responsibility. Even after our contact and constant messages sent by email suggesting how to fix the faults the adhesion was low. The results suggested a notable lack of interest towards the regulation compliance and a strong lack of sensitivity towards people's disabilities.

KEYWORDS

Accessibility Evaluation, Accessibility Tools, Website Accessibility Assessment

1. INTRODUCTION

Providing web accessibility is an important goal that every website should pursue in order to increase the amount of people that can use it effectively. The main beneficiaries of web accessibility are people with vision, hearing or physical disabilities (Cunningham, 2012). A website that provides accessible content allows people with disabilities to assimilate and understand this content, navigate through it, interact with it without technical restrictions, and even contribute to it (Tanaka and Rocha, 2011; Freire et al., 2008b). Applying accessibility rules on websites can make web content available for all users, including people with disability or temporary limitation (Luján-Mora et al., 2014).

Considering the relevance of this issue, some countries created legislations to reinforce and even compel websites to provide full access by people with disabilities. In Brazil, the expansion of the Internet and the dissemination of Brazilian government information and services on the Internet have influenced the decision to create an accessibility regulation, given that this requirement strongly contributes to the digital and social inclusion of citizens (Bach et al., 2009). Indeed, 23.9% of the Brazilian people has visual, auditory, motor or intellectual (temporary or not) disabilities (Oliveira, 2012). Therefore, there is a significant part of citizens that may not access all information provided by non-accessible websites.

Two Brazilian laws define website accessibility as a mandatory requirement of public administration websites. They were introduced in 2000 (Laws 10,048 and 10,098) and they were regulated in 2004 (Decree 5,296). After more than a decade of these laws and regulation be placed, it is very easy to find non-accessible Brazilian government's websites. Even when they have some accessibility certificate, they do not remain accessible over time.

Currently, there are tools available for testing the adherence of websites to accessibility rules. However, people that are responsible for website maintenance usually run these tests only once, at the end of the development process. Afterwards, constant changes implemented daily by the users tend to insert accessibility faults. After these changes, website maintenance-workers often do not revalidate their websites, neither using experts review nor specific tools. This lack of website evaluation process avoids meeting accessibility standards and may cause a regression in website quality.

Aware of this problem, the goals of this work were: (1) to define a continuous accessibility validation process that periodically informs website managers about the compliance of the website with accessibility rules; and (2) to test the hypothesis that adopting this process would motivate those managers to keep websites accessible, despite maintenance and modifications made throughout their existence. We adapted an accessibility tool for doing this kind of validation and executed experiments that helped us to test this hypothesis.

Considering the experiments, we applied tests on two samples. The goal was to identify the faults that are inserted during website maintenances. In addition, an email with a questionnaire was sent to the focused website managers. The results show that feeding the website maintainers with data about accessibility weaknesses tools was not enough for engaging them in a process of accessibility enhancement. We concluded that there is a gap between the enactment of accessibility laws and a real interest of governmental institutions on implementing them.

This paper is organized as follows. In Section 2, the main Web accessibility concepts and related works are presented. The research methodology is explained in Section 3. In Section 4 the experiments' results and discussions are presented. Finally, Section 5 presents the conclusions and future work.

2. BACKGROUND AND RELATED WORK

The investigation of the accessibility during the evolution of websites and the study about the low adhesion to the accessibility regulation have been an important target pursued by several research projects.

Santana and Paula (2013) performed accessibility tests considering two samples. The first one is composed by a selection of 1000 websites, which were chosen in a ranking that classifies the websites based on their quality (popular websites), while the second sample is a random selection of the same amount of websites. Considering the random sample, 14.89% (around 148 websites) are accessible (*i.e.*, compliant with the guidelines); in the other hand, considering the sample with popular websites, only 4.34% (around 43 websites) are accessible. The authors' conclusion refers to the evolution of websites. The accessibility non-conformance is high in the popular websites because their contents are dynamic and constantly change, causing an increase in accessibility faults. Some works are focused on governmental websites. Ferreira et al. (2007) presented an accessibility study based on the websites of Brazilian public organizations. According to the law, these websites must be compliant with the W3C accessibility rules (WCAG) and the Brazilian recommendations (e-MAG). The work evaluates the degree of adherence of these websites to the accessibility guidelines. The authors realized that the number of websites that comply with these guidelines decreased, which can be due to the difficulty of keeping websites accessible when they are constantly updated.

Other countries have low rates of accessibility in governmental websites as well. Shah and Shakya (2007) presented a work that evaluated 27 Nepal governmental websites. They observed a very low compliance with the recommendations as only 11.1% of the websites comply with the regulations. The authors concluded that Nepal, in 2006, needed to make an effort to improve the website accessibility.

Luján-Mora et al. (2014) also addressed the lack of accessibility on governmental websites. They indicate that these sites are not always ready to provide services to people with disabilities. These authors evaluated the accessibility of a group of e-government websites from all South America countries and Spain. Based on the obtained results, they observed that all evaluated websites presented some non-compliance with accessibility laws.

Al-Soud and Nakata (2010) evaluated 30 Jordanian governmental websites in terms of accessibility, usability, transparency and agility. The results show low adherence to the accessibility rules in websites and concluded that those involved in the project are not sufficiently aware of the accessibility guidelines (*i.e.* there is a lack of training).

Freire et al. (2008a) conducted an exploratory research through the application of a questionnaire that involved the 27 Brazilian states. In the project's development, the authors suggested the lack of professional training and information by those responsible for websites development and test. This is the same suggestion presented by Santana and Paula (2013), which also concluded this lack of professional training and observed that between 85 up to 95% of the focused websites present any type of accessibility faults.

There are different ways to evaluate the accessibility of a website. Vu et al. (2012) highlighted the differences between automatic, semiautomatic and manual evaluation. The automatic evaluation considers client-side and display the non-conformity and suggestions to fix the faults. Semiautomatic tools require a personal intervention and accessibility knowledge as it is necessary to interpret the textual recommendation and to identify the items not included in the tool report.

Website accessibility monitoring can be done in different ways, either in real time, regular intervals, or specific stages of the website development. The work of Fong and Meng (2009) stated that governmental websites represent not only a public image but also a reliable service platform for many users. The authors presented the best practices, models, tools and techniques for measuring, monitoring, and maximizing the efficiency and effectiveness of e-Government services. They also created a real time web-based system to monitor the performance and status of public services, given that they consider monitoring as an essential phase of a web system lifecycle.

There are several tools to validate the website accessibility. DaSilva (Acessibilidade Brasil, 2017) was the first tool available to analyze accessibility of the Portuguese language websites. The recommendations considered by the tool are based on the principles of WCAG 1.0 (W3C, 1999) and 2.0 (W3C, 2008) and the Brazilian recommendations (e-MAG), allowing the analysis of all the pages of the website and indicating the non-conformity with the recommendations. The validator VaMoLà (VaMoLà Project, 2010), automatically verifies some accessibility requirements based on the recommendations of WCAG 2.0 and the requirements of Italian laws. Tanaguru (Tanaguru Project, 2014) is a website accessibility assessment tool that tests the recommendations of WCAG 2.0, Section 508 (United States) and AccessiWeb.

The AChecker tool (Inclusive Design Institute, 2017) checks individual HTML pages for compliance to accessibility standards and we elected it to be adapted to support our proposal. The tool supports the international recommendations WCAG 1.0 and 2.0, and regional recommendations such as BITV 1.0 (Germany), Section 508 (United States) and Stanca Act (Italy).

It is worth noting that this review does not found a work that defined a continuous evaluation process, as well as no tool that makes continuous evaluation of accessibility automatically to motivate website managers to ensure the accessibility of their websites. The next section presents the research methodology followed in this work.

3. RESEARCH METHODOLOGY

This section presents the research methodology used for the development of this work. First, we present how we chose the tool and how the samples used in the experiments were composed.

3.1 The Tool Selection

The main characteristic of the tool to be selected is the license type, which must be open source. For the development of this work, it was imperative that the tool can be developed in a collaborative public manner, the source can be available for studies, and modifications and redistribution of the software to anyone and for any purpose be allowed. We considered only open source tools in this work as an imperative requirement. This choice enables a collaborative development of the tool, and the availability of its source code for studies, modifications and redistribution.

Considering the tools presented in Section 2, both VaMoLà and AChecker fit the project requirements. VaMoLà considers the WCAG 2.0 recommendations and it is also customized to Italian law. The AChecker tool is able to test the universal recommendations (WCAG 1.0 and WCAG 2.0), enabling more global information testing report. Additionally, the AChecker tool suggests possible corrections to fix the accessibility faults found. This feature can be considered a support for the training process, which can minimize the weaknesses highlighted by some authors (Al-Khalifa and Al-Khalifa, 2011 and Bailey and Pearson, 2010). Therefore, the AChecker tool was selected to be adapted to fulfill the requirements of this work.

3.2 The Samples Selection

As already discussed, the goal of this work was to test whether adopting a continuous accessibility validation process over time (*i.e.* considering evolution of websites) would help to maintain a website accessible. With that goal in mind, we defined that the first sample is composed by governmental websites that had already undergone accessibility tests. We have chosen these websites because it is assumed that they need to attend the Brazilian accessibility laws (under the decree n°. 5,296). The information about the previous evaluation was extracted from the Clareou website (Santos and Bastos, 2017), which classifies the websites based on their accessibility level. Therefore, 21 websites from the government category considered accessible by the Clareou website were select as this first sample.

The second sample has all of the City Halls' websites of the State of São Paulo. We submitted these websites to a previous evaluation with the support of the AChecker tool, which we adapted in the context of this work. The process of adapting AChecker to make it a continuous evaluation tool involves changing the database structure and the source code of the tool. We developed and added specific classes and methods to meet research needs. For the automation of accessibility tests, a cron job has been configured on the server to run every day. The new classes are responsible for database connection, and for the management of data about the monitored websites and the frequency of monitoring activities.

The first evaluation aimed to record the existent accessibility faults to compare to the evaluation results over time. The initial sample has 645 websites that were submitted to accessibility tests during 45 days in the period of December 2016 through March 2017.

3.3 Experiments using the First Sample

Although Clareou classified the 21 websites used in the first sample as free of accessibility faults, they were submitted to a new test supported by the adapted AChecker tool. The goal of this preliminary test is to reinforce the websites quality under the analysis of the adapted AChecker tool. Thus, the aim is to avoid discrepancy between the implementation of both tools (Clareou and AChecker) which could impact the results. In addition, there was a lack of guarantee that the classification provided by Clareou tool refers to the last version of the focused websites. This procedure showed to be appropriate since there were seven websites unavailable (some files were not found and errors were displayed) and only two websites did not show accessibility faults.

After capturing data from the remaining websites (12 websites), half of them (Group 1) was randomly selected to receive weekly emails informing the research context, the accessibility failures found and suggesting how to fix the corresponding faults.

The reason for choosing half of the sample was to create a control group of websites (Group 2). It would help to verify if the awareness about the accessibility faults would influence the accessibility improvement, allowing a comparison between the aware and the unaware about the accessibility faults.

During 30 weeks, the experiments were performed checking 6 websites and registering the number of accessibility failures found in each week to each website for further analysis.

3.4 Experiments using the Second Sample

We evaluated preliminarily the second sample (City Halls' websites) for 45 days. During these preliminary tests, the number of accessibility failures were recorded for each website in order to compare with the data captured during the tests period. During the test the adapted AChecker sent email to the websites managers to make them aware about the accessibility failures found.

After this period, the websites were grouped considering the size-based distribution of cities according to the last census of the IBGE (*Instituto Brasileiro de Geografia e Estatística* – The Brazilian Institute of Geography and Statistics). We hypothesize that large cities could have more resources available than smaller ones, and that this fact could influence how much effort they could put on accessibility issues. The census classifies 88.3% of São Paulo cities as small cities, 10.3% as medium cities and 1.4% as large and metropolis cities (IBGE, 2010). First, the 645 websites were divided in two groups: the test group and the control group. The test group was divided in other 3 groups. So, each of the tested groups was composed by 99 websites randomly selected, preserving the distribution previously mentioned (*i.e.* 88 small cities, 10 medium cities and 1 large city). The groups have no intersection, *i.e.*, each website belongs to only one group.

On different dates, each group was set up to receive emails reporting the research context, the accessibility failures found by AChecker tool and the suggestion to fix the corresponding faults. The emails were sent weekly during 30 weeks. At the end of this period, all managers of the tested websites received a questionnaire. It highlighted the importance of accessibility and the main goal of the research (*i.e.*, to investigate whether governmental websites take into consideration the WCAG 2.0 recommendations) and invited them to answer a set of questions related to the awareness of this context and of the emails that were sent.

The questionnaire involved multiple choice and open-ended questions. The questions focused on verifying whether the participant was aware of the Brazilian laws that establish a deadline for the accessibility of all public administration sites. In addition, some questions tried to identify which are the difficulties for the adequacy of the websites.

In addition to the questionnaire, as a complementary evaluation, 2.5% of the tested websites of the second sample and 2.5% of untested websites were randomly selected to receive a direct contact (via phone) to understand the accessibility training level, as well as to invite them to participate in the research by answering the questionnaire. The next section presents the results and discussions about the experiments.

4. RESULTS AND DISCUSSION

In the first sample, after testing websites from Group 1 (6 governmental websites) with the adapted AChecker, the results obtained were compared with the results of the training period (*i.e.* the period before the emails were sent to the website managers). It was observed that there was a decrease in the number of failures in 34% of the websites tested, no changes in 16% of them, and an increase in 50% of them. Observing the results in more detail, only one website presented a significant decrease of 65.74% in the accessibility failures. The highest increase was 17.17% in another website. The websites of Group 2, also in the first sample, continued to be tested but no email was sent to the managers. Considering the same period (training and 30-weeks experiment period) it was observed that in 60% of the websites the accessibility failures decreased while there was an increase in 40% of them, and no website (0%) maintained the same number of failures. It is important to highlight that although the percentage of websites with decrease in the number of failures is significantly higher than the websites of Group 1, only one website presented an expressive decrease while the others had a very small decrease. Table 1 presents the results of each group.

Table 1. Comparative failure statistics of first sample

	Group 1	Group 2
Decreased	34%	60%
Increased	16%	0%
Remained	50%	40%

Table 2. Comparative failure statistics of second sample

	Group 1	Group 2	Group 3	Group 4
Decreased	44%	41%	47%	48%
Increased	38%	40%	43%	39%
Remained	18%	19%	10%	13%

In the second sample, as discussed in the previous section, the websites were separated in four groups, and three of them were submitted to accessibility tests. After capturing initial data (training period), the adapted AChecker started to send a weekly email to the website managers. The email reported the accessibility failures found, their severity and suggestions for corrections. Table 2 presents the results of each group. Note that the fourth group is the group of 321 websites that did not receive emails. It is possible to observe that the results are very similar, with a failure decrease percentage varying from 41 up to 48%, a failure increase percentage from 38 up to 43%, and 10 up to 19% remained stable (the same amount of failures). Based on these results it was not possible to identify a significant difference among the groups, even considering the group that received no email. It is worth noting that a stable number of errors does not mean that they are the same faults (it was not checked the faults per se); a more complete checking could check if the same failures remained or not.

After the experiment periods of each group, a questionnaire was sent by email to 297 website managers twice a week during 9 weeks. Amongst those, 2.5 % of the websites that received the failures notification and 2.5% of the websites that received no emails were randomly chosen and their managers were directly contacted (by phone). The purpose of this contact was to raise the awareness of the website managers related to the research and to the accessibility issues. The results obtained in this stage were the following:

- 10% of the emails sent with the questionnaire attached were opened (30 emails)
- 1% of the emails sent were triggered (3 emails)
- 12.79% of the emails received requested removal of the mailing list (38 emails)
- 5.05% of the emails received answered the questionnaires (15 emails)
- 1.34% of the emails were answered after direct contact (phone) (4 emails).

The websites that received emails and the phone calls (8 websites) presented the following results before the calls:

- 75% are interested but asked to forward the email to someone else (6 websites)
- 13% have no interest in the research (1 website)
- 13% had already received the questionnaire and reports (1 website)

The same websites after the phone calls, when the websites manager were re-invited to answer the questionnaire, the same websites returned the following

- 25% answered the questionnaire after the call (2 websites)
- 75% did not respond to the questionnaire even after the call (6 websites)

Other eight websites that were untested (*i.e.* received no email) when directly contacted returned by phone the following results:

- 63% are interested in receiving the notifications and the questionnaire (5 websites)
- 38% have no interest in the research (3 websites).

The emails with the questionnaire in attachment were sent to the website managers after the call and the results obtained are as follows:

- 25% answered the questionnaire after the call (2 websites)
- 75% did not respond to the questionnaire even after the call (6 websites).

According to the received answers (15 answers) of the applied questionnaire, the results indicate that 66.7% of the website managers are aware about the law and tried to apply it, only 26.7% have no knowledge about the laws and 6.6% are aware about the law but are unable to apply it. Considering the participants, 60% already regularly received the accessibility reports generated by the AChecker tool.

Regarding the website improvements during the evaluated period (December 2016 to March 2017), 33% of respondents were unable to justify accessibility improvements made on their website; 26.7% said that the website improvements are due to other institution demands; 13% answered that no improvements were done; 20% stated that the website improvements were done to attend the institution demands and the faults reported by AChecker tool as well; and only 6.7% reported that the improvements were made considering only the report of failures sent by AChecker tool.

When the managers were questioned about the reason why the websites remained with accessibility faults, 40% of them were not able to identify the reason, 20% reported that there were other priorities in the organization, 13.3% answered that they did not receive the accessibility reports that were sent during the experiment period, 6.7% reported that the website was being updated, 6.7% admitted that the website needs to be completely redone and this task will be completed soon, and only 13.4% answered that they fixed the faults responsible by the failures.

Regarding the usefulness of receiving the reports to make accessibility improvements, 80% of the participants thought it was useful to receive them and 20% of them did not know how to answer this question. Moreover, 86.7% of the respondents said that they would like to continue receiving the accessibility reports.

When questioned about the difficulty in adapting accessibility rules, 38.5% of respondents indicated that there are technical difficulties in implementing accessibility improvements, followed by 30.8%, which reported that it was difficult to maintain recommendations during website updates. WCAG accessibility recommendations are difficult to understand to 15.4% of the respondents, 7.7% complained about financial problems and 7.6% indicated lack of knowledge about the recommendations.

5. CONCLUSION

The web is characterized as an important way of communication that promotes the movement of information quickly without people having to move physically. But the lack of accessibility on websites makes it difficult for people with disabilities to navigate, interact with or contribute to it. Accessibility barriers can appear on websites in all stages of their development and especially after their publication. Indeed, daily changes and the insertion of contents by the users tend to place accessibility faults in the website that, if not revalidated (e.g. with the support of accessibility tools), will make the website no longer compliant with the accessibility standards.

The evaluation of the governmental websites was carried out in two samples. The first consisted of 21 websites in the government category that were reported by the Clareou tool website as compliant with the accessibility guidelines. The second sample considered 645 City Halls' websites of the state of São Paulo cities, in Brazil, whose selection was based on IBGE Cidades (IBGE, 2010).

Analyzing the results of the evaluation enabled us to conclude that public Brazilian institutions still have a lack of interest in accessibility. This happens even after more than ten years of the regulation of Decree n°. 5,296 in December 2004, which established a period of 12 months for public administration websites (public interest or government-funded institutions websites) to comply with those recommendations. On the first and second samples, the evaluated websites had low adherence to accessibility standards. When website managers were notified of the problem by email describing the failures and solutions to fix the faults, we observed no interest by the majority of the managers, even after 7 months of monitoring. Unfortunately, we concluded that the effort to report the failures and guide the managers to fix the faults did not work, as the behavior of the notified websites manager and the ones that were not notified were quite similar.

Considering the institutions that were inquired by phone about the research, only 6.7% indicated that the improvements were made as a result of the indications in the report sent by the system. Another 20% reported that there was a lack of priority for these improvements over other tasks. The others considered helpful to receive the reports or advised that they wanted to continue receiving the accessibility reports. However, they did not put any effort to fix the faults.

In addition, it is concluded that there was difficulty in reaching the responsible for the information of the institution on the Internet. In particular, the group of institutions that had direct contacts (phone calls) could not even identify the person responsible for answering the evaluation questionnaire. Thus, the results obtained in this research revealed strong evidence that the hypothesis is false, because even with the continuity of accessibility assessments in websites already published, the faults were still present in the websites of public institutions.

Based on the results, it is possible to assume that the low adherence to the research was due to the lack of priority in the application of Decree no. 5296 that requires that the websites must be accessible. Besides, if an employee participates in the survey and informs that accessibility is not enforced as demanded in regulated laws, he would be admitting to be negligent in their functional responsibility. There was a noticeable lack of interest in the issue of accessibility on websites, even though this is a legal requirement on governmental websites.

Other websites that are not compelled to follow accessibility recommendations could potentially have an even worse accessibility. So, as future work we suggested tests in non-governmental websites in order to identify the knowledge and interest of other areas in relation to the accessibility. In addition, we suggest including the Brazilian recommendations (e-MAG) in the tool for a more comprehensive evaluation.

ACKNOWLEDGEMENT

We thank the grant #2019/04222-4 from São Paulo Research Foundation (FAPESP) and the grant #2232/19 from FAEPEX/PRP/University of Campinas.

REFERENCES

Acessibilidade Brasil, 2017. *DaSilva – Avaliador de Acessibilidade para Websites.* [online] Available at: https://www.dasilva.org.br [Accessed 10 Sep 2017].

Al-Soud, A. R. and Nakata, K., 2010. Evaluating e-government websites in Jordan: Accessibility, usability, transparency and responsiveness. *Proceedings of the 2010 IEEE International Conference on Progress in Informatics and Computing*. Shanghai, China, pp. 761-765.

Al-Khalifa, A. S. and Al-Khalifa, H. S., 2011. An educational tool for generating inaccessible page examples based on WCAG 2.0 failures. *Proceedings of the 2011 International Cross-Disciplinary Conference on Web Accessibility*, Hyderabad, India, Article No. 30.

Bach, C. F. et al., 2009. Diretrizes de acessibilidade: uma abordagem comparativa entre WCAG e e-MAG. *In Revista Eletrônica de Sistemas de Informação*, v. 8, n. 1.

Bailey, C. and Pearson, E., 2010. An educational tool to support the accessibility evaluation process. *Proceedings of the 2010 International Cross-Disciplinary Conference on Web Accessibility (W4A)*. Raleigh, USA, Article No. 12.

Cunningham, K. 2012. *Accessibility Handbook: Making 508 Compliant Websites*. O'Reilly Media, Inc.

Freire, A. P. et al., 2008. A survey on the accessibility awareness of people involved in web development projects in Brazil. *Proceedings of the 2008 International Cross-disciplinary Conference on Web Accessibility (W4A)*, Beijing, China, pp. 87-96.

Freire, A. P. et al., 2008. *Proceedings of the 2008 ACM Symposium on Applied Computing*. Fortaleza, Brazil, pp. 2421-2425.

Ferreira, S. B. L. et al., 2007. E-acessibilidade: tornando visível o invisível. *In Revista Morpheus-Estudos Interdisciplinares em Memória Social*, 6. Article No. 10.

Fong, S. and Meng, H. S., 2009. A web-based performance monitoring system for e-government services. *Proceedings of the 3rd International Conference on Theory and Practice of Electronic Governance*. Bogota, Colombia, pp. 74-82.

Inclusive Design Institute, 2017. AChecker. [online] Available at: https://achecker.ca/. [Accessed 29 May 2019].

IBGE (Instituto Brasileiro de Geografia e Estatística). *Censo 2010*, 2010. [online] Available at: http://www.censo2010.ibge.gov.br [Accessed 29 May 2019].

Luján-Mora et al., 2014. Egovernment and web accessibility in South America. *Proceedings of 2014 International Conference on eDemocracy & eGovernment (ICEDEG)*. Quito, Ecuador, pp. 77-82.

Oliveira, L. M. B., 2012. *Cartilha do Censo 2010 – Pessoas com deficiência*. Brasília: Sdh-pr/snpd, 17. [online] Available at:http://www.pessoacomdeficiencia.gov.br/app/sites/default/files/publicacoes/cartilha-censo-2010-pessoas-com-deficienciareduzido.pdf [Accessed 29 May 2019].

Santos, R. and Bastos, G., 2017. *Clareou*. [online] Available at: https://clareou.com/. [Accessed 29 May 2019].

Santana, V. F. and Paula, R. A., 2013. Web accessibility snapshot: an effort to reveal coding guidelines conformance. *Proceedings of the 10th International Cross-Disciplinary Conference on Web Accessibility*, pp. 2. ACM.

Shah, B. P. and Shakya, S., 2007. Evaluating the web accessibility of websites of the central government of Nepal. *Proceedings of the 1st International Conference on Theory and Practice of Electronic Governance*. pp. 447-448. ACM.

Tanaguru Project, 2017. *Tanaguru Monitor*. [online] Available at: http://www.tanaguru.com/en/. [Accessed 29 May 2019].

Tanaka, E. H., and Rocha, H. V., 2011. Evaluation of web accessibility tools. *Proceedings of the 10th Brazilian Symposium on Human Factors in Computing Systems and the 5th Latin American Conference on Human-Computer Interaction*. Porto de Galinhas, Brazil, pp. 272-279.

VaMoLà Project, 2010. *VaMoLà Monitor*. [online] Available at: http://sourceforge.net/projects/vamola-monitor. [Accessed 29 May 2019].

Vu, T.-H.-G. et al., 2012. Checking and correcting the source code of web pages for accessibility. *Proceedings of 2012 IEEE RIVF International Conference on Computing & Communication Technologies, Research, Innovation, and Vision for the Future*. Ho Chi Minh City, Vietnam, pp. 1-4.

W3C (World Wide Web Consortium), 1999. *Web Content Accessibility Guidelines (WCAG) 1.0*. [online] Available at: http://www.w3.org/TR/WCAG10. [Accessed 29 May 2019].

W3C (World Wide Web Consortium), 2008. *Web Content Accessibility Guidelines (WCAG) 2.0*. [online] Available at: http://www.w3.org//TR/WCAG20. [Accessed 29 May 2019].

INTERACTING WITH RNA SECONDARY STRUCTURE THROUGH SONIFICATION

Andreas Papagiannis, Danyi Liu, Alan Zammit, Alexander P. Gultyaev and Fons J. Verbeek
Leiden Institute of Advanced Computer Science, The Netherlands

ABSTRACT

In this study, sonification strategies are explored by enabling the creation of audio files that represent the RNA secondary structure. A specific rule-set is employed which ensures that audio files generated for different RNA secondary structures will also yield distinct melodies, based on the underlying sound structural rules. The final goal is to create audio files that are constructed in such a way that a user familiar with RNA secondary structure will be able to easily detect audio nuances corresponding to the different RNA structures, as well as understanding which melodies belong to clusters of related RNA secondary structure.

KEYWORDS

RNA Secondary Structure, MIDI, RNA Pseudoknots, Sonification

1. INTRODUCTION

In this work, a novel approach based on standard programming tools and sonification techniques has been used to create non-speech audio for conveying information concerning RNA secondary structure. In addition to listening the outputted audio in a preconfigured way, a user can also use control a purpose-built device to interact with the audio in order to explore and perceptualize the sonified RNA structure.

1.1 Sonification

Sonification is the representation of data in an auditory way. In other words, one can perceive sonification as the equivalent of visualization stimulating our ears instead of our eyes. Sonification has already been used as a tool to help understand obscure datasets, e.g. electrocardiography signals (Kather et al. 2017), or help visually impaired individuals to interpret data (Pereira et al. 2013). In the past, sonification has already been used as a tool to comprehend biological phenomena in a number of projects (Temple, 2017; Shi et al., 2007). It is worth mentioning that sonification can work well in conjunction with traditional visualization techniques, or even a virtual reality environment (Rau et al. 2015), in order to further enhance comprehension by the user (Du et al. 2018). A simplistic example of audio mappings for sonification purposes as described in (Temple 2017) (named Mononucleotides algorithm) is mapping each of the four DNA bases (A, G, C, T) to a different notes (pitch frequencies). So as one can imagine, sonification is about mapping features obtained from data to sound characteristics in a meaningful way.

1.2 RNA Secondary Structure

Two-dimensional (RNA) structure conveys information about the physical conformation that may be attained by biological molecules. This largely depends on whether or not the nucleotide bases present in an RNA biopolymer, and which are located sequentially along the molecule's backbone, are able to interact (pair) with others along the same backbone, creating contiguous double- or single-stranded regions. Classical (*Watson-Crick*) base-pairing, and the set of complex, biochemical rules that drive cellular organisms, act in concert to govern the most stable conformation an RNA molecule can achieve, all derivable from an arbitrarily large set of shapes. In practice, however, natural biological processes tend to favor specific conformations, and -even more so the case- specific modules (*motifs*) that not only denote highly-common 2D structure but also biological function (Hendrix, Brenner and Holbrook 2005). Thus it is common for RNA stems or helices of (paired nucleic acid bases), hairpin loops (a stem with an intervening loop), interior loops, pseudoknots as well as a number of other well-documented structural features. It should be noted that some of these features, such as pseudoknots, fall under tertiary structure, and are typically resolve using 3D probing techniques. *This is particularly relevant to this study, as a complete description of the complex 2D/3D arrangement of RNA molecules motivates for accurate, but more intuitive representations of such structures*. Three of the most common RNA structural models are dumbbell, stem, and cloverleaf structures. In order to represent these structures in an easy way for input to a computer representation, the consensus secondary structure descriptor (CSSD[1]) format is used (Hendrix, Brenner and Holbrook 2005). CSSD is a textual notation for describing RNA secondary structure. This is accomplished is by representing base pairs with '< >' and '( )'. The latter are used for helices closing a multi-branched structure, whereas angled brackets represent base pairs of a terminal stem structure. Unpaired nucleotides in multi-branch loops are represented by the comma symbol ','. Underscores '_' represent hairpin loop residues, dashes '–' for bulge or interior loops and lastly square brackets '[ ]' represent pseudoknot positions in an RNA sequence. Finally, semicolons ':' are used to denote unstructured nucleotides.

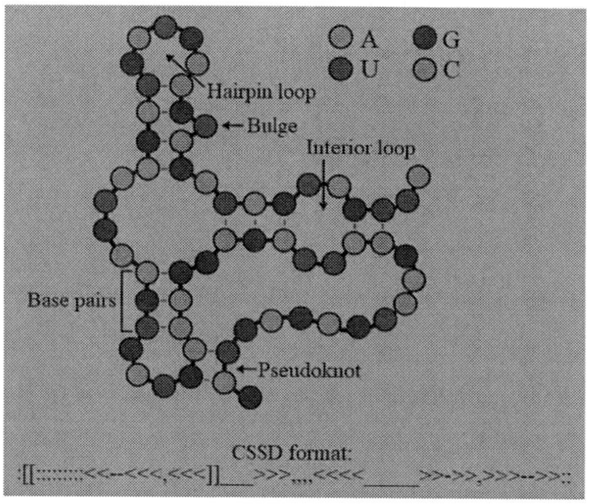

Figure 1. RNA structure example with respective CSSD format

1.3 MIDI Protocol

Musical Instrument Digital Interface (MIDI) is an information protocol used by the majority of synthesizers, audio engines, audio samplers and digital audio workstations. In short, the MIDI protocol can dictate audio generators what notes to play. However, there is a plethora of parameters that can be set by MIDI communication. For our case study, we will use MIDI files generated in Python to drive any sound engine that we will use.

1.4 Aim

The aim of this project is to create audio stimuli that enable listeners to recognize and identify distinct RNA structures. Audio stimuli can serve both as an enhancement for existing visualization of RNA secondary structures as well as for recognition or identification of structure characteristics only with sounds. The sounds sources themselves are not as important as in this study, we focus more on the melodic structure of the respective audio stimuli as well as its sound direction.

---

1 CSSD is an extension of the WUSS notation that supports classic 2D structure in addition to biologically meaningful, tertiary interactions such as pseudoknots and base triples

2. EXPERIMENTS & METHOD

2.1 Experimental Pipeline

In order to achieve the aforementioned aim, the following sequential steps are taken. First, an RNA structure is recruited into the framework. This is done by either creating a random structure or by inputting a known structure in CSSD format. After having the secondary structure in the desired format entered, features of the structure are extracted. Subsequently, depending on the features and the audio mappings in use, a MIDI file specifying audio parameters dictating how the final melody will sound like is created. Lastly, MIDI information must be transferred to an audio generator. This can be done in two different ways. Either the MIDI files created are manually imported to any audio engine in use, or all MIDI information saved in the file are streamed in real time using a virtual MIDI port.

2.2 Audio Mappings in use

After extrapolating and selecting a set of RNA secondary structure features to describe, they are mapped to various MIDI messages that will be saved MIDI files. These MIDI messages occur according to the features extracted previously, such that the final sonified audio files will have a meaning in terms of biology and will not sound totally random. For every MIDI file we are able to change a number of parameters such as pitch or MIDI control messages (MIDI CC) that can be mapped as an audio mapping to any parameter of the target sound engine. In this section, we explain how all audio mappings were made. These can be divided in two categories: mappings altering the frequency of the sound spectrum, i.e. low to high frequencies, and mapping altering the spatial characteristics of any audio.

Pitch: Pitch may be one of the most distinguishable of all audio features when someone listens to a melody. In other words, humans are able to classify low from high pitches. Thereafter, the audio mapping chosen to it must also represent a truly important feature of each RNA secondary structure. In our case pitch frequency is mapped to the kind of connection every nucleotide has in the secondary structure of the RNA sequence. Also, the pitch is depending on the previous pitch of the sequence. More specifically, every time a new base pair appears in the sequence (shown as '(' or '<' in CSSD format), the pitch frequency will ascend a step. That means the if for example the previous note played was C4 (note C of the 4th octave), if the next nucleotide is the first of a base pair of the structure then the note that will represent the current nucleotide will be C#4. If the current nucleotide represents a closing base pair (shown as ')' or '>' in CSSD format), then the pitch will descend a step. In case the nucleotide is an internal loop (shown as '-' in CSSD format), then the pitch will stay the same as the pitch previously played. In case of a hairpin loop '(' in CSSD format) there will be no sound playing. The pitch will supposedly stay same, but since there will be no 'note-on' MIDI message included, it is conceived as a pause. Note that his is the only case where a 'note-off' MIDI message instead of a 'note on' is passed to both the MIDI file as well as the MIDI port. If the corresponding nucleotide represents an unpaired nucleotide in a multi-branch loop or an unstructured one (shown as ',' and ':' respectively in CSSD format), then as it is important identifying these parts of the sequence, the pitch changes to a random note from the selected scale two octaves above the previously played note. This sudden octave ascension results to a change the listener always notices.

Pseudoknots: So far, each nucleotide is assigned to a specific pitch but this is not the case whenever a pseudoknot appears in the sequence. In this case, an arpeggio in the selected scale starts playing. The length, in notes, of the arpeggio is equal to the number of nucleotides tied into the pseudoknot. The arpeggio is split in two halves in the same fashion the nucleotides forming a pseudoknot as split in two groups. The first half of the arpeggio plays the notes in an ascending way, meaning that the first note to be played is of lower pitch than the second pitch, and starts exactly where the first set of nucleotides form the pseudoknot. In the exact same way, when encountering the second set of nucleotides closing the pseudoknot, the same arpeggio plays as before but this time the notes are played in a descending order to indicate that the pseudoknot is now closing.

Table 1. Sonification Pitch strategy

CSSD symbol	Nucleotide action	Pitch
(	helix opening	up
)	helix closing	down
<	base pair opening	up
>	base pair closing	down
[	pseudoknot opening	arpeggio up
]	pseudoknot closing	arpeggio down
_	hairpin loop	pause
:	unstructured	pause
-	interior loop	chord & repeat
,	unpaired	dissonance/random

Reverb: Reverb is an audio effect that add depth to a sound. More specifically it is used to simulate spaces. Imagine shouting inside a huge cathedral, the sound waves of your voice will be reflected to all walls of the cathedral and we hear a mixture of direct sound (sound that travels straight to your ears) and reflected sound (sound that radiates, bounces off of walls and things, and travels back to your ears). In our case, the distance each nucleotide has from the center of the RNA's secondary structure will affect the level of reverb applied to the sound. Nucleotides adjacent to the structure's center will have no reverb on their sound whereas nucleotides far away from the center will have more reverb applied to their sound receptively.

Sound direction: The index of the sequence is always mapped to the direction of the sound no matter how many speakers are included in the setup. In case of two speakers (stereo setup) the audio starts from the left side speaker and following a sigmoid function moves over to the right speaker. When using a four speaker setup (or any setup having placing multiple speakers in a 3D plane), the sound will rotate from the first to the last speaker. These two last mappings are used to help users conceive better the selected RNA structure in a spatial way.

2.3 Framework Tools

2.3.1 Python

Random RNA structures following the Consensus Secondary Structure Descriptor (CSSD) notation as a format are created in Python (https://www.python.org/). This is done in order to test as many RNA secondary structures possible and look in detail every case of RNA structure. Of course, any RNA structure following the same format can be inputted instead of a random one as long as they follow the same notation.

Created random RNA structure had one, two or three stem like branches. In case of having two or three branches, a pseudoknot (holding from four to eight nucleotides) may appear between the first to hairpin loops with probability 0,5. The length or the random structure created was between 100 and 200 (chosen at random) nucleotides. Single-stranded regions of 10 nucleotides were also added at the beginning as well as the end of the randomly created structure. The number of nucleotides forming a closing helix is also randomized to values close to 1/10 of the total length of the structure. More unpaired nucleotides (than the absolutely essential ones) are added to the sequence with probability of 0.14 and number close to 1/22 of the total length of the structure. Lastly the way the random structure is created takes into account that base pairings as well as interior loops tend to group with each other in a meaning that if a nucleotide is forming a base pair, it is highly probable that it's neighboring nucleotides will also form base pairings.

Python 3.7 again is used in order to parse, analyze and extract features out of RNA each sequence concerning its secondary structure. These features consist of nucleic acid pairings or unpairings, hairpin loops or even 'meta-features' such as pseudoknots.

The Mido (short for MIDI Objects) Python library is used in order to create midi files in Python (https://mido.readthedocs.io/en/latest/). There is no restriction concerning the number of MIDI files generated. That means that a single RNA sequence can correspond to multiple time synchronized MIDI files. Every MIDI message contains information about the note frequencies as well as general MIDI information corresponding to a selection of the features extracted. All MIDI files are then transferred to the selected sound engine. This can be done in two ways. Either the associated MIDI files will be inputted manually to any MIDI player, or all information will flow through any of the selected available MIDI ports in the computer running the Python.

2.3.2 Pure Data

After having creating all MIDI messages needed in Python, a Pure Data patch (https://puredata.info/) is made in order to work as an audio engine and MIDI receiver. In this patch, all MIDI CC created before are mapped to audio parameters of the audio engine in use. The Pure Data patch is set up in way that it will store and record all MIDI messages sent to the selected MIDI port. After storing all MIDI information, the whole note sequence can be played once, looped so that it continuously keeps playing and exported as a .wav audio file.

2.3.3 Controller Device

A controller device is built in order to help the user explore the sound file created after its respective MIDI messages has been imported to Pure Data. The user is able to control a number of parameters concerning the playback of the sound.

Firstly, three potentiometers help the user control the overall volume and speed of the sequence to be played as well as the specific index of the sequence. Here speed affects the time period between notes of the sequence. If for example the entered sequence is large, playing it in the predetermined speed may take a lot of time which is not convenient for any user as it is counter intuitive listening to a sound for more than a minute. So, in this case the user can change the speed so the in between notes time will be shorter resulting in a shorter overall sound.

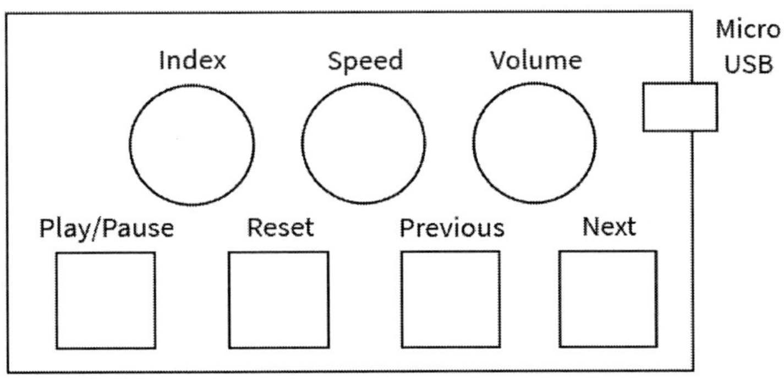

Figure 2. Sketch design of the controller device connectable to computer via USB. There are three potentiometers controlling speed, index and volume of sequence. The four buttons bellow control sequence playback

Figure 2 shows a layout of how the controller device could look like. At the bottom of the device (as seen in 5) four buttons are located. The 'Play' button will start the playback of the sound from the starting point of the sound. As expected, 'Stop' will simply pause any sound currently playing but also set the starting point of the sound at its beginning. The 'Previous' and 'Next' buttons will play the next and previous notes respectively if a sound is already playing. In this way a user can set the speed at its lowest position and explore the whole sound back and forth by using these two buttons. When no sound is playing, these buttons will set the starting point of a sound a note before or a note after from the previous starting point.

The device is powered and programmed in conjunction with an Arduino micro (https://www.arduino.cc/) and is connected to any computer via micro USB. More specifically, it acts as a USB MIDI controller meaning that it can transfer MIDI messages to any MIDI receiver via USB. In our case the MIDI receiver unit is any computer running Pure Data. The MIDI messages transferred are MIDI control changes that are then mapped to any specific values one wishes to control (such as playback speed or volume) inside Pure Data.

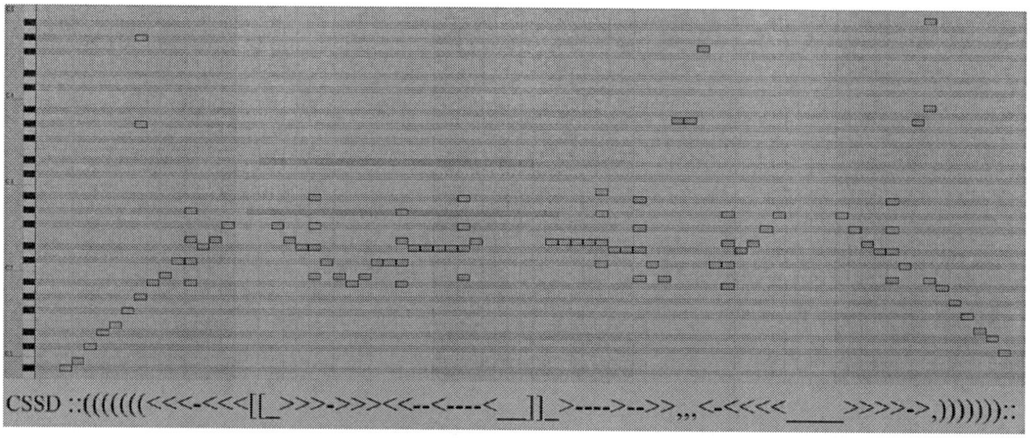

Figure 3. Depiction of generated audio of RNA 2D structure. Y-axis, represents pitch from low to high (keys C1 to C5) while X-axis represents the time domain from start to end of the MIDI file generated. Below the CSSD format of the respective RNA secondary structure is shown

3. CONCLUSION & FUTURE WORK

Sonification as a tool for conceptualizing biological data should be considered as a deep dive exploration in alternative ways of human information perception. In conjunction with visual stimulation, sonification of biological data can possibly help users understand difficult to perceive phenomena in depth. The research project is realized having in mind user experience so that the user is able to interact through the controller device and explore each RNA 2D structure in a comprehensive way. More specifically, in this paper we propose a model based sonification. In other words, we construct a fixed model to sonify structural data. The pitch and sound direction strategies used were built and chosen considering what works best for us in order to classify RNA structural differences by listening to their respective audio generated by MIDI files. However, in order to evaluate this method, a testing procedure should be followed where participants will spend time interacting with the controller built while listening to the audio sequence of a respective RNA structure. After (or even while) auditioning multiple MIDI files, each participant should fill a questionnaire targeted to their understanding of the structural properties of the respective RNAs. Analyzing the answers of such a questionnaire, we will then be able to evaluate if this whole method is suitable for all.

Future work may include embedding this whole experimental pipeline in a micro-controller device such a Bela (https://bela.io/) as well as experimenting with different controller devices such as motion detectors (https://www.leapmotion.com/) in order to further enhance user experience. Moreover, this whole procedure could be replicated sonifying 3D instead if 2D RNA structures and mapping nucleotide position in 3D space to sound direction using eight speakers positioned in a cubic way. Last, relevant to the RNAs structure, visual stimuli can be displayed in order to help the user perceptualize even better the respective structure.

REFERENCES

Temple M. D., 2017, An auditory display tool for DNA sequence analysis. *BMC Bioinformatics, 18. 10.1186/s12859-017-1632-x.*

Shi X. J., Cai Y. Y. And Chan C. W., 2007, Electronic Music for Bio-Molecules Using Short Music Phrases. *Leonardo,* Vol. 40, No. 2 (2007), pp. 137-141.

Pereira F. et al, 2013, Sonified Infrared Spectra and Their Interpretation by Blind and Visually Impaired Students. *J. Chem. Educ., 2013*, Vol. 90, No. 8, pp 1028–1031.

Rau B. et al, 2015, Enhancing visualization of molecular simulations using sonification. *2015 IEEE 1st International Workshop on Virtual and Augmented Reality for Molecular Science.* Arles, France.

Du M. et al, 2018, Exploring the Role of Sound in Augmenting Visualization to Enhance User Engagement. *2018 IEEE Pacific Visualization Symposium.* Kobe, Japan.

Kather J. N. et al., 2017, Polyphonic sonification of electrocardiography signals for diagnosis of cardiac pathologies. *Scientific Reports,* Vol. 7.

Lawrence C. and Ding Y, 2004, A Statistical Sampling Algorithm for RNA Secondary Structure Prediction. *Nucleic Acids Research,* Vol. 31, No. 24, pp. 7280 – 7310.

Hendrix DK, Brenner SE, Holbrook SR, 2005, RNA structural motifs: building blocks of a modular biomolecule. *Quarterly reviews of biophysics*, Vol. 38, No. 3, pp. 221-243.

GESTURE-BASED SMART CAR CONTROL SYSTEM

Yang-Keun Ahn, and Young-Choong Park
Korea Electronics Technology Institute
121-835, 8th Floor, #1599, Sangam-Dong, Mapo-Gu, Seoul
Republic of Korea

ABSTRACT

This article describes a method of controlling a screen showing output information on a transparent display of a car windshield by using a single depth camera without substantial touches made by user. First, this article introduces a smart car menu control system that may be used to control a smart automobile through spatial gesture interaction. Then, the method of extracting user's hand region and recognizing gestures is described. Gesture recognition rate was measured experimentally to verify the reliability of the system proposed in the present study.

KEYWORDS

Hand Detection, Fingertip Detection, Gesture Recognition, Air Touch, Screen Control System

1. INTRODUCTION

As various electronic devices have been developed, smart devices may be easily found in all areas of daily living. A variety of smart devices, including smart phones, smart watches, smart TVs, and even smart cars, have appeared. One representative example of smart car services is Advanced Driver Assistance Systems (ADAS), which allows autonomous driving.

Not only electronic devices but also display technologies have been developed. While conventional LCD monitors were just for viewing information shown on a screen, transparent displays that are currently under development enable driver to view what is behind the screen .

This article proposes a method of replacing the windshield glass of a car with a transparent display and controlling output information shown on the front screen. Direct touching of the information displayed on the windshield while driving may cause safety problems. Therefore, this article proposes a method of controlling the screen with only user gestures, without directly touching the front display.

Figure 1 shows the smart car system that enables user to control the menu through spatial interaction during driving. Figure 2 is the overall system flowchart showing the process of spatial interaction.

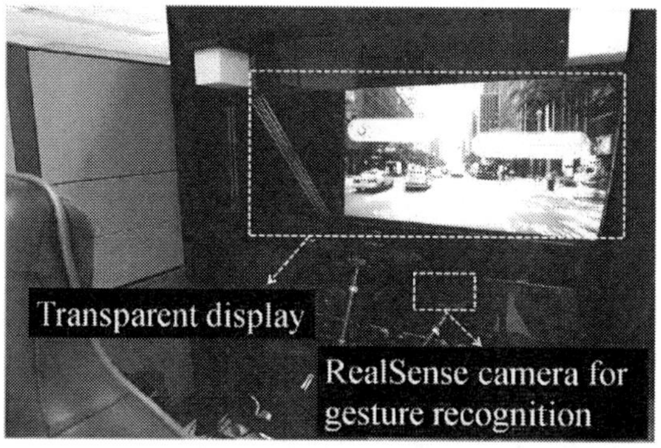

Figure 1. System architecture

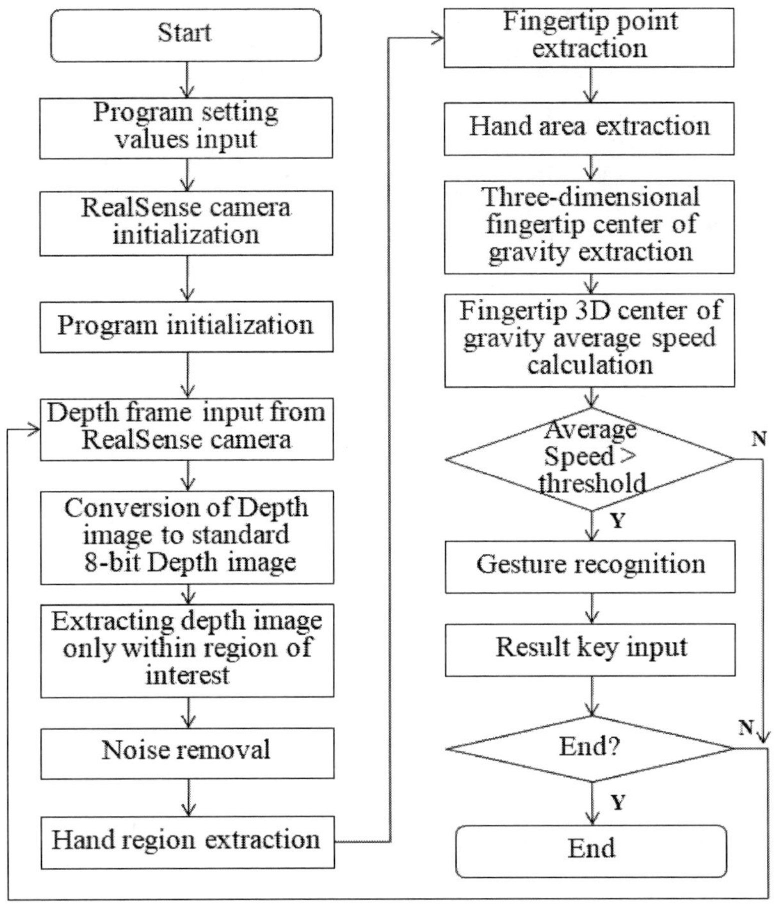

Figure 2. Overall System flowchart

2. REFERENCE POINT EXTRACTION

Before recognizing a user's gesture, a reference point for recognizing gesture speed should be extracted. In the present study, the reference point for measuring hand speed was defined as the center of gravity of the user's hand region.

To extract the hand region, the depth values within the limits of a depth camera were binarized. Widening the allowance limits of the depth camera may cause the image to include a user's elbow region, which causes an erroneous recognition of the elbow as the center of gravity of the hand while the hand region is moving. In the present study, the hand region extraction range was limited to a region within a 40 cm radius with reference to the front center of the depth camera.

A smoothing calculation should be performed to prevent erroneous operation due to motion blur after the extraction of the hand region. In the present study, a dilation calculation was performed eight times to remove noise, and the results showed that almost no erroneous operation was caused by motion blur even in rapid gesture actions.

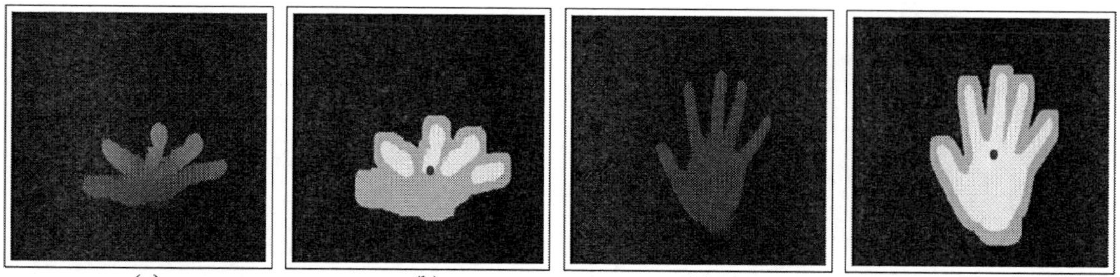

(a) (b) (c) (d)

Figure 3. Extraction of reference point and area
(a) A depth image; (b) reference point and area information of depth image(a);
(c) A depth image; (d) reference point and area information of depth image(c)

The information used for gesture recognition includes the three-dimensional X, Y, and Z coordinate values and the area of the fingertip region. The X and Y coordinate values of the hand region may be obtained by using the secondary moment. The Z coordinate value was obtained by averaging the depth values of the entire extracted hand region. The reference point of the hand region is the gray point shown in Figures 3(b) and 3(d). To extract the information about the area of the fingertip region, adaptive binarization was performed to extract the fingertip region. The fingertip region corresponds to the white regions in Figures 3(b) and 3(d). If the fingertips are toward the camera, only the pixels of the adaptive region of the finger region are extracted with reference to the fingertips (Figure 3(b)). If the fingertips are upward, in other words, if the palm is toward the camera, the entire palm is extracted (Figure 3(d)). The area of the fingertip region was calculated as the number of pixels included in the extracted fingertip region.

3. GESTURE RECOGNITION

The process of controlling a smart car menu by using the spatial interaction proposed in the present study is described here. A user may control the smart car menu by using upward, downward, leftward, rightward, and confirmation gestures. The process of each gesture is described here.

Natural directional gestures are used for gesture recognition. The information used for gesture recognition is the coordinate values of the reference point and the area of the hand region. Only the speed of the hand region reference point is used for the recognition of upward, downward, leftward, and rightward gestures. The method of recognizing the leftward and rightward gestures will be described first.

To recognize the leftward and rightward gestures of the hand region reference point, the speed of the reference point coordinates in the x-axis and the y-axis is measured. To reduce the error, the x and y coordinate values of the reference points are obtained from three consecutive frames and the average speed is calculated. If the calculated average speed is greater than the speed threshold defined respectively for the left or the right in the x-axis and smaller than the speed threshold defined in the y-axis, the gesture is recognized as a leftward or a rightward gesture.

To recognize the upward and downward gestures of the hand region reference point, the speed of the reference point coordinates in the x-axis and the y-axis is measured. To reduce the error, the x and y coordinate values of the reference points are obtained from three consecutive frames and the average speed is calculated. If the calculated average speed is greater than the speed threshold defined respectively for the upside or the downside in the y-axis and smaller than the speed threshold defined in the x-axis, the gesture is recognized as an upward or a downward gesture.

Figure 4 shows a hand gesture to the right side. Figure 4(c) shows the speed plot from the start position of Figure 4(a) to the end position of Figure 4(b). If the speed is greater than the speed threshold defined in Figure 4(c), an event is generated in that direction.

Figure 5 shows a hand gesture to the left side. Figure 5(c) shows the speed plot from the start position of Figure 5(a) to the end position of Figure 5(b). If the speed is greater than the speed threshold defined in Figure 5(c), an event is generated in that direction.

Figure 6 shows a hand gesture to the upside. Figure 6(c) shows the speed plot from the start position of Figure 6(a) to the end position of Figure 6(b). If the speed is greater than the speed threshold defined in Figure 6(c), an event is generated in that direction.

Figure 7 shows a hand gesture to the downside. Figure 7(c) shows the speed plot from the start position of Figure 7(a) to the end position of Figure 7(b). If the speed is greater than the speed threshold defined in Figure 7(c), an event is generated in that direction.

Figure 8 shows a hand gesture to the front. Figure 8(c) shows the speed plot from the start position of Figure 8(a) to the end position of Figure 8(b). If the speed is greater than the speed threshold defined in Figure 8(c) and the fingertip area is greater than the threshold, an event is generated in that direction. The information of the fingertip area is used to prevent an erroneous recognition, because upward, downward, leftward, or rightward gestures may be wrongly recognized as a gesture to the front.

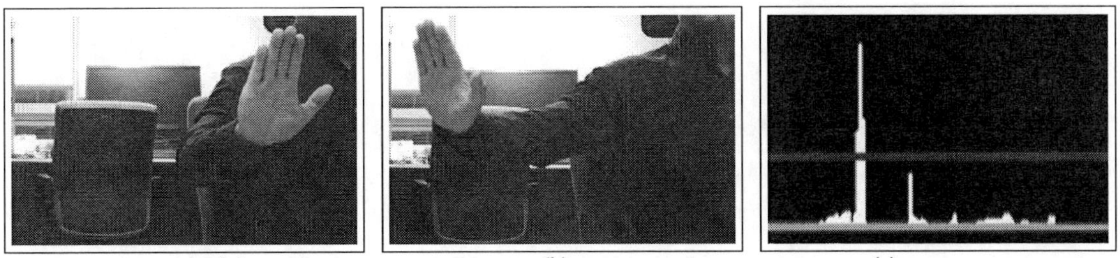

(a) (b) (c)

Figure 4. A rightward gesture
(a) Start position; (b) End position; (c) Speed plot

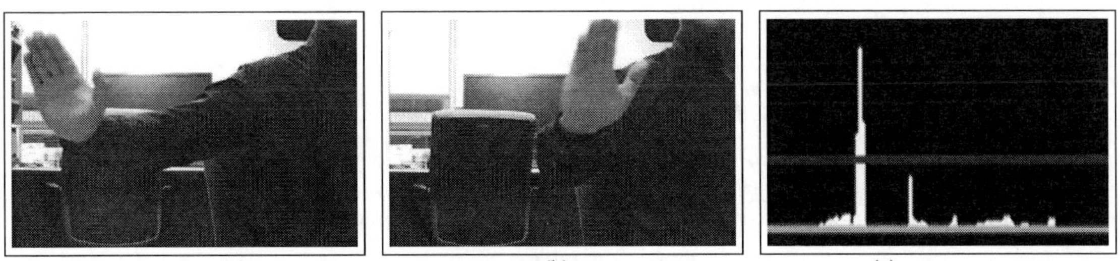

(a) (b) (c)

Figure 5. A leftward gesture
(a) Start position; (b) End position; (c) Speed plot

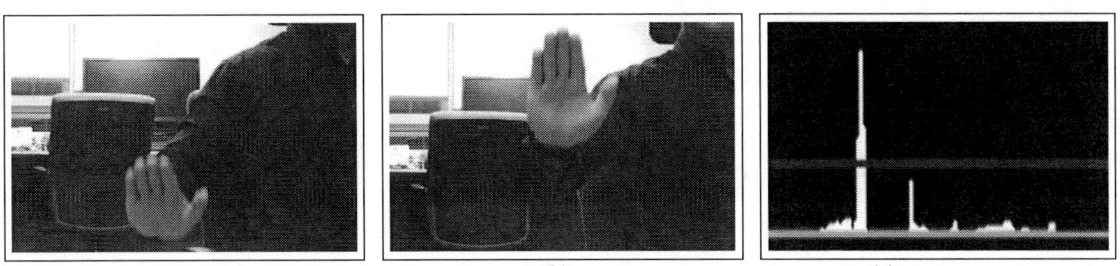

(a) (b) (c)

Figure 6. An upward gesture
(a) Start position; (b) End position; (c) Speed plot

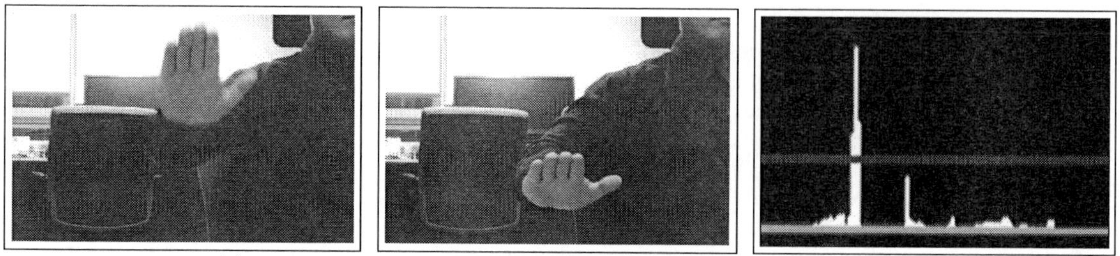

(a) (b) (c)

Figure 7. A downward snap gesture
(a) Start position; (b) End position; (c) Speed plot

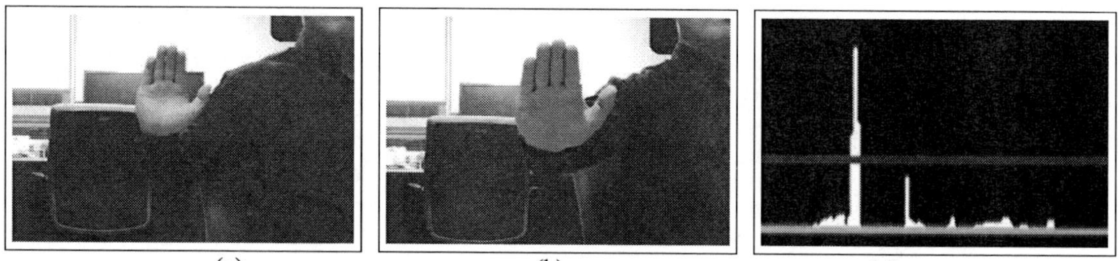

(a) (b) (c)

Figure 8. A gesture to the front
(a) Start position; (b) End positio1n; (c) Speed plot

4. EXPERIMENTAL RESULTS

An experiment to test the system was conducted using a personal computer (Intel® Core™ i7-3770 K 3.5 GHz CPU and 8 Gbyte memory) connected to an Intel RealSense depth camera. The rate of gesture recognition was measured to verify the reliability of the system proposed in the present study.

Table 1. Rate of gesture recognition

	Gesture (Number of times)					Average (%)
	Left	Right	Up	Down	Front	
User 1	100	100	96	98	97	98.2
User 2	99	100	97	98	96	98
User 3	98	98	97	100	95	97.6
User 4	100	100	97	98	98	98.6
User 5	97	98	98	99	99	98.2
-	-	-	-	-	-	98.12%

The rate of directional gesture recognition was measured by counting the number of times of recognition of rapid upward, downward, leftward, rightward, and frontward hand gestures. Each of five users made 100 gestures in the experiment to calculate the average rate of recognition. A total of 2453 gestures were successfully recognized out of 2500 gestures, indicating that the rate of gesture recognition was 98.12% (Table 1).

Figure 9 shows one user's actual spatial interaction with contents shown on the windshield. Figure 9(a) shows the choice of menu through a frontal gesture made by the user. Figure 9(b) shows the driving according to the customized driving information shown on the display screen.

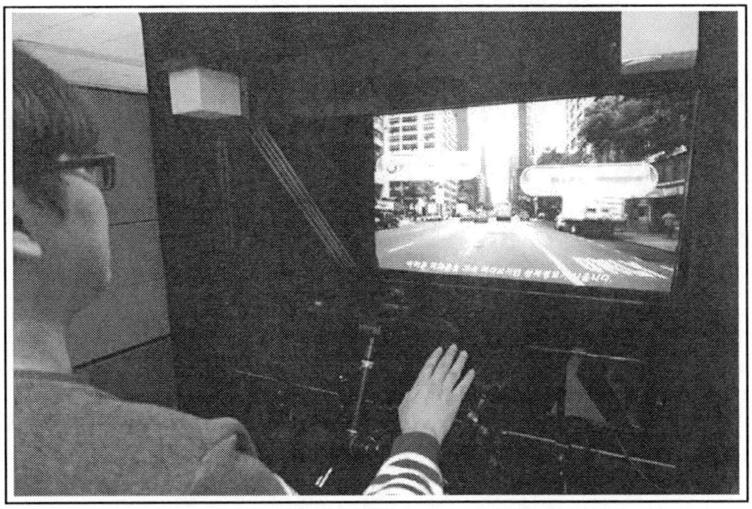

(a)

(b)

Figure 9. User test
(a) Menu choice gesture; (b) Car driving

5. CONCLUSIONS

This article proposes a method of controlling a screen showing output information on a transparent display of a car windshield using a single depth camera without substantial touches made by user. The configuration of the system for implementing the proposed method was described with the overall flowchart of the system. The system proposed in this article may increase driving safety, because a user may manipulate the screen with only natural gestures while looking at the front, without the need for turning the head to press buttons to control the screen while driving.

ACKNOWLEDGEMENT

This research was supported by Korea Creative Content Agency (KOCCA).(No. R2017030009, The development of infotainment contents and interaction for space of movement).

REFERENCES

Sujin Kwak. et al, 2015. Smart Car Technology and Smart Car-Talk Empirical Environment. *Proceeding of Korea Society of Management Information Systems.* Republic of Korea, pp 729-738.

Yejin Shin. et al, 2016. Patent Analysis for Innovative Technology Development of Advanced Driver Assistance Systems (ADAS). *Journal of Information Technology and Architecture.* Vol. 13, No. 1, pp 147-160.

MIAV: AN INCLUSIVE METHOD FOR ACCESSIBILITY ASSESSMENT BY VISUALLY IMPAIRED PEOPLE

Gabriel de Almeida Souza Carneiro and Maria Alciléia Alves Rocha
IFFluminense
Dr. Siqueira, 273, Campos dos Goytacazes – RJ, 28030-130, Brazil

ABSTRACT

Today the Internet is the most popular source of information. Therefore, web content should suit both a general audience and visually-impaired individuals. Consequently, web software products should be assessed to fulfill accessibility standards. This paper introduces an inclusive method for accessibility assessment by visually-impaired users named MIAV. The MIAV enables visually-impaired users to assess the accessibility of web software without supervision. This proposed method complies with the Web Content Accessibility Guidelines (WCAG) and the Brazilian e-Government Accessibility Model (eMAG), combining an automated approach with an approach grounded on the user experience and opinion of visually-impaired individuals. To design this method, we followed a sequence of steps. First, we carried out a pilot test to identify improvements to MIAV. Second, we had three visually-impaired students apply MIAV to assess IFFluminense's portal's, Q-Academico's and Moodle's accessibility. Finally, we ran AccessMonitor, an accessibility assessment tool advised by W3C, to evaluate the same web applications and obtained two indicators: average accessibility index and percentage of nonconformities by accessibility level. Results showed that none of the evaluated web pages met all the accessibility criteria. The resulting average accessibility index for Q-Academico, IFFluminense's portal and Moodle were 4.3 and 5.6 and 6.8 respectively. In addition, the visually-impaired students identified several accessibility issues. Therefore, we suggest improvements for the assessed web applications to provide a better user experience for visually-impaired students.

KEYWORDS

Accessibility, eMAG, Usability, Visual Impairmentand WCAG

1. INTRODUCTION

In Brazil, education provision for people with disabilities has changed dramatically over the years. In the 1980s, the Brazilian Constitution guaranteed disability people attendance, preferably, in regular education. After that, the Brazilian Education Guidelines and Framework Law (LDB) emphasized the need for specialized support services (BRASIL, 1996). Also, LDB enforces and promote, under conditions of equality, exercise of primary rights and freedoms aiming at their social inclusion and citizenship (BRASIL, 2015). The Brazilian population is estimated in 200.6 million, 6.2% of which have at least one of four disabilities (intellectual, physical, auditory or visual) wherein visual impairment (3.6%) is the most representative (IBGE, 2013). These people may face learning issues.

The Internet provides new educational features that people with disabilities could use. In this case, assistive technologies aid the visually-impaired so that they could carry out activities independently (Sartoretto and Bersch, 2017). Web content should be available according to the accessibility recommendations, such as Brazilian eMAG (e-Government Accessibility Model) (BRASIL, 2014) and ISO/IEC 40500: 2012 (ISO/IEC, 2012) which standardized the WCAG (Web Content Accessibility Guidelines). The ISO/IEC 25010 defines accessibility as the extent to which a product or system can be used by the largest number of people regardless of their physical characteristics or capability to achieve a specified goal in a particular context of use (ISO/IEC, 2011).

IFFluminense's (a Brazilian VET school in upstate Rio) students use web applications in their academic activities, such as IFFluminense's Portal (BRASIL, 2018), Q-Academico (QUALIDATA, 2017) and Moodle (MOODLE, 2017). IFFluminense's Portal publishes news on academic activities. Students access information about their grades and attendances using Q-Academico. Teachers can make available educational content and assignment in Moodle. Despite the current Laws, guidelines and NAPNEE's (the Support Center for Students with Special Educational Needs) assistance for IFFluminense's students, blind students face accessibility issues when using those applications. Depending on the activity, accessibility failure can impact these students' learning and academic achievement.

The main objective of this work is to develop a method that allows visually-impaired individuals to assess web applications' accessibility, named MIAV (Inclusive Method for Accessibility Assessment by Visually-impaired Individuals). MIAV complies with WCAG and Brazilian eMAG guidelines. The new method enables the assessment of some accessibility criteria in an automated way by AccessMonitor (FCT, 2012) and others based on the user experience and opinion of the visually-impaired individual. In order to validate the effectiveness of MIAV we asked blind students to identify accessibility and browsing issues and suggest improvements to IFFluminense's Portal, Q-Academico and Moodle.

2. BACKGROUND

In this section, we discuss state-of-the-art web application accessibility assessment, based on the study of standards and tools. Also, we describe some related works identified in literature. Granatto; Pallaro and Bim (2016) performed a systematic review of works published in the Brazilian Symposium on Human Factors in Computational Systems (IHC) between 1998 and 2015. They identified papers focusing on Digital Accessibility, 52% of which are related to web domains and 25% to visual impairment. Accessibility is an important topic that provides many research opportunities (Granatto, Pallaro and Bim, 2016). We conducted an ad hoc literature review and an international standards analysis to identify related works and accessibility criteria. The results show that accessibility assessment is generally carried out through tools, user experience and opinion or checking standards compliance.

From the accessibility standards perspective, WCAG principles are perceivable, operable, understandable and robust. These principles relate to 12 guidelines which contain one or more success criteria, totaling around 60 criteria. Each criterion is assessed against three levels of compliance. Level A is a basic level and does not ensure the accessibility of a web application because each of its pages must meet a success criteria subset. Level AA is an intermediate level that ensures accessibility for most users, since web pages must meet all A and AA success criteria. Level AAA is the highest level and aims to ensure accessibility, since web pages must meet all A, AA, and AAA success criteria. Brazilian eMAG is a tailored version of the WCAG guidelines for accessibility assessment of Brazilian government web applications. It contains sections on markup, behavior, content/information, presentation/design, multimedia and form. These sections list 45 accessibility recommendations.

Considering the number of criteria and web pages to be evaluated in a web application, tools such as AccessMonitor (FCT, 2012) can facilitate accessibility assessment by providing quick insights. W3C lists 122 tools consisting of software or online services that help to determine if web content meets accessibility guidelines. This list includes AccessMonitor with a dynamic logo that summarizes results based on samplings (W3C, 2016). An automatic evaluation method consists of algorithms that search the code of each page and highlight all nonconformities against the standards. However, these tools cannot properly evaluate some criteria. For instance, if the Alt attribute describes an image incorrectly the tool approves it. This case requires human assessment. Visually-impaired individuals could identify this problem, since they consider the context in which an image appears. In addition, evaluation methods that take into account user opinion and experience guarantee language clarity and opportunities to suggest improvements to the evaluated applications.

Visually-impaired users assessed WhatsApp's accessibility and identified several issues. Silva, Ferreira and Ramos (2016) related such issues with WCAG 2.0 success criteria and then reported problems regarding the perception, operation and understanding, except for the robust principle. Another study allowed visually-impaired people to evaluate UOL and Terra chat rooms in order to analyze user interactions (Ferreira, Silveira and Lima (2010). Melo and Baranauskas (2006) presented the Inclusive Participatory User Interface Evaluation (IPE) method. This technique supported the evaluation of the "Todos Nós" portal with the participation of users in an inclusive environment. Finally, Lima et al. (2018) adapted a protocol approach that focused on products and systems for the visually-impaired. This experiment evaluated the usability of the features of three accessibility aids: a Braille keyboard, DOSVOX and JAWS. The last two are screen readers having voice synthesizers. Thirty individuals participated in activities of entertainment, learning and social inclusion to demonstrate the suitability of specific accessibility features (LIMA et al., 2018).

About Moodle, Magalhães et al. (2010) reported usability issues. Also, Franciscato et al. (2008) carried out the suitability and usability evaluation of three virtual learning environments: Moodle, TelEduc and Tidia-Ae. Moodle ranked higher in the analysis of general data and availability of content in a hierarchical way. Neither of the former papers specifically refers to accessibility assessments by visually-impaired users.

3. MATERIALS AND METHOD

In this section, we describe tasks and tools supporting accessibility assessment using MIAV. MIAV aims to assess web pages' accessibility based on the experience and opinion of the visually impaired users when carrying out their activities. Also, we adopted the AccessMonitor (FCT, 2012) tool to test some WCAG 2.0 success criteria and e-Mag recommendations in an automated way. Thus, MIAV involved three stages: the planning, trial and execution stages including data collection and analysis, detailed in Figure 1.

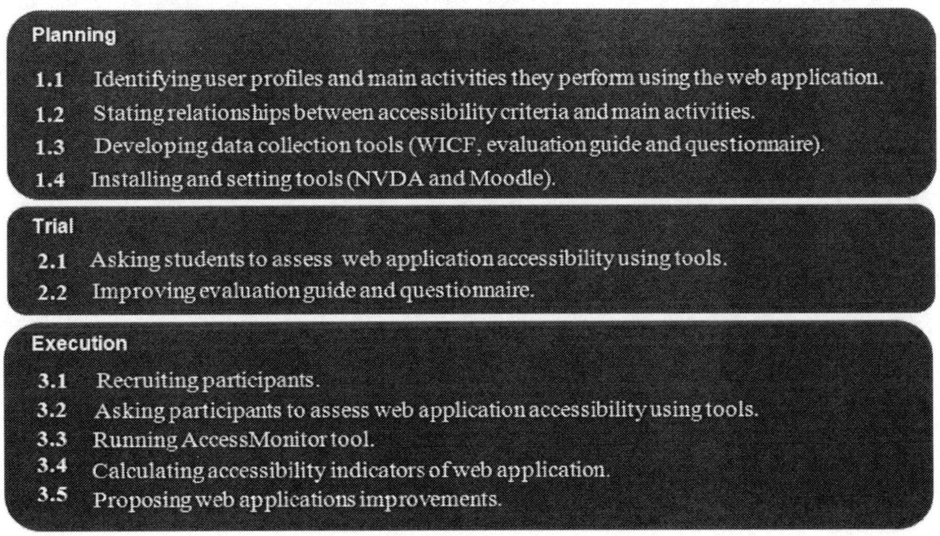

Figure 1. MIAV's overview

During the planning phase, first we screened the visually-impaired user profiles and the main activities they perform using web applications. This screening consisted of a semi-structured interview with NAPNEE's coordinator to identify visually-impaired students' profiles and needs. Second, we assigned WCAG and eMAG criteria to the main activities. In addition, we decided which accessibility criteria would be evaluated using tools or user experience and opinion (questions Q1 to Q14), as in Table 1. Due to paper length limitations, more details on the numbers in Table 1 and WCAG success criteria tests by Access Monitor are available in FCT (2012), W3C (2016) and Brasil (2014). Third, based on the user profiles and the main activities, we developed data collection forms and tools including the written informed consent form (WICF), an evaluation guide and a questionnaire. Questions are in Table 1 plus two open questions to evaluate the screen reader used during accessibility assessment that is NVDA (NV ACCESS, 2017) and questionnaire itself. The evaluation guide lists and details the tasks that participants had to accomplish in the accessibility assessment. On IFFluminense's Portal, participants were asked to choose the news that drew their interests. After reading the news, they were asked to return to the main page and inform news' content. On Q-Academico, participants were asked to choose and inform the name of a course to obtain their attendance rate in percentage and save their enrollment voucher for the current term.

Table 1. eMAG and WCAG criteria evaluation techniques

eMag		WCAG	Techniques
Markup	1.1	4.1.1, 4.1.2	AccessMonitor
	1.2	1.3.1	AccessMonitor
	1.3	1.3.1, 2.4.10	AccessMonitor
	1.4	1.3.2, 2.4.3	AccessMonitor
	1.5	2.4.1	AccessMonitor
	1.6	1.3.1	AccessMonitor
	1.7	1.3.1	AccessMonitor
	1.8	3.2.3	Not evaluated
	1.9	3.2.5	AccessMonitor
Behavior	2.1	2.1.1, 2.1.2	AccessMonitor
	2.2	2.1.1, 2.1.2	AccessMonitor
	2.3	3.2.5	AccessMonitor
	2.4	3.2.5	AccessMonitor
	2.5	2.2.1	AccessMonitor
	2.6	2.3.1	Not evaluated
	2.7	2.2.2	AccessMonitor
Content/ information	3.1	3.1.1	AccessMonitor
	3.2	3.1.2	Q1. Did you notice when there was a language change in the web application's content?
	3.3	2.4.2	AccessMonitor
	3.4	2.4.8	Q2. Did the web application report your location on site?
	3.5	2.4.4, 2.4.9	Q3. Did the web application describe links clearly and succinctly?
	3.6	1.1.1	AccessMonitor
	3.7	1.1.1	AccessMonitor
	3.8		Q4. Did the web application make content available in accessible formats?
	3.9	1.3.1	AccessMonitor
	3.10	1.3.1	AccessMonitor
	3.11	3.1.5	Q5. Did the web application allow reading and understanding the information?
	3.12	3.1.3, 3.1.4	Q6. Did the web application provide an explanation for the acronyms, abbreviations and unusual words?
Presentation/ design	4.1	1.4.3	AccessMonitor
	4.2	1.3.3, 1.4.1	Not evaluated
	4.3	1.4.4	AccessMonitor
	4.4	2.4.7	Q7. Did the web application evidence elements with focus, that is, the selected element was read?
Multimedia	5.1	1.2.1, 1.2.2, 1.2.6, 1.2.8	AccessMonitor
	5.2	1.2.1, 1.2.2, 1.2.6	AccessMonitor
	5.3	1.2.3, 1.2.5, 1.2.7	Q8. Did the web application offer audio description for videos?
	5.4	1.4.2	Q9. Did the web application provide audio control for sound?
	5.5	2.2.2	Q10. Did the web application allow you to pause, stop or hide the video, slideshow or animation available on the homepage?
Form	6.1	1.1.1	Q11.Did the web application provide a text alternative for buttons?
	6.2	1.3.1	AccessMonitor
	6.3	2.4.3	Q12.Did the web application establish a logical browsing order?
	6.4	3.3.2	AccessMonitor
	6.5	3.3.2	Q13. Did the web application confirm the login form information was duly submitted?
	6.6	3.3.1	Q14. Did the web application identify and describe the data entry errors?
	6.7	1.3.1	AccessMonitor
	6.8	1.1.1	AccessMonitor

Whenever needed, we set up the tools to carry out the accessibility assessment. In particular, we installed NVDA and we created a course with three activities in Moodle provided by IFFluminense, to allow students to make the accessibility assessment. In activity 1, we verified if the visually-impaired students were able to access Moodle's content in PDF format, which is often made available by teachers. Activity 2 has an external link to evaluate the HTML content. In activity 3, we investigated if students were able to assess Moodle's and its educational videos' accessibility, observing the audio shift between NVDA and video. Students performed tasks on IFFluminense's Portal and Q-Academico as they were on the assessment date, using their own access credentials.

At the trial stage, after the "Web Accessibility: A Practical Approach" short course was given in July 2018, we asked 7 students to assess a web page's accessibility. As only one participant was visually impaired, we instructed others to turn off their computer monitor and put on their headphones to mimic a blind user experience. We advised them to complete the evaluation guide activities and questionnaire, available in TXT format, using the NVDA screen reader. Also students received a printed list of basic NVDA and computer commands. Based on the pilot-test results, we improved the data collection tools as follows: (i) replacing the multiple-choice questions for open questions because using the screen reader confused participants to choose their answers; (ii) giving easier-to-understand instructions in the evaluation guide.

The data collection and analysis stage begins with the recruitment of the participants. In this research, participants were selected by convenience, specifically partially- or fully-blind IFFluminense students. We sent an invitation with the WICF for five visually-impaired students assisted by NAPNEE, three of whom accepted to assess IFFluminense's Portal's, Q-Academico's and Moodle's accessibility. They completed the evaluation guide and the questionnaire. Next, we ran AccessMonitor on the same pages they evaluated, to evaluate other criteria. AccessMonitor showed the accessibility index and level. We also calculated the average accessibility index for IFFluminense's Portal's, Q-Academico's and Moodle's evaluated pages. Finally, based on the results, we suggest improvements on the evaluated web applications.

4. RESULTS AND DISCUSSIONS

4.1 Participants Characterization

Three visually-impaired students individually assessed IFFluminense's Portal's, Q-Academico's and Moodle's accessibility in August 2018. It took them two hours to complete proposed activities in the evaluation guide and to answer the questionnaire. We named participants P1, P2 and P3. All participants are female, aged between 23 and 26. P1 and P2 were IT professionals and Geography and Information System students respectively. P3 was a computer technician student. They reported being familiar with NVDA and technology-skilled when performing routine and academic activities. They use the smartphone for leisure and communication. They use both the computer and the smartphone to check their academic achievement in Q-Academico. One participant reported using it daily. They read news on IFFluminense's Portal at the computer; two participants reported doing it weekly. Although no participant had used Moodle before, we asked them to assess its accessibility because they might use it in the future.

4.2 Accessibility Level and Related Issues

Table 2 shows the results for each accessibility assessment question in Table 1. Blank cells indicate the question is not applicable to that web application. Participants were comfortable to answer some questions in detail, not following the evaluation guide's directions to type "Y" for Yes, "N" for No, "NA" for "Not Applicable" or "IDK" for "I do not know". In such cases, their answers were adjusted and highlighted (*).

As for IFFluminense's Portal, all participants reported that their location on the web page was not informed (Q2). Two participants stated that no explanation for acronyms, abbreviations or unusual words was provided. P3 reported that she did not know the answer (Q6). For Q10, two participants indicated that it did not apply and P1 gave a negative answer. As for questions Q11 and Q12, two participants answered "Y". However, all participants confirmed that links were described in a clear, direct way (Q3); web content reading and understanding was guaranteed (Q5). On Q-Academico, all participants answered "Y" for Q3, Q7, Q11, Q12 and Q13. Only P3 recalled that the enrollment voucher had not been made available in an accessible format. This document is presented as an image without any text description. As for Moodle, all participants were able to carry out the three activities. They all agreed that Moodle's links were presented in a clear, direct way (Q3). Content was in an accessible format (Q4); web content reading and understanding was guaranteed (Q5); and the selected elements were read and highlighted (Q7 and Q13). However, P1 said that Moodle failed to identify data entry errors (Q14) and on which web page they were (Q2). They all reported that Moodle did not offer audio description for the available videos (Q8). These results demonstrate that none of the evaluated web pages met the accessibility criteria when evaluated by visually-impaired users.

Table 2. Accessibility assessment results

Questions	IFFluminense's Portal			Q-Academico			Moodle		
	P1	P2	P3	P1	P2	P3	P1	P2	P3
Q1							NA*	N	N
Q2	N	N	N	N	Y	Y	N	Y	Y
Q3	Y	Y	Y*	Y	Y	Y	Y	Y	Y
Q4							Y	Y	Y
Q5	Y	Y	Y	Y	Y	N	Y	Y	Y
Q6	N	N	IDK*	NA*	N	Y*	NA*	N	Y
Q7	Y	N	Y	Y	Y	Y	Y	Y	Y
Q8							N	N	N
Q9							Y	N	Y
Q10	NA*	N*	NA*						
Q11	Y	Y	N	Y	Y	Y			
Q12	Y	Y	IDK*	Y	Y	Y			
Q13				Y	Y	Y	Y	Y	Y
Q14				N	Y	Y	N	Y	Y

Other accessibility issues were observed when using the evaluation guide. When participants accessed a link leading to a wrong page, they were not able to return to the previous page by pressing the "Backspace" key. They all had to enter the URL to access the home page again. Q-Academico's login page does not differentiate the fields for login and password. In this case, NVDA informed only "editing", which troubled access by blind users. Similarly, the participants who did not copy and paste the password "Aluno12." from the evaluation guide on Moodle were not able to access it. That happened because NVDA is not case sensitive for letter "A" and does not read the period "." in the password, although capital letters and special characters are required for passwords on Moodle. Also, Moodle request confirming completion of each task. But because NVDA does not read the "Once submitted, you will not be able to change the answers for this attempt" message in the pop-up box, it was not heard by participants. These problems are difficult to detect when blind users do not participate in the accessibility assessment.

When asked how these web applications could be improved, P3 reported that a lot of information is repeated on IFFluminense's Portal and on Moodle's pages. P2 and P3 suggested that web pages' content be provided in a readable format for screen readers. Also, P1 suggested more shortcuts to facilitate information access. However, no participant suggested improvements for NVDA. As for the evaluation guide, all participants found it easy to follow the directions and to understand the questions. Because the guide aimed to evaluate three software products in a row, more questions and directions were given, which caused participants to rate it as long and tiresome. We hope this issue is resolved by using MIAV to evaluate only one web application at a time.

In order to complete the accessibility evaluation, AccessMonitor automatically tested the remaining accessibility criteria in Table 1. AccessMonitor counts nonconformities and calculates the accessibility index for each evaluated web page. Refer to FCT (2012) for more details. Based on these data two indicators for each web application were generated: (i) the average accessibility index and (ii) percentage of nonconformities corresponding to each accessibility level. The average index for the four pages from Moodle was 6.8. The five assessed pages from IFFluminense's Portal resulted in an average index of 5.6. The three assessed pages from Q-Academico were assigned an average index of 4.3. The best result achieved by Moodle matches that reported by Franciscato et al. (2008). That signals a usability and accessibility concern by Moodle's developers.

Table 3 shows the percentage of nonconformities. Blank cells indicate that the assessed web application passed the accessibility test. Items such "markup of links, menus and text links" and "presentation/obsolete elements and attributes" are the most significant, since they impact all evaluated applications. Conversely, issues related to metadata, information contrast, data tables and layout tables were not identified. Yet all assessed pages failed to achieve the A accessibility level provided by AccessMonitor because web applications had at least one nonconformity for levels A, AA or AAA.

Table 3. Percentage of nonconformities by accessibility level (%)

WCAG 2.0	AccessMonitor tests	IFFluminense's Portal			Q-Academico			Moodle		
		A	AA	AAA	A	AA	AAA	A	AA	AAA
1.1.1	Image alternative text	7.0			6.2			6.2		
1.1.1	Markup of Image maps	6.2								
2.4.1, 4.1.2	Insertion of Multimedia	5.9								
1.3.1, 2.4.10	Markup of header				5.9					5.6
2.4.5, 2.4.4, 2.4.9, 4.1.2	Markup of links, menus and text links	5.9		25.0	5.9	100.0				25.0
2.4.1	Links to skip information blocks	12.5			25.0					
1.1.1, 1.3.1, 3.2.2, 3.3.2 , 4.1.2	Markup of forms	2.2			4.3					
4.1.1	Standards W3C: (X) HTML + CSS	12.5			12.5			12.5		
1.3.1, 1.4.1, 1.4.4, 1.4.5, 1.4.9	Presentation/obsolete elements and attributes	4.3			5.8	3.6		5.9	3.6	
1.4.4	Use of absolute units		20.0			40.0				
2.4.2, 2.4.5, 2.4.8	Metadata									
3.1.1	Markup of page primary language				25.0			25.0		
1.4.3, 1.4.6, 1.4.8	Information contrast									
1.4.8	Text formatting			25.0			16.7			
1.3.1	Data tables									
1.3.2	Layout tables									
2.1.1, 2.1.3	JavaScript use				20.0					

From AccessMonitor results and analysis of user experience and opinion, we suggested improvements for the web applications. The enrollment voucher provided by Q-Academico should be compatible with screen readers; the first link on Q-Academico and IFFluminense's Portal should lead users back to the homepage, and provide a shortcut key on the keyboard associated to that link; IFFluminense's Portal and Moodle should have shortcut commands to allow easy access to the main content. Finally, non-textual content should have an equivalent textual description in all web applications.

5. CONCLUSION

This research contributed to MIAV's development, so that visually-impaired individuals identify accessibility fails, according to national and international standards. MIAV proved to be effective in its implementation to assess web application's accessibility and identify significant improvements for IFFluminense's Portal, Q-Academico and Moodle. MIAV strongly contributed to identify major accessibility problems in the assessed web pages. Developers of these software products can solve their accessibility shortcomings to provide visually-impaired students with fully accessible content. In addition, the evaluation guide was considered understandable and easy-to-use by the visually-impaired.

By comparing MIAV against related works, we feature that MIAV combines two techniques for accessibility assessment: an automated one and one based on experience and opinion of visually-impaired users. Franciscato et al. (2008) and Magalhães et al. (2010) evaluated Moodle's usability. However, we suggest MIAV to specifically assess accessibility. Moreover, IFFluminense's Portal's and Q-Academico's accessibility were assessed, which is unprecedented in the literature.

Among this study's limitations, we highlight that in the pilot test most of the participants did not have any visual impairment or experience with NVDA. Due to the limited number of available visually- impaired students, we asked sighted students to experience total blindness by turning off their computer's monitor. This pilot test allowed us to enhance the evaluation guide and questionnaire, and raise participants' awareness about how important web accessibility is, which was the purpose of the short course.

Despite the number of blind participants being very small, Nielsen and Landauer (1993) argued that a single evaluator can identify one-third of usability problems, but three evaluators are enough to map out 70% of them. Indeed, in MIAV's implementation participants pointed out some relevant accessibility problems.

Only a fraction of the pages of each web application was assessed because the web pages are dynamic, which requires that MIAV be applied periodically to assess their current accessibility level. Finally, MIAV proved to be effective in identifying relevant improvements, whose impact can be the object of future study.

REFERENCES

Brasil, 1996. LDB Law of Directives and Bases of National Education, Brazil. Accessed 07-07-2017 at <http://www.planalto.gov.br/ccivil_03/LEIS/L9394.htm>.

Brasil, 2014. eMAG - Accessibility Model in Electronic Government, Brazil. Accessed 07-07-2017 at <http://emag.governoeletronico.gov.br/>.

Brasil, 2015. Brazilian Law on the Inclusion of Persons with Disabilities (Statute of Persons with Disabilities), Brazil. Accessed 07-07-2017 at < http://www.planalto.gov.br/ccivil_03/_Ato2015-2018/2015/Lei/L13146.htm>.

Brasil, 2017. Portal IFF - Federal Institute of Education, Science and Technology Fluminense, Brazil. Accessed 07-07-2017 at <http://portal1.iff.edu.br/>.

FCT, Foundation for Science and Technology, 2013. AccessMonitor. ACCESS Unit of FCT, I.P. Portugal. Accessed 08-06-2018 at <http://www.acessibilidade.gov.pt/accessmonitor/>.

Ferreira, S., Silveira, D., Lima, C., 2010. Accessibility assessment of communication systems with the participation of people with total visual impairment. *Proceedings of National Meeting of Postgraduate Programs in Administration.* Brasília. Brazil. pp. 1-10.

Franciscato, F. et al., 2008. Evaluation of the Virtual Learning Environments Moodle, TelEduc and Tidia-Ae: a comparative study. *In RENOTE*, Vol. 6, No. 1.

Granatto, C., Pallaro, M. A., Bim, S., 2016. Digital Accessibility: Systematic Review of Papers from the Brazilian Symposium on Human Factors in Computer Systems. *Proceedings of the 15th Brazilian Symposium on Human Factors in Computing Systems*. ACM. pp. 1-10.

IBGE, Brazilian Institute of Geography and Statistics, 2013. Perception of health status, lifestyles and chronic diseases Brazil, Major Regions and Federation Units. Accessed 07-07-2017 at <http://www.ibge.gov.br/home/estatistica/populacao/pns/2013/default.shtm>.

ISO/IEC, 2011. ISO/IEC 25010:2011. Systems and software engineering — Systems and software Quality Requirements and Evaluation (SQuaRE) — System and software quality models.

ISO/IEC, 2012. ISO/IEC 40500:2012. Information technology - W3C Web Content Accessibility Guidelines (WCAG) 2.0.

Lima, A. et al., 2018. Evaluation system accessibility using an experimental protocol based on usability. Proceedings 12th International Conference Interfaces and Human Computer Interaction. Madrid, Spain, pp. 85-92.

Magalhães, E. et al., 2010. Impact of Usability in Distance Education: A Case Study in the Moodle IFAM. Proceedings of the Brazilian Symposium on Human Factors in Computer Systems. Manaus. Brazil.

Melo A. M., Baranauskas M., 2006. An Inclusive Option for Cooperative Assessment of User Interfaces. Proceedings of the XXVI SBC Congress. Campinas, Brazil. p. 447-461.

Moodle. Moodle PTCE - Campus Campos Centro. Published 07-07-2017 at <http://ensino.centro.iff.edu.br/moodle/>.

NV Access. About NVDA. Accessed 07-07-2017 at <https://www.nvaccess.org/>

Qualidata. Welcome to Q-Academico Web. Accessed 07-07-2017 at <https://academico.iff.edu.br/>.

Nielsen, J., Landauer, T., 1993. A mathematical model of the finding of usability problems. *Proceedings of the INTERACT'93 and CHI'93 conference on Human factors in computing systems*. ACM. Amsterdam, The Netherlands, pp. 206-213

Sartoretto, M., Bersch, R., 2017. Assistive Technology and Education. Accessed 07-07-2017 at <http://www.assistiva.com.br/tassistiva.html>.

W3C, World Wide Web Consortium, 2008. Web content accessibility guidelines (WCAG), version 2.0. Accessed 07-07-2017 at <https://www.w3.org/Translations/WCAG20-pt-PT/>.

W3C, World Wide Web Consortium, 2016. Web Accessibility Evaluation Tools List. Updated March 2016 at <https://www.w3.org/WAI/ER/tools/>.

HEURISTIC EVALUATION CONDUCTED BY END USERS

Patrik Lif, Jonas Hermelin, Kristofer Bengtsson and Jonathan Svensson
FOI, The Swedish Defense Research Agency, 164 90 Stockholm, Sweden

ABSTRACT

Evaluation of interaction and user interface design is usually carried out by people specialized in usability and/or human factors. However, a common shortcoming for designers and evaluators is limited knowledge about how the systems are used in their context. Usability evaluation with heuristics is a common and rather fast method with which many important design issues and flaws can be discovered. However, it can be challenging to apply in domain-specific systems for non-domain experts. A study was therefore performed to evaluate how end users who are domain experts can be engaged to perform a heuristic evaluation on their main system of use. After being introduced to usability theory, design principles and the method of heuristic evaluation, the end users evaluated their system according to 17 selected usability heuristics. Their evaluation was part of a range of other usability assessments of the system. The results showed that the method is promising and the feedback from the end users was positive. It was also found that there is a need for additional training and more time for the evaluation. In future work, the evaluation method will be modified according to lessons learned and applied in other domain-specific systems.

KEYWORDS

Heuristic Evaluation, End Users, Interaction Design, Usability, Design Guidelines, Human-Computer Interaction

1. INTRODUCTION

Usability is a concept that encompasses a variety of qualities of products, systems and services, that together help users achieve their goals. Nielsen (1993a) described usability both as a method in the design process and as a quality attribute for assessing how easy interfaces are to use in five quality components: learnability, efficiency, memorability, errors, and satisfaction (Nielsen, 2012). There are several definitions of usability that highlight different aspects. One widely spread is described in the ISO standard 9241-11 (ISO, 1998): "The extent to which a product can be used by specified users to achieve specified goals with effectiveness, efficiency and satisfaction in a specified context of use." The purpose of the ISO 9241-11 standard is to focus on the outcome of product use in a specific context with certain goals, rather than describing usability as being a persistent property of a product (or system). The design must be adapted to an intended target group, situation, and the users' expected benefit of the product.

The ISO standard (ISO, 1998) offers a framework for usability, describing important aspects and information that should be included in the description and evaluation of usability, and their relationships. It is necessary to define the users, the product(s) or systems that are evaluated, the goals with the system or presentation, the context and situations in which it is used, and the tasks to be carried out to achieve the users' goals. The outcome of the interaction with the product is compared with the users' intended results of the interaction, which in turn relates to the users' goals. By measuring and evaluating aspects of effectiveness, efficiency and satisfaction, an indication of usability in a given context is provided.

Usability can be divided into the two main parts performance (broken down into effectiveness and efficiency) and satisfaction (Wichansky, 2017). The ISO standard (ISO, 1998) states that effectiveness, efficiency and satisfaction normally need to be measured separately with at least one measure for each component. The choice of measurement method should be adapted to the stated goal of the product or system, but the standard does not give any direct guidelines as to what dimensions should be chosen or how different measures should be combined, as the context may vary.

Different methods and evaluators provide different answers about where usability issues exist. System operators and usability experts may look at a system's usefulness, performance, effectiveness, efficiency and usability in different ways. The current paper concerns how usability can be evaluated by end users (system specialists but usability novices) who are introduced to heuristic evaluation, and what benefits and problems this method may entail. The procedure was performed in the context of other evaluation methods but this paper focuses on the heuristic evaluation.

1.1 Heuristics for Interface Design and Evaluation

The use of heuristics (i.e. principles or broad rules of thumb), to guide the design and evaluation of systems is widespread within the Human-Computer Interaction field. Normally, usability specialists perform a heuristic evaluation by applying a chosen set of proven design guidelines while interacting with the system or device, looking for issues where the design does not adhere to good practice or to the requirements of human perception and cognition. Found flaws can then be remedied early in the design process, avoiding major redesigns or unwanted interaction outcomes later on. Pierre (2015) listed a total of 33 sets of usability heuristics. The existing sets of heuristics are in many cases overlapping, but there are some differences due to diverse foci on specific contexts or types of system. Below are a selection of sets of design principles.

One prominent example of set of heuristics is Nielsen's (1993b, 2017) ten heuristics for user interface design and evaluation. The principles are: (1) visibility of system status, (2) match between system and the real world, (3) user control and freedom, (4) consistency and standards, (5) error prevention, (6) recognition rather than recall, (7) flexibility and efficiency of use, (8) aesthetic and minimalist design, (9) help users recognize, diagnose, and recover from errors, and (10) help and documentation (Nielsen, 1993b).

Norman (2013) has proposed six basic principles of interaction design that mainly focus on interaction with physical objects and how the artefact communicates with the users through its design. Norman's six principles are (1) consistency, (2) visibility, (3) affordance, (4) mapping, (5) feedback, and (6) constraints.

Shneiderman (2017) has put forth a list of eight "golden rules" for design that cover: (1) consistency, (2) shortcuts, (3) feedback, (4) dialogues with closure, (5) simple error handling, (6) easy reversal of actions, (7) internal control, and (8) reduced short-term memory load.

Tognazzini (2018) has given a comprehensive description of principles that are fundamental to the design of effective interfaces that should be both visually apparent and forgiving. In his work, Tognazzini has described a total of 75 principles divided into 19 areas: (1) esthetics, (2) anticipation, (3) autonomy, (4) color, (5) consistency, (6) defaults, (7) discoverability, (8) efficiency of the user, (9) explorable interfaces, (10) Fitt's law, (11) human interface objects, (12) latency reduction, (13) learnability, (14) metaphors, (15) protect users' work, (16) readability, (17) simplicity, (18) state, and (19) visible navigation.

Dix, Finlay, Abowd, and Beale (2004) have described a total of 14 principles in three main categories: learnability, flexibility and robustness. Learnability includes the five principles predictability, synthesizability, familiarity, generalizability, and consistency. Flexibility includes the five principles dialog initiative, multi-threading, task migratability, substitutivity, and customizability. Robustness includes the four principles observability, recoverability, responsiveness, and task conformance.

1.2 Cognitive Walkthrough

Cognitive walkthrough (Wharton et al., 1994) is a method for examining usability aspects by evaluating how participating end users carry out tasks using a given system. In contrast to heuristic evaluation, this is a task-specific approach to usability. The method takes it starting point in defining the task or tasks that users normally perform, which are then divided into simple processes that users follow. Questions during walkthrough entail user's goal, actions available, labelling and feedback. The questions differ both in number and content, depending on cognitive walkthrough variant (Blackmon et al., 2002; Mahatody et al., 2010).

1.3 Usability Questionnaires

User satisfaction is one of three key concepts within usability, and aspects of satisfaction can be measured using questionnaires. One example of a scientifically validated questionnaire is the System Usability Scale (SUS) (Bangor et al., 2008; Brooke 1996). All statements in SUS are to be answered on a five-point scale ranging from "Do not agree at all" to "Agree completely". The score ranges from 0-100. Bangor et al. (2008) collected a multitude of SUS results and recommended a scale for interpreting the score. A result exceeding 90 should be regarded as excellent, 80-90 as good, 70-79 as acceptable, 50-69 as doubtful with further improvement required, and scores below 50 should be considered as unacceptable. Even though SUS is a valuable instrument, it should not be used as the only measure of usability (Bangor et al., 2009) and therefore it needs to be supplemented with measurements of effectiveness and efficiency.

2. CASE STUDY: EVALUATION OF A MARITIME SYSTEM

As part of an evaluation of the usability of a maritime expert system, an adapted method was tested where end users conducted the heuristic evaluation. The system evaluation as a whole was based on the usability framework (ISO, 1998) as a starting point. Heuristic evaluation, cognitive walkthrough and questionnaires (SUS and a custom questionnaire) were used, but since this paper is on the use of heuristic evaluation with end users, only related results and experiences are presented. The end users were given an introduction and tools to evaluate the system in a structured and consistent manner. The clear advantage of this approach is that, unlike system developers and usability specialists, end users have a greater understanding of the actual use of the system and what effects a flaw may have. However, the end users in this paper did not have any prior experience of usability testing.

2.1 Overall System Evaluation Process

The work included task analysis, software review, selection of heuristics, system evaluation, and feedback to various organizations (Figure 1).

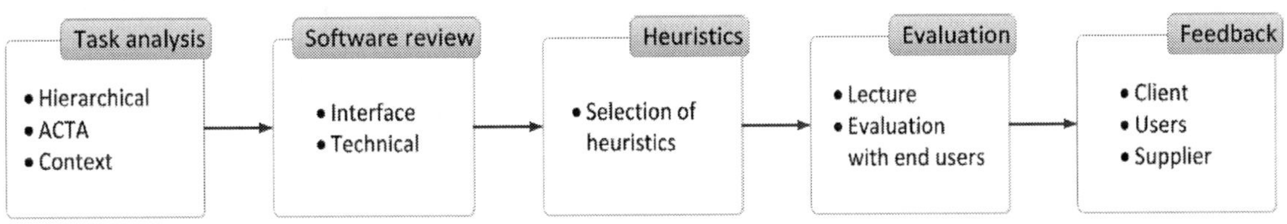

Figure 1. System evaluation process

To understand the context and environment in which the system is used, interviews were first conducted with the end users based on hierarchical task analysis (HTA) and applied cognitive task analysis (ACTA) (Stanton, Salmon, Walker, & Jenkins, 2013). Complex challenging tasks were of particular interest since these imply special requirements for the system to function as intended. Visits were made to both the system supplier and the ships where the system was used, aimed to further understand the system and the context of use. In addition, discussions were held with end users about the strengths and weaknesses of the system.

Second, a software review was conducted where software documentation was studied. Third, a set of heuristics relevant for the system was selected. Fourth, a workshop was held where the system was evaluated through heuristic evaluation, cognitive walkthrough and questionnaires. Fifth, after the results were analyzed feedback was given to the client, users, and supplier.

2.2 Selection of Heuristics

Initially, a compilation of existing usability heuristics were gathered based on a literature review. From this compilation, the researchers selected a more narrow set of heuristics based on relevance to the system type, context and domain. The set of heuristics should (1) contain no duplicates, (2) cover perception, (3) error handling (4) expert systems, and (5) the number of heuristics should be limited. The perception category covered basic heuristics such as visibility, color, and readability. Some system limitations were known from the initial analysis, and therefore it was considered important to ensure good error prevention, error handling and help functions. As this was a system for users with different levels of experience, it was also important to include evaluation of automation, flexibility and shortcuts. The number of heuristics was limited to 17 (as well as the option *Other,* not displayed in Table 1) to ensure that the end users could learn all heuristics and to ensure they had time to analyze the system using them during the evaluation. A pamphlet of the heuristics was printed, containing icon, name, and a brief description of the heuristics (Table 1).

Table 1. Heuristics selected for the evaluation. Icons by Flaticon (2019)

Icon	Name	Description
	Visibility	System status and description of what happens.
	Color & readability	Coloring and readability of text and symbols.
	Delay visualization	Visualization of delays in the system so that users understand the status.
	Autonomy	Current system status. Ensure that users can take control of automatic functions when needed.
	Consistency	Use interfaces and word selection consistently.
	Match between system & real world	Use the users' language. System and reality compliance.
	Users in control	Support undo and redo. If users make a mistake, there should be support to leave the status without redoing everything.
	Flexibility	Support that users use the system differently.
	Error prevention	Prevent users from committing errors.
	Error handling	Error messages should be expressed in a comprehensible manner. Specify the problem and suggest solutions.
	Help	Use proactive help suggestions and clues. The help function should be searchable and focus on tasks. Provide step-by-step instructions.
	Recognition rather than recall	Visible information, easy to perceive and recognize. Users should not have to remember information.
	Feedback	Feedback from the system so that actions are confirmed to the users.
	Aesthetic & minimalism	Use a minimalistic design and avoid information that is irrelevant or rarely used.
	Shortcuts	Shortcuts for frequently used commands.
	Save or send	Save or send information so that users can continue to work from previous status.
	Default settings	Return to the system's default settings. May apply to part or entire system.

2.3 Evaluation with End Users

The evaluated system was a maritime onboard computer system operated by a single operator. The interfaces of the system consist of a main display, a touch-input display, keyboard and trackball. The system is operated by specially trained personnel whose main tasks are performed within the system.

Eleven end users (ten men and one woman) were provided by the client to participate in the evaluation. The end users had one to ten years' experience working with the system. The least experienced individuals had a good overall knowledge of the particular system and a partially good knowledge of the ship's combined activities in daily operations. The most experienced end users can be viewed as experts, not only with regard to operating the designated system, but also with regard to other systems and the ship operations. None of the participants had previous experience of conducting heuristic evaluations.

The heuristic evaluation was carried out as part of a five hour long workshop consisting of five separate sessions. The first session was a 90-minute lecture on usability in general and evaluation methods in particular. During the lecture all the heuristics were explained and exemplified. The three sessions that followed consisted of 60 minutes for heuristic evaluation, 60 minutes for cognitive walkthrough, and 60 minutes for two questionnaires. The participants were divided into three groups and took part in each session in different order. Finally, an open discussion lasting 30 minutes was conducted with all end users and researchers.

The heuristic evaluation session was carried out on a system simulator. This allowed the end users to use the system in a similar way as onboard the ship. Although there were some limitations with stimuli feedback from certain hardware (e.g. sensors) of the system, the end users deemed the similarity to the onboard system to be good enough for this type of evaluation.

As the number of simulators was limited, some participants had to work with the system in pairs. However, the evaluation and documentation of usability flaws in the interface were made individually. Each participant had access to the pamphlet with the 17 heuristics, complemented with a short description (Table 1). They were asked to note each usability flaw they could find for each heuristic in pre-prepared notebooks containing specified pages for each heuristic. If they were unable to match an identified flaw with a suitable heuristic, they were asked to categorize it as *Other*. The notes and categorizations were then submitted to the researchers for later analysis.

3. RESULTS

The results presented in this paper include the number of identified usability flaws the end users found for the 17 heuristics, the researchers' analysis of these flaws, and the participants' opinions of the system's usability and the evaluation method.

3.1 Identified Usability Flaws

The usability flaws identified by the users of the system were analyzed as follows: First, the end users identified, described and categorized usability flaws according to the 17 heuristics or as *other*. Most of the end users' identified flaws (71% of a total of 58) were attributed to *visibility, color & readability, error prevention*, and *other,* while the remaining 14 heuristics (29%) were used to a lesser degree.

Second, the same usability flaw descriptions were interpreted and re-categorized by three researchers with knowledge about usability and heuristic evaluation. The purpose of this re-categorization was to achieve an overall understanding of how well the end users' categorization matched that of the researchers (Table 2). It should be noted that the sum of the number of flaws differs between end users and researchers since some of the end users' descriptions were split into multiple entities if they contained more than one flaw. No statistical analyses were made since only eleven end users and three researchers participated in the evaluation.

An analysis was made to evaluate the overlap between the end users' and the researchers' categorizations of the flaws identified by the end users (Table 2). The overlap corresponds to the proportion of the participants' statements that were categorized in the same way by the researchers. Calculation of overlap was omitted for heuristics with two or fewer statements from the end users. Some categories overlapped while others showed a large discrepancy. The end users' statements in the *visibility* heuristic had low overlap (29%), and statements were mainly re-categorized to the heuristic *color & readability. Error prevention* was erroneously used (20% overlap) and the statements were re-categorized into a number of other heuristics. The heuristic *color & readability* (83% overlap) and *help* (100% overlap) contained fewer discrepancies between the end users' and the researchers' categorizations.

Table 2. Usability flaw categorization in heuristics by end users and researchers

Heuristic	End users	Researchers	% overlap
Visibility	7	12	29
Color & readability	12	20	83
Delay visualization	1	0	-
Autonomy	0	0	-
Consistency	0	2	-
Match between system & real world	0	6	-
Users in control	0	0	-
Flexibility	1	5	-
Error prevention	10	5	20
Error handling	1	1	-
Help	4	5	100
Recognition rather than recall	2	6	-
Feedback	0	0	-
Aesthetic & minimalism	1	7	-
Shortcuts	2	4	-
Save & send	0	0	-
Default settings	0	0	-
Other	9	4	-

3.2 Subjective Feedback from End Users

Overall, the participants verbally expressed that the heuristic evaluation worked well but that improvements could be made. The introductory lecture was found to be informative and the practical evaluation rewarding. The printed pamphlet was particularly appreciated by some participants because they could keep it and continue making evaluations of the system (or other systems) onboard their ship. Some of the end users who also participated in the task analysis that was performed about two months prior to the heuristic evaluation, expressed that it was of great value to conduct the two activities in close connection.

There were also suggestions on how the method could be improved. The respondents suggested that more time should be allocated to conducting evaluations in the simulator since several of them felt that one hour was not sufficient. One contributing aspect for this might be the large number of heuristics.

The respondents also suggested that more time should be allocated to the lecture on usability. Some of them highlighted that they had difficulties performing the heuristic evaluation due to the fact that it was their first time conducting such an evaluation and were lacking in experience. This could possibly be resolved by allocating more time for the lecture, thus giving the respondents more information. Other possibilities to remedy these difficulties are, for example, the development of more refined explanations on each of the heuristics, which in combination with a more extensive briefing could make it easier for the respondents to understand and perform the tasks given to them. According to the respondents, it would have been helpful to use the actual system instead of the simulator, which was not possible at the time of evaluation.

The evaluation workshop was rated highly appreciated as a whole (M=5.8), and the lecture was particularly appreciated (M=6.2). The heuristic evaluation received positive feedback, but the participants' subjective ratings were lower (M=4.6) than the overall and lecture ratings (Figure 2).

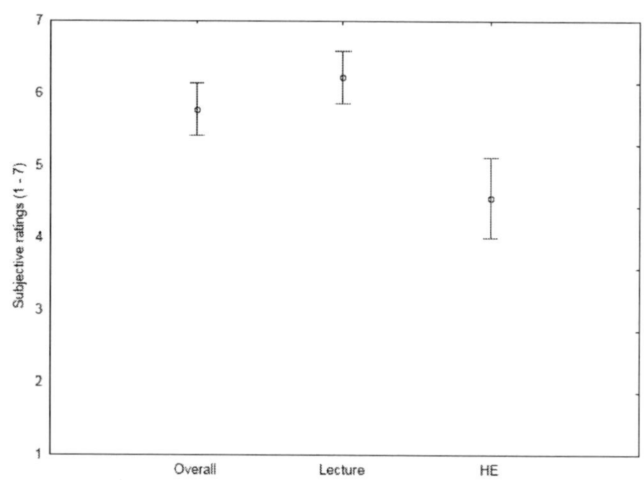

Figure 2. Mean and standard error of mean for subjective ratings of overall, lecture and heuristic evaluation (HE)

4. DISCUSSION

Heuristic evaluation is a well-known and recognized method for assessing the usability of systems, tools and interfaces. It is traditionally performed by designers or usability specialists as a formative evaluation in an iterative design process. Performing heuristic evaluations of specific complex systems in expert domains is difficult since extensive domain expertise is needed to comprehend all tasks and aspects of a system. A domain expert can on the other hand perform realistic tasks and thus identify critical flaws and their potential consequences. In the current study it was therefore evaluated if heuristic evaluation could be performed by end users who underwent a 90-minute introductory lecture on the basic principles of usability and how to perform a heuristic evaluation.

The evaluation results are promising. The eleven end users felt that they were able to evaluate the system's usability to some degree (4.6 on a seven-grade scale) with heuristic evaluation, and they found a total of 58 usability problems or flaws. The researchers then re-coded these into 77 separate flaws into somewhat different categories. End users and usability specialists may complement each other by finding different flaws.

Most of the end users' identified flaws were mainly attributed to four heuristics (*visibility, color & readability, error prevention*, and *other)*. The cause for this distribution has not been investigated, but it is reasonable to assume that some of the heuristics are easier to understand and relate to in the evaluation of the system, while some categories of flaws are more rarely found in a deployed system. Usability flaws for the categories *visibility* and *color & readability* are probably considerably easier to identify than *autonomy* and *consistency* related flaws. For example, it is easier to detect if text is too small or if windows are incorrectly designed, than how the interface is designed with regard to automation. Moreover, identifying usability flaws regarding system consistency can be more time consuming than identification of, e.g. readability flaws. The end users only had one hour to conduct the heuristic evaluation, which is likely to have limited the use of all the heuristics. For future studies, considerations should be made to reduce the number of heuristics and increase the time for the evaluation.

Although the lecture and heuristic evaluation were received positively, the end users reported some shortcomings in the method and process. The most obvious one was the short duration of both the lecture and the heuristic evaluation. In this study, a broad introduction to usability was chosen, including heuristic evaluation, cognitive walkthrough and SUS, as well as an evaluation using cognitive walkthrough, heuristic evaluation, SUS and a post-questionnaire. As the users only had seven hours at their disposal, the time for each activity became limited. Based on the feedback from the end users and according to the authors' own reflections, at least two hours are needed for the lecture and the heuristic evaluation, respectively. However, four hours or more would be adequate in order to give the users the opportunity to go through all relevant parts of the system. In this initial study, both the SUS questionnaire and a second overall questionnaire that together took one hour to answer were used. Future studies should probably focus more on one evaluation method, e.g. heuristic evaluation.

Some participants had problems classifying their identified flaws into the categories provided in the usability heuristics, which could be expected after only a 90-minute lecture. The conclusion is again that the lecture should be extended, and that it can be of value to focus more on the specific guidelines and somewhat less on usability overall during the introduction. However, when possible, an introduction should also include an overview of usability to give the end users a general understanding of the field and purpose, with the benefit of applying the knowledge on different systems they encounter in their work.

Perhaps the greatest benefit of having end users evaluate their own system is that there is no need to introduce them to the system. This is a big difference from when external designers or human factors experts evaluate a new system or design. Evaluating web sites or basic tools or systems is feasible, but evaluating a more advanced system in the context of other systems and a complex organization is considerably more challenging. This requires extensive training and several hours of use to understand the system and the context in which it is used. For some systems, several years of training may be required to become thoroughly knowledgeable. In these cases, it can be significantly more cost-effective to train end users to evaluate their own system under the direction of usability experts. Another option is to perform heuristic evaluation both with end users and usability experts and then cross-examine the outcomes to cover possible gaps in understanding and overcome the differences in perspective. The positive feedback from the participants who wished to keep the set of heuristics for future reference indicates that the heuristics could be useful as a way to guide how flaws in the system can be identified and reported during actual use.

In this initial study, end users' ability to apply heuristic evaluation by analyzing the usability flaws they identified was examined, along with their subjective experiences. In our continued work on methods of usability evaluation the intention is to make a comparison of results from heuristic evaluations conducted by end users, system designers, and usability specialists on an aviation system. The forthcoming study will expand the analysis and examine the differences between groups in more detail. It will also investigate if designers can identify usability flaws in the system they designed themselves.

With the suggested methodological modifications, heuristic evaluation performed by end users could be a favorable and cost-effective way to identify usability flaws in certain complex and domain-specific systems.

REFERENCES

Bangor, A., Kortum, P., & Miller, J. (2009). Determining What Individual SUS Scores Mean: Adding an Adjective Rating Scale. *Journal of Usability Studies*, *4*(3), 114–123.

Bangor, A., Kortum, P. T., & Miller, J. T. (2008). An Empirical Evaluation of the System Usability Scale. *International Journal of Human-Computer Interaction*, *24*(March 2015), 574–594.

Blackmon, M., Polson, P., Kitajima, M., & Lewis, C. (2002). Cognitive Walkthrough for the Web. I *CHI 2002* (s. Vol. 4, No. 1. pp. 463-470). Minneapolis, Minnesota, USA: ACM.

Brooke, J. (1996). SUS -A quick and dirty usability scale Usability and context.

Brooke, J. (2013). SUS : A Retrospective. *Journal of Usability Studies*, *8*(2), 29–40.

Dix, A., Finlay, J., Abowd, G. D., & Beale, R. (2004). *Human-Computer Interaction* (Third Edition). Harlow, England: Pearson Prentice Hall.

Flaticon. (2019). Flaticon. Retrieved 01 februari 2019, from https://www.flaticon.com

ISO. (1998). *ISO 9241-11:1998 - Ergonomic requirements for office work with visual display terminals (VDTs) -- Part 11: Guidance on usability. SIS.* Stockholm.

Lewis, J. R., & Sauro, J. (2009). The Factor Structure of the System Usability Scale (s. 94–103). Springer, Berlin, Heidelberg.

Mahatody, T., Sagar, M., & Kolski, C. (2010). State of the Art on the Cognitive Walkthrough Method, Its Variants and Evolutions. *International Journal of Human-Computer Interaction*, *26*(8), 741–785.

Nielsen, J. (1993a). Iterative user-interface design. *Computer*, *26*(11), 32–41.

Nielsen, J. (1993b). *Usability Engineering*. San Diego: Academic Press.

Nielsen, J. (2012). Usability 101: Introduction to Usability. From https://www.nngroup.com/articles/usability-101-introduction-to-usability/

Nielsen, J. (2017). 10 Usability Heuristics for User Interface Design. From https://www.nngroup.com/articles/ten-usability-heuristics/

Norman, D. (2013). *The Design of Everyday Things* (2nd ed.). Basic books.

Pierre, R.S.D.S.D.Q. (2015). Heuristics in Design: A Literature Review. *Procedia Manufacturing*, *3*, 6571–6578.

Shneiderman, B. (2017). The Eight Golden Rules of Interface Design. Hämtad 15 november 2017, from https://www.cs.umd.edu/users/ben/goldenrules.html

Stanton, N. A., Salmon, P. R., Walker, G. B., & Jenkins, D. (2013). *Human Factors Methods: A Practical Guide for Engineering and Design*. Surrey, England: Ashgate Publishing Limited.

Tognazzini, B. (2018). First Principles of Interaction Design. From https://asktog.com/atc/principles-of-interaction-design/

Wharton, C., Rieman, J., Lewis, C., & Polson, P. (1994). The cognitive walthrough Method: A Parctitioner's Guide. I J. Nielsen & R. Mack (Red.), *Usability Inspection Methods*. New York.

Wichansky, A. (2017). *Hands-On Software Usability Testing Lab and Advanced Methods*. *HCI International.*

MULTIDIMENSIONAL EVALUATION OF USER INTERFACES USABILITY ENRICHED WITH DECISION SUPPORT SYSTEMS ANALYSIS

Mariana Carvalho, Orlando Belo and Saulo Silva
Universidade do Minho, Departamento de Informática, Braga, Portugal

ABSTRACT

Interactive Systems' User Interfaces can be considered as a special type of decision support system, as it exposes system's internal logic for supporting users' decision-making processes. Several evaluation methods can be used for investigating if the behaviour of a user interface complies with the best practices of human interface design. This paper investigates how Decision Support Systems methods and tools might assist in the analysis of Interactive System's User Interfaces. A research instrument is designed, as well as a multidimensional view of the data is created and presented. This work presents an alternative demarche for extending usability measurements of interactive interfaces, seeking to assist system designers and administrators in maintaining and improving their systems.

KEYWORDS

Decision Support Systems, Interactive Systems, User Interfaces, Usability Evaluation, What-If Analysis

1. INTRODUCTION

Decision Support Systems (DSS) materialize a concept about the role of computers within the decision-making processes (Fick and Sprague, 2013). For some researchers, DSS represent a kind of interactive system, i.e., computer systems that managers use for accessing business data. Others focus on DSS as representing analytic models suited for decision-making processes. Regardless of the group and how they understand the concept, its importance is unquestionable, as it intercepts different fields of the modern world. If one looks to decision-making processes from a different angle, an especial kind of DSS is revealed. As interactive systems support interaction between humans and computers, for this reason it should provide a User Interface (UI). In this sense, we can define UI as the part of the system with which humans (the "user" in this context) come into contact, physically, perceptually and conceptually (Benyon, 2014). When such interfaces are graphical (GUI), they provide elements to control the system – e.g., buttons, screens, text boxes, sliders, etc. –, exposing to the user the processes behind the system under control. The user makes use of the UI intending to achieve a goal with the system. If the UI has flaws or problems, the goal is unachieved. Some systems have critical functions, such as medical, energy, aeronautical systems, and in such cases, are referred to as critical interactive systems. For those systems, errors and problems in the UI have the potential for causing losses of different nature, such as financial, environmental or social, which Leveson (2011) characterises simply as accidents. Different kinds of evaluations can be used for ensuring safe and effective operation of UI or special DSS.

In this work we focused our attention in a particular system UI: a university library Web site. Universities' libraries are among the most important resources for students and researchers, as they intend to provide curated and catalogued information for this public. Those libraries provide Web sites for consulting information. Providing a well-designed Web site then has major importance for universities and companies to support their strategic goals. Well-designed Web sites can be valuable tools for its users, fulfilling their needs and expectations and helping them to accomplish their tasks. Several criteria exist to define what a well-designed Web site is, such as reliability and security (Fernandez *et. al.*, 2011); however, from the user point of view, Usability is an important aspect to consider (Djamasbi *et. al.*, 2010; Okhovati *et. al.*, 2017).

Our work was about how to evaluate the referred library Web site, taking into account end user participation. Okhovati *et. al.*, (2017) highlighted that end users expect the library Web site to be easy to use, efficient in performing a specific task and ensure their satisfaction when they use it. Therefore all efforts that can be deployed for ensure the correctness and way of working with the Web site are important, not only in terms of automatic or manual evaluations, considering human factors. This is why a multidimensional view of the usability evaluation might improve the analysis results, allowing for the extraction of additional information from the data, fulfilling the role of DSS for those interested in providing a well-designed UI. We propose the use of a data warehouse (DW) to receive and provide the referred multidimensional data view. Additionally, we applied What-if analysis for enriching the usability evaluation results. Therefore, the contributions of this paper are as follows: to provide a literature review for themes such as DSS, What-If and usability analysis, as well as to provide a clear understanding of how they are related. Our aim was to bring all those concepts without losing sight of its centrality for the evaluation of interactive computer system's interfaces, i.e., its importance on how they can be used for improving those interfaces. The remaining part of this paper is organised as follows: Section 2 addresses some background topics and related work about usability and DSS, Section 3 exposes some considerations about the experiment design, the implementation of the multidimensional and DSS analysis, and, finally, Section 4 presents some conclusions and research lines for future work.

2. BACKGROUND

The literature of libraries evaluation provides evidence that the majority of evaluation studies of digital libraries are related with usability (Kous *et. al.*, 2018). Usability can be seen as a set of multiple constructs derived from various perspectives, such as effectiveness, efficiency, subjective pleasure, or memorability, with large focus on interface design (Jeng, 2006). Nielsen, who in the early 1990s, together with Rubin, developed usability engineering techniques for computer software design applied to Web design (Nielsen, 2003), establishes that usability "is a quality attribute that describes how easy user interfaces are to use" (Kous *et. al.*, 2018). International Organization for Standardization (ISO), in its chapter 9241-11 about Ergonomics of human-system interaction, considers usability as "the extent to which a product can be used by a specified user to achieve specified goals with effectiveness, efficiency and satisfaction in a specified context of use" (ISO/IEC, 1998). More specifically, we can see effectiveness as a reference to the completeness at which users achieve specified goals, efficiency as an allusion to the resources used in completing a task, and satisfaction the construct that reveals positive attitudes toward using the system. The literature provides evidence of strong positive correlation between satisfaction with effectiveness and efficiency (Joo, 2010). Due to these findings, the construct of satisfaction was excluded from the framework used as research instrument. Instead of satisfaction, the construct of learnability is selected as part of the research instrument. This construct is based on software engineering aspects, such as the usability model proposed by Nielsen (Nielsen, 1994), which refers to how easy it is for casual users to learn a system, or ISO/IEC 9126 (ISO/IEC, 2001), referring to the capability of a software product for enabling users to learn how to use it.

The increase in business competitiveness has led to the need of obtaining strategic information, due to its value. In order to achieve this, one possibility was to re-signify pre-existing data in the companies, obtaining multidimensional information from it that might help in a decision-making process. DSS are then characterised by their mission to improve the decision-making process, by providing either interactive systems that managers can use to access data, or analytic models suited for the decision-making process. From the need to re-signify data, the concept of data warehouse (DW) emerged. Muntean & Târnăveanu (2012) highlights that a DW is defined as a special kind of a database, in which atomic data are gathered from several sources in a structured way for creating a multidimensional and oriented version of the corporative truths, which allows for precise initiatives to support decision making processes. There are several divergences about the best approach for defining DW architecture, in terms of quality, high performance or scalability. Ralph Kimball, for instance, supports the idea that each business area should freely implement its own databases, based on their requirements (Matouk & Owoc, 2012). Bill Inmon in contrast, supports a top-down approach, in which the databases are developed according to the DW final project, i.e., a central scheme working as a model for the departments to develop their own databases (Breslin, 2004).

The importance of usability is undeniable. It increases user satisfaction, efficiency and productivity and decreases costs (Mazumder, 2012). Usually, the evaluation of usability involves activities such as collecting, analysing and critiquing usability data (Ivory and Hearst, 1999). The analysis is a crucial phase in this process due to the importance of interpreting data and analysing results. What-If analysis is a technique that can help in this task. By helping the user to simulate scenarios based on human information - modelling a user interaction with a user interface is one of many advantages of the integration of What-If analysis simulation in usability evaluation processes.

Golfarelli, *et. al.* (2006) defines What-If analysis as a method that allows for decision makers to create hypothetical scenarios and analyse possible effects in the behaviour of a complex system caused by changing variables' values. In other words, this technology permits to assess beforehand what might happen in the business as result of manipulating parameters and changing what can be consider as a normal business behaviour without endangering real business. This technology ends up being a useful way for testing and validating business hypotheses and a safer solution to address any doubt, like for instance, answer the What-If type question "What if we pursue a new strategy?". What-If analysis also helps to ensure that the subsequent decisions will have some success, by helping the user to simulate the hypothetical scenarios and analyse the outcome. Moreover, it allows for analysing different scenarios and perspectives of business, anticipating some possible solutions. The process of What-If analysis is made using a simulation model. This model represents the real business model and can be composed by a set of scenarios based on historical data. The user is responsible to delineate the axis of analysis, the set of values for analysing and the set of values of the scenario to change according to his goals. To perform the What-If analysis, it is required to have an appropriate tool, which can perform this technology to get the new (altered) scenario. Goal seek is a Microsoft Office Excel's (Excel, 2019) built-in What-If analysis tool, which helps the user to answer What-If type questions by showing what could be the effects of changing a cells' value in a specific scenario. In other words, it determines what value a user should enter in an input cell to get the desired result in a cell that contains a formula. Goal seek receives a formula cell, the desired value and the cell to change in order to achieve the target and performs all the need calculations giving the user the wanted value. A symbolic example of how goal seek works (Figure 1) is about considering a retail company and a basic model. Giving the number of units sold (1500 units), retail price ($15) and discount (25%), using a calculation formula to calculate the total revenue reveals $16,875.00. The main goal of this analysis is to discover how many units the retail company needs to sell to reach $25,000 of revenue (Figure 1a). To do this, it is important to define the "Set cell", "To value" and "By changing cell" in the goal seek dialog box. The set cell is the revenue cell represented by D5 cell, and we intent to alter this cell to '$25,000', by changing the cell of the '1500' units sold represented by D2. After Goal Seek is performed (Figure 1b), the Excel informs that the Goal Seek provides a solution: 2222 units need to be sold to achieve the target value.

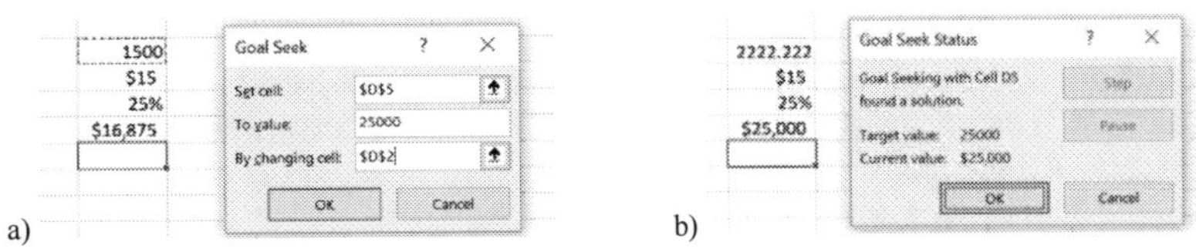

Figure 1. Goal-seek example (a) and results (b)

The literature of What-If analysis provides some relevant references about its use in usability evaluation. For instance, Hearst and Landay (1999) surveys a state of the art of automation of user interface usability evaluation and suggest the use of What-If analysis in an earlier development stage can help to avoid costly mistakes. A simulator named Monte Carlo (Rubinstein and Kroese, 2016), which is a probabilistic simulator model that uses What-If analysis and is frequently used in usability evaluations. Arh and Jerman-Blazic (2007) proposed a complex decision-making solution for the evaluation of learning management systems, by studying and analysing usability, applicability and adequacy of learning management systems. These authors suggest using What-If analysis in the learning management systems evaluation and analysis phase. Eklund *et. al.*, (2008) implement a usability evaluation method for software development using eXtreme Programming (agile methodology for software development). During the usability evaluation setup, the authors use What-If analysis to simulate several types of analysis. What-If analysis is also referred in other Human-Computer Interaction (HCI) literature, such as in aviation safety, where Rungta *et. al.* (2013) presents a formal verification approach based on simulation and on model checking to guarantee the safety in human-machine systems. The models are created using Brahms, which uses What-if analysis and allows for modelling several components using simulation; and in discrete event simulation models with virtual reality integration, Turner *et. al.* (2016) uses What-If analysis in the experimentation and validation of the discrete event simulation model.

3. EXPERIMENT DESIGN

3.1 Gathering, Preparing and Storing Data

The word 'usability' refers to methods for improving ease-of-use during the design process. In general, the usability of a system has the potential to impact how users accomplish tasks in a system. To provide well-designed interactive systems, tools and methods are required for understanding the usability of user interfaces, as well as for improving them (Root and Draper, 1983). In this work, we adopted the usability evaluation model and associated evaluation survey tool proposed by Joo (2011), tailored to academic libraries Web sites. We decided to design our research instrument in the form of a research survey, which is used to obtain necessary data to analyse. The survey uses closed questions to collect the information, as opposed to open-ended questions, where the responder is free to give his own answers to the questions. In this case, we rely in the Likert scale to transform order points into a linear scale (Babbie, 1999) and to address two groups of information: 1) demographic information (filter questions), for exploring the characteristics of the different study groups; 2) research questions information, also referred as to usability evaluation instrument, directly related with the usability evaluation model in the context of academic libraries, proposed by Joo (2011). Typically the scale rating ranges from 5, 7 and 9 points. We decided to use a 7 points scale (Table 1), starting with the alternative *"I strongly disagree"* (1 point), following additional six intervals, until the final interval designated *"I totally agree"* (7 points), respectively. The research survey was designed for collecting information in a monthly basis periodicity.

Table 1. Likert Scale defined for the research instrument (Babbie, 1999)

(1) I strongly disagree	(2) Disagree	(3) Slightly disagree	(4) I do not agree or disagree	(5) Slightly agree	(6) I agree	(7) I totally agree
(Do not answer at all to the required)	*(Serves with failed the minimum required)*	*(Meets partially the expectations)*	*(Neither agree or disagree)*	*(Meets partially the expectations)*	*(Meets completely the expectations)*	*(Above the expectations)*

The research instrument was hosted in a specific computational platform for data gathering and treatment, where university's staff (including master and PhD students, as well as researchers) was invited to participate in the research. Each respondent is required to answer six questions regarding each of the three research constructs (properties), namely effectiveness, efficiency and learnability. A number of thirty-five respondents ($n = 35$) were able to participate. All the answers were collect using a specific Web form and the correspondent data stored in an operational system supported by MySQL (MySQL, 2019).

Based on the data collected and the requisites previously established for user satisfaction analysis we designed a decision support data structure especially conceived for this usability case analysis. This structure includes all the analysis dimensions we considered to be the most relevant for the case, namely "Date", a temporal dimension, "Question", which supports the questions themselves, "Respondent", where we characterized in terms of frequency, skill, or gender, who answered the usability question, and "Property", the dimension that simply describes the property associated with a particular question. These four dimensions were materialized in four relational tables ("Date_Dim", "Question_Dim", "Respondent_Dim", and "Property_Dim") that jointly with a fifth table – a fact table ("Usability_Fact") – formed a relational star-schema (Figure 2), one of the most typical configuration for a data warehouse. The definition of the granularity level of the fact table is an important aspect in the design of the data warehouse, as it impacts directly its performance and analysis capacity. A very high level of granularity might reduce system performance, once it stores a higher number of registers. A very low level of granularity might affect the analysis, since the data are usually shortened. The proposed grain of the analysis is then the classification given by each of the respondents to the specific questions of the research instrument. The field "ScaleValues" in the fact table "Usability_Fact" is responsible for storing this specific information.

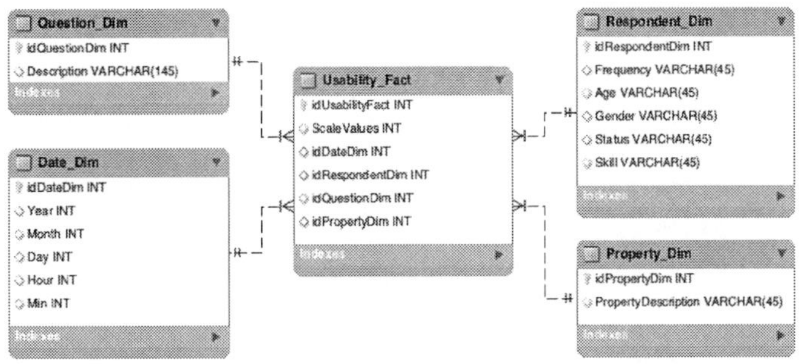

Figure 2. The usability star-schema of the data warehouse

Obtaining the multidimensional data view of the collected data implies the extraction, transformation and loading the data received from the Web-based form into the data warehouse. To accomplish this task we have developed an ETL (extract-transform-load) process. This process is crucial and needs to be performed with attention to ensure the correct introduction of the data into the data warehouse structures, in order that they can be used to identify new strategic information (e.g., tendencies), which can be used to improve the decision-making process. ETL operations are usually performed by a set of tools known as back-end tools, in a reference to the tools used by the engineers in charge of maintenance and management operations of such kind of systems, as opposed to front-end tools, which managers and decision-makers make use for activities such as consulting reports, graphics and information using the DW system. According to Kimbal (1996), the main operations performed by the back-end tools are: 1) extraction of data from internal and external sources; 2) cleaning or normalization of the extracted data; 3) loading data into the data warehouse; and 4) updating data (refresh). During the migration process, different types of needs might exist until the required result is achieved. Therefore, the utilisation of different back-end tools in different phases of the project is frequent. In our case, we choose to work with two, namely: Pentaho Data Integration (Pentaho, 2019), often referred to as *Kettle*, which is the Pentaho component in charge of ETL activities (Casters *et. al.*, 2010); and MySQL Workbench (MySQL Workbench, 2019), which is the database management tool available for MySQL. In Figure 3 we can see the BPMN (Business Process Model and Notation) model proposed to execute the ETL operations. Basically, this process was organized in two different parts. In the first part, the Kettle tool was used to normalise and load the data from the operational system into the data warehouse, namely to populate the dimensions tables and to create data mappings in a staging area, which was used to support all the transformation tasks integrated in the ETL process. In the second part, all the data consolidation tasks are performed, and the fact table is populated.

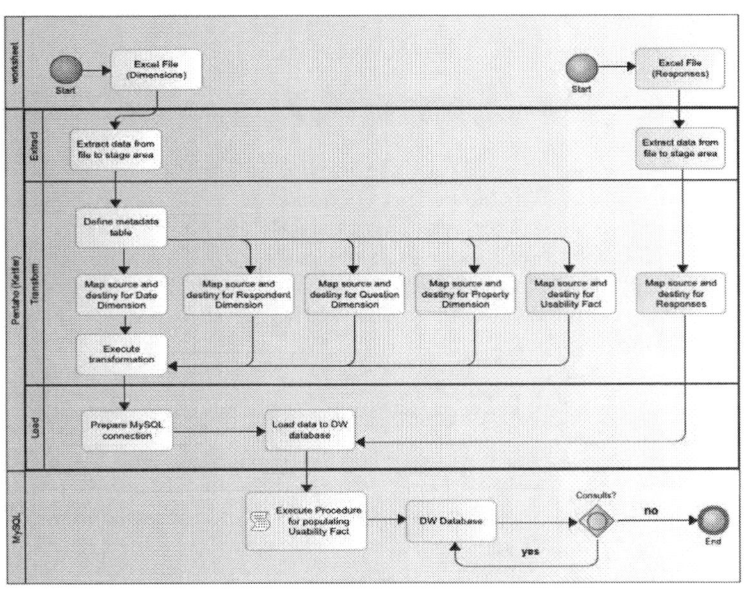

Figure 3. The BPMN Model of the ETL Process

3.2 Usability Analysis

Having the data warehouse fully implemented as a DSS, methods and tools can be used to analyse the results, enriching the value of the multidimensional information. What-If analysis is a valuable method to use in this case. In this work, we use it to verify the outcome of three possible application scenarios. For instance, let's consider the representation for aggregated value of each construct, namely effectiveness, efficiency and learnability. After the data warehouse implementation, those representations can help the designer to understand the user perception for each construct. Therefore, the final evaluation given for the constructs is composed by the pair [order point/representation in the linear scale], in which the order point is obtained by verifying the *mode* value of each construct, and the representation in the linear scale can be obtained by consulting Table 1. Effectiveness and Efficiency constructs are scored 4.0, whereas its respective representation in the linear scale is "*Neither agree or disagree*" to the construct questions. Learnability construct is score 5.0, translating to "*Meets partially the expectations*" in the linear scale of the construct questions. Thus the overall system final evaluation represents the value "*I do not agree or disagree*" in the linear scale. Using the previous rationale, the designer could hypothetically wonder how the system score behaves when one of the constructs is scored maximum classification, indicating final users "*totally agrees*" to the construct questions. Therefore, three applications scenarios are presented: i) effectiveness scores 7, ii) efficiency scores 7 and iii) learnability scores 7. Figure 4a depicts the scenario manager, a tool that works as an interface to the Goal Seek tool. The outcome of the analysis, shown in Figure 4b, presents the possible effects changes in the behaviour of the three scenarios, which are respectively 5.0, 7.0 and 6.0. Based on this outcome, a designer might justify his decisions to change policies or allocate resources to best suit the strategy of improving the Web site.

a)

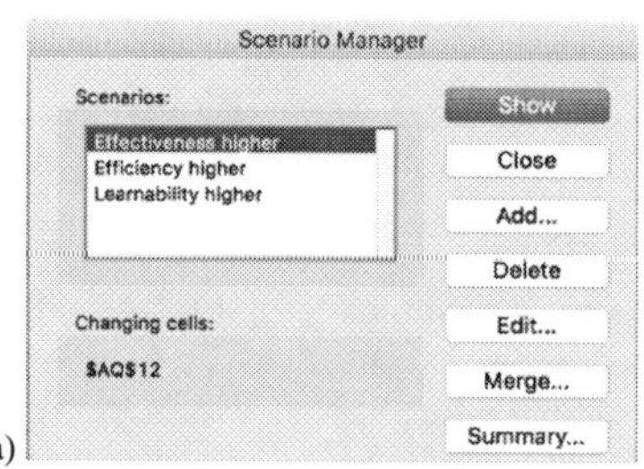

b)

Scenario 1		Scenario 2		Scenario 3	
Effectiveness	7,0	Effectivenes	7,0	Effectivenes	6,0
Efficiency	5,0	Efficiency	7,0	Efficiency	6,0
Learnability	5,0	Learnability	6,0	Learnability	7,0
Result:		Result:		Result:	
5,0		7,0		6,0	

Figure 4. The scenario manager (a) and the outcome of goal-seek application (b)

4. CONCLUSIONS AND FUTURE WORK

In this paper we presented a case study, in which the central library Web site of the University of Minho was evaluated by a group of university students. As result of the analysis, some design improvements about constructs were suggested. We investigated how a research instrument can capture the usability of those Web sites. We also presented a structured methodology to both provide a multidimensional view of the analysis, as well as to perform additional analysis for verifying possible effects in hypothetical scenarios, analysing the system behaviour. We achieved the goals proposed in this paper, providing evidence that the usability of a Web site can be verified in terms of effectiveness, efficiency and learnability. We also provided evidence that DSS methods can be used to help extending the usability analysis, in order to help system designers and administrators to maintain and improve their systems.

In terms of limitation regarding the current research, we highlight the need to extend the end user participation to other university staff (e.g., library and department employees, etc.). This has the potential to increase the feedback regarding the usability aspects considered. Another aspect worth considering is the existing space for methodology improvement regarding the research instrument. While translating linear scale to order points might provide a reasonable simplified method for the respondent to situate his answer for the proposed question, it provides the researcher a smaller universe of space of analysis. Also, providing a non-response option (e.g., "*no opinion*") could provide an alternative for undecided respondents. Additionally automating the evaluation method would allow restoring the respective point scale related to each measurement, presenting order points to the interface designer.

Future work in this research includes using the acquired knowledge for automating the process of analysis and increasing the complexity of the hypothetical scenarios. Additionally, adopting a different methodology for research instrument design might allow a wider range of measurements and therefore less limited universe of space of analysis.

ACKNOWLEDGEMENT

This work has been supported by Conselho Nacional de Pesquisa (CNPq), COMPETE: POCI-01-0145-FEDER-007043, and FCT – Fundação para a Ciência e Tecnologia within the Project Scope: UID/CEC/00319/2013. We also want to thanks to Instituto Federal de Educação, Ciência e Tecnologia de Goiás (IFG).

REFERENCES

Arh, T., & Jerman-Blazic, B. (2007). *Application of Multi-Attribute Decision Making Approach to Learning Management Systems Evaluation*. JCP, 2(10), 28-37.

Babbie, E. (1999) *The basics of social research*. New York, NY: Wadsworth.

Benyon, D. (2014) *Designing interactive systems: A comprehensive guide to HCI, UX and interaction design*.

Breslin, M. (2004). *Data warehousing battle of the giants*. Business Intelligence Journal, 7, 6-20.

Casters, M., Bouman, R., & Van Dongen, J. (2010). *Pentaho Kettle solutions: building open source ETL solutions with Pentaho Data Integration*. John Wiley & Sons.

Djamasbi, S. Siegel, M. & Tullis, T. (2010) *Generation Y, web design, and eye tracking*. International journal of human-computer studies, 68(5), 307-323.

Eklund, T., Tétard, F., Ståhl, P., Hirkman, P., & Back, B. (2008, January). *Usability evaluation of an XP product*. In Proceedings of the 19 th Australasian Conference on Information Systems (ACIS) (pp. 280-289).

Excel (2019). *Microsoft Excel*. Available at https://products.office.com/pt-pt/excel?rtc=1 [Accessed June 19, 2019]

Fernandez, A. Insfran, E. & Abrahão, S. (2011) *Usability evaluation methods for the web: A systematic mapping study*. Information and software Technology, 53(8), 789-817.

Fick, G., & Sprague, R. H. (Eds.). (2013). *Decision Support Systems: Issues and Challenges: Proceedings of an International Task Force Meeting* June 23-25, 1980 (Vol. 11). Elsevier.

Golfarelli, M., Rizzi, S., & Proli, A. (2006). *Designing what-if analysis: towards a methodology*. In Proceedings of the 9th ACM international workshop on Data warehousing and OLAP (pp. 51-58). ACM.

Hearst, M., & Landay, J. (1999). *Improving the Early Phases of Web Site Design via Informal Design Tools and Automated Usability Assessment*.

ISO (2001). *Standard 9126: Software Engineering Product Quality*, parts 1, 2 and 3.

ISO/IEC (International Organization for Standardization) (1998). *Standard 9241: Ergonomic Requirements for Office Work with Visual Display Terminals (VDT)s, Part 11. Guidance on Usability*, Available at: https://www.iso.org/obp/ui/#iso:std:iso:9241:-11:ed-1:v1:en (accessed in 20 Jan 2019).

Ivory, M., & Hearst, M. (1999). *Comparing performance and usability evaluation: new methods for automated usability assessment*. Submitted for publication.

Jeng, J. (2006). *Usability of the digital library: An evaluation model*. College and Research Libraries News, 67(2), 78.

Joo, S. (2010) *How are usability elements-efficiency, effectiveness, and satisfaction-correlated with each other in the context of digital libraries?* Proceedings of the American Society for Information Science and Technology, 47(1).

Joo, S. Lin S. & Lu, K. (2011). *A usability evaluation model for academic library websites: efficiency, effectiveness and learnability*. Journal of Library and Information Studies, 9(2), 11-26.

Kimball, R. (1996). *The data warehouse toolkit: practical techniques for building dimensional data warehouses* (Vol. 1). New York: John Wiley & Sons.

Kous, K. Pušnik, M. Heričko, M. & Polančič, G. (2018). *Usability evaluation of a library website with different end user groups*. Journal of Librarianship and Information Science, 0961000618773133.

Leveson, N. (2011). *Engineering a safer world: Systems thinking applied to safety*. MIT press.

Matouk, K., & Owoc, M. L. (2012, September). *A survey of data warehouse architectures—Preliminary results*. In 2012 Federated Conference on Computer Science and Information Systems (FedCSIS) (pp. 1121-1126). IEEE.

Mazumder, F. K., & Das, U. K. (2014). *Usability guidelines for usable user interface*. International Journal of Research in Engineering and Technology, 3(9), 79-82.

Muntean, M. I., & Târnăveanu, D. (2012). A Multidimensional View Proposal of the Data Collected Through a Questionnaire. Associated Data Mart Deployment Framework. *Database Systems Journal*, *3*(4), 33-46.

MySQL (2019). *MySQL 8.0 Community Edition*. Available at https://www.mysql.com/ [Accessed June 19, 2019]

MySQL Workbench (2019). *MySQL Workbench 8.0*. Available at https://www.mysql.com/products/workbench/. Available at https://www.forbes.com/sites/bernardmarr/2016/04/28/ big-data-overload-most-companies-cant-deal-with-the-data-explosion/#70cbd9506b0d [Accessed June 19, 2019]

Nielsen, J. (1994, April). *Usability inspection methods. In Conference companion on Human factors in computing systems,* (pp. 413-414). ACM.

Nielsen, J. (2003). *Usability 101: Introduction to usability.*

Okhovati, M. Karami, F. & Khajouei, R. (2017). *Exploring the usability of the central library websites of medical sciences universities*. Journal of Librarianship and Information Science, 49(3), 246-255.

Pentaho (2019). *Data Integration – Kettle*. Hitachi Vantara Community. Available at https://community.hitachi vantara.com/docs/DOC-1009855-data-integration-kettle [Accessed June 19, 2019]

Root R. W. & Draper S. (1983). *Questionnaires as a software evaluation tool.* In Proceedings of the SIGCHI conference on Human Factors in Computing Systems, December, pp. 83-87, ACM.

Rubinstein, R. Y., & Kroese, D. P. (2016). *Simulation and the Monte Carlo method (Vol. 10)*. John Wiley & Sons.

Rungta, N., Brat, G., Clancey, W. J., Linde, C., Raimondi, F., Seah, C., & Shafto, M. (2013, May). *Aviation safety: modeling and analyzing complex interactions between humans and automated systems.* In Proceedings of the 3rd international conference on application and theory of automation in command and control systems (pp. 27-37). ACM.

Turner, C. J., Hutabarat, W., Oyekan, J., & Tiwari, A. (2016). *Discrete event simulation and virtual reality use in industry: new opportunities and future trends*. IEEE Transactions on Human-Machine Systems, 46(6), 882-894.

A FOCUS-PLUS-CONTEXT VISUALIZATION FOR STRENGTH EXERCISE TRAINING

Daniel Steffen[1], Florian Kalt[1], Michael Resch[2] and Gabriele Bleser[1]
[1]*Technische Universität Kaiserslautern, AG wearHEALTH, Kaiserslautern, Germany*
[2]*ERGO-FIT GmbH & Co. KG, Pirmasens, Germany*

ABSTRACT

Regular strength exercise training is recommended by the WHO. Users – especially novices or patients – call for intensive supervision to execute strength exercises correctly – even if performed with a fitness device. Usually, a trainer or a physiotherapist provide guidance and assist the user. However, increasing costs and missing experts call for new solutions that support the user to perform strength exercises correctly and without supervision of an expert.
This paper describes the fitness system SMART-FIT. The system comprises a cable machine, a notebook, and a tablet PC providing visual feedback during strength exercise training. 36 participants volunteered in our user study, designed as within-subject experiment. Performing a shoulder exercise, participants tested 3 different visual feedback interfaces: *2-Pillar*, *1-Pillar*, and *Ribbon*. We evaluated the effect of the interfaces on the performance, e.g., Pearson's correlation coefficient. Additionally, we applied the questionnaires Flow-Short-Scale, NASA-TLX, AttrakDiff2, and System Usability Scale among others. The results of our user study will enable designers to make more appropriate design choices for future exercise support systems.

KEYWORDS

Strength Exercise, Focus-Plus-Context, Visual Augmented Feedback, Error Measurements, User Study

1. INTRODUCTION

Physical activity including aerobic and strength training provides many physiological benefits. Regular strength exercise training is recommended by the World Health Organization (WHO) both in prevention and in rehabilitation. It effectively reduces falls and reduces the risk of disease outcomes. However, users – especially beginners or patients during rehabilitation – have to be supervised and supported intensely to ensure correct exercise execution and to avoid infringements. A badly executed exercise can lead to injuries and might delay the recovery. Frequently, a trainer or physiotherapist guides and supports the user in the fitness or rehabilitation center, i.e., a controlled environment. Increasing costs and the absence of qualified personnel call for innovative and flexible solutions that can be used anywhere and even without supervision. Thus, the correct execution of an exercise without supervision is the overall challenge.

There are many fitness devices available in the market, which provide visual feedback to the user through a mounted display (cf. ERGO-FIT 2019). Many of these systems are limited to display only the number of repetitions, the number of sets or the information about breaks. However, additional factors like the range of motion (ROM), the moving amplitude, the speed of eccentric and concentric movements, or the movement smoothness are important variables to guarantee a correct and safe exercise execution.

The problem of executing exercise movements while simultaneously validating the correct execution is a major challenge. Among others, visual feedback can be used to address this problem. Visual feedback for movement tasks can be subdivided into abstract visualizations or natural visualizations (Sigrist et al. 2013). Abstract visualizations – such as lines, curves, bars or points – are being used to provide visual feedback for simple movement exercises. Erikson et al. (2011) evaluated a simple visual feedback for runners. The authors used three bars to visualize the variables vertical displacement, step length, and the mechanical power-consumption, which was a combination of the previous two bars. The height of the bars indicated the values of the parameters at the moment the participant was running. In each bar, a mark was indicating the target level. Morris et al. (2007) evaluated a visualization for learning a sequence of one-dimensional forces.

They used two bars representing target and actual force. Chittaro and Sioni (2014) compared simple abstract visualizations within a mobile breathing app: a circle-based visualization (circle expands and contracts, which suggests the expansion and contraction of human lungs) and a wave-based visualization where a wave-like line illustrates the optimal respiratory cycle.

In contrast, natural visualizations are utilized for more complex movements. A movement is considered complex if the movement consists of several degrees of freedom. Steffen et al. (2011), for example, used wireless movement sensors to track users' movements and to mirror complex exercise movements in VR.

The following sections will describe the SMART-FIT system to support simple movement exercises. We developed 3 training interfaces that belong to the category of abstract visualization for movement exercises.

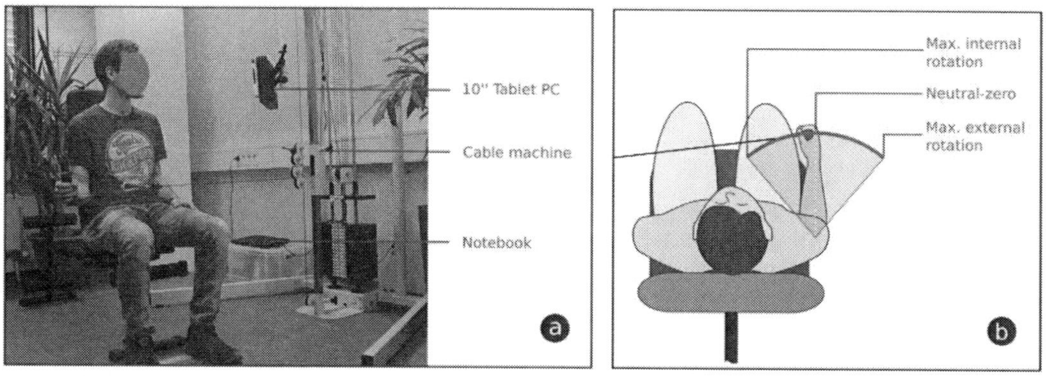

Figure 1. (a) ERGO-Fit's cable machine uses a distance sensor to measure the displacement of the weights. We added a notebook streaming the distance data via Wi-Fi to a 10 inch tablet PC displaying the training interface. (b) Top view of the internal and external rotation of the shoulder exercise in the user study

2. SMART-FIT

Within this paper we present the SMART-FIT system. The SMART-FIT system is displayed in Figure 1. The main component of the system is a cable machine of the ERGO-FIT GmbH & Co. KG. The cable machine utilizes a high performance distance sensor measuring the displacement of the weight in millimeter. The cable machine is equipped with a display that is mounted on a swiveling arm. We enhanced the system with an extra notebook and a 10-inch tablet PC (same display size as the supplied display). The tablet PC is mounted in front of the supplied display. We connected the distance sensor to the notebook and streamed the data over Wi-Fi to the tablet PC. Firstly, we added the extra hardware components to store the movement data for later analysis. Secondly, we aimed for an architecture that is capable of streaming the exercise data to a physiotherapists' smart phone to monitor multiple users, for example.

Figure 2 presents three different training interfaces to support the exercise execution: *2-Pillar*, *1-Pillar*, and *Ribbon* interface. The maximum and minimum displacements for an exercise, i.e., the maximum and minimum flexion / extension, are computed during an initial calibration routine. They define the users' individual range of motion (ROM). The user should not move above or below the maximum and minimum to avoid any injury. A repetition is completed when the user moves the actual from the lower area to the upper area and back again. The target displacement defines speed and position of the exercise, i.e., the displacement of the weight. All interfaces display the number of repetitions and number of sets to perform / performed. Each interface has a stop / pause button to cancel the exercise at any time.

The *2-Pillar* interface uses two animated pillars (see Figure 2, left). The fill level displays the target and actual weight displacement. The pillars are labeled with 'target' and 'actual' to avoid misunderstandings. Using the *2-Pillar* interface might result in a cognitive overload. On the one hand, the user focuses on a correctly executed repetition with respect to the ROM, i.e., moving above and below a specified threshold. On the other hand, he has to pay attention to align actual and target displacement to perform the exercise at the correct speed. This is a dual-task condition which might result in a weak performance while performing the exercise.

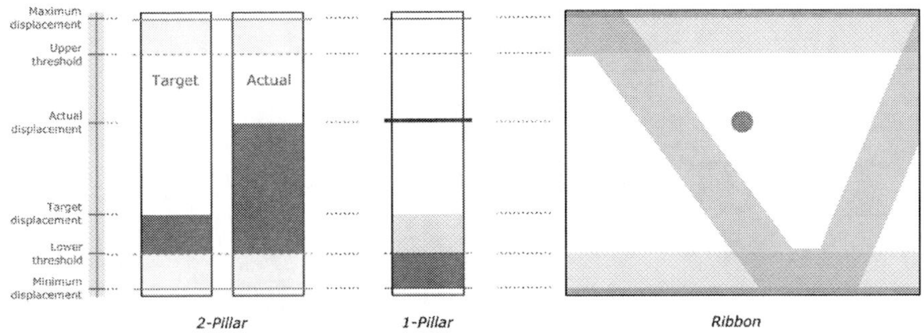

Figure 2. The developed training interfaces: *2-Pillar (left)*, *1-Pillar(center)*, and *Ribbon (right)*. Each interface illustrates maximum, minimum, actual, and target weight displacement. To complete a repetition the user starts below the lower threshold, moves the actual above the upper threshold and back again

To tackle the dual-task condition we developed the *1-Pillar* interface (see Figure 2, center). Target and actual displacement are merged into a single pillar to avoid cognitive overload. The fill level of the pillar illustrates the target displacement. A horizontal bar represents the actual weight displacement.

The idea for the *Ribbon* interface (see Figure 2, right) goes back to wire loop games. Here, the metal loop, i.e., the actual displacement, is a filled circle, which is controlled by the user and moves along the vertical axis. A gray ribbon illustrates the target displacement and moves horizontally from left to right. To perform a correct movement the circle should stay within the ribbon. The *Ribbon* interface is a focus-plus-context visualization. The circle represents the actual displacement, i.e., the temporal focus. The graphical element ribbon visualizes past, current, and future target displacement, i.e., the temporal context. This interface allows the user to perceive the duration of a pause between repetitions. Additionally, the slope of the ribbon provides information about how fast he will have to perform concentric and eccentric movements.

3. USER STUDY

We conducted a within-subject experiment with the independent variable *Training Interface (TI)* with three levels: *2-Pillar*, *1-Pillar*, and *Ribbon*. In order to avoid learning and crossover effects we used a fully counterbalanced setup. To evaluate the performance of the exercise repetitions we used the following error measures as dependent variables: Pearson's Correlation Coefficient (COR), Mean Absolute Error (MAE), Root Mean Squared Error (RMSE), and Russell's Error Measurements (RUS; Russell 1997). Additionally, we used the following questionnaires: Flow-Short-Scale (FSS; Rheinberg, Vollmeyer, and Engeser 2003), Raw NASA TLX (RTLX; Hart 2006), System Usability Scale (SUS; Brooke 1996), and AttrakDiff2 (Hassenzahl, Koller, and Burmester 2008).

In the user study we used the SMART-FIT system as described in the previous chapter. A Samsung Galaxy Tab A10.1 (2016) tablet PC – running Android 7.0 – was used to display the different *TI* conditions. The tablet offers a resolution of 1200 x 1920 pixels.

The participants were students or employees at our University. They were recruited through notices posted on campus or by e-mail. 36 participants (14 female), aged 21 to 66 years (M = 40.22, SD = 15.78) volunteered in the user study. All but one participant were right-handed. 50 % of the participants have never been to the gym, while 20 % visit the gym on a regular basis. The majority of participants (21) were unfamiliar with exercises that involve a smart fitness device while 15 participants had some familiarity with such smart exercise devices. 2 out of 10 participants own a fitness device. Participants did not receive any compensation. No participant has been excluded from the user study.

The experiment was conducted in our laboratory. At the beginning of the experiment the participants signed the informed consent. Furthermore, we gave some general information and explained how to perform the exercise correctly. Figure 1 illustrates the exercise. It is a typical and simple strength exercise that is recommended in the case of the impingement syndrome of the shoulder. The exercise is composed of an external and internal rotation of the shoulder joint. Depending on the users' dominant hand we configured the hardware set up.

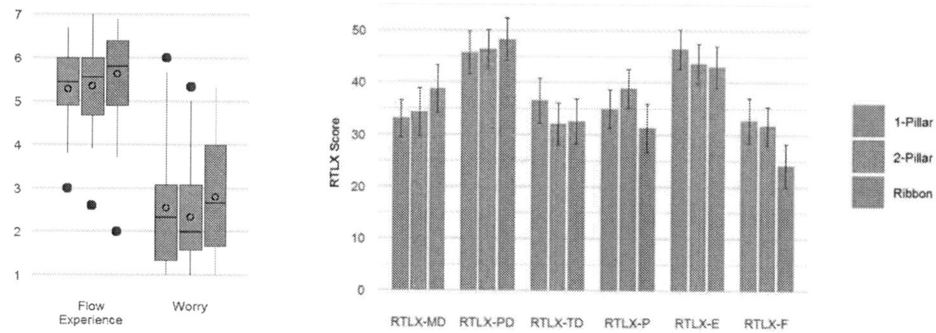

Figure 3. Left: The *Ribbon* interface received the highest mean and median scores in the FSS. Right: Raw NASA TLX (RTLX) scores and standard error bars. No significant differences were found for mental (RTLX-MD), physical (RTLX-PD), and temporal demands (RTLX-TD), performance (RTLX-P), effort (RTLX-E), and frustration (RTLX-F)

Before starting the application, the participants performed the exercise without any interface. By doing this we determined the maximum and minimum displacement of the weight and consequently the participants' individual ROM, i.e., the maximum internal and external rotation. The duration for the internal rotation was set to 3 seconds and the duration for the external rotation was set to 2 seconds. The weight for the exercise was 1kg for all participants. We chose this weight to avoid fatigue and to ensure all participants being able to perform all repetitions.

Before each trial, the participants received a training to familiarize themselves with the selected *TI*. During the training they performed up to five repetitions. Ten seconds after the training had finished the trial phase started automatically. Participants were asked to perform 10 repetitions of the shoulder exercise as correct as possible. The application stopped when 10 repetitions have been performed or the user canceled the application.

After the trials have been finished, we asked participants to rank the *TIs*. Besides their gym habits, participants reported on their demographic variables (e.g. year of birth, gender, etc.). The experimental user study lasted between 31 and 92 minutes ($MD = 45.39$, $SD = 11.42$). The following sections describe the results of the measures taken.

4. RESULTS

4.1 Flow-Short-Scale

Within our experiment we evaluated the effect of the *TI* on the participants' flow state. We used the German version of the FSS questionnaire (Rheinberg, Vollmeyer, and Engeser 2003). The FSS consists of 13 items. Each item is rated on a 7-point Likert scale from 1 ("no agreement") to 7 ("full agreement"). The first 10 items measure the *Flow Experience*. The items 11-13 measure *Worry* someone may have in the situation the measurement is made.

Figure 3 (left) shows the result of the FSS questionnaire. Measuring the participants' flow reveals that the *Ribbon* interface received the highest scores. The average *Flow Experience* using the *Ribbon* interface was larger ($M = 5.62$, $SD = 1.01$) than using the *2-Pillar* interface ($M = 5.35$, $SD = 0.90$) or the *1-Pillar* interface ($M = 5.27$, $SD = 0.92$). The differences between the interfaces conditions were not significant, $F(2, 70) = 2.68$, $p = 0.07$, $\eta^2 = 0.02$.

Furthermore, the factor *Worry* was rated highest when using the *Ribbon* interface ($M = 2.81$, $SD = 1.29$). Participants rated the *2-Pillar* interface lower ($M = 2.33$, $SD = 1.14$) than the *1-Pillar* interface ($M = 2.54$, $SD = 1.34$). Mauchly's test indicated that the assumption of sphericity had been violated, $W = 0.82$, $p < 0.05$, therefore degrees of freedom were corrected using Huynh-Feld estimates of sphericity ($\varepsilon = 0.88$). These differences were significant, $F(1.77, 61.86) = 5.92$, $p < 0.05$, $\eta^2 = 0.02$. Bonferroni post hoc tests revealed a significant difference between the *Ribbon* interface and the *2-Pillar* interface ($p < 0.01$). No other comparisons were significant (all $ps > 0.05$).

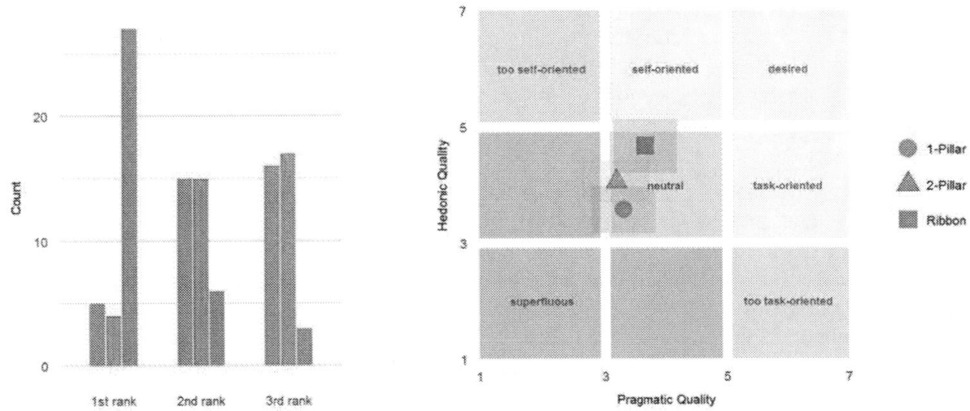

Figure 4. Left: 75% of the participants preferred the *Ribbon* interface over *1-Pillar* and *2-Pillar* when asked "Which training interface do you like best?" Right: The average results for hedonic and pragmatic quality and the 95% confidence intervals of the AttrakDiff2 questionnaire. The training interface had a significant effect on the hedonic quality

4.2 Raw NASA TLX

To measure users' perceived workload we used the NASA Task Load Index (TLX) questionnaire (Hart and Staveland 1988). The NASA TLX is a multi-dimensional scale to obtain workload estimates from users while performing a task or immediately afterwards. We interpret the results of the unweighted, raw NASA TLX (RTLX) data. The RTLX is equivalent to the TLX but eliminating the weighting process (Hart 2006). The questionnaire consists of six subscales: mental (RTLX-MD), physical (RTLX-PD), and temporal demands (RTLX-TD), performance (RTLX-P), effort (RTLX-E), and frustration (RTLX-F).

Figure 3 (b) illustrates the results of the RTLX questionnaire. The results show that the *Ribbon* interface was more mental ($M = 38.75$, $SD = 27.44$) and physical demanding ($M = 48.33$, $SD = 24.38$) than the *1-Pillar* and the *2-Pillar* interface. The temporal effort (RTLX-TD) was highest for the *1-Pillar* interface ($M = 36.53$, $SD = 25.41$). On average, the exercise performance (RTLX-P) was rated best for the *2-Pillar* interface ($M = 38.89$, $SD = 21.89$). Using the *Ribbon* interface the participants had the impression of the lowest performance ($M = 31.39$, $SD = 27.45$). The results of the RTLX-E show that participants described their effort (mentally and physically) to accomplish the exercise goals lowest when using the *Ribbon* interface ($M = 43.06$, $SD = 24.07$). Additionally, the *Ribbon* interface caused less frustration ($M = 24.17$, $SD = 24.85$). Highest frustration was caused by the *1-Pillar* interface ($M = 32.78$, $SD = 25.86$).

One-way repeated measures ANOVAs yielded no significant effects of the *TI* for the variables RTLX-MD ($F(2, 70) = 0.89$, $p = 0.41$, $\eta^2 = 0.00$), RTLX-PD ($F(2, 70) = 0.39$, $p = 0.68$, $\eta^2 = 0.00$), RTLX-TD ($F(2, 70) = 0.60$, $p = 0.55$, $\eta^2 = 0.00$), RTLX-P ($F(2, 70) = 1.22$, $p = 0.30$, $\eta^2 = 0.02$), RTLX-E ($F(2, 70) = 0.48$, $p = 0.62$, $\eta^2 = 0.00$), and RTLX-F ($F(2, 70) = 1.60$, $p = 0.21$, $\eta^2 = 0.02$).

4.3 System Usability Scale and Interface Ranking

The participants evaluated each interface condition of the SMART-FIT system using the System Usability Scale (SUS). Ten items were rated on a 5-point Likert scale from 1 (disagree) to 5 (agree totally). The item scores were totaled to calculate an overall SUS score between 0 and 100, where higher scores indicate better usability (Brooke 1996). A mean SUS score above 72.75 reflects a good usability. A score larger than 85.58 refers to an excellent usability (Bangor, Kortum, and Miller 2008).

One participant forgot to fill in the SUS questionnaire for the *1-Pillar* condition. On average, all three interfaces were rated 'good' or better, i.e., a SUS score above 72.75. Participants perceived the usability of the *Ribbon* interface ($M = 81.14$, $SD = 19.17$) better than the *1-Pillar* ($M = 78.07$, $SD = 13.08$) and the *2-Pillar* interface ($M = 77.00$, $SD = 16.08$). A one-way repeated measures ANOVA showed no significant difference in mean SUS scores, $F(2, 68) = 0.86$, $p = 0.43$, $\eta^2 = 0.01$.

The result of the interface rankings is shown in Figure 4 (left). The ranking was analyzed by assigning scores from 3 to 1 in decreasing order from the highest ranked to the lowest ranked training interface version. 75 % of the participants ranked the *Ribbon* interface on first place. The participants rated the *Ribbon* interface best, following *1-Pillar* on 2nd place and *2-Pillar* on third place.

4.4 AttrakDiff2

To measure pragmatic and hedonic quality of the different *TIs* we used the German version of the AttrakDiff2 questionnaire (Hassenzahl, Koller and Burmester 2008). The questionnaire uses semantic differentials to assess the user experience of a product. From the AttrakDiff2 questionnaire we used the categories pragmatic quality (PQ) and hedonic quality (HQ). The questionnaire consisted of 21 items. The portfolio plot summarizes the results of the AttrakDiff2 questionnaire (see Figure 4, right). Participants rated the *Ribbon* interface best in terms of pragmatic quality ($M = 3.67$, $SD = 1.53$) and hedonic quality ($M = 4.67$, $SD = 1.34$). On average the *1-Pillar* received the lowest values for the hedonic quality. The *2-Pillar* interface got the lowest scores for the pragmatic quality ($M = 3.19$, $SD = 1.58$). A one-way repeated measures ANOVA shows a significant effect of the *TI* on the HQ, $F(2, 70) = 14.40, p <0.01, \eta^2 = 0.12$. Bonferroni post hoc tests show a significant difference between *Ribbon* and *2-Pillar* ($M = 4.06$, $SD = 1.04$, $p <0.01$) and *1-Pillar* ($M = 3.57$, $SD = 1.17$, $p <0.01$), as well as between *2-Pillar* and *1-Pillar* ($p < 0.05$). The differences between the *TI* for the variable PQ were not significant, $F(2, 70) = 1.36, p = 0.26, \eta^2 = 0.02$.

4.5 Error Measurements

To evaluate the effect of the *TI* conditions on the performance we used different error measurements to compare the trajectory of the actual weight displacement with the trajectory of the target weight displacement. The following section will present the results of the calculated error measurements.

COR. The COR measures the linear correlation between two variables, i.e., the actual and the target weight displacement. +1 is a total positive correlation, 0 is no linear correlation. Mauchly's test indicate that the assumption of sphericity has been violated, $W = 0.59$, $p < 0.05$, therefore degrees of freedom were corrected using Greenhouse-Geisser estimates of sphericity ($\varepsilon = 0.71$). The results show that COR was significantly affected by the *TI*, $F(1.42, 49.64) = 3.76, p < 0.05, \eta = 0.01$. Bonferroni post hoc tests revealed a significant difference between COR for *Ribbon* ($M = 0.92$, $SD = 0.22$) and *2-Pillar* ($M = 0.88$, $SD = 0.22$). No other comparisons were significant.

MAE. The MAE measures the difference between the two continuous variables. It includes the comparison between the actual and target weight displacement. Mauchly's test for sphericity is significant, $W = 0.63$, $p < 0.05$. Thus, we corrected the degrees of freedom using Greenhouse-Geisser estimates ($\varepsilon = 0.73$). A one-way repeated measures ANOVA results in a significant effect of *TI*, $F(1.46, 51.15) = 9.27$, $p < 0.01$, $\eta = 0.03$. The comparison of target and actual trajectory yielded the lowest MAE for the interface *Ribbon* ($M= 6.48$, $SD = 6.37$) followed by *1-Pillar* ($M = 7.87$, $SD = 4.66$) and *2-Pillar* ($M = 8.61$, $SD = 5.23$). Bonferroni post hoc tests show a significant difference between *Ribbon* and *2-Pillar* ($p < 0.001$). The differences between 1-*Pillar* and 2-*Pillar* ($p = 0.22$) respectively *Ribbon* ($p = 0.11$) were not significant.

RMSE. When using MAE to compare the trajectories one may neglect the impact of big but infrequent errors, i.e., large deviations from the target trajectory. To address this problem we calculated the RMSE. The lowest RMSE was computed for the *Ribbon* interface ($M = 8.30$, $SD = 8.64$). The RMSE for the *2-Pillar* interface was higher ($M = 11.24$, $SD = 6.67$) than for the *1-Pillar* interface ($M = 10.25$, $SD = 6.22$). Since Mauchly's test of sphericity was significant, $W = 0.71$, $p < 0.05$, we applied Greenhouse-Geisser estimates ($\varepsilon = 0.77$) to correct the degrees of freedom. The one-way repeated measures ANOVA showed a significant difference for the dependent variable RMSE, $F(1.55, 54.14) = 7.89$, $p < 0.01$, $\eta = 0.03$. Again, Bonferroni post hoc tests show a significant difference between *Ribbon* and *2-Pillar* ($p < 0.001$). No other comparisons were significant (all $ps > 0.05$).

Russell's Errors. COR, MAE, and RMSE provide a more general measurement to compare target and actual trajectory. However, those measures do not account for a magnitude error (i.e. an error with regard to the ROM). Additionally, correctly but phase-shifted or asynchronously repetitions will result in a huge error. To tackle this problem, we used Russell's error measurements (Russell 1997). Russell developed a set of magnitude (RUS-M), phase (RUS-P), and comprehensive (RUS-C) error measures that address the limitations of the previous error measurements. Following, we will describe the results for RUS-M and RUS-P using the different *TI*s.

On average, RUS-P is lowest for the *Ribbon* interface (M = 0.0013, SD = 0.0018) followed by *1-Pillar* (M = 0.0022, SD = 0.0014). *2-Pillar* has the highest value for RUS-P (M = 0.0024, SD = 0.0015). Mauchly's test indicate that the assumption of sphericity has been violated, $W = 0.82$, $p < 0.05$, therefore degrees of freedom were corrected using Huynh-Feld estimates of sphericity ($\varepsilon = 0.89$). The results show that RUS-P was significantly affected by the *TI*, $F(1.78, 62.26) = 9.18$, $p < 0.05$, $\eta^2 = 0.03$. Bonferroni post hoc tests revealed a significant difference between RUS-P for *Ribbon* and *2-Pillar* ($p < 0.001$). No effect was found between *Ribbon* and *1-Pillar* ($p = 0.15$) and *1-Pillar* and *2-Pillar* ($p = 0.13$). These results suggest that the phase shift between target and actual trajectory was significantly smaller when participants used the *Ribbon* interface instead of the *2-Pillar* interface.

The lowest average RUS-M value is calculated for the *Ribbon* interface (M = -0.0009, SD = 0.0024). The magnitude error for the *1-Pillar* interface (M = -0.0018, SD = 0.0016) is slightly higher than for the *2-Pillar* interface (M = -0.0016, SD = 0.0016). A one-way repeated measures ANOVA using Huynh-Feld estimates ($\varepsilon = 0.80$) shows a significant difference between the interface conditions, $F(1.61, 56.33) = 3.94$, $p < 0.05$, $\eta^2 = 0.04$. Post hoc comparisons using Bonferroni resulted in no significant differences.

5. DISCUSSION AND CONCLUSION

We used *Flow Experience* and *Worry* of the FSS to evaluate the effect of the training interface. The overall *Flow Experience* during the exercise was between 5 and 6 for all interfaces which is a typical value for engaging in sport activities (Rheinberg, Vollmeyer, and Manig 2005). No significant difference was found for the *Flow Experience*. However, participants were significantly more worried about doing the exercise correctly when using the *Ribbon* interface than using the *2-Pillar* interface. This is in line with the weak performance rating RTLX-P and the larger values for RTLX-MD and RTLX-PD.

The *Ribbon* interface yielded the highest average ratings for the categories RTLX-MD and RTLX-PD. On the one hand, participants perceived the *Ribbon* interface more physical and mental demanding and were less satisfied with their performance during the exercise. On the other hand, they have been less frustrated when using the *Ribbon* interface. This is also reflected in the good usability results and the ranking of the interfaces. As described above, the *Ribbon* interface provides a continuous feedback for all exercise parameters including the target displacement trajectory. Due to this participants might have focused continuously on the correct velocity respectively rotation angle when using the *Ribbon* interface. This might also explain the larger values for the flow experience. In contrast, using the *1-Pillar* and *2-Pillar* interface the user focused primarily on the correct ROM and only then on the correct velocity.

The AttrakDiff2 questionnaire evaluated the hedonic and pragmatic quality of the *TIs*. The pragmatic quality focuses on the usability of the product while the hedonic quality describes how innovative and valuable a product is. Overall, the *TI*s have only a neutral attractiveness and the 95%-CIs is quite large for the hedonic factor. This might be due to our non-homogeneous population in terms of age and gym habits. Future work will have to address this fact.

Although, participants rated the RTLX-P lowest when using the *Ribbon* interface, this fact is not reflected in the error measurements. Statistical analysis revealed significant effects of *TI* for all selected error measurements. Post hoc pairwise comparisons of the interface conditions gave significant lower errors when participants used the *Ribbon* than the *2-Pillar* interface. No significant differences were found between *Ribbon* and *1-Pillar*. *Ribbon* and *1-Pillar* interface combine the relevant exercise parameters – e.g. ROM and velocity – in a single visualization. When using the *2-Pillar* interface participants had to switch continuously the focus between two tasks: (1) align to target velocity in the left pillar and (2) check for the correct ROM in the right pillar. This dual-task problem might be the reason for significantly larger errors when using the *2-Pillar* interface. The errors in the magnitude (RUS-M) were not significantly different, when compared pairwise. Using the developed *Ribbon* interface instead of the *2-Pillar* interface would allow users to focus on the individual ROM and exercise velocity at the same time and to improve their exercise performance.

This paper presented the SMART-FIT system for strength exercise training. The system comprises a cable machine, notebook and a tablet PC. The tablet PC provides visual feedback during exercise training. Within this contribution we presented and evaluated the interface conditions *1-Pillar*, *2-Pillar*, and *Ribbon* to support strength exercise training. We conducted a within-subject user study with 36 participants to evaluate the usability and performance of the developed interfaces. The results of the SUS and AttrakDiff2 questionnaire show a good usability of all interfaces. When asked to rank the interface, 75% of the participants preferred the *Ribbon* interface. Surprisingly, participants perceived their exercise performance (RTLX-P) better when using *2-Pillar* or *1-Pillar* interface. In contrast, the objective error measurements revealed that participants performed the exercise repetitions better using the *Ribbon* interface.

To date, we only evaluated the interface conditions for a simple exercise movement, i.e., the shoulder exercise. Additionally, we did not consider the physical and mental fatigue of users, since we only evaluated 10 exercise repetitions with a weight of 1 kg. Future work should focus on different strength and more complex exercise movements. This should include the personalized selection of the exercise weights to evaluate the different interfaces when muscles fatigue. What about the performance when the user reaches his maximal workload? Furthermore, complex exercises might lead to compensation movements. In our user study we noticed that participants sometimes lifted their elbow or moved their back while performing the exercise. These errors are not reflected in the error measurements. Additional movement sensors fastened to the user's upper arm might address these problems.

ACKNOWLEDGEMENT

We would like to thank all our participants volunteering in the user study. The research group wearHEALTH is funded by the German Federal Ministry of Education and Research (16SV7115).

REFERENCES

Bangor, A.; Kortum, P. & Miller, J. A. (2008), 'The system usability scale (SUS): An empirical evaluation', *International Journal of Human-Computer Interaction* 24(6), 574--594.

Brooke, J. (1996), *SUS - A quick and dirty usability scale*, CRC Press.

Chittaro, L. & Sioni, R. (2014), 'Evaluating mobile apps for breathing training: The effectiveness of visualization', Computers in Human Behavior 40, 56--63.

Eriksson, M.; Halvorsen, K. A. & Gullstrand, L. (2011), 'Immediate effect of visual and auditory feedback to control the running mechanics of well-trained athletes', Journal of sports sciences 29(3), 253--262.

ERGO-FIT GmbH & Co. KG (2019), 'Smart fitness devices. www.ergo-fit.de.

Hart, S. G. & Staveland, L. E. (1988), 'Development of NASA-TLX Results of Empirical and Theoretical Research, Human Mental Workload', *British Journal of Social Psychology*, 139--183.

Hart, S. G. (2006), 'Nasa-Task Load Index (NASA-TLX); 20 Years Later', *Proceedings of the Human Factors and Ergonomics Society Annual Meeting* 50(9), 904-908.

Hassenzahl, M.; Koller, F. & Burmester, M. (2008), Der User Experience (UX) auf der Spur: Zum Einsatz von www.attrakdiff.de, *in* Henning Brau; Sarah Diefenbach; Marc Hassenzahl; Franz Koller; Matthias Peissner & Kerstin Röse, ed., 'Tagungsband UP08', Fraunhofer Verlag, Stuttgart, pp. 78-82.

Morris, D.; Tan, H.; Barbagli, F.; Chang, T. & Salisbury, K. (2007), Haptic Feedback Enhances Force Skill Learning, in 'Proceedings of the Second Joint EuroHaptics Conference and Symposium on Haptic Interfaces for Virtual Environment and Teleoperator Systems', IEEE Computer Society, Washington, DC, USA, pp. 21--26.

Rheinberg, F.; Vollmeyer, R. & Engeser, S. (2003), Die Erfassung des Flow-Erlebens, Hogrefe-Verlag, pp. 261 -- 279.

Rheinberg, F.; Vollmeyer, R. & Manig, Y. (2005), 'DFG-Abschlussbericht zum Projekt Rh 14/11–1: Flow-Erleben: Untersuchungen zu einem populären, aber unterspezifizierten Konstrukt', Psycholog. Institut Universität Potsdam.

Russell, D. M. (1997), Error Measures for Comparing Transient Data: Part I: Development of a Comprehensive Error Measure Part II: Error Measures Case Study, *in* 'Proceedings of the 68th Shock and Vibration Symposium', SAVIAC, Shock and Vibration Information Analysis Center.

Sigrist, R.; Rauter, G.; Riener, R. & Wolf, P. (2013), 'Augmented visual, auditory, haptic, and multimodal feedback in motor learning: A review', Psychonomic Bulletin & Review 20(1), 21--53.

Steffen, D.; Bleser, G.; Weber, M.; Stricker, D.; Fradet, L. & Marin, F. (2011), A Personalized Exercise Trainer for Elderly, in 'Pervasive Health Conference 2011. International ICST Conference on Pervasive Computing Technologies for Healthcare (Pervasive Health-201), 5th, May 23-26, Dublin, Ireland', IEEE Xplore.

DO COMMENTS ON YOUTUBE DIFFER ACROSS GENRE?

Cliff Loke and Anjan Pal
Nanyang Technological University, Singapore

ABSTRACT

This study examines the differences in online comments between educational videos and entertainment videos on YouTube. By employing content analysis of 2,000 comments, it examines the association between the different comment categories and the two genres of videos. For educational videos, the findings suggest that comments were enriching in terms of requesting further information, recommending videos, expressing opinion, commendation, disagreement, and sharing anecdotes as well as personal information. However, for entertainment videos, comments were enriching in terms of reflecting impression, compliments and expressing general sentiments. The potential implications from theoretical and practical perspectives are discussed.

KEYWORDS

User-Generated Content, Content Analysis, Social Media, YouTube, Video Genre, Interface Design, Entertainment Videos, Educational Videos

1. INTRODUCTION

YouTube has been accessed by over one-third of the Internet population (OmniCore, 2018). The website provides Internet users have become keen to use information from various social media platforms such as Facebook and YouTube. Besides communicating with their online peers, users engage themselves in social media in every aspects of their lives starting from education to entertainment. They tend to plug their knowledge gaps from variety of resources that are readily available for access on the Internet. For instance, they use video source repository YouTube, which ranks 2 in terms of getting website traffic after Google, for procedural learning (Alexa, 2018).

Even though the revolution of cutting edge Internet technologies have turned social media into a public space to seek, search, and share information, the exponential growth of information pose serious challenges in terms of evaluating quality, and usefulness in order to make informed decisions in the selection of resources (Rieh, 2002). During information seeking, people make relevance judgement as they attempt to discern and evaluate the content of resource. To some extent, several paralinguistic affordances such as likes and views on Facebook and YouTube provides superficial signs of content popularity. However, user comments offer more in-depth insights about public perceptions about an online content. Online videos have become a popular information resource. With more than a billion user accounts created, YouTube, an online video platform offers paralinguistic affordances such as likes, dislikes, shares and views to indicate users' preferences. It also allows users to comment on videos. Thus, crowdsourced cues that are socially generated can further influence video seekers in their selection of video resources (Loke et al., 2017) and have been a growing part of Internet resources metadata. Metadata are used for subjective relevance judgement and form a basis of recommendations (Bogdanov and Herrera, 2011). To cope with information overloading, such crowdsource cues are often processed heuristically to evaluate and shortlist resources (Zhang et al., 2014). However, users' comments that are usually presented in a chronological thread format, involve extensive efforts to process, and thus cognitively overloaded.

Video is one of the most common form of media sought on the Internet and the video comments facility produces rich socially generated cues. User commenting is a key facility that leverages on social interconnectivity for communication through the resource. It has the potential to support decision making for video seekers. YouTube, with its huge and diverse user base, has an immense amount of user comments have been generated and can contribute to the video experience (Siersdorfer et al., 2010). Any online videos that have comments from a wide user base and often result in very varied perspectives. While user comments can influence the selection of video resource, the sheer amount of comments generated can be time consuming and daunting for video seekers to process. To reduce the time and effort in processing the comments, a summarised view of comments could support video seekers in discerning and evaluate the video. The richness of comments had led to research developing an application based on mining opinions in comments to indicate positive and negative responses (Potthast, 2009). This allowed a large number of comments to be summarized and helped users to sort the comments according to its positive or negative connotations. This afforded users to form some basis of evaluation on the resource. Beyond dichotomous levels of positive and negative, the richness of comments can be explored to provide granular levels of opinions and perspectives.

Research on various social media platforms had drawn out general categories of comments and these provide a useful starting point for analysis (Thelwall, 2018, Madden et al., 2013). Categorical schemas for comments emerged from these studies reflected diversity in granularity and context. While these studies have produced important contributions to the understanding of user behavior and comments relationships, there has not been sufficient research to understand how the comments from different video genres such as educational videos and entertainment videos. These vastly different genres can result in how the comments are used to develop interface features and analyzed. A strong classification scheme for YouTube user comments can open up multiple areas of research and improve the understanding of comment behavior and its potential impact.

Building on the premise that different search goals can result in different curating and evaluating processes, this study examines the differences in online comments between educational videos and entertainment videos on YouTube. For this purpose, the framework of Madden et al. (2013) was leveraged.

By understanding the differences between comments found in educational video resources and entertainment video resources can develop a more robust classification scheme. The more robust classification scheme can better support the development of interface features for video retrieval that leverages on the richness of user comments to evaluate and add value to the video content.

2. RELATED LITERATURE

Interactivity is one of the keys to social media platforms. Many social media platforms afforded interactivity through user comments. Interaction with the online content and other users lead to better user engagement. User comments is a form of user-generated content that can evolve like an online conversation, allowing users to express their opinions and emotions that can be analysed to provide value for businesses and information products (Fan and Gordon, 2014, Yang, 2012). Studies from the business domain investigate social media and user-generated content to improve branding and develop new products (Culnan et al., 2010). A prediction model was developed based on the number of users' comments to forecast the expected popularity of articles published by an online newspaper (Tatar et al., 2014). Businesses and organizations leverage on the understanding of social media interactivity to make predictions and create value propositions.

User-generated comment allows richer analysis as compared to other common social media metrics such as Ratings and Number of Likes. The richer analysis stems from the forms of interaction and the qualitative nature of user-generated comments. The interaction in social media, in particular user-generated comments, reveals interactivity in two forms. The interactivity between the users of the social media platform, user-user interactivity, is captured as conversations in user-generated comments while user-content interactivity are the user-generated comments made directly in reference to the social media content (Ksiazek et al., 2016). The analysis of comments allowed business entities to make sense out of leaner metrics such as a rating system (Stringam and Gerdes Jr, 2010). Other potentials from the analysis of comments that have found success include popularity prediction (Tatar et al., 2011), supporting recommendation systems (Li et al., 2010) and ranking metrics (Tatar et al., 2014). The mining and analysis of comments has created opportunities and supported the development of features for better user interaction.

User-generated comments has shown to influence perception and evaluation of the online resource. For example, research investigating the interplay between public service announcements posted in YouTube and its corresponding user comments has found that both supportive and derisive comments had affected the evaluation of the announcement (Walther et al., 2010). Examining user comments as online reviews on hotel room sales, Ye et al. (2009) suggest online consumer-generated reviews had strong influence on the number of online bookings. These studies suggested that social influence is exhibited through user comments and play a part in decision-making.

Park et al. (2008) explored comments from Digg and del.icio.us and presented categories such as Summary, Additional Information, Impression and Opinion. The categories produced from the study are general and unable to convey the richness of information found in the comments. Jansen et al. (2009) investigated comments on Twitter and produced 23 different comment types. While this study yielded a more granular form of comment classification, they are specific to the context of a marketing study. Content analysis was performed on over 66K of YouTube user comments and derived a more general classification scheme that has ten broad categories and 58 subcategories (Madden et al., 2013). This schema reflects the diversity of comments from the YouTube user base and provides an initial structure upon which other user comment studies can build on.

As one of the largest video platform, researchers are studying YouTube in order to understand video content and usage, video seeking, and user interaction and behavior. Kousha et al. (2012) reviewed the how academics studied YouTube videos across various disciplines and found that there is wide variety of research conducted on YouTube video content. Paek et al. (2014) analysed the content of 365 YouTube videos on e-cigarette and suggested that YouTube videos may play a major role as a promotional medium due to its effective persuasiveness. Madathil et al. (2015) conducted a systematic review on YouTube literature concluded that YouTube is increasingly used as a platform to convey health related information and contains misleading information that could find its way to lay person.

Interaction patterns in YouTube are studied to understand core users and video virality. Abisheva et al. (2014) analysed metrics like view counts, number of comments, favourite markings of the video and set of referrers that led users to the video, in order to understand the factors that impact video popularity. Khan (2017) examined the various motivations for participation and engagement in YouTube. Such studies provide insights to online user behavior and engagement to social metrics.

Given that the use of YouTube has been widely adopted for various purposes staring from education to entertainment (Khan, 2017, Möller et al., 2018), users' comments on videos also helps to make sense about the perceptions of the online community. While YouTube has been abundantly used for the purpose of entertainment (Khan, 2017, Cheng et al., 2013), it has also become a tool for learning (Choi and Behm-Morawitz, 2017). Eventually, YouTube facilitates different media channels for different genres of video. Regardless of different media channels and genre, the comment function on the platform allows users to express their sentiments and much more even beyond the content of the video per se (Choi and Segev, 2016). From astute, reasonable, and well written, they can also be informal, indiscreet or even nonsensical.

Prior works suggest that users' comment can raise relevant issues that can help content creators in developing their content, and can be deemed as valuables to those planning to create an educational video in order to enhance learning in an innovative way. While the interaction through user comments creates valuable insights and conversations, it can also result in arguments and antagonisms. In this vein, little research has been trained on how comments can be differed across different genre. Currently, the lack of structural organization of user comments has limited the utility of users' perceptions for both consumers as well as creators of those videos.

3. METHODOLOGY

To address the research question, comments were required to be collected for educational videos as well as entertainment videos. First, the video channels were determined, then videos from the channels were selected for the harvesting of comments.

Videos were chosen from the two channels (TedEd – Educational; ExplosmEntertainment - Entertainment) that had comparable subscription numbers during the data collection. There is a need to ensure that subscription numbers were similar as this is indicative of the number of video viewers who are viewers of the channel. (Five videos were selected from each channel. The videos were initially sorted to be within the upload period between 6 to 12 months. This is to ensure that there were sufficient comments for the videos.) Then, comments for those videos were retrieved. Figure 1 shows the overview of data collection.

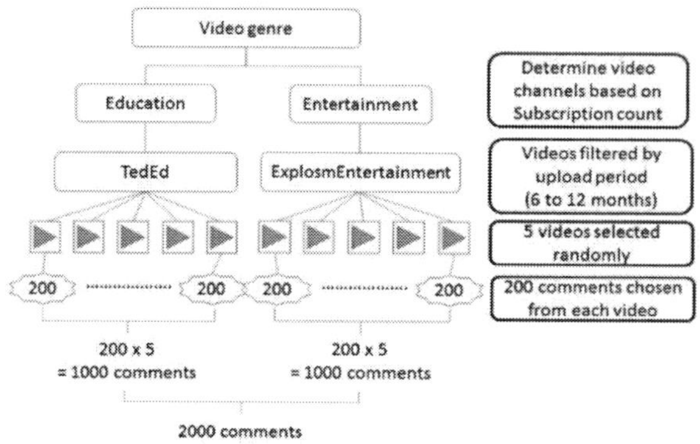

Figure 1. Overview of data collection

For the two types of videos, 200 comments were randomly selected from each of the videos. This led to a set of 1,000 comments (200 x 5) for each of the two types of videos. Thus, a total of 2,000 comments (1,000 comments for educational videos + 1,000 comments for entertainment videos) were admitted for coding.

The coding scheme was adopted from the prior work (Madden et al., 2013). The category for spamming comments is removed in this study as spams may not be user generated and can cause noise within the data. Two coders were involved in the coding process that was done using two phases. In phase I, a subset of 200 comments from each of the two types of videos (thus, a total of 400 comments) was coded independently to establish for mutual agreement of the coding scheme between the coders. A Cohen's Kappa score of 0.7 was used as a threshold for the inter-coder agreement. Disagreements were resolved through discussion. Thereafter, in phase II, the remaining 1,600 comments (2000 - 400) were divided equally between the two coders to complete the coding process.

For the purpose of data analysis, Chi-square tests were employed. The analysis facilitated the examination of the association between the comment types and each of the video types.

4. RESULTS

Overall, a total of 2,000 comments from two YouTube video channels, educational and entertainment were coded. Chi-square test was conducted to assess whether the comments from the educational videos was different from that of the entertainment videos. The results of the test is reported according to the category scheme proposed by (Madden et al., 2013). Table 1 presents the percentage of each category and the chi-square statistic, comparing the comments for educational and entertainment videos. Table 1 presents the percentage of each category and the chi-square statistic, comparing the comments for educational and entertainment videos.

Comments in the Information category provided or requested objective or factual information about the content and context of the video. In this category, Information Request-type comments indicated significant difference between the two video types. Requesting information ($\chi 2(1, N = 2000) = 19.99$, $p < 0.001$) appeared more in the comments for educational videos than for entertainment videos. These comments were asked for details in terms of seeking information or explanation of something related to the video.

Comments in the Advice category either requested assistance or prescribed suggestions or recommendations on what to do in a particular situation. These comments were specifically requesting or giving individuals' judgements, and contained modal verbs such as "should" and "could." In this category, comments on requesting advice, giving advice, and recommending another video indicated significant difference between educational video and entertainment video. In particular, while comments on Requesting advice ($\chi 2(1, N = 2000) = 4.36$, $p < 0.05$) appeared more in the entertainment videos than in the educational videos, Giving advice ($\chi 2(1, N = 2000) = 8.66$, $p < 0.01$) appeared more in the educational videos than in the entertainment videos. Recommendation of another video ($\chi 2(1, N = 2000) = 19.40$, $p < 0.001$) were found more in the educational videos than in the entertainment videos. These comments were included under the category of Advice, because such comments can be interpreted as one person giving advice to another about which videos to watch.

Table 1. Percentage of comments for each category across video genres and Chi-square statistic

		Video Genres		N = 2000 df=1	
		Edu	Ent	χ^2	Cramer's V
Information	Request***	**3.60**	0.70	19.99	0.10
	Make comparison	0.90	1.50	1.52	0.03
	Give (video content)	2.30	2.60	0.19	0.01
	Give (video context)	3.40	2.20	2.65	0.04
	Give (General)	4.90	6.90	3.60	0.04
Advice	Requesting	1.60	3.00	4.36	0.05
	Giving	7.00	4.00	8.66	0.07
	Recommending another video***	**2.20**	0.10	19.40	0.10
Impression	General***	0.90	**6.10**	40.03	0.14
	Positive	4.20	2.00	8.06	0.06
	Negative***	3.60	**10.50**	36.33	0.14
Opinion	Request ***	**8.20**	1.00	59.07	0.17
	Give (General)***	**18.6**	9.80	31.78	0.12
	Give (Positive)***	**2.90**	0.80	12.14	0.08
	Give (Negative)***	**7.60**	1.20	48.69	0.16
	Give (Mixed)	2.90	3.60	0.78	0.02
	Insult	2.30	1.20	3.52	0.04
	Compliment***	3.80	**8.30**	17.81	0.09
	Criticism	7.40	6.00	1.57	0.03
	Tribute	0.30	0.20	0.20	0.01
	Speculate	4.40	7.10	6.73	0.06
Responses	Agree	1.30	0.50	3.59	0.04
	Confirm	0.20	0.70	2.79	0.04
	Disagree***	**3.10**	0.50	19.12	0.10
	Challenge	0.80	0.90	0.06	0.01
Expression of personal feelings	General***	0.40	**4.20**	32.13	0.13
	Positive	2.30	2.40	0.02	0.01
	Negative	6.20	3.50	7.90	0.06
General conversation	Greetings	0.10	0.30	1.00	0.02
	Thanking***	**2.70**	0.40	17.33	0.09
	Joke	3.20	5.60	6.85	0.06
	Apology	0.08	0.10	5.47	0.05
	Reference to offsite communication	1.10	2.60	6.20	0.06
	Status description	2.10	0.40	11.71	0.08
	Anecdote***	**8.10**	0.60	67.60	0.18
	Random off-topic exclamation	1.20	0.10	9.34	0.07
	Request personal information	0.30	0.20	0.20	0.01
	Give personal information***	**2.50**	0.10	22.45	0.11
	Express plans/desires/wishes	4.60	3.10	3.04	0.04

***$p < 0.001$

Comments in the Impression category includes expressing short immediate that has positive, negative or general sentiment. These comments often contains paralinguistic features like emoticons and interjections such as "Yay!" and "Wow!". Positive impressions appeared more in educational videos ($\chi2(1, N = 2000) = 8.06$, $p < 0.01$) while negative impressions ($\chi2(1, N = 2000) = 36.33$, $p < 0.01$) were mostly associated with entertainment videos. General impressions ($\chi2(1, N = 2000) = 40.03$, $p < 0.01$) appeared more in the entertainment videos than the educational videos.

Comments in the Opinion category make request or offer viewpoint on a video, person, object or topic. Opinion comments do not encourage actions and contain explicit and subjective value judgements. Opinion requesting comments ($\chi2(1, N = 2000) = 59.07$, $p < 0.001$) are more prevalent in educational videos. Opinion giving comments (general, positive and negative) appear more in educational videos while more compliments ($\chi2(1, N = 2000) = 17.81$, $p < 0.001$) and speculations ($\chi2(1, N = 2000) = 6.73$, $p < 0.05$) are found in entertainment videos.

Comments in the Responses category are comments that agree, confirm with evidence, disagree, or challenge with evidence the video content. Responses that disagree ($\chi 2(1, N = 2000) = 19.12, p < 0.001$) appear more frequently in educational video than entertainment video. No other responses differed significantly between the two types of videos.

Comments that express personal feelings include positive, negative and general emotional response or personal feeling that are neither positive nor negative. The chi-square test revealed significant difference for having more general responses ($\chi 2(1, N = 2000) = 32.13, p < 0.001$) in entertainment videos while education video garnered more negative personal feelings ($\chi 2(1, N = 2000) = 7.90, p < 0.01$). No significant difference was found between the two types of video for comments that expressed positive personal feeling.

Comments in the form of general conversation encompasses a wide range of comment types that initiate, maintain and terminate conversations. The results showed that educational videos have more comments than entertainment videos comments for thanking ($\chi^2(1, N = 2000) = 17.33, p < 0.001$), describing current status ($\chi^2(1, N = 2000) = 11.71, p < 0.01$), sharing anecdote ($\chi^2(1, N = 2000) = 67.60, p < 0.01$), providing personal information ($\chi^2(1, N = 2000) = 22.45, p < 0.01$) and moving into random off-topic exclamations ($\chi^2(1, N = 2000) = 9.34, p < 0.01$). On the other hand, entertainment video comments appeared more frequently than educational video comments that are joke ($\chi^2(1, N = 2000) = 6.85, p < 0.01$), apologies ($\chi^2(1, N = 2000) = 5.47, p < 0.01$) and refer to offsite communications ($\chi^2(1, N = 2000) = 6.20, p < 0.01$). There were no significant differences for greeting, request for personal information and expressing desire.

5. DISCUSSION

The following findings can be gleaned from this research. For educational videos, comments can be enriching in terms of requesting further information, recommending videos, expressing opinion, commendation, disagreement as well as sharing anecdote and personal information. Comments on educational videos requested more information compared with those on entertainment videos

To plug knowledge gaps, people tend to request or continue for more information until their need is satisfied (Peterson and Merino, 2003). This is evident in *Information Request-type* comments, which showed a significance difference across the genre of videos comments examined. Comments on educational videos shared more related resources compared with those on entertainment videos. When viewing a video with the intention to learn, sharing related resources for further information suggested more meaningful learning behavior (Barak and Rafaeli, 2004). In addition, comments on educational videos were more opinionated, both positive and negative, compared with those on entertainment videos. This suggested that the educational video comments tend to be more expressive. More perspectives on videos were sought, suggesting that educational video viewers are more open to initiate further discussion. Educational videos were used to convey information and for learning. Furthermore, possible discrepancy in educational videos had led to emergence of comments that disagreed with the content. Comments on educational videos tended to exhibit higher level of politeness and gratitude compared with those on entertainment videos. The comments found in educational video had shown to be more cordial and respectful. This study also suggested that educational video viewers were more willing to share personal information as well as content related information.

For entertainment videos, comments were enriching in terms of reflecting impression, compliments and expressing general sentiments. Comments on entertainment videos had more reflection of general and negative impression compared with those on educational videos. Viewers of entertainment videos expressed more impression formation and complimentary comments than those of educational videos. This suggested the appreciation of entertainment value for such videos. Entertainment videos are able to invoke more affective comments than educational videos. In summary, fourteen of the categories of comments showed statistical differences between the two genres of videos. This suggested that the different genres of videos garner different comments for specific comment categories.

6. CONCLUSION

This study examines differences in online comments between educational videos and entertainment videos on YouTube. By employing content analysis, it points out differences between comments for the two types of videos. The findings suggest that comments can be enriching in terms of requesting further information, recommending videos, expressing opinion, commendation, disagreement as well as sharing anecdote and personal information for educational videos. Furthermore, comments can be enriching in terms of reflecting impression, compliments and expressing general sentiments for entertainment videos.

This study has some limitations. The size of the dataset is limited to the randomly selected comments. The volume of comments needs to be increased substantially to facilitate greater generalizability. This study examined comments for two types of video resources obtained from two specific channels. Future investigation could include a list of possible channels to offer a more holistic treatment on the nature of the comments. The study is also limited by the inability to consider cultural differences between the video commenters as the profile of commenters is not captured.

This study has at least two implications. First, it extends the existing literature by distinguishing the video comments' categorical differences across the two genres. This calls further investigation of other video genres such as Sports, Virtual Reality, and News to refine the categorical framework for video comments on YouTube. Second, from the practical perspectives, this study can inform interface design strategies for the YouTube comment section across the different video genres.

REFERENCES

Abisheva, A., Garimella, V. R. K., Garcia, D. & Weber, I. Who watches (and shares) what on youtube? and when? using twitter to understand youtube viewership. Proceedings of the 7th ACM international conference on Web search and data mining, 2014. ACM, 593-602.

Alexa. 2018. *Alexa Top 500 Global Sites on the Web* [Online]. Available: https://www.alexa.com/topsites [Accessed].

Barak, M. & Rafaeli, S. 2004. On-line question-posing and peer-assessment as means for web-based knowledge sharing in learning. *International Journal of Human-Computer Studies,* 61, 84-103.

Bogdanov, D. & Herrera, P. How Much Metadata Do We Need in Music Recommendation? A Subjective Evaluation Using Preference Sets. ISMIR, 2011. 97-102.

Cheng, X., Liu, J. & Dale, C. 2013. Understanding the characteristics of internet short video sharing: A youtube-based measurement study. *IEEE Transactions on Multimedia,* 15, 1184-1194.

Choi, G. Y. & Behm-Morawitz, E. 2017. Giving a new makeover to STEAM: Establishing YouTube beauty gurus as digital literacy educators through messages and effects on viewers. *Computers in Human Behavior,* 73, 80-91.

Choi, S. & Segev, A. Finding informative comments for video viewing. Big Data (Big Data), 2016 IEEE International Conference on, 2016. IEEE, 2457-2465.

Culnan, M. J., Mchugh, P. J. & Zubillaga, J. I. 2010. How large US companies can use Twitter and other social media to gain business value. *MIS Quarterly Executive,* 9.

Fan, W. & Gordon, M. D. 2014. The power of social media analytics. *Communications of the ACM,* 57, 74-81.

Jansen, B. J., Zhang, M., Sobel, K. & Chowdury, A. 2009. Twitter power: Tweets as electronic word of mouth. *Journal of the Association for Information Science and Technology,* 60, 2169-2188.

Khan, M. L. 2017. Social media engagement: What motivates user participation and consumption on YouTube? *Computers in Human Behavior,* 66, 236-247.

Kousha, K., Thelwall, M. & Abdoli, M. 2012. The role of online videos in research communication: A content analysis of YouTube videos cited in academic publications. *Journal of the Association for Information Science and Technology,* 63, 1710-1727.

Ksiazek, T. B., Peer, L. & Lessard, K. 2016. User engagement with online news: Conceptualizing interactivity and exploring the relationship between online news videos and user comments. *New Media & Society,* 18, 502-520.

Li, Q., Wang, J., Chen, Y. P. & Lin, Z. 2010. User comments for news recommendation in forum-based social media. *Information Sciences,* 180, 4929-4939.

Loke, C., Foo, S. & Majid, S. Video Seeking Behavior of Young Adults for Self Directed Learning. International Conference on Asian Digital Libraries, 2017. Springer, 314-324.

Madathil, K. C., Rivera-Rodriguez, A. J., Greenstein, J. S. & Gramopadhye, A. K. 2015. Healthcare information on YouTube: a systematic review. *Health informatics journal,* 21, 173-194.

Madden, A., Ruthven, I. & Mcmenemy, D. 2013. A classification scheme for content analyses of YouTube video comments. *Journal of documentation,* 69, 693-714.

Möller, A. M., Kühne, R., Baumgartner, S. E. & Peter, J. 2018. Exploring User Responses to Entertainment and Political Videos: An Automated Content Analysis of YouTube. *Social Science Computer Review,* 0894439318779336.

OMNICORE. 2018. *YouTube by the Numbers: Stats, Demographics & Fun Facts* [Online]. Available: https://www.omnicoreagency.com/youtube-statistics/ [Accessed].

Paek, H.-J., Kim, S., Hove, T. & Huh, J. Y. 2014. Reduced harm or another gateway to smoking? Source, message, and information characteristics of e-cigarette videos on YouTube. *Journal of health communication,* 19, 545-560.

Park, J., Fukuhara, T., Ohmukai, I., Takeda, H. & Lee, S.-G. Web content summarization using social bookmarks: A new approach for social summarization. Proceedings of the 10th ACM workshop on Web information and data management, 2008. ACM, 103-110.

Peterson, R. A. & Merino, M. C. 2003. Consumer information search behavior and the Internet. *Psychology & Marketing,* 20, 99-121.

Potthast, M. Measuring the descriptiveness of web comments. Proceedings of the 32nd international ACM SIGIR conference on Research and development in information retrieval, 2009. ACM, 724-725.

Rieh, S. Y. 2002. Judgment of information quality and cognitive authority in the Web. *Journal of the American society for information science and technology,* 53, 145-161.

Siersdorfer, S., Chelaru, S., Nejdl, W. & San Pedro, J. How useful are your comments? analyzing and predicting youtube comments and comment ratings. Proceedings of the 19th international conference on World wide web, 2010. ACM, 891-900.

Stringam, B. B. & Gerdes JR, J. 2010. An analysis of word-of-mouse ratings and guest comments of online hotel distribution sites. *Journal of Hospitality Marketing & Management,* 19, 773-796.

Tatar, A., Antoniadis, P., De Amorim, M. D. & Fdida, S. 2014. From popularity prediction to ranking online news. *Social Network Analysis and Mining,* 4, 174.

Tatar, A., Leguay, J., Antoniadis, P., Limbourg, A., De Amorim, M. D. & Fdida, S. Predicting the popularity of online articles based on user comments. Proceedings of the International Conference on Web Intelligence, Mining and Semantics, 2011. ACM, 67.

Thelwall, M. 2018. Social media analytics for YouTube comments: potential and limitations. *International Journal of Social Research Methodology,* 21, 303-316.

Walther, J. B., Deandrea, D., Kim, J. & Anthony, J. C. 2010. The influence of online comments on perceptions of antimarijuana public service announcements on YouTube. *Human Communication Research,* 36, 469-492.

Yang, T. 2012. The decision behavior of Facebook users. *Journal of Computer Information Systems,* 52, 50-59.

Ye, Q., Law, R. & Gu, B. 2009. The impact of online user reviews on hotel room sales. *International Journal of Hospitality Management,* 28, 180-182.

Zhang, K. Z., Zhao, S. J., Cheung, C. M. & Lee, M. K. 2014. Examining the influence of online reviews on consumers' decision-making: A heuristic–systematic model. *Decision Support Systems,* 67, 78-89.

MULTI-USER SCREEN SHARING IN MULTI-DISPLAY GROUPWARE

Choon Jin Ng[1], Masahiro Takatsuka[2] and Tong Ming Lim[1]
[1]*Tunku Abdul Rahman University-College, Malaysia*
[2]*The University of Sydney, Australia*

ABSTRACT

Ever since the idea of computer supported cooperative work (CSCW) was first coined, screen sharing technology has been playing a crucial role in groupware for fostering an environment which enables people to share and exchange information more freely. This is known as a form of What-You-See-Is-What-I-Saw (WYSIWIS) collaboration. Screens can be shared within a group of people in the same room or remotely. As computers are becoming affordable, it is not uncommon to have a collaboration session involving multiple machines. However, existing groupware do not support simultaneous sharing of multiple machines' displays. This limits conference participation in the sense that multi-user participation is confined to only a single machine. This paper intends to present a multi-display groupware (MDG) architecture to make sharing multiple machines' screens possible while enabling true multi-user interaction. This architecture can be configured to be used in co-located, distributed and mixed-presence environment.

KEYWORDS

Multi-display Groupware, WYSIWIS, Remote Collaboration, CSCW, Mixed-Presence Groupware

1. INTRODUCTION

In a computer aided collaboration, being able to share screen content is crucial. Many remote collaboration done today consists not of one but a group of participants located at every site. However, current screen sharing system can only either support a distributed or a co-located environment. That is, screen sharing can only be done remotely between one-to-one participant, or locally between a group of participants. None of them support both environments simultaneously. With computers and monitors becoming increasingly affordable, many home users and organisations can afford several machines with multiple displays. This resulted in the proliferation of various groupware exploiting the availability of these hardware.

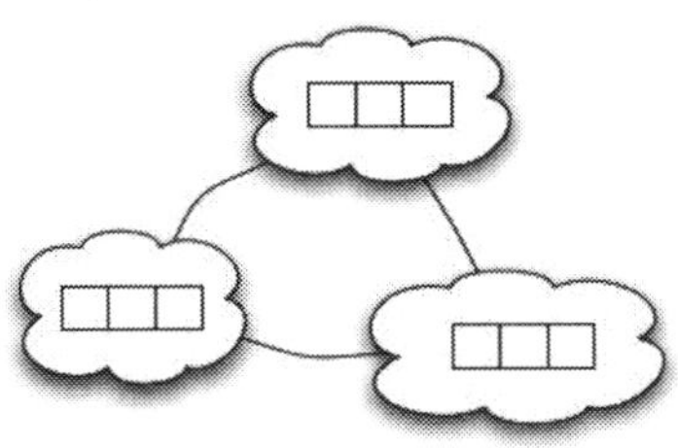

Figure 1. Screen sharing in a mixed-presence multi-display environment. Each cloud represents a site with three machines

Therefore, a groupware for supporting screen sharing in both co-located and distributed environment is important. Such groupware is known as a mixed-presence groupware (MPG) (Tang, Boyle and Greenberg, 2004). Figure 1 shows how we can extend screen sharing support into a mixed-presence multi-display environment. The MDG system comprises of multiple displays shared by multiple users. There are three main challenges posed for such system:

1. Sufficiently integrate display and input control of shared screens in order to create a seamless workspace. The spatial order of displays must be preserved within the local and distributed site. Then, controls such as keyboard and mouse must be unified for seamless navigation.
2. A central architecture for supporting an arbitrary machine configuration for screen sharing.
3. Supporting multi-user inputs in current contemporary operating systems (OS) which inherently only support single-user interaction.

2. RELATED WORK

A single-display groupware (SDG) application uses a single display shared by multiple people (Myers, 1999). Naturally, the environment in which the SDG application operates is called a single-display environment (SDE). Likewise, a multi-display groupware (MDG) operates in a multi-display environment (MDE). In this literature, our definition of MDE comprises of multiple displays over multiple machines shared by multiple users. It does not include the usage of multiple displays over a single machine.

The benefits of MDE are well publicised (Robertson *et al.*, 2005; Biehl *et al.*, 2008). Current MDE research focuses on information organization through specific graphical user interfaces (GUIs) (Jeong *et al.*, 2006; Biehl *et al.*, 2008; Sakurai *et al.*, 2008), interaction technique (Davis and Chen, 2000), scalability and performance (Jeong *et al.*, 2006). However, there is virtually no research in the area of screen sharing in a MDE environment. Most of the existing systems are confined to either a co-located collaboration or a distributed collaboration, but not mixed-presence collaboration.

A collaborative workspace is one public workspace which can be shared to work on problems or to share information. However, Tse et al. found that interference can occur when more than one person is working in close proximity (Tse *et al.*, 2004). To avoid this, spatial separation and partitioning can be employed by partitioning a workspace into personal private space and group space. Then, during a collaboration session, a person can choose to work a sub-problem on his own. The public space can serve as a place to integrate solutions and to exchange information between collaborators. In SDG, if a screen is divided among several participants for personal use, the lack of space not only reduces participant workspace, but it also reduces privacy as participants need to work closer together and this can intrude other participants' privacy (Gutwin and Greenberg, 1998; Booth *et al.*, 2002).

Apart from workspace, the coordination of input controls are also crucial. In this paper, a system control consists of a set of mouse and keyboard inputs supplied on a per user basis. In a co-located environment, the CPNMouse (Westergaard, 2002) can be expanded with several displays while each user is allotted with his or her individual mouse control. However, having the case of multiple screens through multiple machines still poses some challenges. Since each machine has its own separate control system, the controls must be sufficiently integrated to support the notion of single workspace. Several existing collaboration systems such as the Mighty Mouse (Booth *et al.*, 2002), CPNMouse, Synergy, 3D Server (Sakurai *et al.*, 2008), and IMPROMPTU (Biehl *et al.*, 2008) do not allow true multi-user control experience. They either time-slice a cursor between multiple users or uses some kind of floor control.

On the other hand, MPX (Hutterer and Thomas, 2007) enables true multi-user experience by directly supporting multiple mice at system level. It maintained legacy application support. All multi-cursor events are sent directly to the application instead of time-slicing a single OS cursor. It is however tightly tied to the X window system.

The middleware GLIA allows collaborative application development to adopt a multi-cursor approach to co-located collaboration (Yuizono, Nishimura and Munemori, 2006). In GLIA, each user has a mouse cursor and a keyboard. These cursors are managed by its respective mouse agent which can be transported across different machines. A mouse monitor resides at the machine where the physical mouse/keyboard is located. Together with multi-cursor support, this system can support simultaneous work in single co-located environment.

3. MULTI-SCREEN SHARE ARCHITECTURE

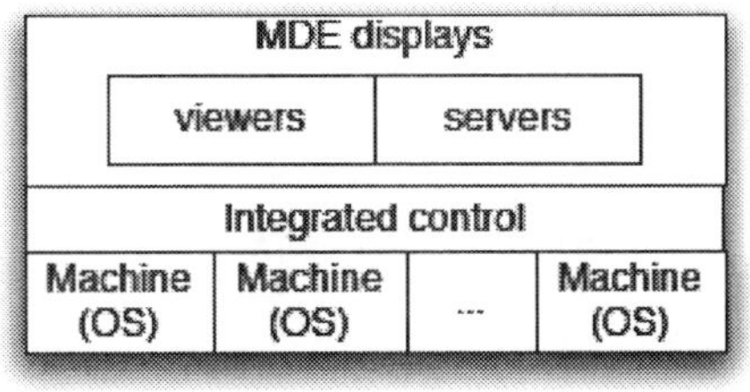

Figure 2. The Multi-Screen Share (MSS) architecture

We have created the Multi-Screen Share (MSS) architecture capable of supporting multi-machine screen sharing in a mixed-presence environment. Figure 2 illustrates the MSS architecture where each site can consists of one or more machines. Cursor communications between machines are peer-to-peer and can migrate across different machines. An aggregation of displays from each machine then forms a MDE display. The display can belong to one of these two components: viewer and server. The server shares its contents to other remote machines while the viewer displays the shared contents.

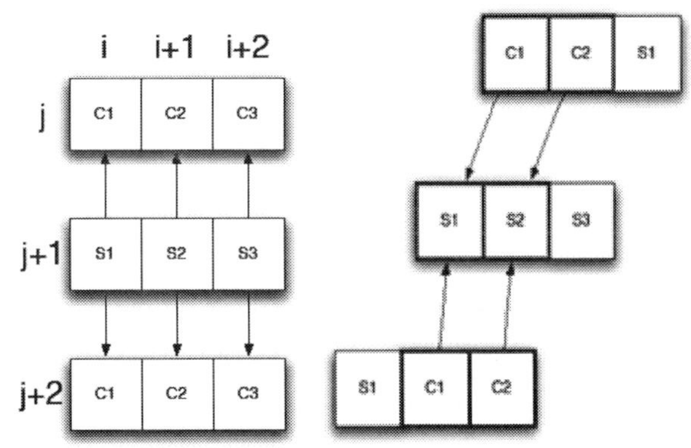

Figure 3. Illustration of MDE screen sharing with (a) strict view –left and (b) mixed view - right

The MDE displays layer is responsible for streaming screen output to the network and receiving them for display. It enables flexible layout through the choice of configuring screens as strict view or mixed view.

A strict view refers to all sites having exactly the same content with the same number of screens arranged in the same position. Hence the collaboration is centred on only one set of workspace. To set up a strict view, for all sites, only one machine at a position can be a server while the rest must be clients. To clarify more, using the example in Figure 3, take i as a position of screen and j as the site number, then X(i,j) is the ith screen position located at site j. Hence for a known position k, X(k,j), only one of the site in j is the server and the rest must be client. On the other hand, for a mixed view, it not only has the same attribute as strict view, but there are additional screens where they are not shared in order to keep them private. However, these screens' controls are still linked together. Hence this allows a single public with one or more private workspaces to be formed.

Again, in Figure 3, the strict view is the server set {S1, S2, S3} placed side by side and the controls are combined as a single workspace. The clients then replicates each server's view in an exact configuration. In a mixed view, the servers {S1, S2, S3} are placed side by side. However, {S3} is not shared to other sites. The client {C1, C2} connects to {S1, S2} respectively to form the public part of the workspace. The screen {C1, C2, S1}, {S1, S3, S3} and {S1, C1, C2} are then aggregated respectively to form a public-private workspace where the controls can be migrated smoothly across different workspaces. A noteworthy fact is that on both view configuration, a mix of clients and servers are possible at any site and the control transition should remain smooth.

At the next MSS level, an integrated control layer is featured to ensure controls across all machines are regulated to produce a seamless workspace. There are two components in the integration layer:

- *Multi-cursor system:* Ensures each physical mouse plugged into any of the machine is detected. This is so that a new control (mouse and keyboard) can be issued to a participant. This layer also determines which machine the control is multiplexed. Therefore, it must be spatially aware of the position of its neighbouring machines.
- *Multi-user input system:* Having multiple cursors for each participant is not enough. When users are performing actions on the same machine simultaneously, the OS must reflect this condition and not simply serialize the commands. We were able to avoid the effects of time-slicing cursor by introducing the "direct-application event injection" mechanism. This mechanism will be described in a later section.

In a mixed-presence environment, sharing multiple screens among several sites consumes tremendous bandwidth. In the worst case of all sites transmitting its own screen at once, the total transmission done is n(n-1) times if unicast connection with n nodes is used. However, if multicast network is employed, then total transmission is reduced to a constant of only n times. Therefore, a multicast version of VNC called MVNC (Ng and Takatsuka, 2009), is incorporated into the MSS system.

To prevent spatial confusion, the positioning of screen should be the same relative to each other regardless of any site. Hence, participants at each site should have its screen position predetermined beforehand.

Lastly, an accompanied screen sharing application, named the M3DESKSHARE, was implemented to demonstrate the MSS architecture.

4. THE MULTI-CURSOR SYSTEM

When sharing screens, different cursor distribution strategy is required for different MDE configurations:

- *Single public space:* Within a local site, cursors should be transferable from one machine to another seamlessly. The cursors are then mirrored to other remote sites.
- *Private-public space:* In addition to the single public space requirements, cursor permission must be enforced to prevent cursors in one private space from intruding other private spaces. Only the mouse cursor in the public space is allowed to be mirrored.
- *Large tile display:* Large tile display usually resides in a public space for centralised monitoring. It aggregates a set of remotely shared screen. Figure 4 demonstrates three standalone machines A, B and C are to have their screen aggregated into a large tile display forming A', B', and C'.

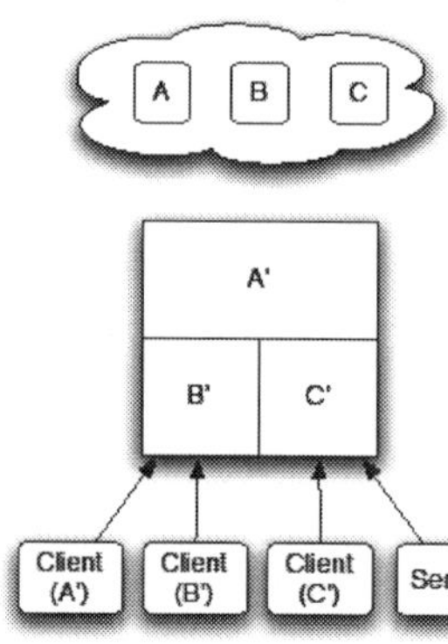

Figure 4. Large-tile display aggregates display from remote host A, B, and C. At the large tile display site, the remote screens are displayed through the clients and each client can access the displays merged as a single tile display. The server does not share any screen but merely plays a role as a controller

The GLIA framework already provides a way to support multi-user collaboration on a set of machines in a single co-located environment. However, to support user control in a mixed-presence MDE environment, the following extensions to the GLIA are required:

- Each site will require its exclusive unit of GLIA environment.

- The agent and monitor behaviour needs to be modified to support this new environment.

To accomplish the abovementioned extensions, the concept of "control mirroring" is introduced so cursors at each site can be mirrored to other distributed sites. This concept is shown in Figure 5 with a purported mirroring between two units of GLIA environments. Each mouse is monitored by a mouse monitor. The management of each cursor and its events are linked to the mouse monitor via the mouse agent. Mirroring is performed when one agent is duplicated and is migrated to a remote target machine.

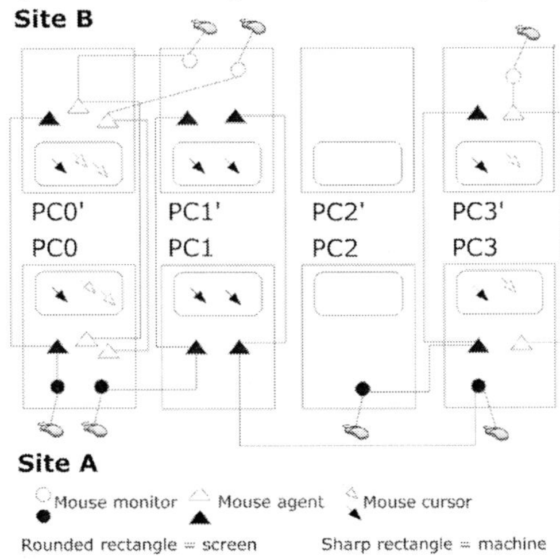

Figure 5. A mirrored GLIA framework between two sites, site A and site B

At each MSS initialisation, the host will wait for any incoming agent migrated from other hosts or any new physical mouse detected locally. Any of these two events will trigger the creation of a mouse agent. From here, it is worth to note that a mouse agent can originates from three different sources:

1. *Local physical mouse:* A physical mouse is plugged into the host.
2. *Remote mouse agent within the same unit GLIA environment:* A mouse agent migrates from one host to another (within the same unit GLIA environment) as its cursor moves from one machine's screen to the other machine's screen.
3. *Remote mouse agent from different unit of GLIA environment:* This is the mirrored cursors from other GLIA environment unit.

For case (1) and (2), the agent is simply duplicated and mirrored to all the hosts' mirrors. However, if case (3) is exercised, the host will have to decide if it has interacted with the incoming agent's machine previously. If it had not, that implies that particular host has no knowledge of any existing external cursor. Therefore, the server will now need to mirror all agents it has in order to initialize the new incoming host. Once that host is initialized, any subsequent new agent from that host will only result in an update to all other connected mirrors.

As mouse activities are performed, the mouse monitor will generate events which in turn are passed to the agent. The agent of course can be located in any machine. As the agent receives the event, the machine will inspect if there is any mirrors associated with that agent. If it has, it will also duplicate those events to the mirror agents.

In the event if the mouse cursor moves beyond the edge of a screen, the mouse agent (which corresponds to the mouse cursor) shall be migrated to another machine. In this case, only non-mirrored mouse agents are migrated. Any mouse agents marked as mirror should not be migrated and should be destroyed immediately.

Initially, GLIA employs relative coordinate (dx,dy) to steer the cursor. Thus if a mouse is moved 10 units to the upper left, (dx,dy) will be (-10, -10). However, this approach is unsuitable for mirroring due to coordinate mismatch between the server (source of cursor) and the mirror. The mirrors simply do not know the initial coordinate of the mouse. Hence transmitting any (dx,dy) will result in the wrong coordinate. Certainly a solution to synchronize initial coordinate can be made, but there is a concern that it can incur overhead to the protocol since a synchronization mechanism needs to be introduced.

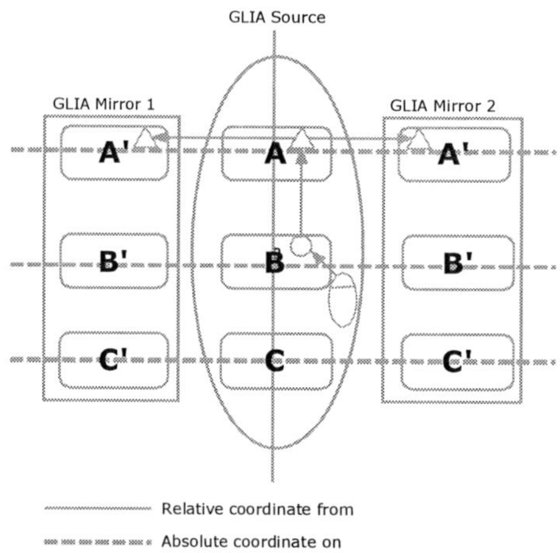

Figure 6. The extended GLIA cursor distribution system: There are 3 sets of GLIA environment. One is the source and the other two are mirrors. Cursor transmission within the same set of GLIA environment employs relative coordinate, while cursor transmission within different sets of GLIA environment employs absolute coordinate

Consequently, a hybrid solution involving both coordinate systems is created. To enable smooth transition within screens of the same GLIA unit, relative coordinate is used. Then each machine will use the relative coordinate to acquire the absolute (x,y) coordinate. The result yielded is then transmitted to its mirrors. As illustrated in Figure 6, the physical mouse is located in host B. The mouse is managed by a monitor (circle), and the cursor is located at host A since the agent is there. The communication and transition from B to A employed the relative coordinate, as shown in the thick bold line. Then host A's agent will calculate the absolute (x,y) position on the screen and distributes them to the mirror agents at A', as shown in the thick dotted line.

Next, for the GLIA to support a true multi-user input in contemporary OS, an "artificial" input injection mechanism is developed. Many OS typically has a main message queue which dispatches OS messages to each application. Using the same message queue, we can inject control input messages directly into the individual application's message queue. This is illustrated in Figure 7.

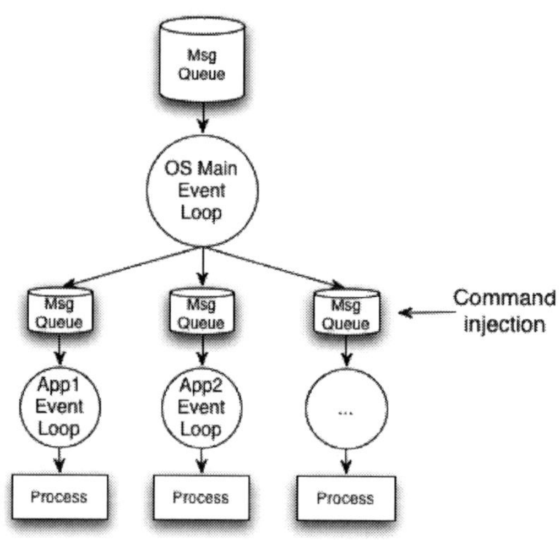

Figure 7. Typical operating system's application event distribution system

5. DISCUSSIONS & RESULTS

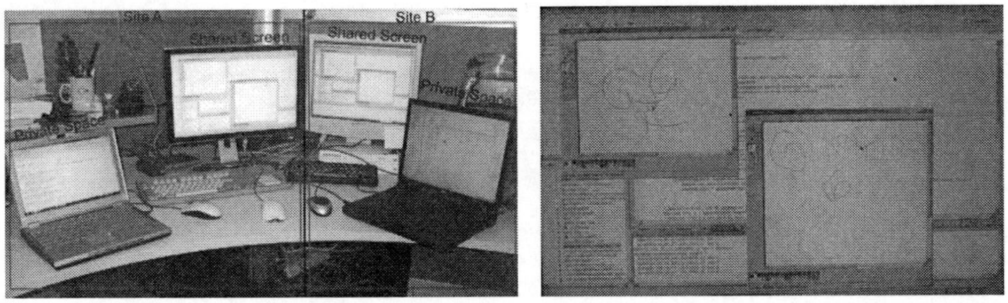

Figure 8. (Left) The M3DESKSHARE prototype in a private-public space configuration; (right) An ongoing M3DESKSHARE collaboration on the shared screen using two Windows Paint programs where two users input their mouse strokes onto both programs simultaneously without complication

Figure 8 (left) shows the M3DESKSHARE prototype which demonstrates the MSS architecture. The configuration set up was a private-public screen sharing between two sites. These sites shared a single common screen labelled "Shared Screen". For each site, a private space was offered. The mouse cursors between the public and private space were linked. That implies the cursor can move from these spaces. As the cursor moved to the public space, it was reflected to the other site as well.

Figure 8 (right) shows the content of the "Shared Screen". There were a total of four cursors. Since each participant had their own control and M3DESKSHARE supports simultaneous multi-user input, users were able to work on separate applications simultaneously even though they belonged to the same desktop. In this example, two Paint programs were launched in Windows. If a time-slicing multi-cursor strategy was used, users would not be able to draw lines on the two paint programs simultaneously. Instead, the lines would have crisscrossed between the paint programs. With M3DESKSHARE, users can exploit desktop level multi-user interaction. That means two users can simultaneously work on their respective application. However, since the application itself does not support multi-user interactivity, users will not be able to enjoy application level multi-user support. If more than one user is controlling the same application, then the result will be unpredictable.

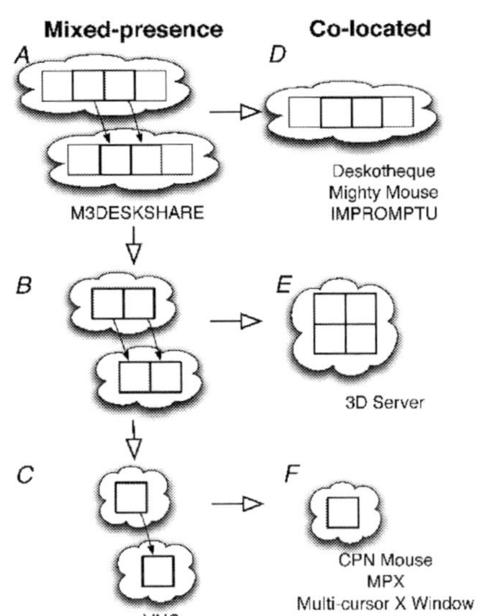

Figure 9. Derivatives of the configurations supported by the MSS architecture

In principle, the MSS architecture supports screen sharing in a mixed-presence private-public configuration. We now show that from this configuration, it is possible to derive all possible configurations arises from the above-mentioned prototypes, which belongs to one of the subset of the private-public configuration.

Figure 9 shows how the MSS architecture, represented by the M3DESKSHARE prototype, can be decomposed into various configurations. The left side of the figure shows collaboration performed over a network remotely. While the right side shows co-located collaboration, the machines are still linked over network in a local environment.

At the first level (A & D), the machines are configured as a public-private space. Figure D shows how multiple machines can be linked together for co-located collaboration. At the next level (B& E), the private space is discarded and all machines are exposed as public. So far, there is virtually no prototype that allows the sharing of multiple machines display remotely among multiple users. Finally, in its most primitive level (C & F), the MSS architecture can be utilized as a VNC-style desktop sharing such as the one illustrated in configuration C. If no remote machine is involved, then the configuration can be simplified to configuration F which is co-located collaboration. Under this configuration, only a single machine is involved and so only multi-cursor is needed in order to support multi-user collaboration.

6. CONCLUSION

In this paper, we have shown the capabilities required for a cursor system to support screen sharing in a multi-user multi-machine MDE in a mixed-presence environment. Apart from the stated capabilities, we have also introduced two primitive cursor functions:

- Cursor transition
- Cursor mirroring

Using these two primitive functions, we showed a cursor distribution system that can support MDE screen sharing in the public and private-public workspace. The system also ensures mouse cursor can navigate through a large tile display. The system is:

1. Cross-platform as it does not requires any modification to any part of the OS or windowing system.
2. Supports multiple machines.
3. Maximize multi-user support without time-slicing cursor.

This architecture does not intend to rival other architectures. Rather, we presented a case on why additional capabilities are required, and how different capabilities can be integrated. We also showed that the MSS architecture does not only support screen sharing in a private-public mixed presence environment, but it also supports screen sharing in any combination of mixed, distributed and co-located environment, single or multiple machines and private-public or public only configurations. This encompasses all scenario described to be supported by other prototypes as discussed previously.

REFERENCES

Biehl, J. T. *et al.* (2008) 'Impromptu: a new interaction framework for supporting collaboration in multiple display environments and its field evaluation for co-located software development', in *Proceedings of the SIGCHI Conference on Human Factors in Computing Systems*, pp. 939–948.

Booth, K. S. *et al.* (2002) 'The mighty mouse multi-screen collaboration tool', in *Proceedings of the 15th annual ACM symposium on User interface software and technology*, pp. 209–212.

Davis, J. and Chen, X. (2000) 'LumiPoint: Multi-User Laser-Based Interaction on Large Tiled Displays', *Displays*, 23, p. 2002.

Gutwin, C. and Greenberg, S. (1998) 'Design for individuals, design for groups: tradeoffs between power and workspace awareness'. University of Calgary.

Hutterer, P. and Thomas, B. H. (2007) 'Groupware Support in the Windowing System', in *Proceedings of the Eight Australasian Conference on User Interface - Volume 64*. Darlinghurst, Australia, Australia: Australian Computer Society, Inc. (AUIC '07), pp. 39–46. Available at: http://dl.acm.org/citation.cfm?id=1273714.1273721.

Jeong, B. *et al.* (2006) 'High-performance dynamic graphics streaming for scalable adaptive graphics environment', in *SC'06: Proceedings of the 2006 ACM/IEEE conference on Supercomputing*, p. 24.

Myers, B. A. (1999) *An implementation architecture to support single-display groupware.*

Ng, C. J. and Takatsuka, M. (2009) 'Method of Frame Buffer Transmission over Reliable Multicast Network', in *CollabTech*. Sydney.

Robertson, G. *et al.* (2005) 'The large-display user experience', *IEEE computer graphics and applications*. IEEE, 25(4), pp. 44–51.

Sakurai, S. *et al.* (2008) 'A middleware for seamless use of multiple displays', in *International Workshop on Design, Specification, and Verification of Interactive Systems*, pp. 252–266.

Tang, A., Boyle, M. and Greenberg, S. (2004) 'Display and presence disparity in Mixed Presence Groupware', in *Proceedings of the fifth conference on Australasian user interface-Volume 28*, pp. 73–82.

Tse, E. *et al.* (2004) 'Avoiding interference: how people use spatial separation and partitioning', in *in SDG workspaces Proceedings of the 2004 ACM conference on Computer supported cooperative work, ACM*.

Westergaard, M. (2002) 'Supporting Multiple Pointing Devices in Microsoft Windows', in *Proceedings of Microsoft Summer Workshop for Faculty and PhDs*.

Yuizono, T., Nishimura, S. and Munemori, J. (2006) 'Development of Middleware GLIA for Connective Wide Collaborative Space with Networked I/O Device', in *Proceedings of the 10th International Conference on Knowledge-Based Intelligent Information and Engineering Systems - Volume Part III*. Berlin, Heidelberg: Springer-Verlag (KES'06), pp. 174–180. doi: 10.1007/11893011_22.

A COLLAGE OF CHANGE: UTILIZING APPRECIATIVE INQUIRY IN A USER EXPERIENCE DESIGN STUDY FOR BIG DATA INTERFACES – A REALITY

Chrisna Jooste
University of South Africa (Unisa), Prodigy Finance
Cape Town, South Africa

ABSTRACT

The significant role that big data interfaces and Business intelligence (BI) play in senior management and their executive decision-making is well known. The topic has become an academic niche area and increasingly research is published on BI, this since the turn of the century. A limitation is research findings on the user experience (UX) of BI interfaces. Literature holds several UX frameworks, however, none pertaining to the UX in relation to BI. This article presents the first phase of a three-stage study and focuses on a revisited systematic literature review (2003-2019). The focuses are on the main elements comprising these UX frameworks and the use of appreciative inquiry to investigate the elements required for the best UX. The article presents a renewed conceptual UX framework for BI interfaces and provides an overview of the subsequent further two phases of the study.

KEYWORDS

User Experience, Usability, Business Intelligence, Big Data, Dashboard, Framework

1. INTRODUCTION

In a world of business optimization and continuous improvement, companies around the globe are embracing big data as it is becoming more readily available (Grover *et al.*, 2018). Companies are also recognizing the need and importance of user dashboards to enable users to make informed decisions and take timely actions (Morabito, Viscusi and Themistocleus, 2016). User experience (UX) is not something unknown anymore in practice, corporates and even start-ups are making an effort to get UX involved throughout the software delivery life cycle (Hokkanen, Xu and Väänänen, 2016). The increase in demand can be seen in the escalation in job adverts, for UX related roles as well as the prominence of the role in the agile team structure (Øvad and Larsen, 2015).

Literature has started to explore how theory informs the practice of UX, and focuses on the links between UX frameworks and design practices (Gegner, Runonen and Keinonen, 2011). Previously literature and research point to the need (of representation and understanding) for UX that is precise, comparable and generalizable that speaks to designing of UX for academia as well as in the industry (Law *et al.*, 2008; Gegner, Runonen and Keinonen, 2011; Kaye *et al.*, 2011).

Following the increase in UX research, contextual factors have shown to have an effect on the user experience (Obrist, 2010; de Kock, van Biljon and Botha, 2016). Context is included in the International Organization for Standardization (ISO)'s definition of usability, as 'the extent to which a product can be used by specified users to achieve specified goals with effectiveness, efficiency and satisfaction in a specified context of use' (ISO, 1998). The need for UX in the context of product development in large organizations are also gaining emphasis (Gegner, Runonen and Keinonen, 2011). Indicating that relevance of context is not only applicable to the context of use but also to the context of software development.

Many UX frameworks have been developed since the call for a unified view on UX (Law *et al.*, 2015), and some have been context specific, for example a UX framework for understanding HCI education (Sari and Wadhwa, 2015), a conceptual UX framework for academic staff in using a learning management systems tool (de Kock, van Biljon and Botha, 2016) and the mobile app usability inspection (MAUI) framework (Cheng,

2016). But no UX framework specific to BI dashboard interfaces could be identified from the literature consulted. This pointed to a gap in the literature and specifically in the context of understanding the elements required for the UX of BI interfaces in a software development environment.

This work forms part of a larger three-stage research study and presents an overview of the research design and focuses on the first stage which includes the systematic literature review, the output of which will serve as input into subsequent two stages of the research (Figure 1). This paper aims to address Phase 1 to contribute by: 1) presenting an updated conceptual UX framework for BI interfaces in an agile software development environment and, 2) using an underlying appreciative inquiry philosophy as a novel approach in the specific field of information systems and user experience.

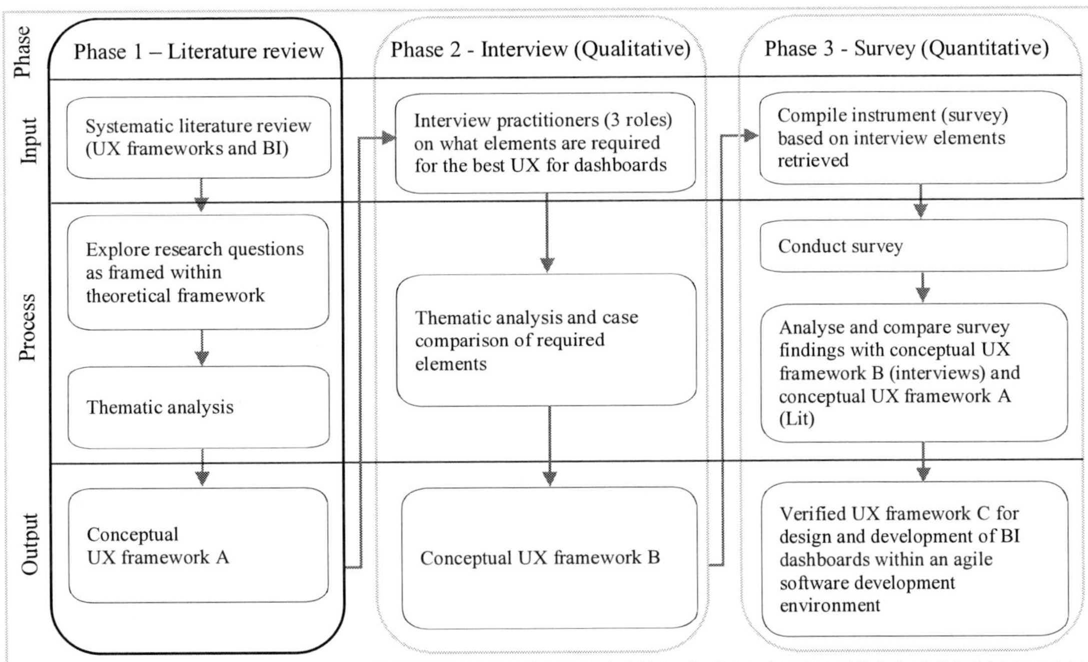

Figure 1. Research design overview

The paper is organized as follows: Section 2 provides an overview of the updated systematic literature review and a revised conceptual UX framework. Section 3 describes the overarching research design and how appreciative inquiry has allowed for the understanding of the context and an improved user experience perspective, while Section 4 concludes with the findings and suggestions for further research.

2. REVISITED SYSTEMATIC LITERATURE REVIEW

A systematic literature review was undertaken in January 2017 to gain visibility of relevant literature to be analysed for the study. The systematic literature review enabled the construction of an overarching conceptualization (Siddaway, n.d.). For the purpose of this study, a systematic review is defined as follows: It is a review guided by plainly formulated question that uses systematic and clear methods to identify, select, and critically review relevant literature (Siddaway, n.d.). The question was constructed to be clear, specific and answerable, with the purpose of scoping the search area in the literature. During March 2019, the systematic literature review was updated, to ensure that the current literature is included in the review, that ensured visibility of the fact that the research problem had not been addressed to date. Revisiting the literature, also made the increase in the number of research articles published since the initial review notably more visible (Table 1).

Table 1. Updated keyword search results across digital libraries

BI	BA	BD	U	V	A	KV	UX	ACM Jan2017	ACM Mar2019	Google Scholar Jan2017	Google Scholar Mar2019	IEEE Explore Jan2017	IEEE Explore Mar2019	Scopus Jan2017	Scopus Mar 2019
x		x						97	173	33700	32900	256	282	228	721
x		x	x					2	3	1890	4710	2	2	3	5
x		x			x	x		1	3	312	110	1	2	6	16
x					x			213	339	25700	60400	279	627	2960	1136
x			x		x			3	6	4200	8800	4	8	5	12
	x	x	x					1	3	581	1600	1	5	0	1
	x	x						104	214	4490	13100	304	798	89	252
		x	x					46	75	13800	35600	113	282	157	453
x			x					52	66	13700	19700	82	108	64	92
	x		x					15	21	833	3210	11	25	3	7
		x		x				316	589	26900	74300	934	2373	997	2936
		x				x		87	144	230	590	128	331	3	6
x				x				234	288	18600	34400	262	430	246	424
x						x		79	92	265	387	61	99	3	5
	x					x		31	42	37	72	31	54	1	1
	x			x				98	141	3280	9000	160	306	27	64
x							x	1	6	n/a	12600	n/a	177	n/a	33
		x					x	2	46	n/a	27000	n/a	657	n/a	353
x					x		x	1	21	n/a		n/a		n/a	
Title search: "BI" and "U"								1	1	n/a		n/a		n/a	
Title search: "BI" AND "UX"								0	0	n/a		n/a	n/a	n/a	n/a

Table 1 legend
BI - Business Intelligence
BA – Business Analysis
BD – Big Data
U – Usability
V – Visualization
A – Analysis
KV – Knowledge Visualization
UX – User Experience

The revisited systematic review as Phase 1 of the study, followed the same process as the initial review and included the following consecutive stages as suggested by Siddaway (n.d): scoping, planning, identification (searching), screening and eligibility as depicted in Figure 2.

Stage 1 (scoping): the research question was used to identify previous research published on the problem. The research question was: What are the elements that influence the UX of BI systems?

Stage 2 (planning): keyword combinations based on the research question were used to refine the search for literature. The keywords used were 'business intelligence', 'big data', 'analytics', 'knowledge visualization', 'usability', 'user experience'. Additionally, as inclusion criteria, the literature had to be written in English.

Stage 3 (identification): the search combinations produced a varying number of search results from the selected digital libraries (ACM, Google Scholar, IEEE Explore, Scopus), see Table 1. The ACM result set was selected to refine the search further, as the ACM contains practitioner and academic literature of high quality, holding comprehensive collections of full-text articles and bibliographic record (ACM, Digital Library).

Stage 4 (screening): duplicate results were removed, records were exported to a spreadsheet and titles and abstracts were screened to identify if the record was suitable for inclusion.

Stage 5 (eligibility): during this stage the full texts of the remaining records were read through quickly to confirm the content of each piece relevance (to the study), resulting in reducing the set from 343 to 197. Thereafter, the remaining records were investigated against inclusion criteria namely, mentioning of theory used, method used, research questions, findings and limitations. The set was then further reduced from 197 to 21 pieces of literature that met the review criteria. Upon revisiting the literature, 2 additional studies were identified to be eligible for inclusion, increasing the final number of records to 23. Figure 2 presents an overview of the filtering process.

Stage 1 Scoping	Research question searched
Stage 2 Planning	Inclusion criteria determined
Stage 3 Identification (keyword combination search)	records increased from 1384 (Jan 2017) to 2273 (Mar 2019)
Stage 4 Screening (duplicates removed, titles and abstracts screened)	Resulting records increased from 343 records (Jan 2017) to 498 (Mar 2019)
Stage 5 Eligibility (full text screened, based on research criteria)	Eligible records increased from 21 records (Jan 2017) to 23 (Mar 2019)

Figure 2. Revisited systematic literature search (March 2019), filtering for suitable records

Once the final set was compiled, the remaining pieces of literature were reviewed again, this time with the aim of identifying UX elements presented as part of the outcome and findings of the literature. A spreadsheet was kept tracking; (i) occurrence of these UX elements across the different literature records (UX elements as column headings, (ii) the names of literature records as rows, and (iii) marking where there was an intersection (occurrence) between the element and the studies. During this new process of literature exploration and elimination, no indication of a previous systematic literature review on the research question (*what are the elements that influence the UX of BI systems?)* could be identified.

The initial set of UX elements was formed by the 217 elements (including duplicates and synonyms) from the different pieces of literature. It was notable that 185 elements covered varying stages of the software development life cycle, their individual research goals were different and had unique framework approaches, resulting in a collection of elements on different levels of abstraction.

To synthesize synonym elements within similar concepts, a card sorting exercise was conducted with three individuals to produce conceptual commonly understood groupings. The card sorting only reduced the number of elements to 183 elements across 10 categories.

3. RESEARCH PROBLEM

The systematic literature review conducted forms part of a larger study (Table 2) that aims to address the research problem that was identified, namely: *Currently there is no UX framework for representing Business Intelligence dashboard interfaces.*

Table 2. Summary of research questions, objectives, data strategies and intended outcomes of the three phases

Phases and questions	Objectives	Data capturing strategy	Outcomes
1. What are the elements that influence the UX of business intelligence dashboard interfaces?	To identify the elements that influence the interface UX of business intelligence dashboards through a systematic literature review.	Systematic Literature Review	A conceptual framework to describe the elements that influence the UX of business intelligence dashboard interfaces.
2. What are the practitioners' perspective on the elements that influence the UX of business intelligence dashboard interfaces?	To identify the practitioners' perspective on the elements that influence the UX of business intelligence dashboards	Interviews to capture practitioners' perspective on the elements that influence the UX of business intelligence dashboards	An intermediate framework to describe the elements that influence the UX of business intelligence dashboards.
3. What are the elements that influen a UX framework for business intelligence?	To develop a validated UX framework for business intelligence dashboards.	Evaluation (quantitative survey) of the factors that emerged from interviews.	Final verified framework to describe the factors that influence the UX of business intelligence dashboards.

The literature review confirmed this is as a reality and that there is a need for consideration of UX in its entirety (Schulze and Krömker, 2010; Fronemann and Peissner, 2014). This first phase of the study aimed to provide a wide and inclusive view on commonly accepted UX frameworks to identify elements required as well as relevance to the business intelligence context.

Table 2 presents the research questions, objectives, data capturing strategies and intended outcomes of the study as a whole. The UX frameworks identified in the literature review are all unique and different, with some similarities in elements, thereby lending itself to the analogy of a collage of information to form a bigger picture. of what is required for

4. RESEARCH DESIGN

The appreciative inquiry paradigm is applied as the underlying philosophical approach in this study. During the systematic literature review a keyword search was also conducted in search for appreciative inquiry studies in the user experience field, and no literature could be identified from the ACM digital library. Literature should encourage researchers to think about and understand research problems from interdisciplinary perspectives where it makes sense and where transferable (Cooper and Klymkowsky, 2013). Research should also present interdisciplinary perspectives as enlightening and a way to be fully engaged in the research (Froneman, 2014).

Appreciative inquiry does not fit into any particular ideology but is known for its inspirational approach and focused on possibilities instead of the customary stage of identification of the problem (Reed, 2007). Appreciative inquiry seeks to engage stakeholders in self-determined change. It also encourages practitioners to move beyond traditional problem-centered methods (Ashford & Patkar, 2001). Appreciative inquiry aims to ascertain the best of 'what is', identifying and building on past achievements, existing strengths, and possibilities of 'what could be'.

This inspirational approach led to the first research question being viewed as: ***What elements would be part of the best UX framework for representing Business Intelligence dashboard interfaces?***

Appreciative inquiry focusses on the workplace setting and understanding of the context (Crotty, 1998). It allows study participants to focus on past achievements, existing strengths and possibilities of what could be (Reed, 2007). Appreciative inquiry as a research method is broken down into four phases: 1) discover; 2) dream; 3) design; and 4) develop. There is also a link between appreciative inquiry and the main concern of pragmatism, being to measure knowledge by what works (Cutchin & Dickie, 2012), for example in an industry.

The study is viewed from a pragmatic approach as pragmatics recognize that there are many ways of interpreting the world and undertaking research, that no single point of view can ever give the entire picture and that there may be multiple realities (Saunders, Lewis & Thornhill, 2009). Pragmatism is also constructionist in that it challenges taken for granted ideas and is therefore a theory that sits well with appreciative inquiry's epistemological roots (Crotty, 1998).

The first phase of the study included a systematic literature review to allow for an in-depth review of existing literature, enabling the identification of gaps in the evidence base (Grant, 2009). From the systematic literature review the UX elements were identified, these elements were organized, themed and grouped by means of a card sorting exercise to identify overlap of elements (where the meaning is similar).

During the planned next Phase 2 of the study, users (practitioners) will be interviewed to find out what these practitioners consider to be required for the best dashboard (as part of the appreciative inquiry approach to find the best of what could be) UX. These interviews will incorporate practitioners from three (3) different roles, UX designers, product owners and developers. Where the interviewees will be probed until information retrieved reaches saturation. The responses from the similar roles will be synthesized as three (3) different perspectives of required elements. These elements will then be synthesized and grouped as a proposed intermediary conceptual UX framework for BI dashboards. The framework will aim to be practitioner specific, where the elements can be used before design, during design pre software release and post software release.

The final phase will employ a survey to validate the elements identified during phase 2 of the study. A statistical analysis of the data collected will follow. As a final step the validated elements from the survey will be compared to the elements identified from the systematic literature review. This will allow the compilation of the verified role specific UX framework for business intelligence dashboards.

5. FINDINGS AND RESULTS

From the revisited and updated systematic literature review an overview was provided on the changes and development in literature on the topic. With the inclusion of two additional pieces of literature, the UX elements were updated from 185 (*un-synthesized*) elements to 183 *reviewed and grouped* elements to make up an updated conceptual UX framework. The elements are on different levels of abstraction and of different weightings and importance and should be viewed as a **collage of elements** that constitute a conceptual UX framework for BI interfaces. This framework will be utilized in subsequent stages of the study to produce a validated framework. The elements and grouping of the conceptual framework can be seen in Table 3. For further research the framework elements would benefit simplification to improve ease of application.

6. CONCLUSIONS AND RECOMMENDATIONS

The updated conceptual framework comprises of 183 elements, grouped into 10 categories, the categories are UX strategy (19), UX goals (13), UX tools (11), Designer (4), UX design (35), Product (22), Technology (7), Interaction (16), Point of interaction (24) and User (32). The categories contain multiple subsets to be explored, refined and grouped in future research, which would improve presentation and use in practice.

The categorization of elements indicates that literature mostly addresses the *design* portion of the software development lifecycle (19%), followed by *user* characteristics and considerations (17%) which is typically encountered as part of the use of the software. This indicates that there is currently a focus in literature on the user and user considerations play a significant part in the design landscape. The Designer category had the lowest number of elements (2%), which contrasts to the vast number of designer related articles on social publication platforms like Medium, indicating to a growing need for research to address all elements of UX in the software delivery lifecycle.

In conclusion, the paper introduced the application of the appreciative inquiry research perspective and confirmed that literature from an appreciative inquiry perspective to identify the best UX elements could not be found. With the set of elements identified from literature being holistic and inclusive, the lack of elements relating to big data is noticeable, this further confirms the need for a UX framework pertaining to BI interfaces specifically.

Further research as part of this study will aim to extend this conceptual framework, by means of conducting interviews through an appreciative inquiry lens to determine what practitioners consider the best of what was for the best UX for BI interfaces, and of what could be in future for the best UX for BI interfaces. Thereafter, the research design will be followed as described in Section 1 of the paper to produce a validated UX framework for BI interfaces.

Table 3. A conceptual framework for User Experience (UX) elements representing Business Intelligence (BI) dashboard interfaces

UX strateg y	**UX goals**	**UX tools**	**Design er**	**UX design**	**Product**	**Technolo gy**	**Inter-action**	**Point of interaction**	**User**
Brand	Brand alignment	Empat hy tools (person a, mood board)	Design er respons ibilities	Standards	Product functiona lity	Technolo gy possibiliti es	Utility	Context physical	Physic al attribut es
UX missio n	Empathy	SUS questio nnaire	Profess ionalis m	Sensory perception layer (design, texture & atmosphere)	Product use	Technolo gy challenge s	Usabili ty	Context related tasks	Mood
UX philoso phy	Design to achieve reasons for product existence	Style guide	Approa chabilit y	Design presentation	Features	Technolo gy and tech support (context)	Efficie ncy	Spatio-temporal effects of place & time of experience	Concer ns

UX principles	Design to assist tech possibilities & challenges	Designer tool: grounded user representation	Design selling the idea	Design attractiveness	Qualities	Security	Flexibility	Usage context – experience driven innovation	Attitude
Accessibility strategy	Scientific understanding of humans (theory)	Interactions flow		Aesthetic & minimalistic design	Intended product character – design, hedonic, stimulation	Devices	Manipulation	Momentary UX – during use (time)	Skills
Measuring achievement of UX goals	Understand design context – what, why, where, whom	UX kpi (accomplishment rate)		Aesthetic layer	Intended product character – design identification	Network infrastructure	Help & documentation	Experience of meaning	Expertise
Data & analytics – UX metrics	Design simple	UX kpi (error frequency)		Function layer	Intended product character – evocation	Source quality	Usefulness	Emotional experience	Experience
Data & analytics – UX kpis	Design intuitive	UX kpi (task time)		Compositional (experience elements fit to form coherent whole)	Intended product character – design pragmatic		Error prevention	Interactions	Know-ledge
Data & analytics capability	What is essential	UCD process		Composition – functional modularity	Meaningful		Recognition over recall	Touch point orchestration	Competence
HR – UX roles	What is needed	Dev – UX process		Composition – distribution of functionality	Security		User control & freedom	Aesthetic experience	Recounting
HR – UX competencies	Test to evaluate	Evaluation process		Interaction layer	Product mobility		Recognize, diagnose, recover from errors	Time cumulative UX – over time	Appropriating
HR - UX responsibilities	Project core			Emotional response layer	Pedagogi-cal appropriateness		Visibility of system status	Time episodic UX – after use	Reflect-ing
HR - training	Design target			Meaning layer	Product information content		Visual attractiveness	User situation consequence – appeal	Interpreting
Change management – roadmap				Design content	Fluency (right data, right time)		Consistency	User situation consequence – pleasure	Expectations
Change management – co-design				Design cross-contextual activities	Product augmentation		Match between system and real world	User situation consequence – satisfaction	Anticipating

Communication strategy				Perceived service coherence	Product context		Navigation	Time anticipated UX before use	Aspirations
Value – worth				Activity evaluation method – communicative	Social context			Benefits – scenario	Desires
Value – strategy				Activity evaluation method – instrumental	Cultural context			Temporality functional dependency (usefulness, long-term usability)	Needs
Organization				Activity evaluation method – psychological	Admin & structural context			Temporality emotional attachment (identification phase: social, personal)	Intention
				Design consistency – semantic	Product presentation			Temporality increasing familiarity (orientation phase: stimulation, learnability)	Perception: thoughts
				Design consistency - perceptual	Service quality			Consequence – appeal	Self-expression / idealism
				Composition – component role allocation	Support			Consequence – pleasure	Autonomy
				Continuity – synchronization				Context aware	Personal
				Continuity – task migration				Cross-platform	Specific
				Continuity – cross platform transitions					Relatedness
				Time dimension					Popularity
				Formalize brainstorming					Competition
				Quick and dirty prototyping					Motivation
				Co-create with end users					Stimulation
				Formalize choice among ideas					Achievement
				Materiality layer					Connecting
				Benefits – design target					Influence
				Experience vision statement					
				Multiple design disciplines					
				Personalization					

REFERENCES

ACM Digital Library, Available at: dl.acm.org/ (accessed 28 July 2017).

Cheng, L. C. (2016) 'The Mobile App Usability Inspection (MAUi) Framework as a Guide for Minimal Viable Product (MVP) Testing in Lean Development Cycle', *Proceedings of the 2nd International Conference in HCI and UX Indonesia 2016 (CHIuXiD '16)*, pp. 1–11. doi: 10.1145/2898459.2898460.

Cooper, M. M. and Klymkowsky, M. W. (2013) 'The trouble with chemical energy: Why understanding bond energies requires an interdisciplinary systems approach', *CBE Life Sciences Education*, 12(2), pp. 306–312. doi: 10.1187/cbe.12-10-0170.

Fronemann, N. and Peissner, M. (2014) 'User Experience Concept Exploration – User Needs as a Source for Innovation', *NordiCHI'14*. doi: 10.1145/2639189.2641203.

Gegner, L., Runonen, M. and Keinonen, T. (2011) 'Oscillating Between Extremes: A Framework for Mapping Differing Views on User eXperience', *ACM Association for Computing Machinery*.

Grover, V. *et al.* (2018) 'Creating Strategic Business Value from Big Data Analytics: A Research Framework', *Journal of Management Information Systems*. Routledge, 35(2), pp. 388–423. doi: 10.1080/07421222.2018.1451951.

Hokkanen, L., Xu, Y. and Väänänen, K. (2016) 'Focusing on User Experience and Business Models in Startups: Investigation of Two-dimensional Value Creation'. doi: 10.1145/2994310.2994371.

ISO W. 9241-11, "Ergonomic requirements for office work with visual display terminals (VDTs)," *Int. Organization for Standardization*, p.45, 1998.

Kaye, J. *et al.* (2011) 'Designing for User Experience: Academia & Industry', *Extended Abstracts on Human Factors in Computing Systems*, pp. 219–222. doi: 10.1145/1979742.1979486.

de Kock, E., van Biljon, J. and Botha, A. (2016) 'User Experience of Academic Staff in the Use of a Learning Management System Tool', *Proceedings of the Annual Conference of the South African Institute of Computer Scientists and Information Technologists on - SAICSIT '16*, pp. 1–10. doi: 10.1145/2987491.2987514.

Law, E. *et al.* (2008) 'Towards a shared definition of User Experience', *CHI 2008 Proceedings - Special Interest |Groups*, pp. 2395–2398. doi: 10.1145/1358628.1358693.

Law, E. L.-C. *et al.* (2015) 'Tracing Links between UX Frameworks and Design Practices: Dual Carriageway', *Proceedings of HCI KOREA 2015*, pp. 188–195.

Morabito, V., Viscusi, G. and Themistocleus, M. (2016) 'Big Data and Analytics Leaders: the Changing Role of CIO'. doi: 10.1145/2890602.2890619.

Obrist, M. (2010) 'Contextual User Experience : How to Reflect it in Interaction Designs ?', pp. 3197–3200.

Øvad, T. and Larsen, L. B. (2015) 'The Prevalence of UX Design in Agile Development Processes in Industry', in *2015 Agile Conference*, pp. 40–49. doi: 10.1109/Agile.2015.13.

Reed, J. (2007). Appreciative inquiry: Research for change. Thousand Oaks, CA: Sage.

Sari, E. and Wadhwa, B. (2015) 'Understanding HCI education across Asia-Pacific', *Proceedings of the International HCI and UX Conference in Indonesia on - CHIuXiD '15*, pp. 65–68. doi: 10.1145/2742032.2742042.

Schulze, K. and Krömker, H. (2010) 'A Framework to Measure User Experience of Interactive Online Products', *MB '10: Proceedings of the 7th International Conference on Methods and Techniques in Behavioral Research*, 2010, pp. 1–5. doi: 10.1145/1931344.1931358.

HOW DO WE PERCEIVE EMOTION FROM A 3-D VIRTUAL TALKING HEAD: EVIDENCE FROM FUNCTIONAL NEAR-INFRARED SPECTROSCOPY

Jianying Wang[1], Jiangtao Chen[1], Nan Yan[1], Lan Wang[1] and Lawrence Ng[2]
[1]CAS Key Laboratory of Human-Machine Intelligence-Synergy Systems, Shenzhen Institutes of Advanced Technology, Chinese Academy of Sciences
1068 Xueyuan Boulevard, University Town of Shenzhen, Xili Nanshan, 518055, Shenzhen, China
[2]Speech Science Laboratory, University of Hong Kong, Hong Kong, China

ABSTRACT

Emotional interaction plays an important role in human-computer interaction. Although more and more virtual heads are endowed with a series of facial expressions under the conversational scenarios, the similarities and differences in neural mechanism underlying emotional perception between virtual head and human are still largely unknown. In the present study, we investigated the activation of emotional perception activities in the dorsolateral prefrontal cortex (DLPFC) region associated with when humans when beings perceiving emotions from 3-D virtual talking heads by using functional near-infrared spectroscopy (fNIRS). Three dynamic emotional stimuli were consisting of 3-D virtual talking head and human face with mute mode or voice presented by twenty participants. The behavioral results showed that participants had lower accuracy watching mute 3-D virtual talking head videos (3DMute) than watching human face videos with voice (HFMute) especially for in anger and happiness stimuli except for neutral emotion. The fNIRS results observed that there was no difference in DLPFC activity area for the observation of 3-D virtual talking head and human face. However, it was found that a stronger DLPFC region had stronger activation was observed for 3-D virtual talking head videos with voice (3DVoice) than 3DMute. In addition, the a stronger activation in DLPFC activation region for affectively angry emotion was videos observed in females was demonstrated, but yet there was no gender difference was found in gender during watching both types for happiness videos. The present results work provided preliminary evidence in physiology mechanism in human-computer interaction.

KEYWORDS

Human-Computer Interaction, Emotional Perception, Function Near-Infrared Spectroscopy, 3-D Virtual Talking Head, Dorsolateral Prefrontal Cortex

1. INTRODUCTION

Emotion perception yields a group of cognitive, physiological and motor changes, based on which an individual could make conscious or unconscious decision (Etkin et al., 2015). Emotion interaction plays an important role in human-computer interaction. Nowadays more and more virtual heads are endowed with a repertoire of facial expressions in conversation scenarios, however, how do humans perceive emotion of a virtual head? Is such emotion perception the same as perceiving emotion from a human face?

Magalie et al. (2015) explored emotive facial expressions using morphological and dynamic characteristics and measured the effectiveness of user's perception of the emotive facial expression during human-machine interaction. Kätsyri et al. (2008) compared emotion recognition using synthetic and natural human facial expressions, they and found a lower accuracy in recognizing synthetic expressions than natural expressions. Such discrepancy was believed to originate from the low intensity of the expressions and the imperfect emotion model of the synthetic expressions.

Despite the studies of behavioral responses associated with emotion perception, the corresponding cortical responses are still largely unknown. Brain functional imaging is a noninvasive method that can be used to record brain activity during emotion processing (Etkin et al., 2011, Glotzbach et al., 2011), and thus provide an objective account of emotion perception by visualizing the neural activity a reality. In comparison to behavioral responses, emotion-related neural activity provides a more solid ground for the study of emotion perception (Ekman et al., 1994). Recently, Wabnegger et al. (2015) applied functional magnetic resonance imaging (fMRI) to study facial emotion recognition in patients with Parkinson. The clinical group showed a generally stronger activation in emotion-related neural activity regions compared to the healthy controls. Balconi et al. (2016) applied functional near-infrared spectroscopy (fNIRS) and electroencephalography (EEG) to explore the cortical lateralization effect in dorsolateral prefrontal cortex (DLPFC) region of the brain with emotional visual and auditory stimulation. They confirmed that the important role of the DLPFC in processing emotional interactions also worked in different species.

fNIRS is a novel, non-invasive brain functional imaging technique with a good temporal resolution (Robert et al., 2016). The technique is mainly used to detect the hemodynamic activity of the cerebral cortex. Despite the limited detection of depth of cerebral cortex associated with fNIRS (Marco et al., 2012), most researches focused on the prefrontal cortex (PFC) which has been confirmed to be involved in emotion processing (Nishitani et al., 2013). Miranda et al. (2015) used images of happy, fearful and angry female facial expressions as stimuli to explore the differences emotion response in infant with focus on the prefrontal cortex when watching the same facial expression. They observed that the activities of PFC were negatively correlated with temperamental factors when the infants watched a happy facial expression. Wrase et al. (2003) studied the difference in PFC activity between genders when reacting to positive and negative emotions, and found a stronger activity in PFC region for happiness videos in men, and stronger activation in PFC region for affectively anger videos in women. The PFC region was demonstrated to be related with emotion.

However, it is not known if similar PFC involvement exists for perception of emotion of a virtual head. Recently, by using fNIRS, Aranyi et al. (2016) observed participants' response in the DLPFC region when perceiving the virtual agent showing different facial expressions. The participants' response showed activation in DLPFC, consistent with what they expected. These findings confirmed the impact of virtual agent on people's emotional perception. Yet, emotion perception of virtual agent with a human face was not included. It is still not known if similar findings could be found for perceiving an emotion from a virtual agent through using a human face. In fact, such emotion perception has been of interest to many researchers nowadays, and some brain regions have been found to be relevant in emotional processing. Matsubara et al. (2014) reported that the DLPFC region played an essential role in the top-down cognitive-emotion control of affect-generating structures. The neural processing of emotion regulation was associated with the model of emotion (Gross, 1998), according to which the ventrolateral prefrontal cortex (VLPFC) region estimates the affection and signals the need for regulatory processing via anterior middle cingulate cortex (aMCC) or its direct anatomical connection to DLPFC. The DLPFC processes the regulation and provides a feed forward signal to angular gyrus, supplementary motor area (SMA), superior temporal gyrus (STG), amygdala and basal ganglia, which in turn executes the emotion regulation (Gross & Thompson, 2007; Kohn et al., 2014).

In our previous work, a 3-D virtual talking head driven by real physical data with human emotions has been developed, and eye tracking experiments found no significant difference in fixation duration when watching 3-D virtual talking head videos and human face videos (Ni et al., 2018). As an extension of such, the present study investigated brain activation when subjects perceived different emotions from a 3-D virtual talking head by using fNIRS technology. Dynamic emotion stimuli (anger, happiness and neutral) conveyed by: (1) mute 3-D virtual talking head videos (3DMute), (2) 3-D virtual talking head videos with voice (3DVoice), (3) mute human face videos (HFMute), and (4) human face videos with voice (HFVoice) were used. The present study set out to confirm that DLPFC, as part of PFC, is an area strongly associated with emotions. In addition, accuracy in recognizing emotions in the above four scenarios was also analyzed. Based on the above discussion, three hypotheses were set up. Firstly, there was no significant difference when people were watching 3-D virtual talking head and human face. Secondly, the previous research by Sharon et al. (2013) found stronger activation in infants when watching the smile of their mother than others. It was also hypothesized that easier distinction of stimuli with improved activation of DLPFC could be found when viewing videos with voice than mute videos. Thirdly, for happiness emotion, it was hypothesized that stronger activation in DLPFC region for affectively when women watched videos of anger emotion.

The rest of this paper is organized as follows: Section 2 and 3 presents the method and data analysis respectively. The results and discussion are presented in Section 4 and 5. The final Section draws the conclusion and the future work.

2. METHOD

2.1 Participants

A group of 20 healthy Chinese college students were recruited in this study including 10 males (age: M = 24.60 years, SD = 1.955 years) and 10 females (age: M = 23.70 years, SD = 1.059 years). All participants were right handed and had either normal or corrected vision. All participants were informed about the purpose and the safety of the experiment, and a written informed consent was obtained. The study was approved by the Institutional Review Board of Shenzhen Institutes of Advanced Technology Chinese Academy of Sciences.

2.2 Experimental Design

For stimulus-induced activation, two experiments from the stimuli material covering two kinds of videos with two different modes, which were 3DMute, 3DVoice, HFMute and HFVoice were selected. A total of 60 videos with different showing time ranging from 2.5s to 10.7s were obtained. They included three emotions (anger, happiness and neutral). Among the videos, each emotion was shown in five videos with different speech content, and the speech content of 3-D virtual talking head videos corresponded to human face videos. The experiment used the event-related design and stimuli were presented randomly. Six conditions (2 renderings: 3-D virtual talking head video and human face video x 3 emotions: anger, happiness and neutral) were set. The block consisted of 60 trails and each trial consisted four epochs including fixation time, viewing time, choose time and blank time. The fixation time was set at 1s and the view time depended on the videos. Participants had the time to choose a right emotion of the presented stimuli. Blank time was set at 20s. To investigate the activation of emotional perception in DLPFC region when human beings perceive emotions from 3-D virtual talking head by fNIRS, the behavioral data and fNIRS data were recorded.

2.3 Instrumentation

To obtain fNIRS data, the NIRScout System (NIRx Medical Technologies, LLC) was used to simultaneously measure changes in concentration of oxygenated hemoglobin and deoxygenated hemoglobin. During the experiment, a plate was attached to the cap made of sturdy fabric to the participants. In each patch, eight detectors and seven light sources were embedded, resulting in 20 measurement channels (CH), as shown in Figure 1. The source detector distance was 3 cm and a sampling frequency of 7.81250 Hz was used.

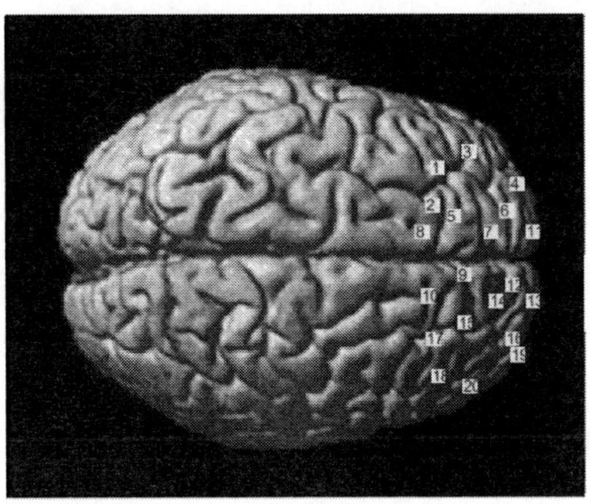

Figure 1. The configuration of channels

2.4 Procedure

During the experiment, the participant was seated in the front of a 22-in screen at the distance of 60 cm from the screen displaying the visual stimuli inside a quiet, dimly lit room. The video stimuli were displayed using E-Prime 2.0 software (Psychology Software Tools, Inc.) with which behavior data were recorded. The participants were first instructed about their task with instructions displayed on the computer screen. The sequence of experiment is shown in Figure 2 and the key frame picture of the animation sequence of happiness and anger emotion perception is shown in Figure 3. The participants were then instructed to carry out the first experiment during which they watched two types of mute videos presented at a random order. After each video stimulus was presented, the participant recognized the emotion and selected their choice by pressing the serial response box with three keys corresponding to three different emotions. The first experiment completed when 60 trials were presented on the computer screen. A brief period of time-out was provided to the participants upon completion of the first experiment. The procedure of the second experiment was similar to the first, except that stimuli with videos and voice were used.

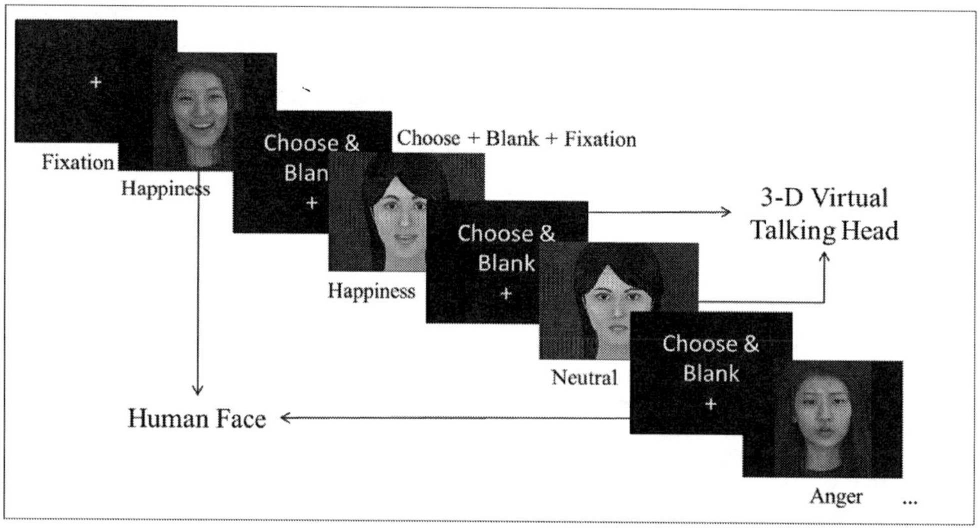

Figure 2. The sample of experiment

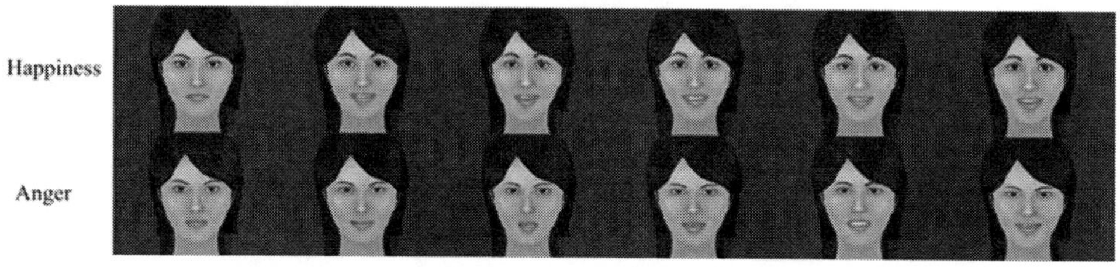

Figure 3. The key frame picture of the animation sequence of happiness and anger

3. DATA ANALYSIS

Before generating hemodynamic states data of each participant, the raw data was preprocessed by using nirsLAB (Xu et al., 2014). Data preprocessing consisted of: (1) interpolation of detector saturation, (2) checking data quality, (3) removal of discontinuities, (4) removal of spike artifacts, and (5) application of frequency filter. The time series of hemodynamic states including oxygenated hemoglobin was computed from the filtered data produced by the preprocessing utility based on the Beer-Lambert Law. Finally, NIRS-SPM

(Ye et al., 2009) was applied to generate a General Linear Model (GLM) matrix and functional data can be modeled using the equation:

$$\mathbf{Y} = \mathbf{X} * \boldsymbol{\beta} + \varepsilon \tag{1}$$

where $\mathbf{Y}$ is the matrix of hemodynamic data, $\mathbf{X}$ constitutes the design matrix containing the respective modeled effects, $\boldsymbol{\beta}$ is the parameter matrix comprising the beta weights to be estimated and the residual term ε. More precisely, the design matrix $\mathbf{X}$ of modeled effects comprises the predicted hemodynamic response function for each experimental condition over time, with stimulus onset as starting point. Hence, the oxyhaemoglobin concentration response of each condition of each participant will be estimated.

To estimate parameter $\hat{\beta}$, some parameters was set: basic function was 'hrf', Filtering was discrete cosine transform (DCT) with cutoff frequency 1/128 s = 0.008 Hz to ensure that the DCT band does not overlap with any event related frequencies. Gaussian smoothing with FWHM 4s to process ship type related noise.

4. RESULT

4.1 The Behavioral Data

Recognition accuracy associated with perceiving different emotions and different types of rendering by males and females are shown in Figures 4 and 5.

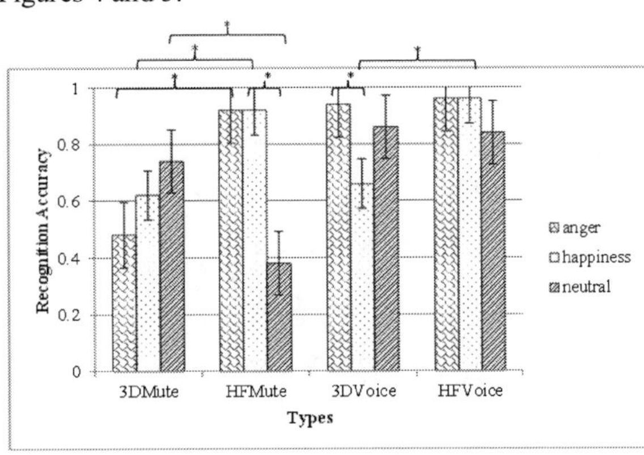

Figure 4. Recognition accuracy of male group

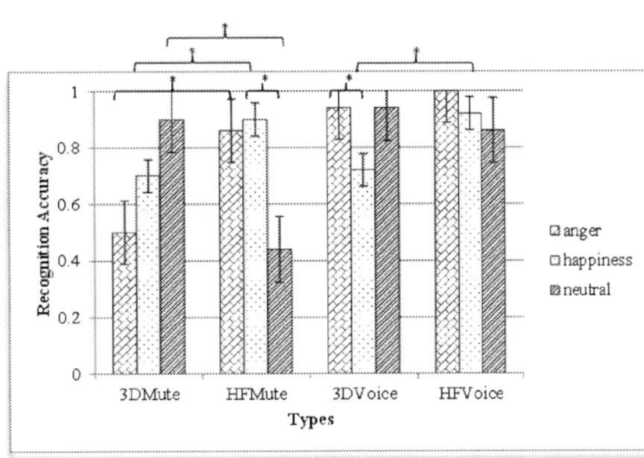

Figure 5. Recognition accuracy of female group

To determine whether the type of rendering (3-D virtual talking head videos and human face videos), mode (videos with voice and the mute videos) and gender (male and female) differed on different emotions, multiple-way analysis of variance (ANOVA) (Emotion * Type * Mode * Gender) was conducted on recognition accuracy of dynamic expressions.

There was main effect in mode ($F(1, 216) = 59.108$, $p < 0.001$) , type ($F(1, 216) = 10.857$, $p = 0.001$) and emotion ($F(2, 216) = 3.788$, $p = 0.024$). But there was no significant difference between the recognition accuracy of male and female.

There was no significant difference between the recognition accuracy of the videos with voice and the mute videos, and watching the videos with voice had higher accuracy than the mute videos ($F(1, 216) = 59.108$, $p < 0.001$). Besides, there was interaction effect between mode and emotion ($F(2, 216) = 10.423$, $p < 0.001$). When watching the mute videos, watching happiness had higher accuracy than neutral ($F(2, 216) = 8.208$, $p < 0.001$). When watching the videos with voice, watching anger had higher accuracy than happiness ($F(2, 216) = 6.003$, $p = 0.002$). There was interaction among type and mode and emotion ($F(2, 216) = 18.320$, $p < 0.001$). When the emotion was anger, watching 3DMute had lower accuracy than HFMute ($F(1, 216) = 45.236$, $p < 0.001$). And for the emotion was happiness, watching 3DMute had lower accuracy than HFMute ($F(1, 216) = 17.670$, $p < 0.001$). However, when the emotion was neutral, watching 3DMute had higher accuracy than HFMute ($F(1, 216) = 47.526$, $p < 0.001$). Watching 3DVoice had lower accuracy than HFVoice ($F(1, 216) = 17.670$, $p < 0.001$) when the emotion was happiness.

4.2 fNIRS Data

Oxyhaemoglobin concentration response was recorded by fNIRS, and the activated region of group can be seen directly as shown in Figure 6.

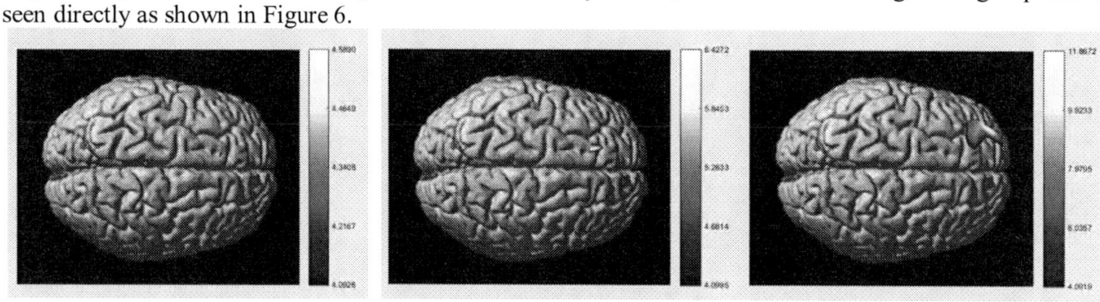

(a) (b) (c)

Figure 6. The group activation patterns ($p < 0.05$, uncorrected) from oxyhaemoglobin concentration response with contrast watching 3-D talking head videos and human face videos with the emotion is anger (a), happiness (b) and neutral (c)

To compare the difference between human face videos and 3-D talking head videos, oxyhaemoglobin concentration response was analyzed with the one way ANOVA in type. It was found that there was no significant difference between watching human face videos and 3-D talking head videos at all channels. Oxyhaemoglobin concentration response for watching human face videos was analyzed with multi-way ANOVA (Emotion*Mode*Gender). There was main effect in gender at CH3($F(1, 34) = 5.089$, $p = 0.039$) and CH6($F(1, 34) = 5.358$, $p = 0.035$). Also emotion had main effect at CH3($F(2, 34) = 5.234$, $p = 0.019$) and CH6($F(2, 34) = 5.437$, $p = 0.017$). Further, there was interaction effect between gender and emotion at CH13($F(2, 34) = 4.109$, $p = 0.038$) and CH18($F(2, 34) = 4.249$, $p = 0.035$). When the female group watched the expression videos, the activation of watching anger videos was higher than watching neutral videos at CH18. Besides, when the participants watched the same anger expression video, the activation of the prefrontal area of the male group was lower than female group. At the same time, there was interaction effect in mode and emotion at CH6($F(2, 34) = 4.276$, $p = 0.0034$) and CH13($F(2, 34) = 6.647$, $p = 0.009$).

Oxyhaemoglobin concentration response for 3-D virtual talking head was analyzed using multiple-way ANOVA (Emotion* Mode*Gender). There was main effect in mode at CH14($F(1, 34) = 5.044$, $p = 0.031$), CH17($F(1, 34) = 9.259$, $p = 0.004$) and CH20($F(1, 34) = 5.246$, $p = 0.028$). And the activation of watching the 3DMute was lower than 3DVoice. When the female group watched the expression videos at CH17, the activation of watching the 3DMute was lower than 3DVoice.

5. DISCUSSION

The present study investigated emotion recognition and activation of emotion perception in the DLPFC region when perceiving different types of emotions from 3-D virtual talking head by fNIRS under twelve conditions - three emotions (angry, happiness and neutral) in mute 3-D virtual talking head videos (3DMute), 3-D virtual talking head videos with voice (3DVoice), human face videos with voice (HFMute) and mute human face videos (HFVoice). The behavioral and fNIRS data were compared to study the similarities and differences in neural mechanism underlying emotional perception between virtual head and human.

From the behavioral data, accuracy of recognizing anger and happiness emotions when watching 3-D talking head videos had lower accuracy than videos of human face. This is in line with the previous findings (Kätsyri et al., 2008). But, for neutral emotion, watching 3-D talking head videos had higher accuracy than human face videos.

Although watching 3-D talking head videos had lower accuracy than human face videos, there was no significant difference of DLPFC activation between human face videos and 3-D talking head videos. This finding reveals a similar cortical mechanism for emotion perception of both 3-D virtual talking head videos and human face videos. This is partly in line with the previous research by Ni et al. (2018), in which no significant difference in fixation duration when watching both types of videos. The present results also shed light in the understanding of the physiology for emotive interaction.

In addition, it is of interest to find that the activation in the DLPFC region when watching 3DVoice was stronger than 3DMute. Results were consistent with previous research (Sharon et al., 2013) with the key finding that infants had stronger activation when watching the smile of their mother than the others. The results indicated that stimuli of easier distinction may be improved to activate the DLPFC region.

Wrase et al. (2003) found that the stronger activity in PFC region for happiness videos in men, and stronger activation in the PFC region for affectively anger videos in women. The present data also showed a stronger activation in the DLPFC region for affectively anger videos perceived by women, but no significant difference in gender during watching both stimuli for happiness videos.

The present is a preliminary study of emotion perception by humans based on different types of renderings. Some limitations are observed. Firstly, the emotional recognition accuracy of 3-D virtual talking head videos was slightly lower than human face videos, the emotion expressed by 3-D virtual talking head should to be improved. Secondly, emotion intensity is important to emotional perception and the influence of emotion intensity of 3-D virtual talking head will be explored in future work.

6. CONCLUSION

Although watching 3-D talking head videos had lower accuracy than human face videos, there was a lack of significant difference of the activation in DLPFC region between human face videos and 3-D talking head videos. The DLPFC region saw a stronger activation when watching 3DVoice than 3DMute. In addition, the stronger activation in DLPFC region for affectively anger videos in female, but there was no difference between genders when watching videos of happiness emotion. The present work provided preliminary evidence in the physiology mechanism in human-computer interaction.

In the future, oxyhaemoglobin concentration response in DLPFC will be observed when individuals with autism spectrum disorders are watching 3-D talking head by fNIRS. As most researches explored the emotion perception of autism spectrum disorders to robots or virtual head by eye tracker (Bekele et al., 2013), these researches may be a new rehabilitation approach for autism spectrum disorders and improve their life.

ACKNOWLEDGEMENT

This study was jointly supported by a grant from National Natural Science Foundation of China (NSFC 61771461 and U1736202), Shenzhen Speech Rehabilitation Technology Laboratory and Health and Health Services Research Fund (HHSRF), Shenzhen Fundamental Research Program JCYJ20160429184226930, KQJSCX20170731163308665, JCYJ20170413161611534 and JCYJ20150330102401089.

REFERENCES

Aranyi G, Pecune F, Charles F, et al., 2016. Affective interaction with a virtual character through an fnirs brain-computer interface, *Frontiers in Computational Neuroscience*, Vol. 10, No. 70.

Balconi, Michela, and Maria Elide Vanutelli, 2016. Hemodynamic (fNIRS) and EEG (N200) correlates of emotional inter-species interactions modulated by visual and auditory stimulation. *Scientific reports*, Vol .6, pp. 23083.

Bekele E, Zheng Z, Swanson A, et al., 2013. Understanding how adolescents with autism respond to facial expressions in virtual reality environments, *IEEE transactions on visualization and computer graphics*, Vol. 19, No. 4, pp. 711–720.

Ekman, Paul Ed, and Richard J. Davidson, 1994. *The Nature of Emotion: Fundamental Questions*, London, U.K.: Oxford Univ. Press.

Etkin, Amit, Christian Büchel, and James J. Gross, 2015. The neural bases of emotion regulation. *Nature reviews neuroscience*, Vol.16, No.11, pp. 693.

Etkin, Amit, Tobias Egner, and Raffael Kalisch, 2011. Emotional processing in anterior cingulate and medial prefrontal cortex, *Trends Cognit. Sci.*, Vol. 15, No. 2, pp. 85–93.

Glotzbach, Evelyn, et al., 2011. Prefrontal brain activation during emotional processing: A functional near infrared spectroscopy study (fNIRS), *The open neuroimaging journal*, Vol. 5, pp. 33–39.

Gross, James J., 1998, The emerging field of emotion regulation: An integrative review. *Review of general psychology*, Vol.2, No.3, pp. 271-299.

Gross, James J., and Ross A.Thompson, 2007. Emotion regulation: Conceptual foundations. *Handbook of Emotion Regulation*, Vol.3, pp. 3-4.

Hu Ni, JianyingWang, LanWang, and Nan Yan, 2018. Track your emotional perception of 3-d virtual talking head in human-computer interaction, *2018 IEEE International Conference on Cyborg and Bionic Systems (CBS)*, pp. 298-303.

Jari Kätsyri and Mikko Sams, 2008. The effect of dynamics on identifying basic emotions from synthetic and natural faces, *International Journal of Human-Computer Studies*, Vol. 66, No. 4, pp. 233–242.

Kohn, Nils, et al., 2014. Neural network of cognitive emotion regulation—an ALE meta-analysis and MACM analysis. *Neuroimage* ,Vol.87, pp.345-355.

Magalie Ochs, Radoslaw Niewiadomski, and Catherine Pelachaud, 2015. 18 Facial Expressions of Emotions for Virtual Characters. The Oxford Handbook of Affective Computing. *Oxford Library of Psychology*, Vol. 261.

Marco Ferrari and Valentina Quaresima, 2012. A brief review on the history of human functional near-infrared spectroscopy (fnirs) development and fields of application, *Neuroimage*, Vol. 63, No. 2, pp. 921–935.

Masataka, Nobuo, Leonid Perlovsky, and Kazuo Hiraki. 2015. Near-infrared spectroscopy (NIRS) in functional research of prefrontal cortex, *Frontiers in human neuroscience*, Vol.9, pp: 274.

Matsubara, Toshio, et al., 2014. Prefrontal activation in response to emotional words in patients with bipolar disorder and major depressive disorder, *NeuroImage*, Vol.85. pp:489-497.

Miranda M Ravicz, Katherine L Perdue, Alissa Westerlund, Ross E Vanderwert, and Charles A Nelson. 2015. Infants' neural responses to facial emotion in the prefrontal cortex are correlated with temperament: A functional near-infrared spectroscopy study, *Frontiers in Psychology*, Vol. 6, No. 922, pp. 922.

Nishitani, Shota, and Kazuyuki Shinohara, 2013. Nirs as a tool for assaying emotional function in the prefrontal cortex, *Frontiers in Human Neuroscience*, Vol. 7, No. 7, pp. 770.

Robert C. A. Bendall, Peter Eachus, and Catherine Thompson, 2016. A brief review of research using nearinfrared spectroscopy to measure activation of the prefrontal cortex during emotional processing: The importance of experimental design, *Frontiers in Human Neuroscience*, Vol. 10, No. 529, pp. 1–7.

Sharon Elizabeth Fox, Jennifer Wagner, Christine L Shrock, Helen Tager Flusberg, and Charles A Nelson, 2013. Neural processing of facial identity and emotion in infants at high-risk for autism spectrum disorders, *Frontiers in human neuroscience*, Vol. 7, pp. 89.

Wabnegger, Albert, Rottraut Ille, Petra Schwingenschuh, Petra Katschnig-Winter, Mariella Kögl-Wallner, Karoline Wenzel and Anne Schienle, 2015. Facial emotion recognition in Parkinson's disease: an fMRI investigation. *PLoS One*, Vol.10, No.8, pp. e0136110.

Wrase J, Klein S, Gruesser S M, et al., 2003. Gender differences in the processing of standardized emotional visual stimuli in humans: a functional magnetic resonance imaging study, *Neuroscience Letters*, Vol. 348, No. 1, pp. 41–45.

Xu, Yong, Harry L. Graber, and Randall L. Barbour, 2014. nirslab: a computing environment for fnirs neuroimaging data analysis, *in Biomedical Optics*. Optical Society of America, pp. BM3A–1.

Ye, Jong Chul, et al., 2009. Nirs-spm: statistical parametric mapping for near-infrared spectroscopy, *Neuroimage*, Vol. 44, No. 2, pp. 428–447.

INTERACTIVE TV USER EXPERIENCE IN BEHAVIORAL SITUATIONS

Seungyeon Lee and Myunghwan Yun
Department of Industrial Engineering, Seoul National University
1 Gwanak ro, Gwanak-gu, Seoul 08826, South Korea

ABSTRACT

Television (TV) is one of the most familiar products in our lives. As TVs evolve into interactive products, the user experience (UX) surrounding TV is also changing. Interactive TV attributes provide new capabilities; however, it is not clear how this affects the TV viewer's experience. The perceived quality of interactive products has two sub-dimensions: ergonomic attributes and hedonic attributes. Users perceive the quality of interactive products differently according to behavioral situations, and have overall experiences through a combination of those sub-dimensions. We hypothesize that a match between an individual's behavior and a particular product's attributes (i.e., ergonomic, hedonic) determine the perceived value of interactive products. Subsequently, we conducted a study with eighty TV viewers, in which half were asked to perform goal-directed tasks with interactive TV and the other half were asked to perform experiential tasks. The results obtained show that interactive TV viewers find interactive TV more appealing when they perform goal-directed behaviors. Regardless of the purpose of use, hedonic attributes were higher than ergonomic attributes on the perceived value of interactive TV. This implies the fundamental purpose of the user-TV interaction is to experience pleasure and achieving the goal is also the pleasure-seeking process as part of the fun. This also implies that hedonic aspect is the important factor than the ergonomic aspect on the TV-viewing experience regardless of the situation. The results demonstrate the potential value of hedonic quality as a measurement factor of interactive TV user experience evaluation and provide implications that interactive TV UX should be designed to enhance the enjoyable experience.

KEYWORDS

Interactive TV, User Experience (UX), Goal-Directed, Experiential, Hedonic Quality, Ergonomic Quality

1. INTRODUCTION

Television (TV) has been loved for a long time as an entertainment medium for relaxation and fun. As TV has become connected to the Internet, and the TV platform has developed to accommodate a variety of applications, it is increasingly becoming an active and interactive medium and the experience of TV viewers is also changing. The key features of interactive TV are, however, focused on new business opportunities (Bellman et al. 2017; Lekakos et al. 2001) or its functional aspects (Morris and Smith-Chaigneau 2012; O'Sullivan et al. 2004), rather than investigating TV viewer's entertainment needs (Chorianopoulos and Spinellis 2004; Livaditi et al. 2003). This diverse function and active usage strengthened by industrial developments obviously differentiates interactive TV from the previous non-interactive TVs (hereinafter "legacy TV"). However, not many studies convince that interactive TV enhances the TV viewer's experience. Instead, there are contrary studies that TV viewers rarely use the interactive TV's new features because they are unnecessary or difficult to use (Darnell 2007; Lee and Lee 1995).

The continuous diffusion of interactive products is possible when people use them casually and frequently. Ardito et al. (2008) stated that experiences are influenced "by the user's psychological state and the context" as well as the characteristics of the interactive system. Chorianopoulos and Spinellis (2004) argued that the evaluation of the traditional user interface might not be adequate for assessing TV applications. Therefore, interactive TV research should also examine the user's experience in terms of "everyday use."

Many studies in human-computer interaction (HCI) have focused on the usability aspects of interactive products. However, studies on everyday products like TV, which are more focused on non-utilitarian tasks, have begun to emphasize the importance of hedonic judgements as important as usability for the overall user experience (Hassenzahl et al. 2000; Hassenzahl and Ullrich 2007; Mano and Oliver 1993). According to those studies, people perceive interactive products in terms of both their ergonomic qualities (EQ) and hedonic qualities (HQ). Hedonic aspects and pragmatic aspects are sub-properties that describe a user's experience, and the user's overall experience is a combination of these sub-experiences. The pragmatic aspects mainly involve the product's utility and usability, including it being simple and predictable. The hedonic aspects include aesthetics, self-assessment, relatedness, novelty, and so on (Jordan 2000). According to Hassenzahl's user experience (UX) research model (2000), the objective quality of the product was judged through the user's perceived hedonic quality and the ergonomic quality and the process of making the overall judgment.

There are also other claims that non-utilitarian factors, such as fun, enjoyment, or aesthetics, are the main factors that affect the user experience (Hartmann et al. 2007; Norman 2004; Tractinsky et al. 2000; Tuch et al. 2012). Tractinsky et al. (2000) argued that the more beautiful the design, the more useful the result. Norman (2004), who emphasized the importance of emotional factors, argued that non-utilitarian aspects play a mediating role in goal-directed activity rather than usability, because the emotional impact through the aesthetic factor has a greater effect on the user experience. Dillon (2002) insisted that aesthetics work as a "driver," enhancing usability. This argument is more convincing as the range of interactive media is increasingly expanding. Bernhoupt and Pirker (2013) also asserted that aesthetics, emotion and stimulation are important UX factors on the interactive TV domain.

The user experience is affected not only by the product's own attributes but also by the user's behavior. According to Apter's (1989) reversal theory, users are affected more pragmatically when they are unconsciously or consciously exposed to a goal-oriented situation. Conversely, if a behavior itself is the goal, the hedonic aspects become more crucial factors to the users. Many studies on consumer experiences in online environments indicate that there are two types of consumption behavior: goal-directed and experiential (Novak et al. 2003; Sánchez-Franco and Roldán 2005). According to Novak et al. (2003), these two categories of behavior have distinct different attributes in important consumer behavior issues such as involvement, search and decision making. Goal-directed behaviors have the following attributes: extrinsic, directed search, and planned purchases. Meanwhile, experiential behaviors have the following attributes: intrinsic, ongoing search, and impulse buys. Hassenzahl et al. (2002) found that the users' evaluations varied depending on whether they had a goal to achieve or not.

TV has been classified as a passive entertainment medium providing relaxation and enjoyment. Interactivity enables more active user participation. People may want to use interactive TV more extensively. On the contrary, people may prefer to just watch TV or may not like the interactive attributes of TV. The purpose of this study is to identify opportunities to see how interacting with TV in the different situations affects the TV viewer's experiences. To do this, we assumed that the match between an individual's motivational orientation and a particular product attribute (i.e., ergonomic or hedonic) would determine the perceived value of the interactive product, and we applied this to interactive TV viewers.

1.1 Research Questions and Hypothesis

The main research question is, when using interactive TV, whether users experience differences between goal-directed behavior and experiential behavior. To answer this research question, two hypotheses were chosen:

H1. The experience aspects users consider will differ between goal-directed situations and experiential situations.

H2. Users will be more appealed in the goal-directed situation than in the experiential situation.

Another research question is what is the main factor affecting the interactive TV-viewing experience? Based on the question, one more hypothesis was set up:

H3. Hedonic quality will affect the interactive TV-viewing experience more than ergonomic quality.

2. METHODS

2.1 User Experience Model

In this study, we employed Hassenzahl and his colleagues' user research model (2000) and adopted it to different situations to investigate how interactive TV viewers' experiences are differentiated in behavioral situations. Hassenzahl et al. (2000) explained that a product has different quality dimensions and suggested a user experience research model consisting of four steps: objective quality, perceived quality, evaluation of the software, and consequences of using the software (or product). They proposed that the process through which the software appeals to users consists of the users' perceptions, evaluation, and the consequences of using the software.

Before starting the main study, we conducted a survey to determine the main behavior of TV viewers. We asked participants about the main purpose of watching TV (N = ninety-nine: female = fifty-eight, male = forty-one, average age = thirty-six years). We created a questionnaire about watching TV and administered the survey through SurveyMonkey.com (San Mateo, CA, USA), which is an online survey site. This survey was conducted for four days in 2017. It was found that sixty-eight percent of the respondents habitually turn on the TV to pass time, or to find "something fun." They search for a TV program by "channel zapping" or by navigating the menu. The average search time was three to five minutes. In addition, thirty-one percent said that they turn on the TV to watch a particular program. They preferred to reach the target content directly and quickly. The average time to reach the intended content was one to two minutes. The results showed that differences exist in the TV viewers' behavior and interaction time based on whether they have a goal. TV viewers usually find interesting content through browsing or menu navigating, whereas when they have specific target content, they go directly to the destination. (Figure 1).

In this experiment, the interactive TV service called Olleh TV, which is provided by Korea Telecom (KT), was used as the material (Figure 1). Olleh TV is a market-leading Internet protocol TV service in Korea that provide thousands of live channels, video content, and applications. The Olleh TV service interface has a hierarchical menu structure. Using a remote control, users navigate the menu in a vertical direction to first search for a category and then select sub-content belonging to the category in a horizontal direction.

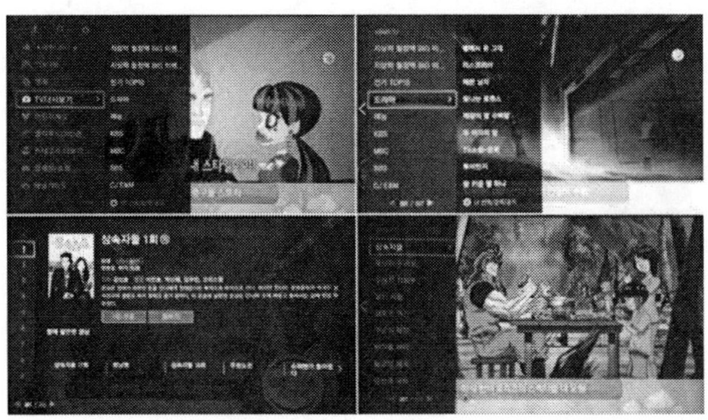

Figure 1. The hierarchy type user interface of Kore Telecom's interactive television service ("Olleh TV"). Clockwise from top left: 1 depth menu, 2 depth menu, 3 depth menu, and content page. Up and down keys on the remote control are used to select categories in the same depth, and left and right keys are used to move between depths

Eighty participants took part in this study (male = forty-four, female = thirty-six, mean age = twenty-nine years). All participants were new employees of KT. We recruited the participants from departments that were not directly related to the interactive TV service to avoid distorting the results of the experiment. All participants were familiar with the use of a remote control and knew how to search for channels and find content. No participation fee was paid to them. To allow participants to watch and manipulate the TV comfortably, a separate room with a comfortable chair was used. The distance between the TV and participants was about two meters. A fifty-inch high definition TV was used in the experiment.

2.2 Measurement of the Hedonic Quality, Ergonomic Quality and Appeal

Regarding the scale for measuring the HQ, EQ, and appeal in terms of the user's experience, we employed the Semantic Differential Questionnaire presented by Hassenzahl (2001). The Semantic Differential Questionnaire is a rating scale to measure the connotative meaning of products and concepts. The hedonic quality (HQ) is composed of seven questions and consists of emotional adjectives such as "interesting - boring," "exciting - dull" and so on. Ergonomic quality (EQ) is composed of eight questions about usability aspects such as "comprehensible - incomprehensible" or "supporting - obstructing." APPEAL is the integrated user feeling consisting of perceived HQ and EQ and has eight questions on dimensions such as "pleasant - unpleasant," or "good - bad." Each item consists of 7 points from -3 to +3, which means that the larger the negative value, the more the users are positively experienced.

2.3 Procedure

All participants signed an agreement to participate before starting the experiment. Eighty participants were divided into two groups. The first group performed three specific goal-directed tasks: (1) searching for a specific program's title through menu navigation, (2) finding specific video-on-demand content, and (3) registering their preferred channels. Each task's time was limited to three minutes in the goal-directed session. The experimental difficulty was adjusted appropriately so that all participants could complete the task in time. We counterbalanced the task order for the goal-directed group. After completing the assignment, the participants completed the semantic differential questionnaire about the perceived quality of the product and SAM questionnaire about their feeling. The second group performed the experiential tasks for ten minutes of freely navigating channels and finding content as they normally do when using a TV. After using the TV, participants also answered the same questionnaires mentioned above.

3. RESULTS

A factor analysis was performed to determine whether TV viewers perceived ergonomic quality (EQ) and hedonic quality (HQ) independently in each task. The factor analysis extracted two EQ factors and a main HQ factor from the semantic differential for the goal-directed tasks. All the sub-attributes of HQ were similar to one another and the eigenvalue of the extracted factor was 6.39 (42.64%); the explanatory range was 42.64% of the total variance. The eigenvalue of factor 1 extracted from EQ was 3.34 (22.26%) and factor 2 was 1.95 (13%); both factors accounted for 35.26% of the total variance. The combined EQ and HQ factors explained 78% of the total variance (see Table 1).

Table 1. Factorial validity of the goal-directed tasks' ergonomic quality and hedonic quality

The user perceived product's attributes	Principal Components with Varimax		
	Factor 1	Factor 2	Factor 3
G_HQ6 original – ordinary	.969	-.039	-.053
G_HQ5 impressive – nondescript	.930	.163	.068
G_HQ4 exclusive – standard	.927	-.029	.003
G_HQ7 innovative - conservative	.924	.136	-.067
G_HQ3 exciting – dull	.919	.159	-.031
G_HQ2 costly – cheap	.870	.030	.072
G_HQ1 interesting – boring	.852	.171	-.101
G_EQ1 comprehensible – incomprehensible	.094	.840	.259
G_EQ3 simple – complex	.250	.834	-.005
G_EQ7 controllable - uncontrollable	.074	.794	.202
G_EQ8 familiar - strange	-.424	.642	.025
G_EQ2 supporting - obstructing	.516	.633	.149
G_EQ4 predictable – unpredictable	-.068	.310	.852
G_EQ6 trustworthy – shady	-.063	.030	.852
G_EQ5 clear – confusing	.128	.544	.585
Eigenvalue	6.396	3.340	1.951
% variance explained	42.641	22.265	13.007

A factor analysis for the experiential tasks extracted a main EQ factor and a main HQ factor from the semantic differential. The eigenvalue of EQ factor was 5.52 (36.81%) and HQ was 5.39 (35.96%) and the combined result explained 73% of the total variance (see Table 2).

Table 2. Factorial validity of the experiential tasks' ergonomic quality and hedonic quality

The user perceived product's attributes	Principal Components with Varimax	
	Factor 1	Factor 2
E_EQ5 clear – confusing	.850	.072
E_EQ4 predictable – unpredictable	.785	.154
E_EQ1 comprehensible – incomprehensible	.782	-.161
E_EQ8 familiar - strange	.885	-.214
E_EQ2 supporting - obstructing	.886	0.1
E_EQ3 simple – complex	.697	.078
E_EQ7 controllable - uncontrollable	.726	-.175
E_EQ6 trustworthy – shady	.804	-.142
E_HQ4 exclusive – standard	.133	.789
E_HQ7 innovative - conservative	.378	.809
E_HQ6 original – ordinary	.1	.877
E_HQ5 impressive – nondescript	-.26	.905
E_HQ3 exciting – dull	-.252	.879
E_HQ2 costly – cheap	-.112	.885
E_HQ1 interesting – boring	-.169	.898
Eigenvalue	5.522	5.394
% variance explained	36.814	35.963

Table 3 shows that each variable had high internal consistency and was reliable to use as a variable in this experiment (Cronbach's α: EQ = .922; HQ = .944; Appeal = .958 in experiential tasks; Cronbach's α: EQ = .840; HQ = .970; Appeal = .958 in goal-directed tasks). According to the results, the HQ, EQ and Appeal were experienced more in the goal-directed tasks (EQ Mean = -1.362; HQ Mean = -.507; Appeal Mean = -.91) than in the experiential tasks (EQ Mean = -.79; HQ Mean = .08; Appeal Mean = -.69).

Table 3. Scale characteristics

Criterion	Scale	Cronbach's Alpha	Mean	Stand. Dev.	Min.	Max.
Experiential Task	EQ	.922	-.79	1.17	-2.63	1.63
	HQ	.943	.08	1.27	-2.71	2.14
	APPEAL	.958	-.69	1.11	-3.00	1.75
Goal-directed Task	EQ	.840	-1.362	.89	-3.00	.63
	HQ	.970	-.507	1.41	-3.00	2.43
	APPEAL	.958	-.91	1.11	-2.88	1.75

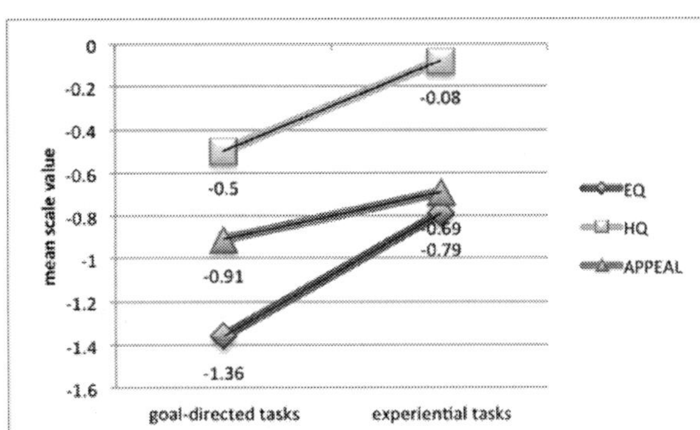

Figure 2. The ergonomic quality, hedonic quality, and appeal of the experiential tasks versus the goal-directed tasks. EQ = ergonomic quality, HQ = hedonic quality

Figure 2 shows the differences for the EQ, HQ, and appeal between the experiential tasks and goal-directed tasks. According to the results, the HQ and EQ were experienced more in the goal-directed tasks than in the experiential tasks. The judgment of the appeal (APPEAL) is a comprehensive evaluation of the product and consists of the individual's perceptions of the EQ and HQ. A regression analysis was performed in order to see the experiential tasks' appeal from the experiential tasks' EQ and HQ, and the goal-directed tasks' appeal from the goal-directed tasks' EQ and HQ (see Table 4).

Table 4. Regression analysis of the ergonomic quality, hedonic quality, and ergonomic quality and hedonic quality interaction on appeal (for the experimental tasks and goal-directed tasks)

	Criterion	Predictors	R^2	Adj. R^2	Beta	Std. error	β	t.	Sig.
Experiential Task	Appeal	EQ			.357	.067	.420	5.303	.000***
		HQ			.635	.062	.807	10.201	.000***
			.770	.758					
Goal-directed Task	Appeal	EQ			.481	.080	.429	6.024	.000***
		HQ			.519	.050	.736	10.334	.000***
			.816	.806					

In the experiential tasks, a significant regression equation was found (F (2, 37) = 61.914, $p < .001$), with an R^2 of .770. It was confirmed that EQ (t(40) = 5.303, p < .001) and HQ (t(40) = 10.201, p < .001) had an effect on appeal. HQ (β = .807) contributed almost twice as much as the EQ (β = .420) to the judgment of the appeal. The explanatory power explaining the dependent variable by the independent variables was 77%. No interaction between the EQ and HQ was found. Similar results were found in goal-directed tasks. A significant regression equation was found (F (2, 37) = 82.166, $p < .001$) with an R^2 of .816 in the goal-directed session. As a result of confirming the significance of each dimension, EQ (t(40) = 6.024, p < .001) and HQ (t(40) = 10.334, p < .001) affected on appeal. As with the experiential tasks results, the influence of HQ (β = .736) on appeal was also higher than that of EQ (β = .429). This result implies that the final judgment of the appeal depends more on the HQ than on the EQ for the TV-viewing experience in both situations. The implications of this will be described further in the DISCUSSION section. Similarly, the correlation analysis results showed a positive linear relationship between the judgement of appeal (APPEAL) and other UX quality dimensions (EQ and HQ) in the experiential session (APPEAL x EQ: r = .351*, APPEAL x HQ: r = .771**) and in the goal-directed session (APPEAL x EQ: r = .535**, ATT x HQ: r = .797**), respectively. In both sessions, the correlation between APPEAL and HQ was higher.

4. CONCLUSION

4.1 Discussion

In this paper, we investigated how the TV viewers experience differs in the experiential situation and the goal-directed situation. First, we confirmed that EQ and HQ are main factors of user experience measurements and independent each other, through factor analysis. Next, we measured whether the experience of both sessions were different each other. The results for the EQ, HQ, and appeal were significantly different according to whether participants were performing goal-directed tasks or experiential tasks; thus, H1 was supported. The hypothesis (H2) that users would be affected more in the goal-directed situation was also proved. As a result of the evaluation of the two sessions, TV viewers were more experienced in the goal-directed situation. Regression analysis showed that both EQ and HQ had a positive effect on APPEAL. The similar results were shown in the correlation analysis that a positive linear relationship between APPEAL and EQ and HQ in the experiential tasks and the goal-directed tasks. These results indicate again that the user perceive the product's character through ergonomic quality and the hedonic quality together. Interestingly, the results of the regression analysis showed that the contribution of the HQ was almost twice as much as the EQ for the APPEAL in both situations; thus, H3 was also supported. This implies the fundamental purpose of the user-TV interaction is to experience pleasure and achieving the goal is also the pleasure-seeking process as part of the fun. This also implies that hedonic aspect is the important factor than the ergonomic aspect on the TV-viewing experience regardless of the situation.

Based on the results of this study, the following constraints need to be discussed. As Chorianopoulos and Spinellis (2004) indicated, the interactive TV experience is influenced by both the interaction with the TV and the TV's contents. Although we tried to focus on the interaction with the TV itself, and minimized the impact of the TV's contents, it may be impossible to fully control the influence of the TV's contents in experiments. The two groups were exposed to different TV contents during the experiment. This implies that participants may have been influenced by the TV's contents while they were evaluating the experience in interacting with the TV. Another constraint is that the "interface" was controlled to focus on the "user experience." All tasks performed in this study were controlled with the four-way buttons of the remote control that have been used so far. We did not include personal computer-like features such as direct text input or pop-up windows. The main features of interactive TVs, so called "smart TV," are focused on its functions and its interface resembles a personal computer or smart phone user interface. This embarrasses users who are accustomed to traditional TV interfaces and they may feel pressured to learn a new way to use the interactive features.

4.2 Conclusion

In this study, we demonstrated that users had a different experience according to the different usage modes. Also, the TV viewers in this study reported having a "better experience" when they could achieve the goals. The goals mentioned here are mainly about pleasure rather than productivity. This finding means that the process of achieving the entertainment goals can also be a part of pleasure, and interactive TV can provide a better experience by providing various ways to experience pleasure corresponding to the user needs.

According to the results, TV viewers were more affected by the hedonic quality than by the ergonomic quality in both situations. TV viewers aspire to have fun and to relax; thus, the way of interacting with the TV should be more focused on enhancing the emotional qualities. As Vorderer (2001) mentioned, TV is not used for work but for entertainment, and research into the entertainment experience should examine ways of moderating the users' moods, focusing on their emotional outcomes.

It is necessary to determine how users' attitudes change based on their experience and the environment surrounding the TV, and to provide users with an optimized TV experience considering the changes in the TV. In particular, continuous and long-term observation is necessary, since hedonic aspects are known to increase as time goes on (Jordan 2000). Good emotions create a favorable experience, and the more that people experience, the deeper the relationship with the medium. In this sense, it is good that there is a growing number of studies employing long-term user experience measures (such as diaries, the experience sampling method, the day reconstruction method, and the user experience curve method) (Drouet and Bernhaupt, 2016; Kujala et al. 2011).

REFERENCES

Apter, M. 1989. *Reversal theory: Motivation, emotion and personality.* Florence, KY, US: Taylor & Frances/Routledge.

Ardito, C. et al, 2008. Combining Quantitative and Qualitative Data for Measuring User Experience of an Educational Game. *Proceedings of the International Workshop on Meaningful Measures: Valid Useful User Experience Measurement (VUUM)*: 27-31.

Bellman, S. et al, 2017. The effects of social TV on television advertising effectiveness. *Journal of Marketing Communications*, 23(1): 73-91.

Chorianopoulos, K. and Spinellis, D. 2004. User interface development for interactive television: Extending a commercial DTV platform to the virtual channel API. *Computers and Graphics* 28(2): 157-166.

Darnell, D. 2007. How do people really interact with TV?: naturalistic observations of digital tv and digital video recorder users. *Computers in Entertainment (CIE) - Interactive TV* 5(2) April/June 2007. doi:10.1145/1279540.1279550.

Drouet, D. and Bernhaupt, R., 2016. User experience evaluation methods: Lessons learned from an interactive TV case-study. In Human-Centered and Error-Resilient Systems Development (pp. 351-358). Springer, Cham.

Dillon, A. 2002. Beyond Usability: Process, Outcome and Affect in human computer interactions. *Canadian Journal of Library and Information Science* 26(4):57-69.

Hartmann, J. et al, 2007. Investigating attractiveness in web user interfaces. In: *Proceedings of the CHI 2007 Conference on Human Factors in Computing Systems*. ACM, Addison-Wesley, New York. 387-396.

Hassenzahl, M. et al, 2000. Hedonic and Ergonomic Quality Aspects Determine a Software's Appeal. *CHI '2000 Proceedings of the SIGCHI conference on Human Factors in Computing Systems*. The Hague, Amsterdam. 201-208.

Hassenzahl, M. 2001. The Effect of Perceived Hedonic Quality on Product Appealingness. *International Journal of Human–Computer Interaction*, 13(4): 481–4.99.

Hassenzahl, M. et al, 2002. The importance of a software's pragmatic quality depends on usage modes. In: Luczak, H., Cakir, A.E., Cakir, G. (Eds.), *Proceedings of the 6th international conference on Work with Display Units. WWDU*, 2002: 275–276.

Hassenzahl, M. and Ullrich, D. 2007. To do or not do to: Differences in user experience and retrospective judgements depending on the presence or absence of instrumental goals. *Interacting with Computers* 19(4): 429-437.

Jordan, P. 2000. *Designing pleasurable products: An Introduction to the New Human Factors*. London: Taylor & Francis.

Kujala, S. et al, 2011. UX Curve: A method for evaluating long-term user experience. *Interacting with Computers* 23(5): 473–483.

Lee, B. and Lee, R. 1995. How and why people watch TV: implications for the future of interactive television. *Journal of Advertising Research* (Nov-Dec 1995): 9.

Lekakos, G. et al, 2001. Information systems in the living room: A case study of personalized interactive TV design. *Global Co-Operation in the New Millennium The 9th European Conference on Information Systems*. Bled, Slovenia (June 27-29): 319-329.

Livaditi, J. et al, 2003. Needs and gratifications for interactive TV implications for designers. *Proceedings of the 36th Annual Hawaii International Conference on System Sciences*, 2003. DOI: 10.1109/HICSS.2003.1174237

Mano, H. and Oliver, R. 1993. Assessing the Dimensionality and Structure of the Consumption Experience: Evaluation, Feeling, and Satisfaction. *Journal of Consumer Research* 20(3): 451–466.

Morris, S. and Smith-Chaigneau, A. 2012. *Interactive TV Standards: A Guide to MHP, OCAP, and JavaTV*. CRC Press, Language Arts & Disciplines.

Norman, D. 2004. *Emotional Design: Why We Love (or Hate) Everyday Things*. New York, Basic Books.

Novak, P. et al, 2003. The Influence of Goal-Directed and Experiential Activities on Online Flow Experiences. *Journal of Consumer Psychology*, 13 (1&2): 3-16.

O'Sullivan, D. et al, 2004. Improving the Quality of the Personalized Electronic Program Guide. *User Modeling and User-Adapted Interaction* 14(1): 5-36.

Pirker, M.M. and Bernhaupt, R., 2011. June. Measuring user experience in the living room: results from an ethnographically oriented field study indicating major evaluation factors. In Proceedings of the 9th European Conference on Interactive TV and Video (pp. 79-82). ACM.

Sánchez-Franco M. and Roldán, J. 2005. Web acceptance and usage model: A comparison between goal-directed and experiential web users. *Internet Research* 15 (1): 21-48.

Tractinsky, N. et al, 2000. What is beautiful is usable. *Interacting with Computers*. 13(2): 127-145.

Tuch, A. et al, 2012. Is beautiful really usable? Toward understanding the relation between usability, aesthetics, and affect in HCI. *Computers in Human Behavior* 28, no. 5: 1596-1607.

Vorderer, P. 2001. It's all entertainment, sure. But what exactly is entertainment? Communication research, media psychology, and the explanation of entertainment experiences. *Poetics* 29, no. 4-5 (November 2001): 247–261.

IDENTIFYING FOREIGN LANGUAGE ANXIETY WHEN USING AN E-LEARNING SYSTEM

Daneih Ismail[1] and Peter Hastings[2]
DePaul University, USA

ABSTRACT

In addition to the cognitive, developmental, and pedagogical challenges of learning a second language, foreign language learners also face emotional obstacles. Negative emotions such as confusion, frustration, and anxiety interfere with the cognitive channels, which in return, moderates the learning. These emotions also diminish the sense of self-efficacy, producing a disinclination toward beneficial practice. In this research, we are focusing on foreign language anxiety (FLA). Our long-term goal is to recognize FLA and overcome it within the context of an intelligent foreign language learning system. As a first step, we are focusing on the recognition of FLA within a simple e-learning system for English language learners. To identify FLA, we correlated physical measurements (eye fixation, heart rate, and blood pressure) with emotional self-report. We found that the compound predictors of self-report of language difficulty, self-report of system difficulty, and exercise score can identify language anxiety. This finding will allow us to build a sensor-free anxiety detector which we will use to help overcome foreign language anxiety in the future.

KEYWORDS

Anxiety, Second Language, Foreign Language, Behavior, E-Learning System

1. INTRODUCTION

Foreign language anxiety (FLA) refers to the learner's feelings of tension, stress, and nervousness while learning a non-native language (Horwitz, Horwitz and Cope, 1986; Maclntyre and Gardner, 1994). Learners with FLA suffer from both reduced performance and achievement (Maclntyre and Gardner 1994), but an intelligent tutoring system which can take into account the affective state can reduce anxiety and increase motivation and self-esteem (Lin, Chao, and Huang 2015). Previous research has shown that there are multiple ways that anxiety hinders learning (Horwitz, Horwitz, and Cope 1986). FLA reduces self-efficacy, motivation and engagement (Van der Meij, Van der Meij, and Harmsen 2015; N. Wang and Lewis Johnson 2008). It interferes with cognitive channels (Castillejo 2018) and decreases foreign language achievement (Onwuegbuzie, Bailey, and Daley 2000). It increases cognitive load and overwhelms working memory (Chen and Chang 2009). Anxious learners shift their cognition from the learning to the threat (Pappamihiel 2002), which obstructs cognitive processes and reduces performance (Maclntyre and Gardner 1994). FLA also interferes with the fluency of speaking the second language (Castillejo 2018; Horwitz, Horwitz, and Cope 1986).

To improve the process of foreign language learning, we need to recognize that anxiety plays a critical role in shaping the learning experience (Horwitz, Horwitz, and Cope 1986). Identifying FLA can alleviate and eventually overcome anxiety, which in return can promote learning (Horwitz, Horwitz, and Cope 1986).

Previous research has described different types of techniques for identifying emotions including self-report (Arevalillo-Herráez et al. 2017; Castillejo 2018; Horwitz, Horwitz, and Cope 1986; Kerns et al. 2014; Maclntyre and Gardner 1994; Monkaresi et al. 2017; Wixon et al. 2014), physical instruments (Fernandes et al. 2018; Gotardi et al. 2018; Kantor et al. 2001; Keil et al. 2018; Krejtz et al. 2018; Mucci et al. 2016; Weeks, Howell, and Goldin 2013; Zhang et al. 2011), and expert observers (Baker et al. 2012; D'Mello and Graesser 2010). The most prominent self-report tool is the Foreign Language Classroom

[1] dismail1@mail.depaul.edu
[2] peterh@cdm.depaul.edu

Anxiety Scale (FLCAS) (Horwitz, Horwitz, and Cope 1986), which has been shown to reliably measure the anxiety level in classroom settings (Park 2014; Rodríguez and Abreu 2003). Other researchers used sliders with emojis on each end to measure emotions such as arousal and pleasure (Betella and Verschure 2016).

Previous research using physical measures to detect anxiety has shown varying results. Some researchers used eye trackers for measuring anxiety, finding that pupil dilation was associated with anxiety (Keil et al. 2018). Anxious participants also had a higher number of fixations with shorter duration (Runswick et al. 2017). On the other hand, (Gotardi et al. 2018) found no correlation between anxiety and saccadic eye movement which should be strongly correlated with fixations. Some researchers used heart rate and facial expression to detect engagement, however, they found that heart rate does not provide significant information (Monkaresi et al. 2017). Other researchers (Gotardi et al. 2018; Kantor et al. 2001; Zhang et al. 2011) found a positive correlation between anxiety and heart rate. Some prior work found a significant association between blood pressure and anxiety (Mucci et al. 2016; Zhang et al. 2011), but others (Howell et al. 2007) found no significant relationship. To label students' emotion, some prior research used observations by expert judges (Baker et al. 2012; D'Mello and Graesser 2010) to identify emotions such as boredom and confusion. These methods were used to measure general anxiety and other emotions, but we are focused on FLA in particular.

Through this study, we want to discover how to detect FLA while using an e-learning system. We addressed four research questions:

1. What is the relationship between classroom anxiety and interaction with the system?
2. Are physical measurements useful to measure FLA?
3. What is the relationship between FLA and the difficulty of the exercise?
4. What sensor-free measures are effective for detecting FLA?

Question 1 addresses the relationship between anxiety in the classroom and anxiety while using an e-learning system. When a participant is anxious in one situation, he is likely to be anxious in a similar context (Maclntyre and Gardner 1994). Understanding the interaction between different anxiety-producing situations could help to overcome anxiety (Huang 2018). We hypothesized that students who are anxious in a foreign language classroom would have the same level of anxiety while using an e-learning system. That would result in differences in interaction behavior which would enable an adaptive tutoring system to detect FLA. This would also validate our choice of emotion self-report as our operationalization of FLA, because we compare it to a previously validated measure of anxiety. In the context of Question 2, some research (Kazdin 2000) has claimed that using physiological measurements is more accurate than using self-report because it does not depend on the truthfulness of the participants and that there is a low correlation between emotion self-report and physiological instruments, but we agree with (Nagane 1990) that using a combination of physical measurements and self-report is better than using one tool. Thus, our hypothesis was that using physical measurements alone would not provide an accurate reading of FLA. For Question 3, (Robinson 2007) showed that language complexity is positively correlated with anxiety. Although (Kim and Tracy-Ventura 2011) found no interaction between task complexity and anxiety, in this study, we hypothesized that more difficult exercises would increase FLA, decreasing participants' assessment of their emotional state. In relation to Question 4, previous research used various metrics of interaction to identify emotion, including mouse behaviors (Azcarraga and Suarez 2012), time on task (Baker et al. 2012; Wixon et al. 2014), the number of wrong answers (Wixon et al. 2014) and emotion self-report (Petrovica, Anohina-Naumeca, and Ekenel 2016; Wixon et al. 2014). We hypothesized that using self-report of language difficulty, self-report of system difficulty, exercise score, time on task, and the number of mouse clicks could predict FLA.

We built a simple e-learning system which provides practice on vocabulary, grammar, listening, and pronunciation at differing levels of difficulty. We observed the learners while using the system and measured their anxiety level using emotion self-report. To detect anxiety, we correlated multiple channels such as fixations, heart rate, and blood pressure with emotion self-report. According to (Cunha-Perez et al. 2018), adopting affect detection on intelligent tutoring system would increase the motivation and learning. The eventual goal of this research is to build an intelligent tutoring system that can recognize FLA and alter its behavior to help the learner overcome their anxiety.

2. METHOD

2.1 Participants

The study consisted of 30 non-native English speakers, 77% (N= 23) female and 23% (N= 7) male, between the ages of 18 and 54 years old. There were 40% (N=12) native Arabic speakers, 37% (N=11) native Chinese speakers, 13% (N=4) native Spanish speakers and 10% (N=3) native Thai speakers. Based on the participants' self-report, their education level was 7% high school, 80% bachelor's degree, 13% master's degree. Their English level was 17% beginner, 53% intermediate and 30% advanced.

2.2 Procedure

We performed three rounds of pilot tests. Each consisted of 1-2 participants. During the pilot test, we tested the physical measurements and self-reports. After each round, we validated the physical measurements settings and self-reports to assure they provide an accurate reading and avoid errors. We observed the participants while doing English exercises on the e-learning system. The participants spent an average 43:41 minutes per session. All sessions were audio and video recorded, and log sheets were used to note any unusual occurrences. To do the observational study, we first asked the participant to read then sign the informed consent, ensuring that they understood. After that, we introduced the physical measurements and the use of each. Next, we requested the participant to complete the demographic survey and FLCAS. Then they followed the directions on the computer while the experimenter was in the observation room. After the participants finished all the exercises and the self-reports, we gave them a $20 Amazon gift card in compensation.

2.3 E-Learning System

The e-learning system consists of 27 exercises concentrated on three topics; greeting, transportation, and emotions. The system was designed to provide practice in English with a focus on vocabulary, grammar, listening and pronunciation. To provide an effective e-learning system, we applied the multimedia, modality, redundancy, coherence, segmentation, and leveraging examples guidelines based on the Cognitive Theory of Multimedia Learning (Mayer 2005). It was implemented in HTML, JavaScript, and included agents using animated agents from Media Semantics.

2.4 Metrics

To measure FLA, we used self-report plus physical monitors. We used two types of self-report in the study, each in the participant's native language (Arabic, Chinese, Spanish, or Thai). The first self-report consisted of demographic information and the FLCAS. The second self-report was collected after each exercise. It consisted of three items: one on system difficulty, one on language difficulty, and one on current emotion. The system difficulty item was *'I felt I knew how to use the interface'* with a five-point Likert scale from strongly agree to strongly disagree. The language difficulty item was *'I felt I knew how to answer the question'* with a five-point Likert scale from strongly agree to strongly disagree. The current emotion question was *'I felt'* with a continuous-valued slider from *'Calm'* to *'Anxious'* with appropriate accompanying emojis.

The physical monitors were the Tobii eye tracker, Polar A370 fitness tracker, and QardioArm blood pressure monitor. The eye tracker was connected to the bottom frame of the screen. It provided us with the number of fixations, the time on task and the number of mouse clicks. The fitness tracker was worn on the left wrist to measure the heart rate. It provided continuous reading for the heart rate for the whole session. We exported the heart rate information from the fitness tracker to a log file and based on the timestamp we paired the heart rate to the exercise. The blood pressure monitor was attached to the left upper arm. We tried to get a blood pressure reading for each of the exercises but were limited in how frequently we could take measurements. On some exercises, we got a couple of measurements while on others we got none based on how long the learner spent per exercise.

2.5 Analyzing the Data

We first calculated the FLCAS score, giving the participants an initial classification as anxious or non-anxious. The participants who scored below 90 were non-anxious and those scoring 90 or above were classified as anxious (Guo, Xu, and Liu 2018).

Language difficulty and system difficulty were coded from the participants' Likert scale responses. The emotion self-report was coded from the participants' continuous-valued slider response. To measure the aggregate exercise difficulty, we calculated the percentage of the correct answers across all participants. Then, we classified the aggregate exercise difficulty into three levels (easy, medium, and hard).

While the participants answered the FLCAS, we measured their blood pressure to record their baseline level. To analyze blood pressure, we calculated the level of change between the baseline and the systolic and diastolic pressure reading for each participant on each exercise. The heart rate was calculated as the difference between the maximum and minimum heart rate per exercise to allow for different base heart rates, and to capture changes that might occur from the exercise itself. We figured that using the average, maximum, or minimum heart rate would not provide us with an accurate reading of the change in heart rate, while the difference would give us an indication of the variance in heart rate. The number of fixations, number of mouse clicks, and time on tasks were provided by the eye tracker device. The score for each exercise for each participant was calculated as the percentage of correct answers for that exercise.

3. RESULTS

3.1 What is the Relationship Between Classroom Anxiety and Interaction with the System?

We did a Mann Whitney U-test comparing the anxious and non-anxious groups as determined by FLCAS with respect to the other measures and found that there was a significant difference between the groups with respect to the emotion self-report, language difficulty self-report, the systolic and diastolic blood pressure relative to baseline. The results of the Mann Whitney U-Test and the median values are shown in Table 1. There was no significant difference between the two groups in the difference of heart rate, score, number of fixation, system difficulty self-report, time on task, nor the number of mouse clicks.

Table 1. Differences between anxious and non-anxious learners

Variable	Anxious Median	Non-anxious Median	Mann-Whitney U	*p*-value
Emotion self-report	14	2	57404.500	< 0.001
Self-report language difficulty	2	1	67585.000	< 0.001
Systolic relative to the baseline	-5	-8	49766.500	< 0.001
Diastolic relative to the baseline	-2.667	-5.2	51734.000	< 0.001
Difference in heart rate	10	10	74523.000	0.067
Self-report system difficulty	1	1	76941.000	0.193
Score	100	95	43037.500	0.554
Time on task	62.61	61.17	78668.500	0.641
Number of mouse click	9	9	78570.500	0.679
Fixations	164	161	80458.500	0.977

3.2 Are Physical Measurements Useful to Measure FLA?

To understand the relationship between FLA as measured by emotion self-report and the physical measurements, we did a Pearson correlation between emotion self-report, number of fixations, difference in heart rate, and the systolic and diastolic blood pressure relative to baseline. We found a significant weak positive correlation between the emotion self-report and the number of fixations $p<0.001$, $r=0.171$. Also, we found a significant weak positive correlation between the emotion self-report and difference in heart rate $p<0.001$, $r=0.166$. We found a significant weak positive correlation between the emotion self-report and the systolic blood pressure relative to baseline $p<0.001$, $r=0.174$. We found a significant weak positive correlation between the emotion self-report and the diastolic blood pressure relative to baseline $p<0.001$, $r=0.149$.

3.3 What is the Relationship Between FLA and the Difficulty of the Exercise?

We measured the exercise difficulty in two ways: learner's "self-report of language difficulty", and "aggregate exercise difficulty" which we calculated based on the score of all the participants. To understand the correlation between the self-report difficulty of the language and anxiety level, we did a Spearman correlation. We found a significant moderate positive correlation between the emotion self-report and the language difficulty self-report $p<0.001$, $r= 0.582$.

We also did a Spearman correlation between the aggregate exercise difficulty, and the anxiety level. We found a significant weak positive correlation between the aggregate exercise difficulty and the emotion self-report $p=0.036$, $r=0.086$.

3.4 What Sensor-Free Measures are Effective for detecting FLA?

To answer this question, we did a multiple regression analysis. The independent variables were language difficulty self-report, system difficulty self-report, score, aggregate exercise difficulty, time on task, and the number of mouse clicks. The dependent variable was the emotion self-report. We found that the model's predictions was not improving with the addition of more predictors. So, we compared all the possible models to find the best fit based on the R^2, adjusted R^2, and predicted R^2. We determined that the best predictors were language difficulty self-report, system difficulty self-report and scores. The other variables did not add power to the prediction. The multiple correlation between emotion and the three predictors provided a good fit $R = 0.554$. The combination of the three predictors accounts for about 30% of the variation in emotion, $R^2 = 30.79\%$, $R^2(adj)=30.45\%$, and $R^2(pred)=29.10\%$. The regression equation, which indicated that the model was a significant predictor of emotion $(F\ 3, 599) = 88.40$, $p < 0.001$ is shown in Table 2.

Table 2. Multiple regression coefficients

Term	Coefficient	Standard Error Coefficient	*t*-value	*p*-value
Constant	15.305	0.663	23.07	< 0.001
Self-report language difficulty	9.659	0.781	12.37	< 0.001
Self-report system difficulty	1.772	0.769	2.30	0.022
Score	-0.580	0.683	-0.85	0.396

4. DISCUSSION

4.1 Question 1: The Relationship Between Classroom Anxiety and Interaction with the System

To initially categorize the participants as anxious or non-anxious in classroom settings, we used the FLCAS score as described above. We did a Mann-Whitney U-test to see if there was a difference between the two groups (anxious/non-anxious) with respect to their system interaction and other measurements. We found that there was a significant difference in the emotion self-report, language difficulty self-report, the systolic and diastolic blood pressure relative to baseline. Our hypothesis that students who suffer from FLA in a classroom situation would also be anxious while using the system was supported.

As we expected, there was a difference in emotion self-report between the anxious and non-anxious groups, with anxious learners reporting a higher anxiety level while interacting with the system. This agrees with (Maclntyre and Gardner 1994), who found that when someone is anxious in one situation he is likely to also be anxious in a similar context. Moreover, the median and average result for the emotion self-report was higher for the anxious group. This indicates that emotion self-report is a valid metric for language anxiety in the context of an e-learning system.

Anxious learners' median self-report of language difficulty was, I *'agree'* that *'I felt I know how to answer the questions'*. While the non-anxious learner median was I *'extremely agree'* that they knew how to answer the questions. This means that anxious learners may have felt the questions were somewhat more difficult than the non-anxious learners did. Or it may indicate that the non-anxious learners were more confident about their answers.

Similar to (Mucci et al. 2016; Zhang et al. 2011), the blood pressure was higher for anxious learners than non-anxious learners. Although both median and average reading for both groups were in the normal range according to (Whelton et al. 2018), there was a slight increase in the average blood pressure reading for anxious learners. This may indicate that non-anxious learners were more relaxed during the exercise.

Similar to (Tanielian and English 2014) the relationship between the anxiety level and the score was inconclusive. This could indicate that anxiety is more related to confidence and self-efficacy than to actual competence with the language.

According to (M. Wang 2014), FLA affects self-confidence and self-esteem. Accordingly, we assumed that there would be differences between anxious and non-anxious learners in the time spent on task and the number of mouse clicks. But we did not find significant differences. Perhaps the anxious learners did not spend significantly more time on the exercises because the difficulty of the exercises was not challenging enough. The number of mouse clicks was the same for both groups which reflects clicking the target button only once when needed.

4.2 Question 2: Identifying FLA Using Physical Instruments

Our hypothesis of having physical measurements alone would not provide an accurate reading of FLA was supported. The physical measurements had low correlations with the emotion self-report. Our results agreed with (Kazdin 2000) that there is low correlation between emotion self-report and the physical measurements.

Our findings agreed with (Runswick et al. 2017) which showed that anxious learners had more eye fixations than calm learners. The results showed us that the increase in the anxiety level would increase the difference between the highest and lowest heart rate per exercise. So, if the learners were calm before starting the exercise their heart rate would be relatively low. Then through the exercise, if the learners become more anxious their heart rate would increase (Gotardi et al. 2018; Kantor et al. 2001; Zhang et al. 2011). We used the blood pressure reading for each exercise relative to the learner's baseline to standardize the measurements. We found a positive correlation between the blood pressure relative to the baseline and the emotion self-report. This finding agree with (Mucci et al. 2016) that showed a positive correlation between anxiety and blood pressure. Based on the blood pressure, anxious participants had a higher rate than non-anxious.

Overall, the physical measurements alone would not suffice to identify FLA within the context of an e-learning system because of the very weak correlation with the emotion self-report. Measuring FLA using physical instrument is inconclusive, some type of self-report is needed to help identify FLA.

4.3 Question 3: The Relationship Between FLA and the Difficulty of the Exercise

We measured the difficulty of the exercise using the language self-report and the average score across participants. The language difficulty self-report represents the user's impression of the exercise while the aggregate exercise difficulty provides a more objective value.

We found that both measurements for difficulty of the exercise language are positively correlated with the emotion self-report. This supports our hypothesis that language difficulty would affect FLA, and replicates the findings of (Robinson 2007) about the relationship between exercise difficulty and anxiety. Similarly,

(Chen and Chang 2009) showed that increased difficulty would increase anxiety, and (Lin, Chao, and Huang 2015) found that providing an easy exercise could decrease anxiety.

4.4 Question 4: Identifying FLA by the Interaction of the Learner with the System

To identify FLA, we did a multiple regression analysis by adapting some of the features used by (Wixon et al. 2014) to identify emotion. The dependent variable was the emotion self-report. The independent variables were language difficulty self-report, system difficulty self-report, exercise score, time on task, number of mouse clicks, and aggregate exercise difficulty. We found, however, that this model was not ideal because the power of the prediction did not improve with the addition of more predictors. So we looked for the best model which used a subset of the predictors.

The factors which appeared to be the most effective predictors for FLA were language difficulty self-report, system difficulty self-report, and exercise score. The other predictors were not dominant. Our explanation of this finding is that participants are aware of their emotions and reported their feelings accurately (Petrovica, Anohina-Naumeca, and Ekenel 2016). They felt more anxious when they believed they didn't know how to answer the question and vice versa. We confirmed that there is a relationship between the complexity of the task and anxiety (Robinson 2007). This relationship led to having language difficulty self-report as the most precise FLA predictor.

The second predictor was the self-report of system difficulty. We assumed this predictor would affect language anxiety because the lack of technical knowledge or of how the e-learning system worked would make the learner confused, which in turn could advance to frustration and anxiety. The system difficulty would also reduce the sense of self-efficacy which in turn increases anxiety (Saadé and Kira 2009). These two predictors replicate the value of self-report as a sensor-free emotion detector as shown by (Wixon et al. 2014). According to (Maclntyre and Gardner 1994), students' performance is affected by FLA. Thus, the third predictor was the learner's score on the exercise. Although the score was not shown to the student in the e-learning system, it predicts their anxiety level. Through this analysis, we could conclude that the calm learners would do better than the anxious learners. More relevant to our long-term goals, it shows that we could use learners' performance in the exercises to help determine their level of FLA.

The other predictors were less important than expected. One of the predictors used by (Wixon et al. 2014) was time on task. We replicated that test, assuming that the time on task would affect language anxiety because we thought the longer the learner took to answer a question, the more anxious he would become. However, we found that time on task had little power in predicting FLA.

We thought that using both measures of exercise language difficulty would add power to the language anxiety predictor. However, the aggregate exercise difficulty did not help predict language anxiety. According to (Robinson 2007), task complexity is determined by the cognitive processing needed for the exercise, which varies from person to person. So although the individual language difficulty self-report did improve the power of prediction of FLA, adding the aggregate exercise difficulty did not.

We hypothesized that anxious learners would click the mouse more than the non-anxious learners. We thought that anxious learners would not be sure about their answer, so they would change their answer which affects the number of the mouse clicks. However, this assumption was wrong. There was no significant correlation between the anxiety level and the number of mouse click, and adding the number of mouse clicks did not affect the power of the prediction of the regression model. This means the number of the mouse clicks would not be a useful component of a sensor-free FLA detector.

5. CONCLUSION

FLA is a major obstacle for foreign language learners. This research showed that emotion self-report is a valid metric for detecting FLA in the context of an interactive system. But we believe that constantly asking the learner how they are feeling is not the best way to help them get over their anxiety. So we have attempted to uncover other measures which will allow an interactive system to detect FLA. We found that the strongest predictors for FLA were the self-report of difficulty of the language in an exercise, self-report of system difficulty, and the exercise score. Finally, we confirmed that physical measurements were not optimal for identifying FLA.

One limitation of the current study is the small range of difficulties of the exercises. We were also unable to evaluate some of the exercises due to technical issues which reduced the total number of available scores and kept us from using the previous exercise score as predictor for FLA.

We need to extend the e-learning system to include a wider range of challenging levels to verify that there are similar responses. Also, we need to determine the best way to intervene when we know the learner is feeling anxious. This research will allow us to build an adaptive tutoring system which includes a sensor-free intelligent FLA detector. We will use the language difficulty self-report, system difficulty self-report, and the score as predictors of the anxiety level. These will trigger the system's anxiety-reduction behaviors, which should help the learners improve the effectiveness of their efforts.

ACKNOWLEDGEMENT

This project was funded in part by a grant from the College of Computing and Digital Media at DePaul University. Also, we are grateful to Media Semantics for providing us with a free license for the animated agent application.

REFERENCES

Arevalillo-Herráez, Miguel, Luis Marco-Giménez, David Arnau, and José A. González-Calero. 2017. "Adding Sensor-Free Intention-Based Affective Support to an Intelligent Tutoring System." *Knowledge-Based Systems* 132: 85–93. https://doi.org/10.1016/j.knosys.2017.06.024.

Azcarraga, Judith, and Merlin Teodosia Suarez. 2012. "Predicting Academic Emotions Based on Brainwaves, Mouse Behaviour and Personality Profile." In , 728–33. Springer, Berlin, Heidelberg. https://doi.org/10.1007/978-3-642-32695-0_64.

Baker, Ryan S.J.d., Sujith M Gowda, Michael Wixon, Jessica Kalka, Angela Z Wagner, Aatish Salvi, Vincent Aleven, Gail W Kusbit, Jaclyn Ocumpaugh, and Lisa Rossi. 2012. "Towards Sensor-Free Affect Detection in Cognitive Tutor Algebra." *Proceedings of the Fifth International Conference on Educational Data Mining*, 126–33. https://doi.org/10.1007/s00192-014-2606-4.

Betella, Alberto, and Paul F.M.J. Verschure. 2016. "The Affective Slider: A Digital Self-Assessment Scale for the Measurement of Human Emotions." *PLoS ONE* 11 (2): 1–11. https://doi.org/10.1371/journal.pone.0148037.

Castillejo, Susana Pérez. 2018. "The Role of Foreign Language Anxiety on L2 Utterance Fluency during a Final Exam." *Language Testing*. https://doi.org/10.1177/0265532218777783.

Chen, I-Jung, and Chi-Cheng Chang. 2009. "Cognitive Load Theory: An Empirical Study of Anxiety and Task Performance in Language Learning." *Electronic Journal of Research in Educational Psychology* 7 (2): 729–46. https://doi.org/10.25115/ejrep.v7i18.1369.

Cunha-Perez, Cristina, Miguel Arevalillo-Herraez, Luis Marco-Gimenez, and David Arnau. 2018. "On Incorporating Affective Support to an Intelligent Tutoring System: An Empirical Study." *Revista Iberoamericana de Tecnologias Del Aprendizaje* 13 (2): 63–69. https://doi.org/10.1109/RITA.2018.2831760.

D'Mello, Sidney K., and Arthur Graesser. 2010. "Multimodal Semi-Automated Affect Detection from Conversational Cues, Gross Body Language, and Facial Features." *User Modeling and User-Adapted Interaction* 20 (2): 147–87. https://doi.org/10.1007/s11257-010-9074-4.

Fernandes, Catarina, Susana Silva, Joana Pires, Alexandra Reis, Antónia Jimenez Ros, Luís Janeiro, Luís Faísca, and Ana Teresa Martins. 2018. "Eye-Tracking Evidence of a Maintenance Bias in Social Anxiety." *Behavioural and Cognitive Psychotherapy* 46 (1): 66–83. https://doi.org/10.1017/S1352465817000418.

Gotardi, Gisele, Paulo Schor, John van der Kamp, Martina Navarro, Dominic Orth, Geert Savelsbergh, Paula F. Polastri, Raoul Oudejans, and Sergio T. Rodrigues. 2018. "The Influence of Anxiety on Visual Entropy of Experienced Drivers." *Proceedings of the 3rd Workshop on Eye Tracking and Visualization - ETVIS '18*, 1–4. https://doi.org/10.1145/3205929.3205936.

Guo, Yan, Jinfen Xu, and Xudong Liu. 2018. "English Language Learners' Use of Self-Regulatory Strategies for Foreign Language Anxiety in China." *System* 76: 49–61. https://doi.org/10.1016/j.system.2018.05.001.

Horwitz, Elaine K., Michael B. Horwitz, and Joann Cope. 1986. "Foreign Language Classroom Anxiety." *The Modern Language Journal* 70 (2): 125–32. https://doi.org/10.1111/j.1540-4781.1986.tb05256.x.

Howell, Carol C., Marti H. Rice, Myra Carmon, and Roxanne Pickett Hauber. 2007. "The Relationships among Anxiety, Anger, and Blood Pressure in Children." *Applied Nursing Research* 20 (1): 17–23. https://doi.org/10.1016/j.apnr.2005.10.006.

Huang, Heng Tsung Danny. 2018. "Modeling the Relationships between Anxieties and Performance in Second/Foreign Language Speaking Assessment." *Learning and Individual Differences* 63: 44–56. https://doi.org/10.1016/j.lindif.2018.03.002.

Kantor, Ludmila, Norman S. Endler, Ronald J. Heslegrave, and Nancy L. Kocovski. 2001. "Validating Self-Report Measures of State and Trait Anxiety against a Physiological Measure." *Current Psychology* 20 (3): 207–15. https://doi.org/10.1007/s12144-001-1007-2.

Kazdin, Alan E. 2000. *Encyclopedia of Psychology*. Washington, D.C., USA: American Psychological Association.

Keil, Verena, Robert Hepach, Severin Vierrath, Detlef Caffier, Brunna Tuschen-Caffier, Christoph Klein, and Julian Schmitz. 2018. "Children with Social Anxiety Disorder Show Blunted Pupillary Reactivity and Altered Eye Contact Processing in Response to Emotional Faces: Insights from Pupillometry and Eye Movements." *Journal of Anxiety Disorders* 58: 61–69. https://doi.org/10.1016/j.janxdis.2018.07.001.

Kerns, Caroline E., Douglas S. Mennin, Frank J. Farach, and Christopher C. Nocera. 2014. "Utilizing an Ability-Based Measure to Detect Emotion Regulation Deficits in Generalized Anxiety Disorder." *Journal of Psychopathology and Behavioral Assessment* 36 (1): 115–23. https://doi.org/10.1007/s10862-013-9372-3.

Kim, YouJin, and Nicole Tracy-Ventura. 2011. "Chapter 11. Task Complexity, Language Anxiety, and the Development of the Simple Past." In , 287–306. John Benjamins Publishing Company. https://doi.org/10.1075/tblt.2.18ch11.

Krejtz, Krzysztof, Katarzyna Wisiecka, Izabela Krejtz, Paweł Holas, Michał Olszanowski, and Andrew T. Duchowski. 2018. "Dynamics of Emotional Facial Expression Recognition in Individuals with Social Anxiety." In *Proceedings of the 2018 ACM Symposium on Eye Tracking Research & Applications - ETRA '18*, 1–9. New York, New York, USA: ACM Press. https://doi.org/10.1145/3204493.3204533.

Lin, Hao Chiang Koong, Ching Ju Chao, and Tsu Ching Huang. 2015. "From a Perspective on Foreign Language Learning Anxiety to Develop an Affective Tutoring System." *Educational Technology Research and Development* 63 (5): 727–47. https://doi.org/10.1007/s11423-015-9385-6.

MacIntyre, Peter D, and R C Gardner. 1994. "The Subtle Effects of LanguageAnxiety on Cognitive Processing in the Second." *Language Learning*. Vol. 44. https://doi.org/10.1111/j.1467-1770.1994.tb01103.x.

Mayer, Richard E. 2005. "Cognitive Theory of Multimedia Learning." In *The Cambridge Handbook of Multimedia Learning*, edited by Richard Mayer, 31–48. Cambridge: Cambridge University Press. https://doi.org/10.1017/CBO9780511816819.004.

Meij, Hans Van der, Jan Van der Meij, and Ruth Harmsen. 2015. "Animated Pedagogical Agents Effects on Enhancing Student Motivation and Learning in a Science Inquiry Learning Environment." *Educational Technology Research and Development* 63 (3): 381–403. https://doi.org/10.1007/s11423-015-9378-5.

Monkaresi, H, N Bosch, R A Calvo, and S K D'Mello. 2017. "Automated Detection of Engagement Using Video-Based Estimation of Facial Expressions and Heart Rate." *IEEE Transactions on Affective Computing* 8 (1): 15–28. https://doi.org/10.1109/TAFFC.2016.2515084.

Mucci, Nicola, Gabriele Giorgi, Stefano De Pasquale Ceratti, Javier Fiz-Pérez, Federico Mucci, and Giulio Arcangeli. 2016. "Anxiety, Stress-Related Factors, and Blood Pressure in Young Adults." *Frontiers in Psychology* 7 (October): 1–10. https://doi.org/10.3389/fpsyg.2016.01682.

Nagane, Mitsuo. 1990. "Development of Psychological and Physiological Sensitivity Indices to Stress Based on State Anxiety and Heart Rate." *Perceptual and Motor Skills* 70 (2): 611–14. https://doi.org/10.2466/pms.1990.70.2.611.

Onwuegbuzie, Anthony J, Phillip Bailey, and Christine E Daley. 2000. "Cognitive, Affective, Personality, and Demographic Predictors of Foreign-Language." *The Journal of Educational Research*. Vol. 94. https://doi.org/10.1080/00220670009598738.

Pappamihiel, N Eleni. 2002. "English as a Second Language Students and English Language Anxiety: Issues in the Mainstream Classroom." *Research in the Teaching of English*. Vol. 36. http://www.jstor.org/stable/40171530.

Park, Gi-Pyo. 2014. "Factor Analysis of the Foreign Language Classroom Anxiety Scale in Korean Learners of English as a Foreign Language." *Psychological Reports* 115 (1): 261–75. https://doi.org/10.2466/28.11.PR0.115c10z2.

Petrovica, Sintija, Alla Anohina-Naumeca, and Hazim Kemal Ekenel. 2016. "Emotion Recognition in Affective Tutoring Systems: Collection of Ground-Truth Data." *Procedia Computer Science* 104: 437–44. https://doi.org/10.1016/j.procs.2017.01.157.

Robinson, Peter. 2007. "Task Complexity, Theory of Mind, and Intentional Reasoning: Effects on L2 Speech Production, Interaction, Uptake and Perceptions of Task Difficulty." *IRAL - International Review of Applied Linguistics in Language Teaching* 45 (3). https://doi.org/10.1515/iral.2007.009.

Rodríguez, Maximo, and Orangel Abreu. 2003. "The Stability of General Foreign Language Classroom Anxiety across English and French." *The Modern Language Journal* 87 (3): 365–74. https://doi.org/10.1111/1540-4781.00195.

Runswick, Oliver R, André Roca, · A Mark Williams, Neil E Bezodis, and Jamie S North. 2017. "The Effects of Anxiety and Situation-Specific Context on Perceptual-Motor Skill: A Multi-Level Investigation." *Psychological Research* 82: 708–19. https://doi.org/10.1007/s00426-017-0856-8.

Saadé, Raafat George, and Dennis Kira. 2009. "Computer Anxiety in E-Learning: The Effect of Computer Self-Efficacy." *Journal of Information Technology Education: Research* 8 (1): 177–91. https://doi.org/10.28945/166.

Tanielian, Adam R, and Disney English. 2014. "Foreign Language Anxiety in a New English Program in Thailand." *The International Education Journal: Comparative Perspectives* 13 (1): 60–81. https://eric.ed.gov/?id=EJ1035913.

Wang, Meihua. 2014. "An Empirical Study on Foreign Language Anxiety of Non-English Major Students: Take the Sophomores in Inner Mongolia University of Technology as an Example." *Studies in Literature and Language* 9 (3): 128–35. http://www.cscanada.net/index.php/sll/article/view/5930.

Wang, Ning, and W Lewis Johnson. 2008. "The Politeness Effect in an Intelligent Foreign Language Tutoring System." *LNCS* 5091: 270–80. https://doi.org/10.1007/978-3-540-69132-7_31.

Weeks, Justin W., Ashley N. Howell, and Philippe R. Goldin. 2013. "Gaze Avoidance in Social Anxiety Disorder." *Depression and Anxiety* 30 (8): 749–56. https://doi.org/10.1002/da.22146.

Whelton, Paul K., Robert M. Carey, Wilbert S. Aronow, Donald E. Casey, Karen J. Collins, Cheryl Dennison Himmelfarb, Sondra M. DePalma, et al. 2018. "2017 ACC/AHA/AAPA/ABC/ACPM/AGS/APhA/ASH/ASPC/NMA/PCNA Guideline for the Prevention, Detection, Evaluation, and Management of High Blood Pressure in Adults: A Report of the American College of Cardiology/American Heart Association Task Force on Clinical Practice Guidelines." *Hypertension* 71 (6). https://doi.org/10.1161/HYP.0000000000000065.

Wixon, Michael, Ivon Arroyo, Kasia Muldner, Winslow Burleson, Dovan Rai, and Beverly Park Woolf. 2014. "The Opportunities and Limitations of Scaling Up Sensor-Free Affect Detection." *Proceedings of the 7th International Conference on Educational Data Mining*, 145–52. https://doi.org/10.1110/ps.073398508.

Zhang, Zhihong, Hai Su, Qiang Peng, Qing Yang, and Xiaoshu Cheng. 2011. "Exam Anxiety Induces Significant Blood Pressure and Heart Rate Increase in College Students." *Clinical and Experimental Hypertension* 33 (5): 281–86. https://doi.org/10.3109/10641963.2010.531850.

RELATIONSHIP BETWEEN TEMPORARY EMOTION OF STUDENTS AND PERFORMANCE IN LEARNING THROUGH COMPARING FACIAL EXPRESSION ANALYTICS

Mahima Maharjan[1], Soo-Hyeong Kim[2], Soonja Yeom[1] and Si Fan[3]
[1]*School of Technology, Environment and Design, Private Bag 87 University of Tasmania, Australia*
[2]*Department of Computer Science, Chonnam National University, Gwangju, South Korea*
[3]*School of Education, Locked Bag 1307, University of Tasmania, Australia*

ABSTRACT

This paper presents a study on temporary emotion of students and their performance related to learning activities. This paper elucidates different kinds of facial expressions elicited during the activities: quiz and a movie trailer with the help of existing facial expression analyzing applications. The user's expressions are recorded as video while watching the movie trailer and doing the quiz. The video is processed by different applications which gives the score for different emotions. The results obtained are studied to find which emotion is mostly prevalent among the user in different situations. From this study, it is shown that students experience seemingly different emotions during the activity. The emotions they portrayed were confusion, sadness, anger and neutral. This study explores the use of affective computing for further comprehension of students' emotion in learning environment.

KEYWORDS

Facial expression, Emotion, Affective computing, Learning

1. INTRODUCTION

Affective issues in learning technologies are concerned with emotional areas such as inspiration, attitudes and feelings (Jones and Issroff 2004). Emotion is one of the most researched topics in the study of psychology (Cho and Heron 2015, Plutchik 2001). Plutchik (2001) notes that over 90 definitions of emotion have been proposed since 20th century; emotion is expressed in terms of anger, despair, joy and grief. Learning strategies like critical thinking (Cho and Heron 2015), and effort contributed less in explaining students' achievement compared to motivation and emotions related to it. Therefore, more motivational and emotional supports are necessary to enhance student's success. Moreover, affective states play a significant role in daily activities of humans, including tasks performed in front of a computer (Jones and Issroff 2005). Objective study of emotion itself is challenging task as several emotions could be experienced at the same time (Plutchik 2001). Emotion can be treated as the on/off switch for learning (Vail 1994). Intellectual energies and capacities are increased/ decreased by positive/ negative emotional states. Having to attend the time limit quiz where there is continuous tension of ongoing time and memory, can impede students' performance increasing anxiety (Jones and Issroff 2005).

LeDoux (2003) noted that the limbic system, also known as the emotional brain is one part of the three-way view of human brain interprets the emotional value of incoming stimuli and decides if they are neutral, good or deadly; controls the ability to learn, memory and make novel connections. The active states of different parts of brain gives different facial expressions. For example: anger result from activation of some parts of brain that help to react with more speed and strength while overpowering prudent things replacing cautiousness with aggressiveness and compassion with resentment. Emotional expressions are states that define different ways of thinking. Furthermore, facial signs are perceived differently than non-facial signs such as audio for the same emotions (Ekman 2003).

Robinson (2008) categorizes interest, curiosity, surprise, joy, and love as positive emotions; while panic, aversion or disgust, fear, anger, anxiety, sorrow, and frustration are considered as negative emotions (Robinson 2008). Positive states like happiness cause positive impacts on learning while negative states like anger and sadness generate negative effects (Macfadden 2005). The theoretical assumption of control-value theory suggest that negative emotions can produce positive outcome (Pekrun 2006). To the contrary, "learning by positive reinforcement" does not account for so much of how people learn.

The relationship between the emotional intelligence (EI) and academic performance (AP) of the students shows substantial positive association between them. EI is ability to perceive and express emotion. It is used to facilitate thought, understand and reason with emotion (Mayer et al. 2001). The technologies which recognize and express emotional states are leading to the development of different algorithms which can provide artificial environment to explore human nature further, control cognition, attention and action. Until now, to enable computers to adapt the human behavior has been the main goal rather than the way round (Minsky 2013).

There have been only limited studies about affective and emotional outcome associated learning. Most of the studies are only focused on positive emotions such as happy portraying positive outcome or success in the overall grade (Macfadden 2005, Fitriani, Apriliaswati and Rosnija 2017); yet the evidence of negative emotion producing success is somewhat limited. In the present study, we would like to investigate if there is correlation between negative emotions and positive outcome.

2. LITERATURE REVIEW

Many facial expressions correspond to emotions. The most commonly used system of facial action analysis was developed by Ekman and Friesan known as Facial Action Coding System (FACS) (Ekman 2003), which determines facial muscular movement based on a set of 46 facial Action Units (AUs). These AUs are automatically related to the contraction of a specific set of facial muscles. For instance, AU0 represents neutral face, AU1 represents inner brow raiser and so on. The six basic emotions: happy, sad, angry, surprised, scared, disgusted, plus neutral are a combination of one or many AUs. FACS intensities are represented by letters A–E (described as maximum, severe or extreme, marked or pronounced, slight and trace respectively), with A being minimal and E as maximal intensity to the action unit number.

Faces contain details about the identity, mood and mind state which are the mechanisms governing the emotions and the most expressive way humans portray emotions is through facial expressions (Sathik and Jonathan 2013). Facial expressions are signaled by different muscle, eye and lip movements (Ekman 2003). Positive facial expressions are indicated by Eyes Opening wide with raising the eye brows which are represented as comprehension. Negative emotions are conveyed by contracting eyes and eye brows raised high, enlarged eyes, curling lips which represent student's incomprehension and confused state (Sathik and Jonathan 2013). Some of the common emotions during the learning process are delight, hope, pride, satisfaction, anger, shame, frustration and boredom. Positive emotions like enjoy, hope associate motivation, effort and learning strategies (Pekrun et al. 2011). Positive affect also increases motivation in learners (Goleman 2006). Negative emotions impact students' performance such as inactive behavior, less concentration, motivation and confidence (Fitriani, Apriliaswati and Rosnija 2017). Emotions upset mental life and those who have negative emotions like anxiety, annoyance and depression are not capable of learning (Goleman 2006). In contrast to conventional classrooms, where lecturers for the most part give direction and structure (both verbal and non-verbal direction), students should exercise self-administrative ability to achieve their learning objectives in today's context (Artino 2010). For example: a person may feel worry or anxiety due to threat of an encounter. Failure leads people to convey negative emotions which as a result outcomes low self-esteem (Schunk 1996). Self-confidence is factor in learning and help to show more perseverance when problems arise. Some researchers also claim that joy and anxiety experienced by the students depends on individual goals (Goleman 2006). If the goal of the student is achieving high marks and if the goal is approaching, the student might feel positive emotions like joy; whereas if the students is not satisfied, the student might experience negative emotions like anxiety (Pekrun 2006). Other research claims that success instigates positive emotions while failure promotes negative emotions (Weiner 1985). Negative states like confusion could prove beneficial because of increased attention on learning activities which consequently gives higher performances (D'mello et al. 2014). Moreover, negative emotion like anxiety is induced if a student expects failure in the quiz or examination, whereas no anxiety will occur if student does not care about it or does not expect failure. Furthermore, Stress which is also a negative state of emotion is considered to encourage or inhibit learning process (Vogel and Schwabe 2016). Surprise is a strange situation which refers an inconsistency among prior and new information (Sathik and Jonathan 2013). While negative emotions are associated with low performance; there is limited research on negative emotions portraying positive outcome. The need for more precise understanding of relation between facial emotion and learning outcome is being driven today by technologies being built to interact with learners.

In this research, four different applications are investigated for analysis of the student's emotions which are explained as below.

OpenFace: It is intended for computer vision and machine learning researchers, affective computing community and people interested in building interactive applications. In this application, facial behavior is composed of facial landmark detection, head pose estimation, facial AU recognition, and eye-gaze estimation (Baltrusaitis, Robinson and Morency 2016).

Noldus Facereader: It has an accuracy rate of 88% (Lewinski, Den Uyl and Butler 2014); allows evaluation of expressions quantitatively. Viola Jones cascaded algorithm with deep face classification for finding the position of the face in an image. Active Appearance Model (AAM) is used to synthesize an artificial model. The expressions are represented as the scale between 0 to 1. The trained artificial neural network is used to classify the six basic or universal emotions (Ekman 2003). Facereader can analyze 20 AUs and 3 affective attitudes (interest, boredom and confusion).

Face Plus Plus: It only supports image. The application analyzes and identifies emotion of detected faces and provides simple and powerful APIs and SDKs to add into deep learning-based image analysis recognition technology (Face++ 2019).

Affectiva: It uses cross platform real-time multi-phase expression recognition toolkit, for research in Emotion AI. Affectiva detects 14 facial actions and 7 different emotional states and has an accuracy of 84.27% and tested for robust databases (Lisetti and Schiano 2000).

Based on the empirical findings of the technologies, our approach is to experiment and get results from various technologies dealing with affect and facial emotions to better comprehend the emotions in learning.

3. MOTIVATION

This paper studies the gap between the students learning and their related emotions. Faces broadcast information about not only emotion but also mood, attitude, character, intelligence, attractiveness, age, sex, race and so on (Ekman 2003). Emotion messages conveyed by facial signals is the primary focus of this study. As mentioned earlier, emotions refer to feelings such as fear, anger, happiness, surprise, confusion etc.; when these feelings occur, they are visible in face in form of facial muscles contractions (Ekman and Keltner 1970). Thus, emotion can be judged from facial signals (Ekman and Friesen 2003). The main significance of this study is to determine if the facial expression correspond to recognized emotions and to what degree do facial emotions predict student accomplishment. This study has been carried to find the correlation between positive as well as negative emotion in learning outcomes. However, this study does not emphasize on any one of those emotions. This paper would help Human Computer Interaction (HCI), Artificial Intelligence (AI) and affective studies understand and respond to the information provided by the face.

4. METHODOLOGY

This section describes the data collection and cleaning to achieve noise free results. An informed consent was obtained from all the participants for the data collection and storage. In this research, the data is collected in the form of video for quiz activity and the movie trailer, which is then analyzed with the help of application described in Section 2. Depending upon the applications, expressions and their understandings may vary. Facereader is commercially trusted and reliable indicator of facial expressions of basic emotions in terms of factors like facial expressions, facial states, AUs, affective attitudes, heart rate and many more. Thus, more analysis is done from Facereader and most of the results are focused based on Facereader. After the analysis, the result of relationship between emotion and the student learning is discussed. Computer-oriented activities generally generates neutral expressions; hence, to study sparse human emotion, movie trailer is used. Since movie trailer comprises of different scenes (action, humor, sad, surprise, fear and so on), we used movie trailer data to study different emotions. Students who are enrolled in one of the Master units are requested to participate in the study by recording their faces during the activities. The participation is voluntary and could be withdrawn anytime without an explanation. A total of 7 students of University of Tasmania, of which 33% of the participants were male and 67% female participated in the research. The participants were mainly international students; among the seven participants, 4 of the participants were from China, the other three were from Hong Kong, Korea and Nepal, aged between 20-30 years. Only those who were enrolled for the summer course are included in the analysis. The University cloud storage is used to store the video recordings from the participants, expression, affective intensity and AUs are recorded during the evaluation. The result obtained from applications are discontinuous; so, it has been resampled to make it continuous. The result of the analysis is then compared with the participant's grade of the quiz as well as overall performance in the unit.

5. EXPERIMENT AND RESULTS

The experiment is performed based on the video sample recorded as mentioned in Section 4. The analysis is broken into three sections: expression, affective attitude and AU intensity analysis.

5.1 Expression Intensity Analysis

The same dataset is used for all the application as mentioned in Section 2 to analyze and compare the effect of participants basic emotions towards the quiz and a movie trailer.

5.1.1 Facereader Results

Among seven participants studied, one of the results is illustrated in Figure 1, which depicts emotions score (0-1) in Y-axis and time (seconds) in X-axis. It is seen that there is a significant effect of participants' neutral, sad and angry emotion throughout the quiz. The other emotions: happy, scared and disgusted are negligible. The highest score is seen for sad emotion. This indicates that participant might have faced difficult questions or unseen questions which participants found tough to answer. Because of difficult questions, the participants' consequence to angry emotion is caused (Macfadden 2005). The neutral emotion could be because the participants are thought to emote to computers and are aware of the video being recorded and therefore the notable facial emotions is rarely shown. Therefore, emotions like fear and surprise are kept away from computers. Techno-phobic people could also experience anger, fear towards computers (Lisetti and Schiano 2000). Ambivalent could be assumed as an impact of happiness, wellbeing and satisfaction. The result of neutral facial expression could infer the ambivalent state (Pekrun 2006). The high score of sad during the quiz indicated that participant might have faced difficult question. As stated by Vogel and Schwabe (2016), negative emotional states like stress represented by sad and angry facial expressions brings positive learning process and memory as well (Vogel and Schwabe 2016).

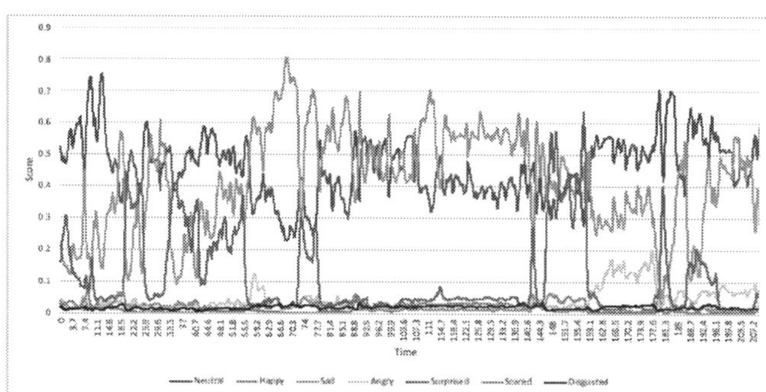

Figure 1. Emotions at quiz by Facereader

Scores for other emotions changed regularly but remained at lower levels. Surprise is a strange situation which refers an inconsistency among prior and new information (Sathik and Jonathan 2013). Thus, surprise emotion could be because of difficult or never seen questions at the beginning of the video. It could also imply that the participant is amazed of the result. In addition, the score for angry with surprise emotion are observed at the end of the quiz. It depicts that the participant is angry as well as astounded during the difficult or unseen question. Delight and surprise are relatively low compared to confusion, boredom and frustration in the complex learning process (D'mello et al. 2014).

In summary, the participant experienced different positive emotions: surprised and happy as well as negative emotions: sad, disgusted and neutral as seen in the Figure 1 and Table 1.

Table 1. The average score of emotions experienced by Participants during the quiz and movie trailer

Expressions	Activities	
	Quiz	**Movie trailer**
Neutral	**0.644914**	**0.675595**
Happy	0.01874	**0.139532**
Sad	**0.161104**	0.073182
Angry	0.070149	0.014673
Surprised	0.046198	0.015427
Scared	0.034932	0.019614
Disgusted	0.010972	0.022628

5.1.2 Face Plus Plus Results

The result obtained from Face Plus Plus insinuates that neutral is dominant expression (Figure 2 (a)) which resembles the result given by the Facereader. The negative emotions like sadness or anger are prominent in the quiz similar to the result demonstrated in Figure 1 and Table 1.

5.1.3 Affectiva Results

The result obtained as demonstrated in Figure 2(b) and Figure 2(c) indicates that disgust expression is dominant over other expressions which is quite different from the other two applications. The other notable emotions are fear and sadness which however matches the result from the Facereader and Face Plus Plus results. The possible reason of variant result could be because of the sensitivity of the mobile phone camera and distance between the camera and data. The result obtained which are disgust, fear and anger could be compared to neutral expressions (Sprengelmeyer et al. 1998).

Figure 2 (a). Realtime facial emotion detection by Face Plus Plus

b) Expressions in Affectiva identified as joy

c) Expressions in Affectiva identified as fear

5.2 Affective Attitude Intensity Analysis

Affective attitudes are complex emotional states that differ from the basic emotions (Ekman 2003). Affective attitudes are associated with a mixture of AUs activations over a time. By examining the participants' responses, a clear distinction of affective intensities like confusion, boredom and interest are found. Interest is induced from occurrence of new incident, intricate and unacquainted and as logical (Silvia 2009). The research also points out that interest is related to physiological activation, behavioral exploration and novelty. As mentioned in Section 1 and Section 2, the emotions such as confusion represents the positive impact on learning because of increased focus (D'mello et al. 2014). Learning comes from confusion, problems, taking risks and discomfort. Learners need to cope with uncertainty which result in negative emotions. Nevertheless, confusion is somewhat made for concentration, worry and skepticism (Rozen and Cohen 2003). In this study, level of confusion as well as interest is observed high in the quiz. Regarding the movie trailer, boredom was more prevalent.

5.3 Action Unit Intensity Analysis

Results from two applications: Openface and Facereader suggest that AU for inner brow raiser are high compared to other AUs. In addition to inner brow, outer brow raiser is also prevalent in Facereader. The action of opening the eyes wider and lifting the eyebrows bear positive emotions; whereas, negative emotions are represented by shrinking eyes with lowering eyebrows and wrinkles on forehead. The raised eyebrows enlarged eyes and curled lips convey negative emotions (Sathik and Jonathan 2013). These negative emotions are the indications of incomprehension and confusion. In this study, lip corner depressor and chin raiser were also detected, in addition to eyebrows movement, which are the indications of negative emotions. The AUs (X-axis) and frequencies of five intensities (Y-axis) of AUs of Facereader are shown in Figure 3.

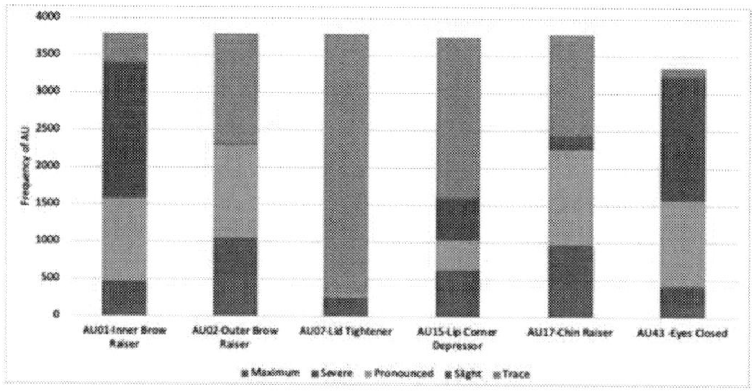

Figure 3. Notable AUs during the quiz by Facereader

6. DISCUSSION

The present study investigated the emotions in learning activities of students. As specified in the Section 1 and Section 2, there is now an agreement and clashed finding on the theory that positive emotions cause positive impact and negative emotions cause negative impact. This study is a slight contribution to the discussion, adding one more voice that suggests, positive emotions or facial expressions do not necessarily give positive outcome. Emotions such as confusion represent the positive impact on learning as a result of increased focus (D'mello et al. 2014). By collating the result of facial expressions and written responses, it is found that learning process brings negative emotions like sad and angry. Another finding of our study is that facial expressions partially corresponded to the result mentioned by the participant. This suggests that facial expressions may not be the only one factor indicating the emotions. Affective attitudes like confusion, boredom and interested is not included but is one of the factors affecting the learning process (Ekman 2003). In the context of learning, higher level of confusion contributes frustration may produce positive outcomes (Rozin and Cohen 2003) which occurred concurrently with negative emotions like angry, sad and neutral. Yet, the paper does not encourage negative emotions while in learning process. Nevertheless, the negative emotions like confusion and worry contributes positive outcome is seen in our study. This has been matched with participant self-reports result and grades of the participants.

The facial actions reported as the most common in confusion involve the eyes and eyebrows: narrowing of the eyes, lowering and bringing together of the eyebrows. These actions, often characteristic of frowns, are seen in several facial expressions. These situations may be related to confusion (Ekman 2003). Results from facial expression study of the movie trailer support the theory of positive emotions such as happiness is directly proportional to outcome. Positive emotions strengthen inspiration while negative can be disadvantageous to learning process. Finally, boredom is also prevalently seen in the movie trailer. As the previous researches regarding the boredom emotion say that boredom is induced from absence of positive and negative emotions (Ekman 2003), the result achieved from the analysis may be because of already watched movie trailer.

7. CONCLUSION AND FUTURE WORK

As mentioned in Section 2, much researches has been done to understand the emotional expressions conveyed by learners. In this research paper, the results of different facial expression recognition applications are studied by recording video of participant's facial expression performing quiz activity and watching a movie trailer. The result shows variant neutral, sad, surprise and disgust emotions during the quiz. Negative emotions like anger, sadness and affective states like confusion has extensive consequences on students learning process. The outcome from the study of the movie trailer is more of a positive facial expression like happy and surprise. The outcome studied are compared to the self-reports and grades of the participants. These reports accompanied the plausible emotions generated by the studied applications. The result of our study might be helpful to enhance the learning setting by comprehending how students react to the learning environment.

The personal attributes and personality of the individuals across the time are not studied. It is assumed that the students who studied the unit with the positive attitude likely maintained high score. The variation of emotions is slightly biased because students are pre-informed about quiz and the movie trailer is old, so they might have already watched that video. It is also reasonable that the graduate students are already motivated to study as participants are in higher level of studies.

Future work will focus on the verification of result from the applications used and determine whether disgust emotion relate to negative emotions like anger and sadness. As the number of participants were low in the research, more participants will be researched in the future. Undeniably, there has been plenty of studies in neuroscience and psychology about the significance of emotional intelligence in rational decision making, performance and adaptation; the aim would be to better comprehend human emotions by building tools with increased awareness of the users' expressions and mental states which would support psychologists to understand more complex processes of human systems with different ethnicity, gender and ages. Besides, as most of the facial expressions are brief, they are missed by observers as well as computers. These micro expressions usually reveal the real emotions a person is trying to conceal, such as delight, hope, pride, satisfaction, anger, shame, frustration and boredom. Automatic recognition procedures need to be studied further.

ACKNOWLEDGEMENT

The research involving human subjects were approved by the Social Science Human Research Ethics Committee (HREC) Tasmania Network (reference H0016953).

REFERENCES

Artino Jr, A.R., 2010. Online or face-to-face learning? Exploring the personal factors that predict students' choice of instructional format. *The Internet and Higher Education*, Vol. 13, No. 4, pp.272-276.

Baltrušaitis, T., Robinson, P. and Morency, L.P., 2016, March. Openface: an open source facial behavior analysis toolkit. *In 2016 IEEE Winter Conference on Applications of Computer Vision (WACV)*, pp. 1-10, IEEE.

Cho, M.H. and Heron, M.L., 2015. Self-regulated learning: the role of motivation, emotion, and use of learning strategies in students' learning experiences in a self-paced online mathematics course. *Distance Education*, Vol. 36, No.1, pp.80-99.

D'Mello, S., Lehman, B., Pekrun, R. and Graesser, A., 2014. Confusion can be beneficial for learning. *Learning and Instruction*, Vol. 29, pp.153-170.

Ekman, P., 2007. *Emotions revealed: Recognizing faces and feelings to improve communication and emotional life.* Macmillan.

Face++, 2019, viewed December 24 2018, <https://www.faceplusplus.com>

Goleman, D., 2006. The socially intelligent. *Educational leadership*, Vol. 64, No. 1, pp.76-81.

Fitriani, I., Apriliaswati, R. and Rosnija, E., Analysis of EFL Students'negative Emotions Towards English Learning Process in SMPN 23 Pontianak. *Jurnal Pendidikan dan Pembelajaran*, Vol. 6, NO. 6.

Jones, A. and Issroff, K., 2005. Learning technologies: Affective and social issues in computer-supported collaborative learning. Computers & Education, Vol.44, No. 4, pp.395-408.

LeDoux, J., 2003. The emotional brain, fear, and the amygdala. *Cellular and molecular neurobiology*, Vol. 23, No. 4-5, pp.727-738.

Lewinski, P., den Uyl, T.M. and Butler, C., 2014. Automated facial coding: Validation of basic emotions and FACS AUs in FaceReader. *Journal of Neuroscience, Psychology, and Economics*, Vol. 7, No. 4, p.227.

Lisetti, C.L. and Schiano, D.J., 2000. Automatic facial expression interpretation: Where human-computer interaction, artificial intelligence and cognitive science intersect. *Pragmatics & cognition*, Vol. 8, No. 1, pp.185-235.

MacFadden, R.J., 2005. *Web-based education in the human services: Models, methods, and best practices*, Vol. 23. Psychology Press.

Magdin, M. and Prikler, F., 2018. Real Time Facial Expression Recognition Using Webcam and SDK Affectiva. *International Journal of Interactive Multimedia & Artificial Intelligence*, Vol. 5, No. 1.

MAVER, J.D., SALOVEV, P., Caruso, D.R. and Sitarenios, G., 2001. Emotional intelligence as a standard intelligence. *Emotion*, Vol. 3, No. 1, pp.232-242.

Minsky, M., 2007. *The emotion machine: Commonsense thinking, artificial intelligence, and the future of the human mind.* Simon and Schuster.

Oudeyer, P.Y., Gottlieb, J. and Lopes, M., 2016. Intrinsic motivation, curiosity, and learning: Theory and applications in educational technologies. *In Progress in brain research*, Vol. 229, pp. 257-284, Elsevier.

Pekrun, R., 2006. The control-value theory of achievement emotions: Assumptions, corollaries, and implications for educational research and practice. *Educational psychology review*, Vol. 18, No. 4, pp.315-341.

Pekrun, Reinhard, et al. "Measuring emotions in students' learning and performance: The Achievement Emotions Questionnaire (AEQ)." *Contemporary educational psychology 36.1 (2011):* pp. 36-48.

Plutchik, R., 2001. The nature of emotions: Human emotions have deep evolutionary roots, a fact that may explain their complexity and provide tools for clinical practice. *American scientist*, Vol. 89, No. 4, pp.344-350.

Robinson, J., 2008. Music and emotions. *Journal of Literary Theory*, Vol. 1, No. 2, pp.395-419.

Rozin, P. and Cohen, A.B., 2003. High frequency of facial expressions corresponding to confusion, concentration, and worry in an analysis of naturally occurring facial expressions of Americans. *Emotion*, Vol. 3, No. 1, p.68.

Sathik, M. and Jonathan, S.G., 2013. Effect of facial expressions on student's comprehension recognition in virtual educational environments. SpringerPlus, Vol. 2, No. 1, p.455.

Schunk, D.H., 1996. Attributions and the Development of Self-Regulatory Competence.

Silvia, P.J., 2009. Looking past pleasure: anger, confusion, disgust, pride, surprise, and other unusual aesthetic emotions. *Psychology of Aesthetics, Creativity, and the Arts*, Vol. 3 No. 1, p.48.

Sprengelmeyer, R., Rausch, M., Eysel, U.T. and Przuntek, H., 1998. Neural structures associated with recognition of facial expressions of basic emotions. *Proceedings of the Royal Society of London. Series B: Biological Sciences*, Vol. 265, No. 1409, pp.1927-1931.

Vail, P.L., 1994. *Emotion: The on/off switch for learning.* Modern Learning Press.

Vogel, S. and Schwabe, L., 2016. Learning and memory under stress: implications for the classroom. *npj Science of Learning*, Vol. 1, p.16011.

Weiner, B., 1985. An attributional theory of achievement motivation and emotion. *Psychological review*, vol. 92, No. 4, p.548.

QEE: VR GAME THAT AIMS TO TEST AND ENHANCE THE PLAYER'S KNOWLEDGE OF TAJWEED

Haya AlKhateeb, Zainab AlSamel, Joud AlBarazi and Evi Indriasari Mansor
Department of Computer Science, College of Computer & Information Sciences, Prince Sultan University, Riyadh, Saudi Arabia

ABSTRACT

This paper aims to provide an effective computer game which, in addition to entertaining players, helps improving their knowledge of Tajweed. Tajweed is an Islamic science that studies the correct recitation of the Qur'an words and letters. It has been proven that learning at an early age gives more reliable and long-lasting knowledge. In addition, teenagers are more capable of controlling their pronunciation and modifying them. For these reasons, *Qee* game targets the ages between 13 and 18. As teenagers nowadays are exposed to a variety of game technologies, which raised their expectations and satisfaction level, a 3D VR game was introduced as an attractive modern solution. A prototype of two levels was developed and tested by 20 participants. The testing session resulted in a successful outcome with some suggestions for future modifications.

KEYWORDS

Tajweed, Gamification, Virtual Reality, Education

1. INTRODUCTION

Teenagers nowadays are spending too much time on their devices, most of the time enjoying games that have no benefit other than entertaining. Therefore, developing an attractive game would be an ideal and effective way to help them make a better use of their time. This research aims to provide this informative and enjoyable game. The content of the game was chosen to be related to the knowledge of Tajweed (the rules of pronunciation when reading the Qur'an). The reason for that is that the teachers of Tajweed are noticed to be facing difficulties in attracting the students and helping them to develop their Tajweed skills. In addition, perceiving information in such an enjoyable way helps retaining and strengthening them. Looking through the applications that are concerned with the knowledge of Tajweed, all are found to be purely educational which is not really the interest of the teenagers. Others may include some gaming, but they are usually of a low quality and don't provide the user with the desired level of interactivity. In general, they are not as attractive as other popular games are. This reduces their popularity among youths. Therefore, the new technology of VR was an interesting idea to apply as it is one of the most appealing and trendy devices used by today's generation. Ultimately, *Qee* - a Virtual Reality (VR) in 3D environment game is proposed to serve as a solution. *Qee* is an Arabic word that means the imperative verb of protection. This name conveys the main task in the game which requires the user to protect himself from the devil. This is done through achieving several tasks in each level (explained in detail throughout the paper). The HTC Vive set is used as the interaction device which allows the player to view the game via a special headset and two hand controllers to interact with the game.

2. RELATED WORK

The topic of this paper can be viewed as a combination of two research areas: e-learning and gaming. The e-learning systems have caught the interests of the researchers many years ago and there are quite a lot of papers considering e-learning for teaching Tajweed. However, very few of them address this issue by providing a solution in the gaming field, which is in most cases not as entertaining as the proposed game in this paper. Several papers worked on speech recognition to correct recitation. Many of them relied on Mel-Frequency Cepstral Coefficient (MFCC) algorithm for feature extraction and Hidden Markov Models (HMM) for classification. Ahsiah et al. (2013) suggested an e-learning technique that applies speech recognition mechanisms to figure out the mistakes made by the students through comparing them with a database of recitations recorded for experienced teachers. This approach applies MFCC and HMM algorithms. Another study that uses these two algorithms was done by Yousfi et al. (2017). They used natural language processing to extract and correct a specific rule of tajweed named Iqlab. In this paper ASR speech recognition system is used to identify the spoken versus. The proposed system is capable of pointing out the mismatch in this rule with an accuracy of 70% obtained for words that were included in the training database of famous reciters and 40% for new words that classifiers was not trained on.

Another educational tool is provided by Ibrahim et al. (2013) and it also uses MFCC and HMM. This system is a Quranic verse recitation recognition system with a function that checks for the rules of tajweed. It was tested on Surat AlFatiha. The resulted recognition rate is 91.95% (ayates) and 86.41% (phonemes). One more purely educational solution is proposed by Marlina et al. (2018). This study is more focused on a specific and basic rule of tajweed which is called Makhraj. Makhraj is the rule that specifies how each letter is correctly pronounced by identifying the speech organ that produces it. Kapi et al. (2017) developed an e-learning application that focuses on teaching the surah of Yassin. A combination of audio, video and animation was implemented in the application. The application focuses on the mistakes of the previous students who have taken the course in the traditional way. By testing the application on 51 students, it was found that the application helps in reducing the number of mistakes made by the students, the instructional time and supports self-studying. A new mechanism that is focused on practically improving the recitation is proposed by Altalmas et al. (2017). This technique uses lips tracking identification methods to extract the correct way of pronouncing the letters from video records for professional reciters. Then the extracted lips movements and final shapes are used to check the recitation of novice readers and figure out their mistakes. It also gives suggestions for improving the recitation.

Furthermore, a study done by Alfaries et al. (2013) applies natural language processing techniques in order to extract the tajweed rules from the Qur'an text and annotate them. In this study, GATE environment was used to develop an application that processes and annotates the text. The followed approach uses two tokenizers (word and letter tokenize) then applies Java Annotation Patterns Engine (JAPE) for annotating the rules. Precision and recall metrics were used to evaluate the application with a 100% result for both metrics. Learning tajweed is also supported through the proposed online portal for all sciences related to Qur'an. This portal is suggested Adhoni et al. (2013) and it is made accessible through different devices. A friendly mobile app is also developed. Ragheb and Mahmoud (2013) have studied the effectiveness of one of the major computer softwares in this area which is The Hafs Tajweed Teacher Software. The software was tested on 200 users in four countries. The experiment proved the important role of Hafs software in accelerating the learning process especially for beginners.

Moreover, researchers have also used deep learning techniques to enhance the solutions provided for teaching tajweed. Al-Ayyoub et al. (2018) proposed an approach that uses Convolutional Deep Belief Network (CDBN) which improved the accuracy of the classification to 97.7%. Support Vector Machine classifier was used to classify the features extracted from thousands of records for reciters from both genders. Moving to the work that integrates some entertaining methods, Tajweed Race Online Game Via Facebook Platform introduced an enthusiastic multiplayer game prototype for children in age range of seven to twelve years old. Its aim is to enrich and assess children's knowledge of Tajweed. It contains highly attractive factors. Children can communicate and at the same time play and compete with their friends. The winner is identified using a specific formula that calculates time, speed and player's correct answers. All these factors energize the game players to participate and consequently learn more about Tajweed rules. An interactive game was proposed by Nurtihah et al. (2018) but has not yet been implemented. This game also includes the use of AR. The approach was designed and developed using an instructional design model (ADDIE) with five basic stages: Analysis, Design, Development, Implementation and Evaluation. Learners can scan a marker in an AR book which leads them to different challenges, videos, animations that explain and examine the learners' knowledge.

A suggested approach by Basuhail (2013) takes into consideration instructors who don't have good IT skills. In his paper, Basuhail, provides a workable model that is simple and straightforward for implementing learning objects. The approach circulates through several steps: planning, interface, visuals, multimedia, texting, formatting, animation, integration and testing. Based on a chosen topic, the instructor can add the suitable buttons, animations, windows and play with many other options to produce an effective teaching object that can be used separately or integrated in an e-learning environment. Most importantly, it satisfies each student's preferable style of learning. For example, the student can listen to a sound of specific letter pronunciation, read its description or see a picture that visualizes the actual positioning of the internal organs with the pronunciation of that letter. As noticed, the uniqueness of this paper comes from the high level of attractiveness and entertainment accompanied by the educational value. The following sections are organized as follows: the first section explains the methodology in detail covering the design, development and testing procedures. The next section includes the results and discussion. Finally, the conclusion section sums up the paper.

3. MATERIALS AND METHODS

The immersive experience in this game is driven to the player using HTC Vive device (Figure 1). It is a wearable device that is mainly composed of a headset, two controllers and two base stations. It requires very powerful computers with at least 4 GB of memory and processors of high performance [Intel® Core™ i5-4590 or AMD FX™ 8350, equivalent or better] (VIVE™|VIVE Virtual Reality System, n.d.). The device is not cheap, but is still affordable. Its downsides mainly include the technical issues that the users face while setting up the device and the time consumed to get it ready. Regarding the software, two main platforms were used: Unity (mainly for the game development) and Blender (for the 3D objects and environment design).

Figure 1. HTC Vive device

4. DESIGN

The first step was conducting a brainstorming session to get the teenagers' preferences (ages 13-18) and consider them in the game design and development. The participants' requirements were mostly focused on a good graphic design quality, immersive music and sound effects and the use of modern technologies such as AR and VR. Based on these results a basic design was proposed. The basic task of the game is for the player to protect himself from the devil (Figure 2a). To do so, the player has to collect an object by the end of each level. This object is symbolised in the *Qee* game logo (Figure 2b). The only way to be able to collect this object is to succeed in each level's challenge. Once all levels are passed successfully, the devil dies and the player gets his freedom.

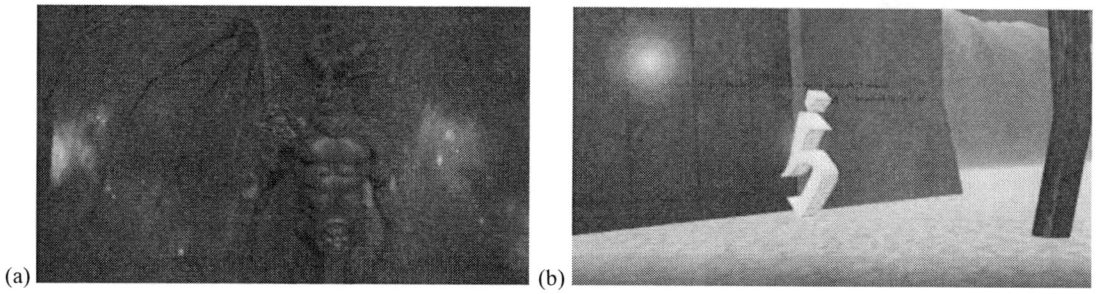

Figure 2. (a) Devil character; (b) Collectable object - the *Qee* game logo

The details of each level are as follows:

4.1 Level 1

This level takes place in a desert setting with trees scattered here and there (Figure 3a). In this level there are six correct collectables (Figure 3b) which are Arabic letters that constitute together the correct answer of the following question: *What are the correct letters of Izhar* (a very well known rule in Tajweed)*? Find them scattered in this level.* This question is displayed to the user on the screen. The level contains a maze that leads to the object required by the devil. The maze gate is locked until the player gets all the collectables. Once he does so, the player can enter the maze, find the object and win the level.

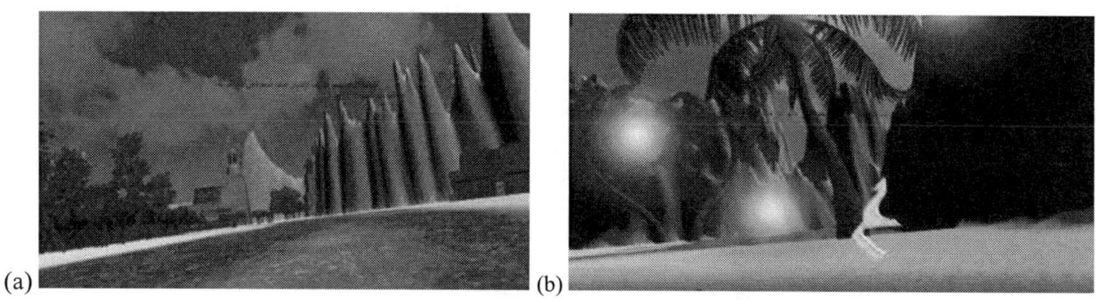

Figure 3. (a) Level 1- Desert setting; (b) Collectable objects

4.2 Level 2

Level 2 takes place in an underground cave setting. This level has a scary theme. The player goes through several paths. There are two questions each with three options. The possible answers are Arabic letters that can be picked up using the controllers. The user has to pick the right letter, or his score will decrease. Once the player answers the two questions, he will be able to collect the object which will be hidden somewhere in the level's environment (Figure 4a & b). By collecting this object, the player wins this level and the game ends with a scene showing the devil dying.

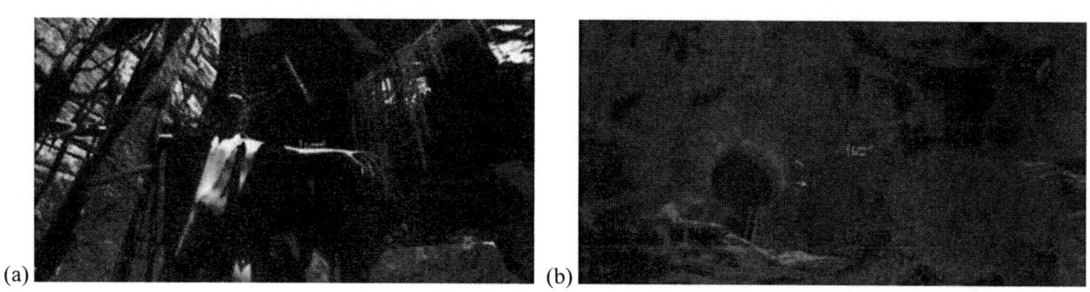

Figure 4. a & b: Level 2 – Cave setting

5. DEVELOPMENT

This game was developed using Unity software accompanied by Visual Studio for the codes. Blender was used for creating 3D models. The game was mainly developed in two stages: building the environment, and creating the required codes according to the player's movement and tasks.

Unity allows the user to come up with a variety of very creative environments. Raising terrains, adding textures, creating particle systems and many other techniques are some of the very powerful design options provided by Unity. Some assets were imported from Unity Asset Store as well (Unity Asset Store - The Best Assets for Game Making, n.d.).

Regarding the coding part, the following functionalities were implemented: walking, collecting by colliding with an object, answering through the laser pointer and grapping. Some important settings needed to be modified for the Vive to work properly such as freezing rotation or checking the gravity option to let the objects behave as if they are in the real world.

6. USER STUDY

The testing was conducted to evaluate the efficiency of the game and get user feedback for improvement suggestions. Two questions were proposed:

- Is the game entertaining enough to attract teenagers?
- Is it helpful in improving the player's knowledge of Tajweed?

To answer these questions the testers' interactions were carefully monitored during the testing session. In addition, a post-testing survey was given to the players to get their neutral opinion and suggestions.

6.1 Setting

Since the target audience of this study is teenagers, the testing was decided to be done in Alfahd private school, Riyadh, KSA, that has students from grade seven to twelve in one campus. The VR device was set up in a room with enough space for the players to move freely while playing (Figure 5). Since some people face motion sickness while using virtual reality technology, a chair was provided if this case was encountered. The laptop, the information sheet, consent form and all the required materials were arranged on a desk beside the device set up. Mobile phones were used for the online survey.

Figure 5. Testing setting

6.2 Participants

The game was evaluated with 20 female participants of ages between 13 and 18, with 59% and 41% percentages for middle and high school respectively. Only female students were recruited in this study due to the gender segregation system at school in Saudi Arabia. Therefore, since all the team members of this research are female, the research team had no access to the male section at the period of the user study. The sample was chosen randomly to cover a diversity of technical backgrounds. A pre-testing survey was conducted to collect demographic information about the players and their backgrounds. The survey shows that 58% of the participants have a previous experience with a VR device. The percentage of using computer games varied between daily, weekly and monthly, with (once a week) option being the most significant (Figure 6). In terms of the tajweed knowledge background, only 15% of them did not have any previous experience in learning Tajweed. Most of those who have learned tajweed previously were taught by a teacher. Some of them used other methods such as books, mobile app. Most of the players were familiar with at least two of the tajweed lessons covered by the game challenges.

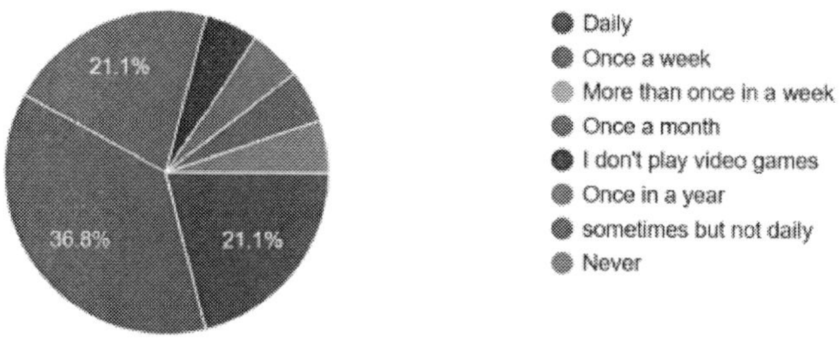

Figure 6. Answering result to question: How often do you play computer games?

6.3 Procedure

The testing session lasted for about 15-20 minutes for each player. After introducing the project and the team to the testers, they went one by one through the following steps:

(a) *Reading information sheet and signing the consent form*

(b) Completing the pre-testing survey

(c) Playing the game

(d) *Completing the post-testing survey*

All participants were notified about the probability of getting dizzy and were requested to note it immediately if it happened. After that, the participant was given the controllers and helped to wear the headset and adjust its size. Then the game was started. Some players managed to win the first level and move to the second one while others only tested the first level.

7. RESULTS

The results were obtained by analyzing the post-testing survey answers and monitoring the players' reactions and attitudes while playing. The survey questions covered three areas: playing experience, game interface and game content. All players tried out level 1 whereas only 42% of them tested level 2.

Based on the players' answers in the playing experience section, 94.7% of the players strongly enjoyed playing the game (Figure 7), 52% of them found it challenging and 100% showed their interest to try it again. When asked to measure the difficulty of each level, most of the testers rated level one as easy, considering its collecting method (i.e. collect by colliding) the most comfortable one. The reason for that is that the player's attention is focused only on walking by touching the controller's forward button. On the other hand, answering with the controller (laser and picking) requires more effort from the player to manage using both controllers, one for walking and the other for answering. Therefore, most players who tried level 2 rated it as medium or hard.

To evaluate the game interface, questions were asked about the creativity and quality of the graphics. As shown in Figure 8, 73.7% of the participants strongly enjoyed the design of the environment. However, it was a common note among testers that the clarity of the displayed texts needs to be increased.

For the last examined area, the game's content, all participants replied positively to the question that asks about their familiarity of Tajweed. However, not all of them managed to answer all the questions. This ensures the role of the game in refreshing and enhancing the players' knowledge of Tajweed. Furthermore, 84.2% of the participants agreed that the game helps supporting their knowledge (Figure 9).

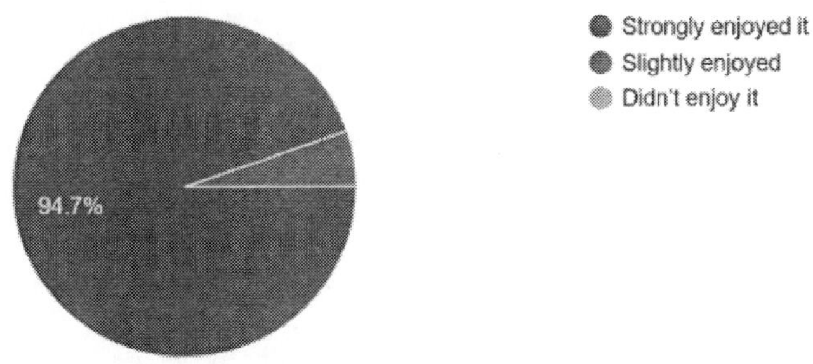

Figure 7. Answering result to question: To what extent did you enjoy playing the game, rather than something you were just doing?

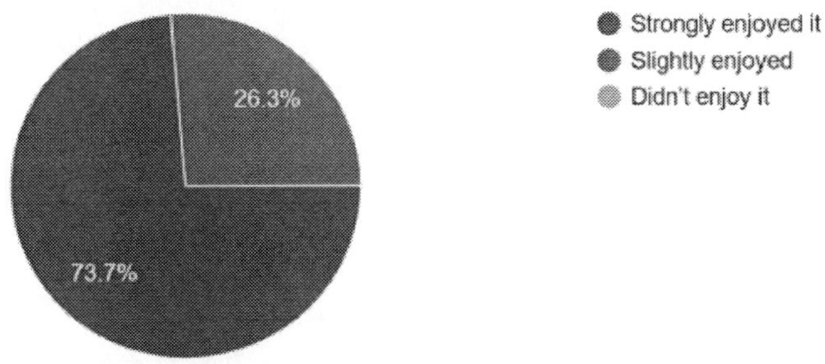

Figure 8. Answering result to question: To what extent you enjoy the graphics and the imagery?

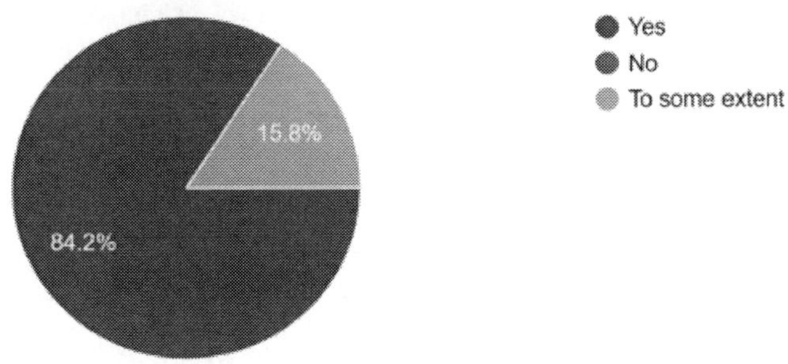

Figure 9. Answering result to question: Did you find the game helpful to support your knowledge of Tajweed?

8. DISCUSSION

Going back to the main proposed questions: "Is the game entertaining enough to attract teenagers?" and "Is it helpful in improving the player's knowledge of tajweed?" and taking the players' feedback into account, many outcomes can be derived. First of all, the testing has proved that the game has an appealing design, and a novel and unique playing technique that catches the player's attention. The immersive experience provided by the game comes from the combination of the realistic environment (Figure 2) with some fantastic characters (Figure 2a) and props (Figure 3 & 4). Secondly, the questions added a sense of challenge and aided in reviewing some Tajweed information, which fulfills the game's purpose.

Beside these remarkable findings, some modifications were extracted from the players' reactions and recommendations. From the user experience perspective, the instructions of using the controllers have to be stated more clearly, especially for those who have not tried a VR device previously. In addition, the font's size and resolution must be increased. Talking about the development aspect, level two has some gaps where the player falls down unexpectedly. These comments will be taken into consideration in future improvements.

9. CONCLUSION

Proceeding from the teenagers' attitude of spending too much time playing computer games and the importance of learning in this age, the idea of developing an entertaining game that at the same time participate in educating an important science was introduced. Noticing teenagers' need for a variety of educational resources and ways in Tajweed science resulted in choosing it for the game content. Tajweed is a science that teaches the correct pronunciation of letters and words in reciting Qur'an. A VR 3D design was chosen for the game to be attracted and satisfying enough for today's teenagers. The testers showed their excitement and enthusiasm towards the game's environment and challenge. Our future work will focus on expanding this game to have more levels and challenges. Furthermore, we plan to test the game with teenage male participants.

ACKNOWLEDGEMENT

We would also like to thank AlFahad School for giving us permission to do the testing in their school. Lastly, we would like to express our gratitude to our families for their permanent support. Indeed, none of this would be possible without them. This work was supported by the Human Computer Interaction Research Group; Prince Sultan University; Riyadh; Saudi Arabia [RG-CCIS-2017-06-01].

REFERENCES

A. Ragheb and A. Mahmoud. 2013. The Role of e-Learning Software in Teaching Quran Recitation. *IEEEXplore.*

A. Alfaries, M. Albahlal, M. Almazrua and A. Almazrua. 2013. A Rule Based Annotation system to extract Tajweed Rules from Quran. *IEEXplore.*

Altalmas, T.M., Jamil, M.A., S. Ahmad, W. Sediono, Salami, M.J.E., Hassan, S.S. and Embong, A.H. 2017. Lips tracking identification of a correct pronunciation of quranic alphabets for Tajweed teaching and learning. *IIUM Engineering Journal*, Vol. 18, pp. 1-15.

Adhoni, Z.A., H. AlHamad, Siddiqi, A.A. and L. El Mortaji. 2013 Towards a Comprehensive Online Portal and Mobile Friendly Qur'an Application. *IEEXplore.*

Basuhail, A.A. 2013. A Model for Implementing E-Teaching Objects for the Holy Quran and Related Sciences Using Animations. *IEEEXplore.*

Beck, K. and Ralph, J., 1994. Patterns Generates Architectures. *Proceedings of European Conference of Object-Oriented Programming.* Bologna, Italy, pp. 139-149.

B. Yousfi, Zeki, A.M and A. Haji. 2017. Isolated Iqlab checking rules based on speech recognition system. *IEEEXplore.*

Ibrahim, N.J., Idris, M.Y.I., Z. Razak and Abdul Rahman, N.N. 2013. Automated Tajweed Checking Rules Engine for Quranic Learning. *Multicultural Education & Technology.*

I. Ahsiah, Noor, N.M. and Idris, M.Y.I. 2013. Tajweed Checking System to Support Recitation. *IEEEXplore.*

Kapi, A.Y., N. Osman, Ramli, R.Z. and Taib, J.M. 2017. Multimedia Education Tools for Effective Teaching and Learning. *Telecommunication, Electronic and Computer Engineering*, Vol. 9, pp. 2-8.

L. Marlina, C. Wardoyo, Sanjaya, W.S.M., D. Anggraeni, Dewi, S.F., A. Roziqin and S. Maryanti. 2018. Makhraj recognition of Hijaiyah letter for children based on Mel-Frequency Cepstrum Coefficients (MFCC) and Support Vector Machines (SVM) method. *IEEEXplore.*

M. Al-Ayyoub, Damer, N.A.M. and I. Hmeidi. 2018. Using Deep Learning for Automatically Determining Correct Application of Basic Quranic Recitation Rules. *The International Arab Journal for Information Technology*, Vol. 15.

Nurtihah, M.N., Yussof, R.L., Yusoff, F.H. and M. Ismail. 2018. Gamification and Augmented Reality Utilization for Islamic Content Learning: The Design and Development of Tajweed Learning. User Science and Engineering.

Unity Asset Store - The Best Assets for Game Making. (n.d.). Retrieved from https://assetstore.unity.com/

VIVE™|VIVE Virtual Reality System. (n.d.). Retrieved from https://www.vive.com/us/product/vive-virtual-reality-system/

RETRIEVAL INTERFACES FOR SUPPORTING EXPLORATORY SEARCHES

Cliff Loke, Schubert Foo and Shaheen Majid
Nanyang Technological University, Singapore

ABSTRACT

Many search engines do not effectively support searches with imprecise or open information needs, such as in the case for exploratory video searches. The information seeker's lack of domain knowledge in exploratory searches convolutes the search process. Search interfaces are generally developed to support high-level search activities like query formulation. The purpose of this study is to gather ideas and opinions from experts from different fields to develop design concepts and interface features for exploratory video search interfaces. The findings suggest that visual maps can be used to present the structure of the domain of interest and to support exploration of the concept of interest. These maps also support knowledge construction and hence aid in the extension of concepts in the search.

KEYWORDS

Exploratory Video Search, Visual Maps, Query Formulation, Knowledge Construction

1. INTRODUCTION

Online information search has become an integral Internet activity. Search activities are broadly classified into lookup and exploratory (Marchionini, 2006). Lookup searches are basic and often return specific and precise objects or resources. Internet search engines have increasingly become more robust and adequately support most searches when information needs are clear and well defined. Through these search engines, information seekers typically issue a query through an interface and search engine returns a set of potentially relevant resources, adopting the query-response paradigm for lookup searches (Ryen W. White & Roth, 2009). Internet search engines cater well to this paradigm, affording effective lookup searches.

Exploratory search is multifaceted as it can get intertwined with other search activities as well as multiple information seeking tasks simultaneously (Ryen W. White & Roth, 2009). Exploratory searches are hence complex and begin with imprecise or open information needs that may become clearer over time (Kim, 2009). Researchers attempt to operationalize exploratory search tasks using two facets: search goal, and complexity (Athukorala, Głowacka, Jacucci, Oulasvirta, & Vreeken, 2016). Exploratory search tasks have vague and open-ended search goal with multiple search paths. During the start of an exploratory search, the information seeker usually lacks the domain knowledge and contextual awareness to formulate adequate queries. When presented with the search results, the information seeker of the complex search problem can be overwhelmed by the selection of resources. Based on the query-responses paradigm, information seekers inability to form adequate queries can lead to an overload of search results that convolutes the search process. The *de facto* standard for Internet search engines - simple keyword or natural language input facility does not adequately support exploratory search. Marchionini (2006) suggested that learning and investigative activities are pertinent in exploratory searches and lookup search can be embedded in exploratory search. This makes exploratory search more complex and cognitively loaded as compared to lookup search. Beyond query specification and results selection, exploratory search tasks require more synergy and interaction between the information seeker and the search system as they learn and improve their knowledge on the domain of interest. Researchers from diverse communities such as information retrieval, user interface design, computer science and library science, are working to improve and evaluate exploratory searches effectiveness. Studies that extend the information seeker's knowledge on the domain of interest during exploratory search are promising (Marie, Gandon, Giboin, & Palagi, 2014; Musetti et al., 2012). The extension of the domain knowledge helps reduce the uncertainty faced by exploratory searchers. The use of visual tools offer the potential to support learning and exploration of the domain of interest.

Videos are heavily used to support learning. The use of multimedia and videos in classrooms change teaching practices (Ottenbreit-Leftwich et al., 2012) and encourage learners to seek videos to support their informal learning (Tan, 2013). The video is useful in supporting learning where a video strengthens learning effectiveness through interactivity (Zhang, Zhou, Briggs, & Nunamaker, 2006). Public available video platforms, such as YouTube, are accepted as part of learner's personal learning environment (Dabbagh & Kitsantas, 2012). While the use of the Internet to seek resources is prevalent, exploratory searches remain challenging for information seekers as they used more trial and error strategies to acquire the resources (Ng, 2012). The advent of user-generated content and the lack of gatekeepers for much of such content compounded the challenge in finding adequate resources to support learning. Learners are often lost in the convoluted exploratory video search due to insufficient support during query formulation (Papadakos, Armenatzoglou, Kopidaki, & Tzitzikas, 2012). Much of the work on exploratory search were done on textual resources. While video retrieval has undoubtedly benefited from these work, the distinctive characteristics of video demand for some work to adapt the findings and ensure applicability. Some work on the exploratory search can be extended from textual resources to video resources. The traditional retrieval interfaces such as keyword and natural language search are ineffective for exploratory search due to uncertainty in expressing the information need and lack of knowledge of the domain.

This paper describes part of a doctoral study that explored the development of video retrieval interfaces and features that support exploratory video searches for learning. Interviews were conducted with academics and industry experts from various fields such as learning and pedagogy, multimedia and information retrieval, learning design, and content development. This study addresses the following research questions:

RQ1: What interface features can support exploratory searches by reducing the uncertainty of searchers during query formulation?

RQ2: What interface features can support the exploration and navigation of the domain of interest?

2. RELATED LITERATURE

People conduct searches to narrow and plug information gaps. Lookup search includes tasks such as fact-finding and searching for known-item. Such searches use specific queries that yield precise results. Using the lookup search model, information search behavior models were developed to promote the understanding of information retrieval. Many of the database management systems and commercial Web search engines used these models to develop their interaction interface and features (Ryen W. White & Roth, 2009). Driven by information retrieval metrics such as precision and recall, these retrieval systems provide perfect results with a well-specified query as in a lookup search. For more complex search tasks, formulating well-specified queries to a level for the retrieval system to handle effectively is challenging (Aula, Khan, & Guan, 2010).

An exploratory search occurs in an information-seeking context that is open-ended with multiple possible aspects. The information seekers in an exploratory search may lack the domain knowledge or contextual awareness to formulate adequate queries with keywords search facility or even navigate through the information space (Ryen W White, Kules, & Drucker, 2006). This results in a complex information seeking process that becomes increasingly challenging as exploratory search involves learning and investigation (Marchionini, 2006) as opposed to searching for known-items. In an exploratory search, the information seeker has a complex search situation and starts with a poor understanding of the domain of interest and information space. Exploratory search often combines several strategies to stimulate learning and investigation to reduce uncertainty (Ryen W. White & Roth, 2009). The information seekers submit a tentative query to navigate the results and explore the information space. As the exploration proceeds, the problem context becomes clearer. This was suggestive of a strong interaction between the search process and problem context when reducing uncertainty.

Interface and features support the interaction between information seeker and retrieval systems. Interface and features make exploratory search more effective by affording a broader range of functionality to aid learning and investigation. Input interface features allow the information needs or intent to be presented to the retrieval system. It is an important interface in the exploratory search for information seekers to overcome the difficulties in specifying the needs and identify the directions for the search (Ruotsalo et al., 2013).

An empirical study showed that information seekers performing exploratory search tasks using a faceted catalog spent more time looking at facets than looking at the query (Kules, Capra, Banta, & Sierra, 2009). Faceted search and categorized overviews support the complex exploratory search by using structured overviews to assist in topical navigation and exploration. The browsing of facets in an image retrieval system allowed image seekers to learn more about the collection (Yee, Swearingen, Li, & Hearst, 2003). Developing search user interface that supports different macro-level stages of complexity, exploratory search tasks, Huurdeman, Wilson, and Kamps (2016) used keyword search textbox and a complementary of input features such as filter using categories, keywords suggestion. This feature reduced the usage of textbox but increased the number of terms per query, suggesting that exploratory activities of the search tasks have improved the understanding of the domain and hence generates more terms when refining the search. Taken together, these studies suggest that faceted search aids exploration and discovery within a collection. However, the design of facets for subject domains that are large and complex might not be as effective.

Keywords search are now the de facto facility in many retrieval systems. The use of natural language to express information needs is common. There is numerous work done on interface and features to support keyword search facility that help information seeker evolve information needs. A study attempted to model the intent of search to direct exploratory search using an interactive visual map with the input of initial keywords (Ruotsalo et al., 2013). These features support information seekers to articulate query statements in exploratory searches based on different techniques, allowing information seekers to visualize the search topic in order to formulate or refine adequate search queries. These studies corroborate that the management of keywords fosters learning and investigation in the domain of interest, citing support in the expression of information needs for exploratory searches.

3. METHODOLOGY

An inductive research approach to explore video retrieval interface and features that can support exploratory video searches for learning was used in this study. Academics and experts from the industry were invited through email to be interviewed to discuss their ideas and perceptions on the development of interface and features for video retrieval system. One-to-one semi-structured interviews were conducted face-to-face or via Skype. The recorded audio were transcribed and were analyzed through thematic analysis. Expert interviews were used in this study as it allows the probing of the experts for in-depth understanding of the ideas for interfaces and features that can support exploratory searches. Based on their domain expertise and experience, new ideas were developed and discussed.

3.1 Selection and Procedure

The selection of interviewees is integral to the research. The success of interview-based research largely depends on how much the interviewees can fulfil the expectations, how well the interviewees understand what is needed, and the extent to which they can articulate their responses (Bogner, Littig, & Menz, 2009). The experts were recruited in several ways. First, the profiles of the experts were studied through published sources such as websites (e.g. academic staff profile in institute websites, industry professionals profile in organization websites). The invitation was extended to academics and experts from the industry who have experience with video or multimedia related work.

The first group were researchers or academics whose research interest is within the field of video and multimedia. They are relevant as their research puts them at the forefront of multimedia processing and indexing landscape. The second group were professionals working in the industry as system developers, web designers and/or user-experience designers who are motivated by practical market demands. These professionals provide insights and ideas from practical perspectives. Subsequent experts were identified by referral through the expert interviewees.

A total of 20 academics and experts from the industry were recruited for the study and interviewed. 6 of the 20 interviews were conducted via Skype. The sample size of 20 balances the resources needed to conduct and analyze in-depth interviews against the return of new insights and ideas from getting more interviewees.

An interview schedule that listed the core and supporting probes was developed to guide the one-on-one interview. The questions from the interview schedule were designed based on the findings of a prior study that investigated the challenges encountered when young adults performed exploratory searches for their learning (Loke, Foo, & Majid, 2017). The interview schedule started off with two opening questions inviting interviewees to share their video related involvement as well as their experience with exploratory video searches. Table 1 lists the core questions asked in the interview.

Table 1. Core interview questions

1	Videos are multi-dimensional, consisting of audio channel and moving images channel as well as is temporal. Do you think the multi-dimensional makeup of video can have richer interface features to be developed to support exploratory video searches for learning?
2	With more complex information needs, expressing exploratory searches can be challenging. For example, a user may be looking for a video but cannot properly define the problem, and/or there is no single correct video. For instance, the user might want to look for video(s) that shows the design factors for a car to have a balance between stability and speed. What new video interface features can allow input and refinement of such exploratory information needs for learning better?
3	Very often, videos can be quite long and there can be so many videos presented in the results list. How can video seekers, be acquainted to the content of the video more efficiently and sufficiently so that they can decide whether the video is relevant for their learning?

The basic protocol is as follows: Permission was sought to audio record the interview session. With face-to-face interviews, an unobtrusive voice recorder was placed between the interviewer and the interviewee. A software that records Skype conversation was used in the Skype interviews. The basic profile of the expert is first collected. Then the research background and objective of the study were explained. The interview began with the core questions according to an interview schedule. The semi-structured interview allowed the experts to share interface design ideas that centered upon their domain expertise.

3.2 Data Analysis

For each interview session, the audio recording was transcribed and the field notes were added to the transcriptions in parenthesis. The transcriptions were guided by seven transcription principles (Mergenthaler & Stinson, 1992) for reliability and quality. A total of 755 minutes of audio recording or 54,939 words was transcribed. The portion of the transcripts discussing on interface and retrieval features were highlighted and extracted. These represented the core of the individual interviewee statements and were coded.

Thematic analysis was conducted to analyze the extracted transcripts (Auerbach & Silverstein, 2003) to identify patterned meaning related to the research questions. Similarly coded sentences were collected from the interview transcripts according to the research questions to form major themes as the interface concepts. The themes were synthesized to propose interface features for the exploratory video retrieval.

4. FINDINGS AND DISCUSSION

The purpose of this study is to synthesize the ideas and opinions of experts within the field of video and multimedia to propose design concepts for interface and features that can improve exploratory video searches. Nine themes that are related to design concepts for video retrieval systems in an exploratory search context were derived from the analysis. The themes are summarised in table 2. Due to the length of the paper, this paper focuses on findings related to the first two themes. Interface features were developed from the themes derived. These themes are presented in this paper focus on the query and input features as well as providing more granular interactivity with videos in the retrieval process.

Table 2. Summary of themes

Improving knowledge on topic of interest	To support information seekers in improving their knowledge in the domain of interest so that better queries can be formulated for exploratory searches.
Video segment interaction	To have more granular video interaction for more focused sense-making of video.
Managing keywords for input	To provide support for handling keywords challenges such as synonyms and homonyms.
Using non-textual input	Options varied means to query the video collection by taking advantage of multi-modal nature of video.
Multiple sources for recommendations	To include different types of recommendations so that different perspectives can be formed.
Richer interaction with video content	Multimodal nature of video offers many means of interaction to cognize video content effectively.
Seeker profile in searching	Having user profile provides support to the preference and possibly context of search.
Relationship between query and video result list	Making sense of the video lists and query relationship allows the exploration of resources more effectively.
Varied input options	Provide exploratory search with advanced search fields and dimensions.

4.1 Improving Knowledge on Topic of Interest

We asked the interviewees for their observations and perspectives on the challenges in performing exploratory searches in learning and how may retrieval systems better support exploratory searches. 14 of the interviewees (IM2, IM3, IF4, IF5, IM6, IM11, RM2, RF3, RM4, RM5, RM6, RM7, RM8, RM9) felt the need for features to support learners in interaction, understanding and exploration of the topic. Visual tools were suggested to present the topic structure can support and refine queries for exploratory searches.

IF4 elaborated on how the visualization of the domain or content area can support her in expanding the search using related terms in the topic. The expert described her idea as '*some kind of content organizer. A visual framework or conceptual framework that I can see and interact with. That might make it easier for me to see how things are associated... That can help me to drill down to the level and content that I need.*' Her experience in developing multimedia learning content allowed her to share how visual organization can aid people in extending the boundaries of existing knowledge. This view is similarly shared by 8 interviewees (IM1, IM2, IM6, IM9, IM10, RM1, RF3, RM4).

RM1 suggested presenting the structure of knowledge in that topic or domain based on initial words available, similar to the semantic web. IM3 felt that semantically related concepts can prompt learners in refining the search: '*For example, when I type "design". The system could pair me with keywords like "learning", because of "design learning", it could also be "Interior design".*' The presentation of semantically related terms allows the learner to establish semantic relationships. Using the semantic relationships, the learner can explore the domain area and navigate towards more specific information gaps.

RM2 proposed the use of concept maps as a modality to navigate information space. He suggested that concept maps support the learners '*to define the key topic that they want to study on a concept map and then use that as a starter to bring them to the right video*'. Based on the initial input of concepts, the visual map presents an overview of the topical structure. From this initial reference concept, the visualization of relationships between sub-concepts in the domain of interest allows the exploration of other related concepts to formulate subsequent queries. A knowledge structure, such as concept maps, can be integrated to the video retrieval system to visualize and allow the exploration of semantic relationships. Keywords extraction is achieved by parsing the query phase to a web application interface. Keywords from the search query are extracted to generate a concept map. A prototype was developed to demonstrate this feature (see Figure. 1).

Different visual maps offer different benefits for learners to explore and understand the domain of interest. Concept and mind mapping has been reviewed on the effectiveness in supporting learner in improving learning of a topic or domain in high education (Kinchin, 2014). Some researchers (Davies, 2011; Eppler, 2006) suggested the integration of various visual mappings in order to leverage on the strength of each method. While the integration of various visual mappings could offer combined benefits from the individual mapping method, further evaluation to understand the effectiveness of different visual maps in extending keywords for information seekers on exploratory searches is required.

A hierarchical classification of a topic can provide the support to explore the specific topical space. For example, Dörk, Riche, Ramos, and Dumais (2012) designed a faceted interface to encourage exploration and make serendipitous discoveries. Visual maps provide an overview of the core concept and the relationships between the main concept and related concepts. A visual map also act as a learning tool that provide opportunities to improve a learner's understanding on the domain of interest. The possible integration of visual map could provide support in exploring domains and improve query formulation.

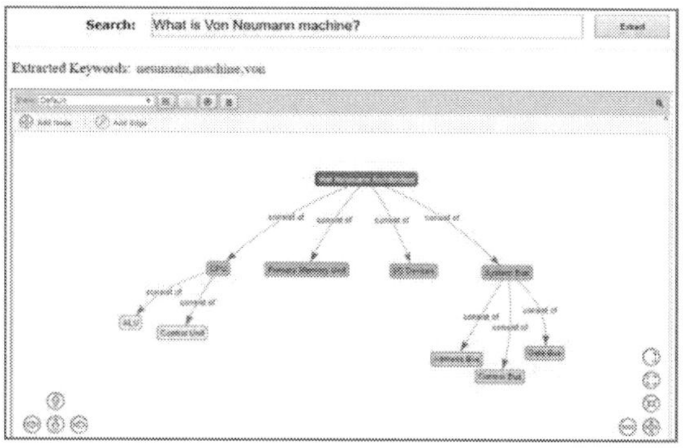

Figure 1. Keywords to concept map

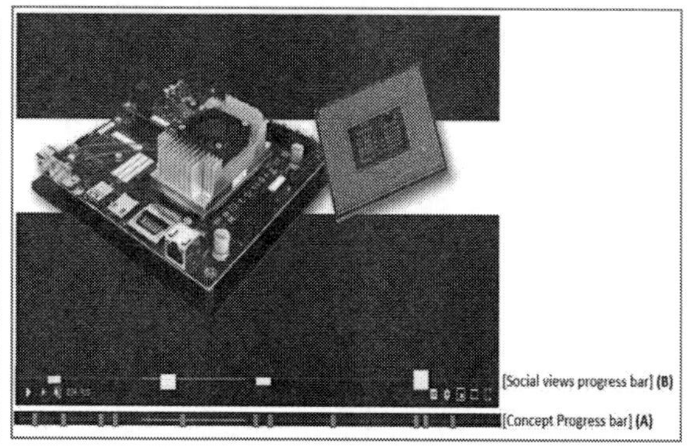

Figure 2. Video progress bar (A) indicating segments emphasizing concept of interest and (B) indicating segments that have high views

4.2 Video Segment Interaction

A video is multimodal and has a temporal dimension. Making sense of the video content can often be time-consuming, especially for long videos. 13 of the interviewees (IM2, IF5, IM8, IM9, IM10, IM11, RM1, RM2, RF3, RM5, RM7, RM8, RM9) suggested various means for more granular video interaction. Video segmentation is an area in the domain of digital video processing research. Their responses indicate that the interaction with video segments can alleviate the temporal dimension challenge encountered with long videos. Using video segments, there were suggestions from the interviewees on how the video segments are searched, displayed, located, represented and managed.

Due to the temporal nature of videos, several interviewees (IM2, IM9, RM1, RM8, RM9) suggested an interface to retrieve video segments rather than to retrieve the whole video. This is summed up by RM8: '.. *very often, I am not going to need the entire video at the end of the search. In an exploratory search, I want very specific information because when I am new to the subject, I want to look at the key things that are going to help me learn more and progress in my understanding. So that does not always come chronologically in a video.*' This granular retrieval allows the learner to locate specific video segments more effectively for their exploratory search. Automatic video segment segmentation strategy has been performed on movies based on logical story units (Hanjalic, Lagendijk, & Biemond, 1999) and more work on segmenting learning videos based on sub-topics is needed. This feature is useful when the learner is able to be more specific in the latter stages of the exploratory search with the interface to support segment retrieval.

RF3 suggested in pre-processing the video and have an abstract representation for each video segment so that the video segments are treated as individual documents. When the video segments are treated as individual documents, existing retrieval interfaces may be enhanced to be used by the learners. Finding keyframes to represent the video segment is useful for learners to visually assessment to segment content (RF3, RM5). Leveraging the temporal nature of video, have dynamic keyframes to represent the segment can improve browsing effectiveness as suggested by RM5: '*Let's say from a 1-minute video, you have five keyframes. ... But I think because of the keyframes made playable, temporal nature will be better....*' This point reveals the use of visual cues for exploratory assessment of the content effectively.

Video segments can be marked or indicated in the video, similar to the index of a book. '*The first thing is that certain videos might be too long and it is very hard to pinpoint exactly on the video where the essence that you want is.... Whereas in a book, I would say that it is well-organized into chapters*' (IM8). The video segments containing the core search concept is marked on a video progress bar, allowing quick navigation to the video segments that have an emphasis on the concept of interest (see Figure. 2(A)).

The number of video views is a common social metadata in video retrieval systems. For more granularity in the interaction, RM8 suggested indicating segments of the video that has high viewing interaction: '... *when I am watching a makeup tutorial and people are always moving back and forth at a particular part of the video. If that is highlighted to me ..then I would know that part of the video is the part where most people find that it is important.*' Using bars of varying height to indicate the relative number of views for the segments, the bars are embedded within the video progress (see Fig. 2(B)). This interface allows learners to know which parts of the video are viewed the most. When the learner synthesizes the two progress bars, the segments that are both viewed extensively and contains the core concept could potentially be the most useful video segment to begin viewing. As the interaction with videos become granular, the need to keep track of the video segments that have been interacted becomes germane. RM7 and RM8 suggested for the video retrieval to be able to keep track of viewed video segments and save video segments when needed. The segmenting of video resulting in more granular interaction can lead to more effective retrieval and learning. This was supported by a study which found that undergraduates achieved better results when using segmented video clips over non-interactive videos (Zhang, Zhou, Briggs, & Nunamaker Jr, 2006).

5. CONCLUSION

Exploratory search tasks often occur during learning. It presents fuzziness and ambiguity as the information seeker ventures into new and unknown domains. Searching for information to support learning is common. People regularly use keywords-based search utility when searching on the Internet. Being not fully conversant with the domain, learners could benefit substantially from some aids or support in their query formulation using their existing knowledge. The objective of this study was to explore the interface and features that can better support exploratory search for video resources in learning. Experts from various fields gave their ideas in the design of retrieval interfaces to alleviate the challenges in exploratory searches.

Visual features such as visual maps is proposed to be potentially useful in supporting learners for understanding the domain of interesting and extending concepts in the search. This reduces the uncertainty in exploratory searches and helps learners to navigate the domain of interest. In visual maps, the display of the relationships between concepts in domain may reveal links to prior knowledge and support deeper learning. More investigations are needed to understand the effectiveness of visual maps during exploratory searching.

The effectiveness of keyword searching is highly dependent on the quality of indexing. Using keywords to represent concepts, language semantic can create confounds during searching. The use of tools like a thesaurus helps define the appropriate concepts to use for the query formulation. This management of keywords helps in reducing fuzziness when refining the queries as well as provide suggestions for similar concepts to extend the search query. Segmented video interaction allows more specific parts of the video to be located, retrieved and manage. Many of the existing video interfaces and features can be used with video segments. However, there is a need to segment the videos logically to prevent incongruence in content otherwise it may be more detrimental.

As part of future studies, the rest of the themes will be synthesized to produce a corresponding list of desirable video retrieval interface and features. Based on the design concepts a prototype on the interface and features will be developed. Subsequently, the interface and features will be evaluated for its effectiveness in supporting the exploratory search for learning. As the number of people using public video repositories to support their learning increases, self-directed learners will find video retrieval more effective with the implementation of appropriate interface features.

REFERENCES

Athukorala, K., Głowacka, D., Jacucci, G., Oulasvirta, A., & Vreeken, J. (2016). Is exploratory search different? A comparison of information search behavior for exploratory and lookup tasks. *Journal of the Association for Information Science and Technology, 67*(11), 2635-2651.

Auerbach, C., & Silverstein, L. B. (2003). *Qualitative data: An introduction to coding and analysis*. New York, NY: New York University Press.

Aula, A., Khan, R. M., & Guan, Z. (2010). *How does search behavior change as search becomes more difficult?* Paper presented at the Proceedings of the SIGCHI Conference on Human Factors in Computing Systems, Atlanta, GA.

Bogner, A., Littig, B., & Menz, W. (2009). Introduction: Expert interviews—An introduction to a new methodological debate *Interviewing experts* (pp. 1-13): Springer.

Dabbagh, N., & Kitsantas, A. (2012). Personal Learning Environments, social media, and self-regulated learning: A natural formula for connecting formal and informal learning. *The Internet and higher education, 15*(1), 3-8.

Davies, M. (2011). Concept mapping, mind mapping and argument mapping: what are the differences and do they matter? *Higher education, 62*(3), 279-301.

Dörk, M., Riche, N. H., Ramos, G., & Dumais, S. (2012). Pivotpaths: Strolling through faceted information spaces. *IEEE Transactions on Visualization and Computer Graphics, 18*(12), 2709-2718.

Eppler, M. J. (2006). A comparison between concept maps, mind maps, conceptual diagrams, and visual metaphors as complementary tools for knowledge construction and sharing. *Information visualization, 5*(3), 202-210.

Hanjalic, A., Lagendijk, R. L., & Biemond, J. (1999). Automated high-level movie segmentation for advanced video-retrieval systems. *IEEE transactions on circuits and systems for video technology, 9*(4), 580-588.

Huurdeman, H. C., Wilson, M. L., & Kamps, J. (2016). *Active and Passive Utility of Search Interface Features in Different Information Seeking Task Stages.* Paper presented at the Proceedings of the 2016 ACM on Conference on Human Information Interaction and Retrieval, Carrboro, NC.

Kim, J. (2009). Describing and predicting information-seeking behavior on the Web. *Journal of the Association for Information Science and Technology, 60*(4), 679-693.

Kinchin, I. M. (2014). Concept mapping as a learning tool in higher education: A critical analysis of recent reviews. *The Journal of Continuing Higher Education, 62*(1), 39-49.

Kules, B., Capra, R., Banta, M., & Sierra, T. (2009). *What do exploratory searchers look at in a faceted search interface?* Paper presented at the Proceedings of the 9th ACM/IEEE-CS joint conference on Digital libraries.

Loke, C., Foo, S., & Majid, S. (2017). *Video Seeking Behavior of Young Adults for Self Directed Learning.* Paper presented at the International Conference on Asian Digital Libraries.

Marchionini, G. (2006). Exploratory search: From finding to understanding. *Communications of the ACM, 49*(4), 41-46. doi:10.1145/1121949.1121979

Marie, N., Gandon, F., Giboin, A., & Palagi, É. (2014). *Exploratory search on topics through different perspectives with DBpedia.* Paper presented at the Proceedings of the 10th International Conference on Semantic Systems.

Mergenthaler, E., & Stinson, C. (1992). Psychotherapy transcription standards. *Psychotherapy Research, 2*(2), 125-142. doi:10.1080/10503309212331332904

Musetti, A., Nuzzolese, A. G., Draicchio, F., Presutti, V., Blomqvist, E., Gangemi, A., & Ciancarini, P. (2012). Aemoo: Exploratory search based on knowledge patterns over the semantic web. *Semantic Web Challenge, 136.*

Ng, W. (2012). Can we teach digital natives digital literacy? *Computers & Education, 59*(3), 1065-1078. doi:10.1016/j.compedu.2012.04.016

Ottenbreit-Leftwich, A. T., Brush, T. A., Strycker, J., Gronseth, S., Roman, T., Abaci, S., . . . Plucker, J. (2012). Preparation versus practice: How do teacher education programs and practicing teachers align in their use of technology to support teaching and learning? *Computers & Education, 59*(2), 399-411.

Papadakos, P., Armenatzoglou, N., Kopidaki, S., & Tzitzikas, Y. (2012). On exploiting static and dynamically mined metadata for exploratory web searching. *Knowledge and information systems, 30*(3), 493-525.

Ruotsalo, T., Peltonen, J., Eugster, M., Głowacka, D., Konyushkova, K., Athukorala, K., . . . Jacucci, G. (2013). *Directing exploratory search with interactive intent modeling.* Paper presented at the Proceedings of the 22nd ACM international conference on Conference on information & knowledge management.

Tan, E. (2013). Informal learning on YouTube: Exploring digital literacy in independent online learning. *Learning, Media and Technology, 38*(4), 463-477.

White, R. W., Kules, B., & Drucker, S. M. (2006). Supporting exploratory search, introduction, special issue, communications of the ACM. *Communications of the ACM, 49*(4), 36-39.

White, R. W., & Roth, R. A. (2009). *Exploratory search. [electronic resource] : beyond the query-response paradigm*: San Rafael, Calif. (1537 Fourth Street, San Rafael, CA 94901 USA) : Morgan & Claypool Publishers, c2009.

Yee, K.-P., Swearingen, K., Li, K., & Hearst, M. (2003). *Faceted metadata for image search and browsing.* Paper presented at the Proceedings of the SIGCHI conference on Human factors in computing systems.

Zhang, D., Zhou, L., Briggs, R. O., & Nunamaker, J. F. (2006). Instructional video in e-learning: Assessing the impact of interactive video on learning effectiveness. *Information & management, 43*(1), 15-27. doi:10.1016/j.im.2005.01.004

Zhang, D., Zhou, L., Briggs, R. O., & Nunamaker Jr, J. F. (2006). Instructional video in e-learning: Assessing the impact of interactive video on learning effectiveness. *Information & management, 43*(1), 15-27.

CYBERBULLYING: EVALUATING AN INSTRUCTIONAL APPLICATION FOR SAFEGUARDING VULNERABLE USERS ONLINE

Marian McDonnell, Breanna Coyle and Irene Connolly
Institute of Art, Design and Technology
Kill Avenue, Dun Laoghaire, Co. Dublin, Ireland

ABSTRACT

Bullying is an aggressive act on a target that is not able to defend themselves easily. Cyberbullying is bullying, when perpetrated through technology online and is a major challenge for adolescents today. Despite the abundance of literature in the area of human-computer interaction (HCI), there is limited HCI research about users with intellectual disability. This research project further evaluates *Let's Be Safe*, an eLearning application in development at the Institute of Art, Design and Technology, Dublin. This application aims to educate young adults with intellectual disability about cyberbullying. Twenty-two individuals with mild to moderate intellectual disability took part in the research. The evaluation investigated preferred learning modes and engagement for this user group. The study employed a mixed-methods design including observational and inquiry methods of usability evaluation. Adapted SUS self- report measures indicated that participants liked the *Let's Be Safe* application. The listening activity was most frequently the preferred learning modality, followed closely by the game activity. Indications are that participants would like to see more games and videos with people in the application. Observational analysis identified occurrences of positive and negative emotional engagement while using the *Let's Be Safe* application. Results revealed more positive emotional responses than negative emotional responses.

KEYWORDS

Bullying, Cyberbullying, Intellectual Disability, eLearning, Emotional Response, Usability

1. INTRODUCTION

1.1 Bullying

Bullying has been described as an aggressive act on a target that is not able to defend themselves easily (Smith, del Barrio, & Tokunaga, 2013). Cyberbullying, perpetuated through technology, is a major challenge for adolescents today (Tokunaga, 2010). 20-40% of youth have experienced cyberbullying, which is associated with academic and psychosocial problems (Tokunaga, 2010). While it is a responsibility of everyone to ensure safety, young people need to be empowered to stay safe online for themselves (Paine, 2009). Listening, empowering and supporting young people to manage risks will help them understand how to stay safe (Paine, 2009). The aim of this study is to evaluate a multiplatform educational intervention designed to empower people with intellectual disability (ID) to stay safe from traditional bullying in order to mitigate against the negative consequences and victimisation of cyberbullying.

1.2 Defining Intellectual Disability (ID)

An intellectual disability (ID) is defined by the American Association on Intellectual and Developmental Disabilities (AIDD), as a significant limitation of adaptive behaviour and intellectual functioning, originating before the age of 18 and is "expressed in conceptual, social and practical adaptive skills" (Schalock, Luckasson, & Shogren, 2007, p. 118). Adaptive behaviour is a term that encompasses the impairments of ID in maturation, learning and social adjustment, as compared to peers (Heber, 1961). ID has replaced the term "mental retardation" frequently used in literature. The AIDD, the International Association have acknowledged ID as a term more appropriate in representing the construct of ID for the Scientific Study of Intellectual Disabilities, and the President's Committee for People with Intellectual Disabilities (Schalock, Luckasson, & Shogren, 2007). ID focuses on the interaction of the person with the environment, i.e. the ecological dimension (Schalock, Luckasson, & Shogren, 2007). The American Psychological Association (APA) guidelines require that the behaviour of an individual be assessed within context, to address the ecological approach (American Psychological Association, 2018). An ecological approach requires assessment of an individual by observation within natural settings, without intrusion and avoids interpretations based on norms (American Psychological Association, 2018). ID as a construct recognises "that the systematic application of individualized supports can enhance human functioning" (Schalock, Luckasson, & Shogren, 2007, p. 117). Recognising and enhancing individual strengths has a positive impact on self-image and the ability to deal with life (Dunn & Dougherty; Dykes, as cited in American Psychological Association, 2018). Interventions are required to support and encourage an individual to live their life to the fullest capacity, independently. The ID construct supports and recognises what is called the disability identity of the individual to include "self-worth, subjective well-being, pride, common cause, policy alternatives, and engagement in political action" (AIDD; Schalock; Vehmas; WHO, as cited in Schalock, Luckasson, & Shogren, 2007, p.117). People with ID are increasingly being recognised for their own unique strengths (Shogren, et al., as cited in American Psychological Association, 2018). Designing an appropriate intervention for individuals with ID will not always take the form of the most explicit needs. Needs of an individual must be addressed without assuming treatment based purely on the diagnosed disability (Butz, Bowling, & Bliss; Mason; Nezu & Nezu, as cited in American Psychological Association, 2018). Interventions must be delivered within an established and secure working relationship. It must be based on an individual's life and disability related experiences. Educational psychology is required to consider the strengths along with the identified limitations of an individual with ID, assessing an individual within a context (American Psychological Association, 2018). Reframing identified difficulties is possible using a social paradigm to encourage a more collaborative relationship between the marginalised community of people with disabilities and the psychologist (Gill, Kewman, & Brannon, 2003).

1.3 Considering Human Computer Interaction (HCI) and User-Centred Design

HCI is an academic discipline contributing to interaction design with a focus on "design, evaluation and implementation of interactive computing systems for human use" and the study of phenomena surrounding them (ACM SIGCHI, as cited in Rogers, Sharp, & Preece, 2015, p.10). Interaction design is defined as "designing interactive products to support the way people communicate and interact" in their lives (Rogers, Sharp, & Preece, 2015, p.8). This involves using theory and research to design user experiences within a specified context and directly relevant to the intended task. Within HCI development, the user-centred approach to development is emphasised (Rogers, Sharp, & Preece, 2015). User centred design considers a system well designed when the real users and not the technology are the driving force in development. A well-designed system will support the user and work in a way that adheres to principles of identified human skills and judgements (Rogers, Sharp, & Preece, 2015). Despite the abundance of literature in the area of human-computer interaction (HCI), there is limited HCI research about users with intellectual disability. This research project evaluates Let's Be Safe, an eLearning application in development at the Institute of Art, Design and Technology, Dun Laoghaire. This application aims to educate young adults with intellectual disability about cyberbullying

1.4 Present Study

Understanding our participants' needs and observing their interaction, within a user-centred approach, this evaluation of the web-based application *Let's Be Safe* will inform the iterative process of development of an appropriate instructional resource intervention to educate the user with ID. The aim is to design an accessible and user-friendly instructional resource to empower and educate about staying safe from bullying and cyberbullying. Using video modelling, picture-based interventions, game-based learning and scripts, through the web-based application *Let's Be Safe*, this study will explore the level of user engagement with the application and the preferred method of learning for participants with ID.

1.4.1 Research Questions

1. Will adults with ID find the Let's Be Safe application engaging?
2. Will adults with ID find the Let's Be Safe application usable?
3. Will adults with ID, demonstrate a clear preference for a learning-modality provided in Let's Be Safe?

2. METHOD

2.1 Design

Advocacy research with marginalised groups needs to be approaches with more mixed methods approaches (Sweetman, Badiee, & Creswell, 2010). Sensitivity within the qualitative approach is based on inquiry and values, with the ultimate goal of social justice (Denzin & Lincoln, 2005). Mixed methods characteristics for participants with disability include focus groups to collect qualitative data and questionnaires in the collection of quantitative data (Boland, Daly, & Staines, 2008). Mixing is seen within the results and discussion sections (Creswell, & Creswell, 2017).A mixed methods design, using transformative theories, in the study of community health issues and marginalised groups has been growing. From a transformative perspective, identification of specific issues of a population, allows identification of issues for the group under investigation (Creswell, & Creswell, 2017). A deeper level of understanding of the issues of this group has contributed to the research by the researchers' eight years of experience working with staff, parents and carers of people with ID, within a facilitative context. Bringing together a group of participants similar in their needs provides the opportunity to conduct a group interview (Coolican, 2004). Engagement in-group conversations stimulated by the questions offer an opportunity to provide insight that may not occur during a one-to-one interview and often provide a starting point for research (Coolican, 2004). Barrett and Kirk (2000) suggest smaller groups allow for the lived-experience of people with ID to come forward. A thematic analysis explored the themes in literature relating to the issues of this this group. Thematic analysis was conducted on the focus group answers based on themes identified in the research of this user group (vulnerability, safe guarding, issues of choice/self-determination, need for skill development).

Let's Be Safe is an eLearning application designed specifically for the use of individuals with intellectual disability. This application intends to educate young adults with intellectual disability about cyberbullying and cybersafety through video, animation, audio, reading and games. There are 6 modules in total: What is Bullying? Cyberbullying, Understanding Bystanders, Resilience, How to tackle Bullying, Respect and Empathy. *Let's be Safe* was designed for people with ID (see figure 1).

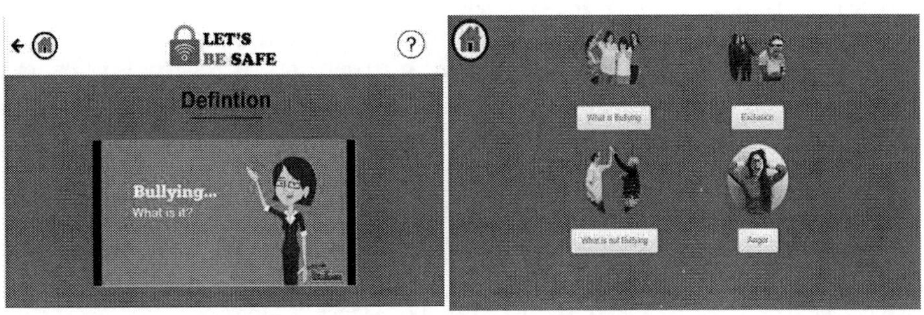

Figure 1. Let's be safe sample screenshots

Kirijian, Myers and Charland (2007) preferred design aspects for this user group were implemented in the final prototype. Fonts with bright colours and outlines were chosen, along with large words with heavy bold treatment. Colour choice was subjective, although nobody was in favour of dull colours. There was strong preference for inclusion of images. Images of young attractive people were included in particular, along with action images. More interest came from images of people of similar age. Animations of bright colour and in motion were included, especially if personalised. Buttons with a clear clickable area are included in the app design. Users like buttons that were very clear in telling what the user is to do. During the undisguised participant observation, participants are aware of being observed for the collection of information when using the application (Shaughnessy, Zechmeister, & Zechmeister, 2003). Undisguised structured observations, were created through observations of interactions with the application Let's Be Safe (Shaughnessy, Zechmeister, & Zechmeister, 2003). Observed instances of categorized behaviours, uses the frequency method of observation within a fixed time to convert observation into a numerical score (Gravetter, & Forzano, 2012). Frequencies of observed behavioural and emotional responses to the learning application Let's Be Safe were recorded. While the contrived observational setting does not allow for a natural observation, it provides an opportunity to observe the behaviour without the need to wait for the occurrence (Shaughnessy, Zechmeister, & Zechmeister, 2003). A verbal summary, identification of themes, categorising information, grouping various pieces of information together and recording observations about the narrative records is a data reduction of qualitative data (Shaughnessy et al., 2003). Coding involves the identification of units of behaviour and antecedents of these behaviours. Learning preferences were identified by indication of what the user liked. Researcher and assistant agreed coding definitions for each category observed. This was based on written definitions indicated prior to the study.

2.2 Participants

A purposive sampling was used to recruit participants of unspecified levels of ID. Recruitment was obtained in accordance with ethical standards of the Psychological Society of Ireland (PSI), Department of Psychology and Technology Ethics Committee (DTPEC) and Carmona House Services (CHS). Inclusion criteria specified an ability to communicate verbally and being over 18 years of age. These criteria were established due to lack of additional support from a speech and language therapist. Although five to eight users with ID have been suggested to identify up to 80% of interface problems (Borsci, Federici, Mele, Polimeno, & Londei, 2012), this study's sample included 22 participants (9=male, 13=female), between the ages of 19-34 years old (M=22, SD=3.72). Levels of ID were not obtained in accordance with Psychological Society of Ireland (PSI) ethics.

2.3 Accessible Materials for People with ID

Materials were designed in an easy to understand format inspired by materials designed by Maloney (2012). Tasks descriptions are used throughout development, involving users early in the development lifecycle of interactive products (Rogers, Sharp, & Preece, 2015). Seven tasks were created to explore the *Let's Be Safe* application, with progressing difficulty to accommodate levels of ability through four modes of learning (game, video, audio, reading). Categories of usability and engagement were adapted from the DEVAN usability and fun coding scheme (Macedo & Trevisan, 2013). A self-report Adapted Usability Questionnaire (SUS) collected data on usability, engagement, preference of learning and post intervention learning consisting of seventeen-items; ten Smileyometer-scale questions; one closed question; six open-ended questions; an adapted four-point

Figure 2. Example of Smileyometer

Smileyometer rating scale was used to limit the cognitive load on participants. Kline (2005) found the Smileyometer-scale to have acceptable reliability, with a Cronbach's Alpha of .706. Reporting for this study focuses on usability, engagement and preference of learning. A Smileyometer is a Likert type scale evaluating people or events of a psychological nature and is often treated as interval data. As distance between each option cannot be measured in this type of scale and may be treated as ordinal data (Shaughnessy et al., 2003). PCs running Windows-10 OS and Chrome browsers were used to run the *Let's Be Safe* application. A mouse was provided for navigation and headphones were available for each participant. Camtasia screen recording software captured participants' interaction with the application, recording screen activity such as the users' navigation of the interface and errors.

2.4 Procedure

Each session took place in a computer laboratory and was two hours in length. Care staff with whom the participants were familiar accompanied them. The participants completed a demographics questionnaire and support was offered, if the individual asked. Participants received a printed number with instructions. This was used to identify them without using their name and thus protect their identity. All participants sat at a PC with headphones and were given instructions on how to use the task sheets. Researchers reminded participants they were observing how easy the application was to use and not the performance of the individual. Observation based on the codebook lasted 10 minutes. Once complete, the Adapted- SUS was filled out by the individual, with assistance as requested. A debrief form with contact details of the lead researcher was given to each participant to take with them and they were thanked for their contribution to the study.

3. RESULTS

3.1 Analysis Procedure

A combination of both inductive and deductive approaches of thematic analysis was used in this research study. The advantage of this approach is the integration of themes derived from literature with themes that emerge from the data examined. The observational method of usability evaluation used in the present research focused on usability and emotional response of users during the interaction. Thematic analysis was conducted on the data collected during the observations. Deductive thematic analysis was applied, using a coding frame from the literature. Prior to the data collection process, ten primary themes were identified. Five themes corresponded to usability and five were representative of the emotional response of users. The inductive approach was utilised when analysing the data collected to identify sub-themes.

3.2 Descriptive Statistics

22 participants (9=male, 13=female), ranging in age from 19-34 years (M=22, SD=3.72) took part in the study. Their use of computers included smartphone, iPad, laptop and PC. Students indicated using the computer everyday (n=14), once a week (n=7), or once a month (n=1). All participants indicated using a computer (n=22) with varying frequency summarized below. Participants reported using the applications Snapchat, Facebook, WhatsApp, Skype, and Facetime. Of those that use Facebook (n=12), 75% found it easy to remember their password (n=9) while 25% (n=3) indicating that it was not easy to remember or that they needed help in remembering their password.

3.3 Findings

3.3.1 Observation of Themes in Engagement and Usability

Definitions of themes were discussed and agreed by researchers and assistants before observations took place. Observed behaviours indicating each theme were agreed prior to observations. Ten themes were used to observe emotional engagement and usability of participants. Five themes for emotional engagement (task completed/stopped before reaching goal, focused, interested/bored; likes/dislikes; positive/negative vocalisation; positive/negative behaviour) and five themes for usability (errors, assistance, confusion, motor difficulties, perception) were identified. The participants were observed while interacting with the application through seven tasks (task 1 =animation video; task 2= reading; task 3= listening to Alice's story about being cyberbullied; task 4= watching the video about cyberbullying; task 5= reading about online safety and playing the game; task 6= watching Strangers and friend video with people; task 7= game). Frequency of overall observed positive emotional responses were 22.43% with 7.22% negative emotional responses observed.

Observations were carried out to understand where further development and design of *Let's Be Safe* could increase usability and accessibility while increasing engagement of the learner. Overall, the observed frequency of positive observed usability was 46.85% and negative was 23.5%.

3.3.2 Preference of Learning Modality

Preference of learning mode in Let's Be Safe was indicated by a four- point Likert type scale (like a lot, like a little, dislike a little, dislike a lot) and a multiple-choice question with six options 'What do you want more of in the app?', with multiple selection options (games, videos with animation, videos with people, sounds/talking, reading, something else). Of the 71.56% indications for like a lot, the listening activity was reported most frequently with 17.43%, followed by 15.60% for the game, 13.76% for the video with animations, 12.84% for the reading activity and 11.93% for the video with people.

3.3.3 Thematic Analysis of Literature and Focus Group

A question led focus group was conducted at the beginning of each session. The discussion was guided by one researcher while the other researchers and assistants took notes. This focus group gathered information from participants about their knowledge and experience of bullying, cyberbullying and cybersafety. Each focus group consisted of between five and nine participants. Thematic analysis of literature revealed four key issues (vulnerability, safe guarding, emotional impact and need for skill development) faced by adults with ID. These themes were identified within the focus group contributions. Literature revealed 17.86% occurrences of vulnerability; 8.33% safe guarding: 30.95% self-determination; and 42.86% need for skill development. The focus group results revealed 20% occurrences of vulnerability, 27% safe guarding, 31% self -determination and 22% need for skill development. The feedback from the focus group supports the research suggesting the need for this population to be informed and educated about cyberbullying and cybersafety. The majority of participants had seen cases of bullying or cyberbullying while some disclosed having personally experienced victimisation. Key themes from literature explored in the focus group contributions revealed participants expressed different needs and abilities than indicated by the research, with self-determination occurring most frequently, followed by safeguarding, the need for skill development and vulnerability respectively. This compared to the literature, where the need for skill development occurred most frequently, followed by self-determination, vulnerability and safeguarding respectively.

4. DISCUSSION

Observations used to identify occurrences of positive and negative emotional engagement while engaging the *Let's Be Safe* application revealed positive emotional responses were more frequently observed than negative emotional responses. Adapted SUS self- report measures indicated participants liked a lot of the Let's Be Safe application, with the listening activity most frequently rated the highest, followed closely by the game activity. Indications of what the participants would like to see more of revealed games and videos with people were most favoured. Overall there was a positive usability experience reported by users. Observations supported these reports with positive observations being reported more frequently than negative occurrences.

4.1 Strengths and Limitations of the Present Study

Continuing to work with the users themselves provided a secure working relationship from which to develop an intervention (American Psychological Association, 2018). Inclusion of support workers gave further clarity to the needs of this group. This project allows for a multidisciplinary approach in development process, utilising psychology and technology skills for a unique perspective to research. A major strength is the involvement of individuals with ID in the development process of a system targeting this user group. The quality of data collected during the user testing suggests the importance of involving the target user group in the development process as well as the need for further research with this user group. Another strength of this study is the large number of participants involved in comparison to previous qualitative research within both the population and research topic. A limitation of this research is that the validity of responses is uncertain as it is unknown whether the responses reflect the actual thoughts and experiences of the individuals. Responses collected may be inaccurate due to the tendency of this population to please those perceived as authority figures (Cáliz et al., 2017). A focus group does not allow for in depth understanding of individual experiences that may help understand why participants accept friend requests from public figures.

4.2 Future Research

Introducing levels to the application would allow for age appropriate or stage appropriate skill development to support independence and social interaction. Engagement in the focus group conversations offer insights stimulated by the questions and offer a starting point for research (Coolican, 2004) and a lived experience can come forward in smaller groups (Barrett & Kirk, 2000). Interviews could provide a richer understanding of the experiences of people with ID that are directly related to bullying and cyberbullying. A semi-structured interview is guided but still informal and can provide "more realistic information on the interviewee's own terms" (Coolican, 2004 p. 155). Audio recording would capture the "exact terms and richness of the interview" (Coolican, 2004 p. 160). Video recording of observation sessions would provide a record of non-verbal communication (Coolican, 2004) and further analysis of responses to the application that are missed through researcher note taking.

4.3 Conclusion

As educational psychology is required to consider the strengths of people with ID (American Psychological Association, 2018), the focus group contributions remind us of what these strengths are. We see the difference between the literature and the voices of this group, what they are capable of, with self-determination and choice, avoiding interpretations based on norms (Shogren, et al., as cited in American Psychological Association, 2018). With users as the driving force in development, an application can be well-designed based on identified skills and judgements (Rogers, Sharp, & Preece, 2015). Understanding users' identified preferences will inform the process of development. This will help to create an appropriate instructional resource intervention with educational value for users with ID, engaging them, to stay safe from traditional bullying and to mitigate against the negative consequences and victimisation of cyberbullying.

REFERENCES

American Psychological Association (2018). *Guidelines for assessment of and intervention with persons with disabilities.* Retrieved from http://www.apa.org/pi/disability/resources/assessment-disabilities.aspx

Barrett, J., & Kirk, S. (2000). Running focus groups with elderly and disabled elderly participants. *Applied ergonomics*, *31*(6).

Boland, M., Daly, L., & Staines, A. (2008). Methodological issues in inclusive intellectual disability research: A health promotion needs assessment of people attending Irish Disability Services. *Journal of Applied Research in Intellectual Disabilities*, *21*.

Borsci, S., Federici, S., Mele, M. L., Polimeno, D., & Londei, A. (2012). The Bootstrap Discovery Behaviour Model: Why Five Users are Not Enough. *Cognitively Informed Intelligent Interfaces: Systems Design and Development: Systems Design and Development*, 258.

Butz, M. R., Bowling, J. B., & Bliss, C. A. (2000). Psychotherapy with the mentally retarded: A review of the literature and the implications. *Professional Psychology*: Research and Practice, 31(1).

Cáliz, D., Martínez, L., & Cáliz, R. (2017). Helping people with down syndrome through a usability testing guide proposal for mobile applications. *International Journal of Computer Science, Engineering and Information Technology, 7*(2), 1-19.

Coolican, H. (2004). *Research methods and statistics in psychology*. UK: Hodder and Stoughton.

Creswell, J. W., & Creswell, J. D. (2017). Research design: Qualitative, quantitative, and mixed methods approaches. Sage publications.

Denzin, N. K., & Lincoln, Y. S. (Eds.). (2005). *The Sage handbook of qualitative research* (3rd ed.). Thousand Oaks, CA: Sage.

Dunn, D. S., & Dougherty, S. B. (2005). Prospects for a positive psychology of rehabilitation. *Rehabilitation Psychology*, *50*(3).

Gill, C. J., Kewman, D. G., & Brannon, R. W. (2003). Transforming psychological practice and society: Policies that reflect the new paradigm. *American Psychologist*, *58*(4).

Gravetter, F. J., & Forzano, L. B. (2012). *Research methods for the behavioral sciences.* International Edition: Wadsworth.

Kline, R., B. (2005). *Principles and Practice of Structural Equation Modeling*, (4th ed.). Montreal, Canada: Concordia University.

Heber, R. (1961). *A manual on terminology and classification on mental retardation* (Rev. ed.). Washington, DC: American Association on Mental Deficiency.

Kirijian, A., Myers, M., & Charland, S. (2007). Web fun central: online learning tools for individuals with Down syndrome. *Universal Usability: Designing Computer Interfaces for Diverse User Populations*, 195-230.

Macedo, I., & Trevisan, D. G. (2013, July). A method to evaluate disabled user interaction: a case study with down syndrome children. In *International Conference on Universal Access in Human-Computer Interaction* (pp. 50-58). Springer, Berlin, Heidelberg.

Moloney, M. (2012). Accessible Information: Advocating the Use of Technology for Individuals with Intellectual Disability on their Path to Individualised Services.

Paine, T. (2009). Virtual violence: protecting children from cyberbullying.

Pallant, J., & Manual, S. S. (2010). *A step by step guide to data analysis using SPSS*. Berkshire UK: McGraw-Hill Education.

Rogers, Y., Sharp, H., & Preece, J. (2015). Experimental design. *Interaction Design: Beyond Human-Computer Interaction*, 486.

Schalock, R. L., Luckasson, R. A., & Shogren, K. A. (2007). The renaming of mental retardation: Understanding the change to the term intellectual disability. *Intellectual and developmental disabilities*, *45*(2).

Shaughnessy, J. J., Zechmeister, E. B., & Zechmeister, J. S. (2003). *Research methods in psychology* (6th ed). New York, N.Y.: McGraw Hill Higher Education.

Smith, P. K., del Barrio, C., & Tokunaga, R. S. (2013). Definitions of bullying and cyberbullying: How useful are the terms. *Principles of cyberbullying research: Definitions, measures, and methodology*.

Sweetman, D., Badiee, M., & Creswell, J. W. (2010). Use of the transformative framework in mixed methods studies. *Qualitative inquiry*, *16*(6).

Tokunaga, R. S. (2010). Following you home from school: A critical review and synthesis of research on cyberbullying victimization. *Computers in human behavior*, *26*(3).

AN EXPERIMENT WITH AN OPTIMIZATION GAME

Ela Pustulka[1], Thomas Hanne[1], Benjamin Adriaensen[1], Stefan Eggenschwiler[1], Egemen Kaba[1] and Richard Wetzel[2]

[1]*FHNW, School of Business, Institute for Information Systems, Olten, Switzerland*

[2]*Lucerne School of Information Technology, Rotkreuz, Switzerland*

ABSTRACT

We aim to improve the teaching of the principles of optimization, including computational intelligence (CI), to a mixed audience of business and computer science students. Our students do not always have sufficient programming or mathematics experience and may be put off by the expected difficulty of the course. In this context we are testing the potential of games in teaching. We deployed a game prototype (design probe) and found out that the prototype led to increased student motivation, intuitive understanding of the principles of optimization, and strong interaction in a team. Ultimately, with the future work we sketch out, this novel approach could improve the learning and understanding of optimization algorithms and CI in general, contributing to the future of Explainable AI (XAI).

KEYWORDS

Computational Intelligence, Optimization Game, TLBO Algorithm

1. INTRODUCTION

We teach optimization in a master level business information systems course alongside business process management, IT management and the cloud, digital economy, business intelligence, and security (FHNW 2019). The optimization course focuses on computational intelligence (CI) approaches and other metaheuristics. Student feedback tells us that some students opt out, as they think they do not have sufficient skills. We want to address such student perceptions by using games to lower the entry barrier. Our scientific interest is the desire to understand the complexity of the learning process and to gain knowledge on how algorithm teaching is best conducted. We presented our course design and the teaching methods in (Dornberger & Hanne 2011, Dornberger & Hanne 2017, Hanne & Dornberger 2017). A broader context for this work is provided by the fields of explainable AI (XAI) (Gunning 2016) and educational game research (Johnson et al. 2016, McGill et al. 2017a, McGill et al. 2017b, Petri & von Wangenheim 2018). On the one hand, computational intelligence games which teach advanced algorithmic techniques contribute to XAI, as they let people experience algorithms in action and further the understanding of computerized decision making. On the other hand, we know educational games have been used as an effective tool for maths teaching (Garneli 2017), but we do not know if this can be transferred to optimization and how to do that as the usefulness of games in optimization teaching has not been studied so far. We want to discover how games could be used in teaching future business leaders, decision makers and engineers who are not all expert programmers or mathematicians. This has the potential to give all students and the general public the ability to learn, use and interpret AI methods, particularly optimization, via challenging games, or, possibly, a mixture of digital and analogue games, visualization, and instruction.

We conducted a successful experiment in teaching the principles of population-based optimization via a game. We observed that an optimization game conveys the idea of optimization successfully while keeping the students motivated and focused on solving the task as a team. The rest of the paper is structured as follows. Section 2 discusses related work. Section 3 presents the methodology and Section 4 the results. In Section 5 we discuss this work, outline our future research and conclude.

2. RELATED WORK

Our work spans optimization, explainable AI and educational games. The Explainable AI (XAI) program (Gunning 2016) has two goals: to use the existing knowledge of the psychology of explanation to deliver a computational model of explanation supported by software; and to design explainable learners allowing us to interpret decisions made by AI tools. This will make sure algorithmic decisions can be properly understood, explained and trusted. ACM, on the other hand, has issued a Statement on Algorithmic Transparency and Accountability (Association of Computing Machinery 2017) which includes seven principles: awareness, access and redress, accountability, explanation, data provenance, auditability, and validation and testing. XAI is a response to new laws, such as the EU General Data Protection Regulation 2016/679 (Calder 2018).

Against this background, we are interested in games for education and knowledge (Schrier 2016), variants of which are called serious games (Abt 1970). This research field can be split into two main camps. The proponents (Gee 2007, Hamari et al. 2016, McGonigal 2011, Schrier 2016) believe that games revolutionize teaching and improve learning (van Gog 2013, Wouters et al. 2013). The critics, however, say that there is little evidence that games improve the educational outcome (Clark et al. 2010). Mayer (2016) promulgates the use of games closely related to the educational content and including personalization, a conversational style and speech instead of text, providing feedback and coaching. He calls for adaptive games which develop as the student learns, to keep motivation high. Kriz (2007) characterizes research into gaming simulation as representing two distinct fields: the design sciences and the analytical sciences. In analytical sciences a game can help to test, justify, or develop theories and can produce new universal knowledge, as in protein structure prediction (Cooper et al. 2010). In design sciences the focus is on design and usability studies which tell us how to design a game that appeals to users and how far the game serves the needs of the users, educators, policy makers or a business in the process of change. In mathematics teaching, there are strong arguments in favor of games (Kiili et al., 2014, McLaren et al., 2017). Also, business schools use simulations to teach business concepts, such as enterprise resource planning (ERP). Legner et al. (2013) report on adapting their course to use an existing simulation and observe clear cognitive gains from simulation and a significant learning effect, with a good understanding of ERP, KPIs and the balanced scorecard.

Foldit, for instance, is a serious optimization game which falls outside the educational agenda. It supports scientists in protein structure modeling (Cooper et al. 2010, Cooper 2014). Players generate new protein models which are then integrated in protein prediction pipelines. The game is based on the following assumptions: a large number of players who like solving 3D puzzles, problems that need a solution requiring human ingenuity (3D matching and modeling skills), a scoring function which has to be minimized (energy function), and scientists who can use the solutions generated by the players to improve their protein structure models. Scoring is analogous to solving complex optimization problems: there is no best score and only ranking is possible. There is strong social interaction and the players are mostly motivated by purpose, immersion and achievement (Cooper 2014). Foldit revealed that players have various strategy preferences and develop many novel valid approaches to solve problems. Players develop recipes and the game supports those via a block-based visual programming interface or scripting. Foldit inspires and informs our work.

3. METHODOLOGY

We follow the design research method (Barab & Squire 2004, Vaishavi et al. 2004). The method situates research in context, considers the complexity of real life situations, uses flexible designs, focuses on social interactions and multiple aspects of design in practice and is interdisciplinary. As part of the awareness phase, we conducted an interview with a part-time Master student attending the optimization module. The goals were: to capture the student's experience in learning algorithms in a traditional lecture environment, to find out how he studies, to learn about his experience with games and about his attitude towards using a game in the future. The student confirmed that when learning algorithms, it is important that one deals with them in depth. The reading of papers and other sources helps to get a first understanding, but an algorithm can only be fully understood by implementing it. The student said that the lectures were highly theoretical and offered little interaction between the student and the lecturer, which is typical of university teaching in many subjects. This made reviewing at home very important. As additional sources, the student used online forums or tech-blog entries. He has tried to read the suggested papers, but found them to be hard to understand. He was comfortable with lecture-based teaching. Due to his technical background (BSc Computer Science), he had no significant problems in understanding algorithms. However, he had not played educational games so far. He stated, he could imagine that a well-developed game that conveys the learning content in an interesting way could certainly be successful.

In teaching optimization, we follow a number of steps representing a growing mastery of the subject.

STEP 1. Realizing the need for algorithmic optimization.
STEP 2. Optimizing manually.
STEP 3. Using a standard optimization solution.
STEP 4. Understanding a number of algorithms and the problems they fit.
STEP 5. Choosing a suitable algorithm, encoding the problem, solving it, and reflecting.
STEP 6. Extending an algorithm, tuning it, and comparing the outcome to the standard version.

All steps can benefit from the use of games. For instance, Step 1 may use an existing "Slick Oil Distribution Game" (Hoorman 2017) which clearly shows that the problem is not easy to solve using pen and paper. Such a game is static and does not demonstrate the use of an algorithm. Standard optimization solutions (step 3) are available from logistics and supply chain management vendors. The issue with most such software is that we have no knowledge which algorithm is being used and cannot modify it. Using open-source software solutions (steps 4 to 6) is often the preferred way but has three prerequisites: understanding the principles of optimization, being able to program algorithms, and understanding some mathematics.

The Teaching-Learning-Based Optimization (TLBO) (Rao et al. 2011) was selected, as it naturally led to a game story involving teaching and learning. TLBO is culture inspired and performs well in engineering and science contexts (Rao 2016). TLBO has a population which takes part alternatingly in teaching and learning. The design variables are represented as subjects the students take and the student grades in all subjects represent their fitness. The teacher is selected as the best learner so far. Learning happens in pairs. The TLBO consists of the following steps.

INITIALIZATION: optimization problem (function), population, design variables (subjects and grades) with constraints, termination criterion

TEACHER PHASE:

a. calculate the population mean of each design variable
b. identify the teacher (best score)
c. modify each student based on teacher and mean, using a random teaching factor tr_i
d. if the solution is better, accept it.

STUDENT PHASE:

a. randomly divide students into pairs
b. in each pair: let the weaker student learn from the better student, using a random learning factor lr_j
c. if the solution is better, accept it.

TERMINATION test (criterion): if satisfied, output the best solution, else start TEACHER PHASE.

Recent work on educational game evaluation comes from Petri et al. (2018), who, however, do not focus on game design. Their model has nine dimensions: usability, confidence, challenge, satisfaction, social interaction, fun, focused attention, relevance, and perceived learning. This mirrors the Octalysis framework (Chou 2015), which we selected, as it supports game development. Octalysis lists eight core motivational drives and specifies how they can be broken down into specific game elements. The drives are: meaning, accomplishment, empowerment, ownership, social influence, scarcity, unpredictability and avoidance. The model sees player experience in terms of two types of outcome: the white hat core drivers enhance well-being and the black hat core drivers provide immersion and can lead to addiction. The model distinguishes between extrinsic and intrinsic drivers, assuming that intrinsic drivers are more effective. The approach links to the classic storytelling concept of the Hero's Journey (Chou 2015). Since improved learning can be linked to intrinsic motivation, our game development focuses on the core drives that directly relate to mastery, autonomy, purpose, and relatedness. Mastery (accomplishment) requires that one gets feedback on game progress. Autonomy (empowerment) is the player's ability to decide on the next action to be taken. Purpose (epic meaning and calling) in the game is contributing to common good. Finally, relatedness (social influence) is based on cooperation and team work. The playing process has four phases. Discovery allows the players to learn why they are playing (the story and purpose). During onboarding the players learn the rules of the game. During scaffolding they build up playing skills and get feedback about the decisions they make. During endgame the goal is achieved. The game should motivate during all four stages and various motivation mechanisms may be needed at various phases.

We chose the TLBO algorithm and designed the game, by applying the Octalysis framework focusing on intrinsic motivation. Then a game with a software back and front end was developed and tested (Adriaensen et al. 2018). Our experimental design comes from design based research (Barab & Squire 2004), as we wanted to assess the feasibility of our approach and to identify the design gaps. The game was evaluated in a two part experiment, with 4 experimental subjects (randomly assigned to two groups). The subjects were not told beforehand what the experiment was about. Their educational backgrounds did not include computer science or optimization. In the first stage (45 min.) two subjects played the game, while at the same time two other subjects studied the optimization algorithm from a two page description and discussed it. In the second stage (30 min.) a non-structured group discussion with four participants was held. Both parts were captured on video.

4. RESULTS

PAPER STUDY. Two male subjects (avg. age 32.5), an MSc student and a BSc student, participated. The master student had a background working with algorithms, and the bachelor student did not. They received a 2-page description of the algorithm and asked to study and discuss it. One of the first reactions of this group was the inquiry about the winning condition. Although there was no gaming/winning incentive, an interesting dynamic in the group developed in which an active shift of knowledge was attempted.

The timeline for this group consists of three phases: *reading* and understanding; *formulation* of the algorithm; and the *exchange of knowledge*. During *reading* we observed silence, concentration and a few frowns and notes on paper. Both participants showed the desire to learn. The paper was the focus of attention. Signs of autonomy and mastery were observable. The *formulation* phase was different. The more knowledgeable participant talked and walked around. The whiteboard was discovered and used to formulate and draw ideas and became the focus. Learning was supported by drawing, talking, and reading, which demonstrated autonomy. However, the autonomy of the BSc student decreased with time, as the MSc student took over control. His engagement and motivation were high. Relatedness rose as the participants started interacting. During *knowledge exchange* (teaching) the moderator tried to confuse the situation in order to raise the engagement of the bachelor student. The MSc student took over the whole process at this point, which led to a teacher/student dynamic. This could also be classified as a sign of purpose as the master student felt the need to explain the algorithm. The MSc student had fully mastered the topic. However, the BSc student struggled with it. At this point, his interest and focus were at its lowest point.

We interpret this as follows. The MSc student had experience of studying scientific papers. He processed new information efficiently, and quickly built a mental model of the algorithm. The BSc student did not have enough background, either technical (algorithms) or scientific (reading papers), to effectively process information. The experiment showed uneven motivation and engagement and serves as a baseline for the second experiment using a game.

GAME EXPERIMENT. The game was designed and implemented as part of an innovation project in an MSc in Business Information Systems by three students (coauthors) using design thinking techniques (Lewrick et al. 2018). The focus was on designing a game that would get the players to understand the principles of population-based optimization. The story involves a population stranded on a desert island, with a plane and no crew, as the crew perished. The way to escape is to repair the plane and learn how to fly it back to safety while controlling fuel consumption. The players assign the passengers to the Campfire (learning), the Plane (teaching) or to Upskilling (stargazing, tinkering, or building sandcastles). Upskilling increases fitness (a small preset reward), whilst gradually nudging the player into discovering that the teaching-learning mechanics are much more effective in improving the score. The learning goal is to realize that population-based optimization can quickly generate a solution with a good score. The game mechanics were designed so that the player can only win if she uses the teaching and learning activities in turn.

The game was implemented in JavaScript. We modified the TLBO algorithm to convey just the essence of population-based optimization. The population size (passengers) and the generation number (days) are set to 10. There are four design variables (engineering, piloting, mechanics, navigation). To motivate the players and keep them guessing the rules, we added Upskilling and Idling. We adapted the algorithm so that at the same time some characters are in the teaching part, some in the learning part, and the rest idling or upskilling. We sum up the four design variables (all with max=25, sum=100). We had two proto- typing sessions and adjusted the design, as simulation showed the need for improvement. We realized the players needed feedback about the fuel efficiency (total score). We numbered the figurines, for easy identification and added an application showing each figurine's skills (Figure 2), to replace scorekeeping on paper. This allowed for fluid play and improved the game experience.

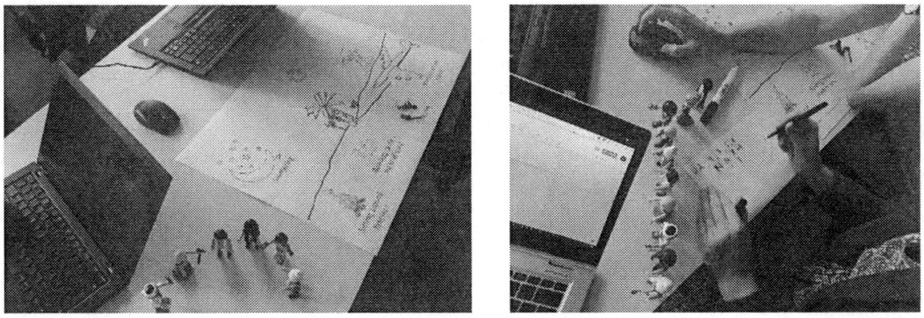

Figure 1. Left: the game with the figurines, the island, and the activities. Right: the game being played

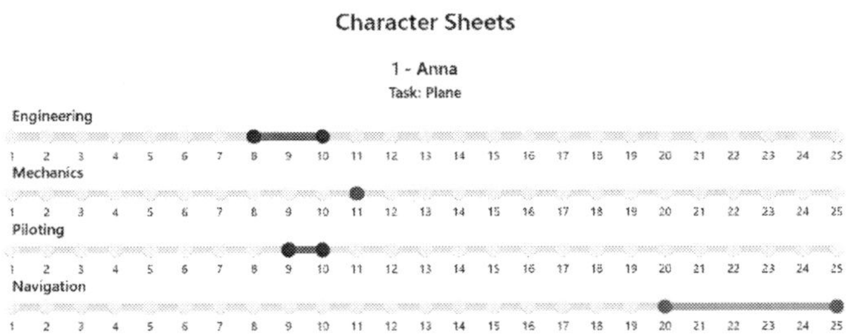

Figure 2. Skill levels (0-25) for one character: green – improving, red – worsening, gray – no change

The game starts when the players sit down at the table with the scenery: an island with a palm tree, five illustrated activity options, and ten small figurines, see Figure 1. The moderator introduces the game by telling the story and the rules, guidelines on how to interact with the characters, and the game objective. From the explanation and the handout, the players learn that they will manage a group of stranded passengers. To escape, the survivors have to learn to use the plane to fly off the island and reach the civilization. To do so, the plane's fuel efficiency needs to be managed. This requires skills that the group currently does not have to the required degree, such as engineering, mechanics, piloting and navigation, which all positively contribute to fuel efficiency. Each turn is a new day where the players allocate the survivors to one of three hubs: Campfire, Plane or Upskilling and select the upskilling activity. The game front end, Figure 2, tells the players how the characters are learning. The goal is to reach a fuel efficiency of 80% within 10 turns. As the players place the figurines on the island activities, the moderator updates the console. She also tells the players what the current fuel efficiency is (the value of the function to be optimized).

Two female subjects (avg. age 26), both holding Master degrees, formed a team. During the introduction both showed interest in the game and asked questions showing motivation (mastery drive), search for meaning, and autonomy. Even before the game started, one suggested that there will be a "pattern to discover". We observed live social interaction. The players discussed strategy, efficiency and possible game mechanics, which showed relatedness and social influence. They formed a strategy: to inventory the skills and assess the impact of various activities. We saw this as empowerment and accomplishment/mastery drive. In rounds 1-2 the participants were playing happily. They were enthusiastic and amazed when they saw their skills improve. After the first round they recognized that the skills evolved differently when the characters were assigned to the campfire (learning). However, they kept their strategy of trying out all activities. By the end of round 2, the excitement peaked. The participants asked for a piece of paper to note their observations, revealing immersion. We saw that not providing writing material was a design weakness. In round 3, the players showed slight disappointment. As they experienced frustration, the social layer became visible, as they interacted more to generate new approaches. One player said that she expected that the characters would have to be moved around constantly, unknowingly referring to the optimization algorithm dynamics. Starting in round 4, the allocation of characters to activities seemed random. The players asked about the upskilling behavior. In round 5, one participant felt "lost". In round 6, the players were told that there was a learning and a teaching activity. This did not help, and the players still aimed at understanding the game. In round 9, the players were told what the teaching and learning activities were. One recognized the influence of the characters on each other's skills at the campfire. When the last round was finished, and the players did not win, they were disappointed, which points to the need for mastery/accomplishment. When asked whether they would like to play again, they replied very positively. The end game was reached in round 11, and a player spontaneously exclaimed that it was an optimization algorithm. The session finished with a brief explanation of the algorithm.

We had to modify the game during the experiment. First, the players were given a pen and paper they asked for (round 2). Soon after the game start we realized we need to impose a time limit for a turn. Then we had a software issue which interrupted the game for 15 minutes, with the subjects asked not to discuss the game during the break. We saw that onboarding was not needed as the game presented no usability problems and the participants were absorbed in the game right from the start.

In terms of the game phases, we saw *exploration* where the players were trying to understand the game mechanics and *discovery*, as they were examining the skill evolution in the game. However, during the 10 rounds we did not see *focusing* which would involve testing the game to maximize the results, as the players did not manage to build a mental game model. In the 10th round, however, they moved to solving with the help of the moderator. We saw that discovery and onboarding happened organically, while scaffolding did not.

During the following non-structured group discussion with all four subjects, the players indicated that they were very engaged and motivated to win the game and that the learning content was valuable. When presented with the description of the algorithm, Player A did not understand one of the visualized explanations used in the paper the study group used, even though the mechanics of optimization were obvious to her after playing the game. This is a very strong indicator that the game significantly lowered the barrier towards integrating the content. The game made the concept of optimization understandable. Another participant added that one learns by failing and recovering, and this dynamic was part of the game. The discussion also revealed some flaws. Player B mentioned that a more extensive explanation of optimization algorithms would be required in order to improve the learning experience. Additionally, the calculation of fuel efficiency was not transparent. This might have led to the occurrence of the "clueless phase" in play rounds 6 to 10. Additionally, the group mentioned that the calculation of the upskilling needed tuning and that the game was too complex.

SUMMARY. We studied two different optimization learning paradigms: self-study and game. The self-study mirrors our current understanding of how optimization can be taught effectively (in the classroom) or less effectively (via self-study or group study). It showed that the less experienced student had too little experience in self-study and in algorithm understanding, and therefore could not master the algorithm, even though the more experienced student was trying to help him. Clearly, an experienced teacher transmits the required knowledge effectively.

The game investigated a new paradigm of optimization teaching. It demonstrated that a game can be an excellent introduction to the topic and can convey an intuitive understanding of the TLBO, without the need to study the code and learn the theory first. The game scenario had a high appeal and brought in strong learning motivation. The first two rounds of the game were very effective. We saw intrinsic motivation to learn, engagement and enjoyment. We expected that to be followed by a scaffolding phase where the players improve in playing and progress in their understanding. However, it turned out that our prototype gave the players too little feedback and they could not construct a mental model of the game. The game was too complex and had too many distractions. We now think, just providing two activities (teaching and learning) in a simpler game would have been more effective. The help given by the moderator in round 6 did not help the players. Once the players were told which activity was learning and which teaching, they started generating a model, but as the game was limited to 10 turns, the players failed to reach the goal of 80% fuel efficiency. So, the number of turns we foresaw was not sufficient to allow for good learning, and the players won by being allowed to do one more turn, in round 11. The prototype needs a moderator, which could be automated in a digital game, to provide for flow. Also, an improved visualization of scores and overall fuel efficiency is needed. In a teaching scenario, we believe, a player should not have time constraints, so that they can totally focus on the game.

The experiment was done collaboratively, in teams of two. This was a good decision, as strong team dynamics were observable, with emotional and intellectual engagement, and the desire to win as a team. This forced the players to talk aloud, express their feelings and observations and share the experience. However, we realize that a game which supports self-study and reinforcement of classroom material, which we envisage as another option, also needs to be supported, and a future game has to allow both team or single-user play, with exchange of strategies and thoughts via a group room, like in Foldit (Cooper et al. 2010).

We note that the effort to construct the game and carry out the experiment was considerable. There is little guidance in the literature on how to design educational optimization games, as this is a new topic, and there are no toolsets we could reuse to build a game quickly, which points to the need for a tooling and methods infrastructure.

5. DISCUSSION AND CONCLUSION

Our starting point was the difficulty of attracting business students to study CI, optimization and algorithms. A teaching solution we propose is to use games to make optimization, and AI in general, more accessible. Our experiment demonstrated that a game can convey optimization ideas while making learning fun in a social context. Next research phases will improve the games, add more algorithms and play scenarios and test them in real life contexts, including both teaching and business and policy making.

To achieve the goals, supporting methods and toolsets are needed. We envisage a conceptual architecture consisting of: a software framework, a set of optimization problems and matching games, a theoretical framework supporting educational goals and teaching strategies, motivation, and evaluation, practical tools including a teaching handbook, ideation cards for game design (Wetzel et al. 2017), and a toolset for game development.

A software framework will support game construction from primitive blocks. This will shorten the development as it will be reused. To derive a framework, we can use an optimization API (Dornberger et al. 2010). We will build an abstraction over the gameplay layer, and a learning level abstraction allowing us to create games with various motivational mechanisms, teaching aims, and strategies. The research will be based on an underlying theoretical framework covering the educational, motivational, and evaluation perspectives.

In summary, we designed and tested an optimization game based on the TLBO algorithm. This first game motivated the players and led to some intuitive understanding of the algorithm. The analysis shows that further research in this direction is needed, and we outline the components for future work, consisting of a software framework, a theoretical framework, games, and tools and materials supporting ideation, game construction, and teaching. We believe optimization games have the potential to reach the student population that might otherwise miss out on the skills our future requires.

REFERENCES

Abt, C.C., 1970. *Serious games: The art and science of games that simulate life*. Viking Press, USA.

Adriaensen, B., Eggenschwiler S., Kaba, E., 2018. Gamification of an Optimisation Algorithm, ITP Project Report, FHNW, https://github.com/EgemenKaba/TLBO-Game, https://github.com/StefanEggenschwiler/TLBO-GameClient.

Association of Computing Machinery, 2017. *Statement on Algorithmic Transparency and Accountability by ACM U.S. Public Policy Council, approved January 12, 2017 and ACM Europe Policy Committee, approved May 25, 2017.* https://www.acm.org/binaries/content/assets/public-policy/2017_joint_statement_algorithms.pdf.

Barab, S. & Squire, K., 2004. Design-Based Research: Putting a Stake in the Ground. *Journal of the Learning Sciences* Vol. 13, No. 1, pp 1–14. https://www.jstor.org/stable/1466930.

Calder, A., 2018. *EU GDPR: a pocket guide*. IT Governance Publishing. https://www.jstor.org/stable/j.ctt1cd0mkw.

Chou, Yu-Kai, 2015. *Actionable Gamification: Beyond Points, Badges and Leaderboards*. CreateSpace.

Clark, R.E. et al, 2010. An analysis of the failure of electronic media and discovery-based learning: Evidence for the performance benefits of guided training methods. In *Handbook of training and improving workplace performance*, Silber, K.H. et al. (ed.). Vol. 1. Pfeiffer, pp 263–297. https://doi.org/10.1002/9780470587089.ch8.

Cooper, S., 2014. *A framework for scientific discovery through video games*. Morgan & Claypool Publishers.

Cooper, S. et al, 2010. Predicting protein structures with a multiplayer online game. *Nature* Vol. 466, No. 7307, pp 756–760. https://doi.org/10.1038/nature09304.

Dornberger, R., Hanne, T., Frey, L., 2010. The Way to an Open-Source Software for Automated Optimization and Learning - OpenOpal. In *Proceedings of the IEEE Congress on Evolutionary Computation*, CEC, pp 1–8. https://doi.org/10.1109/CEC.2010.5586123.

Dornberger, R. & Hanne, T., 2011. E-Learning and Problem-Based Learning in Teaching Information Systems - Changing the Style of Teaching in the Information Systems Programs. In *Proc. of the 2nd International Conference on Education, Training and Informatics (ICETI)*. http://www.iiis.org/cds2011/cd2011imc/iceti_2011/paperspdf/eb183ga.pdf.

Dornberger, R. & Hanne, T., 2017. Problem-Based Learning in Teaching the Module 'Optimization for Business Improvement'. In *ICSIT 2017 - 8th International Conference on Society and Information Technologies, Proceedings, 2017*: 75–79. http://www.iiis.org/CDs2017/CD2017Spring/papers/EB808AV.pdf

FHNW 2019. University of Applied Sciences and Arts Northwestern Switzerland, http://www.fhnw.ch/en/, on 29.5.2019.

Garneli, V. et al, 2017. Serious games as a malleable learning medium: The effects of narrative, gameplay, and making on students' performance and attitudes. *British Journal of Educational Technology* Vol. 48, No. 3, pp 842–859.

Gee, J.P., 2007. *Good video games + good learning: Collected essays on video games, learning, and literacy*. Peter Lang.

Gunning, D., 2016. *Explainable artificial intelligence (XAI)*, Defense Advanced Research Projects Agency, Broad Agency Announcement. https://www.darpa.mil/attachments/DARPA-BAA-16-53.pdf.

Hamari, J. et al, 2016. Challenging games help students learn: An empirical study on engagement, flow and immersion in game-based learning. *Computers in Human Behavior* Vol. 54, pp 170–179.

Hanne, T. & Dornberger, R., 2017. *Computational Intelligence in Logistics and Supply Chain Management*. Springer.

Hoormann (Lewis), S., 2017. Simple Game for Teaching the Value of Optimization, *Blog on Supply Chain Digest*. http://bit.ly/2xLagDY consulted on 28.03.2019.

Johnson, C. et al, 2016. Game Development for Computer Science Education. In *Proceedings of the 2016 ITiCSE Working Group Reports (ITiCSE '16)*, Arequipa, Peru. ACM, pp 23–44. https://doi.org/10.1145/3024906.3024908.

Kiili, K. et al, 2014. Studying the User Experience of a Tablet Based Math Game. *International Journal of Game-Based Learning (IJGBL)* Vol. 4, No. 1, pp 60–77. https://doi.org/10.4018/IJGBL.2014010104.

Kriz, W.C., 2017. Types of Gaming Simulation Applications. *Simulation & Gaming* Vol. 48, No. 1, pp 3–7.

Legner, C. et al, 2013. Designing Capstone Courses in Management Education: Knowledge Activation and Integration Using an ERP-based Simulation Game. In *34th International Conference on Information Systems ICIS*, Milano, Italy. Association for Information Systems. https://aisel.aisnet.org/icis2013/proceedings/ISCurriculum/8/.

Lewrick, M. et al, 2018. *The design thinking playbook: mindful digital transformation of teams, products, services, businesses and ecosystems*. Wiley.

Mayer, R.E., 2016. What Should Be the Role of Computer Games in Education? *Policy Insights from the Behavioral and Brain Sciences* Vol. 3, No. 1, pp 20–26. https://doi.org/10.1177%2F2372732215621311.

McGill, M. et al, 2017a. If Memory Serves: Towards Designing and Evaluating a Game for Teaching Pointers to Undergraduate Students. In *22nd ACM Conference on Innovation and Technology in Computer Science Education*, Bologna, Italy, pp 25–46. https://doi.org/10.1145/3174781.3174783.

McGill, M. et al, 2017b. Game Development for Computer Science Education. In *22nd ACM Conference on Innovation and Technology in Computer Science Education*, pp 385–385. https://doi.org/10.1145/3024906.3024908.

McGonigal. J., 2011. *Reality is broken: Why games make us better and how they can change the world*. Penguin.

McLaren, B.M. et al, 2017. A Computer-Based Game that Promotes Mathematics Learning More than a Conventional Approach. *International Journal of Game-Based Learning* Vol. 7, No. 1, pp 36–56.

Petri, G. & von Wangenheim, C.G., 2017. How games for computing education are evaluated? A systematic literature review. *Computers & Education* Vol. 107, pp 68-90. https://doi.org/10.1016/j.compedu.2017.01.004.

Petri, G. et al, 2018. MEEGA+, Systematic Model to Evaluate Educational Games. *Encyclopedia of Computer Graphics and Games*. Springer, pp 1–7. https://doi.org/10.1007/978-3-319-08234-9_214-1.

Rao, R.V., 2016. Review of applications of TLBO algorithm and a tutorial for beginners to solve the unconstrained and constrained optimization problems. *Decision Science Letters* Vol. 5, No. 1, pp 1–30.

Rao, R.V. et al, 2011. Teaching–learning-based optimization: A novel method for constrained mechanical design optimization problems. *Computer-Aided Design* Vol. 43, No. 3, pp 303–315. https://doi.org/10.1016/j.cad.2010.12.015.

Schrier, K., 2016. *Knowledge games: How playing games can solve problems, create insight, and make change*. JHU Press.

Vaishnavi, V. et al., 2004. Updated 2015. *Design Science Research in Information Systems*. http://desrist.org/design-research-in-information-systems/. Online. Association for Information Systems.

van Gog, T., 2013. Time on task. In *International guide to student achievement*, J. A. C. Hattie & E. M. Anderman (ed.). Routledge, pp 432–433.

Wetzel, R., et al. 2016. Developing Ideation Cards for Mixed Reality Game Design. *DiGRA: Transactions of the Digital Games Research Association* Vol. 3, No. 2. http://todigra.org/index.php/todigra/article/view/73.

Wouters, P. et al, 2013. A meta-analysis of the cognitive and motivational effects of serious games. *Journal of educational psychology* Vol. 105, No. 2, 249. https://psycnet.apa.org/doi/10.1037/a0031311.

FEMININITY IN VIDEO GAMES: AN ANALYSIS OF GENDER IN TERMS OF VISUAL ASPECTS, NARRATIVE AND SOCIABILITY

Mariana Michels Fontoura and Marília A. Amaral
Federal University of Technology - Paraná (UTFPR), Postgraduate Program in Technology and Society, Curitiba, Brazil

ABSTRACT

The role of gender in the design of technologies has been a topic of growing importance in fields such as Interaction Design, HCI and Games. Understanding that technology development and use practices emerge within the cultural processes, we analyze notions of traditional femininity in technology, as well as new approaches to female representation. The issues discussed and briefly analyzed in this essay point to a production and regulation of gender by technologies such as video games. Our goal in this paper, therefore, is to assess how gender impacts design and the use of digital games in terms of visuals, narrative and sociability.

KEYWORDS

Gender, Femininity, Representation, Games

1. INTRODUCTION

This paper starts with the premise that technology development and use practices emerge within social and cultural processes. That means that technology's historical heritage and the developers' context influence its processes and products (Bardzell, 2010). Video games, as technological artifacts, are equally affected by the social, historical and cultural dynamics. The role of gender in designing technologies has been a topic of growing importance in fields such as Interaction design and HCI (Bardzell, 2010; Breslin and Wadhwa, 2014), and Games (Shaw, 2014; Cassel and Jenkins, 2000; Rodrigues, 2014; Goulart and Nardi, 2017). In this paper, our goal is to analyze the influence of gender norms in the development and use of video games. This paper starts with a theorical discussion of essential terms to ground our brief analysis. First, we analyze three characters from the game "Overwatch". Later, we analyze a few players' shared experiences that concerns gender and game discussions. Our analysis takes into consideration: visual aspects, narrative and sociability. The visual and narrative factors are considered relevant because they take part in the development and design of games. The sociability factor is relevant because it focuses on how players act upon gender in video games. Without further ado, we intent to discuss how gender norms, identities and relations shape the design of video games, as well as the ways the notion of femininity can be reinforced or subverted by its use.

2. GENDER

In this paper, gender is approached by denying the ideas that men and women are essentially and naturally different. We understand that this vision would reinforce stereotypes, and would rely on opposing characteristics. Our approach draws on the notion introduced by Simone de Beauvoir, that "one is not born a woman, but rather, becomes a woman" (De Beauvoir, 1989), which provides a distinction between sex (biological sexual identity assigned to one when they were born) and gender (behaviors, values, and other attributes associated to femininity and masculinity). Breslin and Wadhwa (2014[b]) point out that this implies that being female and being a woman do not mean the same thing, and also these categories are not necessarily associated. With this approach to gender as socially constructed, we intent to deviate from universal notions of "men" and "women" and understand that people are able to belong or not to these categories. Still, it is important to acknowledge that in many cultures around the world there are societal norms and habits that associate femininity and being female (Breslin and Wadhwa, 2014[b]).

Besides the notion of gender, in order to theoretically ground the discussion, there is another relevant concept to our analysis. Inspired in the work of Michel Foucault, De Lauretis (1987, pp.38) developed the concept of "technology of gender", that means "the techniques and discursive strategies by which gender is constructed [...]". Rodrigues (2017) provides us the understanding that these techniques and discourses are embed in video games. Based on De Lauretis' concept, Rodrigues (2017) suggests that gender relations are constructed by these gender technologies, therefore creating and reaffirming subject positions. The work of Wajcman (2004, pp.7) presents the notion of technology as a sociotechnical product, that is, "shaped in social relations that use and produce it". Wajcman explains the mutually shaping relationship between gender and technology, comprehending that technology is not only a consequence, but also a source of gender relations.

Based on these concepts, like Rodrigues (2017), we propose to analyze games as technologies of gender that reaffirm notions of femininity and masculinity and produce gender identities. We also highlight the role of institutionalized discourses in the construction of gender, once they have reached the digital space within technologies such as video games.

2.1 Technology

Technology development and use practices emerge within social and cultural processes. That statement leads to the conclusion that values and societal norms may influence the design of technologies. In the HCI field, the works of Breslin and Wadhwa (2014) emphasize the role of gender in the design and use of technologies. The problematics of ignoring gender in the design of technologies are that the artifacts being developed will implicitly embed scripts about play and usage behavior based on the developer's experiences. Since the majority of developers, in the United States and Europe for instance, are white, middle class males, it often leads to hindrances on women's use (Breslin and Wadhwa, 2014[b]). On the other hand, focusing on gender differences, the project tends to reinforce stereotypes tied to ideas of essential and natural differences between women and men (Breslin and Wadhwa, 2014[a]).

Originated from the "girls' game' movement", the pink games are an example of designing technology for women. Often it reaffirms stereotypes tied to the feminine culture, such as fashion, beauty care and motherhood (Rodrigues and Merkle, 2017). According to Rodrigues and Merkle (2017), based on Warren's (2015) work, the separation of games by gender originates from the toys marketing logic. The authors point out that this reiterates not only gender stereotypes, but also expectations based on notions of femininity and masculinity. While "girl games" represent stereotyped notions of femininity, relating women to passive and permissive roles, the categorization of "boy games" present themselves problematic as well, maintaining themes culturally comprehended as masculine, such as competitiveness, war, violence and roles related to domination, tied to boys (Rodrigues and Merkle, 2017). The hierarchy between games understood as belonging to male culture or female culture becomes clear.

The argument used to justify the development of pink games is the notion that it represents girls' tastes, and for that reason are consequently profitable (Rodrigues 2017). Such excuse not only shows the traditional notion of femininity incorporated in the digital realm, but also reinforces values and expectations over the female players. That doesn't mean that women won't or shouldn't play and enjoy these games. What we argue is that their use of technology should not be limited by gender roles, neither by notions of traditional femininity. There should be space for multiple femininities.

Technology is often portrayed as part of a masculine culture. As Wajcman (2004, pp.15) points out, "schooling, youth cultures, the family and the mass media all transmit meanings and values that identify masculinity with machines and technological competence". She describes that as the sex-stereotyping of technology, and argues that it portrays the field as appropriate to men, creating a hindrance for women that want to "enter" technology fields. To enter that world, women must forsake their femininity, in order to belong. We argue that this happens not only in technological work fields, but also with technological products, such as video games. Also, this traces a territory where men and women can enact their masculinity or femininity, as well as when they are able to do that freely. Just like women have to forsake their femininity to enter technological fields, men are also tied to gender norms that require them to forsake their masculinity to enter in fields associated to feminine culture, such as fashion design for instance.

2.2 Femininities

Gender varies cross-culturally, and for that reason there is not a universal model of femininity or masculinity. Notions of what is "natural" or not are constructed in the cultural processes, which means that the notion of natural "gender" identities are also being constructed in the cultural dynamics (Louro, 2000). The cultural context influences the gender identities, notions of femininity/masculinity, and behaviors that are enacted.

According to Louro (2000) the sexology of the 19th century defined what was considered normal/natural masculinity and femininity as distinct characteristics of men and women (as a biological classification[1]). This produced a hierarchy between gender identities, since some values and behaviors are considered appropriate to a specific gender, and not to the other. This distinction also produced notions of normal and abnormal subjects towards gender identities, based on how the person is (or is not) conforming to gender norms. While some values and roles are expected of men, others are expected of women, delimiting how a subject can enact his/her gender. Also, the oppositional binary categories are relevant to understand how the hierarchy of power is grounded, since one is defined by its relation to the norm (Rodrigues, 2014). Femininity is constructed as the opposition to masculinity, so masculinity is taken as the norm, and femininity is a deviation from that same norm.

3. FEMININITY IN VIDEO GAMES

Gender values and norms are tied to notions of femininity and masculinity. The ways this is translated into visual language, narrative aspects of stories and sociability between players are approached in this section. Also, this section is divided into three parts. The first is about the visual aspects of gender representation in video games, focusing on character design. According to Flick (2009) visual content such as films and photos are not only data but instruments of knowledge. A case study described in Flick's (2009) book points to the use of visual material, as complementary documentation to the textual form, on analyzing culture and practices.

Also, we believe that video games contain social reflections and experiences, which are relevant to this paper. The second part is dedicated to the narrative content regarding femininity and gender norms, highlighting plot stereotypes associated to female representation and to the femininity in general. In the third and last part of this section we assess a few gaming informal documentation practices in a brief analysis on how gender roles and relations influences communication among players. The analysis presented in section 3.2.2 and 3.3 rely on the theoretical basis that are grounding this paper.

3.1 Visual Aspects

The visual aspects of femininity are often portrayed as stereotypical elements; the color pink, ribbons, make-up and high heels, for instance. Rodrigues (2014) explains that character design can be a device to reinforce gender stereotypes, pointing out that not only the female representation, but the femininity itself is sexually objectified. These representations are related to societal values and expectations over gender and sexuality. The work of Romanus (2012) discusses the representations of femininities and masculinities in video games. According to Romanus (2012), just like in advertising, the creation and design of characters in video games presupposes a male spectator. Romanus (2012), points out that the way femininities are understood in the popular culture is influenced by the invention and popularization of the computer and the internet, originating images of "digital" women and men. In her essay, Romanus (2012), analyses graphic representations of characters in video games, such as Metroid, Tomb Raider and Devil May Cry. The importance of these analyses is that stereotypes are taken as a place for resistance and questioning of these cultural representations. For that, it must be considered the available social and cultural representations for subjects to identify with, always remembering that these are embedded with values and societal norms.

Video games have shown, throughout the years, a wide range of visual styles for characters, from the abstract designs to the most realistic aesthetics. Hamm (2010) points out that male characters present a large range of body types and facial features, while female characters present a lack of diversity. Even though women are represented in many games, these representations are not diverse. She points out that the game "Team

[1] The original terminology in portuguese is "homens e mulheres biológicos".

Fortress 2", by Valve Corporation, is a good example of variety of character designs. These characters silhouettes can be seen in the figure 1, and are all male. The design of these characters is diverse, and creative. What Hamm intends by showing their silhouettes is to criticize the homogeny in the design of female characters, suggesting that they can be as diverse as the characters represented in Team Fortress 2.

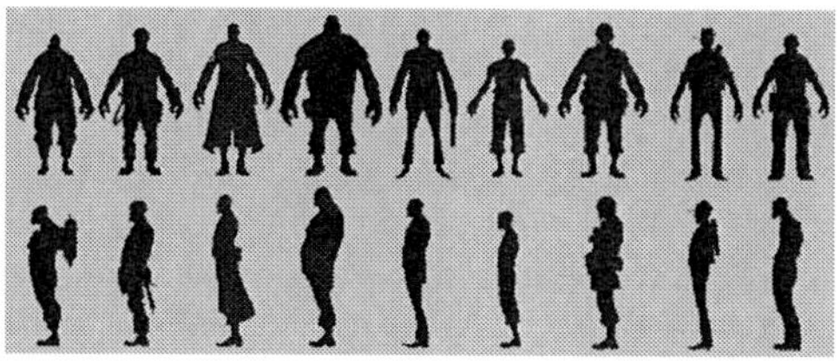

Figure 1. Team Fortress 2 characters silhouettes [2]

The lack of diversity in representing female bodies tends to show only one way of being woman, and that's usually hypersexualized and conforming to the societal standards of female beauty (young, thin...). The hyper-sexualization of female characters is tied to the presumption that gamers are heterosexual males, and for that reason the design is targeted at them. This also works as a mechanism to avoid the homoerotic gaze of male characters, by only sexualizing the female characters (Rodrigues and Merkle, 2017). The many ways of being a man or being a woman are always socially suggested, announced, promoted (Louro, 2000), besides being regulated, condemned and denied. The recurrent eroticized representation of the female characters regulates both genders by constantly representing the imagery of a specific type of desirable woman (large breasts, thin waist, submissive, hero's prize to be won...), as well as the player's expected sexuality (who is supposed to be interested in these representations).

Rodrigues and Merkle (2017) discuss in their essay about the customization tools for characters in video games. The tools are seen as technologies of gender, offering in a scale of masculinities and femininities the ways one can be a man or a woman, producing notions of viable subjects/bodies. According to Rodrigues and Merkle (2017) gender notions are constructed based on the biological sex, and the parameters for customizations of physical attributes and clothing are tied to it, having particular anatomic features.

3.2 Narrative

Femininity is explored in the visual content of games, as it has been argued in the previous section, but the ways in which it is explored in the narrative content tends to be less evident. While visual content is more explicit on representation, narrative content is presented through various means, such as values and ideas on the game's plot. The presence of stereotypes appears not only in the graphic part of the games, but can also be present in the characters' plots, the game's universe and other types of narrative content. This topic is about this regard, focusing on the character's plot.

3.2.1 Damsel in Distress

The role of the damsel in distress can be seen in several prominent franchises, such as Mario, The Legend of Zelda, Dragon Quest, amongst others. Anita Sarkeesian (2013) in her web series "Tropes vs Women" presents several aspects of female disempowerment stemming from this stereotype. According to Sarkeesian (2013), "as a trope the damsel in distress is a plot device in which a female character is placed in a perilous situation from which she cannot escape on her own and must be rescued by a male character, usually providing a core incentive or motivation for the protagonist's quest"[3]. Sarkeesian (2013) analyses the damsel through the subject/object dichotomy, understanding that while subjects act, the objects are acted upon. In the damsel trope, the protagonists are the subjects, and this role is associated to men, while the damsels are the objects, often associated to women. The later most often is reduced to "a prize to be won, a treasure to be found or a goal to be achieved" (Sarkeesian, 2013).

---

[2] Hamm (2010)

[3] Transcription of 3'10'' to 3'39'' from the episode 1, Tropes vs Women: Damsel in Distress. Available in: https://feministfrequency.com/video/damsel-in-distress-part-1/

The damsel role traces expectations and regulations about femininity and gender roles. The mechanism of the damsel trope reaffirms a culture of submission and dependency of the feminine over the masculine (Rodrigues, 2014), representing the feminine culture as lacking of agency. Rodrigues (2014) points out that this stereotype also works as a device to produce ideas of feminine fragility and inexperience, reinforcing a devaluation of femininity. Arantes (2016) discusses the universalization of gender categories (man and woman), pointing out that gender institutes a hierarchical role, which reinforces inequality amongst the notions of femininity and masculinity. Once gender notions reach the "digital realm", they influence not only the technological production, but the very participation in this fields is tied to the hierarchical gender relations

Although the trope of the Damsel in Distress is more evident in women's representations, this trope can also be observed in games that present other types of female characters, such as anthropomorphic animals (as in Starfox Adventures and Sonic CD).

3.2.2 Character's Plot

Productions involving female characters are commonly criticized because of the undeveloped backgrounds and plots, which maintain the representation of them as young, attractive, sidekick or the hero's prize. Hamm's (2010) analysis of the game "Gears of War" point to the very same problem. While the male characters are huge and represented with "battle-scarred forms", Lieutenant Anya Stroud, the only female character in the game, seems to be a lot younger than the male characters, besides having a flawless appearance. According to Hamm (2010) "her personality is calm, her background is undeveloped and she seems very detached from the game, as if she were included only to represent a pretty face".

Even though Hamm's analysis was written in 2010, it remains a fairly current topic. Lima (2018), for instance, discusses gender representation in crowdfounded games. His analysis starts with the hypothesis that independent game producers that rely on crowdfunding have the potential to be more diverse on gender representations than the big names of game industry. At the end of his analysis, the conclusion pointed to the opposite direction. According to Lima (2018), even though independent developers that rely on crowdfounding campaigns have more creative freedom, new constrains arise for them by the backers as they participate on the creation process. Therefore, not only the AAA games, but also independent productions are still below expectations on female representation (Lima, 2018).

Despite this little diverse scenario, there has been some changes. A few games have been moving towards subverting these femininity stereotypes and the lack of female protagonism, featuring stories and plots as well developed as the male characters' have been for years. Blizzard Entertainment's first-person shooter game, Overwatch, is a strong example of that. The game explores multiple platforms to construct its stories and backgrounds, even outside the game itself. Extra content can be accessed through their official website, containing comics, informative pages of each character and cinematic videos. Overwatch stands out because of the diversity represented amongst the female characters, in both visual and narrative aspects, deviating from the traditional notions of femininity. We selected three characters to exemplify this, and also for a briefly analysis.

Figure 2. Overwatch characters: Ana, Zarya and Tracer[4]

Ana Amari, on the left side of figure 2, is one of the founding members of Overwatch[5]. She is an Egyptian ex-commander and snipper, considered to be the world's best. What stands out in Ana's story is her age and high ranking in the hierarchy at Overwatch organization. She remained active until the age of 50, when she got seriously injured in battle, even losing her right eye. Ana represents an elderly woman (now at her sixties) that

[4] All images were taken from Overwatch original comics. From left to right, their titles are: Legacy, Searching and Reflections. These are available at: https://playoverwatch.com/en-us/media/

[5] Available at: https://playoverwatch.com/en-us/heroes/ana/

has severe war injuries and scars, elements that contrasts the notion of flawless beauty commonly depicted in female characters, and the age limit for female characters to remain active in stories.

Aleksandra Zaryanova, also known as Zarya, is represented in the middle of figure 2. According to the official website of Overwatch, she is "one of the world's strongest women, a celebrated athlete who sacrificed personal glory to protect her family, friends, and country in a time of war"[6]. Zarya is a 28-year-old Russian soldier whose goal is to help her people recover from post-war destruction, related to the conflicts that have taken place in the game's universe. The first deviation from the traditional femininity lies in the identification of the character with bodybuilding, in addition to a war-oriented narrative. Her story also influences the character's design, resulting in battle-scarred muscles and scars.

The third character is Tracer, whose full name is Lena Oxton. This character stresses differently the notions of gender and sexuality. First of all, she is a core character, appearing on both the cover of the physical edition of the game and the banner for digital purchase. Since Tracer is one of the most popular characters, it caused great controversy when the Christmas comic "Reflections" came out in December of 2016, and Tracer is shown kissing her girlfriend. Some players responses to that were quite problematic, such as posted in the Blizzard's online forum by the player "IgorJCorrea": "in fact the problem is to meet her as a normal/regular girl, and after almost a year 'out of nowhere' a lesbian kiss scene shows up"[7]. By that reaction, and others presented by players in the official forum, when sexuality is not explicitly shown, the character is considered heterosexual. That is to say, when no sexuality is represented, the character is associated to the normative sexuality. According to this perspective, normal/regular girls are heterosexual, and Tracer, when not conforming to gender/sexuality norms, is pointed as abnormal. That leads us to think that the traditional notion of femininity does not include lesbian women. Therefore, gender regulation itself will also take into account other factors such as sexuality.

3.3 Sociability

As videogames become more and more popular, it is important to understand the ways in which communication and socialization between players have a meaning to the gaming experience. In the 1990s and 2000s, game magazines were very popular ways of sharing passwords, tutorials and even tips on how to surpass challenging parts of a game. At the time, this was not only a popular way to access game content, but also players experiences. Later, another common practice arose from the gaming community, as players started to share content in websites, allowing other players to comment and respond. It is interesting to note that people consume games in different ways, and looking at forms of documentation reveals diverse appropriations of these technologies, as well as unexpected uses. Speedruns are a kind of appropriation practice, that consist in beating a game in the least time possible. There are a lot of categories of speedruns, such as completing the game with a 100% "save" (that is, accomplishing everything that is expected in the game, for instance: collecting all the coins, beating all the bosses…), or even by using glitches to beat the game. Summoning Salt is a Youtuber who documents iconic speedruns on vintage consoles, such as Super Nintendo, and Nintendo64. In one of his videos[8], he explains how the documentation of time records were (and are) done. It started with players contacting each other via email, later becoming more accessible to others by posts in websites, till the uploading or streaming of videos, which is now a popular and more trusting way of sharing time records. Summoning Salt's documentaries are a strong example of how the gaming community can appropriate different ways of playing and even organize itself to document their achievements.

New technologies are being developed, and the exchange of information between players has been facilitated. There are many ways that one can socialize and communicate with other players in the gaming community, such as voice chats, forums, video recording and even streaming live for an audience. Some experiences involving this interaction among players will be highlighted in this topic. The first is a video[9] shared by Glisa, an Overwatch player. Glisa recorded 16 minutes of harassments during a competitive match of the game. By the beginning of the match, Glisa started to be harassed without even contacting her team

---

[6] Available at: https://playoverwatch.com/en-us/heroes/zarya/

[7] In the original language: 'na real o problema é você conhecer ela como uma menina normal e depois de quase um ano "do nada" aparecer uma cena de beijo lésbico...'. Available at: https://us.battle.net/forums/pt/overwatch/topic/20752537624

[8] Summoning Salt. Choco Mountain: The History of Mario Kart 64's Most Infamous Track. Available at: https://www.youtube.com/watch?v=Y99Wj-NStok&ab_channel=SummoningSalt

[9] Available at: https://youtu.be/9f4dW1YpuoA

mates though the voice chat. That means the only representation of femininity associated to her was the character she chose, called Mercy. The provocations directed at Glisa at first concerned her character, like the phrases "I like how Mercy is trying to heal me because she wants me", or about her beauty, as in "Mercy, cure me. I will not call you ugly again. Just kidding, you're probably ugly"[10]. After Glisa contacted her team on the voice chat, the offenses changed from a figurative aggression to the feminine (that is, the female character), and became directed to the player. The offenses documented by Glisa had contents such as: condemning her for being a woman and playing the game, blaming her for the team's failure and associating her with domestic housework spaces (such as laundry room and kitchen). What draws our attention to this video is how the harassment started in the character, and not in the female player, meaning that in order to experience such harassments one can be symbolically associated with femininity, but doesn't require to be a female.

The second example takes place in the in the role-play servers of World of Warcraft, game developed also by Blizzard Entertainment. The tavern known as the "Goldshire Inn" has become a meeting point for players who enjoy erotic role-play, i.e. performing characters for erotic purposes. A problem pointed in the interview conducted by Motherboard with players (Schott, 2017), is the rape fantasies that some players are performing. The role-play is performed through the character's actions and the messages sent by the chat system of the game, which means that, similar to the case described in the previous paragraph, violence is associated with a female figure without necessarily an identification of the player with it. It is important to highlight that even though there is no need to be a woman to experience these harassments, when experienced by one it is very meaningful, since women already experience this type of violence outside the online environment.

This final paragraph approaches the production of online content by people who subvert patterns of femininity and masculinity. The first example is the Brazilian drag queen Samira Close[11], who streams games like Fortnite, Life is Strange and League of Legends. The character is performed by a homosexual man named Wenner Pereira, having a strong relationship with the LGBTQ community and related subjects. Samira is highlighted in this section for playing a female role through drag, in the online game environment. That is, in an environment understood as masculine. Other subversive streamers also considered relevant are: Anaxisde[12], woman who has sought to work as an eSports commentator; and Mandy Candy[13], transgender woman who is a game streamer. What is interesting is how these diverse manifestations of gender have gained space in the context of games through tools for transmitting and publishing videos.

4. CONCLUSION

The issues discussed throughout this essay point to a production and regulation of gender by technologies such as video games. It is important to understand that the cultural and social context, outside the digital environment, influence the production of games, taking into these fanciful universes various gender regulations. It is also emphasized that the consumption and appropriations made by players is quite relevant to understand how femininities and masculinities can be incorporated into the project by the developers, but also can be subverted in the use, and vice versa.

Also, assuming the audience as masculine and heterosexual shapes production, not only in the implicit narratives, but in the design itself. There are many ways to escape from the scope of traditional femininity and present it in a more multiple and diverse way. Allowing characters to be more open to what is understood as feminine and masculine can aid in the process of not producing only one possible form of male / female subject. Promoting positive values linked to femininity can also challenge this hierarchical relation that makes femininity little explored and valued in video games. It is suggested at the end of this essay that if it is possible to think of fanciful universes in games, with mystical creatures, superpowers... it is also possible to detach itself from the traditional stereotypes of femininity and masculinity, and to be creative in the ways of representing these universes.

---

[10] Transcript dialogues from 0'21" to 0'38".

[11] More information available at Samira Close's YouTube Channel: https://www.youtube.com/channel/UCnkhaZ34q4Dw9pgrpBkTcHg

[12] More information available at Anaxisde's YouTube channel: https://www.youtube.com/channel/UCfOpQkN8hNfvNLxqCNRzwhQ?ab_channel=AnaXisde

[13] More information available at Mandy Candy's YouTube channel: https://www.youtube.com/channel/UC0UMjthdcI-0IqgaZaQ5_Ww

ACKNOWLEDGEMENT

This paper is only viable because of the work of Letícia Rodrigues. Her work is responsible for putting Teresa de Lauretis' perspective in game analysis and discussions in Brazil, which provided us with the possibility to analyze games as technologies of gender. We owe her a special thanks.

REFERENCES

Arantes, M. L. P., 2016. *Sexismo nos Campos de Justiça: O Posicionamento de Marca Interferindo na Jogabilidade de League of Legends.* Universidade Federal do Paraná, Curitiba, Brazil.

Bardzell, S., 2010. Feminist HCI: Taking Stock and Outlining an Agenda for Design. *Proceedings of the SIGCHI Conference on Human Factors in Computing Systems.* Atlanta, USA, pp. 1301-1310.

Breslin, S. and Wadhwa, B., 2014. EnGendering Interaction Design. Proceedings of the 3rd International Conference on User Science and Engineering (i-USEr). Shah Alam, Malaysia, pp. 292-295.

Breslin, S and Wadhwa, B., 2014. Exploring Nuanced Gender Perspectives Within the HCI Community. *Proceedings of the India HCI 2014 Conference on Human Computer Interaction*, New Delhi, India, pp. 45-54.

Cassell, J. and Jenkins, H., 2000. *From Barbie to Mortal Kombat: gender and computer games*. The MIT Press, Cambridge, USA.

De Beauvoir, S., 1989. *The Second Sex*. Vintage, New York, USA.

De Lauretis, T., 1987. *Technologies of Gender: Essays on Theory, Film, and Fiction.* Indiana University Press, Bloomington and Indianopolis, USA.

Flick, U., 2009. *Introdução à pesquisa qualitativa.* Artmed, Porto Alegre, Brazil.

Goulart, L. and Nardi, H., 2017, GAMERGATE: digital games culture and male gamer identity. *In Revista Mídia e Cotidiano: artigo seção livre*, Vol. 11. No. 3, pp 250 -268.

Hamm, S., 2010. *The Aesthetics of Unique Video Game Characters.* Available at: http://gamecareerguide.com/features/854/the_aesthetics_of_unique_video_.php?page=1. Last access: 17/09/2018.

Lima, L. A. B., 2018. The struggles of diversity in gaming: an analysis of gender representation in crowdfunded games. *Proceedings of SBGames 2018.* Foz do Iguaçu, Brazil, pp. 902 – 907.

Louro, G. L., 2000. *O corpo educado: pedagogias da sexualidade.* Editora Autêntica. Belo Horizonte, Brazil.

Rodrigues, L., 2014. *Um Estudo em Representações Gráficas nos Jogos Eletrônicos na Perspectiva de Gênero: Os Tipos de Feminilidade em League of Legends.* Universidade Tecnológica Federal do Paraná, Curitiba, Brazil.

Rodrigues, L., 2017. *Questões de Gênero em Jogos Digitais: uma coleção de recursos educacionais abertos de apoio à mobilização.* Universidade Tecnológica Federal do Paraná, Curitiba, Brazil.

Rodrigues, L. and Merkle, L. E., 2017. Tecnologias de gênero na customização de personagens em jogos digitais. *Seminário Internacional Fazendo Gênero 11 & 13th Women's Worlds Congress.* Florianópolis, Brazil. pp. 1-13.

Romanus, J. S., 2012. *Gênero em Jogo: Um olhar sobre personagens e as representações de tipos de feminilidades e masculinidades nos games de ação contemporâneos.* Universidade Tecnológica Federal do Paraná. Curitiba, Brazil.

Sarkeesian, A., 2013 *Feminist Frequency. Tropes vs Women: Damsel in Distress 1.* Available at: http://www.feministfrequency.com/2013/03/damsel-in-distress-part-1/. Last Access: 13/09/2018.

Schott, D., 2017. *'World of Warcraft' Has a Rape Problem. Motherboard.* Available at https://motherboard.vice.com/en_us/article/mb7b9q/world-of-warcraft-has-a-rape-problem?utm_source=mbtwitter. Last Access: 24/10/2018.

Shaw, A., 2014, *Gaming at the edge: sexuality and gender at the margins of gamer culture.* University of Minnesota Press, Minneapolis, USA.

Wajcman, J., 2004. *TechnoFeminism.* Polity Press, Cambridge, England.

Warren, J., 2015. *'Why Do "Girl Games" Matter?'.* Game/Show, PBS Digital Studios. Available at: https://www.youtube.comwatch?v=4GKZ-u0cJsI

IMMERSION DURING DIGITAL MEDIA MULTITASKING

Hao Wang, Chien-Wen Ou-Yang and Chun-Tsai Sun
Department of Computer Science, National Chiao Tung University
1001, Ta Hsieh Road, Hsinchu City, Taiwan

ABSTRACT

In terms of digital media usage, immersion refers to user involvement in and focus on a single activity. It is easy to assume that individuals can only be immersed in one media at any moment, but the commonalty of multi-tasking raises questions regarding whether one media source should be considered the true locus of immersion. Self-report questionnaires and eye trackers were used to measure the immersive experiences of a sample consisting of students (ranging from undergraduate to doctoral candidates) from two universities while playing video games and watching a television program at the same time. Their data were compared with those for a similar group of individuals playing games or watching television only. While we found evidence of immersion across the two activities while multitasking, some immersion dimensions were significantly weaker. We also noted that immersion experiences from multiple media might be cumulative. A possible explanation for our results is that the act of switching between two media compensated for any down time—users could abandon a less attractive medium and switch to the other, resulting in an impression of continuous immersion in the overall multitasking experience.

KEYWORDS

Immersion, Multitasking, Digital Media, Eye-Tracking, User Experience

1. INTRODUCTION

Of the many definitions of immersion found in the literature, one of the most cited is from Murray's work (1997): "The sensation of being surrounded by a completely other reality, as different as water is from air, that takes over all of our attention, our whole perceptual apparatus.... Digital game researchers and designers have long acknowledged the importance of immersion. For example, Jennett, Cox and Cairns (2008) note that immersion in the form of "drawing people in" is an important factor in game design. When proposing their SCI (sensory, challenge-based, imaginative) model for analyzing video game immersion experiences, Ermi and Mäyrä (2005) defined the target concept as "becoming physically or virtually a part of the experience itself." McMahan (2003) also posits that immersion sources can be either diegetic or non-diegetic. The first involves narrative elements such as story and atmosphere, the second involves active play—that is, a "player's love of the game and the strategy that goes into it" (p. 68). Jennett, Cox, Cairns, Dhoparee, Epps, Tijs et al. (2008) performed exploratory analysis to decompose the immersion concept into five dimensions: cognitive involvement, emotional involvement, challenge, real world dissociation, and control.

To date, most studies and experiments on various aspects of immersion have focused on situations in which only one type of media is being used. However, we now live in a period where it is very common for individuals to divide their attention between two or more information sources, sometimes involving more than one outlet of the same media type. Results from a digital consumer survey conducted by the Nielsen Corporation (2014) indicate that 84% of all smart phone/tablet users in their sample used their devices while watching television. It is also increasingly common for game players to watch television or monitor other players' live shows on Twitch or YouTube while playing their own games.

Understanding the potential for immersion among individuals who divide their attention between two or more media is the primary motivation for the present study. Toward that goal, we established four research questions involving two groups of study participants—a multitasking experimental group, and a control group focused on one video or one game:

1. Were immersion levels among participants in the multitasking group lower than immersion levels in control group participants?

2. How do study participants divide their attention between more than one type of media? Do multitasking participants use media in different ways compared to single-task participants?

3. What is the relationship between overall immersion level and immersion levels for each of the two activities? Is the overall immersion level for a single activity close to the average for both, or are immersive experiences cumulative?

4. Are multitasking participants concurrently immersed in both media, or do they tend to be immersed in only one at a time?

2. BACKGROUND

Researchers in digital games often analyze immersion as a natural part of the gaming experience. Carr (2006) has proposed two immersion categories: as a perceptual phenomenon, which emphasizes the way that the human sensory apparatus is occupied by a stimulus or experience; or as a psychological phenomenon, which emphasizes the idea that imaginative play encourages extreme player focus and absorption. Breda (2008) emphasizes emotion when describing immersion as the feeling of connection to a game, especially when deep emotional experiences are involved. As part of their effort to clarify different types of game immersion, Johnson and Wiles (2003) define immersion as deep and effortless involvement in a game, and use the term "engagement" to describe effortful and concentrated play.

Two concepts closely linked with immersion are Flow (Csikszentmihalyi, 1990) and presence (McMahan, 2003; IJsselsteijn, de Ridder, Freeman and Avons, 2000; Lee, 2004). There are important distinctions to note between immersion and presence though. For instance, researchers have noted that it is not necessary for immersion and presence to exist concurrently, and cite as examples those times when players perform repetitive and boring tasks within vivid virtual environments—presence may be strong, but immersion is likely to be low (McMahan, 2003). In contrast, games such as Tetris that are played on handheld devices can be immersive, but without strong feelings of presence.

Csikszentmihalyi (1990) uses the term "flow" to describe optimal experiences when engaging in activities. He summarized optimal experience properties as the existence of conditions for flow to occur (e.g., clear goals, immediate feedback, balance between challenge and skill), plus specific characteristics such as high degree of concentration, sense of control, and the merging of action and awareness, as well as flow-related consequences such as loss of self-consciousness, distorted sense of time, and autotelic activity. Csikszentmihalyi proposed the three-channel flow model shown in Figure 1 to describe changes in mind status among flow, anxiety, and boredom, all of them affected by the balance between challenge and skill.

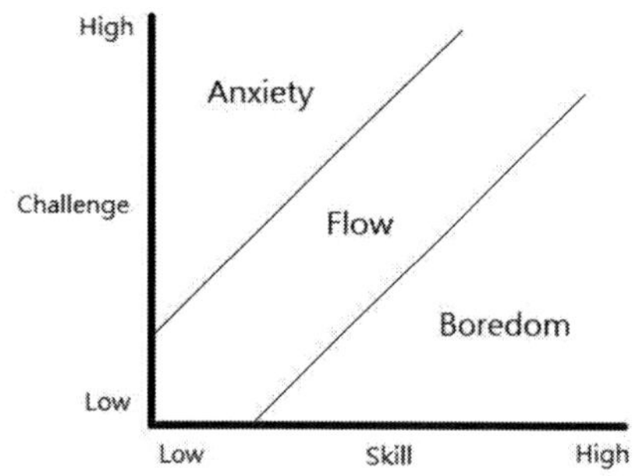

Figure 1. The three channel Flow

Researchers have used both subjective and objective methods to measure immersion experiences. Subjective methods include self-report questionnaires, interviews, and researcher observations (Brown and Cairns, 2004; Csikszentmihalyi, 1990; Sweetser and Wyeth, 2005; Hamari, Shernoff, Rowe, Coller, Asbell-Clarke and Edwards, 2016). These methods have some well-studied limitations—for example, some respondents find it difficult to answer abstract questions that are commonly found in immersion research (e.g., "Do you feel surrounded by another reality?") A second challenge is the ephemeral nature of deep immersion, making it difficult for study participants to be aware of, remember, and report their immersion experiences at the end of game-playing sessions. Objective data collection in immersion studies often entails physiological signal methods (ex. heartbeat rate, perspiration, pupil dilation, electrodermal response, electromyography) that are common to psychophysiological research (Nacke and Lindley, 2009). Objective methods also have shortcomings for gaming experience research, the most important being the complexity and lack of stability in the relationship between physiological signals and psychological phenomena. To overcome the disadvantages of individual methods, researchers suggest using several at the same time to increase analytical effectiveness (IJsselsteijn et al., 2000; Nacke and Lindley, 2009).

3. METHOD

3.1 Participants

Campus-based electronic bulletin board systems were used to recruit study participants from two universities. The final sample consisted of 38 males and 34 females between the ages of 18 and 38 (mean 23.2). Three groups were established from the initial sample, one labeled "multitasking" (30 individuals), one "video-only" (21), and one "game-only" (21). To develop the questionnaire for the formal experiment, we recruited 61 additional participants prior to the formal experiment via the same BBS (37 male, 24 female, age range of 19 to 30, 23.5 year mean).

3.2 Game and Video Selections

We designed our experiment to study a specific multitasking situation: playing a digital game and watching a video at the same time. For selecting specific video and game, several factors dictated our decision. First, the game had to be suitable for multitasking; we rejected real time strategy and multiplayer online battle arena games due to the demands they make for continuous player attention. Puzzle games were considered suitable depending on the level of difficulty in problem solving. The same motivation guided our video selection—watchers had to be able to avert their eyes occasionally and catch up with the video storyline when they returned, therefore programs with intricate plots and exceptionally fast pacing were rejected. FEZ (a casual platformer game that allows for relaxed exploration) and The Mythbusters (a long-running TV program requiring less continuous attention, but with a key question saved for the end) fit our criteria.

3.3 Questionnaires

The game and video immersion-measuring questionnaires used in this study were largely based on the work of Jennett et al. (2008) and Sweetser and Wyeth (2005) plus two additional dimensions: "merging of action and awareness" and "loss of self-consciousness" (Csikszentmihalyi, 1990). The finalized game immersion questionnaire (Cronbach's α .914, proportion of variance explained 60.9%, all question item factor loadings >.400; we didn't append the questionnaires due to page number limitation) has six factors according to the question items they contained: (a) transport, meaning feelings of disconnection with the real world and of being surrounded by a virtual world; (b) enjoyment, or having fun and interest in the activity; (c) cognitive involvement, with a strong focus on thinking and processing in-game information; (d) emotional involvement, including empathy for game characters, anticipation about how a plot will unfold, and emotional changes tied to the game; (e) loss of self-consciousness, such as lower levels of self-awareness and interest in the real-world environment; and (f) merging of action and awareness so that in-game actions feel spontaneous and natural. In light of the study goals, we added a simple statement to measure the participants' sense of immersion: "I felt deeply immersed in the game." This item could be used to check whether questionnaire responses actually reflected the participants' feelings. For the multitasking group, the question "I felt deeply immersed during the activity just completed" was used to measure overall feelings of immersion rather than immersion in either the game or video alone.

The video immersion questionnaire used in the formal experiment (Cronbach's α .893, proportion of variance explained 56.8%, all question item factor loadings >.400). The four extracted factors were labeled according to their associated question items: (a) cognitive involvement, with its focus on thinking and processing information presented in the video; (b) emotional involvement and enjoyment, tied to the content that made the video interesting or that triggered an emotional reaction; (c) loss of self-consciousness, indicating lowered self-awareness of or interest in real world surroundings; and (d) transport, meaning feelings of disconnection from the real world accompanied by a sense of presence in the TV program.

Members of the multitasking group were requested to complete two additional questionnaires, one designed to measure their feelings about multitasking, the other a list of open questions for collecting data on their feelings about the experimental setting.

3.4 Apparatus

A 24-inch LCD display was used to present the dual media content. Eye tracking was performed with a SR Research EyeLink 1000 (1 kHz sample rate). The infrared eye-tracking camera was placed in front of the screen so that the participants' heads could move freely within a limited range. Figure 2 shows the experiment screen containing game and video stimuli.

Figure 2. Multitasking setting screenshot

3.5 Eye Movement Data Analysis

Eye movement data analysis required definitions for three areas of interest (AOI): the game, the main video area, and the video subtitle area. We then used the following features to summarize eye movement data: (a) total length of time that each participant's line of sight fell within an AOI, including fixation and saccades (eye movements across a field without focusing on an object); (b) fixation count, meaning the number of times participants "looked at" a certain AOI; (c) fixation duration, or total length of time spent gazing at an AOI; (d) average fixation duration, calculated as fixation duration divided by fixation count; (e) in-out count, meaning the number of times a participant's eye fixation position moved away from an AOI but returned later; (f) total saccade count; (g) total number of blinks during a session; and (h) average pupil dilation while gazing at an AOI.

4. RESULTS

4.1 Immersion Score Comparison

As shown in Table 1, both instinctive feelings (i.e., responses to the item, "I felt deeply immersed in the game") and overall game immersion scores from the questionnaire were significantly lower for the multitasking group compared to the game-only group (α=0.05)—in other words, a decrease in immersion while multitasking. The largest score differences were for "loss of self-consciousness" (17.4% lower) and "cognitive involvement" (17.1% lower). The video-related data shown in Table 2 indicate significantly lower instinctive feeling and total questionnaire scores for the multitasking group, with "cognitive involvement" and "transport" having the most significant differences compared to the video-only group (35.8% and 16.6% lower, respectively).

Table 1. Game immersion score comparison between multitasking and game-only groups. (${}^{*}p < .05$, ${}^{**}p < .01$, ${}^{***}p < .001$)

Factor	Game-only		Multitasking		t-value	p-value
	M	SD	M	SD		
Game Instinctive Feeling	7.33	1.24	6.40	1.48	2.3700*	.022
Game Cognitive Involvement	8.71	.56	7.00	1.98	4.4860***	.000
Game Emotional Involvement	20.29	4.16	17.30	4.55	2.3880*	.021
Game Transport	17.90	4.81	14.43	4.56	2.6170*	.012
Game Loss of Self-consciousness	14.29	2.43	10.80	3.08	4.3250***	.000
Game Merging of Action and Awareness	10.14	2.56	10.33	2.72	-.2520	.802
Game Enjoyment	24.57	3.92	20.77	4.60	3.0850**	.003
Game Total Immersion Score	95.90	14.61	80.63	15.51	3.5430**	.001

Table 2. Video immersion score comparison between multitasking and video-only groups. (${}^{*}p < .05$, ${}^{**}p < .01$, ${}^{***}p < .001$)

Factor	Video-only		Multitasking		t-value	p-value
	M	SD	M	SD		
Video Instinctive Feeling	7.19	1.63	4.67	2.20	4.4590***	.000
Video Cognitive Involvement	12.48	1.97	7.10	2.51	8.2040***	.000
Video Emotional Involvement and Enjoyment	23.00	4.49	19.43	6.05	2.2920*	.026
Video Loss of Self-consciousness	13.43	2.99	12.70	2.39	.9640	.340
Video Transport	16.90	4.45	12.77	3.95	3.4940**	.001
Video Total Immersion Score	65.81	11.63	52.00	12.24	4.0450***	.000

4.2 Instinctive Feelings of Immersion

Instinctive feelings of immersion were measured according to the statement, "I felt deeply immersed during the activity just completed." We looked for correlations between response scores for this question and total scores from the multi-dimensional immersion questionnaire to determine if the questionnaire accurately measured instinctive feelings about immersion. For the single task groups, Pearson correlation coefficients for the instinctive feeling and total questionnaire scores were .715 for the game-only group and .869 for the video-only group. Among the multitasking study participants, the Pearson correlation coefficients between instinctive feeling and total questionnaire scores were .782 and .863 for the game and video, respectively. These results indicate a high correlation between the instinctive feeling and total questionnaire scores, suggesting that instinctive feeling can serve as an indicator of overall immersion.

Although game and video immersion scores were lower for the multitasking group, the overall instinctive feeling score for the multitasking group was higher (4.04) than those for both single task groups (game=3.67, video=3.60), indicating that immersion values from multiple sources can be summed to some extent, and suggesting that individuals can have strong immersive experiences when multitasking using digital media, even though the degree of immersion from each source is reduced.

4.3 Eye movement and Immersion

AOI time distribution data are shown at Table 3. For multitasking group participants, proportions of time spent in each AOI were .80 for game, .07 for video_main, and .13 for video_subtitle—that is, study participants tended to spend more time playing the game than watching the video. For the video-only group, time proportions were .56 for video_main and .44 for video_subtitle. According to these data, multitasking group participants spent more time reading subtitles than watching the characters in the video—opposite of the video-only group. A likely explanation is that the multitasking participants needed a more efficient method for collecting and processing information.

Comparisons of eye movement data among multitasking and single-task groups are shown in Tables 4 (game) and 5 (video). Total number of blinks was significantly lower for the multitasking group, suggesting greater interest among those study participants who divided their time between the video and the game.

Table 3. Focus time distribution in percentage

AOI	M	SD
Multitasking AOI_Game	.80	.13
Multitasking AOI_Video	.19	.13
Multitasking AOI_Video_Main	.07	.05
Multitasking AOI_Video_Subtitle	.13	.10
Video-only AOI_Video	.99	.01
Video-only AOI_ Video_Main	.56	.11
Video-only AOI_Video_Subtitle	.44	.11

Table 4. Eye movement feature comparison between multitasking and game-only groups. ($^{*}p < .05$, $^{**}p < .01$, $^{***}p < .001$)

Factor	Game-only		Multitasking		t-value	p-value
	M	SD	M	SD		
Total Number of Saccades	3011.39	454.54	3451.60	439.30	-3.0340**	.004
Total Number of Blinks	451.39	298.94	356.65	286.50	.9970	.325
Average Fixation Time (AOI_ Game)	401.93	79.08	386.47	44.98	.7500	.458
Average Pupil Size (AOI_ Game)	1408.06	1377.78	1432.88	1366.85	-.0560	.956

Table 5. Eye movement feature comparison between multitasking and video-only groups. (*p < .05, **p < .01, ***p < .001)

Factor	Video-only		Multitasking		t-value	p-value
	M	SD	M	SD		
Total Number of Saccades	3785.24	605.53	3451.60	439.30	1.938	.061
Total Number of Blinks	780.12	710.52	356.65	286.50	2.303*	.032
Average Fixation Time AOI_Video	299.78	69.18	225.27	45.61	3.795***	.001
Average Fixation Time AOI (Video_Main)	378.99	111.32	256.20	78.64	3.919***	.000
Average Fixation Time (AOI_Video_Sub title)	236.49	47.23	213.55	36.30	1.669	.104
Average Pupil Size (AOI_Video)	1475.25	1429.61	1444.63	1446.30	.065	.949
Average Pupil Size (AOI_Video_Mai n)	1479.08	1431.68	1486.72	1447.17	-.016	.987
Average Pupil Size (AOI_Video_Sub title)	1467.37	1424.16	1425.26	1439.33	.089	.929

5. CONCLUSION

In this paper we compared levels and qualities of immersion in single-tasking and multitasking scenarios involving a game (FEZ) and a popular television program (The Mythbusters). Both self-report questionnaires and eye tracking data were used to measure immersion. We found that immersion levels among the multitasking study participants were significantly lower in most dimensions, especially in dimensions associated with feelings of separation from the real world and level of concentration. We also found that even though most aspects of immersion in two or more kinds of media were negatively affected in the multitasking setting, instinctive feelings of overall immersion were higher in the multitasking group. We interpret this finding as meaning that a cumulative sense of immersion can emerge from multiple media, depending on certain conditions. Our eye-tracking data indicate that multitasking participants spent more time than the video-only group participants reading video subtitles for efficient information consumption. Game/application designers may want to foster multitasking by improving user interface.

We acknowledge that our experiments were limited in terms of material and apparatus, and that results would likely have been different had we used other games or videos. For example, if we chose online chess as the game, participants may have spent more time focusing on the video while their opponents considered their next moves. Factor analysis results for immersion dimensions may have differed because chess matches do not involve storylines or action beyond moving pieces on a board. Another study shortcoming is the use of a single computer display containing more than one task, since most multitasking involves multiple devices and screens.

REFERENCES

Brown, E. and Cairns, P. 2004. "A grounded investigation of game immersion" Human Factors in Computing Systems, pp. 1297-1300.

Breda, L. 2008. "Invisible Walls" Game Career Guide, available at http://www.gamecareerguide.com/features/593/invisible_.php.

Carr, D. 2006. "Games and narrative" Computer games: Text, narrative and play, Carr, D., Buckingham, D., Burn, A. and Schott, G. eds, Cambridge, UK: Polity Press, pp. 30-44.

Csikszentmihalyi, M. 1990. Flow: the psychology of optimal experience. New York, NY: Harper & Row.

Ermi, L. and Mäyrä, F. 2005. "Fundamental Components of the Gameplay Experience: Analysing Immersion" Worlds in play: Int. perspectives on digital games research, S. D. Castell and J. Jenson, eds, Bern, Switzerland: Peter Lang, vol. 37.

Hamari, J., Shernoff, D. J., Rowe, E., Coller, B., Asbell-Clarke, J. and Edwards, T. 2016. "Challenging games help students learn: An empirical study on engagement, flow and immersion in game-based learning" Computers in human behavior, vol. 54, pp. 170-179.

IJsselsteijn, W. A., de Ridder, H., Freeman, J. and Avons, S. E. 2000. "Presence: concept, determinants, and measurement" Proc. SPIE 3959, Human Vision and Electronic Imaging V, pp. 520-529.

Jennett, C., Cox, A. L. and Cairns, P., Dhoparee, S., Epps, A., Tijs, T. and Walton, A. 2008. "Measuring and defining the experience of immersion in games" International journal of human-computer studies, vol. 66, no. 9, pp. 641-661.

Johnson, D. and Wiles, J. 2003. "Effective affective user interface design in games" Ergonomics, vol. 46, pp. 1332-1345.

Lee, K. M. 2004. "Presence, explicated" Communication theory, vol. 14, no. 1, pp. 27-50.

McMahan, A. 2003. "Immersion, engagement and presence" The video game theory reader, Wolf M. J. P. and Perron, B. eds, Psychology Press, pp. 67-86.

Murray, J. H. 1997. Hamlet on the Holodeck: The Future of Narrative in Cyberspace. Cambridge, MA: MIT Press.

Nacke, L. E. and Lindley, C. A. 2009. "Affective ludology, flow and immersion in a first-person shooter: Measurement of player experience" Loading…, vol. 3, no. 5.

Nielsen Corporation, 2014. The Digital Consumer February 2014, available at http://www.nielsen.com/content/dam/corporate/us/en/reports-downloads/2014%20Reports/the-digital-consumer-report-feb-2014.pdf

Sweetser, P. and Wyeth, P. 2005. "GameFlow: a model for evaluating player enjoyment in games" Computers in Entertainment (CIE), vol. 3 issue 3.

DESIGNING IMMERSIVE AND MOTIVATING GAMES WITH HIDDEN THERAPEUTIC BENEFIT TO AID HOME THERAPY FOR STROKE PATIENTS IN RECOVERING HAND FUNCTIONS: A LITERATURE REVIEW

Shauma Hayyu Syakura, Hafiz Aziz Ahmad and Ary Setijadi Prihatmanto
Institut Teknologi Bandung, Bandung, Indonesia

ABSTRACT

Stroke and cerebrovascular diseases are among of the causes for long term disabilities (Harvey et al, 2008). Stroke itself is still becoming a problem in Indonesia, which can be seen from the rise of stroke cases in these recent years. One of the most important needs for stroke rehabilitation is for a home based therapy tool, which can be fulfilled with mobile games technology. Especially for hand function training because it needs more commitment and longer time to recover. This paper reviews research in the field of health, technology, human computer interaction, game design and psychology on how to develop mobile games for home based stroke therapy that trains hand function training emphasizing on patient's immersion and motivation but still has therapeutic benefits for Indonesian stroke patients. First, kinds of therapy for hand function are researched. Second potential technology are reviewed, which ended up as mobile devices chosen because it has high user base, high usage time, and easily obtainable. Game as a type of mobile application is chosen because it is proven to increase motivation in patient. And then factors to create therapeutic games for stroke and how to create highly motivating and immersive games are considered. The conclusion is highly immersive and motivating games can be made but still be able to have therapeutic benefits, as there are some intersecting aspects.

KEYWORDS

Game Design, Stroke Therapy, Stroke Rehabilitation, Mobile Games

1. INTRODUCTION

Stroke and cerebrovascular diseases are among of the causes for long term disabilities (Harvey et al, 2008). One of them is the loss of sensorimotor function caused by brain cells damage occurred during stroke (Goldstein, 2011) (Harvey, 2008). Among lost motoric functions is what termed as the upper extremities (UE) function, which includes upper body parts such as shoulders, arms, hands and fingers. What make UE functions recovery important is because it enables the patient to do activities of daily living (shortened to ADL), eating, wearing clothes, taking care of themselves, and working, so they can support themselves and be productive again. Research by Corr & Wilmer (1977) shows that 77% stroke patients want to return working, while survey done by Timmerman et al (as cited in Curtis et al, 2009) with post stroke patients shows that writing skills are one of the 10 most desired abilities.

Stroke itself is still becoming a problem in Indonesia, which can be seen from the rise of stroke cases in these recent years. Surveys form stroke cases were done by Riskesdas (Riset Kesehatan Dasar) Indonesia—Indonesian government health research organization, from year 2007 to 2013, shows this phenomenon across all age groups. In 2007, stroke cases for 45-55 age group and 55-65 age group, reach 8% and 15% respectively (Riskesdas, 2008), and until 2013, both age group have their cases rising to 15% and 24% (Riskesdas, 2013).

Lost motoric functions, including UE, can be recovered by doing high intensity physical training on affected body parts (Goldstein, 2011). These exercises were primarily done during occupational therapy (OT) done by therapist, a therapy focuses on returning UE and cognitive functions (Alamri et al, 2009). However, for the training to take significant effects, patients can not only depend on therapy sessions with therapist, as it is not enough to reach the intensity needed for significant improvements (Lange et al, 2013). Hence, it is very important for patient to continue training individually outside therapy sessions, which is only in a couple of hours in a few days a week. This is especially substantial for UE functions training since it needs more intense and longer training for significant recovery than LE (Lower Extremity) functions, which includes lower body parts like hips, legs, and feet. Not to mention that the amount of therapy sessions can diminish with increasing medical costs, reduction in paid benefits, longer waiting periods, and a shortage of rehabilitation specialists, (Lange, et al, 2013b).

For home therapy, occupational therapist assists patients' home training by designing training plans for patients to do at home. However, not all patients diligently follow through those training plans, as shown in research done Shaughnessy, et al (2006), which shows that only 31% patients carry out the training plans at home. The prominent cause is the boredom that caused by patients having to do the same motions repeatedly in high numbers. The need of therapy that can keep motivating patients during training is one of the emphasized factors in designing stroke therapy method (Merians, et al, as cited by King, et al, 2012) (Goldstein, 2011). Interview done with therapist in local rehabilitation clinic in Indonesia, and they also expressed the same problems. With stroke cases continuing to rise in Indonesia, there was also a need to solve motivation problems for Indonesian stroke patients.

One of the methods developed to solve motivation problems in stroke therapy is using digital games, as using games for training have been proven to help raise motivations in patients (Shin, et al, 2014). And various researches has been done to develop digital games from stroke therapy, ranging from using sophisticated technology such as robotic equipment (Colombo, et al, 2007) to the usage of commercial technology such as PC and commercial devices like Microsoft Kinect and Nintendo Wii (Lange, et al, 2011), however as of right now both devices have been discontinued. Beside games specifically developed for therapeutic purpose, commercial games were also researched for its potential therapeutic benefits (Lange, et al, 2009).

Seeing the potential of mobile game as another tool to aid home based therapy with for mobile devices are easily obtainable and has large user base (eMarketer, 2014), this paper aims to review research in health, technology, digital games, game design, and psychology to develop motivational mobile games to aid home therapy for stroke patients specifically to aid occupational therapy. Research scope for target users of the mobile game that is going to be researched in this paper was decided after doing a preliminary survey. Preliminary survey was done with 31 patients (15 men, 16 women) in a stroke rehabilitation clinic in Indonesia. Survey result showed that interest for mobile games are shown by patients below 60 years old, because patients in this age range are more used with game and mobile device. Therefore, stroke patients that becomes the target users are stroke patients below 60 years old. Since most stroke patients are elderly, elderly game preference are researched as well in this paper. The result of the research can be used to find what aspects or elements needs to be considered to make motivational game that is suited to the target users, who are stroke patients, and for its function which is as a tool to aid occupational therapy.

2. DIGITAL GAMES IN STROKE THERAPY

Games have been proven to evoke motivations, especially intrinsic motivations (Przybylski et al, 2010), in its players, and numerous researches used games extensively to inject motivations to its targeted players in doing activities that those players found otherwise uninteresting or boring (Baranowski et al, 2008). It is also a method that has been used in health field outside of stroke, such as games to promote changes for better health-related behavior. Examples of this can be seen in "The Asthma Files", a game developed to promote self-management skills related with asthma (McPherson, et al, 2006), "Fun, Food, & Fitness" that promote a healthy lifestyle to eat nutritiously and do exercises (Baranowski, et al, 2007), and "Game Wheels" that encourage wheelchair patients doing physical activity by enabling them to play commercial games using wheelchair interface (O'Connor, et al, 2000). Existing commercial games that have potential for health benefit were also explored, such as the usage of "Dance Dance Revolution" to encourage physical activity (V.B. Unnithan et al., 2006).

As for stroke therapy, various researches have been done to develop digital games employing various technologies. Those games are created to ensure patients doing the required training while also maintain their motivation (Alankus, et al, 2010). Colombo, et al (2007), design a simple game in which patients were asked to move a ball from its initial position to targeted position using robotic hands designed to rehabilitate hand muscles. Yeh, et al (2005) developed a game that involve patients to manipulate objects in 3D World.

Digital games could be a solution to aid patients carrying out training at home, preferably using easily obtainable and applicable technology, as also stated by Lange, et al (2013) that low cost based quality home based sensorimotor rehabilitation is needed. Some of the games for stroke therapy researched in the past involved some quite novel, elaborate, expensive technologies, and/or not commercially available, such as robotic equipment or virtual reality which more suitable for clinic based therapy. However, games that use easily accessible or simpler technology, with focus to assist home based rehabilitation, have also been explored in several research. TheraDrive is driving game built for home PC which was developed as a low cost, commercially viable, home based, game therapy to assist stroke rehabilitation focuses on unilateral and bilateral functional training (Johnson, et al, 2004). Lange, et al (2011) developed low cost game-based balance rehabilitation tool using Microsoft Kinect Sensor, that enables patient to puppet virtual characters on screen using Kinect's motion detection. Customizable games developed by Alankus et al. (2010) mentioned earlier, also developed for the purpose of home therapy using webcam and Nintendo Wii remote which are deemed as devices inexpensive enough for home use but still advanced enough to detect motions needed for therapy. Lange, et al. (2009) also conducted research on commercial video games' suitability for clinical game-based rehabilitation. Among them are sport games using commercial haptic devices like Sony Playstation EyeToy and Nintendo Wii's remote. Lange et al then compared the usability of those commercial video games and devices to prototype game specifically developed for rehabilitation, The Novint Falcon. The conclusion from this research shows that commercial games and devices can be used as therapy tool if they contain appropriate content to fulfill therapeutic goals, and that the Falcon, although built specifically for therapy, has limited workspace and doesn't have as much and as natural movement functions as EyeToy and Nintendo Wii. From this it can be concluded that both type of games, the specifically therapeutic games and conventional games with potential for therapeutic property, and both type of technology used, elaborate or expensive technology with greater or specific therapeutic capability and simpler but cheaper technology with limited capability, are needed and best used in conjunction because each offset each other's weakness.

3. MOBILE GAMES FOR HOME THERAPY

Among commercially accessible, cheap technology, and also the most owned/used device globally, is mobile devices, ranging from smartphone to tablet, which reach 2.56 billion consumers by 2018 (eMarketer, 2014) and 1.51 billion consumers by 2019 (eMarketer, 2015) worldwide respectively according to eMarketer (www.eMarketer.com). Although mobile devices have limited capabilities compared to other commercial devices such as PC/Laptop or commercial game consoles like Nintendo Wii or Microsoft Kinect, but it has larger user base, cheaper and higher active time usage compared to other devices. Therefore, digital games using mobile device technology can be used as another home based stroke therapy alternative tools. Especially in Indonesia, Survey done by Vserv (2015) shows that mobile applications with the highest engagement per day are mobile games, which means Indonesian mobile user is very familiar with mobile games.

Using mobile games, mobile applications, and mobile devices as stroke therapy tools have not eluded researchers' attention. Moreover, there were also some commercial occupational therapy applications available. A pilot study done by Curtis, et al (2009) develops an interactive game to aid handwriting skill rehabilitations using graphic tablet and tablet PC. Hable et al. (2013) create prototype of a tablet application for stroke patients' rehabilitation, using tablet's touch screen to train finger movements. Vandermaesen (2014) developed home based rehabilitation game on Android tablet, Rehoblet. Dexteria Fine Motor Skill Development (www.dexteria.net) is a commercial iPad app targeted at children with special needs comprised of set of therapeutic hand exercises to improve fine motor skills and handwriting readiness, but it could also be used by adults as well. Another commercial mobile application titled iOT Session developed by Dr. Frederick Covington OTD is an app to rehabilitate fine motors/dexterity, visual perceptual, and visual scanning (Harpold, 2013). Doctors and researchers team from John Hopkins University School of Medicine, released an iPhone game titled Bandit's Shark Showdown that utilize iPhone 6S's 3D Touch technology, to see whether pressure sensitive touchscreen can aid patients recover hand force and dexterity (Goode, 2015).

4. DESIGNING MOBILE GAMES FOR THERAPY PURPOSE

Game components appropriate for stroke therapy also have been researched. Flores, et al (2008) researched guide map to design game scenarios for motor impairment rehabilitation and some examples how to use it to develop games for stroke therapy tools. Flores, et al., researched design criteria that satisfy both the nature of a motor rehabilitation program and preference of its most common target users, the elderly users, to entice motivations. From the research, Flores conclude following design criteria for developing games for stroke therapy : (1) The game should be adaptable to patients' motor skill level, (2) Meaningful tasks should be incorporated into the game so that the patient can have a direct correlation between use of their disabled limb during therapy and use in activities of daily living (ADLs), (3) The game should give appropriate feedback to the game on how well the patients improving, (4) The game should include appropriate range of motions needed for patients recovery, (5) the game should divert patient's focus away from conscious effort to move impaired body parts.

Research done by Shin et al. (2014) in developing Rehab Master found following design criteria : (1) Device used should be a stable system with accurate control recognition (2) Game design should contain goal oriented task-specific contents, maintain players interest, interactive and entertaining elements to keep patients immersed, and provide tutorials for the game, (4) Similar to Flores et al., there should be scoring system to evaluate patients performance, but further to also enable to compete with other participants (5) The graphics should be simple and not distractive, using fun elements to provide positive experience.

Alankus et al (2010) in the process of developing stroke therapy games also resulted in elements considered to design games for stroke therapy. Alankus et al concluded the following design criteria: (1) Social context, multiplayer can provide extra motivations compared to single players. However, for stroke therapy games leans more towards collaborative gameplay rather than competitive gameplay, because patients dislike competing with other disabled patient, this is in contrast to Shin et al findings. Collaborative gameplays can also further expand not only with other patients, but with family or caregiver, as Alankus et al pointed out "Perhaps rehabilitation games, in addition to motivating patients to exercise, can also provide a context in which stroke patients and caregivers collaborate as equals." Collaborative games with caregiver can help stroke patients and their caregiver feel greater sense of connection as peers. A finding from Delbressine et al (2012) research also shows that patients would like collaborative games they can play with their grandchildren. (2) Cognitive challenge should be considered when designing stroke therapy games; because many stroke patients has different cognitive issues. (3) Patients motions should be able to be calibrated and suited with the game and ensure patients fully cover their motion range (4) simple games should support multiple modes of user inputs and detect compensatory motions (5) Therapist are able to determine difficulty, also in congruent with Flores et al adaptability criteria (6) NPC and storylines are intriguing, this is a surprising find, but the reason for that is because it's contribute to users' engagement. For future works, Alankus et al suggest to research separate interface for therapist and patients and a model how to build motivating stroke rehabilitations game. Alankus suggestion for future work will be taken into account for the development of this paper's game, it is in line with the main focus of the research which is to design highly engaging and motivating game.

There was another approach in designing game for stroke therapy that is almost a contrast with previous researches, which inspires this research. It is a design approach used by "Bandit's Shark Showdown", a commercial game that could also be used as an aiding tool for stroke therapy (Russel, 2015). This game was developed by BLAM! (Brain, Learning, Animation, Movement Lab), comprised of the original game creator Omar Ahmad, Kat McNally, and Promit Roy, and John Krakauer, neuroscientist at John Hopkins university. This game has double functions, as a commercial game and as "an artistic technology to help heal John's patient", Ahmad said (as quoted from Russel, 2015). A sister version of the game was currently used by Krakauer as a therapy tool for stroke patients with impaired arms. Using a robotic sling, patients can sync their arms movement to the dolphin movement, creating motoric connection, a visceral link between patient's moving body and the simulated dolphin and to make patients rediscover the joy of movement. Krakauer hopes that the game will keep patients engaged in the immersive world for hours.

And thus, a seemingly conventional game can be used as a 'disguise' for a therapy tool. With this knowledge, the goal of this research in the end was to develop a mobile game for stroke therapy by mixing the different approaches: (1) A conventional game which emphasize on patients gaming experience (2) but with hidden therapy benefits by applying the requirements for a stroke therapy game.

5. DESIGN ELEMENTS FOR MOTIVATIONAL AND ENGAGING GAME

To design a stroke therapy game that can motivate users, it is necessary to look for references about motivation and how motivation works to trigger someone to do certain actions. Because the purpose of the application is to increase patient's motivation to do therapy, then BJ Fogg's (2009) behavior model for persuasive design is referenced, which can be a guide for designing persuasive technology. Then the relationship between motivation and games and any elements in the game that can be used to increase motivation to continue playing games, namely by making game players feel immersed/engaged in the game, was also discussed. Theories that are referenced to design immersive games are theory by Fullerton (2018), Flow Theory (Jones, 2009) (Fullerton, 2018), and Motivation Model for Game by Przybylski et al (2010).

5.1 BJ Fogg's Behavior Model for Persuasive Design

According to Fogg (2009), there are three main principles of the FBM theory (Fogg's Behavior Model), namely motivation, abilities and triggers. A behavior or action will be carried out if the offender has motivation, adequate ability, and is triggered by effective trigger.

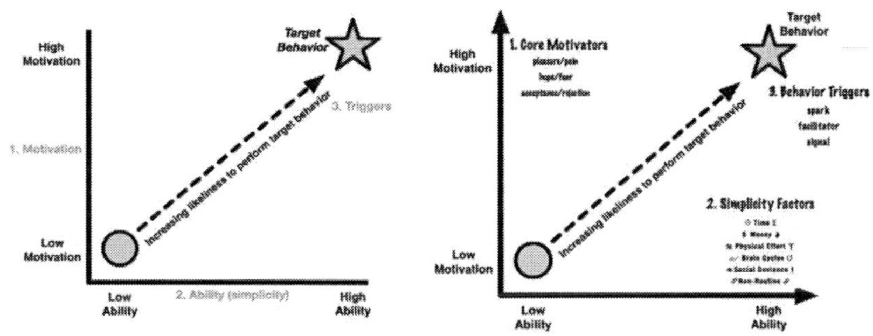

Figure 1. BJ Fogg's Behavior Model for Persuasive Design (Fogg, 2009)

Fogg further described the elements of the three basic factors forming the behavior in Table 1.

Table 1. Elements of Three Basic Factors that forms Behavior (Fogg, 2009)

Factors	Elements
Motivation	Pleasure and Pain Hope and Fair Social Acceptance/Rejection
Ability (Simplicity), the less someone has to invest in this element, the more they are going to do a behavior	Time, Money, Physical Effort, Brain Cycle, Social Defiant, and Non-Routine
Trigger	Spark, Facilitator ,Signal

By considering the characteristics of stroke patients who are targeted by application users and FBM, such as what motivation can be improved by stroke patients, what facilities can be given and what triggers can be used, these factors will be the reference used as the basis for the design of game applications for stroke patients.

5.2 Designing Engaging and Immersive Game by Fullerton (2018)

5.2.1 Dramatic Elements

One way to increase players' immersion in a game is to use dramatic elements. According to Fullerton (2018), the dramatic element of giving context to gameplay, wrapping and combining formal elements of the game so that making moments of playing games becomes a meaningful experience for players. The following are dramatic elements of the game that were referred to in the development of the design for stroke therapy games in this study.

Table 2. Dramatic Elements of a Game (Fullerton, 2018)

Dramatic Elements	
Challenge	Challenge will increase players engagement/involvement in a game by balancing between players' abilities and game challenge.
Premise	Game uses some traditional elements of drama to get players involved with the formal elements of the game. One of the most basic is the premise concept, which places the actions of game players in a setting or metaphor. Without dramatic premise, many games become too abstract for players to be emotionally involved.
Character	Character is an agent in which through its actions a story is told. By identifying with game characters and their goals, the audience internalizes the story and empathizes.

Dramatic elements can be used to trigger a strong emotional reaction from the players. From game design that is inseparable like challenges and gameplay, to complicated integration of the premise, character, etc. Dramatic elements can then be applied in the game in order to make stroke patients immersed in the game as if they were not doing therapy. That's why, in order to design the game premise for stroke patients, it is necessary to consider the premise that will be meaningful to the patient based on the characteristics of the patient.

5.2.2 Flow Theory

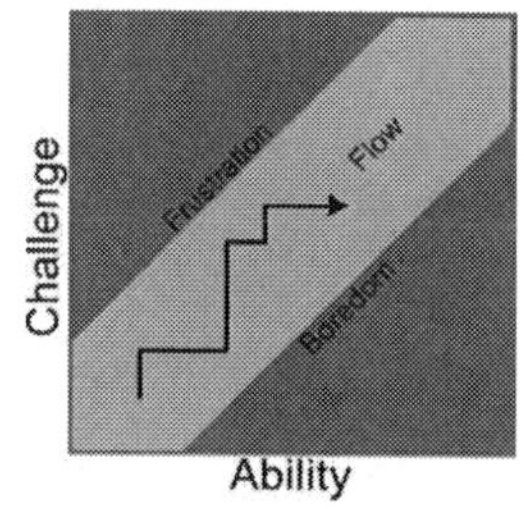

Figure 2. Flow Theory (Fullerton, 2018)

Flow state could also be achieved if there is a balance between challenge and ability (Csikszentmihalyi as quoted by Fullerton, 2018). Jones then describes flow theory, as defined by (Csikszentmihalyi, as quoted from Jones, 1998), a total and total involvement in a particular task. Generally, flow conditions occur when there are no external motivations that affect and occur when people are intrinsically motivated. These are the elements that according to Jones (1998) can create state of flow when playing games.

Table 3. Elements of Flow (Jones, 1998)

Element of flow	Manifestation in a Game
Task that we can complete	The use of levels in a game provides small section that lead to the completion of the entire task.
Ability to concentrate on task	Creation of convincing worlds that draw users in.
Task has clear goals	Survival, collection of points, gathering of objects and artifacts, solving the puzzle
Task has immediate feedback	Find a clue, and you can put it in your bag
Deep but effortless involvement (losing awareness and worry and frustration of everyday)	The creation of environments that are far removed from what we know to be real helps suspend belief systems and take one away from the ordinary
Exercising a sense of control over their action	Mastering the controls of the game, such as mouse movement or keyboard combinations.

Concern for self disappearing during flow, but sense of self is stronger after flow activity.	People can stay up all night to play games. It is the creation of an integration of presentation, problem, and control over the system that promotes this.
Sense of duration of time is altered.	Years can be played out in hours. Battles can be conducted in minutes. People don't feel time flies when playing.

After succeeding in making patients take therapeutic actions with the FJB theory, patients need to be made to continue to carry out these activities. One way is to make stroke patients enter flow conditions or sink into the gaming world so that patients are constantly motivated to keep playing.

5.2.3 Motivation Model for Video Games

Przybylski et al (2010) researched a motivational model for video game engagement based on Self-Determination Theory by Deci & Ryan (as quoted from Przybylski et al), a theory of human motivation that is based on potential social context to provide experiences that satisfy universal human needs. Using the theory, Przybylski et al attempt to understand how video game context satisfy or endanger psychological needs and thus foster or undermine sustained engagement and either positive or negative well-being outcomes of the player. Przybylski et al argues that players are motivated to play games to satisfy their psychological needs specified in SDT. And the needs for gamers can be associated with stroke patient gamer's needs. These needs are as follow:

1) **Competence Need**, is the need for player to fulfill their competence needs that is the feeling that they reach a certain competence. Games fulfill it by having players playing games with rising difficulty as they progressed into the game. If we associate this with stroke patients need, it can be associated with rising difficulty in therapy following patient's improvement.
2) **Autonomy Need**. Games enabling player to make their own choice that can affect the outcome of the game like exploration in RPG Games or sandbox mode in simulation games. This could explain the success of Krakauer's approach for Stroke Therapy games which gives patients freedom of movement instead task based movements.
3) **Relatedness Need**. Social interaction has always been important part of video game, as there are many games employed multiplayer gameplay. The need for multiplayer game was actually expressed by patients from Alankus et al (2010) research.
4) **Mastery of Control**. Players are not immediately able to control the game, they have to learn and master the game mechanic first, and this fulfills players need for mastery of control. This is in conjunction with element of flow in games by Jones (1998) that games enable players to exercise a sense of control over their action.

Therefore, the game will provide motivation for stroke patients to play games if their needs are met, namely the need for competency, autonomy, connectedness and mastery of control, and making a connection from how they progress in the game to how they progress in therapy.

6. ELDERLY & GAMING

Literature on elder players gaming preference were reviewed because most stroke patients are elderly, in order to create games that interest them and suit their skills and capability, which will then motivate them. Although users of digital games generally come from young age groups, there is now an increase in the number of older age group game players. Today's society is more technologically responsive and senior citizens are getting used to technology. In the United States, the population of elderly game players increased from 9% in 1993 to 26% in 2008 (Nep et al, 2009). Research conducted by Hausknecht (2013) also shows that video games have a strong attraction for elderly adults. Several studies have been conducted on the elderly and games, such as the preference of the elderly in games, the motivation to play games, which can be used to identify what elements should be considered in developing games for the elderly.

Unique findings were found in Aison's (2002) study. From his research, he found that Chris Weaver, co-founder of Bethesda Software, created the PC game called "Elder Scrolls". From Aison's personal interview with Weaver, Weaver said that he didn't design games for the elderly, Elder Scroll was designed for players aged 15-30 years. But he was surprised to find players aged 74-75 years, and after interviewing these users,

Weaver found that they were elderly who stayed at home because they could no longer travel often. But by playing games, with the world of games they are free to explore, they can emulate the feeling of traveling in the world. They don't care about the search, for them they just want to get lost in the beauty of the game world. And therefore, for the next Elder Scroll game, "Morrowind", even though elders were not their main target users, they began to be considered in all stages of game creation. He said making games that have elements that can satisfy the older generation can be done.

Games can be a kind of media for 'escape' or 'escapism' for the elderly. For example, participants from Nep et al (2009) reported that some played games to relieve sadness and loneliness after the death of his partner or after learning that one's spouse had dementia.

The most prominent motivation for playing games in addition to fun for parents is the challenge. Research by Nep et al shows that although the elderly become frustrated if they fail to complete their assignments in a game, they quickly motivate themselves and return to playing the game. From the results of a literature study conducted by Hausknecht (2013), it was found that motivation is generally caused by relaxation, opportunities for role play, and challenges especially cognitive stimulation. From one of these studies, from a survey of Baby Boomers by Pearce (as quoted through Hausknecht, 2013) it was found that elderly like games with aspects of the narrative and that provide intellectual challenges.

Most research shows that social factors are one of the most important things to consider in designing games for the elderly. Jisselsteijn (2007) says that many elderly people enjoy games (especially non-digital types) as a means of socializing with others inside and outside their social networks. However, it turns out, Nep et al (2009) study reported that older gamers did not really like playing with multiplayer games, mostly because they did not like the aspect of competition (they did not like to look bad compared to other players). From this, multiplayer games can still be considered but must focus more on cooperation than competition. Research by Nep et al (2009) also shows that elders enjoy teaching games to others, therefore they suggest providing teaching features in games as a way to improve social factors.

Cognitive and physical limitations must be considered in designing games for the elderly. One of the main considerations is when designing user interfaces and game mechanics. The user interface must be clear, easily recognizable, and easy to read by the elderly, for example using larger text or more distinguishable images.

In addition, because the elders are not familiar with technology, this can also make the elderly hesitate to play games. To attract them to play technological games, they must also be designed to suit the abilities of the elderly. Ijsselsteijn (2007) explained that as a result of the elderly being unfamiliar with technology, they became hesitant to use it, therefore they need to be encouraged by giving positive feedback when the user has succeeded in taking an action, which is important to be given on learning success rather than performance. Modifications on the game technology to be more adapted to elderly's capabilities are also worth considering such as adding sensitivity to controllers (Aison, 2002). Providing games with various levels of difficulty in addition to interfaces that can be adapted to the abilities of the elderly also expressed by Nep et al. (2009) and (Gerling et al., 2011). One interesting fact from Nep et al. (2009) is that even though elderly gamers are experienced in the games they play, they don't know much about the rules of the game and most depend on their instincts (heuristic and past experiences). From this it can be concluded that better gameplay has a learning system that is as natural as possible for elderly gamers.

Research has also been conducted on the preferences of old gamers in playing games. Research by Nep et al. (2009) reported that elders mostly played casual games, especially women, while men preferred more challenging games. Research by (Hausknecht, 2013) shows that most elderly game players play casual games, they show preferences for playing games that are familiar to them (such as cards, puzzles, board games), or playing games about activities that are familiar to them (sports, fishing, hunting). Gerling et al. (2011) said because the elderly lack experience in playing games, creating metaphors related to the real world can help to educate the elderly to get to know and play games so that it is easier for the elderly to start playing games. Some older gamers also play games to live out their childhood dreams, for example one participant plays a flight simulator because he wants to be a pilot. Real life graphics and scenarios are preferred by male gamers while female gamers prefer cartoon designs. Research from Nep et al. (2009 and Aison (2002) also show that older people prefer games that have educational value.

From these findings, we can also see that some of the suggestions are almost similar or intersects with the research findings of suggestions to develop game for stroke patients with how it needs to be created to suit the their physical and cognitive ability, and with developing motivating and immersive games, like, providing positive feedback, creating an immersive experience to make the players get in a state of flow and get lost in the game world, creating appropriate challenge with various levels of difficulty, and creating premise that is suitable for them, for example like creating narrative or metaphors related to the real world.

7. CONCLUSION

When accounting to develop games for home based stroke therapy, technology, type of games, therapeutic requirements, game design aspect, and patients' needs, must be accounted. For home based therapy, mobile devices can be used for its commercial, easily obtainable, cheap, has high user base and usage. Secondly, a game for stroke therapy must not always has to be specifically built for therapy, however it can also be a normal game with potential or hidden therapeutic benefits. However, it is still possible to mix both properties by creating a game that emphasize on patients' enjoyment when playing games while still have therapeutic property. In order to do this, first, requirements for therapeutic games must be considered and then elements that make game motivating and immersive, especially for stroke patients, are considered, which are found to actually intersecting with each other.

REFERENCES

Aison, C., Davis, D., Milner, J., & Targum, E. (2008). Appeal and Interest of Video Game Use Among the Elderly. 2002.

Alamri, A., Cha, J., Eid, M., & Saddik, A. E. (2009, May). Evaluating the post-stroke patients progress using an augmented reality rehabilitation system. In Medical Measurements and Applications, 2009. MeMeA 2009. IEEE International Workshop on (pp. 89-94). IEEE.

Alankus, G., Lazar, A., May, M., & Kelleher, C. (2010, April). Towards customizable games for stroke rehabilitation. In Proceedings of the SIGCHI Conference on Human Factors in Computing Systems (pp. 2113-2122). ACM.

Colombo, R., Pisano, F., Mazzone, A., et al. (2007). Design strategies to improve patient motivation during robot- aided rehabilitation. Journal of Neuroengineering and Rehabilitation 4, 3.

Corr, S., & Wilmer, S. (2003). Returning to work after a stroke: an important but neglected area. The British Journal of Occupational Therapy, 66(5), 186-192.

Curtis, J., Ruijs, L., de Vries, M., Winters, R., & Martens, J. B. (2009, April). Rehabilitation of handwriting skills in stroke patients using interactive games: a pilot study. In CHI'09 Extended Abstracts on Human Factors in Computing Systems (pp. 3931-3936). ACM.

Departemen Kesehatan, R. I. (2007). Laporan Nasional Riset Kesehatan Dasar (Riskesdas) 2007. Jakarta: B adan Penelitian dan Pengembangan Kesehatan Depkes RI.

Delbressine, F., Timmermans, A., Beursgens, L., de Jong, M., van Dam, A., Verweij, D., ... & Markopoulos, P. (2012). Motivating arm-hand use for stroke patients by serious games. In 34th Annual International Conference of the IEEE Engineering in Medicine and Biology Society.

eMarketer. (2015). Global Tablet Audience to Total 1 Billion This Year. eMarketer. Retrieved from: http://www.emarketer.com/Article/Global-Tablet-Audience-Total-1-Billion-This-Year/1012451. Access date: December 20th, 2015

eMarketer. (2014). 2 Billion Consumers Worldwide to Get Smart(phones) by 2016. eMarketer. Retrieved From: Consumers-Worldwide-Smartphones-by-2016/1011694#sthash.WXL5Asnv.dpuf http://www.emarketer.com/Article/2-Billion-Consumers-Worldwide-Smartphones-by-2016/1011694. Access date: December 20th, 2015

Flores, E., Tobon, G., Cavallaro, E., Cavallaro, F. I., Perry, J. C., & Keller, T. (2008, December). Improving patient motivation in game development for motor deficit rehabilitation. In Proceedings of the 2008 International Conference on Advances in Computer Entertainment Technology (pp. 381-384). ACM.

Fogg, B. J. (2009, April). A behavior model for persuasive design. In Proceedings of the 4th international Conference on Persuasive Technology (p. 40). ACM.

Fullerton, T. (2018). Game design workshop: a playcentric approach to creating innovative games. AK Peters/CRC Press.

Gerling, K. M., Schulte, F. P., & Masuch, M. (2011, November). Designing and evaluating digital games for frail elderly persons. In Proceedings of the 8th international conference on advances in computer entertainment technology (p. 62). ACM.

Goode, L. (2015, 23 Desember). New 3D Touch apps on iPhone hint at future beyond Peek and Pop. The Verge. Diambil dari: http://www.theverge.com/2015/12/23/10656592/apple-3d-touch-johns-hopkins-medical-games-new-ios-apps, tanggal akses : 11 Januari, 2016.

Goldstein, L. B. (Ed.). (2011). A primer on stroke prevention and treatment: An overview based on AHA/ASA guidelines. John Wiley & Sons.

Hable, R., Pergler, E., and Ram, D. (2013). Prototyping a Tablet Application for the Rehabilitation of Stroke Patients. International Conference on Mobile Business (ICMB 2013). Paper 18.

Harpold, C. L. (2013, November 21st). iOT Session App. OT's with Apps & Technology. Retrieved from: http://otswithapps.com/2013/11/21/iot-session-app/. Access date: January 19th, 2016

Harvey, R. L., Macko, R. F., Stein, J., Winstein, C. J., & Zorowitz, R. D. (2008). Stroke recovery and rehabilitation. Demos Medical Publishing.

Hausknecht, S. N. (2013). Older adult gamers: Patterns of use and opinions on the benefits of digital gameplay (Doctoral dissertation, Education: Faculty of Education).

Ijsselsteijn, W., Nap, H. H., de Kort, Y., & Poels, K. (2007, November). Digital game design for elderly users. In Proceedings of the 2007 conference on Future Play (pp. 17-22). ACM.

Johnson, M. J., Trickey, M., Brauer, E., & Feng, X. (2004, September). TheraDrive: a new stroke therapy concept for home-based, computer-assisted motivating rehabilitation. In Engineering in Medicine and Biology Society, 2004. IEMBS'04. 26th Annual International Conference of the IEEE (Vol. 2, pp. 4844-4847). IEEE.

Jones, M. G. (1998). Creating Electronic Learning Environments: Games, Flow, and the User Interface.

King M, Hijmans JM, Sampson M, Satherley J, Hale L (2012) Home-based stroke rehabilitation using computer gaming. New Zealand Journal of Physiotherapy 40(3): 128-134.

Lange, B., Chang, C. Y., Suma, E., Newman, B., Rizzo, A. S., & Bolas, M. (2011, August). Development and evaluation of low cost game-based balance rehabilitation tool using the Microsoft Kinect sensor. In Engineering in Medicine and Biology Society, EMBC, 2011 Annual International Conference of the IEEE (pp. 1831-1834). IEEE.

Lange, B., Flynn, S., & Rizzo, A. (2013). Initial usability assessment of off-the-shelf video game consoles for clinical game-based motor rehabilitation. Physical Therapy Reviews.

Lella, A., & Lipsman, A. (2015). The US Mobile App Report, comScore, 2014. Retrieved August 1st.

Levesque, C. S., Williams, G. C., Elliot D., Pickering, M. A., Bodenhamer, B., & Finley, P. J. (2007). Validating the theoretical structure of the treatment self-regulation questionnaire (TSRQ) across three different health behaviors. Health Education Research, 21, 691-702

Marin, J. G., Navarro, K. F., & Lawrence, E. (2011, October). Serious games to improve the physical health of the elderly: A categorization scheme. In International Conference on Advances in Human-oriented and Personalized Mechanisms, Technologies, and Services. Barcelona, Spain.

Milward Brown (2014). Adreaction: marketing in a multiscreen world. Retrieved from: http://www.millwardbrown.com/adreaction/2014/report/Millward-Brown_AdReaction-2014_Global.pdf

Nafiah, R. (2015). TINGKAT KEMANDIRIAN PASIEN POST STROKE ISKEMIK DI POLI SYARAF RSUD JOMBANG (Doctoral dissertation, Universitas Pesantren Tinggi Darul Ulum).

Norman, D. A. (1993). Things that Makes Us Smart: Defending Human Attributes in the age of the Machine. Reading, MA: Addison Wesley Publishing Company.

Przybylski, A. K., Rigby, C. S., & Ryan, R. M. (2010). A motivational model of video game engagement. Review of general psychology, 14(2), 154-166.

Ridareneni, Neni. (2014, 2 Februari). Jumlah Penderita Stroke di Indonesia Terus Meningkat. republika.co.id. Diambil dari : http://www.republika.co.id/berita/nasional/jawa-tengah-diy-nasional/14/02/02/n0cz1r-jumlah-penderita-stroke-di-indonesia-terus-meningkat, diakses tanggal : 24 Maret 2015

Russel, K. (2015, November 23). Can Video Games Help Stroke Victims? Retrieved December 30, 2016, from http://www.newyorker.com/magazine/2015/11/23/helping-hand-annals-of-medicine-karen-russell

Selzer, M., Clarke, S., Cohen, L., Duncan, P., and Gage, F. (2006). Textbook of Neural Repair and Rehabilitation: Volume 2, Medical Neurorehabilitation. Cambridge Uni. Press.

Shin, J. H., Ryu, H., & Jang, S. H. (2014). A task-specific interactive game-based virtual reality rehabilitation system for patients with stroke: a usability test and two clinical experiments. Journal of neuroengineering and rehabilitation, 11(1), 32.

Siswanto, Y. (2005). BEBERAPA FAKTOR RISIKO YANG MEMPENGARUHI KEJAIMAN STROKE BERULANG (Studi Kasus di RS Dr. Kariadi Semarang) (Doctoral dissertation, PROGRAM PASCASARJANA UNIVERSITAS DIPONEGORO).

Vandermaesen, Marijke, et al. "ReHoblet—A home-based rehabilitation game on the tablet." e-Health Networking, Applications and Services (Healthcom), 2014 IEEE 16th International Conference on. IEEE, 2014.

VServ. (2015). Smartphone User Persona Report 2015. Retrieved from: http://www.vserv.com/decoding-indonesian-smartphone-user-smartphone-user-persona-report-supr-2015-indonesia/

Yeh, S., Rizzo, A., Zhu, W., et al. (2005). An integrated system: virtual reality, haptics and modern sensing technique (VHS) for post-stroke rehabilitation. Proc. ACM symp. on VR soft. & tech., ACM, 59-62.

IMPROVING GLOBAL NEIGHBORHOOD STRUCTURE MAP DENOISING APPROACH FOR DIGITAL IMAGES

Wasif Shafaet Chowdhury[1], Jia Uddin[2], Hamed Alsufyani[1] and Md. Moinul Hossain[1]
[1]*School of Engineering and Digital Arts, University of Kent, Canterbury, Kent, CT2 7NT*
[2]*Department of Computer Science & Engineering, BRAC University, 66 Mohakhali, Dhaka, Bangladesh*

ABSTRACT

This paper proposes a new noise reduction model for digital images. In the proposed model, the intensity similarity between the center pixel and its neighboring pixels within a certain window for constructing a Global Neighborhood Structure (GNS) using Dominant Neighborhood Structure (DNS) maps of central pixels has been measured. The intensity similarity was calculated by using the Canberra Distance measurement equation; where the conventional GNS map approach used the Euclidean distance principle. To evaluate the performance of the proposed model, several noise attacks were imposed on two public image datasets and experimental results demonstrated that the proposed model outperforms the conventional GNS map based denoising technique by exhibiting higher PSNR and SNR values.

KEYWORDS

Dominant Neighborhood Structure (DNS), Noise Reduction, Canberra Distance Measurement Equation

1. INTRODUCTION

Digital images play a vital role in our daily activities but there is a possibility that the images can get distorted or blurred during the image acquisition process, which is known as noise. These distortion/blurring affects the image pixels, as a result, the original pixel values become inaccurate and escalates the possibility of data loss or can hamper the process of extracting important features from an image. Therefore, noise reduction from digital images is an important factor in the field of image processing (Tin 2011, Chan-yan 2008).

There are several factors that can produce noise in an image such as imperfect instruments, transmission error, compression and etc.(Khellah 2011). These factors result in different types of noises. In this study, five types of noises such as Gaussian Noise, Localvar Noise, Salt and Pepper Noise, Poison Noise and Speckle Noise have been imposed on the tested image datasets. The Gaussian Noise is a randomly generated noise values which affects the image pixels. In a Gaussian Noise added image both the true pixel values and random Gaussian noise added values exists. It distributes the noise values by using the Gaussian probability density function but it is free from the intensity of an image pixel (Hoshyar *et al* 2014, Luisier *et al* 2011). On the other hand, the Localvar Noise is basically a zero-mean Gaussian white noise. The difference lies in the intensity, the Localvar noise is dependent on the pixel intensity of an image (Tin 2011). In addition to that, Salt and Pepper is another type of noise which is the combination of black and white spots in an image. It can occur in an image during the data transmission process because of errors in the image sensors (Hoshyar *et al* 2014). Furthermore, Poison Noise also known as Photon noise is dependent on measurement of light, photon direction and quantized nature of light. Speckle noise is represented on the image by random values which are multiplied by the pixel values of that image. In medical literature, this noise is known as texture (Unser 1995, Rabbani *et al* 2008).

During the last decades, noise reduction has become an important field of research and it is considered as one of the most significant parts of signal processing (Hazavei and Shahdoosti 2017). Various denoising approaches, (known as filters), have been developed and many of them have shown very impressive results. Filters can be divided into Linear and Non-Linear Filters. These filters are usually selected based on the nature and the type of data (Cadena *et al* 2017). Filters like Linear, Median, Gaussian Smoothing and Nonlocal Means are commonly used and well discussed in the literature of (Hazavei and Shahdoosti 2017,

Hoshyar *et al* 2014, Cadena *et al* 2017, Khellah 2014). A brief discussion of some of the popular filters has been presented in this work.

One of the most commonly used filters in image processing is the Linear Filter. The mechanism of this filter is to take an average of the pixels that are situated within a local region. The number of pixels included in the local region is specified by a kernel which can be different in size. It has shown adequate results in case of removing the uniform and Gaussian noise. However, the limitations of this method are blurring and smoothen the edges of an image. In addition, the dominance of the blurring is proportional to the size of the kernel. The bigger the kernel is the predominant the blurring becomes (Hazavei and Shahdoosti 2017, Cadena *et al* 2017).

In the context of noise reduction, median filtering is widely used nonlinear denoising approach, because of the preservation process of edges while removing noise (Hazavei and Shahdoosti 2017). The basic idea of this approach is to replace the center of a window with the median, which is achieved by sorting the pixel values of the window numerically and picking up the center. It is suggested that the window size should be an odd number because it is easier to find the centre value from the sorted numbers. The window slides pixel by pixel through the entire image. It is clear that this procedure is applicable and practical for removing the Speckle and Salt and Pepper noises (Cadena et al 2017, Castro and Donoho 2009, Hsieh *et al* 2013). However, the time complexity is high because of calculating the median of the kernel and process each and every pixel of an image. Additionally, similar to Linear Filter this algorithm blurs the input image even at low densities (Cadena *et al* 2017, Ben 2006, Gonzalez and Woods 2008).

Gaussian Filter is a 2-D convolution operation where each pixel of the image is replaced by a weighted average of its neighbors (Hazavei and Shahdoosti 2017, Mengqi 2011). This filter is similar to the Linear Filter but the kernel is different (Cadena et al 2017). In Gaussian Filter, the convolution operation is based on a Gaussian function which provides an estimation of transformation to be applied at each pixel in an image. The representation of the image is also similar to a collection of discrete values. Therefore, it is essential to produce a discrete approximation to the function before applying the convolution (Pascal 2013). This filtering approach is considered an efficient method but it has some drawbacks such as for noises that are subject to a normal distribution (Wang et al 2014). It is particularly known for blurring and suppressing the noise (Pei *et al* 2007). It also misrepresents the signal, dislocates the edges or vanishes them (Lu and Jain 1989, Clark 1989). As a result, there is a possibility of image distortion or failure to achieve the desired output.

Khellah (2014) reported a nonlocal means filtering approach which produced very impressive outcomes in case of reducing noise from images. This filter is based on an idea that natural and textured images have redundancy and it is not necessary that pixels with similar values should be located in a nearby spatial neighborhood. It uses local neighbourhoods to calculate the similarity of any two given pixels. Additionally, it scans the entire image to calculate the differences between the corresponding neighborhoods for each pixel being processed. Whereas, in windowed nonlocal means filter, the computation is limited within a search window where the processed pixel is at the center (Buades *et al* 2005). The major drawback of this filter is that if noise level increases, the similarity selection also increases. This limitation leads to blurring or strong smoothing. Because, at high noise levels, the averaged intensity values of the pixels in the search window is nearly equal to the restored pixels. The technique proposed by Khellah (2014) addressed the drawback of the windowed nonlocal means filter by using an algorithm that was developed in (Khellah 2011). DNS map was used to determine the most similar pixels surrounding any given pixel within a search window. While filtering a given pixel, the DNS map was applied to exclude any insignificant pixel from the restoration of a given pixel (Khellah 2014). The extracted global image features were then classified using the DNS map (Khellah 2011). Exploiting the high redundancy that exists in texture images in general and specifically inhomogeneous texture images with repetitive patterns are the basis of the DNS map. The DNS map was applied by determining the most similar pixels surrounding any given pixel within a searching window.

This paper presents an improved DNS algorithm for image noise reduction. The improved algorithm has been evaluated by applying different distance measurement principles. The detail implementation of this algorithm has been described and verified through PSNR and SNR. A comparative study has also been carried out to investigate the optimal window sizes and the equation under different datasets and noises. The results obtained from this study have been presented and analysed. The result demonstrates that the proposed algorithm offers the best noise reduction from images in comparison to the conventional DNS algorithm.

2. PROPOSED MODEL

Figure 1 shows the block diagram of the proposed Global Neighborhood Structure (GNS) map using the Dominant Neighborhood Structure (DNS) map. A detail description of the proposed model has been given below.

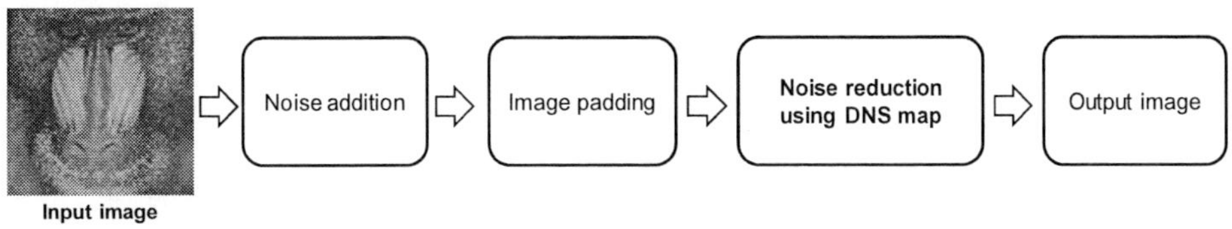

Figure 1. Overview of the proposed noise reduction technique

2.1 Noise Addition

The initial step was to convert the image from RGB to gray scale. The reason was that gray scale based processing techniques provide advantages in case of implementing mathematical equations as the pixel values range between 0 – 255. After the RGB to gray scale conversion, noise has been added on the gray scale image. Figure 2 shows five different noise levels added to the input image. Once the noise addition was completed, the image was padded and the then forwarded to the next step of the algorithm. The proposed DNS algorithm was applied to reduce the noise and their results were analyzed. Similar approach was considered for the rest of the noises.

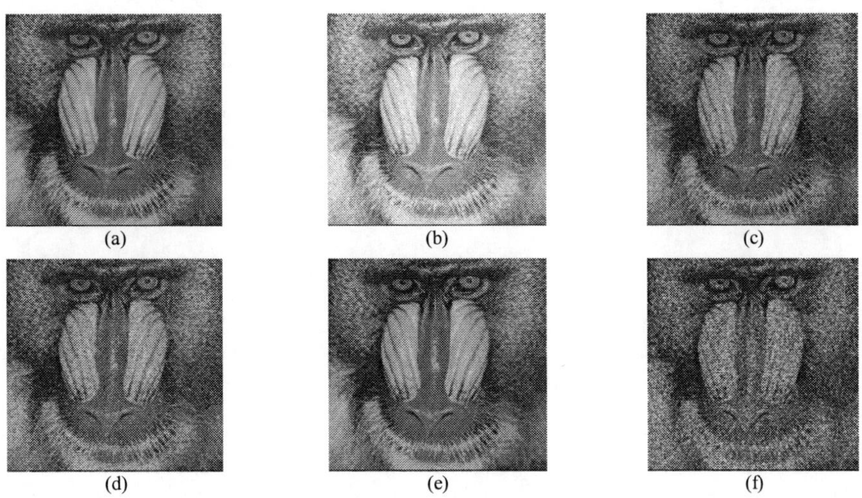

Figure 2. Example of different noise added images: a) Input image, b) Gaussian, c) Salt and Pepper, d) Localvar, e) Poison and f) Speckle

2.2 Image Padding

In this stage, the border of the noise added image was extended. The reason behind extending the border was that at the beginning of the sliding process, the searching window could have ignored the pixels that were situated at the edge of the image in order to provide space to the neighbor window. As a result, the accuracy of the DNS algorithm would have degraded. As depicted in Figure 3, the image was padded by duplicating the pixel values from the upper and lowermost rows and from the left and rightmost columns.

173 170 176 178 177 167
174 164 176 180 174 158
181 159 177 193 177 161
193 171 189 204 190 176
205 198 203 209 209 193
221 214 215 222 226 209

⇨

173 173 170 176 178 177 167 167
173 173 170 176 178 177 167 167
174 174 164 176 180 174 158 158
181 181 159 177 193 177 161 161
193 193 171 189 204 190 176 176
205 205 198 203 209 209 193 193
221 221 214 215 222 226 209 209
221 221 214 215 222 226 209 209

Figure 3. Sample representation of the image padding approach

2.3 Noise Reduction using DNS Map

As described in (Khellah 2014, Uddin *et al* 2014), there are two windows that should be built to construct the DNS map. The first one is the searching window and the second one is the neighborhood window. The searching window slides the entire image and at the same time, the neighborhood window scans the searching window. The sliding process of the searching window starts from the first pixel of the padded image. During the scanning process, the differences of pixel values between the neighborhood and the central pixel window were calculated by using the Canberra equation (6). Here, the result of Canberra replaces the central pixel of the neighborhood window. It is clear that the neighborhood window does not scan the central pixel window while going through the searching window. The reason is the difference in pixel value between these two windows would always be zero. Figure 4 illustrates a graphical representation of the proposed DNS map.

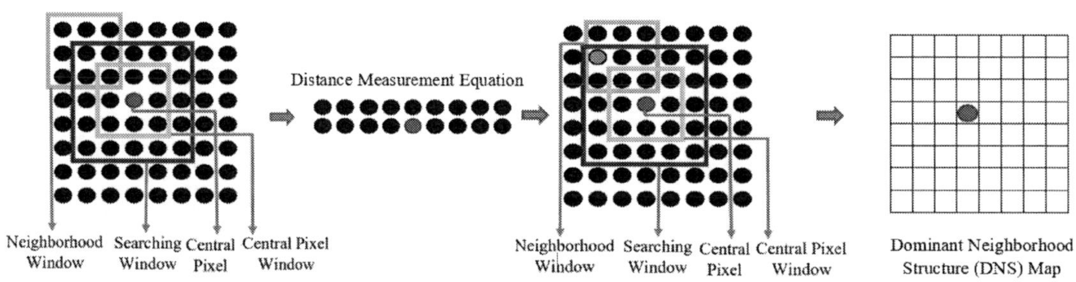

Figure 4. Graphical representation of the DNS map

The size of the searching window, neighborhood window and the gap between the central pixels are the three important factors that can affect the result of the proposed denoising approach (Uddin and Kim 2014). Therefore, the sizes have been calculated by adopting a try and error procedure. The outcome of the try and error process exhibited that the optimal size for the searching and the neighborhood windows were 21x21 and 19x19 respectively. As the size of the neighborhood window was 19x19, the size of the central pixel window was set to 19x19. An analysis of the window size determination has been discussed in Section 3.

Six distance measurement equations were taken under consideration to determine the optimal one. Table 1 shows the list of the selected equations. In these equations *d(x, y)* represents the central pixel of the neighborhood window and x_i represents the pixels within the neighborhood window and y_i represents the pixels located in the central pixel window. According to the experimental results of this study, the Canberra Distance equation provides the best results for the denoising approach. A detail explanation of the outcomes of these distance measurement equations has been presented in Section 3.

Table 1. List of distance measurement equations

Equation Name	Equation	
Euclidean Distance	$d(x,y) = \sqrt{\sum x_i - y_i}$	(1)
Squared Euclidean distance	$d(x,y) = \sum (x_i - y_i)^2$	(2)
Manhattan Distance	$d(x,y) = \sum \lvert (x_i - y_i) \rvert$	(3)
Bary Curtis Distance	$d(x,y) = \frac{\sum \lvert x_i - y_i \rvert}{\sum x_i + y_i}$	(4)
Cosine Correlation Distance	$d(x,y) = \frac{\sum x_i \times y_i}{\sqrt{\sum (x_i)^2 \sum (y_i)^2}}$	(5)
Canberra Distance (Proposed scheme)	$d(x,y) = \frac{\sum \lvert x_i - y_i \rvert}{\sum \lvert x_i + y_i \rvert}$	(6)

2.4 Dataset

In order to analyse the efficiency of the proposed model two public datasets have been used in this study. The first one was the 'Face Recognition ORL Database' (Petitcolas access 2019) and the second dataset is the texture images from (Brodatz 1966). Figure 5 shows some sample texture images that have been used in this study.

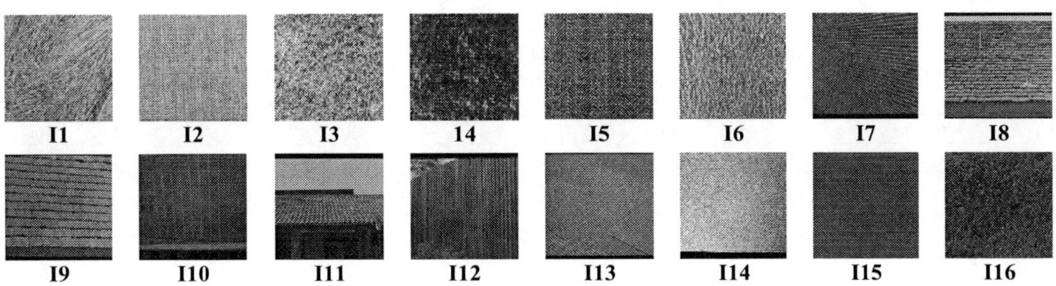

Figure 5. Sample texture images used in this experiment

3. RESULTS AND DISCUSSIONS

The results analysis has been divided as follows. Firstly, while calculating the distance between the pixels within the neighborhood and central pixel window, six distance measurement equations (1) - (6) have been implemented, where the equation (1) is the traditional one. A comparative study has been carried out to investigate the best equation based on higher PSNR and SNR results. Secondly, the try and error procedure has been undertaken to determine the optimal window sizes for both the searching window (SW) and the neighborhood window (NW). Table 2 demonstrates the outcomes of the six distance measurement equations for the try and error approach on Speckle noisy image.

3.1 Determining the Optimal Equation

From Table 2, it can be seen that for the first three equations (Euclidean, Squared Euclidean and Manhattan) the PSNR values fluctuates within the range of 47.05 to 54.39 with respect to the changes in window sizes.

Another noticeable point is that the PSNR results of equation (2) and (3) are similar to the PSNR results of equation (1) for most of the cases. It evident that equations (2) and (3) did not provide any significant changes while measuring the intensity similarity for DNS map. Looking more closely, the PSNR values for the last three principals (Bary Curtis, Canberra and Cosine Correlation), ranges between 49.53 to 62.99, which are significantly higher than the first three equations. Therefore, equation (4), (5) or (6) are the candidate equations, to be the optimal ones for the DNS map. Additionally, the PSNR results that were obtained for the proposed equation (Equation 6) was higher than equations (4) and (5) and the Euclidean equation as well, for all sizes of SW and NW. Moreover, as the window sizes increase the results of Equation (6) also increases and get noticeably higher in comparison with all the other equations. Hence, the Canberra equation (Equation (6)) has been selected as the optimal equation in order to measure the intensity similarity between the center pixel and its neighboring pixels within a certain window for the DNS map based GNS algorithm.

Table 2. PSNR results of distance measurements against different window size

Window Sizes SW x NW	Euclidean	Squared Euclidean	Manhattan	Bary Curtis	Cosine Correlation	Proposed (Canberra)
5x5 & 3x3	54.39	47.05	47.05	56.80	56.89	**57.18**
7x7 & 5x5	49.29	48.78	48.78	54.53	54.63	**55.27**
9x9 & 7x7	48.75	48.75	48.75	52.72	52.80	**53.71**
11x11 & 9x9	49.31	49.31	49.31	52.26	52.34	**53.49**
13x13 & 11x11	48.52	48.52	48.52	53.35	53.44	**55.59**
15x15 & 13x13	48.26	48.26	48.26	54.09	54.19	**56.92**
17x17 & 15x15	47.81	47.81	47.81	55.10	55.21	**59.68**
19x19 & 17x17	48.85	48.85	48.85	52.99	53.08	**57.05**
21x21 & 19x19	**47.83**	**47.83**	**47.83**	**55.07**	**55.18**	**62.99**
23x23 & 21x21	48.50	48.50	48.50	53.36	53.45	**58.95**
25x25 & 23x23	49.05	49.05	49.05	52.75	52.83	**61.75**
27x27 & 25x25	49.55	49.55	49.55	51.79	51.87	**59.27**
29x29 & 27x27	49.56	49.56	49.56	51.87	51.95	**59.47**
31x31 & 29x29	49.88	49.88	49.88	51.60	51.67	**61.22**
33x33 & 31x31	51.84	51.84	51.84	49.63	49.69	**57.69**
35x35 & 33x33	51.58	51.58	51.58	49.53	49.59	**57.22**
37x37 & 35x35	50.64	50.64	50.64	50.65	50.72	**55.82**

3.2 Optimal Window Size Determination

In order to determine the optimal window sizes, a try and error approach has been carried out. Initially, the window sizes of SW & NW were set to SW 5x5 & NW 3x3 and then they were increased gradually by adding two pixels in both the windows. Table 2 demonstrates the gradual increment of the window sizes and represents their corresponding PSNR results. The peak PSNR value of 62.99 was observed for SW 21x21 & NW 19x19. Therefore, these window sizes have been considered as the optimal sizes for the proposed model. Note that, the results presented in Table 2 were obtained from the outcomes of the proposed model on a Speckle Noise added image.

As five types of noises were imposed on the tested dataset images. Therefore, further analysis of the proposed algorithm has been done for the other types of noises. Table 3 demonstrates the results of the traditional equation (Euclidean equation) and the proposed equation (Canberra equation). From the table (Table 3) it is clear that the proposed model of the DNS map exhibits better results in comparison with the traditional algorithm for all types of noises based on PSNR and SNR results.

Table 3. Comparison between proposed and Euclidean equation

	Noise	Gaussian	Salt and Pepper	Localvar	Poisson	Speckle
PSNR	**Euclidean**	48.02	48.81	47.23	48.24	47.83
	Canberra	55.76	54.55	54.16	55.42	62.99
SNR	**Euclidean**	42.65	43.44	42.11	42.80	42.49
	Canberra	50.39	49.18	49.04	49.97	57.65

Further to validate the proposed algorithm, the Canberra (Can) and Euclidean (Euc) were explored for 16 different texture images as shown in Figure 5. The five different noises were applied to the texture images. The optimal window sizes of SW 21x21 & NW 19x19 was used to calculate the PSNR and their results have been presented in Table 4. It is clear that the proposed scheme provides better performance compared to the traditional equation. For example, a significant difference can be seen for the images I3, I4, I5, I6, I7, I9, I10, I11, I12, I13, I14, I15 and I16, and almost 82% improvement was achieved by the proposed model. Hence, it is suggested that the Canberra principal can be used to measure the intensity similarity between the center pixel and its neighboring pixels within a certain window for constructing the DNS map instead of Euclidean equation.

Table 4. A PSNR based comparison between the Euclidean and Canberra equations on texture images

Img	Equ	Gau	S&P	Loc	Poi	Spe	Img	Equ	Gau	S&P	Loc	Poi	Spe
I1	Euc	50.37	49.17	50.20	50.21	50.14	I9	Euc	46.62	46.25	46.93	46.40	46.16
	Can	50.79	51.25	49.90	50.55	50.08		Can	**57.05**	**59.12**	**56.00**	**58.30**	**58.99**
I2	Euc	49.64	49.68	50.11	50.87	50.85	I10	Euc	45.60	45.39	45.28	46.81	47.03
	Can	51.74	51.00	49.73	50.47	49.97		Can	**64.31**	**67.07**	**64.33**	**68.24**	**68.10**
I3	Euc	49.73	50.55	49.91	49.91	50.20	I11	Euc	47.38	47.52	49.92	47.55	47.53
	Can	**53.31**	**52.54**	**53.92**	**52.92**	**52.84**		Can	**54.26**	**61.51**	**50.45**	**61.67**	**63.43**
I4	Euc	47.30	47.54	47.11	47.08	46.98	I12	Euc	48.04	48.03	48.59	47.96	47.51
	Can	**59.41**	**55.83**	**55.43**	**65.95**	**63.74**		Can	**62.14**	**57.72**	**52.74**	**58.68**	**62.67**
I5	Euc	50.82	50.12	52.37	50.27	49.93	I13	Euc	45.63	45.62	46.65	45.52	45.46
	Can	**52.41**	**52.10**	**48.96**	**53.37**	**55.82**		Can	**63.92**	**64.53**	**55.83**	**65.55**	**66.39**
I6	Euc	50.46	50.50	48.24	50.65	50.37	I14	Euc	45.14	45.04	46.01	46.79	47.90
	Can	**53.71**	**52.99**	**57.32**	**52.37**	**53.41**		Can	**67.57**	**56.89**	**57.43**	**54.25**	**58.42**
I7	Euc	45.72	45.35	45.98	47.34	47.20	I15	Euc	50.06	49.56	48.21	49.95	49.92
	Can	**61.21**	**67.15**	**60.09**	**65.34**	**65.62**		Can	**54.58**	**53.78**	**57.74**	**53.35**	**55.20**
I8	Euc	50.50	50.17	50.73	49.91	50.42	I16	Euc	47.92	48.88	48.20	48.84	48.50
	Can	50.71	51.39	49.37	51.66	50.71		Can	**63.58**	**55.79**	**55.40**	**56.24**	**59.15**

4. CONCLUSION

A noise reduction model for the digital image has been developed and implemented by constructing a GNS map based DNS algorithm. Various distance measurement equations and noises were used to verify the model. Their PSNR and SNR values were calculated. Optimal window sizes for the proposed model was also been investigated. The difference between the central window pixels and the neighbourhood window pixels were calculated by using the Canberra distance measurement technique. A comparative study has been carried out to further verify the proposed algorithm. The results obtained from the comparative study demonstrates that the proposed model is capable of reducing the noise ≈82% for texture images in comparison to the conventional DNS algorithm.

REFERENCES

Ben, W., 2006. Fast median and bilateral filtering. *ACM SIGGRAPH 2006 Papers*, pp. 519-526.

Brodatz, P., 1966. Texture: A Photographic Album for Artists and Designers, Dover, New York.

Buades, A. et al, 2005. A non-local algorithm for image denoising. *Proceedings of the International Conference on Computer Vision and Pattern Recognition*, pp. 60–65.

Cadena, L. et al, 2017. Noise reduction techniques for processing of medical images. *Proceedings of the World Congress on Engineering 2017*, London UK, Vol. I, pp. 496-500.

Castro, E. A. and Donoho, D. L., 2009. Does median filtering truly preserve edges better than linear filtering?. *The Annals of Statistics*, pp. 1172-1206.

Chang-yan, C. et al, 2008. Study on methods of noise reduction in a stripped image. *The International Archives of the Photogrammetry, Remote Sensing and Spatial Information Sciences*, China, Vol. XXXVII, pp. 213 – 216.

Clark, J. J., 1989. Authenticating edges produced by zero-crossing algorithms. *IEEE Transactions on Pattern Analysis and Machine Intelligence*, Vol. PAMI-1 1, pp. 43-57.

Gonzalez, R. C. and Woods, R. E., 2008. *Digital Image Processing*. Prentice Hall, Upper Saddle River, New Jersey, USA, ch. 5.

Hazavei, S. M. and Shahdoosti, H. R., 2017. A new method for removing the moire' pattern from images. *CoRR*, Vol. abs/ 1701.09037, pp. 1-6.

Hoshyar, A. N. et al, 2014. Comparing the performance of various filters on skin cancer images. *International Conference on Robot PRIDE,* Vol. 42, pp. 32-37.

Hsieh, M. H. et al, 2013. Fast and efficient median filter for removing 1–99% levels of salt-and-pepper noise in images. *Engineering Applications of Artificial Intelligence*, Vol. 26, pp. 1333-1338.

Khellah, F. M., 2011. Texture classification using dominant neighborhood structure. *IEEE Transactions on Image Processing*, Vol. 20, No. 11, pp. 3270-3279.

Khellah, F. M., 2014. Textured image denoising using dominant neighborhood structure. *Arabian Journal for Science and Engineering*, Vol. 39, No. 5, pp. 3759–3770.

Lu, Y. and Jain, R. C., 1989. Behavior of edges in scale space. *IEEE Transactions on Pattern Analysis and Machine Intelligence*, Vol. PAMI-I 1, pp. 337-356.

Luisier, F. et al, 2011. Image denoising in mixed Poison-Gaussian noise. *IEEE Transaction on Image Processing*, Vol. 20, No. 3, pp. 696-708.

Mengqi, L., 2011. Research on Image De-Noising Enhancement. *Savonia University of Applied Sciences, Bachelor's thesis*.

Petitcolas, F. a. p. (n.d.). Face recognition ORL database. Retrieved April 29, 2019, from https://homepages.cae.wisc.edu/~ece533/images/

Pascal, G., 2013. A Survey of Gaussian Convolution Algorithms: Main Page. (2019). Retrieved from http://dev.ipol.im/~getreuer/code/doc/gaussian_20131215_doc/.

Pei, Y. H. et al, 2007. Generic 2D Gaussian smoothing filter for noisy image processing. *IEEE Region 10 Conference (TENCON)*, pp. 1-4.

Rabbani, H. et al, 2008. Speckle noise reduction of medical ultrasound images in complex wavelet domain using mixture priors. *IEEE Transactions on Biomedical Engineering*, Vol. 55, No. 9, pp. 2152-2160.

Tin, H. H. K., 2011. Removal of noise by median filtering in image processing. *The 6th Parallel and Soft Computing (PSC)*, pp. 1-3.

Uddin, J. and Kim, J. M., 2014. A Reliable Fault Detection and Classification Model of Induction Motors using Texture Features and Multi-class Support Vector Machines. *The 2014 FTRA International Workshop on Advanced Multimedia Computing (AMC - 14) Proceedings*, pp. 1- 6.

Uddin, J. et al, 2014. Accelerating 2D Fault Diagnosis of an Induction Motor using a Graphics Processing Unit. *International Journal of Multimedia and Ubiquitous Engineering*, Vol. 9, No. 7, pp. 1 – 13.

Unser, M., 1995. Texture classification and segmentation using wavelet frames. *IEEE Transactions on Image Processing*, Vol. 4 (11), pp.1549-1560.

Wang, M. et al, 2014. A new image denoising method based on Gaussian filter. *International Conference on Information Science, Electronics and Electrical Engineering (ISEEE)*, Japan, pp. 163-167.

MACHINE LEARNING CONTENT ADAPTIVE FILTERS FOR IMAGE DE-BLURRING

Pradip Mainali
OneSpan, Belgium[1]

ABSTRACT

This paper proposes a novel algorithm to recover blindly a sharp image from its degraded form by pixel pattern classification and filtering by using the deconvolution filters trained for the corresponding pixel pattern. Noise amplification is a well-known phenomenon that arises due to an ill-posed nature of the deconvolution, which is tackled better with the pattern classification, thereby state-of-the-art image de-blurring quality is demonstrated, yet at the very low complexity. For the computational efficiency, the pixel pattern classes are learnt in a multi-layer structure consisting of the coarser and the finer patterns, reducing the pattern search complexity in the dictionary by a factor of 6 without losing any quality. As compared to deep-learning based methods, the proposed approach provides a smaller memory footprint and lightweight implementation. For lightweight and real-time implementation, the paper also validates a simple class matching metric of l_1-norm. The proposed method is suitable for embedded applications such as camera, TV systems, etc.

KEYWORDS

De-blurring, Deconvolution, Restoration

1. INTRODUCTION

Images are degraded with blur and noise during an image formation process for a number of reasons. The degradation process is expressed as:

$$\mathbf{I}_m = \mathbf{I}_a \otimes \mathbf{h} + \eta \tag{1}$$

where $\mathbf{I}_m$ is a measured blurry and noisy version of an actual image $\mathbf{I}_a$, $\mathbf{h}$ is a PSF (Point Spread Function) or blurring kernel and η is the noise of the camera system. To recover an actual image from the measured image, a deconvolution/inverse filtering of the measured image is required with the filter $\mathbf{h}$. The inverse filtering is in general an ill-posed problem in presence of the noise (Bertero, 1998), hence some regularization is required (Bertero, 1998; Hansen, 1998; Vogel, 2002). Regularization is studied extensively to alleviate this problem and the proposed scheme provides regularization with training.

This paper proposes a low-cost algorithm to recover blindly a sharp image from a single blurry image based on the pixel pattern classification as shown in Figure 1. The pixel p_1 shown in Figure 1 is recovered by extracting the pixel feature by using the pixels in the $n \times n$ aperture in the blurry image. Subsequently, the m nearest matching pixel patterns are searched in the dictionary and then the pixel is filtered with the filters trained for the corresponding pixel classes. Finally, the responses from the filters are combined by weighting with their class similarity distances. The noise contribution in the restored image can be reduced, if the deconvolution filters are adapted to the local SNR (signal-to-noise-ratio) of the pixel regions. For example, the low SNR region such as flat pattern p_0 shown in Figure 1 needs less enhancement to avoid noise amplification whereas the higher SNR region such as edge pattern p_1 can be enhanced more.

This paper reduces the computational complexity of the method based on pixel classification proposed in (Mainali, 2015) by using multi-layer pixel structure in the dictionary as shown in the right side of Figure 1, reducing significantly the class search complexity in the dictionary. With the two layer class structure

[1] This work was carried out while the author was working at TPVision, Belgium.

consisting of the $r = 96$ coarse classes and each coarser classes clustered into the $f = 8$ finer classes for the 5×5 aperture, achieves 6 times less complexity as compared to the algorithm proposed in (Mainali, 2015) having the single layer of the 768 pixel classes in the dictionary. Second, matching the pixel class in the dictionary is also a complex operation depending on the similarity metric that is used. In this paper, l_1-norm is selected as the similarity metric as compared to l_2-norm in (Mainali, 2015). The experimental results also show that no noticeable visual loss on the image sharpness was observed. The main advantage of the proposed approach as compared to the deep convolutional neural network based approaches (Schuler, 2013; Xu, 2014; Hradi, 2015; Kupyn, 2017; Nah, 2017) is that the proposed method has smaller memory footprint of the parameters and the better computational efficiency, requiring no multiplier in searching pixel class in the dictionary. Therefore, opening up a lightweight implementation of the algorithm in the FPGA device for a real-time video processing for the application such as TV, camera systems etc. The proposed scheme is mainly suitable to remove the optical blur in the image, while the methods based on the deep convolutional neural network based approaches can be used to remove many different types of artifacts such optical blur, motion blur, etc.

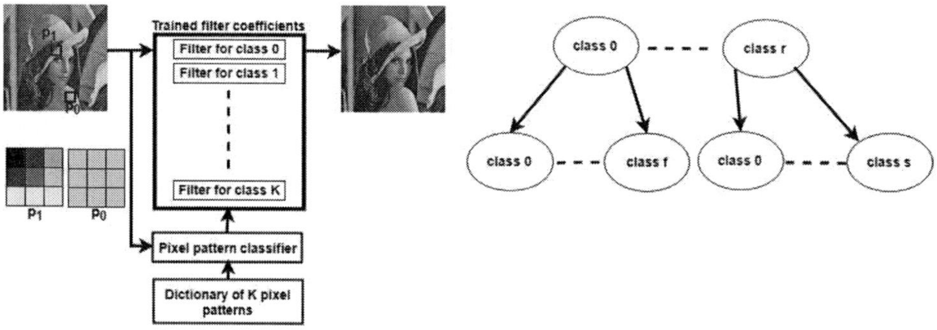

Figure 1. Recovering a sharp image with the pixel pattern classification and the trained filters (left) and multi-layered pixel patterns with the coarser and finer patterns (right)

The paper organization is as follows. Sec. 2 provides a quick survey of the image de-blurring algorithms and comparison with the proposed approach. The proposed image de-blurring algorithm is explained Sec. 3. The experimental results are given in Sec. 4. Sec. 5 concludes the paper.

2. RELATED WORK

In the past, several image de-blurring algorithms are proposed. The methods can be broadly categorized into four different categories. These methods in the first category proposed in (Bilcu, 2008; Horiuchi, 2007; Nam, 2012) inject a high frequency details derived from the original image by filtering it with the derivative filter. Historically, this category of the methods appeared as the first step in developing the deblurring algorithms. These methods are still very widely used in many applications such as in the TV systems, photo-shop, camera etc. due to their low complexity and lightweight implementation for real-time applications. However, the same filter is used to filter every pixel, which enhances only the frequency details that are inside the frequency spectrum of the filter and also leads to the amplification of the noise in the flat region.

The methods in the second category are based on the iterative approach with some priors. Most of the methods in this category also assumes that a PSF is known. The methods based on probabilistic image priors are proposed in (Levin, 2007; Joshi, 2009; Krishnan, 2009; Levin, 2009; Schmidt, 2011; Zoran, 2011; Xu, 2014). They seek a maximum posteriori (MAP) estimate of the clean image, given a blurry (and noisy) version and a PSF. The iterative approach for the deconvolution by using the sparsity constraint in the wavelet transform domain were proposed in (Daubechies, 2004; Figueiredo, 2003; Vonesch, 2008). However, due to an iterative nature of the algorithm, the methods in this category are generally not suitable for the real-time implementations.

The methods in the third category are based on the two step approach. First step is an inverse filtering in the frequency domain followed by the second step of denoising (Foi, 2006; Dabov, 2008; Schuler, 2013). Most of the methods in this category also assumes that a PSF is known. These methods apply a regularized inversion of the blur with a known blur PSF in the Fourier domain. This results in the sharper image, but it also has an effect of the noise amplification. The method in (Schuler, 2013) uses a neural network to clean the noise.

The methods in the fourth category are based on the machine learning approach. The image de-blurring algorithms based on machine learning using a deep convolutional neural network were proposed in (Xu, 2014; Hradi, 2015; Kupyn, 2017; Nah, 2017). The methods based on the pixel pattern classification were proposed in (Kondo, 2002; Ling, 2008), using handcrafted binary coded pixel classes. The main contributions of this paper compared to the previous works based on the binary coded pixel classes is that the proposed method automatically learns the pixel pattern classes from the images in the database instead of hand-crafting them.

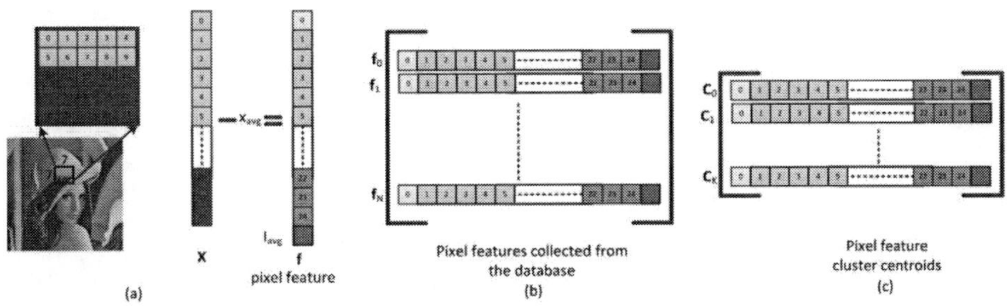

Figure 2. (a) Pixel feature extraction from the aperture of size 5 × 5. (b) Feature matrix of all the pixels in the database. (c) Learnt dictionary of pixel feature vectors (cluster centroids)

3. PROPOSED ALGORITHM

The blur phenomenon during the image acquisition is often modelled by the forward Gaussian convolution (Horiuchi, 2007; Joshi, 2009) and noise with an additive white Gaussian noise. The images in the training database consists of various scene types such as the indoor, outdoor, natural, dark/bright images etc. The degraded images are computed by applying the Gaussian blur and additive white Gaussian noise (AWGN) for the images in the training database. In the training database, there are 8×10^9 number of the pixels for the training. The training is performed for various blur ($\sigma_b = [0.8, 1.1, 1.4, \ldots, 5.0]$) and noise settings ($\sigma_n = [0.0, 1.0, 2.0, \ldots, 5.0]$). The offline learning and on-the-fly filtering stages are explained in Secs. 3.1 and 3.2 respectively.

3.1 Offline Learning

In the offline training, the algorithm learns the dictionary of pixel classes and the corresponding deconvolution filter kernels. The pixel feature consisting of the dynamic information and the average value is extracted by using the pixels within an aperture of size $n \times n$ as shown in Figure 2(a) as in (Mainali 2015), with the dynamic information computed as:

$$\mathbf{f} = \mathbf{X} - x_{avg} \quad (2)$$

where $\mathbf{X}$ and x_{avg} are the pixels within the aperture and the average value of the pixels respectively. This type of pixel feature is suggested because after many experiments it was observed that it works very well for the sharpness enhancement as compared to the other features such as using pixel values, gradients etc. It is also simple to compute. The feature vector captures varying (i.e. ac) and fixed (i.e. dc) part of the pixel. Theoretically, for the sharpness enhancement, the varying part needs to be modified and hence is well suited for the sharpness enhancement.

To learn the dictionary, the clustering algorithm is used to cluster the pixel feature vectors as shown in Figure 2(b). For the computational efficiency, the dictionary of the pixel patterns is learnt in a multi-layer structure consisting of the coarser and finer pixel classes. For our application for TV, the two layered network is used to de-blur image/video. The single layer of pixel classes with $K = 768$ classes for the 5×5 aperture size was used in (Mainali 2015). For the two layer pixel classes, a solution consisting of the 96 coarser pixel classes with each coarse pixel class divided over 8 finer pixel classes was observed to be suitable for the de-blurring application. Once the dictionary is learnt, the next step is training the filters for each pixel pattern for the different blur and noise model parameters. The filters are trained only for the finer pixel pattern classes, as the filtering of a pixel with the coarser filters are not yet explored.

To train the filter h_c for each class c, the least mean square error optimization cost function between the source pixels (x_s) and the degraded pixels (x_d) is used:

$$e_c^2 = \sum_{j=1}^{N_c} \left(x_s - \sum_{i\epsilon(n\times n)} h_c(i) x_d(j,i)\right)^2 \tag{3}$$

where N_c is the total number of the pixels that belongs to the class c. The degraded image is generated as: $I_d = I_s \otimes G + \eta$, where G is the Gaussian blurring kernel of standard deviation σ_b and η is Gaussian noise of standard deviation σ_n and zero mean.

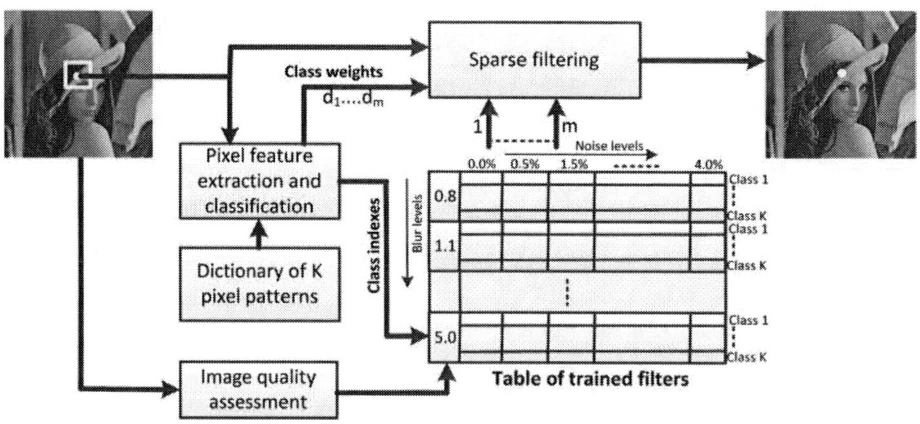

Figure 3. Recovering the image sharpness with the image quality estimation, the pixel pattern classification and the pattern adaptive trained filters

The optimal values of the filter coefficients for the class (c) is estimated by taking the first derivative of e_c^2 and by setting it to zero. After simplification, the following linear equation is solved to estimate the filter coefficients ($\mathbf{h}_c$) for each class (c) (Mainali 2015):

$$\mathbf{A}_c \mathbf{h}_c = \mathbf{b}_c \tag{4}$$

where,

$$\mathbf{A}_c = \sum_{j=1}^{N_c} \mathbf{X}_{d,j} \mathbf{X}_{d,j}^T, \; b_c = \sum_{j=1}^{N_c} x_{s,j} \mathbf{X}_{d,j} \tag{5}$$

where $\mathbf{X}_{d,j}$ is the lexicographically arranged pixels in the aperture as the column vector from the degraded image, $x_{s,j}$ is the jth pixel from the source image and N_c is the total number of pixels belonging to the class c. The least square solution for the filter coefficients ($\mathbf{h}_c$) for the class c is computed by using SVD. The training process is repeated for the different Gaussian blur (σ_b = [0.8, 1.1, 1.4,...5.0]) and noise (σ_n = [0.0, 1.0, 2.0,...5.0]) values. So, in total 6 MB of data including dictionary and trained filters needs to be stored, with the data values stored in the 16-bit precision format.

3.2 On-the-fly Filtering

Figure 3 shows the block diagram for filtering the image. The algorithm consists of image quality assessment, the pixel feature extraction and classification blocks. The image quality assessment block is used to select the correct filter set (i.e. (σ_b, σ_n) used in training) that is most suitable for the input image.

To measure the blur and noise impacts present in the input image, the cumulative histogram of pixel transition delta (i.e. difference between maximum and minimum value within the 3×3 aperture) value is computed over the whole image. The transition delta values at 0.98 and 0.02 in the cumulative histogram are used to select the filter set. The former value (i.e. fluctuations of larger values) indicates the sharpness and the later one indicates the noise (i.e. fluctuations of small values) in an image. Once the global blur and noise impacts present in the input image is measured, the filter set trained with the nearest blur and noise model parameters is selected. The former value indicates that the 98% pixels in the image have transition delta below this value. The higher value indicates the sharper picture whereas the lower value indicates the blurry image. The experiment is also carried out to check how this value is changed due to the blur impact. Figure 4a shows the cumulative histogram of the transition delta values for the images blurred with the Gaussian blur values of $\sigma = 1.0, 2.0, 3.0$. The transition delta values at 0.98 cumulative histogram decreases with the increasing blur values. Figure 4b shows the cumulative histogram of the transition delta values for the image by adding the AWGN for the noise levels of σ: 2.0, 3.0, 5.0. The transition delta values at 0.02 cumulative histogram increases, indicating that the flat and texture regions in the image are corrupted more with the noise. The appropriate setting for the noise model parameters are derived by using the translation table from the measured values. It is also interesting to note that the measurement of the blur impact (i.e. values at 0.98) is less influenced with the addition of noise.

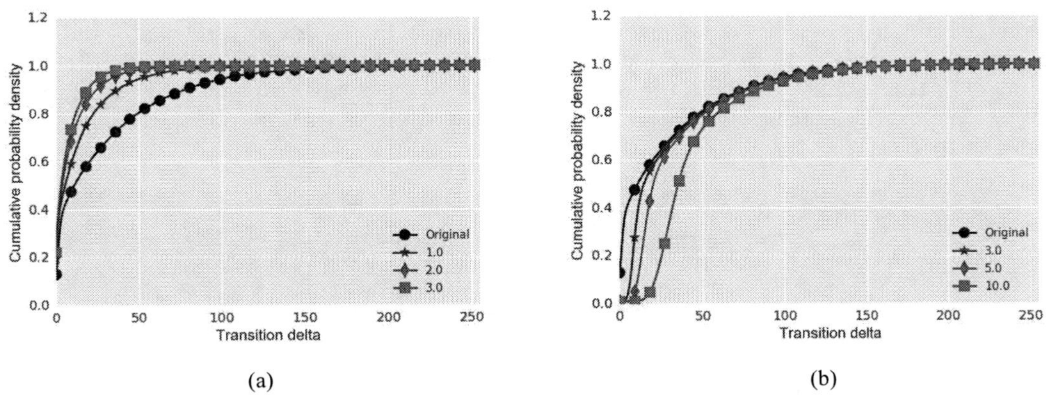

Figure 4. (a) Cumulative histogram for the Gaussian blur 1.0, 2.0 and 3.0. (b) Cumulative histogram for noise of 2.0, 3.0 and 5.0

The pixel feature vector is computed exactly as during the training stage and the nearest matching pixel feature patterns are searched in the dictionary. As the dictionary is organized in the coarser and finer pixel patterns, the m nearest matching coarse pixel classes are searched. In this paper, $m = 4$ is chosen. Once the coarse pixel classes are selected, the class distances are computed with all the finer pixel classes belonging to these m coarser pixel classes. The class distances are normalized. The filters corresponding to the finer pixel classes are used to filter the pixel. The filtering results from these multiple filters are combined by weighting the filtered results with the class similarity distances (d_c).

In this paper, l_1-norm is used as a similarity metric to find the nearest matching coarse pixel classes as compared to l_2-norm in (Mainali, 2015), which requires only the subtract and add operations, hence eliminates the complex and scarce multiplier operations in the FPGA device. Figure 5 shows the visual comparison of the results obtained with l_2-norm and l_1-norm search technique, where no visible loss on the perceived image quality was observed.

To filter image the algorithm only needs to load 768 different pixel classes, hence the method requires a very small footprint while the methods based on deep convolutional neural network has very high memory footprint requiring to load millions of parameters. Also, filtering is needed to perform with only small set of 32 filters, hence requiring a very low computational cost.

Figure 5. The image sharpness restored with (left) l_2 and (right) l_1 techniques

4. EXPERIMENTAL RESULTS

In this section, the experimental results are given to compare the quality of the image sharpness recovered by the state-of-art methods: BM3D (Dabov, 2008), the peaking approach (Rieder, 2001) and the method proposed in (Mainali 2015) using a single layer of pixel classes. The peaking approach is widely used in the TV system, photo-shop etc. and hence included in the comparison. The computational complexity is also compared with the single class layer approach in (Mainali 2015). For the BM3D algorithm, the default settings of the *alpha sharp* = 1.4 and the noise $\sigma = 1.0$ are used. The algorithm proposed in (Mainali, 2015) is configured with $K = 768$ pixel classes for the 5×5 aperture size and $m = 32$. The proposed algorithm is configured with the two layers of the pixel classes consisting of the 96 coarser pixel classes and the 8 finer pixel classes for each coarser pixel class, $m = 4$ and the aperture of size 5×5 is used. The blur meter proposed in (Crete, 2007) is used to measure quantitatively the sharpness of the original and recovered images. The blur measurement results are provided in the range [0, 1], with a lower value indicating the higher sharpness.

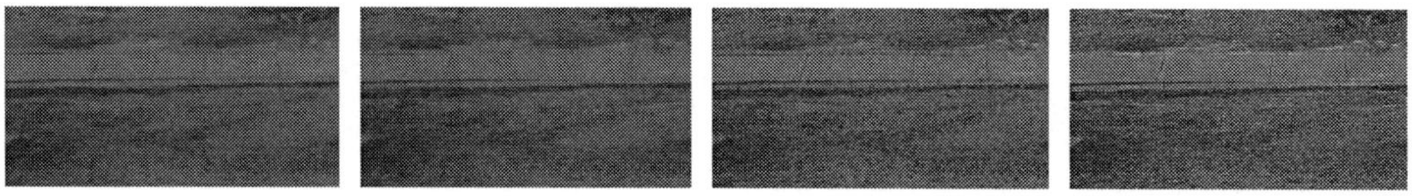

(a) (b) (c) (d)

Figure 6. (a) The original blurry image with blur index 0.36. The image sharpness restored with: (b) peaking with blur index 0.21 (c) BM3D with blur index 0.19 and (d) the proposed method with blur index 0.14

Table 1 gives the mean and the variance of the blur index values of the original and sharper images that were recovered by the proposed algorithm, BM3D, the peaking approach and the method given in (Mainali, 2015), evaluated over 50 different real-life images. These test images were not present in the training database. Table shows that the proposed method achieves the lowest blur index values, indicating the more sharply recovered images.

Figures 6 and 7 show visual comparison for the two different test images, the small extracted portion of the original blurry image and the images after the sharpness restoration by BM3D, the peaking and the proposed algorithm. The blur measurements are 32, 44, 63 and 55 respectively. The noise measurements are: 0, 0, 4, 9 respectively. With these measurements from the quality assessment block, the algorithm selects the filter set of pairs trained with (σ_b, σ_n) of (3.5, 0) and (2.3, 2.0) respectively for these images. The visual results in the figures show that the proposed method generates visually sharper images. It is also observed that the proposed method recovers the finer details more sharply in the grass region in Figure 6 and also without noticeably enhancing the noise. On the other-hand, noise is amplified in the stone region by BM3D. Finally, for the challenging image in Figure 7 consisting of significant amount of noise, the proposed method enhances very little noise whereas the BM3D algorithm enhances the noise much more. For example, in the sky and the red tower of the bridge regions in Figure 7, the noise is enhanced much less by proposed algorithm as compared to the BM3D algorithm.

Table 2 gives the execution time comparison with the method in (Mainali, 2015) for the aperture sizes 3×3 and 5×5 on an Intel Xeon 2.1 GHz CPU with 4GB RAM for the UHD image of the size 3840×2160. The proposed method in this paper achieve 3 and 6 times less complexity respectively as compared to approach in (Mainali, 2015), as the complexity in searching the nearest matching pixel class in the dictionary is reduced significantly. The method proposed in this paper consists of the 32 coarser, the 4 finer classes, the 96 coarser, and the 8 finer pixel classes for the former and the later aperture sizes. The method proposed in (Mainali, 2015) consists of the 128 and 768 pixel classes respectively for these two aperture sizes.

(a) (b) (c) (d)

Figure 7. (a) The original blurry image with blur index 0.18. The image sharpness restored with: (b) peaking with blur index 0.17 (c) BM3D with blur index 0.15 and (d) the proposed algorithm with blur index 0.12

Table 1. Blur index before and after sharpness restoration

Original	Umask	BM3D	Proposed
0.38±0.16	0.22±0.019	0.19±0.020	0.13±0.018

Table 2. Execution time (secs.) for 3840 × 2160 image size

	3 × 3	5 × 5
Proposed algorithm	1.70	6.80
(Mainali, 2015)	5.62	43.84

5. CONCLUSION

The paper proposed an image de-blurring algorithm based on the pixel pattern classification. To sharpen the image with different amount of blur impacts, the algorithm also integrates the image quality assessment block to measure the blur impact. The best matching filter sets from the pool of trained filters is selected for filtering. The mechanism for a low computational cost is also presented, resulting on 6 times less complex algorithm and a simple l_1-norm metric for class matching, without having any loss in the quality. This also paved the way for a lightweight real-time implementation of the algorithm in the resource-limited devices.

REFERENCES

Bertero, M., Boccacci, P., 1998. Introduction to Inverse Problems in Imaging. *CRC Press*.

Bilcu, R., Vehvilainen, M., 2008. Constrained unsharp masking for image enhancement. *In: Image and Signal Processing*, vol. 5099, pp. 10–19.

Crete, F., Dolmiere, T., Ladret, P., Nicolas, M., 2007. The blur effect: perception and estimation with a newno-reference perceptual blur metric. *In: SPIE Conference Series Society of Photo-Optical Instrumentation Engineers*. vol. 6492.

Dabov, K., Foi, A., Katkovnik, V., Egiazarian, K., 2008. Image restoration by sparse 3D transform-domaincollaborative filtering. *In: SPIE Electronic Imaging*.

Daubechies, I., Defrise, M., De Mol, C., 2004. An iterative thresholding algorithm for linear inverse problems with a sparsity constraint. *Comm. Pure Appl. Math.* 57(11), 1413–1457.

Figueiredo, M., Nowak, R., 2003. An em algorithm for wavelet-based image restoration. *IEEE Transactions on Image Processing,* 12(8), 906–916.

Foi, A., Dabov, K., Katkovnik, V., Egiazarian, K., 2006. Shape-adaptive DCT for denoising and imagereconstruction. *In: PROC. SPIE Electronic Imaging.*

Hansen, P.C., 1998. Rank-deficient and Discrete ill-posed Problems: Numerical Aspects of Linear Inversion. *Society for Industrial and Applied Mathematics.*

Horiuchi, T., Watanabe, K., Tominaga, S., 2007. Adaptive filtering for color image sharpening and denoising. In: *International Conference on Image Analysis and Processing Workshops*. pp. 196–201.

Hradi, M., Kotera, J., Zemk, P., roubek, F., 2015. Convolutional neural networks for direct text deblurring. *In: Proceedings of the British Machine Vision Conference (BMVC).*

Joshi, N., Zitnick, C., Szeliski, R., Kriegman, D., 2009. Image deblurring and denoising using color priors. *In: IEEE Conference on Computer Vision and Pattern Recognition*. pp. 1550–1557.

Kondo, T., Kobayashi, N., Takahashi, K., Watanabe, Y., 2002. Picture converting apparatus, picture converting method, learning apparatus, learning method, and record medium, US Patent 6,414,717.

Krishnan, D., Fergus, R., 2009. Fast Image Deconvolution using Hyper-Laplacian Priors. *In: Advances in Neural Information Processing Systems 22*, pp. 1033–1041.

Kupyn, O., Budzan, V., Mykhailych, M., Mishkin, D., Matas, J., 2017. Deblurgan: Blind motion deblurringusing conditional adversarial networks. *ArXiv e-prints.*

Levin, A., Fergus, R., Durand, F., Freeman, W.T., 2007: Deconvolution using natural image priors. *ACM Trans. Graphics* 26(3), pp. 0–2.

Levin, A., Weiss, Y., Durand, F., Freeman, W., 2009. Understanding and evaluating blind deconvolutionalgorithms. *In: IEEE Conference on Computer Vision and Pattern Recognition*. pp. 1964–1971.

Ling, S., Hui, Z., de Haan, G., 2008. An overview and performance evaluation of classification-based leastsquares trained filters. *IEEE Transactions on Image Processing* 17(10), pp. 1772–1782.

Mainali, P., Wittebrood, R., 2015. Machine learning deconvolution filter kernels for image restoration. *In: Proc. SPIE. Electronic Imaging* vol. 9401, pp. 940104–13.

Nah, S., Kim, T.H., Lee, K.M., 2017. Deep multi-scale convolutional neural network for dynamic scenedeblurring. *In: The IEEE Conference on Computer Vision and Pattern Recognition (CVPR).*

Nam, M., Ahuja, N., 2012. Learning human preferences to sharpen images. *In: International Conference onPattern Recognition*. pp. 2173–2176.

Price, J., Gee, T., Tobin, K., 2001. Blur estimation in limited-control environments. *In: IEEE International Conference on Acoustics, Speech, and Signal Processing.* vol. 3, pp. 1669–1672.

Rieder, P., Scheffler, G., 2001. New concepts on denoising and sharpening of video signals. *IEEE Transactions on Consumer Electronics* 47(3), pp. 666–671.

Schmidt, U., Schelten, K., Roth, S., 2011. Bayesian deblurring with integrated noise estimation. *In: IEEE Conference on Computer Vision and Pattern Recognition.* pp. 2625–2632.

Schuler, C.J., Burger, H.C., Harmeling, S., Scholkopf, B., 2013. A machine learning approach for non-blindimage deconvolution. *In: Proceedings of IEEE Conference on Computer Vision and Pattern Recognition*. pp. 1067–1074.

Vogel, C.R., 2002. Computational Methods for Inverse Problems. *Society for Industrial and Applied Mathematics.*

Vonesch, C., Unser, M., 2008. A fast thresholded Landweber algorithm for wavelet-regularized multidimensional deconvolution. *IEEE Transactions on Image Processing* 17(4), pp. 539–549.

Xu, L., Ren, J.S., Liu, C., Jia, J., 2014. Deep convolutional neural network for image deconvolution. *In: Advances in Neural Information Processing Systems 27*, pp. 1790–1798.

Xu, L., Tao, X., Jia, J., 2014. Inverse kernels for fast spatial deconvolution. *In: 13th European Conference on Computer Vision ECCV*. pp. 33–48.

Zoran, D., Weiss, Y., 2011. From learning models of natural image patches to whole image restoration. *In: IEEE International Conference on Computer Vision*. pp. 479–486.

HYBRID SCHEDULING FRAMEWORK FOR PARALLEL VISUALIZATION OF LARGE-SCALE MULTIPHYSICS SIMULATION DATA

Yi Cao, Zeyao Mo, Zhiwei Ai, Huawei Wang and Li Xiao
High Performance Computing Center
Institute of Applied Physics and Computational Mathematics
Beijing, China

ABSTRACT

Following the recent rapid growth in supercomputer performance, many real-world problems in fields such as climate change and weather forecasting, nuclear energy, and electromagnetic environments can be solved via multiphysics simulation. However, current multifield visualization has difficulty handling multiphysics parallel simulation data. First, it is difficult to correctly visualize overlapping multifield data with semitransparent properties because of the complex distribution of partitioned data domains across multicore processors. Second, the interactive visualization performance of large-scale multifield data in serial processing mode on a personal computer is often slow because multiphysics simulations can produce large-scale data sets, i.e., of the order of gigabytes to terabytes. This paper introduces a hybrid scheduling framework for parallel visualization of computational multifield data, which is used to overcome problems both in correct visual representation and in efficient visualization of large-scale computational multifield data. The proposed framework supports scalable in situ visualization of 8.5 billion mesh cells on the 10 k cores of China's TianHe-2 supercomputer, which could help domain scientists understand multiphysics phenomena more clearly and with greater accuracy.

KEYWORDS

Multiphysics, Multifield Visualization, Parallel Visualization, In Situ Visualization

1. INTRODUCTION

In real-world applications, simulation of large numbers of complex physical phenomena that are usually composed of various tightly coupled physical processes is known as multiphysics simulation. Multiphysics simulation can reveal new physical phenomena that cannot be elucidated via single physics simulation in the fields of science and engineering. Following the recent rapid growth of supercomputer performance, many multimaterial, multiscale, and multidiscipline real-world problems can now be overcome using multiphysics simulation. The demand for visualization of coupled multiphysics fields has emerged in several important application domains, e.g., climate change, weather forecasting, electromagnetic (EM) environments, and nuclear energy. The data sets output by such applications usually contain physical multifield data such as scalar fields, vector fields, or tensor fields that describe multiphysics processes. However, most existing research in the visualization community is limited to single-field visualization problems. Multifield visualization currently faces two considerable challenges. First, it is difficult to correctly visualize overlapping multifield data with semitransparent properties because of the complex distribution of partitioned data domains across multicore processors. Second, the interactive visualization performance of large-scale multifield data in serial processing mode on a personal computer is slow.

To help domain scientists understand accurately and efficiently the complex phenomena behind multifield data, we present a scalable parallel visualization framework for large-scale computational multifield data. The main contributions of this paper comprise the following:

- A multiplex visual-channels-based visualization strategy to encode multifield data based on a proper combination of visual channels that could enable scientists to correctly decode phenomena from the resultant images.

- A hybrid scheduling framework for parallel visualization that improves the efficiency of large-scale multifield visualization, by taking advantage of data locality within multiple visual channels.

This parallel visualization framework improves the interactive visual analysis of computational multifield data in fields such as fusion energy and EM environments, supporting scalable in situ visualization of 8.5 billion mesh cells under the 10 k cores of China's TianHe-2 supercomputer. This framework can satisfy the larges-scale visualization needs of typical multiphysics simulation applications.

2. RELATED WORK

In the field of science and engineering computing, multiphysical simulation is involved in many complex applications (Lethbridge, 2015), e.g., fusion and fission energy, EM environments, global climate change, and weather forecasting. Most of these typical applications still use traditional single-field visualization methods to support multifield data analysis because of the limitations of multifield visualization. Ensemble visualization (Phadke et al., 2012) supports exploration and comparison of a collection of single-field data produced by simulations for the same physical phenomenon with different initial conditions or parameters. Furthermore, constrained by the interactive performance of large-scale data analysis, domain-driven applications rely primarily on 2D cross-section based visualization to reveal spatial trends in 3D space.

Volume rendering is one of the most difficult methods to implement in multifield visualization. Multifield data require a stage of visual fusion within the visualization pipeline. Traditional rendering methods only support visual fusion between volume data and opaque geometric data (Kreeger et al., 1999; Insley et al., 2011). Jacq et al. (1997) mapped the attributes of multifield data into color space and implemented fusion at the color level. However, the new color generated by color fusion tends to confuse the visualized results. Translucent fusion based on the ray-accumulation-level method can represent more accurately the depth relationship (Cai et al., 1999), but it relies on visually accurate sorting of all the objects within the scene.

Existing sorting methods have certain limitations in terms of both fidelity and efficiency. (1) Z-buffering (Eberly, 2006) does not support sorting between translucent objects. (2) The painter algorithm (Porter et al., 1984) cannot handle the sort of intersecting objects with ambiguity. (3) Backface culling (Eberly, 2006) cannot be used to sort concave objects. (4) Depth peeling involves high computational complexity of the algorithm and relies on hardware acceleration. 5) Mesh subdivision relies on a large number of newly generated convex mesh cells for overlapping mesh regions, which makes it unsuitable for large-scale multifield data visualization. Considering the fidelity and efficiency of visualization, a new parallel visualization framework is required for multiphysics simulation data that can maintain the original mesh data generated by the multiphysics simulation.

3. COMPLEX MESH SYSTEMS IN MULTIPHYSICS SIMULATION

Popular parallel visualization system for scientific data considers only simple types of mesh systems, e.g., convex meshes or domains, in which each domain consists of one or more mesh cells. However, mesh data of multiphysics simulations are more complicated. Some typical mesh data characteristics of multiphysics simulations are listed below.

3.1 Irregular and Adaptive Mesh System

Computational problem solving for real-world applications often involves complex boundary conditions of physical models. Therefore, the numerical solver of an application often uses a complex mesh system with specific characteristics (e.g., irregular and adaptive meshes) for improved adaptation to complex boundary problems. Often, these types of mesh system present complex domain features such as concavities and holes.

3.2 Domain Decomposition

Domain decomposition is also often used to solve boundary value problems in numerical partial differential equations. This method can decompose a complex boundary value problem into a boundary value problem of a smaller subdomain, which is solvable using adjacent subregions. As problem solving for such subdomains is reasonably independent, it is highly suitable for parallel computing. However, the region shapes of the decomposed domain might become more complex. For example, an original convex domain could be decomposed to several concave subdomains.

3.3 Load Balancing

Applications in the field of parallel computing often use static or dynamic load balancing to achieve efficient large-scale numerical simulation. However, load balancing can change the connectivity of the original problem domain. For example, if a parallel process is newly allocated mesh data from another process during the load-balancing strategy, both the newly allocated and the original mesh data on this parallel process might constitute a new complex domain with concave, disconnected, or non-manifold features. Figure 1 shows the load distribution of a multiphysics simulation in the field of laser plasma interaction (Ren et al., 2012). Mesh cells with the same color are assigned to the same processor core. It can be seen that many domains distributed on same processor core have concave or even disconnected features.

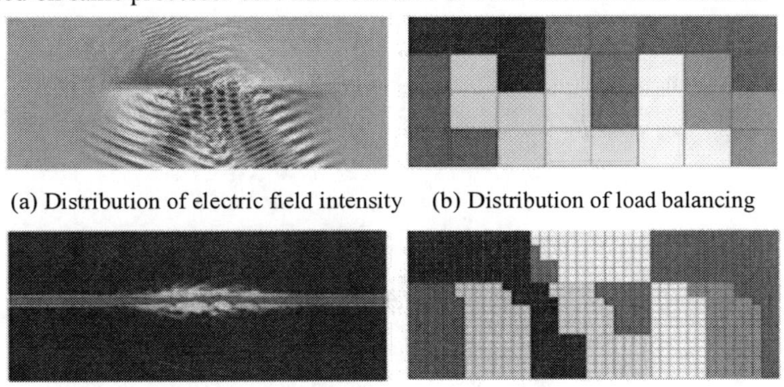

(a) Distribution of electric field intensity (b) Distribution of load balancing

(c) Distribution of particle density (d) Distribution of load balancing

Figure 1. Complex distribution of Mesh Data in Laser Plasma Interaction Simulation

4. HYBRID SCHEDULING FRAMEWORK FOR PARALLEL VISUALIZATION

4.1 Multiplex Visual Channels Based Multifield Visualization

For visual representation of computational multifield data, we introduced multiplex visual channels (Bertin, 1983). Taking advantage of the multichannel characteristics of human vision system (HVS, 2019), we consider multifield visualization as a coding process. By properly encoding multifield data through a combination of multiple visual channels, domain experts could correctly decode phenomena from resultant images. The visual channels defined in the proposed framework are divided into two types: geometric and optical. Figure 2 represents multifield data containing four different physics fields and the operations that act between them. The geometric channels, which provide a means for distinguishing visual objects based on geometric properties, are designed for dealing only with opaque geometry. The optical channels provide a means for distinguishing visual objects based on optical effects. Different operation of visual fusion is defined in different channels, which can be used to separate opaque and transparent objects during visualization. For example, the rendering of opaque objects in geometric channels only needs a simple depth comparison test, whereas the rendering of translucent objects in the optical channels uses the over operator introduced in the painter's algorithm.

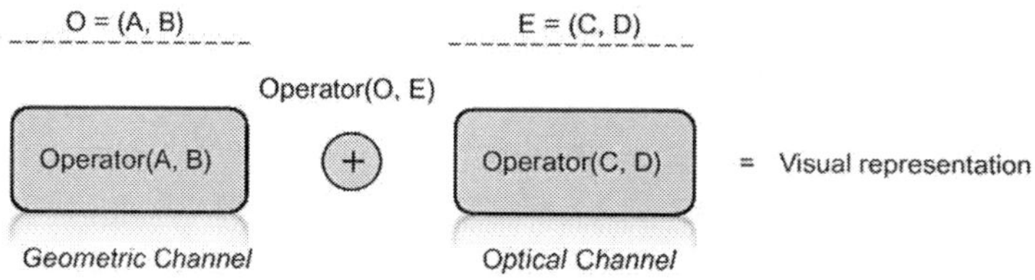

Figure 2. Multiplex Visual Channels for Multifield Visualization

4.2 General Parallel Rendering

A parallel visualization pipeline usually employs a five-phase process: data partitioning, data distribution, rendering, image composition, and display. The domain decomposition strategy of the numerical simulation determines how the global data are divided and distributed. Although visualization can regenerate the partitioned data that are more suitable for visualization, it is not feasible for large-scale simulation applications. Therefore, the parallel visualization pipeline discussed in this paper does not consider changing the original data partitioning.

For general parallel rendering (Molnar et al., 1994), the rendering is considered a sort problem based on screen space. Mainstream visualization systems often use sort-last rendering to achieve efficient visualization. Because the sort object of sort-last rendering is pixel-level data, it can only provide correct rendering when each domain distributed in the processor cores behaves as a convex set. The sort objects of sort-middle rendering are the primitives transformed from the physical space into the screen space. Therefore, correct sorting of primitives can be achieved in the form of sampling points converted in the 3D screen space. However, global sampling and communication within sort-middle rendering, whether for opaque or semitransparent objects, can seriously affect parallel rendering performance.

Considering the fidelity and efficiency of multifield visualization, the proposed framework utilizes a hybrid sort-last and sort-middle parallel rendering scheme based on multiple visual channels. The framework introduced in this paper is shown in Figure 3, in which G represents the geometric processing and F represents the rasterization process. This scheme can separate opaque and transparent objects within the visualization pipeline, and then the most suitable parallel rendering method is selected according to the operation feature of visual fusion for each channel. Thus, accurate and scalable visualization of multifield data can be achieved.

4.3 Hybrid Scheduling for Parallel Rendering

The hybrid scheduling scheme can be represented as a two-way hybrid parallel rendering algorithm. The first way is the parallel rendering pipeline for the geometric channels that uses sort-last rendering, and the output pixel is used as part of the input data for the second way. According to the predefined conditions above, only opaque geometric objects that exhibit strong data locality for parallel rendering are processed in the geometric channels. Therefore, parallel rendering in the first way does not involve a sorting problem and it is independent of the complex mesh data characteristics of multiphysics simulations. Thus, the parallel rendering process in this way does not require data communication until the image is synthesized.

The second way is the parallel rendering pipeline in the optical channel. It adopts sort-middle rendering, in which the final subimage is generated locally in a processor core by communicating the sampling data of local mesh cells with each of the other processor cores. When the processor core completes data communication and performs local rendering, the original mesh cells will have been transformed into a series of sampling points in 3D screen space. At this point, the sorting problem between the subdomains in the original physical space is converted to a sorting problem between the sampling points in the 3D screen space. The sorting of the sampling points considers only the depth comparison test and it is also independent of the complex mesh data characteristics; therefore, there will be no ambiguity error regarding the sorting of scene objects. Thus, it can solve the parallel translucent rendering problem of complex domains in multiphysics simulations.

The two-way hybrid parallel rendering is performed during the ray-accumulation level of volume rendering within the optical channels. Since both the geometric and the optical channels can obtain linearized depth information in the rendered scene, the visual fusion between multiplex visual channels can be performed correctly. This hybrid scheduling scheme not only improves parallel visualization efficiency by taking advantage of data locality in the geometric channels, but it also provides accurate visualization results for the complex mesh data of multiphysics simulations. The hybrid parallel rendering introduced in this paper takes place in the uniform 3D sampling space; therefore, it can be used not only for CPU based rendering but also for GPU based rendering to meet the interactive analysis needs of different domain users.

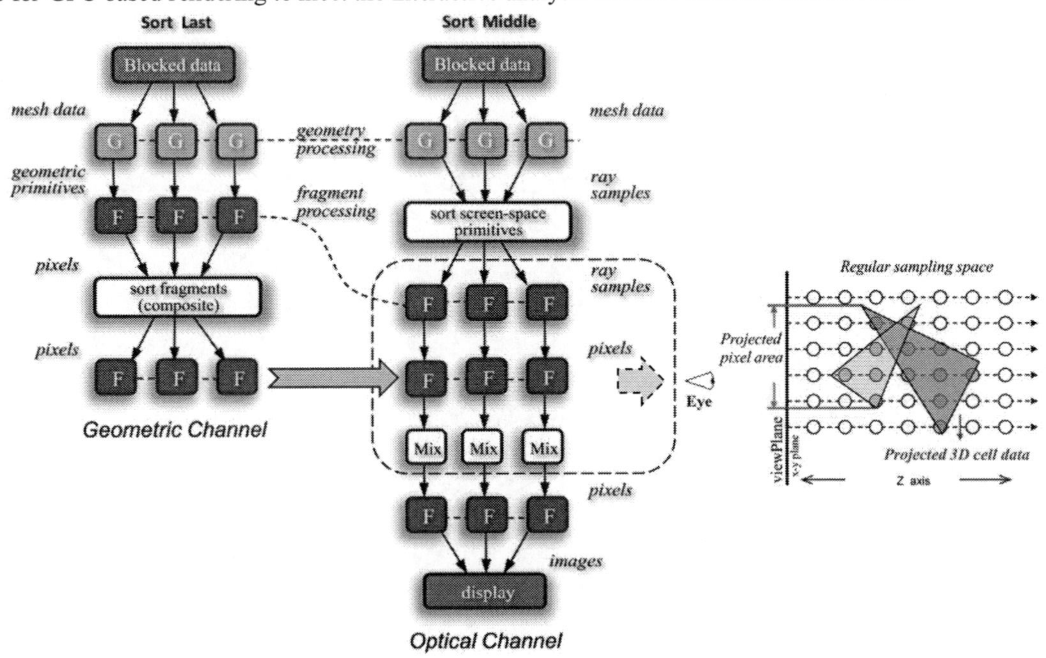

Figure 3. Hybrid scheduling for Parallel Rendering

5. RESULTS AND DISCUSSION

In this section, we discuss the application results of the proposed parallel visualization framework in several typical multiphysics simulation fields.

5.1 Inertial Confinement Fusion

Inertial confinement fusion (ICF) is controlled nuclear fusion that can provide a clean and sustainable energy supply for humans. This process involves cross-coupling relations among multiple physical processes. For example, one of the core scientific problems of ICF is laser-plasma instability or, more specifically, the mechanisms causing the instability and how best to control them. The cause of the instability is interaction between the laser beam and the plasma, which is affected by the coupling of multiple physical processes such as stimulated Raman scattering, stimulated Brillouin scattering, and the filament.

Currently, ICF radiation hydrodynamics 3D applications, based on the JASMIN parallel programming framework (Mo et al., 2010), can generate time-varying data sets of the scale of terabytes through fine physical modeling and simulation of billions of mesh cells. Without a method for multifield visualization that is intuitive and efficient for interactive data analysis, it will be difficult for ICF scientists to analyze and recognize the potential physical phenomena of interface instability. To visually analyze such multiphysics phenomena, traditional visualization (Figure 4c) uses a single-field geometric rendering method to represent the instability interface of the target region. However, because opaque geometry rendering can cause spatial structure occlusion, it is also necessary to use isovolumetric extraction to derive important information regarding the material interface. Nevertheless, it remains difficult to reflect fully the feature-rich trend of fluid interface in the original multiphysical field.

Compared with the results of traditional visualization, the multiple-CPU based multifield visualization supported by our framework could provide a more intuitive and clear representation of the interface instability for ICF domain scientists on 128 CPU cores. As can be seen in Figure 4a, pseudocolor-based cross-section rendering is adopted in the geometric channels to represent the instability distribution in the axial center of the physical field. The volume rendering method is used in the optical channels to represent the 3D distribution of interface instability. Our multifield visualization framework could help ICF experts achieve rapid comparison of ensemble simulation results to deepen their understanding of hydrodynamic instability issues.

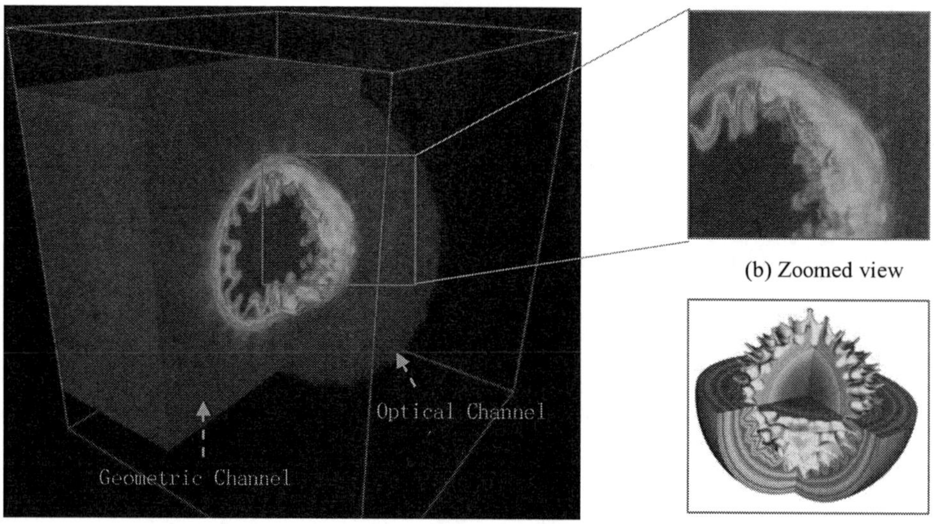

(b) Zoomed view

(a)Multiplex multifield visualization result

(c) Traditional visualization

Figure 4. Multiple-CPU based multifield visualization of fluid instability in ICF

5.2 Electromagnetic Environment

The EM environment refers to the overlapping of multiple EM signals distributed in the airspace, time domain, frequency domain, and energy domain, which has certain influence on both equipment and personnel. Computational EM modeling is a typical multiphysical techniques often used in the simulation of real-world EM applications, e.g., EM pulse radiation and scattering with irregular geometric structures.

Applications in the EM environment can be divided into three different scales of simulation: the device level, platform level, and regional level. Platform-level simulation is used mainly for multiscale electrical targets such as aircraft and ships. Regional-level simulation is used for regional scenes on the scale of square kilometers, and device-level simulation is used for components and devices on the meter–millimeter scale. Currently, simulations of platform- and regional-scale applications based on JASMIN can achieve the fine physical modeling and simulation of billions to tens of billions of mesh cells. EM experts need intuitive visualization methods to support the analysis of the very large-scale multifield data sets.

For the interactive analysis requirements of device-level EM applications, we adopt GPU-based multifield visualization using the multifield visualization framework proposed in this paper, and we realize real-time interactive visual analysis of high-power microwave simulation data using an NVIDIA k6000 graphics card. Figure 5 shows the multifield visualization results of tens of millions of particles, the electric field intensity and complex device models that satisfy the EM analysis demand of a device-level application.

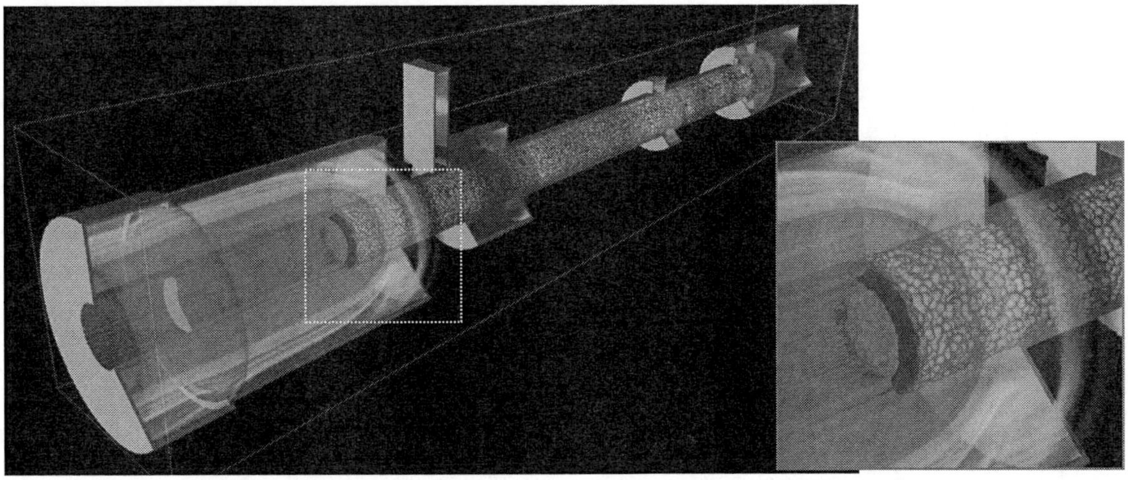

Figure 5. Hardware accelerated multifield visualization of device-level EM application

5.3 Large-Scale EM Simulation Application

An in situ visualization method (Cao et al., 2017) has also been employed for the ultra-scale simulation data of EM radiation shielding for an unmanned aerial vehicle with 8.5 billion mesh cells. This simulation used 8192 CPU cores of China's TianHe-2 supercomputer with a total simulation comprising 15,000 time steps and 187 time steps for the in situ visualization. The total time of the simulation and visualization was close to 120 min. In terms of visualization, the in situ visualization of this example adopted the multifield visualization method presented in this paper. It completed the multifield visualization of three physical fields, including the aircraft model, cross-section surface of the 3D electric field, and energy distribution of the 3D electric field. The image resolution reached 1024 × 1024 pixels. The multifield visualization results of this application are shown in Figure 6. In this figure, geometric rendering of the model of the unmanned aerial vehicle and cross-sectional surface rendering of the energy distribution of the electric field was adopted in the geometric channels, and volume rendering of the energy distribution of the electric field was adopted in the optical channels. The multifield visualization framework proposed in this paper clearly reveals the wavefront distribution in the physical field, which would help accelerate the understanding of EM experts regarding EM mechanisms such as radiation and scattering.

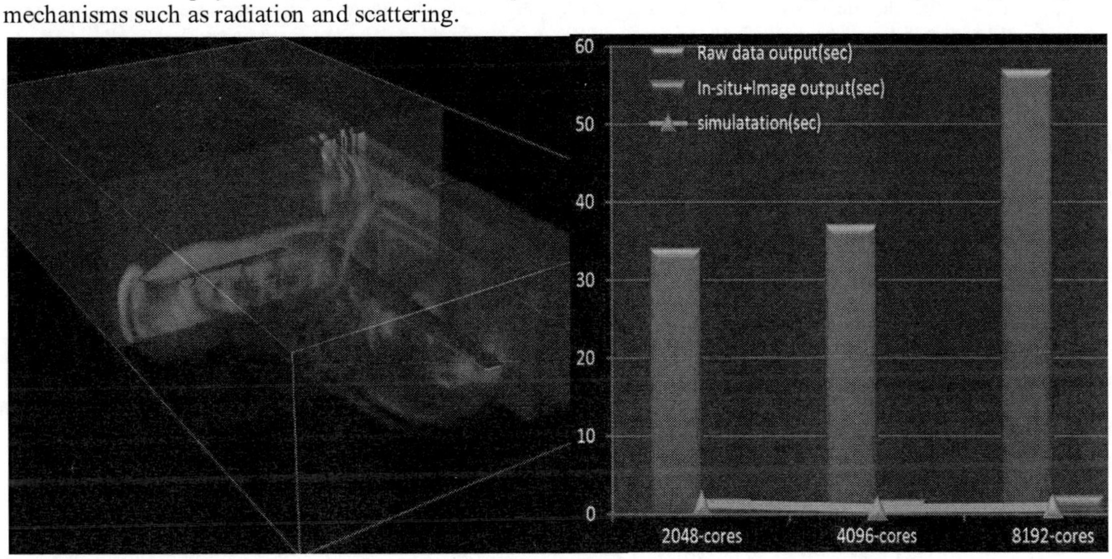

Figure 6. In situ visualization result (left) and scalable performance measurement (right) of the simulation of EM radiation shielding for an unmanned aerial vehicle on the Tianhe-2 supercomputer

In terms of in situ visualization performance, it required 56 s per time step of the EM simulation to output the raw data to disk in the traditional off-line data analysis mode. Conversely, in situ visualization and image output only required 1.8 s per time step. Therefore, it can be seen that the efficiency of data analysis can be increased by at least 25 times by in situ visualization, demonstrating the scalability of our proposed hybrid scheduling scheme for parallel visualization of large-scale multiphysics simulations. The detailed test results of this large-scale simulation are presented in the right-hand panel of Figure 6.

6. CONCLUSIONS

In this paper, we proposed a hybrid scheduling framework for parallel visualization of computational multifield data, which can overcome the two fundamental problems of multifield visualization. A multiplex visual-channels-based multifield visualization scheme was introduced, which was used to solve the visual representation problem of complex multiphysics phenomena. A hybrid scheduling framework for parallel rendering was also presented, which was used for scalable visualization of large-scale multifield data. The framework has been applied in typical applications, e.g., fusion energy and EM environments. Compared with the traditional method, the visualization images obtained using our proposed framework are considered more intuitive and of higher fidelity. Our proposed parallel visualization scheme is scalable because it preserves the original mesh partitioning, making it suitable for applications involving large-scale multiphysics simulation and data analysis.

ACKNOWLEDGEMENT

This work was supported by the National Key R&D Program of China under grant NO.2017YFB0202203, and the Defense Industrial Technology Development Program of China (Grant No. C1520110002).

REFERENCES

Bertin J.,1983. *Semiology of graphics: diagrams, networks, maps*. University of Wisconsin Press, London.

Cai W. et al, 1999. Data intermixing and multi-volume rendering. *Computer Graphics Forum*, 18(3):359-368.

Cao Y. et al, 2017. In situ visualization infrastructure for large scale simulations with structured meshes. *International Conferences Computer Graphics, Visualization, Computer Vision and Image Processing*. IADIS Press, Portugal, Lisbon, pp.139-146.

Eberly D.H., 2006. *3D Game Engine Design: A Practical Approach to Real-Time Computer Graphics*, pp. 69. Morgan Kaufmann Publishers, United States.

HVS model, 2019. https://en.wikipedia.org/wiki/Human_visual_system_model

Insley J.A. et al, 2011. Viusalizing Multiscale, Multiphysics Simulation Data:Brain Blood Flow. *IEEE symposium on Large-Scale Data Analysis and Visualization*, pp. 3-7.

Jacq J. et al, 1997. A Direct Multi-Volume Rendering Method Aiming at Comparisons of 3-D Images and Models, *IEEE Transactions on Information technology in Biomedicine*, Vol.1, pp. 30-43.

Kreeger K.A. et al, 1999. Mixing translucent polygons with volumes. *Proceedings of IEEE Visualization*, pp. 191-198.

Lethbridge P., 2005. *Multiphysics Analysis*. The Industrial Physicist, udson, Ohio.

Molnar S. et al, 1994. A Sorting Classification of Parallel Rendering. *IEEE Computer Graphics and Applications*, 14(4), pp. 23–32.

Mo Z.Y. et al, 2010. JASMIN: A parallel software infrastructure for scientific computing. *Frontiers of Computer Science in China*, 4(4):480-488.

Phadke M.N. et al, 2012. Exploring Ensemble Visualization. *Proceedings of SPIE*. Vol. 8294, pp.1–12.

Porter T. et al, 1984. Compositing digital images. *SIGGRAPH'84: Proceedings of the 11th annual conference on Computer graphics and interactive techniques*. ACM Press, New York, NY, USA, pp. 253–259.

Ren J. et al, 2012. Composition Computation of Radiation Hydrodynamics and Particle Transport Based on JASMIN. *Chinese Journal of Computational Physics*, 29(2): 205-212.

IN SITU VISUALIZATION FOR LASER PLASMA INTERACTION SIMULATIONS

Zhiwei Ai, Yi Cao, Huawei Wang and Li Xiao
Institute of Applied Physics and Computational Mathematics, Beijing 100094, China
CAEP Software Center for High Performance Numerical Simulation, Beijing 100088, China

ABSTRACT

In situ visualization is important to meet the needs of scientific visualization for exascale computing in diverse areas of science and engineering. Knowledge discovery from such simulations remains challenging and it is becoming increasingly urgent as the trend toward ultrascale computing with millions of cores continues. Under current trends, most simulated data could be lost if in situ visualization is not deployed. Therefore, traditional numerical simulation data output and post-processing visualization might be unsustainable. In situ visualization in this paradigm will gain unprecedented access to simulation output, potentially being able to process all relevant simulation output at every simulation time step, allowing for very high temporal fidelity compared with traditional post-processing visualization. The solution is to minimize data storage by extracting important features of the data at high temporal resolution using in situ visualization of tight coupling (on the same resource as the simulation), and saving them rather than the raw data. This paper adopts the component-based software engineering mode to realize tight coupling of in situ visualization with a simulation program. It resolves key technological issues of in situ visualization processing, e.g., data access, load balance, and predefined visual analysis patterns. This paper presents preliminary results of in situ visualization of a simulation of large-scale filamentous phenomena in laser plasma under the black cavity physical condition. This simulation is used to study the beam divergence phenomenon after laser filament formation. Moreover, we examine the overheads and effects on code performance associated with inline computations associated with in situ visualization.

KEYWORDS

In Situ, Visualization and Analysis, Laser Plasma Interaction

1. INTRODUCTION

As the computing power of high-performance supercomputers becomes ever more powerful, scientific simulation programs running on such machines are generating increasingly larger amounts of data. However, the increased time overhead of data movement, especially the movement of data to disk, increasingly limits the ability to process, analyze, and fully understand the simulation results (Ahern et al. 2011), thereby hampering knowledge cognition. Although the I/O bandwidth increases steadily as each new generation of supercomputer appears, these increases are much smaller than the corresponding increases in computing power and generated data, and this trend is expected to continue into the foreseeable future. Many scientific fields need to process petabyte-level data in simulation processes; however, currently, data movement, storage, and analysis constitute the main obstacles facing exascal computing.

The above trends have created problems for traditional post-processing visualization methods. The traditional visualization workflow performs visualization as a post-processing task in which data need to be output from the simulation program, read from disk into the memory of the visual analysis software, and then the visual analysis software is used to perform data visualization and analysis. Visualization of post-processing modes is usually limited by I/O bandwidth (Childs et al. 2010). Specifically, there are two prominent problems in the post-processing visualization mode. The first is that disk I/O performance is limited. Therefore, operations such as transmission and management of hyper-large-scale data between computing nodes, disk arrays, and visualization nodes that consume substantial amounts of system resources mean that processing time, which greatly affects visualization efficiency, cannot meet the requirements of real-time and efficient data analysis. The second problem is that numerical simulation data must be output at a certain interval of simulation time to match the limited storage capacity of the computing resources.

Thus, effective information of physical features in the numerical calculation could be discarded, meaning that the integrity of the visual data cannot be guaranteed.

In situ processing presents many new challenges for simulation and visualization scientists. This article focuses on solving some of the problems facing in situ techniques including the integration of in situ routines with simulations, the transformation of data from analog description representations into visual representations, and the distribution of data between simulation and visualization modes.

The remainder of this paper is structured as follows. Section 2 discusses the history of in situ visualization, the paradigms of two in situ techniques, and related work on tightly coupled in situ visualization techniques. Section 3 introduces the 3D laser plasma (Lap3D) simulation program and visualization effects. The architecture of the in situ visualization technology of the tight coupling method, the realization of in situ visualization and the details of three key technologies in Section 4. Section 5 describes the in-situ visualization results for LAP3D application and performance tests.

2. RELATED WORK

Visualization is enabling technology used to gain insight into data in various scientific fields. It constitutes an important tool that can help domain scientists and general users understand data (Childs et al. 2013). Traditional scientific visualization is generally performed as a post-processing task, whereby all simulation data are written to the persistent store, and then analyzed and visualized after completion of a simulation. Although this model is well adapted to the petascale era, it has begun to collapse (Wong et al. 2012). The total amount of data generated by a supercomputer through simulation far exceeds the capability of writing all that data to persistent storage. This indicates the difficulty of processing all scientific data to disk before performing visualization, which has prompted the development of another visualization model that bypasses this limitation, called in situ.

Many large-scale simulations attempt to bypass the I/O bottleneck through use of in situ visualization and analysis, which handles simulation data at build time. In a broad sense, two paradigms have emerged. One constitutes a collaborative or tightly coupled approach in which the simulation and visualization codes run in the same process using the same resources. The other is a method of concurrent processing or loose coupling in which the simulation transmits data over a network to a separate set of visualization nodes for processing. The most important concern with the implementation of tight coupling is the full utilization of resources. Clearly, the simulation should be run with as much capacity as possible, rather than retaining nodes for visualization or I/O operations. This implementation has the advantage that the visualization routine can directly access the full analog output and simulate the full parallel capacity of the machine.

Woodring et al. (2011) described an in situ workflow for simulating time-random sampling of large-scale particle data from a cosmological simulation. Lorendeau et al. (2013) reported a workflow used the Catalyst in situ visualization library for visualizing a computational fluid dynamics code. Ahrens et al. (2014) described a tightly coupled system that uses a number of images from many angles of a simulation rather than writing simulation data to disk. Rivi et al. (2012) reviewed instrumenting two simulation codes with ICARUS and another with Libsim and presented some parallel performance analysis of ParaView and VisIt. They exploited different visualization tools on both techniques using a ParaView (Ahrens et al. 2005) plug-in, ICARUS, and a library, VisIt (Childs et al. 2012). Larsen et al. (2015) presented Strawman, a system designed to explore the in situ visualization and analysis needs of simulation code teams planning for multi-physics calculations on exascale architectures.

3. LASER PLASMA SIMULATION

Laser plasma interaction involves coupling multiple temporal- and spatial-scale nonlinear processes with very important physical phenomena. Laser filament instability is caused mainly by the inhomogeneity of laser irradiation. With the development of instability, the amplitude of the disturbance increases continuously, eventually causing the beam to break into a filamentous structure with high intensity and disorder, through which a large amount of laser energy is lost. To study the generation and development of laser filament instability in the black cavity, a propagation model of the spatial beam uniform beam was established. The Lap3D (Hu et al. 2015) simulation program was used to simulate large-scale filament formation under the physical conditions of the black cavity. The simulation results can correctly describe the beam divergence and spectral spatial intensity distribution characteristics of the light intensity after filament formation. We used Lap3D to simulate the evolution of filament instability under different parameters. In this example, simulating a physical time of 56.6 ps requires 16,384 CPUs with 1024*1024*2048 cells (approximately 21 billion cells). The total time-varying data of the analog output of the entire process of 104 steps is 1.74 TB. Volume rendering with laser intensity reveals significant filamentation in Figure 1; a partial slice at x = 512λ is displayed in Figure 2.

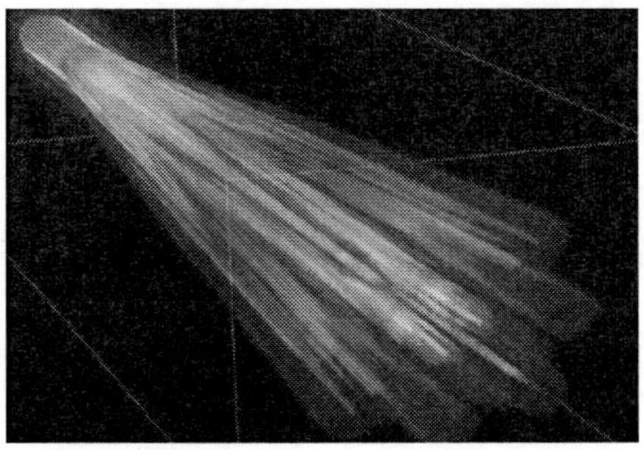

Figure 1. The Volume Plot of the Laser Intensity in 3D

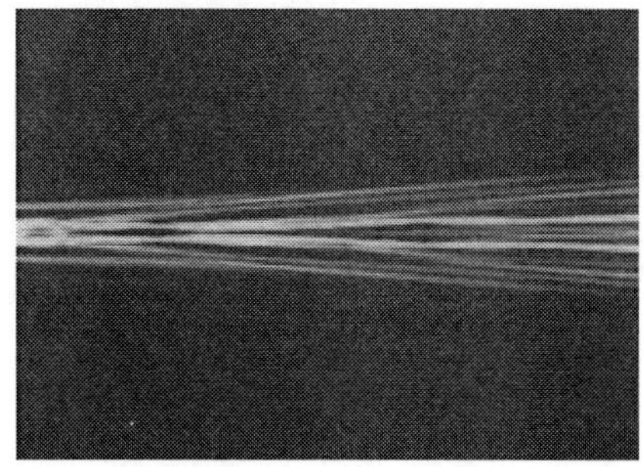

Figure 2. The Filametation Phenomenon in 2D

4. TIGHTLY COUPLED IN SITU ARCHITECTURE

The in-situ visual analysis technique of tightly coupled mode is to simulate and visualize shared computing node resources, share memory data, establish data connection channels for simulation results and visual analysis, and realize online integration of embedded applications in structural grids. Depending on the analysis, it meets the real-time and efficient visualization requirements of ultra-large-scale numerical simulation data results, while avoiding the time overheads introduced by big data I/O operations.

In situ visualization has several design goals: (1) to minimize the modification of the numerical simulation program code, achieve maximum support for in situ visualization of the application with minimal code modification, and spend the least amount of time reusing code for new numerical simulations to maximize the use of the in situ visual analysis engine for high-performance scientific and engineering calculations; and (2) to minimize the impact of in situ visualization technology on the performance of the numerical simulation during runtime. Ideally, the decision of whether to use and run in situ visualization technology should have little effect on the efficiency of the simulation program.

4.1 In Situ Component

As shown in Figure 3, the core components of in situ visualization technology include data adapters, data access modules, and in situ visual analysis engines. The data adapter is embedded in the simulation program code in the form of componentized module instrumentation, which is referred to as the in situ visual analysis component. Its main functions include encapsulating the data slice pointer of the simulation program, and providing a data access interface to realize data management and interaction based on the hierarchical structure of the mesh slice. The data access module is the production plant for the data source. The module obtains data pointers from the data adapter and it generates metadata information, grid information, and physical quantity information required for the visualization pipeline. The in situ visual analysis engine is a lightweight engine for online visualization of very large-scale data with minimal operational overheads. The engine uses the VTK data model (Schroeder et al. 2004) as its underlying data structure to create a visual pipeline that provides a variety of common visual analysis capabilities. Its functions include various graph drawing methods (e.g., pseudo color maps, volume plots, and isosurfaces), data manipulation methods (e.g., cutting operations and threshold filtering). The output of the in situ engine can be divided into pictures or into reduced data. Data communication and data exchange between processes are implemented by MPI (Message Passing Interface).

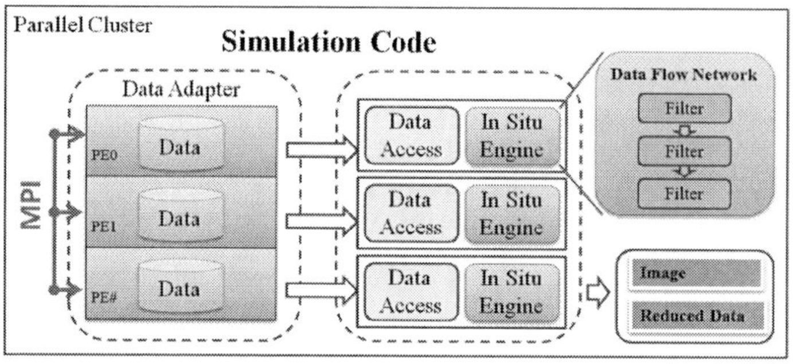

Figure 3. In-Situ Visualization Hierarchy Diagram

4.2 Data Accessing Component

The data access module is designed to obtain data pointers from the data adapter, and to generate metadata information, grid information, and physical quantity information required for the visualization pipeline. Metadata comprise lightweight information about the real data, such as the data type, dimensions, and spatial extent. Grid data represent a spatial distribution carrier of the real data, describing the spatial distribution of the physical quantity data. According to the grid space dimensions, it can be divided into one-dimensional, two-dimensional, or three-dimensional grids, and according to the topological relationship of the grid, it can be divided into a uniform linear grid, structural grid, unstructured grid, or point grid. The grid data callback function needs to fill the dimensions of the grid, define the topological relationship of the grid, and fill the coordinates of the node space that constitute the grid. After the numerical simulation program registers the grid data callback function, it returns a handle to the grid data access. The in situ engine is accessed via the handle, and the mesh data of the simulation program are accessed seamlessly, as shown in Figure 4. The variable callback function of the simulation program is called by the in situ visualization engine, and the field data (e.g., scalar, vector, or tensor) are required for the visualization process at any time. The variable callback must create a variable data object and initialize it using the memory array of the emulator. This mode simply passes the analog data array back to the in-place engine for creating the VTK object, as shown in Figure 5.

```
InsituSetMeshData(DataAdapter)
{
    teravap_handle h, hxc, hyc;
    teravap_VariableData_alloc(&hxc);
    teravap_VariableData_alloc(&hyc);
    teravap_VariableData_setDataF(hxc,
          DataAdapter->rmesh_dims[0],
          DataAdapter->rmesh_x);
    teravap_VariableData_setDataF(hyc,
                DataAdapter->rmesh_dims[1],
                DataAdapter->rmesh_y);
    teravap_RectilinearMesh_setCoordsXY(h, hxc, hyc);
    ... ...;
}
```

Figure 4. Mesh Data Callback Function

```
InsituSetVariableData(char *name ,DataAdapter)
{
    teravap_handle h;
    if(strcmp(name, "pressure") == 0)
    {
      TeraVap_VariableData_alloc(&h);
      TeraVap_VariableData_setDataD(h,
           DataAdapter ->nx* DataAdapter ->ny,
           DataAdapter ->pressure);
    }
    ... ...;
}
```

Figure 5. Variable Data Callback Function

4.3 Data Loading Component

The in situ engine data come from the memory data of the numerical simulation program. As the numerical simulation program provides a dynamic load balancing strategy, the simulated program's in-memory data are migrated between processes based on the calculated load threshold. This will result in diversity of the data distribution. As shown in Figure 6, the in situ visual analysis is the exponential value calculation and the in situ engine is part of the same process sharing the memory data. To ensure the integrity of the data, the numerically calculated memory data block must notify the process to which the in situ engine belongs of the need to process the data block with the corresponding ID, thereby implementing visualization. The numerical calculation module adjusts the distribution of the data slices on the respective processors according to the load balancing strategy, although the distribution of the data blocks on the respective processors might be uneven and irregular. The in situ engine obtains the ID index of the data block that is processed by its own process, and it implements the data block "load data on demand". Therefore, the in situ engine's data loading strategy adapter satisfies the custom data allocation strategy for matching the data block distribution in the numerical calculation module to ensure the integrity of the in situ engine data processing.

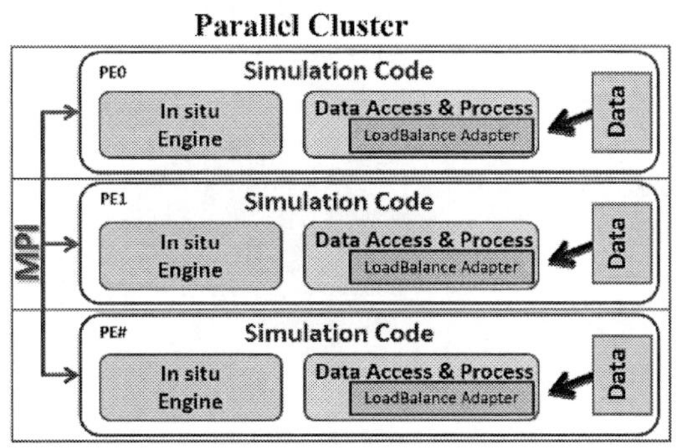

Figure 6. Data Load Policy Adapter for the In-Situ Engine

4.4 Visualization Pipeline Configuration

The visual analysis pipeline of the batch mode uses its predictive experience to configure its parameters for automatic visualization and analysis. Therefore, we consider the design and implementation of a visual analysis mode based on user semantics, set parameters through standardized user semantic description, guide the in situ engine to establish a visual analysis process, and realize batch processing of data visualization and analysis. The in situ visualization template based on user semantics is described in the InSituVisPattern data structure. The data structure includes elements such as physical quantity names, data operation types, and spatial location information. The parameter description of the in situ visualization template exists in the input file of the simulation program. The visual analysis module of the in situ engine obtains the visual analysis description from the input file, and it constructs the visualization process of the in situ engine through semantic analysis, as shown in Figure 7.

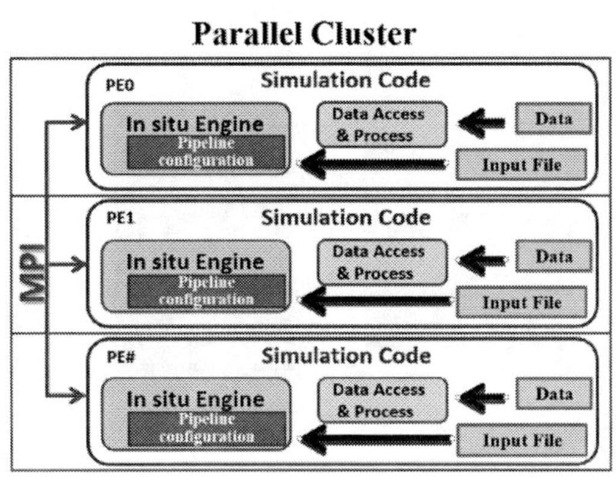

Figure 7. Modular Implementation of Visualization Pipeline Configuration

5. RESULTS AND DISCUSSION

5.1 In Situ Visualization in LAP3D

The results of this research have been simulated successfully using the laser plasma interaction in the Lap3D application. The program studied the spatial transmission characteristics of a uniform beam and the dependence of laser energy related parameters on filament instability caused by the spatial characteristics of the uniform beam. The Hawk parallel machine 62 CPU core was used to realize the in situ visualization of the electric field intensity amplitude distribution of the cutting drawing beam in the plasma, and to obtain a high confidence visual image, as shown in Figure 8.

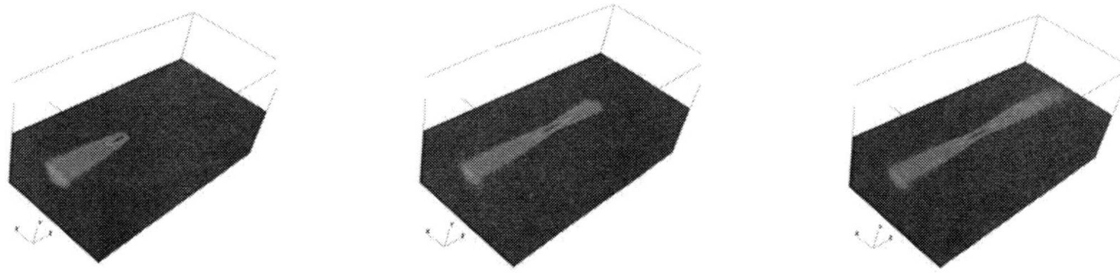

(a) step 201 (2) Step 401 (3) step 601

Figure 8. Visualization of the Transmission Characteristics of a Single Gaussian Beam

5.2 Visualization Pipeline Configuration based on user semantics

Cut-out data plotting is one of the most important diagnostic methods for Lap3D, and most of the physics is discovered via slice content. Therefore, rapid generation of slice data is very important for physical diagnosis. As shown in Table 1, the model in this case was a Gaussian beam-forming example, and the spatial distribution effect of the laser intensity amplitude is shown at 1000 and 2000 time step. The user defines the 50% cross section of the y-axis to analyze the law of laser amplitude propagation along the z-axis. Then, 20%, 40%, and 60% of the x-y plane perpendicular to the z-axis shows the laser exit surface, and the laser intensity amplitude distribution on each section can be analyzed.

Table 1. Visual Analysis of User-Defined Cross-Sectional Spatial Position

step	Y:50%	Z:20%	Z:40%	Z:60%
1000	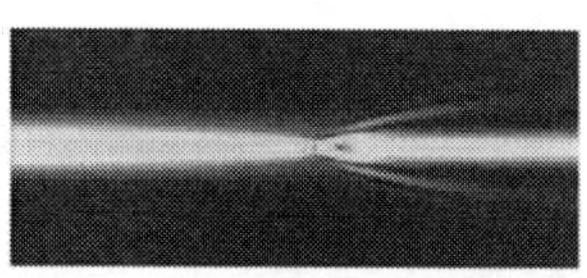	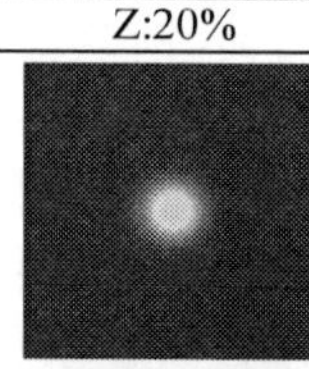	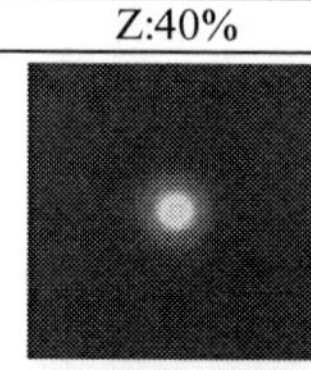	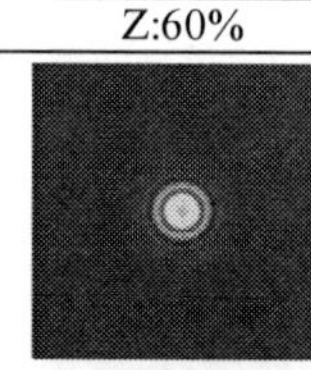
2000		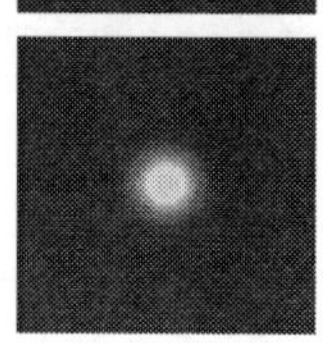	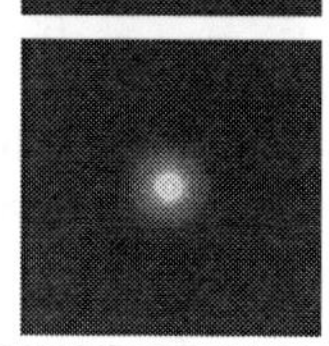	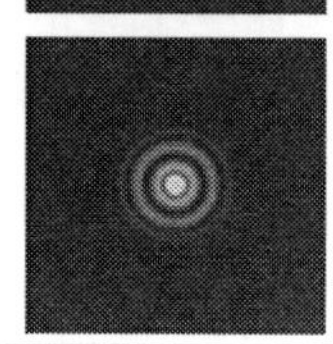

5.3 Performance Testing

The result of the in-situ visualization of the lap3d code is to process the image of the laser electric field intensity amplitude slice at each time step. A number of parametric studies were conducted to understand the performance and memory impact of in-situ visualization of the code. The results and analysis are as follows.

The first aspect of the study was the memory overhead and wall clock time of the simulated in-situ visualization. The simulation runs with an increased core count and the grid is added accordingly (weakly scalable). For a fixed grid size, the memory overhead for each core comparison of 100 steps of in-situ and non-in-situ operation is given in Table 2.The results show that the memory overhead of the simulated non-in-situ is fairly stable at around 610MB / core, and the memory overhead of the simulated in-situ is fairly stable at around 710MB / core. The simulation process increases the extra memory overhead of the visual pipeline, and the in-situ visualization adds about 100 MB of memory compared to the in-situ numerical simulation. In addition, we also studied the impact of using all cores on a node versus computing tasks using 32 cores/nodes. The non-in-situ running time of the simulation program is maintained at about 200 seconds, while the in-situ running time is also maintained at about 250 seconds. Table 2 shows the wall clock time variation for different core numbers, fixed grid size (128x128x64) / core. The results show that for 32 core/node run the performance impact is ~16-32% when we write the in-situ output every time step. In this test case, it should be noted that an extreme example of writing a file very time step is considered for the in-situ case (where as the non-in-situ case only writes 1 file per 100 steps) and practically the run will be down with lower write frequency of writes. The key result is that the performance and memory impact of each core is consistent with an increase in the number of cores, up to 1k core. This will enable the use of in-situ visualization on a larger scales.

Table 2. The Memory Overhead of the Simulated Non-In-Situ and In-Situ Visualization

Cores	Grid Size	MB RAM/Core(MB)		Wall-clock time(sec)	
		Non-in-situ	In-situ	Non-in-situ	In-situ
64	512*512*256	661.87	756.65	206.27	239.74
256	1024*1024*256	613.98	703.99	196.34	240.38
1024	1024*1024*1024	616.44	713.39	201.89	266.49

The second aspect of the study is the evolution of memory usage as time steps increase. The test case uses a 512*512*256 grid with 128 cores. This is done to ensure that there is no significant increase in the memory used, as it can lead to resource exhaustion. Figure 9 shows how the memory usage of each core changes over time. The results show that the increase in memory usage is very small (1.25%) and is expected to not affect any long-term evolutionary simulation runs.

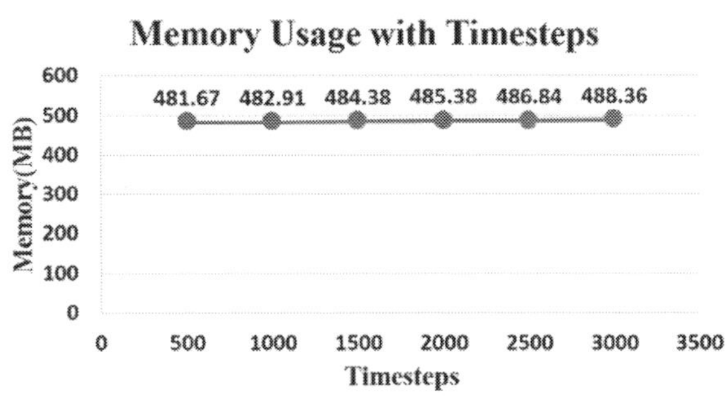

Figure 9. Variation of Memory Usage with Time Step for the In-Situ Visualization Test Case

In addition to the weak scaling run, we also performed strong scaling runs. The test case uses a 1024*1024*1024 grid to do a strong scaling study with 256-1024 cores. The results are shown in Table 3. The results show that in this case, the non-in-situ strong scaling is better than the in-situ strong scaling. Again, it should be aware that the in-situ run is to write one file per time step and the I/O overhead will be higher. When using 256 cores, the simulated wall clock time is too long because the memory has reached the maximum memory of a single compute node. When using 512-1024, the simulated wall clock time drops linearly.

Table 3. Wall Clock Time and Memory Overhead (for 100 Time Step Run) Variation with different Core Counts (Fixed 8 Cores/Node). Grid Size Fixed at 1024*1024*1024

Cores	Grid Size	MB RAM/Core(MB)		Wall-clock time(sec)	
		Non-in-situ	In-situ	Non-in-situ	In-situ
256	1024*1024*1024	1835.82	2003.62	1275.68	1652.13
512	1024*1024*1024	1137.09	1257.10	418.70	470.63
1024	1024*1024*1024	615.532	713.395	204.31	271.89

6. CONCLUSION

To support the Lap3D simulation in the study of the large-scale filament formation under black cavity physical conditions, and to analyze the beam divergence phenomenon and spectral spatial light intensity distribution characteristics after filament formation, this work used in situ component technology to achieve coupling of the Lap3D program and a general visualization software package. The three key technologies of data access, data loading, and in situ visual analysis mode based on user semantics were adopted to resolve the critical problems of "data loading－data visualization－data analysis" and to apply them to an actual numerical simulation. The efficacy of the demonstrated approach means it could be used both to help researchers understand fundamental physics problems and to improve the accuracy and efficiency of data analysis.

ACKNOWLEDGEMENT

This work was supported by National Key R&D Program of China (No. 2017YFB0202203) and the Defense Industrial Technology Development Program of China (Grant No. C1520110002).

REFERENCES

Ahern, S. et al., 2011. Scientific discovery at the exascale. *Report from the DOE ASCR 2011 Workshop on Exascale Data Management*.

Ahrens, J. et al., 2005. Visualization in the paraview framework. *In The Visualization Handbook*, Hansen, C. and Johnson, C. editors, pp. 162–170.

Ahrens, J. et al., 2014. An image-based approach to extreme scale in situ visualization and analysis. *Proceedings of the International Conference for High Performance Computing, Networking, Storage and Analysis*. IEEE Press, pp. 424-434.

Childs, H. et al., 2010. Extreme scaling of production visualization software on diverse architectures. *In IEEE Comput. Graph. Appl.*, Vol. 30, No. 3, pp. 22-31.

Childs, H. et al., 2012. VisIt: An End-User Tool For Visualizing and Analyzing Very Large Data. *In High Performance Visualization–Enabling Extreme-Scale Scientific Insight*, pp. 357-372.

Childs, H. et al., 2013. Research challenges for visualization software. *In Computer*, Vol. 5, pp. 34-42.

Hu, X. et al., 2015. The development of laser-plasma interaction program LAP3D on thousands of processors. *In Aip Advances*, Vol. 5, No. 8, pp. 87174.

Larsen, M. et al., 2015. Strawman: A Batch In Situ Visualization and Analysis Infrastructure for Multi-Physics Simulation Codes. *Proceedings of Workshop on in Situ Infrastructures for Enabling Extreme-scale Analysis & Visualizaiton*, pp. 30-35.

Lorendeau, B. et al., 2013. In-situ visualization in fluid mechanics using catalyst: A case study for code saturne. *Proceedings of LDAV '2013*. pp. 53-57.

Rivi, M. et al., 2012. In-situ Visualization: State-of-the-art and Some Use Cases. *Prace White Paper*.

Schroeder, W. et al., 2004. *The Visualization Toolkit*. Kitware.

Wong, P. et al., 2012. The top 10 challenges in extreme-scale visual analytics. *In IEEE Computer Graphics and Applications*, Vol. 32, No. 4, pp. 63.

Woodring, J. et al., 2011. In-situ sampling of a large-scale particle simulation for interactive visualization and analysis. *In Computer Graphics Forum,* Vol. 30, pp. 1151-1160.

POLAR SORT: COMBINING MULTIDIMENSIONAL SCALING AND POLAR COORDINATES FOR MATRIX REORDERING

Celmar Guimarães da Silva
School of Technology, University of Campinas, R. Paschoal Marmo, 1888. Jardim Nova Itália. Limeira, SP, Brazil

ABSTRACT

Matrix reordering algorithms aim to permute rows and columns of a matrix (or a matrix-based visualization, such as a heatmap) in order to reveal data patterns that could not be perceivable in some orderings of its columns and rows. Finding a good permutation, according to some evaluation criteria, is not straightforward, and many approaches try to find out a good tradeoff between algorithm execution time and output quality. This work argues that using multidimensional scaling and polar coordinates helps to find row and column orderings that reveal Band and Circumplex patterns if they are present in some permutation of a matrix. The proposed $O(n^3)$ method – Polar Sort – uses classical MDS to find an initial 2-dimensional projection of rows (or columns) of the input matrix. After that, the method sorts the projected points according to their angular coefficients in a polar coordinate system whose center is the barycenter of these points. The algorithm then replicates this order to the correspondent rows (or columns). Experiments with synthetic data indicates that Polar Sort produces high-quality results for uncovering Band and Circumplex patterns, and that its mean execution time is as fast as the fastest tested methods for matrices with size 200 × 200. This paper also presents real-world examples in which Polar Sort shows those patterns.

KEYWORDS

Heatmaps, Information Visualization, Visualization Design and Evaluation Methods

1. INTRODUCTION

Matrix reordering algorithms (also called seriation algorithms) tries to permute rows and columns of a matrix in order to enable users to have a better comprehension about the data it contains, when it is presented as a visual structure (such as a heatmap, a Table Lens display etc.). A general principle is that similar rows (or columns) should be closer. Researchers have been trying many approaches to solve matrix reordering problems, such as dimensional reduction and spectral approaches (Behrisch et al., 2016); and some of them focus on unveiling specific sets of patterns (Rocha et al., 2017; Medina et al., 2016). In this work, we prove the Wilkinson's untested hypothesis (Wilkinson, 2005) that doing a bidimensional projection of rows and columns of a reorderable matrix, and ordering them according to the angles of their projected points in a polar coordinate system would be able to reveal Band and Circumplex patterns. We formalize and implement his idea as a matrix reordering algorithm called Polar Sort.

We used Matrix Reordering Analyzer tool (Silva et al., 2014) to compare Polar Sort to other algorithms that produce good results (in terms of output quality and execution time) regarding those focus patterns. We conclude that the proposed algorithm recompose those patterns even when the tested matrices have high noise ratios. Besides, its execution time is as fast as the ones from the other algorithms that reveal these patterns, for the tested scenarios.

We organize this paper as follows. Section 1 presents theoretical background about matrix patterns and matrix evaluation functions. Section 2 briefly presents other related reordering algorithms. Section 3 defines Polar Sort and exemplifies its outputs for the mentioned patterns. Section 4 evaluates our algorithm with synthetic data, compares its asymptotic complexity with other algorithms, and illustrates its output for real-world data. Section 5 presents conclusions and future work.

2. THEORETICAL BACKGROUND

In this section, we define matrix concepts and patterns, and then we present some functions to evaluate a permuted matrix.

A *reorderable matrix* $R_{m\times n}$ is a matrix that supports row and column permutations. It may be defined by a non-permutable matrix N and by two permutation vectors: *rowOrder* and *columnOrder*, in such a way that $r_{i;j}=n_{rowOrder[i];columnOrder[j]}$. Permuting rows or columns of R demands only permuting its permutation vectors.

Wilkinson (2005) and Behrisch et al. (2016) present a list of nine patterns that matrices may present. This paper focuses only on Wilkinson's Band and Circumplex patterns. In a matrix with a Band pattern, the closer the cells are to the diagonal, the higher their values. If we consider a matrix as a torus and draw a diagonal band on it, similarly to the Band pattern, we generate the Circumplex pattern. Table 1 exemplifies both patterns. One may configure the bandwidth of Band pattern to a thin or large band. Circumplex has no configuration parameter.

The formal definition of Band and Circumplex patterns (Wilkinson, 2005) begins with the definition of a matrix $X_{n\times p}$ whose cell values are $x_{i;j} = e^{-t^2} + u_{i;j}$. For Band pattern, $t=(j/p-i/n)/b$, where $1\leq i\leq n$ and $1\leq j\leq p$; in other words, t measures the distance to the main diagonal, and b defines how sharp is the boundary between low and high values, and also the bandwidth. For Circumplex pattern, $t=\cos(\Pi(j/p-i/n))$. For both patterns, $u_{i;j}$ is a random error; in our case we replaced it by a salt-and pepper error.

We call *pre-Circumplex* and *pre-Band* a matrix whose one or more permutations reveal its Circumplex and Band structure, respectively. We also call Circumplex (or Band) matrix a matrix that obeys the definition of Circumplex (or Band) pattern.

One may use evaluation functions to assess a permuted matrix. Those functions either analyze the data matrix itself, or distance matrices of rows and columns of this matrix (i.e., proximity matrices). Here we focus on the three functions used in this work. *Moore neighborhood stress* (Niermann, 2005) (*Moore stress*, for short) measures how similar each cell is in comparison to all its eight neighbors in a matrix. Given a matrix $X_{m,n}$, this measure is defined as $stress = \sum_{i=1}^{m}\sum_{j=1}^{n} s(i,j)$, where $s(i,j) = \sum_{k=\max(1,i-1)}^{\min(m,i+1)} \sum_{l=\max(1,j-1)}^{\min(n,j+1)} (x_{i,j} - x_{k,l})^2$. *Minimal Span Loss Function* (*MSLF*) (Wu et al., 2008) sums the distances of each pair of neighbor rows (or columns) of a matrix. MSLF may use Euclidean Distance as proximity coefficient to measure distance; indeed, one may calculate MSLF directly in a proximity matrix if it is already available. Given a proximity matrix $P_{n,n}$, MSLF is defined as $\mathrm{MSLF} = \sum_{i=1}^{n-1} p_{i,i+1}$. Both measures may help to assess permutation quality in a pre-Band matrix, but according to Rocha et al. (2017), they do not fit evaluation needs of a pre-Circumplex matrix. Those authors propose using *Circular Correlation* as a quality measure. Rocha et al. define this measure as the highest possible absolute Spearman correlation between rows (or columns) of a matrix $A_{m,n}$ and their respective ordering in all possible shifted versions of rows (or columns) in a matrix $B_{m,n}$.

Text citation patterns and data about subjects' preferences for sets of objects are examples where band patterns arise. Circumplex patterns are present in a diversity of psychology phenomena, such as classification of emotions and color perception (Wilkinson, 2005).

Table 1. Examples of synthetic matrices with Band and Circumplex patterns

Band (bandwidth=0.2)	Band (bandwidth=0.5)	Circumplex	Band (bandwidth=0.2)	Band (bandwidth=0.5)	Circumplex
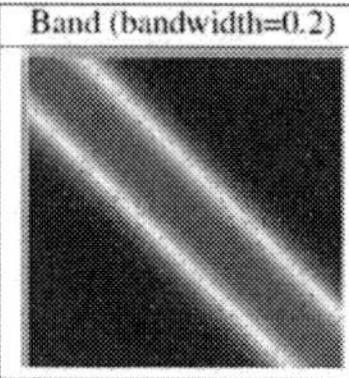	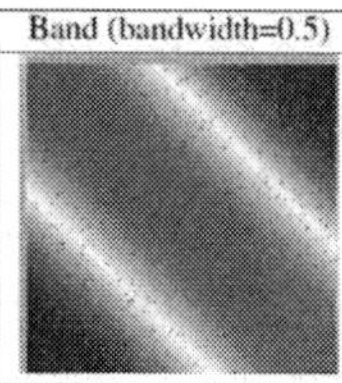		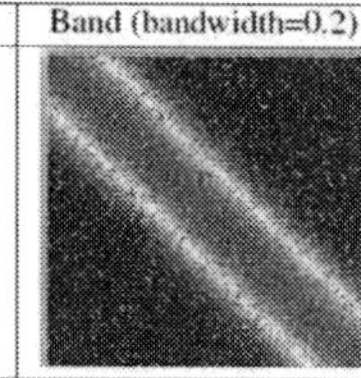	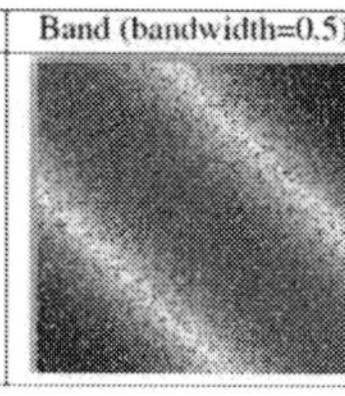	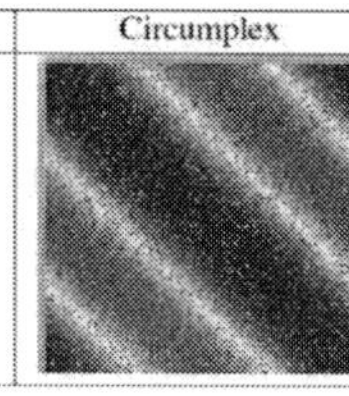
Noise ratio 0.05			Noise ratio 0.3		

3. RELATED WORK

In this section, we classify and exemplify some matrix reordering algorithms (Sect. 3.1). Then we present the research gap related to the use of multidimensional projection approaches for matrix reordering (Sect. 3.2).

3.1 Matrix Reordering Approaches

Behrisch et al. (2016) present seven classes of matrix reordering algorithms. In this work, we highlight the classes of *dimensional reduction* and *spectral* algorithms, due to their strong relation to our approach.

Spectral algorithms calculate permutations based on eigenvalues and eigenvectors of proximity matrices of rows (or columns). As an example, Chen (2002) uses a correlation operator φ that calculates the correlation matrix of a given matrix (which may be the original matrix or another correlation matrix); he also defines D as the original data matrix, $R^{(1)} = \varphi(D)$, and $R^{(n+1)} = \varphi(R^{(n)})$. Chen projects the columns of a correlation matrix as points in a bi-dimensional space defined by the first two eigenvectors of this matrix. When doing this for many values of n, he perceived that $R^{(i)}$ may place the projected points into an ellipse, and in an extreme case (R^{∞}) they are projected into two opposite parts of this ellipse. Chen uses both facts to develop approaches for finding a one-dimensional order for points (and their respective columns or rows), and for applying a hierarchical divisive clustering.

Friendly and Kwan (Friendly, 2002) (Friendly & Kwan, 2003) present another spectral algorithm for reordering a variable-per-variable correlation matrix C, which they call "correlation ordering". They use eigen decomposition to calculate the two first eigenvectors of C: e_1 and e_2. They define α[i] as the angle of the vector (e_1[i], e_2[i]) for each row i of C. They order the rows of C according to the values of α. This circular order is linearized by defining its beginning and ending point where the difference between α[i] and α[i+1] is maximum. C is symmetric, so the order of its columns and rows is the same. Their works exemplify how their method reorders real-world correlation matrices, but they do not use their approach to reorder data matrices.

Dimensional reduction algorithms reduce the number of dimensions d of a dataset to n dimensions, $n \ll d$. Outside matrix reordering context, it is usual to define n=2, and therefore the dataset is projected into a plane. However, when n=1, these algorithms find a linear order of elements, i.e., an order of rows or columns in the reorderable matrix. This approach may use rows' and columns' proximity matrices.

Wilkinson (2005) uses dimensional reduction algorithms for reordering matrices. In his experiments, he compares Singular Value Decomposition (SVD), iterative non-metric MDS (iMDS) (both with n=1), Locally Preserving Projection (LPP) and a clustering approach. Wilkinson concludes that SVD and iMDS produce the best results for reordering pre-Band and pre-Circumplex matrices (among other types of matrices), in terms of average Spearman Correlation of indexes of rows and columns. However, it is worth noting that Spearman Correlation is not appropriate for Circumplex pattern (see Rocha et al. (2017)).

Apart from those papers, it is worth noting two works from Rehm et al. (2005, 2006) that combines MDS and polar coordinates in order to provide dimensional reduction. Both are based on the algorithm MDS_{polar}, which projects d-dimensional points in two dimensions. It preserves the distance between pairs of data points and tries to preserve the angle between those pairs when projecting them to the lower dimension. While they use polar coordinates for projecting points from d to n dimensions, our approach first project points from d to n and then finds a circular ordering of these points by using polar coordinates.

3.2 Research Gap

In this section we detail a research gap related to the works of Wilkinson (2005), Friendly (2002), and Friendly & Kwan (2003). Despite a good evaluation of SVD and iMDS for revealing Band and Circumplex patterns, Wilkinson criticized both methods because they failed on revealing the intrinsic unidimensionality of these patterns. Wilkinson tried to show that this unidimensionality could be captured by using SVD and iMDS with n=2 instead of n=1. He used two matrices as input: one Band matrix and one Circumplex one. Then he projected their rows and columns in $\Re^2$ with SVD and iMDS. He was not interested in the matrix reordering itself at this time, but in showing the resulting projections. The results were four 2D projections (two for SVD, two for iMDS) that we classify into one of the following situations:

1. The proximity of the d-dimensional points in the $\Re^2$ space defines a circular order (forming an arc or a circle), which corresponds to a good approximation of the correct order of columns (or rows) in the pattern. However, a 1D projection of the same d-dimensional points would not be able to reveal this order. It happens for Circumplex and Band matrices when using SVD, and for Circumplex when using iMDS.
2. The d-dimensional points fall within a "football-shaped envelope", and the direction of its major axis reveal a good approximation of the correct order of columns (or rows). Therefore, a 1D projection probably would reveal it. It happens for Band matrices when using iMDS.

Regarding SVD and Circumplex pattern, Wilkinson writes, "Unfortunately, we cannot detect its unidimensionality unless we convert to polar coordinates, and we cannot know that in advance" (Wilkinson, 2005). Regarding Band pattern, we point out in Section 4 that the projections of its columns (or rows) in 2D also define a circular ordering (given by an arc). Wilkinson states that the projection of the rows or columns of a Band pattern should be unidimensional, but that projection constraints forced the projected points to be in an arc format.

Note that Wilkinson did not use SVD with n=2 or iMDS with n=2 for reordering matrices. He just indicated that these 2D projections are of interest to observe circular ordering, but he did not reorder matrices based on these projections or evaluate his proposal. Therefore, his idea remains as a hypothesis.

On the other hand, Friendly and Kwan (Friendly, 2002; Friendly & Kwan, 2003) applied an approach that is similar to Wilkinson's proposal. As already presented in this section, they proposed to order variables of a variable-per-variable correlation matrix according to the angles formed by the first two eigenvectors of this matrix. They present examples of their technique but a formal evaluation is absent. Besides, they cite neither Band nor Circumplex patterns.

In summary, these authors propose the use of algorithms that do a bidimensional projection of rows and columns of a matrix, and uses the circular order of the projected points to sort the rows and columns that they represent. The research gap is that: (1) Wilkinson did not implement and evaluate his bidimensional projection proposal; and (2) Friendly and Kwan did not evaluate their proposal. In order to fill this gap, in this work we propose, implement and evaluate the use of a bidimensional projection in order to generate a circular order to be used for reordering rows and columns of pre-Band and pre-Circumplex matrices.

4. POLAR SORT

Based on the research gap, we derived a method for revealing Band and Circumplex patterns in reorderable matrices. Our approach (Polar Sort) analyzes the radial layout of points in 2D projections of rows (or columns) of a pre-Band or pre-Circumplex matrix given as input. First, the method projects the rows (or columns) in $\Re^2$. Then it converts the Cartesian coordinate system into a new polar coordinate system whose center is the barycenter of the projected points. Then the method sorts the points by their angular coordinates and replicates this order for rows (or columns) of the matrix.

Instead of using SVD for producing projections with circular order, we opted by using classical MDS (Torgerson, 1952). Table 2 shows the projections for six distinct Band and Circumplex matrices. Color intensity indicates the indexes of rows in the matrix. Each projection helps to note the similarity of order among neighbor points, and that a barycenter of these points would be a possible candidate for the origin of our polar coordinate system. Note that these projections are very similar to those presented by Wilkinson (2005) for SVD outputs and do not produce the undesired football-shaped envelope of the iMDS output for Band.

In order to enhance the output for the case of pre-Band matrices, Polar Sort uses the same strategy of the correlation ordering algorithm (Friendly, 2002). Given the angular ordering of the list of projected points, the method considers this list as circular, and finds the more distant pair of adjacent points in the list. They become the first and the last points of the ordered list that the algorithm will use to reorder rows (or columns). This procedure is needs for Band patterns because of the horseshoe curve of pre-Band projected points. This step does not damage pre-Circumplex ordering.

Regarding asymptotic complexity, Polar Sort algorithm is influenced by the asymptotic complexity of the classical MDS algorithm. Given an input matrix with dimensions $n \times n$, executing the classical MDS algorithm is $O(n^3)$ (Tzeng et al., 2008). Sorting a list of projected points by angle is $O(n \log n)$. The remaining steps are linear procedures. Therefore, Polar Sort algorithm is also $O(n^3)$. A way of improving it is to replace classical MDS by another faster dimensional reduction algorithm that preserves the quality of the output.

We exemplify the results of our algorithm in Table 3. It presents synthetic matrices with dimensions 200×200 with Band and Circumplex patterns (marked as "Original") and the result of using Polar Sort for reordering a shuffled version of them, i.e., a version with rows and columns randomly permuted. Observe that each pair of original and reordered matrices are quite similar, even for the largest noise ratio presented (0.3). Flipped columns (or rows) do not hamper users to observe Band or Circumplex pattern. Idem for shifted columns (or rows) and Circumplex pattern.

Table 2. 2D projections of rows of Band and Circumplex matrices with size 200 × 200

Band (bandwidth=0.2)	Band (bandwidth=0.5)	Circumplex	Band (bandwidth=0.2)	Band (bandwidth=0.5)	Circumplex
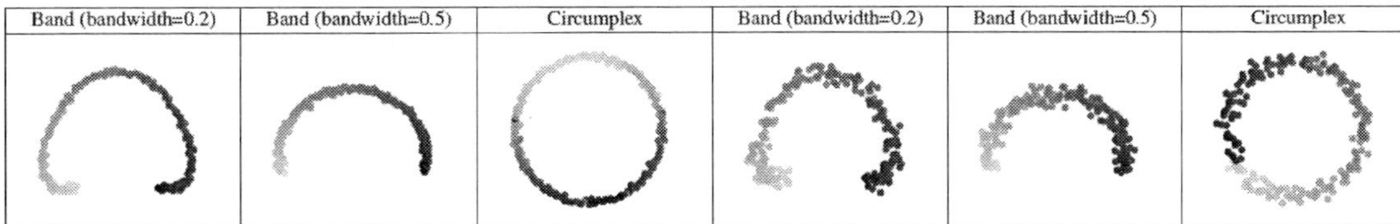					
Noise ratio 0.05			Noise ratio 0.3		

Table 3. Examples of synthetic matrices with Band and Circumplex pattern and their shuffled version after reordering

Noise ratio	Band (bandwidth=0.2)		Band (bandwidth=0.5)		Circumplex	
	Original	Reordered	Original	Reordered	Original	Reordered
0.05	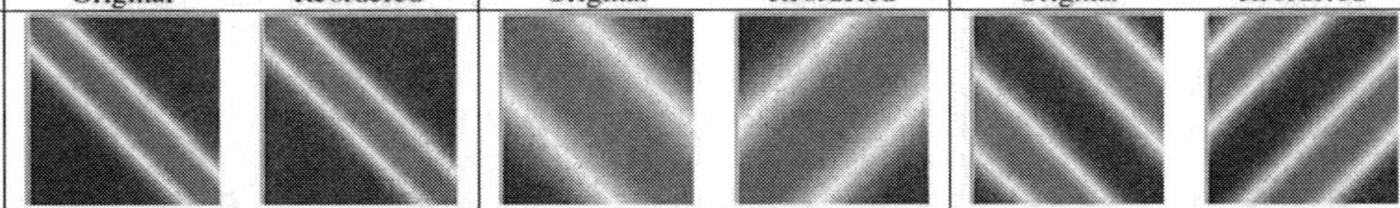					
0.3	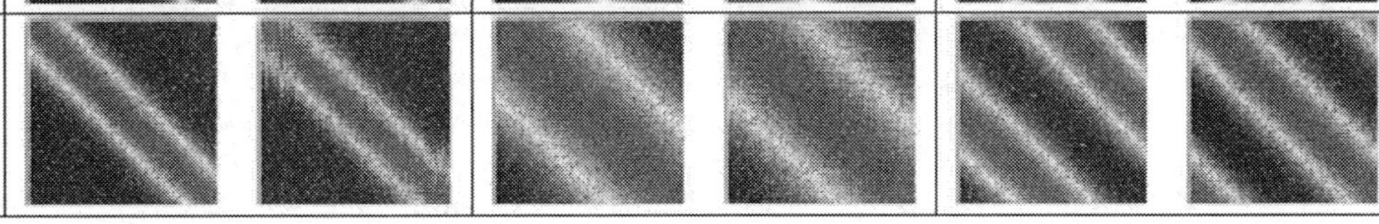					

5. EVALUATION

In this section, we present how we evaluated our method. First, we assess the output quality and execution time of our algorithm and other related reordering algorithms from the literature. Second, we compare its asymptotic complexity to these algorithms. After that, we show Polar Sort applied to real world data.

5.1 Synthetic Data

In this section, we compare reordering algorithms from the literature with our proposal. First, we present MRA tool, used for the comparison process. Then we define how we configured our experiment. We also show and discuss our results in the last part of this section.

We used Matrix Analyzer Reordering tool (MRA) (Silva et al., 2014) to compare our method to other relevant reordering methods from the literature. We inform to MRA the data pattern to use for creating the input matrices, a list of pattern configuration parameters, a list of matrix sizes, a list of salt-and-pepper noise ratios, and a list of reordering algorithms to compare on the test. We also inform the evaluation function and the proximity coefficients for comparison. MRA creates a set of K matrices according to the input parameters, shuffles these matrices (in other words, it transforms them in pre-Band and pre-Circumplex, in our case), and uses each reordering algorithm to reorder each shuffled matrix. It uses as shuffling approach the Knuth's unbiased shuffling algorithm (Knuth, 1981). The tool measures the execution time of each reordering algorithm. MRA also evaluates the quality of the output matrices according to the evaluation functions and the proximity coefficients. The tool generates files with time and quality measures per output matrix, together with mean and standard deviation values for each matrix type. MRA also executes paired t-tests that helps to analyze the winning algorithm for a given evaluation function and a set of matrices.

We configured MRA for executing two experiments, one for Band and other for Circumplex patterns. For both experiments, we defined the matrix size as 200 × 200; and we used noise ratios 0.01, 0.05, 0.1, 0.3, and 0.5. We tested four configurations of the Band pattern, with bandwidth 0.2, 0.5, 1.0, and 1.5. The Circumplex pattern has no configuration to be set. We also defined $K = 50$. In total, we tested a set with 1000 Band matrices (5 noise ratios × 4 bandwidths × 50 matrices) and with 250 (5 noise ratios × 50 matrices) Circumplex matrices.

We chose the following reordering algorithms to be compared, due to similarity to Polar Sort or to good previous results related to Band or Circumplex patterns (Rocha et al., 2017): Classical MDS (n=1), Eigen Decomposition (correlation ordering of Friendly (2002)), SVD (with n=2, in order to improve the results),

SMB+FV+Median (Medina et al., 2016), Entropy Minimization (EM-ordering), and Circumplex Sort. The strings "(n=1)" and "(n=2)" indicate algorithms that projects data into one and two dimensions, respectively.

We defined Moore stress and MSLF (with Euclidean Distance as proximity coefficient) as evaluation functions for the Band experiment. Both functions indicate differences to be reduced as much as possible among neighbour elements (cells, rows, and columns), in order to reveal a Band pattern. We used Circular Correlation as evaluation function for the Circumplex experiment, according to Rocha et al. (2017).

The evaluation results for Band experiment reveal that all the tested algorithms produce outputs with quite similar values of Moore stress and MSLF, so it is difficult to observe a clear winner in most scenarios. Nevertheless, paired t-tests' results show that Polar Sort and EM-ordering win the other algorithms. Besides, the execution time data indicates that in most scenarios Polar Sort and Classical MDS were the fastest algorithms in our tests, with mean execution time around 0.5 s (exemplified in Figure 1). We also note that EM-ordering had a mean execution time of 1 s or more in most scenarios.

The evaluation results for Circumplex experiment (exemplified by the circular correlation for rows in Figure 1) show that Polar Sort and Eigen Decomposition produced the highest correlation values and lowest standard deviations in each scenario of this experiment. Regarding execution time, Polar Sort and Classical MDS have the lowest execution times (~ 0.6 s), while Eigen Decomposition spent around 1.1 s in each scenario.

Given these data, we conclude that Polar Sort is very competitive with respect to other algorithms for revealing Circumplex and Band patterns in pre-Circumplex and pre-Band matrices with size 200 × 200.

It is worth noting that we executed our experiments as jobs on a high processing cluster, which has 160 cores Power 755 3.3 GHz, 8 cores Power 720 3.0 GHz, and 24 cores Intel X5650 2.6 GHz.

For the sake of completeness, we list the asymptotic time complexity of the reordering algorithms used at our experiments: Circumplex Sort – $O(n^2)$ (Rocha et al. 2017); Classical MDS – $O(n^3)$ (Tzeng et al., 2008), EM-ordering – $O(n \log n)$ (Djuric & Vucetic, 2013), Polar Sort – $O(n^3)$, SMB+FV+Median – $O(n^2\alpha(n^2))$ (Medina et al., 2016), Eigen Decomposition $O(n^3)$ (Dubrulle et al., 1971). We could not find a reliable reference with the asymptotic time complexity of SVD. Note that α is a function that grows very slowly, known as the inverse of Ackermann's function.

Despite having the highest time complexity when compared to most of the analyzed algorithms, the analysis presented at this section indicates that Polar Sort produces high quality outputs in a short time for the evaluated cases. An open question is how to produce such kind of result with a faster time complexity, in order to reduce the expected increasing of time for bigger matrices.

5.2 Real World Data

We present two examples of real world data reordered by Polar Sort. The first one is the Iris data set (Fisher, 1936), available at UCI Machine Learning Repository (Dheeru & Taniskidou, 2017). It has data about 150 flowers of three distinct classes. In this set, one class (*Iris setosa*) is completely distinct from the other two, which are not linearly separable; so, the set has two natural clusters. First, we created a dissimilarity matrix of flowers, based on Euclidean distance. Then we normalized it and converted it into a similarity matrix.

Figure 2 (left) presents the original matrix (top-left), and the results of reordering it by each algorithm used in our experiments. Red, white and blue stands for high, mean and low similarity values, respectively. Note that the results of Eigen Decomposition, Polar Sort and SVD methods show the expected two red clusters, and present less noise than the other results (see the stress measures below each matrix).

Our second example is Russell's dataset about classification of words (Russell, 1980). A set of 36 volunteers received a list of 28 expressions ("words or phrases that people use to describe their moods, feelings, temporary states, affect, or emotions", as Russell wrote). Each volunteer classified each expression into one of the following eight emotion categories: arousal, contentment, depression, distress, excitement, misery, pleasure, and sleepiness. Russell create an expression-per-category matrix, whose cells are the frequency in which volunteers classified an expression into a given category. He argues that one may use this matrix "to estimate the order of the eight categories". Figure 2 (right) presents a heatmap of this matrix, after shuffling, in order to simulate how the real data would be received by a researcher. The rightmost heatmap is how Polar Sort reorders this shuffled matrix. Note that the answer has a quasi-Circumplex pattern. Also note that Circular Correlation measures for the Polar Sort output, when compared to the original Russell's matrix, are 1.0 for columns and 0.997 for rows, which indicates that this output has the same pattern than the manually ordered matrix.

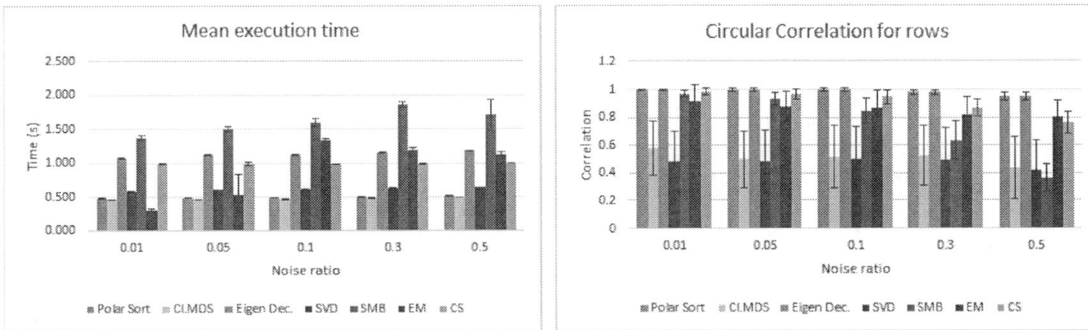

Figure 1. Left: mean execution time for Band experiment (b=0.5). Right: circular correlation for rows in Circumplex experiment.

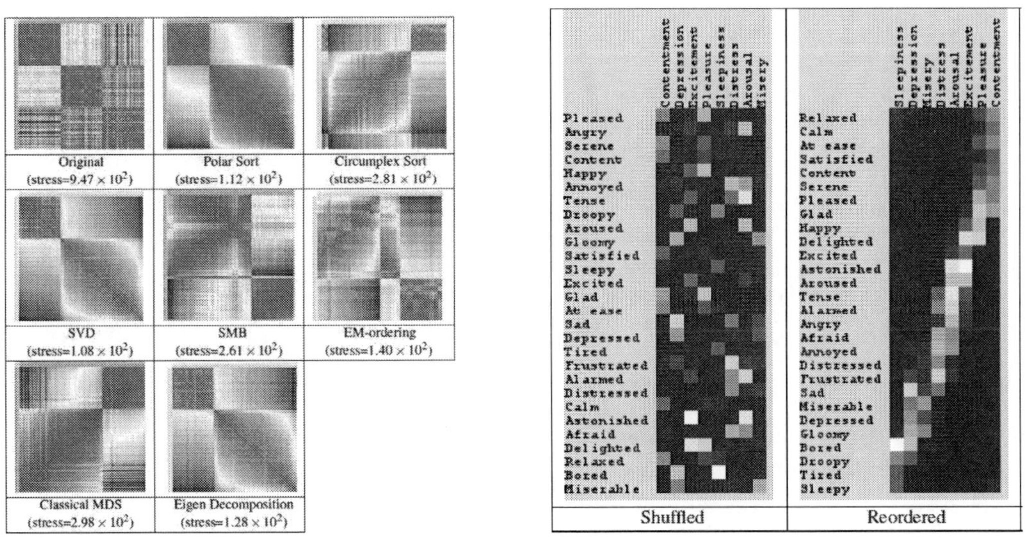

Figure 2. Left: Similarity matrices of Iris dataset, with distinct permutations of rows and columns. Right: Russell's matrix of expressions-per-categories (shuffled and ordered by Polar Sort)

6. CONCLUSION

We presented Polar Sort as a fast and high-quality method for reordering both pre-Band and pre-Circumplex matrices. Some reordering methods produce good results only for pre-Band matrices, but not for pre-Circumplex ones; other methods produce good results for both types of matrix, but these methods are time-consuming. Our synthetic experiments revealed that Polar Sort produces high-quality results for both patterns, according to MSLF, Moore stress, and circular correlation, for matrices with size 200 × 200. Besides, despite its $O(n^3)$ time complexity, its mean execution time is as fast as the fastest tested methods: it spent less than 1 s for reordering a 200 × 200 pre-Band or pre-Circumplex matrix, which is an acceptable time for providing a quick answer for users.

A limitation of our work is that one must presume that the matrix to be reordered is pre-Band or pre-Circumplex, given that most of the time there is no information about this classification *a priori*. Besides, given that our algorithm is $O(n^3)$, another limitation is regarding scalability. Future works may analyze alternative approaches to classical MDS for dimensional reduction, in order to reduce asymptotic complexity without losing quality of the output matrices.

ACKNOWLEDGEMENT

We thank the grant #2019/04222-4 from São Paulo Research Foundation (FAPESP) and the grant #2232/19 from FAEPEX/PRP/University of Campinas.

REFERENCES

Behrisch, M. et al., 2016. Matrix reordering methods for table and network visualization. *Computer Graphics Forum*, Vol. 35, No. 3, pp. 693–716.

Ben-Dor, A. et al., 2003. Discovering local structure in gene expression data: The order-preserving submatrix problem. *Journal of Computational Biology*, Vol. 10, No. 3-4, pp. 373–384.

Bar-Joseph, Z. et al., 2001. Fast optimal leaf ordering for hierarchical clustering. *Bioinformatics*, Vol 17 (Suppl. 1), pp. S22–29.

Chen, C.-H., 2002. Generalized association plots: information visualization via iteratively generated correlation matrices. *Statistica Sinica*, Vol. 12, pp. 7–29.

Dheeru, D. and Taniskidou, E. K., 2017. *UCI machine learning repository*. Available at: http://archive.ics.uci.edu/ml [Accessed 01 March 2019].

Dubrulle, A. et al., 1971. The Implicit QL Algorithm. *Handbook for Automatic Computation*. Springer Berlin Heidelberg, Berlin, Heidelberg, pp. 241–248.

Silva, C. G. et al., 2014. PQR sort: using PQR trees for binary matrix reorganization. *Journal of the Brazilian Computer Society*, Vol. 20, Issue 1, Article 3.

Silva, C. G. et al., 2017. A fast feature vector approach for revealing simplex and equi-correlation data patterns in reorderable matrices. *Information Visualization*, Vol. 16, No. 4, pp. 261–274.

Djuric, N. and Vucetic, S., 2013. Efficient visualization of large-scale data tables through reordering and entropy minimization. *Proceedings of IEEE 13th International Conference on Data Mining 2013*, pp. 121–130.

Fisher, R.,1936. The use of multiple measurements in taxonomic problems. *Annual Eugenics*, Vol. 7, Part II, pp. 179–188.

Friendly, M. and Kwan, E., 2003. Effect ordering for data displays. *Computational Statistics and Data Analysis*, Vol. 43, No. 4, pp. 509–539.

Friendly, M., 2002. Corrgrams. *The American Statistician*, Vol. 56, No. 4, pp. 316–324.

Knuth, D. E., 1981. *The Art of Computer Programming*, Vol. 2. Addison-Wesley.

Lenstra, J. K., 1974. Clustering a data array and the traveling salesman problem. *Operations Research*, Vol. 22, No. 2, pp. 413–414.

Medina, B. F. et al., 2016. Smoothed Multiple Binarization – Using PQR tree, smoothing, feature vectors and thresholding for matrix reordering. *Proceedings of 20th International Conference Information Visualisation* (IV), pp. 88–93.

Mäkinen, E. and Siirtola, H., 2000. Reordering the reorderable matrix as an algorithmic problem. *Theory and Application of Diagrams*. Springer, pp. 453–468.

Niermann, S., 2005. Optimizing the ordering of tables with evolutionary computation. *The American Statistician*, Vol. 59, No. 1, pp. 41-46.

Rehm, F. et al., 2005. MDS_{polar}: A new approach for dimension reduction to visualize high dimensional data. *Advances in Intelligent Data Analysis,* LNCS, Vol. 3646, pp. 316–327.

Rehm, F. et al., 2006: Polarmap - efficient visualization of high dimensional data. *Proceedings of the 10th International Conference on Information Visualisation* (IV'06), pp. 731–740.

Rocha, M. M. N. et al., 2017. Circumplex sort: a two-phase method for revealing circumplex data patterns in reorderable matrices. *Proceedings of International Conferences Computer Graphics, Visualization, Computer Vision and Image Processing 2017 and Big Data Analytics, Data Mining and Computational Intelligence 2017*, pp. 181–188.

Russell, J., 1980. A circumplex model of affect. *Journal of Personality and Social Psychology*, Vol. 39, No. 6, pp. 1161–1178.

Tzeng, J. et al., 2008. Multidimensional scaling for large genomic data sets. *BMC Bioinformatics*, Vol. 9, Article 179.

Torgerson, W. S., 1952. Multidimensional scaling: I. theory and method. *Psychometrika*, Vol. 17, No. 4, pp. 401–419.

Wilkinson, L., 2005. *The Grammar of Graphics*. Springer Science & Business Media.

Wu, H.-M. et al., 2008. Matrix Visualization. *Handbook of Data Visualization*. Springer, pp. 681–708.

INTRA-CLASS CONSTRAINED SPARSE REPRESENTATION WITH GRADIENT FEATURE FOR OCCLUDED FACE RECOGNITION

Qinqin Ma and Xiang Ma
School of Information Engineering, Chang'an University, Xi'an 710048, China

ABSTRACT

A novel occlusion face recognition method based on gradient feature and intra-class constrained sparse representation classification is proposed in this paper. We propose a second-order gradient feature to extract the texture and contour of images, which is more robust to occlusion than the original pixel of the face image. Intra-class constraint sparse representation is designed to make the test image close to the specific class by minimizing intra-class error. Furthermore, intra-class error is used as classification criteria. Experiments on the Extended Yale B and AR face databases prove the superiority and robustness of the proposed method for occluded face recognition, especially for the real world occlusion.

KEYWORDS

Occluded Face Recognition, Intra-Class Constraint

1. INTRODUCTION

Face recognition technology has achieved remarkable achievements and has been applied in many aspects of social life, including online verification, secure payment, access control system and so on. In the real situation, face occlusion is very common and the factors that cause occlusion are various, for instance, external obstacles such as scarves and glasses, as well as shadow occlusion caused by illumination. Figure 1 shows face images with different types of occlusion. Diversified occlusion types, uncertain occlusion areas, and random occlusion positions have a huge impact on the accuracy of face recognition. Considering the difficulty of face recognition due to the randomness and complexity of occlusion, this paper focuses on the problem of occlusion face recognition.

In recent years, occlusion face recognition methods can be roughly divided into two categories: robust feature extraction and robust classifier. The core idea of robust feature extraction methods is to separate the occlusion region from the overall face images and reduce or even ignore the weight of the occlusion region in the recognition process. A key-points descriptor of the Gabor ternary pattern for partial face recognition was proposed (Liao et al., 2013). Lu et al. (2015) reduce the difference in the feature level between face images by learning a compact binary face descriptor. An directional illumination estimation set algorithm (Cheng et al., 2017) was proposed to improve the method of multiscale principal contour direction (Cheng et al., 2010), which greatly alleviates the false contours of shadow edges and preserves the basic characteristics of the face. Robust feature extraction methods achieve good results for the certain type of occlusion, but can not fundamentally remove occlusion from the face image. In the existing feature extraction methods, region division and weight setting are still issues that need to be explored.

The second category mainly focuses on training robust classifiers. Wright et al. (2009) have proposed a sparse representation classification (SRC) method to represent test samples through sparse linear combination of training dictionaries. The cooperative representation classification (CRC) (Zhang et al., 2011) and the probability CRC (ProCRC) (Cai et al., 2016) are more conducive than the SRC. The robust version of ProCRC (R-ProCRC) is valid for occlusion. Since the occlusion portion contains structural information, the SRC does not effectively simulate the occlusion portion of face images. A structural constraint based on the dictionary learning method is proposed to deal with occlusion (Ou et al., 2014). Recently, Huang et al. (2017) proposed a kernel extended occlusion dictionary to improve efficiency. In real-world occlusion situations, since occlusion pixels have spatial continuity rather than being isolated from each other, Zhou et al. (2009) used Markov random field to describe the spatial correlation of occlusion pixels. The half-quadratic based iterative minimization method used a semi-quadratic minimization framework and iteratively restored occluded data (He et al., 2014). Inspired by robust principal component analysis, extracting sparse error of robust PCA is used to compute descriptors for face recognition (Luan et al, 2014). Li (2013) proposed a structured sparse error coding algorithm. A further improvement is to establish a model based on structured sparse error coding with discriminant error, structural error and occlusion support (Liang et al., 2015). At present, the use of sparse representation methods to deal with the face occlusion problem has received great attention, but further improvement of the recognition performance is needed.

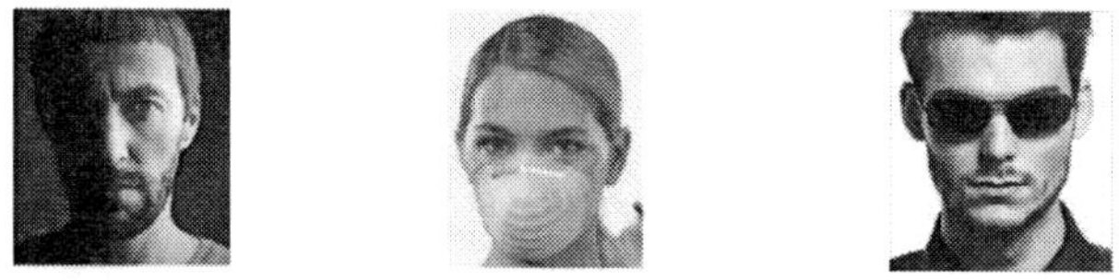

Figure 1. Face images with different occlusion types, from left to right: shadow occlusion, mask occlusion, sunglasses occlusion

Inspired by the above two types of methods, we propose a gradient feature-based intra-class constraint sparse representation method that combines robust features with robust classification. We extract the second-order gradient feature of the face image as the basis of recognition process. The gradient feature can better describe the edge and texture, and has better occlusion robustness than the original pixels of the face image. The intra-class error is finally used as a classification criterion. The contributions of this paper are as follows:

1) Fully exploit the performance of robust feature extraction and the error representation and detection capabilities of robust classifiers by combining robust feature extraction techniques with robust classifiers.

2) The second-order gradient feature is used to describe the edge and texture of the face image, which has better occlusion robustness than the original pixels of the face image, and contributes to the understanding and analysis of the face image.

3) Intra-class constraint is introduced in the sparse representation classification method to expand inter-class differences and reduce intra-class variations.

2. PROPOSED METHOD

In this part, we propose an intra-class constrained sparse representation method based on gradient feature, which specially describes the process of extracting second-order gradient feature and how to model the intra-class constrained sparse representation. The framework of the proposed algorithm is shown in Figure 2.

2.1 Second-Order Gradient Feature

Since the gradient feature can better describe the edge and texture of the face image, we propose to replace the original pixel of face images with the gradient feature. The second-order vector gradient $\nabla^2 I$ of the face image is calculated by the following formula:

$$\nabla^2 I = [G_{r2}, G_{c2}]^T = [\frac{\partial^2 I}{\partial r^2}, \frac{\partial^2 I}{\partial c^2}]^T \tag{1}$$

where r and c represent the row and column direction of the face image I . G_{r2} and G_{c2} respectively represent the second-order gradient of the horizontal and vertical direction.

$$g(\theta(I)) = 1 + \frac{2}{1 + e^{s*(\theta(I) - v)}} \tag{2}$$

where s and v represent the scaling and offset factor, respectively. In order to ensure the convergence of the optimization process, the formula (2) is used to map the second-order gradient direction of the face image into second-order gradient features $g(\theta(I))$. When the gradient direction $\theta(I) = G_{r2} / G_{c2}$ approaches infinity, the mapping function can make the second-order gradient feature close to a constant value.

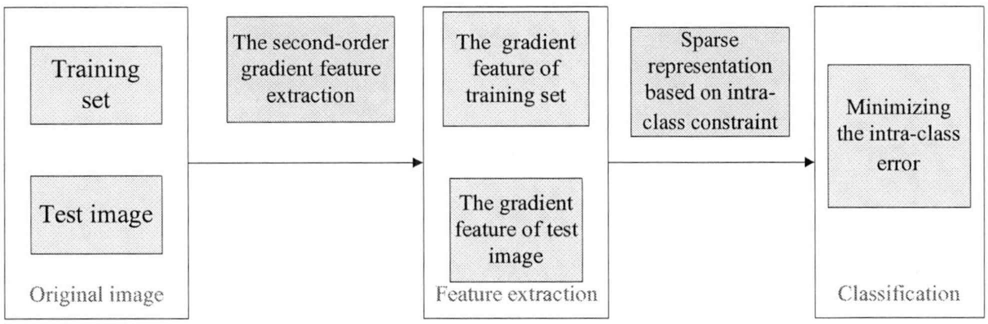

Figure 2. The framework of the proposed algorithm

The second-order gradient feature can describe the edge and texture information of the face image, and has better occlusion robustness than the image intensity domain feature. By extracting the contour and texture, structural features of the face image can be obtained, which provide a robust feature for subsequent classification and reduce the influence of occlusion on face recognition. Therefore, we propose to use the second-order gradient feature information instead of the intensity domain feature of the original image as the basis for the sparse representation classification.

2.2 Intra-Class Constrained Sparse Representation

SRC is a popular classification method and many extensions have been proposed. It mainly represents the test image by sparse linear combination of training samples, and uses the reconstruction error to achieve classification. It is assumed that the training set includes face images belonging to K classes, denoted as $X = [X_1,...,X_k,....,X_K]$, where X_k represents the k-th class face sample matrix of size $d \times m$, m represents the number of k-th class samples and d represents the dimension of the face image column vector. The test image y can be represented as $y = Xw$ by the SRC method, where w is a sparse representation vector. Since the l_0-norm cannot be directly solved, the sparse representation vector is calculated by relaxing it as a l_1-norm convex optimization problem:

$$\min_w \lambda \|w\|_1 \quad s.t. y = Xw \tag{3}$$

where λ is a constant. According to the proposed second-order gradient feature extraction method in Section 2.1, the gradient feature of training set and test images can be obtained as $G = [G_1,...,G_k,....,G_K]$ and $g(\theta(y))$, respectively. For convenience, we define $g(\theta(y))$ as y_g. G_k indicates the gradient feature of the k-th class sample X_k. We replace the original image pixels with the second-order gradient feature obtained in Section 2.1, and the formula based on the sparse representation of gradient feature is:

$$\min_w \lambda \|w\|_1 \quad s.t. y_g = Gw \tag{4}$$

The l_1-norm in the SRC method guarantees the sparsity of the linear representation vector. In order to make the reconstruction error of the test image as small as possible, we improve the performance of face recognition by introducing an intra-class constraint. The equation for the sparse representation method based on intra-class constraint with gradient feature is defined by:

$$\min_w \lambda \|w\|_1 + \frac{\beta}{K} \sum_{k=1}^{K} \|Gw - G_k w_k\|_2^2 \quad s.t. y_g = Gw \tag{5}$$

where $w=[w_1;w_2;...;w_k;...;w_K]$ and w_k is a representation coefficient corresponding to G_k. λ and β are balance factors for adjusting sparsity and intra-class constraint. Intra-class constraint can make test images close to the specific class by minimizing intra-class errors while maintaining sparsity. The intra-class constraint continuously adjusts the representation coefficient w_k according to the k-th class gradient feature to obtain the optimal solution.

We use the augmented Lagrangian multiplier method to optimize equation (5) to obtain the solution of w :

$$(\hat{w}) = \arg\min_w \left\{ \left\| y_g - Gw \right\|_2^2 + \lambda \left\| w \right\|_1 + \frac{\beta}{K} \sum_{k=1}^{K} \left\| Gw - G_k w_k \right\|_2^2 \right\} \quad (6)$$

After obtaining the solution of the sparse representation vector w, the intra-class error $r(y)$ is finally used as a classification criterion:

$$r(y) = \arg\min_k \left\{ \left\| Gw - G_k w_k \right\|_2^2 \right\} \quad (7)$$

The proposed method combines the advantages of robust feature and robust classifier. The second-order gradient feature extracts the edges and contours of face images, which helps to reduce the impact of occlusion on recognition performance. The SRC method based on intra-class constraint simultaneously guarantees sparsity and intra-class constraint, making the test image close to the specific class and minimizing the reconstruction error. In the next section, we will verify the effectiveness and robustness of the proposed method through sufficient experiments.

3. EXPERIMENTAL RESULTS

In this section, we evaluated the effectiveness and robustness of the proposed method for occlusion face recognition by conducting experiments on Extended Yale B (Georghiades et al, 2001) and AR face database (Martinez and Benavente, 1998). To illustrate the superiority of the proposed method, the proposed method was compared with some related representative methods, including SRC, CRC, ProCRC, the robust version of SRC(R-SRC) (Yang and Zhang, 2011) and R-ProCRC. For fair comparison, all methods of comparison use the optimal parameter settings. The two balance factors λ and β in the proposed method are determined by cross-validation, so we set $\lambda = 1$ and $\beta = 0.01$.

3.1 Experiments on Extended Yale B Face Database

In order to verify the recognition effect of the proposed algorithm on the occlusion factor, the algorithm was tested on the Extended Yale B face database of Yale University. There are 38 different categories of face images in the Extended Yale B face database, each class containing 64 different lighting conditions. All face images used in the experiment are manually aligned and cropped, leaving only the face area. And the resolution of face images is also adjusted to 32×32. In this experiment, each class randomly selects 30 images as the training set, and the remaining images as the test set. In addition, the recognition rate is the average of 5 test results, and each time different training set and test set were randomly selected. We determine the second-order gradient feature parameters $s = 2.8$ and $v = 0.28$ through experiments. Each image in the test set is randomly occluded by uncorrelated images, as shown in Figure 3. The occlusion ratio from left to right is 10%, 20%, 30%, 40%, respectively.

Figure 3. Sample images with different sizes of occlusion. From left to right, the ratio of occlusion is 10%, 20%, 30%, 40%, respectively

Table 1 shows the recognition rates of different methods under different occlusion rates. It can be seen from Table 1 that compared with other methods, the proposed method achieves the best recognition results under different block sizes, which fully demonstrates the effectiveness of the proposed method. The performance of ProCRC decreases sharply with the increasing occlusion area, indicating that the ProCRC is sensitive to corruption and occlusion. R-ProCRC is an improved version of ProCRC, which achieves robustness to occlusion, and its recognition rate is only lower than the proposed method. However, the decline trend of R-ProCRC recognition performance is still relatively obvious compared to the proposed method as the occlusion ratio increases. The proposed method still achieves a recognition rate of 89.64% at the occlusion rate of 40%, which proves that the occlusion factor has little effect on the proposed method. When the occlusion rate is 0, the recognition rate of the proposed method is still the highest, indicating that the recognition performance of the proposed method is excellent regardless of whether the face image is occluded or not.

Table 1. Experimental results with different sizes of block occlusion on the Extended Yale B database

Occlusion rate	0	10%	20%	30%	40%
SRC	95.97%	89.84%	83.06%	73.61%	62.33%
CRC	96.83%	93.65%	85.13%	72.80%	60.02%
R-SRC	96.28%	90.36%	86.13%	78.44%	69.79%
ProCRC	97.65%	81.93%	72.77%	63.70%	54.65%
R-ProCRC	98.22%	97.76%	90.87%	83.42%	75.47%
Proposed method	99.69%	98.51%	97.88%	96.38%	89.64%

3.2 Experiments on AR Face Database

In the previous section, the robustness of the proposed method is tested mainly by adding occlusion to the face image. To further verify the applicability of the proposed method, we test it on the AR face database with real guise. There are 100 different classes in the AR database, including 50 males and 50 females. Each category has two subsets, and the two subsets are taken at different times. Each subset consists of 7 unoccluded face images, 3 sunglasses occluded images, and 3 scarves occluded images. All face images are preprocessed and their resolution is set to 42×30. In this experiment, 7 unoccluded face images of the first subset are used as the training set, while 6 sunglasses occlusion images and 6 scarf occlusion images from the two subsets are used as test sets, respectively. As shown in Figure 4, the training set samples, the glasses occlusion test samples, and the scarf occlusion test samples are sequentially arranged from top to bottom. For the AR face database, we adjust the parameters $s=7.3$ and $v=0.51$.

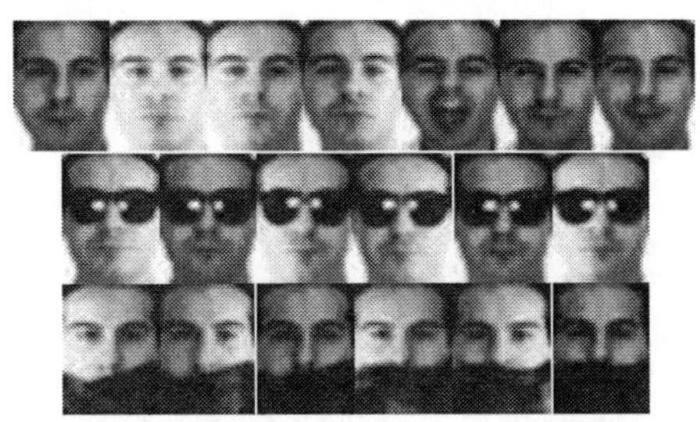

Figure 4. Sample diagram of AR face database (From top to bottom, the face images are from the training set, the glasses occlusion test set, and the scarf occlusion test set, respectively)

Table 2. Recognition rates of different methods on the AR face database

Occlusion type	Glasses	Scarf	Average
SRC	67.50%	61.83%	64.67%
CRC	68.83%	63.00%	65.92%
R-SRC	70.33%	64.33%	67.33%
ProCRC	53.33%	49.83%	51.58%
R-ProCRC	71.67%	65.00%	68.34%
Proposed method	87.00%	78.00%	82.50%

Table 2 shows the recognition rates of all methods for different occlusion types. The results in Table 2 show that all methods have better peformance on the glasses occlusion than the scarf occlusion. Because the scarf has the larger occlusion area, and it blocks some discriminative facial features. ProCRC has obtained the lowest recognition rate in all methods of comparison, indicating that it is sensitive to occlusion. The performance of CRC is slightly superior to SRC. The proposed method has obvious advantages, and it improves the recognition rate by about 14% compared with R-ProCRC. The experiments on the AR database fully demonstrate that the proposed method is also robust to real-world occlusion.

4. CONCLUSION

We propose a novel method using gradient feature and intra-class constrained sparse representation classification to solve the occlusion problem of face recognition. The second-order gradient feature is proposed as a robust feature for extracting the texture and contour of the face image. It is more robust than the original pixels of the face image and can effectively reduce the influence of occlusion. Intra-class constrained sparse representation is used as a robust classifier to minimize intra-class errors, making test images close to the specific class. Intra-class constraint achieves the purpose of expanding the differences between classes and narrowing the distance within the class. We use the intra-class error as a classification criterion. We have carried out sufficient experiments on the Extended Yale B face database and AR database, and compared the proposed method with some representative methods. Experimental results demonstrate the superiority and robustness of the proposed method for occlusion face recognition.

The proposed algorithm in this paper has achieved good recognition results on the standard face database. How to apply the proposed algorithm to face recognition in unconstrained natural scene is the research direction of future work.

ACKNOWLEDGEMENT

This work was supported in part by the National Natural Science Foundation of China under Grant 61771075, and in part by the China Fundamental Research Funds for the Central Universities under Grant 300102249203.

REFERENCES

Cai S. et al, 2016. A probabilistic collaborative representation based approach for pattern classification. *Proceedings of the IEEE Computer Society Conference on Computer Vision and Pattern Recognition.* Las Vegas, USA, pp. 2950–2959.

Cheng Y. et al, 2010. Multiscale principal contour direction for varying lighting face recognition. *In Electronics Letters.* Vol. 46, No. 10, pp. 680-682.

Cheng Y. et al, 2017. Directional Illumination Estimation Sets and Multilevel Matching Metric for Illumination-Robust Face Recognition. *In IEEE Access.* Vol. 5, pp. 25835-25845.

Georghiades A.S. et al, 2001. From few to many: illumination cone models for face recognition under variable lighting and pose. *In IEEE Transactions on Pattern Analysis and Machine Intelligence.* Vol. 23, No. 6, pp. 643-660.

He R. et al, 2014. Half-quadratic based iterative minimization for robust sparse representation, *In IEEE Transactions on Pattern Analysis and Machine Intelligence.* Vol. 36, Vo. 2, pp. 261-275.

Huang K. et al, 2017. Learning Kernel Extended Dictionary for Face Recognition, *In IEEE Transactions on Neural Networks and Learning Systems*, Vol. 28, No. 5, pp. 1082-1094.

Li X. et al, 2013. Structured Sparse Error Coding for Face Recognition with Occlusion. *In IEEE Transactions on Image Processing.* Vol. 22, No. 5, pp. 1889-1900.

Liang R. et al, 2015. Mixed error coding for face recognition with mixed occlusions. *Proceedings of the International Joint Conf. Artificial Intelligence*, pp. 3657–3663.

Liao S. et al, 2013. Partial face recognition: alignment-free approach, *In IEEE Transactions on Pattern Analysis and Machine Intelligence.* Vol. 35, No. 5, pp. 1193–1205.

Lu J. et al, 2015. Learning Compact Binary Face Descriptor for Face Recognition. *In IEEE Transactions on Pattern Analysis and Machine Intelligence*. Vol. 37, No. 10, pp. 2041-2056.

Luan X. et al, 2014. Extracting sparse error of robust PCA for face recognition in the presence of varying illumination and occlusion, *Pattern Recognit*. Vol. 47, No. 2, pp. 495–508.

Martinez A. and Benavente R., 1998. The AR face database. *CVC Technical Report*, No. 24.

Ou W. et al, 2014. Robust face recognition via occlusion dictionary learning. *Pattern Recognition*. Vol. 47, No. 4, pp. 1559–1572 .

Wright J. et al, 2009. Robust face recognition via sparse representation, *In IEEE Trans. Pattern Anal. Mach. Intell*. Vol. 31, No. 2, pp. 210–227 .

Yang J. and Zhang Y., 2011. Alternating direction algorithms for ℓ_1-problems in compressive sensing. *In SIAM journal on scientific computing*. Vol. 33, No. 1, pp. 250–278.

Zhang L. et al, 2011. Sparse representation or collaborative representation: which helps face recognition? *In: Proceedings of the IEEE International Conference Computer Vision*. Barcelona, pp. 471–478.

Zhou Z. et al, 2009. Face recognition with contiguous occlusion using markov random fields. *Proceedings of International Conference on Computer Vision*. Kyoto, pp. 1050-1057.

AUTOMATING USABILITY EVALUATION OF VISUAL USER INTERFACES IN THE TILE LOGIC

Vladimir V. Devyatkov and Evgeny A. Tipsin
Bauman Moscow State Technical University, Russia

ABSTRACT

This article presents the methodology of formal automated evaluation of user interface usability. The tiles logic was selected as the language for solving problems in formal usability verification. The paper contains an overview of the related works, explains the reasons for using the tile logic, and considers the principles of verification (proof) of usability as validation of agent's interaction. The differences and advantages of the developed approach from the well-known are shown. A description of the agents interaction in the tile logic is used to automate usability evaluation. The methodology of formal automated usability evaluation is demonstrated by describing the interaction of two simple agents in the tile logic. In conclusion, we present future of use and development of the proposed approach.

KEYWORDS

Tiles Logic, Verification of Properties, Graphical User Interface, Usability, Usability Evaluation, Intelligent Agents, Automating Usability Evaluation, Human-Machine Interactions

1. INTRODUCTION

There was introduced the term of usability in the standards ISO / IEC 25010, which is defined as "convenience and ease of use, degree of convenience", as well as suitability of use, ergonomics (the ability of an application to be understood, be studied, be used and attractive for a user in the specified conditions to achieve a set goals with necessary efficiency, effectiveness and satisfaction.

There is a wide range of traditional means of usability evaluation: standards/guidelines review, heuristic evaluation, cognitive walkthrough, pluralistic walkthrough, feature inspection, task analysis (Hackos and Redish, 1998), focus groups (Nielsen, 1997), surveys, interviews, questionnaires and benchmarking, eye tracking (Jacob and Karn, 2003), analysis of user's electroencephalogram (Alfimtsev et al., 2015) and others. However, all these usability evaluations are rather labor-intensive. This is reflected in spending time for preparing for benchmarking, selection of respondents and further analysis of obtained results by the experts of human-machine interaction. In some cases, availability of special equipment is necessary. In order to reduce complexity and amount of manual work, the direction of automated usability evaluation is relevant. In this direction, there are three basic approaches to automating evaluation of visual user interfaces usability:

1. Analysis of user logs properties (Approach 1). Analysis of logs (files) that contains entries of user's actions in process of interaction with real applications or dynamic prototypes in chronological order. Typically, these actions are motion of a mouse cursor; a time spent on page, transition between pages and other.

2. Parametric analysis of page properties (Approach 2). The analysis of parameters the particular pages of the application for compliance with the best practices in design, visual noise and interface complexity, also identifying the page areas that the user will draw attention primarily (Alfimtsev et al., 2016).

3. Model-oriented proof of the properties existence. (Approach 3) In the paper (Devyatkov, 2016) considered the properties of multimodal intelligent interfaces, implementation of which, according to the authors, provides a "barrier-free" user interaction with application (Sakulin et al., 2018).

In the first column of table 1is the list, according to an analytical review, containing 10 selection criteria an approach to usability evaluation. In the other columns, for each approach, a "+"sign indicates that criterion is met in approach, and a " - " sign indicates that criterion is not met. This table shows that the most number of criteria is met in the model-oriented approach. There are three criteria that is not met: the explanation of user's behavior, no need to invite human-machine interaction experts, the lack of the subjective factor.

Despite the dissatisfaction of the three criteria, the model-oriented approach is preferable. Model-oriented approach uses models of architecture and system behavior in which interaction is implemented. If the model developer believes, that its architecture and behavior has all necessary objective properties, that provide necessary degree of usability, then remains to prove that this architecture and behavior is met of these properties.

The authors believe that the address these drawbacks (explanation of user behavior, no need to invite human-machine interaction experts, the lack of a subjective factor) is possible by automated model-oriented proof of objective property presences in architecture and interacting models of user behavior and an application within adequate calculus, including:

– formal language of adequate patterns description of user behavior and executor in interaction process;

– formal description of the objective properties of the architecture and interacting models behavior that ensures a high degree of usability in this language;

– many consistent inference rules in this language;

– output strategy to ensure completeness proof of architecture properties and interacting models behavior.

A formal description of objective architecture properties and interacting models behavior, that ensures high degree of usability, will obviate need to invite human-machine interaction experts and, as a result, their subjective opinion (Chernenkiy et al, 2018).

Table 1. Approaches and criteria

Criteria \ Approaches	1	2	3
Carrying out at an early stage of development	-	-	+
Explanation of user behavior	-	-	-
Ease of use rating after making changes to the interface	-	+	-
No need to invite human-machine interaction experts	-	-	-
Time executions	-	+	+
Considering the context of using the application	-	-	+
User experience considering	-	-	+
Dynamic page analysis	+	-	+
The lack of the subjective factor	-	-	-

A strategy for ensure completeness proof of architecture properties and interactive models behavior based on inference rules will allow to identify an application usability and disadvantage reasons of usage of application.

Automation of output strategy will ensure ease of evaluating usability after changes in interaction process.

According to the author's opinion, language of tile logic is the most appropriate to automation of evaluation usability. In particular, this opinion is based, on the fact that a tile, as a construction, allow to display the elements of pages naturally and transitions between the elements, implemented as a result of certain user actions. In addition, acceptable tiles sequences of user interaction with system can be put together, according to certain rules, that serve as a means of usability evaluation.

The principles of proving any properties of systems based on the tiles logic have been known for a long time (Bruni et al, 1998). In order to create a language of the tile logic for our case, it is necessary to create a basic tiles set that allow to represent application behavior (Ivashkin et al, 2018). Further in this article, an application will be called the agent-executor and a respondent will be called the agent-user.

Below are the basic concepts of the tile logic. Then a formal description of application (agent-executor) and respondent (agent-user) models will be provided. After that, usability criteria will be introduced. The example of usability evaluation of the application will be shown. In conclusion, directions of further work of automation usability evaluation of applications are given.

2. THE TILES AND TILE OPERATIONS

Rules structure of inference is an advantage of the tile logic, each of rules can be represented as a tile. A tile structure in general form is shown on Figure 1.

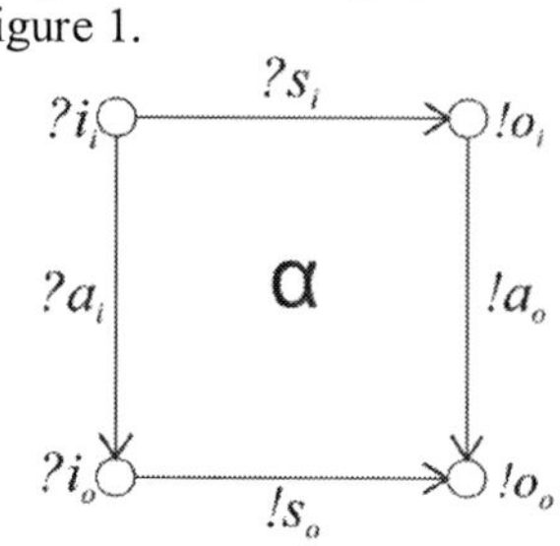

Figure 1. The tile: α – the tile name; $?s_i$ – the tile initial configuration; $!s_o$ – the tile final configuration; $?a_i$ – the tile perception; $!a_o$ – the tile reaction; $?i_i$ – the tile initial input interface; $?o_i$ – the tile initial output interface; $?i_o$ – the tile final input interface; $!o_o$ – the tile final output interface.

Tile allows to describe system components behavior that contain variables called configurations. This behavior is described in terms of possible interactions with the external or internal environment. System behavior is a coordinated interaction of individual tiles. Tile interfaces define interaction format with the external environment. Tiles can be composited horizontally (denoted by symbol $*$), vertically (denoted by symbol $\bullet$), and in parallel (denoted by symbol $\otimes$) to define complex behavior of systems. The tile logic is obtained by introducing a set of basic tiles and a certain set of auxiliary tiles. Tile operations can be performed leading to various kinds of tile compositions, in particular, in order to prove the user interfaces properties.

3. AGENT ARCHITECTURE FOR AUTOMATION USABILITY EVALUATION

An architecture, consisting of the agent-executor and the agent-user, is used to demonstrate method of automated usability evaluation process (Vorotnikov et al., 2018).

The agent-executor (*AE*) has two channels. The input channel (*UE*) is the output to the agent-user and the output channel is the input to the agent-user (*EU*). The agent-user can put a message to the input channel of the agent-executor. The agent-executor can take this message. The agent-executor can put a message to the agent-user on it output channel. Further, the agent-executor and agent-user will be called the executor and the user.

If the channels UE and EU compare to the variable *c* (from *channel*), and the messages in channels compare to the variable m (from message), then the set of all channel states is $c(m)$, where $c \in \{UE, EU\}$, $m \in \{m(UE) \cup m(EU)\}$, $m(UE)$ – the set of messages in the channel UE, $m(EU)$ - the set of messages in the channel EU. The couple $[UE(m_u), EU(m_e)]$ is a configuration. If no matter message in the channel EU for the executor, then configuration will be denoted as $[UE(m_u), EU(\_)]$, and conversely, if no matter message in the channel UE for the user, then configuration will be denoted as $[UE(\_), EU(m_e)]$.

The executor performs internal behavior in accordance with own convictions after receiving a message from the user. The executor and the user interaction begins after receiving a notification of start of interaction from the user. If the executor has concurred to interaction, then it continues. In other case, an interaction terminate. The user stops an interaction by sending an appropriate message to the executor.

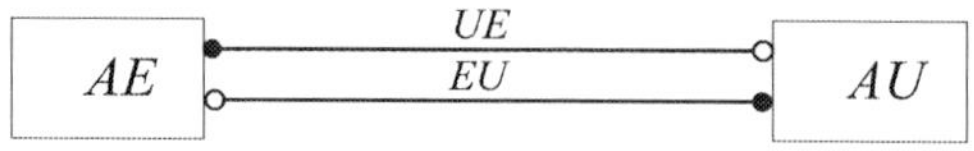

Figure 2. User and executor interaction channels

4. USABILITY EVALUATION CRITERIA

Usability evaluation criteria can be qualitative and quantitative and allow to conclude about interface usability, as well as comparing user interface with other projects or previous versions of the design.

According to Nielsen's approach (Nielsen, 1994), there are three types of evaluation:

– completed the task without difficulty - 100%;
– had difficulties, but completed the task - 50%;
– did not complete the task - 0%.

The problem that we placed in this article does not include a detailed consideration of all evaluation criteria. Therefore, in article will be focus on calculus of tile logics.

5. MODEL OF THE USER INTERFACE

An application can be represented as a collection of pages. Each page has own user interface, which includes various types of elements: navigation elements, specifying possible movements between pages; control elements to perform actions, such as sending an email, attaching files, or changing content; content items.

Thus, each user interface consists of certain interface elements — primitives of a graphical user interface that have a standard appearance and perform standard actions. Interface elements include: edit fields (textbox), buttons, radio buttons, checkboxes, icons, and others.

Related elements grouping is using to improve usability, for example: alignment, grouping, highlighting, indents, pins, element sizes and spacing. Usually grouped interface elements are named as blocks. Introduce the following notation to proceed to the developed approach specification with the tile logic.

An application I consists of a finite set of pages P. A page $p \in P$ consists of at least one block $b \in B$, which may consist of blocks $b_1^{'},...,b_j^{'} \subset b$ and/or interface elements $e_1,...,e_k \in E$ $e_1,...,e_k \in b$. Thus, application can be represented as $I = \{P, B, E\}$: P – a set of pages, which contains the application $\{p_1,..., p_k\} \in P$; B – a set of blocks $\{b_1,...,b_m\} \subset B$; E – a set of interface elements $\{e_1,...,e_l\} \in E$.

Each page $p \in P$ has the following attributes: c_1^p – a name of the page; c_2^p – a set of blocks $\{b_1,...,b_n\} \in B$ that contains page.

Each block $b \in B$ has the following attributes: c_1^b – a set of blocks $\{b_1^{'},...,b_j^{'}\} \subset B$, that contains the block $\{b_1,...,b_j\} \subset b$; c_2^b – a set of interface elements $\{e_1, e_2,..., e_k\} \subset E$, that contains the block $\{e_1, e_2,..., e_k\} \subset b$.

Each interface elements $e \in E$ has the following attributes: c_1^e – type that can be one of eight values: *text*, *input* (single line input field), *textarea* (multiline input field), *button*, *image*, *select* (drop-down list), *video*, *audio*; c_2^e – hint/ user interface label; c_3^e – content; c_4^e – size, represented by the corresponding pair of values, in the format (width, height); c_5^e – form; c_6^e – color; c_7^e – brightness; c_8^e – an additional attribute that can contain a description of reactions when interacting with an element, for example, notification of incorrect format of entered data in text field (Sakulin et al., 2018).

6. AGENT-EXECUTOR REPRESENTATION IN THE TILE LOGIC

The executor is on interface object, receiving messages from the user, it changes contents of objects (inserts data) or moves to another object.

In order to set the executor behavior, horizontal and vertical tiles compositions are applied. A horizontal composition simulate an action on side of the executor. A vertical composition is to exchange messages with the user (receiving and placing messages in interaction channels).

The executor behavior depends on perception (message from the user in his input channel). It performs a reaction (place message to the user in output channel) in response to communication. The executor analyzes the current configuration $[UE(m_u), EU(\_)]$ (the "Getting an action on an object" tile), perform perception of message m_u from the channel $UE(m_u)$, sets the initial output interface $s\_i(m_u)$ (from set interface) depending on message m_u, as a result, the configuration $[UE(m_u), EU(\_)]$ remains unchanged.

The «Object reaction» (Figure 3b) tile describes the reaction on message in the output channel. The tile perception is not set. It perform reaction (place message in output channel to the executor) in response. The executor analyzes the current configuration $[UE(m_u), EU(\_)]$, generates a reaction m_e (message) that puts into the channel $EU(m_e)$, as a result, the configuration $[UE(m_e), EU(\_)]$ goes into the configuration $[UE(m_u), EU(m_e)]$.

Blocks and interface elements have a similar description, so let's call them general concept – object.

The user and application interaction may be the following in real situation. The user scans each new page and clicks on the first link similar to that he were looking for. If a result did not meet expectations, user goes back to the previous page and continues scanning (Mahyavanshi et al, 2017). Thus, main types of user interaction with application can be identified: a transition from one object to another; performing actions on an element (click, double click, entering data); return to previous page.

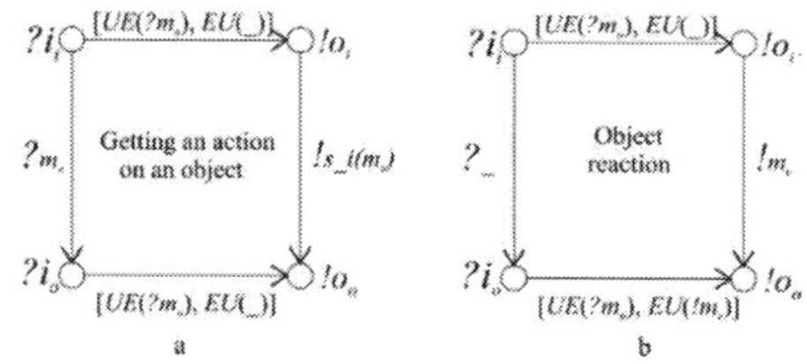

Figure 3. Agent-executor tiles

$left$ – move to left object of the current $object$; up – move to upper object of the current $object$; $right$ – move to right object of the current $object$; $down$ – move to bottom object of the current $object$; $single\_click$ – single click on the $object$; $double\_click$ – double click on the $object$, $back$ – return to previous page, $data$ – data to enter into interface element.

Perceptions $single\_click$, $double\_click$ are available only for interface elements E.

A message (reaction) can be the following type: $object\_info$ – a set of interface object characteristics (block, interface element); $notification$ – notification of correct or erroneous entry of data into interface element.

7. THE SELECTION PRINCIPLES OF THE AGENT- USER

Define user groups, to which an application is focused, is performed in selection an user for usability testing. Agent user is a collective character of users group. Agent-user must have behavioral features of selected user group. Agent tiles should take into account features, as well as the goals that need to be identified and reflected by selected user. Thus, the user is a model of behavior for a certain users group, and behavior characteristics are represented in the tile logic. Tile or set of tiles describes characteristics.

In addition to the tiles of behavior patterns, the user have a certain set of attributes that represent the necessary information to interaction. For example, the user should to know a login and a password, which are agent's attributes, when it authorizing in an application. Without these attributes, the user cannot complete a task. Given applications and tasks diversity, it is impossible to set all possible user attributes in advance. Therefore, attributes is set expertly.

8. AGENT-USER IN THE TILE LOGIC

In this paper, the simple user behavior, which receives a message from the executor (the «Receiving object» tile), will demonstrate. The user goes to another interface element (puts the message on the output channel with the transition direction) or puts the data on the interface element (puts the message on the output channel with the data), depending on the message. Transition to another element (the «Performing action» tile) is performed if the message is a notification of correct data entry into an element or interface object description that is not an input field. Otherwise, it is entered data into interface element (the «Goal achievement» tile). Tiles, describing various characteristics and user behavior patterns, will not be considered in this article.

Horizontal and vertical composition is applied to set user behavior, similar the executor. Horizontal composition is an action on side of the user. A Vertical composition is exchange of messages with the executor (receiving and putting messages in interaction channels).

The following five tiles are used to describe user behavior.

1. As stated earlier, the executor and the user interactions begins after receiving notification of start of interaction from the user. The «Interaction initialization» (figure 4a) describes the placement of a message of start of interaction from the user to the executor. The user analyzes the current configuration $[EU(\_),UE(\_)]$, generates a response m_u (notification of the start of interaction), which is placed in the UE channel, as a result, the configuration $[EU(\_),UE(\_)]$ goes into the configuration $[EU(\_),UE(m_u)]$.

2. The «Receiving object» (figure 4b) tile describes the receipt of a message from the executor. Similarly, the user uses a perception (message) in the input channel placed by the executor. Perception sets the initial output interface and determines the subsequent agent behavior. The initial output interface imposes restrictions on horizontal composition with other tiles that limits the user's acceptable actions. The user analyzes the current configuration $[EU(m_e),UE(\_)]$, perform the perception of the message m_e from the channel $EU(m_e)$, establishes interfaces $s\_i(m_e)$ (from *set interface*) depending on message, as a result, the configuration $[EU(m_e),UE(\_)]$ remains unchanged.

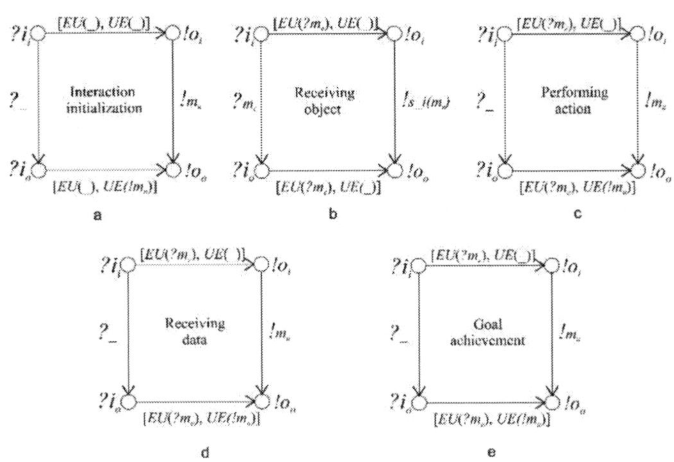

Figure 4. Agent-user tiles

3. The «Performing action» (figure 4c) tile describes the placement in the output channel of transition direction to another interface element. The tile perception is not set. The reaction is to put a message in output channel to the executor. The user analyzes the current configuration $[EU(m_e),UE(\_)]$, generates a reaction m_u (message) that puts into the channel $UE(m_u)$, as a result, the configuration $[EU(m_e),UE(\_)]$ goes into the configuration $[EU(m_e),UE(m_u)]$.

4. The «Receiving data» (figure 4d) tile describes the data acquisition for entering into an interface element. The tile perception is not set. The reaction is to put a message in output channel to the executor. The user analyzes the current configuration $[EU(m_e), UE(\_)]$, generates a reaction m_u (message) that puts into the channel $UE(m_u)$, as a result, the configuration $[EU(m_e), UE(\_)]$ goes into the configuration $[EU(m_e), UE(m_u)]$.

5. The «Goal achievement» (figure 4e) tile describes check the goal achievement. The tile perception is not set. The reaction is to put a message in output channel to the executor. The user analyzes the current configuration, generates a reaction m_u (message) that puts into the channel $UE(m_u)$, as a result, the configuration $[EU(m_e), UE(\_)]$ goes into the configuration $[EU(m_e), UE(m_u)]$.

9. SIMPLE EXAMPLE OF AUTOMATING USABILITY EVALUATION IN TILE LOGIC

In this section, the simple example of usability evaluation, that demonstrate a general approach to automating usability evaluation, are shown.

The developed approach of automation of usability evaluation has been demonstrated for the one-page application (figure 5). The application is a service for translating numbers between systems of positional numbers. Application page contains 5 interface elements: page name e_1; input field for the initial number system e_2; input field for source number e_3; input field for the number system to which the initial number will be translated e_4; output field for result of conversion e_5. After filling in the fields e_2, e_3, e_4 the initial number is transferred to the specified numeral system, the result is placed in the field e_5.

A developer, who performs usability evaluation, presents an application as a set of tiles. More detailed an application, the higher accuracy of usability evaluation, because each element can affect user behavior. The application can be represented as $I = \{P, B, E\}$, where $P = \{p_1\}$; $B = \{b_1\}$, $b_1 \subset p_1$; $E = \{e_1, ..., e_5\}$, $\{e_1, ..., e_5\} \subset b_1$.

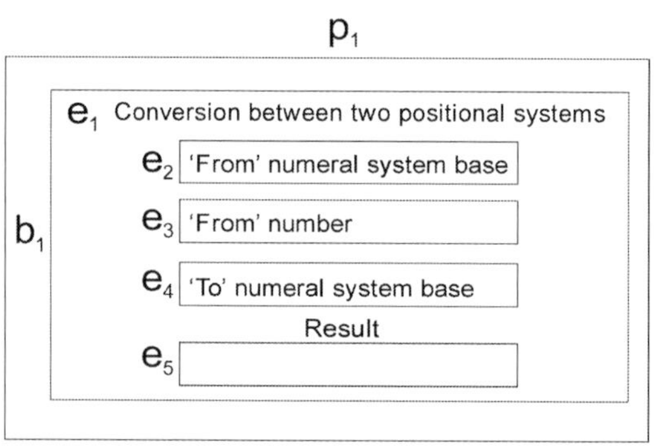

Figure 5. User interface

The sequence of actions is given below, that an expert should perform:

1. The creation of a set of tiles and attributes for each page p_1, block b_1 and interface element $e_1, ..., e_5$.

2. Choice of usability criteria to evaluate application. In this paper, only one criterion is considered, which usability evaluation based on result of task (completed - an application has a high degree of usability, otherwise low).

3. Assigning a task to the user to solve it by interacting with the executor.

4. A user type determines user behavioral characteristics. Various types of user agents (behavior model of user's specific groups) are not considered in this article. The user interacts with the executor through the tiles presented in the previous section.

5. Setting necessary attributes of the user to solve task. For this application: “From” numeral system base – 5; “From” number – 10; “To” numeral system base – 2.

Consider a sequence of composition of the executor and the user tiles as they interact.

After the user has put a message to the channel UE , the user is described by the «Getting an action on an object» tile. Similarly, the executor has put a message to the channel EU , the executor is described by the «Receiving object» tile.

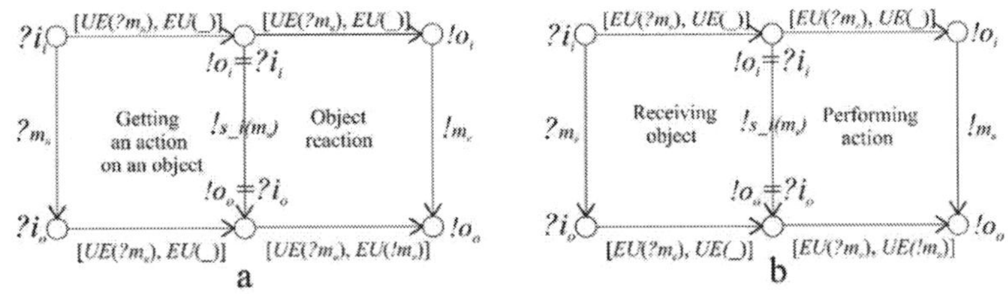

Figure 6. Tiles composition

User (step 1). «Initialization interaction»

Executor (step 2). «Getting an action on an object» * «Object reaction», as it shown on the figure 6a (e_1).

User (step 3). «Receiving object» * «Performing action», as it shown on the figure 6b.

Executor (step 4). «Getting an action on an object» * «Object reaction», as it shown on the figure 6a (e_2).

User (step 5). «Receiving object» * «Receiving data»

Executor (step 6). “Getting an action on an object» * «Object reaction», as it shown on the figure 6a.

User (step 7). «Receiving object» * «Performing action», as it shown on the figure 6b.

Further steps 4-7 are performed similarly for the elements e_3, e_4.

Executor (step 8). «Getting an action on an object» * «Object reaction», as it shown on the figure 6a.

User (step 9). «Receiving object» * «Goal achievement»

According to the usability criteria, it can be concluded that the interface has a high degree of usability.

10. CONCLUSIONS

In this paper provides an analytical review of approaches to automating usability evaluation of applications, in which the advantages and disadvantages of each approach were identified. The formal model-oriented method of automated usability evaluation based on tile logic was proposed to address existing deficiencies, in which an application and user model is created. Valid user interaction sequences with an application are assembled from tiles according to certain rules that provide a means for usability evaluation. The use of the method was shown by the example of the one-page application. In future work, the application model will be improved, namely, the addition of new tiles describing transitions between interface elements. Full-on user model, describing characteristics and behavior while scanning the application page, will be created in the tiles logic. User model behavior will compare with the behavior of a real user. Number of usability evaluation metrics will be increased. After the improvements, the usability of the multi-page application will be evaluated. In fact, automating usability in the tile logic is the knowledge extraction of the interacting agents. User behavior is the subject of analytics in a wide variety of applications. It is demand at the present stage of intelligent information systems development. This paper outlines the principles of interacting agents behavior based on the use of processes local behavior patterns in the tile logic. Composition of tiles forms the interacting agents general behavior. The presentation of principles is carried out at a general level, allowing the tiles composition, but without formal proof of properties of the interacting agents actual behavior. In [Devyatkov, 2016], a properties proof concretization is given for the case of proving the presence of intelligent interfaces certain properties and the proof implementation in the logic language PROLOG. Since the basis of the proof procedures in the PROLOG language is unification. Unification can serve as a means of detecting the presence of specific behavior in the tiles composition. In addition, by analogy with the same work, if it is know that interacting agents behavior are most interested, then the properties of this behavior can be formulated in the modal logics languages, and then they will be checked. In the future, it is supposed to be implemented.

REFERENCES

Alfimtsev, A. N., Basarab, M. A., Devyatkov, V. V., & Levanov, A. A. (2015). A new methodology of usability testing on the base of the analysis of user's electroencephalogram. Journal of Computer Sciences and Applications, 3(5), 105-111.

Alfimtsev, A., Sakulin, S., & Levanov, A. (2016). Formalization of expert knowledge about the usability of web pages based on user criteria aggregation. International Journal of Software Innovation (IJSI), 4(3), 38-50.

Bruni, R., Meseguer, J., & Montanari, U. (1998). Process and term tile logic.

Chernenkiy, V., Gapanyuk, Y., Terekhov, V., Revunkov, G., & Kaganov, Y. (2018). The hybrid intelligent information system approach as the basis for cognitive architecture. Procedia computer science, 145, 143-152.

Devyatkov V.V. Verification of Intelligent Interface Properties in the Tiles Logic. Vestn. Mosk. Gos. Tekh. Univ. im. N.E. Baumana, Priborostr. [Herald of the Bauman Moscow State Tech. Univ., Instrum. Eng.], 2016, no. 3, pp. 65–87.

Hackos, J. T., & Redish, J. (1998). User and task analysis for interface design.

Ivashkin, Y. A., Blagoveschensky, I. G., & Nikitina, M. A. (2018). Neural network and agent technologies in the structural-parametric modeling of technological systems. In 2018 School-Seminar on Optimization Problems and their Applications, OPTA-SCL 2018 (pp. 169-180).

Jacob, R. J., & Karn, K. S. (2003). Eye tracking in human-computer interaction and usability research: Ready to deliver the promises. In The mind's eye (pp. 573-605).

Mahyavanshi, N., Patil, M., & Kulkarni, V. (2017). Enhancing Web Usability using User Behavior and Cognitive Study. International Journal of Computer Applications, 164(2).

Nielsen, J. (1997). The use and misuse of focus groups. IEEE software, 14(1), 94-95.

Sakulin, S., Alfimtsev, A., Solovyev, D., & Sokolov, D. (2018). Web page interface optimization based on nature-inspired algorithms. International Journal of Swarm Intelligence Research (IJSIR), 9(2), 28-46.

Sakulin S. A., Alfimcev A. N., Tipsin E. A. (2018). Verification of user interface distribution based on π-calculus. Bulletin of Bryansk state technical university, (9), 56-65.

Vorotnikov, S., Ermishin, K., Nazarova, A., & Yuschenko, A. (2018). Multi-agent Robotic Systems in Collaborative Robotics. In International Conference on Interactive Collaborative Robotics (pp. 270-279). Springer, Cham.

ANIMATING AN AUTONOMOUS 3D TALKING AVATAR

Dominik Borer[1], Dominic Lutz[2], Robert W. Sumner[2] and Martin Guay[2]
[1]*ETH Zürich, Disney Research*
[2]*Disney Research*

ABSTRACT

One of the main challenges with embodying a conversational agent is annotating how and when motions can be played and composed together in real-time, without any visual artifact. The inherent problem is to do so—for a large amount of motions—without introducing mistakes in the annotation. To our knowledge, there is no automatic method that can process animations and automatically label actions and compatibility between them. In practice, a state machine, where clips are the actions, is created manually by setting connections between the states with the timing parameters for these connections. Authoring this state machine for a large amount of motions leads to a visual overflow, and increases the amount of possible mistakes. In consequence, conversational agent embodiments are left with little variations and quickly become repetitive. In this paper, we address this problem with a compact taxonomy of chit chat behaviors, that we can utilize to simplify and partially automate the graph authoring process. We measured the time required to label actions of an embodiment using our simple interface, compared to the standard state machine interface in Unreal Engine, and found that our approach is 7 times faster. We believe that our labeling approach could be a path to automated labeling: once a sub-set of motions are labeled (using our interface), we could learn a prediction that could attribute a label to new clips—allowing to really scale up virtual agent embodiments.

KEYWORDS

Conversational Embodiment, Interactive Conversational Agent, Parametric Body Motion

1. INTRODUCTION

Intelligent avatars that can talk and interact with people offer a natural and friendly way to interface with autonomous systems—may they be cars, televisions, food dispensers, phones, maps, and so on. While this vision is not new, machine perception and natural Language processing has evolved rapidly in recent years, causing a re-visitation of this vision by various companies, each releasing voice-based assistants such as Alexa, Siri, or AliGenie and some embodied systems with digital displays such as Gatebox, Jibo and Baidu.

One of the main challenges with embodying an agent is annotating how and when motions can be played and composed together in real-time, without any visual artifact. The inherent problem is to do so—for a large amount of motions—without introducing mistakes in the annotation. To our knowledge, there is no automatic method that can process animations and automatically label actions and compatibility between them. In practice, a state machine, where clips are the actions, is created manually by setting connections between the states with the timing parameters for these connections, together with other state parameters such as body part mask, clip start and end time, as well as whether the motion is looping or not. For example, consider an action that has the arm waving in the air, while a new action requests a beat gesture that starts with the arm pointing on the floor. The sudden jump to the other motion will cause a visual artifact. Hence in this case the state machine would have a transition between both gestures, and the timing would be set to the end of the first clip, forcing the embodiment to finish the first clip before playing the next (assuming they have a compatible pose at their respective extremities).

Authoring this state machine for a large amount of clips requires repetitive labour for many actions, and can grow exponentially for certain types of behaviors that require transitions between them, as shown in Figure 1. Hence the possibilities of introducing mistakes is very high. In consequence, conversational agent embodiments are often left with little variations, and quickly become repetitive and predictable. In this paper, we address this problem with a compact taxonomy of chit chat behaviors, that we can utilize to simplify and partially automate the graph authoring process. We observed from casual dyadic conversations that people are mainly in stances, fidgets, gestures and transitions (between stances). Stances are synonymous to idle (e.g. arm on waist, or body weight on one side), fidgets are ticks and small subtle gestures, while gestures are more functional. The final element are the transitions between the stances such as changing the body weight to another side, or having a hand going from the waist to a shoulder.

With our taxonomy, we propose a more abstract and partially automated interface for the state machine authoring, where animation clips are dragged and dropped onto one of the action types (gesture, fidget, stance, transition), as shown in Figure 2. We asked an animator to create animations guided by our taxonomy, and to utilize our interface to populate the graph. In total, 152 animations were created, and labeling all the motions (or authoring the graph) was 7 times faster than using the traditional interface in Unreal Engine (see our comparison discussion for more details Section 7.1). We believe that our labeling approach could be a way to automated labeling via a bootstrapping phase: once a sub-set of motions are labeled (using our interface), we could learn a prediction that could attribute a label to new clips—allowing to really scale up virtual agent embodiments.

We additionally report on our best practices for embodiment decision making (Section 6, which we learned during a collaborative project for embodying an agent. We found that in practice agents operate at different levels of abstraction. For example, one agent might output high-level actions such as "say line 279", or lower level commands such as "nod here". To cope with different levels of abstraction, we designed a motion planner that can filter, as well as synthesize actions, if needed. Our planner takes sequences of abstract actions and outputs a sequence of specific actions. In the case of too few actions, the planner can generate natural sequences using probability distributions conditioned on the previous action, which we compute from video recorded human performances.

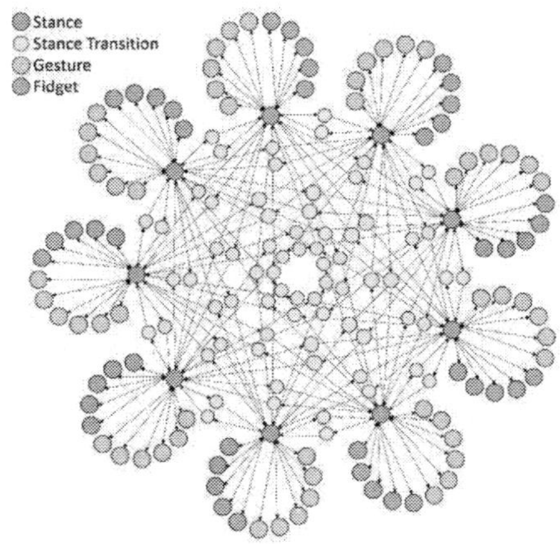

Figure 1. Explicitly creating the animation state machine with all connectivity information quickly becomes complex and prone to errors. Since the logic for all transitions is the same (up to some motion-specific parameters), there is a lot of redundant information, which we can reduce to a simple interface as shown in Figure 2

2. RELATED WORK

2.1 Agency, Planning and Architecture related to Embodiment

Over the past years there have been many works on turning text and other modalities into actions. The seminalwork by Casell et al. on text to motion [Cassell et al. 1998, Cassell et al. 1999, Cassell and Vilhjálmsson 1999], culminating in [Cassell et al. 2001], use natural language processing together with manually designed rules and heuristics to create a sequence of nonverbal behaviors from text. Similarly rule based approaches have been used to create talking head animations from chat text in online games [Vilhjálmsson 2004]. The realization of the motions is often performed for the whole body, without advanced additive composition [Thiebaux et al. 2008] and the interface for the action specification is often the Behavior Markup Language BML [Kopp et al. 2006]. Similar recent work use besides text also speech (audio) features [Marsella et al. 2013], and have been applied to a virtual therapist conducting a depression screening therapy [DeVault et al. 2014]. Other works on text to motion, build a probabilistic model of gestures for a specific speaker from annotated video [Neff et al. 2008].

To play animation clips, often state machines are used, which can conceptually be viewed as graphs. The works [Arikan and Forsyth 2002, Kovar et al. 2002] focuses on automatically building such a graph based on similarity between poses

in large data-sets.To match animations to action specifications more accurately in time, others have investigated optimal matching with dynamic programming [Stone et al. 2004, Bozkurt et al. 2016], which requires allowing re-timing of the clips via warping. In our experiments, we found that the warpings cause the resulting motion to look unnatural.

2.2 Engineering Feature-based Maps

When the motion can be generated from a set of features, or parameters known to the agent, such as the audio (the speech), or high-level parameters such as the gaze direction, or even a part of the motion specified otherwise, such as the head orientation for gaze, then a large amount of variations can be synthesized automatically, especially when the parameter and the mapping are continuous.

Lip sync is one case where audio is analyzed and corresponding lip shape parameters are computed over time [Digital 2017, Entertainment 2018]. In the case of the body, recent work has explored to map audio features to the trunk motion of the character— mapping the volume of the audio to the trunk and head arc [Sakai et al. 2016]. Adding arm gestures in an override fashion from the shoulder downwards, removing essentially all spine motion from the arm's action, results in a motion that looks uncanny. Hence some map the arm motion back to the spine motion to bring back some of the missing dynamics, as described in chapter 9 of [Tanenbaum 2018].

2.3 Machine Learning

Mapping audio or speech to lip motion is a relatively well defined problem as strong correlations exist between the speech and mouth shape used to produce the sounds, resulting in many methods and papers on the topic, summarized in [Mattheyses and Verhelst 2015]. Researchers have pushed the envelope with speech-driven eyebrow motion [Ding et al. 2013], and more recently with speech-driven facial animation, which can produce motions in a given expression [Karras et al. 2017, Taylor et al. 2017, Sadoughi and Busso 2017]. In case of the body, experiments have been conducted to learn a mapping from speech to body motion, by first capturing the motion of an actor while talking [Levine et al. 2009, Levine et al. 2010]. Similarly an interesting recent work seeks to map music audio to body motion performed while playing the instrument to produce the sounds [Shlizerman et al. 2017].

But generally the results are poor, perhaps due to the articulated nature of the human body, but most likely due to the lack of powerful latent structures that can model the natural gestures that accompany speech content. Recent works experimented with the idea that additional modality, such as the face of the person talking to the avatar, together with audio and transcripts, could improve the results in a deep learning setting [Chu et al. 2018].

3. OVERVIEW

It is not possible to simply play any motion at any point in time when using the standard joint space interpolation provided in game engines such as Unity or Unreal Engine. For example, consider a gesture that moves the arm up, and then a sudden request for an action that starts with the arm pointing downward. Interpolating between both motions will cause a visual jump.

To avoid these artifacts, engineers and designers encode which motion can be played when or after which other motion as connections in a state machine, where the states are the motion clips. For example, consider arm motions and following our taxonomy guideline: stances for the arms such as hands on the hips, transitions between different stances, and all the gestures and fidgets that can be played from those stances. Imagine we have 9 stances, and about 5 gestures and fidgets on each stance. We would end up with a graph that looks like Figure 1. Authoring and maintaining these connections, requires exponential effort as the number of animations grows, and the probability of making mistakes gets increasingly high. In consequence very few embodiments scale up to rich and highly varied conversation behaviors. When looking at this large graph, we can observe the self-similarities between the sub-structures of the graph. We can generalized these sub-structures into meta nodes, as shown in Figure 2. This generalized graph is a perfect fit for a simplified drag-and-drop interface that automates the connectivity logic, while animators focus on the motions (Section 4).

To this point, we discussed arm motion, but when people are talking, they perform head motions such as nods, while doing different hand gestures and occasionally changing body postures such as shifting the weight to one side of the body. Creating all the combinations of head motions with gestures, fidgets and weight shifts leads to exponential content authoring. To cope with this complexity, we break down the motion space into body part layers (we call body, arms, head), and compose them in an additive fashion (Section 5). Note that our taxonomy still holds for the different body parts. Hence, the graph on each layer is the same, and we explain in Section 4 how the interface for specifying the motions on each layer works.

Finally, we tackle the problem that different agents can operate at different levels of abstraction, which makes it difficult for the embodiment to be used in practice. An agent might specify action types such as "beat" gesture at a given time, or have specific gestures it wants to play. Another agent might want to simply send dialogue lines without any actions. By modeling the probability distributions of the gestures, we designed a planner that can translate action sequences at different levels of abstraction into specific action sequences without conflicts (Section 6). In other words, our planner can generate plausible action sequences when none provided, and can avoid repetitive gestures when more abstract actions are specified. That said, we begin by describing the user interface for specifying the graph.

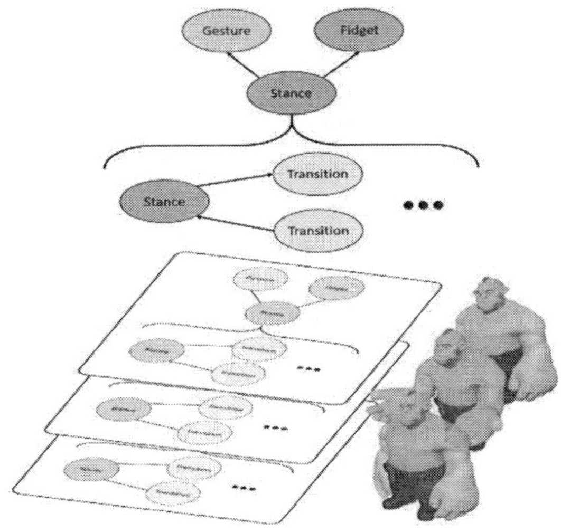

Figure 2. We can observe the self-similarities in the full graph (Figure 1), and generalize the connections between meta nodes corresponding to our taxonomy (stance, gestures, fidgets and stance transitions). This abstract graph, we call the meta-graph, naturally leads to a simplified interface for users to simply drag-and-drop animation clips over the nodes, as described in Section 4 and shown in Figure 3

4. USER INTERFACE

Based on the generalized meta graph shown in Figure 2 we devise a simple drag-and-drop interface to automate the connectivity logic between the animations as illustrated in Figure 3.

First the current stance, which is the central piece, is specified either by selecting an existing one or by drag-and-dropping a new one. Gestures and fidgets are then simply added by drag-and-dropping them onto the propper nodes. Similarly transitions are added, but first the other stance has to be selected. Any additional properties such as layer masks and timing together with optional details such as semantic information or base likelihood are specified in the properties panel on the right. By drag-and-dropping animations we fill the graph data structure, which is a multi-index map, where for each stance and meta-node type (taxonomy element type), we have a list of compatible motions. Additionally for each transition motion we also store in which stance it ends. Next we detail the inner workings of the state machine playback, together with the additive layer composition.

5. ANIMATION COMPOSITION

Creating all combinations of head motions with gestures, fidgets and weight shifts is not feasible and we therefore break the motion space down into body layers. Specifically we decompose the motions into three layers: body, arms, and head. Simply composing the layers by masking, results in robotic and uncanny motions, because the dynamics for other body parts is lost. Instead, by composing the motions for the different layers additively, we can maintain this dynamics. From analyzing the motions we observed the following influences between the three layers (body, arms, head) and the four body parts (legs, spine, arms and head):

$$body \rightarrow head, spine, legs$$
$$arms \rightarrow head, spine, arms$$
$$head \rightarrow head, spine$$

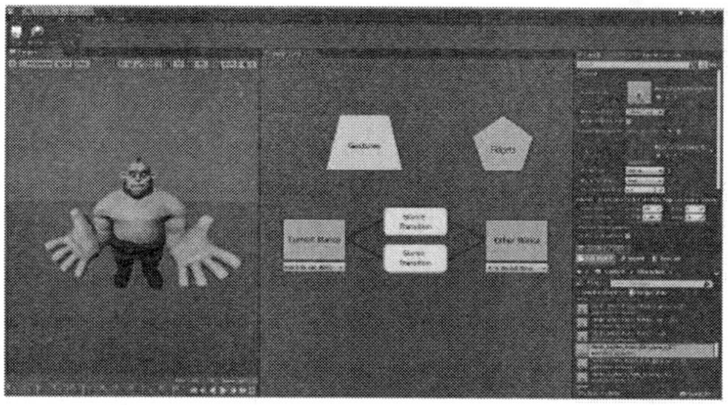

Figure 3. To add new motions, users drag-and-drop animation clips onto the corresponding meta nodes. Additional properties such as layer masks and timings can be specified in the properties panel

The final pose for each body part is thus composed as the additive combination of these three layers as visualized in Figure 4. The base pose used for this is a neutral pose, where the character has the hands at his side. To create an additive animation, all joint.

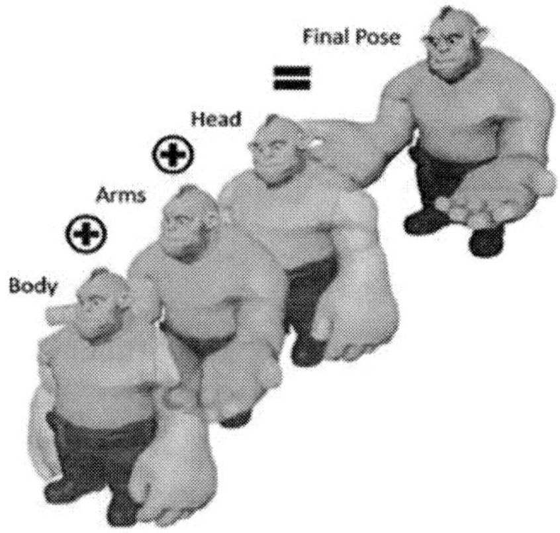

Figure 4. The animations triggered on the different layers head, arms, and body, are composed additively to build the final pose. The influences of the layers on the different body parts are highlighted in green

Transforms Q_{anim} are converted into offsets $\tilde{Q}_{relative}$ to those of the base pose Q_{Base} such that $Q_{anim} = Q_{Base} \otimes \tilde{Q}$ where $\otimes$ is the additive operator (multiplication for orientations and addition for translations). The final poses for all layers are then composed as:

$$Q_{Head} = Q_{Base} \otimes \omega_b \tilde{Q}_b \otimes \omega_a \tilde{Q}_a \otimes \omega_h \tilde{Q}_h ,$$
$$Q_{Spine} = Q_{Base} \otimes \omega_b \tilde{Q}_b \otimes \omega_a \tilde{Q}_a \otimes \omega_h \tilde{Q}_h ,$$
$$Q_{Legs} = Q_{Base} \otimes \omega_b \tilde{Q}_b ,$$
$$Q_{Arms} = Q_{Base} \otimes \omega_a \tilde{Q}_a ,$$

where ω are influence weights, $\tilde{Q}$ additive offsets, Q final poses and $\{h , a , b\}$ refer to the *head*, *arms* and *body* layers. For the influence weights we used $\omega = 1.0$ for all layers. Despite not normalizing the weights, we did not observe any visual artifacts. We assume that with more extreme motions, it might be necessary to perform some normalization, possibly through optimization.

A final note: to make the character more alive we apply a breathing motion that affects spine, head and arms (slight shoulder motion), lip-sync for the speech and life-like eye motion, further detailed in Appendix A. These are applied in the same additive fashion as the other motions. Now that we have a lively character, we look at how to combine it with the agents actions.

6. PLANNING AND MOTION SYNTHESIS

In practice it may be hard to predict at which level of abstraction an agent is going to operate: will it be at the level of *"say line X"*, or will it be at the level of *"lift right hand index finger by 10 degrees"*? To support the various levels of abstraction, we designed a *planner* that first converts streams of actions from the agent, into *meta actions,* which are a unified representation containing all required meta data.

The meta actions (shown in Figure 5) contain an abstract action field with values that match our taxonomy: "gesture, fidget, stance transition", as well as a specific action field, together with an additional property field for dimensions such as positive - negative, and finally a timing field. This tuple of abstract and specific allows to accept both, more specific actions, as well as more abstract actions.

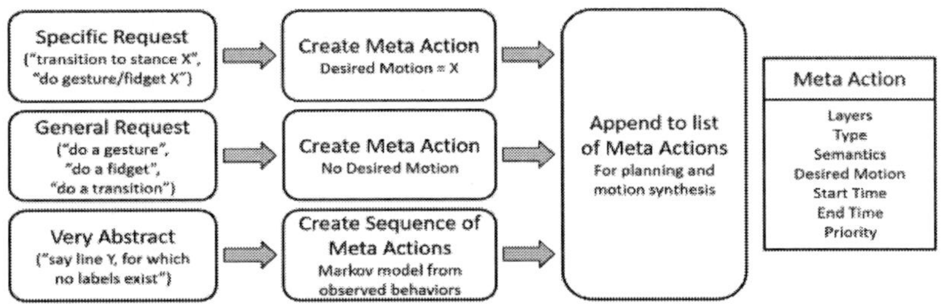

Figure 5. Action requests at various levels of abstraction are converted into meta actions, a unified representation containing all required data for further planning (Section 6.1) and motion synthesis (Section 6.2)

The next ingredient to our planner are probabilistic models of the gestures and actions. In the event of unusually absent actions, or when an agent acts only at a very high level such as "utter line X", the planner generates sequences of *meta actions* using a sequential probability distribution. We compute a Markov model from *labeled* real world casual conversations, which we detail further in Section 7.3.

Once we have the sequences of *meta actions*, our planner turns them into specific actions: first by resolving temporal conflicts, then by making sure gestures don't repeat using a probability distribution of the actions conditioned on past actions.

6.1 Temporal Replanning

Besides potential conflicts among the input meta actions, there may be conflicts with an already existing *meta plan*, which is a conflict-free sequence of meta actions as shown in Figure 6, created at an earlier timestep. From the existing plan we first recover all meta actions that start after the currently active action and merge them with the inputs. Through temporal replanning we then create a meta plan by adjusting the timings of the meta actions in a greedy way according to start time and action priority as illustrated in Figure 6.

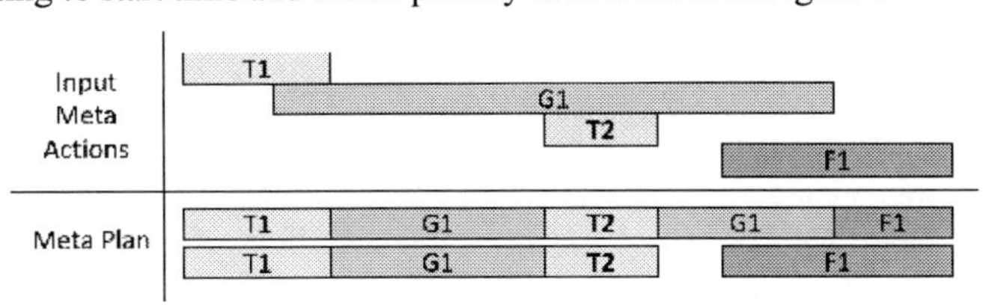

Figure 6. Through temporal replanning the meta actions are converted into a meta plan, a conflict-free sequence of meta actions, by adjusting the timings greedily according to start time and priority. For long actions interrupted by shorter actions of higher priority we either continue with the remaining part after the cut or discard it

6.2 Sampling Specific Actions

In the last stage, the meta plan is translated into a sequence of specific actions (animation clips). For a given meta action, we first retrieve all potential candidates by matching meta action properties against the specific motion data set. The possible actions may introduce conflicts temporally, as the three cases shown in Figure 7. We remove these from the possible actions.

From the final set of possible actions, we sample according to a distribution that is conditioned on past actions. We assume here that all actions are uniformly distributed, unless specified differently through the interface, but modulate the distribution to reduce the probability of having recurrent motions. We also consider the three cases illustrated in Figure 7 in our sample selection.

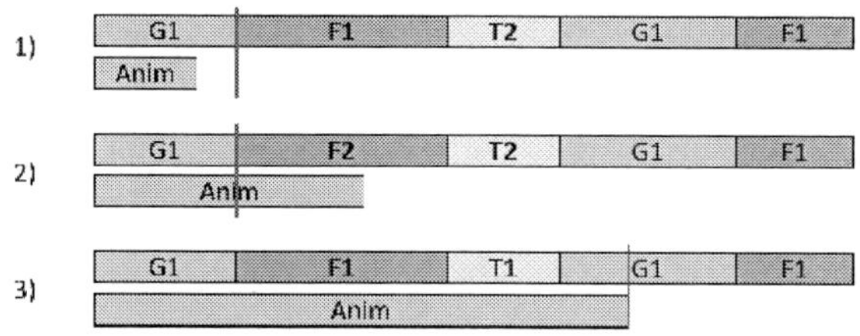

Figure 7. To synthesize a motion, animations are sampled according to the meta action properties. We distinguish three cases during this process: 1) If the animation ends before the meta action, we continue at the begin of the next meta action. 2) The animation has to end before a meta action with higher priority. If none is compatible, the meta action is discarded. 3) Meta actions completely overlapped by the animation are discarded and we continue at the end of the animation

Given a count of past actions $\{c_i\}$ for the n candidates, the probability of picking candidate k is:

$$p_k = \frac{\frac{1}{\max(c_k,1)}}{\sum_{i=1}^{n} \frac{1}{\max(c_k,1)}}$$

When an animation has been used, its counter is updated as:

$$c_k = c_k + a,$$

where a is a weight determining how quickly the probability decreases the more often a motion is used. We used $a = 4$ .Now that we have the agent connected to the animation system, we continue with experiments and results.

7. EXPERIMENTS AND RESULTS

One of the benefits of our taxonomy is to effectively guide animators and artists on which motions to create: stances, stance transitions, gestures and fidgets. However, it is quite challenging to evaluate these benefits, as creating the animations for an embodiment each time represents months of labor.

That said, we could leverage our taxonomy into automation, and the time required to populate the state machine with actions is much lower than with the standard state machine utilities in a game engine. In practice, the state machine increases in complexity as the number of motions increases, and requires engineering skills to find problems (see Section 7.1 for additional discussion on authoring state machines). To confirm this reality, we conducted an evaluation by measuring the time taken for an animator to populate the state machine using our interface, and the time taken using the standard state machine utilities in Unreal Engine.

Our animator has three years' experience with the Maya software, and has no engineering background. We first explained the interface with an example of 2 stances, 1 gesture, 1 fidget and 2 stance transitions, each explaining the layers for the body parts and motion-specific parameters. It required a total of 8 hours spread over two days (1.5 days of work) to We conducted several experiments to demonstrate the look and feel of our embodiment, which can be viewed in our accompanying video. However, we did additional work to accommodate agent actions at different levels of abstraction. To demonstrate this capability we conducted 3 experiments. First we hand-labeled videos of dyadic conversation with meta labels (see Section 6) and show that the embodiment can generate variations of the same meta action sequences (Section 7.2). A second experiment demonstrates the combination of two different streams of actions: a meta-actions stream together with specific actions coming from an interactive mimicry module (Section 7.4). Finally, we learned probability distributions of the meta actions and show that we can generate plausible performances in the absence of actions from the agent (Section 7.3).

Populate the state machine with our 152 animation clips. Using directly Unreal Engine, our animator had a 1 week tutorial on authoring state machines with frequent help required to accomplish tasks. After this 1 week tutorial, our animator started creating a state machine manually. It took 63 hours (8.5 days) of work to finalize an equivalent state machine. The resulting motion holds several jumps and artifacts and it holds many more mistakes.

7.1 Discussion on State Machine Authoring

When authoring a state machine in Unity or Unreal Engine (or any modern game engine), motions are added by creating a new state. Several properties such as looping or not, start and end times, and so on, have to be specified. To use this state, all the connections to other states (clips) have to be established, which as the state machine grows, becomes more and more demanding. The growing number of connections shown on screen quickly leads to a visual overflow, making it highly prone to errors. For example, forgetting a connection or connecting to the wrong state leads to visual artefacts in the performance. Additionally, a transition requires transition logic such as the time at which it is possible to transition, and the type of blend between clips. This process is quite redundant as actions of the same meta class, all behave the same in terms of transitions. In contrast, our interface has transition logic pre-defined for the meta action classes: stance, stance transitions and the gesture/fidget categories.

Figure 8. Face-to-face conversation between a user and the virtual character. To generate the action sequences, we annotated audio as shown in Figure 10

Figure 9. Due to the probabilistic nature of the motion synthesis, for the same abstract action sequence different performances emerge. This includes using different animations as well as different timings

7.2 Annotating Dyadic Conversations (Video)

We video recorded two hours of dyadic conversation: 2 times 1 hour, each with 2 subjects. A list of casual topics was given to each subject in case conversation runs dry. We captured the upper body above the knees, as can be seen in our accompanying video and Figure 10.

To annotate the videos with our abstract action labels (stance, stance transition, gesture or fidget), we used the ELAN software [Max Planck Institute for Psycholinguistics 2018], shown in Figure 10. To capture the different combinations of actions, we created labels for multiple body layers: two layers for the head (one for stance and one for action such as nodding), one layer for each arm, and one layer for the body, legs and spine. For the arms, the labels included gesture, fidget and stance-transition. For the head action, the labels included nodding and shaking. And for the head stance and body layers, the labels only included stance-transition.

Given these sequences of abstract action labels, we can synthesize a performance by feeding them to our planner. Since the labels remain abstract, we can synthesize different performances for the same input sequence. Figure 9 shows an example of various hand gestures, synthesized from the same input.

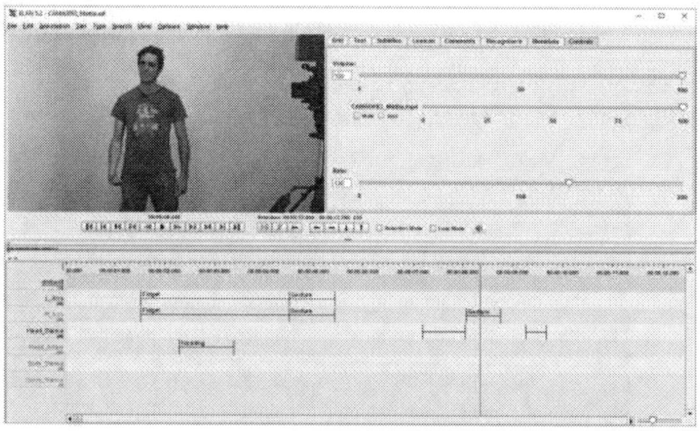

Figure 10. To create action sequences for casual conversations, we annotated the recorded dyadic conversations using the ELAN software [Max Planck Institute for Psycholinguistics 2018]. These annotations include abstract actions for different body part layers, which include head stance, head action, left arm, right arm and legs. These annotations can then be used either directly as actions (Figure 8), or to learn a Markov model (Section 7.3)

7.3 Modeling Action Distributions with a Markov Model

In the absence of labels, the embodiment can generate plausible conversation motion by leveraging the label distributions. We build a first-order Markov-model from the labeled video and sample the distribution to generate actions sequences. The possible states of the Markov model are the abstract actions gesture, fidget and stance transition. When additional semantic information is required such as positive for nodding, we can either randomly pick a semantic label when landing in a gesture state, based on its distribution in the annotations, or we can include it into the Markov model as additional states (gesture-without-semantics, positive-gesture, negative-gesture etc.). Then at generation time, we take the current Markov state and sample the next state based on the observed transition probabilities. Figure 11 shows a possible transition matrix for the different Markov states and Figure 12 shows different generated performances. The full performances can be seen in the accompanying video.

	L, G	L, F	L, T	R, G	R, F	R, T	LR, G	LR, F	LR, T
L, G	25%	37.5%	12.5%	12.5%	0%	0%	12.5%	0%	0%
L, F	26.7%	33.3%	6.7%	13.3%	20%	0%	0%	0%	0%
L, T	20%	20%	0%	0%	60%	0%	0%	0%	0%
R, G	0%	28.6%	0%	42.9%	0%	0%	14.3%	0%	14.3%
R, F	0%	42.9%	14.3%	0%	0%	0%	14.3%	14.3%	14.3%
R, T	0%	0%	100.0%	0%	0%	0%	0%	0%	0%
LR, G	25%	0%	0%	25%	25%	0%	0%	25.0%	0%
LR, F	0%	33.3%	33.3%	0%	0%	0%	33.3%	0%	0%
LR, T	0%	0%	0%	0%	20%	20%	0%	0%	60%

Figure 11. Using the labeled audio, we can build a first-order Markov-model. The transition matrix, in this example for the arms, shows the probability between the different states of the model, which consist of the left hand (L), right hand (R) and both hands (LR) together with the actions gesture (G), fidget (F) and transition (T)

Figure 12. Using the learned Markov model, we can generate new action sequences that look natural. Since the generated actions are still abstract, the resulting performances will vary

7.4 Video-based Mimicry

To demonstrate combining two streams of actions, one abstract and one specific, we took as input a mimicry module that reads the pose of a person in a video and classifies the stance, together with the stream of actions for the arm and head gestures. Given the detected stances, we pass an action of the form "transition to the detected stance" to the planner. If the stance is different from the current stance, the planner then finds the corresponding transition to trigger. Similarly the mimicry module also detects the orientation of the spine and head and then passes an action of the form "shift weight to the detected side" or "tilt head to the detected side". Again, if the requested side for weight shift or head is different from the current, the planner finds the corresponding motion to trigger.

8. CONCLUSION

We introduced a compact action taxonomy for chit chat embodiment, together with a fast interface for labelling motion clips at a large scale (152 actions in our experiment). Users require no engineering skills to connect hundreds of motions, with regard to their body part and action type (stance, gesture, fidget and stance transition): they simply drag-and-drop clips onto the corresponding sheet and adjust timings in a side window. Compared to the standard state machine authoring system, our interface avoids many human mistakes and requires significantly less time (7 times faster by our measurement). Holding a large number of motions and variations yields richer and more natural looking performances, as can be seen in our accompanying video. Finally, our fast labeling interface could lead to additional automation: given a large set of labeled actions, we could investigate training a predictor to label new similar motions—allowing to fully automatically add motions to the agent's embodiment.

REFERENCES

Arikan, O., 2002. Interactive motion generation from examples.ACM Trans. Graph Publishers New York USA pp. 483-490.

Bozkurt, E., 2016. Multimodal analysis of speech and arm motion for prosody-driven synthesis of beat gestures. Speech Commun. Vol. 85 C pp. 29–42.

Cassell, J., March 1999. Fully embodied conversational avatars: Making communicative behaviors autonomous. Autonomous Agents and Multi-Agent Systems. KluwerAcademic Publishers Vol. 2, Issue 1, pp. 45–64.

Cassell, J., 1998. An architecture for embodied conversational characters. MIT Media Laboratory Publishers Cambridge Massachusetts USA.

Bickmore, T. September 1999. Requirements for an architecture for embodied conversational characters. In Computer Animation and Simulation, Eurographics Publishers Italy, pp. 109–120.

Cassell, J., January 2001 Beat: The behavior expression animation toolkit. New York, USA, pp. 477–486.

Chu, H. 2018 A face-to-face neural conversational model. Toronto, Canada. pp. 7113-7121.

Devault, D. January 2014 .Simsensei kiosk: A virtual human interviewer for healthcare decision support. AMAS Paris France. Pp. 1061–1068.

Ding, Y. 2013. Speech - driven eyebrow motion synthesis with contextual markovian models. Houston USA pp. 3756–3760.

Lehtinen, J. July 2017 Audio-driven facial animation by joint end-to-end learning of pose and emotion. ACM Trans. Graph. Publisher New York USA. Vol. 36, No. 94.

Rick, J. 2007. The behavior markup language. In Intelligent Virtual Agents, Springer Publisher, Berlin Germany.

Kovar, L. July 2002. Motion graphs. ACM Trans. Graph Publisher New York USA. vol . 21, pp. 473–482.

Levine, S., December 2009 Real-time prosody-driven synthesis of body language. ACM Trans. Graph Publisher California USA. vol. 28, pp. 172.

Levine, S. July 2010. Gesture controllers. ACM Trans. Graph Publisher. vol. 29, pp. 124.

Marsell A. 2013. Virtual character performance from speech. In Proceedings of the 12th ACM SIGGRAPH/Eurographics Symposium on Computer Animation. New York USA. pp. 25–35.

Mattheyses, W. February 2015. Audiovisual speech synthesis: An overview of the state-of-the-art. Ghent Belgium vol. 66, pp. 182–217.

Coutrot, A., February 2015 Saccadic model of eye movements for free-viewing condition.

Hans, P. March 2008 Seidel Gesture modeling and animation based on a probabilistic recreation of speaker style. ACM Trans. Graph. Publisher vol. 27 no. 5.

Sadoughi, N 2017. Speech-driven animation with meaningful behaviors. Texas USA

Sakai, K. 2016. Speech driven trunk motion generating system based on physical constraint. New York pp. 232–239.

Mattheur S. 2004. Speaking with hands: Creating animated conversational characters from recordings of human performance.ACM Trans. Graph Publisher vol. 23 no. 3 pp. 506–513.

Tanenbaum, J 2014. Nonverbal Communication in Virtual Worlds: Understanding and Designing Expressive Characters. ETC Press Publisher Pittsburgh USA.

Taylor S. July 2017. A deep learning approach for generalized speech animation. ACM Trans. Graph Publisher Vol. 36 no. 4 pp. 93.

Thibeaux, M. 2008. Smartbody: Behavior realization for embodied conversational agents. In Proceedings of the 7th International Joint Conference on Autonomous Agents and Mul-tiagent Systems – Estoril Portugal vol. 1 pp. 151–158.

Almsson, H. 2004. Animating conversation in online games.In Entertainment Computing – Publisher Springer Berlin Germany pp. 139–150.

FASTER RENDERING OF LARGE PSEUDO-DYNAMIC SCENES USING HIERARCHICAL DYNAMIC LODS

Vitaly Semenov[1,2,3], Vasily Shutkin[1] and Vladislav Zolotov[1]
[1]*Ivannikov Institute for System Programming of the Russian Academy of Sciences*
25, Alexander Solzhenitsyn st., Moscow, 109004, Russia
[2]*Moscow Institute of Physics and Technology (National Research University)*
9 Institutskiy per., Dolgoprudny, Moscow Region, 141701, Russia
[3]*National Research University Higher School of Economics*
20 Myasnitskaya Ulitsa, Moscow, 101000, Russia

ABSTRACT

Rendering of large dynamic scenes with a convincing level of realism is a challenging problem of computer graphics. One of the promising approaches to rendering such scenes is a simplification of models and the use of multiresolution series of models with levels of detail (LOD) appropriate for the current view-dependent context. Nowadays, different simplification techniques, including hierarchical level of details (HLOD), have been proposed and widely applied. However, these techniques face dramatic difficulties when scenes undergo modifications. Known attempts of their adaptation for dynamic scenes have not resulted in significant progress. In the paper an alternative approach to rendering pseudo-dynamic scenes is presented. Such scenes have numerous industrial applications, in particular, visual spatial-temporal modeling of complex construction projects, city infrastructure programs, and machinery assembly production. A concept of hierarchical dynamic levels of details (HDLOD) is introduced and complementary methods for generation of HDLODs and their visualization are proposed. The results of computational experiments are also presented.

KEYWORDS

Rendering, Dynamic Scenes, Polygonal Models, Level of Details

1. INTRODUCTION

In recent years, the problem of rendering of large dynamic scenes with a convincing level of realism has received increasing attention. Often such scenes are composed of thousands and millions of polygonal models created or acquired at a very high resolution level. Being scene objects, the models can be supplemented by dynamic behaviors assuming their appearance, movement or disappearance in accordance with a deterministic schedule or randomly occurring events.

Highly detailed models with accurately specified schedules are not always required, but prevent effective rendering of scenes by current graphics systems at reasonable interactive frame rates. This observation is critically important for many CAD/CAM/CAE applications whose functions involve both display of complex scenes and manipulation of individual objects in space and time dimensions.

One of the promising approaches to rendering complex scenes is a simplification of models and the use of multiresolution series of models with appropriate levels of detail (LOD) for the current view-dependent context. This research topic has a long history in computer graphics which began with the introduction of the LOD concept by James Clark in 1976. The concept realization assumes the appropriate LODs should be selected and rendered so that finer representations are used for the nearest objects and coarser approximations are applied to the farther objects. Although this concept allows broader interpretations, including simplifications of spatial-temporal models, the main efforts of researchers focused on polygonal meshes and sometimes on meshes with colors and textures.

Numerous simplification algorithms have been proposed following the same goal: to reduce the number of polygons of the mesh while preserving details and characteristics of the original as much as possible. Generally, the algorithms differ in the underlying decimation operation used to transform the mesh and the error metric used to measure the introduced geometric error. By decimation operations the algorithms can be categorized into the following classes: vertex removal, edge collapse, face collapse, vertex clustering and vertex merging. Vertex removal algorithms commonly use an iterative prioritization and retriangulation scheme within which the vertices are sequentially selected, their adjacent faces are removed and the resulting holes are retriangulated (Schroeder 1992; Soucy and Laurendeau 1996). Vertex clustering algorithms employ an auxiliary grid surrounding the simplified mesh. Within each cell, the cell's vertices are clustered together into a single vertex, and the incident faces are updated accordingly (Rossignac and Borrel 1993). Edge removal algorithms iteratively choose an edge to be contracted into a single point and degenerate the adjacent faces (Hoppe 1996; Ronfard and Rossignac 1996; Guéziec 1995). None of these algorithms provides the combination of efficiency, quality, and generality which would be desired for complex objects and scenes. We highlight the algorithm most relevant to our goals (Garland 1997). By leveraging both edge contraction, vertex aggregation and quadric error metrics, the algorithm exhibits good performance and quality for non-manifold and unconnected meshes.

The aforementioned algorithms help in the generation of LODs for single polygonal objects, but are quite limited to manage complex scenes. Nowadays, hierarchical level of details (HLOD) techniques are widely employed for such purposes (Erikson 2001). Unlike traditional ones, HLODs provide simplified representations not of the individual objects, but of the entire groups of objects organized into multilevel hierarchies. Instead of analyzing individual objects and displaying appropriate LODs, it becomes possible to render the entire groups of objects at once when traversing HLOD hierarchies and analyzing descending nodes. Processing of all individual objects is generally unnecessary.

However, HLODs face dramatic difficulties when scenes undergo modifications. Their representations should be recomputed whenever the objects are added, deleted or moved in the scene. The CPU time required for recomputations is typically greater than that for rendering the scene on GPU, which makes HLODs useless for dynamic scenes. Known attempts to optimize HLODs by using incremental updates and their asynchronous parallel execution on shared memory multiprocessor systems, haven't resulted in significant success (Erikson 2001).

In the paper we present an alternative approach to rendering large dynamic scenes for which the following two assumptions are made. The first assumption concerns the deterministic nature of the events in the scene, which allows you to analyze them before modeling the scene. The second assumption concerns the dominant number of events associated with the appearance and removal of objects relative to the number of the object movements. We call such scenes pseudo-dynamic ones and claim a large number of industrial applications that operate with just such scenes. In particular, these are visual planning and modeling of complex construction projects, city infrastructure programs, and machinery assembly production.

We also propose hierarchical dynamic levels of details (HDLOD) for rendering such scenes and specify an algorithm for generation of HDLODs. The results of preliminary computational experiments are also presented in the paper.

2. HIERARCHICAL DYNAMIC LODS

Let the scene $S(t)$ be defined in three-dimensional Euclidian space E^3 on the model time period $t \in [0, T]$ and be represented as a flat composition of objects $s(g_s, f_s) \in S$ having fixed spatial positions and unchangeable geometry representations $g_s \subseteq E^3$. The presence status of objects and their groups in the scene is determined by the behavior functions $f_s(t): [0, T] \to \{0,1\}$ so that the function $f_s(t)$ takes the unit value if the object s is present in the scene at the time t and the zero value if the object is absent. Throughout the work we call such scenes deterministic pseudo-dynamic. It is worth mentioning that continuously moving objects can be modelled through the discretization of a continuous path and simulation of successive events of the appearance and removal of object instances along this path. We suggest that relatively few objects are continuously moved or even that such movements are completely absent in the scene.

Contrary to this limitation, the considered class of scenes has numerous industrial applications. Figure 1 shows an example of a scene simulating the construction of a stadium in accordance with a preliminary prepared project schedule. As modeling time changes, building elements and pieces of equipment are mounted, installed on a construction site or removed. The landscape elements remain unchanged throughout the entire modeling period. Such behaviors are reproduced by standard functions presented in Figure 2.

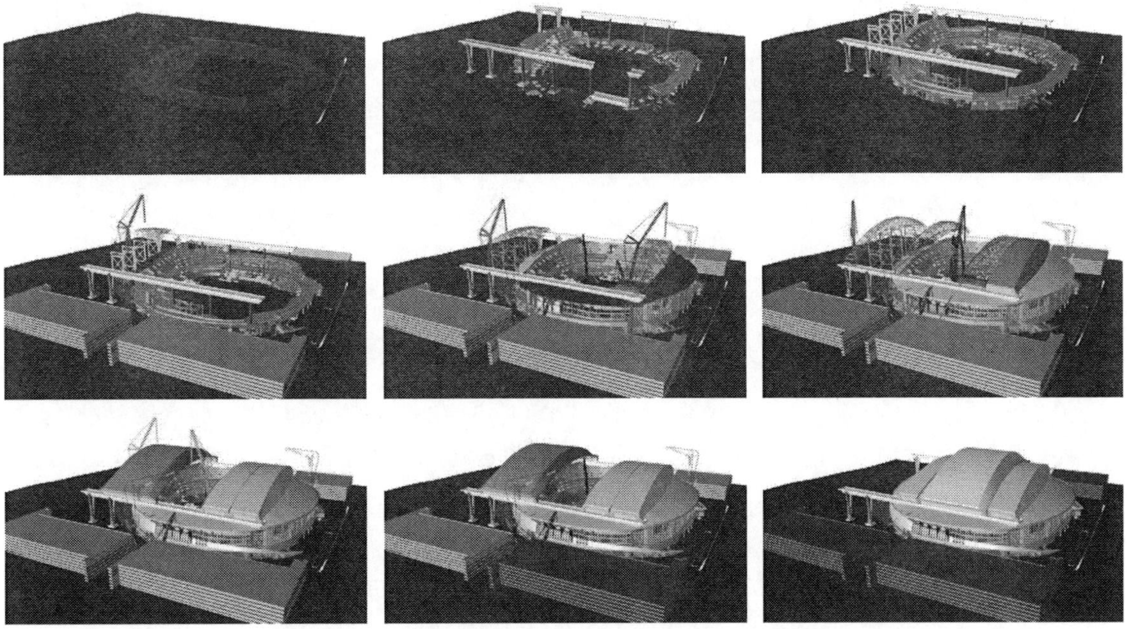

Figure 1. Example of a pseudo-dynamic scene simulating the construction of a stadium

In the following discussion we assume that the scene objects are geometrically represented as triangle sets with vertices referring to common set of points. No assumptions about solidness of the objects and manifoldness of their boundary representations are made because often only "polygon soups" are provided for rendering purposes without any guarantees of regular topological properties.

We also do not impose any restrictions on the coherence of the scenes, although we expect that in the industrial project scenes with proper organization of workflows this factor can be relatively high. By spatial-temporal coherence σ we mean the difference $1-\rho$ where ρ is the average distance between objects participating in subsequent events related to the size of the entire scene. Being defined in this way, the introduced coherence factor lies in the following range: $0 \leq \sigma \leq 1$.

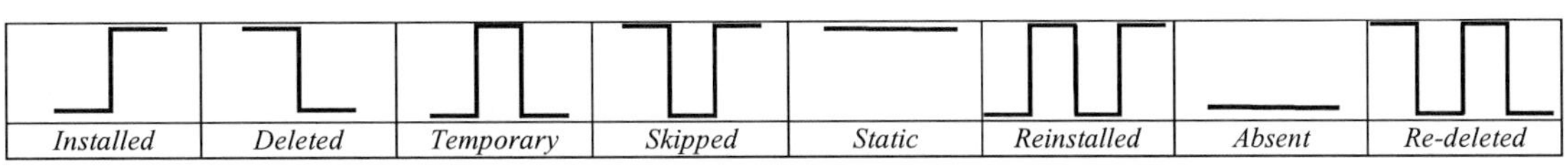

Figure 2. Some typical behavior functions

We will call the HDLOD a cluster tree $C(G,F) = \{c(g_c, f_c), \prec\}$ represented by a set of clusters $c(g_c, f_c)$ with prescribed geometry representations g_c and behavior functions $f_c(t): [0,T] \rightarrow [0,1]$. Unlike the object functions $f_s(t)$, which take values 0 or 1, the cluster functions $f_c(t)$ take values in the range between 0 and 1 thereby employing the concept of partial truth. Indeed, since some of the cluster objects may be present in the scene at some time point, while others may be absent, an unambiguous verdict on the presence status of the entire cluster cannot be made. For the clusters an agglomerative relation $\prec$ is also defined so that $c' \prec c$ only if the cluster $c' \in C$ is a direct child of the parent cluster $c \in C$. The leaves of the tree are the precisely defined individual objects. Interior nodes represent clusters aggregating the geometries and behaviors of the objects in corresponding subtrees. The root is the cluster containing the least accurate and most simplified representation of the entire scene. No assumptions are made about the degree of nodes and the balance of the tree. Figure 3 provides an example of unbalanced HDLOD tree with the nodes of varied degree.

Each cluster $c \in C$ stores not only the geometry and behavior representations but also such derived attributes as axis-aligned or oriented bounding box b_c, size or strength w_c, spatial tolerance ε_c, temporal tolerance γ_c as defined below. Basically, these attributes are computed when generating HDLODs and are applied when displaying HDLODs. Thus, each HDLOD cluster is represented as a tuple $c(g_c, f_c, b_c, w_c, \varepsilon_c, \gamma_c)$.

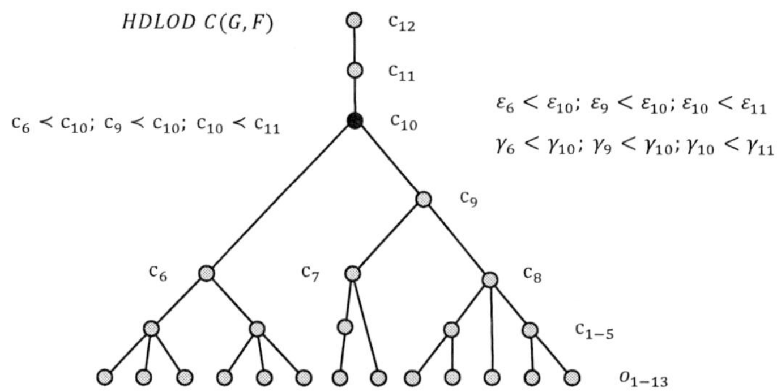

Figure 3. HDLOD tree and some agglomerative and algebraic relations

Let us dwell on the aforementioned parameters in more detail since they are important for displaying scenes with a given accuracy. Although these parameters allow different interpretations, we define ε_c as an absolute tolerance which establishes the possible maximum local deviation of the geometric representation of the cluster c from an aggregated representation of the originating objects $o \prec .. \prec c' \prec c$:

$$\varepsilon_c = \max_{c' \prec c}(\varepsilon_{c'}) + D_H\left(g_c, \bigcup_{c' \prec c} g_{c'}\right)$$

Here, the tolerance ε_c is recurrently defined using the Hausdorff distance $D_H(A, B)$ that is the greatest of all the distances from a point in one set to the closest point in the other set:

$$D_H(A, B) = max\{max_{x \in A}\, min_{y \in B}\, D(x, y), max_{y \in B}\, min_{x \in A}\, D(x, y)\},$$

where A, B are closed sets of points and $D(x, y)$ is a metric function in Euclidian space.

The temporal tolerance γ_c is defined as a maximum deviation of the cluster behavior from individual behaviors of the originating objects:

$$\gamma_c = \max_{c' \prec c}\left(\gamma_{c'} + D_F(f_c, f_{c'})\right),$$

where the distance $D_F(f_A, f_B)$ is determined using the functional metric:

$$D_F\left(f_A(t), f_B(t)\right) = \frac{1}{T}\int_0^T |f_A(t) - f_B(t)| dt$$

Thus, the introduced parameters are used to estimate the spatial proximity of objects, the geometry deviations and the proximity of temporal behaviors. The spatial tolerances are evaluated during the geometry simplification using one of the methods mentioned in the introduction. The temporal tolerances should be evaluated simultaneously with the simplification of behavioral functions. We propose the following computation method:

$$f_c(t) = \frac{\sum_{c' \prec c} w_{c'} f_{c'}(t)}{\sum_{c' \prec c} w_{c'}}$$

The use of the weighted sums enables us to take into account the behavior of significant objects to a greater degree and to reproduce the cluster behavior in the most relevant way. If the function $f_c(t)$ takes the unit value then all the cluster objects are present in the scene at the time t and the cluster should be displayed as a simple object. If the function takes the zero value then all the objects are absent at the time t and should be ignored completely. Otherwise, the spatial time-dependent tolerance (spatial error induced by both geometrical and temporal simplifications) should be estimated to decide whether to display the cluster or to ignore the cluster or to use more accurate descending representations. The resulting time-dependent spatial tolerance $\delta_c(t)$ can be directly expressed through the cluster behavior function as follows:

$$\delta_c(t) = \begin{cases} 0, & if\ f_c(t) = 0 \\ \varepsilon_{c'}, & if\ f_c(t) = 1 \\ \varepsilon_c + (1 - f_c(t)) \sum_{c' < c} w_{c'}, & if\ \frac{1}{2} \leq f_c(t) < 1 \\ \varepsilon_c + f_c(t) \sum_{c' < c} w_{c'}, & if\ 0 < f_c(t) < \frac{1}{2} \end{cases}$$

When visualizing a scene, the cluster tree is traversed starting from the root and descending to the leaves. At each node the cluster attributes are analyzed to determine the necessity of the further traversal of the subtree. It is checked whether the cluster is present in the scene at a specified model time, whether the cluster bounding box falls into the view frustum, and whether the tolerances are small enough to obtain the required resolution. If all the conditions are satisfied, the cluster representation is applied for rendering immediately. In such case, a whole subtree can be pruned from the traversal, which decreases the number of visualized objects and accelerates the rendering process. If the third condition is not met, the traversal of the cluster subtree continues and descending nodes are underwent to similar checks until the leaves with precisely given scene objects are reached.

Pseudocode of the specified algorithm is presented in Figure 4. The main procedure DISPLAY invokes DISPLAY CLUSTER for the root cluster with the given parameters of camera view, current modeling time and graphics system resolution. This procedure in turns traverses descending nodes by calling itself recursively. The visited clusters are rendered with the required accuracy when it becomes possible and reasonable. The purpose and use of auxiliary functions are quite transparent.

```
PROCEDURE DISPLAY (HDLOD tree, VIEW view, TIME time, RESOLUTION resolution)
{
DISPLAY CLUSTER (ROOT (tree), view, time, resolution)
}

PROCEDURE DISPLAY CLUSTER (CLUSTER node, VIEW view, TIME time, RESOLUTION resolution)
{
IF (VALUE OF (BEHAVIOR FUNCTION (node), time) EQUAL 0)
        RETURN
ELSE IF (IS OUTSIDE FRUSTUM (BOUNDING BOX (node), view))
        RETURN
ELSE IF (VALUE OF (DELTA FUNCTION (node), time) / DISTANCE (node, view) < resolution)
        RENDER (GEOMETRY (node), view))
ELSE
        {
        SET OF CLUSTER children = CHILDREN NODES (node)
        FOR_EACH (CLUSTER child IN children)
                DISPLAY CLUSTER (child, view, time, resolution)
        }
}
```

Figure 4. Pseudocode for displaying HDLODs

3. HDLODS GENERATION

The HDLODs can be generated automatically using the proposed method that leverages both hierarchical (bottom-up) clustering and multi-level accuracy control. The method is effective for both view-dependent rendering and view-frustum culling purposes. The method starts with the individual objects and progressively groups these together into larger and larger clusters until the desired number of levels is achieved. The root clusters can be further simplified as a series of LODs if it is planned to render the scene as part of a more complex composition. Clustering should be carried out under strict control of accuracy, and the resulting HDLOD tree should meet numerous requirements and conditions regarding the expected number of levels of details, the degree of nodes, the spatial density and overlap of sibling clusters, the temporal proximity of sibling clusters, and the descent of the cluster complexity with increasing levels.

Unfortunately, classical clustering methods cannot be directly applied to the HDLOD generation problems. The imposed requirements are quite complex and can contradict to each other. That hinders the mathematical formalization of metric functions and linkage criteria necessary for the clustering methods (Xu 2015). Unacceptably high computational complexity of the methods is another reason preventing the adaption of classical results.

```
PROCEDURE GENERATE HDLOD (SCENE scene, INTEGER levels, HDLOD tree)
{
SET OF CLUSTER active = NULL, next = NULL
FOR_EACH (OBJECT object IN OBJECTS (scene))
        {
        CLUSTER cluster = FORM CLUSTER (object)
        ADD TO (cluster, tree)
        ADD TO (cluster, active)
        }
FOR_EACH (INTEGER step = 1 TO levels)
        {
        REAL epsilon, gamma
        COMPUTE LEVEL THRESHOLDS (scene, levels, step, epsilon, gamma)
        WHILE (NOT EMPTY (active))
                {
                CLUSTER representative = SELECT REPRESENTATIVE (active)
                SET OF CLUSTER neighbors = FIND NEIGHBORS (active, representative, epsilon,
                                                        gamma)
                IF (IS EMPTY (neighbors))
                        {
                        ADD TO (representative, next)
                        REMOVE FROM (representative, active)
                        }
                ELSE
                        {
                        SET OF CLUSTER children
                        ADD TO (representative, children)
                        FOR_EACH (CLUSTER neighbor IN neighbors)
                                 ADD TO (neighbor, children)
                        CLUSTER cluster = CREATE CLUSTER (children)
                        SIMPLIFY (cluster, epsilon, gamma)
                        ADD TO (cluster, tree)
                        ADD TO (cluster, next)
                        REMOVE FROM (representative, active)
                        FOR_EACH (CLUSTER neighbor IN neighbors)
                                REMOVE FROM (neighbor, active)
                        }
                }
        COPY (next, active)
        EMPTY (next)
        }
}
```

Figure 5. Pseudocode for generating HDLODs

For example, a naïve implementation of agglomerative clustering has a time complexity of $O(n^3)$ and requires $O(n^3)$ memory, which makes it useless for even simple scenes. Faster hierarchical clustering with a time complexity of $O(n^2)$ and memory consumption $O(n^2)$ is also not feasible for the problems discussed (Xu 2015).

Therefore, we prefer to form HDLOD trees by employing other principles. The clustering process is divided into steps, at each of which the formed clusters satisfy certain requirements for accuracy. As new steps are taken, the requirements are weakened in such a way that the process is guaranteed to terminate after a specified number of steps equal to the number of levels of details L. Only active clusters are involved in the clustering process as opposed to passive clusters that have already been analyzed and grouped.

At each planned step l of the method ($1 \le l \le L$), an attempt to form new clusters with the tolerances $\varepsilon_c \le \varepsilon(l), \gamma_c \le \gamma(l)$ is made. For this purpose threshold values $\varepsilon(l), \gamma(l)$ are preliminary computed in such a way that the thresholds increase monotonously with increasing levels $\varepsilon(l-1) < \varepsilon(l), \gamma(l-1) < \gamma(l)$. For example, the tolerance thresholds can be chosen as follows:

$$\varepsilon(l) = 2wl/R, \quad \gamma(l) = 2\tau l,$$

where w is the size of the smallest scene object related to the size of the entire scene (e.g. diagonal of the box bounding all the scene objects over the modeling period, including temporally installed and removed ones), R stands for the effective display resolution (the typical number of pixels along one of the axes divided by the camera field of view) and τ is the effective temporal discretization used for the animation purposes (the typical time step between successive events related to the entire modeling period).

Once the tolerance thresholds have been determined, clusters can be formed step by step. At each planned step, representatives among active clusters are selected using space-filling curves and corresponding orderings by Hilbert (Samet 2006). On the one hand, it allows representatives to be chosen throughout the entire volume of the scene, and on the other hand, to localize them in densely filled regions. Then, for each representative the neighbors are sought in both spatial and temporal dimensions. The neighbors should satisfy the conditions of spatial and temporal proximity as well as ensure the formation of parent clusters with the planned accuracy. If no proper neighbors are found for the selected representative, it is excluded from the analysis at the current step, but participates in the succeeding cluster formation. The parent cluster behavior is determined using computations of the weighted behavior function as specified above. The resulting geometry representation of the parent cluster is merged from polygonal models of the originating clusters and then is simplified using the highlighted algorithm (Garland 1997). Pseudocode of the specified algorithm is presented in Figure 5.

Using indices preliminary computed and deployed, clustering can be done in $O(n\log n)$, where n is the number of the scene objects. This is a promising result compared to the classical clustering methods mentioned above. Although many different techniques can be used for spatial-temporal indexing (Samet 2006), in particular, regular dynamic octrees exhibiting good performance for pseudo-dynamic scenes (Morozov 2018), we utilized simple indexing structures to search for objects (more exactly, centers of their bounding boxes) in each dimension separately.

4. COMPUTATIONAL EXPERIMENTS

To validate the introduced HDLODs concept and the proposed method for their automatic generation and visualization, a series of computational experiments has been carried out. Display frame times were measured when navigating across a given scene at fixed modeling times and when animating and viewing the scene from fixed camera positions throughout the modeling period. As a benchmark, the presented in Figure 1 dynamic scene of the stadium construction was explored. The stadium model consisted of 52630 building elements represented by polygonal meshes totally containing 9799257 triangles. The construction schedule consisted of 48902 activities each of which was responsible for certain works on the construction site and induced related events in the dynamic scene. The spatial-temporal coherence factor σ for the scene was evaluated and amounted to 0.78. This factor is usually quite high for typical industrial scenes and leads to higher performance of visualization facilities.

To evaluate the effectiveness of the HDLODs with eliminated frustum culling factor, the experiments were repeated for a camera located at different distances from the scene. In the first position, the camera was placed at the closest distance, at which the entire scene was visible. In other positions, the camera was placed at the distances, at which the scene was occupying one-fourth and one-sixteenth of the screen area correspondingly. The times were chosen at the start and end of the modeling period as well as on one third and two thirds of the modeling period. The computational experiments have been carried out on a typical hardware configuration: Intel Core i7-4790 CPU (3.6 GHz), 16 GB of RAM, GeForce GTX 750 Ti (2 GB).

Table 1 showcases the rendering performance results obtained during the specified experiments. The last column provides the results obtained using direct rendering methods without HDLODs. As seen, the use of HDLODs significantly increases the rendering performance compared to traditional techniques. The farther from the scene the camera is placed, the greater is the achieved effect. It is exhibited both when navigating the static scene fixed at the chosen times, and when animating the scene. It is worth mentioning that the dependence is super-linear and this gives reason to make conclusions about the scalability of the method with respect to the complexity of both static and dynamic scenes. Compared to traditional HLODs which would lead to excessive computing costs for updating, even with minor local changes in the scene, HDLODs are prepared beforehand and do not require any updates when animating the scene throughout the entire modeling period.

Table 1. Frame times (in milliseconds) during the visualization of the stadium construction scene

	1/1 screen view	**1/4** screen view	**1/16** screen view	No HDLODs
Start time	0.37	0.32	0.31	26.81
1/3 of the period	7.17	3.31	1.38	31.36
2/3 of the period	21.9	7.35	4.4	124.8
End time	1.73	0.79	0.6	142.4
Animation	20.01	12.91	6.63	86.35

5. CONCLUSION

Thus, the concept of hierarchical dynamic levels of details has been introduced and the complementary methods for their automatic generation and visualization have been proposed in the paper. As opposed to traditional LODs techniques suitable only for static scenes, the developed methods are applicable to a wide class of deterministic pseudo-dynamic scenes arising in numerous industrial applications, including visual modeling of complex construction projects, city infrastructure programs, and machinery assembly production. The results of conducted computational experiments have confirmed high efficiency of HDLODs. Future research will focus on different algorithmic options for the developed methods, as well as on generalizations necessary for applying to scenes with continuously moving objects and objects with complex materials.

REFERENCES

Erikson, C. et al., 2001. HLODs for Faster Display of Large Static and Dynamic Environments. *I3D '01 Proceedings of the 2001 symposium on Interactive 3D graphics*. New York, USA, pp. 111-120.

Garland, M. and Heckbert, P.S., 1997. Surface simplification using quadric error metrics. *SIGGRAPH '97 Proceedings of the 24th annual conference on Computer graphics and interactive techniques*. New York, USA, pp. 209-216.

Guéziec, A., 1995. Surface Simplification With Variable Tolerance. *2nd Annual International Symposium on Medical Robotics and Computer Assisted Surgery*, Baltimore, USA, pp. 132-139.

Hoppe, H., 1996. Progressive Meshes. *SIGGRAPH '96 Proceedings of the 23rd annual conference on Computer graphics and interactive techniques*. New York, USA, pp. 99-108.

Morozov, S. et al, 2018. Indexing of Hierarchically Organized Spatial-Temporal Data Using Dynamic Regular Octrees. *In: Petrenko A., Voronkov A. (eds) Perspectives of System Informatics. PSI 2017. Lecture Notes in Computer Science*, vol 10742, pp. 276-290.

Ronfard, R. and Rossignac, J., 1996. Full-range approximation of triangulated polyhedra. *In Computer Graphics Forum*, Vol. 15, No. 3, pp. 67-76.

Rossignac J. and Borrel P., 1993. Multi-resolution 3D approximations for rendering complex scenes. *In: Falcidieno B., Kunii T.L. (eds) Modeling in Computer Graphics*. IFIP Series on Computer Graphics. Springer, Berlin, Heidelberg, Germany.

Samet, H., 2006. *Foundations of Multidimensional and Metric Data Structures*. Morgan Kaufmann, Burlington, USA.

Schroeder, W.J. et al., 1992. Decimation of Triangle Meshes. *SIGGRAPH '92 Proceedings of the 19th annual conference on Computer graphics and interactive techniques*. New York, USA, pp. 65-70.

Soucy, M. and Laurendeau, D., 1996. Multiresolution Surface Modeling Based on Hierarchical Triangulation. *In Computer Vision and Image Understanding*, Vol. 63, No. 1, pp. 1-14.

Xu, D. and Tian, Y., 2015. A Comprehensive Survey of Clustering Algorithms. *In Annals of Data Science*, Vol. 2, pp. 165-193.

BUTTERFLY-ORTHOGONAL LOOP SUBDIVISION WAVELETS

Huawei Wang [1, 2, 3], Guiming Qin [2, 3], Li Xiao [2, 3] and Yi Cao [2, 3]

[1] *Laboratory of Computational Physics, 6 Huayuan Road, Haidian, Beijing 100088, China*

[2] *Institute of Applied Physics and Computational Mathematics, 2 Fenghao East Road, Haidian, Beijing 100094, China*

[3] *CAEP Software Center for High Performance Numerical Simulation, 6 Huayuan Road, Haidian, Beijing 100088, China*

ABSTRACT

In this paper, we have proposed a new butterfly-orthogonal Loop subdivision wavelet based on the lifting scheme. We use a butterfly-style local orthogonalization structure to optimize the free parameters introduced in the wavelet transforms so as to obtain a very stable and nearly semi-orthogonal wavelet. Although it takes a little more computation time than the existing Loop subdivision wavelets, the proposed wavelet possesses a better fitting quality as well as performance of denoising, as demonstrated in the experiments. Similar to the other Loop subdivision wavelets, the butterfly-orthogonal wavelet has a linear computing complexity, because all lifting operations in the wavelet transforms are of perfect in-place computing and relate to only local vertex points or edge points. The proposed wavelet analysis can be used in a wide range of applications, including progressive transmission, shape approximation, data compression and multiresolution rendering.

KEYWORDS

Wavelet Analysis, Butterfly-Orthogonalization, Loop Subdivision Wavelet, Lifting Scheme

1. INTRODUCTION

Multiresolution modeling techniques attract much attention in recent decades, because they can address the challenge of modeling massive polygons obtained by high-resolution 3D scanning and have a wide range of applications such as progressive transmission, data compression, level-of-detail control and multiresolution rendering. Among multiresolution techniques, wavelet is a commonly-used tool, and subdivision is another powerful tool for representing smooth surfaces of arbitrary topology in multiple resolutions. By combining them naturally, people have focused on subdivision-based wavelet analyses for efficiently representing highly-detailed geometric models. The key to constructing such wavelets is to decompose the subdivision rules into a series of reversible local operations and then convert the forward and inverse subdivisions into wavelet transforms. Usually, the reconstruction and decomposition algorithms of subdivision-based wavelets are very simple, quite efficient and practical.

Subdivisions and wavelets are joined smoothly by the lifting scheme (Schröder and Sweldens, 1995; Sweldens, 1996), which is an efficient technique for constructing second-generation wavelets. A simple wavelet, e.g. a lazy wavelet, can be improved according to users' design requests by several steps of lifting. Schröder and Sweldens showed an example of constructing lifting wavelets on the sphere with customized properties (Schröder and Sweldens, 1995). Lounsbery et al. proposed a class of wavelets based on subdivision surfaces so as to generalize wavelet analysis to functions defined on compact surfaces of arbitrary topology (Lounsbery et al., 1997). Based on the hierarchical Delaunay triangulation, a multiresolution analysis on planar or spherical meshes of irregular connectivity is proposed in (Bonneau, 1998). By generalizing the uniform subdivision to a new irregular subdivision scheme in topology, Valette and Prost extended the work of Lounsbery et al. and proposed a wavelet-based multiresolution analysis that can be applied directly to irregular meshes, thus the connectivity of the processed mesh keeps unchanged (Valette and Prost, 2004).

Samavati and Bartels showed how to reverse subdivision rules and construct the wavelets by straightforward matrix observations (Samavati and Bartels, 1999). By using a quadrature mirror construction, Khodakovsky et al. constructed a Loop wavelet transform (Khodakovsky et al., 2000). Samavati et al. proposed multiresolution surfaces of arbitrary topology by locally reversing the Doo subdivision scheme (Samavati et al., 2002; Doo and Sabin, 1978). Wu and Amaratunga used the wavelets based on the butterfly scheme (Zorin et al., 1996) to deal with GIS data (Wu and Amaratunga, 2003). Using local lifting operations performed on polygonal meshes, Bertram et al. gave a new construction of lifted biorthogonal wavelets on surfaces of arbitrary two-manifold topology (Catmull and Clark, 1978) and presented generalized B-spline subdivision surface wavelets (Bertram et al., 2004). Based on local orthogonalization using discrete inner products, Bertram presented a biorthogonal wavelet construction for Loop subdivision (Bertram, 2004). Li et al. independently proposed another unlifted Loop subdivision wavelets by optimizing free parameters in the extended subdivision steps (Li et al., 2004). Later, Wang et al. proposed an effective wavelet construction for general Catmull-Clark subdivisions (Wang et al., 2006), and the resulting wavelets have better fitting quality than the existing Catmull-Clark-like subdivision wavelets (Bertram et al., 2000, 2004). Such wavelet construction methods based on local lifting operators are very efficient, e.g., usually in linear-time complexity as well as fully in-place operations, and thus do not need to solve global sparse linear systems.

In order to improve the stability of Loop subdivision wavelets, we present a new Butterfly-orthogonal wavelet in the paper by using the lifting scheme. Compared with the previous Loop subdivision wavelets, the wavelet has better stability as well as fitting quality. The resulting wavelet transforms still have a linear computational complexity because they are composed of local and in-place lifting operations. The wavelet analysis can be used in a variety of applications such as progressive transmission, data compression, shape approximation and real-time multiresolution rendering.

2. LOOP SUBDIVISION

Subdivision is attractive due to its powerful ability of modeling smooth surfaces of arbitrary topology as well as its multi-resolution representation format. Loop subdivision is designed to generalize the recurrence relations for the three-directional quartic box splines to triangular meshes of arbitrary topology (Loop, 1987). As triangular meshes arise in many applications, Loop subdivision becomes one of the most popular subdivision schemes. A Loop surface is defined as the limit of a sequence of finer and finer meshes produced in the recursive subdivision of an initial control mesh.

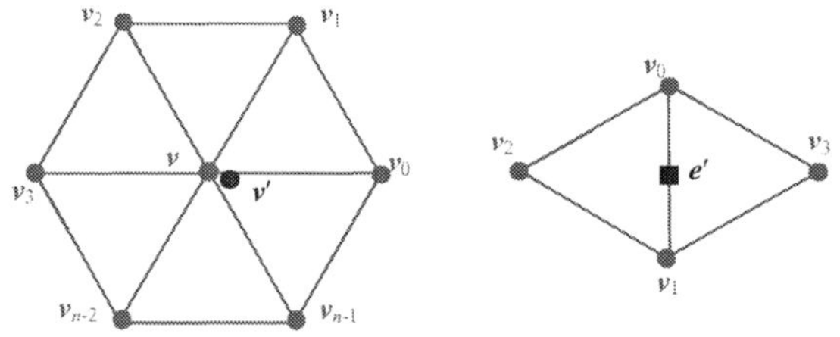

Figure 1. Local structures: (Left) updating an old vertex; (Right) computing the new vertex for an edge

In a refinement step, a triangle is divided into four pieces by updating every old vertex and introducing a new vertex for each edge. The local structures of control vertices for updating an old vertex and computing the new vertex for an edge are shown in Figure 1, and the corresponding computing formulae are given as follows:

$$v' = a(n)v + b(n)\sum_{i=0}^{n-1} v_i, \quad e' = \tfrac{3}{8}(v_0 + v_1) + \tfrac{1}{8}(v_2 + v_3), \qquad (1)$$

where $n \geq 3$ is the valence of v and

$$a(n) = \frac{3}{8} + \frac{(3 + 2\cos(2\pi/n))^2}{64}, \quad b(n) = \frac{1 - a(n)}{n}.$$

v' and e' are usually called the vertex point and the edge point, respectively. Each vertex point has the same valence as the corresponding old vertex while all edge points are of valence 6. A vertex with valence other than 6 is regarded as an extraordinary point. After one step of refinement, all extraordinary points will be isolated.

3. IMPROVED SUBDIVISION OPERATIONS AND WAVELETS

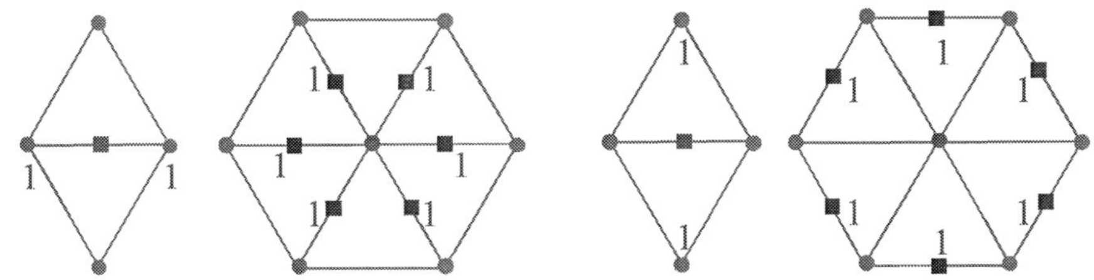

(a) $v \triangleright e$ (b) $e \triangleright v$ (c) $s \triangleright e$ (d) $e \triangleright s$

Figure 2. Un-normalized masks for local operators

The key idea for constructing subdivision-based wavelets is to decompose a complicated wavelet transform into a series of reversible simple local operations (also called lifting operations). The four local operators used in (Li et al., 2004) are listed in Figure 2, where the operator $\boldsymbol{v} \triangleright \boldsymbol{e}$ means "take the average of the two vertex points adjacent to an edge point", $\boldsymbol{s} \triangleright \boldsymbol{e}$ means "take the average of the two sideling points adjacent to an edge point", the operator $\boldsymbol{e} \triangleright \boldsymbol{v}$ means likewise "take the average of the edge points adjacent to a vertex point" and $\boldsymbol{e} \triangleright \boldsymbol{s}$ is defined similarly. Using these local operators, the rules of Loop subdivision (1) can be expressed equivalently as the following two steps of local operations:

$$\text{i)} \quad \boldsymbol{e} \leftarrow \tfrac{3}{4}(\boldsymbol{v} \triangleright \boldsymbol{e}) + \tfrac{1}{4}(\boldsymbol{s} \triangleright \boldsymbol{e}),$$

$$\text{ii)} \quad \boldsymbol{v} \leftarrow \alpha \boldsymbol{v} + n\beta(\boldsymbol{e} \triangleright \boldsymbol{v}), \qquad (2)$$

where $\alpha = \alpha(n) = [8a(n) - 3]/5$ and $\beta = \beta(n) = [1 - \alpha(n)]/n$. By introducing a vector $\boldsymbol{e}$ for each edge point initially and then adding an additional lifting operation, one can extend the above subdivision (2) into an in-place reversible transform (Li et al., 2004):

$$\text{i)} \quad \boldsymbol{v} \leftarrow \boldsymbol{v} + \eta_0(\boldsymbol{e} \triangleright \boldsymbol{v}) + \eta_1(\boldsymbol{e} \triangleright \boldsymbol{s}),$$

$$\text{ii)} \quad \boldsymbol{e} \leftarrow \gamma \boldsymbol{e} + \tfrac{3}{4}(\boldsymbol{v} \triangleright \boldsymbol{e}) + \tfrac{1}{4}(\boldsymbol{s} \triangleright \boldsymbol{e}), \qquad (3)$$

$$\text{iii)} \quad \boldsymbol{v} \leftarrow \alpha \boldsymbol{v} + n\beta(\boldsymbol{e} \triangleright \boldsymbol{v}),$$

where η_0, η_1 and $\gamma(\gamma \neq 0)$ are free parameters and can be adjusted later. Note that the forward subdivision (3) is equivalent to the original Loop subdivision expressed by Eq. (1) or (2) when all $\boldsymbol{e}$ are initially equal to $\boldsymbol{0}$. Since each step is reversible in Equation (3), by inverting the steps and arranging them in the reverse order, we have

$$\text{i)} \quad \boldsymbol{v} \leftarrow [\boldsymbol{v} - n\beta(\boldsymbol{e} \triangleright \boldsymbol{v})]/\alpha,$$

$$\text{ii)} \quad \boldsymbol{e} \leftarrow [\boldsymbol{e} - \tfrac{3}{4}(\boldsymbol{v} \triangleright \boldsymbol{e}) - \tfrac{1}{4}(\boldsymbol{s} \triangleright \boldsymbol{e})]/\gamma, \qquad (4)$$

$$\text{iii)} \quad \boldsymbol{v} \leftarrow \boldsymbol{v} - \eta_0(\boldsymbol{e} \triangleright \boldsymbol{v}) - \eta_1(\boldsymbol{e} \triangleright \boldsymbol{s}).$$

Equations (3) and (4) are forward and inverse subdivision processes, respectively, which actually constitute the multiresolution synthesis and analysis framework of a Loop subdivision wavelet (Li et al., 2004). The initial vectors $\boldsymbol{e}$ can be regarded as wavelet coefficients accordingly. They will contribute to the resulting limit surface as surface details at each resolution level.

In order to achieve better stability, we will improve the construction of the Loop subdivision wavelet in two aspects. At first, we will introduce a new local operator $\boldsymbol{e} \triangleright \boldsymbol{f}$, which means "take the average of the farther-sideling edge points adjacent to a vertex point", as shown in Figure 3. The forward subdivision is then improved as

$$\text{i)} \quad \boldsymbol{v} \leftarrow \boldsymbol{v} + \eta_0(\boldsymbol{e} \triangleright \boldsymbol{v}) + \eta_1(\boldsymbol{e} \triangleright \boldsymbol{s}) + \eta_2(\boldsymbol{e} \triangleright \boldsymbol{f}),$$

$$\text{ii)} \quad \boldsymbol{e} \leftarrow \boldsymbol{e} + \tfrac{3}{4}(\boldsymbol{v} \triangleright \boldsymbol{e}) + \tfrac{1}{4}(\boldsymbol{s} \triangleright \boldsymbol{e}), \qquad (5)$$

$$\text{iii)} \quad \boldsymbol{v} \leftarrow \alpha \boldsymbol{v} + n\beta(\boldsymbol{e} \triangleright \boldsymbol{v}),$$

where the free parameter γ is omitted because it is usually set to 1 as shown in (Li et al., 2004). Afterwards, we will turn the three free parameters in the first step of (5) into more free parameters so that we have more degrees of freedom to optimize the resulting wavelet. We will assign a distinct coefficient respectively for each of the $4n$ edge points instead of one for each type of edge points. Therefore, we number the n adjacent edge points, the n sideling edge points and the $2n$ farther-sideling edge points as 0, 1, …, n-1, …, $2n$-1, …, $4n$-1, and the coefficient for the edge point e_i is denoted by $\omega(\boldsymbol{v},\boldsymbol{e}_i)$. Note that $\omega(\boldsymbol{v},\boldsymbol{e}_i)$ depends on the connection relation of local vertices around $\boldsymbol{v}$ and $\boldsymbol{e}_i$. Thus, we can finally rewrite the improved subdivision as

$$\begin{aligned} &\text{i)} \quad \boldsymbol{v} \leftarrow \boldsymbol{v} + \sum_{i=0}^{4n-1} \omega(\boldsymbol{v},\boldsymbol{e}_i)\boldsymbol{e}_i\,, \\ &\text{ii)} \quad \boldsymbol{e} \leftarrow \boldsymbol{e} + \tfrac{3}{4}(\boldsymbol{v} \triangleright \boldsymbol{e}) + \tfrac{1}{4}(\boldsymbol{s} \triangleright \boldsymbol{e}), \\ &\text{iii)} \quad \boldsymbol{v} \leftarrow \alpha\,\boldsymbol{v} + n\beta(\boldsymbol{e} \triangleright \boldsymbol{v}), \end{aligned} \tag{6}$$

and its inverse is given as follows:

$$\begin{aligned} &\text{i)} \quad \boldsymbol{v} \leftarrow [\boldsymbol{v} - n\beta(\boldsymbol{e} \triangleright \boldsymbol{v})]\,/\alpha, \\ &\text{ii)} \quad \boldsymbol{e} \leftarrow \boldsymbol{e} - \tfrac{3}{4}(\boldsymbol{v} \triangleright \boldsymbol{e}) - \tfrac{1}{4}(\boldsymbol{s} \triangleright \boldsymbol{e}), \\ &\text{iii)} \quad \boldsymbol{v} \leftarrow \boldsymbol{v} - \sum_{i=0}^{4n-1} \omega(\boldsymbol{v},\boldsymbol{e}_i)\boldsymbol{e}_i\,. \end{aligned} \tag{7}$$

Obviously, all lifting operations in the forward subdivision (6) and its inverse (7) are of perfect in-place computations, and relate to only the local vertex points or edge points, so the computations of wavelet synthesis and analysis are very efficient.

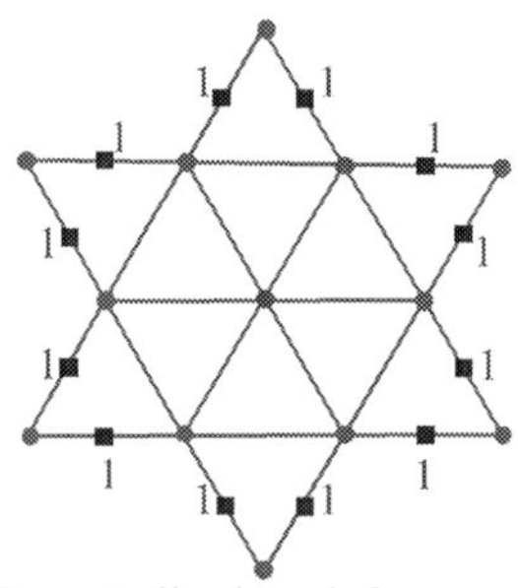

Figure 3. Un-normalized mask for a new local operator

4. OPTIMIZING THE FREE PARAMETERS

In the section, we will choose proper free parameters to optimize the performance of the resulting wavelet analysis. From the point of view of data reduction, the orthogonality of wavelets with scaling functions is a main goal of custom design of lifted wavelets to eliminate the data correlation. It is known that the last two steps of the forward subdivision (6) define a lazy wavelet synthesis (Bertram, 2004), and the basis functions corresponding to $\boldsymbol{e}$ (lazy wavelet ψ) and $\boldsymbol{v}$ (scaling function ϕ) are defined naturally by the two steps of lifting operations. The first lifting operation in (6) is equivalent to a lifting step of the lay wavelet as follows:

$$\psi' = \psi + \sum_{k=0}^{7} \omega(\boldsymbol{v}_k,\boldsymbol{e})\phi_k\,, \tag{8}$$

and the local situation of the wavelet function and related scaling functions is shown in Figure 4. Since the final wavelet function is ψ' after the lifting (8) and the scaling functions are not changed, the eight free parameters in (8) may be used to force the following eight orthogonality constraints:

$$<\phi_k,\psi'>=0, k=0,1,\cdots,7, \tag{9}$$

By substituting Eq. (8) into (9), we can easily obtain the eight parameters:

$$[\omega(\boldsymbol{v}_0,\boldsymbol{e}),\omega(\boldsymbol{v}_1,\boldsymbol{e}),\cdots,\omega(\boldsymbol{v}_7,\boldsymbol{e})]^{\mathrm{T}} = \boldsymbol{A}^{-1}\boldsymbol{B}\,, \tag{10}$$

where

$$\boldsymbol{A} = \left(A_{i,j}\right)_{8\times 8} = \left(<\phi_i,\phi_j>\right)_{8\times 8},\quad \boldsymbol{B} = -\left(<\phi_0,\psi>,<\phi_1,\psi>,\cdots,<\phi_7,\psi>\right)^{\mathrm{T}}.$$

The above computing process actually corresponds to a local orthogonalization (Lounsbery et al., 1997, Bertram, 2004) of the lazy wavelet, which will produce a nearly semi-orthogonal wavelet. The more scaling functions the wavelet orthogonalizes with, the more close to the global semi-orthogonal one the wavelet transform is. The local structure used in the orthogonalization is just like a butterfly, as shown in Figure 4, thus the resulting new wavelet is called the butterfly-orthogonal Loop subdivision wavelet in the paper.

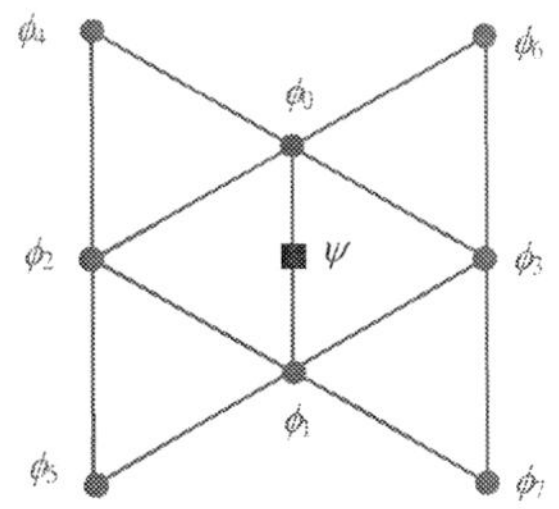

Figure 4. Local butterfly structure for orthogonalizing a lazy wavelet

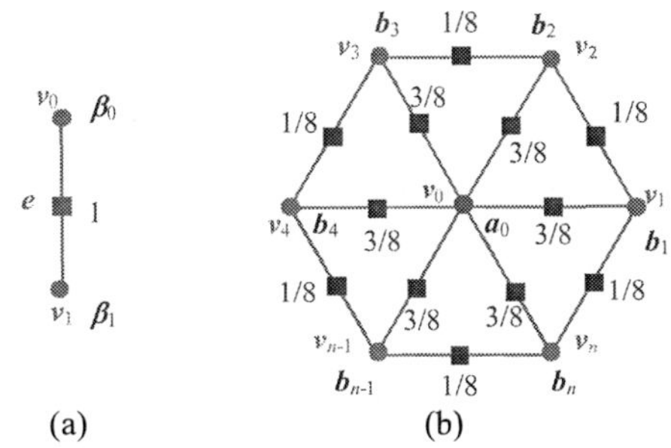

Figure 5. Discrete basis functions: a) wavelet ψ; b) scaling function ϕ_0

Next, we will discuss the computation of the inner products of basis functions in the matrices ***A*** and ***B***. In order to enhance the efficiency of wavelet transforms, we do not use the continuous shape of wavelets and scaling functions directly but adopt a discrete inner product operating on the subdivision masks (Bertram, 2004; Samavati and Bartels, 1999). As shown in Figure 5, the discrete masks of lazy wavelets and scaling functions can be obtained from the subdivision formulae in the last two steps of Eq. (6) and are exactly the same as those presented in (Bertram, 2004). Here, $a(n_i)$ is simplified as a_i where n_i denotes the valence of the vertex $\boldsymbol{v}_i$, and b_i, α_i and β_i are defined analogously. If n is 6, $a(n)$ is simplified further as a for short, and $b(6)$, $\alpha(6)$ and $\beta(6)$ are abbreviated similarly. Then, if supposing all nearby vertices other than $\boldsymbol{v}_0 \sim \boldsymbol{v}_7$ to be regular and the local structure to be nondegenerative, we can deduce the following formulae:

$$A_{i,i} = \begin{cases} \frac{5}{32}n_i + a_i^2 + b_{1-i}{}^2 + b_2{}^2 + b_3{}^2 + b_{4+i}{}^2 \\ \qquad + b_{6+i}{}^2 + (n_i - 5)b^2, \text{if } n_i > 4, \\ \frac{5}{32}n_i + a_i^2 + b_{1-i}{}^2 + b_2{}^2 + b_3{}^2 + (1-\delta_i)b_{4+i}{}^2, \text{otherwise,} \end{cases}$$

$$A_{2+i,2+i} = \tfrac{5}{32}n_{2+i} + a_{2+i}^2 + b_0{}^2 + b_1{}^2 + b_{4+2i}{}^2 + (1-\delta_{2+i})[b_{5+2i}{}^2 + (n_{2+i} - 4)b^2],$$

$$A_{2j+i,2j+i} = \tfrac{5}{32}n_{2j+i} + a_{2j+i}^2 + b_i{}^2 + b_j{}^2 + (n_{2j+i} - 2)b^2 + \pi_i(b_{2(5-j)+i}{}^2 - b^2) + \chi_i(b_{5-j}{}^2 - b^2) + \chi_j(b_{2j+1-i}{}^2 - b^2) + \delta_j(b_{1-i}{}^2 - b^2),$$

$$A_{0,1} = \tfrac{21}{64} + a_0 b_0 + a_1 b_1 + b_2{}^2 + b_3{}^2 + \delta_2(\tfrac{1}{64} + b_4{}^2) + \delta_3(\tfrac{1}{64} + b_6{}^2],$$

$$A_{i,j} = \tfrac{21}{64} + a_i b_i + a_j b_j + b_{1-i}{}^2 + b_{2j+i}{}^2 + \delta_{1-i}(\tfrac{1}{64} + b_{5-j}{}^2) + \delta_{2j+i}[\tfrac{1}{64} + b^2 + \pi_i(b_{2(5-j)+i}{}^2 - b^2) + \chi_i(b_{5-j}{}^2 - b^2) + \chi_j(b_{2j+1-i}{}^2 - b^2) - \delta_j b^2],$$

$$A_{i,2j+i} = \tfrac{21}{64} + a_i b_i + a_{2j+i} b_{2j+i} + b_j{}^2 + b^2 + \delta_j(\tfrac{1}{64} + b_{1-i}{}^2) + \pi_i[b_{2(5-j)+i}{}^2 - b^2 + \delta_{2(5-j)+i}(\tfrac{1}{64} + b_{5-j}{}^2)] + \chi_i[b_{5-j}{}^2 - b^2 + \delta_{5-j}(\tfrac{1}{64} + b_{1-i}{}^2)],$$

$$A_{i,2j+1-i} = \begin{cases} A_{i,2j+i}, \text{if } n_j = 3, \\ \frac{1}{64} + b_{1-i}{}^2 + b_j{}^2 + \chi_{1-i}(\frac{1}{64} + b_{5-j}{}^2) + \chi_j(\frac{1}{64} + b_{2j+i}{}^2), \end{cases}$$

$$A_{j,2j+i} = \tfrac{21}{64} + a_j b_j + a_{2j+i} b_{2j+i} + b_i{}^2 + b^2 + \chi_j(b_{2j+1-i}{}^2 - b^2),$$

$$A_{5-j,2j+i} = (1-\chi_i)b_i{}^2 + \chi_i A_{5-j,2(5-j)+i},$$

$$A_{2,3} = \tfrac{1}{64} + b_0{}^2 + b_1{}^2 + \chi_0(\tfrac{1}{64} + b_4{}^2) + \chi_1(\tfrac{1}{64} + b_5{}^2) + (\delta_0 + \delta_1 - \delta_0\delta_1)(\tfrac{21}{64} + a_2 b_2 + a_3 b_3 + b^2) - \delta_0\delta_1 b^2,$$

$$A_{2j,2j+1} = \begin{cases} \frac{21}{64} + a_{2j}b_{2j} + a_{2j+1}b_{2j+1} + b_j^2 + b^2, \text{if } n_j = 4, \\ \delta_j A_{2j,2j} + \pi_j(\frac{1}{64} + b_j^2 + b^2) \\ \qquad + (1-\delta_j)(1-\pi_j)b_j^2, \text{otherwise,} \end{cases}$$

$$A_{4+i,6+i} = \begin{cases} A_{4+i,4+i}, \text{if } n_i = 4, \\ \frac{21}{64} + a_{4+i}b_{4+i} + a_{6+i}b_{6+i} + b_i^2 + b^2, \text{if } n_i = 5, \\ \frac{1}{64} + b_i^2 + b^2, \text{if } n_i = 6, \\ b_i^2, \text{otherwise,} \end{cases}$$

$$A_{4,7} = \begin{cases} \chi_0 A_{6,7} + \chi_1(1-\chi_0)A_{4,5}, \text{if } n_0 = 4 \text{ or } n_1 = 4, \\ \delta_2 A_{5,7} + (1-\delta_2)\delta_3 A_{4,6}, \text{if } n_2 = 3 \text{ or } n_3 = 3, \\ \chi_2\pi_1 b_5^2 + \chi_3\pi_0 b_6^2, \text{otherwise,} \end{cases}$$

$$A_{5,6} = \begin{cases} \chi_0 A_{4,5} + \chi_1(1-\chi_0)A_{6,7}, \text{if } n_0 = 4 \text{ or } n_1 = 4, \\ \delta_2 A_{4,6} + (1-\delta_2)\delta_3 A_{5,7}, \text{if } n_2 = 3 \text{ or } n_3 = 3, \\ \chi_3\pi_1 b_7^2 + \chi_2\pi_0 b_4^2, \text{otherwise,} \end{cases}$$

$$<\psi,\phi_i> = \tfrac{3}{8} + a_i\beta_i + b_{1-i}\beta_{1-i}, \quad <\psi,\phi_j> = \tfrac{1}{8} + b_0\beta_0 + b_1\beta_1,$$

$$<\psi,\phi_{2j+i}> = b_i\beta_i + \delta_j b_{1-i}\beta_{1-i} + \chi_i\delta_{5-j}[\tfrac{1}{8} + (1-\delta_j)b_{1-i}\beta_{1-i}],$$

$\forall\, i \in \{0, 1\}$, $\forall\, j \in \{2, 3\}$, where $\delta_k \equiv \delta(n_k)$ is equal to 1 if $n_k = 3$ and 0 otherwise; $\chi_k \equiv \chi(n_k)$ is equal to 1 if $n_k = 4$ and 0 otherwise; $\pi_k \equiv \pi(n_k)$ is equal to 1 if $n_k = 5$ and 0 otherwise.

As a result, we can obtain all free parameters by computing the formula (10) after the matrices $\boldsymbol{A}$ and $\boldsymbol{B}$ are computed, and thus we obtain a new butterfly-style wavelet analysis based on Loop subdivision, which has an in-place and linear-time computation. Since extraordinary points are enough far from each other after two subdivision steps, there is at most one extraordinary point in the local structure shown in Figure 4. Therefore, in order to enhance the real-time computing efficiency, we can pre-compute the free parameters for the cases of the local structure containing at most one extraordinary point.

5. EXPERIMENTAL RESULTS

We will carry out the noise-filtering experiment (Bertram, 2004; Bertram et al., 2004) to check the stability of the wavelet proposed in the paper. Firstly, we subdivide a triangular mesh six times by the original Loop subdivision rules (1), and then add white noise to the vertices of the resulting mesh. The mesh obtained finally can be regarded as the fully detailed model, which will be analyzed step by step using the proposed wavelet analysis algorithm (7). The noise-filtered versions of the model at each level are shown in Figure 6 from level 6 to level 0, respectively. It is obvious that the wavelet analysis has a very good stability because the influence of the white noise on the model decreases gradually with the increase of the filtering time.

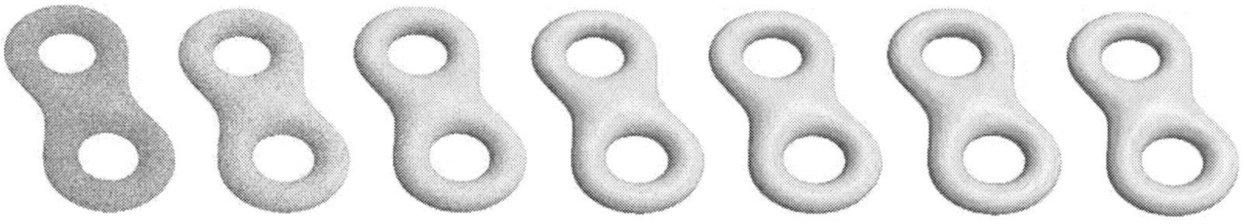

Figure 6. Wavelet analysis from level 6 to level 0

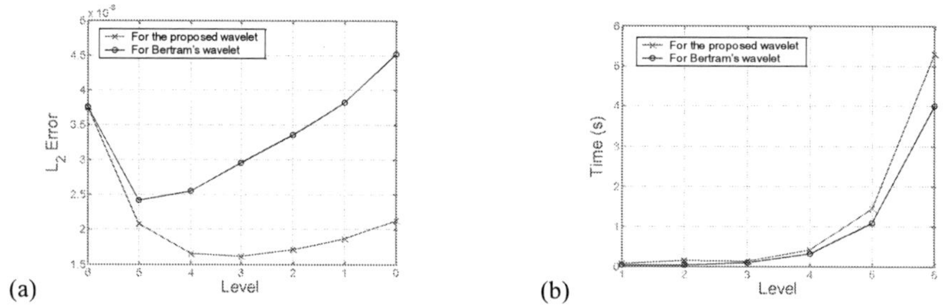

Figure 7. Sketch maps of (a) noisy errors and (b) computation times varying with levels

Furthermore, we have computed the L_2 norm error of each low-pass filtered noisy mesh with respect to the undisturbed model. The errors for Bertram's Loop subdivision wavelet (Bertram, 2004) are also computed for comparison in the condition of the same model and the same noise. The varying sketches of the errors with regard to the levels are shown in Figure 7(a) for the two wavelets, respectively. It is shown that the noisy error for the proposed wavelet is always less than that for Bertram's wavelet at each level and actually equal to about a half of that for Bertram's wavelet after three times of filtering. The overall denoising ratio, or the ratio of the noisy error at level 0 to the initial error, is equal to 0.5680 for the proposed wavelet, which is obviously smaller than the overall denoising ratio 1.2053 for Bertram's wavelet. Thus, compared with Bertram's wavelet, the wavelet proposed in the paper has a better stability as well as a better performance of noise reduction.

In addition, we have also recorded the computation times when the wavelet transforms are performed. The platform is a PC equipped with a 2.8 GHz Pentium 4 CPU and 512 MB RAM and running Windows XP Professional. We measure the computation time at each step for the proposed wavelet as well as Bertram's one when reconstructing the model from level 0 to level 6. The comparison of the computation times for the two wavelets is shown in Figure 7(b). In general, the wavelet synthesis or analysis algorithm proposed in the paper needs a computation time about 1/3 more than Bertram's one, which on the other hand brings better stability and fitting quality.

The analysis effects of three actual highly-detailed models are shown in Figures 8, 9 and 10, respectively, where all resulting meshes at each level are subdivided again to the highest level without considering wavelet coefficients to show their fitting quality relative to the original models. Note that the model meshes are required to have the subdivision connectivity of Loop subdivision, i.e. 1-to-4 triangle splitting. Such subdivision connectivity can be obtained conveniently by some remeshing algorithms (Lee et al., 1998; Eck et al., 1995). On the surfaces of the original models, we have rendered the borderlines of each triangular region corresponding to the coarsest mesh so as to make the connectivity of the meshes clear. The computation times of the wavelet analyses and the numbers of triangles at each level are listed in Table 1 for the three models in detail. These examples have shown sufficient stability and good fitting quality of our wavelet transforms. Progressive transmission of highly-detailed geometric models on a network will be a direct application of the wavelet proposed in the paper. Other applications of the proposed wavelet include shape approximation, data compression, multiresolution rendering, etc.

Table 1. Computation times (seconds) in wavelet analyses

	Venus		Horse		Feline	
Level	Triangle Num.	Cost time	Triangle Num.	Cost time	Triangle Num.	Cost time
6	1589248	-	901120	-	2064384	-
5	397312	1.337149	225280	0.759805	516096	1.737340
4	99328	0.367125	56320	0.206454	129024	0.474483
3	24832	0.106602	14080	0.059295	32256	0.138144
2	6208	0.033035	3520	0.018766	8064	0.043531
1	1552	0.037539	880	0.021010	2016	0.048779
0	388	0.017256	220	0.008990	504	0.022508

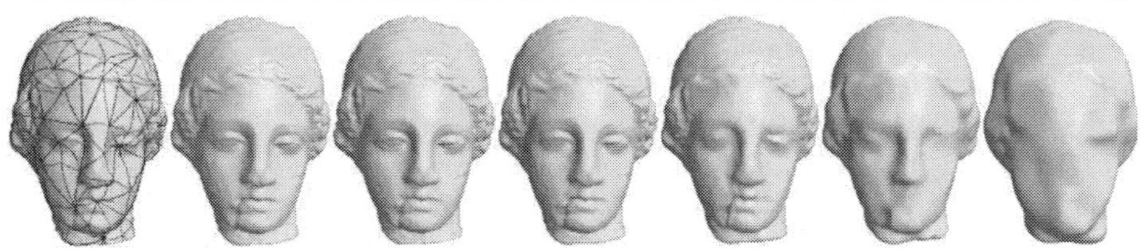

Figure 8. Wavelet analysis for the Venus model

Figure 9. Wavelet analysis for the horse model

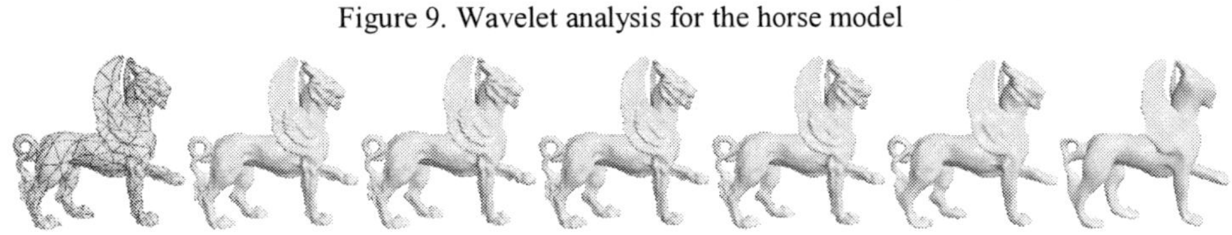

Figure 10. Wavelet analysis for the feline model

6. CONCLUSIONS

In this paper, we have proposed a new butterfly-orthogonal Loop subdivision wavelet based on the lifting scheme. We use a butterfly-style local orthogonalization structure to optimize the free parameters introduced in the wavelet transforms so as to obtain a very stable and nearly semi-orthogonal wavelet. Although it takes a little more computation time than the existing Loop subdivision wavelets, the proposed wavelet possesses a better fitting quality as well as performance of denoising, as demonstrated in the experiments. Similar to the other Loop subdivision wavelets, the butterfly-orthogonal wavelet has a linear computing complexity, because all lifting operations in the wavelet transforms are of perfect in-place computing and relate to only local vertex points or edge points. The proposed wavelet analysis can be used in a wide range of applications, including progressive transmission, shape approximation, data compression, multiresolution rendering and editing of complex models.

ACKNOWLEDGEMENT

This work was supported by National Key R&D Program of China (No. 2017YFB0202203), the Defense Industrial Technology Development Program of China (Grant No. C1520110002) and Foundation of Laboratory of Computational Physics.

REFERENCES

Bertram, M., 2004. Biorthogonal Loop-subdivision wavelets. *In Computing*, Vol. 72, No. 1-2, pp. 29-39.

Bertram, M. et al., 2004. Generalized B-spline subdivision-surface wavelets for geometry compression. *In IEEE Transactions on Visualization and Computer Graphics*, Vol. 10, No. 3, pp. 326-338.

Bonneau, G., 1998. Multiresolution analysis on irregular surface meshes. *In IEEE Transactions on Visualization and Computer Graphics*, Vol. 4, No. 4, pp. 365-378.

Catmull, E. and Clark, J., 1978. Recursively Generated B-spline Surfaces on Arbitrary Topological Meshes. *In Computer Aided Design*, Vol. 10, pp. 350-355.

Doo, D. and Sabin, M., 1978. Behavior of Recursive Division Surfaces near Extraordinary Points. *In Computer Aided Design*, Vol. 10, pp. 356-360.

Eck, M. et al., 1995. Multiresolution analysis of arbitrary meshes. *Proceedings of SIGGRAPH '1995*, pp. 173-182.

Khodakovsky, A. et al., 2000. Progressive geometry compression. *Proceedings of SIGGRAPH '2000*. New Orleans, Louisiana, USA, pp. 271–278.

Lee, A. et al., 1998. MAPS: multiresolution adaptive parameterization of surfaces. *Proceedings of SIGGRAPH '1998*. Orlando, Florida, USA, pp. 95-104.

Li, D. et al., 2004. Unlifted Loop subdivision wavelets. *Proceedings of Pacific Graphics '2004*. Seoul, Korea, pp. 25-33.

Loop, C., 1987. *Smooth subdivision surfaces based on triangles*. M.S. Thesis, Department of Mathematics, University of Utah.

Lounsbery, M. et al., 1997. Multiresolution analysis for surfaces of arbitrary topological type. *In ACM Transactions on Graphics*, Vol. 16, No. 1, pp. 34-73.

Samavati, F. and Bartels, R., 1999. Multiresolution curve and surface editing: reversing subdivision rules by least-squares data fitting. *In Computer Graphics Forum*, Vol. 18, No. 2, pp. 97-119.

Samavati, F. et al., 2002. Multiresolution surfaces having arbitrary topologies by a reverse Doo subdivision method. *In Computer Graphics Forum*, Vol. 21, No. 2, pp. 121–136.

Schröder, P. and Sweldens, W., 1995. Spherical wavelets: efficiently representing functions on the sphere. *In Computer Graphics (Proceedings of SIGGRAPH '95)*, pp. 161-172.

Sweldens, W., 1996. The lifting scheme: a custom-design construction of biorthogonal wavelets. *In Appl. Comput. Harmon. Anal.*, Vol. 3, No. 2, pp. 186–200.

Valette, S. and Prost, R., 2004. Wavelet-based multiresolution analysis of irregular surface meshes. *In IEEE Trans. on Visualization & Computer Graphics*, Vol. 10, No. 2, pp. 113-122.

Wang, H. et al., 2006. Efficient wavelet construction with Catmull-Clark subdivision. *In Visual Computer*, Vol. 22, No. 9-11, pp. 874-884.

Wu, J. and Amaratunga, K., 2003. Wavelet triangulated irregular networks. *In International Journal of Geographical Information Science*, Vol. 17, No. 3, pp. 273-289.

Zorin, D. et al., 1996. Interpolating subdivision for meshes with arbitrary topology. *Proceedings of SIGGRAPH '1996*, pp. 189-192.

UNSUPERVISED PEDESTRIAN SAMPLE EXTRACTION FOR MODEL TRAINING

Hao Yu[1,2], Daryl Maples[2], Ying Liu[1] and Zhijie Xu[2]
[1]*Xi'an University of Posts and Telecommunications, Xi'an, China*
[2]*University of Huddersfield, Huddersfield, UK*

ABSTRACT

Many researches on pedestrian detection use benchmarking datasets such as INRIA for model training. However, models trained with standard video database do not usually obtain satisfying performance in real-life conditions. Hence, supervised training through manually labelled instances is often required to help achieving better detection result. In this research, an innovative unsupervised training approach is proposed. By analyzing the histogram of adjacent pixels modelled from the video sequences, separated pedestrians can be extracted without manual intervention. Experiments have shown consistent performance that is superior over the state-of-the-art methods.

KEYWORDS

Pedestrian Detection, Crowd Analysis, Unsupervised Learning

1. BACKGROUND

For approaches using classifiers for detection, the positive and negative samples are often manually labelled for model training. Most benchmarking datasets contain the annotated positive and negative samples. Thus, the acquirement of sampling information is usually ignored in the task of pedestrian detection. For example, INRIA set is used to train the detection model in approaches such as HOG (Dalal & Triggs, 2005), FPDW (Dollar et al. 2010) and PLS (Schwartz et al. 2009). TUD-MP is used by MUTLIFTR-CSS and MUTLIFTR-MOTION (Walk et al. 2010). The PASCAL set is used by LATENT-SVM (Felzenszwalb et al. 2008). However, cameras in real-life applications are installed at varied height and angles with different perspective and effective distances. Most of the time, a model trained with samples from standard datasets do not perform as well in real-life if without additional parameter adjustment processes, which could be tedious and problem-prone. Therefore, manual labelling is often required when a new pedestrian detection system is installed. Researches have been conducted to simplify the labelling process. In the research of Davide et al. (2013), a so-called Weak-supervised annotation approach is devised to automate the extraction of positive and negative samples of pedestrians. In the work, simulated virtual video footages are firstly exploited to generate positive samples for the initial support vectors (SVM-based) training. With the trained classifier, various samples are extracted from the real-life footage and sorted with the confidence score. Next, the true positive samples of pedestrian will be manually labelled alongside the true negative samples. These weakly-supervised samples are again sent to the classifier for the second-round of training. With this process, it claims to have obtained a fine miss-rate/FPPI curve. However, the weakly-supervised labelling process is still time consuming, and requires professional personnel to operate in order to achieve the optimal detection result.

In order to address this issue, a novel unsupervised pedestrian sampling approach is proposed in this research. The devised method is capable of automatically extracting the positive and negative samples from the detected targets without the need for manual intervention. Details of the work is organized as follows: Section 2 introduced the technical design of the proposed method, including the positive and negative sampling techniques. Section 3 investigated datasets adopted for modelling and validation. The efficiency of the new approach is also analyzed in comparison with the result acquired from annotated model-based methods. Section 4 concludes the work with anticipated future improvement.

2. UNSUPERVISED SAMPLING OF PEDESTRIAN TARGETS

The training of machine learning model for pedestrian detection requires two types of sampling data - positive and negative samples. The positive sample is an image patch of pedestrian with the optimal position, which could be used to extract the most representative patterns of the pedestrian. The negative samples usually are the opposite. Benchmarking dataset holds the advantage of the large number of manually labeled sample data. Take INRIA as an example, thousands of positive samples of pedestrians have been annotated.

In order to obtain as many positive samples in the unsupervised sampling process, the strategy adopted in this research is to analyze a consecutive video sequence with proper length, and to probe pedestrians who are 1) not occluded with others, 2) separable from the crowd. A histogram based positive sampling method is developed based on the principle that with sufficient video data, positive samples of large quantity can be extracted. Pilot tests demonstrated promising recall rates for extracting positive samples. In general, the number of negative samples is more important than the number of positive samples. The proposed approach consists of two parts, which are focused on the extraction of positive pedestrian samples and negative pedestrian samples separately.

2.1 Positive Target Sampling

The procedure of positive sampling contains three main phases. In the first phase, the foreground is subtracted from the original image. Then a histogram is modelled with the foreground pixel clusters. An average estimated cluster size to represent a pedestrian is obtained from the histogram. In the final phase, positive samples with proper foreground cluster size could be extracted from the training video sequence. The devised procedure is illustrated in the Figure 1 below.

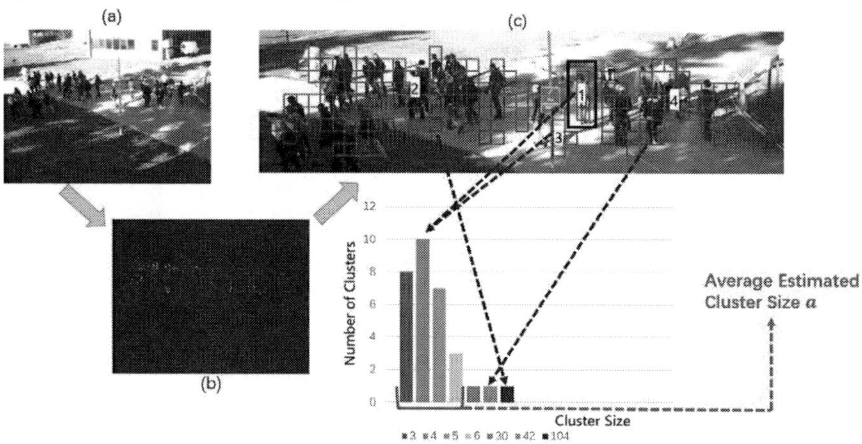

Figure 1. The procedure for estimating the average cluster size of pedestrian bounding box. (a) Original image (b) Subtracted foreground image. (c) Clustered foreground image patches

The subtracted foreground could be obtained with either the Mixture of Gaussian segmentation (KaewTraKulPong and Bowden, 2002) or through standard threshold filtering. Next, a grid of blocks is mapped to the foreground image, any block not completely covering the foreground will be discarded. As shown in Figure 2(c) below, the red block marks the clustered foreground. A pedestrian separated from the crowd usually occupy several coherent blocks. In the training process, an image patch consists of these coherent blocks can be considered as a positive sample of a pedestrian. As shown in Figure 2(c), the pedestrian in red jacket that is marked by a black box occupies four adjacent blocks. When the position of a camera is known, one can assume that the number of coherent foreground boxes for a single pedestrian will be limited in a certain range. As aforementioned procedures that two steps will be needed to obtain various positive samples in a video sequence through, estimating of the block range, and searching for clusters within this range.

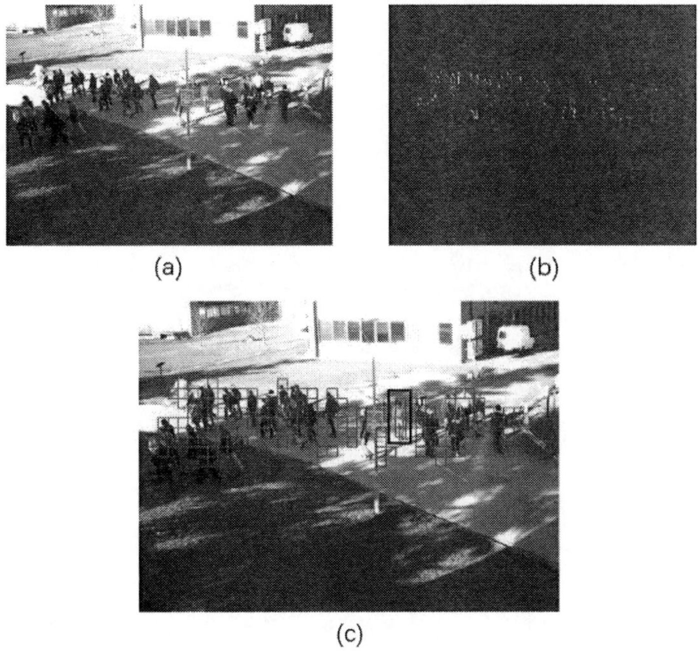

Figure 2. (a)Original image. (b) The Subtracted Foreground. (c) The marked pedestrian separated from the crowd occupies four coherent foreground blocks

2.1.1 Estimating of the Block Range

Based on the assumption that the cluster size for each pedestrian separated from the crowd will locate in certain range, the accumulative quantity of clusters of size within this range during certain period of time should be significantly higher than the quantity outside this range. Therefore, a histogram of cluster size and its accumulative quantity can be modelled for analysis. In order to model the histogram, adjacent blocks within a frame are labeled with numbers. As illustrated below, Figure 3(a) contains clusters with 4, 4, 104, and 42 adjacent blocks. By iteratively apply this process for several frames, a histogram can be modelled with the total number of groups of same number of blocks. The modeled histogram using 10 consecutive frames as illustrated in following Figure 3(b). It can be observed that the detected clusters with block numbers ranged from 4 to 15 are heavily grouped together and have significant higher values than clusters of different sizes. Therefore, the size of these clusters can be used to represent a separated pedestrian. Next, the average size of the cluster is calculated as the estimated patch size of a separable pedestrian target.

2.1.2 Searching for Clusters

Before modelling the histogram, clusters with less than 2 blocks are removed, since they are most likely generated by the background noise. Next, a 2-dimensional histogram $h = \{v_1, v_2, \dots, v_i\}$ is modelled, in which $v_i = [n_i, m_i]$, n indicates the cluster size, and m indicates the quantity of clusters with size n. The modelled histogram will be sparser as long as the value of n become larger. The reason is when various pedestrians are occluded, the size of its derived cluster has a high probability of variation from a norm in a large scale. On the contrary, separable pedestrians in the same camera view will occupy areas within certain range. Thus, the value m for separable pedestrian will be significantly larger. Next, by applying a typical classifier such as k-nearest-neighbor (KNN) on h, value n of this histogram can be readily classified into two clusters. It is expected that the initial n with larger m will be determined as the first cluster C_1 and the rest n as the second cluster C_2. Once $\{v\} \in C_1$ is determined, the average cluster size can be estimated. The average cluster size a for a single pedestrian is expressed by the following equation (1).

$$a = \frac{\sum_{v_i \in C_1}(m_i \times n_i)}{\sum_{v_i \in C_1} m_i} \qquad (1)$$

After the average cluster size a of a separable pedestrian target is determined, any cluster of similar size will be considered as a potential pedestrian and the corresponding image patch selected as a candidate of positive sample. When the qualified clusters are located, the image patch is extracted by a bounding box with the 0.4 width/height ratio. The size is determined by a, and the center of this bounding box is set as the center of the located cluster.

The samples extracted from 27 consecutive frames from the PETS09 dataset are illustrated in Figure 4(a). During the test, 9 separable pedestrians are successfully located. Figure 4(b) shows the 2 false positives, which are caused by occlusion from the signpost. In the following process, the annotated samples will be sent to the SVM model for training.

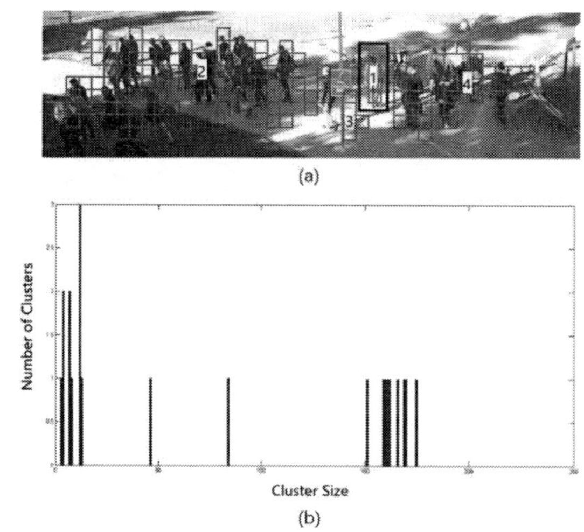

Figure 3. (a) Clustered coherent blocks. (b) Histogram modelled with clustered blocks from several consecutive frames

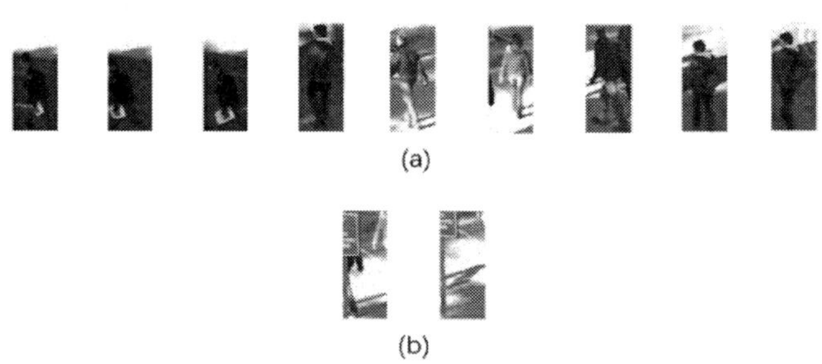

Figure 4. Extracted positive samples using the proposed approach. (a) True positive samples. (b) False positive samples

2.2 Negative Target Sampling

In order to improve the classification performance, the selection of negative samples is also crucial in the training phase. Most of the time, negative samples must significantly outnumber positive samples. By using a sliding window on the image, any obtained patch with certain patterns will be labelled as negative samples by the proposed approach. These patterns will be derived from 3 different circumstances, 1) a patch contains pure static background; 2) a patch contains part of pedestrians and part of background; 3) a patch contains multiple overlapped pedestrians.

In the first circumstance, the patch with pure background will be considered as a negative sample. Approaches on background segmentation are widely studied such as Mixture of Gaussian (MoG) (KaewTraKulPong and Bowden, 2002) (ZoranZivkovic and Ferdinandvan, 2006) (Andrew et al. 2012) and the gray-scale threshold segmentation (Milan et al. 2007). In the proposed approach, the MoG model is used for the background segmentation. In the second circumstance, the image patch contains a portion of foreground information. In this case, a threshold T has been applied whose values will be estimated empirically among the range 0 to 1. If the foreground occupies a ratio of the entire patch that is less than T, it will be considered as a negative sample. A practical range of T is set between and 0.2 to 0.4 based on experiments. In the last circumstance, the patch contains multiple but occluded pedestrians. In this case, the patch of this type will not be qualified as an appropriate positive sample since at most of the frames, individual pedestrian do not occupy a premier lactation on the patch. However, this scenario will not be appropriate if all classified as negative samples due to it mixed nature. Thus, this type of patches will be ignored in the training phase. The following Figure 5 illustrates the negative sample selection procedures encompass different circumstances.

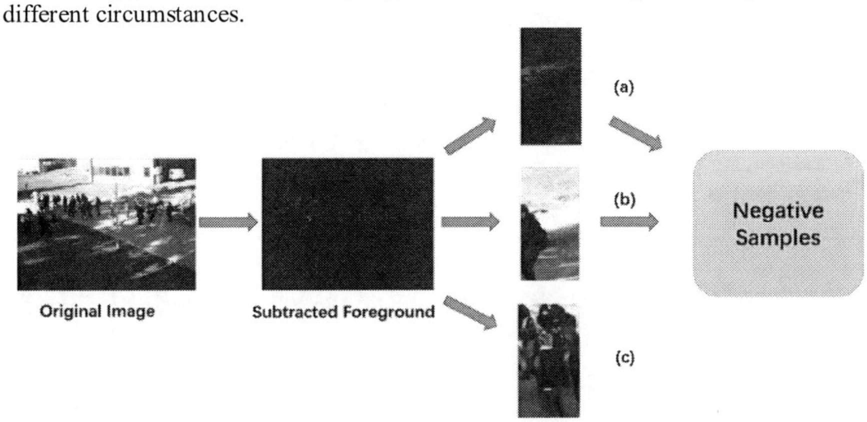

Figure 5. The procedure of selecting negative samples. (a) Pure background is categorized as solid negative. (b) Patch contains partial foreground with lower ratio than threshold will be categorized as negative. (c) Patches contain multiple overlapped objects are ignored

Once completed, a set of positive and negative samples will be automatically annotated from a video sequence and feed to classifiers for training.

3. EXPERIMENT AND EVALUATION

In this section, experiments are carried out to evaluate the performance of the proposed approach. In the first experiment, the efficiency of unsupervised positive sampling is assessed by benchmarking tests on four video clips from PETS2009. In the second experiment, a comparison has been made to prove the detection model trained by the unsupervised approach can outperform the model trained by the standard INRIA video dataset.

3.1 Benchmarking and Datasets

In the following experiments, benchmarking datasets are utilized to evaluate the performance of the developed unsupervised pedestrian detection approach. One of the most used pedestrian detection datasets is INRIA dataset (Dalal and Triggs, 2005). The INRIA set contains thousands of positive and negative data for training and testing. All pedestrians in the testing set are annotated with the co-ordinates. However, the INRIA set is not appropriate for the testing in this case due to, 1) the proposed approach is devised to handle data from the same camera that the INRIA was from different camera sources; and 2), the approach is devised to handle the pedestrian in mid-to-high density with frequent occlusive scenes that the INRIA does not satisfy.

Another widely used dataset for pedestrian detection is PETS2009. PETS set contains crowd videos collected with static cameras from various perspectives, which is most suitable for testing the developed approach. There are three sub-categories in PETS2009 namely, person counting, tracking, and event recognition. In the person counting subset, video footages contain walking and running individuals within a mid-to-high crowd setting that are ideal for the assessment of the developed techniques and are used for both training and testing in this research.

3.2 Positive Sample Extraction Efficiency

In the first experiment, performance of the unsupervised sampling approach is evaluated. All 4 subsets of PETS_S1_L2 at time 14-06 are used to mine positive samples. Each subset contains 200 frames of same pedestrians from different view perspective. The sampling results vary with cameras as illustrated in Figure 6. Take camera 1 as an example, 117 samples are extracted, which consists of 55 samples of separated pedestrians and 62 samples of occluded pedestrians. 47 percent of total extracted samples are optimal/desired for training. According to the devised rule of positive sampling, most samples with clustered pedestrians are discarded. However, significant portion of samples are composed with occluded pedestrians. These samples are exploited for training process along with the desired ones, since most of them successfully captured at least a pedestrian despite of the occlusion. Another noticeable issue is the abnormality of the sample number and the low rate of desired samples. The main reason is the camera distance is too far for the accurate optical flow calculation. The inaccurate optical flow would eventually cause the false estimation of a, and sampling failure. This result reveals a weakness of the proposed approach that in order to achieve the best performance, the distance between camera and pedestrian need to be controlled.

	View1	View2	View3	View4

Detected	117	111	426	129
Samples				
Desired	55	71	52	51
Occlude	62	40	374	78
Rate	47%	64%	12%	39%

Figure 6. Sampling results of the same crowd from different cameras

3.3 Evaluation against the Manually Labelled Dataset

In this experiment, the performance of unsupervised sample extraction is evaluated by comparing to the detection result using the same detection procedure with manually labelled training data. Total 540 positive and 300 negative samples in a subset of INRIA are exploited to train the classifier. Figure 7 illustrates the annotation results from different perspectives of the same image frame. The results show that training using unsupervised approach is capable of achieving better performance than the standard manually based ones such as the HoG-LBP method (Xiaoyu, Tony, and Shuicheng, 2009).

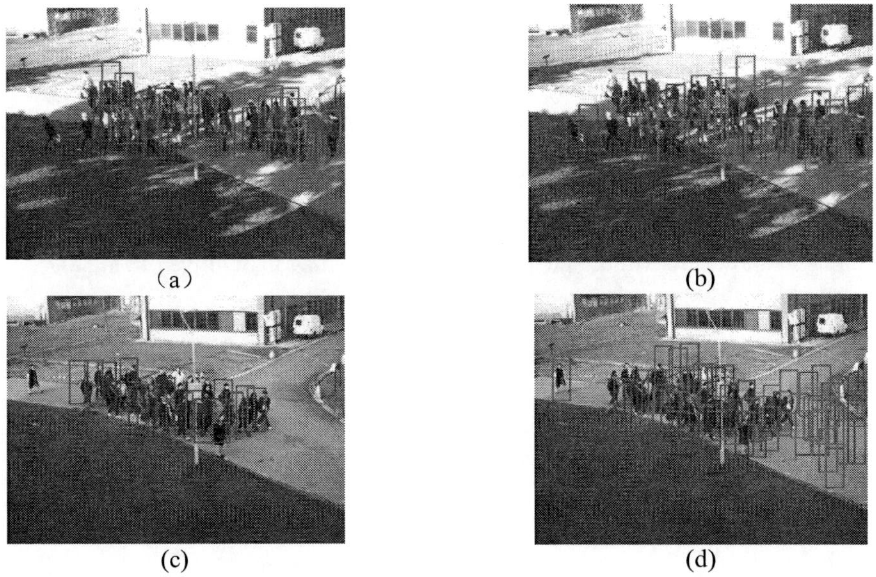

Figure 7. (a) (c) Trained with unsupervised extracted samples. (b) (d) trained with INRIA

In the next experiment, the performance of the devised approach is evaluated based on different combinations of patterns following the same unsupervised training paradigm. In the training phase, data from subset S1-L2-Time_14-06 of each camera is used for positive and negative sampling. This subset contains 200 consecutive frames, all of which will be fed to the unsupervised sampling model. The size of an image patch is set to 18 by 18 pixels. The calculated average cluster size is 10 for total 200 frames. In the detection phase, subset S1-L2-Time_14-31 is used for the detection. This subset contains 130 frames which has the identical view perspective but different illumination settings to the training data. According to the estimated pedestrian size, the bounding box is empirically set as 100 by 40 pixels. The linear SVM is trained and applied for the detection. The step of sliding window is set to 5 pixels.

As the detection result illustrated in Figure 8, the performance of pedestrian detection using unsupervised training data is slightly lower than the supervised data in all three approaches. Despite the approach using HoG-LBP pattern with Motion Rescoring and Soft-NMS techniques exhibits the best miss-rate/FPPI curve, the same approach with unsupervised training data still has high performance.

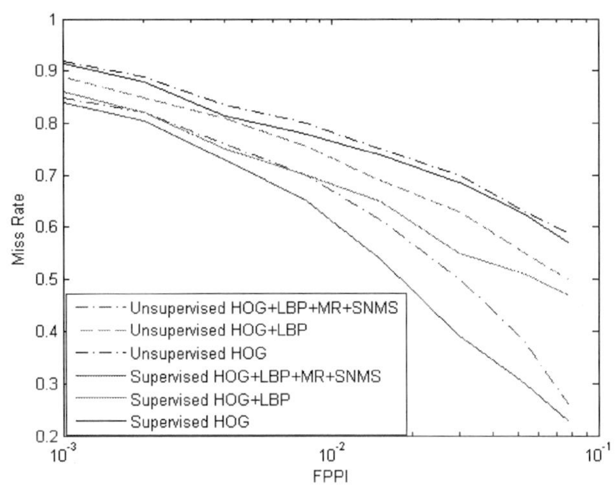

Figure 8. Comparison of detection results using the unsupervised and supervised training data

4. CONCLUSIONS AND FUTURE WORK

In order to avoid the tedious and erroneous operations for training pedestrian detection systems using manually labelled dataset, this research has developed an unsupervised training approach to automatically extracting separable pedestrian targets. The experiments show the positive samples of pedestrians can be efficiently extracted by this cost-effective and efficient approach. However, due to the nature of the cluster size-based detection mechanism, the proposed solution only applies on the static camera and constant scene conditions, which is a major limit to be addressed in the further research. To improve the robustness of the proposed model, future work will see the investigation of homographic-driven frame transformation to cope with video data from different camera sources and parameter settings.

ACKNOWLEDGEMENT

This research is funded by Key Research and Development Program of Shaanxi (2019GY-054), the Sichuan Science and Technology Program (2019YFH0187) and Shaanxi Smart City Technology Project of Xianyang (No. 2017k01-25-5).

REFERENCES

Andrew, B. G. et al. (2012). Visual tracking of human visitors under variable-lighting conditions for a responsive audio art installation. In 2012 American Control Conference (ACC). Montreal, QC, Canada.

Dalal, N. and Triggs, B. (2005). Histograms of Oriented Gradients for Human Detection. In Proc. IEEE Conf. Computer Vision and Pattern Recognition, San Diego, CA, USA.

David, V. et al. (2013). Weakly Supervised Automatic Annotation of Pedestrian Bounding Boxes. In the IEEE Conference on Computer Vision and Pattern Recognition (CVPR) Workshops. Oregon, Portland.

Dollar, P. et al. (2010). The Fastest Pedestrian Detector in the West. In Proc. British Machine Vision Conf. Wales, UK.

Felzenszwalb, P. et al. (2008). A Discriminatively Trained, Multiscale, Deformable Part Model. In Proc. IEEE Conf. Computer Vision and Pattern Recognition, Anchorage, Alaska, USA.

KaewTraKulPong, P. and Bowden, R. (2002). An Improved Adaptive Background Mixture Model for Real-time Tracking with Shadow Detection. In Video-Based Surveillance Systems. Boston, MA.

Milan, S. et al. (2007). Image Processing, Analysis, and Machine Vision. Brooks/Cole, USA.

PETS 2009 Benchmark Data. Retrieved from http://www.cvg.reading.ac.uk/PETS2009/a.html

Schwartz, W. et al. (2009). Human Detection Using Partial Least Squares Analysis. In Proc. IEEE Int'l Conf. Computer Vision. Kyoto, Japan.

Walk, S. et al. (2010). New Features and Insights for Pedestrian Detection. In Proc. IEEE Conf. Computer Vision and Pattern Recognition, San Francisco, CA, USA.

Xiaoyu, W., Tony, X. H. and Shuicheng, Y. (2009). An HOG-LBP Human Detector with Partial Occlusion Handling. In the IEEE 12th International Conference on Computer Vision. Kyoto, Japan.

ZoranZivkovic, and Ferdinandvan, H. (2006). Efficient adaptive density estimation per image pixel for the task of background subtraction. Pattern Recognition Letters. 27(7), 773-780.

FACIAL RECOGNITION, AUTONOMOUS LEARNING, BASED ON IMAGE FRAGMENTATION

Danilo Daniel González Guacte and Diego Alberto Aracena Pizarro
Department of Computer Engineering and Informatics, University Tarapacá, Chile

ABSTRACT

This paper uses variations in the image fragmentation approach, considering the number of fragments, number of samples per person, number of hyperplanes and size in the region of interest. Computational vision techniques, in particular gradient histogram (HOG) as feature space descriptor, automatic learning methods, such as vector support machines (SVM) for model construction and a face detection algorithm, are used to replicate these experiments in a real time context. Tests are performed on a population of 40 people, samples taken in uncontrolled situations, in this way some states are discarded, refining the parameters until arriving at a configuration that complies with delivering the best results in this experiment and under these conditions.

KEYWORDS

Facial Recognition, Image Fragmentation, HOG, SVM, Region of Interest, Hyperplanes

1. INTRODUCTION

At present, crime and recidivism rates reflect no less growth and, as a direct consequence, the population's distrust of its safety (Unidas, 2015) (Dammert & , 2012). This type of problem is mitigated in many ways: use of personal weapons, greater penalties for those caught, greater security personnel, among others (Dammert, 2004). One of the solutions that has given greater security to the population according to some studies (Cordero Vega, 2015) (Dammert, 2004), is use security cameras, also known as CCTV[1].

The aim is to provide a solution oriented towards use automatic recognition techniques based on biometric features. This allows the identification of individuals in a non-invasive way, since it does not need more information than that contained in the inherent traits of each individual (Viola & Jones, 2001).

The search for new ways to improve the people recognition by means of machines has been under study for several years. This work focuses on the use of fragments, motivated by the article written by: Tetyana Baydyk, Ernst Kussul and Sandra Bonilla Meza (Baydyk, et al., 2016). This paper uses SVM [2] for sample classification, but there are also papers that use ANN[3] under the same sample fragmentation approach (Salyut & Kurnaz, 2018).

2. FACIAL RECOGNITION

Facial recognition (RF) is a technique that has been widely used even before the development of automatic recognition systems. RF has long generated the interest of the scientific community, as it has led to good levels of efficiency in this area (Hu, et al., 2017).

The face is an inherent and very discriminatory element by which individuals can be identified with the naked eye and is used for identification in various fields (Díaz Moreno, 2004). A facial recognition system can be described in five main stages (see Figure 1).

---

[1] Closed Circuit Television
[2] Support Vector Machine
[3] Artificial Neural Network

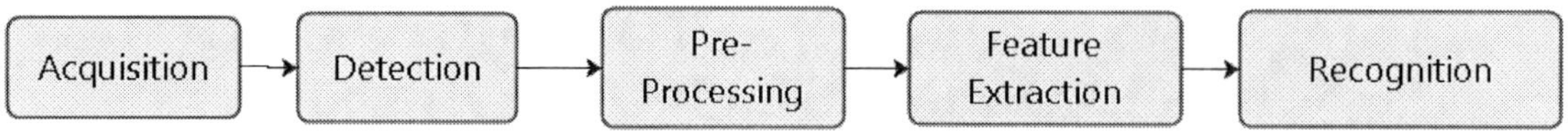

Figure 1. General diagram of an object recognition system

3. SYSTEM ARCHITECTURE

The system architecture is presented in Figure 2, having as its core the processes of search and identification. These require at least two input channels (camera data and people registration).

The first input flow corresponds to the registers (learning models) of people that one tries to recognize, requires at least one sample or image per person, although there are techniques to solve this problem (Hu, et al., 2017) is not the purpose of this work. The second channel corresponds to the data provided by the camera, the objective of the application is to contrast these two inputs and through a threshold of acceptance, make a decision. If the defined threshold is exceeded, the information of the localized person is provided and in this way automate these processes.

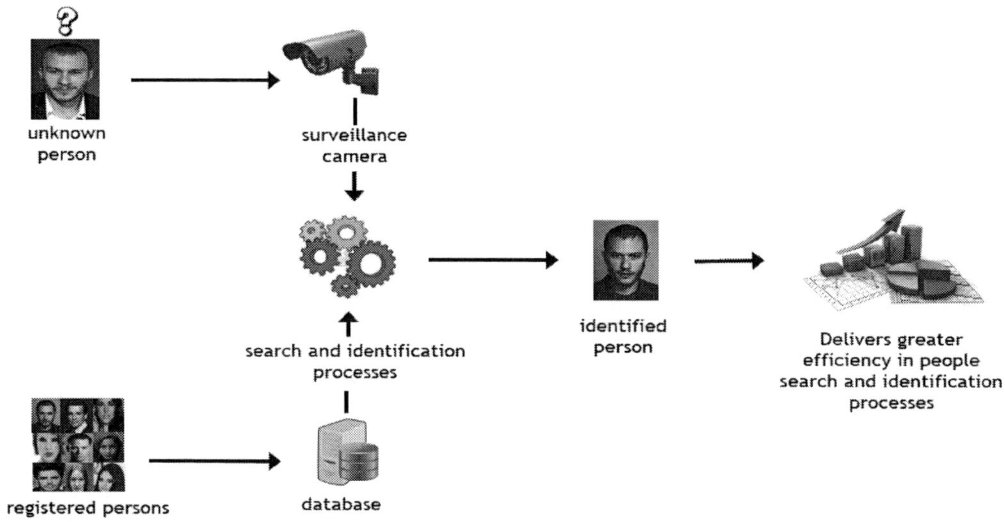

Figure 2. General system architecture

The architecture based on layers, allows to structure the different components of the system, in such way that each component is in a layer that depends only on the lower layers and not on the upper ones. This more restrictive variant of the traditional architectural abstraction model of layers, allows the future evolution of the software through the definition of new components in higher layers. The architecture presented in Figure 3 is defined as follows:

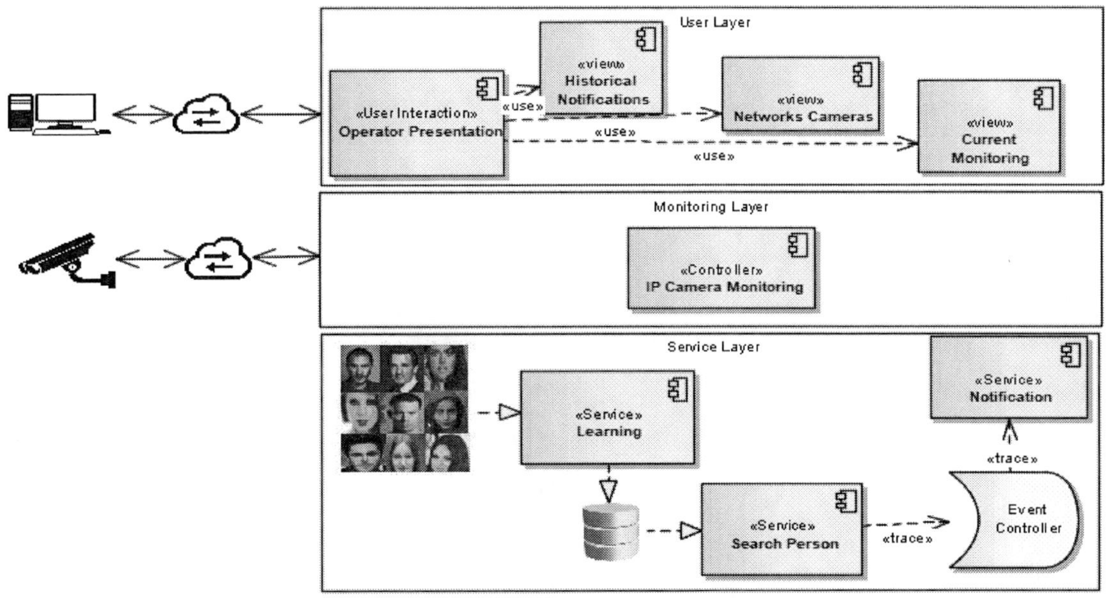

Figure 3. Layer-based system architecture

- **Layer 1**. Level service. Layer that composes the services of the system, camera management, user management, person search, learning and notification.

- **Layer 2.** Level monitoring. That supports the monitoring component (IP camera) the component hosted in this layer requires the services of the service layer.

- **Layer 3**. Layer User. Layer that supports user interaction.

3.1 Learning Module

This module is in charge of carrying out the whole process of sample training and model generation. Figure 4 defines the learning module in 6 sub-modules: loading, detection, pre-processing, fragmentation, extraction of characteristics and classification.

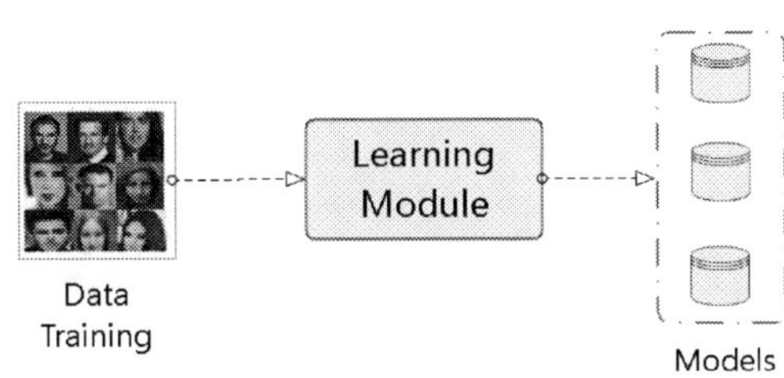

Figure 4. Module diagram, for the sample training service

- **Load.** Responsible for sample reception and organization (labelling).

- **Detection.** Responsible for the detection of one face per sample (using the algorithm proposed by P. Viola y M. Jones) (Viola & Jones, 2001).

- **Pre-Processing.** In charge of "refining" the samples, he basically performs three activities: trimming, equalizing histogram and eye alignment (Viola & Jones, 2001).

- **Fragmentation.** In charge of partitioning each of the samples (four fragments, sixteen fragments or sixty-four fragments). Other works use three areas of fragmentation (eyes, nose and mouth (Baydyk, et al., 2016) (Singh, et al., 2014)).

- **Characteristics extraction.** In charge of calculating the characteristics space for each one of the fragments, using the HOG method.

- **Classification.** In charge of classifying the samples, according to the vector of characteristics and labels.

3.2 Person Search Module

Figure 5 presents the organization of the sub-modules for the search of people. This diagram shows seven sub-modules, several of which are shared with the learning module.

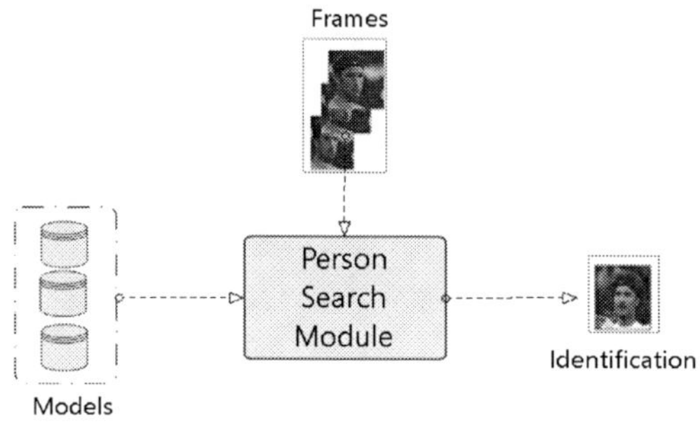

Figure 5. Module diagram, for the person search service

The sub-module added to this diagram is the prediction sub-module, which takes the results provided from the classification sub-module (based on the already trained models of the learning module) and evaluates the entered sample. For this, it makes use of two extra activities:

- **Merge predictions**. Accumulates predictions made by all models.

- **Prediction evaluation.** According to some criteria (75% agree in the prediction of the models (Singh, et al., 2014)) determines if this sample is possible to recognize.

4. IMPLEMENTATION

4.1 Sample Filtering

The cleaning process allows filtering those samples that will not be useful for the training of the models. The LFW[4] database is a large facial data set containing 13.233 images, 5.749 people for an uncontrolled environment and is the data source used for static testing (Columbia, 2009) (Kumar, et al., 2009).

The following criteria are considered for this process: A single face per sample, exactly seven samples, exactly ten samples, exactly thirteen samples and more than thirteen samples. Working with 1835 samples for test execution.

[4] Labeled Faces in the Wild

4.2 Fragmentation of Samples

The fragmentation process is worked with at least three degrees of fragmentation, factor 4, 16 and 64. This means that for factor 4, a face is fragmented into four parts and for each of these fragments, a learning machine is trained, specialized in the region of interest assigned (see Figure 6).

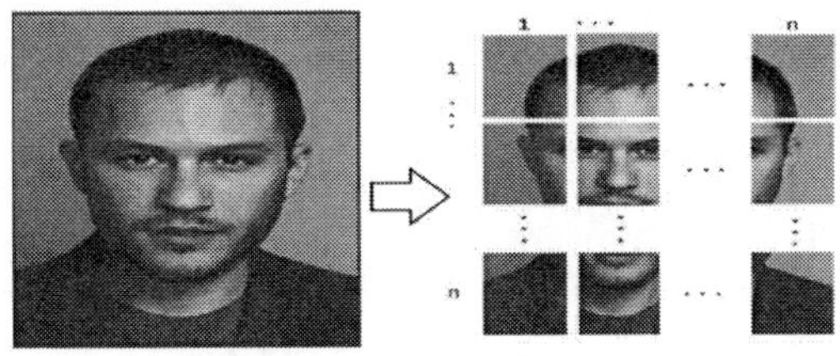

Figure 6. Example of face fragmentation

4.3 Calculation of HOG Descriptors

To use the HOG method as descriptor, enter a grayscale image (matrix of pixels with values between 0-255). The output of this method delivers what is known as vector descriptor or feature vector. Each of the components of this vector reflects the final value of the histogram associated with a cell (equation 1). The dimension of the vector depends on the number of blocks, number of cells and the orientation angle, with or without sign.

$$h((k) = \sum_{(x,y)\epsilon\, C} w_k(x,y) * g(x,y) \quad (1)$$

This means that the calculation of the histogram is given by the sum of each gradient multiplied by a weighting factor associated with the pixel. Tables 1, 2 and 3 present the configuration used for three region sizes of interest tested, depending on each degree of fragmentation.

Table 1. Parameters for a HOG object, with degree of fragmentation 4

Roi (px)	Win size (px)	Block size (px)	Cell size (px)	N° bins
64x64	32x32	16x16	8x8	9
128x128	64x64	32x32	16x16	9
64x128	32x64	16x32	8x16	9

Table 2. Parameters for a HOG object, with degree of fragmentation 16

Roi (px)	Win size (px)	Block size (px)	Cell size (px)	N° bins
64x64	16x16	8x8	4x4	9
128x128	32x32	16x16	8x8	9
64x128	16x32	8x16	4x8	9

Table 3. Parameters for a HOG object, with degree of fragmentation 64

Roi (px)	Win size (px)	Block size (px)	Cell size (px)	N° bins
64x64	8x8	4x4	2x2	9
128x128	16x16	8x8	4x4	9
64x128	8x16	4x8	2x4	9

5. RESULTS

Tests are performed on a random population of 40 people, the categories are: seven samples per person, ten samples per person, thirteen samples per person and more than thirteen samples per person (and less than 20 samples). According to this categorization, tables 4, 5, 6 and 7 describe the recognition success rate, considering only the number of hyperplanes and degrees of fragmentation.

Table 4. Average of results carried out on the population, for category 7 samples per person, evaluating degrees of fragmentation and number of hyperplanes

N° hyperplanes	Frag. 4 (%)	Frag. 16 (%)	Frag. 64 (%)	Score
4	60	80	80	220
9	65	65	50	180
14	43,33	50	40	133,33
19	40	40	40	120

Table 5.Average of results carried out on the population, for category 10 samples per person, evaluating degrees of fragmentation and number of hyperplanes

N° hyperplanes	Frag. 4 (%)	Frag. 16 (%)	Frag. 64 (%)	Score
4	45	60	60	165
9	60	70	45	175
14	40	63,33	36,67	140
19	47,5	55	32,5	135

Table 6. Average of results carried out on the population, for category 13 samples per person, evaluating degrees of fragmentation and number of hyperplanes

N° hyperplanes	Frag. 4 (%)	Frag. 16 (%)	Frag. 64 (%)	Score
4	55	55	35	145
9	60	60	45	165
14	56,67	50	43,33	150
19	45	45	30	120

Table 7. Average of results carried out on the population, for category +13 samples per person, evaluating degrees of fragmentation and number of hyperplanes

N° hyperplanes	Frag. 4 (%)	Frag. 16 (%)	Frag. 64 (%)	Score
4	80	100	60	240
9	65	70	45	180
14	56,67	66,67	40	163,33
19	52,5	57,5	40	150

These tests suggest the use of between 4 to 9 hyperplanes per learning machine, i.e. 4 to 10 people per model. Tables 8, 9 and 10 describe the success rate considering the size of the region of interest (64x64 pixels, 64x128 pixels and 128x128 pixels) and the degree of fragmentation.

Table 8. Average results obtained for tests carried out on a degree of fragmentation 4

Roi (px)	7 samples (%)	10 samples (%)	13 samples (%)	+13 samples (%)	Score
64x64	65	60	60	65	250
128x128	75	60	60	70	265
64x128	60	55	50	70	235

Table 9. Average results obtained for tests carried out on a degree of fragmentation 16

Roi (px)	7 samples (%)	10 samples (%)	13 samples (%)	+13 samples (%)	Score
64x64	65	70	60	70	265
128x128	60	55	65	70	250
64x128	70	55	55	70	250

Table 10. Average results obtained for tests carried out on a degree of fragmentation 64

Roi (px)	7 samples (%)	10 samples (%)	13 samples (%)	+13 samples (%)	Score
64x64	50	45	45	45	185
128x128	55	50	55	50	210
64x128	55	45	65	65	230

These results make it possible to approximate a suitable type of configuration when working with HOG descriptors and SVM-based learning machines. Using an orientation based on fragments, number of samples per person, number of hyperplanes per learning machine and size of the region of interest. In this sense and supported by the different tests carried out, it is possible to conclude a suitable configuration for the parameters that were part of the experimentation (see Table 11).

Table 11. Result of better configuration

Parameter	Configuration
Fragmentation	16
N° hyperplanes	4-9
N° Samples	+13
Region of interest	64x64

6. CONCLUSIONS

This work allows to know an effective configuration, verified with samples of people in an uncontrolled context. Allowing to establish the number of fragments, number of samples per person and size of the region of interest that provides the best results for people recognition.

The use of HOG as a method to describe an image is mainly due to the great use of it in different approaches in recognition work, its low computational cost and because it was necessary to opt for some method and lay the groundwork to empirically demonstrate the use of image fragments. Being a method that works on contours in an image, it was possible to predict that, by fragmenting one more face, the HOG method would not have many features to highlight and, therefore, the models would not be robust.

Likewise, the parameters for the configuration of each learning machine were adjusted thinking about a later application in real time, so a best option is to use a linear kernel to find an optimal hyperplane and with certain slack or slack variables. While this configuration is not the best for sample separation, it has a low computational cost. From this point of view, the integration of more CPUs or even GPUs could be worked on, since the fragmentation process allows exclusive work between fragments (parallelization of processes). This would allow to work with a better image resolution, and use methods that require a higher computing power and not be so restricted by the hardware.

REFERENCES

Baydyk, T., Kussul, E. & Meza, S. B., 2016. Facial Recognition on the Basis of Facial Fragments. *International Journal of Computer and Information Engineering,* 10(12).

Columbia, U., 2009. *www.cs.columbia.edu.* [Online] Available at: http://www.cs.columbia.edu/CAVE/databases/pubfig/ [Accessed 13 05 2019].

Cordero Vega, L., 2015. Videovigilancia e intervervención administrativa: las cuestiones de legitimidad. *revistatrabajo.uchile,* pp. 359-376.

Dammert, L., 2004. ¿Ciudad sin ciudadanos? Fragmentación, segregación y temor en Santiago. *EURE,* 30(91), pp. 87-96.

Dammert, L. & L. M., 2012. *La Seguridad Ciudadana: El problema principal de América Latina.* Santiago de Chile: Corporación Latinbarómetro.

Díaz Moreno, A. B., 2004. *Reconocimiento Facial Automático Mediante Técnicas de Visión Tridimensional.* Madrid: Universidad Politécnica de Madrid.

Hu, X., Peng, S., Wang, L. & Lo, Z., 2017. Surveillance video face recognition with single sample per person based on 3D modeling and blurring. *Elsevier,* pp. 113-117.

Kumar, N., Berg, A. C., Belhumeur, P. N. & Nayar, S. K., 2009. Attribute and Simile Classifiers for Face Verification. *International Conference on Computer Vision (ICCV),* pp. 365-372.

Salyut, J. & Kurnaz, C., 2018. Profile Face Recognition using Local Binary Patterns with Artificial Neural Network. *2018 International Conference on Artificial Intelligence and Data Processing (IDAP),* pp. 1-4.

Singh, A. K., Kumar, A., Nandi, G. C. & Chakroborty, P., 2014. Expression invariant fragmented face recognition. *2014 International Conference on Signal Propagation and Computer Technology,* pp. 184-189.

Singh, A. K., Kumar, A., Nandi, G. C. & Chakroborty, P., 2014. Expression invariant fragmented face recognition. *2014 International Conference on Signal Propagation and Computer Technology,* pp. 184-189.

Unidas, N., 2015. *Naciones Unidas.* [Online] Available at: http://www.un.org/es/sections/issues-depth/population/index.html [Accessed 13 05 2019].

Viola, P. & Jones, M., 2001. Robust Real-Time Face Detection. *Computer Vision and Pattern Recognition,* pp. 747-747.

Short Papers

PROTOTYPE ULTRASONIC WAYFINDER WITH HAPTIC FEEDBACK FOR AN IOT ENVIRONMENT

Soonja Yeom[1], Riseul Ryu[1], Eunbin Pak[2] and Pankoo Kim[2]
[1]School of Technology, Environment and Design, University of Tasmania, Sandybay, Hobart, Australia
[2]Department of Computer Engineering, Chosun University, Gwangju, Republic of Korea

ABSTRACT

Sensor technology for small mobile devices is developing quickly, prices for equipment are dropping rapidly and IoT infrastructure is increasingly accessible. These developments have made it possible to build a haptic glove with a vibrating interface to help a person with visual impairment to move around. This haptic sensing glove will guide the user as an additional device – on top of what they use for guidance at present. This article describes a prototype which is undergoing user testing and can be further tied into a smart home environment.

KEYWORDS

Sensor Technology, Haptic Feedback, Wearable Technology

1. INTRODUCTION

Pervasive computing and the Internet of Things (IoT) have stimulated the development of many new assistive devices. It is possible to incorporate sensors such as acoustic, inductive, capacitive, temperature, humidity, pressure, location, and many more. Haptic feedback provides a person with sensory information through the skin using vibration or force-feedback responses. Commercial organizations have moved very quickly into this design space, particularly Sunu (smart-watch), HandSight (cameras on glove), and others. Arduino and Raspberry Pi are examples of the computing platforms currently in use. Sonar or ultrasonic transducers enable the production of lighter equipment with improved functionalities. Sonar as a means of assistive navigation has been used extensively in maritime environments to detect animals (D'Amico and Pittenger, 2009, Evans and Awbrey, 1988). As an assistive technology, there are projects for the blind which upgrade their walking sticks with an ultrasonic sensor (Amemiya and Sugiyama, 2010).

Similar projects have been undertaken worldwide and most devices can only provide one or two designated functions. The size of the completed device is small enough to embed on a shoe, a walking stick, or on a wheelchair. A sonar sensor can detect something less than a meter from an individual user. This study uses a glove to attach a sonar sensor on a Raspberry Pi 0, whereas the Tacit glove (Hoefer, 2011) carries two sonar sensors with an Arduino controller actuating vibrating motors on a glove.

2. BACKGROUND

The Raspberry Pi is a small, powerful, cheap, hackable and education-oriented computer board introduced in 2012 (Vujović and Maksimović, 2014, Nikhade, 2015). It has the capacity to build a wireless sensor network (WSN), with a sensing unit, processor, storage, and transceiver.

The project was to design and build a device worn on a single hand by a visually impaired person. Each wearable glove carries a sonar sensor and a set of haptic feedback devices, connected to a Raspberry Pi Zero (RPi0). As the RPi0 has minimal mass, size, and power which combines with a minimal mass and size 5V power pack. One of the limitations of the Raspberry Pi for this kind of application is its relatively large power consumption (Vujović et al., 2014). The glove would provide haptic feedback to the wrist/hand of the wearer, via vibration, on the relative positional-distance of objects. The positional-distance would be calculated through data provided by sonar sensors contained on the glove. The sonar sensors should have a documented range of up to 4 metres, however they worked up to a distance of 1.5 meters in the test. Some of the contributing factors include distance, angle, signal absorbency, and power input (Borenstein and Koren, 1988).

The RPi0 would operate headless – that is, without any screen or keyboard which reduces the need for peripheral components. The aim is to provide:

(a) A wearable platform that can be used by sight-impaired persons to sense their immediate environment by hand-waving.

(b) A device which can be modified by software to provide a wider range of functions compared to other similar devices.

A similar haptic handheld wayfinder for people with visual impairment was reported in 2010 (Amemiya and Sugiyama, 2010). This was positively evaluated by people with visual impairments. It needed extra devices and a miniaturized force display. Adding the device to a glove produced a similar project, Tacit Glove, which was tested in 2011 (Hoefer, 2011). Another approach is putting the device on cane. The Raspberry Pi was compared with other wireless sensor nodes such as MicaZ, TelosB, Iris, Cricket, and Lotus in terms of size, cost, power, memory, and flexibility (Vujović & Maksimović, 2014). The Raspberry Pi has better processing power, memory, connectivity, and multipurpose usage (USB) with a cheaper cost. However, power consumption was the area identified for improvement. In the prototype, Python 2 was used for programming instead of Python 3, since some libraries have not yet been ported to Python 3.

3. PROTOTYPE

3.1 What it does?

The Raspberry Pi 3 (RPi3) is the fully functional current model that is widely available. The Raspberry Pi Zero (RPi0) is lighter than the RPi3 as well as less power demanding. In the project, the RPi0 is used with an ultrasonic sensor powered by an auxiliary 5V battery pack. It also supports a WIFI dongle for connectivity in headless configuration. For haptic feedback, a micro servomotor, 'SG90' was tested, followed by a vibration module, with the thought that vibration module would be an easier option to use.

The board was modified as shown in the diagram below (Figure 1) and connected to the ultrasonic sensor via the 5V General Purpose Input/Output (GPIO) pin. The 5V pin of the ultrasonic sensor is connected to GPIO Pin 2 (which is for 5V power) on the RPi0. The trigger signal is connected to Pin 16 (GPIO23), the Echo line is connected to Pin18 (GPIO24) and Ground to Pin6 (Ground).

A USB hub board (Figure 2) was attached to the Raspberry Pi so that the WIFI dongle could be attached to the top of the RPi0, rather than protruding from a side (where it is easily brokened or damaged).

Figure 1. Assembled version before putting it on glove

The prototype uses the ultrasonic sensor for object recognition, while the existing systems in this field commonly use the fixed cameras (Wang et al., 2017, Yi et al., 2013) or radio frequency (Dionisi et al., 2012).The ultrasonic sensor was successfully assembled on the RPi0 by using the breadboard and jumper cable through an expanded GPIO board (BreakHAT). A switch and a vibrator were placed on the board and the circuitary test was performed.. A way is currently being sought to add the servomotor or vibrator or LCD screen to the glove. But the LCD screen was found to be too large and impractical for use, so the project switched to a virtualised screen through VNC viewer. It should be noted that the virtualised screen is only for developers as an auxiliary visual aid for use when testing. More experiments are needed to determine whether RPi0 can provide enough power for two different sensors. The ultrasonic sensor needs a pair of resistors to lower the input 5V voltage to 3.3V.

All the devices, including ultrasonic sensors and High-Definition Multimedia Interface (HDMI) will be connected to a small LCD display and battery pack when completed, excluding keyboard, mouse and WIFI dongle. Power was supplied with a 5V battery kit with USB charging input and a switch attached (Figure 3). If running more than just the WIFI dongle the battery pack will need to be upgraded - which could be a powerbank or any external portable battery suitable for a mobile phone. The input should be about 1A to source enough power to the RPi0.

In the experiment for measuring distance, a WIFI dongle with a battery pack was used due to a need for lesser than 5V supplied from the 5V battery. It was controlled via Secure Shell (SSH) through the phone hotspot WIFI and the Android application 'connectbot'. The ultrasonic sensor works well and updates the distance reading as it changes. The vibrator or servomotor produces haptic feedback when the distance is closer than 30 cm or 100 cm. Detecting an obstacle at 30 cm may be too short to avoid when the user is walking, hence different signals can be given to the user at 1 meter and again at 50 cm with a longer and stronger vibration. The simple on/off switch is attached to the prototype so that a user who is visually impaired can turn the prototype on and off without entering the commands on the device through a keyboard. It needs further work to implement a mobile application so that the user can issue voice commands to connect to the device, run the system, and turn the device off.

Due to power concerns, it is proposed that the prototype uses a bigger battery such as a small mobile phone battery or dedicated battery pack to replace current small 5V battery for further development work. It will support the vibrator and ultrasonic sensor as well as the extra USB hub board for the WIFI dongle.

3.2 Difficulties

One of the major difficulties is the power consumption of the device (Vujović & Maksimović, 2014). This may be addressed in future through programming to reduce clock cycles when not in motion, or by choosing lower power consumption sensors and actuators.

Further testing by the Tacit Project looked at various implementations of haptics on devices like headbands and vests and highlighted several problems related to cost (vest) and object height (headband) (Hoefer, 2011). While the Tacit Project finally settled on a wrist and glove mounted device, of which this project shares a similar design, some problems were identified with range of movement that need to be addressed in future research.

One such issue relates to the physical action of 'searching' using a wide straight-arm motion which can produce variable results between 80 and 120 degrees. A bent arm at the elbow can account for a greater range of motion but is still blocked by the body and range of motion issues that may be present. Further physical issues with the device and range of motion come from the height of the device in the sweep. Which may exclude objects that are nearby but out of the cone. Furthermore if the sensor is pointed near the ground then objects that are further up may be excluded. Simple testing resulted in the use of a figure-eight like motion to scan distant and near objects, but prolonged use will result in discomfort.

Another broader problem comes from the use of ultrasonic sensors which have technical difficulties that present problems in this style of device, like smoothness of surface, softness of surface, and size of the object (Borenstein and Koren, 1988). A solution for this is to use the properties of RPi0 to run algorithms to increase the effectiveness of the ultrasonic sensors, with the possible inclusion of different sensor types to counteract the negative traits.

4. CONCLUSION

The purpose of this project is to create a prototype device that uses ultrasonic sensors in a lightweight environment to provide haptic feedback based on environmental cues. This was achieved through using an RPi0 mounted on a glove, which has the benefit of being extensible through software and added to smart home environments. Extending on the features of the device in a smart home environment will be the focus for further research after the functionality of the device has been tested.

The vibration gives feedback to the users in terms of the distance from an object; however, this design has yet to be validated in the project group. Full user testing will evaluate the system's feasibility which will require social science ethics approval. This will require permission to undertake usability trials for a community group with visual difficulties. User testing will be conducted to evaluate the accuracy of the system by comparing the real distance and the distance of feedback vibration. The prototype needs a glove or bracelet to put on (Figure 1). The prototype also needs to be used in conjunction with a cane, as it is currently unable to detect obstacles under knee level.

Because the platform can be extended by software, it can arrange to collect data about personal mobility and safety. The infrastructure can be expanded to provide an alarm when the person is assumed in trouble, by identifying an abnormal pattern of movement. The alarm can also be issued to a pre-arranged destination (remote receiver). This extension of the project can be beneficial to the user and caretaker but will require additional ethical approvals. Security and privacy are other important issues to be considered as the project moves forward.

Microcontrollers (MCUs) have a purpose-driven, low-cost nature. Wearable technology combined with a cloud-based wellness program enables individuals to self monitor manage and share their data with healthcare providers and others. By leveraging the properties of IoT and smart homes, the device can be used to build up an environmental pattern of object layout within the home. By using a central storage device to communicate with the RPi0, it is possible to map the environment, resulting in a finely-tuned system with location awareness.

ACKNOWLEDGEMENT

This research was supported by the Korean MSIT (Ministry of Science and ICT), under the National Program for Excellence in SW , supervised by the IITP (Institute for Information & communications Technology Planning&Evaluation)(2017-0-00137).

REFERENCES

amemiya, T. & Sugiyama, H. 2010. Orienting kinesthetically: A haptic handheld wayfinder for people with visual impairments. *ACM Transactions on Accessible Computing (TACCESS),* 3, 6.

Borenstein, J. & Koren, Y. 1988. Obstacle avoidance with ultrasonic sensors. *IEEE Journal on Robotics and Automation,* 4, 213-218.

D'amico, A. & Pittenger, R. 2009. A brief history of active sonar. Space and Naval Warfare Systems Center San Diego Ca.

Dionisi, A., Sardini, E. & Serpelloni, M. Wearable object detection system for the blind. 2012 IEEE International Instrumentation and Measurement Technology Conference Proceedings, 13-16 May 2012 2012. 1255-1258.

Evans, W. E. & Awbrey, F. T. 1988. Natural history aspects of marine mammal echolocation: feeding strategies and habitat. *Animal Sonar.* Springer.

Nikhade, S. G. Wireless sensor network system using Raspberry Pi and zigbee for environmental monitoring applications. Smart Technologies and Management for Computing, Communication, Controls, Energy and Materials (ICSTM), 2015 International Conference on, 2015. IEEE, 376-381.

Vujović, V. & Maksimović, M. Raspberry Pi as a wireless sensor node: performances and constraints. Information and Communication Technology, Electronics and Microelectronics (MIPRO), 2014 37th International Convention on, 2014. IEEE, 1013-1018.

Wang, H., Katzschmann, R. K., Teng, S., Araki, B., Giarré, L. & Rus, D. Enabling independent navigation for visually impaired people through a wearable vision-based feedback system. 2017 IEEE International Conference on Robotics and Automation (ICRA), 29 May-3 June 2017 2017. 6533-6540.

Yi, C., Flores, R. W., Chincha, R. & Tian, Y. 2013. Finding Objects for Assisting Blind People. *Network modeling and analysis in health informatics and bioinformatics,* 2, 71-79.

LIGHT AS A LONG-TERM VISUALIZATION METHOD OF THE TRAINING STATUS FOR PATIENTS IN HOME TRAINING IN REHABILITATION

Mareike Gabele[1], Andrea Thoms[2], Dominik Schumacher[3], Steffi Hußlein[3] and Christian Hansen[1]
[1]*Otto von Guericke University Magdeburg, Germany*
[2]*HASOMED GmbH, Paul-Ecke-Straße 1, 39114 Magdeburg, Germany*
[3]*Magdeburg-Stendal University of Applied Sciences, Germany*

ABSTRACT

The continuation of training at home after a stay in a rehabilitation clinic requires motivation and personal responsibility. However, patients do often not achieve the required training frequency. In this work, we propose a method to visualize the training status based on light, which can be integrated into the rehabilitation process. Integrated into the personal environment, feedback is generated if training is necessary or not. Based on a first prototype, we evaluated the impact on a patient in a qualitative experimental pilot study over four weeks and the expected overall effect on patients by an expert interview. The results show an animating and rewarding impact on the patient, as well as an orientation for scheduled training days and supporting effect for regular training. This work provides a basis for further research to improve the integration of home training into the everyday life of patients and the use of feedback.

KEYWORDS

Light, Feedback, Rehabilitation, Hometraining, Motivation, Tangible

1. INTRODUCTION AND RELATED WORK

A rehabilitation clinic enables effective progress in cognitive and / or motor rehabilitation in a short period of time (Yoo et al. 2015: 2487, Hatem et al. 2016: 442). However, training often has to be continued at home to support long-term effects. At home, the patients are responsible for their own motivation and for carrying out the training. In home training, less than half of all patients train sufficiently (Knop 2014). One problem may also be an excessively high training frequency. The feedback given to patients usually refers to performance or physical movements. (Kearney et al. 2018:1, Ginis et al. 2016:28). However, feedback between training sessions in everyday life has been neglected. To address it, we suggest to visualize whether a training session is currently to be performed, or whether no training is currently required according to the training plan. Our research questions were: a) How can the training status be visualized outside of training in patient's personal environment? b) How does a physical permanent visualization affect patients? c) Are patients guided by the frequency of feedback? d) Is the visualization of the training status perceived as support to conduct training?

We suggest light as a feedback to provide patients with information about their training status. This is based on easy comprehensibility and a positive influence on the mood by constantly illuminated elements (Wardono et al. 2015: 342). Light is used as safety feedback on machines according to DIN EN 60204-1 or to visualize current biological data (Snyder et al. 2015). However, this is limited to the time of use. By changing the light, a nudge effect may be created. The view of vegetation or garden-like elements has a pleasant promoting effect and reducing sadness (Ulrich 2002). We propose to integrate this. The contributions are the prototypical development of a method to visualize feedback on training status in the patients' environment and the evaluation of the effect on patients for further HCI research to support patients in rehabilitation.

2. DESIGN CONSIDERATIONS AND PROTOTYPE

A set of user-centered requirements and restrictions was identified by literature research and expert review to inform the development of a prototype (research question a). This was done with a focus on the medical aspects of rehabilitation and the emotional needs on the patient. The requirements and restrictions were developed in cooperation with interaction designers, psychologists and patients and are presented in Table 1.

Table 1. Requirements and separated restrictions for the visualization of feedback external to training sessions

Requirements	Restrictions
- transfer of feedback to a physical object - visually harmonious integration into the patient's personal environment - technical elements shall not be in the foreground - indirect interaction (visualization based on patient's interaction with training) - creating a connection between training and everyday life - can be combined with various rehabilitation trainings (software / physical) - giving feedback on when training is needed to motivate and minimize one's own cognitive memory requirements - giving feedback when no training is necessary to give the patient a sense of security regarding the training plan and to avoid too high training frequency - promoting a sense of self-efficacy - positive reinforcement in the assumption of personal responsibility - easy to clean / disinfect and easy to grab (also for patients with motor limitations)	- a supplement to training / therapeutic feedback, not a substitution - no visual effect like a medical object to prevent stigmatization - not integrated into a smartphone, as feedback would require conscious interaction - no or little interaction by the therapist required - non-valued visualization of training performance to avoid negative feedback

This resulted in the prototypical combination of a light, initially in the form of a light-emitting diodes (LED), with a plant placed in a glass corpus in a closed physical system. Based on Arduino, HTML and Javascript, an ESP12e Wifi module is used as web server to control the light status (on / off) (Figure 1 (1)). The Wifi module is powered by a rechargeable battery. The technology is hidden in the prototype (Figure 1 (2)).

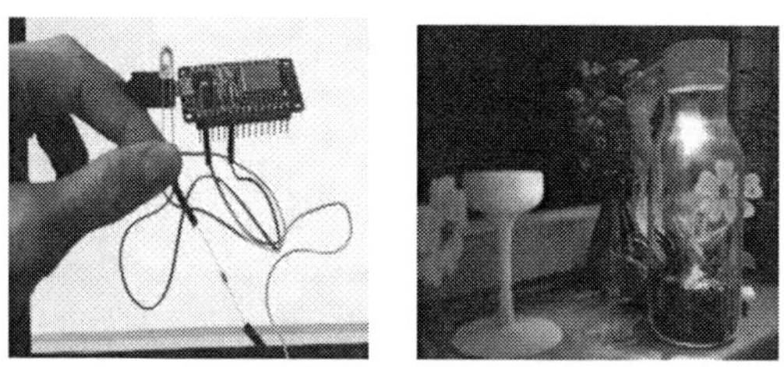

Figure 1. (1) Left: Technical base of the prototype, (2) Right: Prototype during use by the patient

3. EVALUATION

The first use of the system by a patient and an expert evaluation allows to consider subjectively perceived effects and therapeutic aspects for use in rehabilitation. The study was conducted in Germany.

3.1 User Test

We conducted a qualitative explorative pilot study over 4 weeks. The participant was female, 52 years old, undergoing medical treatment and has an acquired long-term physical impairment. In consultation with her doctor, light physical training several times a week to improve strength and endurance promotes her health. The selection of the age based on the increasing frequency of illnesses and rehabilitation in older patients.

Method and Material: The participant was informed about the prototype and instructed to place it visible at home as preferred. The training days chosen by the participant were Tuesday, Thursday and Sunday. There was no direct control by the participant, but by her husband who works from home and acted as our test assistant by observing her training routine. He changed the status of the LED (on/off) via web server (Wizard of Oz): On training days the LED was switched off and switched on after training. It remained switched on until the next training day began. The test assistant moved a training day once to another day and observed the participant's training behavior. Finally, the participant answered open questions on her subjectively experienced impressions during the use of the prototype and the meCue questionnaire to record user-centered evaluations in the experience of interactive technical products (Minge et al: 2013:89). Statements were evaluated on a 7-point Likert scale between strongly object (1) and agreeing completely (7). Thus a minimum of 3 and a maximum of 21 could be achieved per category. Overall rating was between bad (-5) and good (5).

Results: The participant perceived the switching on of the light as training success (b) and described the subjectively experienced emotions 'proud' and 'satisfied'. With the light switched off, her emotional response was reported as 'spurred on' and 'prompted'. The meCue questionnaire scored the following ratings: Usefulness (20), Usability (18), Visual Aesthetics (21), Status (16), Binding (17), Use Intention (16) and Product Loyalty (18). Furthermore, for positive emotions AP (18) and DP (16) and for negative AN (3) and DN (3). The overall rating was 4. The participant did not indicate that she arranged her training behavior according to the day of the week, but rather according to the light status (c). The test assistant also reported that after changing the training day, the participant trained on the day indicated by the light rather than her schedule training day. The participant stated that the light had a supportive effect on conducting the training (d). By positioning the light in the personal living space, it was often perceived when walking past. The technique of the system was not consciously perceived during use.

3.2 Expert Interview

The expert interview was conducted with the head psychologist of an outpatient clinic.

Method and material: The prototype was demonstrated to the expert and explained to him with a video recording. An oral, semi-structured expert interview was conducted afterwards.

Results: The expert rated the method as a good, coherent and functioning system (a). The interviewee stated that the system transfers responsibility to patients and thereby inspires confidence (b). He indicated that it may have a life-affirming effect and, in combination with the plant, conveys a lively atmosphere. This is important for diseases that may be fatal despite rehabilitation. The interviewee also stated that the system communicates, in a positive way, that the patient is being involved in therapy and achieved something. The feedback is presented in an easily understandable way. The expert assumed that the system supports and motivates patients to conduct training (d). He concluded that it can be used in this way for patients.

4. DISCUSSION

The visualization of the training status is feasible by means of light (a) and can be used in the presented form. Due to individual preferences and personalization, different elements may be used in combination with light. It should be noted that there is no guarantee for the survival of the plant, which may have a negative effect on the motivation of patients. To counteract this, a drought tolerant semi-arid plant can be used. The encouraging and rewarding effect beyond training (b) shows that the desired effect has been achieved. This is also shown by the participant following the light with her training times (c). This is particularly relevant when no training is necessary, as this enables a confirmation of the training behavior for patients in the rehabilitation process. A risk factor, however, is whether the patient positions the object at a visible place. The pilot study shows that feedback outside the training shows the potential to support the regular conduction of the training (d). A long-term effect over several months or years should be further tested. The presented system can be connected with devices for motor training or software for cognitive training via Wifi, but it requires the existence of wifi. However, a stand-alone version would probably require a direct interaction.

5. CONCLUSION AND FUTURE WORK

The visualization of the personal training status by means of light is perceived as animating and rewarding. It is easy to understand and is perceived as support to conduct the training regularly. The feedback on the training status is used as an orientation for when a training session has to be conducted. The advantage of the presented method is that it can be used for different types of rehabilitation after the clinical stay.

The pilot study shows not only the impression of a single use, it shows the results after four weeks and thereby a tendency towards long-term use of the system. Due to the small sample size, however, this cannot be generalized. In this work we show a first approach to supporting patients in rehabilitation in home training beyond of clinical training, which is geared towards improving the health and thus also the emotional situation of patients in the long term. In the next step, the method and prototype will be further developed and evaluated with a larger sample size without requiring a test assistant. The development of a concept to strengthen the emotional connection of patients to the training and thus to oneself is currently in progress.

ACKNOWLEDGEMENTS

This work was funded by the European Social Fund (ESF) of Saxony-Anhalt (under the operation number CCI 2014DE05SFOP013) as part of the initiative “Sachsen-Anhalt WISSENSCHAFT Chancengleichheit” with the program title "FEM-Power". This work was also funded by the European Regional Development Fund under the operation numbers ZS/2016/04/78123 and ZS/2017/01/83843 as part of the initiative ”Sachsen-Anhalt WISSENSCHAFT Schwerpunkte”.

REFERENCES

Ginis, P. et al., 2016. Feasibility and effects of home-based smartphone-delivered automated feedback training for gait in people with Parkinson's disease: A pilot randomized trial. *Parkinsonism & Related Disorders*, Vol. 22, pp. 28-34.

Hatem S. et al, 2016. Rehabilitation of Motor Function after Stroke: A Multiple Systematic Review Focused on Techniques to Stimulate Upper Extremity Recovery. *Frontiers in human neuroscience*, Vol. 10, pp. 442.

Kearney, E. et al, 2018. Augmented visual feedback-aided interventions for motor rehabilitation in Parkinson’s disease: a systematic review. *Disability and Rehabilitation*, pp. 1-18.

Knop, A., 2014. Hometraining kognitiver Störungen mit RehaCom. *Presentation at GNP Tagung 2014.*

Minge, M. et al, 2013. meCUE – Ein modularer Fragebogen zur Erfassung des Nutzungserlebens. *Tagungsband MuC 2013.* Munic, Germany, pp. 89-98.

Snyder, J. et al, 2015. MoodLight: Exploring Personal and Social Implications of Ambient Display of Biosensor Data. *Proceedings of the 18th ACM Conference on Computer Supported Cooperative Work & Social Computing.* Vancouver, Canada, pp. 143-153.

Ulrich, R. (2002). Health Benefits of Gardens in Hospitals, *Plants for People - International Exhibition Floriade 2002.*

Wardono, P. et al, 2015. Effects of Luminous Furniture on Mood, *Procedia - Social and Behavioral Sciences,* Vol.22, pp. 342-350.

Yoo, C. et al 2015. Effect of computerized cognitive rehabilitation pro-gram on cognitive function and activities of living in stroke patients. *Journal of Physical Therapy Science.* Vol. 27(8), pp. 2487–2489.

DESIGNING FOR QUANTUM COMPUTING

Andrea Alessandro Gasparini
Department of Informatics & University of Oslo Library,
University of Oslo, P. Boks 1080, 0316 Blindern, Oslo, Norway

ABSTRACT

During the last few years, quantum computing seems to have become a reality. Some few companies have developed quantum computers, and are in use in some large institutions and Universities, while other public organizations have made a similar attempt, but on a smaller scale. Promising to solve otherwise intractable problems for normal supercomputers, companies like Google are already using quantum computers to design solutions, including one allowing the software to distinguish cars from landmarks. However, after numerous and different empirical tests the results are not unanimous, resulting in new attempts to figure out what it is the best way of using this new type of machine that exhibits quantum properties. Developers and scholars argue for the need to redesign quantum computer to achieve full use of this new technology in computers. Proposing a designerly perspective on quantum computing seems a novel and interesting possibility to allow researchers fully taken advantages of this technology. This theoretical paper suggests the use of Design Thinking, and how it is used to solve wicked problems, to re-think how to approach quantum computing. For the design community, understand how to approach, understand and design for quantum computers, may open for a new field of research.

KEYWORDS

Quantum Computing, Design, Design Thinking, Wicked Problems

1. A NEED FOR DESIGN IN QUANTUM COMPUTERS

During the last few years, quantum computing seems to have become a reality. The Canadian company D-Wave (2019) has developed a quantum computer which is in use in few large institutions and Universities, while other public organizations have made similar attempts, but in smaller scale (Thompson 2014). The American company IBM has launched in 2017 an online service running on a quantum computer processor giving the possibility to the public to develop services (Lubensky 2017). In addition, both D-Wave and Berkeley based Rigetti (2019) has developed the same platform of services lately. The first commercial quantum super computer, the IBM Q System One, is also ready. Promising to solve otherwise intractable problems for normal supercomputers, companies like Google are already using a quantum computer to design solutions, including one allowing the software to distinguish cars from landmarks. On the other hand, after numerous and different empirical tests the results are not unanimous, resulting in new attempts to figure out, what it is the best way of using this new type of machine that exhibits quantum properties (Cusumano 2018; Grossman 2014). Quantum computers exploit proprieties of quantum mechanics laws, and, unfortunately, they are difficult to grasp as they show non-logical characteristics. As pointed by Coffey (2014) the need for a design approach is highly needed: "Physicists are making progress toward this goal every day, but nearly every part of a quantum computer still needs re-engineering or redesign to make it all work." Also, Google wrote in their research-blog a quest for new perspectives: “The design of next generation annealers must facilitate the embedding of problems of practical relevance.” (Denchev et al. 2015; Google 2015) The idea of using a designerly way of thinking, to fully take advantages of this technology is novel. As an approach the paper uses Design Thinking (Brown 2009), as it has interesting elaborative forces aiming to define and solve problems. The design community has long traditions in approaching, analyzing and trying to solve complex problems (Dorst 2006), emphasizing on the creative designers activity between the problem space and solution space (ibid.) One category of problems of interest are those difficult or impossible to solve because of incomplete, contradictory, unbalanced and changing requirements (Rittel & Webber 1973), they are named wicked. Using Design Thinking to solve ill-defined problems has proven as a viable way to develop solutions to them

(Brown & Wyatt 2010; Buchanan 1992; Jobst & Meinel 2014; von Thienen, Meinel, & Nicolai 2014). This theoretical paper suggests the use of Design Thinking, and how it is used to solve wicked problems, to re-think how to approach quantum computing.

2. QUANTUM COMPUTING FOR DESIGNERS

Quantum computing relays on theories of quantum mechanics, and unfortunately, they are difficult to grasp as they are often contradictory. They are non-logical. Quantum mechanics explain the rules working in the subatomic world. Thus, understanding quantum computing and the theories behind is not an easy task, and those limitations and constraints posed by technology need to be addressed properly. The design of the processor to be used in the quantum computer relays on the properties of some of the law of quantum mechanics. The first one, named *superposition*, is when, in the subatomic world, an electron acquires a state not positive or negative but in between, i.e. neither the one nor the other. In the world of computers, this corresponds to having a third-bit value in addition to 0 and 1. When designing a processor, using the quantum bits named qubit, gives an exponential possibility of computation. The second property, *entanglement*, is when two entities, like electrons, after an interaction, becomes entangled, then a change in one entity will have an effect on the other one, regardless of distance. The last one is quantum *decoherence* of the state of superposition, where observation of the state in which the electron is resting down in one of the two possible positions. In quantum processor, the qubit decay from a fluid non-binary identity to one of the possible output. The superposition, entanglement, and quantum decoherence properties are needed to ensure maximal effectiveness in the quantum computer processor (Grossman 2014). In addition, there is a need to use an additional process so errors can be detected and corrected after decoherence.

2.1 Superposition

The most interesting propriety is superposition and implies a third position a particle can have in addition to a positive and negative state. This position is both negative and positive at the same time, but an uncertainty. The Schrödinger cat paradigm (Monroe, Meekhof, King, & Wineland 1996) is an example often used to explain to non-scientist how superposition function. Inside a closed box, where the cat is, there is a radioactive item and a poison container. At some point, the radioactive item can activate and open the poison container with a beam. The observer outside cannot see if the beam has occurred, thus the cat is both alive and dead at the same time. For instance, in science, if a particle can have a spin left or right, a superposition implies that it has both simultaneously. Applied to computer science, a bit having the possibility to be in a superposition, can be represented by a quantum bit (qubits), and have as values 0 or 1 or both at the same time, representing a superposition. There are several types of processors using the laws of quantum mechanics, although they are using different hardware techniques (Ladd et al. 2010). The aforementioned D-Wave uses a niobium (a type of metal) based chip, where the spin of the atoms in one or the other direction represent the 0 or 1 used in normal computer processors. When elevated into a superposition, exponential quantity of data can be uploaded into the processor. This type of quantum computers uses "adiabatic quantum computing," also known as "quantum annealing." Common for all quantum processor is the problem with reading the state of the qubits (quantum decoherence), since it may happen uncontrolled by external temperature variation and noise, and therefore the processor need to be kept at the lower temperature possible and away of all form of noise.

2.2 Entanglement

The quantum property named entanglement implies a non-locality connection after an interaction has occurred between two particles (typically an electron). This connection acts counter-logical since it implies that each of the two particles are connected even if they are far away. Thus, changes made to one of the particles will affect simultaneously the other one. This fuzzy property act also when the two particles are moved far away from each other after the first interaction, leading to paradoxes (Rieffel 2000). Entanglement is often explained as a spooky action at a distance. Lately, tests have confirmed entanglement property of particles over large distances (Ursin et al. 2007). The implications of entanglement open for, among others, to quantum cryptography and quantum network (Sangouard, Simon, de Riedmatten, & Gisin 2011).

2.3 Quantum Decoherence

Decoherence is a quantum behavior happening when a particle (typically an electron) in superposition do rest down to a classical state, as a reaction to an interaction, like observation or noise. In a qubits decoherence results in moving from a state of quantum superposition back to one of the two states e.g. 0 or 1. If not controlled properly, the effect of decoherence may cause insecurity in regards to the validity of the answer, since the way the observation is done will reflect on the result.

2.4 How a Quantum Computer Works

Summing up, the quantum computer uses processor where "entanglement makes it possible for quantum bits to work together and represent multiple combinations of values simultaneously, rather than represent one combination at a time." (Cusumano 2018) Qubits, in addition to being entangled, when in a superposition state, they can store and represent an exponential quantity of data. The aforementioned niobium processor supports this feature. The combination of representing and storing an exponential amount of values make the quantum computer extraordinary powerful. The values represented can be a complete set of solutions or answers to a given problem. The clue of the niobium processor is the ability to analyze all the possible answers at the same time, and at the end, the answer with the highest cumulative probability will be the correct answer (Trabesinger 2017). Rephrased, when decoherence is performed on all the qubits of a quantum processor the correct answer will be discovered among all answers. However, several iterations of the same process are needed to achieve a relevant cumulative probability.

3. DESIGN THINKING AND QUANTUM COMPUTING

Design Thinking uses a combination of immersive understanding of context and users and their needs in the problem space. The rapid prototyping act during a Design Thinking process fosters the best possible solution. Abductive reasoning (Brown 2009; Kolko 2012) is one of the elaborative force behind Design Thinking, which helps define the solution space. This way of thinking helps redefine the problem while finding a solution. The elaborative force behind this activity support a converge toward to a solution and in doing so, a redefinition of the problem (Kolko 2009).

The rapid prototyping act in the Design Thinking process, rely upon a divergent thinking act (Cropley 2006), adding insight in the process where the outcome is a high quantity of results and prototypes. This activity of making alternative solutions is mediated by "a variety of tensions between possibilities and constraints." (Liedtka 2015) Convergent thinking is then needed to support an abductive reasoning process narrowing the results, and giving at the end a handful of viable ideas. Rowe (Rowe 1987) says also that the action (of designing) and the problem definition becomes intertwined, as the problem become defined simultaneously with the proposal of a solution. Overall, the process of Design Thinking, allows the result to be a technically viable solution, a desirable output for users and an economically feasible project (Brown 2009).

Another strength Design Thinking has, is the possibility to solve complex and ill-defined problems (Brown & Wyatt 2010; Rittel & Webber 1973), ranging from business to social context. Usually problems in science have a single goal and predefined rules enabling a clear solution (Coyne 2005); they can be defined as tame. Mathematics is one example, where solving an equation require little creative effort as one need to follow a clear predefined rule in how to solve them. On the contrary, wicked problems belongs to the architectural, social and organizational sphere. Wicked problems are complex, ill-defined and are hardly to fully be solved. Those problems have no stopping rules, and they are always changing and evolving, driven by a variety of stakeholders (Churchman 1967; Rittel & Webber 1973). Rittel has identified ten properties of wicked problem, where two are relevant in regards to quantum computing: solutions to wicked problems "are not true-or-false, but good-or-bad", and every solution to a wicked problem is a "one-shot operation". In the next section, a discussion will clarify how to apply the designedly approach used to solve wicked problems, to exploit the possibility quantum mechanics give when developing a quantum computer.

4. DISCUSSION

Wicked problems show signs of good analogies with quantum computing, especially with superposition, entanglement, and decoherence. As a possible solution to wicked problems, Buchanan (1992) use the "concept of placements" which bring to the design process insight and different perspectives. Constructing a design situation with different "placements", the problem formulation and the solution coincide (Johansson-Sköldberg, Woodilla, & Çetinkaya 2013).

In Design Thinking, the problem formulation and the solution are described as the result of abductive reasoning. Abduction in reasoning was first described by Pierce as the "step of adopting a hypothesis as being suggested by the facts" (Pierce 1974). One of the relevant points from a design perspective is the fact that abductive reasoning function also as a generator of new knowledge and insight (Fischer 2001; Kolko 2009). The solution is not part of the premises, but as a result of an educated guess, based on observations, data, and insight (Kolko 2009). In other words, the problem becomes re-defined at the same time as the proposed solution (Khisty 2000; Rowe 1987). New understandings are created. This framework relates with Buchanan "placements", and explains why it is possible to argue that Design Thinking can solve wicked problems.

As mentioned the niobium processor can analyze all the possible answers of a problem at the same time (Trabesinger 2017). However, applying how Design Thinking can solve wicked problems, can inform how to exploit the full potential of the quantum processor. During the process of redefining the problem, new data are created (e.g. knowledge) and are needed to be used in the same process. The design of the quantum processor should take this into account.

5. CONCLUSION AND FUTURE WORK

The field of quantum computing is still at the first steps toward a promising new future, as researchers are still trying to figure out what it's in for them and how to use it properly. The analogy between how the Design Thinking approach can be used to solve wicked problems, and the different quantum mechanics properties presented in this paper, gives a new understanding in how to address and adapt design methods to quantum computing. Future work should analyze other types of quantum processor and how Design Thinking can help a redesign.

REFERENCES

Brown, T 2009, *Change by design: how design thinking transforms organizations and inspires innovation*, HarperCollins Publishers, New York.

Brown, T & Wyatt, J 2010, 'Design Thinking for Social Innovation (SSIR)' *Stanford Social Innovation Review*, vol. 30, no. 5.

Buchanan, R 1992, 'Wicked Problems in Design Thinking' *Design Issues*, vol. 8, no. 2, pp. 5–21, doi: 10.2307/1511637.

Churchman, CW 1967, 'Guest Editorial: Wicked Problems' *Management Science*, vol. 14, no. 4, pp. B141–B142.

Coffey, VC 2014, 'The Incremental Quest for Quantum Computing' *PHOTONICS SPECTRA*, vol. 48, no. 6, pp. 36–41.

Coyne, R 2005, 'Wicked problems revisited' *Design Studies*, vol. 26, no. 1, pp. 5–17, doi: 10.1016/j.destud.2004.06.005.

Cropley, A 2006, 'In Praise of Convergent Thinking' *Creativity Research Journal*, vol. 18, no. 3, pp. 391–404.

Cusumano, MA 2018, 'The Business of Quantum Computing' *Communications of the ACM*, vol. 61, no. 10, pp. 20–22.

Denchev, VS, Boixo, S, Isakov, SV, Ding, N, Babbush, R, Smelyanskiy, V, Martinis, J, & Neven, H 2015, 'What is the Computational Value of Finite Range Tunneling?' *ArXiv:1512.02206 [Quant-Ph]*

Dorst, K 2006, 'Design Problems and Design Paradoxes' *Design Issues*, vol. 22, no. 3, pp. 4–17.

D-Wave 2019, 'D-Wave Systems', viewed 10 October 2018, http://www.dwavesys.com/.

Fischer, HR 2001, 'Abductive Reasoning as a Way of Worldmaking' *Foundations of Science*, vol. 6, no. 4, pp. 361–383,

Google 2015, 'When can Quantum Annealing win?', Retrieved from http://googleresearch.blogspot.com/2015/12/when-can-quantum-annealing-win.html.

Grossman, L 2014, February 6, 'The Quantum Quest for a Revolutionary Computer' *TIME*, Retrieved from http://time.com/4802/quantum-leap/.

Jobst, B & Meinel, C 2014, 'How Prototyping Helps to Solve Wicked Problems' in L. Leifer, H. Plattner, & C. Meinel (eds.), *Design Thinking Research: Building Innovation Eco-Systems*, pp. 105–113, Springer International Publishing, Cham, doi: 10.1007/978-3-319-01303-9_8.

Johansson-Sköldberg, U, Woodilla, J, & Çetinkaya, M 2013, 'Design Thinking: Past, Present and Possible Futures' *Creativity and Innovation Management*, vol. 22, no. 2, pp. 121–146, doi: 10.1111/caim.12023.

Khisty, C 2000, 'Can Wicked Problems Be Tackled through Abductive Inferencing?' *Journal of Urban Planning and Development*, vol. 126, no. 3, pp. 104–118, doi: 10.1061/(ASCE)0733-9488(2000)126:3(104).

Kolko, J 2009, 'Abductive Thinking and Sensemaking: The Drivers of Design Synthesis' *Design Issues*, vol. 26, no. 1, pp. 15–28, doi: 10.1162/desi.2010.26.1.15.

Kolko, J 2012, *Wicked problems: problems worth solving: a handbook and call to action*, Ac4d, Austin Center for Design, Austin, Texas.

Ladd, TD, Jelezko, F, Laflamme, R, Nakamura, Y, Monroe, C, & O'Brien, JL 2010, 'Quantum computers' *Nature*, vol. 464, no. 7285, pp. 45–53, doi: 10.1038/nature08812.

Liedtka, J 2015, 'Perspective: Linking Design Thinking with Innovation Outcomes through Cognitive Bias Reduction' *Journal of Product Innovation Management*, vol. 32, no. 6, pp. 925–938, doi: 10.1111/jpim.12163.

Lubensky, D 2017, March 6, 'Quantum computing gets an API and SDK', Retrieved from https://developer.ibm.com/dwblog/2017/quantum-computing-api-sdk-david-lubensky/.

Martin, R 2009, *The design of business: why design thinking is the next competitive advantage*, Harvard Business School Press, Boston.

Monroe, C, Meekhof, DM, King, BE, & Wineland, DJ 1996, 'A "Schrödinger Cat" Superposition State of an Atom' *Science*, vol. 272, no. 5265, pp. 1131–1136, doi: 10.1126/science.272.5265.1131.

Pierce, CS 1974, *Collected Papers of Charles Sanders Peirce* ed. C. Hartshorne, Harvard University Press, Boston, Mass., Retrieved from http://www.hup.harvard.edu/catalog.php?isbn=9780674138001.

Rieffel, E 2000, 'An Introduction to Quantum Computing for Non-physicists' *ACM Comput. Surv.*, vol. 32, no. 3, pp. 300–335, doi: 10.1145/367701.367709.

Rigetti 2019, 'Rigetti Computing', Rigetti Computing, viewed 30 May 2019, https://www.rigetti.com/news.

Rittel, HWJ & Webber, MM 1973, 'Dilemmas in a general theory of planning' *Policy Science*, vol. 4, pp. 155–169.

Rowe, PG 1987, *Design thinking*, MIT Press, Cambridge, Mass.

Sangouard, N, Simon, C, de Riedmatten, H, & Gisin, N 2011, 'Quantum repeaters based on atomic ensembles and linear optics' *Reviews of Modern Physics*, vol. 83, no. 1, pp. 33–80, doi: 10.1103/RevModPhys.83.33.

Stewart, J, Gold, J, Gold, J, Walton, J, Cureton, P, & Anderson, L 2011, 'Theorising and practitioners in HRD: the role of abductive reasoning' *Journal of European Industrial Training*, vol. 35, no. 3, pp. 230–246

Thompson, C 2014, May 20, 'The Revolutionary Quantum Computer That May Not Be Quantum at All' *WIRED*, Retrieved from http://www.wired.com/2014/05/quantum-computing.

Trabesinger, A 2017, 'Quantum leaps, bit by bit.' *Nature*, vol. 543, no. 7646, pp. S2–S3, doi: 10.1038/543S2a.

Ursin, R, Tiefenbacher, F, Schmitt-Manderbach, T, Weier, H, Scheidl, T, Lindenthal, M, Blauensteiner, B, Jennewein, T, Perdigues, J, Trojek, P, Ömer, B, Fürst, M, Meyenburg, M, Rarity, J, Sodnik, Z, Barbieri, C, Weinfurter, H, & Zeilinger, A 2007, 'Entanglement-based quantum communication over 144 km' *Nature Physics*, vol. 3, no. 7, pp. 481–486, doi: 10.1038/nphys629.

von Thienen, J, Meinel, C, & Nicolai, C 2014, 'How Design Thinking Tools Help To Solve Wicked Problems' in L. Leifer, H. Plattner, & C. Meinel (eds.), *Design Thinking Research: Building Innovation Eco-Systems*, pp. 97–102, Springer International Publishing, Cham, doi: 10.1007/978-3-319-01303-9_7.

METHOD-MIX FOR THE DEVELOPMENT OF INTERCULTURAL USER INTERFACES EXEMPLIFIED

Rüdiger Heimgärtner
Intercultural User Interface Consulting (IUIC), R&D HMI
Lindenstraße 9, 93152 Undorf, Germany

ABSTRACT

In this paper, a method-mix for intercultural user interface design (IUID) is explained and exemplified by an application example to elucidate why and how cultural aspects play a role in UI design and usability/UX engineering. The readers are sensitized to the challenges of intercultural usability/UX engineering and intercultural UI design and will be equipped with methodological knowledge relevant to the derivation of recommendations for user interface design in their desired cultural contexts.

KEYWORDS

Culture, Human Factors, UX, Intercultural User Interface Design, Method Mix, HMI Dimensions

1. INTRODUCTION AND RELATED WORK

Intercultural user interface design (IUID) is a prerequisite for improving the intercultural usability of software, which in turn is a prerequisite for global sales opportunities. Using methods of intercultural usability engineering, further design guidelines can be iteratively derived from the results of the tests and the feedback of potential users from all over the world for intercultural user interface design. Based on feedback from tutorials and workshops on IUID (M&C, Interact, IHCI, SouthCHI, ICCHP, HCII) and the revised summary of the state of research on IUID in (Rüdiger Heimgärtner, 2013a), the author has reviewed the synopsis of well documented IUID methods in academic literature to construct a corresponding method-mix for IUID. This method-mix for the development of intercultural user interfaces will be presented and exemplified by an application example in this paper.

The internal model of the user about the system is shaped by the culture of the user, his expectations about the characteristics of the system and his interaction experience with the system. Differences between cultures can be found by analyzing critical interaction situations between people (Thomas, Kinast, & Schroll-Machl, 2010). (Honold, 2000) made this method available for cultural differences in Human-Machine Interaction (HMI). Consequentially, critical interaction situations that arise due to problematic user interfaces or are based on the given system functionality must be analyzed. For example, (Vöhringer-Kuhnt, 2002) found that Hofstede's cultural dimension of "Individualism Index" (cf. (Hofstede, Hofstede, & Minkov, 2010) is related to user satisfaction and usability of the product and has a significant influence on intercultural usability. (Röse, 2002) proposed the "Method for Culture-Oriented Design" (MCD), which integrates cultural differences into existing concepts of HMI design. Relevant cultural variables for intercultural HMI design must be determined analytically based on literature and requirement studies. Their values represent culture-dependent variations that occur at all levels of HMI localization (interface, functionality and interaction) and can be used for IUID. Similarly, (Shen, Woolley, & Prior, 2006) focus on culture-oriented design. Further methods are applying user interface characteristics by (Marcus, 2006) or cultural markers by (Badre & Barber, 1998). More recent approaches e.g. by (Castro Salgado, Leitão, & Souza, 2013) are based on semiotic theory, such as (Pereira, Baranauskas, & Liu, 2015) or (Zheng, Rau, Yueh, Chen, & Huang, 2018). One of the most promising methods to preserve cultural differences in HMI is the observation and analysis of user interaction with the system (cf. (Rüdiger Heimgärtner, 2012)). The results of these observations in the form of cultural variables and their manifestations serve as a basis for IUID recommendations and guidelines.

2. IUID METHOD-MIX

The IUID method mix (Rüdiger Heimgärtner, 2017) consists of a combined and hybrid use of cultural dimensions, intercultural variables, user interface characteristics, and HMI dimensions within the method of culture-oriented design. These core concepts of the IUID method-mix are introduced briefly.

The characteristics of cultural dimensions influence the user experience and provide orientation for the usability engineering process. Differences between cultures can be found by analyzing critical interaction situations between people (cf. (Thomas et al., 2010)) expressed by cultural dimensions (cf. (Hofstede et al., 2010)) that serve to describe and compare cultural systems (cf. (Hall & Hall, 2009)). Using the "Method for Culture-Oriented Design" (Röse, 2002), relevant cultural variables for intercultural HMI design can be determined analytically based on literature research and requirement studies. Their values represent culture-dependent variations that occur at all levels of HMI localization (surface, functionality and interaction) describing the differences in HMI design with respect to the preferences of users from different cultures. "Visible" intercultural variables are immediately perceptible at any certain time (font, color, window size, navigation, etc.). In contrast, "invisible" (or "hidden") intercultural variables are only recognizable over a certain period (interaction speed, information display duration, dialogue display frequency, use of the navigation bar, etc.). The user interface characteristics "Metaphor", "Mental Model", "Navigation", "Interaction" and "Presentation" (Marcus, 2006) are linked to five of Hofstede's cultural dimensions (Hofstede et al., 2010) (cf. (Röse, 2002)). User interface characteristics can be used in conjunction with empirical surveys on their characteristics for the corresponding cultural target context to derive recommendations for the development of intercultural user interfaces. HMI dimensions describe the behavior of a user (i.e. the HMI style) with an interactive information processing system (Rüdiger Heimgärtner, 2013b). HMI dimensions and those of their values useful for HMI design are operationalized by means of interaction indicators representing HMI metrics. Cultural interaction indicators represent the correlations between the user's interaction behavior and his culture as well as the correlation of HMI dimensions such as information speed (speed of dissemination and frequency of occurrence of information), information density (number and distance of information units) or information order (sequence of occurrence and arrangement of information) with culturally different basic patterns of behavior (Rüdiger Heimgärtner, 2012). HMI dimensions consistently represented based on cultural variables can be called "(Inter-)Cultural HMI Dimensions", which express the culturally influenced HMI style of the user in the respective cultural context, i.e. how the user interacts with the system. Using the method of the culture-oriented HMI design (MCD, see (Röse, 2002)), cultural differences are identified based on cultural dimensions and cultural variables are derived for the project. With this knowledge of cultural differences and affected aspects of the HMI system, further effects on the HMI design have been determined and supported by hypothesis-driven data transmission using user interface characteristics (see (Marcus, 2006)) and HMI dimensions (see (Rüdiger Heimgärtner, 2012)) and thereby to obtain recommendations for intercultural UI/UX design and for intercultural usability engineering (e.g. via cultural interaction indicators and a corresponding model of culture-dependent HMI (cf. (Rüdiger Heimgärtner, 2013b)).

The IUID method-mix integrates the concepts above to derive design recommendation for the designated cultural context before doing any empirical studies from scratch in order to estimate the labor expenditure in advance. The procedure of applying the IUID method-mix is as follows:

First, the application, main uses cases and the desired target cultures are chosen. Depending on the use case, the respective UI elements (e.g. layout, buttons, text fields) have to be determined and mapped to the category of the cultural variables (direct, indirect, visible, hidden) as well as to the user interface characteristics (presentation, interaction, navigation, mental model and metaphor). Using this information, the time and space related HMI dimensions concerned must be analyzed (such as information density or interaction frequency). Via the rules and the variables in the explanatory model for culturally influenced HMI, the detected HMI dimensions can be related to the cultural dimensions in order to obtain the related cultural interaction indicators. Design recommendations for intercultural user interfaces can be drawn as well (cf. (Rüdiger Heimgärtner, 2012)). For example, the higher the density of an information network (e.g. as in China compared to Germany according to (Hall & Hall, 2009)), the stronger the values of the HMI dimensions (such as information density and interaction frequency according to (Rüdiger Heimgärtner, 2013b)), cf. Figure 1.

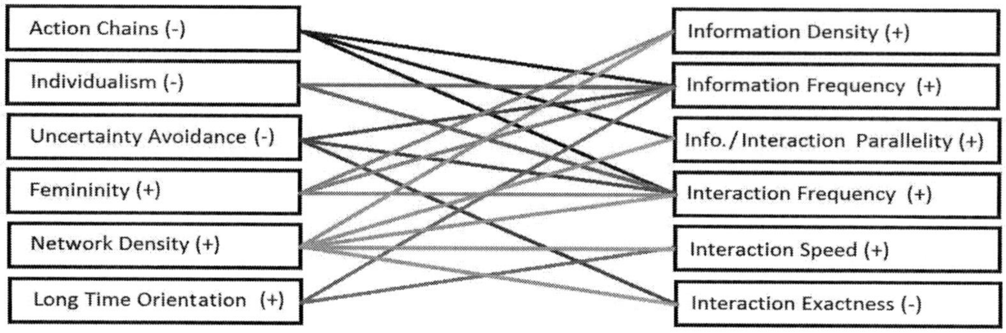

Figure 1. Model of the hypothetical relationship between cultural dimensions and HMI dimensions according to (Rüdiger Heimgärtner, 2013b)

3. APPLICATION OF THE IUID METHOD-MIX

Table 1 shows the results obtained by the application of this systematic procedure using the IUID method mix for some examples of applications representing the characteristics of decisive variables for the development of intercultural user interfaces.

Table 1. Application of the IUID method mix (extract of the results from IUID method mix workshops by the author)

Application / Use Case	Cultural aspect / Cultural dimension	UI Character-istics	Cultural variable	HMI dimension	Cultural interaction indicator	IUID implication
Word processing / Filling in a form	Language / Communicat-ion network density	Presentation, Interaction	Direct (word length), layout	Information density, Interaction frequency	Average number of chars per word, page	Resizing, calculate size of display according to language
E-learning system / Learning content	Communicat-ion speed, power distance, uncertainty avoidance	Presentation, Navigation	Visible (character set, buttons)	Information presentation speed	Dialogues per minute, Number of breaks in interaction	Adapt speed of guided dialogues (wizards) and button size
Phone / Looking up, dialing via name or number	Communica-tion speed, density of the information network	Interaction, Mental model	Indirect (online operating manual)	Interaction speed and interaction style	Number of pressing buttons per task	Choose appropriate input method editor (IME) and sorting algorithms
Word processor on a mobile phone / Sending a short text message via SMS	Power distance, individualism, uncertainty avoidance	Presentation: text, character, character set, layout, skin, edit field, send button, receiver list box	Direct, visible, surface (color, skin, language)	Information density, interaction frequency and speed, Information and interaction parallelism, interaction exactness	Number of pieces of information per space, Number of SMS per day, Number of saved contacts	Adapt system memory / Choose appropriate input method editor (IME) and sorting algorithms / allow customization of the number of entries in lists

Assume, an UI designer wants to identify design recommendation for IUID for users from China or Germany regarding an application with the use case “sending a short text message via SMS on a mobile phone” (cf. last example in Table 1)!

The first step is to identify the cultural dimensions representing the highest cultural distance between the target cultures. The values of the cultural dimensions can be looked up in literature of cultural research (as absolute numeric values from (Hofstede et al., 2010) (cf. retrieved from https://www.hofstede-insights.com/product/compare-countries/, last access 5|4|2019) or (Schwartz, 2004) or as relative categorial numbers by other authors of cultural dimensions such as (Hall & Hall, 2009)).

The relationship between cultural dimensions and HCI dimensions comes into play by following the rules of the explanatory model expressing the connection between the values of the cultural dimensions and the values of the HCIDs (Rüdiger Heimgärtner, 2013b). IDV is related to information and interaction frequency. UAI is related to information and interaction frequency as well as to interaction exactness (cf. Figure 1). Hence, information frequency and interaction frequency tend to be high (e.g. for China in contrast to Germany), when individualism in a culture is low (e.g. for China (IDV=20) in contrast to Germany (IDV=67) (cf. (Hofstede et al., 2010) and (Rüdiger Heimgärtner, 2013b), cf. also Figure 1).

The next step is to identify the UI elements (e.g. text, characters, character set, layout) that are involved by the use case and to relate them to the user interface characteristics (e.g. presentation - concerning direct, visible cultural variables on the surface of the user interface (such as language, color, layout)). For example, information density is affected by the cultural presentation requirements (cf. culturally different communication patterns, (Lewis, 2006)). This different communication behavior can be expressed using adequate cultural interaction indicators such as the number of pieces of information per space, the number of SMS sent per day or the number of contacts, which in turn leads to the subsequent requirements for system design and recommendations for IUID: The HCI system needs to have enough memory for storing contacts and sent short messages.

Furthermore, it needs an input method editor for the different character sets in China and Germany in order to quickly choose and select the desired receiver name from an adequately sorted list. Hence, the user interface should be customizable to the number of presented pieces of information, e.g., the number of entries in lists or menus (cf. hierarchical versus flat menu structure, (Gould, Marcus, & Chavan, 2006)).

These anticipated results allow the project manager to plan the most important work packages and do the related time and cost estimations for future intercultural user interfaces projects in advance.

4. DISCUSSION

The perception and consideration of the customs and requirements of other cultures by the developers of intercultural user interfaces is one of the main tasks within intercultural user interface design. The localization of hidden intercultural variables is very difficult to realize because the contextual relation to the cultural background as well as to the product is very strong for interaction and dialogue design. However, precisely this culturally distinct context and consequently its cultural dependency is why these patterns and non-visible intercultural variables are so important for information architecture as well as for interaction design and, hence, for the resulting dialogues (cf. (Röse, 2002), p. 98).

Although cultures are constantly changing, for a product life cycle of a few years at least trends can be determined, and for special cases of application even selective parameters can be determined which serve the intercultural user interface design. There must be at least one potential indicator as a measurement variable in order to be able to represent the character of an HMI dimension. For real use, however, several empirically proven indicators should be used.

Successful explanatory models can be applied to new examples, use cases or products and thus empirically verified, which in turn allows predictive design recommendations. The investigation and consideration of hidden cultural variables for intercultural HMI design is still ongoing. This is particularly the case in relation to the lack of research, which relates to culturally shaped interaction and dialogue design and is based on empirical research.

Nevertheless, applying the IUID method-mix is a reasonable approach towards an explanatory model for culturally influenced HMI, where areas such as intercultural usability engineering and intercultural user interface design (IUID) can benefit to the extent that the model (cf. Fig. 1) is further developed and validated.

5. CONCLUSION AND OUTLOOK

Applying the IUID method-mix allows the derivation of predictive and anticipatory UI design recommendations for systems in cultural contexts in advance. Even if the IUID method-mix is at its beginning and it still must be improved upon in terms of the separability of variables and the validity of the resulting design recommendations, it represents a reasonable hybrid approach integrating several concepts to reach recommendations for intercultural user interface design. It is planned to repeat the study described in (Rüdiger Heimgärtner, 2012) to check the persistency of the relationship between cultural and HMI dimensions and therefore, the reliability of the presented model, as well as to implement an application providing the IUID method-mix for practitioners.

REFERENCES

Badre, A., & Barber, W. (1998). Culturabilty: The Merging of Culture and Usabilty. In *Proceedings of the 4th Conference on Human Factors and the Web*. NJ, USA: Basking Ridge.

Castro Salgado, L., Leitão, C., & Souza, C. (2013). Semiotic Engineering and Culture. In *A Journey Through Cultures* (pp. 19-42): Springer London.

Gould, E. W., Marcus, A., & Chavan, A. L. (2006). *International usability evaluation SIG: issues and strategies*. Paper presented at the CHI '06 Extended Abstracts on Human Factors in Computing Systems, Montréal, Québec, Canada. http://delivery.acm.org/10.1145/1130000/1125537/p399-gould.pdf?ip=93.209.99.96&acc=ACTIVE%20SERVICE&CFID=205638749&CFTOKEN=35037099&__acm__=1353416358_b94cfdac326fc273d6cec6d251f95cb8

Hall, E. T., & Hall, M. R. (2009). *Understanding cultural differences : Germans, French and Americans*. Boston, Mass. u. a.: Intercultural Press.

Heimgärtner, R. (2012). *Cultural Differences in Human-Computer Interaction* (Paperback B: Einband - flex.(Paperback) ed. Vol. 1): Oldenbourg Verlag.

Heimgärtner, R. (2013a). *Intercultural User Interface Design*. In K. Blashki & P. Isaias (Eds.), *Emerging Research and Trends in Interactivity and the Human-Computer Interface*.

Heimgärtner, R. (2013b). Reflections on a Model of Culturally Influenced Human–Computer Interaction to Cover Cultural Contexts in HCI Design. *International Journal of Human-Computer Interaction, 29*(4), 205-219. Retrieved from http://dx.doi.org/10.1080/10447318.2013.765761. doi:10.1080/10447318.2013.765761

Heimgärtner, R. (2017). *Using Converging Strategies to Reduce Divergence in Intercultural User Interface Design* (Vol. 05).

Hofstede, G. H., Hofstede, G. J., & Minkov, M. (2010). *Cultures and organizations : software of the mind* (3. ed.). Maidenhead: McGraw-Hill.

Honold, P. (2000). Intercultural Usability Engineering: Barriers and Challenges from a German point of view. In D. Day, E. d. Galdo, & G. V. Prabhu (Eds.), *Designing for Global Markets 2. Second International Workshop on Internationalisation of Products and Systems* (pp. 137-147).

Lewis, R. D. (2006). *When Cultures Collide: Leading Across Cultures* (Vol. 3rd Ed.): Boston/MA: Brealey.

Marcus, A. (2006). Cross-Cultural User-Experience Design. In D. Barker-Plummer, R. Cox, & N. Swoboda (Eds.), *Diagrammatic Representation and Inference* (Vol. 4045, pp. 16-24): Springer Berlin Heidelberg.

Pereira, R., Baranauskas, M., & Liu, K. (2015). *The value of values for HCI: an informed discussion beyond philosophy*. Paper presented at the Proceedings of the 14th Brazilian Symposium on Human Factors in Computing Systems, Salvador, Brazil.

Röse, K. (2002). *Model of Culture and Their Applicability for Designing User Interfaces*. Paper presented at the Paper presented at the Conference WWDU 2002- World Wide Work, Berchtesgaden.

Schwartz, S. H. (2004). Mapping and interpreting cultural differences around the world. In H. Vinken, J. Soeters, & P. Ester (Eds.), *Comparing cultures, Dimensions of culture in a comparative perspective* (pp. 43-73). Leiden, The Netherlands: Brill.

Shen, S.-T., Woolley, M., & Prior, S. (2006). Towards culture-centred design. *Interact. Comput., 18*(4), 820-852. doi:10.1016/j.intcom.2005.11.014

Thomas, A., Kinast, E.-U., & Schroll-Machl, S. (2010). *Handbook of intercultural communication and cooperation. Basics and areas of application*. Göttingen: Vandenhoeck & Ruprecht.

Vöhringer-Kuhnt, T. (2002). *The Influence of Culture on Usability*. (M.A. master thesis), Freie Universität Berlin,

Zheng, Y.-L., Rau, P.-L. P., Yueh, H.-P., Chen, P.-H., & Huang, D.-L. (2018). *An Exploratory Study on Design and Implement an Emotional Karaoke Robot (EKR)*, Cham.

AUGMENTED REALITY BOOK AS A NARRATIVE MEDIUM

Jan K. Argasiński[1] and Jakub Woynarowski[2]
[2]*Jagiellonian University in Krakow*
Faculty of Physics, Astronomy and Applied Computer Science, ul. Łojasiewicza 11, 30-348, Krakow, Poland
[2]*Academy of Fine Arts (ASP) in Krakow, plac Jana Matejki 13, 31-157 Krakow, Poland*

ABSTRACT

The article takes a critical aim at one of the most popular uses of Augmented Reality technology – that is enriching literary works. The authors look at popular publications by analyzing the methods of communication used in them. Next, an art project called "Stilleben" is presented. It is an attempt to create a work that is essentially coherent with the medium. The inspirations, motivations and implementation of the "Stilleben" are presented.

KEYWORDS

Augmented Reality, Movable Books, 3D Interaction, Visual Storytelling, Graphic Novel, Virtual Exhibition

1. INTRODUCTION

Augmented Reality – as a hybrid environment – could be the best example of "Mixed Reality", described by Paul Milgram and Fumio Kishino. Of course, it's just the one of many technologies of visual displays, "that involve the merging of real and virtual worlds somewhere along the 'virtuality continuum' which connects completely real environments to completely virtual ones" (Milgram, and Kishino, 1994).

AR printed publications are frequently described as 21st century 'pop-up' books, which places them in the context of very vivid and rich tradition. Some of AR books remind also different kinds of ludic, playable literature or interactive board games with virtual 'pawns'. Another possible context and source of inspiration for performative AR books – as a new-old genre – could be the universe of artist's books (or books-as-exhibitions) and liberature – literary genre, combining the form and content of the book (Lat. *liber*) into an inseparable whole. As Katarzyna Bazarnik and Zenon Fajfer states: "Hence, the material book, which can be of any shape and structure, ceases to be a neutral container for a text, but becomes an integral component of the literary work. It becomes its spatial-temporal foundation shaped by authors just as they shape the fictional world represented through language" (Fajfer, 2010)

Recalling these contexts is necessary to understand the wide range of possibilities opening for the authors creating the new generation of AR art books, laying particular stress not only on the evolving digital technology, but also on the communication tactics and conceptual content of their works

2. LITERATURE REVIEW

A literature review of the topic shows that the main areas of interest in Augmented Reality are: specialized applications of AR interfaces in industry, medicine, rescue etc. (Jetter, 2018), education (Kidd 2015), (Chen 2016), (Lai 2018), digital entertainment (Von Itzstein, 2017), retail (Bonetti 2017), (Yung, 2017).

A separate extremely interesting topic is "expanding" the so-called old media using virtual content. Experimenting with the traditional press and the book becomes especially popular. The earliest experiments can be noted in specialist (medical, engineering) literature and in books for children and adolescents (Vanderschantz, 2018), (Cheng, 2019), (Yilmaz 2016). This probably results from the fact that this type of work contains traditionally and indispensable, illustrative material - important for pragmatic or aesthetic reasons.

One of the main topics of the article below is to look at selected cases of the use of technological enhancement in modifying literary content and to present one special case of the "Stilleben" project.

3. CASE STUDIES: COMMUNICATION STRATEGIES IN CONTEMPORARY AR BOOKS

Focusing not only on the technological, but also on the artistic point of view, the most important aspects of AR experience could be:

– aesthetic layer of the work (including 'internal' visual cohesion between printed and virtual elements and its compatibility with contemporary trends in art and design),
– advantage of book's communicative function over its decorative aspect (is AR 'appendix' only a tautological reflection of material layer of the work? Does it create any new meanings, storylines?),
– deep understanding of 'material' layer of the book (does the author take into the consideration not only visual, but also haptic aspect of the book?).

The following brief review of selected AR projects presents how various communication tactics could be applied to projects designed for different audiences. All recalled examples are grouped into four categories: educative and entertaining books intended for immature readers, comics books, literary works (focused on the mutations of traditional text), art books.

The first group contains books created for children and youth – despite the huge amount of such publications, it seems the variability of their visual forms isn't so high. One of the emblematic examples could be "iDinasaur", published by Carltonbooks (Carlton Kids, 2013). This non-narrative, educational book, is aiming to digitally 'reconstruct' prehistoric environment supported by simple interactions and „natural" soundtrack, intended to create immersive effect. Unfortunately, rather low graphic quality and very small amount and limited range of digital augmentation makes it probably less more attractive to the targeted audience than it was expected. Another popular AR book created for young readers is an adaptation of "The Litte Prince", the classical philosophical tale by Antoine de Saint-Exupéry (2015). Interesting initial idea – animating the world of "The Little Prince" and making it more accessible through simple games – collides with very low design quality of the book. Even though the publisher decided to preserve the iconic illustrations created by the writer himself, the chaotic typography and incoherent aesthetics of digital augmentation (also tautologically reflecting the original images) doesn't fit to the imagery of the original concept by Saint-Exupéry. The last example recalled in this section is Skip Brittenham's novel for teenanagers, under the significant title "Between Worlds", in which the augmentation supports the fantastic, alternative reality, making it more accessible to the reader/viewer. (Brittenham, 2016) Although the number of interactions is highly limited, it's worth to appreciate the old-style, ascetic layout of the book, far from usual 'horror vacui' effects, typical for this kind of publications.

The second group of books contains popular graphic novels, enriched by multilayered digital augmentation. The first one is "Anomaly: The Rubicon – Special Collector's Edition", invented by previously mentioned author Skip Brittenham (2017). From the formal point of view, it represents definitely different approach towards book design than projects such as "Between Worlds". It's extremely dense composition, overloaded with variable graphic effects and supported by many interactive augmentations coherent with the 3D-style illustrations, starts to be problematic at some point, but it's worth to mention that the book is designed mainly as a gadget for "Anomaly" fans and for sure it fulfills its function. Similar way of augmented storytelling can be find in "Black Eye Peas presents Master of the Sun – Zombie Chronicles". (will.i.am et al., 2017) In this case the augmentation covers the whole pages and it's almost as dense as the material layer, which causes a 'conceptual' dissonance: the overstimulating 2-D animation, accompanied by the full cast reading looks rather as an intermedial webcomic and it seems that the internet could be more appropriate distribution channel for such projects than the book. Paul Gravett discusses this way of storytelling in his "Comics Art", asking the questions: "With these advances, or gimmicks, does there comes a point when a comic is no longer a comic? What happens when 'motion graphics' recycle and convert pre-existing printed comics into limited animation by moving elements of the artwork in layers to suggest depth and movement, perhaps adding some lip-sync simulation? A few motion comics, like 'Watchmen', quirkily retain the balloons and captions alongside the voice-acting, music and sound effects, but most are an entirely audiovisual experience. Does it matter that the reader no longer reads, and the viewer is no longer in constant control of what to take in next?" (Gravett, 2013) This approach could be linked to effects of 'convergence culture' visible in US comics industry: "What is clear is that many consumers, especially of America's massive superhero brands, come to these characters first through their much more hyped film, television and game adaptations than through their printed or digital comics, so motion comics may more than satisfy their need for something that resembles a comic." In addition Gravett points out that the "parallel and perhaps counter to these digital innovations has been a resurgence of the book as a covetable, tactile object"; spectacular examples of this non-linear, yet analogue models of visual storytelling could be such projects as Richard McGuire's „Here" (a hyperemic inspired by Windows interface) (2014) and Chris Ware's „Building Stories" (resembling multilayered narrative board game). (2012)

The third group of AR books contains literary works. The first example – "Notebook" by polish author Tomasz Lipko – represents the highly commercial branch of literature (2015). In this case using the AR technology is rather a gimmick supporting the publisher's marketing strategies than the real revolution in literary narration. Unfortunately all the additional elements – mainly photos and videos – does not enrich the basic storyline, thus they're rather a distraction than the attraction. It's not difficult to imagine the better solution: the source of inspiration could be beautifully and wisely edited "S" project, created by J.J. Abrams and Doug Dorst – another book, although not virtually augmented, based on 'investigation' concept (2013). Another interesting example, referring to avant-garde tradition of concrete poetry (or, even, ancient poesia visiva) is literary project, entitled „Between Page and Screen", written and designed by Amaranth Borsuk & Brad Bouse. (2012) The initial idea is obviously self-referential: and exchange of love letters between the 'Page' and the 'Screen'. Despite the high conceptual value of the work, the subtle imbalance between its two parts is quite visible: the 'page' section (filled with QR codes) is completely illegible without digital tools, belonging to the 'screen' section. In fact, 'the page' is just an interface between the screens.

The last group contains the selection of AR art books. One of the possible sources for the inspiration in this area could be location-based AR, present in contemporary art institutions. "Pop-Up (AR)t book", published by CoCA Center on Contemporary Art in Seattle, is a good example of adaptation of this strategy (2016). This "Augmented Reality Pop-Up Book", featuring 3D Artwork by 18 Artists, becomes a portable virtual sculpture exhibition. At the book release, the institution organized an exhibition displaying each AR digital object for interactive public viewing. Lacking deeper conceptual structure or storyline, the project is focused mainly on highly formal values.

4. THE „STILLEBEN" PROJECT: ARTISTIC CONCEPTION

The "Stilleben" project is a collective work of Jakub Woynarowski and Jan K. Argasiński, the members of a group of polish researchers, artists and programmers affiliated with the Ubu Laboratory at the Jagiellonian University in Cracow, who focus their research on creative computing and platform studies. They also study ways for curating, presentation and preservation of such works.

"Stilleben" consists of two parallel yet interconnected visual stories. One of them is contained in the AR artbook, which could serve as "operating manual" of brand new visual language. The second version of the story is presented in the form of VR interactive installation, which can be seen as a form of exploratory game or non-linear visual poem. Its idea was inspired by 17th century still life paintings (german: "Stilleben"), depicting mostly inanimate subject matter, in which the state of 'death' reveals also to be a kind of 'silent life'. In fact, many of these compositions were allegorical visual essays, which could be compared with early modern cabinets of curiosities – encyclopedic collections of objects, regarded as memory theaters or microscopic reproductions of the world, which could be treated also as a prototypes of a contemporary art galleries. The word "cabinet" can be understood in two ways: as a room, a unique environment in which the various elements that make up the collection become integrated into an organic whole, or as an object, a piece of furniture, associated with Duchamp's "Green Box" or Breton's "poem-objects". Some of these cabinets, enclosed in the form of fine furniture, bring modern computers to mind. A good example would be a piece of furniture commissioned in the 17th century by Philipp Hainhofer, which was equipped with all the functions found in a modern computer, such as a catalogue system, writing and music playing applications, or even a variety of games. This parallel could be taken to a further step – quite a few researchers have pointed to the similarities between contemporary internet blogs and curio cabinets.

Multilayered storytelling of "Stilleben" is founded on "cosmological" way of thinking, present in two significant examples of early modern synthetic visual "hexamerons", which describe God's work on the six days of creation: Michael Wolgemut's Genesis sequence for "The Nuremberg Chronicle" and Matthaus Merian's illustrations for Robert Fludd's treatise "Utriusque cosmi... historia" (1617-24). In both cases, we encounter a presentation of the Genesis creation myth in a form that could be described as a semi-abstract comic strip, a sequence of images circumscribed around the figure of a circle. The first drawing in Robert Fludd's cycle presents the original chaos and it is nothing but a black square, captioned with a formula "Et sic in infinitum" (And so on to infinity). This print, created in 1617 is deceptively similar to Malevich's Black Square on White Ground. It's possible to compare these works with another examples of "cosmological" visual stories created in the 20th century (mostly based on architectonic metaphors), such as El Lissitzky's "A Suprematist Tale of Two Squares in Six Constructions". According to Odile Belkeddar, the author of introductory note to Lissitzky's book: "Transformed into a visual object, the book is constructed as a building in which volume and movement are represented. As a designer of exhibitions, El Lissitzky would even use walls, floor and ceiling, like six faces of a cube" (2014). Very similar intuition was expressed by Paul Gravett, who described British narrative "PoCom-UK-001" (2003) as the interference between contemporary „hyper comics" and „gallery comics": "The originators' ambition, still to be realised, is to extend PoCom around another three walls of the gallery and then connect panels with further stories across the floor and ceiling, and cutting diagonally across the gallery space, to burst out beyond this cube to create a blossoming organic nest of stories, achievable only in virtual space".

In "Stilleben's" sterile and claustrophobic space, a mysterious "para-matter" sets ordinary objects in motion, causing their spectacular deconstruction in the course of time. The white color of the walls, fabrics and electrical appliances may be associated with the illusory peace and quiet of a home, but they become black in the final stage of the story, annexing the spaces which follow. The appearance of danger in a "tamed" space implies a certain conventionality of the territory delineated by humans, constituting both an asylum and prison.

5. THE CREATION OF THE "STILLEBEN"

The "Stilleben" AR application was created using Vuforia Augmented Reality SDK and Unity Engine. These are state of the art technologies available for free for educational use. App was build using Android SDK. The implementation of Jakub Woynarowski's design was quite standard for this type of software development.

6. THE „STILLEBEN" PROJECT: VISUAL COMMUNICATION TACTICS

The whole multilayered narrative of "Stilleben" refers to the tradition of visual "hexamerons", depicting the stages of Genesis process. The gallery-like white cube space can be seen as a reference to The Cube of Space - an occult concept that was popularized by Paul Foster Case. It associates the three axes, the center point, the six sides and the twelve edges of the cube, with the 22 letters of the hebrew alphabet. The Cube of Space is based upon the verses of the proto-cabbala text called the Sepher Yetzirah, which describes directly the Genesis process. Similar concept was also introduced by Jay David Bolter in his book "Writing Space: Computers, Hypertext, and the Remediation of Print", where the alchemical and cabalistic codes are compared with contemporary digital interfaces (Bolter, 2001).

This kind of procedure could also describe very well the way how the user of "Stilleben" opens up new chapters of the story, following semi-abstract icons placed inside the white cube. The process of communication is repeatedly interrupted by rebellious black matter – this strategy is present also in two early examples of "interactive" literature: "The Life and Opinions of Tristram Shandy, Gentleman", a novel by Laurence Sterne (full of narrative „blackouts") (1759-1767) and Gustave Doré's graphic book "History of Holy Russia" (where the abstract ink blots take over the pages of historical treatise) (2017).

In the "Stilleben" augmented reality book three-dimensional white cube space (which appears in VR version of the project) is translated into the form of flat, two-dimensional white square of hermetically closed book – once it's opened, the viewer/reader enters the wordless universe of objects and symbols. 64-pages storyboard-like graphic novel is divided into 32 units: two-pages spreads, presenting variable 'iterations' based on the same group of elements. On each spread, the right side represents the isometric, hexagonal view of the cubic living space; the diagram is always accompanied by pictograms, linked to certain details of the interior. All of these objects could be symbolically 'animated' by the viewer by interacting with the images on the left side of each spread. The interaction reflects the next steps of user's exploratory activity. Every simplified, graphic element on the left side represents the chosen part of the interior; the augmentation reveals the three-dimensional view of the objects, hidden behind the semi-abstract drawings. Most of them are supported by simple animations, accessible by touching the 'button' also located on the page. By following this visual 'guide' the user stays in permanent movement between the visible surface of the world represented in the story and its hidden, organic interior, which remains a secret 'still life', not accessible for everyone.

7. SUMMARY

The article discusses the phenomena of augmented reality books as a new artistic and literary medium, however, rooted in the deeper tradition of non-linear, tactile – yet analogue – models of visual storytelling, appearing in movable books, board games, liberature, concrete poetry, experimental graphic novels and artists' books. Today, at the early stage of development of the genre, the authors of AR books frequently face fundamental problems, reflecting the imbalance between aesthetic layer of the work, book's communicative function and its haptic aspect. Also, if AR books should be something „more than a gimmick", there's a need for more minimalist approach, focused on detail, to oppose the common tendency towards intermedial overstimulation, present in contemporary augmented reality projects. It seems that possible centers able to support this tendency and educate the potential viewers/readers are universities and art schools, treated as laboratories for high-quality AR visual storytelling, focused both on aesthetic and conceptual values of the work.

ACKNOWLEDGEMENT

The Stilleben is part of Creative Computing. The laboratory (Twórcze programowanie. Laboratorium) K/PMI/000260 National Programme for the Development of Humanities grant funded by the Polish Ministry of Science and Higher Education.

REFERENCES

Abrams, J.J. and Dorst, D., 2013. *S.* Mulholland Books, New York

Barker, J. M., 2009. *The Tactile Eye. Touch and the Cinematic Experience.* University of California Press, Berkeley - Los Angeles – London

Bolter, J. D., 2001. *Writing Space: Computers, Hypertext, and the Remediation of Print, Second Edition.* Lawrence Erlbaum Associates, Mahwah

Bonetti, F. et al, 2017. Augmented Reality and Virtual Reality in Physical and Online Retailing: A Review, Synthesis and Research Agenda, In: Jung T., tom Dieck M. (eds) *Augmented Reality and Virtual Reality. Progress in IS.* Springer, Cham

Borsuk, A. and Bouse, B., 2012. *Between Page and Screen.* Siglio Press, Los Angeles

Bouchardon, S., 2008. *The aesthetics of materiality in electronic literature.* https://elmcip.net/sites/default/files/media/critical_writing/attachments/bouchardon-bergen-materiality.pdf (access: 1 April 2019)

Brittenham, S., 2016. *Between Worlds.* G.P. Putnam's Sons Books for Young Readers, New York

Brittenham, S. et al, 2017. *Anomaly: The Rubicon - Special Collector's Edition.* Anomaly Publishing, Los Angeles

Carlton Kids, 2013. *iDinasaur (AR).* Carltonbooks, London

Center on Contemporary Art, 2016. *Pop-Up (AR)t book. An Augmented Reality Pop-Up Book Featuring 3D Artwork by 18 Artists.* CoCA Center on Contemporary Art, Seattle

Chen, P. et al, 2016. A review of using Augmented Reality in Education from 2011 to 2016. In: Popescu E. et al. (eds) *Innovations in Smart Learning. Lecture Notes in Educational Technology.* Springer, Singapore

Cheng, K.-H., 2018. Parents' user experiences of augmented reality book reading: perceptions, expectations, and intentions. *Education Tech Research Dev*, 67: 303

Doré, G., 2017. *The Rare and Extraordinary History of Holy Russia.* Pallas Athene Arts, London

Fajfer, Z., 2010. *Liberature or Total Literature. Collected Essays 1999–2009.* Korporacja Ha!art, Kraków

Fludd, R., 1617-24. *Utriusque Cosmi ... metaphysica, physica atque technica Historia. &c.,* Aere Johan-Theodori de Bry: Typis Hieronymi Galleri, Oppenhemii

Gazcón, N. and Castro, S., 2015. ARBS: An Interactive and Collaborative System for Augmented Reality Books. In: De Paolis L., Mongelli A. (eds) *Augmented and Virtual Reality. AVR 2015. Lecture Notes in Computer Science,* vol 9254. Springer, Cham

Gartner, 2018. *Gartner Identifies Five Emerging Technology Trends That Will Blur the Lines Between Human and Machine.* https://www.gartner.com/en/newsroom/press-releases/2018-08-20-gartner-identifies-five-emerging-technology-trends-that-will-blur-the-lines-between-human-and-machine (access: 1 April 2019)

Gravett, P., 2013. *Comics art.* Yale University Press, London

Haining, P., 1979. *Movable Books: An Illustrated History.* New English Library, London

Hügli, M. and Kovacovsky, M., 2010. *Jekyll and Hyde Augmented Reality Book,* Hochschule für Gestaltung und Kunst (HGK), Basel

Jetter, J. et al, 2018. Augmented reality tools for industrial applications: What are potential key performance

indicators and who benefits?. *Computers in Human Behavior*, Volume 87, October 2018, Pages 18-33

Kidd, S. H. and Crompton, H., 2015. Augmented Learning with Augmented Reality. In: Churchill D., Lu J., Chiu T., Fox B. (eds) *Mobile Learning Design. Lecture Notes in Educational Technology.* Springer, Singapore

Lai, A.-F., 2018. An augmented reality-based learning approach to enhancing students' science reading performances from the perspective of the cognitive load theory. *Br J Educ Technol,* 50: 232-247. doi:10.1111/bjet.12716

Lindberg, S. G., 1979. *Mobiles in Books: Volvelles, Inserts, Pyramids, Divinations, and Children's Games.* The Private Library, 3rd series, vol. 2, Private Libraries Association

Lipko, T., 2010. *Notebook.* Wydawnictwo Literackie, Kraków

Lissitzky, E., 2014. *A Suprematist Tale of Two Squares in Six Constructions*. Tate, London

McCloud, S., 200. *Reinventing Comics,* William Morrow Paperbacks, New York

McGuire, R., 2014. *Here.* Pantheon, New York

Miligram, P. and Kishino, F., 1994. *A Taxonomy of Mixed Reality Visual Displays.* IEICE Transactions on Information Systems, Vol E77-D, No.12

Phoenix, W., 2008. *Rumble Strip: If You Want to Get Away with Murder, Buy a Car.* Myriad Editions, Brighton PoCom-UK-001, 2003, http://e-merl.com/pocom.htm (access: 1 April 2019)

Rüegg, N., 2004, *SPUK*, Edition Fink, Zürich

Saint-Exupéry, A. de, 2015. *The Little Prince: Augmented Reality,* Design Media Publishing Limited, London

Scherrer, C., 2008. *Le Monde des montagnes.* The École cantonale d'art de Lausanne (ECAL), Lausanne

Sterne, L., 1759-1767. *The Life and Opinions of Tristram Shandy, Gentleman.* Ann Ward (vol. 1–2), Dodsley (vol. 3–4), Becket & DeHondt (vol. 5–9), London

Ware, Ch., 2012. *Building Stories.* Pantheon, New York

will.i.am et al, 2017. *Black Eye Peas Present: Master of the Sun – Zombie Chronicles,* Marvel Comics, New York

Vaughn-James, M., 1975. *The Cage,* Coach House Press, Toronto

Vanderschantz, N., 2018. Using augmented reality to enhance children's books. *Working paper series. University of Waikato, Department of Computer Science*. No. 02/2018. Hamilton, New Zealand

Von Itzstein, G. S., Augmented Reality Entertainment: Taking Gaming Out of the Box. In N. Lee (Ed.) *Encyclopedia of Computer Graphics and Games.* Cham, Switzerland: Springer

Yilmaz, R. M. et al, 2016. Are augmented reality picture books magic or real for preschool children aged five to six?. *Br J Educ Technol,* Vol. 48, Issue 3

Yung, R. and Khoo-Lattimore, C., 2017. New realities: a systematic literature review on virtual reality and augmented reality in tourism research. *Current Issues in Tourism,* Routledge

EMULATION OF HUMAN ATTENTION FOR EXPLORATION OF VIRTUAL ARCHITECTURAL ENVIRONMENTS. APPLICATION TO LE CORBUSIER'S *PROMENADE ARCHITECTURALE* OF A VIRTUAL *VILLE SAVOYE*

Viviana Barneche-Naya and Luis A. Hernández-Ibáñez
Universidade da Coruña, Spain

ABSTRACT

This paper describes the use of *Paseante*, an autonomous agent for real-time assisted navigation inside virtual environments. In order to carry out its implementation, theories of human attention and environmental psychology were considered. This work describes the application of the system for the emulation of one of the mythical experiences of the theory and history of Architecture: *La Promenade Architecturale* inside the *Ville Savoye.*

KEYWORDS

Human Computer Interaction, Human Attention, Aided Navigation, Real-time Visualization, Architectural Visualization

1. INTRODUCTION

For some years, real-time technologies for architectural visualization have been used, mainly motivated by the possibility of traveling and interacting with the virtual environment. Every day real-time simulations acquire a greater realism, however, natural navigation forms are still lacking, closer to human movement than to the mechanical sequence of turns and movements, which characterize current forms of movement.

Research conducted on navigation has found strong correlations between real-world and virtual navigation (Richardson et al, 1999; Gaunet et al, 2001; Claessen et al, 2016) which has led to virtual environments being used to investigate spatial cognition in simulated real environments. This has been applied to particular cases such as Alzheimer's, people with brain injury or orientation activities in elderly people (Foreman et al, 2005; Plancher et al, 2012; Cogné et al, 2017).

A detected deficiency arises in the navigation of non-expert users in virtual environments since their attention is focused in the first instance on learning the maneuvers of navigation itself (Waller, 2000; Smith & Du'Mont, 2009). This greatly affects their ability to understand what you are seeing; so many inexperienced visitors may feel somewhat lost or not be very clear what to do or where to look. Because of this, it was necessary to first identify what are the elements that define the experience of navigation in the real architectural space. This research analyzed what aspects related to human perception and attention affect the ways of navigation of human beings within the built environment in real life.

2. METHODOLOGY

The implementation of this system has required the creation of an autonomous agent endowed with criteria to obtain the most interesting point of attention for each position and visual orientation of the user in the virtual environment. For this, it was necessary to enter into the analysis of human perception of space.

Lewin's field theory (Lewin, 1938) was considered in the first place. It explains human movement in an environment in terms of forces acting on it from different directions and with different intensities. The work also considers the affordance theory (Gibson, 1979), which describes the potential capacity of any element of the environment to attract attention and be used by the perceiver. The system also implements the concept of attentional focus, especially the metaphor of the focus of light (Posner et al, 1985) and the metaphor of the attentional gradient as a variation of assigned resources in the visual field as a function of the origin position of the gradient (LaBerge & Brown, 1989).

Related to the navigation design, two concepts were considered: the attentional value of the reference points according to their visual, cognitive and structural characteristics (Sorrows & Hirtle, 1999) and the concept of enriched space (Raubal & Winter, 2002). The system is implemented as an autonomous agent inside the character representing the user in the Unreal Engine 4 game engine. This agent subtly modifies the view and movement direction based on the presence of attracting elements in the scene.

On a given environment, the analysis of the presence of landmarks in a zone surrounding the user can be used to model the amount of attention that the area that contains every element may arise from the user.

We have implemented this by designing an element that can be placed anywhere in the virtual model called attractor. This element is defined by several parameters that include interest, range of attraction, decay and other variables that describe the willingness to look at it based on the distance to the user and direction in the scene relative to the character's sight direction.

The presence of several attractors in the viewable area surrounding the user can be weighted using models from the field of Psychology of Perception such as the one proposed by Lewin. This model defines a *hodological* space (the space surrounding the user that contains zones that push or pull his or her attention based on personal interest related to each one). In Lewin's model, every area has a valence that quantifies the attractive effect to the user.

The resultant of all forces of attraction describes the final intention of the subject to point his or her attention to a particular direction. Our solution, as described in figure 1, weights the attracting forces by turning the continuous Lewin's space into a discrete one, populated with attractors (**A**) with given interests, and considering every attractor as generator of a field of attractive force, being the geometry of this field a function that involves distance, direction relative to user's sight and two values of willingness for distance and angle (q). Then, a vector of attention of this attractor ($\mathbf{F_A}$) is defined, being the valence the value of its module.

The center of attention (**C**) is then calculated as a center of force, and will be used to drive smoothly the user sight toward it when no turning input is detected in a given time. By placing attractors in every interesting point, the movement of the user can be controlled. Interest of attractors can decay with exposure to the user contemplation. The center of attention is being recalculated every frame considering the change in location and orientation of the user.

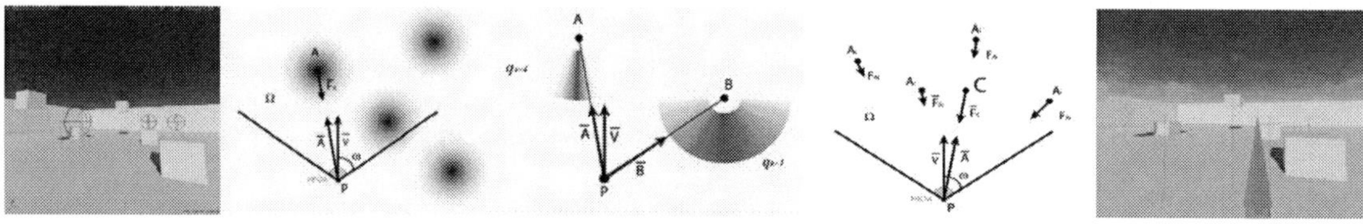

Figure 1. Left to right: Attractors placed on a virtual environment. Field of attention. Parameters for calculation of the attention of attractors. Center of attention. Debug representation of forces and direction to the center of attention

3. RESULTS

This new metaphor for the navigation through virtual architectural environments was used to emulate one of the most paradigmatic experiences of architectural walkthrough: *La Promenade Architecturale* proposed by Le Corbusier for his famous *Ville Savoye*. (Figure 2).

Figure 2. Virtual model of Le Corbusier's Ville Savoye made by the authors for this work

The intended way of perceiving this house is not completely open to the freedom of the visitor, but is mediated by the work of its architect, who defined a priori the sequence of the itinerary. The concept of architectural walk was materialized in an interior ramp that makes possible the continuous perception of living spaces from the main access to the house to the landscape seen from the terrace, establishing different visual and spatial relationships through movement.

The walk is assisted by the attractors that the authors placed inside the building. Attractors are placed in those locations or spaces that the designer of the walk considers that deserve special attention (Figure 3). Objects with special meaning can also be augmented with attractors (Figure 4). By fine-tuning the values related to their intensity, willingness, decay, etc, the authors seek to reproduce the desire of the architect regarding the sequence to follow in the discovery and contemplation of the spaces. While no input from the visitor is detected, *Paseante* checks the surroundings and evaluates the influence of all attractors in the user's field of view, locates the center of interest and drives the view to focus on this point. Therefore, the user can devolve to *Paseante* the task to find every interesting part of the building and perform the turns and camera pointing when needed. If the user takes full control of the movement, *Paseante*, will wait for him or her to stop, then it will visually suggest new places and things to look at in the actual location. In this regard, assisted navigation based on the use of attractors is a valid alternative for space exploration, closer to the human way in which a building can be experienced.

Paseante is well suited to be used in conjunction with natural interaction schemes and devices. The authors are actually making UX test combined with the use of Kinect driven navigation in virtual architectural spaces (Hernandez-Ibáñez, Barneche-Naya, Mihura-López, 2016).

Figure 3. Entrance. Above: Interior space. Below: Attractors located in the areas of interest affecting the view direction

Figure 4. Living-room. Above: View of the space. Below: Attractors located on the objects of interest. Transparency means attention decaying with time

REFERENCES

Claessen, M. H., Visser-Meily, J. M., de Rooij, N. K., Postma, A., & van der Ham, I. J., 2016. A direct comparison of real-world and virtual navigation performance in chronic stroke patients. *Journal of the International Neuropsychological Society*, 22(4), 467-477.

Cogné, M., Taillade, M., N'Kaoua, B., Tarruella, A., Klinger, E., Larrue, F., ... & Sorita, E., 2017. The contribution of virtual reality to the diagnosis of spatial navigation disorders and to the study of the role of navigational aids: A systematic literature review. *Annals of physical and rehabilitation medicine*, 60(3), 164-176.

Foreman, N., Stanton-Fraser, D., Wilson, P. N., Duffy, H., & Parnell, R., 2005. Transfer of spatial knowledge to a two-level shopping mall in older people, following virtual exploration. *Environment and Behavior*, 37(2), 275-292.

Gaunet, F., Vidal, M., Kemeny, A., & Berthoz, A., 2001. Active, passive and snapshot exploration in a virtual environment: influence on scene memory, reorientation and path memory. *Cognitive Brain Research*, 11(3), 409-420.

Gibson, J., 1979. *The Ecological Approach to Visual Perception*. Hillsdale, NJ: Lawrence Erlbaum Associates.

Hernandez-Ibáñez, L.A., Barneche-Naya, V., Mihura-López, R., 2016. A comparative study of walkthrough paradigms for virtual environments using Kinect based natural interaction. *22nd International Conference on Virtual System & Multimedia (VSMM) pp 210-2177*. IEEE

LaBerge, D., & Brown, V., 1989. Theory of attentional operations in shape identification. *Psychological review*, 96(1), 101.

Lewin, K., 1938. The conceptual representation and the measurement of psychological forces. *Duke University. Contributions to Psychological Theory*.

Plancher, G., Tirard, A., Gyselinck, V., Nicolas, S., & Piolino, P., 2012. Using virtual reality to characterize episodic memory profiles in amnestic mild cognitive impairment and Alzheimer's disease: influence of active and passive encoding. *Neuropsychologia*, 50(5), 592-602.

Posner, M. I., Rafal, R. D., Choate, L. S., & Vaughan, J., 1985. Inhibition of return: Neural basis and function. *Cognitive neuropsychology*, 2(3), 211-228.

Raubal, M & Winter S., 2002. Enriching wayfinding instructions with local landmarks. *International conference on geographic information science*. 243-259. Springer, Berlin, Heidelberg.

Richardson, A. E., Montello, D. R., & Hegarty, M., 1999. Spatial knowledge acquisition from maps and from navigation in real and virtual environments. *Memory & cognition*, 27(4), 741-750.

Smith, S. P., & Du'Mont, S., 2009. Measuring the effect of gaming experience on virtual environment navigation tasks. *2009 IEEE Symposium on 3D User Interfaces*, pp. 3-10.

Sorrows, M. E., & Hirtle, S. C., 1999. The nature of landmarks for real and electronic spaces. *International Conference on Spatial Information Theory*. pp. 37-50. Springer, Berlin, Heidelberg

Waller, D. (2000). Individual differences in spatial learning from computer-simulated environments. *Journal of Experimental Psychology: Applied*, 6(4), 307.

MLV-VIEWER: ADVANCED GRAPHICS FOR VISUALIZATIONS IN DECISION SUPPORT SYSTEMS

Carlos Manuel Oliveira Alves[1], Manuel Pérez Cota[2], María Díaz Rodríguez[3] and Miguel Ramón González Castro[4]

[1]*Instituto Politécnico de Castelo Branco, Av. D. Pedro Álvares Cabral 12, Castelo Branco, Portugal*

[2]*Dr, Universidade de Vigo, Rúa Torrecedeira 86; 36208 -Vigo, Spain*

[3]*Universidade de Vigo, Rúa Torrecedeira 86; 36208 -Vigo, Spain*

[4]*Dr., Universidade de Vigo, Rúa Torrecedeira 86; 36208 -Vigo, Spain*

ABSTRACT

Abstract. Information visualization (InfoVis) is defined as "the use of visual, interactive and visual representations supported by computer, to increase cognition". InfoVis tools and methods help us accelerate our understanding of a large amount of data. Data visualization improves understanding, especially with multidimensional data sets. Visual analysis methods allow decision makers to combine their human flexibility, creativity and knowledge with the huge storage and processing capabilities of today's computers for information about complex problems. Using advanced visual interfaces, humans can interact directly with the data analysis, adding more to their liking and need. The MLV-Viewer prototype will be described in this article.

KEYWORDS

Multi-Level Visualization on DSS, DSSM, Big Data Visualization

1. INTRODUCTION

In the late 1960s a new type of information system oriented to practical models, or decision support systems (DSS) or management decision systems (MDS) emerged. Peter Keen and Charles Stabe, pioneers of the DSS concept, point out that the concept evolved from theoretical studies of organizational decision making conducted at the Carnegie Institute of Technology. The origin of the DSS dates back to the beginning of the mid-20th century when the military objective was dominant. One of the oldest DSS was the SAGE (semi-automatic Ground Environment) designed to unify different images over the wide area and used in the cold war. SAGE was the largest computer ever built. According to another approach, the first DSS can originate in LEO I (Lyons Electronic Office) in 1951.

In this article, we will introduce the theme, followed by a review of the literature Madureira, Gomes, Cunha, Pereira, Santos, and Pereira (2014) on the theme "Multi-level Visualization in Decision Support Systems", with a main focus on the state of the art and finally we will describe the prototype performed and brief conclusions and future work.

2. LITERATURE REVIEW

According Siddiqa, A., Niazi, Mustafa, M. F., Bokhari, H., Hussain, A., Akram, N., Shaheen, S., Ahmed, F. and Iqbal, S. (2009) and Alves, C. M. O. and Cota, M. P. (2018) DSSs provides semi-structured and unstructured decision-making problem support, usually interactive, computer-based systems to assist decision-makers using various tools (such as communication, data, document, knowledge and modeling technologies) to aid in decision-making in a variety of areas, and the main components are: decision maker; data base; models and procedures; software.

FUMAHES, NED-2 in Modi, D., Fabregas, A. and Otero, L. (2015), AgMine in Anadiotis, G., Hatzoplaki, E., K. Tsatsakis K. and Tsitsanis, T. (2015), DISASOR in Bencsik, G., Bacsárdi, L. (2015), ViDSS in Müller, H., Reihs, R., Posch, A.E., Kremer, A., Ulrich, D. and Zatloukal, K. (2016), Ma, H., Yan, L. and Wang, T. (2011), ADSyS in Lee, H., Kang, N., Han, J., Kim, J., Kim, K. H., Kim, J. D.K. and Kim, C. Y. (2013), 16Dawood, I. and Alshawi, M. (2009), ADSyS in Ni, J., Zhang C. and Ren, L. (2009), Trase, K. and Fink, E. (2014), Wang, L., Wang, G. and Alexander, C.A. (2015), Armstrong, L.J. and Nallan, S.A. (2016), Kos, L. (2014), Cota, M. P., Rodríguez, M.D., González-Castro, M. R. and Gonçalves, R. M. M. (2018), Cota, M. P., Castro, M. R. G. and Domínguez, J. A. (2014), Cota, M. P. and Castro, M. R. G. (2012), UDSS in Pankratova, N. D. and Nedashkovskaya, N. I. (2017), DISASOR in Groumpos, P. P. (2016), VMAG in Nina, R. and Yurii, T. (2015), Imen, S., Chang, N. B., Yang, Y. J. and Golchubian, A. (2016), InVEST in Henriques, S., Antunes, M. B. B., Rodrigues, C. S. C. and Werner, C. M. L. (2016) are some examples of DSSs.

3. A NEW APPROACH: MLV-VIEWER

The developed prototype allows the user, in a dynamic and interactive way, to select what to view and how to visualize. It starts by selecting which database, then which table (s), and finally the column (s) and their contents. If the database does not already exist in the MySQL DBMS, you can import both the logical structure (contained in an XML Schema file) and the data (contained in an XML file). If the following are displayed: 1D; 2D; 2D + 1; and 3D.

3.1 MLV-Viewer Architecture

The developed prototype needs a MySQL server as well as a PHP server, in addition to these requirements can be used by a user with a web browser. It should also be noted that by the calculation requirement the PC must have a high processing capacity.

3.2 Visualizations with MLV-Viewer

After selecting the table (s), the user can choose to view the data in the format (1D) CSV, XML or Listing, or if the user chooses a 2D view, it has a "Bar" view, "Lines", "Donut", or "Pyramid". The view “Bar” uses the bars format with the image of the respective product at the base of each bar, while the quantity for each reference of each product is presented either quantitative (left scale) or qualitative (image size).

So far nothing new has been added to the "usually" used for data visualization. The prototype allows a set of "smart" views with the possibility for the user to decide what to view and how to view. In this context, the user can choose which fields of a table to view as well as which "part" of the column of the table shows, and if more than one "part" is chosen, the corresponding information will be displayed in a "paired" form (see Figures 1 and 2).

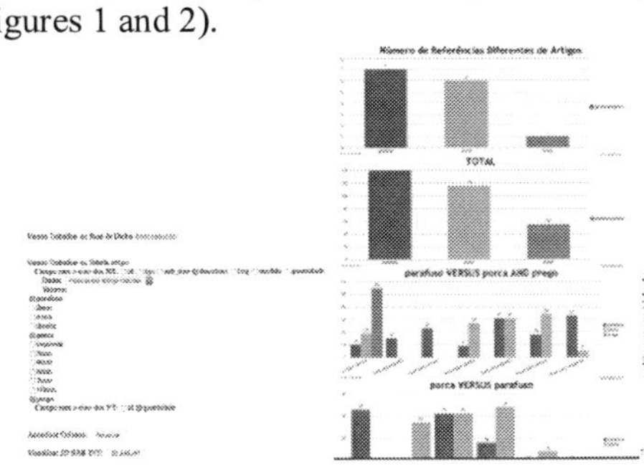

Figure 1. 2D Bars “Intelligent"

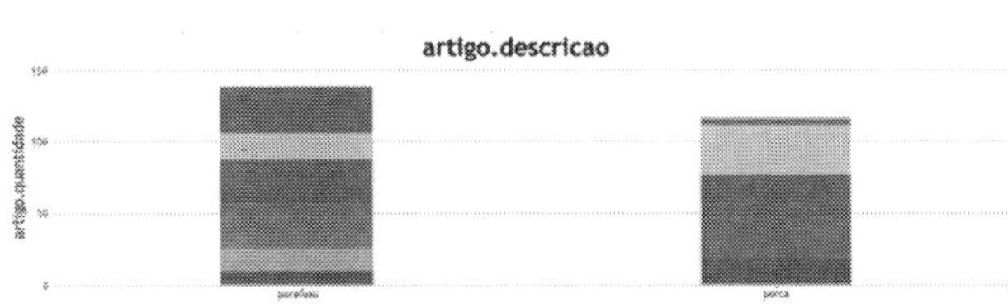

Figure 2. 2D View Stacked "Intelligent"

It should be noted that in the following figures, classified as 2D + 1, the dimension of bubbles (Figure 3) reflects the dimension "+1", as well as the size of the images (Figure 4).

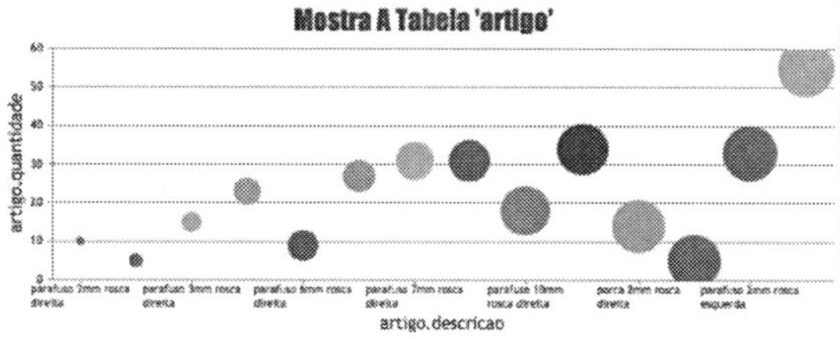

Figure 3. 2D View Bubble "Intelligent"

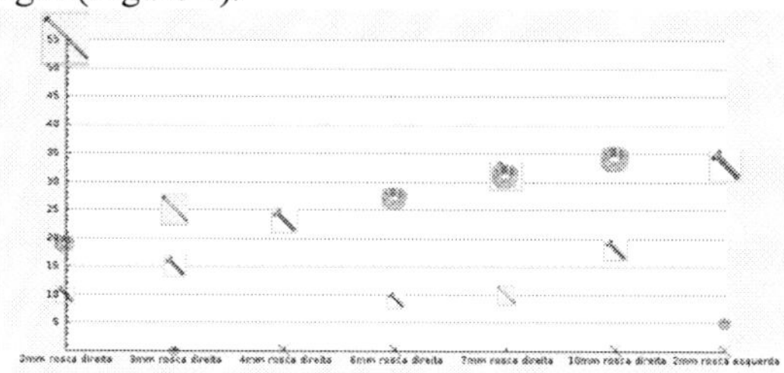

Figure 4. 2D View Line "Intelligent" with image

In Figures 5 ("Points"), 6 ("Stacked"), 7 ("Line") and 8 ("Bars") 3D visualizations are presented that allow the user to visualize interactive 3D (enabling, viewing angle change rotation).

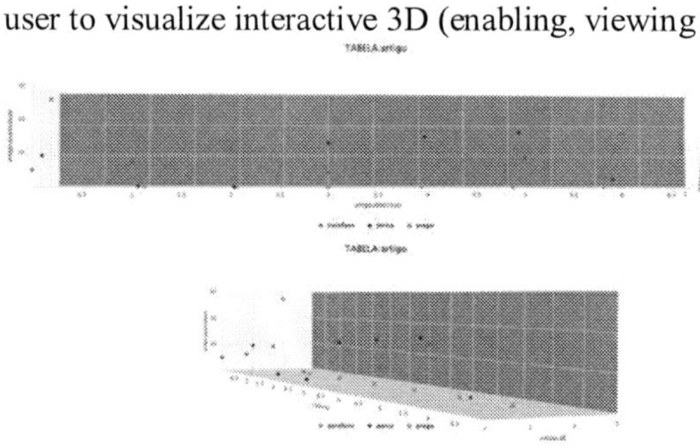

Figure 5. 3D View "Points"

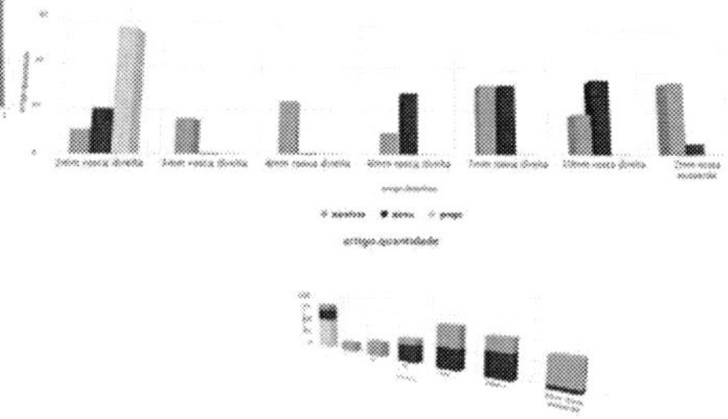

Figure 6. 3D View "Stacked"

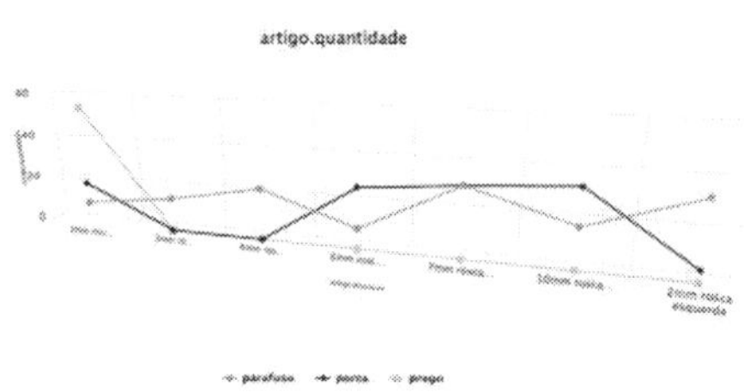

Figure 7. 3D View "Line"

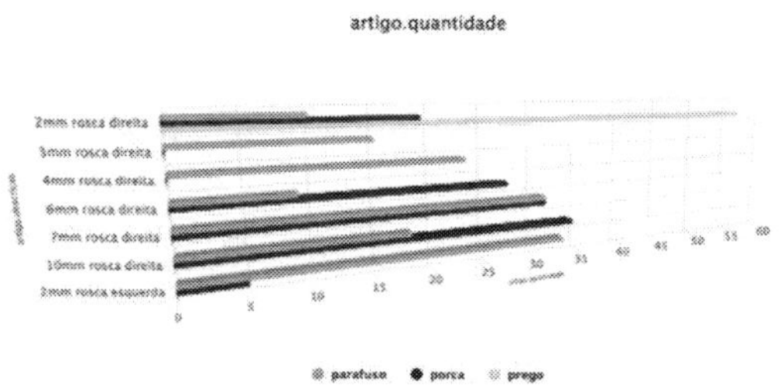

Figure 8. 3D View "horizontal Bars"

At this stage of the implementation of this prototype the objective was to allow the user, regardless of their competencies and privileges within the company, to visualize in the way that they would like the data they select.

4. CONCLUSION AND FUTURE WORK

All alike, all different. More, even "inside" the same individual we have differences (if the reader has doubts try to visualize the same scenario with one eye at a time). The whole computer system must be prepared to respond as widely as possible to all these vicissitudes of the most varied users. It's not easy, of course not. It is so important to allow a user to choose what to view so much, or more, to let them choose how to view those same data. A wrong choice of display type may inhibit obtaining the desired information.

The development of a software tool to support the design of the user interface of a DSS is not enough by itself, and should as far as possible meet the specifics of each user. For example, while the information may be displayed graphically, users may not be able to understand everything that is being displayed, or they may be overloaded with too much data to be displayed on the monitor. As we know, in any system we have input and output data, however the output / presentation of data to the user through a set of symbols is more easily understood by the user. A good system, therefore, should support users in finding meaningful information, Kos, L. (2014), in a simple way, which system should be user friendly and customizable, also suggesting the best visualization to obtain this information.

The visualization of information contained in the data through graphics or images is a developing technology transforming traditional methods of observation and analysis of relational data tables so that people can discover relationships and structure in a more intuitive way. Thus, hidden information can be easily discovered in Xin Yan, X., Qiao, M., Li, J., Simpson, T. W., Stump, G. M. and Zhang, X. (2012). A DSS visualization tool can be very important and advantageous, in Ye, X., Dai, Z., Qiu, J., & Fang, F. (2008), in decision making, supporting managers and leaders to reach the right decision as well as ensuring business continuity and, most importantly, ensuring customer satisfaction. It is also important that the choice of DSS is correct from the outset to reduce time and cost in making the right decisions and quality. As much as possible, DSS should be easy, simple, effective and customizable. Data visualization and hence information play a key role in decision making supported by decision support systems, but we believe the challenges are still in the beginning.

With the MLV-Viewer it was intended to implement a dynamic, interactive system in which the user can choose the best way to visualize the data.

As future work is intended to make this prototype in an application advise the user on a set of views that are more recommended / advised for the branch of activity in question (but if you want, others may be chosen). On the other hand, it is intended that there are users with different profiles, and consequently with different levels of data access, which will be visualized with 3D images, following the construction of a query dynamically and with interpolation of the missing data, as well as conduct tests with data from various business areas.

REFERENCES

Alves, C. M. O. & Cota, M. P. (2018). Multi-level visualization in decision support systems: Literature review, 2018 13th Iberian Conference on Information Systems and Technologies (CISTI).

Anadiotis, G., Hatzoplaki, E., K. Tsatsakis K. & Tsitsanis, T. (2015). A Data Model for Energy Decision Support Systems for Smart Cities - *The Case of BESOS Common Information Model.*

Armstrong, L.J. & Nallan, S.A. (2016). Agricultural Decision Support Framework for Visualization and Prediction of Western Australian Crop Production, 2016 3rd International Conference on Computing for Sustainable Global Development (INDIACom).

Bencsik, G. & Bacsárdi, L. (2015). Towards to decision support generalization: the Universal Decision Support System Concept, 2015 IEEE 19th International Conference on Intelligent Engineering Systems (INES).

Cota, M. P. & Castro, M. R. G. (2012). Problems with the use of 3D environments in DCS: New model of visualization in operation displays, 7th Iberian Conference on Information Systems and Technologies (CISTI 2012).

Cota, M. P., Castro, M. R. G. & Domínguez, J. A. (2014). Importance of visualization usage in enterprise decision making environements, 2014 9th Iberian Conference on Information Systems and Technologies (CISTI).

Cota, M.P., Rodríguez, M.D., González-Castro, M. R. & Gonçalves, R. M. M. (2018). Massive Data Visualization Analysis, 2018 13th Iberian Conference on Information Systems and Technologies (CISTI).

Dawood, I. & Alshawi, M. (2009). Decision Support Systems (DSS) Model for the Housing Industry, 2009 Second International Conference on Developments in eSystems Engineering.

Groumpos, P. P. (2016). Conceptual modeling and decision making support systems for complex dynamical systems: A critical overview, 2016 ELEKTRO.

Henriques, S., Antunes, M. B. B., Rodrigues, C. S. C. & Werner, C. M. L. (2016). Supporting System Modeling Learning Using Gestures for Visualization Control as Method of Immersion, 2016 XVIII Symposium on Virtual and Augmented Reality.

Imen, S., Chang, N. B., Yang, Y. J. & Golchubian, A. (2016). Developing a Model-Based Drinking Water Decision Support System Featuring Remote Sensing and Fast Learning Techniques, IEEE Systems Journal.

Kos, L. (2014). Visualization Support for Code Development in EUROfusion Integrated Modelling, MIPRO 2014.

Lee, H., Kang, N., Han, J., Kim, J., Kim, K. H., Kim, J. D.K. & Kim, C. Y. (2013). Interactive Manipulation and Visualization of a Deformable 3D Organ Model for Medical Diagnostic Support, The 10th Annual IEEE CCNC Conference- 3D Imaging & Processing & Communication and Display Track.

Ma, H., Yan, L. & Wang, T. (2011). Dynamic Model for Enterprise Human Resources Decision SupportSystem, 2011 3rd International Workshop on Intelligent Systems and Applications.

Madureira, A., Gomes, S., Cunha, B., Pereira, J.P., Santos, J.M., & Pereira, I. (2014). Prototype of an Adaptive Decision Support System for Interactive Scheduling with MetaCognition and User Modeling Experience, 2014 Sixth World Congress on Nature and Biologically Inspired Computing (NaBIC 2014)

Modi, D., Fabregas, A. & Otero, L. (2015). Requirements and decision model for a taxiway route support system, 2015 Annual IEEE Systems Conference (SysCon) Proceedings.

Müller, H., Reihs, R., Posch, A.E., Kremer, A., Ulrich, D. & Zatloukal, K. (2016). Data Driven GUI Design and Visualization for a NGS based Clinical Decision Support System, 2016 20th International Conference Information Visualisation.

Ni, J., Zhang C. & Ren, L. (2009). An Intelligent Decision Support System of Lake Water Pollution Control Based on Multi-agent Model, 2009 International Conference on Computational Intelligence and Security.

Nina, R. & Yurii, T. (2015). Simulation Model of the Decision-Making Support for Human-Machine Systems Operators, 2015 IEEE Seventh International Conference on Intelligent Computing and Information Systems (ICICIS'15).

Pankratova, N. D. & Nedashkovskaya, N. I. (2017). A Decision Support System for Evaluation of Decision Alternatives on Basis of a Network Criteria Model , 2017 IEEE First Ukraine Conference on Electrical and Computer Engineering (UKRCON).

Siddiqa, A., Mustafa, F., M. F., Bokhari, H., Hussain, A., Akram, N., Shaheen, S., Ahmed, F. & Iqbal, S. (2009). A new hybrid agent-based modeling & simulation decision support system for breast cancer data analysis, 2009 International Conference on Information and Communication Technologies.

Sugiarto Hartono; Evaristus Didik Madyatmadja, "Decision support system model to determine contribution of own source revenue towards regional government", 2016 22nd Asia-Pacific Conference on Communications (APCC), 2016.

Tieming Liu, Qinyue Pan, Javier Sanchez, Shuzhen Sun, Ning Wang, and Hongbo Yu: Prototype Decision Support System for Black Ice Detection and Road Closure Control, IEEE Intelligent transportation systems magazine,2017

Trase, K. & Fink, E. (2014). A Model-Driven Visualization Tool for Use with Model Based Systems Engineering Projects, 2014 IEEE Aerospace Conference.

Wang, L., Wang, G. & Alexander, C.A. (2015). Big data and visualization: Methods, challenges and technology progress. http://pubs.sciepub.com/dt/1/1/7/.

Xin Yan, X., Qiao, M., Li, J., Simpson, T. W., Stump, G. M. & Zhang, X. (2012). A Work-Centered Visual Analytics Model to Support Engineering Design with Interactive Visualization and Data-Mining, 2012 45th Hawaii International Conference on System Sciences.

Ye, X., Dai, Z., Qiu, J., & Fang, F. (2008). A Metadata-Based Flexible Function Model of Decision Support Systemfor Emergency Management, 2008 4th International Conference on Wireless Communications, Networking and Mobile Computing, 2008

AN ALTERNATIVE INTERACTION PARADIGM FOR DNA-SEQUENCE DATA

Loes Dekker, Max Peeperkorn, Danyi Liu and Fons J. Verbeek
LIACS, Leiden University, The Netherlands

ABSTRACT

From several online resources DNA-sequence data is available. In using these resources, none of them offer intuitive interactions. It is, moreover, inconvenient to use multiple resources to find data for a DNA sequence. This research investigates whether an interaction mechanism from another domain can help solve these existing usability issues. We show that the interaction mechanism of Google Maps is suitable for more inclusive and intuitive DNA sequence exploration. Applying an interaction mechanism to another domain has the potential to lead to new insights and to develop new, and better operational mental models. It is important though to consider all factors that make the interaction mechanism successful in order to apply it to the target domain.

KEYWORDS

User Interface, Interaction, Infovis, Deoxyribonucleic Acid, Bioinformatics, Sequence Software

1. INTRODUCTION

The current visualization tools for DNA and protein sequences are very technical. These tools, for example ORFfinder (Fig. 1) or BLAST, neither offer intuitive interactions nor do they visualize the data in an accessible way. Our goal is to create a new intuitive tool that allows for better visualization of DNA data as well as at the same time find new ways of interaction in exploring DNA sequences with a visual searching paradigm for patterns.

Our research mainly focuses on the possibility to take the interaction mechanism from one domain and apply it on another domain. To this end we have investigated the interaction mechanism from Google Maps and look at the implications of transferring this interaction mechanism for application to DNA sequence data.

In order to find out if the “Google Maps”-like interaction mechanism can be applied to DNA sequence data we identified our user group and conducted two surveys within the user group. One of these surveys was focused on our central idea and we used it mainly to get insights as to whether or not our envisionment of the tool would be appreciated. The second survey was focused on a prototype of the tool and will provide insight in how the tool is received and how well the interaction mechanism and visual cues work in practice.

The remainder of this paper is structured as follows. In section 2 we discuss the problems we think exist in current visualization tools and give a user analysis of our focus group. In section 3 we discuss our form of solution for interactive DNA visualization. The results of the evaluations of our prototype are given in section 4. In section 5, we present our conclusions through which we try to answer our research question. Finally, future work is presented in section 6.

2. DNA SEQUENCE INFORMATION AND VISUALIZATION TOOLS

In the field of Biology and Bioinformatics, there are several tools dedicated to find information in DNA sequences (Fig. 1). These tools have emerged from DNA research over the past decades and they are connected to a range of services, meaning that all information regarding DNA sequences that is known to man can be found somewhere. In reviewing tools for interactive visualization and information retrieval of DNA structures we conclude that the usability of these tools is rather low. They are engineered and were never designed. In order to find different sorts of data points in one sequence, multiple tools need to be addressed; this is inefficient and moreover, it does not appeal to a good mental model (Norman, 1988).

In solving the observed issues, we state that our approach to visualization will probably save time for the professionally engaged part of our user group. For the less experienced part of our user group it will facilitate an easier understanding of the information presented. We therefore are in the opinion that solving these issues is beneficial to the fields of Biology and Bioinformatics. By introducing an interaction mechanism from another domain we want to provide the possibility obtaining different and new insights in the data and create a better mental model for DNA sequence visualization.

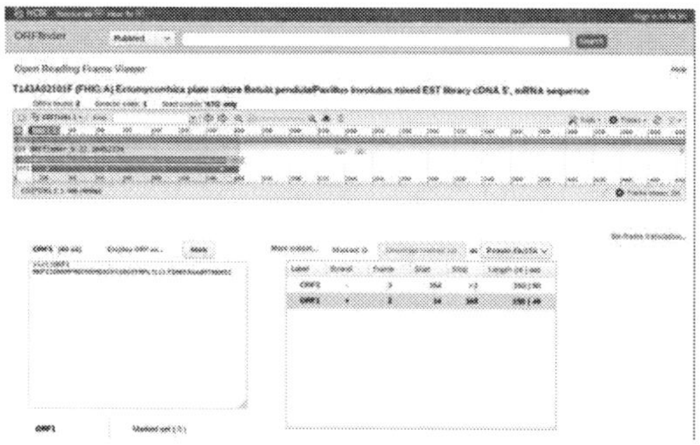

Figure 1. ORFfinder an example of a current DNA-sequence data application.

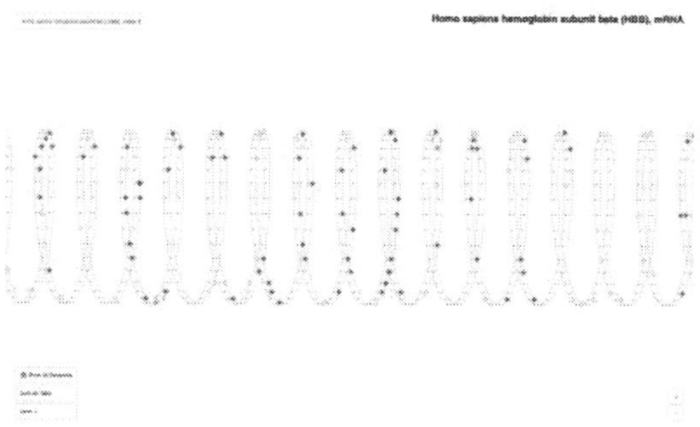

Figure 2. DNA Maps, a new application for browsing DNA-sequence data

3. GOOGLE MAPS FOR DNA SEQUENCES

We have taken the interaction paradigm of Google Maps and considered the tasks that can be completed with it. In Google Maps, one can zoom out to get a global view of a town, while zooming in reviews individual streets and buildings. This mechanism is in correspondence with the focus and zoom paradigm of Shneiderman (Card et al., 1999). We consider this interaction mechanism to be very applicable to DNA sequences. A zoomed out view would show the open reading frames (DNA regions that code for a protein) in a sequence for example, zooming in on can show the user introns and exons, and further zooming would then reveal individual enzyme cutting sites and the nucleotides (Alberts, 2014).

Using Google Maps as a metaphor for DNA sequence visualization might provide a solution to the usability issues that exist in current tools. The tool would namely combine a lot of different data points and we believe that the interaction mechanism could greatly improve the usability of the product by increasing its intuitiveness. DNA is double stranded, but we would like to visualize on the gene level as well. In our prototype both the sense and the antisense are visible. In addition, it even supports mRNA sequences.

In order to create a Google Maps like mechanism, we defined four different zoom levels for ourselves and decided what sort of data points would be displayed in each level:

- Level 1: *The Base/Global overview* (Figure 2 & Figure 3). The Base/Global overview level will enhance the Google Maps metaphor and might lead to new insights in data point patterns.
- Level 2: *The Open Reading Frames* (Figure 4). Open Reading Frames can be hundreds of nucleotides long, and we figured that these are the data points one would come across first when zooming in. That is why we put the Open Reading Frames in the 'second level'.
- Level 3*: Introns/Exons* (in Higher Organisms only) (Figure 5). In an Open Reading Frame, introns and exons can exist. These are thus always smaller than Open Reading Frames, but are still significantly larger than single nucleotides. That is why we decided to make a separate level for these data points.
- Level 4: *Cutting Sites and Individual Nucleotides* (Figure 6). Enzyme cutting sites are five to six nucleotides long and can be displayed on the level where the individual nucleotides are shown.

In general, our main goal for usability is a soft transition of data in the maps-like interaction mechanism. The zoom should feel like it takes you along and should not be like a bumpy ride in the bus. It has been shown that smooth transitions assist in spatial navigation (Rutherford, 2008). Therefore, once this is achieved, the main interaction mechanism will be sufficient.

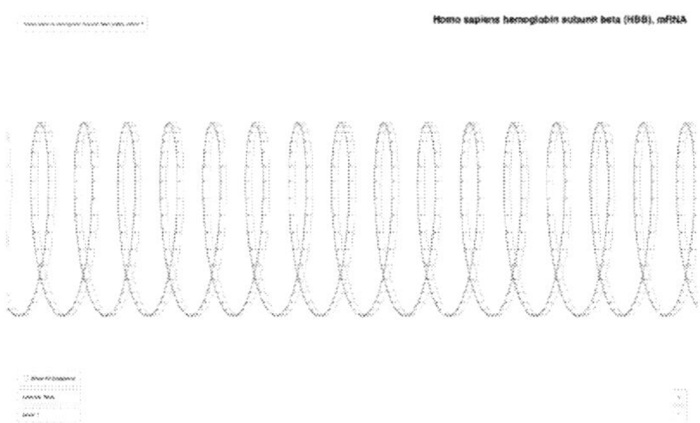

Figure 3. The base level: DNA folded

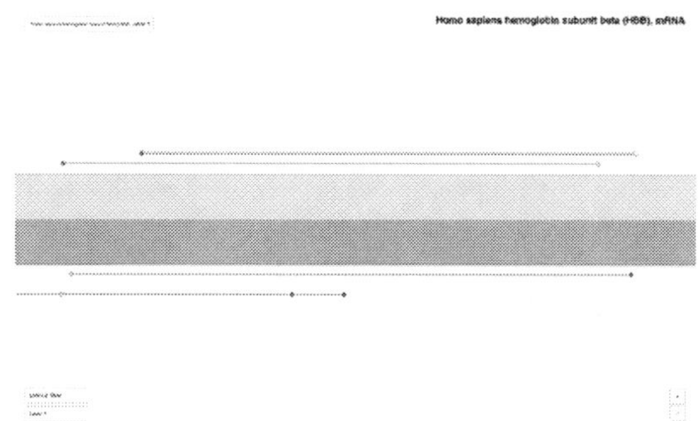

Figure 4. The second level: open reading frame data

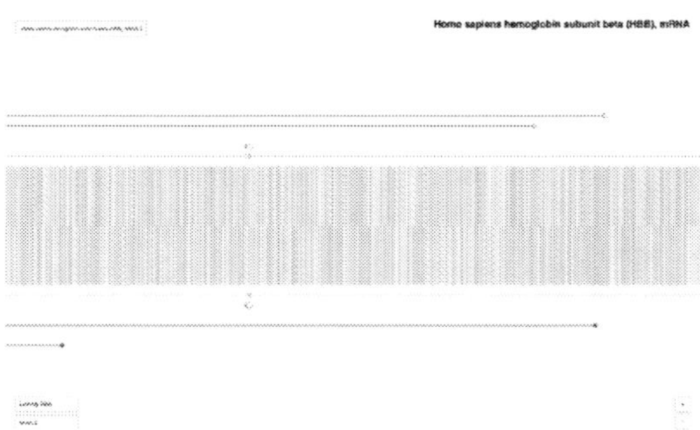

Figure 5. The third level: intron/exon data

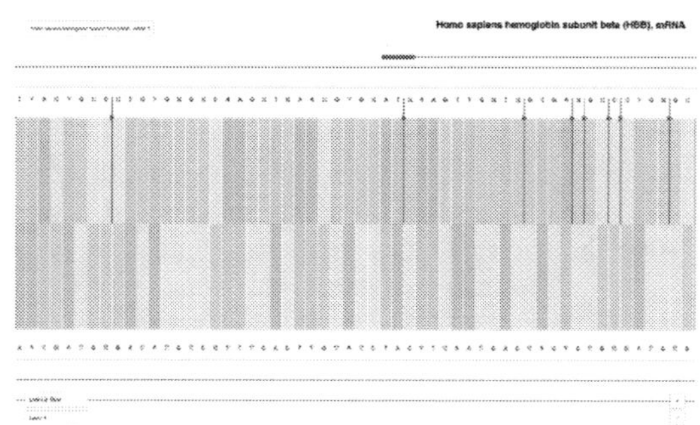

Figure 6. The fourth level: enzyme cut site and nucleotides

4. EVALUATION

4.1 Surveys

In order to evaluate the prototype, we conducted two surveys. In the first survey our questions were mainly aimed at finding out the general satisfaction with current available tools and the interest in using a DNA visualization tool with a "Google Maps"-like interaction mechanism. We also tried to find information about more technical aspects, like: where would our user group want to use such a tool, what minimum number of nucleotides displayed would still be useful and what colors and shapes do they find suitable for different data points. We conducted the first survey on students (undergrad/grad) from Bio-informatics and Biology.

In a second user evaluation our main aim was to find out how usable our application was and thus how well the interaction mechanism of one domain could be transferred to another. We also hoped to learn out how to further enhance the usability of our application. In order to find these results, we made 5 test subjects do several small tasks in the application before we had them fill in a usability survey and a more in depth survey about the application. In this user evaluation participants were both professional and student users.

4.2 Focus Group Presentations

In addition to the survey a focus group presentation session was held with students from bioinformatics and computers science. During this session valuable feedback was received. We were asked if other information like transposons (jumping genes) could be included. It was suggested that such information would not work with the Google Maps mechanism. We think it could work with our prototype, since the prototype works with sequenced DNA strands, meaning that transposons, if there, are at a fixed position for that particular sequence. We have decided to not yet include transposons in our prototype, since this is beyond the scope of the current research as our focus is mainly on the implementation of the interaction mechanism and to find visual cues that are suitable in this mechanism and suitable for the type DNA characteristic it represents. Others asked about the parts of the DNA sequence would be presented as tertiary structures (3D). Our initial design focused on the global level in 2D. However, we eventually settled on a simplified visualization in pseudo-3D for the global level.

5. RESULTS

From the first survey we gained the insight that the students believe that there is improvement to be seen in the current tools. Some of the users mentioned the usefulness of having one global place to find different data types. The majority is interested in using a "Google Maps"-like interaction mechanism for DNA sequence exploration, and half of the group thought that it might be possible to obtain new insights and find new patterns from the proposed tool. Though novice users might not have the best overview of the available tools, the overall consensus is that the proposed product is a valuable addition to the current landscape. We have used the answers from the more technical questions in our prototype.

The professional users who took part in the second survey found that the Google Maps interaction mechanism is well suited to DNA sequence exploration. This test group also believed that visualizing DNA sequence data in this way could lead to new insights. There were however some remarks on the way our prototype was implemented. Some users felt disoriented while navigating through the different levels, it was unclear to some users when a level transitioned into another or/and felt that it would be better if data from previous levels would also be displayed in the current level. The scrolling direction was not intuitive everybody. There was a dependency on operating system regarding the scrolling direction. We have fixed these issues in our 'final' prototype. This evaluation included short discussions with the participants and it became clear that the participants had not encountered an application like this before. They found the base level visualization especially interesting as it brings together multiple data points.

Based on the results of the user evaluation we have made further improvements to the design elements of the prototype, i.e. colors and shapes. In consecutive prototype the inclusion of these design choices showed to work out very well. In order to make sure that data points from previous levels are visible on the current level we made the scrolling direction dependent on the operating system. This contributed to a better orientation of the navigation through the zoom levels. In earlier prototypes disorientation was experienced by some testers.

6. CONCLUSION & DISCUSSION

From our first user evaluation we have gained the insight that, though there is not a lot of dissatisfaction with the current DNA sequence tools, there certainly exists an interest in a DNA exploration tool with a "Google Maps"-like interaction mechanism.

During our second evaluation it became clear that the researchers (and research assistants) did show some dissatisfaction with current tools and were enthusiastic about our visualization. Based on this evaluation and the discussion this interaction mechanism is a good step in providing new mental models about how to look at DNA sequence data. It also became evident that the visual cues were not as intuitive as the visual cues in Google Maps, since our test subjects needed the look-up table to understand them.

With this application we intended to increase the intuitiveness compared to other DNA sequence visualization tools. Some of our test subjects found themselves disoriented in the application since the scrolling direction was not very intuitive on every operating system (on one OS scrolling up was zooming in while on another scrolling up was zooming out). This issue is easily resolved however, namely by swapping the scrolling direction for these operating systems. We conclude that this application is intuitive, though more research is necessary on the mapping of the Google Maps interaction to the DNA sequence visualization. In the original domain the metaphors are well defined which is not the case in the target domain yet. The metaphors are not fully formed in the target domain, but the fact that this approach delivers a new model for this kind of data unambiguously concludes that it is possible and useful to take the interaction mechanism from one domain and apply it to another.

7. FUTURE WORK

7.1 Translating Interaction Mechanisms

To further develop this visualization, more research is needed. For example, more user evaluations, to find out how to translate the interaction mechanism more efficiently and with better integration. Especially the design of visual cues for a specific domain require extra attention find out if it is possible and how to construct new cues and build the metaphors for the target domain.

7.2 DNA Maps

The current prototype offers a design basis the build upon to extend the application for consistent DNA visualization. There are several things that are important for any future research. Including the transposon and find a way to make it fit the mechanism (cf. section 4) and translation options to protein sequences (from nucleotides to codons (translated nucleotide triplets). Our prototype does not have a search function, meaning that currently a *fasta*-file is required to display sequences. In future implementations a search function should be added and linked to the common sequence databases. It might also be interesting to implement a gesture driven interaction so that the tool can be used in a lab environment for example. When gestures are implemented, a 3D visualization could provide a more intuitive visualization than our current 2D approach. To find out whether this would be more usable it would require more user evaluations. At the moment RNA is visualized with both the sense and the antisense. For further work should be done to investigate the possibility to view RNA as a pure single strand. Another thing to consider for future research is the possibility of customization. Within the constraints of accurate visualization of DNA sequence data not every bioinformatician or biology researcher has the same requirements for which data will be represented when and where.

REFERENCES

Alberts, B. et al, 2014. *Molecular Biology of the Cell* (6th Edition). Garland Science, New York, USA.

Card, K., Mackinlay, J., Shneiderman B., (1999) *Readings in Information Visualization: Using Vision to Think*. Academic Press, San Diego, 1999

Norman, D. A., 1988. *The psychology of everyday things* (Vol. 5). Basic books, New York, USA.

Rutherford, P., 2008. *Usability of Navigation Tools in Software for Browsing Genetic Sequences*. Master Thesis at Lincoln University

CHANGEIT: TOWARD AN APP TO HELP CHILDREN WITH AUTISM COPE WITH CHANGES

Vivian Varnava, Aurora Constantin and Cristina Adriana Alexandru
University of Edinburgh, School of Informatics
10 Crichton Street, Edinburgh EH89AB, United Kingdom

ABSTRACT

The use of technology-based interventions for ameliorating Autism Spectrum Disorder (ASD) core deficits has been growing in popularity. However, limited technologies are available that can help children with autism (aged 6 to 11) cope with changes, and these do not typically incorporate the methods used or recommended by practitioners. Our project addresses this gap through the design, development and evaluation of a prototype app to support children with ASD overcome their difficulties with changes. We report on preliminary work in developing this app, in which we decided not to involve children with ASD before getting some evidence that the app may be useful and suitable for them. Therefore, the design at this stage was informed by the research literature and design studies involving typically developing (TD) children, practitioners and researchers. The evaluation studies revealed that: 1) the app is easy to use; 2) the activities are perceived as fun and engaging; 3) the app may be suitable for children with ASD. Future work will extend the evaluation studies to include children with ASD and more practitioners.

KEYWORDS

Autism, Coping with Changes, Assistive Technology, Interface Design

1. INTRODUCTION

Autism Spectrum Disorder (ASD) is a lifelong neurodevelopmental disorder characterized by deficits in social interaction and communication and the appearance of repetitive patterns of behaviour and interests, including resistance to change (APA, 2013). The use of technology-based interventions for ameliorating ASD core deficits has been growing in popularity, and a variety of technologies such as mobile computing, virtual reality or robotics have been introduced to improve social communication skills and support practitioners' work (Grynszpan et. al, 2014, Morin et al. 2018).

Visual Activity Schedules are often used to help children with ASD cope with the challenges posed by various activities or behaviours during an individual task or throughout the day (Dettmer et al. 2000). For children with autism, they promote independence and predictability, and help with transitioning between activities (Banda et al. 2009). Changes may also be introduced into the routine schedule, which is encouraged to alter constantly, so that children can develop adapting skills (Mesibov et al. 2005). *Social Stories™* - first introduced by Gray (2019) - represent short stories describing certain situations, events or activities which are following a set of criteria. They aim to teach children with learning disabilities of certain situations or events, such as getting dressed, and also prepare them for novel events, such as moving house. A series of applications have been developed to support practitioners in creating and children in working with Visual Activity Schedules (Cramer et al., 2011) and Social Stories™ (Constantin, 2015).

However, limited technologies are available that can help children with autism cope with changes, and these do not typically incorporate the methods used or recommended by practitioners. Therefore, this project explores how technology can be best designed to help children with autism cope with changes. We designed and developed an app called *ChangeIt*, which may enhance the work of practitioners in helping children with ASD cope with changes. This paper reports on preliminary work, in which we decided not to involve children with ASD before getting some evidence that the app may be useful and suitable for them. Instead, we involved typically developing (TD) children, as well as practitioners and researchers in ASD and Human-Computer Interaction (HCI) as proxies in the initial design and evaluation of the app. The results of the evaluation were very promising, suggesting that the app has potential in helping children with autism cope with changes. However, more studies for the app design and evaluation, involving children with ASD, are necessary until these results can be considered generalisable.

2. METHODOLOGY

We used a User-Centered Design (UCD) framework, in which users are involved in every stage of the design process (Norman et al., 1986). However, despite children with autism being the end users of our proposed app, involving them in empirical studies can cause distress, and is moreover very time and resource consuming. Instead, we involved TD children, as suggested by other reports (Frauenberger et al., 2012), because they could bring their age-related expertise in the design of technology with good usability for children. Moreover, we involved HCI experts with general experience in usability, and ASD practitioners and experts, who could advise what is appropriate to help children with ASD cope with changes.

The project followed a methodology which is represented in Figure 1 and is detailed in the next sections.

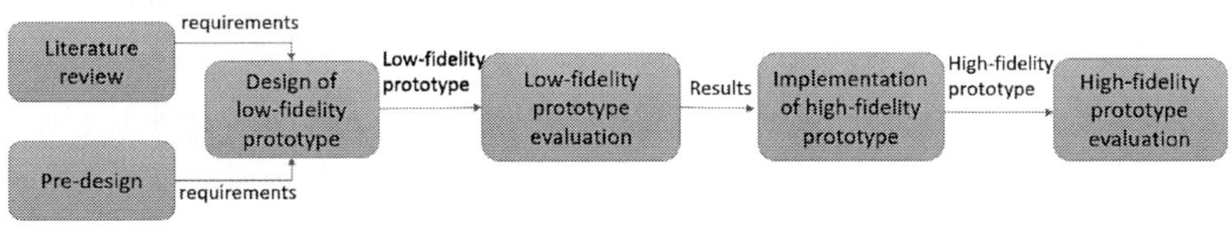

Figure 1. Methodology

2.1 Pre-Design

During the pre-design stage, we conducted one-to-one semi-structured interviews with one ASD practitioner and 2 researchers on HCI/ASD with the aim to gather their practical experience with helping children with ASD deal with changes. This stage also involved a workshop using pens and paper with 2 TD children with the aim of identifying the reaction of children to undesirable changes and their strategies to cope with them.

Based on the literature review and interviews, three main methods for helping children with autism cope with changes were identified: Visual Activity Schedules (Dettmer et al., 2000), Social Stories™ (Gray, 2019) and a list of Coping Strategies. *Coping Strategies* are used to overcome the difficulties after changes occur and were revealed at the pre-design stage. We decided that our app should support all of these methods.

The literature review and pre-design studies resulted in a list of requirements for the user interface design of the app. Nielsen's 10 Usability Heuristics (Nielsen, 1994) and autism-specific guidelines for user interface design (Bartoli et al, 2014; Pavlov, 2014) helped add requirements to ensure that the app has good usability- both in general and for autistic users. For example, one of the autism-specific guidelines recommends the use of visual cues to improve reading comprehension, and a simple design with contrast between background and font, few and clear elements on screen, and simple graphics (Pavlov, 2014).

Overall, the most important requirements were that the app should:

1. Have two distinct interfaces: one of practitioners and one of children.
2. Allow practitioners to create/edit/delete Social Stories™, Schedules and Coping Strategies.
3. Allow children to view the Social Stories™, Schedules and Coping Strategies which had been created by practitioners.
4. Provide simple templates for filling information by practitioners.
5. Provide examples of Social Stories™, Schedules and Coping Strategies to the practitioner.
6. Include a fictional character, a pet. Using stories with anthropomorphic animals and fantasy can enhance learning, as also suggested by Weisberg et al. (2015).

2.2 Low-Fidelity Prototype Design and Evaluation

Using the list of requirements, we designed a low-fidelity prototype using the Figma design tool (Figma, 2019). TD children and experts on HCI/ASD were invited to individually evaluate the low-fidelity prototype. We used task-based Evaluation and Cooperative Evaluation (Dix et al., 2004), respectively, followed by a post-task semi-structured interview (for TD children) or online questionnaire (for HCI/ASD experts). The aim was to gather feedback on the app's usability and its suitability for the target population and for helping children with ASD cope with changes. The qualitative data gathered from the studies was analysed using Thematic Analysis (Braun & Clarke, 2006), following a top-down approach. In terms of usability, results helped identify some issues such as misleading elements of the design and inconsistencies. For example, there was some inconsistency between buttons and the appropriate message after adding/deleting actions. Also, some suggestions for more functionalities were collected (e.g. a reward system to encourage children on ASD to use the app). In terms of suitability, all the experts agreed that the prototype is suitable for autistic children and may help them cope with changes. The app was perceived as easy to use both by children with ASD and practitioners. The evaluation results helped refine the requirements and prototype.

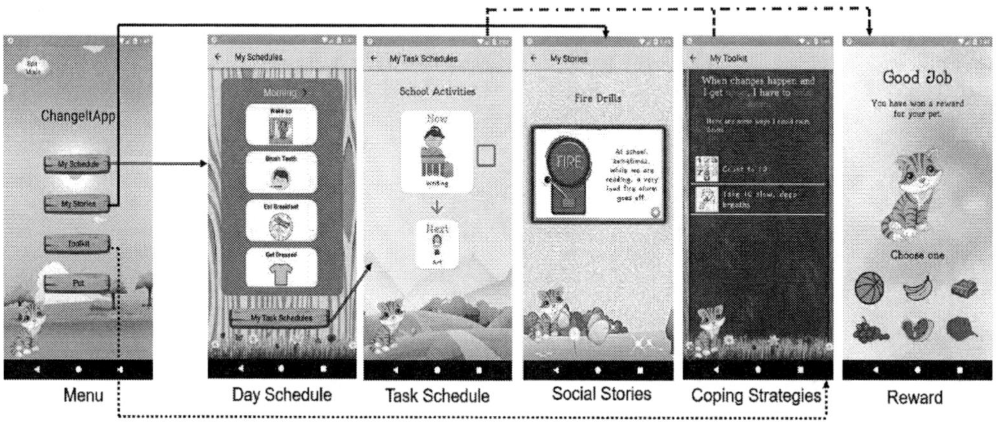

Figure 2. The child interface to the ChangeIt app

2.3 High-fidelity Prototype Implementation

A high-fidelity prototype was developed using Android Studio (2019). The child interface opens with the 'Menu' screen which contains three buttons which, when clicked, take the child to either the 'Day Schedule' screen (with the schedule of the day), 'My Stories' (where stories about changes can be read) or the 'Coping Strategy' screen (see Figure 2). In each section, after completing a series of tasks, the child is presented with the 'Rewards Screen' in which they can choose a reward for their pet.

Clicking on the 'Edit mode' button from the Menu Screen leads to the practitioner interface (Figure 3). To create a new task schedule, the practitioner has to add tasks, and to create a new Social Story™, the practitioner has to add pages. Icons are provided in each screen to add (plus icon), save (floppy disk icon), delete (trash icon) elements. An element can be edited by clicking on it.

2.4 Evaluation

In the evaluation stage for the high-fidelity prototype, we first conducted a **study with students and staff from the University of Edinburgh**, with the aim of assessing the app's general usability**.** We first asked university students and staff to freely interact with the app and fill in a small online questionnaire consisting of a combination of Likert scale questions and optional open-ended questions. The data was analysed using Descriptive Statistics and Thematic Analysis (Braun & Clarke, 2006). The majority of the participants agreed that the app is easy to use and suitable for the target population. The app was rated overall as 'Very Good' (4/5) or 'Excellent' (5/5). A participant mentioned that ChangeIt is a brilliant idea and she suggested that it should be tested further and released to the market.

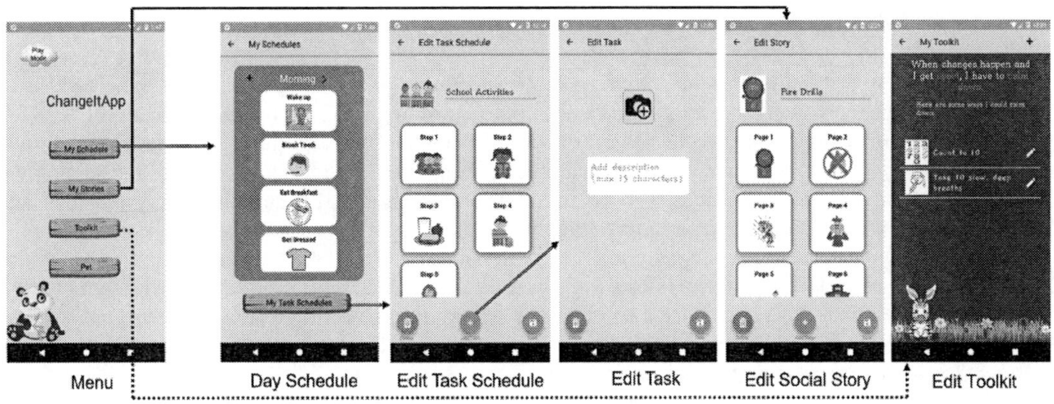

Figure 3. The practitioner interface to the ChangeIt app

We then conducted a **study with 5 TD children** (3/5 having also participated to the low-fidelity prototype evaluation), with the aim of assessing the ChangeIt app's suitability, whether the app's activities are fun and enjoyable, and the children's perceptions of its usability. The study consisted of a combination of task-based Evaluation and free exploration followed by a post-task semi-structured interview, and involved children individually or in pairs. The qualitative data was analysed using Thematic Analysis (Braun & Clarke, 2006). All of the children found the ChangeIt app very easy to use and its activities fun. The majority (4/5) of the children rated the app as 'Excellent' and for the majority (3/4) the favourite functionality was the reward system. One of the children commented liking that the pet was present in every interface.

Finally, we conducted a **study with 6 experts on HCI/ASD**, with the aim of assessing the app's suitability and the experts' perceptions of its usability. The study consisted of a combination of Cooperative Evaluation (Dix et al. 2004) followed by a small questionnaire. The data was analysed using Thematic Analysis (Braun & Clarke, 2006) and Descriptive Statistics. All the experts found the ChangeIt app easy to use and suitable for the target population. A practitioner remarked: *"I think it is really easy to use....but I think there are some little things that can be added and enhance the usability of the app, overall. But I don't think it is difficult at all, it's not.*". They found the methods used in the app effective in helping children with autism cope with changes. However, 3 out of the 6 experts expressed some doubts with regards to the appropriateness of Coping Strategies. One of them remarked: *"When they are upset, the children will not really go and look at something to calm them down"*. On the other hand, another expert mentioned: *"I think you have to train them to go and grab this toolkit. I think this is a great way for them, to remind them what they could do if they get upset"*. This was a controversial issue but it was agreed that the specific section needs more functionality.

The most important suggestions that were identified after analysing the data of the studies were:

- Adding more interaction with the pet and a high-level reward system to increase motivation (5/5 children, 3/6 experts).
- Adding interaction when clicking on the Coping strategies (5/6 experts). One expert explained: *"It ['Coping strategies' page] doesn't say much. So maybe if you could click and say a bit more...Maybe you need to include some audio, maybe an option is to listen to a song he likes or pictures or videos of their favourite cartoons."* Also one of the children stated: *"Honestly, I think of what I want and that is what calms me down...I want a cat so I might think about a cat or me getting a cat...One of the things could be a picture of a cat down here (as a coping strategy)"*.
- Making the app more customizable by allowing practitioners to upload images of pets (2/5 children, 2/6 experts), videos or music (3/6 experts), choose interactions for the pet as rewards (1 child, 1 expert), choose the colour scheme (1/6 experts), as well as provide text-to-speech functionality (1/6 experts). One of the experts remarked: *"I think if the child has a pet, they can put their own picture or something like that. I think given more customization it's always a good thing."*
- Extending the day schedule to a calendar one, to prepare children for changes in advance (1/6 experts).

3. CONCLUSION

This paper presented a preliminary investigation of how technology can be best designed to help children with ASD cope with changes, which resulted in the development of an Android app called ChangeIt. The app was designed and evaluated by involving HCI/ASD experts, practitioners, TD children and general users, following the UCD framework. The results from its evaluation suggested that ChangeIt has potential for helping children with autism cope with changes, it is easy to use, fun and engaging. Furthermore, they led to a series of suggestions that will be considered for improving the app for children with ASD and practitioners.

Nevertheless, any conclusions should be taken with caution. Although the participation of TD children in the development of technology for children with disabilities is useful and important (Grynszpan et. al, 2014), involving children with ASD and a larger sample size would give clearer outcomes. For our next step, we plan to recruit children with ASD, as well as more ASD practitioners, from schools and organisations for children with ASD from across Edinburgh, United Kingdom.

REFERENCES

American Psychiatric Association (APA). 2013. Diagnostic and statistical manual of mental disorders (DSM-5®). American Psychiatric Pub.

Android Studio, 2019 – last update, Android Studio. [System Software]. Available: https://developer.android.com/studio/, [2019, 1st May]

Banda, D.R., Grimmett, E. and Hart, S.L. 2009. Activity schedules: Helping students with autism spectrum disorders in general education classrooms manage transition issues. Teaching Exceptional Children, 41(4):16-21.

Bartoli, L., Garzotto, F., Gelsomini, M., Oliveto, L. and Valoriani, M. 2014, June. Designing and evaluating touchless playful interaction for ASD children. In Proceedings of the Interaction design and children 2014: 17-26, ACM.

Braun, V. and Clarke, V. 2006. Using thematic analysis in psychology. Qualitative research in psychology, 3(2): 77-101.

Carol Gray, Social Stories™, 2019 – last update, Carol Gray, Social Stories™ [Online]. Available: https://carolgraysocialstories.com/social-stories/what-is-it/, [2019, 1st May]

Constantin, A. 2015. Supporting practitioners in social story interventions: the ISISS Authoring Tool.

Cramer, M., Hirano, S.H., Tentori, M., Yeganyan, M.T. and Hayes, G.R. 2011, May. Classroom-based assistive technology: collective use of interactive visual schedules by students with autism. In CHI, 11:1-10.

Dettmer, S., Simpson, R.L., Myles, B.S. and Ganz, J.B. 2000. The use of visual supports to facilitate transitions of students with autism. Focus on Autism and Other Developmental Disabilities, 15(3):163-169.

Dix, A., Finlay, J., Abowd, G. and Beale, R. 2004. Evaluation techniques. Human-computer interaction.

Figma. 2019 – last update, Figma: the collaborative interface design tool. [Online]. Available: https://www.figma.com/, [2019, 1st May]

Frauenberger, C., Good, J. & Alcorn, A. 2012, June. Challenges, opportunities and future perspectives in including children with disabilities in the design of interactive technology. In Proceedings of the 11th International Conference on Interaction Design and Children, 367-370, ACM.

Grynszpan, O., Weiss, P.L., Perez-Diaz, F. & Gal, E. 2014. Innovative technology-based interventions for autism spectrum disorders: a meta-analysis. Autism, 18(4):346-361.

Mesibov, G.B., Shea, V. & Schopler, E. 2005. The TEACCH approach to autism spectrum disorders. Springer Science & Business Media.

Morin, K. L., Ganz, J. B., Gregori, E. V., Foster, M. J., Gerow, S. L., Genç-Tosun, D., & Hong, E. R. 2018. A systematic quality review of high-tech AAC interventions as an evidence-based practice. *AAC*, *34*(2):104-117.

Nielsen, J. 1994, June. Heuristic evaluation. In Usability inspection methods, 25-62, John Wiley & Sons, Inc.

Norman, D.A. & Draper, S.W. 1986. User centered system design: New perspectives on HCI. CRC Press.

Pavlov, N. 2014. User interface for people with ASD. Journal of Software Engineering and Applications, 7(02):128.

Weisberg, D.S., Ilgaz, H., Hirsh-Pasek, K., Golinkoff, R., Nicolopoulou, A. & Dickinson, D.K. 2015. Shovels and swords: How realistic and fantastical themes affect children's word learning. Cognitive Development, 35:1-14.

A PROCEDURE FOR AUTOMATIC ADAPTATION TO THE USER IN INTELLIGENT VIRTUAL AGENTS

Mattias Wahde
Department of Mechanics and Maritime Sciences, Chalmers University of Technology
412 96 Göteborg, Sweden

ABSTRACT

This paper describes procedures for improving the functionality of task-oriented intelligent virtual agents (IVAs) and carrying out adaptation to the user in such agents. The functionality improvement is based on automatic extension of input patterns (rules), using a database of interchangeable phrases. This extension results in greater flexibility both regarding the user's input and the agent's output. The adaptation to the user relies on a complexity measure, allowing the agent to assess the level of complexity of the user's input and thus to adapt the complexity level of its response. For the case of a simple travel information agent, the pattern extension procedure resulted in an increase in the number of available patterns of around a factor 20, greatly enhancing the agent's capacity of adapting its output to the user.

KEYWORDS

Task-Oriented Agents, Intelligent Virtual Agents, User Adaptation

1. INTRODUCTION

Intelligent virtual agents (IVAs) are systems that allow a human user to interact with a computer in a natural way, for example using speech and gestures, and receiving speech output in return, often along with an animated three-dimensional on-screen avatar. Such systems are becoming increasingly important in many different application fields including, but not limited to, customer service, automatic booking systems for restaurants, transportation etc., health care and elderly care, travel information systems, and so on (see e.g. Laranjo et al, 2018; Chen and Cheng, 2010). However, an important aspect of such systems which is sometimes overlooked is their ability to adapt their (spoken) output to the user. At a first glance, this might seem like a minor point, but the manner in which a person is addressed, whether by an agent or a human, does in fact have a large impact on the person's perception of the interaction: Some users may prefer an agent that gives very brief, factual answers, whereas others may prefer more verbose and affective speech. Moreover, the suitable manner of speech may also depend on the user's age. That is, if two users are, say, 8 and 88 years old, respectively, an IVA should ideally be able to address them in different ways, focusing on simplicity when interacting with the 8-year old and clarity when interacting with the 88-year old user.

Broadly speaking, IVAs can be divided into two main categories, task-oriented agents and chatbots (Jurafsky and Martin, 2018), where the former are intended to interact with users on a specific task (such as, for example, a reservation request), giving accurate, reliable, and relevant information to the user, whereas chatbots are focused on maintaining a discussion over a large range of topics, but in a more vague and non-committal manner. A currently popular approach to IVAs is to build end-to-end systems using neural networks and deep learning (see e.g. Wen et al, 2016). However, due to their black-box nature, such systems are very difficult to analyze and to modify in a controlled fashion, for example in order to achieve user adaptation as described above. On the other hand, IVAs with more traditional approaches often rely on the identification and interpretation of dialogue acts that classify a speaker's intent into a finite set of classes (Stolcke et al, 2000), and is used when parsing the user's input and determining the appropriate response. While there has been a considerable amount of work on automatic recognition of dialogue acts, the accuracy of that process is around 77% at best (Mezza et al, 2018) over a large benchmark corpus (the Switchboard dialogue act corpus, SWDA), even though higher accuracy has been achieved on smaller data sets or using fewer classes than the 42 used by Stolcke et al (2000). In addition to the limited recognition accuracy for dialogue acts, it is also not clear how to achieve controlled adaptation to the user in an IVA based on dialogue acts.

A simpler approach is to use a set of specific input patterns or rules (typically hand-crafted) for matching user input, coupled with a set of output patterns for generating the agent's output. Such approaches were used in many early IVAs but have fallen out of fashion, in favor of IVAs based on the two approaches described above. Indeed, it is hard to specify input patterns in a sufficiently general way to handle the great variability in possible user inputs (i.e. the many ways in which a given query can be phrased). However, starting from a rather small set of hand-crafted rules, a procedure (introduced in this paper) can be devised for *automatically* extending the set of allowed inputs, as well as the set of possible outputs, using dictionary information. Applying this procedure, one can thus obtain an IVA that can both handle input and output variability *and* dynamically adapt its speech complexity to that of the user, with the help of a complexity measure for the user input, also defined below. The purpose of this short paper is twofold, namely (1) to introduce a procedure for extending a limited set of hand-crafted rules to a more complete set (see Section 3.1) and (2) to describe a method for adapting an agent's output to the user's input (see Section 3.2), in both cases using the framework of the DAISY dialogue manager, which will now be described briefly.

2. THE DAISY DIALOGUE MANAGER

In this work, a dialogue manager (DM) for task-oriented agents known as DAISY (an abbreviation of *Dialogue Architecture for Intelligent Systems*) has been used. DAISY operates in three stages: First, the system processes the user's input (either speech or text). DAISY allows several methods for input processing (including, for example, the use of dialogue act recognition). However, for the purpose of this study, and motivated by the considerations in the previous section, a rule-based approach has been used, where the user's input is matched to a set of input patterns (exemplified below). Next, if the user's input matches any of the allowed input patterns, cognitive processing takes place, in the form of a sequence of elementary actions that make use of data in the agent's long-term memory (LTM), working memory (WM), or both. Finally, the agent formulates the output using patterns of a similar kind. A typical user-agent interaction thus consists of a triplet I-C-O, where I represents the input processing, C the cognitive processing, and O the presentation of the agent's output.

Note that the patterns need not be rigid, neither for input nor for output: They can (and often do) involve so called query tags for the variable parts of the user's input. As a simple example, a travel information agent may have an input pattern (one among many) of the form "*When is the next bus to <Q1>?*" where the contents of <Q1> would be compared to a set of bus stops, providing a match if the name of the bus stop is available in the agent's database. In DAISY, patterns can be condensed, allowing several options to be represented in a compact fashion. For example, the condensed pattern "*[Can, Would] you [help, assist] me, please?*" is a short-hand representation of four specific patterns ("*Can you help me, please?*", "*Would you help me, please?*" etc.).

An agent based on DAISY also maintains information about the context of conversation and can thus, for example, interrupt an ongoing dialogue, answer an unrelated question, and then return to the original dialogue. Furthermore, DAISY features *inference* from context, allowing an agent to respond to questions that require knowledge of the current (or previous) context of conversation. A full description of DAISY will not be given in this short paper; see instead Wahde (2019).

3. ADAPTATION TO THE USER

The procedure for the agent's adaptation to the user takes place in two stages. First, there is an offline stage in which the patterns (both for user input and agent output) are extended to maximize the capability of the agent to understand the user's input and give it opportunity for user adaptation, something that requires that the agent should be able to formulate its output, in a given situation, in several different ways. Second, during interaction with the user, the agent measures the complexity of the user's input, and attempts to adapt its output accordingly.

3.1 Pattern Extension

For this stage, it is assumed that a developer has first generated a rather small set of hand-crafted input patterns, which will act as a starting point. Typically, with the authoring tool that has been implemented for DAISY, such a specification can be completed quite rapidly. For the next stage, i.e. extending the set of input patterns to handle the great variability in user input, the original intention was to use a synonym dictionary on a word-by-word basis. However, even though it is easy to take into account word classes (for example, distinguishing the verb "present" as in "present a paper" from the same noun, meaning "gift"), many words have, of course, several meanings within the same word class, thus making it difficult to automatically extend patterns using synonyms (Ferret, 2010). Thus, the automatic pattern extension procedure was instead implemented on the level of synonymous *phrases* that typically consist of more than one word.

In order to achieve maximum accuracy, crucial for a task-oriented agent, the procedure is based on a new pre-defined database of interchangeable (i.e. synonymous) phrases[1], rather than making use of a corpus-based automatic approach as was done by Manishina et al (2016) and Pavlick et al (2015). Moreover, the dictionary features *dynamic phrases*, i.e. phrases containing unspecified words. For example, the phrase "*the next <Q> departs*" is synonymous with "*the next* <Q> *leaves*", regardless of whether <Q> represents (for example) "train", "flight", "bus", or "tram". Such constructs provide higher accuracy than just (in this example) replacing the word "*departs*" by "*leaves*", without considering the context.

The construction of the phrase synonym database involves a considerable effort, but on the other hand it can be done once and for all. In order to make sure that the phrases are relevant for human-agent dialogue, a pre-processing method can be applied by which the words in the phrases are checked against a large corpus of spoken dialogue, retaining only phrases containing words that appear frequently in speech. A simple example of a pattern extension is as follows: Starting from the original pattern "*When would you like to go?*", and using phrase substitutions such as "*when would you => at what time would you*", "*like to go => wish to go*" etc., an extended pattern was generated that, in condensed form (see also Section 2 above), takes the shape "*[When, At what time] [would, do] you [like, wish, want, prefer] to [go, depart, travel]?*".

3.2 Complexity Matching

In order to adapt to the user's way of speaking, the agent must somehow measure, or at least estimate, the level of complexity of the user's speech. A coarse-grained option for doing so would be to equip the agent with a camera, allowing it to assess the approximate age of the user. While possible as a *complement* to the approach described below, camera-based user age estimation would only provide partial information, at best. Thus, a more reliable approach would be to infer the level of complexity of the user's input.

Several measures of speech complexity (or quite often the reverse, i.e. speech simplicity) exist, one of the most well-known, and thoroughly validated, being the Flesch-Kincaid (F-K) readability measure (Kincaid et al, 1975). However, this measure is primarily intended for analyzing a body of text spanning many sentences, and can give inaccurate or at least counter-intuitive results when applied to single sentences. Moreover, the F-K measure is not designed specifically for use with *spoken* input, where sentences are often very short, sometimes just a single word. Thus, while the F-K measure is indeed implemented as an alternative in DAISY, here a much simpler complexity measure has been used, namely the number of syllables in the user's input. One could also have used the number of words, but this measure was deemed too primitive and coarse-grained (keeping in mind, again, that the user's input often consists of only a few words). With the chosen syllable-based measure, a better estimate is obtained. For example, compare the two semantically equivalent user-input sentences (in response to a statement by the agent regarding, say, a museum): (I) "*Can you show an image of it?*" (8 syllables), and (II) "*Can you please display a visual representation of the museum?*" (19 syllables). Even though the second sentence is perhaps a bit too contrived to be a likely user input, it illustrates the complexity measure quite well, when contrasted with the first sentence.

The complexity matching procedure operates as follows: For a given user input, the agent registers the level of complexity (denoted c) using the measure just described. Next, if a matching pattern is found, the agent computes its relative complexity, by first sorting the complexity values for *all* versions of the matching

---

[1] The database is available at http://www.me.chalmers.se/~mwahde/DoIP/doipDescription.html

pattern (expanding the condensed pattern as illustrated in Section 2) in ascending order, and then computing the rank of the user input.

For example, if a condensed pattern can be expanded to 48 different specific patterns (which is the case for the condensed pattern shown at the end of Subsection 3.1), and the *actual* user input would be ranked (for example) as the 39th, the relative complexity r is computed as $r = 39/48 = 0.8125$. This relative measure is used instead of the absolute complexity value c, since there is no reason to believe that the agent's selection of possible outputs would cover the same complexity range as the inputs. Instead, when responding to the user (after processing the input), the agent would repeat the procedure, ranking the complexity values of the possible *output* patterns, and selecting (for output) the pattern whose relative complexity is closest to that of the user input. Continuing the example, if the condensed output pattern (not shown here) allows for 16 different specific patterns, ranked in ascending order of complexity, the output would in this example be chosen as the pattern with index 16 x 0.8125 = 13. Of course, if the index thus computed is not an integer, the index should be set as the nearest integer.

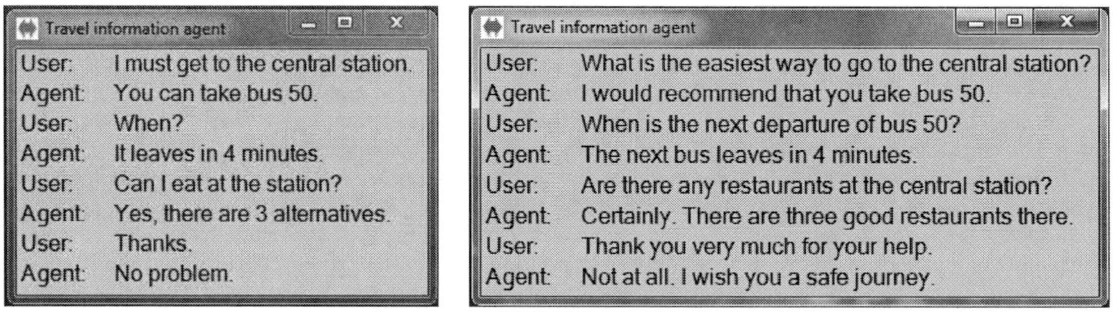

Figure 1. Left panel: A dialogue between an agent and a user who is in a hurry, and therefore expresses requests in a very brief manner. Right panel: A dialogue between *the same* agent and a more verbose and relaxed user. As can be seen in the dialogues, the agent adapts its output to the user's input in both cases, using the procedure described in Subsection 3.2

4. PRELIMINARY RESULTS AND DISCUSSION

The methods for pattern extension and complexity matching described above have been implemented and are currently undergoing testing. In order to test the pattern extension method, a travel information agent was implemented with the capability of giving information of the kind exemplified in Figure 1. The phrase synonym dictionary is not yet complete (i.e. covering phrases useful in *any* topic). Instead, in its current form, it contains a set of basic phrases that are relevant in any context and a set of phrases specifically relevant for a travel information system of the kind exemplified in the figure.

For the sample dialogue in Figure 1, the hand-crafted agent (i.e. the starting point) contained a total of 7 input patterns and 7 output patterns, distributed over the various user-agent interactions defined in the dialogue. Next, the pattern extension procedure was applied, resulting in a total of 118 input patterns and 165 output patterns, representing a combined increase by a factor of 20.2. The magnitude of the increase in the number of patterns depends on several factors, but the numbers just given provide an indication of the typical magnitude. Moreover, in this agent, rather than rigidly selecting the output pattern index as described in Section 3.2 above, a modification was implemented such that the output pattern is selected from a range of indices centered on the computed index, to allow also greater *variability* in the agent's output, which is an important factor to consider in task-oriented agents.

The initial results regarding adaptation to the user, which are qualitative in nature, show that the agent does indeed generate output that matches the level of complexity of the user's input rather well. These initial tests will be followed by a more rigorous examination, where a large group of users will be exposed to agents either with or without user adaptation, and will then give (subjective, but detailed) feedback on the user experience for the two cases. Another rather natural observation is the fact that the complexity matching works well only if the agent has a large set of specific patterns (both for input and for output) to choose from, thus making the first step (pattern extension) a crucial component of the system.

5. CONCLUSION

A procedure for automatic extension of patterns (rules) for intelligent virtual agents has been introduced, allowing greater variability in the user's input and also making it possible for an agent to adapt the complexity level of its output to that of the user, provided that a database of synonymous phrases is available. Such a database is currently under construction. Once it has been completed, it should prove useful in many different task-oriented agents. A specific method for adaptation to the user's style of speech in task-oriented agents has also been introduced and briefly described. Preliminary results, for the case of a simple travel information agent, indicate that the pattern extension method leads to a large increase in the set of patterns, and that the method for adaptation to the user achieves the intended objective of automatic matching to the user's style of speech.

REFERENCES

Chen, B. and Cheng, H. H., 2010. A review of the applications of agent technology in traffic and transportation systems, *IEEE Transactions on Intelligent Transportation Systems,* Vol. 11, No. 2, pp. 485-497.

Ferret, O., 2010. Testing semantic similarity measures for extracting synonyms from a corpus. *Proceedings of the Seventh International Conference on Language Resources and Evaluation (LREC'10),* Malta, pp. 3338-3343.

Jurafsky, D and Martin, J.H. 2018. *Speech and Language Processing* (3rd ed.), Prentice-Hall, New Jersey.

Kincaid, J.P. et al 1975. Derivation of new readability formulas (automated readability index, fog count, and Flesch reading ease formula) for Navy enlisted personnel. *Research Branch Report 8–75. Chief of Naval Technical Training.*

Laranjo, L. et al 2018. Conversational agents in healthcare: A systematic review. *Journal of the Americal Medical Informatics Association,* Vol. 2, No. 9, pp. 1248-1258.

Manishina, E. et al 2016. Automatic corpus extension for data-driven natural language generation. *Proceedings of the Tenth International Conference on Language Resources and Evaluation (LREC'16),* Paris, France, pp. 3624-3631.

Mezza, S. et al 2018. ISO-standard domain-independent dialogue act tagging for conversational agents. *Proceedings of the 27th International Conference on Computational Linguistics,* Santa Fe, NM, USA, pp. 3539-3551

Pavlick, E. et al 2015, PPDB 2.0: Better paraphrase ranking, fine-grained entailment relations, word embeddings, and style classification. *Proceedings of the 53rd Annual Meeting of the Association for Computational Linguistics and the 7th International Joint Conference on Natural Language Processing,* Beijing, China, Vol. 2, pp. 425-430

Stolcke A. et al 2000 Dialogue act modeling for automatic tagging and recognition of conversational speech. *Computational Linguistics*, Vol. 26, No. 3, pp. 339-373

Wahde, M. 2019. A dialogue manager for task-oriented agents based on dialogue building-blocks and generic cognitive processing. *Proceedings of the 9th Workshop on Applications of Software Agents* (in press)

Wen, T.-H. et al 2016. A network-based end-to-end trainable task-oriented dialogue system. *arXiv preprint arXiv: 1604.04562.*

GESTURAL LOCOMOTION IN 360° VIRTUAL TOUR OF COIMBRA

Mariana Santos, Solange Santos, Carolina Cerqueira, Maria Pedroso, Inês Lopes and Luís Duarte
Department of Informatics Engineering, University of Coimbra
P-3030-790 Coimbra, Portugal

ABSTRACT

The locomotion between 360° images in virtual reality environments can be challenging due to the limited types of possible movements. In this work we created a virtual tour of the city of Coimbra to study the locomotion between 360° images through the usage of gestures. To accomplish this, we resorted to the usage of the Myo armband which can read up to 5 pre-defined gestures. These gestures allow the navigation between images, such as go to the previous location, to the next location or look at a map and select a location to go to. It is also possible to trigger other types of actions that do not involve locomotion such as, for example, open pop-ups containing information. We ran usability tests to evaluate the experience of this virtual visit, which allowed us to conclude that the majority of the participants believed they were in a virtual environment but felt some vision related discomfort. Not only that, but users thought that the gestures used to trigger the features of the application were natural and intuitive.

KEYWORDS

Virtual Reality, 360° Images, Locomotion, Myo Armband, Gesture Control

1. INTRODUCTION

Virtual Reality (VR) is a concept that was defined by Ivan Sutherland, in 1965, by presenting *The Ultimate Display*. The VR experience consists of placing the user in a world generated by a computer. Through this unique experience, you participate by interacting with virtual objects that can simulate the physical world, which are not limited by the same constraints, such as laws of physics and time. To improve the interaction within a virtual environment the contact with the virtual world must be as natural as possible, unlike what happens with conventional hardware. With the introduction of gesture identifying devices, the user can select and manipulate objects in an intuitive fashion. The tools used for the execution of our software were a VR headset alongside a Myo armband. The Myo armband is a bracelet capable of detecting the user's movement and up to 5 pre-defined gestures, allowing interaction without the need of touch. Our solution was to develop an application that allows its user to virtually visit Coimbra's emblematic locations. Through the usage of VR headsets, the user can view every detail of the 360° images of the selected locations, while also being able to interact with them through the usage of the Myo armband.

2. RELATED WORKS

In virtual reality environments, locomotion and interaction have been the subject of many studies, and as such, are regularly evaluated in order to verify potential solutions.

One of these solutions is the use of the Myo armband, which, since its launch, has roused a great interest in this field. Below, we describe some works that benefited from using Myo in VR.

McCullough et al proposed a navigation technique to explore virtual environments, by detecting the movement of the arm using Myo, this movement is then translated as a walk through the virtual space. This is a good method, however, it is not applicable in the context of our work because it implies locomotion in a 3D VR environment built in such a way that allows free movement through the space, while our objective is to navigate between various 360° images.

Bonome et al. also explored the use of Myo in VR, however, focused on its ability as an interaction and feedback tool as opposed to its locomotive use. They tested the usability of Myo in the selection and manipulation of 3D objects in a virtual environment and used the armbands vibrations as a feedback system. They concluded that the use of the Myo with this purpose in mind could enrich the user experience, making it more realistic, by using the measure of the force applied to a gesture and using Myo vibrations as a feedback system. This study shows interesting results relative to the usability of the armband to interact with objects, however it does not address the question of locomotion, which is our main focus.

When it comes to locomotion between 360º images in VR, some works approach solutions that do not utilize Myo.

Bozgeyikli et al. describe the technique “Point Teleport” and compare it to other more common usages - walking in place and joystick. With this technique the users simply point to where they want to go in the virtual world and then are teleported to said point. Their analysis of this technique showed that it is a user friendly form of locomotion that does not induce nausea caused by the movement unlike other techniques they compared. This a solution comparable to our solution of locomotion through Myo.

Another study by Pai et al. proposes the “GazeSphere” which provides a smooth transition between locations in a 360º video environment, through the usage of the movement in orbit, considering the head rotation and eye gaze tracking. This approach has several advantages, such as the usage of the human's natural sense of rotation used for locomotion that makes the actions intuitive and the use of eye tracking allows locomotion without the use of any extra device and in a more discreet manner.

Considering all these references, we gained knowledge of various forms of benefitting from Myo in VR environments and also other solutions that do not utilize Myo, but allow the locomotion between 360º images which are comparable to our approach. We also learned that our work is distinguishable from others due to the use of the Myo armband, specifically for the locomotion between 360º images in VR which requires jumping from one point to the other and, therefore, is a different approach from the others.

3. METHODOLOGY

Our system contains multiple high quality 360º pictures of the most well-known places located in the city of Coimbra which can be viewed by the user in a virtual environment in order to have a better idea of how Coimbra truly looks like compared to simple 2D pictures. The system also enables a natural navigation between the images of each location by using a map as a menu for navigation, as well as navigation with hand gestures. These methods were selected so as to not distract the user from the purpose of the system which is to view the most famous locations of the city of Coimbra.

The development of the application was not a simple and immediate software implementation process. It was divided by tasks, which we present below:

3.1 Creation of Personas and Scenarios

With the intention of minimizing the amount of complex alterations needed in the more advanced development phase, we started by creating personas and realistic scenarios involving the usage of the application, with the intention of focusing on our target audience in the context of the usages of the application. It was created a persona who was a potential tourist who goes to a travel agency to plan a trip to Coimbra, Portugal. It is in the travel agency that the application and the necessary equipment for its use are available and where the potential tourist uses the developed application.

3.2 Tasks and Cognitive Walkthrough

After we defined where the application will be accessible, the necessary accessories and who we are designing it for, the next step was designing the application itself, keeping the necessary functions and execution of said functions in mind.

In order to facilitate the development of the application, a task list was created that would always be accessible and would allow the team to confirm which features the application should have in order to meet the projected tasks. The cognitive walkthrough allowed the group to predict how to carry out interactions between future users and the application, along with the ability to foresee possible interaction issues in the future.

3.3 Development of a Prototype

Having the application's features and interactions with the system specified, we started developing a system prototype. This prototype allowed us to verify the feasibility of the features we had planned to implement in the system and to discover usability issues that would later be resolved. The following is a brief description of the application's components that were used to develop the prototype:

3.3.1 A-Frame

Our application uses web pages built using the A-Frame framework. They are 360° web pages with interactions triggered by the users focus (where they are looking), making use of the 3D object positioning provided the A-Frame. The user can trigger an informative pop-up of the location, of the map and of a specific point at which they are looking at.

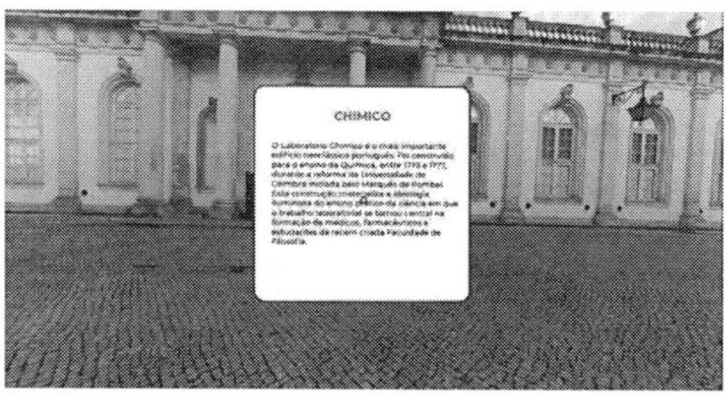

Figure 1. Pop-up with information of the location

Figure 2. Map with points of interest

3.3.2 MYO Armband

In our application, actions are triggered even when not wearing the VR headset. With a higher quality level of interaction and a better immersion experience inside the virtual environment in mind, we resorted to the Myo armband. Between the 5 pre-defined gestures, we picked 4 of them. Each of the 4 recognized gestures (fist, wave left, wave right and spread fingers) was associated with an action, which the system recognizes as a keyboard or mouse input. The fist gesture corresponds to a click in a location of the map (in which the focus of the VR headset and the direction the user is looking at function as a mouse pointer). The wave left gesture allows the user to return to the previous image (the location previous to the one they are in). The wave right gesture allows the user to continue to the next image (the next location). Finally, the spread fingers gesture first allows the user to open a pop-up with information on the location and, if that pop-up is already visible, allows the user to close it.

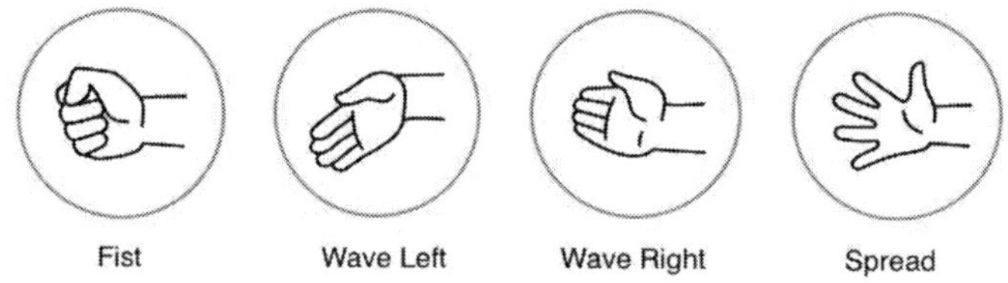

Figure 3. Myo Armband gestures used in the application

3.4 Performing Usability Tests

The prototype was then subjected to usability tests, which allowed us to reach conclusions regarding the experience of virtual reality, the ease of interaction, the possible side-effects and the limitations of the technology used in order to ensure the efficient use of the system. Ten participants took part in the test and in the end they had to answer two questionnaires adapted to our project: the Simulator Sickness Questionnaire and the Slater-Usoh-Steed Questionnaire. The tested users started off by receiving a tutorial on how to use Myo armband and what gestures corresponded to what features. After the tutorial, the user had the opportunity to explore the application a little more freely. Sometimes the person giving the tutorial asked the users to perform certain actions so the evaluators could take notes of how the user proceeded, if he remembered what he learned in the tutorial and whether the navigation through the environment was intuitive. Finally, the user answered the two usability questionnaires.

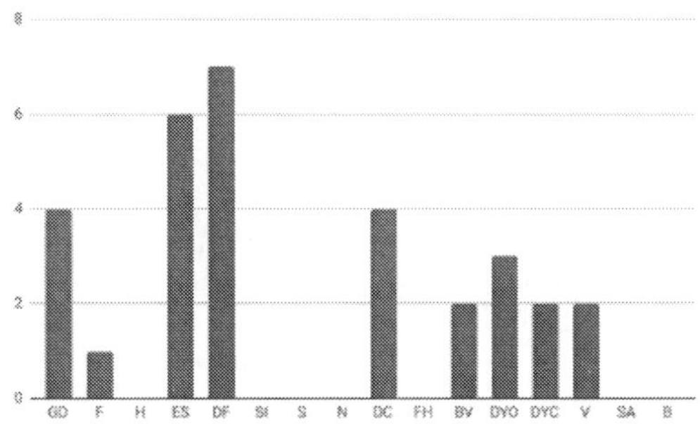

Figure 4. Simulator Sickness Questionnaire

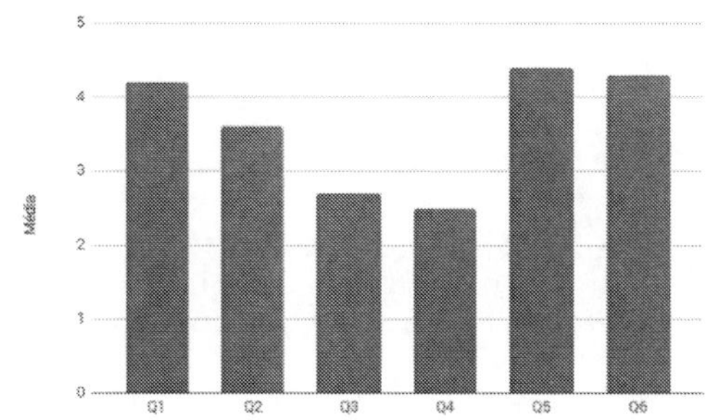

Figure 5. Slatrer-Usoh-Steed Questionnaire

The first questionnaire's objective is to determine whether the tester felt any type of physical discomfort or other symptoms during the usages of the software, like Headache (H), Salivation increasing (SI), Sweating (S), Nausea (N), Fullness of the head (FH), Stomach awareness (SA), Burping (B), Eye strain (ES), Difficulty focusing (DF), General discomfort (GD), Fatigue (F), Difficulty concentrating (DC), Blurred vision (BV), Dizziness with eyes open (DYO), Dizziness with eyes closed (DYC) and Vertigo (V).

The second questionnaire evaluates how immersive the VR environment is, the efficiency of the gesture execution and if the selected gestures are intuitive enough for the average user. The following questions were the ones in the questionnaire:

- Q1: Evaluate the virtual reality experience.
- Q2: During the experiment, how much did you believe to be in a virtual environment?
- Q3: When you recall the experience, do the memories remind you of just images, or a sense of having actually visited the sites?
- Q4: During the experiment, did you feel as if you were in a virtual environment or another kind of reality?
- Q5: During the experiment you used Myo to perform certain actions. Assess how intuitive the interactions were.
- Q6: Actions performed through Myo are triggered by gestures performed. Assess how effective (in the sense of being intentional) were the gestures you made.

4. CONCLUSION

After finishing the tests, it was clear that not all participants adapted well to using the Myo and the device would often not detect the gesture that they were performing, or it detected a different gesture. Furthermore, some gestures were less intuitive than others.

Some participants reported that the transition time between images was long and that it broke the immersion of the 360º environment.

Finally, we noticed that after the tutorial, when the users were allowed to use the program freely, they felt lost, since they knew that wave right led them to the next location and wave left returned them to the previous location, but after selecting a location in the map many users expected that wave left would bring them to the location they were previously in instead of the previous one in the route defined by the program, that is, the wave gestures were predefined, a fact that was not obvious to the users. A possible solution to mitigate this problem would be to color code in the map, the next and previous locations in the predefined route starting from the location that the user is in, so that they do not get lost navigating through the application.

The development of this application has allowed us to not only study the planning and development of the software, but also to analyze technologies that we had never had access to before to develop content, namely the Myo armband and the HTC Vive VR headset.

In general, despite the problems we identified, we believe that approaching locomotion in a virtual reality setting with the Myo armband vastly enriches the experience of the user. The interaction between the 360° images through gestures using the armband doesn't break the immersion and allows the user to control their surroundings, using hardware that does not require extensive time to learn how to use.

REFERENCES

Bonome, Y., Mondéjar, A., Oliveira, R., Albuquerque, E. and Raposo, A., 2018. Design and assessment of two handling interaction techniques for 3D virtual objects using the Myo armband. *Virtual, Augmented and Mixed Reality: Interaction, Navigation, Visualization, Embodiment, and Simulation*. Las Vegas, NV, USA, pp. 30-42.

Bozgeyikli, E., Raij, A., Katkoori, S. and Dubey, R., 2016. Point & Teleport Locomotion Technique for Virtual Reality. *Proceedings of the 2016 Annual Symposium on Computer-Human Interaction in Play*. Austin, Texas, USA, pp. 205- 216.

McCullough, M., Xu, H., Michelson, J., Jackoski, M., Pease, W., Cobb, W., Kalescky, W., Ladd, J. and Williams, B., 2015. Myo arm: swinging to explore a VE. *Proceedings of the ACM SIGGRAPH Symposium on Applied Perception*. Tübingen, Germany, pp. 107-113.

Pai, Y., Outram, B., Tag, B., Isogai, M., Ochi, D. and Kunze, K., 2017. GazeSphere: Navigating 360-Degree-Video Environments in VR Using Head Rotation and Eye Gaze. *ACM SIGGRAPH 2017 Posters*. Los Angeles, California, USA.

Sutherland, I., 1965. The Ultimate Display. *Proceedings of IFIP Congress*. pp. 506-508.

NATURAL USER INTERFACE-BASED CAR INFOTAINMENT CONTROL SYSTEM

Yang-Keun Ahn and Young-Choong Park
Korea Electronics Technology Institute
121-835, 8th Floor, #1599, Sangam-Dong, Mapo-Gu, Seoul
Republic of Korea

ABSTRACT

This article proposes a natural user interface (NUI) system for the control of infotainment content in a smart car that recognizes a user's emotions and gaze with a 2D camera, an eye camera. The configuration of the system used to recognize a user's emotions and gaze is introduced. The methods for recognizing a user's emotions and gaze are described. An experiment was performed to evaluate the performance of emotions and gaze recognition, and to demonstrate the user performance of the system proposed in this article.

KEYWORDS

Smart Car, Natural User Interface, Face Recognition, Eye Tracking

1. INTRODUCTION

Smart cars (autonomous vehicles) have recently attracted attention as products in the era of the Fourth Industrial Revolution. When the smart car is completely realized, the environment in automobiles will be changed from a driver-centered focus to a passenger-centered one. As a result, smart cars will become a new space for consuming infotainment content. Various methods of handling infotainment content in smart cars have been suggested, and one of them is the natural user interface (NUI) technology.

The NUI technology has previously been applied as a controller for multiple functions. For example, the 'Golf R Touch' system by Volkswagen is used to control the audio volume, sun roof, and windows of vehicles through the recognition of user gestures. Panasonic employs a system that can measure the number of eye blinks of a driver, extract the facial state, recognize the driver's drowsiness, and control the indoor space accordingly.

This article proposes a NUI-based system that allows infotainment contents to be managed in a smart car through the recognition of emotions and gaze.

2. SYSTEM

The system proposed in the present study has the configuration shown in [Figure 1], and includes two user interfaces (UI).

The face UI for recognizing a user's emotions includes a 2D camera that receives images of a user's face. The 2D camera used in this study was a Logitech 920C Webcam, which was separated from a user by a distance of less than 60 cm. The front face images were extracted to determine the emotions.

The gaze UI includes a Tobii Eye Tracker 4C, a gaze tracking camera for the tracking the user's gaze, is installed at the lower end of the monitor pointing toward the eyes of a user who is looking at the monitor.

[Figure 2] shows a demonstration of the emotion recognition feature. The user at a distance of about 60 cm from the 2D camera has made a surprised facial expression. Among different emotions the surprise emotion was recognized at the highest rate of 80%.

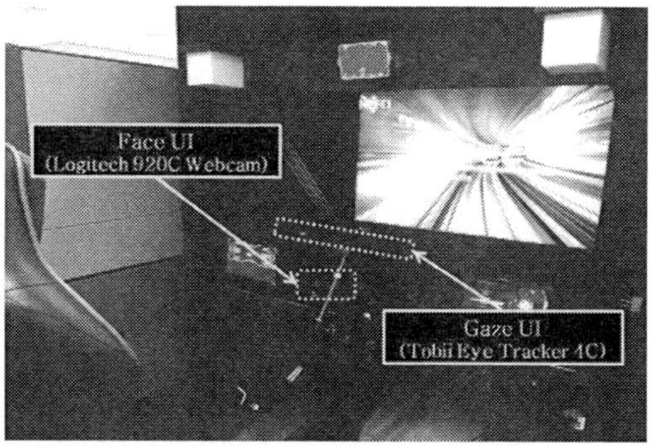

Figure 1. System configuration

Figure 2. Demonstration of emotion recognition

3. EMOTION RECOGNITION

The 2D camera (Logitech 920C Webcam) is located at a position about 60 cm away from a user so that the front face of the user is shown on the screen. The face is detected from the video input from the 2D camera. After detecting the face, 68 feature points are extracted from the face outline and the area around the eyes, eyebrows, nose, and mouth. The user's emotion is recognized by using the extracted feature points. Seven kinds of emotions may be recognized: Neutral, Happiness, Surprise, Fear, Sadness, Anger, and Disgust. The seven emotions are evaluated by a numerical value ranging from 0 to 100, and a higher value means that the facial expression is closer to the corresponding emotion.

The emotion recognition software recognizes a user's face. After the face is detected, the user may enter a number from 1 to 9 to connect an ID to the user's face. Later, if the user's face with a predetermined ID is detected, the face ID number is shown on the screen through template matching.

The actions using the facial information, including face detection, feature point extraction, emotion recognition, and face ID recognition, were performed using the functions provided by Verilook SDK (Neurotechnology). [Figure 3] shows the overall flowchart of the emotion recognition software.

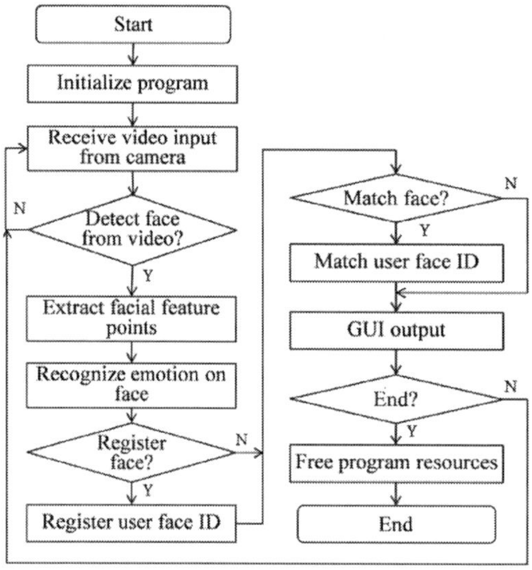

Figure 3. Flowchart of emotion recognition software

[Figure 4] shows the screen in which a user's surprise emotion was recognized. The image on the left shows the user information and the image on the right shows the face information output displayed on the video received from the 2D image. The face information is of a 28-year old man whose ID was not registered. Among the seven emotions, the recognition values were 95 for surprise, 53 for disgust, and 16 for sadness. The size of the circle in the left image is determined by the numerical values of each emotion. The circle was the largest for the surprise emotion with the highest numerical value.

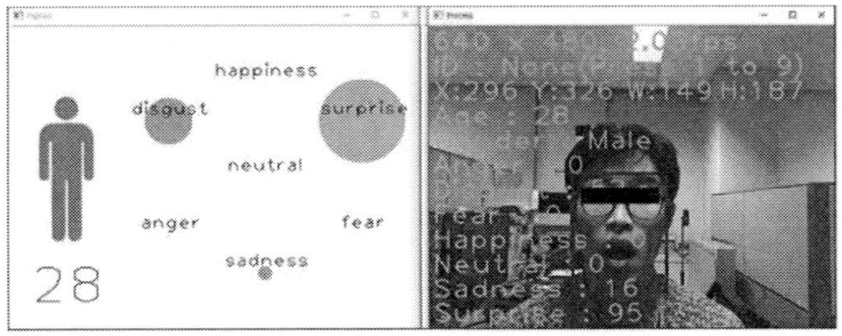

Figure 4. Emotion recognition

4. GAZE RECOGNITION

Gaze recognition is performed using Tobii Eye Trakcer 4C, a gaze tracking camera. The position coordinates of the user gaze were obtained by using the function provided by Tobii Eye Tracking Core Software v2.10.0.

The gaze tracking camera was installed at the lower part of the monitor pointing toward the user's eyes. The gaze tracking camera tracks the user's eyes by using the pupil center corneal reflection (PCCR) technology. After the camera is connected, a reflection is produced by a user illuminated with a near-infrared ray, and the camera detects the reflection pattern on the cornea and the pupil. Then, a vector is calculated based on the angle between the cornea and the pupil reflection, and the gaze direction is calculated by combining the vector direction and other geometrical features of the reflection. After that, the point of intersection between the extension line of the user's gaze and the plane of the screen is calculated to obtain the user's gaze coordinates and to output the gaze coordinate information. [Figure 5] shows the overall flowchart of the gaze recognition software.

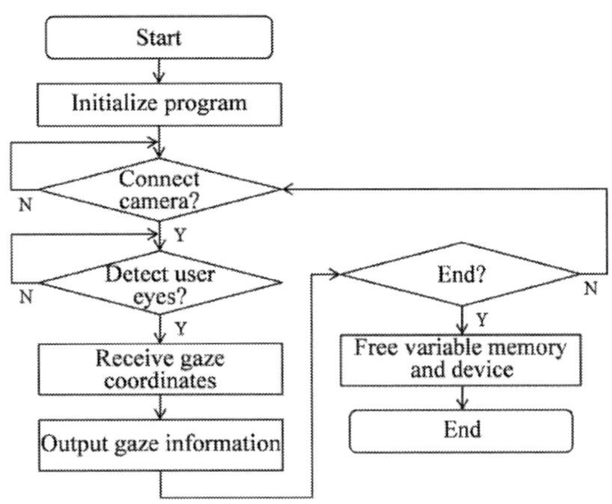

Figure 5. Flowchart of the gaze recognition software

Before using the gaze recognition function, the gaze tracking camera is adjusted to each user by using the calibration function provided by the Tobii Eye Tracker 4C software. The gaze coordinates values are adjusted to the screen resolution, where the x-coordinate ranges from 0 to 1919 and the y-coordinate ranges from 0 to 1079. When a user's gaze is outside the screen it is specifically processed so that the coordinate values do not exceed the range of the screen resolution.

When the calibration was normally performed for a user, the error of the gaze coordinates was about 1.5 cm with reference to the screen size (53×30 cm).

[Figure 6] shows the screen representing the user gaze recognition results. The user's gaze was directed toward the center of the screen, and the x-coordinate and the y-coordinate of the gaze were 304 and 217, respectively. The point corresponding to the gaze coordinates represents the user's gaze.

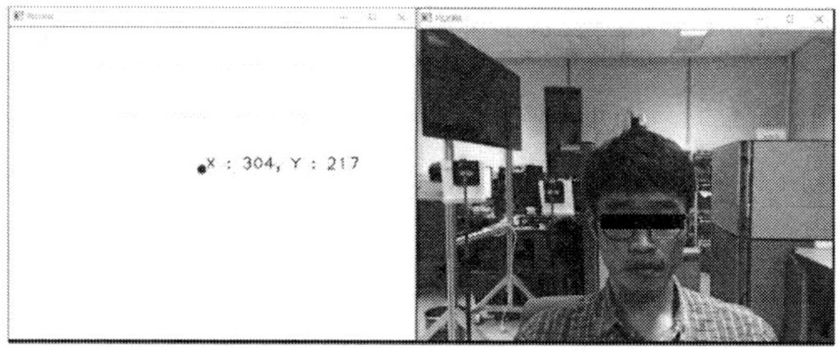

Figure 6. Gaze recognition

5. EXPERIMENTAL RESULTS

The performance of the system was tested by connecting the 2D camera and gaze tracking camera to a PC (Intel(R) Core(TM) i7-3770K 3.5 GHz and 8 Gbytes memory).

The emotion and gaze recognition rates were tested to show the performance of the system proposed in this study. Each experiment was performed with five users. The distance between the system and the user was about 60 cm. The 2D camera was installed to view the front face of a user, and the gaze tracking camera was installed at the lower end of the monitor.

The experiment for testing emotion recognition was performed while the five users made the facial expressions for three emotions, of Happiness, Sadness, and Disgust, among the seven kinds of emotions, a hundred times for each emotion. The average of the number of times when the emotion was rightly recognized was calculated. Among the emotions showing a numerical value over 50, if the emotion recognized with the highest numerical value was the same as the user's facial expression, the recognition was considered to be the right recognition.

The emotion recognition experiment showed that the average emotion recognition rate was about 80.13% [Table 1].

Table 1. Emotion recognition rate

User	Emotion (No. of times)			Average (%)
	Happiness	Sadness	Disgust	
1	76	86	82	81.33
2	93	77	73	81.00
3	85	72	76	77.67
4	68	83	93	81.33
5	74	89	75	79.33
-	-	-	-	80.13

Table 2. Gaze recognition rate

User	Gaze (No. of times)				Average (%)
	Quadrant 1	Quadrant 2	Quadrant 3	Quadrant 4	
1	83	88	93	92	89.00
2	86	96	95	93	92.50
3	94	92	91	88	91.25
4	85	84	87	89	86.25
5	93	87	89	97	91.50
-	-	-	-	-	90.10

The gaze was recognized by quartering the screen and letting five users gaze at the centers of the Quadrants 1, 2, 3, and 4, a hundred times for each quadrant. The number of times when the user's gaze point was rightly included in the corresponding quadrant was averaged. The allowed error was about 1.5 cm from the centers of the quadrants in the screen (53×30 cm). The average gaze recognition rate found in the experiment was about 90.1% [Table 2].

6. CONCLUSION

The present article proposes a NUI technology-based method of handling infotainment content in a smart car by recognizing a user's emotion and gaze with cameras. This article introduces the system configuration to use the proposed system, and describes the overall flowchart of the software programs for the emotion and gaze recognition UIs, as well as the recognition results. The proposed system does not require a controller with direct contact, such as a mouse and keyboard, but is handled by a user's natural facial expressions and gaze as inputs, and as a result the system may provide convenient and new user experiences.

ACKNOWLEDGEMENT

This research was supported by Korea Creative Content Agency. (Project No. R2017030009, The development of infotainment contents and interaction for vehicle).

REFERENCES

Dongmin Shin. et al, 2017. Development of emotion recognition interface using complex EEG/ECG bio-signal for interactive contents. *Multimedia Tools and Applications*. Vol. 76, No. 9, pp 11449-11470.

Fernández. et al, 2016. Natural user interfaces for human-drone multi-modal interaction. *2016 International Conference on Unmanned Aircraft Systems (ICUAS).* Arlington, VA, USA, pp. 838-848.

Sujin Kwak. et al, 2015. Empirical Environment for Smart Car Technologies and Smart Car Talk. *Proceeding of Korea Society of Management Information Systems.* Republic of Korea, pp. 729-738.

Yejin Shin. et al, 2016. Patent Analysis for Innovative Technology Development of Advanced Driver Assistance Systems (ADAS). *Journal of Information Technology and Architecture.* Vol. 13, No. 1, pp 147-160.

TRUST IN SYNTHETIC TRAINING ENVIRONMENTS: APPLICATIONS FOR MILITARY SOLDIERS

Michael Boyce[1], Ericka Rovira[2], Joshua Rea[2], Payton Rengel[2], John Emezie[2], Christian Ackerman[2] and Camilla Knott[3]

[1]*Simulation and Training Technology Center – West Point Field Element, West Point, NY, USA*
[2]*U.S. Military Academy, West Point, NY, USA*
[3]*TiER1 Performance Solutions, Washington, DC, USA*

ABSTRACT

Familiarity with simulations and game-based environments, including the use of technologies like Augmented Reality (AR) and Virtual Reality in which these games are played, may make young Soldiers more willing to use training approaches that leverage the use of gaming technologies. The goal is to introduce sophisticated training technologies and to use technological developments to tailor training to Soldier needs. AR/VR technologies have been identified as a low-cost solution to enhance training. However, little is known about the impact of AR/VR technology system reliability as well as how best to use VR for training. Decades of human automation interaction research suggests that technology reliability impacts trust in the system which then impacts SA and task performance. An understanding of how trust in VR interplays with performance outcomes is critical for enhancing Soldier performance with VR technology. Concurrently, individual differences will impact responses to new technologies and should therefore be accounted for in the introduction of new forms of technology and training. Thus there is a need to understand (1) the impact of trust in VR-based training on training objectives, e.g., situational awareness (SA) or performance, given challenges with reliability of the technology, and (2) how to optimize the use of VR given individual differences in trust in technology. Thirty-six participants volunteered and participated in a single factor three level within subjects design tactical mission simulation. Results indicate less trust with Microsoft HaloLens technology as compared to a tablet or ARES table.

KEYWORDS

Augmented Reality, Virtual Reality, Training, Military, Usability, Trust, Individual Differences

1. INTRODUCTION

1.1 Synthetic Training Environment

All soldiers are expected to perform to a designated level of performance to achieve an accepted standard. This is often represented by creating training environments that mimic military operation conditions, also known as "training as you fight" (ADRP 7.0). This extends to the military classroom where performing exercises aimed at specific learning objectives and realistic training scenarios can enhance learning experiences for situated learning. The Synthetic Training Environment (STE) has been identified as one of the key priorities in the U.S. Army Modernization strategy. The STE refers to having a collective training capability to conduct complex, diverse and multi-domain battles at the point of need. The STE will leverage technologies like artificial intelligence (AI), machine learning (ML), and augmented reality to reduce the cost of executing collective training events. Developed products from the STE will have a strong emphasis on augmented reality technology, such as the Microsoft HoloLens ®. Hence it is important to establish how the technical capabilities and weaknesses of these technologies impact usability, soldier technology acceptance, and trust.

1.2 Trust and Automation

There is a vast literature on how humans interact with automation. Traditional automation is static, in contrast synthetic training environments are designed to learn and adapt based on the knowledge of the user as well as display vast amounts of information that would support the operator in decision-making.

The literature has demonstrated that the reliability of automation impacts human trust and reliance in automation (Parasuraman & Riley, 1997; PSW, 2000; Wickens & Xu, 2002; Parasuraman, Sheridan, & Wickens, 2008). And further suggests that with highly reliable, but imperfect automation, there is a differential cost associated with automation that supports operator decision making versus perceptual processes (Rovira, McGarry, & Parasuraman, 2007). It is unknown if this finding would apply to a synthetic training environment or more specifically to STE in the context of a military task.

Existing literature has conclusively shown the explanatory power of trust (Lee & See, 2004; Hoff & Bashir, 2015) in human automation interaction. According to Lee & See (2004) model of appropriateness of trust and automation, the key elements to develop trust consist of information simulation, trust evolution, intention formation and reliance action. To provide appropriate calibration, mixed reality devices will need to understand the soldiers trust in the system and its own limitations in terms of the current environment.

1.3 Human Partner Characteristics

The human factors literature suggests that the human element is a critical factor when designing technology. However, there has yet to be a thorough exploration of the factors that impact successful AR/VR in training. Given that the goal of STE is to act flexibly and adaptively i.e. more human like, human partner characteristics are likely to be helpful in understanding trust and performance with STE.

A small yet growing body of literature has explored cognitive individual differences with automation (perceived attentional control: Chen & Terrence, 2009; working memory: de Visser et al., 2010; Rovira et al., 2016; genetics: Parasuraman et al., 2012). STE are designed in some instances are similar to the highest types of automation, hence understanding the role of trust in performance with STE is imperative.

1.4 Research Questions

This research focuses on AR/VR technology, individual differences, and multimodal interaction with different combinations of technology to assess trust, usability, workload and performance while conducting a simulated attack. The primary research questions guiding this line of research include:

1. Does trust in VR-based synthetic training systems impact performance on training objectives, e.g., situational awareness (SA) or performance?
2. Do individual differences predict trust in AR/VR equipment?

2. METHOD

2.1 Participants

Thirty-seven cadets from the U.S. Military Academy volunteered and received extra credit in introductory psychology courses for their participation.

2.2 Equipment

2.2.1 ARES

The Ares Sandtable is an advanced battlespace visualization framework; a traditional sand table, filled with play sand, augmented with a commercial, off the shelf (COTS) projector, LCD monitor, laptop, and Microsoft Kinect and Xbox Controllers. Ares was developed internally at ARL, and has been used in previous experiments (Boyce, Reyes, Cruz, Amburn, Goldberg, Moss, & Sottilare, 2016; Boyce, Rowan, Amburn, Shorter, Moss, Goldberg, & Sottilare, 2018). The sandtable can be used in conjunction with the HoloLens peripherals to provide multi-modal visualization of the terrain, urban structures, and assess above/below the terrain.

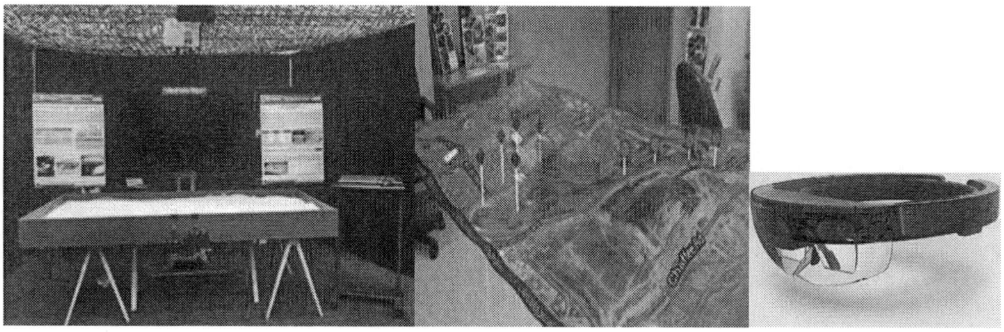

Figure 1.

2.2.2 Microsoft HoloLens

The Microsoft HoloLens is an AR HMD that creates images through a projection system with holographic high-definition in full color with low latency in real time. The headset can capture photos, record video and allow users to navigate with air tap gestures With the Microsoft HoloLens in ARES users can see urban structures, artillery visualization, and other elements above the terrain.

2.3 Materials, Tests, Tasks, and Stimuli

Individual differences in attitudes (trust) towards technology will be assessed with Automation Induced Complacency Potential – Revised Scale (AICP-R). The AICP-R assesses propensity to trust technology. It is a ten item scale using a five point likert rating. The scale was administered at the start of the experiment. The following scales are used in between each condition. The System Usability Scale (SUS) uses a Likert scale format consisting of 10 questions that range with five responses from "strongly agree" to "strongly disagree". The SUS can be utilized as a tool to cover system usability, support and training. Analysis across ten years of research indicated that the SUS demonstrated strong reliability for measuring usability of a system, Cronbach's $\alpha = .91$ (Bangor et al., 2009). The technique captures examples of extreme expressions on a spectrum. For example, the individual might be asked to respond to statements such as "I thought the system was easy to navigate" or "I can't imagine myself using something like this". The Lee and Moray Trust Scale is a multi-item scale that examines the operators trust in automated systems specifically process control of an experimental task. A subjective 10 point rating scale measures participants' perception of the trustworthiness and reliability of the technology.

2.4 Experimental Design

A single factor three level within subjects design was employed. The first condition is using the ARES tablet tactical planner by itself, the second is to use the tablet tactical planner in conjunction with the ARES table, and the third is to use the tactical planner app in conjunction with the Microsoft HoloLens.

2.5 Procedure

Participants first completed the AICP-R scale. Participants then observed a map of a company attack and answered two types of questions. One type of question was what they observe in front of them at the given time. For example these questions consisted of asking "What phase line did the company just cross?" or "Where is the enemy location?" The second set of questions test what the participant anticipated would happen next according to the display in front of them. For example these questions consisted of asking "What is the enemies' most likely course of action?" or "Where should you place the FO?"After each condition, the participants were given a series of surveys: the SUS, the NASA-TLX, the SEQ, TAM, and trust questions modeled after Lee & Moray (1994). Performance time was measured via stopwatch. Accuracy was measured by percentage correct of the scenario- based questions.

3. RESULTS

All dependent variables were checked for outliers and one extreme outlier was removed. This left a total of 36 data points. Testing for normality was accomplished via histograms and assessing the shapiro-wilk test since the sample was less than 50. Although the Shapiro-Wilk showed violations of normality for two of the dependent variables, (Time on Task Sandtable, and Accuracy Tablet) inspection of both the histogram plots and QQ plots, along with the robustness of the ANOVA to withstand violations of normality it was decided to continue with the analysis.

A repeated-measures analysis of variance (RM ANOVA) was conducted to assess the effect of technology on Time on Task, Accuracy, Workload according to the NASA TLX, System Usability according to the System Usability Scale, and Automation Aid Trust using the four question Lee & Moray Questionnaire. Upon running an RM ANOVA, there is a need to check Mauchly's test for Sphericity. Only one of the dependent variables (SUS) violated sphericity (p = .023), but upon checking the corrections, all the corrections demonstrated significance ($p < .001$).

Analysis were completed by looking at within-subject Helmert Contrasts. The reason for this is that due to our population (West Point Cadets) familiarity with both flat maps as they are shown in the classroom, the fact that every cadet has a tablet, and our primary research interest of understanding how the additional technology (hololens / sandtable) would impact our outcome variables. Below is a table of those contrasts that were significant at the .05 threshold.

Table 1. Contrasts

Tests of Within-Subjects Contrasts				
Source			F	Sig.
condition	Time_On_Task	Tablet vs. Later	25.328	0.000*
		Sandtable vs. HoloLens	4.739	0.036*
	SUS	Tablet vs. Later	14.826	0.000*
		Sandtable vs. HoloLens	16.126	0.0008
	Lee_Moray_Q2	Tablet vs. Later	0.003	0.954
		Sandtable vs. HoloLens	4.831	0.035*
	Lee_Moray_Q4	Tablet vs. Later	0.986	0.328
		Sandtable vs. HoloLens	7.029	0.012*

3.1 Time on Task

Planned contrasts indicated a significant difference in the predicted direction for both Tablet versus the experimental conditions $F(1,35) = 25.328$, $p < .001$. Further, there is also a significant difference between the two experimental conditions in the predicted direction Sandtable vs. Hololens, $F(1,35) = 4.739$, $p < .04$. Taking the means and standard deviations of the three conditions and comparing them:

Tablet (M = 78.44, SD = 16.34) and Sandtable (M = 89.00, SD = 22.91), Cohen's d=.53 (medium)
Tablet (M = 78.44, SD = 16.34) and Hololens (M = 96.84, SD = 21.85), Cohen's d = .95 (large)
Sandtable (M = 89.00, SD = 22.91) and Hololens (M = 96.84, SD = 21.85), Cohen's d = .35 (small)

3.2 System Usability Scale

Planned contrasts indicated a significant difference in the predicted direction for both Tablet versus the experimental conditions $F(1,35) = 14.826$, $p < .001$. Further, there is also a significant difference between the two experimental conditions in the predicted direction Sandtable vs. Hololens, $F(1,35) = 16.126$, $p < .001$. Taking the means and standard deviations of the three conditions and comparing them:

Tablet (M = 75.90, SD = 11.68) and Sandtable (M = 74.16, SD = 12.56), Cohen's d=.14 (below small)
Tablet (M = 75.90, SD = 11.68) and Hololens (M = 61.95, SD = 15.63), Cohen's d = 1.01 (large)
Sandtable (M = 74.16, SD = 12.56) and Hololens (M = 61.95, SD = 15.63), Cohen's d = .86 (large)

3.3 Lee & Moray Question 2: To what extent did you rely on the automation aid in this scenario?

Planned contrasts indicated a significant difference between the two experimental conditions in the predicted direction Sandtable vs. Hololens, $F(1,35) = 4.831$, $p < .04$. Taking the means and standard deviations of the conditions and comparing them:

Sandtable (M = 7.97, SD =1.40) and Hololens (M = 7.39, SD = 1.38), Cohen's d = .41 (small)

Follow on analysis looking at the correlation between the alleviating workload factor of the AICP and reliance on the automated aid indicate a significant moderate positive correlation $r(34) = .50$, $p < .01$. Therefore participants who answered that they relied more on the automation also rated more highly that they use automation to relieve workload.

3.4 Lee & Moray Question 4: To what extent do you think the automation aid improved your performance in this scenario compared to performance without the automation?

Planned contrasts indicated a significant difference between the two experimental conditions in the predicted direction Sandtable vs. Hololens, $F(1,35) = 7.029$, $p < .02$. Taking the means and standard deviations of the conditions and comparing them:

Sandtable ($M = 7.47$, $SD = 1.46$) and Hololens ($M = 6.53$, $SD = 2.12$), Cohen's $d = .52$ (medium)

4. CONCLUSION

Our data suggests that as compared to other technologies the HoloLens results in less trust and worse performance as measured by time on task. This is a first in a series of studies scheduled to investigate trust in AR/VR technology.

REFERENCES

Bangor, A., Kortum, P., Miller, J. (2009). Determining what individual SUS scores mean: adding an adjective rating scale. *Journal of Usability Studies, 4:* 114-123

Boyce, M.W., Reyes, R. J., Cruz, D. E., Amburn, C. R., Goldberg, B., Moss, J. D., & Sottilare, R. A. 2016. Effect of Topography on Learning Military Tactics - Integration of Generalized Intelligent Framework for Tutoring (GIFT) and Augmented REality Sandtable (ARES). Technical Report AD1017876.

Boyce, M. W., Rowan, C. P., Moss, J. D., Amburn, C. R., Shorter, P. L., Garneau, C. J., & Sottilare, R. A. (2018). The Impact of Surface Projection on Military Tactics Comprehension. *Military Psychology, 31:*45-59.

Chen, J.Y.C., and P.I. Terrence. 2009. "Effect of Imperfect Automation and Individual Differences Concurrent Performance of Military Robotics Tasks in a Simulated Multitasking Environment." *Ergonomics 52:* 907–920.

de Visser, E., T. Shaw, A. Mohamed-Ameen, and R. Parasuraman. 2010. "Modeling Human-Automation Team Performance in Networked Systems: Individual Differences in Working Memory Count." In Proceedings of the Human Factors and Ergonomics Society 54th Annual Meeting, 1087–1091. Santa Monica, CA: Human Factors and Ergonomics Society.

Hoff, K.A., and M. Bashir. 2015. "Trust in Automation Integrating Empirical Evidence on Factors That Influence Trust." *Human Factors* 57 (3): 407–434.

Lee, J.D., and N. Moray. 1994. "Trust, Self-Confidence, and Operators' Adaptation to Automation." *International Journal of Human-Computer Studies* 40 (1): 153–184.

Lee, J., & See, J. (2004). Trust in automation and technology: Designing for appropriate reliance. *Human Factors, 46,* 50–80

Merritt, S. M., Ako-Brew, A., Bryant, W. J., Staley, A., McKenna, M., Leone, & Shirase, L. Automaiton-Induced Complacency Potential: Development and Validation of a New Scale. *Frontiers Psychology, 10:*225

Parasuraman, R., E. de Visser, M.-K. Lin, and P.M. Greenwood. 2012. "Dopamine Beta Hydroxylase Genotype Identifies Individuals Less Susceptible to Bias in Computer-Assisted Decision Making." *PLoS ONE 7* (6): e39675.

Parasuraman, R., & Riley, V. (1997). Humans and automation: Use, misuse, disuse, abuse. *Human Factors, 39,* 230–253.

Parasuraman, R., T.B. Sheridan, and C.D. Wickens. 2000. "A Model of Types and Levels of Human Interaction with Automation." *IEEE Transactions on Systems, Man, and Cybernetics – Part A* 30: 286–297.

Parasuraman, R., T.B. Sheridan, and C.D. Wickens. 2000. "A Model of Types and Levels of Human Interaction with Automation." *IEEE Transactions on Systems, Man, and Cybernetics – Part A 30*: 286–297.Savoy: University of Illinois, Aviation Research Lab.

Rovira, E., K. McGarry, and R. Parasuraman. 2007. "Effects of Imperfect Automation on Decision Making in a Simulated Command and Control Task." *Human Factors 49:* 76–87.

Rovira, E., Pak, R., McLaughlin, A. (2017). Effects of individual differences in working memory on performance and trust with various degrees of automation. *Theoretical Issues in Ergonomics Science, 18*: 573-591.

Wickens, C.D., and X. Xu. 2002. Automation Trust, Reliability and Attention (Tech. Rep. AHFD02-14/MAAD-02-2).

A STUDY TO FURTHER UNDERSTAND THE LINK BETWEEN IMMERSION AND FLOW

Ehm Kannegieser[1], Daniel Atorf[1] and Josua Meier[2]
[1]*Fraunhofer Institute of Optronics, System Technologies and Image Exploitation*
Fraunhoferstraße. 1, 76131, Karlsruhe, Germany
[2]*Karlsruhe Institute of Technology, Kaiserstraße. 12, 76131, Karlsruhe, Germany*

ABSTRACT

Flow and Immersion are states of extreme concentration on an activity. For Serious Games, games which focus on achieving learning effects in players, high Flow and Immersion during gameplay can help improve these learning effects. Both Flow and Immersion are currently only measured using questionnaires, which is both delayed and subjective. This work introduces a study which aims to further the understanding of how Flow and Immersion are linked and to ease future work towards a new measurement method using physiological data.

KEYWORDS

Flow, Immersion, Combined Model, Correlation, Measurement, Physiological

1. INTRODUCTION

The design of Serious Games still presents an active field of research. Especially important are techniques to increase the learning rate of these games. Previous studies find in their research that high focus helps to transmit learning material through Serious Games (Deci and Ryan, 1985; Krapp, 2009). Two terms used to measure high focus are Flow and Immersion. These terms describe states of great focus on an activity or game. They are currently measured using questionnaires (Nordin, Denisova and Cairns, 2014), which have a range of problems. A participant cannot fill out a questionnaire without interrupting the concentration state, meaning there must be a delay when gathering data. Additionally, questionnaires are inherently subjective, adding additional bias to the measured results. The solution to this problem would be to measure changes in the player's body and derive Flow and Immersion from that. This work tries to present a step towards this solution. In order to better understand how Flow and Immersion interact, a combined model is established. Afterwards, based on previous work (Atorf et al., 2016; Kannegieser et al. 2018), a study is presented, which attempts to validate the model and link it with physiological measurements taken from players.

2. PREVIOUS WORK

Flow was first described by Csikszentmihalyi as the state of the optimal experience of an activity (Csikszentmihalyi, 1991). When entering a state of Flow, even taxing activities like work no longer feel taxing, but rather feel enjoyable. However, the Flow state cannot be achieved for every activity. Csikszentmihalyi bases flow on the model of extrinsic and intrinsic motivation. Only intrinsically motivated actions, which are not motivated by external factors, can reach the Flow state. Flow is reachable when the challenge presented by such an intrinsically motivated action is balanced with the skill of the person performing the task. All this makes Flow an interesting point of research in regard to games, as playing games is usually intrinsically motivated. Flow is mapped to games in the GameFlow questionnaire (Sweetser et al., 2005).

There exist two concurrent definitions of Immersion. The first definition is called presence-based Immersion and refers to the feeling of being physically present in a virtual location. The second definition is known as engagement-based Immersion. It defines Immersion based on the strength of a player's interaction with the game. The model given by Cairns et al. in their series of papers (Cairns et al., 2006; Jenett et al., 2008), defines Immersion as a hierarchical structure, with different barriers of entry. Figure 1 left shows this hierarchy. The lowest level, Engagement, is reached by interacting with the game and spending time with it. Engrossment is reached by becoming emotionally involved with the game. During this state, feelings of temporal and spatial dissociation are starting to appear. The final state, Total Immersion, is reached by players having their feelings completely focused on the game. Cheng et al. improve upon this hierarchical model by adding dimensions to the three levels of the hierarchy (Cheng et al., 2015). The Engagement level is split into the three dimensions: Attraction, Time Investment and Usability. The second level, Engrossment, is split into Emotional Attachment, which refers to attachment to the game itself, and Decreased Perceptions. Finally, Total Immersion is defined by the terms Presence and Empathy.

Flow and Immersion share many similarities. Both have similar effects, such as decreased perceptions of both time and the environment, and refer to a state of focus. Georgiou and Kyza even take the empathy dimension in the immersion model by Cheng et al. and replace it with Flow (Georgiou and Kyza, 2017). There are two main differences between the two: First, Flow does not define an emotional component, while Immersion is focused heavily on the emotional attachment of players to the game. Second, while Flow refers to a final state of complete concentration, Immersion refers to a range of experiences, ranging from minimal engagement to complete focus on the game. This is reflected in how those two psychological states are described in their introduction. Csikszentmihalyi describes Flow as the "optimal experience of an activity", while Cairns et al. describe Immersion as the "sub-optimal experience of an activity".

3. MODEL

The model used in the study is based on the Flow model presented by Csikszentmihalyi (Csikszentmihalyi, 1991) and the Immersion model by Cheng et al. (Cheng et al., 2015), which itself is a refinement of the hierarchical model presented by Cairns et al. Flow, as the optimal experience of an action, is considered the highest point in the Immersion hierarchy, which implies that Total Immersion and Flow are regularly experienced together. Figure 1 center presents the Immersion hierarchy imposed on top of the three-channel model by Csikszentmihalyi. As Immersion grows, the possibility to reach the Flow state increases. It must be noted that the diagram is only meant to be a qualitative visualization, as Immersion is not dependent on the challenge/skill balance.

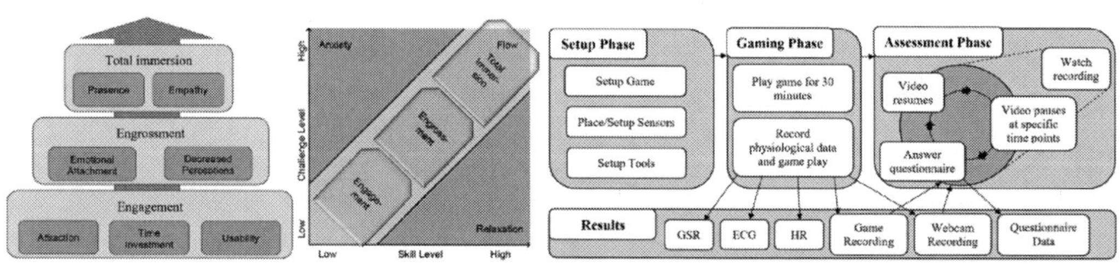

Figure 1. Left: Levels of the Immersion model by Cairns et al., with dimensions for each level by Cheng et al. (Cairns et al., 2006; Cheng et al., 2015). Center: Hierarchical Immersion model on top of the three-channel Flow model by Csikszentmihalyi (Csikszentmihalyi, 1991). Right: Stages of the study described in section 4

4. EXPERIMENT

The study was designed to both gather data to link physiological measurements with Flow and Immersion, as well as validate the Flow/Immersion model presented in section 3. 40 participants took part in the study. Participants were self-selected. This method was chosen to help observe higher levels of Immersion and

Flow. The study is split into three phases. During the Setup Phase, a game is selected. Free choice of game makes finding links between physiological measurements harder, but was chosen to help participants reach the Flow state more easily. During the Gaming Phase, participants play the game for 30 minutes. For 30 minutes, physiological measurements are taken. The physiological measurements used in this study were used due to being non-intrusive and not hindering the immersion of players. Galvanic skin response, Electrocardiography, gaze tracking and web cam footage for emotion analysis were used. A facial EMG would be more precise for analyzing displayed emotions, however, placing electrodes on the face of the player would distract from the gameplay experience and make it harder to reach the flow state. For the same reasons, EEG measurement was not chosen for the study. After the Gaming Phase has concluded, participants enter the Assessment Phase and watch their previous gaming session, while answering questionnaires about Immersion and Flow periodically. This setup was chosen to get more exact results and because it does not interrupt the Flow experience. Three questionnaires are used during the study. The first questionnaire used is the Immersion questionnaire described by Cheng et al (Cheng et al., 2015). As the questionnaire was too long to be measured multiple times without worsening the results, it was split into an Immersive Tendency questionnaire asked at the beginning of playback and an iterative questionnaire asked every three minutes during playback. For Flow, the Flow Short Scale questionnaire by Rheinberg et al. was used (Rheinberg et al., 2003). It was originally designed for being used multiple times in a row, making it perfect for this iterative approach. During playback, it is asked every six minutes. The final questionnaire used is the Game Experience Questionnaire (IJsselsteijn, de Kort and Poels, 2013). It measures a more general set of questions and is asked once after playback is over. Figure 1 right shows the three phases of the experiment as well as the activities of each phase.

5. PRELIMINARY RESULTS

The first step of the analysis is to check for correlations between Flow and Immersion. The results from both the Flow and Immersion questionnaires do not follow a normal distribution. For that reason, Spearman correlation was chosen. The correlation analysis found a strong correlation between all three levels of Immersion and Flow. The strongest correlation was found between Engagement and Flow ($R = 0.69$, $p = 8.536e-30$), which makes sense, knowing that Flow encompasses all features making up Engagement. The second strongest correlation exists between Total Immersion and Flow ($R = 0.652$, $p = 1.91e-25$). This is caused by the fact that players who played games without clear avatars, such as strategy games, found it difficult to emphasize with their avatar in the game, leading to reduced Total Immersion. The least correlated level of the three is Engrossment ($R = 0.56$, $p = 1.829e-18$), which can be explained as Engrossment puts strong emphasis on emotional attachment of the player to the game, something Flow does not elicit. All three show strong correlation to Flow, meaning the relation between these two psychological states explained in section 3 is likely. Table 1 displays the Rho coefficients for all states. Direct correlation between normalized physiological data and answers of the Flow/Immersion questionnaires show no meaningful correlation. The direct correlation results are shown in table 1. This means a more advanced method has to be employed. The first advanced method tried was using expert rules and fuzzy logic to create rules and activation methods based on an approach used by Goshvarpour et al. (Goshvarpour et al., 2017). Using this approach did not lead to meaningful results either, as it was difficult to create useful rules from the raw data and direct correlation results between physiological measurements and Flow/Immersion.

Table 1. Spearman Rho correlation coefficients for Flow/Immersion and physiological measurements

	Flow	Engagement	Engrossment	Total Immersion	GSR	Heartrate	Restpoints Per minute
Flow	1	0.69	0.57	0.65	-0.02	-0.03	-0.07
Engagement	0.69	1	0.45	0.58	0.01	-0.08	-0.02
Engrossment	0.57	0.45	1	0.62	-0.04	-0.09	0.05
Total Immersion	0.65	0.58	0.62	1	-0.15	0	0.06

6. CONCLUSION

With this work, an attempt was made to link physiological reactions in players to the states of Flow and Immersion. Furthermore, a second aim was to get a clearer understanding of how Flow and Immersion are linked, and present a unified model. In order to reach these goals, a study was performed and the results evaluated. As far as the link between Immersion and Flow is concerned, the results back up the model presented in section 3. The data shows strong correlation between high Flow and high Immersion for all three Immersion levels, which would imply Flow to be situated at the highest point of the Immersion hierarchy, along with total Immersion. Results are less clear for the link between physiological measurements and the Flow/Immersion model. Direct correlation did not find any connection between the recorded data. This also made creating an advanced rule-based system, as explained in chapter 4, difficult to achieve. Future research will be aimed at further analyzing the connection between physiological measurements and Flow with other more advanced techniques.

REFERENCES

Atorf, D., L. Hensler, and E. Kannegieser (2016). "*Towards a concept on measuring the Flow state during gameplay of serious games*". In: *European Conference on Games Based Learning (ECGBL). ECGBL 2016*. Paisley, Scotland, pp. 955–959. isbn: 978-1-911218-09-8. url: http://publica.fraunhofer.de/documents/N-438328.html.

Kannegieser E., Daniel Atorf and Josua Meier (2018). "*Surveying games with a combined model of Immersion and Flow*". In: MCCSIS 2018 Multi Conference on Computer Science and Information Systems, Game and Entertainment Technologies 2018.

Cairns, Paul (2006). "*Quantifying the experience of immersion in games*".

Cheng, M.-T., H.-C. She, and L.A. Annetta (June 2015). "*Game Immersion Experience: Its Hierarchical Structure and Impact on Game-based Science Learning*". In: J. Comp. Assist. Learn. 31.3, pp. 232–253. issn: 0266-4909. doi: 10.1111/jcal.12066. url: http: //dx.doi.org/10.1111/jcal.12066.

Csikszentmihalyi, Mihaly (Mar. 1991). *Flow: The Psychology of Optimal Experience*. New York, NY: Harper Perennial. isbn: 0060920432. url: http : / / www . amazon . com / gp / product/0060920432/ref=si3_rdr_bb_product/104-4616565-4570345.

Deci, Edward and Richard Ryan (Jan. 1985). *Intrinsic Motivation and Self-Determination in Human Behavior*. Vol. 3.

Georgiou, Yiannis and Eleni A. Kyza (Feb. 2017). "*The Development and Validation of the ARI Questionnaire*". In: Int. J. Hum.-Comput. Stud. 98.C, pp. 24–37. issn: 1071-5819. doi: 10.1016/j.ijhcs.2016.09.014. url: https://doi.org/10.1016/j.ijhcs.2016.09.

Goshvarpour, Atefeh, Ataollah Abbasi, and Ateke Goshvarpour (2017). "*An accurate emotion recognition system using ECG and GSR signals and matching pursuit method*". In: Biomedical Journal 40.6, pp. 355–368. issn: 2319-4170. doi: https://doi.org/10. 1016/j.bj.2017.11.001. url: http://www.sciencedirect.com/science/article/pii/ S2319417016301056.

IJsselsteijn, W.A. et al. (2008). "*Measuring the experience of digital game enjoyment*". English. In: Proceedings of Measuring Behavior 2008, 6th International Conference on Methods and Techniques in Behavioral Research, August 26-29, 2008, Maastricht. Ed. by A.J. Spink et al. Noldus, pp. 88–89. isbn: 978-90-74821-81-0.

Jennett, Charlene et al. (Sept. 2008). "*Measuring and Defining the Experience of Immersion in Games*". In: Int. J. Hum.-Comput. Stud. 66.9, pp. 641–661. issn: 1071-5819. doi: 10. 1016/j.ijhcs.2008.04.004. url: http://dx.doi.org/10.1016/j.ijhcs.2008.04.004.

Krapp, Andreas, Ulrich Schiefele, and Inge Schreyer (2009). *Metaanalyse des Zusammenhangs von Interesse und schulischer Leistung*. postprint

Nordin, A. Imran, Alena Denisova, and Paul Cairns (Oct. 2014). "*Too Many Questionnaires: Measuring Player Experience Whilst Playing Digital Games*".

Rheinberg, F., R. Vollmeyer, and S. Engeser (2003). "*Die Erfassung des Flow-Erlebens*". In: Diagnostik von Motivation und Selbstkonzept. Göttingen: Hogrefe, pp. 261–279.

Sweetser, Penelope and Peta Wyeth (July 2005). "*GameFlow: A Model for Evaluating Player Enjoyment in Games*". In: Comput. Entertain. 3.3, pp. 3–3. issn: 1544-3574. doi: 10.1145/1077246.1077253. url: http://doi.acm.org/10.1145/1077246.1077253.

EXPLORING TO LEARN WINNING STRATEGY

Samuel Lee
SFHS
Sunnyvale, California, USA

ABSTRACT

This paper presents a novel algorithm "*UCB**" (called "UCB star") to make "intelligent" decisions, enhancing the winning chances within games through the utilization of a well-known tree search algorithm, "Monte Carlo Tree Search (MCTS)". In the typical setting of a MCTS, exploration and exploitation are well balanced to propose "optimal" decisions, given the game status of a board. This happens through the use of the "Upper Confidence Bound (*UCB*)."
In this paper, a new form of *UCB* is formulated by taking into account the "posterior" of the parameters, allowing "bias" to be minimized from the observations.
Based on the experiments this paper performed, our *UCB** has shown statistically significance of its effectiveness, compared to a traditional *UCB* algorithm within the MCTS.

KEYWORDS

Board Game, MCTS, Game Strategy, A.I.

1. INTRODUCTION

In the past decades, games, ranging from board games, such as Go, to real time strategy (RTS) games, like StarCraft, have been an interesting topic to explore for both research communities and entertainment industries (Bourg and Seemann 2004; Ontanon et al. 2013). Finding "the best" strategy given a state of a game is often considered a challenging task due to the complexity behind most of games. "Go" is a game with such complexity, requiring a space complexity of 10^{171} space complexity and tree complexity of 10^{360} (Robson 1983). Due to the copious amount of calculations needed, it is not feasible for an A.I. agent to consider all possible movements in a given state. Thus, heuristics and other machine learning algorithms are often utilized (Bouzy and Cazenave 2001; Wang, Wang, and Gao 2017).

MCTS is one of the well-known methods; it is an algorithm used to find the "optima" action by taking random movements in an action space and building them into a tree structure. An example of this is illustrated in Figure 1.

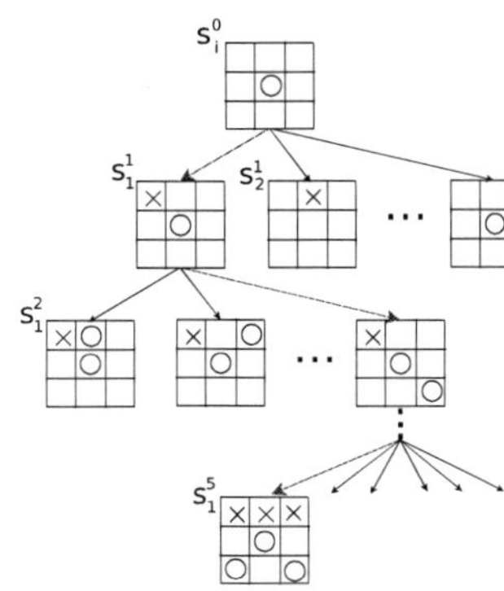

Figure 1. A tree with possible moves given a starting state. Blue arrows are the path of sequential movements

Note that the figure is based on a well-known simple board game, Tic-Tac-Toc. Each level in Figure 1 shows the possible movements given a state defined in the upper level (known as the parent node).

MCTS is applicable to many different types of games (Sievers and Helmert 2015), particularly ones with decision making processes. The overview of MCTS's process is very straightforward; it is essentially decomposed into four steps – 1) Selection; 2) Expansion; 3) Simulation; and 4) Backpropagation. (The details are found in a survey article (Browne et al. 2012).) For each iteration in building a search tree subject to a constraint (e.g. budget of computations), the first action is to select a "most promising" next movement that balances exploration and exploitation. Note that "exploitation" is to look for the best decision based on learned examples so far, while "exploration" is to try a new probing that has not been known to the space of the learned examples. $S^1{}_1$ is the example of an action from starting state S^0, where $S^l{}_m$ denotes a state with m^{th} possible movement in l level spawned from $(l\text{-}1)^{th}$ parent node. Among possible movements $S^l{}_i$ at level l, where $i \in \{1 \ldots m\}$, an "optimal" movement is selected based on a function that quantifies each action w.r.t. the likelihood of winning. Upper Confidence Bound (*UCB1*) (Auer, Cesa-Bianchi, and Fischer 2002) is an example of such functions quantifying "optimality" by balancing exploitation in the first term and exploration in the second term in Eq. (1). The details of explanations are followed in the next section.

$$UCB1(S_i^{l-1}, S_j^l) = \frac{w(j)}{n(j)} + C \times \sqrt{\frac{2 \ln n(f_j)}{n(j)}} \qquad (1)$$

2. SMOOTHED UPPER CONFIDENCE BOUNDS: *UCB**

In Eq. (1), the first term $w(j)/n(j)$ is interpreted as an estimator for winnings – Bernoulli $n(j)$ trials with $w(j)$ winnings observed. For each trial $x_t \in \{0, 1\}$, the maximum likelihood estimator $\hat{\theta}$ is calculated as

$[\Sigma(I\ (x_t == 1))]/N$ by maximizing the likelihood $\Pi_{t=1}\ \theta^{x_t}\ (1 - \theta)^{(1-x_t)}$, which corresponds to $w(j)/n(j)$ in Eq. (1). Note that I(c) is an indicator function that returns 1 when condition c meets true. By extending the likelihood with prior over θ, the posterior mean, $E[\theta|w(j), n(j), \alpha_0, \alpha_1]$ is

$$E[\theta|w(j), n(j), \alpha_0, \alpha_1] = \frac{w(j) + \alpha_1}{n(j) + \alpha_0 + \alpha_1} \qquad (2)$$

Substituting the first term in Eq. (1) with the posterior mean derived in Eq. (2) formulates a new *UCB*, which is smoothed by consider the conjugate prior beta distribution $B(\alpha_0, \alpha_1)$.

3. EXPERIMENTS

In this section, I report experimental results to show the effectiveness of *UCB**.

Figure 2 shows statistical significance as *UCB** outperforms *UCB1* at a p-value of 0.05 from cumulative winning rate results for over 50 runs, where each run is a game played with 2 for α_0 and 5 for α_1 and 10 as the simulation budget in a typical MCTS.

In order to see the consistency of the robustness of *UCB** over *UCB1*, more experiments are performed in Figure 3, showing the win rate differences between *UCB** and *UCB1* through 700 runs, where each run is the cumulative win rate from 50 games played. The areas on the right side of the blue line indicates the winning chances of *UCB** over *UCB1*.

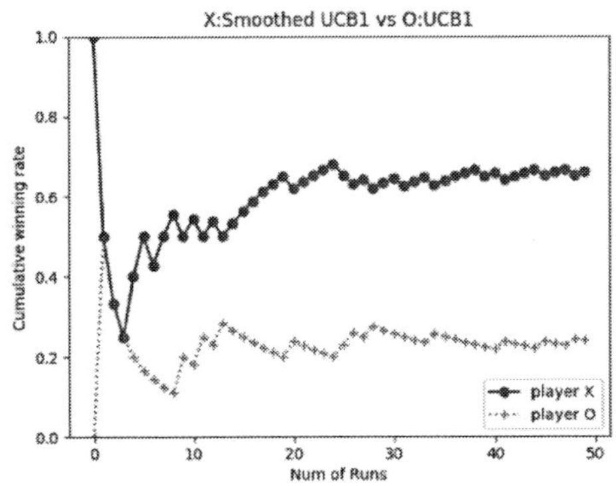

Figure 2. Cumulative win rates by increasing the number of runs to 50. Y axis shows the cumulative win rate to each run in the X axis

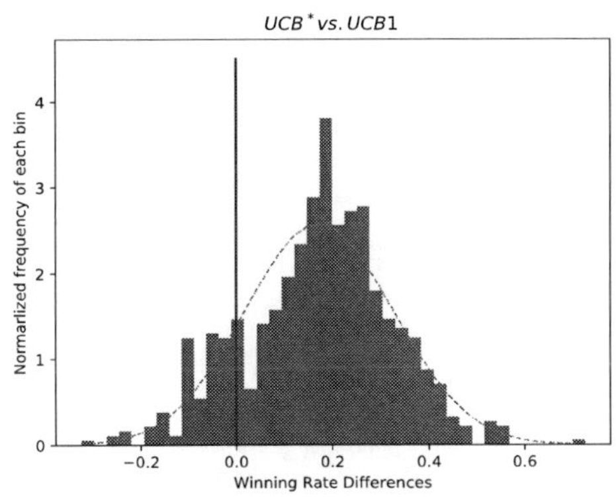

Figure 3. Normalized winning rates in histogram after 700 runs, where each run is the cumulative winning rate from 50 games played

4. CONCLUSION

In this paper, a new formulation UCB* is proposed, and its performance has been proven effectively through the statistical significance over many simulations. For future work, I will investigate 1) how to tune the hyperparameters -- α_0, α_1 -- for automatic learning; 2) how to balance exploration and exploitation for better effectiveness as well as faster decisions; and 3) applying the UCB* to many other use cases.

ACKNOWLEDGEMENT

I appreciate valuable comments from the anonymous reviewers, which provides many insights for the future endeavors.

REFERENCES

Auer, P.; Cesa-Bianchi, N.; and Fischer, P. 2002. Finite-time analysis of the multiarmed bandit problem. *Mach. Learn.* 47(2-3):235–256.

Bourg, M., and Seemann, G. 2004. *AI for Game Developers*. O'Reilly Media, Inc.

Bouzy, B., and Cazenave, T. 2001. Computer go: An ai oriented survey. *Artificial Intelligence* 132(1):39 – 103.

Browne, C.; Powley, E.; Whitehouse, D.; Lucas, S.; Cowl- ing, P. I.; Tavener, S.; Perez, D.; Samothrakis, S.; Colton, S.; and et al. 2012. A survey of monte carlo tree search methods. *IEEE T-CIAI.*

Ontanon, S.; Synnaeve, G.; Uriarte, A.; Richoux, F.; Churchill, D.; and Preuss, M. 2013. A survey of real-time strategy game ai research and competition in starcraft. *IEEE T-CIAIG* 5(4):293–311.

Robson, J. M. 1983. The complexity of go. *Congress,* 413–417.

Sievers, S., and Helmert, M. 2015. A doppelkopf player based on uct. In Holldobler, S.; Penaloza, R.; and Rudolph, S.,eds., KI 2015: *Advances in Artificial Intelligence*, 151– 165.

Wang, J. W. W.; Wang, R.; and Gao, W. 2017. Beyond monte carlo tree search: Playing go with deep alternative neural network and long-term evaluation. CoRR abs/1706.04052.

HOW GAMING EXPERIENCE INFLUENCES NEW GAME LEARNING

Hao Wang, Wen-Wen Chen and Chun-Tsai Sun
Department of Computer Science, National Chiao Tung University
1001, Ta Hsieh Road, Hsinchu City, Taiwan

ABSTRACT

A large number of new video games are specially designed to meet the needs of players with different levels of gaming experience. To provide ideal learning environments, designers must understand differences in how experienced/less experienced players learn new games. Using a sample of players with different experience levels, our goal is to understand learning processes for a new real-time strategy game. Data from observations, post-game interviews, and eye movement recordings indicate that the majority of study participants relied on a trial-and-error approach, with more experienced gamers using a structured mental model involving feedback and expectations about making progress. Specifically, experienced gamers in the sample tended to use a top-down learning style emphasizing connections between goals and available actions, and to focus on the functions of game objects. In comparison, players with little or no gaming experience were more likely to focus on appearance and textual descriptions. Our findings suggest that in-game information interface designers need to consider player experience level in order to facilitate learning. Our results raise questions about whether gaming experience affects student classroom learning styles, as well as expectations regarding teachers and curriculums.

KEYWORDS

Learning Strategies, Mental Model, Game Interface, Eye-Tracking

1. INTRODUCTION

Despite the large body of research on the positive learning aspects of playing digital games, few efforts have been made to understand the processes involved in learning a new game—an important issue for game designers in light of the large number of new games entering the market. For commercial game designers it is important to understand how individuals in specifically targeted populations learn to play their products so as to increase the potential for pleasant learning experiences; without such experiences, players may quickly move on to other games that offer faster and more pleasing results. Further, in game based learning (GBL) and health care environments, it is important to ensure that the interests of users are quickly captured and held. Such efforts require an understanding of player learning style, with prior experience possibly influencing how players learn in other environments. If gaming does in fact exert an effect on player learning models, understanding the underlying mechanisms may support the design of more suitable curriculums, especially for students with considerable gaming experience. In this study we address two issues—learning behavior and the use of game information interfaces (i.e., interfaces that provide alerts and text regarding game rules)—to determine how gaming experiences affect learning behaviors, and how players use interfaces to learn. We invited study participants to learn a game they had never played before, and gathered data on their learning techniques (especially those associated with in-game information) by conducting post-game interviews and recording eye movements with an eye tracker.

2. METHOD

We chose a RTS game for our experiments because RTS is considered a mainstream game genre with clearly defined structural concepts to be learned. Although they are considered complex in terms of strategy, RTS game concepts can be summarized as follows:

1. Players are initially given several worker units and a command center that can produce additional worker units.
2. Worker units visit resource locations and deliver collected resources to a command center.
3. The purpose of producing additional worker units is to collect resources more quickly. However, worker unit production also consumes resources.
4. Resource-consuming worker units can also be used to construct buildings for military purposes.
5. Military buildings can be used to produce military units, a task that also consumes resources.
6. Military units can be used to destroy enemy units and buildings—two tasks that are considered the ultimate game goals.

We analyzed progress in terms of how and how quickly study participants learned each game concept. To keep mechanics as simple as possible, we used the game making tool that accompanies the mainstream RTS game Starcraft 2 to create an original RTS game.

To analyze eye gaze data, multiple areas of interest (AOI) are sometimes assigned to different parts of content material based on research objectives.

A primary study goal is to determine differences in new game learning behaviors among players with various gaming experience levels. We created three categories: "RTS players" who describe themselves as having played games two or more times per week on average for three years or more, and who are therefore very familiar with real time strategy games; "Experienced players" who describe themselves as having played games two or more times per week on average for three years or more, but who have never played RTS games; and "Inexperienced players" who describe themselves as playing games less than one time per month on average. We focused on differences in learning processes between experienced and inexperienced players, based on our assertion that they reflect how gaming experience influences the learning of new games. For experienced RTS players, recognizing that a new game is an RTS game is sufficient for their needs, and not much new learning is required. We therefore studied recognition processes rather than learning processes for the RTS player group.

Study participants were recruited through the Internet bulletin board system of a public university located in north-central Taiwan. Based on self-reports of gaming experiences, our final sample of 30 participants (22 male, 8 female) included 7 RTS players (6 male, 1 female), 14 experienced players (10 male, 4 female), and 9 inexperienced players (6 male, 3 female). Ages ranged from 18 to 26.

3. RESULTS

We will present our results in three stages corresponding to the above-described RTS game learning checkpoints:

Stage 1: Initial screen browsing. We found that all of the participants quickly focused on worker objects after noticing them, and then immediately tried to manipulate them with the computer mouse. None of them read directions or tried any other screen objects at the start. We found that the largest fixation count involving worker unit AOIs for all three player groups occurred during the first 20 seconds. This is consistent with previous video game research findings indicating that most people learn through trial and error rather than systematic reading or observing. We noticed that RTS players made inferences based on contextual information rather than graphical clues, and identified the game as an RTS game by acknowledging a building-like structure surrounded by objects that might be considered valuable at the screen center—two characteristics typical of RTS settings. From this they apparently inferred that the human-like objects must be workers that could be used to collect resources (another typical RTS feature), and therefore did not bother to take a closer look. This observation underscores the need for careful game design in support of correctly perceived affordances for first-time game users.

Stage 2: Resource collection. The behaviors of experienced and inexperienced players diverged during this stage. All of the experienced players moved worker objects so as to explore maps until their expectations regarding progress were satisfied—that is, when they felt a lack of potential for something new to happen, raising the possibility that they were playing incorrectly. At this point they started reading the directions on worker unit actions and discovered the capability of those units to collect resources. Upon this discovery, all of the experienced players assigned all of the worker units to collect resources, regardless of whether or not they understood the purposes of those resources. During post-game interviews these players described their expectations that everything in a game should be meaningful, therefore they collected as many resources as possible because they were confident that the resources would be useful at a later time. We observed two types of learning patterns among the inexperienced players during this stage. One type turned to the written directions after playing with worker units for a short while, and then tried actions one-by-one. These were the only players in the entire sample to quickly rely on written directions. During interviews they described themselves as trying to learn the game and to make progress as quickly as possible. Another type completely ignored the written instructions and instead moved the worker units around the screen until the end of the play session. During interviews they described themselves as bored due to the lack of any on-screen action, but unconcerned by the thought that they might be playing incorrectly.

Stage 3: Discover worker unit construction powers and resource usage. The experienced players quickly discovered the ability of worker units to construct objects after looking at the written directions, but only when they felt that they were progressing in the right direction and had sufficient time to read those directions. In most cases they described themselves as believing that things were going well once they had assigned all of their worker units to collect resources, and when resources were flowing into their stocks—in other words, when all of their worker units were optimized. Among the inexperienced players, only those who systematically read the written directions discovered the construction function, and only after trying the "move action" button located to the left of the resource-collection button.

We summarize the above findings in Figure 1. The main difference between experienced and inexperienced players was their expectations regarding progress and feedback. The observed actions of experienced players suggest that they quickly constructed mental models using past gaming encounters that could be applied to new ones, even in unfamiliar game genres. Their expectations regarding progress and feedback encouraged them to refer to written directions much more quickly than some of the inexperienced players in our sample, who had no such models to rely on. The above-described differences partly explain the top-down versus bottom-up characteristic observed in the learning styles of the study participants. According to the eye-tracking data, when experienced goal achievement-oriented players read game directions, they compared several actions to determine which one was best to try first. In contrast, inexperienced players appeared to view the game either as a toy to mindlessly play with or to be mastered through the use of written directions. Whereas experienced players maintained and updated a mental model of relationships between actions and goals (a top-down learning approach), inexperienced players apparently did not acknowledge or did not care about connections between goals and available actions. Instead, their approach was similar to someone reading instructions to operate a machine without knowing (or even wondering) what the machine is for—a bottom-up approach.

Both experienced and inexperienced players primarily focused on worker units during the first 20 seconds of each session, which is consistent with our interview data. Further, the experienced players spent more time than the inexperienced players focusing on other game objects. After the first 20 seconds, the percentage of experienced player fixation on worker units decreased by 46.8% (from 32% to 17% of total fixation) between the 60- and 120-second time points. For the inexperienced players the decrease was only 27.5% (from 40% to 29% of total fixation).

Our index of the average number of transitions between AOIs is analogous to the regression behavior mentioned in reading eye movement research. In the present study, transitions were assumed to indicate the degree to which players had learned or were checking relationships between two AOIs. According to the RTS game concept list, resources are clearly at the center of concept learning. We therefore focused on transitions between the resource stock AOI and related AOIs in the resource collection system, including the command center, worker units, resource mines, and action buttons. We found that experienced players had significantly higher counts for all transitions connected to their resource stocks (Table 1), suggesting that they were building mental models of the resource collection system.

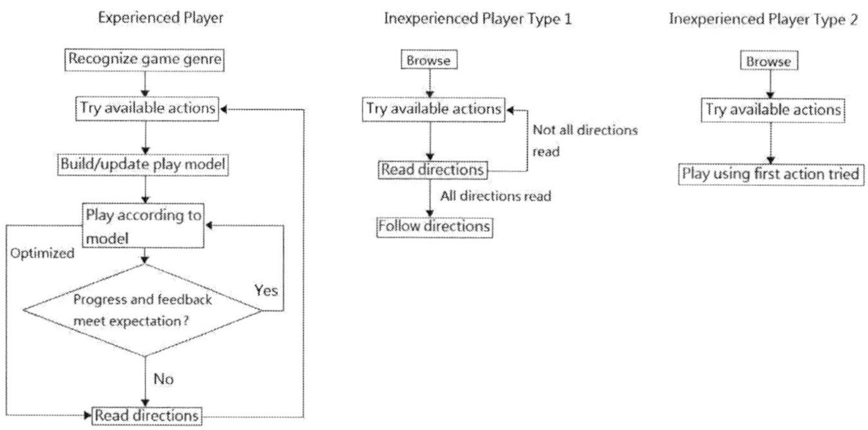

Figure 1. RTS game learning flowcharts

Table 1. Average numbers of fixation transitions between resource stock (RS) AOIs and related AOIs

Group	RS <-> command center	RS <-> Action buttons	RS <-> Worker units	RS <-> Resource mines
RTS players	4.14	2.43	4.00	3.00
Experienced players	6.07	5.07	11.78	3.42
Inexperienced players	0.77	0.55	1.44	0.55

4. CONCLUSION

The goal of this paper was to use interview-based and data-driven approaches to clarify how learning behavior is affected by gaming experience. We noted several significant differences between players with a great deal of experience and those without, and suggest that of these, the most important are expectations concerning feedback and progress—factors that may be generalizable to classrooms, skill training programs, software applications, and other learning situations. This assertion is consistent with previous descriptions of players being accustomed to receiving feedback and quick rewards in both digital game and physical worlds (Koepp et al., 1998; Reeves and Read, 2009). Another important finding is that participants with more gaming experience favored a top-down learning style, while inexperienced players favored a bottom-up style. There are two possible explanations. First, most games have goals that players try to achieve, which encourages them to create mental models (Gee, 2007). Second, the "active processing assumption" associated with multimedia learning states that individuals actively engage in cognitive activity leading to coherent mental connections with past experiences (Mayer, 2005). Accordingly, experienced players may actively process a new game in a manner that fits with a familiar goal-achieving model. This preference may be tied to another observation: experienced players tend to be functionalists who care more about what in-game objects can do rather than text descriptions or external appearances. To transfer such a characteristic to classrooms, teachers need to clearly state the purposes of lessons in order to attract and maintain student interest—an important top-down instructional tactic.

We also looked at how and when players used the game information interface, and found that they tended to completely ignore it at the start of a playing session in favor of experimenting with worker objects. Our data indicate that affordance is an important factor in terms of intuitive learning, and that game designers need to acknowledge how players prefer contextual information to appearances when learning a new game. In game design, creating a sense of affordance requires taking advantage of players' physical world experiences to create interest and to support expectations; this is especially true for inexperienced gamers.

REFERENCES

Blumberg, F. C. and Randall, J. D. 2013. "What do children and adolescents say they do during video game play?" Journal of Applied Developmental Psychology, vol. 34, no. 2, pp. 82-88.

Blumberg, F. C. and Sokol, L. M. 2004. "Boys' and girls' use of cognitive strategy when learning to play video games." The Journal of General Psychology, vol. 131, no. 2, pp. 151-158.

Clark, W., Logan, K., Luckin, R., Mee, A. and Oliver, M. 2009. "Beyond Web 2.0: mapping the technology landscapes of young learners." Journal of Computer Assisted Learning, vol. 25, no. 1, pp. 56-69.

Coller, B. D. and Scott, M. J. 2009. "Effectiveness of using a video game to teach a course in mechanical engineering." Computers and Education, vol. 53, no. 3, pp. 900-912.

Dalgarno, B. and Lee, M. J. 2010. "What are the learning affordances of 3-D virtual environments?" British Journal of Educational Technology, vol. 41, no. 1, pp. 10-32.

Gee, J. P. 2007. What Video Games Have to Teach Us about Learning and Literacy. Second Edition: Palgrave Macmillan.

Gibson, J. 1977. "The concept of affordances." Perceiving, acting, and knowing, 67-82.

Greenfield, P. M., Camaioni, L., Ercolani, P., Weiss, L., Lauber, B. A. and Perucchini, P. 1994. "Cognitive socialization by computer games in two cultures: Inductive discovery or mastery of an iconic code?" Journal of Applied Developmental Psychology, vol. 15, no. 1, pp. 59-85.

Hamlen, K. R. 2011. "Children's choices and strategies in video games." Computers in Human Behavior, vol. 27, no. 1, pp. 532-539.

Hwang, G.-J., Yang, L.-H., and Wang, S.-Y. 2013. "A Concept Map-Embedded Educational Computer Game for Improving Students' Learning Performance in Natural Science Courses." Computers and Education, vol. 69, pp. 121-130.

Koepp, M. J., Gunn, R. N., Lawrence, A. D., Cunningham, V. J., Dagher, A., Jones, T., Brooks, D. J., Bench, C. J. and Grasby, P. M. 1998. "Evidence for striatal dopamine release during a video game." Nature, vol. 393, issue 6682, pp. 266-268.

Mayer, R. E. 2005. "Cognitive theory of multimedia learning." The Cambridge handbook of multimedia learning, pp. 31-48.

Norman, D. 1999. "Affordance, conventions, and design." Interactions, vol. 6, no. 3, pp. 38-43.

Novak, J. D., Bob Gowin, D. and Johansen, G. T. 1983. "The use of concept mapping and knowledge vee mapping with junior high school science students." Science Education, vol. 67, no.5, pp. 625-645.

Reeves, B. and Read, J. L. 2009. Total Engagement: How Games and Virtual Worlds to Change the Way People Work and Businesses Compete: Harvard Business Press.

Sancar, H., Karakus, T. and Cagiltay, K. 2007. "Learning a New Game: Usability, Gender and Education." Paper presented at the Young researchers furthering development of TEL research in Central and Eastern Europe.

Taylor, T. L. 2006. Play between worlds: MIT Press.

EMPATHETIC GAMES: MAKING MEANINGFUL EXPERIENCES FOR OTHERNESS PROMOTION

Daniel de Sant'anna Martins[1], Alexandre Magalhães Rangel[2] and Joshua Kritz[2]
[1]*Escola Técnica Estadual Cícero Dias - NAVE Recife, Pernambuco, Brazil*
[2]*Colégio Estadual José Leite Lopes - NAVE Rio, Rio de Janeiro, Brazil*

ABSTRACT

Empathy is the ability or attitude of putting yourself in someone else's shoes, using imagination to understand their actions and motivations. It is the art of understanding the other's feelings and thus, knowing their real needs and desires. Our empathic capacity allows us to identify the way or the learning path of the others, and enables the teacher-facilitator to guide their actions based on this understanding (KRZNARIC, 2015). It facilitates and promotes collaboration between people, leading them to build projects and realities together, as it assists in understanding behaviors, ideas, dreams, values and needs. As games are a medium or even a language that can serve as a powerful tool to promote meaningful experiences, the present work studies the conjugation of these with empathy, investigating the advent of a new genre or class of digital games: the empathetic games. The investigation of its possibilities is still expressed in the case study of a didactic practice guided by project based learning methodology (PBL), in a context of technical high school technical development of games.

KEYWORDS

Empathy, Education, Project Based Learning, Game Development, Empathetic Games

1. INTRODUCTION

The World Development Report 2019 - The Changing Nature of Work, promoted by the World Bank, shows above all that it is with young people and children that "the main challenge is to equip them with skills that they will need to use regardless of the nature of the work of tomorrow, (this includes) above all the ability to solve problems and exercise critical judgment, as well as interpersonal skills such as empathy and the spirit of collaboration," says World Bank Group President Jim Yong Kim.

Empathy is one of the conditions or interactions between teacher-learning facilitators and learners, so that there is a creative trust environment that enables a true "freedom to learn" experience (ROGERS, 1977). In total, for this type of learning to occur, six are the conditions described by Rogers (1977), namely: a) confrontation with a real problem; b) trust in the human organism; c) teacher authenticity; d) acceptance; e) empathy; f) provision of resources ".

Speaking of experiences, games are, so far, one of the most effective tools for producing meaning. Zimmerman and Salen tell us that "a game is a system in which players engage in an artificial, rules-based conflict that implies a quantifiable outcome." (SALEN & ZIMMERMAN, 2012). In this context, game design activity directs this result since "design is the process by which a designer creates a context to be found by a participant, from which the meaning emerges" (SALEN & ZIMMERMAN, 2012).

Based on this, the development of an empathic game project was proposed for students of NAVE - Núcleo Avançado em Educação (Advanced Nucleus in Education), a high school educational program of Oi Futuro, in partnership with Rio de Janeiro and Pernambuco government, transforming the particular school in full time and integrated school with technical-professional courses in the area of digital game programming, powered by CESAR - Centro de Estudos e Sistemas Avançados do Recife (Recife Center for Advanced Studies and Systems) - a research and innovation institute - aiming to promote a significant experience whose subject matter is related to a difficult theme for empathy promotion in its users. It became clear after the development of the project that the experience of developing a game with this premise, promoted changes not only in its end users, but in students and faculty.

2. DEFINING EMPATHY

Empathy enters as a powerful tool, not as an emotional, affectionate, and vague feeling, but as a transforming attitude, capable of promoting a revolution in the relationships between teachers, apprentices, communities, and institutions. This is what Krznaric (2015) says when teaching. Canada, New Zealand, Germany and Britain have hundreds of thousands of learners benefiting through the Roots of Empathy program. This Canadian program, created in 1995, is an empathic teaching method for five- to twelve-year-olds with a baby as a teacher. Trainees should observe a baby and try to understand their emotional relationships with the world and with others, including their parents through an empathic practice (Krznaric, 2015). The results of several studies have shown that the program was able to reduce bullying practices, stimulate cooperation, improve the learner's relationship with his parents and raise his grades (Krznaric, 2015).

Child education specialist and program creator Mary Gordon believes “that empathy education is vital to children's well-being and a cornerstone of emotional intelligence," and continues her statement that she is essential in the formation of " global citizens "capable of solving the world's problems," from child poverty to armed violence "(Krznaric, 2015). These are also objectives that are present in the Report to UNESCO of the International Commission on Education for the 21st Century and the 17 UN Sustainable Development Goals. Empathic people have what Krznaric (2015) calls the "creative spirit," a sort of curiosity that encourages research from the other person's point of view on the world, causing the researcher to develop new thoughts and perspectives through interaction (Krznaric, 2015). This creative spirit can certainly aid in the development of skills for the 21st century and facilitate learning.

The Universities of Eastern Finland, Jyväskylä and Turku jointly conduct research on the use of empathy by teachers. The studies revealed that "empathic teachers promote children's motivation and the development of academic skills, such as reading, writing and arithmetic skills" (University of Eastern Finland, 2015). The Finnish First Steps research has further shown that empathic relationships and interactions between apprentices and teachers are more relevant to learning than physical structures or the provision of educational materials. The conclusion of the research is that the practice of empathy is capable of increasing motivation for learning (University of Eastern Finland, 2015).

Krznaric (2015) gives some tips on how we can learn to develop an empathic practice, namely: 1) Understand that we can expand our empathy; 2) Recognize the perspective, humanity and individuality of the other as true; 3) Do not judge the cultural experiences of others, but explore them; 4) Exercising "radical listening" and curiosity, being authentic in relation to the other; 5) Transport yourself imaginatively to the minds of others with the help of tangible artifacts; 6) Use empathy, to understand others.

This skill is particularly useful in game design and development activities, as in a game we’re trying to deliver an experience, based on a player specific profiles with needs and personal interests.

3. SERIOUS GAMES

Serious games also known as games with purpose, represent a category of games. We then have a definition of serious game: "What separates serious games from the rest [of games] is the focus on a specific and intentional learning outcome to achieve serious, measurable, and continuous performance and behaviour changes." (Carryberry, 2008) In other words, these games have a purpose beyond entertainment. They seek to use all the power of this media to provide more than fun, conveying knowledge, learning and empathy. Other authors agree with this association of serious games to an educational objective and clarifying that the term serious does not go back to a dull or demotivating game, but rather reflects only the purpose of the game created (Michael; Chen, 2005).

The Serious Games theme is not relatively new, the 1970s being considered one of the first times it was mentioned (ABT, 1970), being defined as games that are committed to the educational and training character. With the development of digital technologies there is an emergence of digital players. Greater access to games in a personal environment has made it possible to create serious digital games that can reach a much larger number of people than analog ones. These new possibilities have led to a great increase in serious games studies and their importance.

3.1 Classification of Serious Games

The growth of serious games in both studies and in quantity of games leads to efforts to classify these. There arc several classifications in the literature, generally according to the purpose present in the games. The proposal of an example classification is, to take into account the main objectives (purpose) of the game, used media, applied technologies, gender, area, expected impact, transmitted values, results of abilities or by the type of behavioral change (Connolly et al., 2012).

Even with these classification efforts there is still no one widely accepted by serious game scholars. However, it is possible to recognize similarities in various classifications with respect to the purpose of the game. Common names given to various forms of serious games are: Newsgames, Training and simulation, Persuasive, Organizational dynamic, Games for health, Art games and Militainment (Edgar Alves, 2013).

3.2 Empathetic Games

There isn't yet no consensus on the classification of this new genre - or whether it is in fact a new genre - but what really matters is that empathic games figure as a significant tool in promoting alterity between people and in solving other issues associated with empathy. According to the Game designer Mary Flanagan, in 2018 annual meeting of the World Economic Forum in Davos, Switzerland. "Normally, we tackle the world's biggest problems through treaties, through policy, through careful laws, through design, but history keeps repeating itself [...] And could we use - games - something fundamental to human history to do? [...]"(FLANAGAN, 2018).

These games aspire to enhance a player's understanding of an outside perspective, particularly those pertaining to real-world struggles and inequalities, through interactive experiences. In the game industry there are a few successful cases, like Papers, Please (by 3909 LLC) and That Dragon, Cancer (Numinous Games) showing that this emerging genre is here to stay. For Vander Caballero, the designer of Papo & Yo (Minority Media Inc.), the reason these games work so well is because they are endowed with four key elements: Personal Story, which gets people to identify with the narrative; Metaphors, which softens the weight of sensitive issues; it is equally important to Give Closure allowing the player to reflect on the experience; and finally, the Beat Chart, which are keywords or key concepts that define the structure of the game. Through these immersive experiences, players often acquire or enhance a whole bunch of important skills, such as agency. How does agency play a role in empathy? Agency is "the satisfying power to take meaningful action and see the results of our decision and choices" (Murray, 2017, p. 159). Agency is defined as the understanding that "actions taken by the player [will] result in significant changes within the world" (Gibbs, 2011, para. 4).

4. METHODOLOGY

4.1 Case Study: Games with Empathy

The PBL method is generally guided by a step-by-step approach consisting of seven of them, which will be presented and contextualized with the case study, below. First, it was necessary to "clarify the difficult terms," contextualizing to the students what was empathy, followed by a debate for a common understanding. There was also a presentation on empathy with a guest expert, where the students were able to delve deeper into the subject. The second step was to list the social issues related to the theme, such as racism, femicide, xenophobia, urban violence, among others. We continue to discuss possible diagnoses and means to prove them, through research on news, media (films, novels, documentaries, etc.) and sharing personal experiences; this was the third step in the process. It is worth highlighting the whole process, but mainly in the initial stages, was also guided by the design thinking method, where the students used some tools to assertively understand the context.

To move to the fourth step we summarized in shared documents the information collected and make it publicly accessible by all. The class self organized into thematic interest groups. In the fifth stage a specific learning objective related to the proposal of the technical course of the college - multimedia (basically digital art and design) and game programming - was defined: the development of a short digital games as tools to promote positive impact in society, through the reflection caused by its emergent narrative and through gameplay. This objective was accompanied by technical restrictions such as specific gaming genres aligned with the students' technical ability limitations and a game scope consistent with the time they possessed. To reduce the impact on students, the three subjects of the technical year of the school year in question (in this case, the second year of high school) were integrated to evaluate the project as a unique production.

In the sixth stage, usually of study and complementary research, the development of the game projects was given; the search for knowledge was specific to the technical issues of each project. In group, students sought to complement the technical content of game development in a specific engine, viewed in the classroom, as well as other content inherent to the activity, such as technical documents of game design, organization and management of agile projects with tools online and even pixel art for digital games, which was not initially part of the scope of the digital game programming course. The projects were also developed through iterative prototyping and guided by agile design reasoning, using Scrum as a production framework.

Finally, in the seventh and final stage, the groups presented their solutions - four digital empathetic games - in pitch presentation for a group of professionals from the regional game development market.

5. RESULTS

As a result of the case study four prototypes of relatively good games were produced, very well evaluated by the bank of external professionals. Students have engaged exceptionally and developed a collaborative culture across the class. It also became apparent that all groups were self-educated on topics not covered by the course syllabus proactively.

One of the teams, which had the topic of "abusive relationships between teenagers," developed an online survey form during the preliminary stages and obtained almost one hundred responses and eventually developed a network of sorority with the people interviewed (mostly girls). In a particular case, a subject of research contacted the girls, and inspired by them, identified that she was having an abusive relationship and created the courage to bring an end to it. During the pitch presentation day, a very significant feedback came from one of the evaluating teachers (who also participated in the game's mentoring process), who reported ignoring the relevance and particularities of the topic "abusive relationship" and showed how much that experience had "changed" him, making him rethink his paradigms.

Figure 1. Gameplay screen of True Colors digital game, visual novel about abusive relationships between teenagers

The other games used the elements exposed by Caballero (2014) to classify the empathic games: in the visual novel "Space Between Us", students use the metaphor of a human astronaut who is harassed by aliens residing in a distant galaxy because it is different of them and is considered inferior by the simple fact of being human, even while it tries to warn them about an imminent supernova of its Sun - a clear reference to xenophobia. In the action adventure "Sound of the War", the player is exposed to a reality, that was common among the participants of the team: the urban violence that slum dwellers experience in Rio de Janeiro. The goal of the game was to divert from various hazards and save children in a scenario depicting a favela with top-view camera. Already in "RunFugiada", an action runner, the narrative was about a girl from the Middle East region, who must flee the war and its dangers. Although it looks like the endless runner genre, the game GIVE CLOSURE to the player, when it reached a certain stretch of the scene, which caused its immediate defeat, followed by news and statistical data on the impact of the wars in the region.

Figure 2. Gameplay screen of Space Between Us digital game, visual novel uses narrative metaphors to talk about xenophobia

6. CONCLUSION

It is clear from the case study that empathic games, without value judgment as to their gender classification, are powerful tools for promoting positive impact on society. Even games being considered by many as an "escapist" activity, they are also "returnist" (McGonigal, 2012), ie: the player, after playing them, returns to "real life" with real abilities, which were more or less developed through the emergence of the lived narratives. The activity of developing empathic games through the pbl by the students was fundamental not only to enable them technically in the task, but also to make them reflect on their role in society, to develop criticality and to connect with other time, either by sharing difficult personal experiences or by listening attentively to the anguishes of their peers' difficulties. It is clear to the authors the reflexive potential that this type of game has in relation to its players, since the agency that normally the act of throwing caused that subjects previously ignored by some of them, were evidenced and paradigms were revised.

REFERENCES

ABT, C. C. Serious Games. 1st edition ed. New York: The Viking Press, 1970.

Connolly, T. M. et al. A systematic literature review of empirical evidence on computer games and serious games. Computers & Education, set. 2012. v. 59, n. 2, p. 661–686.

Edgar Alves. Jogos Sérios para Ensino de Engenharia de Software. Portugal: Faculdade de Engenharia da Universidade do Porto, 2013. Dissertação de Mestrado.

Krznaric, Roman. *O poder da empatia*: a arte de se colocar no lugar do outro para transformar o mundo. Rio de Janeiro: Zahar, 2015.

Michael, D.; Chen, S. Serious Games: Games That Educate, Train, and Inform. 1. ed. [S.l.]: Course Technology PTR, 2005.

Rogers, Carl R. *Liberdade para aprender*. Belo Horizonte: Interlivros, 1977.

Salen, Katie; Zimmerman, Eric. *Rules of play: Game design fundamentals*. MIT press, 2004.

University of Eastern Finland. *Empathetic teachers enhance children's motivation for learning*. 2015. Retrieved from <https://www.sciencedaily.com/releases/2015/11/151103064738.htm> Accessed on June 22, 2017.

Farber, M.; Schrier, K. The limits and strengths of using digital games as empathy machines. MGIEP Working Paper 5, 1–35, 2017.

A Question of Empathy - Are There Positive Effects from Gaming? - Extra Credits. 2015. Retrieved from <https://www.youtube.com/watch?v=fftjo1CepQE>. Accessed on February 27, 2019.

Bartelson, Eric. *Empathetic games: birth of a genre?*. CONTROL500. Retrieved from <https://ctrl500.com/developers-corner/empathy-games-%E2%80%A2-fighting-tears/>. Accessed on February 27, 2019.

Ratner, Paul. *Video games can have a meaningful social impact.* Big Think. 2018. Retrieved from <https://bigthink.com/paul-ratner/video-games-can-have-a-meaningful-social-impact?fbclid=IwAR32fbafI8Ht3CgYq548ctJNAWinQJv95vAHC52I1egI6B4WrUHdm9nCrXc>. Accessed on February 27, 2019.

Caballero, Vander. *Empathetic games are here to stay! What's next?*. GDCVault. 2014. Retrieved from <https://www.gdcvault.com/play/1020598/Empathetic-Games-Are-Here-to>. Accessed on February 27, 2019.

Bennet, Chris. *Designing for difficult subjects*. Stanford education. 2018. Retrieved from <http://gdt.stanford.edu/designing-for-difficult-subjects/>. Accessed on February 27, 2019.

Farber, Mathew. *Teaching Empathy with Video Games*. Edutopia. 2018. Retrieved from <https://www.edutopia.org/article/teaching-empathy-video-games>. Accessed on February 27, 2019.

http://www.gamesforchange.org/studentchallenge/la/kindness-empathy/ (?)

Pedersen, Traci. *Can A Video Game Boost Empathy in Teens?* Psych Central. 2018. Retrieved from <https://psychcentral.com/news/2018/08/11/can-a-video-game-boost-empathy-in-teens/137794.html>. Accessed on February 27, 2019.

STUDY OF DEVELOPMENT OF CREATIVITY THROUGH DIGITAL GAMES

Werner W. Marin and Pollyana Notargiacomo
Faculty of Computer Science and Technology - Mackenzie Presbyterian University (UPM)
Higienópolis Campus - 0132-907 - São Paulo - Brazil

ABSTRACT

The interest in creativity has grown steadily in the last decades. Amidst this surging interest is the question of whether it is possible to aid the development of creativity. This study investigates the possibility of developing a digital game with just such objective. Therefore the game Luovus was created, utilizing previous research on the subject of creativity and digital games as learning aids. The game has been tested with a group of users and seems to be an effect on the player's self perceived creative capabilities and society's impact on their creativity.

KEYWORDS

Creativity, Digital, Games, Development, Test

1. INTRODUCTION

Although studies on creativity have been ongoing since 1950 by Maslow (1943) and others, this area has been given increasing importance, not only in the context of individual life, but also the benefits it brings to society (Alencar 2010). With this came the desire to find ways to develop and improve creative thought. Past studies show this is not a fruitless endeavor and that it is indeed possible to develop and individual's creative thought. In an experiment conducted by Azevedo et al. (2017) a group of teenagers showed significant progress after going through the *Future Problem Solving* program, for instance.

As comprehension of the subject grew, came a search for tools to aid in the development of creative thought. Some experiments studied workplace activities (Wang 2013) and pedagogical activities with children (Coppi 2015).

Following this path, this research proposes to study the viability of developing creative thought through digital games. Prior studies corroborate the supposition that this is possible. FLIGBY, a serious game studied in the research of Buzady (2017) has shown itself successful in inducing the state of flow in the player, this state being important to incentivise creative thought.

To reach the goals of this research, the game Luovus was developed in parallel. Luovus will be further elaborated on in the Method section of this paper.

2. LITERATURE REVIEW

2.1 Definition of Creativity

Creativity is the result of a mutually beneficial interaction between person and environment, interaction which needs autonomy and resistance to excessive social control. Associated to creativity are aspects of cognitive skills, personality traits, motivation, learning style, strategy, decision making, thought management, amongst others. Creativity is a psychosocial ocurrance, expression of characteristics both of the individual and the social environment or ecosystem (Alencar 2010). In other words, an individual's creative thoughts are consequences of the environment they are found in as well.

2.2 Developing Creativity

The experiment led by Azevedo et al. (2017) with the *Future Problem Solving Program International* had positive results. All competencies showed significant increase on the experimental group. This indicates a promising possibility of developing creative thought.

Moffat and Shabalina (2016) studied the relationship between imposed restrictions on the solution of a task and the levels of creativity reached in finding a solution to the desk. It should be noted that a game with the purpose of aiding the development of creative thought on the player should present challenges with some form of constraint or rule so that the player has some guidance on how to practice their creativity. That said, it is important that the game is not so strict as to limit the player's freedom in pursuing their ideas and keeping them from engaging their creativity.

An individual may reach a more creative solution by spending a longer time thinking about the task (Zhang 2014). On the other hand, an overly long session of creative thinking may lead to cognitive exhaustion and unsatisfactory results (Coppi 2015), influencing the ability to focus on a specific task. It seems that minimum amount of time a player must engage with a game designed to aid the development of creative thought must be intentional and calculated.

A superior's feedback has a positive impact on an employees' ability to engage in creative thought, but that depends largely on the employee's capacity to monitor themselves (Zhou 2013). The impact is more significantly positive when the employee practices self-monitoring. When aiding the development of creative thought, it is important not only to give constructive feedback, but also stimulate self critique.

A player's final experience with a game is influenced by their age. Vella et al. (2013) conducted a study with people with ages ranging from 12 to 52 years. They found a positive relation between age and the player's feelings wellbeing. Therefore, the same game will have a different effect on different aged players (Vella 2013). It would be unlikely to design a game that had equally satisfactory results spanning all age groups.

2.3 Measuring Creativity

There are multiple tools to measure creative thought. The most famous is possibly the *Torrance Tests for Creative Thinking*, on which was based the *Abbreviated Torrance Test for Adults*. The TTCT is well trusted and often mentioned when talking about measuring creativity (Cramond 2005).

Besides the TTCT and the ATTA there is also the *Abedi Test for Creativity*, what is a self-evaluation test, making it useful as a way to understand an individual's own self perceived ability to think creatively. The test created by Alencar et al. (2010) is also self-evaluative, with the advantage of being designed in the language spoken by the experimental group studied in this research.

3. METHOD

Luovus was made in JavaScript (using the PixiJS graphical engine) and considering the ease of accessing a web page and multiplatform application. Modules are added to the main *.html* page of the game. Modules are activated and deactivated as needed. Each module corresponds to a questionnaire, a scene or a menu screen. To manage the modules, an engine called *Voorhees* was written in JavaScript (Figure 1). This engine initializes PixiJS and decides which modules will be activated and deactivated based on game states.

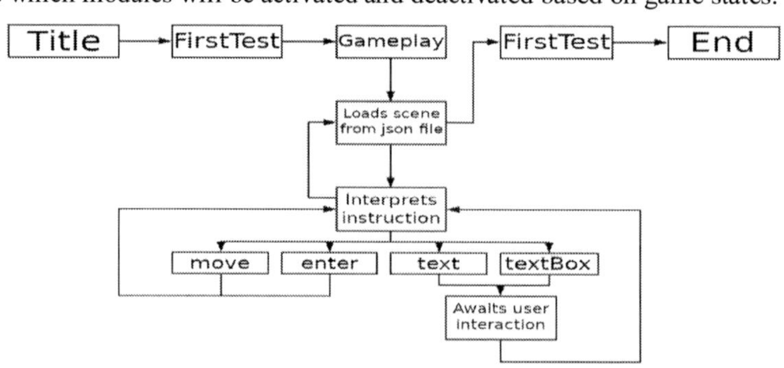

Figure 1. Functioning of the *Voorhees* engine

When a scene module is loaded, *Voorhees* load a corresponding *.json* file containing the scene information, like appearing characters, dialogue and background art. *Voorhees* then interprets this information and, working in tandem with PixiJS, draws the scene on the screen. Then, *Voorhees* interprets player interactions and reacts accordingly.

When the game is first accessed the user is presented with the main screen, containing the options "start" and "about". Upon choosing "start" the user is asked to answer the self-evaluative creativeness questionnaire created by Alencar et al. (2010) (Figure 2). Since the game will be tested with portuguese speakers, this specific test was chosen for being written originally in portuguese. The questionnaire consists of 66 questions in the format "*I would be more creative if...*" followed by a statement. For instance "*I would be more creative if I were less afraid to share my ideas*". For each statement the user must inform if they "*completely disagree*", "*partially disagree*", are "*undecided*", "*partially agree*" or "*completely agree*". The results are analyzed on a Likert Scale. The questionnaires purpose is to understand how the user perceives their own creativity in a self-evaluation. According to Zhou (2013), as important as giving positive feedback to the player is, it is also important to lead the player into monitoring their own creative engagement and find ways to further develop their own creativity.

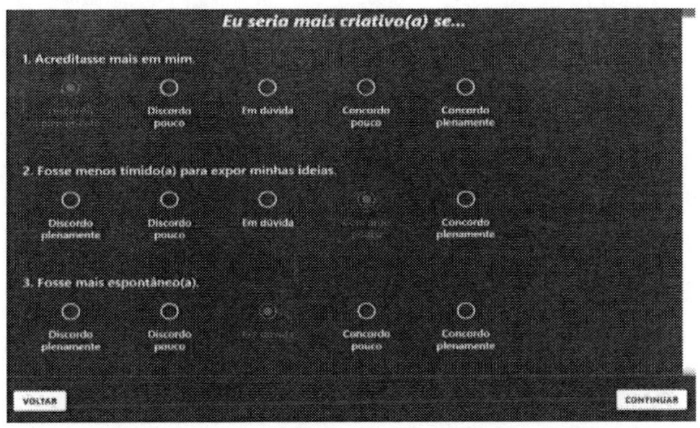

Figure 2. Likert Scale with translation of questions and metric ("I would be more creative if… 1. I believed more in myself. 2. I were less afraid to share my ideas. 3. I were more spontaneous.") The scale used was "Completely disagree | Partially disagree | Undecided | Partially agree | Completely agree"

After the questionnaire, the player is taken to the game. At a first moment the player is presented to the Artist, a character that will serve as a guide to the player during the game. After the Artist explains the story of the game to the player, a second character appears. This character will be the first amongst others to ask the player for help (Figure 3a). In this first instance it is made clear to the player they are welcome to respond in the most outlandish way possible. Shortly after, in the same scene, the player's response is reacted to by the characters present, so as to show the player that the game world will react to their choices.

a)  b)

Figure 3. a) "(...) What do you think would grab the attention of anyone who came through here?"; b) "I come from"

Throughout the game the player will meet other characters with whom they will interact (Figure 3b). At each interaction the player is presented with the opportunity to come up with a solution to a problem. At the end, the Artist will present the player a story he wrote. This story changes based on the interactions the player had with the world.

After the game, the player is asked to answer the questionnaire again. This is done to analyze the impact the game had in the player's perception of their own creativity, besides their approach to each question in the questionnaire. The results of the questionnaires answered by the players are saved on a *.json* file without any information that might compromise the player's anonymity. Each file is identified by a unique random id.

4. RESULTS

The sample group comprises of 7 male participants and 8 female participants, for a total of 15 participants. Participants were chosen by age group and degree of academic education. The youngest participant was 20 years of age and the oldest participant was 25 years of age, for an average of 22 year of age in the sample group. When comparing the results between the pretest and the post test for the creativity test, there was found no significant variation in the scores for the subjects perceived creativity, with an average variation of -6 on a scale of -132 to 132 (Figure 4).

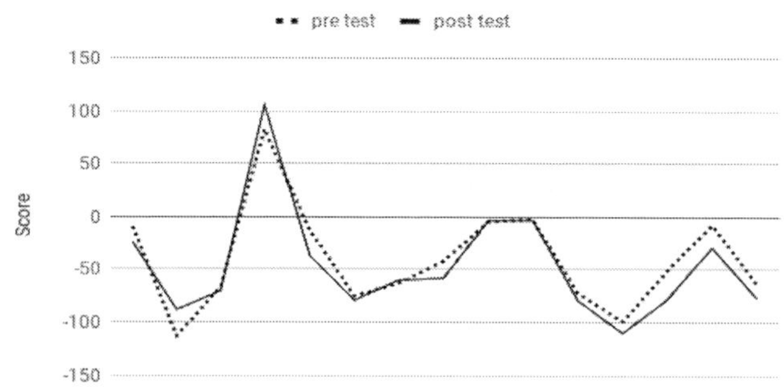

Figure 4. Score variation on the creativity test between the pretest and the post test for each player

The variation on the answers for each question between the pretest and the post test was also analyzed (Figure 5). In other words, if the subjects scored higher or lower on each given question on the post test in relation to the pretest.

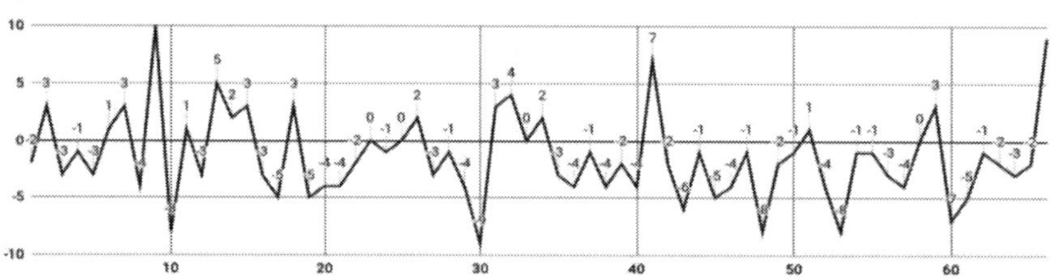

Figure 5. Average score variation for each question of the creativity test between the pretest and the post test

Most questions showed no relevant variation in their scores, with a variation of 5 points or less. Some questions, on the other hand, showed a more relevant variation, variating up to 10 points, namely questions *9*, *10*, *30*, *41*, *43*, *48*, *53*, *60* and *66*.

Table 1. Questions on the creativity test with the most relevant score variation

Question	"I would be more creative if.."	Variation
9	**"I had more initiative"**	10
10	**"I wasn't afraid of contradicting people"**	-8
30	**"I wasn't afraid of being misunderstood"**	-9
41	**"I had more resources to put my ideas into practice"**	7
43	**"I hadn't been put down by my teachers"**	-6
48	**"There was more cooperation between people"**	-8
53	**"People valued more new ideas"**	-8
60	**"I had a sense of humor"**	-7
66	**"I had more knowledge"**	9

5. CONCLUSION

When asked about their experience with the game, 11 of the players reported having found the game "fun", "pleasant" or "interesting", which indicates that over two thirds of the subjects reported having a positive experience interacting with the game. Additionally, five of the subjects reported that they found the game too short, which could possibly aid the player in reaching a state of flow. It is possible the results would be more enlightening if the game was longer.

Analysis of the results does not indicate that game has aided in developing the players' creative thought. As the test is of the self-evaluating kind, it is possible the negative average score variation is due to the players evaluating themselves more criteriously after having played the game. In other words, roughly half the participants complained that the test is too long. This would be similar to the problem found by Coppi (2015), in which it's duration affected negatively the results. A test reduced in size or integrated seamlessly with the game could have mitigated this effect, and this might be further investigated in future research with more users and application of telemetry of the game combined with neural networks to explore how different they are.

While the average variation of the results for each individual question has been, for the most part, insignificant, it is interesting to note the questions that had an average variation of over 5 points. When looking at positive and negative variation, it is possible to speculate that the game had the effect on the players of giving them some confidence in not needing outside material and intellectual resources to be creative, but less confident in how others and society would react to their ideas. Questions such as "I would be more creative if I had more initiative" and "I would be more creative if I had more knowledge" had a notably positive variation, which may signal that the experience of practicing their creative skills made the players feel more confident in their capability of producing creative ideas without the need of outside assistance.

REFERENCES

Ahmadi, G. A.; Abdolmaleki, S.; Khoshbakht, M. 2011. Effect of computer-based training to increase creativity and achievement science, students in fourth grade of elementary. *In Procedia Computer Science*, pp. 1551-1554.

Alencar, E. M. L. S.; Fleith, D. S.; Bruno-Faria, M. F, 2010. *A Medida da Criatividade: Teoria e Prática*. Artmed, Porto Alegre, Brazil.

Azevedo, I.; Morais, M. D. F.; Martins, F. 2017. Educação para a Criatividade em Adolescentes: Uma Experiência com Future Problem Solving Program International. *In REICE*, pp.75-87.

Buzady, Z. 2017. Flow, leadership and serious games – a pedagogical perspective. *In World Journal of Science, Technology and Sustainable Development*, Vol. 14 Issue: 2/3, pp.204-217.

Coppi, A. E. 2015. Fostering creativity through games and digital story telling. *2015 International Conference on Interactive Technologies and Games*, Nottingham, England, pp. 17-21.

Li, Zhang; Qiong, Bu; Wee, Sooyeon. 2014. Impact of Job Control on Employee Creativity: The Moderating Effect of Cognitive Irritation. *Proceedings of the 21th ICMSEM* , Helsinki, Finland, pp.873-878.

Maslow, A. H. 1943. A Theory of Human Motivation. *In Psychological Review*, pp. 430-437.

Moffat, David C.; Shabalina, Olga. 2016. Student Creativity Exercises in Designing Serious Games. *European Conference on Games Based Learning*, Paisley, Scotland, pp.470-478.

Vella, Kellie; Johnson, Daniel; Hides, Leanne. 2013. Positively playful: When videogames lead to player wellbeing. *Proceedings of the Gamification 2013*, Stratford, Canada, pp. 99-102.

Wang, Kai. 2013. The Effect of Autonomy on Team Creativity and the Moderating Variables. *2013 Proceedings of PICMET '13: Technology Management for Emerging Technologies*, San Jose, USA, pp.1156-1160.

Zhou, Ming-Jian; Li, Shu-Kun. 2013. Can Supervisor Feedback always Promote Creativity? The Moderating Role of Employee Self-Monitoring. *Proceedings of the ICIII 2013*, Shenzhen, China, pp.510-512.

AN ADAPTIVE IMAGE SHARPENING SCHEME

Tzong-Jer Chen
School of Information Engineering, Baise University, Baise, Guangxi, 533000 China

ABSTRACT

Image enhancement is one important process for digital images. This processing gives a better subjective visual appearance. The contours and texture are key features that contain important information essential to the visual quality aspect. Adaptive image enhancement schemes are proven better than global methods. An adaptive image sharpening method based on spatial statistics is proposed in this report to effectively sharpen image structures. A noisy Lena was pre-filtered using a low-pass filter to produce a blurred Lena. The residual image was obtained using average filtering and then subtracted from the original image. The high-pass residual image should be a combination of structure and noise. The autocorrelation of each pixel is calculated on the residual image and the image then is sharpened using a nimble filter based on the adaptive autocorrelation values. The PFOM results show that the similarity of adaptive sharpening is better than the global scheme. The proposed method will be further developed and applied to improve image acuity, de-noising and image quality improvement.

KEYWORDS

Image Sharpening, Spatial Statistics, Nimble Filter, PFOM

1. INTRODUCTION

Significant growth in digital image technology development in a wide range of fields has led to rapid expansions in applications. In many usage areas, digital image improvement technology behavior depends on the input image quality [Chen, T.J. et al, 2016.]. Image enhancement is one of the areas of digital image processing that involves altering the pixel intensity so that the processed image gives a subjectively better visual appearance. This is an essential pre-processing stage for various image processing systems. For different kinds of images, various image enhancement methods have been proposed. There is no unique algorithm that can provide the best visual output on a wide variety of input images [Neeraj K.S. and Arun K.S., 2017].

In digital images the key features are the contours, edges, and textures essential to the visual quality aspect [Fu, S. et al., 2007, Zohair A.A., 2018]. The visual appearance of an image may be improved by emphasizing its high frequency parts to enhance the edges and detail information. High frequency content enhancement, such as edge and detail information may significantly improve the visual appearance of an image [Polesel A. et al., 2000, Chen T.J. et al., 2017].

Image sharpening changes the visual quality without altering the content of the processed image. This is a computer vision and image processing scheme [Cao, G. et al., 2011]. Image sharpening can be defined as the improvement of apparent sharpness in an image that is supposed to be blurred [Haq N. et al., 2011]. Unsharp masking-based schemes have been widely used in increasing the sharpness of images. However, image sharpening is still an active research area due to the existence of various effective challenges, including the amplification of latent image noise [Sheppard A.P. et al., 2004], the introduction of overshoot [Kheradmand, A., & Milanfar, P. (2015)], and over-sharpening effects [Zohair A.A., 2018].

A fast, efficient and simple filter for image sharpening sufficient for achieving satisfactory results was proposed. This work showed that the effect of this nimble filter is better than traditional Laplacian and unsharp mask filters [Zohair A.A., 2018.]. It was, nevertheless, a non-adaptive and global scheme. This may amplify the noise pixels as sharpened structures.

Adaptive schemes for image enhancement were recently proposed [Polesel A., et al., 2000, Fu S. et al., 2007, Gui Z.G. et al., 2012]. These algorithms enhance images while effectively decreasing the noise concurrently. The development of adaptive modules for image enhancement may be a good scheme [Chen

T.J. et al, 2016.]. Recently, Chen et al. proposed using spatial statistics (SS) as a threshold for adaptive filtering and work well [Chen T.J. et al, 2016, 2017, Chen T.J. 2018, Lu R.H. and Chen T.J. 2018].

The SS calculation was initially direct on a noisy image. Categorizing the pixel belongs to noise or structure based on the SS calculation results. This method successfully accomplishes the dual objectives of amplifying the detailed areas and not increasing noise. [Chen T.J. et al, 2016, 2017]. Afterwards, the SS calculation was applied to a residual image [Chen T.J. 2018, Lu R.H. and Chen T.J. 2018]. A residual image is obtained using average filtering and then subtracted from the original image. The high-pass residual image should be a combination of boundary and noise. The SS is calculated on each pixel of the residual image, and the noisy image is then adaptively filtered using a low pass filter based on the SS values. The PSNR results in their report showed that image quality using adaptive filtering is significantly better than that obtained from global filtering [Chen T.J. 2018, Lu R.H. and Chen T.J. 2018].

In this paper SS is applied on a residual image and then sharpened using a nimble filter adaptively. Images were processed through the proposed sharpening approach followed by an edge map calculation using Canny's approach [Bao P., Zhang L. and Wu X., 2005., Neeraj K.S. and Arun K.S., 2017]. The edge map is also reported quantitatively in terms of Pratt's Figure of Merit (PFOM) [Chabrier S. et al., 2006, Neeraj K.S. and Arun K.S., 2017]. The PFOM results show that the adaptive sharpening similarity is better than that obtained with the global scheme.

2. METHODS AND MATERIALS

A Lena image was used in this report to prove the assumption. Gaussian white noise was added to this image ($\mu = 100$, $\sigma = 10$) first. The residual image may be obtained by subtracting the noisy Lena from the smoothed pre-filtered image (3×3 and 5×5 average filter) [Roychowdhury S. et al., 2015].

2.1 The Spatial Statistics

The SS named Moran statistics are used to evaluate the mapped data randomness by measuring the spatial autocorrelation [Cliff A.D .and Ord J.K., 1981]. This SS is a Z score of spatial correlation in a window. This Z value was proven to be a good index for determining image smoothness or sharpness [Chen T.J. et al, 2006, Shiao Y.H. et al, 2007]. This SS also showed that it has been shown to have ability to distinguish between image noise and edges [Chen T.J. et al, 2016]. Both Chen et al. and Hung et al. recently proposed adaptive filters using Moran statistics [Chen T.J. et al, 2016, 2017, 2018, Hung C.C. and Chang E.S., 2017]. Pixels with higher Z score are likely to be structured areas and lower Z is possible for noise. To improve image acuity, a pixel will perform sharpening if the Z score at this position is higher than a preset value. A pixel Z score lower than the preset is thought to be noise.

2.2 A Sharpness Filter

A new nimble filter was recently proposed to improve the sharpness of medical images utilizing specific spatial image information with a distinct tuning weight. This filter is described below:

$$k_{(x,y)} = \left(\varphi \times f_{(x,y)}\right) + \left((1-\varphi) \times \left[\frac{\left(f_{(x,y+1)} + f_{(x,y-1)} + f_{(x+1,y)} + f_{(x-1,y)}\right)}{4}\right]\right) \quad (1)$$

where $k_{(x,y)}$ is the resulting image; x,y are spatial coordinates, $f_{(x,y)}$ is the original degraded image, φ is a tuning weight that controls the amount of produced sharpness. It should fulfill ($\varphi>1$), where higher values lead to shaper results. $f_{(x,y+1)}$, $f_{(x,y-1)}$, $f_{(x+1,y)}$, $f_{(x-1,y)}$ are horizontally and vertically shifted version of the original image [Zohair A.A., 2018].

2.3 Pratt's Figure of Merit (PFOM)

Pratt processes an empirical measure for two pixel sets comparison. This measure is one of the most commonly used. Given scaling factor a (a = 1/9), and separation distance of d, PFOM can be calculated as follows: [Chabrier S. et al., 2006, Neeraj K.S. and Arun K.S., 2017]

$$\text{PFOM} = \frac{1}{I_N}\sum_{i=1}^{I_A}\frac{1}{1+a\times d^2} \quad (2)$$

where $I_N = \max\{I_I, I_A\}$, I_I and I_A are the ideal and actual edge maps, respectively. Higher PFOM value indicates the similarity between the ideal edge map and the candidate map.

3. RESULTS

3.1 SS on Residual Images

The Moran *Z* value of each pixel in the residual image was calculated with a 5×5 sliding window. A *Z* histogram was produced by collecting the *Z* values from all pixels. This *Z* histogram has proven that the image noise and edges are individually in lower and higher areas [Chen T.J. et al, 2006, Shiao Y.H. et al, 2007]. The *Z* histograms for two residual images from a noisy Lena was filtered using 3×3 and 5×5 average filters each, as noted in Figure 1. This figure shows that the histogram (winsz = 5) is shifted to areas with higher Z values compared to winsz =3. This effect also indicated that a residual image from a bigger window (5×5) had higher structural information than a smaller one (3×3). The smaller window has contained more noise than the big one.

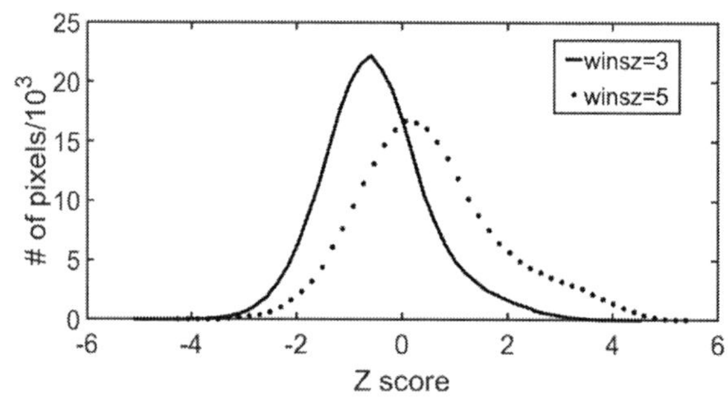

Figure 1. Histogram of Z score for two residual images, ie.winsz=3 (3×3)

3.2 Adaptive Image Sharpening

It is known that various medical devices introduce blur to recorded images due to many factual yet inevitable limitations. This nimble filter was originally applied to naturally blurred medical images [Zohair A.A., 2018].

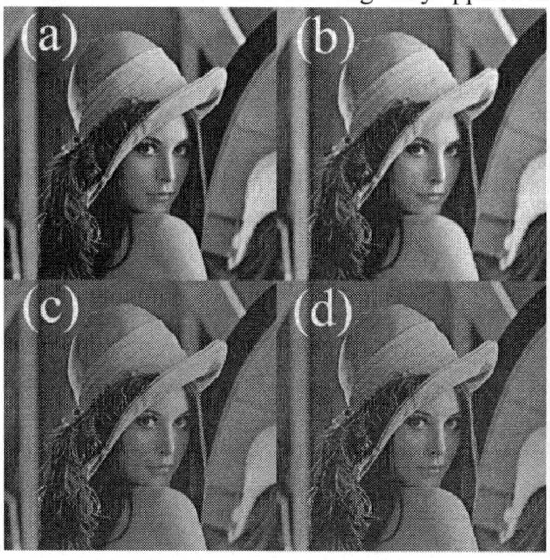

Figure 2. Lena images (a) original, (b) noisy, (c) Nimble filtered with Z adaptive (φ=6, Z>0), (d) Nimble filtered (φ=6)

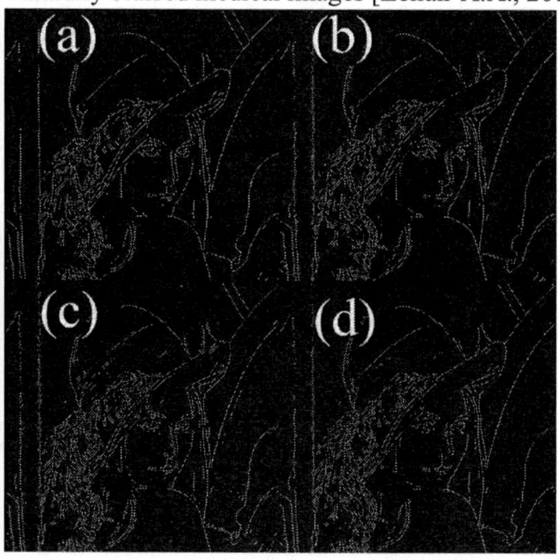

Figure 3. Edge map of Lena images (original), (b) noisy, (c) Nimble filtered with Z adaptive (φ=6, Z>0), (d) Nimble filtered (φ=6)

This new scheme was tested on a low-pass filtered noisy Lena image (3×3 average filter). The tuning weight φ=6 and 7 for nimble filter were used based on previous work [Zohair A.A., 2018]. Figure 2 shows the original Lena image, noisy (μ = 100, σ= 10), nimble filtered with Z adaptive (φ=6, Z>0), and Nimble filtered (φ=6). Figure 3 shows an edge map of the images in Figure 2. These edge maps were obtained using Canny's approach with code support [Bao P., Zhang L. and Wu X., 2005.].

The PFOM calculates quantitative effects of sharpening scheme on the edge map, as noted in Table 1. The higher PFOM indicates the similarity between the ideal edge (original Lena) and the edge map using the proposed scheme. The first row in Table 1 shows the PFOM values for the noisy Lena and those non-adaptive sharpening include φ=6, 7. The (3×3) means the SS calculation was on a residual image produced using a winsz=3 average filter. Equally, the (5×5) means that the SS calculation was on a residual image produced using a winsz=5 average filter. The highest PFOM in this table is obviously at Z>0.0 and Z>1.0 for φ=6 (3×3) and for φ=7 (5×5), individually. We found that the curve peaks are located around Z=0.0 and 1.0 for winsz=3, 5 individually, as shown in Figure 1. This effect indicates that sharpening on half of pixels may produce the best results.

Table 1. Quantitative performance (in terms of Pratt's Figure of Merit) PFOM

Noisy Lena	Nimble φ=6 (3×3)	Nimble φ=7(5×5)
Non-adaptive 0.895	0.9187	0.8950
Adaptive (Z>0.0)	**0.9397**	0.9142
Adaptive (Z>1.0)	0.8416	**0.9387**
Adaptive (Z>2.5)	0.7612	0.8711

4. DISCUSSIONS

This report proposes a new adaptive image sharpening scheme based on the results from spatial statistics. The SS Z score was applied to determine if an area belongs to the edge or noise before filtering. The PFOM calculation shows that the similarity between the edge maps is improved over the global image sharpening method. This scheme is effective for further image sharpening technology studies and improving image acuity.

The weight (φ) and Z score turning on the variation of acuity and PFOM will be addressed in future works. This proposed scheme will also be applied to much more different images to verify the effectiveness. A noise model such as the Poisson distribution will be considered to simulate medical imaging systems and applied to medical images.

ACKNOWLEDGEMENT

This work was supported in part by grants from Baise University, Guangxi, China:

1. Construction project of characteristic specialty and experimental training teaching base (center) of Guangxi colleges and universities from 2018 to 2020: characteristic specialty of Electronic Information Engineering of Baise university (approval number: 52, Guijiao higher education [2018]; number: 119).

2. Project grant of master of engineering professional degree authorization point (electronic information) of School of Information Engineering, Baise University in 2019.

REFERENCES

Bao P., Zhang L. and Wu X., 2005. Canny edge detection enhancement by scale multiplication, IEEE. Trans. on Pattern Analysis and Machine Intelligence. 27, pp. 1485-1490.

Cao G. et al., 2011. Unsharp masking sharpening detection via overshoot artifacts analysis. IEEE Signal Processing Letters, 18 (10), pp. 603–606.

Chabrier S. et al., 2006 .Supervised evaluation of synthetic and real contour segmentation results. European Signal Processing Conference (EUSIPCO) 2006, Florence, Italy.

Chen T.J. et al., 2006. A blurring index for medical images. J Digital Imaging, 19, pp. 118-125.

Chen T.J. et al., 2016. A pilot study on a new image enhancement method using spatial statistics. Joint International Information Technology, Mechanical and Electronic Engineering Conference (JIMEC 2016), Xian, China, pp. 33-38.

Chen T.J. et al., 2017. A NOVEL EDGE-PRESERVING FILTER FOR MEDICAL IMAGE ENHANCEMENT. Computer Graphics, Visualization, Computer Vision and Image Processing 2017, Lisbon, Portugal, pp. 279-384.

Chen T.J. et al., 2017. Compressed Medical Image Quality Determination Using the Kolmogorov Smirnov Test. Current Medical Imaging Reviews, 13 (2), pp. 204-209.

Chen T.J., 2018. MORAN'S Z BASED ADAPTIVE IMAGE FILTER. Computer Graphics, Visualization, Computer Vision and Image Processing 2018, Madrid, Spain. pp. 382-386.

Cliff A.D. and Ord J.K., 1981. Spatial process: models and applications. Pion, London, UK.

Fu S. et al., 2007. A feature-dependent fuzzy bi-directional flow for adaptive image sharpening. Neurocomputing, 70 (4), pp. 883–895.

Gui Z.G. et al., 2012. An X-ray image sharpening algorithm using nonlinear module. The Imaging Science Journal, 60: pp. 3-8.

Haq N. et al., 2011. Image sharpening by DWT-based hysteresis. In International conference on advanced concepts for intelligent vision systems . Ghent, Belgium, pp. 429–436.

Kheradmand A., & Milanfar P., 2015. Non-linear structure-aware image sharpening with difference of smoothing operators. Frontiers in ICT, 2 (22), pp. 1–12.

Lu R.H. and Chen T.J., 2018. Adaptive Image De-noising Method Based on Spatial Autocorrelation. ISICDM 2018, Chengdu, China, pp. 125-128.

Neeraj K.S. and Arun K.S., 2017. An adaptive image sharpening scheme based on local intensity variations. SIViP, 11: pp. 777–784.

Polesel A. et al., 2000. Image Enhancement via Adaptive Unsharp Masking. IEEE Transactions on image processing , 9, pp. 505-510.

Roychowdhury S. et al., 2015. Blind analysis of CT image noise using residual denoised images. 2015 IEEE Nuclear Science Symposium and Medical Imaging Conference, San Diego, CA, USA.

Sheppard A. P. et al., 2004. Techniques for image enhancement and segmentation of tomographic images of porous materials. Physica A: StatisticalMechanics and its Applications, 339(1), pp. 145–151.

Shiao Y.H. et al., 2007. Quality of Compressed Medical Images. J of Digital Imaging, 20, pp.149-159.

Zohair A.A., 2018. Sharpness Improvement for Medical Images Using a New Nimble Filter. 3D Res, 9:12, pp. 2-12.

JIM DINE AND THE ARC DETECTOR

Richard Nau
Carleton College
Northfield MN USA

ABSTRACT

Heart shapes are ubiquitous. Among the numerous places they appear are in the artworks of famous artists as well as children. One of Jim Dine's favorite subjects for print making early in his long career was hearts. Most of his hearts are shaped differently from the usual hearts found in most designs or those given by mathematical formulas. In comparing heart shapes we naturally considered their underlying characteristics, especially those related to smoothness and curvature. To that end, some standard image processing procedures were used, and specialized ones developed and applied.

KEYWORDS

Arc Detection, Heart Shapes, Curvature, Jim Dine

Figure 1. (a) Orange Heart, (b) Outline, (c) Piecewise Linear, (d) Piecewise Arcs

1. INTRODUCTION

Consider the heart shapes in Figure 1. The one on the left is from a large poster of an orange heart. Its shape is typical of those that appear in many of Jim Dine's 40-some heart prints. His orange heart was selected for its size and because it is relatively well formed as Dine's hearts go. Our goal is to obtain outlines for the shapes, such as shown in Figure 1b, and use them for analytic and comparative purposes. A simple piecewise linear model for the outline is shown in Figure 1c together with the 14 points used. Figure 1d shows a much smoother model using the same points connected by circular arcs. Half of the arcs are dashed for clarification. We will use the term arcs to mean circular arcs, which may simplify to straight line segments, as happened in the longer line at the lower right. It is our contention that the heart shapes in Dine's art can be effectively modeled by such arcs. Of special interest will be the smoothness and curvature exhibited in the models. Although the outline in Figures 1b and 1d seems satisfactory, one might argue that there were too few points used and that they were not chosen arbitrarily. Using standard techniques of image processing as well as some especially developed routines to detect arcs, we aim to overcome such issues in this paper. First, to establish some bases for comparison, we will consider some heart shapes defined by mathematical formulas. Next we will establish the means for comparing the shapes' features such as smoothness and curvature. Then the routines will be applied to Dinc's hearts. Finally, finer points in the methods and artworks will be examined.

The artworks considered are prints or photographs, and as such there's not a precise location where they are found. D'Oench (see References) incudes 40-some different images for our selection. The two main ones presented here will be referred to as the orange heart and the snowy heart. D'Oench discusses mainly artistic considerations other than shape. Similarly there are many educational articles and projects available that employ Dine's hearts without being particularly concerned with the shape, which in this study is the only concern.

Most of our techniques are familiar in image processing circles. We employed *Mathematica* for its image processing routines and ability to develop our own. See the References for the author's earlier methods on the radome for the Boeing 747. A recent work (Futterlieb, 2017) studying cloud shapes is similar to ours but on a much larger scale with respect to as the amount of data, the hardware, and the sophistication of its techniques.

2. DESIDERATA

Because the interest is in the shape of the curves outlining the hearts, especially considered will be:

1) The fit. How well does the model fit the image? As the piecewise linear model above demonstrates one can fit the points exactly, but still not provide a good outline to the heart.
2) Continuity. Unless there is an obvious discontinuity in the artwork itself, the model should be continuous.
3) Smoothness, i.e. the continuity of the slope of the curve, and hence its tangent and normal vectors. With just a few points as in the example above, it's possible to obtain a model using piecewise arcs that fits the points without the terrible disruptions in the smoothness that the piecewise linear model exhibits.
4) Convexity. The model should be convex wherever the heart shape is. Of course there is the concavity at the cusp at the top that should be met and perhaps some slight concavity near the bottom.
5) Curvature. This will be the foremost objective. Curvature is, by definition, the change in the tangent direction with respect to change in arc length. For a straight line there is no change so the curvature is zero. For a circle the curvature is constant and works out to be the reciprocal of the radius. That's a reason for considering only circular arcs and line segments.
6) Size does not matter. To be able to compare the shapes for hearts of various sizes, we usually will normalize all distances in terms of the radius of the topmost arc of the right lobe, which will be considered to be of radius one. Thus the goodness of fit will be measured by the average absolute deviation between the original points and its approximating curve. Angles and percentages are unaffected by this scaling. Smoothness is measured as the percentage of the turning which is accomplished smoothly.

3. SMOOTHNESS AND CURVATURE OF SCRIPTED HEART SHAPES

Figure 2 shows three shapes based on mathematical formulas. Figure 2a shows a heart that commonly is used in elementary schools to familiarize students with circles and lines, perhaps using disks and triangular wooden blocks.. Most all heart shapes include a right lobe and a left lobe and two cusps. The upper cusp we will refer to as the cleft and the lower one as the tip. The exterior angle at the cleft will be denoted by α, and the interior angle at the tip by β. Whereas the elementary heart is upright and balanced those of artists are often slightly askew and asymmetrical. As ones eye traces the right edge of the elementary heart in Figure 2a from top to bottom one reaches the point where the circular arc and the slanted line meet. At this join there's a disturbing discontinuity in the slope, a jerk if you will. The smoothness of that edge is approximately 83%. To determine whether Dine's hearts also often lack smoothness will require close inspection. By matching the tangents at the join the jerk can be removed yielding the "smooth" heart in Figure 2b.

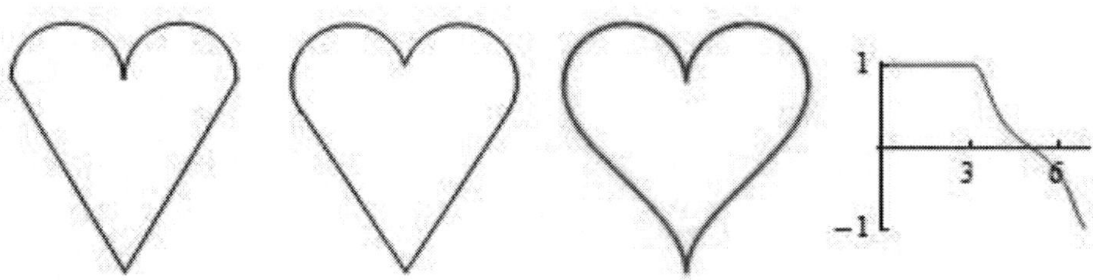

Figure 2. (a) Elementary Heart, (b) Smooth Heart, (c) Ideal Heart, (d) Ideal Heart Profile

The so-called Ideal Heart in Figure 2c combines a semi-circular arc with an arccosine for each lobe. Not only is the curve for each half smooth, i.e. no jerk, but furthermore it has a continuously changing curvature, which among heart aficionados is a highly desired property

Consider again the right lobe of the elementary heart. It starts straight up, bends to the right along the unit circle a distance of π units until the joining with the line. From there we travel 4 units straight ahead without curving, i.e. curvature 0. Thus the motion of the trace for the elementary heart shown can be summarized by (0, 1, π), (30°, 0, 4). A *trace* in general will be specified as a sequence of triples, (Θ, K, L), in which Θ is the clockwise turn, K (kappa) is the curvature, and L the distance to be traveled on that segment.

Derivable from the trace is the *curvature profile*, i.e. the curvature as a function of arc length. This is shown in Figure 2d for the Ideal Heart. The profiles for the elementary and smooth hearts (not shown) are simply step functions. Expressing the curvature in terms of arc length was trivial for the two simpler cases; not so for the Ideal Heart where numerical evaluation of an elliptical integral was required.

4. MODELING THE DINE HEARTS°

Our attempt to model the Dine hearts is intended to remove some of the subjectivity in the choices made. In general, the procedure is to:

1) Obtain an image and crop it to include mainly the heart.,
2) Apply an edge detector.
3) Identify the relevant larger connected components.
4) For each such component, fit a circular arc to it,
5) Assemble the arcs into an outline of the heart.
6) Evaluate the result for fit, smoothness, and curvature.

The sources for the first step varied from a 3 meter square poster of the orange heart to 5 cm square images in an art book. For steps 2 and 3 we used several of the appropriate routines in *Mathematica*'s Image Processing suite. Steps 4, 5, and 6 will be demonstrated more thoroughly in the context of the next example, which is the snowy heart depicted in Figures 3a, b and c. What's being modeled is a snow covered statue. In considering the right lobe notice a short line segment at the cleft, a large circular arc at the top, another short line segment, a large arc on the right side, then a long line towards where the tip would be. The left lobe is less complicated, consisting of a short line, two arcs, and a long line. The edges in the image as detected result in Figure 3b.

Figure 3. Snowy Heart. (a) Photo, (b) Edges detected, (c) Outline

Then many smaller components were removed. Next the nine major components were identified, dealt with individually and combined into the outline shown in Figure 3c.

The first connected component considered and set was the large arc on the right shoulder. See Figure 4. This component consisted of about 230 points (pixels). It was fit using only five points. If the points selected were too close together, overfitting and scattering could result. So the points used were separated by about 40 pixels. Call these points 1, 2, 3, 4, 5. Three points determine a circle, so the points were grouped (1,2,3), (2,3,4), (3,4,5). Rather than using the equation for a circle one can use the fact that the center of a circle is at the intersection of the perpendicular bisectors of any two chords, as in Figure 5. In this manner three centers could be obtained and averaged to form a common center. The average distance to the five points, or all 230 points for that matter, could be used for the common radius. Although this may seem complicated it is made computationally quite simple by using the generalized matrix inverse.

Suppose there were n perpendicular bisectors each of the form of a line and assumed to go through the common center (h, k); i.e, $a\,h + b\,k = c$. Collectively the set of linear equations as a matrix equation is simply $A\,(h, k)^t = C$, where A is an n by 2 matrix containing columns of a's and b's, C is n by 1 for the c's, and t denotes the transpose. The generalized solution for this over-determined system is simply $(h,k)^t = A^g\,C$ where $A^g = (A^tA)^{-1}A$ is the generalized matrix inverse. Please note this works very efficiently for any n (>=2).

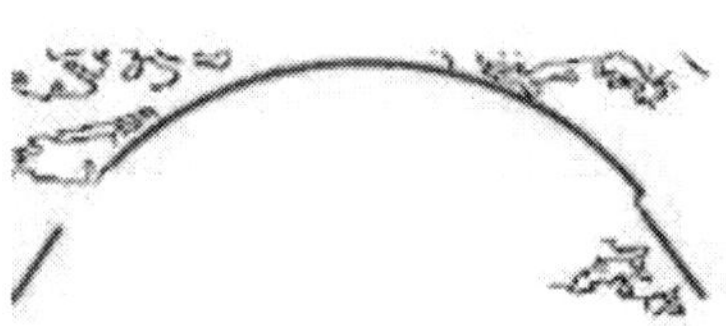

Figure 4. Snowy right top.

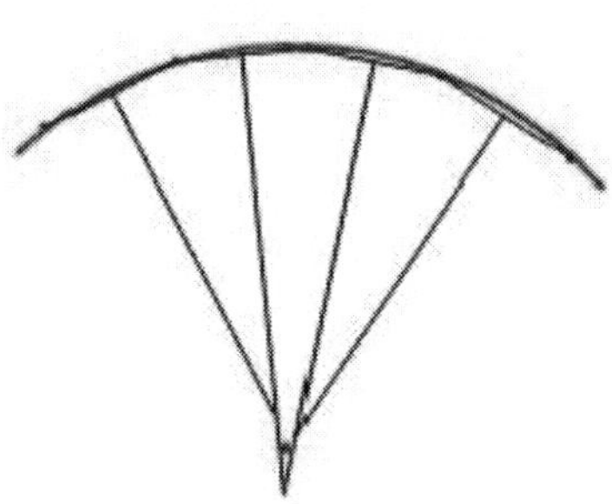

Figure 5. Four bisectors.

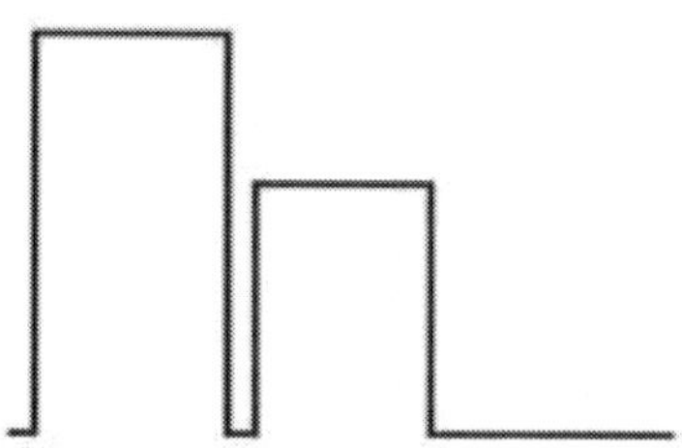

Figure 6. Snowy Right Profile

The bulb at the left lobe was handled similarly to that on the right. The connected components for the two long lines at the tip can be easily dispatched. Shorter ones require more explanation. Consider the two short components in the lower corners of Figure 4. If the arc were extended it would undershoot the one on the left and overshoot the one on the right. These situations are often referred to as an under-bite and an overbite, resp. The short component at the left in Figure 4, i.e. the one near the cleft, when blown up reveals its linear fit. Any closer fit would result in a concavity, which is unjustified considering the few points involved. The connections between the top arcs and the long lines required some intervention. Looking closely at those areas it is clear that those components are not as well defined as for the top arcs and the long lines. A single arc on the left lobe connected its top arc and long line. On the right lobe an intervening short line segment was discerned there. The curvature profile for the right lobe showing the curvature is given in Figure 6.

In analyzing other Dine hearts there were many similarities. The larger hearts were generally elongated and had a right lobe slightly larger than the left and were tilted by a few degrees to the right which gave an illusion that added to the apparent asymmetry. Again large components were obtained and fitted by arcs with little error. Joining the arcs often required compromises among the fit, curvature and smoothness. However in all cases the fitness on the main components was within a percentage or two and the amount of jerkiness limited to less than 20%, Smaller hearts studied were often so well formed that the largest component was in fact an entire outline by itself and the main task was to separate it into adjacent circular arcs.

5. RESULTS AND CONCLUSIONS

Applied to Dine's hearts the generalized matrix inverse based arc detector proved to be a very efficient and effective tool for obtaining the arcs and their curvature as well as to measure their fitness. It would be informative to apply it to more artworks and other areas where circular arcs are known to exist or suspected.

Visually piecewise arcs, requiring very few arcs, fit the heart images tested, at least their major edge detected components. It's not a surprise that arcs would fit, but what is surprising is how few were sufficient, how few points were needed from each arc, and how well they fit, often within 1%. .Furthermore, the resulting curvatures were constant over fairly large regions. Trade-offs between the fit and smoothness were possible although a smoothness of at least 80% was always achievable.

More accuracy and smoothness could be obtained using more arcs. One could also eliminate some of the jerkiness by sacrificing some fit. However closer examination shows that much of that jerkiness is really there, i.e. it is an artifact in the art, not a consequence of the algorithms. We should not blame the algorithm. Even more fit could be expended to get a more smoothly changing curvature as well. But generally, the tight fit indicates that that curvature obtained, or something very close to it, is really there.

Some smaller anomalies in the artworks were detected, such as a slight discontinuity or a small unexpected concavity. Although the larger arcs and longer lines were well defined, where they joined was often somewhat obscure. Indeed a detailed inspection of the artworks reveals that those areas were subjected to shadowing, over-sketching and what might be considered patching. But that, together with such irregularities as the tilting and asymmetry, is what makes it art rather than computer graphics. Jim Dine, when asked about the rationality behind his work is said to have quipped "I have never had a rational thought".

ACKNOWLEDGEMENT

The support of Carleton College to present this work is greatly appreciated. I also wish to thank the reviewers for their thoughtful and constructive advice.

REFERENCES

D'Oench, E.G. and J. E. Feinberg, 1986. *Jim Dine Prints 1977-1985,* Harper & Row, New York, NY, USA.

Futterlieb, J. et al, 2017. Smooth Visualization of Large Point Clouds. *IADIS Journal on Computer Science and Data Visualization* Vol 11, No 2, Porto, Portugal, pp 146-156.

Nau, R, 1966. Generalized Radome Incidence Analysis. *Boeing Reports*, Seattle, WA, USA.

OBJECT-LOCATING VIA OBJECT RECOGNITION AND INDOOR POSITIONING

Chuan-Kai Yang and Hsuan Chin
National Taiwan University of Science and Technology, Taipei, Taiwan

ABSTRACT

Object locating has been a problem in our daily lives, and some techniques have been proposed to address this issue. However, there are still some drawbacks with previous methods. This paper proposes to use two techniques to make object locating easier through object recognition and indoor positioning, so that not only a picture containing the desired object can be shown to help recall where the object was placed, but also the location or room can be shown to help guide where to retrieve the desired object.

KEYWORDS

Object Locating, Indoor Positioning, Object Recognition

1. INTRODUCTION

Modern people tend to become more forgetful as there are too many things to remember, and this is especially true when we tried to recall where a particular object was finally placed. The problem, termed as object locating, has become an issue that the paper tries to address. Existing techniques mostly resort to particular devices or multiple cameras. However, the involved hardware either causes higher cost or lacks particular orientation or positioning information, thus making the corresponding solutions less attractive. We propose to make use of a commonly available mobile phone to develop two versions for locating a desired object. The first version of our system takes a picture of a desired object, sends the picture for object recognition, and stores the returned recognized object name with the picture so that later on such a picture can be retrieved through a voice command to help recall where the object was finally put. The second version, aims to further improve the first one, by taking a picture of the object attached with a specially designed paper tag so that we could infer the relative distance and orientation of the object with respect to the mobile phone. Together with the use of some indoor positioning technique to record the position of the mobile phone when taking the picture, we later on could guide a user to the location/room where the object was placed last time. The rest of the paper is organized as follows. Section 2 reviews work related to this paper. Section 3 describes how the first version of our system is implemented. Section 4 details how we based on the first version to further improve it to develop our second version. Section 5 presents some of our results. Section 6 concludes this paper and hints for possible future directions.

2. RELATED WORK

Regarding object locating, there exist several systems, as surveyed by Koyuncu and Yang, (Koyuncu and Yang, 2010), while most of them applied some specific hardware to help locate desired objects. Another representative work, done by Frank et al. (Frank et al., 2007), is also to make use of RFID/Bluetooth technique for object locating. Although the work is quite complete, the lack of orientation information and limitation of the sensing range for using a mobile phone as a signal reader has made the system more complicated. To resolve these issues, as mentioned previously, this work applies basically two techniques, i.e., object recognition and indoor positioning, to help address the object locating problem. We therefore also briefly review these two fields of study respectively.

In terms of object recognition, there are many related studies using robots to identify objects. In 2016, Rafsan et al. (Rafsan et al., 2016) proposed a human-robot interaction framework. Robots can detect specific objects at home according to the needs of users. They use Haar classifiers to identify them. For Objects at home, they can distinguish specific objects based on their colors, sizes, or positional information. In addition to using robots, cameras can also be used to identify objects. In 2015, Liaquat et al. (Liaquat et al., 2015) proposed a single camera-based depth estimation technique. After detecting different objects in the room, they calculate their areas, and then estimate the distance between the camera and the object based on the training data and a polynomial curve fitting method. In 2012, Mustafah et al. (Mustafah et al., 2012) proposed a more accurate measurement of the distance and size of objects in the "field of view" using a stereo vision system of two cameras.

In terms of indoor positioning, since the GPS positioning system cannot be used indoors, other positioning technologies have been proposed, such as iBeacon, geomagnetic positioning, Bluetooth, and wifi.iBeacon: In 2017, Dalkılıç et al. (Dalkılıç et al., 2017) tested the accuracy of the distance between two devices communicating via iBeacon technology. The results of the study indicate that iBeacon technology is suitable for indoor positioning systems where accuracy is not critical. The placement of iBeacons and environmental conditions are important for obtaining more accurate distance estimates. Regarding geomagnetic positioning, in 2014, Pritt (Pritt, 2014) investigated the possibility of using indoor geomagnetism to enhance the accuracy of wifi indoor positioning. The results show that the combination of geomagnetic and Wi-Fi fingerprint recognition can improve the accuracy of indoor positioning. Regarding Bluetooth, in 2018 Satan (Satan, 2018) used a Bluetooth beacon to transmit RF signals for distance calculation. Based on the distance from the beacon, the user's position is estimated and Dijkstra's shortest path algorithm is used for route planning.

3. OBJECT INFORMATION COLLECTION AND RETRIEVAL

3.1 System Flow for Object Information Collection

The object detection and positioning process is divided into three phases:

(1) First, take a picture of the desired object.

(2) Use Tensorflow Mobile to detect/recognize the object on the mobile phone, and also detect the marker on the object.

(3) Combine the direction sensor of the mobile phone itself to know the positioning coordinates of the object relative to the mobile phone.

3.2 Object Recognition

Google's object detection API – Tensorflow is an open source software library for high performance numerical computation. Its flexible architecture allows easy deployment of computation across a variety of platforms (CPUs, GPUs, TPUs), and from desktops to clusters of servers to mobile and edge devices. If we use/download an engine that can recognize the desired object already, then we don't need to perform any training. However, if the object in question cannot be recognized, then we need to train the engine ourselves.

3.3 Calculation of Distance

Figure 1

In order to quickly and easily know the distance of the object, we designed a marker as shown in Figure 1 to be attached on the object. As this marker is with a fixed size, its distance, as well as its orientation, to the camera, can be calculated according to the pin-hole camera formula.

3.4 Calculation of Orientation

Once we know the distance of the object, denoted as r in Figure 2, and then we can use the direction sensor of the mobile phone to obtain the current directional angle of the mobile phone, and the trigonometric function can be used to obtain the X, Y coordinates of the object relative to the mobile phone (user).

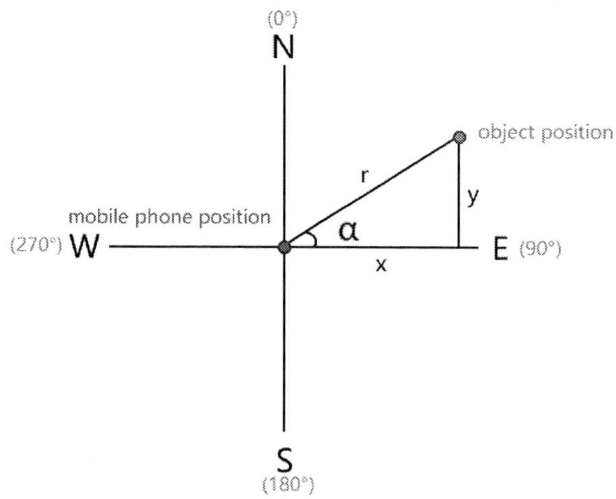

Figure 2

3.5 Voice Retrieval

The image, name, distance, orientation and coordinate information of the object are stored in the database. Users can use voice command to retrieve to find the objects they are looking for.

4. INDOOR POSITIONING

4.1 Geomagnetic Indoor Positioning Technology

The Earth itself is a giant magnet that forms a magnetic field between the geographic north and south. However, the earth's magnetic field is disturbed by metal objects, which creates a unique magnetic force map inside each building, can cause the different magnetic field differences at various points in the room for indoor positioning. The advantage is that we can use existing equipment without deploying other hardware infrastructure. The disadvantage is that the magnetic field changes must be actually collected at various locations in the room, and the preparation process is troublesome.

4.2 Indoor Atlas

IndoorAtlas is a Finnish start-up that offers a geomagnetic indoor positioning platform. It is expected to provide users with indoor positioning services with an accuracy of 1 meter by effectively utilizing the functions of the smart phone built-in magnetometer and through its cloud-based geomagnetic map service.

IndoorAtlas Business Director Daniel Patton said, "This technology is very simple, because modern buildings have a unique magnetic field feature." The structure and materials of the building interact with the

Earth's magnetic field, creating a unique magnetic map on each floor. Once this magnetic map is recorded and stored in the cloud, it can be used to accurately find and track the individual's position indoors.

4.3 Indoor Positioning Process

The process of indoor positioning is divided into 5 steps:

(1) First upload the indoor floor plan to the IndoorAtlas platform.

(2) Using the MapCreator app provided by Indooratlas to actually visit the entire indoor environment and collect geomagnetic data from various locations in the room.

(3) The collected geomagnetic data will be uploaded to the IndoorAtlas platform and converted into different X, Y coordinates according to the change of geomagnetism.

(4) Then according to the difference of geomagnetism, we can use the API provided by IndoorAtlas to get the X, Y coordinates of the current position.

(5) Finally, the technique of walking and painting can be implemented according to the user's movement. And in such a manner a user can be aware where he/she is and as long as the location (room) of the object is known, this can be used to guide the user to the reach where the object is placed.

5. RESULTS

Table 1. Development Environment

Development Platform	Android Studio
Program language	Java
Use Packages	(1) Object detection library：library 'org.tensorflow:tensorflow-android:+' (2) Indoor positioning package：Package 'com.indooratlas.android.sdk'
Phone specifications	Sony Xperia Z3+

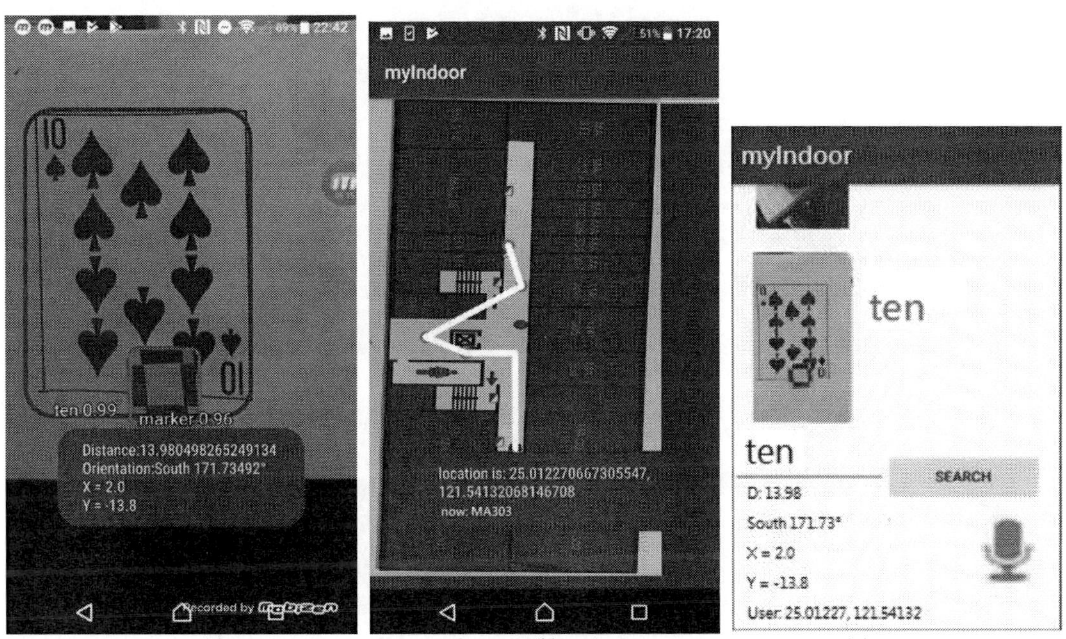

(a) (b) (c)

Figure 3

Table 1 shows our development environment. The testing environment is the 3rd Floor in our school, and the Figure 3(a) shows the object detection result, which recognizes the playing cards 10 and markers in the picture, and shows that the distance from the mobile phone (user) is 13.98 cm, located at 171.73° in the south, and the coordinate relative to the mobile phone (user) is (2.0 , -13.8).

Figure 3(b) shows the result of the painting while walking. The gray point is the location where the user visited. The blue point is the user's current position, and the white line segment is the line segment formed by walking. Figure 3(c) shows the result of the voice retrieval. A user can press the red microphone icon to enter the name of the item by voice. He/she then presses the search button to display the photo containing the desired object.

6. CONCLUSION AND FUTURE WORK

We have proposed two versions for object locating. The first one makes use of object detection by taking a picture of a desired object and recording the recognized name into a database so that later on the associated picture can be retrieved through a voice command to help recall where the object was placed last time. The second version improves the first one by incorporating the relative distance and orientation of the object with respect to the image-capturing mobile phone, together with the location of the mobile phone and a third-party indoor positioning system to guide the user to where the object was finally put.

There are still some limitations in our current system. First, to make sure that our system works, a user needs to take a picture of an object each time it is moved to a new place. Second, even though an object may stay where it is, it is still possible that some other object is placed in front of it to prevent it from being seen. Third, currently our system can only show a user where the object was placed without actively guiding the user toward the object. In the future, to address the first two issues, one or more surveillance cameras could be installed to keep track of how and where the objects are displaced. To address the third issue, we believe some other functionality of third-party indoor positioning tool can be employed to achieve this.

ACKNOWLEDGEMENT

This work was supported in part by the Ministry of Science and Technology of Taiwan under the grants MOST 104-2221-E-011-083-MY2, MOST 105-2218-E-011-005, MOST 105-2218-E-001-001, MOST 106-3114-E-011-003, and MOST 106-2221-E-011-148-MY3.

REFERENCES

Dalkılıç et al., 2017. An Analysis of the Positioning Accuracy of iBeacon Technology in Indoor Environments, *International Conference on Computer Science and Engineering (UBMK)*, pp. 549-553.

Pritt, 2014. Indoor Navigation with use of Geomagnetic Anomalies, *IEEE Geoscience and Remote Sensing Symposium*, pp. 1859-1862.

Satan, 2018. Bluetooth-based Indoor Navigation Mobile System, *19th International Carpathian Control Conference (ICCC)*, pp. 332-337.

Rafsan et al., 2016. Design a Human-Robot Interaction Framework to Detect Household Objects, *International Conference on Informatics, Electronics and Vision (ICIEV)*, pp. 973-978.

Liaquat et al., 2015. Object Detection and Depth Estimation of Real World Objects using Single Camera, *Fourth International Conference on Aerospace Science and Engineering (ICASE)*, pp. 1-4.

Mustafah et al., 2012. Stereo vision images processing for real-time object distance and size measurements, *2012 International Conference on Computer and Communication Engineering (ICCCE)*, pp. 659-663.

Frank et al., 2007. Objects Calling Home: Locating Objects Using Mobile Phones, *Pervasive Computing. Pervasive 2007*.

Koyuncu and Yang, 2010. A Survey of Indoor Positioning and Object Locating Systems, International Journal of Computer Science and Network Security, Vol. 10, No. 5, pp. 121-128.

VISUALIZATION AND ANALYSIS OF MOLECULAR POTENTIAL ENERGY SURFACE (PES) AND ITS MINIMA

Eugene Popov[1], Anatoly Batiukov[1], Natalja Vogt[2], Tatyana Popova[3] and Jürgen Vogt[2]
[1]*Nizhegorodsky State Architectural & Civil Engineering University, 65, Ilyinskaya Street, Nizhny Novgorod, 603950, Russia*
[2]*University of Ulm, Albert Einstein Allee 47, D-89069 Ulm, Germany*
[3]*National Research University Higher School of Economics, 25/12, Bolshaja Pecherskaja Ulitsa, Nizhny Novgorod, 603155, Russia*

ABSTRACT

The study of the potential energy surface (PES) of a molecule is of fundamental importance in structural chemistry. PES, being a function of torsion angles describing the internal rotation of different fragments in the molecule, is usually calculated by means of standard programs for quantum-chemical calculations (for instance, by GAUSSIAN). The supplementing program (GAUSSVIEW) suggests the visualization of PES with not more than two torsional coordinates (3D PES). The visualization of four-dimensional and more complex hypersurfaces is still a challenge for structural chemists. Another problem is finding all local minima of hypersurfaces corresponding to the conformational landscape of the molecule. This paper describes how a specially designed multidimensional postprocessor can be used to solve these problems. It also demonstrates the postprocessor capabilities by presenting a few examples.

KEYWORDS

Multidimensional Postprocessor, Visualization and Analysis of Multidimensional Function, Java, Java3D, Conformations of Molecules with Several Internal Rotors

1. INTRODUCTION

Understanding and predicting the properties of chemical compounds are of paramount importance both from technological and academic points of view. Quantum chemical computational methods become the useful tools for solving some chemical problems and studying the reaction mechanism prior to difficult, expensive or even impossible experiments.

There are several computer program packages applied to solve this problem, for example, GAUSSIAN, GAMESS, MOLPRO, SPARTAN, CFOUR, etc. The widely used program GAUSSIAN is supplemented by the visualization tool (GAUSSVIEW) which allows the graphical presentation of obtained results, for instance visualization of the potential energy surface (PES) of the molecule. As a function of torsion angles describing the internal rotation of the different fragments in the molecule, PES yields the information concerning the stable conformations of the molecule (conformers), corresponding to minima on PES, and the barrier height of interconversion between the conformers. However, the graphical presentation of PES is limited by two geometrical variables (3D PES). The visualization of four-dimensional and more complex hypersurfaces is still a challenge for structural chemists. Therefore, there is a need to create a reliable and affordable post-processor for visualization and minima finding of complex hypersurfaces. In the present work, we used the output of GAUSSIAN 03 program package (Frisch, 2003).

2. DISPLAING MULTIDIMENSIONAL PES

The multidimensional postprocessor should carry out two main duties, namely: searching all the minima on multidimensional PES calculated by GAUSSIAN program and their visualization. The main requirements for visualization are the clarity of the surface and its behavior in the considered range, the ability to display all the minima found in its area, and the ability to observe the obtained results from any point of view. The PES calculations are usually associated with extremely high computer time. Therefore, they are usually made on a sparse grid. In the case of the function of 4 variables, the dimension of the grid cannot be made more than $6\times 6 \times 6 \times 6$. In addition, the program leads to multidimensional tables that are extremely difficult to analyze in terms of finding energy minima. The only way to improve the situation is to increase the grid density at the postprocessing stage. We have developed a reliable and efficient algorithm for such increasing.

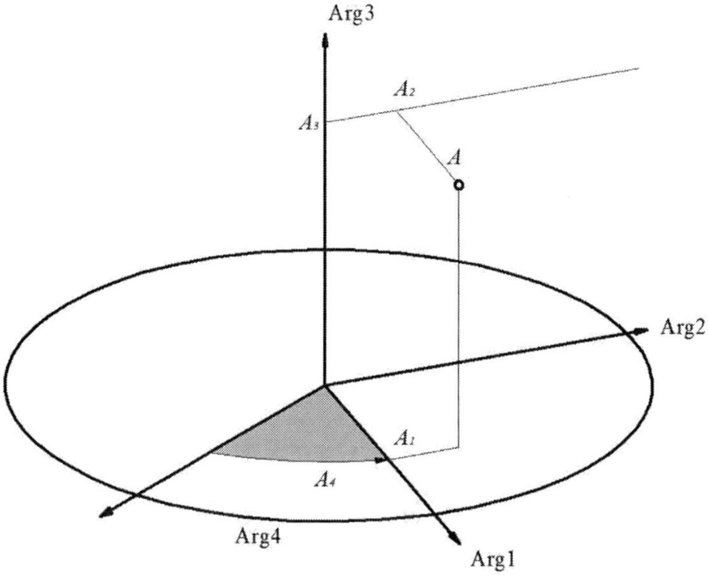

Figure 1. Special co-ordinate system to display 5D function (Four arguments + color)

We have developed a postprocessor that allows us to visualize and find the minima of 3D, 4D and 5D hypersurfaces. Visualization of the three-dimensional surface is carried out by the NURBS approximation and it is not difficult. To visualize 4D function we apply the voxel representation as introduced, for example, by James Foley (Foley et al, 1990). A much more complex problem is to visualize 5D function. Often, when analyzing multidimensional data, dimensionality reduction (DR) techniques are displayed in form of 2D or 3D scatterplots that project the multidimensional points onto a lower-dimensional visual space (Etemadpour R. et al, 2016). One can also reconstruct 5D function to 4D function with energy level represented by color and apply the model called Lumigraph by S.Gotler (Gotler, 1996). The Lumigraph is a subset of the complete plenoptic function that describes the flow of light in all positions and in all directions. Unfortunately, though such representation is very simple and convenient it is poor for perception. An example of multidimensional visualization is the Self-Organizing Map (SOM). The SOM algorithm is a special type of neural network developed by Kohonen (2001) in the 1980s. The SOM algorithm creates a two-dimensional layout in which multidimensional data is presented, so that similar data elements are located close to each other. The SOM technique can be used to visualize large multidimensional data sets (by projecting data into low-dimensional space) and for clustering.

There are many other methods to generate 2D similarity-based layouts from a higher-dimensional space. For example, the method of paired distances between points by I. Borg, et al (see Borg, (2010)) implemented with multidimensional scaling (MDS), taking into account the distances within the cluster or the distances between the clusters (Tenembaum, 2000). Sometimes Principal component analysis (PCA) is applied to generate similarity layouts by reducing data to lower dimensional visual spaces (Jollife, 1986). Some methods, such as isometric object mapping (Isomap), preferably use distances between data clusters. However, all of them are insufficient in our case for solving the problem of minima finding of the hypersurface and its visualization.

In our turn, we applied a special coordinate system to solve this problem (see Figure 1), which includes four independent variables. Such co-ordinate system makes point A in Figure 1 a five-dimensional point including its color. To visualize 5D function we introduce a set of 5D elementary hyper volumes (tetraxels) (Vogt, 2009).

To develop multidimensional postprocessor we choose Java language as a programming tool (Niemeyer, 2013) in conjunction with the Java 3D extension (Selman, 2003). The selected API provides a set of high-level tools for creating and manipulating three-dimensional geometry, as well as for pleasant rendering.

3. MINIMA FINDING OF MULTIDIMENSION PES

PES calculated and tabulated by GAUSSIAN has no analytic expression, which seriously complicates the search for its minima. Therefore, we developed the approach for PES local minima finding consisting of two stages:

1. We need to replace the initial multidimensional function defined as a regular grid of calculated points by more condensed regular grid. The function values at the nodes of condensed grid are calculated by multidimensional spline interpolation. In this version of the post-processor, we apply a recursive cubic spline interpolation procedure developed by Flanagan M. (2014) that allows interpolating the values of a function specified in a table of any dimension.

2. Further, we need to consistently compare the function values at each grid node with the function values at the neighboring nodes surrounding it. If this value is the smallest one, then we consider this value as a local minimum. The number of neighboring nodes depends on the dimension of the problem being solved. In 3D case, such nodes are 8, in 4D case - 26, in 5D case, such nodes are 80 (See Figure 2). To make minima more accurate we should condense the grid as much as possible.

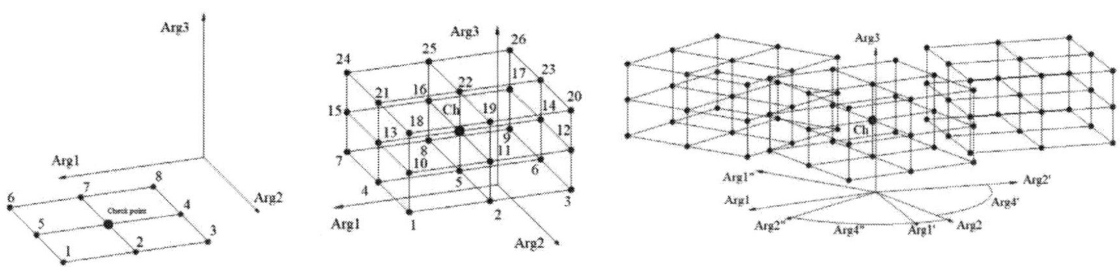

a) b) c)

Figure 2. The scheme of minima finding. a) 3D case; b) 3D + color = 4D; c) 4D + color = 5D

This approach allows the finding of energy function minima at the sufficient accuracy level. Figure 3 shows the first 11 found minima together with a 5D hypersurface.

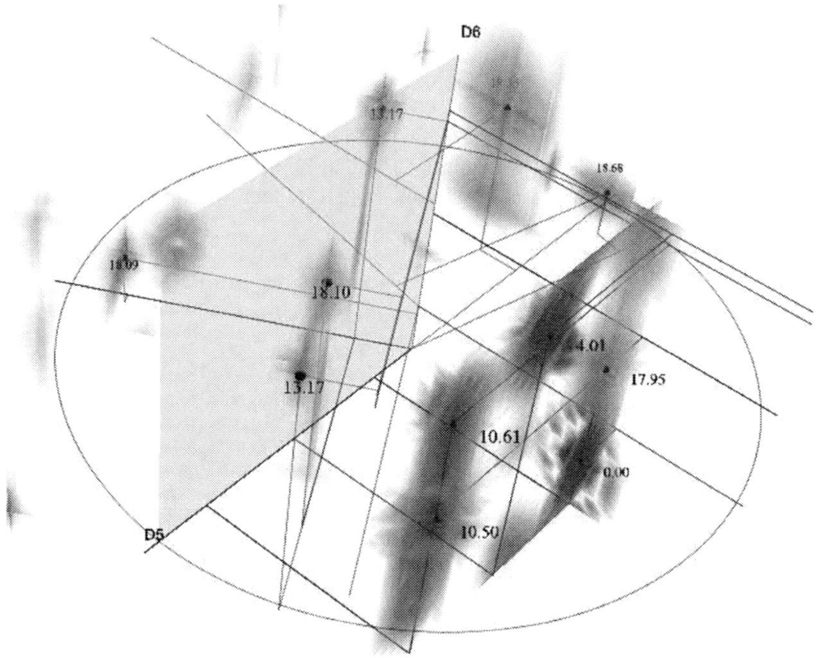

Figure 3. Part of 5D PES with the first 11 minima for glyceraldehyde

4. SOME EXAMPLES FOR COMPLEXE CONFORMATIONAL LANDSCAPE OF MOLECULES

We investigated conformational landscapes of a number of molecules by the developed postprocessor. Glyceraldehyde and fumaric acid with four and succinic acid even with five axes of internal rotation were predicted to exist in the form of several conformers.

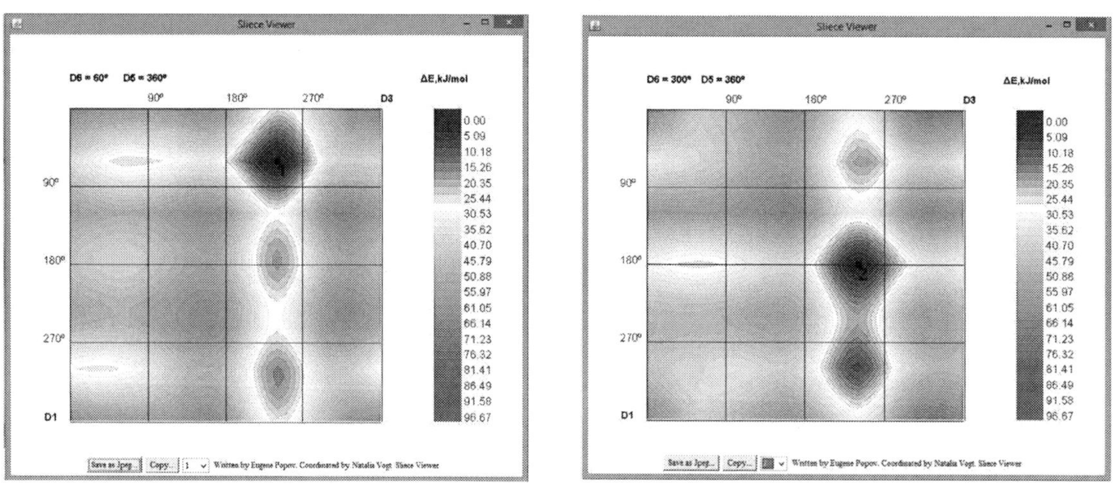

Figure 4. PES slices for 2 most stable conformers of glyceraldehyde

Finding the stable conformers of several molecules in the gas phase was carried out in several experimental and computational studies (Vogt et al, 2007 - 2011). The developed post-processor was benchmarked by results of these studies and applied for finding stable conformations (Vogt et al, 2009). Its application helped to find 36 and 18 stable conformations for glyceraldehyde (Vogt, 2009) and succinic acid (Vogt, 2011), respectively. The post-processor permits automating the analysis of a multidimensional energy hypersurface and it looks as a systematic and reliable tool for conformer finding. Figure 4 demonstrates the sample slices of energy hypersurface (see hypersurface in Figure 3) through two stable conformers of glyceraldehyde.

5. CONCLUSION

The multidimensional postprocessor is aimed at processing potential energy hypersurface calculated by GAUSSIAN program. It also provides a systematic analysis of multidimensional energy hypersurfaces for minima finding. The solution of this problem is important for the study of the complex conformational landscape (for instance of biomolecules). The grid condensation technology significantly improves the accuracy of the PES minima finding. Besides, the post-processor has a very attractive visualization platform that allows the user to analyze the complete conformational landscape. In addition, it seems promising to use the postprocessor for solving other problems, for example, for searching the lowest-energy path between the local minima of multidimensional hypersurface, *i.e.* for finding the way of the interconversion between the conformers. This purpose can be challenge for the further research.

ACKNOWLEDGEMENT

The work was supported by the Dr. B. Mez-Starck Foundation (Germany).

REFERENCES

Borg I. et al, 2010. *Modern Multidimensional Scaling Theory and Applications.* Springer Series in Statistics. Springer, 2nd edition.

Etemadpour R. et al, (2016). Choosing Visualization Techniques for Multidimensional Data Projection Tasks: *A Guideline with Examples.* 166-186 pp 598. 166-186. 10.1007/978-3-319-29971-6_9.

Flanagan, M. T. 2014. *Java Scientific Library* http://www.ee.ucl.ac.uk/~mflanaga/java/index.html.

Foley J. D. et al, 1990. *Computer Graphics: Principles and Practice.* Addison-Wesley. ISBN 978-0-201-12110-0

Frisch M.J. et al, 2003. *GAUSSIAN 03, Revision E.01.* – Pittsburgh PA : GAUSSIAN , Inc.,Wallingford.

Gotler S. et al, 1996. The Lumigraph. *In Computer Graphics, Annual Conference Series* (Proc. SIGGRAPH '96):43-54.

Jollife I. T., 1986. *Pincipal Component Analysis*. Springer-Verlag.

Kohonen T., 2001, *Self-Organizing Maps*, Third edition, Berlin: Springer-Verlag.

Niemeyer P. et al, 2013. *Learning Java, 4th Edition. A Bestselling Hands-On Java Tutorial.* O'Reilly Media, Inc.

Selman, D. 2003. *Java3D. Programming.* – Manning Publications Co Austin,– 302 p.

Squire R. 1997. *Fundamentals of Radiology*. 5th edition – Harvard, UniversityPress.

Tenembaum, J. B. et al, 2000. A global geometric framework for nonlinear dimensionality reduction. *Science*, 290:2319-2323.

Vogt N. et al, 2007. Molecular Structure and Conformational Composition of 1,3-Dihydroxyacetone Studied by Combined Analysis of Gas-Phase Electron Diffraction Data, Rotational Constants, and Results of Theoretical Calculations: Ideal Gas Thermodynamic Properties of 1,3-Dihydroxyacetone. *Physical Chemistry A.* – 2007. № 111. – P. 6434–6442. 2.

Vogt N. et al, 2009. Equilibrium structure and relative stability of D-glyceraldehyde conformers: gas-phase electron diffraction (GED) and quantum-chemical studies. *Molecular Structure* – The Netherlands, Elsevier, № 936. P. 125–131. 1.

Vogt N. et al, 2011. Determination of molecular structure of succinic acid in a very complex conformational landscape:Gas-phase electron diffraction (GED) and ab initio studies. *Molecular Structure – The Netherlands,* Elsevier, 2011. – № 996. – P. 120–127. 4.

Vogt N. et al, 2011. Molecular structure and stabilities of fumaric acid conformers: gas phase electron diffraction (GED) and quantum-chemical studies. *Molecular Structure* – The Netherlands, Elsevier, 2011. – № 987. – P. 199–205. 3.

ESP: EUCLIDEAN SPHERES PACKING IMPLEMENTATION FOR VOLUME DATA USING SLICER3D

Anod Alhazmi and Sudhanshu Semwal
Computer Science Department, University of Colorado at Colorado Springs
Colorado Springs, USA

ABSTRACT

The Gamma Knife radiosurgery treatment involves geometrically mapping for covering the tumor area in three dimensions so that the gamma rays can provide precise treatment to the affected area. The entire process has to be accurate in order to prevent the exposure of the gamma rays to the neighboring healthy tissues. When the tumor shape is irregular, it is difficult to ensure the coverage of the tumor region. We present, in this paper, a new approach to fit spheres in a bounded region based on maximum distance. Our proposed method for automating the gamma knife surgery planning is by using a geometrically-based Euclidean sphere packing optimization method. We implement our algorithm in Slicer3D using Python libraries. Experiments show that our algorithm produces reasonable dense packing of different irregular shapes.

KEYWORDS

Euclidean Distance, Slicer3D, Sphere Packing, Gamma Knife, Stereotactic Radiosurgery

1. INTRODUCTION

Spheres packing is a venerable topic in mathematics. Researchers have been interested in packing spheres into regions since the time of mathematician and astronomer Johannes Kepler (Szpiro, 2003). Different sphere packing problems have been studied depending on the shape, type, and position of objects. Our study is motivated by medical applications in radiosurgery. Gamma knife is one type of the radiosurgery that is a minimally invasive procedure uses radiation to kill tumor tissue inside the human brain. A main geometric problem in Gamma knife treatment planning is to fit multiple radiation shots into a 3D irregular shaped tumor. The Gamma Knife works by a process named Stereotactic Radiosurgery (SRS) where each shot is consisting of gamma-ray beams coming from different sectors with different collimation that can be represented as spheres of diameters (Ferris & Shepard, 2000).

Performing shape approximations are required to ensure that the dosage does not go outside the geometric coverage area to preserve as many normal tissues as possible. The general approach to generate spheres or approximate shape in Gamma knife is by placing random spheres or by using skeleton (Wu, Q. Jackie & Bourland, 1999; Wu, Qingrong J., Bourland, & Robb, 1996). These approaches can significantly change the behavior in Gamma Knife surgery. The reason for that is because the skeleton algorithms check only the end points and cross points of the skeleton at each iteration to place a sphere without caring about the other object's points. As a complete algorithm for arbitrary shapes that uses the only *minimum* number of spheres based on maximum distance is NP-Complete, taking exponential time in the worst case.The radiation planes are only targeting tumor tissues that need to be eliminated and destroy their DNA, so it limits the intensity so that tumor tissues will be affected more than the normal tissues. Margins around the tumor volume are strongly depend on the clinical assessment of risk and extent of spread, such as in the case of benign and malignant tumors. In addition, there are two different types of radiotherapy, frame-based and frameless system. In the frame-based SRS system, a fixed immobilization frame is used to position the patient's head to the correct coordinates for each shot, so the dose is delivered to tumor using MRI without margins. In the frameless, margins are necessary around tumors in case of target motion occurs. Adding many margins could expose more normal brain tissue to radiation and increase the risk. In this paper, we only focus on the frame-based SRS that target the tissues that are to be eliminated without margins, which could be added later by the radiologists. Moreover, certain sizes of shots (spheres) could be hard to get or unavailable because of physical constraints. In our case, we choose the placement covering the largest number of voxels inside the tumor no matter what is the size of the spheres. This is because our goal is to design the treatment planning system that optimize the target coverage, not proposing a design suitable for routine clinical practice. Optimizing conformity, where finding number of beams needed with their weights and angles, are not our focus, which in other word are determined by a dosimetrist.

Our *approximate* algorithm for sphere packing provides the possibility to group several spheres together to cover complex structures based on the maximum distances to the object boundary. Distance transformation is not new but when used in our algorithm it creates a way to generate spheres iteratively, which is different than the existing methods. We place the spheres such that they do not overlap and do not intersect with healthy tissues surrounding the tumor since overlapping may cause an overdose. The proposed algorithm offers a novel method to create multi-spheres for the given arbitrary shapes for more than 90% of the tumor coverage and terminates in a reasonable time based on the number of spheres and coverage desired.

2. THE CREATION OF ESP

The spheres are placed into the tumor target one-by-one, starting with the largest sphere based on the maximum Euclidean distance to tumor boundary. Our main goal is that the treated volume (covered by the spheres) matches the tumor shape by placing spheres that cover as many tumor pixels as possible to ensure the coverage of tumor tissues. The total sphere coverage density and radii can be adjusted to obtain different purposes such as in Gamma Knife surgery. Three objectives need to be fulfilled for sufficient approximation: using the minimum number of spheres is required for saving computation time, the applicability of the algorithm for different arbitrary shapes, and the number of spheres must be enough to accomplish an adequate surface representation. Our ESP algorithm consists of:

A. Find the Segmented Region:

Medical imaging is given as a 3D surface representation by using medical imaging techniques. The standard file format in this context is DICOM that represent the images as a complete 2D slices. We access the segmented tumor image (label map) as an array. The label map data is composed of a 3-D array of data, which specify the *x*, *y*, and *z* coordinates for each data point while the background value=0.

B. Get Range of Region:

It is necessary to mark the region boundary since that characterizes the volume surface. We get the boundaries of our region of interest (tumor) by excluding the object's pixels that are outside of our region of interest. To do that, we first use a bounding box by extracting both the minimum (*xmn, ymn, zmn)* and the maximum (*xmx, ymx, zmx)* non-zero cubic values of the corresponding coordinate (Figure 1) for faster geometrical operations and reducing the calculation time. Second, we delete all zero's pixels, which are background pixels.

C. Apply Distance Transform:

Calculate the 3D exact Euclidean distance transformation of each pixel as explained in our paper in O(n) time (Alhazmi & Semwal, 2018).

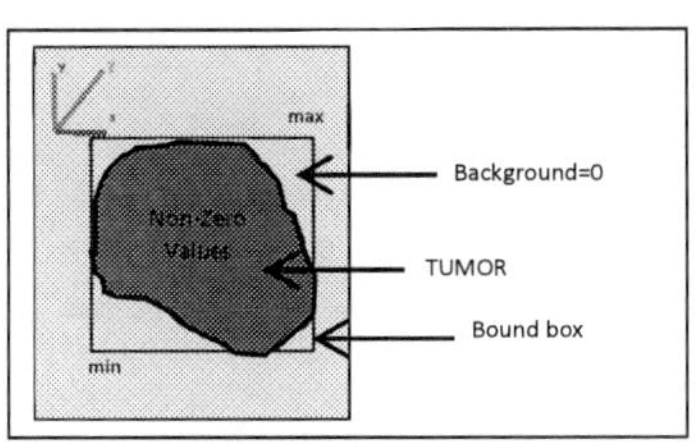

Figure 1. The segmented region that shows the tumor region before and after the bounding box

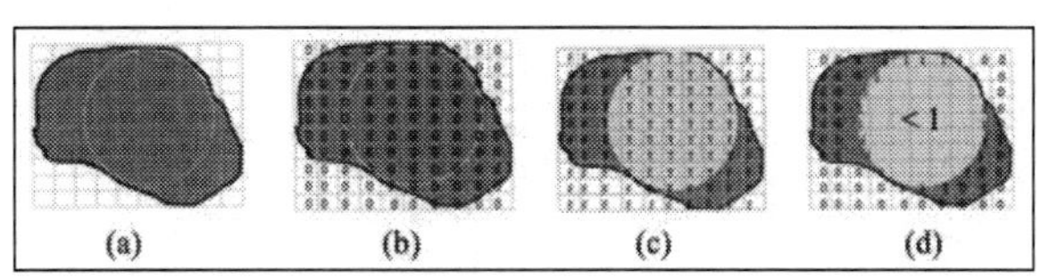

Figure 2. Find the coordinates of points within a sphere bounded by shape. (a) grid points. (b) mask of value=0. (c) The Boolean distance of all points from the center (d) The inner part of sphere will have distance < 1 and border =1

D. Record the center and radius of sphere.

Determine the biggest sphere by using the maximum distance value as a radius "*r*" and its location as center "*c*". To find the exact location of the sphere's center, the distance between the center of the sphere and the center of each bounding cell is computed. So, the minimum coordinate values along each axis (*xmn, ymn, zmn*) is added to the center value, as in: *center = [c[0][0] + xmn, c[1][0] + ymn, c[2][0] +zmn]* *(1)*

Then, save these sphere's information into two lists: one for radiuses *"r_list[]"* and the other one for the centers *"c_list[]"*.

E. Getting further spheres:

Generate a center-based grid, which is a grid constructed around the sphere's center, stretched by the shape of the segmented region (Figure 2 (a)). In the grid, each voxel represents a volume of fixed size. Then, we use a mask of the same size with zero values (Figure 2 (b)) to calculate the Boolean distance of each point from the sphere's center scaled by the radius (Figure 2 (c)). Positive voxels (sphere's voxels) are labeled by the distance of these voxels while surrounding tissue voxels are represented by zero (Figure 2 (d)). The area of the sphere by definition is:

$$(x-x_c)^2+(y-y_c)^2+(z-z_c)^2=r^2 \qquad (2)$$

Where (x,y,z) is a point, (x_c,y_c,z_c) is the center, and r is the radius. So:

$$((x-x_c)/r)^2 + ((y-y_c)/r)^2 + ((z-z_c)/r)^2 = 1 \qquad (3)$$

Points inside the sphere will have the lowest values (below 1), and points on the border will have the highest value (equal to 1) (Figure 2 (d)). After that, we need to exclude the first sphere's pixels from the segmented region to start placing the next sphere, so we subtract one from the previous mask in (Figure 2 (c)) as in (Figure 3). The final result is as in (Figure 4).

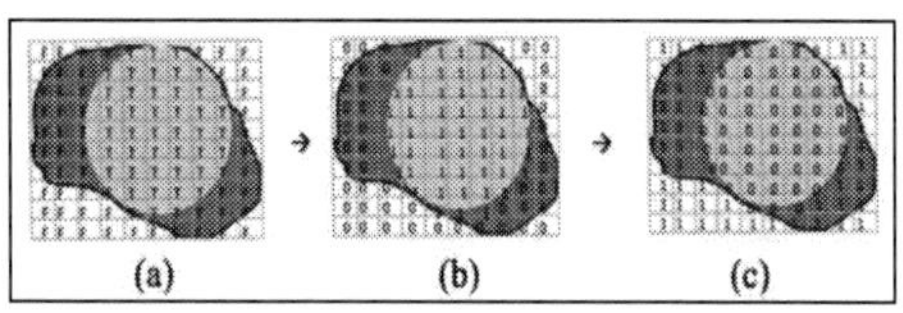

Figure 3. (a) mask of the sphere's shape. (b) converting (a) to float type. (c) the result after subtracting 1 from (b) with sphere's points=0

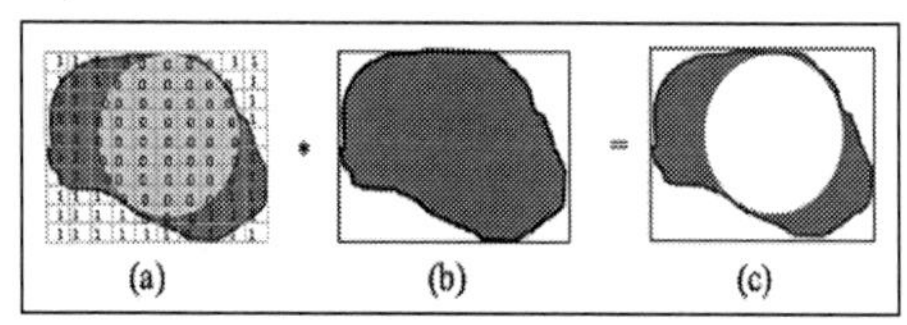

Figure 4. (a) sphere's shape =0, multiply by (b) segmented region. (c) the result of the segment region without the pixels/voxels of the first sphere

F. Calculate the approximation error:

The ratio between current non-zero volumes and original non-zero volumes. This ratio is used to find when our algorithm terminates based on the number of spheres and coverage (*accuracy rate)* desired. If the: *approximation error < (accuracy rate * original non-zero volume),* then draw all spheres, otherwise, go to step C. The complete algorithm of approximation is shown as pseudo code, as follow:

```
1.  Input volume as nrrd file
2.  SegmentedRegionOrigin= Volume (nrrd)
3.  Create Bounding Box
4.  SegmentedRegion= Bounded Regions with margins
5.  OriginalVolume= SegmentedRegion(true)
6.  Distance= EuclideanDistance(SegmentedRegion)
7.  Max= maximum distance
8.  Sphere_radius= max
9.  Sphere_center= location(max)              // center inside bounding box
10. Sphere_acccenter= (Sphere_center + nrrd)   // center inside nrrd volume
11. Sphere_grid= (distance, radius, center)
12. SegmentedRegion= (1- Sphere_grid)
13. While (pixels not covered > pixels in desired coverage)    do
            Repeat 6, 7, 8, 9, 10, 11, 12
14. Draw MultiSpheres()
15. Update volume (outputVolume)
```

3. RESULT AND DISCUSSION

We implement our algorithm as a new module in Slicer3D (Fedorov, 2012) (Figure 5). It is an open-source medical visualization application that builds on top of different libraries and provides a variety of tools or as in Slicer3D called modules. Our Experiments on MacBook 10.12.6 is based on the BRATS dataset (Menze, Bjoern H and Jakab, 2015) that contains large brain tumor MRI scans with ground truth. The MRI scans and all the ground truth labels are manually revised and delineated by experts broad-certified neuroradiologists. In our study, we did our experiments on 3 datasets, each with 10 patients, with different tumor size, intensity, and shape. The acceptance rate of the coverage that been used in medical applications is above 90% (Wang, 1999), the remaining voxels can still be covered by the beams defined by those spheres (multiple beams create a dose like a cloud that cover the gaps in between spheres). The resulting dose distribution shows that gaps between shot boundaries (spheres) are covered in most cases with adequate dose, when using 50% isodose line (Landberg et al., 2016). In this paper, due to the fact that overlapping is not allowed, we believe that our sphere packing algorithm usually requires much higher number of spheres to reach the desired density instead of using overlapping spheres.

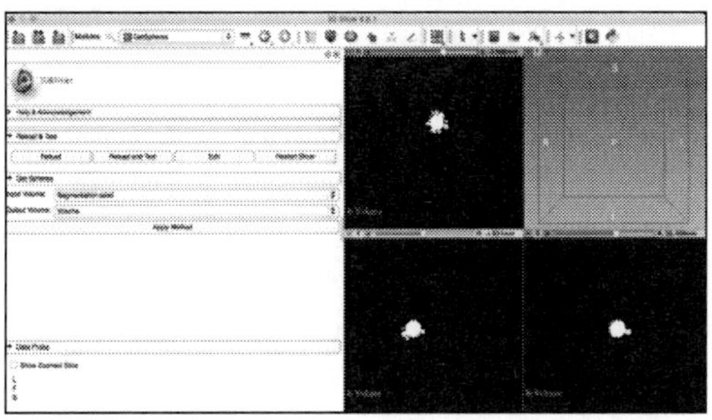

Figure 5. Sphere packing module GUI in Slicer3D

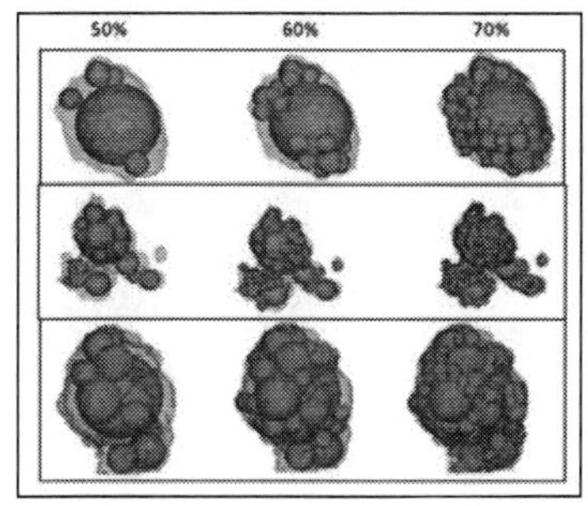

Figure 6. ESP 3D result in Slicer3D with 50%, 60%, 70% of packing density

The creation of multiple spheres or isocenters is always a compromise between the total number of spheres and accuracy (packing density) (Figure 6). Increasing the approximation accuracy implies to increase the number of spheres (Figure 7). In other words, the approximation accuracy can be assumed as a score of similarity to the original shape. More spheres give better shape approximation, and an infinite number of spheres will give an identical shape approximation. Moreover, the minimum spheres' radii decrease when more spheres are added because adding more spheres leave a small free area that needs to be covered to give more dense packing. Therefore, a number of small spheres (1 pixel) are distributed around the 3D shape especially around its boundary.

Depending on the total number of pixels/voxels in the shape, the number of the filled spheres and radii may vary significantly. The maximum spheres radii increase with the increase of tumor size. Increasing the tumor size also leads to increase the number of spheres with respect to the shape complexity. Complex tumor shape affects the result such as increasing the number of spheres. Regular tumor shape, on the other hand, decreases that number of spheres because large spheres can cover a large amount of the tumor's pixels.

The computation time of the sphere packing algorithm depends on different criteria such as the total number of pixels/voxels in the shape and accuracy (density). From (Figure 8), we can see that time increases rapidly when increasing the dense packing from 50% to 70%. Our algorithm sometimes takes long time in case of high dense packing such as in 90%. This long time is because of the need of computing the 3D arrangement of O(n) complicated surfaces while nontrivial numerical manipulations are needed.

4. CONCLUSIONS AND FUTURE WORKS

Gamma knife currently produces spheres of three different radii (4mm, 8mm, and 16 mm). In our method, we present a new approach to fit spheres in a bounded region based on maximum distance. Due to the shape irregularity of the 3D object (tumor), approaches such as using skeleton and grassfire may fragment the object into small disconnected regions that remain eventually with no further packing. The ESP is a novel technique to approximate a shape to be used in Radiosurgery. Experiments show that our algorithm produce reasonable dense packing of different irregular shapes. Using the grid of shape ensure that the shape is appropriately filled. The coverage percentage of the shape grid points is adjustable to reach a variant density with a sufficient number of spheres for any arbitrary shape. The radii of all spheres are computed as the maximum Euclidean distance to the shape boundary.

For the future works, using machine learning and optimization algorithms in the future could reduce the number of spheres, such as using clustering algorithms to cluster multiple spheres into one sphere such that those sphere's centers are very close to each other. There is another criterion that would give better results such as controlling spheres allocation and spacing between spheres at fixed distances. In addition, using a tight margin around the shape could also be considered especially in the case of very small shapes to ensure accurate coverage. Moreover, further investigations into Gamma Knife treatment planning, doses size, and weights need to be pursued in the future as well.

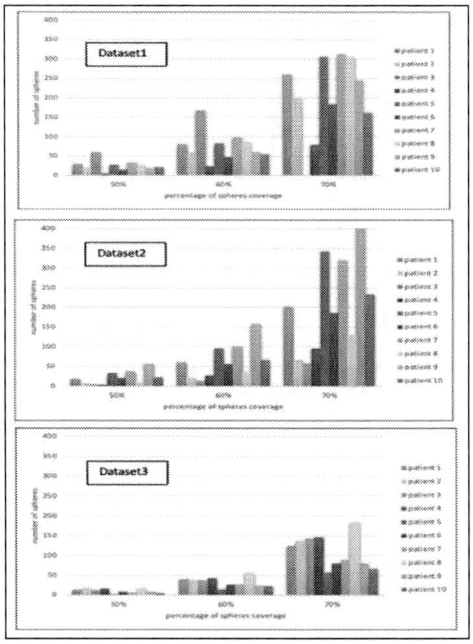

Figure 7. Increasing the number of spheres when more dense coverage is required

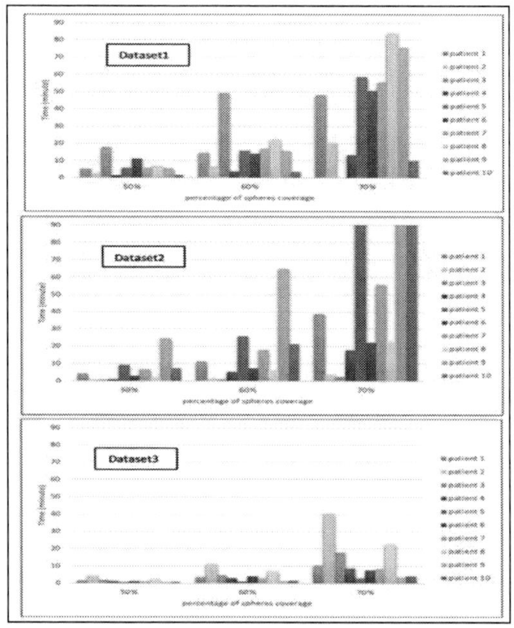

Figure 8. Execution time increases for dense spheres packing

REFERENCES

Alhazmi, A., & Semwal, S. (2018). Implementation of linear time exact euclidean distance transform in 3D slicer. *Journal of Computing Sciences in Colleges, 34*(2), 117-124.

Fedorov, A. a. B. (2012). 3D slicer as an image computing platform for the quantitative imaging network. *Magnetic Resonance Imaging, 30*(9), 1323-1341.

Ferris, M. C., & Shepard, D. M. (2000). Optimization of gamma knife radiosurgery. *Discrete Mathematical Problems with Medical Applications, 55*, 27-44.

Landberg, T., Chavaudra, J., Dobbs, J., Hanks, G., Johansson, K. -., Möller, T., et al. (2016). Report 50. *Journal of the International Commission on Radiation Units and Measurements, os26*(1), NP.

Menze, Bjoern H and Jakab. (2015). The multimodal brain tumor image segmentation benchmark (BRATS). *IEEE Transactions on Medical Imaging, 34*(10), 1993.

Szpiro, G. G. (2003). Kepler's conjecture. *Hoboken: Wiley,*

Wang, J. (1999). Packing of unequal spheres and automated radiosurgical treatment planning. *Journal of Combinatorial Optimization, 3*(4), 453-463.

Wu, Q. J., & Bourland, J. D. (1999). Morphology-guided radiosurgery treatment planning and optimization for multiple isocenters. *Medical Physics, 26*(10), 2151-2160.

Wu, Q. J., Bourland, J. D., & Robb, R. A. (1996). Morphology-guided radiotherapy treatment planning and optimization. *Medical Imaging 1996: Image Display, , 2707.* pp. 180-190.

SHAPE CONTEXT BASED CLUTTER DEFIANCE IN LOGARITHMIC CORRELATION FILTERS

Ahmed Bilal Awan[1], Asim D. Bakhshi[2], Farhan Riaz[1] and Saad Rehman[1]
Department of Computer Engineering, EME College,
[1]National University of Sciences and Technology (NUST), Islamabad, Pakistan
[2]Department of Computer Engineering, Abasyn University, Islamabad, Pakistan

ABSTRACT

Correlation based classification decisions are challenged by the occurrence of clutter in the real life input scenes. Clutter tends to cause side-lobes in the output correlation plane thus making correlation based classification decision nontrivial. The pronounced side-lobes may dominate correlation peak for true class objects leading to a false alarm. We propose a new hybrid scheme involving shape context and correlation filters to avoid impact of clutter in correlation output. The proposed combination provides a dual validation strategy where presence of true class object in test image is confirmed at two different stages before final class decision. Clutter participation in correlation process is denied by matching shape contexts of each object in test image with the true class object. The recommended addition in optimal logarithmic maximum average correlation height filter (LMACH) results in a performance gain ranging from 30% to 70% in peak to side-lobe ratio leading to a correct classification decision. The improvement remains consistent throughout the range of in-plane angular distortions against synthetically cluttered challenging images.

KEYWORDS

Correlation Filters, Object Recognition, Correlation Pattern Recognition (CPR), MACH, LMACH, Shape Context

1. INTRODUCTION

Although being a basic mathematical operation, correlation function has become an important component of computer vision techniques to resolve object recognition problem. A comprehensive machine vision capability still remains a challenge thus needing an appropriate pre-processing coupled with correlation operation to answer some essential questions. A number of such algorithms have been devised in the past resulting in various brands of correlation filters that show a promising recognition performance against relatively complex input scenes (Vijaya Kumar et al. 2005, Mahalanobis et al. 1994 & Alkanhal et al. 2000). Further optimization of correlation filters is achieved by inculcating logarithmic translation in the design (Ho et al. 2002), thereby accumulating rotation (both in-plane and out-of -plane) and scale invariance capability in a single solution (Bone et al. 2006). However, the task of recognition becomes significantly complex in real time due to the frequent occurrence of clutter alongside presence of background. Recently, a remarkable technical advancement has been viewed in the recognition domain while employing feature based methods. One of the most convincing methods involved shape contexts as descriptors for the object identification.

The logarithmic correlation filters being a composite package for distortion invariance is challenged by the occurrence of clutter and backgrounds that indirectly tend to impact classification decisions by distorting correlation output through occurrence of side lobes (Vijaya Kumar et al. 2005). Whereas, the feature based methods can supplement correlation filters to evade clutter while maintaining distortion invariance. This study is focused on utilizing strengths of techniques based upon correlation filters and feature based classifiers to augment each other.

The proposed hybrid scheme titled as "Shape Context based Logarithmic Maximum Average Correlation Height Filter" (SC-MACH) uses shape contexts by Belongie et al. (2002) as features to ascertain the presence of target object in the input scene with subsequent validation by the correlation filter. The presence of target is determined on the basis of shape contexts specific to that particular object. This process also entails a mechanism of discarding false objects/ clutter during the course of ascertainment of true object. Resultantly, a clean test image is reconstructed before carrying out correlation with the reference image.

We evaluate logarithmic Correlation filter design with a focus on optimal MACH filter in Section 2. The next section covers an overview of shape context alongside histogram matching and optimal cost assignment. Adopted methodology is discussed in section 4, followed by the performance evaluation, results and discussion. Some conclusive remarks are given in the end.

2. LOGARITHMIC CPR FILTERS

CPR adopts a statistical pattern recognition technique to generate a reference image that enables machines to identify presence of the target object in input image by observing the level of matching with the reference image. The degree of resemblance observed in output correlation-plane, is used to classify images. A variety of filter designs have been discovered so far with some common goals such as distortion invariance, noise tolerance and clutter rejection (Vijaya Kumar et al. 2005). A basic optimal MACH filter in frequency domain (Hanying and Tien-Hsin 1999) can be represented as following:-

$$H = \frac{M^*}{\alpha C + \beta D_x + \gamma S_x} \qquad (1)$$

Where M is average of all training images $(X_1, X_2, \ldots\ldots, X_N)$ in frequency domain, and α, β and γ are non-negative parameters. The diagonal power spectral density matrix of additive input noise represented by white noise covariance matrix $C = \sigma^2 I$. D_x is the diagonal average power spectral density of the training images, which can be represented as:-

$$D_x = \frac{1}{N} \sum_{i+1}^{N} X_i X_i^* \qquad (2)$$

Where, X_i corresponds to the ith training image in frequency domain, N represents total number of training images, and * depicts conjugate. S_X stands for the similarity matrix of the training images:

$$S_x = \frac{1}{N} \sum_{i=1}^{N} (X_i - M)^* (X_i - M) \qquad (3)$$

Varying the image representation from 2D Cartesian plane to a logarithmic plane allows us to view the angular rotation and scale alterations in the target object as equivalent shifts in memory (Ho et al. 2002), which are better understood by the machines. CPR filters when coupled with logarithmic conversions, yield some remarkable advantages. The blend of techniques has been profitably undertaken in the past (Bone et al. 2006 and Rehman et al. 2013), while joining log-polar mapping with different versions of CPR filters known as correlation filters. These filters with an inherent invariance to the out-of-plane rotations are augmented by the logarithmic mapping which caters for the complete range of in-plane rotations alongside scale changes (ranging between 0.5-2.5 times object size) and illumination effects. Although these filters have a good response against occlusions but presence of clutter distorts the recognition performance of log-CPR filters.

3. SHAPE CONTEXT BASED MATCHING

Object matching based on the shape context explores the similarity measure by correspondence between points on the two shapes. These correspondences are used to estimate alignment cost of two objects. Interest points are selected on each object. The distribution of all other points on the same object to the reference point is unique for each shape and this context can be effectively used as a descriptor of a specific shape. Shape context of two objects having similar shapes is identical.

For each point on object-1 we calculate shape contexts in the form of distribution of vectors joining nth point with all other n-1 points on the same object. This distribution of vectors for each point at object-1 is translated into histogram having log-polar bins. Consequently we get n number of histograms for n interest points on object-1 and n' histograms for n' number of points at object-2 (where n and n' can or cannot be equal). The histogram cost matrix is obtained by computing pair wise cost between all shape contexts represented by log polar histogram arrays of reference and test images.

$$C_{ij} = C(p_i, q_j) = \frac{1}{2}\sum_k^K \frac{[h_i(k) - h_j(k)]^2}{[h_i(k) + h_j(k)]} \quad (8)$$

Where $h_i(k)$ and $h_j(k)$ are k-bin histograms (normalized by mean distance) for a point p_i on object-1 and q_j on object-2. Optimal cost assignment using Hungarian algorithm (applying row and column reductions) yields cost vector carrying coordinates of best matching points (Belongie et al.2002).

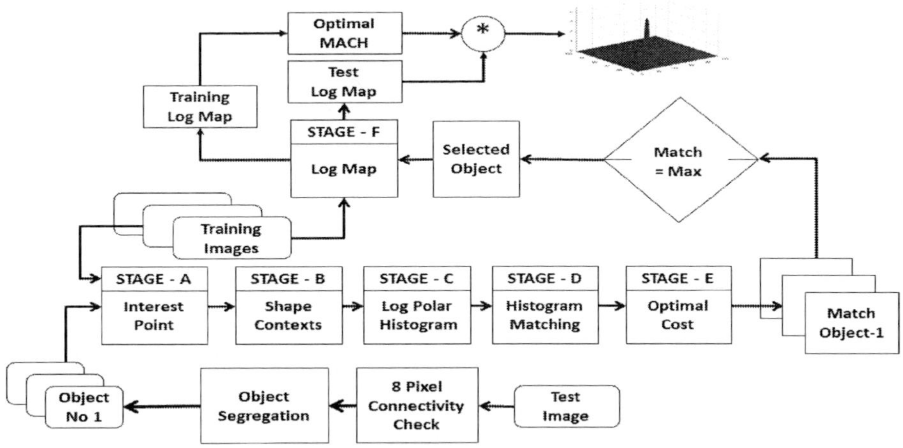

Figure 1. Block Diagram – Proposed Methodology

4. METHODOLOGY

We recommend image set having out-of-plane rotated versions of the target object shown in Figure 2a for training purpose. As in-plane rotation and scale invariance is inherently achieved by logarithmic mapping, training of correlation filter with out-of-plane rotated examples of target caters for other angular distortions.

Test image set includes synthetically cluttered images with added distortions as shown in Figure 2b. Object segregation in test image is performed through 8-pixel connectivity check before subsequent processing. The separated objects are independently passed through the stages A to E to learn level of matching of each object with the target object. As shown in block diagram (Figure 1), all training and test images are processed through stage A to stage E leading to the selection of test image containing target object. The log map of selected object (generated at stage F) are subsequently correlated with reference image (generated by LMACH) to validate results. Processing at each stage is elaborated below.

Stage-A: Segregated objects in test image alongside training images are input to this stage. Interest points are calculated for each object in the image. Sampled points on edges describe the presence of each object in the image. Coordinates of each interest point of segregated objects in test image and target objects in training images are output of this stage. As training images contain out-of-plane rotated views of target object, interest points that tend to exist in multiple views are identified. These common interest points accumulate to represent training data. Whereas, test data set is sequentially built by recording the set of interest points separately for each object in test image.

Stage-B: Training and test data in the form of coordinates of interest points is input to this stage. Each interest point in a single combined training image and multiple test objects participate to generate independent shape contexts respectively. The set of distance vectors originating from each interest point in an image to all other points within the same image form shape context as a specific representation of the object present in that image. As output of stage B, training and test data set is translated into the shape context information.

Stage-C: Shape context information is further transformed into logarithmic polar histograms at Stage C using 5 bins for log r and 12 bins for θ. This provides us 60 bins representation against each interest point where descriptors for both training and test data are more sensitive to the nearby interest points than the farther points.

Stage-D: All descriptors in training data are matched with the descriptors in test data pertaining to all separated objects in test image using (Equation 8). Histogram cost matrices for all separated objects in test image are obtained, where each element in a matrix represents matching cost of a training interest point with a specific test interest point.

Stage-E: This stage involves solving optimal cost assignment problem using Hungarian algorithm (Belongie et al. 2002). Cost matrices are squared by adding dummy elements before carrying out cost assignment. For each cost matrix pertaining to a specific test object, the best matching interest points are identified with the points in training data based upon lowest matching cost. The points matching to the dummy elements are discarded and only good matches against each test object are recorded. Information regarding number of good matches is observed against each segregated test object and the one having maximum number of good matches is picked up as a selected object in the test image. The remaining objects in test image with lower number of matches are discarded while considering these objects as clutter.

Stage-F: After the relevant test object selection based on matching shape context, the selected test object alongside a complete set of training images are input to logarithmic polar transformation. Logarithmic polar maps for the test and training images are separately obtained. The training logarithmic maps are used to carry out training of MACH filter. Consequent to the output of correlation between MACH filter and logarithmic map of the selected test object, we can undertake the final detection decision.

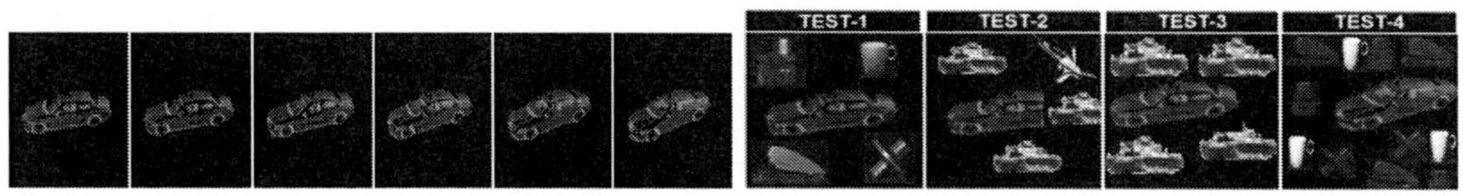

(a) (b)

Figure 2. Data Set, (a) Training Images (0°-25°out-of-plane rotated versions of a car), (b) Synthetically cluttered Test Images with added complexity level

5. PERFORMANCE EVALUATION

The training set (shown in Figure 2a) contains out-of-plane rotated images each having 5° angular differences (0°- 30°). Whereas, synthetically cluttered test images with multiple distortions (shown in Figure 2b) were used for performance evaluation of the proposed design. To evaluate for the whole angular distortion range, test images were exposed to in-plane rotations ranging from 0-360° with 45° separation. Rotated versions of Test-2 are shown in Figure 3a. Objects were segregated based upon 8-pixel connectivity in each in-plane rotated test image. The separated objects in the example test image are displayed in Figure 3b. Each of the segregated objects was passed through Stage A to C for generation of test data in the form of 60 bin log-polar histograms accrued from shape context information of that object. On the parallel, training images were consolidated as a single training image based upon accumulated common interest points after Stage A and the same was passed through Stage B and C for obtaining training data.

Histogram matching between test data pertaining to the segregated object and training data of consolidated training image was carried out at stage D. Subsequently, Hungarian optimal cost assignment algorithm was applied on cost matrices (against each object in Figure 3b) to determine the perfect match of each interest point. Based upon maximum number of matching interest points, the valid test object was selected out of test image and remaining objects were discarded. Figure 3c displays the selected object for the example test image, where other non-target objects/ clutter are wiped off. All training images and selected test object were logarithmically transformed to produce training and test logarithmic maps. The reference image was constructed by applying optimal MACH on training logarithmic maps (referred as Optimal LMACH in Figure 1). Logarithmic map of the selected object in test image was correlated with the reference image to validate detection of target object.

The correlation output peak intensity (COPI) corresponding to the selected image was compared to a pre-selected threshold value and occurrence of the target object was registered. The performance of CPR filters is benchmarked by a conventional parameter COPI (Vijaya Kumar et al. 2005). Peak performance of filter is captured while inducing in-plane angular rotations (ranging from 0° to 360°) in the test image.

6. RESULTS AND DISCUSSION

The example test image (Figure 3a) carries multiple distortions including in-plane and out-of-plane angular rotations, scale changes and synthetically embedded occlusion in the scene. The selected test object shown in Figure 3c portrays removal of clutter from the test image based upon matching of shape context information. As logarithmic versions of correlation filters are enabled to cater for multiple distortions, therefore distortion invariant technique like shape contexts provides us with an additional layer of validation. Apart from defiance of clutter/ non-target objects from the test image, we get enhanced results in correlation output leading to an improved classification decision.

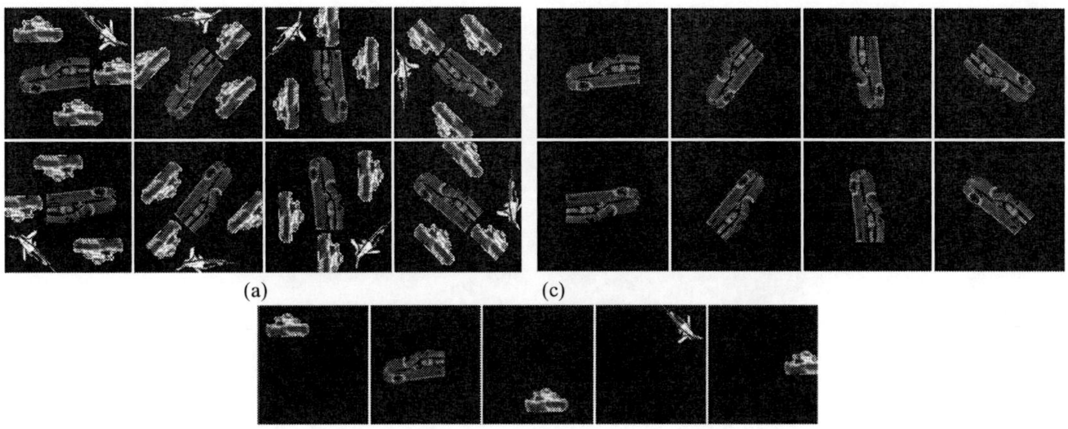

(a) (c)

(b)

Figure 3. Example Test Image. (a) Rotated versions of Test-2 (0-360 degrees in-plane rotations). (b) Segregated Objects in Test-2. (c) Output Images (Reconstructed images after Clutter Removal)

Figure 4 displays a combined COPI difference plot against test images shown in Figure 2b. The COPI difference is calculated by subtracting the pre-selected threshold value from the correlation peak height and the difference is obtained in percentage form. A remarkable COPI difference percentage can be viewed in all 4 test cases, which is attributable to removal of clutter in the test image.

Clutter impacts on correlation output through occurrence of side lobes. These side-lobes in the correlation plane tend to distort output thus effecting classification decisions. The proposed treatment of clutter through shape context matching enables us to reduce the side-lobe contribution leading to a considerable improvement in peak to side-lobe ratio (PSR). PSR is a conventional benchmark parameter for ascertaining efficiency of the correlation filters.

PSR plots for all test images are displayed in Figure 4b. The prominent increase in PSR for all the test cases manifests efficacy of the proposed scheme. Percentage gain in peak to side-lobe ratio is also displayed against each angle for all 4 test images. Overall gain ranging from 30% to 70% can be viewed in peak to side lobe ratio in Table-1 below.

Table 1. % Gain in Peak to Side Lobe Ratio for all test images in figure 2b

In-Plane Rotation (Degrees)	**% Gain Peak to Side Lobe ratio**			
	Test Image-1	**Test Image-2**	**Test Image-3**	**Test Image-4**
5°-30°	70.24 %	46.13 %	29.99 %	65.84 %

7. CONCLUSION

An appropriate addition in the optimal LMACH design causes a considerable improvement in the results. The proposed filter SC-MACH effectively denies clutter thus making the classification decision free from any participation of clutter in the correlation output. This yields a performance gain ranging from 30% to 70% in the PSR, thus allowing correct classification of true class objects. The improvement remains consistent throughout the range of in-plane angular distortions against synthetically cluttered challenging images.

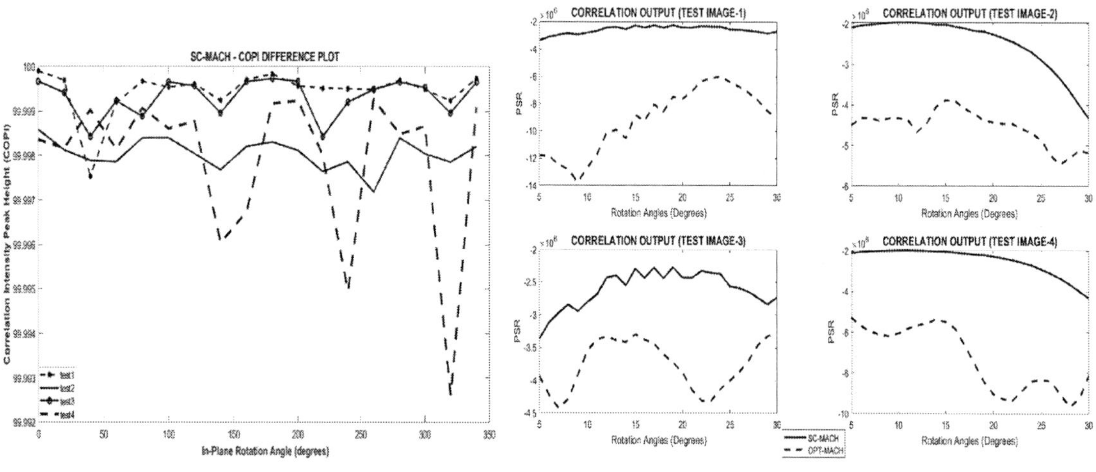

(a) (b)

Figure 4. (a) COPI Difference Plot for SC-MACH Filter. (b) PSR Plots for Test Images, a PSR Plot test image-1, b PSR Plot test image-2, c PSR Plot test image-3, d PSR Plot test image-4

REFERENCES

Vijaya Kumar B.V.K., Mahalanobis A., Juday R.D., 2005. *Correlation pattern recognition*. Cambridge University Press, New York, USA.

Mahalanobis A., Vijaya Kumar B.V.K. and Song S., 1994. Unconstrained correlation filters. *In Appl. Opt.*, 33, (17), pp. 3751–3759.

Alkanhal M., Vijaya Kumar B.V.K. and Mahalanobis A., 2000. Improving the false alarm capabilities of the maximum average correlation height correlation filter. *In Opt. Eng.,* 39, (5), pp. 1133–1141.

Vijaya Kumar B.V.K. and Alkanhal M., 2001. Eigen-extended maximum average correlation height (EEMACH) filters for automatic target recognition. *Proceedings of SPIE*, Orlando, Florida, USA, pp. 424–431.

Hanying Zhou and Tien-Hsin Chao., 1999. MACH filter synthesizing for detecting targets in cluttered environment for grayscale optical correlator. *Proceedings of SPIE - The International Society for Optical Engineering*. 3715. 394-398. 10.1117/12.341322.

Bone P., Young R. and Chatwin C., 2006. Position, rotation, scale and orientation-invariant multiple object recognition from cluttered scenes. *In Opt. Eng.*, 45, (7), p. 077203.

Ho C.G., Young R.C.D. and Chatwin C.R., 2002. Sensor geometry and sampling methods for space-variant image processing. *In Pattern Anal. Appl.*, 5, (4), pp. 369–384.

Rehman S., Bilal A. and Javed Y., 2013. Logarithmically pre-processed EMACH filter for enhanced performance in target recognition. *In Arab. J. Sci. Eng.*, 38, (11), pp. 3005–3017.

Rodriguez A., Boddeti V.N. and Vijaya Kumar B.V.K., 2013. Maximum margin correlation filter: a new approach for localization and classification. *IEEE Trans. Image Process.*, 22, (2), pp. 631–643.

Fernandez J.A. and Vijaya Kumar B.V.K., 2015. Partial-aliasing correlation filters. *IEEE Trans. Signal Process.*, 63, (4), pp. 921–934.

Tehsin S., Rehman S. and Bilal A., 2017. Comparative analysis of zero aliasing logarithmic mapped optimal trade-off correlation filter. *Pattern Recognition and Tracking XXVIII*, Anaheim, California, USA, p. 1020305.

Ahmed B. Awan, Saad Rehman and Asim D. Bakhshi, 2018. Composite filtering strategy for improving distortion invariance in object recognition. *IET Image Processing*, Online ISSN 1751-9667.

S. Belongie, J. Malik and J. Puzicha, 2002. Shape matching and object recognition using shape contexts. *In IEEE Transactions on Pattern Analysis and Machine Intelligence*, vol. 24, no. 4, pp. 509-522.

SEMI-AUTOMATIC MULTI-CAMERA VIDEO ANNOTATION TOOL FOR OBJECT TRACKING AND OPTICAL FLOW BENCHMARK CREATION

Vladimir V. Devyatkov and Igor I. Lychkov
Bauman Moscow State Technical University, Vtoraya Baumanskaya 5, Moscow, Russia

ABSTRACT

This paper addresses a problem of video annotation for object tracking evaluation. Contemporary object tracking methods relies heavily on optical flow calculation techniques. State of the art optical flow calculation methods are not enough to provide robust and accurate tracking under object occlusion and shading conditions. Thus, comprehensive visual object tracking datasets are required for deep analysis, benchmarking and improvement of object tracking methods. In most cases publicly available real video datasets does not include ground truth for optical flow evaluation, so new datasets might be in demand. Public video annotation tools for object tracking dataset labeling were reviewed. Lack of open source video annotation tools with functions of automatic optical flow markers and object bounding box visual tracking was noticed. In this work we developed a new open video annotation tool that is suitable for object bounding box labeling as well as optical flow annotation in multicamera video recordings. This tool makes it possible to specify the feature point and/or moving object position on the first video frame and track its position automatically in the subsequent video frames. This tool supports manual adjustment of the tracked position if needed. Multi-layer modular architecture of the annotation tool simplifies its testing, maintenance and further extension by the community.

KEYWORDS

Moving Object Tracking, Multi-Camera Video, Optical Flow, Video Annotation Tool

1. INTRODUCTION

Visual object tracking is a challenging task related to various problem domains including self-driving cars, security, robotics, etc. Broad scientific research in visual object tracking started in 1980s and is still in progress (Anishchenko, 2018; Deviatkov and Lychkov, 2017; Lychkov et al, 2018; Morozov et al, 2015; Taranyan et al, 2018) because real videos include many issues that are difficult to deal with, e. g. moving object occlusion, drastic illumination changes, video noise and blur. Main approaches to visual object tracking are blob-tracking (Wu et al, 2018), optical flow based tracking (Du et al, 2018), neural network tracking (Price et al, 2018), contour-based tracking (Allili and Ziou, 2006), 3D model based tracking (Yu et al, 2018), etc. Neural networks outperforms other approaches in terms of accuracy but they require special hardware for real-time operation. Object tracking methods implemented in real-time embedded systems are mostly based on optical flow techniques which are less computationally expensive. This paper considers optical flow based object tracking as the most promising approach to visual object tracking.

Comprehensive video datasets are required for comparative studies of existing object tracking methods and development of novel methods. There are some publicly available video datasets created for object tracking methods evaluation: OTB (Wu et al, 2013), VOT (Kristan et al, 2016), KITTI Vision (Geiger et al, 2013). There are some publicly available video datasets intended for optical flow benchmarking: Middlebury (Baker et al, 2011), Sintel (Butler et al, 2012), Flying Things 3D (Mayer et al, 2016). These video datasets are synthetic, they lack real camera noise and blur distortions. The only real video dataset that includes optical flow ground truth is KITTI Vision dataset (Geiger et al, 2013). Thus development of object tracking methods for particular applications may require creation of new video datasets. Summary of the publicly available visual object tracking datasets is presented in Table 1.

A video dataset must include ground truth for automatic evaluation of object tracking results. This ground truth information is usually specified manually by human using special video annotation software. Among special video annotation tools one can mention ViPER (Mariano et al, 2002), Ground Truth Editor (Sarvanko et al, 2013), Phylosis Label Editor (Philosys, 2018), ViTBAT (Biresaw et al, 2016) and Dark Label (DarkLabel, 2018). ViPER (Mariano et al, 2002) was designed in the University of Maryland. It requires manual annotation of an object bounding box in every video frame. Ground Truth Editor (Sarvanko et al, 2013) provides more comfortable user interface however it assumes user to annotate the whole video frame by frame. Phylosis Label Editor (Philosys, 2018) makes it possible to specify the bounding box corners in several video frames, then automatically calculates the bounding boxes for all the rest video frames using interpolation technique. Some restrictions of the software usage are implied by its commercial license. ViTBAT (Biresaw et al, 2016) is an open source analog of Phylosis Label Editor. It also uses interpolation, besides it makes it possible to label moving objects with point markers. Dark Label (DarkLabel, 2018) is a powerful proprietary tool that provides automatic tracking of the object bounding box from frame to frame and operates fairly well, thus user only needs to specify the object bounding box in the first video frame. Summary of the publicly available video annotation tools is presented in Table 2.

Table 1. Summary of public visual object tracking datasets

Dataset	Optical flow ground truth	Moving objects	Genesis
OTB	–	miscellaneous	Reality
VOT-IR	–	miscellaneous	Reality
Kitti Vision	+	cars, pedestrians	Reality
Middlebury	+	toys, etc.	Synthetic
Sintel	+	human, birds	Synthetic
Flying Things 3D	+	miscellaneous	Synthetic

Optical flow tracking approach consists in object feature points detection and tracking within the video image. This approach involves several issues related to the feature point tracking. Some object feature points may be lost or move to background. Some background feature points may be picked up by the moving object. Besides the feature points may slide from the front part of the moving object to its back part while tracking. All these issues can cause inaccuracy in results of tracking algorithms. In order to deal with such issues one must prepare a video tracking dataset with optical flow measurement ground truth. There are few real video datasets that include such ground truth information, for instance KITTI Vision dataset (Geiger et al, 2013). Some problem domains can require creation of new video datasets that meet application-specific requirements. However, there are no publicly available video annotation tools for automatic object feature points markup which is critical for the optical flow ground truth specification. Indeed, ViTBAT (Biresaw et al, 2016) makes it possible to specify the object feature point position using interpolation which is not accurate enough and may require much manual adjustment efforts. Dark Label (DarkLabel, 2018) can automatically track the whole object bounding box but cannot track its distinct feature points. Besides, Dark Label is a proprietary software and cannot be easily extended by the scientific community.

Table 2. Summary of public video annotation tools

Annotation tool	Point markers	Interpolation	Automatic tracking	License
ViPER	–	–	–	Open
Ground Truth Editor	–	–	–	Open
Phylosis Label Editor	+	+	–	Commercial
ViTBAT	+	–	–	Open
Dark Label	–	+	+	Proprietary
Our Tool	+	+	+	Open

In this work we create a new video annotation tool for semi-automatic annotation of the object bounding boxes and its feature points position within the video thus providing ground truth information for the optical flow evaluation on real videos. New video annotation tool can cope with multicamera recorded videos such that user can identify and mark a distinct moving object on several camera views corresponding to the same time moment. Finally, the developed video annotation tool is open source so community can extend its functionality anyway.

2. VIDEO ANNOTATION TOOL OVERVIEW

The video annotation tool was developed using OpenCV library (Bradski and Kaehler, 2016) and Microsoft .NET Framework. The Windows Forms application loads four dynamic libraries with a managed C# code: DisplayControl.dll, ObjectTracker.dll, MarkupProvider.dll, CameraProvider.dll. The DisplayControl.dll implements a Windows Presentation Forms visual control that makes it possible to display multiple camera views simultaneously and draw a rubber band selection interactively using mouse events. The ObjectTracker.dll implements an optical flow based object tracking method for automatic bounding box calculation in a sequence of video frames. The MarkupProvider.dll manages video annotation data in memory and provides service functions for loading and storing annotation data into an XML text file. The CameraProvider.dll provides a program interface to a dynamic library OcvWrapperMfc.dll with unmanaged native C++ code that makes it possible to open and decode video files and calculate optical flow for automatic image feature points tracking using OpenCV library functions. All dynamic link libraries of the application can be tested independently using custom testbench applications.

The source code of the application is divided into five major classes: FileManager, DisplayManager, TraceManager, MarkupManager and CameraManager. All these classes are related to one another by means of inheritance relationship. All together the classes comprise some kind of a service stack, such that any user command initiated by a button click, a mouse movement or a menu selection can be processed sequentially by all classes of the service stack. Each class of the service stack incapsulates some part of the application functionality and has links only to those visual controls of the main form it is responsible for. Such a program code organization makes it possible to hold the visual controls close to the business logic they are supported by and to simplify the source code testing and maintenance.

The FileManager class is responsible for open and save operations as well as initialization of all the rest classes of the service stack. The DisplayManager class receives data from the lower stages of the service stack and loads data into the DisplayControl visual control. The TraceManager class implements video playback, fast forward and backward, switches between trajectory edit and view modes as well as creation of new object categories, tags and trajectories. It also implements the automatic object tracking method in its private instance of the ObjectTracker class. The MarkupManager class integrates the MarkupProvider class instance into the user interface application. The CameraManager class integrates the CameraProvider class instance. The ObjectTracker, MarkupProvider and CameraProvider classes are called from corresponding service stack classes by means of documented program interfaces. The application can be easily extended with alternative implementation of these classes thus providing support of new video sources, annotation database engines and automatic object tracking methods.

Our video annotation tool has two tracking modes. In the first mode the user specifies the feature point marker position in the current video frame. The specified feature point is automatically tracked in the subsequent video frames using pyramidal Lukas-Kanade optical flow (Bouguet, 1999) implemented in OpenCV library. In the second mode the user specifies the object bounding box corners in the current video frame. The position of the bounding box in the subsequent video frames can be estimated in three ways. In the first way the bounding box for the subsequent video frame is initialized in the same position as in the previous video frame, then the user can manually adjust its corners to fit the actual object location within the video frame. In the second way the user must specify the object bounding box corners in several distinct video frames, then its positions in the intermediate video frames are calculated using interpolation. In the third way the user can specify several object feature points along with the object bounding box, then the position of the object bounding box in the subsequent video frames is automatically calculated given the positions of the object feature points tracked using optical flow in the following way.

Let $p(i,t) = \{x(i,t), y(i,t)\}$ be a 2D co-ordinate vector of the i-th object feature point in the t-th video frame. Let $P(t)$ be a 2D co-ordinate vector of a mean object feature point position in the t-th video frame. Let D(t) be a object feature points standard deviation in the t-th video frame.

Let $C(t)$ be a 2D co-ordinate vector of the object bounding box center in the t-th video frame. Then 2D co-ordinate vector of the object bounding box center in the $(t+1)$-th video frame can be calculated as follows: $C(t+1) = C(t) + P(t+1) - P(t)$.

Let $S(t) = \{w(t), h(t)\}$ be a 2D vector of the object bounding box width and height in the t-th video frame. Then 2D vector of object bounding box width and height in the $(t+1)$-th video frame can be calculated as follows: $S(t+1) = S(t) * D(t+1) / D(t)$.

The architecture of the application makes it possible to easily extend its functionality with alternative object bounding box tracking methods if necessary.

3. CONCLUSION

In this work we presented a brief overview of contemporary methods for automatic object detection in videos. Despite neural network methods produced a great breakthrough in recent years, optical flow based tracking methods are still promising due to their real-time performance for embedded systems. A short survey of open video datasets for visual object tracking was also presented. There are few publicly available video datasets that provide optical flow ground truth information for optical flow algorithm benchmarking and contain real life videos that include actual camera noise and blur. New video datasets should be created for testing and improvement of optical flow based tracking methods in order to meet application-specific requirements. Publicly available video annotation tools were also revised. Lack of open source video annotation tools with functions of automatic optical flow markers and object bounding box visual tracking was noticed. Thus a new video annotation tool with such functions was proposed. The proposed video annotation tool has a five layer architecture that simplifies its testing and maintenance. Video source decoding, markup database management and visual tracking program units were implemented as a separate dynamic link libraries and are called from the main application through the documented program interfaces. This approach makes it possible to add new tracking methods, video sources and markup database engines with minimal modifications of the main application source code. The source code of the new video annotation tool will become publicly available on https://github.com/lychkovi/multicam-annotation repository when the article will be published.

ACKNOWLEDGEMENT

This research was supported by Ministry of Science and Higher Education of the Russian Federation, R&D state project №2.5048.2017/8.9.

REFERENCES

Allili, M.S. and Ziou, D., 2006. Object contour tracking in videos by using adaptive mixture models and shape priors. *Proceedings of the International Symposium on Computational Modelling of Objects Represented in Images. Fundamentals, Methods and Applications*. Coimbra, Portugal, pp. 47-52.

Anishchenko, L., 2018. Machine learning in video surveillance for fall detection. *Proceedings of 2018 Ural Symposium on Biomedical Engineering, Radioelectronics and Information Technology*. Yekaterinburg, Russia, pp. 99-102.

Baker, S. et al, 2011. A database and evaluation methodology for optical flow. *In International Journal of Computer Vision*, Vol. 92, No. 1, pp. 1-31.

Biresaw, T.A. et al, 2016. Vitbat: Video tracking and behavior annotation tool. *Proceedings of 13th IEEE International Conference on Advanced Video and Signal Based Surveillance*. Colorado Springs, CO, USA, pp. 295-301.

Bouguet, J.Y., 1999. Pyramidal implementation of the affine lucas kanade feature tracker description of the algorithm. Technical Report, Intel Microprocessor Research Labs.

Bradski, G. and Kaehler, A., 2016. *Learning OpenCV 3. Computer Vision in C++ with the OpenCV Library*. O'Reilly Media.

Butler, D.J. et al, 2012. A naturalistic open source movie for optical flow evaluation. *Proceedings of European Conference on Computer Vision*, Florence, Italy, pp. 611-625.

DarkLabel 1.3. Image Labeling and Annotation Tool. https://darkpgmr.tistory.com/16

Deviatkov, V.V. and Lychkov, I.I., 2017. Recognition of Dynamical Situations on the Basis of Fuzzy Finite State Machines. *Proceedings of IADIS International Conferences Computer Graphics, Visualization, Computer Vision and Image Processing 2017 and Big Data Analytics, Data Mining and Computational Intelligence 2017*. Lisbon, Portugal, pp. 103-109.

Du, B. et al, 2018. Object Tracking in Satellite Videos Based on a Multi-Frame Optical Flow Tracker. arXiv preprint arXiv:1804.09323.

Geiger, A. et al, 2013. Vision meets robotics: The KITTI dataset. *In The International Journal of Robotics Research*, Vol. 32, No. 11, pp. 1231-1237.

Kristan, M. et al, 2016. A novel performance evaluation methodology for single-target trackers. *In IEEE transactions on pattern analysis and machine intelligence*, Vol. 38, No. 11, pp. 2137-2155.

Lychkov, I.I. et al, 2018. Tracking of Moving Objects With Regeneration of Object Feature Points. *Proceedings of 2018 Global Smart Industry Conference*. Chelyabinsk, Russia, pp. 1-6.

Mariano, V.Y. et al, 2002. Performance evaluation of object detection algorithms. *Proceedings of IEEE International Conference on Pattern Recognition*. Quebec City, Quebec, Canada, pp. 965-969.

Mayer, N. et al, 2016. A large dataset to train convolutional networks for disparity, optical flow and scene flow estimation. *Proceedings of the IEEE Conference on Computer Vision and Pattern Recognition*. Las Vegas, NV, USA, pp. 4040-4048.

Morozov, A.A. et al, 2015. Development of concurrent object-oriented logic programming platform for the intelligent monitoring of anomalous human activities *In Biomedical Engineering Systems and Technologies. Communications in Computer and Information Science*, Vol. 511, pp. 82-97.

Philosys Label Editor. https://www.philosys.de/en/products/label-editor

Price, E. et al, 2018. Deep Neural Network-based Cooperative Visual Tracking through Multiple Micro Aerial Vehicles. arXiv preprint arXiv:1802.01346.

Sarvanko, J. et al, 2013. Consumer video dataset with marked head trajectories. *Proceedings of the 4th ACM Multimedia Systems Conference*. Oslo, Norway, pp. 84-89.

Taranyan, A.R. et al, 2018. Selective Covariance-based Human Localization, Classification and Tracking in Video Streams from Multiple Cameras. *Proceedings of the 9th International Conference on Bioinformatics Models, Methods and Algorithms; Part of the 11th International Joint Conference on Biomedical Engineering Systems and Technologies*. Funchal, Portugal, Vol. 3, pp. 81-88.

Wu, J. et al, 2018. Study of multiple moving targets' detection in fisheye video based on the moving blob model. *In Multimedia Tools and Applications*, pp. 1-20.

Wu, Y. et al, 2013. Online object tracking: A benchmark. *Proceedings of the IEEE conference on computer vision and pattern recognition*. Portland, Oregon, USA, pp. 2411-2418.

Yu, Y. et al, 2018. HeadFusion: 360° Head Pose tracking combining 3D Morphable Model and 3D Reconstruction. *In IEEE Transactions on Pattern Analysis and Machine Intelligence*. Vol. 40, No. 11, pp. 2653-2667.

Reflection Papers

ELICITING USER REQUIREMENTS FOR CRITICAL COMMUNICATIONS IN PUBLIC SAFETY USING ACTIVITY THEORY AND SYSTEMISM

Débora Vanessa Campos Freire[1], Alessandra Callado Bezerra de Mello[2] and Ana Clara Cândido[1]
[1]Federal University of Santa Catarina, Brazil
[2]Federal University of Pernambuco, Brazil

ABSTRACT

The decision to adopt a technology is a problem that includes different aspects of information. This view, considering not only the technical aspects, but also economic factors and social context, is the definition of Technological Assessment (TA). This work is an applied exploratory research based on primary and secondary data. It focuses on user requirements capture based on understanding the activity system's context and user-related task analysis as a resource for developing or adjusting the Critical Communication (CC) systems used in Public Safety (PS). The collected was analyzed data with the worldview of Systemism, which considers that everything is either a system or a component of a system, and every system has peculiar properties. This work also proposes a system characterized by their mechanism, using the construction logic of Composition–Environment–Structure-Mechanism (CESM) to represent the problem. Starting from a theoretical framework regarding resource information on Activity Theory (AT) and Usability, in order to identify methods of data collection for generating information on user requirements, and Systemism in order to build a System, this work aims to improve Human Computer Interaction (HCI) design through user requirements to support the development or improvement of a computer system regarding the activities developed by CC users in the field of Public Safety.

KEYWORDS

User Requirements, Activity Theory, Systemism, Critical Communication, Information Science, Public Safety

1. USER REQUIREMENTS

Solutions for informational problems cannot be developed isolated from other actors and mechanisms of the ecological chain. As a rule, they require the consideration of several other actors and mechanisms in the larger set of informational ecology (SARACEVIC, 1996). According to Leventhal & Barnes (2008), in Software Engineering, a computerized solution is required in order to solve a system or process problem, while, in Usability, the user context and its tasks are the focus of the problem. Usability considers the actors are the users of the system. The incorporation of AT in HCI design aims to include the user's context in social, cultural and psychological aspects, helping the understanding of human activities related to the problems and focusing on the actors involved, being these subjects and members of the system (MELLO & NEVES, 2018). Regarding the construction of a broad representation, Systemism is related to information concepts, seeking a better understanding of the system, its actors, processes, environment and relationships between them. Both AT and Usability have elements that are deeply related to Systemism, and therefore can be used together in order to capture user requirements and build a system representation.

2. INFORMATION SCIENCE, USABILITY, ACTIVITY THEORY AND SYSTEMISM

Although there are various definitions of the term 'information', this study appropriates the concepts consolidated in the field of Information Science. According to Buckland (1991), 3 meanings can be identified: information as a process, as knowledge and as a thing. In this context, the tools used in CC activities – for example, radio equipment – are information, and they can be categorized as “information-as-thing”, assuming that they will be an object of analysis. Radio interfaces should be built in such way that allows the user to use the device efficiently, effectively and satisfactorily; therefore, interfaces can be understood as “information-as-process”. User perception can be understood as “information-as-knowledge”, or what is perceived from the information-as-process that can be measured through the application of usability and user experience.

Performing a task using a product or system can be challenging; what will make this task easier or not is the relationship between user and system. According to Jordan (1998), usability should not be considered isolated from other factors, since it’s a property of the interaction between product, user and environment. Usability addresses this relationship, being a determining factor for user satisfaction over various consumer products. According to Falcão & Soares (2013), consumer products are predominantly three-dimensional objects, used in a determined environment, that have gone through the project conception and development for industrial manufacturing. Radio equipment is one of the tools that can be analyzed within this definition. Different radio models provide different functionalities and interfaces; thus, users must have a wide range of options, focused not only on the product, but also on improving efficiency and effectiveness in PS actions.

In order to understand the problem, the adopted strategies consider user requirements as a basis information. The first step for a system’s design and construction is to collect data. For this, this work used an activity analysis, based on AT, that considers that activities are developed through action (conscious) and operations (unconscious), while individuals interact with the activity’s environment considering social relations. Mwanza (2001) proposed a methodology that guides the process of data collection and interpretation of requirements, using Engeström System Model of Activities (1987) as a heuristic model. The method makes possible the analysis of activities and the understanding of the community’s social and cultural context, considering aspects of mediation through tools, rules and division of labor.

The process of operationalization is applied in 6 stages: modeling of the situation; production of the activity system; decomposition of the activity system; generation of research questions; conducting of detailed research; and interpretation of the findings. From the interviews, it was possible to identify components and produce the Activity System. Mello & Neves (2018) present an adaptation of the Mwanza (2001) method, proposing a hexagonal diagram representation system based on Amstel (2010), instead of the second-generation diagram of Engeström (1987). The authors propose a Canvas diagram, named "Canvas Activity Analysis". Through the understanding of the activity with the identification of its components and the relations between them, this method can contribute as a subsidy for TA in CC for Public Safety.

For a broader system view, this paper uses Systemism concepts from Bunge (2000, 2005). Bunge opposes approaches that are too reductionist, reducing what should be irreducible; the author proposes the CESM model, which describes a system at a certain level of its composition. Each Component is an atom of the system; the Environment are the external items that act upon or suffer action from a component; its Structure are the connections between components and between those and the environment; and the Mechanism are the processes that act on transformations, causing, for example, the growth or collapse of a system. The epistemology adopted by Bunge is scientific realism, with Systemism as the ontological foundation. The systemic approach could be summarized in 7 general rules: put all social facts into a broader context; divide each system into its composition, environment and structure; distinguish the system’s various levels and display their relationships; seek the mechanisms; verify the hypothesis by experimental manipulation; prefer dynamic hypothesis to phenomenological models; in case of system mal function, check the C, E, S, M (SILVA, 2016).

3. METHODS

The present work is an applied research, characterized as exploratory and descriptive, using quantitative and qualitative approaches. Secondary data were obtained through a Systematic Review of Literature and bibliographical review. Primary data were obtained from interviews and data treatment based on Mwanza (2001) and Mello & Neves (2018), applied to 10 system users who were also experts from industry, PS agencies and the Ministry of Science, Technology and Innovation of Brazil. This work aims to represent, through the interviews’ answers, the perception of specialists, society members, technical teams, users, government and manufacture companies. The CESM representation also allows the visualization of the innovation ecosystem.

4. EXPERIMENT APPLICATION

This research applied stages 1 and 2 of the Mwanza (2001) method with contributions from Mello and Neves (2018), in order to understand the components and the context of the activity. The questions applied were: 1. How would you describe CC activity? 2. What is the purpose of CC? 3. Who is involved in CC? 4. What resources are used for CC? 5. What are the social norms, rules or regulations that influence or govern the performance of CC? 6. What is the role of each individual in CC and how do they organize themselves? 7. What is the environment in which CC is carried out? 8. What is the desired result when performing CC? 9. If you could solve any aspect related to the activity, what would it be? In addition, we proposed other questions to the model, in order to assist in the elucidation of difficulties encountered in the activities system: 10. What are the main difficulties you identify in the current CC scenario in Brazil? 11. What opportunities do you perceive in the advancement of technologies for CC in Brazil and in the possibility of partnerships with other countries? 12. What legal, economic and social implications do you consider relevant for this decision to implement new technologies for CC? 13. What is your opinion on the possibility of interoperability between Public Safety organizations, using technologies in LMR and LTE? 14. In your opinion, which would be an ideal model for CC in Brazil, considering current and future technologies?

5. CANVAS OF CRITICAL COMMUNICATION´S ACTIVITY SYSTEM

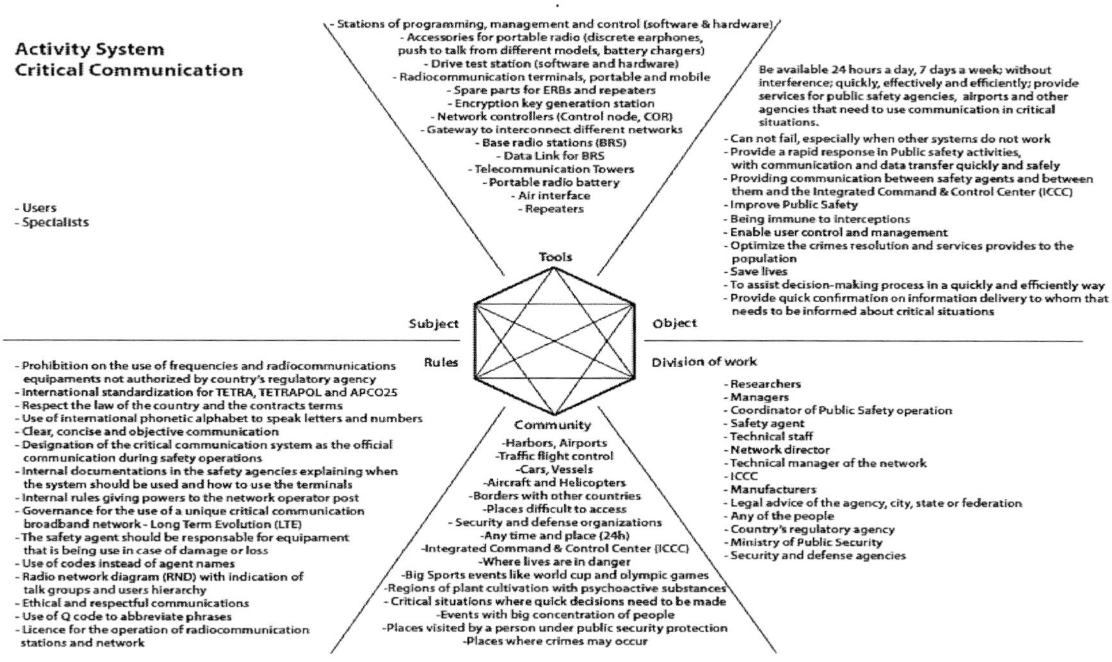

Figure 1. Critical Communication's Activity System, based on the Diagram from Mello & Neves (2018)

With the canvas, one can identify, for example, the governmental institutions and their respective actions that make possible for the actors to execute the objective of the activity.

6. SYSTEM CONSTRUCTION

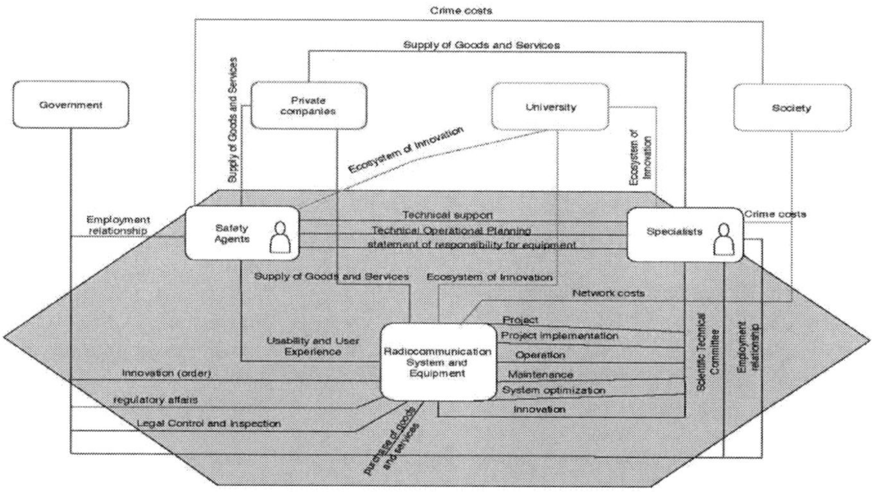

Figure 2. Critical Communication's System based on Critical Communication's Activity System and CESM concept

7. CONCLUSION

The results above present data that helps identifying, in the context of the organization, the actors, the means and the purpose of the activity. The "rules", "community" and "division of labor" fields provide important elements for understanding which entities may be relevant for creating an innovation ecosystem. The "tools" section enables a look over possible target elements for innovation. This work applied methods to collect user requirements that assist in a Technological Assessment exercise of Critical Communication in Public Safety, through the analysis of the Activity System and considering user requirements as a basis.

REFERENCES

Amstel, F. M. C. van., 2010. *Interaction Design Yearbook*. Faber-Ludens Institute for Interaction Design.

Buckland, M. K., 1991. Information as thing. *American Society for Information Science*, v. 42, n. 5, p. 351 – 360.

Bunge, M., 2000. Systemism: the alternative to individualism and holism. *Journal of Socio-Economics*, v. 29, n.2, p. 147-157.

Bunge, M., 2005.*Diccionario de filosofía*. 3. ed. Buenos Aires: Siglo XXI.

Engeström, Y., 1987. *Learning by Expanding: An Activity Theoretical Approach to Developmental Research*. Helsinki: Orienta-Konsultit.

Falcão, C. S; Soares, M. M., 2013. Usability of Consumer Products: an analysis of the concepts, methods and applications. *Estudos em Design*, Rio de Janeiro, v. 21, n. 2.

Jordan, P. W., 1998. *An Introduction to Usability*. London: Taylor & Francis.

Leventhal, Laura; Barnes, Julie, 2008. *Usability Engineering: Process, Products and Examples*. Pearson Education, Inc., New Jersey.

Mello, A. C. B. De; Neves, A. M. M. das, 2018. Eliciting Requirements for Digital Systems Using Activity and Task Analysis. In: (IADIS), I. A. for Development of the I. S. (Ed.). *Multi Conference on Computer Science and Information Systems*. Madrid: IADIS Press, p. 329 – 333. ISBN 978-989-8533-79-1.

Mwanza, D., 2001. Where Theory meets Practice: A Case for an Activity Theory based Methodology to guide Computer System Design. In: HIROSE, M. (Ed.). Proceedings of INTERACT'2001: *Eighth ifip tc 13 international conference on human-computer interaction.* Tokyo, Japan: IOS Press Oxford, UK.

Saracevic, T., 1996. Information Science: origin, evolution and relations. *Perspec. Ci. Inf.*, Belo Horizonte, Brazil, v. 1, n. 1, p. 41 – 62.

Silva, L. M., Vianna, W. B., & Kern, V. M. (2016, mai/ago.). O sistemismo de Bunge como base teórico-metodológica para pesquisa em Ciência da Informação. *Em Questão*, 22(2), 140 – 164.

THE FALLACIES OF MDA FOR NOVICE DESIGNERS: OVERUSING MECHANICS AND NEGLECTING AESTHETICS

Kenneth Chen
Drexel University, 3501 Market Street, Philadelphia, PA, 19104, USA

ABSTRACT

Ever since MDA was publicized by Hunicke et al. in 2004, it has become a building block for game developers and scholars. However, it has also incited several misconceptions that have spread among students and the gaming community. For example, players have overused the term "mechanics," to the point that it is virtually meaningless. On the other side, the terms "dynamics" and "aesthetics" have been comparatively neglected, despite their value. Building upon my experiences of teaching an undergraduate game design course, I argue that these misconceptions stem from the ways that consumers have misinterpreted the MDA framework. Game educators are not necessarily working with experienced designers: they are working with students who are often more passionate about playing games than making them. Thus, game educators need to target this misconception in order to shed light on preconceived biases.

KEYWORDS

Game Design, Teaching, Mechanics, Dynamics, Aesthetics

1. INTRODUCTION

With the rise of game development as a viable career choice, more and more students are entering game design programs for higher education. Decades ago, potential designers were seen as solitary tinkerers, but now, they are players who feel inspired by games and have paths to turn that inspiration into production. However, this introduces a new problem: these players often develop misconceptions about game design based on their experiences from consuming games rather than creating them. On the academic level, instructors need to be aware of these misconceptions and specifically target them.

The misconception I want to discuss is the concept of mechanics. This word was popularized by Hunicke et al. in a 2004 workshop paper at GDC, along with dynamics and aesthetics in their foundational MDA model (Hunicke et al, 2004). MDA argues that game design can be understood as the connections among mechanics (data, formulas, rules), dynamics (behaviors, interactions, decisions), and aesthetics (emotions, reactions, feelings). Since its inception, MDA has been appropriated by players and morphed into an amalgamation of different definitions. In its current state, the word "mechanics" is nearly meaningless, and has lost all of its insight into the MDA framework. Despite this, the word is still extremely common not only among players, but also among students who are relying on their previous experience as players.

For instructors in game development, it is not sufficient to teach students how to make games. They also need to unteach students how they thought games were supposed to be made. Many of the students who are entering university-level game design programs are primarily inspired by playing games rather than making games. Even though MDA was originally developed as a means to bridge this divide, I argue that it has unintentionally yet ironically widened it. However, if we become more aware of the problem, we can take steps to fix the situation.

2. THE GAP BETWEEN DEFINITIONS

Some of the more experienced and established members of the industry and academic communities might not be familiar with the ways in which the gaming community has twisted the word "mechanics." Although there isn't exactly a true dictionary definition, players have generally taken the term to mean something along the lines of the expression of skillful play through controlled intentional inputs. This is often paired with a positive connotation.

In some online gaming communities, mechanics are considered as an element of skill, separated from tactics or communication or foresight. Thus, mechanics in this sense become more closely related to reflexes or precision in timing and aiming. For example, the following quote refers to a player's reaction to the boss monster Kushala Daora in *Monster Hunter World*:

"Technically among the worst designed enemies in the history of video games. Design and execution-wise obviously. Really*****ty and meaningless enemy design; sloppy hitboxes and stagger. This is how you literally ruin a mechanical game and turn it into a cheese/equipment fest." - Anonymous

This quote from a gaming wiki forum illustrates a different use of "mechanics" than the one seen before in the player analysis. We can reinterpret this passage to mean that the stifling of player skill is an indication of poor design.

And yet, that is false, because the stifling of player skill is an important part of a game designer's toolbox. Perhaps the designer has decided that this is the point at which players should stop trying to muscle their way through a fight with quick reflexes, but rather take a more deliberate and methodical approach. Many game design principles discuss the idea of increasing difficulty over time and forcing players to develop new skills to approach new problems. This is the core concept of psychological flow (Chen, 2006) and the reason why learning is fun (Koster, 2003). The player has used the concept of mechanics in terms of skill in order to discuss the concept of mechanics in terms of design. Since these two concepts are different, the player fails to realize some of the most basic principles of game design.

Clearly, the player is just frustrated and most likely not actually trying to conduct an insightful design analysis. This is just an exaggerated example of the overreaching mentality that I want to expose. When students emphasize the importance of mechanics as a skill, they fail to recognize the larger design implications behind these decisions. Even though both players and designers are saying "mechanics," they are not communicating the same meaning. If this anonymous player were a college-bound game design major, we as educators cannot teach them the formal definition of a mechanic until we first address their misconception of that definition.

Moving away from the game consumer community, the game development community also suffers from the ambiguity circling the word "mechanics." We can see an especially odd use of this term in Martin Sahlin's GDC 2017 talk "*Unravel - Using Empathy as a Game Mechanic*" (Sahlin, 2017):

"Unravel turned empathy into a game mechanic. I wanted players to fall in love... Then break their hearts! Then we make it all worth it." - Martin Sahlin

While these are certainly interesting and valuable goals for a game designer, the use of the word "mechanic" just invites even more confusion. Moreover, this is a point at which the term "aesthetics" from the original framework would have been perfectly appropriate. It is doubtful that Sahlin was unaware of the MDA framework. The word "mechanic" just communicated the point better, because the word has expanded to mean practically any part of a game.

When Sahlin uses the term "mechanics" instead of the more appropriate term "aesthetics," he reflects a similar shift in public perception. People are putting less emphasis on dynamics/aesthetics and more emphasis on mechanics, and then expanding the definition of mechanics to include dynamics/aesthetics. The whole purpose of MDA was to separate these three concepts so that designers could intelligently discuss how they interacted with each other. But the direction of modern discourse seems to indicate the opposite effect. Greg Costikyan wrote "I Have No Words and I Must Design" in 2002 about this exact problem. If he had no words to design with, we may end up with only one, which isn't a much better situation (Costikyan, 2002).

3. MISCONCEPTIONS AND MISTAKES

Although MDA is a victim of misinterpretation, I argue that it is also a perpetrator. I do not attack developers/academics/players for misinterpreting MDA out of faith in the framework. Rather, I believe that MDA cannot be treated as a truth of game design, and that we need to consider it along with other approaches. However, we cannot teach students how to deconstruct MDA if they did not understand MDA in the first place.

One of MDA's arguments is that designers experience games from mechanics to dynamics to aesthetics, whereas players experience games from aesthetics to dynamics to mechanics. The terms of mechanics, dynamics, and aesthetics are insightful and valuable. However, I believe that the illustrated progression from one to the next is not only false, but also a reason why the words have become so severely misinterpreted.

Players who want to talk about games in a more intelligent manner will try to use more advanced language, which from this perspective, is the word "mechanics." Anonymous could have written "Kushala Daora beat me and I felt weak and helpless" and that would be an illustration of game aesthetics, but that's not how humans express frustration. Likewise, designers who want to appeal to players will use the same language that they use, as seen in Sahlin's GDC talk about empathy as a game mechanic.

We have ended up in a situation where we use the word "mechanics" far too often, and the word "aesthetics" far too rarely. It doesn't help that the word "aesthetic" is already commonly used to refer to artistic quality, which causes people to think that "game aesthetics" means "game art." I believe that the aesthetics are the most important part, and that we must not neglect the value of this term.

3.1 Players: From Mechanics to Aesthetics

Hunicke et al. state that "From the player's perspective, aesthetics set the tone, which is born out in observable dynamics and eventually, operable mechanics."

On the contrary, players need to first learn the mechanics and then the dynamics in order to properly appreciate the aesthetics. For example, let us examine chess. The mechanics of chess cover the core rules and the movement for each piece. The dynamics of chess illustrate different strategies, openings, counterattacks, sieges, and all the other types of events that can happen during play. The aesthetics represent the final experience: not only the joy of winning or the sadness of defeat, but also the cleverness of a tricky move, or the bravery of a reckless assault, or the desperation of an unlikely plan.

But when a player first sits down at the chess board, they cannot experience these emotions directly. They cannot be told to feel clever, or brave, or desperate, or joyful or sad. Those emotions need to be earned through gameplay. If the player does not know the rules, then they are not responsible for their actions. And if they are not responsible for their actions, they will not have an emotional attachment. Imagine a player who loses because they do not know the rules. Such a player will not feel disappointed: they will only feel bored. Thus, it makes more sense to say that players experience games from mechanics to dynamics to aesthetics: the complete opposite of what Hunicke et al. described.

The original players-from-aesthetics-to-mechanics position can be understood as a product of its time. MDA was first publicized in 2004, around the period of the ludology vs narratology debate (Aarseth, 2012). This was a period when mainstream AAA games operated primarily through cutscenes, and the indie market with more experimental narrative formats was still growing. Cutscenes can be interpreted as a shortcut to aesthetics which bypasses mechanics and dynamics (Klevjer, 2002). If the player watches enough cutscenes of their character being powerful, eventually they will feel powerful too despite never touching a button. In this context, it is understandable that Hunicke et al. said that aesthetics set the tone.

But today, long after ludology vs narratology, the field of game development has generally settled into the agreement that players are an important part of their own experience. We are seeing more and more games, AAA games even, which are breaking away from the strict cutscene-gameplay-cutscene-gameplay rhythm. Clint Hocking's work on ludonarrative dissonance (Hocking, 2007) has illustrated the importance of guiding players through mechanics to dynamics to aesthetics, rather than just forcing an aesthetic directly. The IMP framework (Elson et al, 2014) is better suited to understand how cutscenes and other external forces influence the experience outside of the MDA loop.

3.2 Designers: From Aesthetics to Mechanics

Hunicke et al. state that "From the designer's perspective, the mechanics give rise to dynamic system behavior, which in turn leads to particular aesthetic experiences."

This progression from mechanics to dynamics to aesthetics can also be seen as a product of its time, although the argument is weaker. Modern approaches to game design have shown the importance of working backwards from a strong aesthetic goal. Matt Thorson, creator of *Towerfall* and *Celeste* described his process in a GDC talk in 2018 (Thorson, 2018). He starts with the experience that he wants players to have and then iterates his levels until they properly evoke the intended reaction. Each mechanic in *Celeste* such as dashing or climbing up walls is reverse-derived from the final aesthetic experience.

However, this was a popular view even around the 2004 period. Tracy Fullerton's book "Game Design Workshop" quickly emphasizes that the first thing a designer should do is set "player experience goals": the type of experience that players will have during the game, or in other words, aesthetics (Fullerton, 2004). This is mirrored in Jesse Schell's "Art of Game Design," where the very second chapter is titled "The Designer Creates An Experience" (Schell, 2008). Even outside of games, we can see the same kind of division between aesthetics/experiences and mechanics/handicraft in Scott McCloud's "Understanding Comics", where out of six steps, the idea is first and the form is second (McCloud, 1993). All of these established works of knowledge focus on the designer's ability to conceptualize a central vision and lay out the path carefully and deliberately.

Hunicke et al.'s argument, that designers start with mechanics which lead to dynamics which lead to aesthetics, seems haphazard in comparison. Is the designer supposed to throw together a bunch of mechanics with no plan or direction and just hope that it ends up being fun? There are several prominent modern designers who are exploring that exact question. Frank Lantz casts doubt on "the iconic image of the designer - smart, confident, sophisticated, stylish, informed" in his post "Against Design", and argues that perhaps we should say that games are discovered or composed rather than designed (Lantz, 2015).

This perspective exists because it is built on top of the previous one. There cannot be an "Against Design" if there is not a "Design" in the first place. Once we realize the limits of our ability to build aesthetics, we can come back to the mechanics-first approach. But starting with mechanics from the very beginning is hardly designing: it is only throwing a game together and hoping it sticks (Pulsipher, 2016).

Naturally, every game production has a different process: some start with aesthetics, some start with mechanics, some with a different approach altogether. However, when Hunicke et al. propose that designers start with mechanics, they don't acknowledge this full range of possibilities. They would not have been able to do so in a short workshop paper, but unfortunately that short workshop paper seems to have developed more traction than expected.

4. CONCLUSION

MDA has been one of the most prominent game frameworks in not only industry and academia, but also player communities. We need to properly assess the impact of MDA in order to teach the next generation of game designers how to use it more effectively. In programming, we call this effect a "tech debt," when a whole system is built on top of a piece of outdated legacy code. Removing or refactoring that code could end up sending the whole system crashing down, but then you would be able to rebuild it stronger than before. The burden of handling this tech debt should fall to university teachers, who are in the best position to pinpoint this problem and turn it into a learning opportunity. MDA should be taught as one type of approach, rather than as an incontrovertible truth. Educators can use other models such as SSM (Grip, 2017) or DDE (Walk, 2017) as juxtapositions to better understand MDA and its relation to game design.

REFERENCES

Aarseth, E. (2012). A narrative theory of games. In Proceedings of the international conference on the foundations of digital Games. ACM, 129–133.

Anonymous. (2018). Kushala Daora - Monster Hunter World. https://monsterhunterworld.wiki.fextralife.com/Kushala+Daora

Chen, J. (2006). Flow In Games. Master's thesis. University of Southern California.

Costikyan, G. (2002). I Have No Words And I Must Design. The game design reader: A rules of play anthology (2005).

Elson, M., Breuer, J., Ivory, J.D., & Quandt, T. (2014). More Than Stories With Buttons: Narrative, Mechanics, and Context as Determinants of Player Experience in Digital Games. Journal of Communication 64, 3 (2014),521–542.

Fullerton, T. (2004). Game Design Workshop: A Playcentric Approach To Creating Innovative Games. CRC Press.

Grip, T. 2017. The SSM Framework of Game Design. Blog.

Hocking, C. (2007). Ludonarrative Dissonance in Bioshock. https://clicknothing.typepad.com/click_nothing/2007/10/ludonarrative-d.html

Hunicke, R., LeBlanc, M., & Zubek, R. (2004). MDA: A formal approach to game design and game research. In Proceedings of the AAAI Workshop on Challenges in Game AI, Vol. 4.

Klevjer, R. (2002). In Defense of Cutscenes. In CGDC Conf.

Koster, R. (2003). A Theory of Fun for Game Design. O'Reilly Media.

Lantz, F. (2015). Against Design. http://gamedesignadvance.com/?p=2930cpage=1

McCloud, S. (1993). Understanding Comics: The Invisible Art. Tundra Publishing.

Sahlin, M. (2017). Unravel - Using Empathy as a Game Mechanic. https://www.gdcvault.com/play/1024661/-Unravel-Using-Empathy-as.

Schell, J. (2008). Art of Game Design: A Book of Lenses. CRC Press.

Thorson, M. (2018). Level Design Workshop: Designing Celeste. In GDC.

Pulsipher, L. (2016). Are you designing a game, or throwing one together? You can't design a game as though you were playing a video game. Gamasutra.

Walk et al. (2017). Design, Dynamics, Experience (DDE): An Advancement of the MDA Framework for Game Design in Game Dynamics. Best Practices in Procedural and Dynamic Game Content Generation.

MIXED REALITY AS ONE OF MAIN COMPONENTS OF THE SCIENTIFIC GATEWAY

Eva Pajorová and Ladislav Hluchý
Institute of Informatics, Slovak Academy of Sciences
Bratislava, Slovakia

ABSTRACT

Data visualization and mixed reality is incredibly important as a tool of communication - whether for hard or softer data. A Science Gateway is a connection between scientists and their computational tools in the form of web portal. It creates a space for communities, collaboration and data sharing and visualization in a comprehensive and e-client manner. The main purpose of such a solution is to allow users to access the computational resources, process and analyze their data and get the results in a uniform and user friendly way. It is very important for us, researcher to communicate our science to non-scientists. Our paper deal with position the ***mixed reality*** as a one of main component the scientific gateway and portals. The scientific portals and gateways are cumulative all classes of ***visualization and Mixed reality.***

KEYWORDS

Mixed Reality, Scientifics Gateway, Research Results, 3D Visualization

1. INTRODUCTION

Science gateways provide access to advanced resources for science and engineering researchers, educators, and students. Through streamlined, online, user-friendly interfaces, gateways combine a variety of cyberinfrastructure (CI) components in support of a community-specific set of tools, applications, and data collections. In general, these specialized, shared resources are integrated as a Web portal, mobile app, or a suite of applications. Through science gateways, broad communities of researchers can access diverse resources which can save both time and money for themselves and their institutions. Mixed reality is used as an independent concept, or to classify the spectrum of reality technologies. The area between the two extremes, where both the real and the virtual are mixed is called *mixed reality*. This in turn is said to consist of both *augmented reality,* where the virtual augments the real, and *augmented virtuality*, where the real augments the virtual. Augmented reality (AR) supplements the real world with virtual objects, such that virtual objects appear to coexist in the same space as the real world. Mixed reality called as mixed because it is regarded as a system in which augmented reality (AR) and virtual reality (VR) technologies are combined.
For example some experts present the framework for mixed reality agents, i.e. agents that exist in both the real and virtual space. These agents combine the physical presence of a robot with the adaptability and expressivity of a virtual character. The architecture can be employed in the context of a mobile collaborative mixed reality environment that is cohabited by both robots and humans. As an example application they applied the framework to a museum virtual presence of the mixed reality agent to convey an individual and personalized learning experience. Through user-friendly web interfaces integrated into the same environment, researchers and scientists can securely and transparently access to computational and data sources, services, tools, sensors, etc. Scientific portals and gateways are able to provide a community-centric view, workflow/dataflow services and a strong support in accessing to the cyber infrastructure including grid and cloud based resources. In each of Science contexts, scientific gateways play a key role since they allow scientists to transparently access to distributed data repositories (across several domains and institutions), metadata sources, carry out search & discovery activities, as well as ***visualization and mixed reality*** and analysis ones, etc. Finally, Scientific Gateways can play an important role for training students (at the academic level) in the different sciences disciplines, attract new users and representing a relevant centralized knowledge repository in the Sciences context.

Currently they are lot of communications framework and gateways. For example Story telling (Kosara, 2017) is an art and free form mostly used as entertainment in the arts. The framework of storytelling can be applied very effectively to scientific data to make it intelligible to those learning and those who are not scientists. To allow users to interact remotely with future supercomputers and large-scale computing environments in a more interactive and visual manner we present a tool called Vine Toolkit that has been successfully used as a core web platform for various gateways (Song, 2016) . Also Vine Toolkit is a modular, extensible and easy-to-use tool as well as high-level Application Programming Interface (API) for various applications, visualization components and building blocks to allow interoperability between many different HPC and grid technologies.

P-GRADE is a good example of highly integrated parallel application development web-based system for Grid and clusters (P-GRADE Grid Portal). It uses Globus, Condor-G, ARC, BOINC and MPICH-G2 as grid-aware middleware to conduct computations. The framework supplies a repository of gems enabling scripts to interface low-level resources such as PBS queues, EGEE computing elements, LFC directories and other types of Grid resources. Moreover, GridSpace2 provides a Web 2.0-based Experiment Workbench supporting joint development and execution of virtual experiments by groups of collaborating scientists. GridSpace2 main idea to enable HPC environments via web interface is very similar to Vine Toolkit main idea, however GridSpace with its scripts is more like programming environment for the Grid {suitable for advanced users or programmers; on the other hand, Vine Toolkit Applications do not require from the user knowledge of scripting languages and focus on delivering ready to use GUIs. Moreover, thanks to Vine Toolkit native JSDL and BES support and the QosCosGrid middleware stack used in the prototype portal can be easily changed to any type supported by Vine middleware's without changes in code or even the need to restart the portal. Our contribution is in Astro Portal: A Science Gateway for Large-scale Astronomy Data Analysis. We have developed mixed reality visualization tools. One of them is mixed reality visualization tool of dynamical evolution of Oort cloud as a part of Protoplanetary disk. Second our contribution is in *Water HUB is a Science Gateway for Water Research and Education* when we are working on mixed reality tools for water management?

2. MIXED REALITY (MR) AS A WAY OF REPRESENTATIONS OF DATASETS

There are some main reasons for that scientist are using VR as visual representations of datasets.

1. For visual control in High performance computing (HPC) of the execution proces
2. For presentations the research academic results in different disciplines
3. For publication of research results
4. For scientists and non-scientist, students as a directly visual education form

2.1 MR as Visual Control of the Execution Process

MR and *visualization* have the main position as a way to control execution process. The visualization tool is designed as a plug in module. Client asking for visualization is as a "visualization client". Output data on the storage element are the inputs data for visualization jobs. Visualization workers are to modify data to the visualizable formats, but also to prepare the typical visualization scenes.

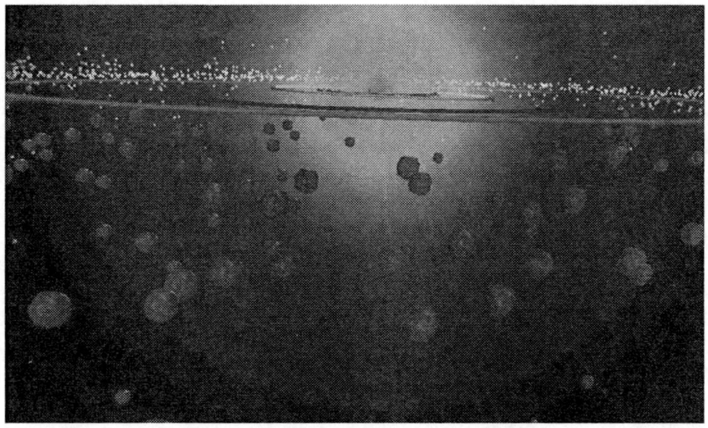

Figure 1. Example when is MR and Visualization using as a Control of Execution Process

2.2 MR Tools as a Presentations Form

The Science Gateways Research Center develop and use open source software to create user tools and environments that help scientific communities do what they could not otherwise do. The Science Gateways Research Center researches, develops, and operates science gateways in collaboration with many clients and partners. Advance in sciences and engineering has put high demand on tools for high-performance large-scale visual data exploration and analysis.

2.3 Formal Publication of Research Results

The goal of MR and scientific visualization is to help scientists view and better understand their large data. (Šipková, 2016).There are data from computing, experiments or numerical simulations. Directly the output data are difficult to understand. MR and scientific visualization can help with these difficulties. Using mixed reality techniques, the data can be viewed naturally. Viewing the data as MR can quickly draw the scientist's attention to interesting and/or anomalous portions of the data. Scientists to use MR from the beginning to end of their experiments and simulations. This also allows the scientists to develop a set of MR tools and techniques that will help them understand their data. We have developed lot of MR tool in different disciplines for better understand the research results. Such as MR tool for natural disasters, VR tool for astronomical research, MR tool for water management and so on.

For example VR tool for water management are using for better understand the process of water simulation in different research goals (Pajorová, 2016). Our MR tool is composed from 5 modules which all have different mission. They can work separately or together as a one framework. See some outputs from MR tool for water management. *Water HUB is a Science Gateway for Water Research and Education*, is a global communication and research platform for research, education, knowledge sharing and global outreach (Cuckerberk, 2017). Built on the HUB zero cyberinfrastructure for scientific collaboration, Water HUB develops and makes available modeling and data sharing tools used in water related research and education activities. Among its tools, the SWAT Share online application not only allows users to run and calibrate their SWAT models, it also supports sharing of models and output data visualization through web browsers.

Figure 2. Pictures Shows the Water Simulation Research Results

2.4 MR Tools as a Visual Teaching and Education Form

Educational visualization is using a simulation normally created on a computer to create an image of something so it can be taught about. This is very useful when teaching about a topic which is difficult to otherwise see, for example, atomic structure, because atoms are far too small to be studied easily without expensive and difficult to use scientific equipment. It can also be used to view past events, such as looking at dinosaurs, or looking at things that are difficult or fragile to look at in reality like the human skeleton, without causing physical or mental harm to a subjective volunteer or cadaver.

3. CONCLUSION

The goal of our paper is to demonstrate the some examples and to support the mixed reality and visualization as an essential component in new portals and gateways technologies. For a future we want to create a scientific gateway for some scientific disciplines as are naturel disasters sciences with all *visualization* aspects by using mixed reality and all new one visualization technologies.

ACKNOWLEDGEMENT

This work is supported by projects VEGA 2/0167/16 and U – COMP: APVV – 17-0619.

REFERENCES

Cuckerberk, M. F., 2017. How the WaterHub Works http://www.campserv.emory.edu/fm/energy_utilities/water-hub/how%20it%20works. https://www.facebook.com/zuck/posts/10101319050523971.

Kosara, R. and Mackinlay, J., 2017. Storytelling: The Next Step for Visualization. Computer (Special Issue on Cutting-Edge Research in Visualization https://www.bing.com/search?q=Story+telling+papers&form=PRUSEN&pc=UE07&mkt=en-us&httpsmsn=1&refig=0fdab404c62d411d80bb6139a1549183&sp=-1&pq=story+telling+papers&sc=7-20&qs=n&sk=&cvid=0fdab404c62d411d80bb6139a1549183).

Pajorová,, E. and Hluchy, L., 2016. Water management - 3D visualization of research results. In Inovatívne informačno-komunikačné technológie vo vodnom hospodárstve. - Bratislava: STU Bratislava, p. 53-58. ISBN 978-80-89535-19-4.

Song, C., Zhao, L. and Biehl, L., 2016. New Science Gateways for Advanced Computing Simulations and Visualization Using Vine Toolkit in Pl-Grid.

Šipková, V., Hluchý, L., Dobrucký, M., Bartok, J., Nguyen, B. M., 2016. Manufacturing of weather forecasting simulations on high performance infrastructures. In ECW 2016 Environmental Computing Workshop: 12th International IEEE Conference on eScience. - Baltimore, USA: IEEE, 2016, p. 432-439. ISBN 978-1-5090-4273-9. ISSN 2325-372X.

TOWARDS 3D FACIAL RECONSTRUCTION USING DEEP NEURAL NETWORKS

Hafiz Muhammad Umair Munir and Waqar S. Qureshi
Department of Mechatronics, National University of Sciences and Technology, H-12 Islamabad

ABSTRACT

3D facial reconstruction is an emerging and interesting application in the field of computer graphics and computer vision and is been used for 3D printing, creating avatars etc. It is difficult and challenging to reconstruct the 3D model of face from a single photo because of arbitrary poses, non-uniform illumination, expressions and occlusions. None of algorithm provides detailed 3D facial model because every algorithm has some limitations related to profile view, fine detail, accuracy and speed. The major problem is to develop 3D face with texture of large poses, wild faces and occluded faces. Mostly algorithm is used convolution neural network (CNN) and deep learning frameworks to create facial model and 3D dense face alignment (3DDFA) is the first algorithm that constructed the database consisting of 2D images and 3D facial model. In this paper we review 3D face reconstruction algorithm for application such as 3D printing, creating avatars and facial recognition. Different issues, problems and their proposed solutions are discussed in this paper while advantages and disadvantages are highlighted. A comparison of different algorithms is described in the context of texture and poses to find the best solution regarding reconstruction of 3D facial model from single photo.

KEYWORDS

3D Facial Model, Computer Vision, Convolution Neural Network, Deep Learning Frameworks

1. INTRODUCTION

Mostly algorithms for 3D facial shape is used only for small poses, medium poses, and uniform illumination but challenge comes when there is profile view and occluded view. Current algorithms and system are using multiple images as an input and getting more fine details as compared to using single image as an input. The computational cost of multi-view algorithm is always high. Constructing the 3D facial model from a single photo is still a problem and researchers are going to solve that problem. Existing algorithms of facial reconstruction are designed that are based on variety of models such as landmark-based face model and 3D Morphable Models (3DMM). This paper focuses on 3D facial reconstruction from single image using deep neural network architecture. Single photo face reconstruction is rarely employed by modern face recognition systems. 3DMM is the most popular method for reconstructing the full 3D facial model from a single photo. CNN has applications in the field of image classification, object detection and extract meaningful information from photos.

The earliest approaches is utilized the reference 3D faces (Hassner, Basri, 2006) (Hassner, Basri, 2013) to adjust the shape estimated for an input face image. These old methods are emphasized on robustness rather than fine details. Later methods are designed to construct the 3D face model by detection of facial landmarks (Jourabloo, Liu, 2016) (Zhu, 2016) and these algorithms give importance to accuracy regarding detection of landmarks. The 3DMM fitting methods are widely used which is originally proposed by Blanz and Vetter (Blanz, Vetter, 1999). Shape from shading techniques (Kemelmacher-Shlizerman, Basri, 2011) (Li, 2014) showed accurate and detailed 3D face reconstruction. Now a day deep neural networks (Jackson, 2017) (Tran, 2017) (Tran, 2018) are used for the estimation of 3D face shape with an unconstrained images. These deep 3D face estimation methods are still challenging and focus on speed, accuracy and low computational cost. Nikolai et al. (Nikolai, 2018) proposed mobile based 3D facial reconstruction which is fast. Coarse-to-fine method is used to reconstruct a high-quality 3D facial model from a single photo (Jiang, 2018) but whole face is reconstructed during reconstruction. Self-supervised bootstrap method (Xing, 2018) and model free approach (Feng, 2018) is new technique for 3D face reconstruction. The four algorithms with their features, pros and cons will be explained later.

There are four main challenges that are occurring now a day in 3D face reconstruction methods. Firstly, commonly landmark-based face model is used but this method is not suitable for profile views because appearance of face dramatically changes from frontal view to profile view. Secondly, in large poses landmark labeling is extremely challenging task that invisible landmarks have to be guessed. Thirdly, 3D estimates of wild facial faces are unstable and change for different photos while the last one is need of robustness and detailed 3D facial reconstruction. Different algorithms are described later which are used to reconstruct the 3D facial model from single photo using deep CNN and 3DMM and their comparison too. Pros and cons are explained briefly and then explained the selected different features for analyzing these algorithms. Finally, experimental setup and results of methods are described.

The four different algorithms that have been deployed for solving the above four challenges are as follows:

1. 3D dense face alignment (3DDFA).
2. Regressing robust and discriminative (RRD).
3. Volumetric regression network (VRN).
4. 3D detailed reconstruction (3DDR).

2. METHODS

This section describes the different methods which are designed for 3D facial reconstruction from an input single photo.

2.1 3D Dense Face Alignment (3DDFA) and Regressing Robust and Discriminative (RRD)

3DDFA (Zhu, 2016) is used to fit the face model to the image via convolution neural network with project normalized coordinate code (PNCC). This algorithm is solved the first challenge that is listed above. An evaluation is conducted on 300W, AFLW and construction of AFLW200-3D database. This algorithm estimates the 3D facial reconstruction and facial alignment across large poses by using convolution neural network and landmarks. The input is the 100 × 100 × 3 color image stacked by PNCC and the architecture consists of four convolution layers. Framework of face profiling is used to creating the large poses from medium poses to solve the second challenge.

When applied the single view 3D face reconstruction on wild facial faces, their 3D estimates are either unstable and change for different facial poses. So, Tran et al. (Tran, 2017) proposed to solve the problem described in third challenge. This algorithm has tested on LFW, YTF and IJB-A while best for face recognition in case of wild faces. This algorithm estimates the 3D facial shape and texture directly from an unconstrained 2D face image. For a given input image, it produces a standard .ply file of the face shape and texture. ResNet-101or Caffe deep network is used for regressing 3DMM shape and texture parameters under Linux.

2.2 Volumetric Regression Network (VRN) and 3D Detailed Reconstruction (3DDR)

Jackson et al. proposed method (Jackson, 2017) approaches the problem of reconstruction regarding segmentation. This algorithm specially estimates large pose 3D facial reconstruction using simple CNN architecture bypassing the training and testing of 3DMM. This method also performs direct regression of a volumetric representation of the 3D facial geometry from single input photo. The images are unconstrained and downloaded from websites that including arbitrary facial poses, expression and occlusion. Evaluation of this method is conducted on three different databases, namely AFLW2000-3D, BU-4DFE, and Florence. This method is developed under Linux and Torch 7 deep neural network framework is used. This architecture does not need accurate alignment but performs direct regression of a volumetric representation.

Tran et al. proposed method (Tran, 2018) has ability to reconstruct the 3D facial model in detail under extreme conditions such as wearing glasses, hide by hairs etc. The algorithm is motivated by old age computer graphic concept named bump mapping (Blinn, 1978) that is used to separate the global shape from local details (wrinkles etc.). It naturally creates plausible details and better capability to produce the 3D facial with good texture model for out of plane rotations and occluded facial regions. The references set of this algorithm consists of 12K unoccluded face images that are selected from the VGG and CASIA sets. The recent method of Sela et al. (Sela, 2017) close to this method that produces good detailed results when face become unoccluded but fails completely on occluded faces because of weak regularization. This algorithm estimate a coarse 3D face shape which acts as a foundation and then separately layer this foundation with details represented by a bump map. This method is developed under Linux and Pytorch deep neural network framework is utilized.

3. DISCUSSION

All the algorithms are state of the art on reconstruction of 3D face model by using deep neural network that are described above. We used Intel Core i7-7700K and NVIDIA GeForce GTX 1050 for the analysis of and generation of 3D facial model of different algorithms. 3DDFA method is the first algorithm which is used to reconstruct the 3D face model from single image using cascaded CNN. This algorithm has solved the problem of invisible landmarks in large poses and face alignment across large poses as well. The areas around mouth and nose are more sensitive while texture of 3D face shape is not so good. This method takes more than a minute to build one 3D solid facial model with pose and slightly texture to small extent.

The second algorithm is accurate, fast and robust that is used for estimating the parameters of 3DMM face shape from an input image using a deep CNN architecture. The areas around nose and mouth have very low errors and texture of 3D facial model is better than 3DDFA algorithm. This method is robust to recognize faces in the wild setting. This method takes less than 1 minute to build a 3D facial model with texture and slightly pose to some extent. It is failed in some cases when reconstructing the facial model such as beard hairs or facial hairs. This method is faster to predict the 3DMM parameters than 3DDFA.

The third approach works with unconstrained facial images of different poses, occlusions and facial expressions downloaded from the websites and reconstruct 3D face shape from single image. This CNN architecture for 3D segmentation is based on hourglass network (Newell, 2016). The volumetric architecture consists of two hourglasses modules.

Table 1. Comparison of Algorithms

Algorithms	3DDFA	VRN	RRD	3DDR
3D Morphable Model (3DMM)	Yes	Yes	Yes	Yes
Convolution neural Network (CNN) Architecture	Yes	Yes	Yes	Yes
Deep Neural Framework	No	Torch 7	Caffe	Pytorch
Operating System	Windows	Linux	Linux	Linux
Graphic Processing Unit (GPU)	No	Yes	Yes	Yes
Robustness	Low	Medium	Fast	Fast
Complexity	Low	Medium	Medium	High
Runtime	75.7ms	69ms	88ms	50s

The last method is complex than others but more efficient and robustness for 3D facial reconstruction from single photo by using deep neural frameworks with wild setting while using bump mapping concept and mid-level details. You can see the wrinkles and expression in every facial model as in the facial image while result seems good. It takes 50s per image producing 3D facial model and producing beautiful texture as compared to other methods. This algorithm is better for 3D printing faces, visual speech recognition and facial recognition, facial augmented reality and virtual reality. The comparison of different algorithms is shown in Table 1.

4. CONCLUSION

The state of art methods regarding detailed 3D facial reconstruction from single image using deep neural network are explained. The recent approaches play an important in the field of computer vision community, graphics and deep learning field. Some algorithms produce better result across large poses, some better for robustness regarding texture parameter, some for occlusions and utmost conditions. Benefits and proposed solution of different problems is described. The performance of all the deep networks is used for different purposes such as facial expressions, occluded images and wild photos are discussed. Future work may include reviewing the 3D hair reconstruction from a single photo and developing a method and application as well for the reconstruction of 3D facial shape with hairs from single image by using deep neural networks.

REFERENCES

Blanz, V. and Vetter, T., 1999. Morphable model for the synthesis of 3D faces. *In Proc. ACM SIGGRAPH Conf. Comput. Graphics,* 1999.

Blinn, F. J., 1978. Simulation of wrinkled faces. *Proc. ACM SIGGRAPH Conf. Comput. Graphics,* 12(3):286-292, 1978.

Chinaev, N. et al, 2018. MobileFace: 3D face reconstruction with efficient CNN regression. *arXiv preprint arXiv:1809.08809,* 2013.

Feng, M. et al, 2018. 3D face reconstruction from light field images: A model free approach. *In European Conf. Comput. Vision*, 2018.

Hassner, T. and Basri, R., 2006. Example based 3D reconstruction from single images. *In Proc. Conf. Comput. Vision Pattern Recognition (CVPR) Workshops, IEEE,* 2006.

Hassner, T. and Basri, R., 2013. Single view depth estimation from examples. *arXiv preprint arXiv:1304.3915,* 2013.

Jackson, A. S. et al, 2017. Large pose 3D face reconstruction from a single image via direct volumetric CNN Regression. *Proc. Int. Conf. Comput. Vision*, 2017.

Jiang, L. et al, 2018. 3D face reconstruction with geometry details from a single image. *arXiv preprint arXiv:1702,05619,* 2018.

Jourabloo, A. and Liu, X., 2016. Large-pose face alignment via cnn based dense 3D model fitting. *In Proc. Conf. Comput. Vision Pattern Recognition (CVPR),* 2016.

Kemelmacher-Shlizerman, I. and Basri, R., 2011. 3D face reconstruction from a single image using a single reference face shape. *Trans. Pattern Anal. Mach. Intell.,* 33(2):394-405, 2011.

Li, C. et al, 2014. Intrinsic face image image decomposition with human face priors. *In European Conf. Comput. Vision,* pages 218-233. Springer, 2014.

Newell, A. et al, 2016. Stacked hourglass networks for human pose estimation. *In European Conf. Comput. Vision*, 2016.

Sela, M. et al, 2017. Unrestricted facial geometry reconstruction using image-to-image translation. *In Proc. Int. Conf. Comput. Vision*, 2017.

Tran, T. T. et al, 2017. Regressing robust and discriminative 3D morphable models with a very deep neural network. *In Proc. Conf. Comput. Vision Pattern Recognition (CVPR),* 2017.

Tran, T. T. et al, 2018. Extreme 3d face reconstruction: Seeing through occlusion. *In Proc. Conf. Comput. Vision Pattern Recognition (CVPR),* 2018.

Xing, Y. et al, 2018. A self-supervised bootstrap method for single-image 3D face reconstruction. *arXiv preprint arXiv:1812.05806,* 2018.

Zhu, X. et al, 2016. Face alignment across large poses: A 3D solution. *In Proc. Conf. Comput. Vision Pattern Recognition (CVPR),* 2016.

AUTOMATIC HUMAN HEART SEARCH ON CT-SCANS

Mariya Dubrovskaya
Lobachevsky State University of Nizhni Novgorod
Russian Federation, 23 Prospekt Gagarina (Gagarin Avenue)

ABSTRACT

Here is proposed a solution for actual problem of heart allocation on tomography data. One of the most popular tomography types used for various heart investigations is CT, thus the technology proposed here is initially developed for CT data. The main part of the algorithm consists of four stages: preliminary source volume limitation, forming hypotheses of lungs location, determination of approximate surrounding heart cube and searching for a point within the cube which is for sure inside the heart. The algorithm also includes a preliminary stage: coordinate system allocation. This stage is essential when position of a scanned patient is unknown relative to a tomograph. During the stage we find, where are left and right, top and bottom, front and back sides of human body. The stage consists also of four parts itself: definition of Ox and Oy axes and determination of Oy, Oz and Ox directions, by analyzing anatomy of a patient, with regard to standard human anatomy. The method is fast and doesn`t require any human guidance and preliminary adjustment. The whole method is convenient as automatic preprocessing for unlimited scope of problems, e.g. segmentation, surface or solid model reconstruction, etc. The proposed method provides flexible way for further local heart positioning refinement and works even for static, not timed, tomography data.

KEYWORDS

Localization, Surrounding Cube, Hypothesis, Preprocessing, Approximation, Cardiac

1. INTRODUCTION

Almost every task of heart processing on tomography data starts with attempts to understand where the heart locates. Investigation problems, such as segmentation, surface reconstruction, etc. often allow to guide heart position for an algorithm manually. On the contrary, in real clinical applications it becomes more and more inconvenient and hard to make these actions every time. Therefore, it is useful to have a tool, able to find a target organ, heart, without user guidance.

Currency of the examined problem remains due to insufficient experience in automatic heart search. Investigated methods are mostly limited to requirement of time scale in data. There are attempts to use entropy of the intensity changes (Atehortua, 2016a) and center-surround principle (Atehortua, 2016b). Absolute difference between the first and the following frames (Fadil, 2017) is also computed. Furthermore, mean image and absolute error (Ma, 2016) were calculated. These inventors tried heart search on MR data, so that the methods require timed tomography, because they detect regions changing in time. Similar methodologies were invented by the following researchers. Background estimation and Laplacian pyramid (Hoffmann, 2016) were used, linear combination of time functions was researched with 3D labeling in order to ensure spatial continuity (Constantinides, 2010), simple technique of subtracting (Farag, 2012) was applied, differences between images (Sorgel, 1997) were computed together with automatically determined intensity threshold, standard deviation was used (Hadhoud, 2011) and optical flow (Saleh, 2016) was tried. These methods are based on MR data and the assumption that heart is the strongest moving structure in the CMR (Cardiovascular magnetic resonance imaging) data, hence they impose a requirement of time dimension presence. Big amount of methods for MR imaging and of their usages demonstrate their easiness and the fact that such methods are classical for MR. There is also a work with 3D data field (Lei, 2016), however time-domain characteristics of 3D data for heart ROI extraction are used there as well. Another research (Huang, 2007) is also based on spatio-temporal data and on motion and is tested on 4D MRI and tagged MRI images of heart. Heart region localization on chest X-rays (Candemir, 2016) was introduced. The author tried intensity histogram analysis in accordance with anatomy knowledge. The method uses existing chest X-rays and their manually marked heart boundaries as models, and estimates the heart boundary of a patient X-ray by registering the model X-rays to the patient X-ray. A heart localization method based on Computed Tomography Angiography (CTA) images and Generalized Hough Transformation (Saalbach, 2011) was proposed. The method implies templates and learning usage and sufficiently time-consuming execution. Automatic heart localization, based on machine learning (Zheng, 2008), was provided. A recursive ray casting mechanism for cardiac CTA scans (Kim, 2009) and thoracic CT data (Lorenz, 2005) was also used. The method is based on intensities analysis and anatomy knowledge. Unfortunately, recursion implies memory dependence. Motion fields in CT images (Tavakoli, 2013) were tried.

The method, proposed here, doesn`t depend on time scale. The input of the method is CT data without any preprocessing, and the result is a point, that for sure belongs to heart (is positioned inside this organ).

2. METHODOLOGY

The whole method consists of the four main sequential stages (2.2 – 2.5) and an auxiliary stage 2.1, explained in detail below. Here is presented the chronological order of all stages` start (Figure 1).

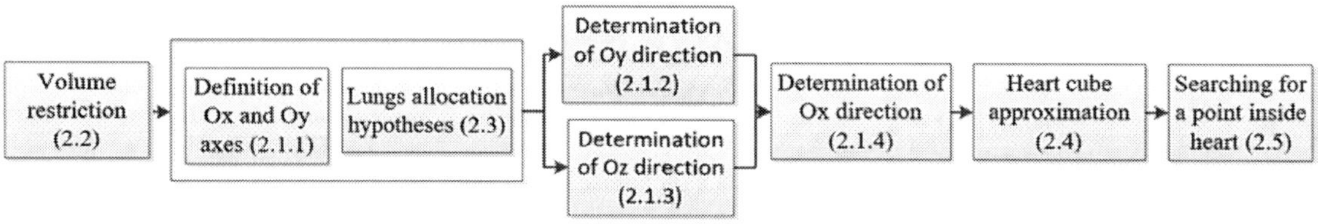

Figure 1. Methodology Sequence Diagram

2.1 Axes Allocation

The main heart search mechanism is preceded by establishment of accordance between orthogonal axes and the body sides. This step is essential for fully automatic algorithmic search and is automatic itself. Requirement of the stage is explained by the fact that we must navigate within CT-scans volume in order to find a desired object. In theory, a tomograph can scan a patient starting with any of eight angles of the scanned volume. Additionally, the patient can be disposed differently concerning the tomograph, that`s why at first it is required to understand, where each side of the body locates. After that, it is possible to process further anatomical peculiarities of a human body for the search. The single assumption of algorithm declares that body lies along Oz axis. I define direction of Oz, location of Ox and Oy axes and their directions.

2.1.1 Definition of Ox and Oy Axes

First of all, we need to define the rest of axes directions within Oxy plane. In fact, the stage 2.2 of the main search mechanism is applied before this step. Then executions of this (2.1.1) and 2.3 sections are combined. According to 2.1.1, the stage 2.3 is implemented twice, concerning two possible allocations of Ox and Oy axes within a slice. In order not to destruct primary logic, descriptions of stage 2.3, as well as of 2.2, are retained in appropriate sections below, therefore it`s suggested to get acquainted with 2.2 and 2.3 first, and then continue reading from here. So, here I try to construct hypotheses of lungs along both axes within a slice. Distance inside a lung is relatively long along the direction between breast and spine in comparison with another orthogonal direction within Oxy. The axis, along which there are more hypotheses, is named as Oy. The latter means, that we dispose Oy axis along direction between breast and spine.

2.1.2 Determination of Oy Direction

Now, when all three axes are located, we need to define their directions. Let the direction of Oy be pointed from spine towards breast. Therefore, we need to distinguish both appropriate sides of the body (which contain accordingly spine and breast). In order to find this direction, the spine location is detected. Here results of 2.3 together with 2.1.1 are used as well. The middle Oy coordinate of lungs hypotheses is used in order to subdivide an experimental slice of the chest onto two halfs, as only one such half can contain spine anatomically. Such a slice must contain chest, so that any of slices with successful lungs hypotheses can be chosen for this objective, e.g. the middle of them. Within each half of the slice, limited to the body cube, I move a little square frame of size comparative to spine`s 2D trace in Oxy. This shape of frame was chosen because spine trace in Oxy is similar to such symmetric shape as a square, for instance. For each half of slice I look for the frame with the biggest number of bone densities. Then I compare the maximum frames` counters of both halfs. The half with the biggest of maximums is declared as the side which contains spine.

2.1.3 Determination of Oz Direction

In this step the results of 2.3 together with 2.1.1 are also used. Let Oz be directed from legs towards head. Therefore, we need to understand, where legs and head are. I assume that both lungs` size in body in the direction between arms widens from lungs` highest part (nearest to head) towards the lowest (nearest to legs). Thus, I compare distances along Ox axis (between arms) in the hypotheses of the highest and lowest slices with successful lungs hypotheses. The one of them with the biggest distance is determined as nearest to legs.

2.1.4 Determination of Ox Direction

Now, when we know all three orthogonal axes` locations and directions of two of them, we can calculate direction of the latter. If you look attentively at the human body coordinate system, where Oz is directed along the body from legs towards head and Oy is directed from spine towards breast, you can see, that the vector from axes` center towards the left arm is located unambiguously with regard to two other axes, because they form a left-hand triple. I just let the direction towards the left arm be a positive direction of Ox (which means, that Ox is directed from the right arm towards the left). Using mixed product we easily determine the side of the left body half in CT volume.

2.2 Volume Restriction

This step is executed before 2.1.1 (read 2.1.1 for details). The main algorithm begins with source volume limitation for more efficient search. It doesn`t make sense to process the volume that is known not to contain the desired object. Thus, surrounding volume including only air-like substances, are excluded from consideration. It is the first stage of the main algorithm. In order to reach such result the algorithm runs along each of three axes from both endings and stops when it meets any density of either muscle or bone. Hounsfield unit (HU) nature allows such references to different tissues and densities of many objects, because the ranges of various substances are computed and known. All the six spaces between each CT volume`s border and an appropriate coordinate of stop are excluded. Hence, the volume for further processing includes whole scanned human body, so that the space that doesn`t include it for sure is ignored.

2.3 Lungs Allocation Hypotheses

This step is executed along with 2.1.1 (read 2.1.1 for details). Hypotheses of lungs allocation are formed at each slice of reduced volume. Algorithm casts parallel rays through data volume within Oxy and detects sufficiently long continuous distances of lungs densities, which lie between shorter, but thick enough, distances of body tissues densities. Note, that both lungs must present at CT-scans. Each hypothesis is represented as a couple of points that denote the start and the end of approximate lung position. Examples of hypotheses are demonstrated in the figure (Figure 2, a). When all hypotheses are found, their connectedness is checked up. There shouldn`t be long intervals between hypotheses along Oz. Only that largest subset of hypotheses is chosen as successful, where all of them locate close to one another along Oz.

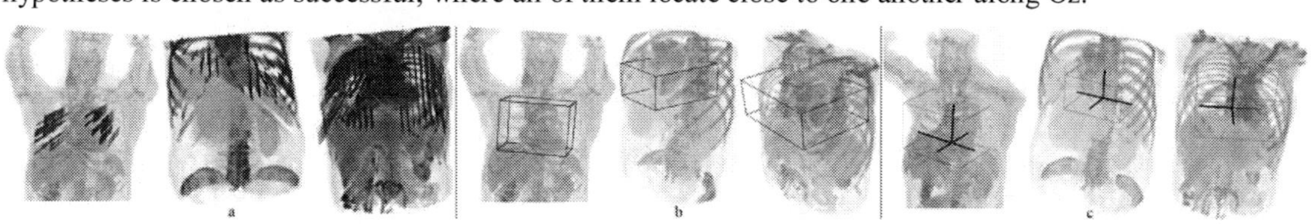

Figure 2. a) Hypotheses of hearts` allocations; b) Surrounding hearts` cubes; c) Determined points inside hearts

2.4 Heart Cube Approximation

From slices, which contain hypotheses, those are chosen, where there are two hypotheses or more. Then only those are retained, that contain at least one couple of neighbor hypotheses, divided by long enough distance. The first such pair is chosen for each slice. Then extreme coordinates are chosen from successful hypotheses collected from all slices, along both horizontal orthographic axes: the least and the biggest along each axis. Extreme coordinates along vertical axis are defined below. All the limits are used for surrounding heart cube (to be precise, parallelepiped) to be built, where six coordinates are required, two for each axis. These coordinates are very approximate limits, containing heart inside. However, it is necessary to consider several anatomical peculiarities. Firstly, it is necessary to correct the surrounding box along direction between arms. We have to expand the left extreme border proportionally towards the left in order to include Apex for sure (all such proportions are described in section 2.6, identification between body sides and axes is described in 2.1). Note, that patient`s body mustn`t locate at CT-scans at significant angles with orthogonal axes (usually, it doesn`t). Secondly, both extreme coordinates along another horizontal direction (between spine and breast bone) should be proportionally enlarged towards breast, because heart is shifted towards breast bone with regard to lungs and spine. Thirdly, the middle coordinate along vertical axis is chosen from successful hypotheses, and then similar indents are added in both directions from this center. Sample surrounding hearts` cubes are shown in the figure (Figure 2, b) for several CT-scans.

2.5 Searching for a Point inside Heart

The algorithm searches for sufficiently long continuous distances, comparable to heart size (about it`s half or less; this proportion is also described in section 2.6), of such tissues as muscles, blood and blood contrast along all three orthogonal axes within found heart cube. Thus, as a result, here is detected some point, which for sure lies inside heart. After this step more precise and full characteristics of heart can be determined, for any purpose. By moving out of the point, it is possible to approximate position of the whole heart, build heart surface or solid heart model, etc. Such points inside hearts are denoted as intersections of three lines inside hearts` cubes in the figure (Figure 2, c) for some CT-scans.

2.6 Experiments

All parameters, used in the algorithm, are considered to satisfy every concrete patient body`s proportions. Formally, each of the parameters can be tuned in case of misses in proportions, however in this work I examine only the solution, that doesn`t include user`s manual postprocessing. General necessary body proportions were considered as mutual relations taken from several CT-scans. The relations turned out to be similar, but they still were averaged. All proportions have a single and simple base: surrounding body box. I took the following proportions: *threshold for necessary (minimal) lungs` length (lungs_len_thres)* is: body cube dimension in the direction between arms (dim_arms) divided by 5; *threshold for necessary heart size* (among distances between rays) is: lungs_len_thres divided by 2; *heart cube limit in the direction between head and legs, nearest to legs* is: middle lungs` coordinate extended in the direction from head to legs by "lungs_len_thres divided by 4"; *heart cube limit in the direction between head and legs, nearest to head* is: middle lungs` coordinate extended in the direction from legs to head by "lungs_len_thres divided by 4"; *both heart cube limits in the direction between breast and spine* are: shift in the direction from spine towards breast by "(dim_arms divided by 25) and multiplied by 2"; *heart cube limit in the direction between arms, nearest to the right* is: the coordinate from hypotheses, nearest to the right arm (without additional adjustment); *heart cube limit in the direction between arms, nearest to the left* is: the coordinate from hypotheses, nearest to the left arm, extended in the direction from the right to the left by "dim_arms divided by 25"; *the frame side for skeleton* search is: dim_arms divided by 10. The parameters were taken for processing of these and all other CT-scans. Given parameters don`t require repeated adjustment, as they are based on standard anatomy, so they can be taken from here as ready constants. All iterations along rays should have sizes, that intersect all considerable tissues` passages. Intensities` thresholds for tissues and substances must conform with HU standards.

3. CONCLUSION

The search method, presented here, results in a point, which belongs to heart or any of tissues inside heart. Additionally, approximate bounding box is built around heart, which is a bit wider than the heart itself. Outputs of all algorithm`s stages mostly agree with visual intuitive analogues, which could be implemented manually. The method is convenient as preliminary stage for any heart processing, such as surface or solid model reconstruction, etc. Instead of manual specification of heart location on CT-scans for each person and for each task, it is possible to set real heart position quickly using proposed method of automatic heart search.

The method is simple, fast (about a few seconds for a single full-body CT-scans on Intel®Core™i7-7700HQ 2.80 GHz processor), fully automatic and doesn`t require human guidance, preliminary adjustment and time scale. This method is convenient as automatic preprocessing for unlimited scope of problems regarding human heart. Proposed method provides flexible way for further local heart positioning refinement.

REFERENCES

Atehortua, A. et al, 2016. Automatic segmentation of 4D cardiac MR images for extraction of ventricular chambers using a spatio-temporal approach. *Medical Imaging 2016: Image Processing*, vol. 9784.

Atehortua, A. et al, 2016. Automatic segmentation of right ventricle in cardiac cine MR images using a saliency analysis. *Med Phys*, 43(12):6270.

Candemir, S. et al, 2016. Automatic heart localization and radiographic index computation in chest x-rays. *Medical Imaging 2016: Computer-Aided Diagnosis*, vol. 9785.

Constantinides, C. et al, 2010. Automated heart localization for the segmentation of the ventricular cavities on cine magnetic resonance images. *2010 Computing in Cardiology*, 37. 911 - 914.

Fadil, H. et al, 2017. 4D Automatic Centre Detection of the Right and Left Ventricles from Cine Short-Axis MRI. *Statistical Atlases and Computational Models of the Heart. Imaging and Modelling Challenges. STACOM 2016. Lecture Notes in Computer Science*, vol. 10124.

Farag, A. and Fakhreldin, M., 2012. Heart Localization from Magnetic Resonance Images Sequence. *Journal of Computer Science*, 8(4), 499–505.

Hadhoud, M. M. A. et al, 2011. Automatic global localization of the heart from Cine MRI images. *2011 IEEE International Symposium on IT in Medicine and Education*, vol.2, 35-38.

Hoffmann, R. et al, 2016. Automated Heart Localization in Cardiac Cine MR Data. *Bildverarbeitung für die Medizin 2016*, pp. 116-121.

Huang, J. et al, 2007. Dynamic texture based heart localization and segmentation in 4-D cardiac images. *2007 4th IEEE International Symposium on Biomedical Imaging: From Nano to Macro*, 852-855.

Kim, J. et al, 2009. Automated 3D heart segmentation by search rays for building individual conductor models. *Medical Imaging 2009: Visualization, Image-Guided Procedures, and Modeling*, 72611W.

Lei, R. et al, 2016. A Novel Approach For 3D Surface Reconstruction Of LV Endocardium Based On SPCNN. *2016 4th International Conference on Electrical & Electronics Engineering and Computer Science (ICEEECS 2016)*, vol. 50.

Lorenz, C. and von Berg, J., 2005. Fast automated object detection by recursive casting of search rays. *International Congress Series*, 1281, 230–235.

Ma, Y. et al, 2016. An SPCNN-GVF-based approach for the automatic segmentation of left ventricle in cardiac cine MR images. *International Journal of Computer Assisted Radiology and Surgery*, 11(11), 1951–1964.

Saalbach, A. et al, 2011. Optimizing GHT-Based Heart Localization in an Automatic Segmentation Chain. *Medical Image Computing and Computer-Assisted Intervention – MICCAI 2011*, 463–470.

Saleh, R. H. et al, 2016. An innovate automatic heart localization method in cardiac Cine MRI using optical flow. *2016 8th Cairo International Biomedical Engineering Conference (CIBEC)*, 106-109.

Sorgel, W. and Vaerman. V., 1997. Automatic heart localization from a 4D MRI data set. *Proc. SPIE 3034, Medical Imaging 1997: Image Processing*, vol. 3034, p. 333-344.

Tavakoli, V. and Sahba, N., 2013. Cardiac motion and strain detection using 4D CT images: comparison with tagged MRI, and echocardiography. *The International Journal of Cardiovascular Imaging*, 30(1), 175–184.

Zheng, Y. et al, 2008. Four-Chamber Heart Modeling and Automatic Segmentation for 3-D Cardiac CT Volumes Using Marginal Space Learning and Steerable Features. *IEEE Transactions on Medical Imaging*, vol. 27, no. 11, pp. 1668-1681, doi: 10.1109/TMI.2008.2004421.

Posters

FUNDAMENTAL STUDY ON NONINVASIVE BCI COMMUNICATION USING CHECKERBOARD PATTERN REVERSAL STIMULUS

Ingon Chanpornpakdi[1], Junya Enjoji[1], Tatsuhiro Kimura[2], Hiroshi Ohshima[1] and Kiyoyuki Yamazaki[1]
[1]*Department of Biomedical Engineering, Tokai University,*
143 Shimokasuya, Isehara-shi, Kanagawa 259-1193, Japan
[2]*Department of* Medical Care and Welfare Engineering, *Tokai University,*
9-1-1 Toroku, Higashi-ku, Kumamoto-shi, Kumamoto 862-8652, Japan

ABSTRACT

The objective of this research is to develop a new noninvasive method of a non-verbal communication system for the patients those who are struggling with a total locked-in syndrome, such as Amyotrophic Lateral Sclerosis (ALS) patient in the final stage and etc., using Brain-Computer Interface (BCI). In this research, the experiment was divided into two parts, 8x8 and 32x32 matrix checkerboard pattern stimuli reversed at frequencies of 3 and 6Hz. The most remarkable result from this data was that the significant differences between not attending to the stimulus and attending to each stimulus were observed with the p-value below 0.005 in the case of 8x8 matrix checkerboard pattern stimulus. Based on the results, the feasibility of using the checkerboard pattern as a stimulus in BCI, when it is used as a visual stimulus for BCI, was also discussed in this paper.

KEYWORDS

Electroencephalogram (EEG), Brain-Computer Interface (BCI), Total Locked-in Syndrome, Neurotechnology, Welfare Technology

1. INTRODUCTION

There are numbers of communication options for ALS patients such as electric eyes gaze devices, which still can be used in locked-in syndrome stage. However, when it comes to total locked-in syndrome, ALS patients lose their eye mobility too. In that case, there is still no communication way for ALS patients to communicate with the people, although they still can think and have intact consciousness of what is going on around them.

In order to help these patients to be able to communicate once again by developing a new non-verbal communication system using BCI is the aim of this study. There are many researchers devoted to investigate on the similar objective. Most works, for example Sato and Washizawa (2016), only employed with the analysis of N100 and P300 of the evoked potentials, in which signal averaging is commonly used as an analysis method. In that respect, it requires a large capacity for data storage, and take long time to process. On top of that, the flashlight-like LED Steady State Visual Evoked Potential (SSVEP) stimulus was mainly utilized, which can cause dizziness and vertigo to the patients when it flickered at very high frequency for a long time. Thus, the checkerboard pattern reversal stimulus and the fast Fourier Transform (FFT) were introduced to solve these problems.

2. EXPERIMENTAL METHOD

Two experiments were performed on 8 healthy participants (7 male and 1 female) with the mean age of 22 years old under the same conditions, same reversal frequencies at 3 and 6Hz (figure 1), but different number of matrix of the checkerboard pattern. Obata et al. (2015) claimed that the evoked potential appeared to be larger when the more number of the matrix size of the checkerboard were used. Waytowich et al.'s (2017) also found that the checkerboard pattern with spatial frequency of 2.4 cycles per degree (32x32 matrix) yielded the maximum information transfer rate with lower subjective visual irritation as compared to the lower spatial frequencies. According to Ryan D.B., et al. (2013), the color paradigm gave higher accuracy over the black and white checkerboard when it was used in an ALS population. On those accounts, the checkerboard pattern stimuli were adapted as 8x8 matrix, used in experiment 1, and 32x32 matrix, used in experiment 2 and shown on the light green background for the better contrast in both the experiment.

To record the EEG, each volunteer was asked to sit at 60cm away from the screen monitor, placed at the eye level, in the shielded room. The EEG device utilized in this study was brain vision V-AMP (Brain Products) and the band pass filter of 0.53-30Hz with 0.3s time constant was applied during the measurement. The electrodes were placed according to 10-20 system at the position of C3, C4, P3, P4, O1 and O2 as the recording electrodes while A1 and A2 were the reference electrodes. The measured conditions were as follows; each stimulus was displayed independently and the participant concentrated on the stimulus reversed at 1) 3Hz, 2) 6Hz and both reversal stimuli were displayed side by side (figure 1) and the subject were asked to focus on 3) neither of them, 4) 3Hz and 5) 6Hz stimulus.

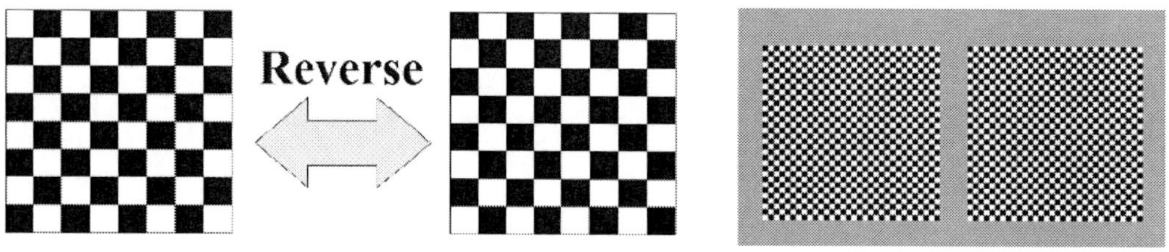

(a) (b)

Figure1. Reversal checkerboard pattern stimulus
(a) How the stimulus reversed (8x8 matrix)
(b) Checkerboard pattern stimuli displayed side by side with light green background (32x32 matrix)

Apart from those conditions, the EEG of resting opened eyes was also taken down as a reference for examining spectral changes. Each condition was recorded in the shielded room for two minutes with one minute of resting time in between. The obtained data was analyzed by offline fast Fourier transform (FFT) analysis method and the power spectral changes of each condition were calculated. Finally, the statistically significant was performed out using Wilcoxon Signed-rank Test.

3. RESULTS

The peaks generated around the frequency of attended side were investigated from the power spectral changes in each condition of each experiment. The criterion adopted to identify the peak area was between the range 2.5 to 3.5Hz for 3Hz reversal stimulus and 5.5 to 6.5Hz for 6Hz reversal stimulus. The data taken from electrode O1 and O2 conveyed the most significant among all, hence their results were selected for data analysis.

The 8x8 matrix size of checkerboard pattern was used in experiment 1 while the matrix size of the checkerboard stimulus employed in experiment 2 was 32x32 matrix. Figure 2 showed the participant's power spectral changes when the subject was asked to attend to 3 and 6Hz reversal stimulus. The graph highlighted that as the subject concentrated to the reversal stimulus, there were changes in amplitude at the frequency of the focused stimulus in both of the experiments. Nevertheless, the changes were noticed on both figure (a) and (b), the result is significant exclusively at experiment 1 that used 8x8 matrix checkerboard pattern.

The average amplitude of peaks of all the subjects in each condition of both experiments were determined and shown in figure 3. From the graph, they were clear that the average peaks of 3Hz in condition 1 and 4 were larger than that of in condition 2 and 5 and vice-versa for the condition 2 and 5. However, when compared the results of the two experiments, the amplitude of 3 and 6Hz in the experiment 1 was larger than the experiment 2. By considering both the figure 2 and 3, it can be presumed that the results of 8x8 matrix checkerboard pattern is more remarkable.

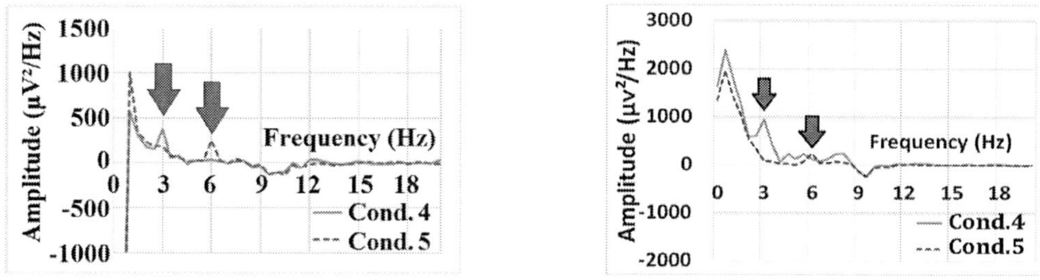

(a) (b)

Figure 2. The EEG power spectrum of a subject in condition 4 (focused on 3Hz) and 5 (focused on 6Hz)
(a) 8x8 matrix
(b) 32x32 matrix

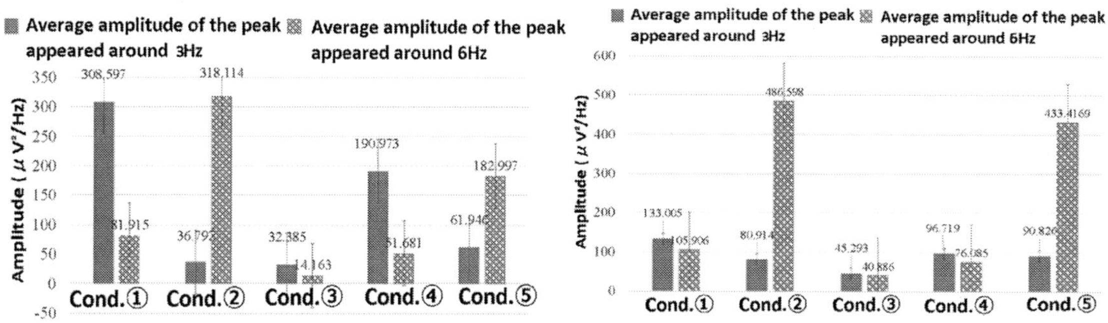

(a) (b)

Figure 3. The average amplitude of the peaks in each condition
(a) 8x8 matrix
(b) 32x32 matrix

As a consequence, Wilcoxon signed-rank test was introduced to calculate the significant differences of all the cases. The statistically significant results were listed below. The significant difference of condition 1 was determined by comparing the peaks formed around 3Hz in condition 1 and 2. Conversely, the significant difference of condition 2 was done with the same comparison but at 6Hz. In condition 4 and 5, condition 3 was taken as a controlled condition. Then, the significant differences was calculated by comparing the amplitude magnification of peaks formed at the corresponding frequency, similar to the procedure done in condition 1 and 2.

Table 1. The significant differences of condition 1 and 2 when compared the peaks formed at corresponding frequencies between two conditions

Experiment	Condition	P-value
Experiment 1	Condition 1	0.005
	Condition 2	0.005
Experiment 2	Condition 1	0.010
	Condition 2	0.005

Table 2. The significant differences of condition 4 and 5 when compared the peak amplitude magnification formed at corresponding frequencies between two conditions, having condition 3 as a controlled condition (*nonsignificant)

Experiment	Condition	P-value
Experiment 1	Condition 4	0.005
	Condition 5	0.005
Experiment 2	Condition 4	NS*
	Condition 5	0.025

From the table 1 and 2, the utility of 8x8 matrix checkerboard pattern is thus proved that it conveyed better strength of induced response on EEG over 32x32 matrix checkerboard pattern. However, there were some problems in data processing that showed the lack in time. Therefore, the future work should concentrate on the development of data analysis method such as the utility of python.

4. CONCLUSION

From the results, the peak of the EEG spectral changes obtained corresponding to the focused frequencies. In contrast to Waytowich et al.'s (2017), it was found that the 8x8 matrix checkerboard pattern produced the result, which revealed the significant differences in all conditions carried out in the experiment. This may have occurred due to the different size of the checkerboard pattern stimulus, which caused the deviation in spatial frequency, even though the matrix size was made with the same 32x32 matrix. Besides, some limitations in our research were also recognized. Since the EEG is a sensitive bio-signal, the most appropriate region to record the EEG varies in each person. Therefore, the most suitable electrode region should be identified individually. In fact, the lack in time, while the FFT and spectral changes analysis was processed, also cannot be neglected. The data analysis procedure should be further investigated in the future, in order to develop new communication system for the practical use.

However, there is a definite probability that the power spectral changes of checkerboard pattern reversal stimulus might be usable for noninvasive BCI communication in the future. This can be applied to develop the BCI communication system using binary selective method such as yes or no question. In this method, the caregiver can ask the patient a question and inform the patient that which stimulus related to which answer. By looking at the corresponding stimulus, the EEG of the patient is sent and the answer of that question could be shown on the PC monitor in front of the caregiver.

ACKNOWLEDGEMENT

A part of this research was supported by Fujikura Foundation.

REFERENCES

Obata, M., et al, 2015. Frequency Entrainment of EEG Induced by Checker-flag reversal stimuli, *Proceedings of the 28th SAS Symposium*. Kanagawa, Japan. (In Japanese)

Ryan D.B., et al, 2013. Enhancing Brain-Computer Interface Performance in an ALS Population: Checkerboard and Color Paradigms. *Proceedings of the Fifth International Brain-Computer Interface Meeting*. Article ID: 026, DOI: 10.3217/978-3-85125-260-6-26.

Sato, H. and Washizawa, Y., 2016. An N100-P300 Spelling Brain-Computer Interface with Detection of Intentional Control, *Computers 2016*. Vol. 5, pp. 31.

Waytowich, N.R., et al, 2017. Optimization of Checkerboard Spatial Frequencies for Steady-State Visual Evoked Potential Brain–Computer Interfaces, *IEEE Transactions on Neural Systems and Rehabilitation Engineering*, Vol. 25, No. 6, pp. 557-565.

ON THE WAY: DEVELOPING AN APP FOR DELIVERY MEDIATION WITHIN THE SHARING ECONOMY CONCEPT

Cláudio Souza, Eleonor Silva, Emanuel Azevedo and Sydney de Almeida Neto
University of Aveiro, Portugal

ABSTRACT

This paper reports on a human-centric development of a digital prototype of a delivery mediated mobile application within the concept of "sharing economy". The application 'On The Way' was developed by the authors in the Multimedia Communication Masters Programme in a Project Based Learning (PBL) process. The goal of the application is to promote 'hitchhiking' for deliveries with bicycles, motorcycles, cars, vans or even by public transport or by foot. The development of the project, included User Experience design and evaluation techniques, which will be explained in this paper, as well as the description of the digital prototype itself available for hands-on exploration in the InVision platform.

KEYWORDS

App, Transportation, Sharing Economy, User Experience, UX Design and Mobile

1. INTRODUCTION

Mobile transport apps have changed the way people have moved around in major cities in the world during the last decade. Two of the biggest examples are Uber, founded in 2009 in California, and BlablaCar, founded in 2006 in France. As part of its concept of carpool apps, which already have more than 20 million users worldwide, the idea of the *On The Way* application is to connect people willing to carry out orders in their vehicles, or even on public transport or on foot, with users who want to receive their purchases or other products in their homes or work by affordable means.

This APP can constitute a contribution to some business models considering it can optimize the retail logistics chain and provide a new experience for small businesses that do not have a delivery service in their business. It can also help people to make some money from product deliveries and, on the other hand, allow people to save money on ordering deliveries. The other advantage is the environmental gains, reducing the number of delivery trips.

The application is conceptualized in the peer-to-peer ecosystem, a growing business model already studied by researchers Botsman and Rogers that state in their studies, according to BOTSMAN & R., Rogers, R. (2010, apud Rodrigues, 2017, p.3), "*we are saving money, time and space, leading people to build closer relationships and to pass from passive consumers to active employees*."

In this paper we will show the features of the app, the steps of the app's development process, following the practices and concepts of human-centric design, using User Experience methods and techniques and the conclusions, which also point out the next steps to be taken.

2. THE APP AND ITS FUNCTIONALITIES

The *On The Way* app connects previously registered couriers to users willing to request deliveries. In the developed digital prototype, to be presented, the registered couriers create trips, with routes, approximate dates and times in which they will be available to deliver goods. Users enter their orders, with dates on which they would like to have parcels delivered and the route. The system makes a match between available trips and requests. The price for the delivery is defined by the delivery person in the act of creating the trip. There is a system of mutual reviews of user and deliverer to contribute to building trust in the system.

2.1 User Experience

The User Experience (UX) concept is very popular nowadyas to the development of any technology-based system, product, or service. In order to understand its strategic influence in the development of the app, we chose one of the several existing definitions of the term UX. "*All the aspects of how people use an interactive product: the way it feels in their hands, how well they understand how it works, how they feel about it while they're using it, how well it serves their purposes, and how well it fits into the entire context in which they are using it*". (Alben, L. 1996, apud Effie Law, 2008)

The application began to have its characteristics defined based on studies raised in initial research, with the aid of benchmarking analysis, and a first stage of UX testing with the low fidelity prototype, still on paper wireframes. At this stage, the tests provided information that was decisive throughout the process of conceptualizing the application's identity: the feeling of trust.

The digital prototype was developed in two phases. The first consisted of the definition of the design system. Its construction took into account the concept of the application, the logo, the icons and other graphic elements. For the user interface (UI) development, we used the program ILLUSTRATOR. In a second moment, to allow navigation in the digital prototype, the mockups were inserted into InVision quick prototyping web platform, tested, and then taken to the UX evaluation phase.

The UX tests were performed also in two phases in the months of November and December of 2018, at the University of Aveiro, Portugal. According to Nielsen (2000), "*the best results come from testing no more than five users, running as many small tests as you can afford*". So, for this alfa moment (aka first conceptual prototype) of the app, we chose an intentional sample of five people for each phase of the test, all with the same characteristics of the app's target audience.

The average duration of each test was five minutes, with one and a half minute to navigate in the app prototype and the rest of the time to give feedback. The idea was to have an informal conversation with the participants to get their impression about the app's flow and affordance. The tests were performed in different parts of the university, like class rooms and cafes, but always to keep the participant in his own interaction comfort context.

Questionnaires and semantic scales, like Hassenzahl and Hassenzahl (2016), besides Cavalcante, Rivero and Conte (2015), were used with the purpose of evaluating the experiences present in verbal and non-verbal communication. Another preselected design method was the 3E, reported by Tähti and Niemelä (2008) as a sensitive design aid in cards that illustrate the option of emotional exercise. However, because of the level of the literacy in this intentional sample, the cards were not used, but their commitments were kept on the numerical and semantic scales, from 1 to 5 (1 is the weakest and 5, the strongest).

During all the tests, we were able to assess the emotional reactions of the participants. One of the most important attributes in the application, trust, was well evaluated in the tests. On a scale of 1 to 5, with 5 as the maximum confidence level and 1 the minimum, the prototype received four scores of 4 and one 5.

Another result was related with the expectations. Before the test, the authors asked the participants what was their expectations concerning such an app. The result were that 60% pointed number 3 (neutral, in a scale from 1 to 5). After the test, we asked how was the experience using the app and the results were 80% scoring on 5 (whith 1 as the most unpleasant and 5 the most pleasant) and 20%, scoring on 4. Another result from the tests was the input related to the meaning of some buttons, that some participants found confusing, like the evaluation process of the delivery. So, we improved that, making it clearer that what was being evaluated was the delivery process not the product.

All participants in the tests signed an Informed Consent, in accordance with the recommendations of the Declaration of Helsinki.

3. CONCLUSIONS

After a second round of UX tests, with the digital prototype in the INVISION (https://projects.invisionapp.com/share/VPPP7D1F834#/screens/337794767) the app took shape and the programming phase of a Minimum Viable Product (MVP) started. The first MVP version was up and going on February, but still needs to be tested and improved in a continuous human-centric iterative development process, depending on the future financing opportunities.

The UX tests were very important for the development of the app. Mainly the last UX phase, with extremely pertinent contributions, especially in the trust attribute, with 4 or 5 scores in a scale from 1 to 5, where five is the highest grade.

The tests also pointed out other features to be developed in the application in a second stage, such as linking user profiles with social networks, to increase the trust on users and couriers. Other features, like a list of user request alerts for couriers, would also be included in the app after the first MVP deployment.

REFERENCES

Cavalcante, e.; Rivero, L.; Conte, T. Max: A Method for Evaluating the Post-use User eXperience through Cards and a Board. p. 495–500, 2015.

Effie Law, L. et al, 2008, *Towards a shared definition of user experience.* Extended Abstracts Proceedings of the 2008 Conference on Human Factors in Computing Systems, CHI 2008, Florence, Italy, April 5-10. pp: 3.

Hassenzahl, M.; Hassenzahl, M. User experience (UX): Towards an experiential perspective on product quality. n. April, 2016.

Nielsen, J. Why You Only Need to Test with 5 Users. 2000 (Retrieved in 2019). https://www.nngroup.com/articles/why-you-only-need-to-test-with-5-users/

NNGroup. (2016). Nielsen Norman Group. Retrieved December 4, 2018, from https://www.nngroup.com/articles/which-ux-research-methods

Rodrigues, Catarina, 2017. Práticas de consumo colaborativo e de economia da partilha: o caso de um grupo de boleias entre Porto e Lisboa. *Master's Degree dissertation for Universidade Católica Portuguesa.* Porto. pp: 237.

A STUDY ON ELECTRIC PROSTHETIC HAND CONTROL INTERFACE USING EEGS GENERATED BY RECALLING IMAGES FOR DISABLED PEOPLE

Tomoyuki Gunge**, Ingon Chanpornpakdi**, Junya Enjoji**,
Kiyoyuki Yamazaki*and Yosiyuki Kageyama*
** Tokai University, ** Graduate school, Tokai University*
**143 Simokasuya Isehara city, Kanagawa, 259-1193, Japan*

ABSTRACT

The purpose of this study is to develop an interface to control the electric prosthetic hand using electroencephalogram (EEG) analysis by recall memorized image. In this study, whether it is possible to distinguish among EEGs for each recalling image was investigated. Canonical discriminant analysis was used as a discrimination method. The measurement of EEGs was conducted in healthy volunteers. Two experimental conditions of three types of numerical character images and geometric images were used to create a video for image recall. As a result, both of the two experimental conditions were able to discriminate the EEG for each image. From this result, it was suggested that EEGs generated by recalling images can be used as the electric prosthetic hand commands. Discrimination by machine learning is underway to introduce the electric prosthetic hand control using EEGs generated by recalling images.

KEYWORDS

Electroencephalogram (EEG), Prosthetic Hand, Canonical Discriminant Analysis, Welfare Technology, Neurorehabilitation

1. INTRODUCTION

Electric prosthetic hands, which are on the market, mostly using electromyogram (EMG) as a control command. However, the possible movement of these prosthetic hands are only grasp or release, and multiple operations are difficult. Depending on the amputated position of the arm, the measurement of EMG becomes more difficult.

Therefore, EEG was focused instead of EMG. The EEG can be measured noninvasively and hardly affected by the physical characteristics of the user. In this study, based on the mentioned points, the EEG was adopted to control of the electric prosthetic hand. The EEG obtained from recalling memorized images was utilized for making various types of commands. The feasibility of the method using EEGs by recalling images as control commands were discussed based on the result of canonical discriminant analysis.

2. EXPERIMENTAL METHOD

The volunteers of healthy three male and one female (mean age of 22yrs) participated in the experiment. The EEG was measured in the shielded room. To record the EEG, based on 10-20 system, electrodes were placed on Fp2, F4, C4, F8, O1, O2 positions for measurement and A1, A2 as references. The videos were created for the stimulus. Figure 1 shows the loop of the video playing. The loop started with a gazing point of 2 seconds, then the stimulus to memorize was displayed for 3 seconds. The stimuli used were a set of numeric characters (1, 2, 3) and a geometric figures (circle, triangle, square), splitted into two videos respectively. All the stimulus in each set were shown randomly for six time. Finally, the gazing point was displayed again for 2 seconds, and a stimulus was recalled in the image recollection period. Thus, this loop was repeated 18 times.

The bandpass filter was set from 0.15 to 100 Hz. The EEG at the image recollection part was as shown in the "EEG of the stimulated section" in figure 2. The section was resampled from the 400ms and marked at every interval of 25ms for 15 points. The data were obtained from the electrode Fp2. The electrode O2 were also chosen and analyzed considering the ease of application for the actual use in future. For each set of numeric characters and geometric figures, 15x18 matrix data were processed by the canonical discriminant analysis software (College Analysis version 6.8).

Given a nominal classification ($Y_{1\text{-}3}$) variable and interval variables ($X_{1\text{-}15}$), Canonical discriminant analysis is derived by the following plural equations (1), (2), and (3).

$$Y_1 = a_1X_1 + a_2X_2 + \ldots + a_{15}X_{15} + a_0 \quad (1)$$
$$Y_2 = b_1X_1 + b_2X_2 + \ldots + b_{15}X_{15} + b_0 \quad (2)$$
$$Y_3 = c_1X_1 + c_2X_2 + \ldots + c_{15}X_{15} + c_0 \quad (3)$$

Each stimulus applied to nominal classification variables. In these equations, coefficients ($a_{0\text{-}15}$, $b_{0\text{-}15}$ $c_{0\text{-}15}$) were determined so as to maximize the ratio of variance between groups to variance within groups. Two canonical variables can be obtained from these three equations. They were outputted from the software and named Discrimination Score 1 and Discrimination Score 2 respectively. Multiple scatter plots were created using the discrimination score 1 on the horizontal axis and the discrimination score 2 on the vertical axis. In addition, an established 1.5σ ellipse was also created when the distribution of each group was considered bivariate normal.

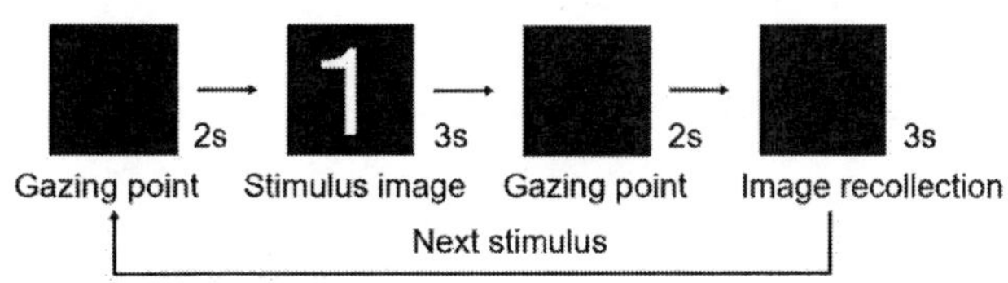

Figure 1. Schematic illustration of the video loop

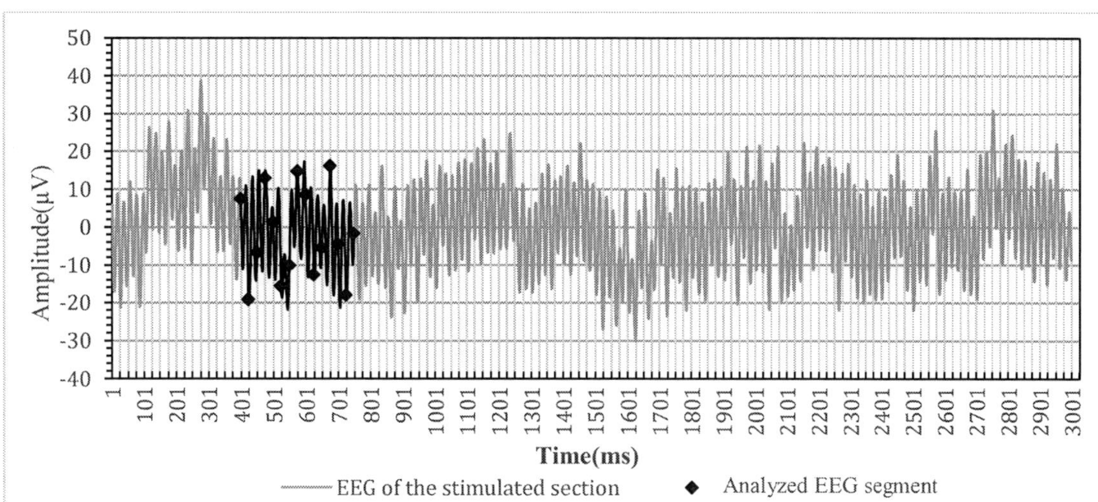

Figure 2. An Example of the EEG waveform

3. RESULTS AND DISCUSSION

Figure 3 shows an example of the determination result of the EEG in the electrode Fp2 of the recalling numeral characters. The ellipse represented each group of the EEG of the recalling images were independent. Figure 4 shows an example of the determination result of the EEG in the electrode O2 of the recalling numeral characters. Similarly, the ellipses were independent. In addition, the analysis results of the data from both electrodes, obtained by recalling the geometrical images were also presented the independence of the ellipses. The independence of the ellipses means that the EEG of each stimulus image by recalling has different characteristics. From the results, it can be considered that both the EEGs of the recalling numeral characters and the EEGs of the recalling geometric images have different characteristics and it can be used as operation commands of the electric prosthetic hand. However, with some results, the ellipse was not outputted and could not be discerned. Therefore, it is necessary to discuss about the improvement of canonical discriminant analysis, or else alternative discrimination method is needed for the investigation.

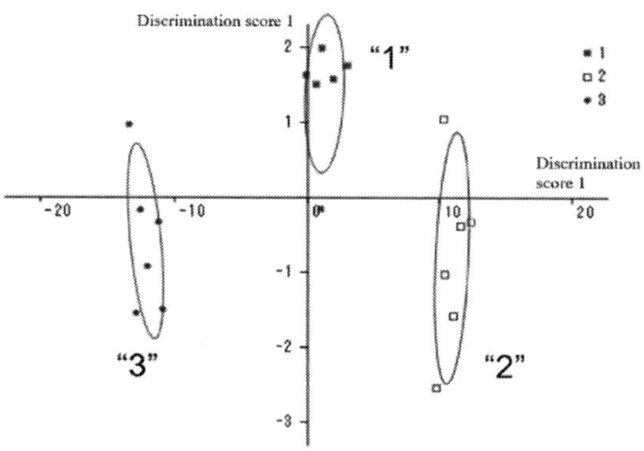

Figure 3. The EEG of the recalled numerical character condition (Fp2)

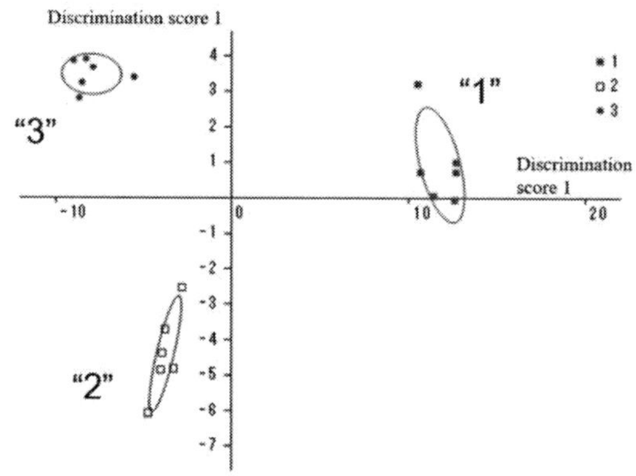

Figure 4. The EEG of the recalled numerical character condition (O2)

4. CONCLUSION

From this result, it can be suggested that each the EEG by recalling image is usable for further application in commanding of the electric prosthetic hand. However, the discrimination method needs to be optimized. In future, it is necessary to discuss a simple way of the EEG measurement that can be connected wirelessly for practical application. In addition, the discrimination method by machine learning using Python is underway.

REFERENCES

Yamanoi,T. et al, 2016. Discrimination of plying cards by EEGs during recognizing and recalling-Playing cards estimation magic without a trick-. *Japan Society for Fuzzy Theory and Intelligent Informatics*, Vol.28, No.3, pp.639-646.

Nakazawa,M. et al, 2015. Implementation and it's Evaluation of Autonomous Moving Wheel Chair System using EEG. *Information Processing Society of Japan*, Vol.2015-DPS-163, No.14.

Tomoyuki.G. et al, 2018. Canonical Discriminant Analysis of EEG Obtain by Image Stimulation for Controlling Electric Upper Limb Prosthesis. *Japan Society for Welfare Engineering,* Vol.22, pp.51-52. (In Japanese).

AN EMPIRICAL INVESTIGATION OF THE ORGANIZATIONAL IMPACTS OF A SALES SUPPORT APP

Michal Levi-Bliech, Nava Pliskin and Lior Fink
Department of Industrial Engineering and Management, Ben-Gurion University of the Negev
1 Ben-Gurion Ave., Beer-Sheva 84105, Israel

ABSTRACT

This study empirically explores and documents the organizational impact of implementing a sales support app that complements face-to-face interaction of a salesperson with a customer in the process of purchasing a new car. Two consecutive periods were investigated. Compared to the first period of conventional car buying, the study's results confirm that the sales support app in the second period added business value to the implementing organization via increased visits and car purchases.

KEYWORDS

Mobile Application, Conventional Buying Process, Showroom Visit, Innovative Buying Process, Sales Support App, App Visit

1. INTRODUCTION

App implementation within organizations is increasing since apps serve as enablers of information sharing, communication, and automation (Turban et al., 2017) which, in turn, help generate business value (Zhang et al., 2016) and facilitate innovative services and processes beyond those enabled by a computer (Singh et al., 2017). Despite their considerable potential, only a few studies have explored the business value of apps that support (rather than substitute) face-to-face interaction (Knoesen and Seymour, 2016). To meet the study's goal, the following research question is empirically explored in a case study of a large-scale car importer that implemented a new sales support app: Can implementation of a sales support app add business value via increased visits and purchases?

After the implementation of the sales support app, a customer could fill in personal details and the scan driver's license to trigger an innovative buying process. A customer can then choose a location and schedule a time for face-to-face interaction with the salesperson. Finally, if the customer decides to purchase a car, it is ordered and the sales support app can be used for signing the required documents. Toward exploring this question, data from the organizational database by the organization studied were collected and analyzed.

The results of the empirical analysis confirm that the sales support app added business value compared to conventional car purchasing via increased car purchases and visits in the innovative buying process. This study contributes to the literature on information systems (IS) by referring to the hardly-explored before implementation of apps (Heinze and Matt, 2018) that complement rather than substitute face-to-face interaction of the employee and the customer.

2. THEORETICAL BACKGROUND

This study is about an app that supports a business process where face-to-face interaction is necessary rather than apps that can substitute a human agent completely. Such apps, with a substitution role, are prevalent in banking, navigation, healthcare, ticketing, shopping, hospitality, marketing, appointment scheduling, and insurance (Chhonker et al., 2017; Turban et al., 2017).

Of the scarce research about apps that support face-to-face business processes, Taylor and Levin (2014) and Heinze and Matt (2018) identified a lack of research in this unique fields, with previous research studies shedding light neither on the supportive role of a sales support apps, nor on how these apps affect business value in contemporary organizations.

In response to this gap in previous research, the present research explores the business process of purchasing a new car via sales support app that complements face-to-face interaction between a salesperson and a customer rather than presumes complete substitution. The secondary-data analysis is used as a basis for testing the hypotheses formulated next.

In a sales process, substitution of face-to-face interaction by a mobile app is more likely for a simple retail product that does not demand significant search efforts as the case, with grocery store customers who have all the information they need about the product and a strong intention to buy (Moe, 2003). The search process is more demanding for banking, taking a mortgage, and buying houses (Yu and Chantatub, 2015), insurance policies (Heinze and Matt, 2018; Knoesen and Seymour, 2016), or cars (Moe, 2003). Customers using mobile technologies to visit a digital store have lower transportation costs than customers visiting a regular store (Turban et al., 2017). Most customers presently prefer to search online for information via mobile technologies (Chaffey, 2017; Taylor, 2015). App visits thus can help trigger the selling process by facilitating showroom visits and/or test drives. Hence, the next hypothesis is proposed.

H1: Customers make more app visits for information search than showroom visits.

A car salesperson can use the sales support app in response to app visits of a customer in two possible ways. One way is via face-to-face interaction, either in the showroom or during a test drive at the customer's location. Another way is by collaborating via the app with a customer remotely, within seconds after a customer's app visit, to provide specific details such as quotes, design information, or technical answers to customer questions. By reducing search costs, by triggering face-to-face interaction between customer and salesperson, perhaps even close to a customer's home, without decreasing her intention to buy, app visits by a customer can thus accelerate sales opportunities compared to showroom visits. It is therefore reasonable to expect an increase in the number of customers who eventually purchase a car due the feasibility, accessibility, ease of use, and ubiquity of app visits (Turban et al., 2017). Hence, the next hypothesis is proposed.

H2: Compared to showroom visits, customers make more purchases following app visits.

3. METHODOLOGY

A large-scale importer of over 30 car models provided access to data records collected during two periods. In the first period, from January 2018 until April 2018, cars were sold via showroom visits under a conventional buying process. In the second period, from April 2018 to August 2018, the importer implemented a sales support app and, for a single car model that was taken out of all showrooms, conducted a pilot of an innovative car buying process. Data records collected from the organizational databases included for each customer activity, like a visit, a purchase or a cancellation, the fields: date, week, day of the week, and current order status. Other customer demographics, as age and gender, were omitted from the activity records collected in the 3149 activity logs in 207 days. The visits recorded in the organizational databases were period-dependent. To test Hypotheses H1 and H2, Poisson regression was used with two numeric dependent variables- Visits and Purchases. App Usage was recorded as a period-dependent binary variable that assumed the value of 1 in the second period and of 0 in the first period. Week was recorded as an ordinal variable that represented the week in which visits/purchases occurred, denoting the first week as Week 1, the second week as Week 2, etc. Day of the Week was recorded as a categorical variable (Sunday = 1… Saturday =7) and used as a control variable.

4. RESULTS

Providing support for H1 and H2, App Usage was found to have a significant positive effect on Visits and Purchases. To better understand the nature of these significant results, t-tests indicate that the slop for Visits (slope_H1 =3.723, *t*=-15.625, *p*<0.001) and the slop for Purchases (slope_H2 =1.035, *t*=-11.024, *p*<0.001) were significantly different from zero. The averages for Visits are 5.166 and 168.842 and for Purchases are 3.91 and 19.947 respectively via the conventional buying process in the first period (from Week 1 to Week 12) and via the innovative buying process in the second period (from Week 13 to Week 31). Between Week 14 and Week 16 Visits increased, at the beginning of the innovative buying process, possibly as a result of aggressive advertisement. It decreased later on, but stayed higher than under the conventional buying process in the first period. Almost the same result is found for Purchases.

5. CONCLUSION

The innovative buying process investigated in this work not only shortens the search time, but also cuts down on hassle of physically visiting a showroom. This study is among the first to report that using a sales support app increased purchases by triggering an innovative mobile buying process and, thus, adding business value.

The first limitation of this study refers to external validity. The app was studied based on data provided by a single organization about one car model over a limited time period without any other external validation. The second limitation refers to causality since app use was not randomly manipulated.

The theoretical contribution of this research is to the IS literature, with regard to the influence of a mobile sales support app on purchasing decisions. This research has empirically confirmed the importance of exploring the impacts of a specific mobile app. It shows how such a technology, which complements rather than substitutes face-to-face interaction, can generate business value.

REFERENCES

Chaffey, D., 2017. Statistics on Consumer Mobile Usage and Adoption to Inform Your Mobile Marketing Strategy Mobile Site Design and App Development. URL: https://www.smartinsights.com/mobile-marketing/mobile-marketing-analytics/mobile-marketing-statistics/

Chhonker, M. S. et al., 2017. Review of Technology Adoption Frameworks in Mobile Commerce. *in Procedia computer science,* Vol. 122, pp 888-895.

Heinze, J. and Matt, C., 2018. Reducing the Service Seficit in M-Commerce: How Service-Technology Fit Can Support Digital Sales of Complex Products. *in International Journal of Electronic Commerce,* Vol. 22 No. 3, pp 386-418.

Knoesen, H. and Seymour, L. F., 2016. Designing a Process for Identifying and Managing the Benefits of Mobile Enterprise Applications in the Insurance Industry. *Proceedings of the annual conference of the south african institute of computer scientists and information technologists*. Johannesburg, South Africa, pp. 1-10.

Moe, W. W., 2003. Buying, Searching, or Browsing: Differentiating between Online Shoppers Using in-Store Navigational Clickstream. *in Journal of consumer psychology,* Vol. 13 No. 1-2, pp 29-39.

Singh, H. et al., 2017. Assessment of E-Governance Projects: An Integrated Framework and Its Validation. *Proceedings of the Special Collection on eGovernment Innovations in India*. New Delhi, India, pp. 124-133.

Taylor, D. G. and Levin, M., 2014. Predicting Mobile App Usage for Purchasing and Information-Sharing. *in International Journal of Retail & Distribution Management,* Vol. 42 No. 8, pp 759-774.

Taylor, G., 2015. More Than 90% of Consumers Use Smartphones While Shopping in Stores. URL: https://www.retailtouchpoints.com/topics/mobile/more-than-90-of-consumers-use-smartphones-while-shopping-in-stores

Turban, E. et al., 2017. *Electronic Commerce 2018: A Managerial and Social Networks Perspective*. Springer, Cham, Switzerland.

Yu, C.-S. and Chantatub, W., 2015. Consumers' Resistance to Using Mobile Banking: Evidence from Thailand and Taiwan. *in International Journal of Electronic Commerce Studies,* Vol. 7 No. 1, pp 21-38.

Zhang, C. et al., 2016. Developing a Geopackage Mobile App to Support Field Operations in Agriculture. *2016 fifth international conference on agro-geoinformatics (Agro-Geoinformatics)*. Tianjin, China, pp. 1-4

A STUDY ON CRUTCH DESIGN FOR THE WALKING ASSISTANCE OF THE HANDICAPPED IN THE LOWER EXTREMITY

Sung-Ho Yang
Dept. of Design Engineering, Inje University, 197, Inje-ro, Gimhae-si, Gyungnam, 50834, S. Korea

ABSTRACT

This study aims to draw objective results on walking with a crutch, present a realistic alternative based on the drawn results, and develop crutch design from the industrial aspect. The innovative crutch, TOGO, developed as a result of this study, has the following characteristics: (1) minimization of impact occurring due to contact between a crutch and ground through the improvement of shape and structure of the crutch tip and auxiliary pad, (2) ergonomic structure rationally responding to user's body, (3) easy and quick crutch length adjustment for portability and mobility, (4) minimization of safety risk factors during walking, (5) sufficiently attractive shape so that users can have dignity. The patent application for the new crutch produced through the study has been completed, and company search for mass production and commercialization measures are sought, following the review of potential problems that may occur in the mass production environment.

KEYWORDS

Axillary Crutches, Crutch, Crutch Design

1. INTRODUCTION

Even though many studies on crutches and walking using crutches have been carried out thus far, it is not easy to find the cases in which the study results have been applied to crutch design. Since a patent for a crutch was registered for the first time in 1917, design improvement has been insufficient, and many crutches distributed in the markets are similar, irrelevant of manufacturers (Sungho, 2016). This study is a part of long-term study to present the basics and cases of walking assistance device development helping the walking of the handicapped in the lower extremity and is the latter part of the entire study. As the study results of initial stage, the guidelines[1] that can be the guide to ensure the stability and use convenience of walking were developed (Sungho, 2015). This study, the latter part of the entire study, aims to develop the design of a crutch in line with the characteristics of walking using a crutch and that ensures study result utilization from the industrial aspect.

2. FINAL DESIGN; TOGO

This study was focused on (1) how to minimize the impact caused by contact of a crutch with ground during walking with a crutch and (2) how to secure mobility by effectively adjusting the length of a crutch when it is not used. The reason is that these two questions include most of problems that existing crutches have among the 10 developed guidelines.

---

1 Absorbing shock to minimize the vertical motion of the upper body, Minimize the shock associated with planting of the crutch tips, Maximum mobility and Maneuverability, Ergonomically designed crutch, Durable and Support the weight of the user, Lightweight, Remaining attached during reaching object, Keep user self-esteem, Minimize possibilities of safety hazards, Economically feasible and highly marketable

The finally developed crutch was named TOGO (to go) to express the lower extremity-handicapped users' smooth walking desire. The logo design emphasizing the crutch's movement as a walking assistance device reflects the characteristics of TOGO well, and the characteristics are presented below:

Crutch's basic structure using extruded Aluminum; TOGO's major components are manufactured through cutting and bending processing after extrusion molding to meet requirements, such as easy and quick crutch length adjustment for mobility and lightweight suitable for durability and long-time walking that can bear user's weight during walking. Although the components manufactured by extrusion molding have a limit to have the same cross section in any parts, they have many advantages for manufacture of a structure in which one part moves into another part to adjust length like a crutch. Figure 1 shows the final prototype and cross section to show the basic structure of TOGO manufactured with aluminum extrusion molding.

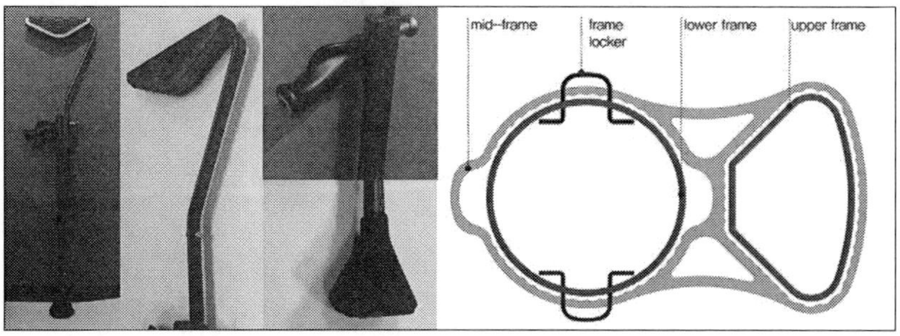

Figure 1. Final prototype and cross section to show structure

Mobility consolidation with quick and easy length adjustment; TOGO's length can be easily adjusted if the user rides a vehicle with a crutch or if the crutch is stored for long period without walking, since TOGO's portability and mobility are high. Upper frame's tightening is released by pulling the fixing lever at the back of the crutch, and if the fixing lever is released for fixing the location again, it can be easily fixed with internal spring and magnet. The total length of TOGO shows a large difference between TOGO's short-adjusted length (965mm) and long-adjusted length (1390mm) (Figure 2).

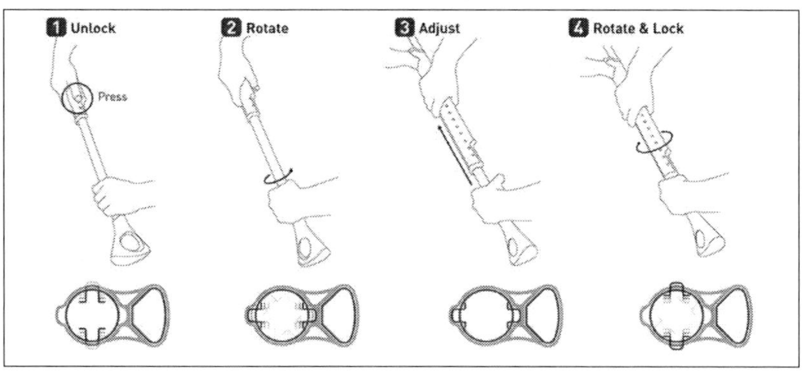

Figure 2. TOGO's easy length adjustment

Minimization of impact occurring with the contact of crutch with ground; TOGO's crutch tip is soft and flexible to minimize the impact occurring when a crutch contacts ground. The central part of the tip has a cobweb-shaped structure, and thus it is partially open, and therefore it plays a role in offsetting impact delivered from user's weight to the crutch or delivered from the ground. The fan-shape crutch tip enhances walking stability by making the contact side with ground larger and improves an ability to stably contact the crutch with the flat ground. The shape of the auxiliary pad and the shape of the entire crutch minimize the impact occurring when the crutch contacts the ground, which is delivered to a user.

Ergonomic structure rationally responding to user's body while walking; TOGO's auxiliary pad and grip are ergonomically designed. The auxiliary pad's contacting side with armpit is designed to have a net shape and thus the contacting part can flexibly respond to human body, and makes pleasant walking with a crutch possible through natural flow of air. The auxiliary pad is designed to tilt six degrees forward/backward to naturally respond, according to body movement during walking. TOGO's grip is connected 15 degrees downward, which makes the wrist maintain in the natural state (Figure 3).

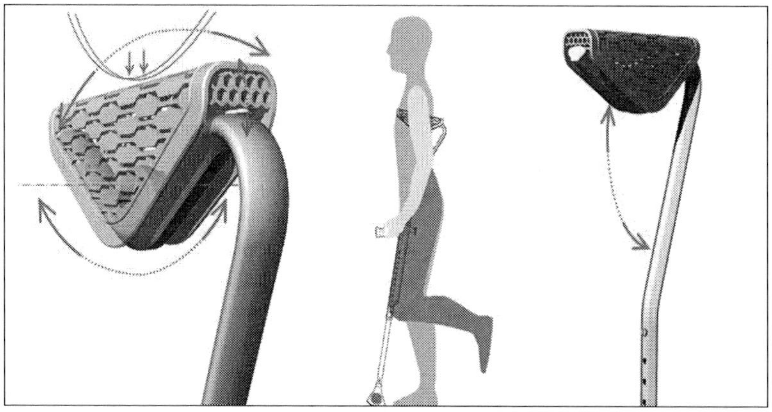

Figure 3. Auxiliary pad and entire shape of the crutch to properly respond to human body

Safety factors and attractive shape during walking; Because TOGO is manufactured with cutting and bending processing, after extrusion molding, it has durability enough to support user's weight and it is light enough to reduce energy consumption during walking. TOGO has an attractive shape for a user to have dignity unlike existing crutches, and risk factors in terms of safety that may occur when a user uses the crutch have been minimized. TOGO's tip is much larger than general crutch's tip, which can prevent the crutch's tip from being stuck up with a small gap or manhole cover during walking. The grip fixing screw cap and the upper frame's fixing lever cap at the back emit light at night, which can ensure crutch user's safety.

3. CONCLUSION AND FUTURE WORK

TOGO, the outcome of this study, needs to verify its utility through usability evaluation. To this end, a walking comparative evaluation experiment with existing crutches using a 3D motion analyzer can be a rational means as in the experiment carried out in the basic research step. However, for practical walking evaluation experiment, a prototype needs to be manufactured by using the same material(aluminum) as the actual design. An opportunity for subsequent research for a new prototype manufacture and walking evaluation to verify TOTO's utility is currently explored.

ACKNOWLEDGEMENT

This work was supported by the 2018 Inje University research grant.

REFERENCES

Yang Sungho, 2016. Comparative Evaluation Study with Axillary Crutch Design Variations, Design Convergence Study, Vol. 15, No. 6. pp.245~255

Yang Sungho, 2015. Development of the Design Guideline for a Crutch as Mobility Aids for the Handicapped in the Lower Extremity, Journal of Digital Design, Vol. 15, No. 3. pp.37-48

CROSS-CULTURAL GAME DESIGN: HOW DIFFERENT STUDENTS SEE THE SAME DEVELOPMENT

João Gabriel Guedes Pinheiro and Marco Aurélio Soares dos Santos
Universidade do Vale do Itajaí, 5 ª Avenida, 110 – Balneário Camború, SC, Brazil

ABSTRACT

This paper discusses how two groups of students, with different nationalities and academical backgrounds develop the same game. Through literature review, the author profiled the groups and identified five differences on how they work. Results point towards a structured process by bachelor`s students, with master`s taking more liberties in their design process.

KEYWORDS

Game Development, Students, Methods Comparison

1. INTRODUCTION

Digital games are a new type of entertainment, even more when compared to cinema or theater: while there are records of Greek plays from the 6th century BCE (Cartwright, 2016), and a predecessor of films from 1872 (Encyclopaedia Britannica, 2018) only 1958 the first digital game was made (APS News, 2008). As games are still new, designers are still building a base of knowledge on game creation, with an example being author who defend a linear approach to game design (Novak, 2010) and others defending an approach based on cycles (Chandler, 2012). These different approaches were observed on a internship opportunity given to bachelor`s students of game design by a company that employs master`s students of game design.

This study is in progress, as the game is being developed, but early results point towards the bachelor`s group having an approach closer to a waterfall method (Hiwiller, 2015) while the master`s group tends more towards the feature driven development (Meravý, 2013). Understanding those differences allows the bachelor`s university to better understand the game development process in an international context, while guiding students towards more effective methods of game design.

2. METHODOLOGY

This work is based on a case study, as proposed in (Liem, 2017), of a game in development by master`s students, that the group of bachelor`s students joined in a later date. To perform the analysis, the authors utilized as reference for methods adopted by both groups in bibliography cited by the two game development programs, while also utilizing authors that refers to methods used by the teams, but not found in their references: an example of this is (Goodwin, 2016), that while not used as a reference in the design programs analyzed, discuss version control, a system used during the project development.

3. DEVELOPMENT CULTURES

It's undeniable that the north-American game industry is a reference for Brazilian game developers: according to (Gamedevmap, 2019), United States has 1634 game companies, developing areas varying from serious games to mobile. Brazil is in a different stage: while it's going through a growth in number of game companies of 164%, (Wakka, 2018), the number of formal game development studios is still 276.

To understand if there is a difference between how game development is thought, the authors used an ongoing project that involves master's students from an american university, and bachelor's students from a brazilian university. Although there could be an innate difference in how the two groups operate through their previous experiences, not every master's student have a background on game development, and some of the bachelor's students had it. It's also important to comprehend that as bibliographies in universities programs doesn't vary too much throughout time, they can be used to make a case for their practices being similar to how games are made within those cultures.

This study uses a table, based on literature review, to identify some of the differences between the two groups of students. As the game is still in development, and more features are expected to be implemented, it`s not possible to emphasize all the differences observed between both teams. Instead, the authors focus on five elements observed during development of most games, from subjects of how they create their visions, to how they approach the game documentation and their views on playtesting. Only in the future, after the game is complete, a more detailed analysis can be made on which of those two different views on game design provided the best results, or had a better use of resources to achieve the results desired.

3.1 On their Practices

As (Brathwaite & Schreiber, 2009) discusses different approaches in game design, this view was adopted to identify how, from a creative view, their games are made and their different priorities. In the groups observed in this study, two main views were observed, the *blue-sky* and the *mechanic-driven* design. The first approach is more creative when compared to the second, where the designers allow themselves to pursues different ideas, ignoring constraints such as time or resources. For a *mechanic-driven* design, the game is made around one idea, with the remaining aspects following it. So if a game is focused on the idea of racing, every mechanic and system will be build to better deliver the experience of racing.

About documentation, (Novak, 2010) discusses the use of a single design document, that contains every material needed for designers, artists and developers to create their game. While this view is more common within the industry, (Adams, 2013) comments on the use of different documents that fulfill different needs. This analysis can be used to not only identify the best way to introduce a new team member to a project, but also how to keep track of development: a centralized document may make it easier to understand the project, as it contains the entire process, whle different documents can provide a better comprehension of different aspects of the game.

As games are made of features, it`s also valid to identify the main tool in which those features were thought of, as there are methods that can use existing games as a reference, with SCAMPER being an example of it (Brynteson, 2012), to creating user stories that define what the user would like to do, and then creating a system to assure him that experience (Maioli, 2018). This difference can also be used to exemplify how different their processes are when making a game: SCAMPER is better used with an existing design, where you reorganize their elements in order to improve it, while user stories doesn't depend on existing systems to be used.

Comparing how each team uses version control can also explain their views on the process, as working on the main branch only may indicate some lack of concern with stability of the build, as some of the work that`s done may cause a negative impact on the game (as creating major bugs), while worrying about side branches may indicate that the team is concerned to not affect the main branch if some asset creates unexpected results (Goodwin, 2016).

The last comparison is between tests: playtesting throughout the development is a practice encouraged, as it allows the team to understand how the game is played, and where it is when compared to their goals (Kramarzewski & De Nucci, 2018). This can be used to measure how progress is being tracked: if the game is tested frequently, it can be assumed that the team has a better idea of where the game is in its pipeline, while not testing may indicate possible issues on its quality control.

3.2 Comparison

The Table 1 contains a comparison between the groups of students, based on the criteria specified previously. It can be noted that they have major differences in how they think of features in their games: the Master`s group tends to think more towards the user experience, while losing some structure in the process, that may create obstacles along the development, from levels being added to the build without being tested to the usage of outdated documents in the game.

The Bachelor`s group, instead, follows a more rigid structure: instead of only focusing on the user experience, there`s a bigger concern with the formality of the design, through the use of a single document, the use of different branches as was asked by the Master`s group, to the use of tests to identify problems before they are added to the main branch of the game. Such a view does present a concern, that their view of the game is not open to expansions when compared to the Master`s group, as their system is more defined, and for that reason less open to the creation of new features, or changes to existing ones.

Table 1. Comparison of the groups

	Master`s	Bachelor`s
Game design approach	Blue-sky	Mechanic
Documentation	Different documents	A single document
Methods for concept creatio	User Stories	SCAMPER
Version control	Main branch	Different branches
Testing	Not usual	Frequent tests

4. CONCLUSION

This study attempts to profile groups of students, from different nationalities and academical experiences, to better understand how games are made, and how bachelor`s students can experience a different view on game design, from developers with more experience in it. Through literature review, and the use a game in which bachelor`s students joined a project in development by master`s students as a case study, the authors profiled both groups using concepts of game creation, allowing them to understand the differences between the two groups, and how the bachelor`s education can be adapted to better fit the industry expectations.

ACKNOWLEDGEMENT

The authors are grateful for the support of Zygobot, that kindly gave the team of students from Univali an opportunity to work in their game, allowing the authors to start this study. They are also grateful for Univali allowing students to take part in such an opportunity, and offering its space and resources.

REFERENCES

Adams, E., 2013. *Fundamentals of Game Design.* 3 ed. s.l.:New Riders.

APS News, 2008. *October 1958: Physicist Invents First Video Game.* [Online] Available at: https://www.aps.org/publications/apsnews/200810/physicshistory.cfm [Accessed 3 January 2019].

Brathwaite, B. & Schreiber, I., 2009. *Challenges for Game Designers.* Boston: Cengage Learning.

Brynteson, R., 2012. *Innovation at Work.* s.l.:Amacom.

Cartwright, M., 2016. *Ancient Greek Theatre.* [Online] Available at: https://www.ancient.eu/Greek_Theatre/ [Accessed 3 January 2019].

Chandler, H. M., 2012. *Manual de producao de jogos digitais [The game production handbook].* Porto Alegre: Bookman.

Encyclopaedia Britannica, 2018. *Eadweard Muybridge.* [Online] Available at: https://www.britannica.com/biography/Eadweard-Muybridge [Accessed 2 January 2019].

Gamedevmap, 2019. *Gamedevmap.* [Online] Available at: https://www.gamedevmap.com/index.php?country=United%20States&state=&city=&query=&type= [Accessed 16 March 2019].

Goodwin, S., 2016. *Polished Game Development: From First Steps to Final Release.* London: Apress.

Hiwiller, Z., 2015. *Players Making Decisions: Game Design Essentials and the Art of Understanding Your Players.* s.l.:New Riders.

Kramarzewski, A. & De Nucci, E., 2018. *Practical Game Design.* s.l.:Packt Publishing.

Liem, A., 2017. *Prospective Ergonomics.* London: Wiley-ISTE.

Maioli, L., 2018. *Fixing Bad UX Designs.* s.l.:Packt Publishing.

Meravý, J., 2013. *Effective Leadership in Game Industry using Agile Methods.* Brno: s.n.

Novak, J., 2010. *Desenvolvimento de games [Game development essentials].* Sao Paulo: Cengage Learning.

Ratcliffe, L. & McNeill, M., 2011. *Agile Experience Design: A digital designer's guide to agile, lean, and continuous.* Berkeley: New Riders.

Scolastici, C. & Nolte, D., 2013. *Mobile Game Design Essentials.* Birmingham: Packt Publishing.

Wakka, W., 2018. *Cresce número de empresas de jogos no Brasil, mas salário ainda é baixo.* [Online] Available at: https://canaltech.com.br/games/cresce-numero-de-empresas-de-jogos-no-brasil-mas-salario-ainda-e-baixo-126545/ [Accessed 16 March 2019].

WINE LABEL IMAGE RECOGNITION USING CONVOLUTIONAL NEURAL NETWORK WITH AUGMENTED DATA

Mei-Yi Wu
Graduate Institute of Food Culture and Innovation, National Kaohsiung University of Hospitality and Tourism, Taiwan

ABSTRACT

Wine label information was found to have a positive effect on consumer choice. However, it is not easy for consumers to read the information on wine labels since these texts are usually not print in English. Wine label information system with visual recognition function seems to be important as an auxiliary reading tool for customers. In this paper, we proposed an efficient wine image label recognition method using convolutional neural network(CNN) algorithms. Data augmentation techniques for machine learning with different image manipulation such as cropping, rotation and hue modification were applied to enlarge the dataset. Experimental results show a high accuracy on 130 different wine label images using the proposed CNN model with mixing different image manipulation.

KEYWORDS

Wine Label Image Recognition, Convolutional Neural Network, Augmented Data, Deep Learning

1. INTRODUCTION

In order to encourage consumption in a country without a strong culture of wine drinking, the expanding wine producers put their efforts on the design of wine labels. Some wine marketing studies make reference to the importance of wine labels and the information they contain. The information content of wine labels can be grouped under seven information positioning statements: namely, parentage, nonpareil, manufacture, attributes, endorsements, end user and end use. Nested within some of these statements is other information commonly associated with wine labels (Thomas et al., 2003,). However, it is not easy for consumers to read the information on wine labels since these texts are usually not print in English. A simple approach to solve this problem is to develop a mobile wine label image recognition system. Customers can take a shot of wine label photograph with mobile phone camera and the related information about the wine label will be displayed on the mobile phone.

Two different approaches, traditional image recognition and deep learning algorithms, are generally applied in the implementation of image recognition systems. Traditional image recognition schemes are based on specific handcrafted feature extraction. On the contrary, deep learning schemes optimize the features that are extracted. The major difference between deep learning and conventional methods is that deep learning automatically learns features from big data, instead of adopting handcrafted features, which mainly depends on priori knowledge of designers and is highly impossible to take the advantage of big data. Deep learning can automatically learn feature representation from big data, including millions of parameters which largely explains why these deep learning perform better (Liang et al., 2017). Although great achievements and perspectives, deep learning algorithms have some relevant challenges to tackle. The most frequently mentioned problem in the field of machine learning is the lack of sufficient amount of the training data within the datasets (Mikołajczyk et al., 2018,). In this paper, we have compared and analyzed multiple methods of data augmentation like cropping, rotation and hue modification to enlarge the dataset. More details about the proposed method and experimental results can be found in the next session.

2. PROPOSED METHOD

The implementation of proposed wine label image recognition system can be divided into four steps (1) Build a small-size wine label image dataset (2) data augmentation (3) Design CNN algorithms (4) Wine label recognition. The flowchart of proposed system is illustrated in Figure 1.

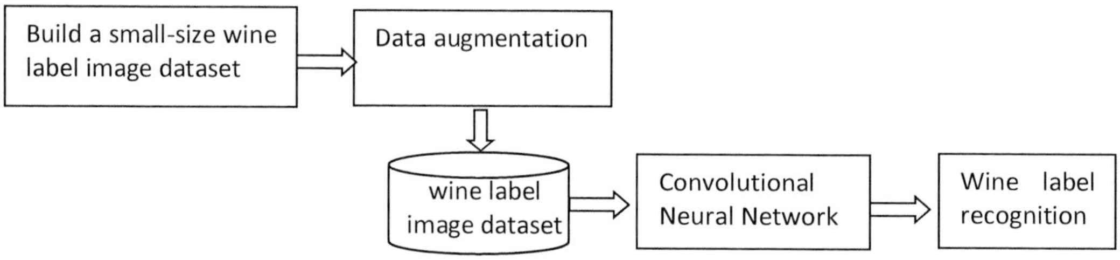

Figure 1. The flowchart of proposed wine label image recognition system

2.1 Build a Small-Size Wine Label Image Dataset

To fit the need of user's convenience, camera of mobile phones is preferred in proposed system to capture wine label photos. In building the wine label image dataset, we have selected 130 different wine bottles from wine retailers and taken 5 photos in different views for each wine bottle. Figure 2 shows the process to build the small-size wine label image dataset.

Figure 2. Build a small-size wine label image dataset. (a) a wine label image shot by mobile phone camera (b) an wine label image example (c) 5 images captured in different views for each wine bottle

2.2 Data Augmentation

Three different image manipulations were used to enlarge the small-size dataset (including cropping, rotation and hue modification). Figure 3 shows an example for image manipulation with cropping, rotation and hue modification, respectively. In this study, each image sample in small-size dataset was modified in 2 factors.

Figure 3. An example for image manipulation with cropping, rotation and hue modification

2.3 Convolutional Neural Network and Experimental Results

The CNN offers a state-of-the-art technique for image recognition (Zhang et al. 2018). In this study, images were resized into 64 × 64. The proposed CNN model comprises 4 convolution layers and 2 pooling layers, with a fully connected layer to produce the final result of the task. In image classification, each unit of the final layer indicates the class probability.

Three different image manipulations were used to enlarge the small-size dataset(including cropping, rotation and hue modification). There are totally 130 classes of wine label images in the original dataset. Each class has 5 different view images. In this study, each type of image manipulation will generate two times of "similar" images. We performed the proposed CNN model to train the dataset with different image manipulations. The original method without performing any data augmentation obtained 0.4 test accuracy rate. The test accuracy rates are 0.96, 0.83 and 0.88 with hue modification, rotation and cropping, respectively. And the best performance is obtained by mixing all types of augmentation operations and the accuracy rate can achieve 0.98. Figure 4 shows these experimental results.

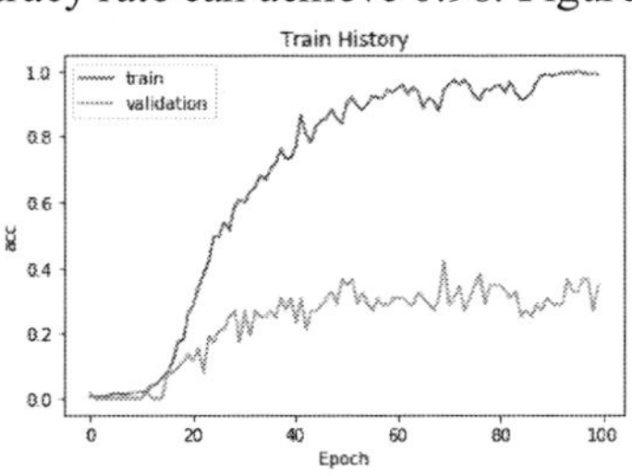

Original: accuracy 0.4

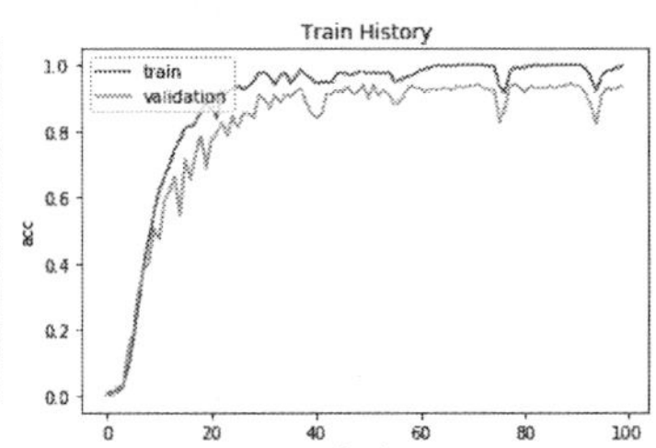

Hue modification: accuracy 0.96

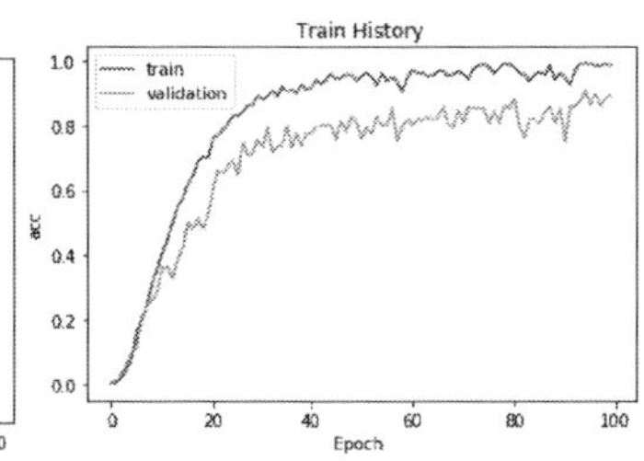

Rotation: accuracy 0.83

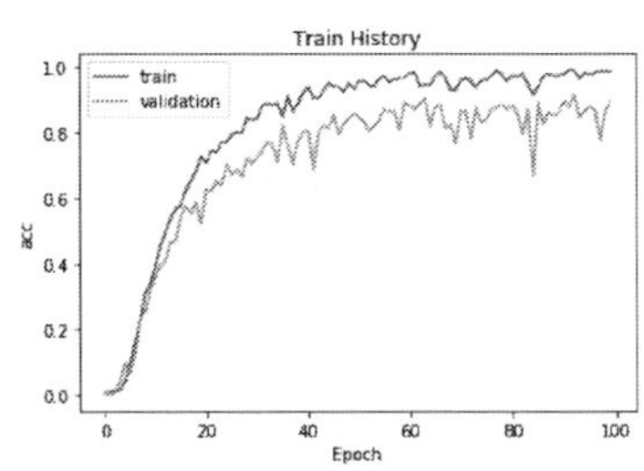

Cropping: accuracy 0.88

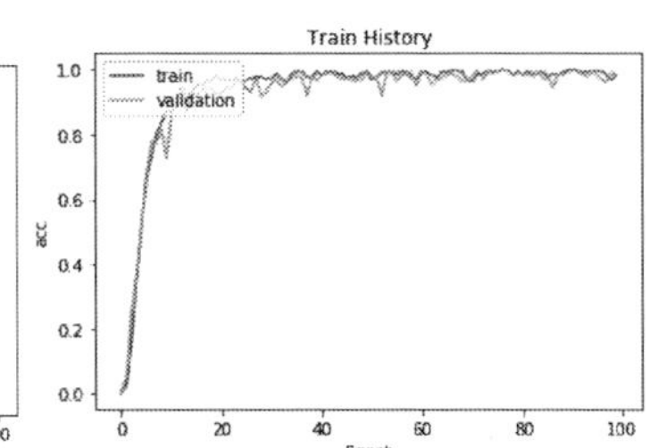

Mixed all: accuracy 0.98

Figure 4. Test accuracy using different manipulations

ACKNOWLEDGEMENT

We would like to thank the Ministry of Science and Technology of ROC for supporting this work in part under Contract MOST 107-2637-E-328-001.

REFERENCES

Thomas, A., & Pickering, G., 2003, The importance of wine label information. International journal of wine marketing, 15(2), pp. 58-74.

Liang, H., Sun, X., Sun, Y., & Gao, Y., 2017, Text feature extraction based on deep learning: a review. EURASIP journal on wireless communications and networking, 2017-211, pp.1-12.

Mikołajczyk, A., & Grochowski, M., 2018, Data augmentation for improving deep learning in image classification problem. In 2018 international interdisciplinary PhD workshop (IIPhDW), pp. 117-122.

Zhang, X., Xv, C., Shen, M., He, X., & Du, W., 2018, Survey of Convolutional Neural Network. In 2018 International Conference on Network, Communication, Computer Engineering (NCCE 2018).

AN INDOOR NAVIGATION SYSTEM FOR THE VISUALLY IMPAIRED USING HOLOLENS

Chien-Yi Lee[1], Jia-Hong Lee[1] and Mei-Yi Wu[2]
[1]*Department of Information Management, National Kaohsiung University of Science and Technology, Taiwan*
[2]*Graduate Institute of Food Culture and Innovation, National Kaohsiung University of Hospitality and Tourism, Taiwan*

ABSTRACT

The technological progress has brought us many new discoveries and better facilities, but it has also changed our daily lives. Recently, with the rapid development of augmented reality and virtual reality techniques, there has been a lot of business opportunities through the perception of context to make human senses have new experiences. The mixed reality device such as Microsoft HoloLens can detect the 3D environment and respond to the user via voice instructions. This technology can be applied to blind people for more convenience in their daily moves. In this paper, we have implemented a blind indoor navigation system using Microsoft HoloLens. With the proposed system, we can get the camera's coordinates and direction and detect distance from obstacles via the HoloLens functions such as gaze detection, image recognition, audio recognition and output. This system can also provide various blind guidance functions such as planning of safety paths, display the name of near targets, and BB sound warnings when walking beyond the safe path range. The system mainly controls the activities and functions through voice commands. To evaluate the system performance, we invited 8 testers to use the indoor navigation system to guide users through voice commands. After the experiments, the testers filled in the scores and opinions of a questionnaire. The experimental results show that the proposed system has good performance and provides a potential indoor navigation application for the visually impaired.

KEYWORDS

Augmented Reality, Indoor Navigation System, Microsoft Hololens, The Visually Impaired

1. INTRODUCTION

There are more than 57,291 visually impaired people in Taiwan, and the number is continued to rise rapidly in recent years. The visually impaired people might suspect their work abilities and affect the employment selection due to their visual disabilities. In a civilized society, in order to help visually impaired people to carry out safe activities, many barrier-free living spaces and environments have been established. So that visually impaired people can get more fair opportunities in this society. The visual problems of blind people rely on other sensory organs for identification such as sound, touch, smell, etc., in their daily lives.

The possibility of creating technology which simplifies the daily life of visually impaired people with their needs is easier today. Technologies that are able to analyze the surrounding environment and produce useful and interactive information are definitely an added value. Toyota developed a high-tech vest for the blind. This piece is called "BLAID"(Toyota project, 2016). It has a built-in camera to detect the surrounding environment, and combines map and image recognition, including image recognition. The face is detected, and when the current party detects the obstacle of the object, it will remind the blind person through the vibration, avoiding hitting the obstacle, etc. The vest also has a microphone and navigation system, and navigates through simple voice commands to lead the blind person to walk. Filipe et al.(Filipe et al. 2012) proposed a system to assist blind users. The system can provide information about the surrounding environment, in real time, based on depth data acquired by Microsoft Kinect sensor. It is able to detect different patterns in the scene like no obstacles, obstacle ahead, and stairs. In addition, neural network is applied and proved to be efficient in the classification of lines profiles extracted from depth images in the system. Wang et al.(Wang et al. 2017) presented a real-time wearable system, which includes a camera, an embedded computer and a belt with embedded vibration motors that provides vibration feedback to signal obstacles to its users. Using depth information from a camera, the system distinguishes walkable free space from obstacles and can identify a few important types of objects such as the location of a chair. In this paper, we have implemented a blind indoor navigation system using Microsoft HoloLens to achieve a more effective and convenient purpose.

2. PROPOSED INDOOR NAVIGATION SYSTEM

The proposed indoor navigation system using Hololens consists of 8 function modules: gaze cursor, distance computation, spatial mapping, speech recognition, target object recognition, route plan & display, warning sound and navigation platform modules. The architectures of the system is shown in Figure 1. Using the real-time mapping capabilities of Hololens, the headset can create a spatial map of a campus building. The headset's speaker, which has a surround sound quality, acts as a dynamic audio guide, navigating the blind person through the building by telling them when to turn right or left. The headset's speaker can also start a warning BB sound if the tester is walking outside the range of safe path regions. Figure 2 shows the actual route paths and the spatial mapping in a building.

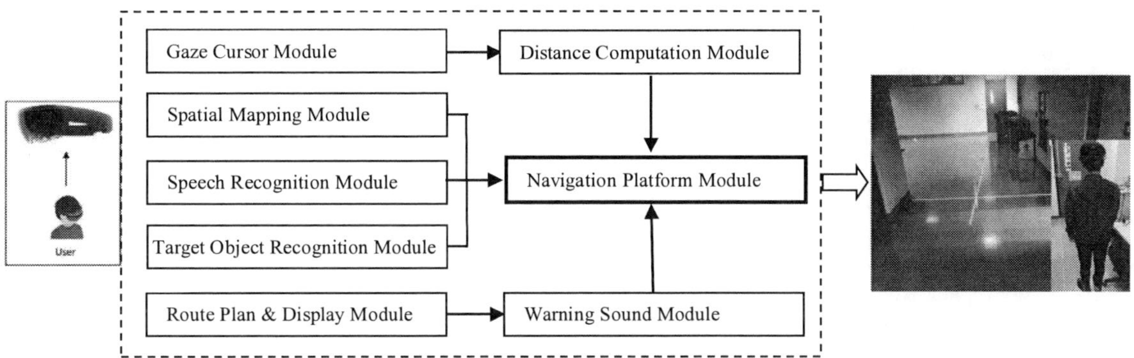

Figure 1. Function modules of the proposed indoor navigation system

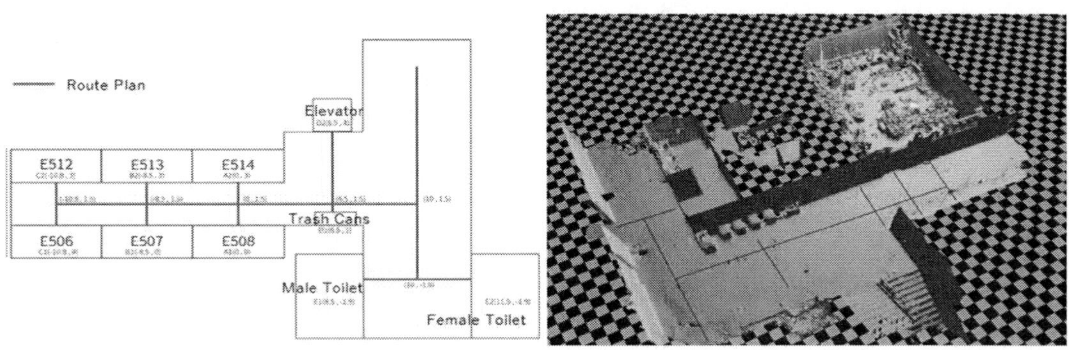

Figure 2. The actual route paths and the spatial mapping in a building

To evaluate the proposed system, 8 testers joined the navigation test and answered questions about user satisfaction. In satisfaction questions, 5 levels: "Not at all Satisfied," "Partly Satisfied," "Satisfied," "More than Satisfied," "Very Satisfied," numbering 1 to 5 as an interval scale are applied. Figure 3 shows the actual walking tracks and statistics of user satisfaction in our system tests. The experiments illustrate that the system can act as a reliable navigator and achieve a high user satisfaction.

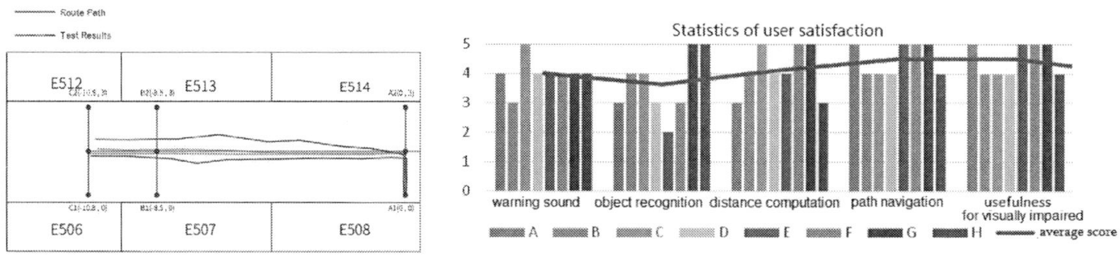

Figure 3. The actual walking tracks and statistics of user satisfaction in our system tests

ACKNOWLEDGEMENT

We would like to thank the Ministry of Science and Technology of ROC for supporting this work in part under Contract MOST 107-2637-E-992 -015.

REFERENCES

Toyota Project Blaid Wearable Set to Help Blind and Visually Impaired People, march 7, 2016. http://blog.toyota.co.uk/toyota-project-blaid-blind-visually-impaired-people

Filipe, V., Fernandes, F., Fernandes, H., Sousa, A., Paredes, H., & Barroso, J., 2012, Blind navigation support system based on Microsoft Kinect, *Proceedings of the 4th International Conference on Software Development for Enhancing Accessibility and Fighting Info-exclusion*. Porto, Portugal, pp. 94-101.

Wang H. C., Katzschmann R. K., Teng S., Araki B., Giarr´e L., Rus D., 2017, Enabling Independent Navigation for Visually Impaired People through a Wearable Vision-Based Feedback System, I*EEE International Conference on Robotics and Automation.* Singapore, pp. 33-40.

GENERATING DYNAMIC 3D SCENES FOR RENDERING BENCHMARKS

Vyacheslav Gonakhchyan, Oleg Tarlapan and Vitaly Semenov
Ivannikov Institute for System Programming of the Russian Academy of Sciences
109004, Moscow, Alexander Solzhenitsyn st., 25, Russia

ABSTRACT

Performance comparison of different rendering methods is either based on synthetic 3D scenes or commonly used 3D scenes. A lot of static scenes exist but dynamic scenes are not common. Performance of modern rendering methods depends on the dynamic state of objects and varies with an increasing number of objects, degree of scene volatility. In this paper, two new methods of dynamic scene generation are proposed. We consider the bottlenecks of common rendering methods, based on which the parameters of the proposed methods are selected. We propose a method for dynamic scene generation, which allows to create scenes with a specified number of objects, vertices, different appearance order, temporal coherence of visibility, degree of spatial coherence of appearance and other parameters. We propose a method for converting of static scenes into dynamic scenes using space-filling curves to determine the order in which objects appear in a scene. The proposed methods will fill the gap in the field of rendering benchmarks and will allow to use the proven static scenes when evaluating the performance of methods with dynamic objects.

KEYWORDS

Test set Generation, Dynamic 3D Scene, Space-filling Curve, Spatial Coherence

1. INTRODUCTION

Capabilities of GPUs are constantly evolving, which allows for rendering of scenes with an increasing number of polygons and objects. Existing methods usually use static scenes and do not take into account the characteristics of scenes that are important for rendering: gradual appearance of new objects, spatial coherence of the appearance in time, the order of object appearance (Bittner et al., 2004; Guthe et al., 2006). We propose a new method for dynamic 3D scene generation with a large number of parameters that allows to vary the computational load on various subtasks of rendering methods.

Rendering of large 3D scenes with dynamic behavior of objects is used in many applications. Although a lot of static 3D scenes exist that are commonly used for performance evaluation, there are no common dynamic 3D scenes. In this paper, we propose a method to convert static scenes to dynamic scenes, where object visibility is determined based on space-filling curves.

Let's consider common static scenes that are used as benchmarks. Following datasets are widely used when testing mesh simplification, mesh compression, surface restoration, and rendering methods (Turk, G. and Mullins, B., 2003; The Stanford 3D Scanning Repository, 2014). Proposed models have a large number of polygons, however, rendering tasks usually also have individual objects with different materials. Following datasets have a large number of different objects, which makes them more suitable for rendering tests, but they consist of static scenes only (Power Plant Model, 2001; Havran, V. et al., 2010; SPECviewperf 13, 2018).

Let's consider existing approaches to performance evaluation when dealing with dynamic objects. Objects can be moved along a path that causes the rebuilding of a hierarchy (Sudarsky & Gotsman, 1999). In some papers animated data was created using specialized software like Poser and DAZStudio (Wald et al., 2007). Lext et al. (2001) proposed benchmarking datasets and a method for ray-tracing performance evaluation when rendering animated scenes. However, authors have not considered methods of scene generation with a large number of primitives, temporal and spatial coherence.

Let's consider the space-filling curves in two-dimensional space. Given a square grid with N^2 cells, space-filling curve is a numbering of grid cells, in which numbers vary from 1 to N^2. In the limit N→∞, the curve passes through each point of a given region of space. Described properties allow space-filling curves to be used for indexing of complex n-dimensional data, including the clustering of objects in 3D scenes (Lawder & King, 2000; Pantaleoni & Luebke, 2010). The most common space-filling curves are Hilbert curve, Morton curve (z-order curve), Row-prime order (see figure 1). In this paper, space-filling curves are used for clustering and calculation of appearance time of resulting objects.

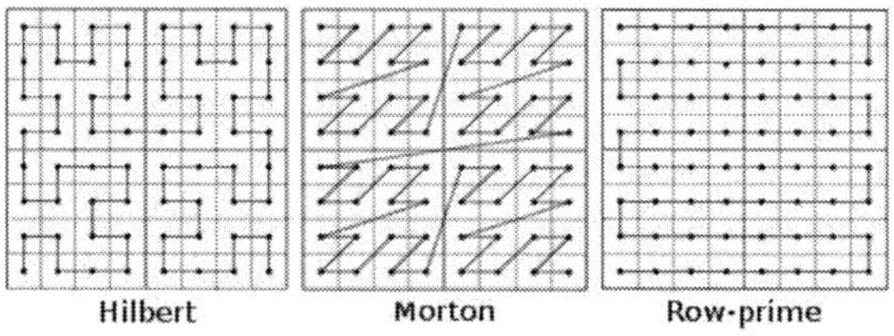

Figure 1. Two-dimensional space-filling curves

2. DYNAMIC SCENE GENERATION

Let's consider the bottlenecks in the work of common computer graphics methods to derive the main parameters of proposed methods of dynamic scene generation.

Traditional rendering of polygonal scenes performs the following steps: command recording and submission, vertex transformation, rasterization, fragment shading, blending and output to frame buffer. Each of them might be a bottleneck. To evaluate the performance of command recording and submission, we need to create a large number of objects (entities requiring different pipeline state). To evaluate the performance of vertex transformation, we need a large number of vertices. To evaluate the performance of fragment shader, we need a large number of overlapping surfaces, which generate a lot of pixels on the screen, or expensive shader calculations. The dynamic behavior of objects might cause command buffer overwriting, hierarchy rebuilding. So, the following parameters are required to evaluate the rendering performance: the number of objects in the scene, the number of vertices, the number of overlapping surfaces.

Many rendering methods assume that during animation, when going from frame to frame many objects remain visible (temporal coherence of visibility) (Bittner et al., 2004; Guthe et al., 2006). As a result, visibility calculations can be performed once per multiple frames. In practice, coherence of visibility is achieved when objects are located inside containers (buildings). To generate such scenes, we need to build exterior first and then fill the interior. In order to do that, we identify relatively large objects in a scene. A large object is an object with a diagonal value that is much higher than the average value in a scene. We propose a parameter to output large objects first by traversing the set of objects multiple times until large objects remain in the scene. We also propose a parameter to output small objects first to stress test methods that perform a lot of computations when new objects appear inside view.

In dynamic scenes the order of appearance of objects affects the performance of hierarchical LOD generation. If neighboring objects appear at the same time, then methods can use less levels of detail and reduce the amount of consumed memory. We propose a parameter specifying the degree of spatial coherence of the displayed objects. The parameter ranges from 0 (random appearance of objects) to 1 (appearance of objects along a space-filling curve).

Let's consider the parameters that determine the order of appearance of objects: grid size, traversal order, time interval, space-filling curve. Grid size specifies the granularity of appearance in time, where small size can be used to increase the number of objects appearing at once. We use the right-handed coordinate system, where Z axis is directed upwards. Traversal order allows to change the direction of traversal for each axis (e.g. XYZ is bottom-up, XY-Z is top-down traversal order). Each cell of the grid contains a set of objects, which become visible at time $n * \Delta t$, where n is the cell number, Δt is time interval. We use a space-filling curve (Hilbert, Morton, Row-prime) and traversal order to calculate n.

We propose a method for dynamic scene generation that is based on the described parameters. The method creates the file in FBX format with polygonal objects and visibility information. It creates a scene with different number of objects and vertices, spatial dimensions, degree of coherence. It can generate a square block of buildings with a given number of buildings with specified number of floors, windows, additional objects per floor, distance between the buildings (see figure 2). It allows to evaluate the performance with a large number of overlapping surfaces. When the number of additional objects is set, it positions them inside the buildings according to the specified traversal order (see figure 3). When visibility coherence is set, it displays large objects (walls, slabs) along a curve in several iterations, and then places additional objects inside the buildings (see figure 4). When a space-filling curve is set, it displays the objects in time calculated from the specified curve (see figure 5). When a degree of spatial coherence is set, it displays the objects with the given degree of randomness along the space-filling curve (see figure 6).

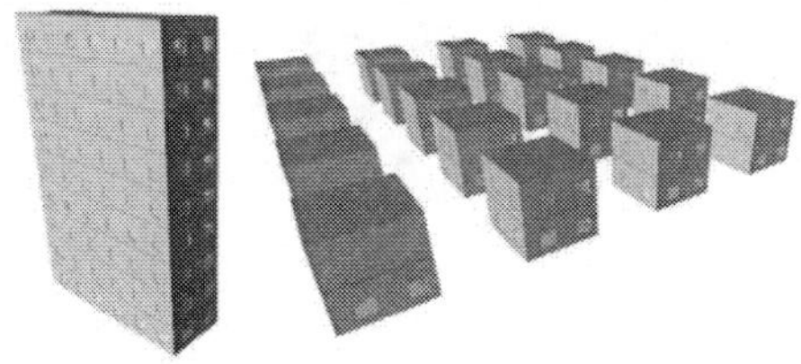

Figure 2. One tall building (left). Block of small buildings (right)

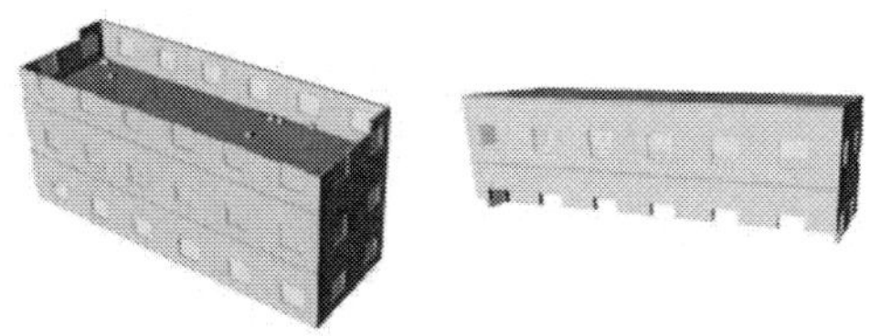

Figure 3. Bottom-up traversal order (left), top-down traversal order (right)

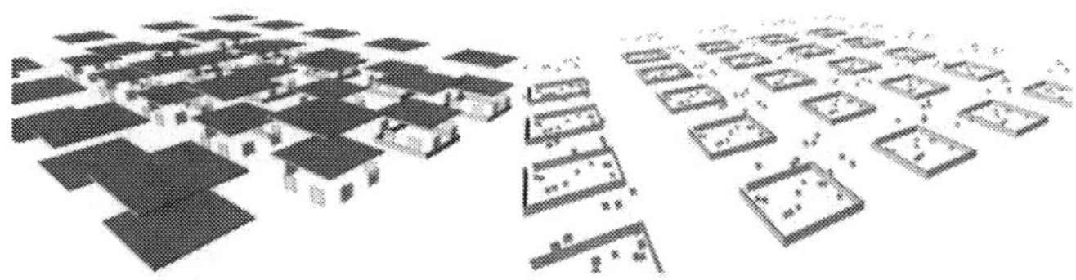

Figure 4. Big objects appearing first (left), small objects appearing first (right)

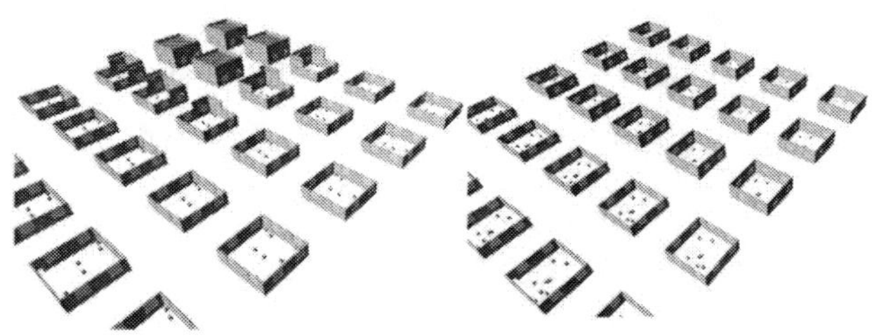

Figure 5. Objects appearing according to Hilbert curve (left) and row-prime order (right). Shown for the same moment of time

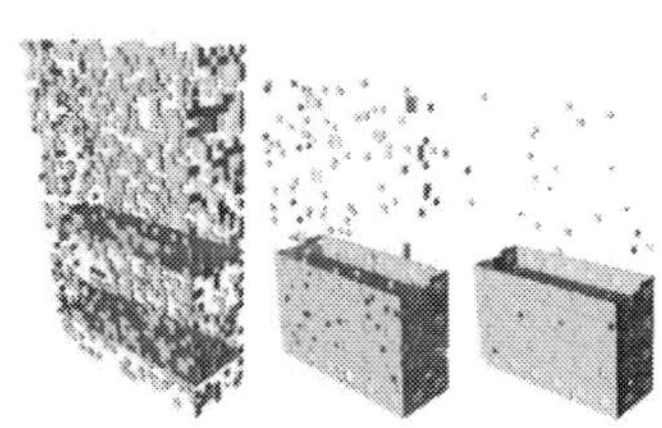

Figure 6. Objects appearing with increasing spatial coherence (0.1, 0.95, 0.99) along the row-prime curve. Shown for the same moment of time

We propose a method that converts static scene to dynamic scene, which takes as input a file in FBX format. As output, the method creates a file in FBX format with original objects and visibility information. The method uses all the described parameters except the parameters that specify additional objects. Figure 7 shows an example where a large static scene is converted to the dynamic scene by displaying objects in row-prime order.

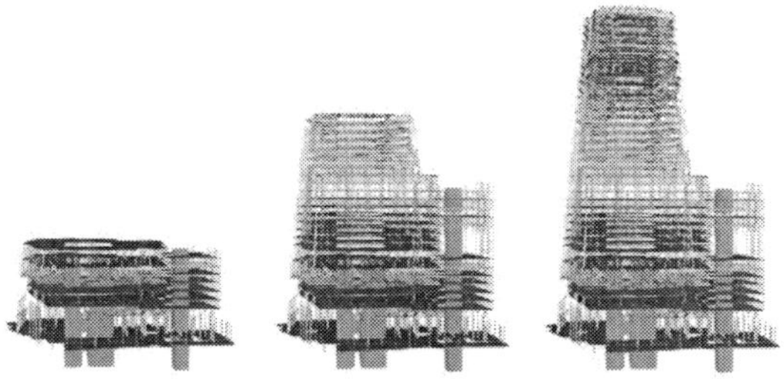

Figure 7. Generation of the dynamic scene from the static scene. Objects gradually appear along the row-prime curve

3. CONCLUSION

We developed two methods of dynamic scene generation. The first method generates a block of buildings with a given number of buildings, additional objects, temporal coherence of visibility, spatial coherence of appearance. It can be used for performance benchmarking of different rendering methods with an increasing number of objects. The second method takes a static 3D scene and converts it into a dynamic 3D scene, using space-filling curves to determine the order of appearance of objects. It allows to create dynamic scenes from widespread static scenes.

REFERENCES

Bittner, J. et al., 2004. Coherent hierarchical culling: Hardware occlusion queries made useful. In *Computer Graphics Forum*, Vol. 23, No. 3, pp. 615-624.

Guthe, M. et al., 2006. Near Optimal Hierarchical Culling: Performance Driven Use of Hardware Occlusion Queries. In *Rendering Techniques*, pp. 207-214.

Havran, V. et al., 2010. MPI Informatics Building Model as Data for Your Research (online). Available online: http://resources.mpi-inf.mpg.de/mpimodel/v1.0/

Lawder, J. K. and King, P. J., 2000. Using space-filling curves for multi-dimensional indexing. In *British National Conference on Databases*, pp. 20-35.

Lext, J. et al., 2001. A benchmark for animated ray tracing. *IEEE Computer Graphics and Applications*, Vol. 21, Issue 2, pp. 22-31.

Pantaleoni, J. and Luebke, D., 2010. HLBVH: hierarchical LBVH construction for real-time ray tracing of dynamic geometry. In *Proceedings of the Conference on High Performance Graphics*, pp. 87-95.

Power Plant Model, 2001. Available online: http://gamma.cs.unc.edu/POWERPLANT/

SPECviewperf 13, 2018. Available online: https://www.spec.org/gwpg/gpc.static/vp13info.html

Sudarsky, O. and Gotsman, C., 1999. Dynamic scene occlusion culling. *IEEE Transactions on Visualization and Computer Graphics*, Vol. 5, Issue 1, pp. 13-29.

The Stanford 3D Scanning Repository, 2014. Available online: http://graphics.stanford.edu/data/3Dscanrep/

Turk, G. and Mullins, B., 2003. Large Geometric Models Archive. Available online: https://www.cc.gatech.edu/projects/large_models/

Wald, I. et al., 2007. Ray tracing deformable scenes using dynamic bounding volume hierarchies. *ACM Transactions on Graphics (TOG)*, Vol. 26, Issue 1, Article 6.

AUTHOR INDEX